EUROPE

1815 TO THE PRESENT

Combining

EUROPE 1815–1914

and

EUROPE AND THE WORLD SINCE 1914

by

Ernest John Knapton

Thomas Kingston Derry

CHARLES SCRIBNER'S SONS   *New York*

1815 **EUROPE** *1914*

Ernest John Knapton   Wheaton College, Norton, Massachusetts

Thomas Kingston Derry   Visiting Professor of History, Wheaton College

CHARLES   SCRIBNER'S   SONS   NEW   YORK

E U R O P E

1815 - 1914

ACKNOWLEDGMENTS

Grateful acknowledgment is made to the following publishers and authors for granting
permission to quote at the pages indicated from their copyright works:

COLUMBIA UNIVERSITY PRESS: Alexis de Tocqueville, *The Recollections of Alexis de Tocqueville*
(1949), on pp. 34–35, 57.

CORNELL UNIVERSITY PRESS: Charles Morazé, *The French and the Republic* (1958), on
p. 361. English translation © 1958 by Cornell University. Used by permission of Cornell
University Press.

HARVARD UNIVERSITY PRESS: Lawrence Steefel, *The Schleswig-Holstein Question* (1932),
on p. 147.

THE MACMILLAN COMPANY: Koppel S. Pinson, *Modern Germany, Its History and Civilization*
(1954), on pp. 143, 310, 326.

OXFORD UNIVERSITY PRESS: Lewis B. Namier, *1848: The Revolution of the Intellectuals*
(1946), on p. 92.

PRINCETON UNIVERSITY PRESS: T. S. Hamerow, *Restoration, Revolution and Reaction:
Economics and Politics in Germany, 1815–1871* (1958), on pp. 85, 94.

THE REV. F. A. SIMPSON, *Louis Napoleon and the Recovery of France* (Longmans, Green & Co.,
2nd ed., 1930), on p. 70.

UNIVERSITY OF NOTRE DAME PRESS: Hans Kohn, *Pan-Slavism: Its History and Ideology*
(1953), on pp. 96–97.

The illustrations on the title page are as follows:

A SOLDIER ON HORSEBACK, taken from a steel engraving of the Battle of Mondovi,
April 22, 1796. Courtesy of the Picture Collection, New York Public Library.

THE GREAT STACK, SHEFFIELD, 1909, an etching by Joseph Pennell, reproduced from the
Collections of the Library of Congress.

TO THE MEMORY OF
GEOFFREY MAY

Pro Amicitia

PREFACE

This book deals with the history of nineteenth-century Europe—that well-defined period which lies between the Congress of Vienna and the First World War. It is a continuation of *Europe: 1450–1815* by one of the present authors, and will be followed by a further volume written in collaboration to cover the years from 1914 to the present day. The general policy of the book is to adopt the pattern of the *New Cambridge Modern History* and much other recent historical writing in attempting to enlarge and enrich the central themes of European political life by allocating substantial space to economic, social, and cultural developments. Attention has also been paid to the interaction of Europe and the overseas world as seen in colonization, trade, and diplomatic and military rivalries. The center of interest, nevertheless, is placed throughout in Europe, for, whatever the subsequent changes of fortune, Europe's leading role during the nineteenth century can hardly be questioned. Moreover, within the field of European political life, the authors have thought it best to deal separately with the development of the principal states, not because the growth of international movements has been disregarded by them, but because the divisions of nineteenth-century Europe played a far larger part in its life than did any notion of a united continent.

The maps, charts, and illustrations are designed to elucidate the text, of which they form an integral part. The Reading List which appears at the end of each chapter consists of carefully selected and reasonably short items from sources that are likely to be widely accessible. These will serve both to amplify the text and to stimulate further reading. Although some biographical material is given in special footnotes throughout the book, biographies are not usually cited in the lists, their existence being sufficiently obvious to the reader; for much the same reason no specific references are made to compilations of source material, except for a general list of them in the Bibliography which indicates the most useful books available in English. A Comparative Chronological Table has also been included.

The authors, who have planned and written the book as a common enterprise, express their joint appreciation of help received from various sources. They thank the Trustees, President, and Faculty of Wheaton College for much general encouragement and for very helpful grants from their faculty research fund. Among their Wheaton colleagues and friends they thank in particular Professors Mary Heuser, Henrietta Jennings, Bojan Jennings, Frank Ramseyer, and Arthur Martin for their suggestions and help. Similar help was generously rendered by the late Dr. Geoffrey May. They thank Miss Hilda Harris, Librarian of Wheaton College, and members of her staff for their cordially rendered assistance. They thank the college department staff of Charles Scribner's Sons for advice at all stages in the execution of their plans; Professor Goldwin Smith, college consultant of the publishers, for saving them from many mistakes; and Miss Nancy Foster, who has typed and re-typed the manuscript with exemplary patience. Finally, they thank their students at Wheaton College for the stimulus they have given to this work in the lecture room and elsewhere.

E. J. K.

T. K. D.

September, 1964

x

CONTENTS

		Page
LIST OF ILLUSTRATIONS		xv
LIST OF MAPS		xvii

Part I   *Nationalism in the Ascendant, 1815–1871*

PROLOGUE: THE CONFLICT OF OLD AND NEW   2
Some Basic Trends
"A World Restored"
The European Scene
Constitutionalism and Autocracy
The Guarantee of European Stability
The Conflict of Two Worlds in the Arts
Prospects of the Nineteenth Century

CHAPTER 1   THE YEARS OF UNCERTAINTY, 1815–1848   16
The European Territorial Settlement
Authority as a Principle of Rule
The Congress System
First Breaches in the Established Order
Social Unrest and Its Causes
Liberalism
The Beginnings of Modern Socialism
Nationalism

CHAPTER 2   FOUR REGIMES IN FRANCE, 1814–1870   50
The Bourbon Restoration, 1814–1830
The July Monarchy of Louis Philippe, 1830–1848
Revolution and Second Republic, 1848–1852
The Second Empire: Domestic Policies, 1852–1870
The Second Empire: Foreign Policies, 1852–1870
The Second Empire: Finale, 1870–1871

CHAPTER 3   THE STRUGGLE FOR POWER IN CENTRAL EUROPE, 1848–1851   82
From Unrest to Revolution
The First Revolutionary Wave in Central Europe
Revolutionary Frustrations
Resurgence and Repression, 1849–1851
The Balance Sheet of Revolution

CHAPTER 4   ITALY AND ITS UNIFICATION   106
Italy from 1815 to 1846
Reform, Revolt, and Reaction, 1846–1850
Italy and the French Alliance
1860: The Impact of Garibaldi
The Continuing Struggle: Venetia and Rome
An Imperfect Union

CHAPTER 5   THE UNIFICATION OF GERMANY
AND THE EUROPEAN BALANCE, 1849–1871   132
Aftermath of the Revolution of 1848
The "Bach System" in the Hapsburg Empire, 1851–1859
Creation of the Dual Monarchy in Austria-Hungary, 1859–1867
The German Problem During the 1850's
Bismarck's First Approach to the German Problem
The Impact of Foreign Affairs: Poland and Schleswig-Holstein
Defeat of Austria and Formation of the North German Confederation
The Franco-Prussian War and the Creation of the German Empire

CHAPTER 6   CHANGING RUSSIA, 1815–1871   158
The Reign of Alexander I
The Decembrist Conspiracy
Nicholas I: Orthodoxy, Autocracy, and Nationality
Foreign Policy: Russia and the Ottoman Empire
The Liberation of the Serfs by Alexander II
Concomitant Reforms
Problems of Polish and External Relations, 1855–1871
Conclusion

CHAPTER 7   BRITAIN—THE EPOCH OF REFORM   188
Postwar Distress
Reforms of 1832–1850
The Politics of the Poor and the Growth of Free Trade
Foreign and Imperial Policy
The Second Era of Reform
Mid-Victorian Britain

CHAPTER 8   THE INDUSTRIAL REVOLUTION IN EUROPE TO 1871   214
Conditions in 1815
Economic Development, 1815–1850
Economic Development, 1850–1871
Armaments
Social Consequences of Technological Change
The Life of the Masses

CHAPTER 9   MOVEMENTS OF THOUGHT AND CULTURE, 1815–1871   238
A Retrospective Glance: Reaction and Romanticism
The First Great Scientific Advances
Mid-Century Transition to Realism in the Arts
Darwinism, Science, and Life
Science and the Study of Society
Religion, Science, and Social Issues

Part II The Uncertain Balance, 1871–1914

PROLOGUE: THE FORTY YEARS' PEACE, 1871–1914   262

Political Trends
The Course of Economic and Social Development
The International Anarchy
Cultural Changes

CHAPTER 10 THE TRIUMPH OF MACHINE INDUSTRY, 1870–1914   274

Introduction
Increase in Industrial Production
Transport and Communications
The Growth of World Trade
Urbanization and Emigration
European Agriculture
The Growth of Armaments
The Role of Government

CHAPTER 11 THE GERMAN POWER IN EUROPE   304

The Political Structure of Imperial Germany
The Party System
Political Developments Under Bismarck
Economic Growth and Its Consequences, 1871–1890
Germany and the European Balance, 1871–1890
Transition to a New Age
Economic and Social Growth Under William II
Imperial Germany and the World Stage

CHAPTER 12 REPUBLICAN FRANCE, 1870–1914   336

The Aftermath of Defeat
Establishing the Republican Constitution
Parties and Politics
Stresses and Strains in the Third Republic
Problems of Church and State
Socialism and the Social Problem
France Overseas
"La Douce France"

CHAPTER 13 BRITAIN AND HER EMPIRE   364

Introduction
Limits of Victorian Reform Programs
The Problem of Ireland
Imperialism and the Empire
The South African War and Its Consequences
The Liberal Revival
The Years of Increasing Strain
Foreign Policy and Imperial Defense

CHAPTER 14   RUSSIA AT THE PARTING OF THE WAYS   390

Introduction
Alexander II: The Last Decade
The Reign of Alexander III
Nicholas II and the Russo-Japanese War
The Growth of Opposition
Revolution and Reaction, 1905–1907
The Stolypin Regime and Its Development to 1914

CHAPTER 15   AUSTRIA-HUNGARY, ITALY, AND THE LESSER POWERS   416

Intermediate Status of Austria-Hungary and Italy
Lands of the Dual Monarchy
Turkey and the Balkans
The Kingdom of Italy
The Iberian Peninsula
Stabler Small Powers North of the Alps
Conclusion

CHAPTER 16   EUROPEAN CULTURAL INFLUENCES AT THEIR ZENITH   444

A Generation of Materialism
Changing Concepts in Physical Science
Man and Nature
Man and Society
Socialist Interpretations of Society
Religion in the New Age of Science
Literature and the Arts
Crosscurrents

CHAPTER 17   THE ROAD TO WAR   472

Introduction
The Heritage of Bismarck
Alliances and Regroupings, 1890–1907
Conflicts and Compromises, 1908–1913
Underlying Causes of War
1914: Events Leading to War
Conclusion

BIBLIOGRAPHY   507
COMPARATIVE CHRONOLOGICAL TABLES   528
INDEX   539

LIST OF ILLUSTRATIONS

Last Page of the Final Act of the Congress of Vienna, June 9, 1815   18

Classic and Romantic   22

The Bourgeoisie   39

Bust of Guizot, by Honoré Daumier   58

Louis Philippe in Cartoons   59

Cross Section of a Parisian Apartment House Under the Second
Empire   71

The King of Prussia Offering His Help to His Fellow German Rulers,
1848   84

Meeting of the German National Assembly in St. Paul's Church,
Frankfurt, 1848   90

Garibaldi in 1860, Wearing a "Puncio"   114

The Plebiscite in Naples, October, 1860   122

The Aftermath of Battle   137

Napoleon III and Bismarck at Biarritz, October, 1865   147

"The Prussian Hercules"   156

Pushkin: Self-Portrait and Page of Manuscript   168

"Turkey in Danger"—Threats from the Russian Bear   171

The Bolshoi Theater in Moscow   179

The Petersfield Massacre, Manchester, 1819   191

A British Election Handbill of 1834   197

Gladstone in 1859   200

Building the Mont Cenis Tunnel   218

The "Great Transept" of the Crystal Palace, London, on Opening
Day, May, 1851   222

Departure of the *Great Western* from Bristol for New York in 1838   225

Michael Faraday Lecturing at the Royal Institution, London   244

Justus Liebig's Laboratory at Giessen in 1842   249

Darwin, Age Thirty-Five, with His Son   250

"Over London by Rail," an Engraving by Gustave Doré   276

Tramcars on the First Electric Street Railway in Europe,
Frankfurt-am-Main, 1884   280

Bismarck in Middle Age   307

The Krupp Steel Works at Essen, in the Ruhr   316

"Dropping the Pilot," from *Punch*, March 29, 1890   323

The Problem of Monarchy in France, 1871   348

The Dreyfus Case: "*J'Accuse!*"   351

An Irish Eviction   369

London, the Heart of an Empire   374

Burslem, a Staffordshire Pottery Town   383

Convicted Nihilists Leaving for Siberia   399

Tsar Nicholas II of Russia and the Tsarina Alexandra in Court Robes   403

Bombing of King Alfonso XIII's Wedding Procession, 1906   432

Henri Dunant   436

Pope Leo XIII   460

Prospectus for *The Daily Express*, 1900   466

H.M.S. *Dreadnought*   474

Russian Prewar Maneuvers   483

The Austro-Hungarian Declaration of War on Serbia, July 28, 1914   495

LIST OF MAPS

Europe in 1815	19
The *Zollverein*	36
France at Mid-Century	66
Linguistic Divisions in the Hapsburg Possessions	95
Areas of Revolutionary Unrest, 1847–1849	102
Italy in 1815	118
Proposed Confederation of Italy	119
Stages in Italian Unification, 1859–1870	119
Unification of Germany (The Schleswig-Holstein Affair)	152
Western Borderlands of Russia	162
The Russian Advance in Asia	182–183
Britain at Mid-Century	209
The European Railway Network, 1848–1877	233
The Changing Face of Europe to 1914	290
Colonizing Activities of Modern Europe	300–301
Growth of German Cities in the Nineteenth Century	331
The Partition of Ireland	385
The Struggle for the Balkans, 1876–1887	394
The Russo-Japanese War, 1904–1905	405
Austria-Hungary in 1914	422
The Small Powers North of the Alps, 1914	435
Growth of Mediterranean Rivalries in the Nineteenth Century	476–477
The Balkans After the Balkan Wars	488
The Burden of Armaments, 1914	493
Territorial Changes Affecting the European Powers, 1815 to 1914	498–499

NATIONALISM

IN THE ASCENDANT

1815–1871

"Europe is racing towards democracy. . . .

France and England, like two enormous battering-rams,

beat again and again upon the crumbling ramparts

of the old society. The most audacious

doctrines concerning property, equality, and liberty

are proclaimed night and morning

in the face of monarchs trembling behind a

triple guard of unreliable soldiers."

CHATEAUBRIAND in the *Revue des deux-mondes*, April, 1834

Prologue: The Conflict of Old and New

The most striking feature of European history in the nineteenth century was the rapid transformation of the major aspects of life as a result of the forces of a new industrial age. In western Europe a preponderantly agrarian society gave way to a society dominated by urban interests. New forms of industrial production and finance capitalism developed. A Europe dependent for centuries upon poor roads and slow, horse-drawn vehicles saw the growth of an elaborate railway network which, from its modest beginnings in the 1830's, soon developed at an impressively accelerated pace. The older system of dynastic states, most of them largely autocratic in character, was followed by a new pattern of nation states with elected legislatures. Political power began to reside much less exclusively in the hands of a hereditary governing class and much more in the hands of a steadily enlarging middle, bourgeois class.

Not content with this growing bourgeois leadership, the common man, whom we visualize less as the country worker, or peasant, and much more as the factory hand, the shop assistant, and the office clerk, began to demand his just rights. In addition to the vote, he sought public education for his children and a larger range of government activity in the field of social legislation. In many cases he began to give allegiance to new doctrines of socialism, some of them evolutionary and reformist, others revolutionary in character. Spectacular developments in the field of science enormously increased both man's knowledge and control of his environment. The world exterior to Europe, long regarded as a colonial subsidiary intended for European exploitation rather than for large-scale settlement, grew in importance. Finally, the relationships between European states, powerfully affected by the new drive of national, industrial, and imperial forces, grew in complexity and produced new tensions. Ever more

3

dangerous crises were created, of which the war of 1914 was to be the ultimate outcome. Such are the major themes of this volume.

■ "A WORLD RESTORED"

As much as any year can, 1815 marked the beginning of a new age in Europe. Yet the people of that day could hardly be expected to realize the vast changes that were in store for them, and indeed to many the new age must surely have looked like the restoration of the old. After more than two decades of war and change, the Continent at last returned to a condition of general peace. Although these preceding decades had not witnessed the total war of our own age, yet millions of men had been under arms, savage battles had been fought all over Europe from Lisbon to Moscow, revolutionary doctrines of the rights of man had been proclaimed, old regimes had been replaced by new, and old frontiers had been redrawn. For more than ten years Napoleon Bonaparte, as Emperor of the French, had held the greater part of Europe in subjection. Now the mighty adventurer was defeated and sent into distant and permanent exile. At the very center of what had been Napoleon's power sat installed on a royal throne in the Tuileries Louis XVIII, brother of the ruler who had been guillotined in 1793.

The best conservative view of this period was expressed by the British foreign minister, Lord Castlereagh: "It is not our business to collect trophies," he wrote, "but to . . . bring back the world to peaceful habits." The substantial gains made by the principal European powers after their victory over Napoleon were intended, as far as possible, to restore and preserve the old order. No widespread protests against such restoration were immediately evident. In time, to be sure, Italians in Lombardy and Venetia would show that they were as little satisfied to be under the rule of Austria as the three million Belgians were to be united with two million Dutch, or the inhabitants of Poland to be partitioned among Russia, Austria, and Prussia. Yet these dissatisfactions were questions of the future rather than of the immediate present, for national aspirations were slow to find concrete expression. Since modern means of mass communication, such as the daily newspaper and the radio, were absent, public opinion was not easily whipped up, and great causes sometimes remained without a spokesman.

■ THE EUROPEAN SCENE

The man of 1815 lived in a world of stagecoaches and sailing ships, of dirt paths and graveled roads, of canals where slow barges carried much of the coal, grain, timber, and other bulk commodities. It was a world lighted with torches, oil lamps, and candles, a world of books whose type was set laboriously by hand, of newspapers small in size and sparsely furnished with news, often passed from hand to hand among those who could comprehend them. Such readers in most countries were never more than a small fraction of the total population, since at this time more than half the population of Europe could neither read nor write. Even as late as 1860 it was estimated that the proportion of literate persons in Italy, Spain, Portugal, Austria, Russia, and the Balkans was one in ten.

Though the proportion was declining, most Europeans were still concerned with work on the land, whether as owners of great estates, freeholders, tenant farmers, sharecroppers, day laborers, or, in eastern Europe, still as serfs. The picture varied enormously, from the well-to-do yeomen and tenant farmers of England at one extreme to the illiterate serfs of Russia (nine-tenths of its forty million people) at the other. In France the majority of country folk were becoming petty proprietors, cultivating their small holdings in time-honored fashion. In western Germany the peasant farmers were much better off than their fellows east of the Elbe River, where the newly freed serfs of Prussia and Pomerania were still for the most part laborers on the large estates of their former masters. In Spain and the Mediterranean lands, the peasants continued their agelong struggle with poverty. In Austria, Hungary, and Poland the system of dependent tenure on large estates accompanied by compulsory labor (known as *Robot*) was such that the term serfdom could still be applied to it.

Europe's cities and towns were pre-eminently filled with small shops and, in major part, handicraft industries. In their narrow streets skilled artisans and craftsmen turned out their wares, notably the elegant furniture, the fine fabrics and upholsteries, the potteries and porcelains, the handsome silver and glassware, the leatherwork, the jewelry, enamels, swords, firearms, clocks, chronometers, and other instruments of precision, all testifying to the long traditions of European manufacture and intended for a privileged class of purchasers. Steam was in the slow process of being harnessed, so that it would become, in addition to wind and water, the means of driving the new machines developed by the ingenuity of man. The new factories were increasing in size. In England, and to a lesser degree Belgium, the factory chimneys and the ever-increasing number of industrial establishments indicated that the new age of coal and iron was at hand.

Though cities had grown larger, they were not industrialized as we know them today. Alexander I of Russia returned in 1815 to a St. Petersburg where the fine mansions of the aristocracy, the imperial palaces, the great churches, and the buildings housing the ministries dominated the scene as they had done since Peter the Great founded the city. In 1814 Frederick William III rode through the streets of a flower-decked Berlin which still had more suggestion of a market town than of a great capital. The Paris of Louis XVIII, with the exception of a few broad avenues and public squares and the magnificent sweep of the River Seine, was still a maze of narrow, cobbled, badly kept, and poorly lighted streets. Yet changes everywhere were in the making, and not all of these were necessarily for the better. More in the new western centers of industry than in the famous old capitals, industrial workers—the urban proletariat —were beginning to crowd into miserable living quarters adjacent to their employment and to create the slums that in time would disfigure almost every large city of the Continent.

The Europe of 1815, taking the Urals as its eastern boundary, was estimated to have a population of about 200,000,000, the largest number for any state—40,000,000—being found in Russia. France's population was nearly 30,000,000, Austria and Hungary together numbered about the same; the population of Great Britain with Ireland was about 19,000,000, and that of Prussia about 10,000,000. These five powers, then, accounted for well over half the population of Europe. The well-being of these great populations lay much less in their own hands than in those of their masters, for, despite what the French Revolution had done, the social and political system of Europe in 1815 still remained one of privilege.

■ CONSTITUTIONALISM AND AUTOCRACY

Important political legacies had come out of the revolutionary era. The old regime in Europe had made possible a long period of royal and aristocratic pre-eminence in which a minority had monopolized the benefits of wealth and power. The French Revolution had overthrown privilege in France, proclaimed new doctrines of the Rights of Man, and carried much of the new creed abroad to France's neighbors. By the close of 1799 Napoleon Bonaparte had become the master of France. The empire that he proceeded to construct was regarded by the conservative European powers both as a device for imposing his will upon Europe and also as a means for disseminating some of the basic innovations of the French Revolution. They had opposed it and, understandably enough, they took his downfall in 1815 to be a signal for a return to the old order.

Though the past can seldom if ever be restored, men have often been willing to act as if it could. The monarchs who had joined in the last coalition against Napoleon saw no reason to doubt the justice of their traditional authority. Legitimacy was in the ascendant, and many dispossessed rulers—"like worms after the rain," as the German historian, Heinrich von Treitschke, puts it—came forth to assert their old claims. Talleyrand said that the Bourbons who returned after an exile of more than twenty years had learned nothing and forgotten nothing. Victor Emmanuel I of Piedmont and his staff appeared at Turin in 1815 wearing the powdered wigs and the costumes of the old regime. The botanical gardens and the very street lighting introduced at Napoleon's orders were stupidly removed. In France the nobility soon clamored to be compensated for the lands which they had lost under the revolution. "Govern and change nothing," commanded the Emperor Francis I of Austria. Cavour, living in Piedmont, said that in these first years he found his land "an intellectual hell."

Those in authority spoke frankly in support of actual repression. Frederick William III of Prussia, who in the spring of 1815 had promised his people a constitution, a few months later gave his blessing to a ministerial memorandum which quite clearly revoked his earlier pledge. "One must not allow the hotheads," he wrote, "those very active and loud groups of persons who for some years have set up as the nation and cried for a constitution—a gathering place where extreme ideas and feelings would be furthered." The Austrian foreign minister, Metternich, soon declared that the trouble lay with presumptuous men who aspired to do too much and with governments who attempted too little. "When passions are aroused," he told the Austrian emperor, "one must not think of *reforming:* wisdom requires that at such times one limits himself to *maintaining.*" Metternich's friend, Friedrich Gentz, put it more crudely when he wrote, no doubt with conscious exaggeration: "In an age of decay the sole function of a statesman is to prop up moldering institutions." Even so, the monarchies and the aristocracies of 1815 soon found that they could not assert their privileges with quite the same arrogant confidence that they had exhibited before 1789.

The most powerful social force of the new age was to be the rise of a prosperous bourgeois class—the bankers, the manufacturers, the merchants, and the professional men of an increasingly industrialized society. Not yet in control of political power, they were moving in this direction. Even though some of them would acquire titles, it could hardly be expected that titles alone would perpetuate the outlook of an older aristocracy. Many bourgeois leaders were champions of political change, associated with new liberal movements for national unification. The lower middle classes—petty tradesmen, craftsmen, and the like—to say nothing of the new urban proletariat and the peasants, could hardly be expected to play a dynamic role. Yet they in time were to be drawn along by new currents.

The American Revolution and the French Revolution had proclaimed a new concept of the individual in relation to the state—the idea of the *citizen,* a person who has rights guaranteed to him by law and who participates in the work of government through the process of voting and holding office. Constitutionalism had been very much in the air as the eighteenth century progressed, and in America the Thirteen Colonies had triumphantly vindicated their faith in it by establishing the written constitution of the United States of America. France had completed its first written constitution in 1791, prefaced by the famous Declaration of the Rights of Man; between then and 1814 France produced at least six more written constitutions.

Such developments in America and France had widespread and profound effects elsewhere. The Napoleonic kingdom of Italy was equipped with a written constitution in 1805, as was Switzerland by the Act of Mediation in 1803. In 1812 the Spanish liberals drew up a constitution for their country, only to have it repudiated by Ferdinand VII when he returned in 1814. Norway obtained a constitution in the same year providing in effect a single-chamber national assembly and denying the king an absolute veto. A moderately liberal constitution was granted by its ruler in 1815 to the joint kingdom of the United Netherlands, comprising both Holland and Belgium. When Napoleon returned from Elba in March of that year he promised by his Additional Act to give France truly representative, liberal institutions. So likewise Frederick William III of Prussia in that same spring promised a constitution to his country—a pledge not fulfilled until 1848, and not by him. Those parts of Poland which Russia had taken over were promised by the Congress of Vienna a liberal, constitutional regime as a kingdom within the Russian Empire. Under the direction of the distinguished Polish patriot, Prince Adam Czartoryski, Congress Poland obtained, on paper at least, as liberal a constitution as any in Europe. For the German Confederation of 1815 a constitution was provided which contained the vague stipulation that in each of the thirty-nine member states a constitution providing for an assembly should be established.

When the Bourbons returned to France in 1814, Louis XVIII was shrewd enough to promise his people a written constitution. It was quickly drafted by the provisional government—the famous Charter of 1814. Great Britain, much more than France, had its long tradition of parliamentary liberties secured by those historic victories, beginning with Magna Carta, which had been won at critical points in its history. These traditions were none the less genuine, although in 1815 control of the House of Commons still lay very largely in the hands of the landed gentry—a relatively small fraction of the total population. And in many rural constituencies a handful of men, or even one very wealthy man, could control the election.

Granted that constitutionalism, however defective in practice, was a substantial reality in the Europe of 1815, the prevailing winds were blowing in a different direction. The great empires of Russia and Austria were absolutisms untouched by parliamentary restraints, as also were Prussia, Denmark, Spain, Portugal, the Ottoman Empire, and most of the component states of the Germanic Confederation. Political control was still exercised by the hereditary dynasties; they were thoroughly entrenched and they intended to remain. Thus it fell upon a new generation to attempt in some cases to limit the power of the dynasties and in other cases even to upset them.

■ THE GUARANTEE OF EUROPEAN STABILITY

The peacemakers of 1815 had the problem of finding some way to guarantee the security of their arrangements. This was no unique problem, for again and again in its history, though seldom on so large a scale as in 1815, Europe has faced the uncertainties of peace following an age of war. Major threats to the peace have commonly arisen from the rivalries of great dynasties, most notably the Hapsburgs and the Bourbons. Attempts to create a European order which would preserve the peace have all too frequently sprung from the ambitious mind of one dominating figure—a Charles V or a Philip II, a Louis XIV or a Napoleon. Time and again great coalitions have sprung up, seeking a balance of power adequate to curb the overweening ambitions of one such overmighty ruler. But the most typical feature of any coalition is its impermanence. The revolutionary era had seen France burst out beyond her borders. Then Napoleon, the heir of the Revolution, had created his mighty empire consisting of a dramatically enlarged France, a fringe of client states, and then other states—Spain, Italy, Prussia, Austria, and what had been Poland—either allied to him or subject to his will. Five successive coalitions had been needed before Napoleon's overthrow was complete and his empire shattered. Once this was done, diplomats had the double task of rebuilding the European states system and, somehow, ensuring its permanence.

The Congress of Vienna undertook the first of these tasks, and its territorial rearrangements were embodied in the Final Act of the Vienna Congress (June 9, 1815). Following the defeat of Napoleon at Waterloo, the Second Treaty of Paris (November 20, 1815) imposed new terms upon France somewhat less lenient than those of 1814.[1] The second problem was to make the last settlement stick. How were all these arrangements to be made secure? Proposals for a general guarantee of the settlement of Vienna, though raised by Castlereagh, fell through. It is notable that the great powers thought first of the old technique of alliances. They had signed the Treaty of Chaumont in March, 1814, before Napoleon's fall, agreeing to an armed alliance for twenty years against a warlike France. They had renewed this treaty in 1815 on the news of Napoleon's return from Elba. The sword, quite clearly, was to be their first protection.

This was not all. In September, 1815, Tsar Alexander of Russia had surprised the European leaders at Paris by presenting them with his Treaty of Holy Alliance. This document, couched in religious language, was in part the outcome of a not uncommon tendency of people in an age of revolution and upheaval to find comfort and take refuge in a mystical faith based upon

---

1. For the details of this settlement see ch. 1, pp. 17–20.

biblical prophecy. The Treaty of Holy Alliance, which Alexander surprisingly presented in the first instance for the signature of the emperor of Austria and the king of Prussia, urged his brother monarchs to recognize the sublime truths of the Christian religion, to look upon all men as brothers, to view themselves in relation to their subjects as fathers of families, to render mutual service to each other, and to govern their various states as three branches of the same Christian community. It was Alexander's hope that once the rulers of Austria and Prussia had joined with him in this treaty, other monarchs would adhere and "be received into this Holy Alliance with as much cordiality as affection."

The Holy Alliance as Alexander intended it probably does not deserve the contemptuous terms in which Castlereagh and Metternich damned it. Our own age is not unfamiliar with sincere efforts to obtain from political leaders solemn statements of their good intentions. But the greater significance of the Holy Alliance lay in its auspices and surroundings: it was for signature only by *rulers;* it was at first kept secret; and it was quickly and inaccurately rumored to be connected with wicked schemes on the part of Alexander to extend his power in Europe with the backing of his brother monarchs. It therefore stood condemned by liberals from the start. In actuality nearly all European rulers gave perfunctory adherence to the document and went their worldly ways as before. Castlereagh explained to Alexander that the prince regent of England could constitutionally do no more than send a personal letter that did not commit his ministers. Pope Pius VII tartly declared that he did not need instruction in his Christian duties; and the sultan of Turkey, for obvious reasons, made no claim to be admitted to signature of a document so exclusive of his own beliefs. In general the Holy Alliance unhappily created the impression in the minds of European liberals that the monarchs of Europe were united in a sinister league against them.

Far more important as a guarantee of the peace was the Quadruple Alliance signed at Paris in November, 1815. Largely a product of Castlereagh's initiative and welcomed by Metternich, this treaty pledged Britain, Austria, Russia, and Prussia to maintain for twenty years the military alliance secured at Chaumont and renewed at Vienna, and to take action immediately in the event that a return of Napoleon threatened the peace settlement just completed. The new element in this treaty appeared in Article VI. By it the signatories agreed—

> to renew their Meetings at fixed periods, either under the immediate auspices of the Sovereigns themselves, or by their respective Ministers, for the purpose of consulting upon their common interests, and for the consideration of the measures which at each of these periods shall be considered the most salutary for the repose and prosperity of Nations, and for the maintenance of the Peace of Europe.

More than one interpretation is possible of this historic document. In one sense it marks an effort on the part of the great powers to avert the danger of war by holding periodic reunions at which they would consider any dangers to the peace settlement. Thus the treaty can be seen as an early step in the construction of the elaborate machinery of international cooperation as we know it today. On the other hand the Alliance was limited to the four great powers, its scope was not defined, and time was to show that the leaders of Austria, Russia, and Prussia (in other words, a kind of eastern bloc) were increasingly disposed to use this arrangement as a justification for interfering in the internal affairs of any country where a threat to the *status quo* could be detected. Such was not the original purpose of Castlereagh; and, as the conservative aspects of the treaty became more prominent, its prime purpose of concerning itself with the "repose and prosperity of the Nations" became clouded. As the year 1815 closed, nevertheless, European statesmen might well have had some justification for thinking that they had at last succeeded in inaugurating an era of enduring peace.

■ THE CONFLICT OF TWO WORLDS IN THE ARTS

While it is easy to see that an age of revolution and war may speed up social and technological change and introduce dramatic innovations in politics, corresponding changes do not always occur in the realms of literature and the arts. An era of revolution, indeed, may well throw serious obstacles in the way of cultural advance. The Jacobins of the French Revolution sent the poet, André Chénier, and the great chemist, Antoine Lavoisier, to the guillotine. Napoleon's policies drove into exile the two greatest literary figures of his age, Chateaubriand and Madame de Staël, and his despotism did little to encourage anything save "official" art. Even so, the closing decades of the eighteenth and the opening decades of the nineteenth centuries together make up a transitional period of enormous importance in the general progress of European culture.

Europe entered the age of the Restoration with its conservatively organized state-system apparently thriving and, it was hoped, adequately safeguarded. But the intellectual climate of 1815 was still marked by the conflict between two generations, if not between two worlds. "I call Classic that which is healthy," declared Goethe, "Romantic, that which is sick." The persistence of the European classical tradition in painting, sculpture, architecture, and to a lesser degree in literature is an extraordinary tribute to its vitality. The neoclassicism of the late eighteenth century represented an effort to return to those purer forms which had undergone a veritable transformation in the baroque and rococo eras. This renewed classicism assumed a new form in what has come to be called the "Empire style" of the Napoleonic age—that heavy, gilded, imperial style in which the Egyptian elements, such as sphinxes' heads and claws, took their place among the urns, cameos, and pilasters of the traditional classical *décor*. Some of the great monuments of Paris today—the Church of the Madeleine, the Vendôme Column, the Carrousel Arch, and the Arch of Triumph—have their origins in this lavish imperial period. The architecture of the classical revival, so evident in the imposing public buildings and monuments of cities such as Berlin and Munich, carried on this tradition into the opening decades of the nineteenth century. Yet with this persistence of traditionalism, most evident in the solid field of architecture, powerful new forces were at work which soon took dramatic shape in the various cultural aspects of the Romantic Revolution.

The arts showed a genuine ferment. In literature the departure from the classical conventions had been foreshadowed in some of the poetry and prose of the mid-eighteenth century. Gray's "Elegy in a Country Churchyard" was composed in 1750. Rousseau's great works were written chiefly in the 1760's. The publication by Coleridge and Wordsworth of *Lyrical Ballads* in 1798 and the appearance of the first part of Chateaubriand's *Genius of Christianity* in 1800 opened the door to a new romantic age. Madame de Staël's *On Germany* (1810) first suggested the richness of a German culture that had long been regarded as almost barbaric. In 1814 Sir Walter Scott turned from his career as a poet to publish *Waverley*, the first of the long list of historical novels that captivated Europe and did so much to romanticize the past. Beethoven's *Eroica Symphony* (1804) likewise was the harbinger of a new age in music. Some of the paintings of the Spanish artist, Goya—his moving "Third of May," for example—stir profound human emotions in dramatic contrast with classical art. At Paris, Géricault's "Raft of the Medusa," a tormented painting of human beings suffering and dying on a raft at sea, created a sensation when it was shown at the Salon of 1819. The long reign of classicism in architecture was challenged by the Gothic revival, anticipations of which emerged earlier when, for example, Horace Walpole had begun in mid-century to remodel his villa, Strawberry Hill, in mock Gothic style. This addition of battlements, gargoyles, oriel windows, and Gothic arches to buildings of another era, whether churches, villas, or domestic interiors, was evidence of a kind of conscious artificiality— a deliberate attempt to manufacture an unreal, romantic past.

Side by side with these artistic changes were comparable developments in other fields which gave men a much richer appreciation of their past. The decade of the 1820's was to be one of the most fruitful in the growth of modern philology, most notably in the studies made by the brothers Grimm of German language and folklore, and the great work of Bopp in comparative philology, a work which brought out the basic similarity of Sanskrit, Greek, Latin, and

Germanic verb forms. Like studies were made of the Romance languages. Historical scholars, emulating the fantastic erudition of the Italian Muratori in the eighteenth century, began to compile the sources dealing with their country's history. The first volume of the great German source collection, *Monumenta Germaniae Historica*, appeared in 1826 and the first volume of the French *Documents inédits* in 1833. This growth in historical studies was accompanied by the growth of a new concept of law—a law not based exclusively on the logical maxims of the great Roman texts but founded instead upon the past life and customs of each separate people. It is striking to see how these technical and scholarly achievements, many of them remote from the busy currents of public life, contributed to the surging growth of nationalism as a major force during the nineteenth century.

In 1815 such developments were not as yet in full tide. Yet the beginnings had been made, so that the great decades of the 1820's and 1830's were able to display a kaleidoscope of color in the fields of culture and learning and the arts which made a striking contrast to the prevailing gray traditionalism of political life.

■ PROSPECTS OF THE NINETEENTH CENTURY

The immediate problems encountered during the first years of peace can give at best only a partial suggestion of the enormous changes that were in store for Europe. The history of the period from 1815 to 1871 shows clearly that the conservative order of European society was unable to maintain itself when faced with so many new challenges. Despite the ingrained habits of life and livelihood which went back for centuries, Europe experienced a transformation which was in part evolutionary and in part revolutionary in nature. It is a commonplace to say that the steadily accelerating tempo of such changes, beginning in the nineteenth century and continuing into the twentieth, was of a kind to which earlier centuries could offer no parallel.

In the economic sphere, the Industrial Revolution was to set its mark upon one country after another. Spurred on by continued advances in technology and by the vigorous efforts of a new class of business leaders, this great acceleration in industrial production—to single out only one of its aspects—was associated with, and at least partly responsible for, political and social changes of major proportions. And it is also true that industrial advances made possible new weapons of mass destruction and new methods of military transportation that were to transform the accepted techniques of warfare.

Political changes were soon to appear. The constitutional doctrines of the French Revolution were reasserted, despite all efforts of the conservatives to suppress them. The relatively moderate demands of the liberals for political rights met not infrequently with stubborn opposition, soon to be followed by revolutionary efforts intended to speed up the process by which such rights could be acquired and to enlarge the objectives of the movement. Whatever the failures of such revolutions—and they were many—by 1871, parliamentary regimes, based on a more or less representative franchise, were the rule in Europe rather than the exception.

Nationalism was to become one of the most powerful of all the new forces at work. The French Revolution had been the period during which nationalism first assumed a truly militant form. As one subject people after another felt the power of its doctrines, vague national aspirations gradually crystallized into programs of action. This was true of some parts of the Balkans and also of Italy; new national states were born of the sword and baptized in blood. Elsewhere the once loosely associated German states were united by the same ruthless process.

Economic and political changes were accompanied by an active concern with the continuing problem of social justice. Here the Industrial Revolution placed new strains upon the fabric of European society by dramatizing the great disparities of wealth, by bringing into prominence a new and powerful business class, and by replacing the peasant with the "wage slave"—the individual whose problems loomed largest on the social horizon. New views of human society became common, whether in the benignly utopian schemes of a Robert Owen or a Charles Fourier, or the militantly revolutionary theories of Karl Marx. Not only an enormous literature of discussion and propaganda, but also the active organization of men to attain new social goals became characteristic of this period. But the movement from theory to realization was certainly not a stampede. Marx's *Communist Manifesto* appeared in 1848; the International Workingmen's Association was organized in 1864; and a lone socialist deputy sat in the first parliament of the North German Confederation in 1867.

Since the middle decades of the nineteenth century were a dramatic period of state-making, it is hardly surprising that they witnessed the new leadership of vigorous and astute men in the age-old game of international politics. Metternich, with all his great abilities, had moved through the first half of the century with the airs and viewpoint of a seigneur of the *ancien régime*. Lord Palmerston, perhaps more than any other, combined something of this same tradition with a peculiarly British self-confidence and assertiveness that enabled his country to play a vigorous and effective role in European affairs. Napoleon III of France and Count Cavour of Italy were in truth men of a new age. This latter-day Napoleon combined a dramatic sense of France's destiny with a genuine concern for national aspirations and for the creation of a European order. His failures should not obscure the virtues of many of his proposals. Cavour used every diplomatic wile and expedient to make the unity of Italy a triumphant reality. More spectacularly successful than either, Otto von Bismarck displayed during the decade of the 1860's a ruthless virtuosity in diplomacy and war that enabled him to unite his country, using techniques to which the German word *Realpolitik* is still commonly applied.

The transition from romanticism to realism in the arts marked these same decades. The basic scientific discoveries of the period were to make possible the dynamic technological advances which enlarged man's control over nature and vastly added to the world's material wealth and population. In this age of political realism many disputants employed the new theories concerning man's evolutionary place in the world of nature to challenge traditional religious views. In the world of politics itself a new emphasis was given to the conviction (much older, to be sure, than the nineteenth century) that in human affairs the race was to the swift and the battle to the strong.

Chapter 1

The Years
of Uncertainty, 1815–1848

The European Territorial Settlement
Authority as a Principle of Rule
The Congress System
First Breaches in the Established Order
Social Unrest and Its Causes
Liberalism
The Beginnings of Modern Socialism
Nationalism

■ THE EUROPEAN TERRITORIAL SETTLEMENT

The territorial arrangements made in the great European peace settlements of 1814 and 1815 were the outward signs of the permanent order which the leading powers hoped they had successfully established. Such permanence was to be assured in three ways: first, by augmenting the strength of those major states who were taken to be the principal guardians of the peace; second, by restoring wherever possible or by compensating those legitimate rulers who had been dispossessed; and, third, by setting up special bulwarks against any new aggression from France. These complex arrangements are the obvious starting point for the history of the nineteenth century.

The negotiations were threefold. After Napoleon's first defeat and abdication the Treaty of Paris (May, 1814) drew up terms of settlement with France. A year later the Final Act of the Vienna Congress (June, 1815) embodied all

16

SIGNIFICANT EVENTS

1815   Final Act of the Congress of Vienna (June)
        Treaty of Holy Alliance (September)
        Treaty of Quadruple Alliance (November)
1818   Prussian Tariff Act
        Congress of Aix-la-Chapelle
1819   Carlsbad Decrees
1820   Revolution in Spain (January) and Naples (July)
        Congress of Troppau
1821   Revolution in Moldavia and Greece; Congress of Laibach
1822   Congress of Verona
1823   President Monroe's message to Congress
1825   Decembrist Revolt in Russia
1827   Battle of Navarino
1830   London Protocol recognizing Greek Independence
        Bourbon monarchy replaced by Orleanist line in France (July)
        Revolution in Belgium (August) and Poland (November)
1833   Treaty of Unkiar-Skelessi between Russia and Turkey
        Zollverein established in Germany
1841   Straits Convention

the elaborate provisions agreed upon by the European powers, large and small, in the course of their nine-months negotiations at Vienna. Finally, the Second Treaty of Paris (November, 1815) imposed more severe terms upon France in consequence of her rallying to Napoleon during the Hundred Days.

The total effect of these various treaty arrangements can be briefly summarized as follows. France went back roughly to the frontiers of 1792. She was forced to give up some frontier fortifications allowed her in 1814, to cede French Savoy to the kingdom of Piedmont, to pay a 700,000,000-franc indemnity, and accept an army of occupation of 150,000 men for five years. She subsequently was required to return some, but by no means all, of the art treasures she had seized throughout Europe. Yet clearly she remained a great power, regaining most of her colonies except Tobago, St. Lucia, and Mauritius. As for the general European settlement, the powers at Vienna tried to restore as

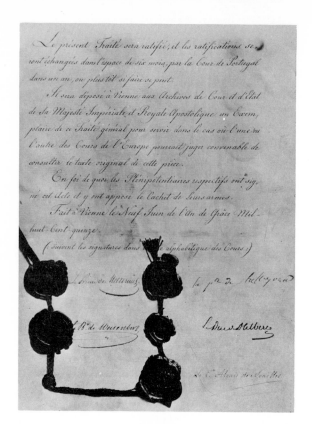

much as they could of the old order ("legitimacy") and, when they could not, to provide an adequate alternative ("compensation"). Their interests were largely selfish, and thus, since these were broadly satisfied, it was clearly to their advantage to maintain what they had restored.

The new European map of 1815 was largely redrawn in the interests of the great powers. Russia, whose Tsar Alexander I regarded himself with some reason as the central figure in the overthrow of Napoleon, made impressive gains in the northern, central, and southern parts of her western borders. She kept Finland, won from Sweden in 1809; she obtained the greater part of Poland; and she kept Bessarabia, that Black Sea province won from the Turks in 1812 which brought her one step nearer to Constantinople. Austria consolidated her power in central Europe by regaining the Tyrol, Polish Galicia, and the lost portions of Carinthia and Carniola. Salzburg, Venetia, Istria, and Dalmatia, which she now also regained, had been acquired under Napoleon and then quickly taken from her. Lombardy, now substantially larger than the duchy of Milan, which the Hapsburgs held throughout the eighteenth century, was joined with Venetia to form a new kingdom under the Hapsburg crown. Thus, by moving down through the Brenner Pass, Austria stood guard in northern Italy against any future threat from France and at the same time exercised a powerful influence over the mosaiclike pattern of small states into

18

EUROPE in 1815

	MILES
0 100 200 300 400 500	

GAINS BY:

▨ PRUSSIA

▥ AUSTRIA

▦ RUSSIA

— GERMAN
CONFEDERATION

FINLAND

SWEDEN
and NORWAY

DENMARK

RUSSIAN
EMPIRE

NETHERLANDS

HANOVER

P R U S S I A

POSEN

KINGDOM
OF
POLAND

LUXEMBOURG

RHINELAND

SAXONY

BAVARIA

GALICIA

BESSARABIA

FRANCE

SWITZ.ᴰ

BADEN

SALZBURG

TYROL

AUSTRIAN

EMPIRE

LOMBARDY

VENETIA

PIEDMONT

DALMATIA

OTTOMAN

EMPIRE

SARDINIA

TUSCANY

PAPAL
STATES

SPAIN

CORSICA

KINGDOM OF SARDINIA

SARDINIA

KINGDOM OF
THE TWO
SICILIES

which the rest of the peninsula was divided: the kingdom of Piedmont (enlarged by gains from France and by the former Republic of Genoa), the duchies of Parma, Modena, and Lucca, the grand duchy of Tuscany, the Papal States, and the kingdom of Naples.

Prussia likewise was compensated for the deep humiliation Napoleon had caused her. She won substantial territories from two of her neighbors, Poland and Saxony. The province of Posen and adjacent land, now regained, constituted those areas won in the Polish partitions of 1772 and 1793, and subsequently taken by Napoleon to create the grand duchy of Warsaw. Some scattered Prussian territories lying between the Rhine and the Elbe and lost at Tilsit were now restored. The Saxon provinces (amounting to about two-fifths of that kingdom and having about 850,000 subjects) were a new acquisition, as were the important areas of Westphalia and Rhenish Prussia, standing guard across the Rhine against France. Great Britain's gains were colonial: Malta, Mauritius, Tobago, St. Lucia, Ceylon, and the Cape of Good Hope.

The creation of a German Confederation of thirty-nine states under Austrian presidency was, though lamentably weak, intended as some contribution to European order. The inclusion of the former Austrian Netherlands (Belgium) in the new kingdom of the United Netherlands was designed to set up a bulwark in the north against French aggression. The guarantee of Swiss neutrality, the extension of Prussian control in the Rhineland and of Austrian control in northern Italy, and the enlargement of Piedmont were all for this same purpose of resisting any dangerous advance on the part of France.

The Treaty of Holy Alliance, which the Tsar Alexander persuaded his brother monarchs to sign at Paris in September, 1815, was not, save through the misinterpretations and fears which it aroused, an active element in European policy. The Quadruple Alliance, on the other hand, played a most significant role during the first years of peace.[1] It will be important, therefore, to investigate the degree of success obtained by the European powers in maintaining the settlement which they had so laboriously created.

■ AUTHORITY AS A PRINCIPLE OF RULE

Though the nineteenth century has quite generally been regarded as a period of steady and impressive progress, its first decades following the defeat of Napoleon saw the rulers of states, almost without exception, dedicated to maintaining things as they were. "When I was at the top of the St. Gothard pass," the poet Heine wrote, "I heard Germany snoring." The dramatic interest of the decades between 1815 and 1848 is that gradually a challenge to this system of somnolent authority developed. In some cases rulers made changes voluntarily and peaceably. Some lesser revolts failed. By 1848 the tensions

1. For these two documents see pp. 9–11.

were such that a dramatic series of explosions introduced the revolutionary struggles which for more than a year were to affect large areas on the Continent.

What the conservative statesmen were seeking to do in practice found justification in the arguments of some remarkably eloquent theorists. Much earlier, in the background of the American and French revolutions, the names of Locke, Montesquieu, Rousseau, and Jefferson had stood out as the most distinguished champions of the doctrines of natural law, natural rights, and individual liberties. Their writings now came under heavy attack. The great starting point of the literature of the conservative era had been the publication in 1790 of Edmund Burke's *Reflections on the Revolution in France.* This member of the British House of Commons profoundly disliked what he saw across the Channel. Society, he protested, is not a mechanical structure that can be altered at will whenever some clever man produces new blueprints. It is not like a business partnership that can be reconstituted whenever the members choose to do so. It is rather a living organism, like a tree, with its roots deep in the past. Change will come about slowly through natural growth and not through the wild-eyed schemes of those whom Burke called "Cannibal philosophers."

Burke's volume was translated into German and his ideas popularized by Friedrich von Gentz, a publicist of great fluency, a friend of Metternich, and one of the principal secretaries of the Congress of Vienna. Another distinguished German theorist, Adam Müller, preached similar doctrines in which he visualized the state as an organic unity directed by absolute power. The greatest German philosopher of this period, Friedrich Hegel, saw the state in somewhat the same light. "The state," he wrote, "is not an artificial creation, but a natural organism which represents one phase in the historical evolution of the world." Also in Germany other writers combined authoritarian views of the state with a desire to re-establish the Christian pattern of life as it had once existed, so they believed, in the unity of medieval Roman Catholic Europe.

Conservative writers in France pleaded for a close alliance between "the Throne and the Altar." If all power comes from God, men need no longer believe that political societies are built, as Rousseau taught, on the will of men and the social contract. No position was too extreme for some of these conservative theorists. Joseph de Maistre placed central in his political scheme the grim figure of the executioner. "All greatness, all power, all order," he wrote, "depend upon the executioner. He is the tie that binds society together. Take away this incomprehensible force and at that very moment order is suspended by chaos, thrones fall, and states disappear." Such extreme views were not characteristic of England, yet even there a strong appeal to tradition was obvious in the novels of Sir Walter Scott, as it also came to be in the political views of members of the Lake School of poetry—Wordsworth, Southey, and

CLASSIC AND ROMANTIC. The classic interior of the Pantheon in Paris, designed by Soufflot and completed in 1789, contrasts strikingly with the neo-Gothic design prepared in 1810 by the German architect, Schinkel, for the tomb of Queen Louise of Prussia.

Coleridge—particularly in their aging years. Whether fanatics or moderates, the common element of these conservative theorists is found in their desire to stress unity and stability in the social structure and to take a determined stand against the advocates of radical change.

Such theoretical views were borne out in the practice of governments. In England the conservative prime minister, Lord Liverpool, viewed with frank alarm the unrest arising from bad harvests, the enclosure of the old open fields of the villages, the wretched conditions of the new factory workers, and the generally hard times. Firm action was felt to be necessary. In 1817 the Habeas Corpus Act had been temporarily suspended so that individuals could be held in prison without trial, and old laws had been refurbished in order to ban "seditious" meetings and put heavy penalties on "disloyalty." In 1819 an even more rigorous code of legislation was passed.[2]

In France the restored Bourbon monarchy, while playing its hand cautiously and not unskillfully, was quite clearly on the conservative side. In the elections of 1815 a majority of Ultras, as the extreme royalists were called, was chosen. They moved at once to produce a law forbidding divorce, a strict censorship of the press, and the creation of special courts to try cases of treason. In 1816 Louis XVIII dissolved the Chamber which had actually embarrassed him by its excessive zeal. The king was still on the side of authoritarianism, yet he was shrewd, and in a practical sense moderate; like Charles II of England he had no desire to go on his travels again. The new elections brought in a less reactionary group, yet the Ultras persisted as a vigorous opposition. When Louis XVIII died in 1824, his brother and successor, Charles X, made it clear that he was emphatically on the side of conservatism. Thus the Ultras now had some expectation of realizing their full program, an example of their success being that within a year the government had authorized the payment of financial compensation with a capital value of a billion francs to former *émigrés* who had lost their landed property during the Revolution.

This pattern of conservatism was widespread. In Spain the reaction was complete. Ferdinand VII, restored to the throne in 1814, repudiated the constitution which the Spanish parliament had proclaimed two years before. He established a severe censorship, restored lands to the Church, reintroduced the Inquisition, and granted landlords important judicial powers over their tenants. The same pattern of conservatism, though on a lesser scale, could be seen in the kingdom of the United Netherlands, where King William I of the House of Orange, though ruling by means of a moderately liberal constitution, insisted on maintaining an unquestioned Dutch supremacy over three million resentful and irreconcilable Belgians. In Switzerland, where the federal Diet

2. See p. 191.

operated under the new Constitution of 1815, principal power still lay with the governments of the twenty-two cantons, which were preponderantly conservative and oligarchic in nature. The "Era of Regeneration" in Switzerland did not begin until 1828.

In Scandinavia, conservative tendencies were less emphatic. Denmark saw some growth of liberal and national feeling. Norway, whose union with Sweden was approved by the Congress of Vienna, had obtained a constitution in 1814 guaranteeing some degree of parliamentary government. In Sweden, however, King Charles XIV (Bernadotte) engaged in a vigorous conflict with the estates after his accession in 1818, trying to extend his royal prerogatives.

The conservative reaction was strongly in evidence throughout Italy. Repression was at its worst in the kingdom of the Two Sicilies, where Ferdinand I abolished the Constitution of 1812 and launched a veritable reign of terror. The Papal States were steeped in reaction, as to a somewhat lesser degree were Parma, Modena, and Lucca. In Tuscany the despotism was at least benevolent. Austria ruled the kingdom of Lombardy and Venetia with the combined forces of the soldier, the customs official, and the policeman. Austrian influence, moreover, was spread widely throughout the entire peninsula. Even in Piedmont—the most advanced territory of Italy—despotism was in operation, though here a certain degree of economic progress gave evidence of a vitality lacking elsewhere except in Lombardy.

In the great areas of Central Europe which composed the rest of the Hapsburg Empire, the "Metternich system" was soon in full flood. The Austrian foreign minister was a man of high intelligence, a cosmopolitan of the eighteenth century, who had played a major role in the overthrow of the Napoleonic Empire. His system was based on a frank recognition of the conflicting German, Italian, Slavic, and Magyar elements which only an absolute monarchy, so he believed, could successfully direct. He would be willing to accept the work of local diets, but never to introduce parliamentary institutions on the topmost level. Metternich knew all too well the limitations imposed upon him by having to serve an autocratic emperor of limited intellectual abilities and having to depend on a host of incompetent officials. "I have governed Europe sometimes," Metternich once wrote, "Austria never." In 1819, after the outbreak of student disturbances and unrest in the German Confederation, Metternich summoned representatives of the nine principal German states to Carlsbad, where they drew up a series of decrees which within a month were submitted to the Diet of the German Confederation and promptly ratified. These Carlsbad Decrees dissolved many student societies, imposed inspectors on the German universities, and authorized a very strict censorship of the press. At a conference of the German states at Vienna in 1820 the Decrees were reasserted. Their effect was to create an atmosphere of intolerance, to drive many distinguished professors from their posts into exile, and to fetter liberal opinion for a generation.

The German Confederation, of which Austria was perpetual president, had a Diet sitting at Frankfort which was really a congress of delegates of the thirty-nine governments, acting under instructions and powerless to legislate on its own. The imposition of the Carlsbad Decrees was an example of the way in which Metternich could use this Diet to maintain the whip hand of Austria over Germany. Article XIII of the Federal Act of 1815 had provided that in each of the member states a constitution with assemblies of estates "will be established." This, it was wryly said, gave the states little more than the unlimited right of expectation. In point of fact, beginning with Saxe-Weimar in 1816, eight constitutions had been granted by 1820.[3] These, to be sure, were all royal grants. They were limited with respect to suffrage, and did not notably moderate the general conservative pattern in the Confederation as a whole. Frederick William III of Prussia had promised in 1815 to summon a representative assembly for his kingdom, but he failed to do so, and, indeed, made it clear to his ministers and to the public that he proposed to continue in the absolutist tradition of his Hohenzollern ancestors.

In Russia the paradox existed of an absolutist tsar who had permitted a constitutional regime, created in earlier times, to continue in Finland after he annexed it in 1809. He also established a constitutional regime, as he had promised by the Vienna settlement, in Congress Poland. Between 1816 and 1819 he abolished serfdom in the Baltic Provinces. Yet these actions represented only one aspect of his policy. Alexander's interests were much more in the field of European affairs than in domestic matters; and when, at length, he did look homeward he was soon shaken by the signs of disaffection which he discovered. The mutiny of the crack Semenovsky Regiment in 1820 was a shock and a decisive turning point; henceforth he depended increasingly upon his brutal and reactionary minister, Alexander Arakcheev, for advice.

Few periods are absolutely uniform in nature. These years in which conservatism was so obviously in the saddle were marked by occasional unrest. If Germany was asleep, the note of protest was soon to be heard in the Balkans, in Italy, and in Spain. The machinery of the congress system had been set up by the great powers in 1815 to take account of such unrest and to consider from time to time those measures "most salutary for the peace of Europe." In the workings of this system, which had been authorized in the Quadruple Alliance of 1815, we may observe some striking examples of the conflict between peoples beginning the struggle for freedom and rulers whose purpose it was to resist change.

3. The states, in chronological order, were: Saxe-Weimar, Baden, Württemberg, Bavaria, Hesse-Darmstadt, Lippe-Detmold, Nassau, and Hanover.

■ THE CONGRESS SYSTEM

In international affairs, the principal powers who had defeated Napoleon were likewise determined to maintain the settlement they had made. While Alexander I's nebulous Holy Alliance may be regarded as a pious expression of good intentions, accepted skeptically by realistic rulers, Castlereagh's[4] Treaty of Quadruple Alliance was real enough. As we have seen, it bound together Great Britain, Austria, Russia, and Prussia in a twenty-year alliance, one feature of which was to be the holding of periodic reunions to consider any possible threats to the peace of the Continent.[5] The first meeting was held at Aix-la-Chapelle, in the Rhineland, in 1818. France, having paid her indemnity, was quickly freed from the army of occupation. As a respectable, conservative power, France was admitted to what now became a Quintuple Alliance, though the original members saw fit secretly to renew their original alliance against a still-possible Napoleonic return. All members were satisfied—"I have never seen a more charming little congress," Metternich wrote—and, indeed, never again during the nineteenth century did the diplomatic machinery apparently function so smoothly.

The almost immediate sequel to this idyllic picture was sensational. In 1819 Germany was thrown into an uproar when Karl Sand, a young divinity student, murdered August von Kotzebue, a German dramatist and conservative, reputed to be a Russian spy. Early in 1820 the Duke de Berri, nephew and heir of Louis XVIII, was assassinated in Paris. In London a plot was discovered to blow up the entire British cabinet while at dinner. Yet these events, however alarming, were mere episodes in contrast to the actual revolts which flared up in 1820, first in Spain and then in Southern Italy and Portugal. These were quickly followed in 1821 by three further revolts, in Piedmont, in the distant Ottoman provinces of Moldavia-Wallachia and in southern Greece.

A second meeting of the powers was held at Troppau, in Silesia, where the British and French representatives came as observers without plenary authority. Here, late in 1820, the divergence between the moderate views of the English, who did not wish the congress system to become a machinery for automatic intervention and repression, and those of Metternich and Alexander I became apparent. In November, Austria, Russia, and Prussia issued the famous Troppau Protocol, a document which declared bluntly that they would not recognize changes brought about by revolutionary means, and, moreover,

---

4. 1769–1822. As secretary of state for war under William Pitt, he absorbed many of Pitt's views concerning the remaking of Europe. He fought a duel with Canning, was foreign secretary from 1812 until his death in 1822, and worked hard at the Congress of Vienna to establish a "just equilibrium." He was principal architect of the congress system following 1815, by which the major powers were to keep the peace by retaining effective control of international affairs in their own hands.
5. See pp. 10–11.

that they would claim the right to intervene with force if these changes threatened neighboring countries. The revolt at Naples had forced the unspeakable Ferdinand I to accept a constitution. At Madrid and elsewhere in Spain military risings had compelled Ferdinand VII to accept a wildly democratized version of the constitution of 1812. Risings similar in nature occurred in Portugal. Castlereagh, whose views were moderate, fought hard to prevent the congress from becoming a mere instrument of repression. "The Great Alliance," he had explained in May to British missions abroad, ". . . never was intended as a Union for the Government of the World, or for the superintendence of the internal affairs of other states." The Troppau Protocol, he told Parliament, "was destitute of common sense." Yet he fought in vain. When wintry weather set in, the Congress left Troppau for the sunny skies of Laibach, further south. Here, where the injured Ferdinand of Naples turned up in person, it was agreed that the rising in Naples was the principal danger. Hence Austria, with her special interests in Italy, was authorized to send an army to the south. She quickly did so, restoring Ferdinand to an absolutist throne. On its way back this army then helped to put down a constitutional revolt that had flared up in the kingdom of Piedmont. Despite Castlereagh's wishes and warnings, the policy of military intervention and repression was a fact.

By 1822 the questions of Greece and Spain were both urgent. Greece presented a particularly vexing problem, for a large "philhellenic" emotion had grown up in western Europe, and it was hard for the most dedicated reactionary to feel indifferent when the presumed descendants of Plato and Pericles struggled to free themselves from the non-Christian Turk. Yet the Greeks were revolutionaries, and the western powers had good reason to fear that if Russia joined in helping them the outcome might be more favorable to the Russian than to the Greek cause. Broken by the strain of his duties, Castlereagh cut his throat in 1822. His successor, George Canning, had no use for the congress system. A meeting had, nevertheless, been summoned for Verona in October, 1822. When it convened, the British representative, the Duke of Wellington, carried out the instructions written by Castlereagh and approved by Canning, making it clear that if intervention by force was planned in Spain, then, "come what may," Britain would not be a party. France, understandably concerned about the revolutionary fires burning on her neighbor's soil, obtained the approval which she desired from Austria, Russia, and Prussia. In April, 1823, a French army crossed the Pyrenees, marched to Madrid, and restored the incompetent Ferdinand VII to absolutism. The parallel to Austrian action in Naples was striking. Soon thereafter the king of Portugal, encouraged by the successful venture of the French in Spain, felt strong enough to revoke the constitution which the Portuguese revolutionaries had proclaimed in 1820.

The meetings at Verona marked the definite end of the congress system, which in point of fact had begun to fall apart much earlier. Canning soon demonstrated how England could, if need be, act on her own. The Spanish colonies of South America, with whom England had built up a very profitable trade, one by one asserted their independence. The real danger in 1823 was that Spain, helped by what were loosely described as the powers of the Holy Alliance, might try to win them back. Canning first had proposed a joint statement from Great Britain and the United States against this, and had warned Polignac, the French ambassador at London, in a famous memorandum that the British fleet would forcibly oppose any French attempt to restore Spanish dominion in the New World. The United States chose not to associate itself with Canning, John Quincy Adams, the secretary of state, not wishing to be like "a cock-boat in the wake of the British man-of-war." Acting separately, President Monroe sent his famous message to Congress in December, 1823, stating that European intervention in the western hemisphere could not be viewed "in any other light than as the manifestation of an unfriendly disposition toward the United States." This was Monroe's great contribution. With it must be linked Canning's Polignac Memorandum. Yet emphasis on Canning's role should not obscure the fact that the independence of South America was won largely by South Americans themselves.

■ FIRST BREACHES IN THE ESTABLISHED ORDER

Evidence soon grew that the maintenance of the established order would not be easy. The European powers had the problem of the Ottoman Empire, where Serbian revolts, beginning in 1804 in the northern limits of Turkish territory, had led by 1817 to a practical condition of Serbian autonomy—a state of affairs much less, to be sure, than independence. Early in 1821 other revolts, far more serious in their consequences, broke out in the extreme north and the extreme south of Turkey's European possessions. These were the outcome of a Greek cultural revival in the eighteenth century which had as one consequence the organization at Odessa in 1814, with Russian assistance, of a secret society, the *Hetairia Philike*, for the purpose of resurrecting the medieval Greek Christian Empire. The revolt began in March under the leadership of Prince Alexander Ypsilanti in Moldavia, a principality bordering on Russia's newly acquired province of Bessarabia. The Turks quickly brought this revolt under control and imprisoned Ypsilanti. Then a second revolt flared up in the southernmost area of Greece known as the Morea. This the Turks began to put down with great savagery, massacring large numbers of civilians and going so far as to hang the Greek patriarch of Constantinople in his sacred vestments outside his palace and to throw his body into the Bosphorus. Alexander I of Russia understandably wished to intervene, but was opposed by Metternich, the foe of all revolutions, who proposed quite cynically that the Greek revolt should be permitted "to burn itself out beyond the pale of civilization." When the Greeks, unfortunately for Metternich, continued to show a remarkable capacity to strike back, European sympathy for them rose in a loud chorus. In March, 1823, Canning went so far as to recognize the Greeks as belligerents. Volunteers began to go to Greece, among them Lord Byron, whose death at Missolonghi on the Gulf of Corinth in the following year caused a European sensation. He had written his own best epitaph:

> The mountains look on Marathon—
>   And Marathon looks on the sea;
> And musing there an hour alone,
>   I dreamed that Greece might still be free;
> For standing on the Persians' grave,
> I could not deem myself a slave.

The barbaric fury of the Greeks almost equaled that of the Turks; when, for example, they captured the Turkish fortress of Tripolitsa they massacred the more than ten thousand captives whom they took.

A new turn came in 1825 when the Turkish sultan, now in danger of defeat, summoned aid from his powerful vassal, Mehemet Ali, Pasha of Egypt. The Turkish-Egyptian successes were so great that the European powers once more became gravely concerned. Despite his aversion to the congress system, Canning in 1826 sent the Duke of Wellington to St. Petersburg to see whether England and Russia together could find some way to secure Greek autonomy within the Ottoman Empire. By the Treaty of London (1827) France joined Britain and Russia in agreeing to establish this autonomy by enforced mediation. A combined British, French, and Russian squadron was dispatched and, when fired upon, it destroyed a large Egyptian fleet of warships and transports that had arrived in Navarino Bay on the west coast of the Morea (October, 1827). This disaster for Turkey was followed by a Russian declaration of war in the following spring. After a slow start the Russian armies, to the alarm of Europe, advanced almost to the gates of Constantinople.

No European concert in the formal sense now existed, yet clearly some kind of joint action was essential. An ambassadorial conference of Britain, Russia, and France, meeting at London in March, 1829, agreed that southern Greece, below a line running from Arta on the Mediterranean coast to Volo on the Aegean (see map, p. 394, should be autonomous. This led to the Treaty of Adrianople between Russia and Turkey (September, 1829) by which autonomy was conceded to Greece, Serbia, and the principalities of Moldavia and Wallachia. Russia won slight frontier extensions in the Danube delta and in the Caucasus.

Greek independence—the first breach in the *status quo* since 1815—was formally agreed upon by Britain, France, and Russia in February, 1830. Not until 1832, however, were Greece's boundaries defined, and a ruler found in the person of Otto, son of King Ludwig of Bavaria, who was prepared to accept the Greek crown. Though the Greek state was much smaller than its people had hoped for, independence had been won and recognized by the powers. These changes, moreover, had come about in a Europe where the maintenance of the established order had been for more than a decade very close to being an article of religious faith.

Belgian independence represented a direct breach in the treaty structure of 1815. The union of the Belgians and the Dutch had not worked; indeed, one may question whether it ever had the slightest prospect of success. Overwhelmingly Roman Catholic, sympathetic to France, much more advanced industrially than the Dutch, different in law and language, the Belgians bitterly resented the new regime imposed upon them. It took only the outbreak of revolution in Paris in July, 1830, to trigger a similar explosion in Brussels. Fighting against the Dutch authorities broke out in August, and by October independence had been proclaimed. An international conference was held at London where Lord Palmerston, fearing that the new French government might interfere on behalf of the Belgian revolutionaries with deep designs to place a son of King Louis Philippe on the throne, or even to annex Belgium, sought quick recognition of Belgian independence. He succeeded, and a provisional agreement of 1831 recognized Leopold of Saxe-Coburg as king of an independent Belgium. Dutch opposition necessitated some slight naval and military action by the French and British—pressure rather than actual war. Few international settlements, however, have taken longer to complete, and the stubborn Dutch did not finally agree until eight years later. Then, in 1839, the five great powers signed the London Treaty which, with its guarantee of "perpetual neutrality" so fateful in its ultimate consequences, placed the seal of European approval upon Belgian independence.

The revolutionary disturbances of 1830 in France helped also to provoke disturbances elsewhere. In Italy revolts against the heavy hand of Austria broke out in the little duchies of Modena and Parma. Then those parts of the Papal States lying east of the Apennines tried to throw off papal control. The revolutionaries hoped that help might be obtained from the new liberal regime of Louis Philippe in France, even as Metternich hoped that France could be persuaded to help Austria to put down the revolts. Neither expectation was realized; the outcome simply was that Austrian troops alone were sent southward as they had been in 1820, and by their help the old regimes were restored.

A vigorous wave of liberal unrest in some parts of the German Confederation, stimulated by the news from Paris, led to isolated disturbances and to the proclamation of new constitutions for Brunswick, Hanover, Hesse-Cassel, and Saxony. This meant that some kind of limited constitutional regime now existed in eleven out of the thirty-nine German states. Intervention was not possible for Metternich here as it had been in Italy; nevertheless, he took the lead in securing the passage, in 1832, at the Frankfort Diet, of legislation authorizing rulers of states having legislatures to override action by those legislatures if need be, and to exercise large powers in lawmaking, taxation, and censorship. In this way the principle of authority was once more asserted.

Revolution, begun by leaders of secret societies and by university students, broke out in Warsaw, the Polish capital, in November, 1830. The unrest soon spread throughout the kingdom in protest against the harsh policies of the new Russian tsar, Nicholas I. When the Polish Diet voted the deposition of Nicholas as king of Poland, a Russian army was sent in and a savage repression was launched, the liberal Constitution of 1815 abrogated, and a new Organic Statute issued by the tsar. The unhappy outcome was that Poland was governed like an occupied country during a state of war, the universities of Vilna and Warsaw were closed, intellectuals were forced into emigration, and thousands of rebels were executed, imprisoned, or driven from their homeland.

Still more troubles, further affecting the stability of Europe, arose in 1831. Mehemet Ali, ruler of Egypt and vassal of the sultan, sought to wrest Palestine, Syria, and Arabia from his master by sending an army commanded by his son Ibrahim against them. Egyptian victories were so great that Turkey, like a drowning man, turned desperately to Russia for help. This help in a military sense was most effective and had striking political results. The Treaty of Unkiar-Skelessi (1833), ostensibly establishing a defensive alliance between the two, gave Russia a virtual protectorate over the Ottoman Empire, with the right to insist on the closing of the Straits by Turkey at Russia's demand. This state of affairs, so contrary to historical precedent, lasted until 1839, though it is worthy of note that the Russians complained that the responsibilities assumed under the Treaty were as great as the advantages gained. Then Turkey, fearing another Egyptian attack, decided to anticipate it by striking the first blow. The result was a Turkish disaster, for the Egyptians, victorious in the field, advanced to the gates of Constantinople. Now it was the turn of the British foreign secretary, Lord Palmerston, who was convinced that it was a British interest to maintain Turkey against either Egyptian or Russian threats. He welcomed a Russian proposal to invoke some kind of European concert for this purpose. Metternich, always opposed to revolutionary change, was agreeable. Nicholas I of Russia likewise agreed. The one real objector to all this was France, whose interests seemed tied to the Egyptians as Russia's had been to the Turks. Yet France was unwilling to flout the powers and so in July, 1841, they all signed with Turkey the famous Straits Convention stipulating that the sultan was not to permit "vessels of war belonging to foreign powers" to enter the Dardanelles and Bosphorus in times of peace. Whether we regard this as the joint action of the powers or the personal victory of Palmerston, it is clear that a new period of stability, if only temporary, had been established in the Near East.

The verdict upon the complicated diplomacy of these years would seem to be that on the whole the interests of the conservative powers had been successfully asserted. In most cases when revolution had come it had been fairly quickly controlled or stamped out. In the case of Belgium and Greece, the revolutions that could not be averted had been steered and assisted in directions least harmful to the general public order. In the case of the Ottoman Empire, both Russia and France had been prevented from capitalizing on internal dissent in order to score great individual victories. In contrast to our own twentieth century, where local crises have twice exploded into great European wars, these first decades of the nineteenth century had witnessed no international crisis so far out of hand as to endanger the general European peace.

■ SOCIAL UNREST AND ITS CAUSES

Whatever hopes the conservative governments may have had that they could maintain unchanged the European political structure which they had taken such pains to safeguard in 1815 were soon belied by the course of events. By and large, those in authority were much more successful in maintaining the general peace of the Continent than they were in preserving the governmental and social systems of their states. Grievances felt *within* states, far more than any desire for sweeping alterations of the European map, led to a mounting volume of unrest.

Basically, western Europe was experiencing the inevitable economic stresses and social dislocations arising out of the shift from a preponderantly agrarian society to the society of a new industrial age. Concomitantly, governments had to grapple with the vast unfinished business of political reform. With the American Revolution as one source of its inspiration, the French Revolution had familiarized Frenchmen with the concept of constitutional regimes in which citizens could genuinely participate. Such goals had not been attained. Furthermore, in this general atmosphere of frustration and dissatisfaction, an additional cause of unrest arising from the growth of national sentiment began to show itself.

Social unrest arose chiefly from changing economic conditions. A veritable agricultural revolution—involving the development of new crops, new methods of cattle breeding, new tools, and new methods of soil utilization—had come about in the more advanced parts of western Europe during the late eighteenth century. Its effects were important. At the same time great changes were beginning in industry—changes that involved the growing use of steam power, the development of more efficient machinery, especially for textiles, the widespread exploitation of coal and iron, and the emergence of much more rapid systems of transportation. These developments were most advanced in England, spreading from there to Belgium and more slowly to some parts of France and Germany. It seemed to some observers that the spectacular prosperity of the new lords of industry was closely involved with the poor housing, the low wages, and the long hours which were the lot of the steadily increasing masses of factory workers. Clearly not so basic, yet of immediate and pointed significance at the beginning of this period, were the bad harvests of 1816 and 1817, as well as the phenomenally severe winters that went with them. The first years of peace, unhappily, were the "hunger years," marked by great economic misery in France, Switzerland, Piedmont, and south Germany. In some areas the situation was that of veritable famine. A cycle of business depressions running at ten-year intervals can be charted in 1815, 1825, 1835, and in a most acute form in 1846–1847. By 1848 Germany, for example, was experiencing the most severe economic crisis it had known since Napoleon had imposed his Continental System upon Europe.

In Great Britain the agricultural and industrial worlds were both subject to many stresses and strains. For centuries the English villages had gone their way under a system whereby the peasant farmers cultivated their separate holdings and in addition shared in the use of certain common lands. A widespread process of "enclosure" in the eighteenth century had resulted in the fencing of these "commons" and removing them from general village use to the great advantage of the lords of the manor. Much hardship was thus imposed upon the villagers who, if they did not seek their fortunes in the new industrial centers, became the renters of farms or, in many cases, simply day laborers. They could not easily make use of the new scientific techniques of farming available to the wealthy tenant farmers, and they resented even the new types of machinery which only the richer farmers could afford.

Not surprisingly, therefore, recurrent waves of rioting had to be put down. In 1816 there were revolts in the eastern counties which had to be repressed by yeomanry and dragoons. In 1830 even more serious riots flared up in the southern and western counties and then spread still further afield. The demand basically was for a living wage; some of the rioters were charged with breaking the new threshing machinery that took their jobs; others simply attacked the property of their landlords. As significant as the uprisings were the ruthless means employed to put them down.

Paralleling this was much unrest in the industrial centers. The Luddite riots against certain types of new machinery led to stern repression. The Peterloo Massacre of 1819 showed local police methods at their worst, and a plot of the following year to blow up the British cabinet is a contrasting example of the extremes to which radical agitation could go.[6] As magistrates continued unavailingly to hand down their heavy punishments, it became increasingly evident that England needed enlightened measures of reform rather than an unintelligent program of repression to meet a situation of this kind.

France never went through an Industrial Revolution like that in England. Down to the late nineteenth century it was still preponderantly a land of country dwellers and small farms. Even so, a substantial industrial growth took place in the major cities. This created serious stresses and strains. Paris, with a population of 600,000, counted in 1830 one-tenth of this total population as indigent. It was estimated that one-fifth of the working class was criminal. All associations of working men were forbidden and it was necessary for each worker to carry a passbook and have it signed by his current employer before he could seek work with another. Food shortages, miserable wages, and wretched housing were all prevalent in the large cities. In 1832 Paris experienced a terrible epidemic of cholera; from March to September there were 18,400 deaths, the figure for these deaths rising as high as an appalling 1800 in one day. Under such complex circumstances the beginning of organized agitation for better conditions is understandable. Despite the prohibition against workers' associations many secret societies existed. These *compagnonnages*, some originating in the Middle Ages, ostensibly were for charitable and social purposes; actually they became connected with widespread disturbances. Rioting and strikes were common at Lyons, an important textile center, as they were also in Paris and other industrial cities in the 1830's and the 1840's.

Since the government seemed to be largely indifferent to workers' grievances in France, sensitive observers were not slow to detect signs of coming trouble. On the very eve of the revolutionary disturbances of 1848, a distinguished public figure, Alexis de Tocqueville,[7] addressed the French Chamber in words which showed an unusual grasp of the true situation and a deep concern over the state of mind of the working class. De Tocqueville spoke in part as follows:

> You say there is no peril since there is no uprising. . . . I believe that you are mistaken. . . . Look at what is going on in the hearts of the working classes, who today, I acknowledge, are quiet. . . . Cannot you see that there is spreading little by little in their minds ideas which will not merely overthrow this law or that,

6. See p. 191.
7. 1805–1859. A French judge, he wrote his *Democracy in America* (1835–1840) after a two-year stay in this country, one of the first and most penetrating analyses of the American political system. As a member of the French Chamber from 1839 to 1851, he warned of the danger to liberty of a too-rapid growth of democracy, of growing social evils, and of the threat of dictatorship. His *Ancien Régime* (1856) is one of the first substantial studies of the French Revolution. He was also responsible for the prophecy that ultimately there would be only two great powers, Russia and the United States.

this ministry or that, this government or that, but will overthrow society itself, and will shatter the bases on which it stands today? . . . Cannot you see that the working class is gradually saying to itself that property rests upon foundations which are not just?

Only one other major area, the German Confederation, showed any industrial development comparable to that of England and this was on a much smaller scale and only in some parts. The economic separatism of the thirty-nine states, the different currencies, and the various business codes were among the substantial obstacles to economic progress. In 1815 it is estimated that four-fifths of the population of the German Confederation was agrarian; by 1848 the figure was still as much as two-thirds. Industrial growth was limited to the Rhineland, the Berlin area, and Saxony. The great Krupp works had their modest beginnings at Essen in 1827. Just ten years later the Borsig machine works were founded at Berlin. With the growth of industry, the beginning of railways, and the rise in population (from 25,000,000 in 1815 to 34,500,000 in 1848), the inevitable problems of an industrial society appeared. Though industrial wages were better than in agriculture, they were clearly inadequate. The working day ranged from twelve to eighteen hours; and even women and children were expected to work from twelve to sixteen hours. When Frederick William III of Prussia, for example, issued his cabinet order of 1839 concerning child labor, he did no more than forbid children under the age of nine to work, and restricted to ten hours a day the labor of children between the years of ten and sixteen. And even this was not stated to be a humanitarian measure but rather a means to guarantee physical fitness in future army recruits!

Following the example of France, state after state in the German Confederation abolished the rights of the ancient gilds which for so long had dominated the handicraft system of production. The process began in Prussia in 1811 and reached its culmination in Hanover in 1847. It was not undertaken without serious protest. There were riots in Hesse-Cassel in 1832 and others in the Rhineland. "Things are for the moment peaceful," an agent reported to Metternich, "but fire glows beneath the ashes." Riots occurred in the Palatinate in 1833, and much more serious outbreaks in 1844 among the Silesian weavers, who fought vainly against the new manufacturing techniques. Ringleaders in Silesia were punished by public lashings and by long terms of imprisonment.

A development most significant for German unification had its beginnings in Prussia. Under the strong pressure of the free-traders, a law of 1818 had abolished all customs barriers between the Prussian provinces and established a uniformly low tariff wall around the kingdom as a whole. Since a number of other states or parts of them (enclaves) were completely surrounded by Prussian territory, and since high duties were retained on goods in transit to these and adjoining areas, the pressure to form a customs union with Prussia was very

THE ZOLLVEREIN

- ▤ Prussian Tariff Union of 1818
- ▦ Accessions to 1828
- —— Bavarian~Wurtemberg Union, 1828~1833
- ----- Central German Commercial Union, 1828~1833
- ▥ Accessions to Prussian Tariff Union, 1828~1834
- ▨ Accessions to Prussian Tariff Union, 1835~1854
- ▧ Accessions to Prussian Tariff Union, Since 1866

The law of 1818 removed tolls within Prussia; the first areas to accede were small states completely surrounded by Prussian territory; in 1834 a struggle among three rival unions ended with the accession of Bavaria and Württemberg to the Prussian Customs Union.

real. By 1828 a number of small states and one larger state, Hesse-Darmstadt, had joined with Prussia, and two other rival customs unions had come into existence. By January, 1834, Prussian negotiations with Bavaria, Württemberg, and the central German states led to the creation of the *Zollverein*, a free-trade area of well over twenty million people and eighteen states with a relatively low external tariff on manufactured goods. Its subsequent development was to be a major contribution to the growth of German unity.[8]

No open disturbances marked German agriculture, where the landlords maintained their favored position, whether as absentee owners of the small farms typical of western Germany or as direct operators of the great estates in Pomerania and Prussia. Nevertheless, the number of landless agricultural

8. See pp. 139 ff.

laborers tended to increase, and many of them, as they failed to get jobs on the farms, simply were added to the unskilled population of the cities where they struggled along at a bare level of subsistence. After centuries of bondage, the newly emancipated German peasants were largely left to shift for themselves in an increasingly industrialized world.

The phenomenon of the "hungry forties" in Germany affected town and country alike. One of the last major famines in Europe broke out in 1845, beginning in Ireland with the failure of the potato crop and spreading as far away as Silesia and Poland. In many areas foodstuffs had to be imported. Between 1844 and 1847 the average prices of food increased by 50 percent. The price of rye and potatoes was doubled. Silesian weavers sold their hand looms to obtain cash, and then were required to rent them back to use for the short periods when work was available. In the city of Solingen, famous for its cutlery, one out of three families in those years was destitute. Begging, vagabondage, vice, and crime increased in the German cities. An immediate consequence was a dramatic rise in emigration to America—a phenomenon which preceded, rather than followed, the Revolution of 1848. During the "hungry forties" half a million Germans went to America, and doubtless many others, if they could have afforded it, would have done likewise. On the eve of 1848 hunger riots occurred in almost every state of Germany, as they did in foreign cities, such as Cracow, Prague, and Pilsen. In Berlin, cavalry were used in 1847 to disperse the mobs. Under such circumstances it is perhaps not surprising that a meeting of German liberals held at Offenburg, in Baden, in 1847 should have adopted a program demanding in addition to political reforms a complete economic transformation—the end of all privilege—in Germany.

No widespread pattern of economic unrest and social protest was to be found during these years in Italy. Throughout most of the peninsula the settlement of 1815 meant in oversimplified terms that an Austrian master had been substituted for a French. During the Napoleonic period opposition to the conqueror had centered in the secret societies, of which the *Carbonari* was the most famous. Some of this opposition continued during the years of peace. When it flared up in the form of the revolts of 1820 and 1830, it was largely constitutional in nature, seeking political safeguards against absolutism. Its leaders came from the enlightened bourgeoisie and from a new class of businessmen who saw progress elsewhere and wished to see it likewise in Italy. The Lombard journals of the 1830's, for example, were greatly impressed by the progress of the Prussian Customs Union. Yet the growing force in Italy was that of nationalism which, coupled with the movement for constitutional government, sparked the revolts of 1848 and 1859. In other countries, such as Spain, Portugal, and Poland, economic conditions changed so little during these decades that social unrest and protest could hardly be expected. Here, as in

Italy, the major ferments were those which demonstrated the wish for constitutional reform and national self-determination.

■ LIBERALISM

Liberalism is a key word for the understanding of progress in the nineteenth century. Though its significance varied somewhat from country to country, it had a common core which enabled men to have some measure of agreement and understanding when they spoke of a "liberal" program, a "liberal" constitution, a "liberal" statesman, or a "liberal" party. In essence liberalism has its roots in certain eighteenth-century ideas. One of these is that individual men are entitled to seek their freedom in the face of arbitrary or tyrannical restrictions imposed upon them. Men have certain natural rights, so it was held by the eighteenth-century theorists, which it is the purpose of governments to guarantee. Prominent among these rights is *property*. Other rights are those of *freedom of speech, freedom from excessive punishment, freedom of meeting*, and *freedom of worship*. These rights are best provided for by a constitutional form of government with a careful definition of the limits to which governmental action may go. Both the American Declaration of Independence (1776) and the French Declaration of Rights of Man (1789) were great affirmations of such liberal principles.

Another view of liberalism was presented by men who came to be known as the utilitarians. These denied the existence of natural rights, substituting for them the principle of utility—"the greatest happiness of the greatest number." "Natural rights," scornfully declared Jeremy Bentham,[9] "are natural nonsense—nonsense on stilts." Whether or not liberals believed in "natural" rights, their principal concern was to clear away the obstacles to man's freedom of action and to remove the vast jungle of privilege which had flourished so luxuriantly in the eighteenth century.

Liberalism was quite clearly reformist and political rather than revolutionary in character. The name had been adopted in Spain where in conservative eyes it seemed identical with revolution. The word first appeared as a political designation in England about 1816. Its effects were seen in the increase in the number of states with some kind of constitutional guarantees of at least minimum political rights. By 1815 this number was substantial.[10] The creeds

9. 1748–1832. A youthful prodigy who took his degree at Oxford at the age of fifteen, he founded Utilitarianism, insisting that the object of all legislation is the greatest happiness of the greatest number, and devised the word "international," to be applied to the law of nations. He believed in the humane treatment of criminals, invented the Panopticon jail where all prisoners could be observed from a central point, helped to found University College, London, to which he bequeathed his skeleton, and worked long at the simplification and codification of English law. His disciple John Stuart Mill wrote: "There is hardly anything in Bentham's philosophy which is not true."
10. *Supra*, pp. 6–8.

THE BOURGEOISIE. This drawing of the Gatteaux family, done about 1850 by Jean Dominique Ingres, skilfully characterizes the substantial bourgeois society that was beginning to dominate the nineteenth century.

of liberalism were modified by the new economic conditions of the nineteenth century—by the spread of industrialism and the growth of a new bourgeois class of businessmen. When Adam Smith wrote his *Wealth of Nations* in 1776, he had argued for a policy of laissez-faire ("let things alone") in the hope that this policy would end the strangling restrictions of the old mercantile system. He could hardly have anticipated the need for so elaborate a pattern of legislation as the liberals in time actually produced.

One of the first great manifestations of liberalism came in the growth of constitutional governments, based on a restricted franchise and frequently granted by the king rather than resting on popular sovereignty. The French Charter, the Federal Act of 1815 creating the German Confederation, the Swiss Federal Act, the Polish Constitution of 1815, the short-lived Spanish and Neapolitan constitutions, those in Belgium, Greece, and South America, and that vainly sought in the Russian Decembrist revolt of 1825 are all manifestations of this principle. It is noteworthy that the most substantial treatises of this period on constitutionalism were written by an Englishman, Jeremy Bentham, a Frenchman, Benjamin Constant, and a German, Karl von Rotteck. New constitutional governments were associated with the older ideas of separation of powers, cabinet government, responsibility of ministers to the legislature, and the party system.

Liberalism was prolific in its manifestations. It also concerned itself with the rights of man and with civil liberties. Equality before the law, no taxation without representation, freedom of thought and worship, civil marriage, easier divorce laws, the demand for universal state education—are all examples of the variety of demands arising in the new creed.

Still another important new area for the liberal program came in the field of economics. The starting point—the idea of freedom and laissez-faire—had been enunciated by Adam Smith and by such disciples as J. B. Say in France. They attacked mercantilism with arguments in favor of free competition, and these arguments won considerable acceptance. Thus the famous *Petition of London Merchants* presented to the House of Commons in 1820 declared: "The maxim of buying in the cheapest and selling in the dearest market which regulates every merchant in his individual dealings is strictly applicable as the best rule for the trade of the whole nation." Economic liberalism claimed to be based on the realities of a new industrial era. The so-called "classical economists," such as Thomas Malthus and David Ricardo, insisted there were certain inescapable forces at work: competition, the pressure of population growth, the iron law of wages, the law of supply and demand, in accordance with which economic life must function. The animating principle would be that of "enlightened self-interest." Hence it was the duty of the government to clear away the dead wood, to end rules and privileges which obstructed the operation of these natural forces, and then stand aside.

Jeremy Bentham, from his liberal-utilitarianism viewpoint, would repeal the Navigation Acts and the Corn Laws; he would favor electoral reform, poor law reform, and revision of the legal codes; but he would not support an elaborate program of factory legislation. The state's duty is like that of a referee who keeps the ring under certain simple and clearly recognized rules. So the French Benjamin Constant wrote in his *Course on Constitutional Politics:* ". . . there is a part of human life which necessarily remains individual and independent, and has the right to stand outside all social control." John Stuart Mill, in his famous essay *On Liberty* (1859), declared himself to be opposed to government schools for everyone. "If the government," he wrote, "would make up its mind to *require* for every child a good education, it might save itself the trouble of *providing* one." Such liberalism would go so far and no further. Lord John Russell, who in 1832 had secured passage of the Great Reform Bill, extending the suffrage to the English middle class, was nicknamed "Finality John," because he promised that his reform would mark the limit of his action. Mill laid down three principles to determine when the government should not interfere: (1) when matters are done better by individuals; (2) when matters, although not done as well, are educative to those doing them; (3) when there is danger of adding unduly to the concentration of governmental power. The individual, Mill argued, is accountable to society for actions prejudicial to others; he is not accountable for actions harmful only to himself.

The liberalism that could give its sanction to the various kinds of freedom —personal, fiscal, civil, religious, or economic—could hardly divorce itself from another great area where, during the course of the nineteenth century, the principle of freedom was to be asserted. Nationalism as a force which impelled people having a common language, a common soil, and common traditions to seek some kind of political unity had been aroused by the French Revolution. Its manifestations in the early nineteenth century, which can only be referred to here as an aspect of the regenerative force of liberal thought, are discussed later in this chapter.

Liberalism was involved in the various revolutionary movements of 1820 and 1830 in France, Italy, Spain, Portugal, Poland, Russia, and the Balkans. It found concrete expression in the ten or so constitutions secured between 1815 and 1848 in states of the German Confederation. Its power was manifest in the reform measures which successive British governments adopted in these same decades. It affected German student groups and it raised its head on more than one occasion in Prussia. For a great many Germans, the liberal hopes which slowly developed were to find temporary victory in the Revolution of 1848.

■ THE BEGINNINGS OF MODERN SOCIALISM

The creeds of liberalism were not enough to satisfy all reformers of the nineteenth century. The widespread development of socialist systems through-out the world in the twentieth century gives special interest to the opening decades of the nineteenth century, for it was here that such ideas, strongly critical of the current organization of society, began to take shape. Since biblical times, to be sure, men have been concerned with the problem of social justice, and men have long tried their hands at sketching the outlines of Utopia. It was, however, the active concern of the eighteenth-century *philosophes*, with their questions concerning natural rights, individual freedom, justice, and the place of man in organized society, that gave the first impetus to the develop-ment of modern socialist doctrines, and one must look to such writers as Rous-seau, Mably, and Morelly for the first tentative statement of such views. Broadly, these theories have arisen as a protest against what were considered to be the injustices and inefficiencies of capitalistic society. The common elements in the various programs are the desire for the widespread establish-ment of human equality, and the extension of state ownership of property and state control over the means of production in order to secure this end.

During the French Revolution occasional measures were adopted which could be regarded as socialist in nature, even though the movement as a whole was largely bourgeois in character and asserted property to be one of the sacred rights of man. Yet modern socialism could hardly have developed apart from those aspects of the Industrial Revolution which largely follow the years of revolution in France, for it was the growth of industrial capitalism which seemed to intensify the gap between the rich and the poor and to create in many instances appalling conditions of life and labor for the working class. The tradition of critical enquiry, long established in both England and France, led to the emergence of the Utopian Socialists in the 1820's. These men showed an astonishing fluency in proposing schemes which, so they argued, if adopted would bring about a new golden age for men. A study of Utopian Socialism tends, consequently, to be a study of books. In the first half of the nineteenth century few if any of these schemes found concrete embodiment in legislative proposals or in the platforms of organized parties. Militant activity on the part of the working class was to come later.

The ferment of new ideas was affected by events in France. As early as 1819 the Swiss writer, Jean Charles Sismondi, pointed out that the Industrial Revolution had divided modern society into two classes, the capitalists and the proletariat. "If the government," he declared, "should set as its goal the advantage of one class of the nation at the expense of others, it is the working-man that it would have to favor." This, clearly, is a departure from the laissez-faire principles of the classical economists. Sismondi differs significantly from Adam Smith in insisting that political economy, instead of being only a science of *wealth*, has as its true object the study of *well-being* for everyone.

A French nobleman, Count Henri de Saint-Simon, a figure of eccentric adventure who claimed descent from Charlemagne and who had taken part in the American and in the French Revolution, looked searchingly at the organization of industrial society in his day and declared it to be impossible of acceptance. "A system is needed to replace a system," he wrote, and in various books he proposed that the old "Christian and feudal" order be replaced by a new scheme of things, based on a new faith and a new ordering of abilities. The candidates for authority in this new industrial age were quite clearly those who labored in order to produce, whether they were manufacturers, farmers, sailors, locksmiths, or merchants. In Saint-Simon's new world the old rulers of society would be replaced by the industrialists, the scientists, and the artists (*industriels, savants, artistes*). There could be no idlers. How this new society would come about, and how it would operate, Saint-Simon did not explicitly say. Some have denied him the title of socialist. Certainly he was chiefly concerned in painting the picture of a society organized so that the right to property would be based on contributions to the general welfare, and especially on contributions intended to improve the lot of the poorest classes. From Saint-Simon and his followers have come some of the most famous phrases in the socialist vocabulary, such as "the right to work," and "from each according to his capacity, to each according to his needs."

The Saint-Simonians, followers of this unusual figure, were far more eccentric than their master. They grew long beards, dressed in costumes of red, white, and violet, and designed a special waistcoat which, being buttoned up the back, emphasized the dependence of man upon man; and they set out to find a female Messiah on the banks of the Nile. Yet they included some very able men, such as Ferdinand de Lesseps, later the builder of the Suez Canal, Franz Liszt, the composer, and Michel Chevalier, negotiator in 1860 of the free-trade treaty with England. Saint-Simon remains one of the first men seriously to advocate the peaceful transition by the method of persuasion from what he considered to be a society based upon exploitation to one which would not be crudely egalitarian but so organized and planned by technicians as to bring the greatest possible benefits to all its members.

If Saint-Simon and the Saint-Simonians appeared eccentric, then surely a taint of madness hangs over another Frenchman, Charles Fourier.[11] A man of lower-middle-class origin, whose life was one of penury, his books picture a society which defeats its own ends by accepting human exploitation, suffering, ill-gotten wealth, and waste. Fourier saw competition as a great evil. He proclaimed a law of "universal attraction" by which men can be led through their natural passions to live and act in certain constructive ways. They should seek to do so by organizing themselves in social groups called phalansteries, or phalanxes, each numbering around 1,800. (The reason for this number, so Fourier explains, is that 2,000 would be too large and 1,600 too small to provide the needful variety of human capacities.) In time the earth would be peopled with precisely 2,985,984 phalansteries, this number being the cube of 144. Within their phalanxes men would work freely and happily at the tasks they desire, and the fruits would be distributed to Capital (4/12), Labor (5/12), and Talent (3/12).

The nineteenth century did see numerous attempts to form modified Fourieristic communities, both in Europe and in the United States. Few succeeded. It is striking that some of Fourier's ideas were adapted by Robert Owen, who, as a poor Welsh boy of nine, had begun work as a shop clerk. By the age of nineteen he was manager of a factory and at twenty-six became the owner of the New Lanark cotton mill in Scotland—an enterprise so revolutionary and successful that it attracted world-wide attention. Mill owners are seldom socialists. Owen's importance was that he was an *environmentalist*, be-

---

11. 1772–1837. At the age of five he is said to have taken a vow of hatred against commerce. He predicted a future period of harmony when a luminous ring, forming around the North Pole, would turn the oceans to lemonade; when ships would be drawn by the greatest of living creatures, the whales; and lions would be harnessed for the service of man. He combined these eccentric predictions with powerful criticisms of an unbridled industrial society and, by his proposals for a new form of organization, stimulated the discussion of social reforms that would recognize individual needs and capacities.

lieving that by creating the proper conditions of working, housing, clothing, and schooling, he would produce a model community. In such a community men would replace competition by cooperation. New Lanark, indeed, became just such a model under the paternal hand of its owner. In his famous *Report to the County of Lanark* (1820), Owen laid it down as his first principle that "manual labor, properly directed, is the source of all wealth and of national prosperity." Owen entered the ranks of the Utopian Socialists by employing a substantial part of his wealth (some forty thousand pounds) to establish a cooperative community, New Harmony, Indiana, on the banks of the Wabash and encouraging the founding of others. Within three years New Harmony had failed and Owen turned more successfully to advocate the formation of cooperative societies in England. One outcome was the appearance in 1844 of a little store in Toad Lane, Rochdale, founded by twenty-eight Lancashire weavers to sell goods cooperatively to the members. Out of this grew the great cooperative movement in England and Scotland, which by the end of the century had become a major business concern. Owen also attempted to combine the working classes in his Grand National Consolidated Trades Union (1833)—a movement soon ended by internal disruption and by savage punishments inflicted by the government. Owen was an odd combination of capitalist and labor champion moving in his old age into a sadly confused atmosphere of religious eccentricity. It seems true that the very word "socialism" occurs for the first time in an Owenite journal as a vague name for communal solidarity in opposition to the principle of private gain.

A figure paralleling Robert Owen, but taking us into the larger sphere of state socialism, was a French journalist, Louis Blanc, who, living in Paris in the 1830's, was deeply shocked at the world he saw around him. He was a keen critic of social abuses. In his *Organization of Labor* (1839) he called for government action which would transform society by doing what individuals had failed to do—creating model factories, model banks, model enterprises of every kind on a limited scale. "You tell the poor man that he has the *right* to improve his position," Blanc asked. "What good is that to him if you do not give him the power to do it?" In 1848 Blanc's proposals were caricatured in the ill-fated experiment of the National Workshops.[12]

Still another critic of the new industrial age was Pierre Joseph Proudhon. In 1840 he wrote *What is Property?* giving the answer in a famous phrase, "Property is theft." How great a departure this is from the Declaration of the Rights of Man in 1789 which declared property to be a basic right of mankind is obvious. Proudhon, a somewhat unclear thinker, seems actually to have been chiefly concerned with the problem of justice. This concept he found to be violated whenever the possessors of property made use of it to exercise power

12. See pp. 65–67.

over others. Hence, since the state is the guarantor of property rights, Proudhon becomes an enemy of the state, and thus this man—"the most difficult and the most elusive of all the great figures in the history of socialism"—becomes associated with later doctrines of anarchism.

Such ideas of socialism, most commonly expounded in England and France, had echoes in Germany and Italy and even as far afield as Poland and Russia. They have been labeled "Utopian" because they were based on the idea of the essential goodness of man. Since they believed that man was suffering greatly under the evils of the new industrial system, it became the duty of socialists to stress the moral value of cooperation and the need for association. Thus Utopian Socialists advocated some kind of harmonious society, some form of model communities, social workshops or the like, where the ruthless qualities of an individualistic capitalism would disappear. These utopian hopes were replaced after 1848 by the militant doctrines of "scientific socialism"—Marx's communist theory of revolution that would undertake to destroy the capitalist regime by brute force.

■ NATIONALISM

Still another force developing in these complex years remains to be described. Nationalism is a word easily understood in general terms and yet difficult of precise definition. It is not altogether a phenomenon of the modern world. Englishmen fighting at Agincourt in the Hundred Years' War were conscious that they were one breed and their French opponents another. Dutchmen fighting for their freedom from the Spain of Philip II knew what it meant to have endured the rule of the foreigner. Not, however, until the time of the French Revolution, when Frenchmen became citizens of their country as they had never been before, could they identify themselves completely with *la patrie* and develop that sense of pride, tradition, and common purpose which is an essential ingredient of modern nationalism. A national flag, the tricolor, and a national anthem, the Marseillaise, were outward symbols of new and profound emotions.

During these revolutionary years one of the greatest voices in the history of nationalism had spoken with another emphasis. Johann Gottfried Herder, who had gone as a student from Königsberg to teach in the cathedral school of Riga, became interested in the folklore and songs of the Baltic peasants. Having translated some of this material into German, he went on to a lifelong study of German language and culture, in the course of which he came to regard the national identity of any people as an outcome of their historic traditions and literary evolution. Thus he regarded nationalism as essentially a cultural phenomenon which was both healthful and benign. All national groups he took to be parts of that greater whole which is humanity. Herder's writings had a powerful influence in stimulating a whole breed of German historians, philologists, linguists, and publicists. In 1827 Edgar Quinet translated one of his major works into French. Herder had his greatest influence possibly among the Slavs, who, under Austrian or Ottoman rule, found in him both an inspiration and a program.

Other tendencies soon transformed the cosmopolitan nationalism of Herder. The deeply felt reaction of the Spanish people against Napoleon's domination of their country, and the even more deeply felt emotions of the Prussians at the humiliation which he had enforced upon them, suggest the beginnings of a new and more militant form of national sentiment. In Germany these feelings were proclaimed eloquently by a group of patriotic poets, not all of them Prussians, and in the burning pages of Johann Fichte's *Addresses to the German Nation*, originally lectures given in 1807 and 1808 on the eve of the founding of the University of Berlin and just before the great national uprising against Napoleon.

Conditions immediately following 1815 were not favorable to the peaceful growth of nationalistic views. France and England, to be sure, were countries where national identity was securely established. Yet, in general, the map of Europe, as it had been drawn up in 1815, gave a very imperfect expression to national groupings. Statesmen had set the boundaries for strategic or political reasons, keeping in mind dynastic interests, and souls were freely bartered by the hundreds of thousands following the technical work of the statistical committee at the Congress of Vienna. The German Confederation was a poor substitute for a genuine national state. The Austro-Hungarian monarchy was an extraordinary hodgepodge of linguistic, ethnic, and cultural groups. A disunited Italy was largely under the hand of Austria. The Russian Empire included Estonians, Latvians, Lithuanians, Finns, Poles, and Bessarabians. The various peoples of the Balkans—Greek, Serb, Croat, Montenegrin, Albanian, Bulgarian, and Rumanian—were beginning to stir under the alien rule of their Turkish masters.

Such repression was in itself some contribution to the growth of nationalism, for history shows clearly enough that the subjection of people to an outside rule will in itself stimulate the development of national consciousness. The Italian resentment at Austria's interference in 1821 to put down the revolts in Naples and Piedmont was real enough, as was Polish resentment at Russia's harsh repression of 1831. Fear of outside intervention works potently in the same direction. The war scare of 1840 which blew up between France and Prussia prompted the Rhineland poet, Nikolaus Becker, to compose his famous *German Rhine*, with the lines—

> They shall not, shall not have it,
> Our free, our German Rhine
> Though hoarse as famished ravens
> They round it croak and whine,
> So long its winding current
> Shall wear its dark green vest,
> So long as splashing boat-oar
> Shall cleave its rippling breast.

King Ludwig of Bavaria sent Becker a golden goblet with the message, "From this gold and silver tankard, a gift from me to you, drink often, singing the while, 'They shall not, shall not have it!' " In the same year Max Schneckenburger wrote the poetically less distinguished *Watch on the Rhine*, destined thirty years later for even greater fame as a popular anthem in imperial Germany.

Perhaps the best way to illustrate the steadily increasing significance of nationalism in the years between 1815 and 1848 is to list a number of examples, many of which will reappear later in the discussion of the appropriate countries. In France, for example, Jules Michelet published in 1833 the first volume of his *History of France*, a work of literature as much as of history and suffused with a deeply felt national pride. In 1826 scholars at Berlin began publishing the famous series of the *Monumenta Germaniae Historica*, a huge collection of medieval sources with the motto, *Sanctus Amor Patriae Dat Animum*. In the 1820's the patriotic Russian historian, Nicolai Karamzin, was at work on his *History of the Russian State* and the poet, Alexander Pushkin, was becoming famous. The poet himself called Karamzin "the Columbus of ancient Russia" and a modern Soviet historian has written of Pushkin, "Without 1812 there would have been no Pushkin." In Poland the historian, Ignaz Lelewel, and the great national poet, Adam Mickiewicz, are of this period. In Bohemia the historian, Frantisek Palacky, and the poet, Jan Kollàr, were beginning to establish their reputations. The appearance of students devoted to the language and traditions of the Serbs, Croats, and Slovenes marks a parallel phenomenon. The Greek scholar, Adamantios Koraés, brought out new editions of the Greek classics, and, as we have seen, in 1814 a secret society, the *Hetairia Philike*, was reorganized at Odessa to work for Greek independence. Italians could read the works of Giacomo Leopardi and Alessandro Manzoni, finding in them veiled attacks upon Austrian rule. Above all, this period marks the rise of the great Italian figure of Guiseppe Mazzini. In 1829 he joined the *Carbonari*, a secret society, and in 1831 he founded Young Italy, which, with the motto, "God and the people," became one of the great forces in the Italian struggle for national unity. In Denmark the name of Bishop Grundtvig is associated with the revived interest in the nation's past. In Finland the scholar, Elias Lönnrot, brought together a mass of traditional folk songs to create the *Kalevala* (1835), one of the great epic poems of the world. These scattered examples indicate the growth of national sentiment at a time when reaction outwardly prevailed and Metternich, the dedicated foe of all nationalist aspirations, was the master of central Europe. Much of this national sentiment flowed in literary, historical, and philological channels. Yet it became eventually a force that was to explode with revolutionary violence throughout large parts of the Continent. If any illustration can serve to show that in these decades of conservative authority new forces were germinating, the example of nationalism, surely, is one of the most striking.

Reading List: Chapter 1

Nicolson, H., *The Congress of Vienna* (1946; paperback, 1961), ch. 16. Failure of the congress system.

Webster, C., *The Foreign Policy of Castlereagh 1815–1822* (1925), pp. 490–505. An estimate of Castlereagh.

Woodward, E. L., *Three Studies in European Conservatism* (1929), part I. Metternich.

Viereck, P., *Conservatism Revisited* (1950), ch. 2. "Union of Europe: Some History Lessons from 'Professor' Metternich."

Kann, R. A., "Metternich: A Reappraisal of His Impact on International Relations," *Journal of Modern History*, vol. XXXII (1960), no. 4.

Artz, F. B., *Reaction and Revolution 1815–1832* (1934 and frequent reissues), chs. 3–5. "Search For a Principle of Authority"; "Creeds of Liberalism"; "Rise of a New Generation."

Schapiro, J. S., *Liberalism and the Challenge of Fascism* (1949), ch. 1. "What is Liberalism?"

Hayes, C. J. H., *Nationalism: A Religion* (1960), ch. 6. Deals with European nationalism, 1800–1870.

Royal Institute of International Affairs, *Nationalism* (1939), chs. 4–6. German, Russian, and other European national movements.

Gray, Alexander, *The Socialist Tradition: Moses to Lenin* (1946), chs. 6–8. Saint-Simon, Fourier, Owen.

Manuel, F., *The Prophets of Paris* (1962), chs. 3–5. Saint-Simon, the Saint-Simonians, Fourier.

Markham, F. M. H., "Saint-Simon," *History Today*, vol. IV (1954), no. 8.

Chapter 2

Four Regimes
in France, 1814–1870

The Bourbon Restoration, 1814–1830
The July Monarchy of Louis Philippe, 1830–1848
Revolution and Second Republic, 1848–1852
The Second Empire: Domestic Policies, 1852–1870
The Second Empire: Foreign Policies, 1852–1870
The Second Empire: Finale, 1870–1871

■ THE BOURBON RESTORATION, 1814–1830

The France to which the Bourbons came back in 1814 was, despite all the confusions inherent in the overthrow of the Napoleonic regime, a going concern. Even the temporary excitement of Napoleon's return from Elba in March, 1815, and the tense drama of the Hundred Days were, if not forgotten, at least soon over. "We are a tranquil people with agitated legislators," a French critic once wrote; indeed, in the first years of peace not even the agitation of the reactionary Ultras could prevent the return of a majority of moderates in the new elections of 1816. The machinery of administration so masterfully organized by Napoleon continued to function. Despite the residual effects of the wartime blockade and the new hardships of the bad winters of 1815 and 1816, France gave many signs of being a thriving country. The peasantry, to be sure, who constituted more than 75 percent of the population, could not claim to be as well off as their English counterparts, and the progress of industrialization, even if slow, brought hardships to many urban workers. Yet Paris, with

50

SIGNIFICANT EVENTS

1814	The Charter granted by Louis XVIII (June)
1824	Accession of Charles X
1830	Beginning of French occupation of Algeria (July)
	July Revolution replaces Bourbon with Orleans line (Louis Philippe)
1848	Revolution in Paris
	Election of Louis Napoleon Bonaparte as President of Second Republic (December)
1850	Falloux Law
1851	Coup d'Etat of December 2
1852	Proclamation of the Second Empire (December 2)
1856	Congress of Paris
1859	Austro-Sardinian War
1860	Commercial Treaty with Great Britain
1862–1867	French acquire Cambodia and Cochin China
1870	Proclamation of the "Liberal Empire"
1870–1871	Franco-Prussian War

its more than 600,000 inhabitants, was a splendid capital in which the fine buildings erected by Napoleon, even if not completed, added to the distinguished monuments of his predecessors.

The Revolution had not ended the sharp cleavages in French society. Even though the nobility had suffered heavily, losing many of their ancient privileges and much of their landed wealth, they still asserted their social claims and with the return of the Bourbons exercised a powerful influence on politics. From the nobility came the strongest support of the Roman Catholic religion. Talleyrand and Polignac, both of them princes, as well as Richelieu and Broglie, both of them dukes, played leading roles under the restored monarchy. They were required, however, to share the limelight with the leaders of the newly rising bourgeoisie, later to be so mercilessly depicted in the cartoons of the great satirist, Honoré Daumier. Adolphe Thiers was a journalist who also distinguished himself as a great historian of the Napoleonic era; François Pierre Guizot, the son of a lawyer, moved into political life from a chair in

history at the Sorbonne. In time leaders would arise who would identify themselves actively with the cause of the people, but it remains true that in 1815
the great mass of the peasants and urban workers were still largely illiterate
and deprived of any significant role in the political life of France.

The Bourbons returned with little fanfare or splendor, and yet with few
signs of protest from a people who had loyally accepted the Revolution and
the Empire. The king who waited impatiently in the Tuileries, while the
Napoleonic bees embroidered on the palace furniture were covered over by the
Bourbon lilies, had within a year to flee ingloriously at the outset of the Hundred
Days to Ghent. After Waterloo he was brought back, as the phrase had it, "in
the baggage wagons of the Allies." Yet, however ungraceful the process,
legitimacy was re-established. The king's excessive stoutness, his fifty-nine
years, his gout, his odd habit of wearing a costume part military, part naval,
and part civilian, and his completely empty past were offset by a native dignity,
a moderation, and a shrewdness that stood him in good stead. He presided over
a threadbare and aging court altogether lacking in the glamour of the splendid
Napoleonic regime.

The Charter, hastily drawn up in April, 1814, by a commission of former
ministers, public servants, and deputies of the Napoleonic Empire, strikingly
illustrates the way in which constitutional principles, first affirmed by the men
of the Revolution, persisted into the new age. To be sure, hereditary monarchy
and the ancient titles of nobility were restored. The Charter was "given at
Paris, in the year of grace 1814 and of our reign the nineteenth." Along with
this assertion of traditional rights, the Napoleonic pattern of administration, the
great imperial law codes, the nation-wide educational structure, and such institutions as the Legion of Honor were kept. There was to be a legislature of
two chambers somewhat like the British Parliament. The Senate was to consist
of no more than two hundred hereditary peers, nominated by the king. The
Chamber of Deputies was elected in two stages for five years on the basis of a
very restricted suffrage, one-fifth of the deputies retiring annually. Voters had
to be aged thirty and deputies forty. Many details were left to be filled in later
and many points, for example, the questions of freedom of the press and
ministerial responsibility, were left obscure. Under the actual regulations of
1815 about 78,000 adult males out of a total French population of nearly
30,000,000 could vote.

Louis XVIII reigned for ten years and on the whole managed well. It
is true, he began harshly by approving a wave of prosecutions against leading
Bonapartists who had turned to Napoleon again during the Hundred Days.
As a result, a number of distinguished figures including Marshal Ney—"the
bravest of the brave"—were shot. In various parts of France, royalist mobs
launched a "White Terror" against individuals who had been prominently

identified with the Revolution. The revolutionary and imperial painter, David, found it advisable to spend his declining years in Belgium. Yet the period of reprisals was soon over and it was clear that the monarchy had strong, perhaps even dangerous, support. When the first elections were held, a majority of ultra royalists, soon simply known as the Ultras, were returned. These would gladly have turned back the hands of the clock in every respect; they disliked Louis XVIII and gave their support much more to his brother, the Count of Artois. The groups in the Chamber ranged from these Ultras on the right to the moderate Royalists who supported the existing Charter, then to the more liberal reformists or Doctrinaires next to them, then to the Orleanists, the Bonapartists, and, on the extreme left, to the small group of Republicans. The atmosphere in the capital was not without its strains, for it was quite possible for a regicide who had voted for the execution of Louis XVI to rub shoulders with an *émigré*, whose devotion to the monarchy had led him to spend long years of exile in the Rhineland city of Coblenz.

The desire of the Ultras to undo all the work of the Revolution led Louis XVIII to outmaneuver the Ultra majority in the Chamber and call for new elections in September, 1816. Since these were less conservative in their outcome, the political history of the next four years ran fairly smoothly. The Ultras, curiously enough, were in favor of manhood suffrage on the assumption that the common people would give support to their betters. The moderate Royalists, however, who benefited by the election and depended on middle-class support, were satisfied to extend the electorate to the neighborhood of 100,000. The army was reorganized, the war indemnity paid off, and France admitted in 1818 to the Quadruple Alliance.[1] Liberal sentiment began to grow and liberal newspapers to appear, most notably the *Globe*, founded in 1824. Yet the revolutionary troubles of 1820, marked by the assassination of the Duke de Berri, had challenged this assertion of liberalism. The Ultras won control of the Chamber, and conservative religious groups, the Clericals, worked to restore the ancient power of the Church and establish closer ties with Rome. While moderates, such as Frayssinous, a teacher at the seminary of Saint-Sulpice, championed the historic Gallicanism of the French monarchy, others, most notably the Vicomte de Bonald and Joseph de Maistre, supported an extreme ultramontane position.[2] A Catholic organization of clerics and laymen, the Congregation, established in 1814 was denounced by the Liberals as being ultramontane and closely connected with the Jesuits who, once banned, were now coming back into France. In the field of foreign affairs the Liberals could see little to approve

1. See p. 26.
2. Gallicanism is that view which accepts the teachings of Roman Catholicism but puts the organization and discipline of the Church largely in French hands. Politically it is the opposite of ultramontanism.

in the conservative pressures, which in 1823 forced Louis' minister Villèle to send French troops into Spain and restore the absolutist rule of King Ferdinand VII.

In 1824 the sixty-seven-year-old Count of Artois, who reigned as Charles X, succeeded his brother. The policy of the regime was now clearly designed to restore the monarchy to a position as much as possible like that before the Revolution. "Each year," it was said, "had its memorable anachronism." The coronation ceremony at Rheims suggested the Middle Ages in its neo-Gothic splendor, and, following it, Charles gave the royal touch to more than a hundred sufferers afflicted with scrofula. Money compensation (in the form of annual interest payments on a total of one billion francs) was voted for nobles who had lost property during the Revolution; and, in deference to the Church, the crime of sacrilege was made punishable by death. Severe censorship, fines levied on publishers, and the attacks on certain university lecturers announced the beginnings of a veritable persecution. The few reforms offered by the moderate ministry of 1828 could not allay discontent.

The downfall of Charles X followed within a year his summoning the Prince of Polignac—an Ultra of the deepest dye—to head the ministry. It appeared that the king was now seeking to establish a despotism. In order to defend the Charter the Liberals became more active, making greater use of a political organization, founded in 1827, with the strange name, "Heaven Helps Those Who Help Themselves." Bitter conflicts followed in the Chamber of Deputies, and new elections strengthened the opposition. The crisis came to a head in July, 1830, when Polignac persuaded Charles to let him invoke Article XIV of the constitution, empowering the king to issue special ordinances "for the safety of the state." These July Ordinances, which spelled disaster for Charles X, authorized a severe new censorship of the press, dissolved the Chamber, called for new elections, and, most shocking of all, reduced the electorate from 100,000 to a mere 25,000. This last would have greatly increased the voting power of the conservative landed class at the expense of the wealthy bourgeoisie.

On the news of these measures Paris rose in revolt. Barricades appeared in the narrow, stone-paved streets, and contemporary drawings show these barricades manned much more by respectable bourgeoisie in frock coats and top hats than by the "men of the people." In the famous "Three Glorious Days" that followed, Paris fell into the hands of the liberal leaders, and Charles X, watching the city from Saint-Cloud through a spyglass, saw the tricolor floating over the towers of Notre-Dame. Soon afterwards he fled to England—the last Bourbon to have ruled on the throne of France.

Politically the Bourbon Restoration had ended in catastrophe for the legitimate monarchy. Yet France in many respects had thrived under Bourbon rule. Since 1815 the population had grown by three millions, finances were stable, budgets yielded surpluses, banks grew, and joint stock companies began to appear. Better roads, better canals, the beginnings of steamboat transportation on the Loire, paved streets, horse omnibuses in Paris, and gas lighting on the streets—all these were marks of substantial material progress. In the arts the advance was phenomenal. An age that had Chateaubriand, Hugo, Dumas, Musset, Sainte-Beuve, Lamartine, and Vigny for its writers, Ingres, Géricault, and Delacroix for its painters, Rossini, Auber, and Berlioz for its musicians could surely claim to be one of the great periods in the modern development of the arts. This period showed a striking reawakening of religious faith. In interior *décor* the Gothic revival was in full swing. In the drama the struggle led by the champions of the romantic movement had its climax in the uproar at the Comédie Française in 1830 when the traditionalists tried to jeer Hugo's new play, *Hernani*, off the stage. Their failure, a landmark in the history of French romanticism, meant in effect that the champions of the new order had won their battle.

■ THE JULY MONARCHY OF LOUIS PHILIPPE, 1830–1848

The Revolution of 1830 was quick, relatively bloodless, and in its outcome somewhat accidental. Responding to the disturbances in Paris, and rapidly discovering that the dismissal of Polignac was not enough, Charles X had wished to abdicate in favor of his grandson. The deputies assembled in Paris were unwilling to accept this succession as were other influential figures who, urged on by a rising young journalist named Adolphe Thiers,[3] sought also to avoid the danger of a republic. This latter danger was real, for at the Hôtel de Ville the republican crowds were acclaiming the venerable Lafayette, hero of the American and the French revolutions, as their commander. Meanwhile, a group of moderate deputies had invited Louis Philippe, Duke of Orleans and distant cousin of Charles X, to come to Paris and act as lieutenant-general of the kingdom.

This Duke of Orleans was, to say the least, unusual. His father had been a prominent Freemason, had intrigued against Louis XVI, had accepted the Revolution, had taken the new name of "Philippe Egalité," had voted for the execution of the king, and had eventually himself been guillotined. The son had fought with the Republican armies in the great victories of Valmy and

3. 1797–1877. He founded the *National* in 1830, a journal opposing the Bourbons, served in various ministries, and for a time was prime minister under the July Monarchy. A conservative republican in 1848, he voted for Louis Napoleon, then opposed the Second Empire. Head of the provisional government in 1870, he served from 1870 to 1873 as president of the French Republic. His twenty-one-volume *History of the Consulate and Empire*, a main factor in the growth of the Napoleonic legend, was called by Lamartine the book of the century. Suspicious of democracy, he once compared universal education to "building a fire under a great pot that is empty."

Jemappes in 1792, and later had lived blamelessly in exile. He had given French lessons in rooms situated above the Old Union Oyster House in Boston. In the tradition of his family he was not without political ambition. Yet, as it has been put, he chose to aspire rather than to conspire. Though royal blood flowed in his veins, there were few marks of the Old Regime about Louis Philippe. He did not care, like his predecessors, for uniforms. He had the habit of wandering amiably on the boulevards, carrying a green umbrella. He sent his children to public schools, lit his own fire of a morning, and had a bourgeois fondness for soup. His curiously pear-shaped head later became the delight of hostile cartoonists. Would not this modest man, who seemed happy to accept the tricolor flag of the Revolution and the limited monarchy envisioned in the Charter, be the ideal head of a stable, bourgeois regime? His cause had been secretly encouraged by Talleyrand and other nobles. With some courage he rode through the crowded streets of an uncertain Paris to the Hôtel de Ville, where the Republican Lafayette was now prepared to accept him as an alternative to the dangers of the extreme Jacobin left. The pair appeared together on a balcony, Louis Philippe holding the tricolor. When they embraced, the outcome was certain. Although Charles X still tried to abdicate in favor of his grandson, it was too late. Within a few days 252 deputies of the old Chamber met, declared the throne vacant, undertook to revise the Charter, and formally offered the crown to Louis Philippe. He accepted, assuming the title, "Louis Philippe, King of the French People," agreed to a revised Charter and to substituting the tricolor for the white flag of the Bourbons. A monarchical compromise had been achieved by leaders who in essence represented the bankers, property owners, industrialists, bondholders, and professional men—leaders who were equally distrustful of the Ultras on the right and the Republicans on the left. The mass of the nation still had no voice in politics.

Some significant changes were made in the Charter. The preamble, which implied divine right, was dropped. Roman Catholicism, no longer "the religion of the state," was declared to be "the religion of the majority of Frenchmen." Royal power to issue ordinances and impose press censorship was restricted. Seats in the Chamber of Peers were no longer hereditary, and the franchise was extended to include altogether about 200,000 people. Municipal government was reorganized so as to place it more firmly in the hands of the bourgeoisie and country gentry. Service in the National Guard was restricted to those paying direct taxes and purchasing their own uniforms. Seeing that Louis Philippe was required to *accept* the Charter and did not *grant* it, his status was clearly different from that of his Bourbon predecessors. Even so, it is proper to stress the element of continuity which stretches from the Bourbon Restoration through these decades. Though workingmen had joined in the fighting, actually they gained very little from the Revolution of 1830. The upper bourgeoisie had prevailed, and the core of the Charter, with its restricted suffrage, remained intact.

The system of political parties now emerging demonstrated this truth. On the extreme right were the small group of Legitimists who still clung to their Bourbon hopes. On the extreme left were the Republicans, whose leader, Godefroy Cavaignac, had explained, "We only gave way because we were not strong enough. Later on it will be different." Gathered between these wings were two groups: the Party of Resistance and the Party of Movement. Both were essentially bourgeois in outlook. The former, led by François Guizot,[4] was satisfied that revolution had gone far enough: "Peace abroad and peace at home, the maintenance of law and order, and no encouragement for democratic passions" sums up its program. It represented pretty clearly the governmental policy of the reign. The Party of Movement, initially led by the venerable Lafayette and by the banker, Laffitte, was aware of the need for further changes. It professed to be willing to extend the franchise, sought individual freedom in the state, and demanded a vigorous foreign policy. In the phrase of Victor Hugo, it held that "1830 is a revolution stopped half-way." Clearly, the spokesmen representing the new doctrines of socialism and the revolutionary, republican "tradition of 1789" would find no welcome in this new legislature.

The first decade of this July Monarchy saw some alternation of rule between the Party of Movement and the Party of Resistance. Not surprisingly, the latter was more usually in office. While these two parties disagreed as to how liberal the monarchy should be, they had no other thought basically than to maintain the authority of the prosperous middle class. Alexis de Tocqueville shrewdly evaluated the situation in his *Recollections:*

> Posterity will perhaps never realize to what an extent the government of the time had come to resemble a limited liability company in industry which undertakes all its operations with a view to the profit to be exacted from them by the shareholders.[5]

These "shareholders," to be sure, would tolerate a certain modest measure of reform. The threat of a conservative alliance between the Throne and the Altar was gone. Qualifications for voting and serving as deputies had been broadened somewhat. Threats to freedom of speech had been reduced. Guizot's education law of 1833 provided for state-aided primary schools, where the clergy could give religious instruction, in every commune; the grave defect was that attendance at them was not compulsory. In some of the early cabinets

4. 1787–1874. Son of a victim of the guillotine, he began to lecture on history at the Sorbonne in 1812. One of the *Doctrinaires* in the French Chamber, he feared both absolutism and democracy. Virtual prime minister under the July Monarchy from 1840 to 1848, by his conservative policies he became identified with its unpopularity. A prolific historian, he was along with Lamartine and Thiers one of the distinguished small group combining careers in literature and politics.
5. A. DE TOCQUEVILLE, *The Recollections of Alexis de Tocqueville* (1949), p. 3.

BUST OF GUIZOT, by Honoré Daumier. Daumier's ability to use his satirical gifts in sculpture as well as in drawing is demonstrated in this striking characterization of Guizot.

the names of Thiers, the revolutionary journalist of 1830, and Guizot, the brilliant historian of the Sorbonne, were associated in a common support of the Party of Resistance. By 1836 they had split, Guizot taking a determinedly conservative stand and Thiers becoming a more vigorous supporter of parliamentary government. Their disagreements have been epitomized in two famous phrases: "The king reigns but does not govern" was the formula of Thiers; "The throne is not an empty chair," that of Guizot.

From 1840 to 1848 the hand of Guizot, more than any other, guided the destinies of France. The old Napoleonic soldier, Marshal Soult, was prime minister until 1847, when Guizot took over, but throughout all these years Soult's authority had been nominal. Guizot had regarded himself as a liberal, and in his great work on the history of civilization in Europe he had taken the emergence of a middle class and the struggle for representative institutions as his central themes. During the 1840's he maintained himself in office, despite growing criticisms, by taking advantage of the steady support of the king, by encouraging business expansion, by shamelessly manipulating the electoral machinery, and by offering fat jobs to those who supported him in the Chamber. When Thiers tried in 1845 to increase the electorate by a modest 15,000, Guizot refused. "There are in France," he argued, "no more than 180,000 men capable of voting intelligently and independently." His favorite retort to those asking for an extension of the franchise was, "Get rich!" (*Enrichissez-vous!*). In foreign policy, likewise, he saw no need for adventure. "Let us not talk about our country having to conquer territory, to wage great wars, to undertake bold deeds of vengeance. If France is prosperous, if she remains free, rich, peaceful, and wise, we need not complain."

The significance of this period of the July Monarchy lies less in the

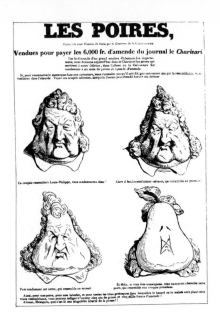

LOUIS PHILIPPE IN CARTOONS. The French satirical weekly, *Charivari*, in which these famous pear drawings appeared was frequently in trouble with the authorities. The printing makes an appeal for freedom of the press.

pattern of its policies than in the forward march of industrialism and in the social problems thereby created. It was to the credit of the regime that the government showed itself ready to help commerce by enlarging the network of good roads, by canal building, and (after much hesitation) by subsidies to railway and ship building. A fair amount, too, was done in erecting or restoring public buildings. A high tariff was maintained to protect French industry.

With such assistance the economy of France made substantial progress. The principal areas of growth were the cotton and textile industries, silk manufacture, and metallurgy. After a slow start in 1828, railway building forged ahead so that by 1848 there were 1322 miles of track in operation. The first transatlantic steamer sailed from France in 1840. Cities, such as Paris, Lyons, Roubaix, and St. Etienne, grew rapidly in size. Even so, true factory conditions were exceptional in the France of 1848. The urban population which had accounted for 15 percent of the total in 1830 had risen only to 25 percent in 1848. Steam power was introduced very slowly, and the workshop and small, family-owned establishment continued to be typical of business organization. This did not mean that the hardships associated with economic change were absent. On the contrary, they were the source of a mounting volume of protest, and on numerous occasions of actual violence.

The literature of protest which began to grow in France under the July Monarchy was in part the product of disillusioned liberals and republicans, in part also the product of radical groups looking for a drastic transformation of society. Saint-Simon had died in 1825 and Fourier in 1837; their direct disciples included some brilliant young men who were nevertheless unable to develop any important organization. The creed of active, revolutionary violence was preached by Philippe Buonarrotti (he, like Fourier, died in 1837) and by

59

Auguste Blanqui, whose career was one long series of violent episodes interrupted by terms in prison.

Such attitudes encouraged violence. In 1831 revolts occurred among the silk weavers of Lyons. Disturbances in Paris which led to the use of troops broke out in 1832 and again in 1834. A general strike was attempted by the workers of Lyons in the latter year, and there were strikes in St. Etienne, Clermont, Grenoble, and Marseilles. Millions of republican pamphlets were circulated, and a variety of secret organizations, such as The Seasons and The Society of the Rights of Man, were formed. One should not exaggerate the extent of these subterranean forces—Lavisse calls them "a handful of unfortunate and passionate men"—but they were real. Low wages, miserable housing, food shortages, and such tragedies as the shocking cholera epidemic of 1832 which claimed twenty thousand victims in Paris alone, all contributed to the unrest. Between 1835 and 1846 there were six attempts on the life of the good bourgeois monarch, Louis Philippe. Writers of the romantic generation could appeal to emotions of pity, as Victor Hugo was able to do with the characters of Fantine, Cosette, and Valjean in *Les Misérables*.

When Louis Blanc[6] published his *Organization of Labor* in 1839, he made his points with passages such as the following: "The other day a child was frozen to death behind a sentry box in the heart of Paris and no one was shocked or surprised at the event." "Walk through an industrial city at five in the morning," he wrote, "and observe the crowd that presses about the entrance to the mills. You will see miserable children, pale, puny, stunted, dull-eyed, livid-cheeked, breathing with difficulty, bent over like old men. Listen to the talk of these children: their hoarse voices [are] hollow, as if muffled by the noxious atmosphere which they breathe in the cotton mills." In such a situation the passage of a factory act in 1841 which forbade children under eight to work in factories, and limited to eight hours daily the work of children from eight to twelve, must be looked upon as the feeblest kind of palliative, all the more so since there were no effective provisions for inspection and enforcement. In 1840 nine thousand out of ten thousand men called up for military service in manufacturing areas were rejected as physically unfit. The years 1846 and 1847 were years of bad harvests and of a most severe economic depression. In 1847 one-third of the population of Paris was said to be in receipt of charity. Partly in consequence of this the persistent unrest of the previous decades had as its outcome the explosive situation of the year 1848.

6. 1813–1882. Lawyer's clerk and journalist, his *Organization of Labor* (1839) and *History of Ten Years* (1841) indicted the July Monarchy for its failure to legislate for the new industrial age. He advocated the right to work and the government's responsibility for economic planning and welfare services. He served as member of the French provisional government that in 1848 initiated the experiment of National Workshops for unemployed labor—a fiasco which he claimed was due to the government's lack of sympathy with the project.

Questions of foreign policy likewise contributed to the growing sense of unrest. Plenty of Frenchmen could remember the heady days of the Napoleonic Empire. Those who could not do so hardly needed to be reminded of the dominant role which France had then played in European diplomacy. By contrast the record of the July Monarchy seemed at best undistinguished and at worst almost catastrophic. Some regretted that Louis Philippe, under pressure from England, had refused in 1831 the proposal of the Belgian Congress that his son accept the offer of the Belgian crown. Many regretted France's failure to support the Polish revolutionaries of 1831. When Mehemet Ali, Pasha of Egypt, tried to take Syria from the Ottoman Empire in 1831, he had much backing in France. Yet the government of the Duke de Broglie was unwilling to antagonize Russia, now posing as the protector of Turkey. So likewise France would give no help to the Italian revolutionaries of 1831 for fear of antagonizing Austria. The most that Louis Philippe would do in deference to the Clericals was to send French troops to Ancona in 1832, where for six years a watchful eye was kept on the affairs of Rome and the papacy.

When a further war between Mehemet Ali and the sultan broke out in 1839, France's interests were again on the side of Egypt, as they had been since the days of Napoleon. For the other western powers, however, it seemed that the time had come for Turkey to free herself from the threat of Mehemet Ali. By the London Treaty of 1840, England, Austria, Russia, and Prussia offered to guarantee Mehemet Ali possession of Egypt if he would withdraw from Syria. France was furious and Thiers, who was prime minister, made preparations for war. This was the war scare of 1840 which likewise aroused German fears along the Rhine. A British squadron bombarded the Egyptian forces in Beirut; they withdrew; Thiers was forced to resign as premier; and a new French government signed with the other four powers the celebrated Straits Convention of 1841 by which the Straits were to be closed to all foreign warships in times of peace. It is a significant commentary on French policy that Guizot, whose major diplomatic interest was to avoid all foreign adventures, should have succeeded Thiers at this point.

Another source of blunder lay in relations with Great Britain. In 1834 France had joined England in an early Entente Cordiale designed to support the legitimate governments in Spain and Portugal. The Entente was broken in 1846 over the intricate affair of the Spanish marriages. In order to prevent another French succession to the Spanish throne (as in 1700), England had objected to the queen's sister marrying a French prince until Queen Isabella herself had married a Spanish prince and borne children. Such was the first agreement. The sordid arrangement of 1846 which so infuriated Palmerston and Queen Victoria was that Isabella married the Duke of Cadiz, reputedly unable to become a father, and that her sister was then married to Louis

Philippe's son, the Duke de Montpensier. Franco-British relations were seriously compromised and France's diplomatic isolation made even more striking.

The one area of progress was Algeria. The city of Algiers had been occupied by Charles X in 1830 as a last desperate attempt to achieve a popular victory that would save his regime. Little had been done to expand in face of the opposition from the native leader, Abd-el-Kadir. By 1840 it was clear that the policy of "restrictive occupation" had been a failure. A drive therefore was undertaken for full occupation of Algeria and by 1847 had made significant progress, with 100,000 French settlers established. Many of the problems of occupation became the concern of the French army which, with its Foreign Legion and Zouave regiments, took on a new color and developed a high degree of experience and technical competence in the increasingly important field of colonial warfare.

The years before 1848 are a good point at which to assess the position of the Roman Catholic Church in France. An overwhelmingly Catholic country (there were only about 680,000 Protestants and 60,000 Jews in 1815), France lived under the religious regime established by the Napoleonic Concordat of 1801. This clearly recognized the supremacy of the state, which paid clerical salaries, shared in appointments, directed educational life, and set clear limits upon papal authority in France. The king, the ministry, and the Chamber in 1815 could be counted upon as Gallican. A significant tendency of the years after 1815, however, was the growth of a more ardent Roman Catholicism, associated with that aspect of romanticism which looked for a return to the Christian unity of medieval life. This envisaged a close alliance of the Throne and the Altar, it hailed the return of the Jesuit order to France, and it likewise was associated with the growth of that combined lay and clerical organization known as the Congregation, to which an exaggerated and supposedly sinister importance was attached by liberal thinkers. Under Charles X the post of minister of education was held by a bishop. The combination of such tendencies, seeing that it implied the policy of looking beyond the Alps to Rome for assistance and strong papal leadership, was known as "ultramontanism." The conflict between ultramontanism and Gallicanism was profoundly significant in the history of nineteenth-century France, for it introduces the long struggle which under the banners of clericalism and anticlericalism has continued to our own day.

A still further complication arose in the late 1820's with the emergence of the Liberal Catholic movement. The purpose of its leaders—Lamennais, Lacordaire, and Montalembert—was to "liberate" the Catholic Church in France from Gallican control by a separation of church and state. This policy they advocated in their newspaper, L'Avenir, claiming particularly that the clergy should be free to teach the faithful in their own schools. This kind of

Liberal Catholicism was ultramontane in the sense that it appealed to Rome for leadership against state control. Lamennais' views, however, developed so far in the direction of a sort of mystical Jacobinism that in 1832 Pope Gregory XVI was led to denounce the Liberal Catholics in an encyclical. Lamennais, in turn, denounced Rome as "the most infamous sink of iniquity that ever defiled the eyes of man." Although Liberal Catholicism thus separated itself from Rome and declined as a movement, it had served to detach some Roman Catholics from the conservative policies of the regime and put them in touch with certain tendencies of nineteenth-century liberalism.

A final illustration of the unrest haunting the July Monarchy is the phenomenon of Bonapartism. The tremendous legend of the great Napoleon began to take shape from the first moment of his exile to St. Helena. Hundreds of thousands of Frenchmen had worn his uniform. Amid all the changes of this new, bourgeois age, many Frenchmen looked back nostalgically and, no doubt, garrulously to the glamour of imperial days. The moving prose and poetry of Béranger, of Lamartine, and, above all, of Victor Hugo intensified such feelings. Napoleon died in 1821 and the flood of memoirs soon pouring from the pens of those who had shared his exile—Las Cases, Montholon, O'Meara, Bertrand, and Gourgaud—gave further substance to the legend. In 1831 the statue of Napoleon, taken down in 1814, was restored to the top of the imposing column in the Place Vendôme. In 1840 Guizot arranged to have the body of Napoleon brought back to France; and in a solemn ceremony it was placed under the great dome of the Invalides, as Napoleon himself had stipulated in his will, "On the bank of the Seine in the midst of the French people whom I have loved so well."

Legends, if they are to serve, sooner or later must become personified, and it was the fortune of France that the Napoleonic legend eventually became embodied in a remarkable figure destined to leave a lasting mark upon his country. Louis Napoleon Bonaparte was the son of Hortense Beauharnais, daughter of the Empress Josephine by her first marriage, and of Louis Bonaparte, brother of Napoleon. Born in 1808, he had, like all the Bonapartes, gone into exile in 1815. In 1831, while in Italy, he was connected with the revolutionary organization, the *Carbonari*. In 1839 he published an eloquent little book, *Napoleonic Ideas*. "The Emperor Napoleon," he wrote, "has contributed more than any other person to hasten the reign of liberty by preserving the moral influence of the Revolution and diminishing the fears which it inspired." France should once again undertake a vigorous foreign policy that would establish a truly European order, beneficial to all peoples, as Napoleon had been on the point of doing at the time of his overthrow.

Louis Napoleon made two attempts to rally the French in support of such ideals. In October, 1836, he crossed into France at Strasbourg and attempted to win over the garrison there. His failure led to his arrest, brief imprisonment, and deportation to America. In August, 1840, he tried again, crossing the Channel from England in a chartered steamer and landing at Boulogne with a tame vulture—supposedly an eagle—in a cage. With him was a small group with whom he hoped to win over the local garrison. Though he again failed and was arrested, at his trial before the Chamber of Peers in Paris he made a deep impression:

> One last word, gentlemen. I stand before you the representative of a principle, a cause, a defeat. The principle is the sovereignty of the people; the cause is the cause of Empire; the defeat, Waterloo. That principle *you* have recognized, that cause *you* have served, that defeat *you* would revenge. No, there is no disagreement between you and me.[7]

Despite his eloquence, he was sentenced to life imprisonment in the ancient fortress of Ham, where he was able to receive visitors, including, interestingly enough, Louis Blanc. From prison he published another pamphlet, *The Extinction of Pauperism* (1846), which, reflecting current socialist ideas, declared that the government could and should end poverty by colonizing large tracts of untilled land with men lacking means of subsistence. From this prison also he escaped in 1846 by dressing in workman's clothes, putting a pipe in his mouth and a plank over his shoulder, walking out of the main gate, and buying a ticket to England. He had established a name and revived a cause, both of which were to serve him well in 1848.

■ REVOLUTION AND SECOND REPUBLIC, 1848–1852

The revolution which broke out in Paris in February, 1848, was quickly followed by a spectacular wave of revolutions spreading over Italy and central Europe. Constitutional and political demands, national aspirations, and social unrest were the general contributory forces. In France, already unified as a nation, the precipitating factors were essentially political and social. Quite clearly the July Monarchy was not prepared to extend the franchise and liberalize the constitution; it was unwilling to meet even the moderate social demands made by the spokesmen of the working classes; and it had no solution for mounting food prices and unemployment.

The precipitating circumstance came on February 21, 1848, when the government of Guizot banned a huge reform banquet planned by constitutional monarchists and republicans to further the cause of parliamentary reform. The crowds which quickly gathered in the streets to demonstrate against Guizot soon became menacing. Though the king dismissed Guizot in favor of Thiers, the rioting grew worse, and on the twenty-third troops fired into the crowds and sixteen people were killed. The old cry, "*A bas Guizot!*" was now replaced

7. F. A. SIMPSON, *The Rise of Louis Napoleon* (1909), p. 191.

by the cry, "*Vive la République!*" When the National Guards began to fraternize with the people, the seventy-five-year-old Louis Philippe announced his abdication in favor of his young grandson, the Count of Paris. This was on February 24. By now the mobs had driven out all but a minority of the Chamber, and an improvised revolutionary assembly had gathered at the Hôtel de Ville. Two groups emerged. The one, associated with Thiers' newspaper *Le National*, had as its leaders moderate republicans, such as Lamartine, Arago, and Marie. The other, associated with the more radical journal, *La Réforme*, included socialists, such as Louis Blanc, Albert, and Ledru-Rollin. Some of these, indeed, wished to raise the red flag of socialism. Together both groups proclaimed the Republic and quickly formed a provisional government.

This provisional government had at least four main concerns. First, it had to maintain order. Second, it announced plans for the early election of a constituent assembly, and by its decree of universal male adult suffrage at one stroke technically enlarged the electorate from 250,000 to 9,000,000. This, to be sure, was no guarantee that democracy had won the day, as subsequent developments would show. One-third of the prospective voters were still illiterate. Yet France had obtained universal suffrage, even if many of these votes might well be cast on the conservative side, at a time when the electorate in England still remained between 500,000 and 600,000. In the third place, the provisional government was concerned with its reception abroad. The poet, Alphonse de Lamartine,[8] serving as foreign minister, issued an important manifesto in March, assuring the European powers of France's peaceful intentions. Since, however, the revolution was based on the principle of popular sovereignty, he declared that France could not accept the territorial arrangement made in 1815 and would regard herself as the ally of every people aspiring to determine its own fate. She would, however, accept provisionally the present state of Europe in a peaceful sense "as a base and a point of departure."

In the fourth place, and most striking of all, it had to deal with the demands of the socialists that the government tackle the social problem by nationalizing railways, canals, insurance companies, mines, and salt works. The right to work was proclaimed and a permanent commission with Louis Blanc as chairman was set up at the Luxembourg Palace by the constituent assembly to investigate social problems. This soon grew into a veritable parliament of nearly eight hundred members. In order to deal with the acute unemployment in Paris, the famous National Workshops were authorized. These, although faintly echoing the plan devised by Louis Blanc in his *Organization of Labor*,

8. 1790–1869. Romantic poet, historian, and politician, he refused a government post under the July Monarchy declaring, "France is bored." He was foreign minister in the provisional government of 1848. His *History of the Girondins* (1847) was said to be the first historical work eagerly read by women. Within a year of its publication, a rival historian compiled a monograph listing 113 pages of errors of fact in it.

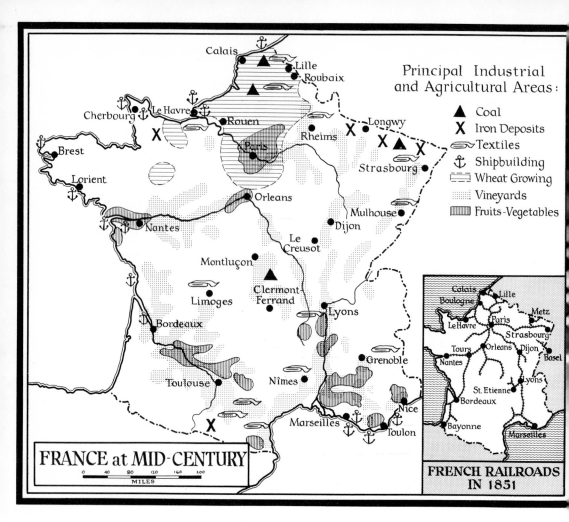

Principal Industrial
and Agricultural Areas:

▲ Coal
✕ Iron Deposits
〰 Textiles
⚓ Shipbuilding
▭ Wheat Growing
░ Vineyards
▦ Fruits-Vegetables

FRANCE at MID-CENTURY

0   40   80   120   160   200
MILES

FRENCH RAILROADS
IN 1851

Note the concentration of French industrial resources near the northeast frontier. In the insert Paris clearly represents the center of the rail network, which by mid-century has reached the frontiers.

were much more of an improvised expedient than they were the state-aided social workshops, or factories, which Blanc had originally envisaged. It is possible indeed that some members of the government hoped from the beginning that the plan would fail. The number of men so employed soon rose from 8,000 to 115,000, though many were simply put to work with pick and shovel leveling the Champ de Mars at two francs a day.

The elections of April for a provisional constituent assembly saw 7,800,000 voters, about 84 percent of the total, go to the polls. The results gave 500 seats to Lamartine and his moderate republicans and only 100 seats to Louis Blanc and the socialists. The Orleanists won 200 seats and the Legitimists, or Bourbon supporters, 100. Resentful at this, to them unsatisfactory, outcome, mobs threatened the new assembly on May 15, which thereupon voted to bring the experiment of the National Workshops to a close. This quickly provoked the great insurrection of June 23 to 26, by far the greatest eruption of violence that Paris had seen since the Revolution of 1789. Troops under the direction of General Cavaignac were poured into the city, fighting went on for three days, and at the end 15,000 were arrested and 4,000 deported. Nine hundred soldiers and nearly 1,500 rioters died, and the Archbishop of Paris was killed as he tried to mediate. Unlike the situation in 1830, a genuinely proletarian element had injected itself into the street fighting and its cry was as much for social, as it was for political, equality. General Cavaignac, who put down the revolt and followed it with a program of repression, carried the stigma of these days for the rest of his life. Truly, the dreams of a republic of socialists had been shattered.

By November the Assembly had created the constitution for what is known as the Second Republic. It provided for a single assembly to be elected by universal suffrage for three years. The president was to be elected by universal suffrage for four years, and not to be eligible for immediate re-election. He named his own ministers and was given very wide executive powers. Members of parliament were to be paid, and individual rights included the usual rights of speech and assembly, but not, despite the socialist theorists, the right to work.

Four candidates for the presidency appeared. General Cavaignac was the candidate of the moderate republicans, Ledru-Rollin, of the radical republicans, and Raspail, of the extreme socialists. But the candidate who flashed into a blaze of prominence was none of these. The man of the hour was Louis Napoleon Bonaparte, who had returned to France from London as heir of the great imperial tradition and who was able to captivate Frenchmen by his promises of a new and glorious age. Some of Napoleon's old soldiers, indeed, were said to have believed that the great emperor himself had returned. "Why should I not vote for him," one of them asked, "I, whose nose was frozen at Moscow?" For clearer heads he could point out that he had the backing of Thiers, the spokesman of the conservative republicans. The results of the voting were as follows:

Cavaignac	1,448,107 votes
Ledru-Rollin	370,119 votes
Raspail	36,329 votes
Louis Napoleon	5,434,226 votes

Elections for the Assembly were held in May, 1849, and again proved a startling reversal for the hopes of the republicans. The moderates won 80 seats and the socialists 180. This last figure, it should be noted, was almost twice that of the socialist membership in the provisional assembly. But the men of the left were a minority when set against the 450 monarchists, either Orleanists or Legitimists, chosen by the electorate. Thus it came about that the Second Republic had as its president an adventurer dedicated to the Bonapartist imperial tradition and a legislature the majority of which had repudiated as clearly as could be the republican cause. Under such circumstances a vigorous republican program was a vain hope.

In domestic matters the new president of France moved slowly. He appointed an Orleanist, Odilon Barrot, as his prime minister; most of his cabinet were men who had served under Louis Philippe. In October the ministry was replaced by a group of untried men, devoted only to himself and in some measure, therefore, to a dictatorship. In March, 1850, the legislature passed the Falloux Law, which made it much easier for Roman Catholic schools to be established, and gave the Church a substantial influence in the governing bodies of all French universities and schools. An electoral law of May, 1850, stiffened the property and residence requirements for voting, with the result that the electorate was cut down from nine to six millions. Other laws, inspired by fear of the left, suppressed radical journals, limited free speech, and forbade republican emblems and clubs. Something that could be called "Caesarism" was in the making.

Equally significant moves were made in the field of foreign affairs where, to be sure, a Bonaparte could hardly remain long silent. In February, 1849, Mazzini and Garibaldi had proclaimed a republic in Rome, whence Pius IX earlier had fled. From the kingdom of Naples he appealed to the European powers for help. When Austria sent troops to the Romagna, concern arose in France lest the Austrians take the lead over the French. Hence Louis Napoleon, who wished to win Clerical support, was able to disembark French forces (April, 1849) in the Papal States. At the end of June French forces broke into the Eternal City, overthrew the Roman Republic, and re-established the authority of Pius IX. Louis Napoleon had moved into the European limelight; he had kept Austria from playing a lone hand, and he had delighted the Clericals in France. Yet he had alienated the republicans whose cause he had sworn to uphold.

Louis Napoleon's writings had made it clear that he wished to play the role of a Caesar, and the elections seemed to imply that France had little enthusiasm for a republic. By December, 1852, the president's term would be up, and under the constitution he could not succeed himself. When the Assembly refused Louis Napoleon's request to restore the vote to the three millions who had been disfranchised, he had maneuvered that parliamentary body nicely into a corner. Conditions were now ripe for a coup d'état.

On December 2, 1851, shrewdly picked as the anniversary of the Battle of Austerlitz—one of Napoleon I's greatest victories—the blow fell. The key ministers were privy to the secret. Large loans had been obtained from abroad, placards and posters printed, and lists made of hostile soldiers and deputies who were to be temporarily arrested. Paris awoke to find the city covered with announcements saying that the Assembly was dissolved, universal suffrage restored, and a new constitution promised. Seventy-eight of Louis Napoleon's leading opponents had quietly been arrested. For most workingmen the old Assembly, dominated by royalists, hardly seemed worth saving. The coup had succeeded and it was therefore something of an accident that on December 4 the crowds assembled on the Boulevard de Montmartre tangled with the troops. A shot rang out, the troops fired back, and before the rioting ended an undetermined number of Parisians, certainly rising into the hundreds, were dead. On a smaller scale, similar troubles occurred in the provinces. Louis Napoleon's authority was not seriously in danger, yet throughout the next two decades he was never able to remove the stigma of being the Man of December. A plebiscite on December 21 authorized Louis Napoleon by a majority of 7,500,000 to 640,000 to draw up a new constitution for France. To all intents the Second Republic was dead, and, in the words of F. A. Simpson, "If the coup d'état was a crime, France was less its victim than its accomplice." This Constitution of 1848 was the ninth which France had scrapped since 1792.

■ THE SECOND EMPIRE: DOMESTIC POLICIES, 1852–1870

The result of the plebiscite of December, 1851, was to turn France into a legalized dictatorship. The arrest of over 25,000 accused persons throughout France, the expulsion of 88 deputies from the country, and the deportation overseas to Algeria of some 9,000 others, to say nothing of muzzling the press, closing political clubs, dissolving the National Guard, and imprisoning thousands for terms of varying length, all were clear marks of the autocratic hand. Very quickly, in January, 1852, a revised constitution was proclaimed. Prince Louis Napoleon Bonaparte was named in it as president for ten years, with very wide executive powers. He initiated, sanctioned, and promulgated the laws, appointed ministers, and received an oath of fidelity from all public officials. He could appeal at any time to the people by plebiscite. A Council of State, nominated by the president, was to draft all legislation. A Senate most of whose members were appointed by the president for life watched over the constitution. The Legislature was to be elected by universal manhood suffrage for six years on the basis of one deputy for every 35,000 voters. It could reject, but not amend, the bills submitted to it; it was to sit for only three months yearly; and its debates could not be published. Save for the provision of universal suffrage, this structure was closely reminiscent of the constitution which the first Napoleon had drawn up in 1800.

With such a constitution it was easy to proceed with elections. A circular sent to all prefects in February, 1852, announced that there need be no secrecy as to the government's intentions: "The people must be in a position," it said, "to discern who are the friends and who are the enemies of the regime which they have created. Consequently take measures to make clear to the electors in each constituency who are the candidates that the government of Louis Napoleon considers the most suitable to help him in his work of reconstruction." For the Senate, 72 of its 84 members were direct nominees of Louis Napoleon and in the Legislature 251 out of the 261 elected were "official" candidates. It is not surprising, therefore, that the prince-president should have quickly moved to re-establish the Empire. In a tour through the provinces in the autumn of 1852 he was greeted with cries of "*Vive l'Empereur!*" At Bordeaux, in a famous speech in October, he recognized this situation and eloquently stated what he considered his goals to be:

> There are some who doubt, and say, "The Empire, that means war." I tell you, the Empire means peace. . . .
> We have immense waste territories to cultivate: roads to open, harbors to deepen, canals to complete, rivers to render navigable, railways to link in one. Facing us across from Marseilles we have a vast dominion [Algeria] to assimilate to France. We have all our great ports of the west to bring near to America by speed of communications which as yet they lack. Everywhere we have ruins to raise again, false gods to tread underfoot, truths to make triumphant. That is how I would interpret the Empire, if the Empire is indeed to be restored. Such are the conquests I contemplate.[9]

The plebiscite which soon followed gave 7,824,189 votes for, and 253,145 votes against, the Empire. In December, 1852, once again on the Day of Austerlitz, it was proclaimed. The title "Napoleon III" indicated that Louis Napoleon considered the son of Napoleon I, the Duke of Reichstadt who had died in 1832, likewise to have been the embodiment of the imperial dignity.

Between 1852 and 1862 the rule of Napoleon III was such as to justify the phrase, the "Authoritarian Empire," which has been attached to it. His first aim was to establish the brilliance of an earlier period. Hence his search for a bride, resulting in his marriage in 1852 to a beautiful Spanish countess, Eugénie de Montijo, whose titian hair and sapphire eyes compensated for her lack of royal descent and gave gaiety and charm to the gaslit splendors of the Tuileries. Those who surrounded the emperor were of many types: able civil servants, such as Baron Haussmann, who rebuilt Paris; parvenus, such as Persigny, the tax-collector's son whom Napoleon III made a duke; adventurers and dandified types such as the Duke de Morny (illegitimate son of Hortense Beauharnais and half-brother to Napoleon III); and Count Walewski (son of the beautiful Polish Countess Walewska by Napoleon I), foreign minister from 1855 to 1860, then senator and president of the Chamber. The Second Empire was never free from an atmosphere of peculation and scandal. Despite his radiant empress, so perfectly depicted in the paintings of Winterhalter, Napoleon kept up the

9. F. A. SIMPSON, *Louis Napoleon and the Recovery of France*, (2nd ed., 1930), pp. 194–195.

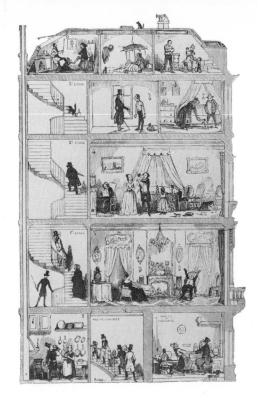

CROSS SECTION OF A PARISIAN APARTMENT HOUSE UNDER THE SECOND EMPIRE. Note that, unlike England, families of different social status live under the same roof, and that as one climbs higher prosperity declines.

long list of gallantries that had marked his earlier years. In the eyes of Europe the new imperial court was widely regarded as trivial and suspect. The Tsar Nicholas I was reluctant to change the conventional greeting "Dear Friend" into "Dear Brother." When the Empire fell in 1870, one of its minor French beneficiaries wrote its epitaph in a sentence that many would agree to accept as accurate. "It wasn't much of an Empire," he declared, "but we had a devilish good time." (*Ce n'était pas un Empire comme il faut, mais nous nous sommes diablement bien amusés.*)

The reasons for this inability to appreciate Napoleon's qualities are clear. He was suspect to the Republicans for having overthrown the Republic. Many of them chose to go into exile. He was suspect to the Orleanists and to the Legitimists. He was suspect, even, to some Bonapartists, such as Victor Hugo, who regarded him as a pygmy in comparison with the mighty figure of Napoleon I. Hence the contemptuous phrases about the new master of France: "Napoleon the Little," "The Man of December," "The sphinx without a secret," "A vast, unfathomed incapacity." Yet the outward appearances and contemptuous verdicts concealed many of the intelligent purposes and the substantial achievements of Napoleon III.

The expression, "Authoritarian Empire," as applied to the decade of the 1850's in France, is wrong if it implies that there was little more to it than political repression; and even these measures could be understood, if not approved, as part of Napoleon's overwhelming desire for order. Police supervision, press censorship, arrests, exilings, and rigid control of education were only one part of the picture. Recognizing the authoritarian color of political life, which was drained of all popular vitality, one must see also a remarkable grasp on the part of the emperor of the economic and social trends of the times. Albert Guérard has written that Napoleon III had a sense of the future which compelled him to steer and not to drift. His genuine concern was for the prosperity and welfare of his people. He had written of such goals, albeit crudely, in his *Extinction of Pauperism;* he had, as we have noted, talked to Louis Blanc while in prison; and he drew many members of the Saint-Simonian circle to support his regime. The great French critic, Sainte-Beuve, indeed, called Napoleon III "Saint-Simon on horseback." Earlier, perhaps, than any other major European figure, Napoleon III was able to fix his policies in relation to the tremendous forward march of the Industrial Revolution.

The decade of the 1850's showed remarkably vigorous government action in economic matters. Credit for business enterprises was made possible through two agencies, the *Crédit Foncier* and the *Crédit Mobilier,* both chartered in 1852. The former, by obtaining funds through land mortgages, stimulated urban rebuilding. The latter helped to finance railways, shipping companies, gas lighting companies, and mining companies. Government assistance was given to railroad building; the many small companies were merged into six great regional networks and subsidies were provided for their operation. Similar arrangements were made for steamship companies. Tariffs were reduced to stimulate trade. Beginning with the English treaty of 1860, others quickly followed with Belgium, Switzerland, the Netherlands, Sweden, Italy, Spain, and Prussia. The result was a substantial increase in the French export trade. The Universal Exposition of 1859, like the famous Crystal Palace Exhibition of 1851 in England, was a spectacular testimonial to the regime's new concerns. Napoleon III likewise initiated an active social policy. Mutual aid societies, government-owned pawnshops, and improvements in workers' dwellings were undertaken. In 1854 committees were authorized to undertake conciliation in disputes between workers and masters. Baron Haussmann,[10] appointed prefect of the Seine in 1853, undertook a spectacular rebuilding of Paris, creating wide streets and boulevards, elegant public squares, new or refurbished public buildings, such as the Opera and the Markets, elaborate new drainage systems and water supplies, new bridges over the Seine, and a great development in the Bois de Boulogne. Few reigns have seen so much material improvement in so short a time.

---

10. 1809–1891. Of German extraction, he served as prefect of the Seine under Napoleon III. He laid out the Bois de Boulogne and many of the boulevards, was responsible for beginning the construction of the Paris Opera and for several bridges, and reorganized the capital's water supply. He is one of the pioneer city planners of modern times.

Napoleon was anxious to improve his relations with the Roman Catholic Church, a policy in which the empress, an ardent Clerical, steadily encouraged him. While president of the Second Republic he had helped in 1849 to restore the pope to Rome. He extended the concessions initiated by the Falloux Law of 1850, which extended the role of the Church in primary and secondary education. The religious orders needed for these purposes steadily added teachers. Meanwhile, the Liberal Catholics, led by Montalembert, were reluctant to give their support to a regime not based on genuine principles of freedom.

The virtue of these various programs is much more evident in retrospect than it was to many Frenchmen in the 1850's. Criticism of the political regime went on apace, and when Victor Hugo, living in self-imposed exile on the island of Jersey, wrote his account of the coup of 1851 he entitled it *History of a Crime*. Passive resistance came from the Royalists and from such Republicans as Cavaignac, who chose rather to forfeit his seat in the Legislature than to take an oath of loyalty to the regime. French participation in 1859 with Piedmont in the war against Austria resulted indirectly in the loss of papal territories to the new kingdom of Italy. This offended many of Napoleon's supporters among the French Catholics. While a "war of epigrams" was carried on against him by moderates, such as Thiers, Guizot, and Broglie, a more ominous opposition came from secret societies and radical revolutionaries hoping to overthrow the regime by violence. In 1858 one of them, an Italian anarchist named Orsini who looked upon Napoleon III as an obstacle to the unification of Italy, threw three bombs at the imperial coach as it arrived at the Opera. Though the emperor and empress escaped, their escape was narrow. In the elections of 1857 the opposition parties who had cast only 250,000 votes in the plebiscite of 1852 now, though still only one-tenth of the total, cast 665,000 votes. The unrest in Paris found an echo in many of the provincial cities.

By 1860 a combination of pressures arising both from domestic and foreign matters led Napoleon in the direction of the Liberal Empire. The phrase is a misnomer if it suggests a sudden and complete transition, yet the steps are evident. In 1859 an amnesty was accorded to all political offenders. In 1860 a decree provided that the Senate and Legislative Assembly could discuss the address from the throne freely and reply to it; their debates were to be published; and ministers without portfolio could be questioned in parliament. Prefects were instructed to be more lenient toward the press, and in subsequent years this freedom was enlarged. The relaxation of press controls in 1868, for example, led to the appearance of 140 new journals in Paris alone within a year. In 1861 legislative control over the steadily mounting expenditures of the state was enlarged. In 1864 the rights of workers to combine and even to strike were recognized.

None of these steps allayed the opposition, which in the elections of 1863 polled nearly two million votes, a threefold increase since 1857. This opposition came together in a broad coalition known as the Liberal Union. Thiers, who had been re-elected to the Chamber, was the center of one group demanding the "indispensable liberties" (that is, the basic parliamentary rights enjoyed by Englishmen). French socialists issued in 1864 their Manifesto of the Sixty. This landmark in their cause declared that, while universal suffrage had brought *political* maturity, it had not brought *social* emancipation. "Equality," the Manifesto said, "which is stated in the law is not a part of our customs and has not been realized in fact." By 1867 the emperor was led by pressure at home and failures abroad to promise still further reforms. Not even this would suffice. Within the legislature a Third Party arose, separate from the Republicans, and inspired by Thiers. It was supported by some Catholics, by businessmen, disgruntled officials, and others, all seeking a more genuinely parliamentary regime.

VOTING IN NATIONAL ELECTIONS UNDER THE SECOND EMPIRE[11]

OCCASION	FOR THE GOVERNMENT	AGAINST, WITH % OF TOTAL
Plebiscite on accepting the empire, 1852	7,824,189	253,145 (3.1%)
Elections of 1857	5,471,000	665,000 (10.8%)
Elections of 1863	5,308,000	1,954,000 (26.9%)
Elections of 1869	4,438,000	3,355,000 (43.0%)
Plebiscite on liberal constitution, 1870	7,358,000	1,572,000 (17.6%)

The steady increase of the opposition, despite the concessions of the 1860's, is notable, as well as the overwhelming majority for the liberal constitution of 1870.

Further concessions, such as a more liberal press law and greater freedom of assembly, were granted in 1868. The unrest, nevertheless, continued, some of it taking an outspokenly republican form. The elections of 1869 revealed 43 percent of the voters in opposition to the government. In January, 1870, the emperor approached Emile Ollivier, one of the leaders of the Third Party, to form a ministry. Ollivier did so, though it was not clear that Napoleon was genuinely ready to turn over his authority to a prime minister armed with constitutional powers. By a *senatus consultum* of April, 1870, the emperor had announced a further revision of the constitution of 1852 which would truly have created a liberal empire. Authority taken from the Senate would be given to the Legislature, which was granted the right to amend, to question all ministers,

11. Derived from the several accounts in E. LAVISSE, ed., *Histoire de la France contemporaine* (1921), vols. VI and VII.

and to vote the budget chapter by chapter. Ministers would be responsible to the Legislature. The plebiscite of May, 1870, gave the constitution a five-to-one approval—well over seven million ayes to one and a half million noes.[12] Ollivier professed to be delighted. Had not France met military disaster within a year, one may still ask whether a limited monarchy might not conceivably have prospered. One may ask, but the answer is not clear. Statistics in favor of a monarchical constitution do not tell the whole story. In the late sixties republicanism found some eloquent champions: Jules Favre, Jules Simon, Jules Ferry, and, above all, Léon Gambetta. This young lawyer from Marseilles made a name for himself by defending some journalists in a press trial of 1868. Elected for Belleville, a working-class suburb of Paris, in 1869, Gambetta issued the famous Belleville Manifesto of 1869, calling for universal manhood suffrage in both local and national elections; complete freedom of the press, of meetings and of associations; total separation of church and state; free, compulsory, universal primary education; suppression of standing armies; the abolition of all privilege; the election of all public functionaries; and a wide program of social reforms. This was the new force that was to sweep Gambetta into prominence as the Empire fell. In the first session of the Chamber elected in 1869, Gambetta boldly addressed the majority who had accepted the Liberal Empire in eloquent and prophetic words:

> If you count on our support in order to establish liberty and Empire together, you will wait in vain. . . . In our eyes universal suffrage is not compatible with the form of government that you advocate. Between the Republic of 1848 and the Republic of the future, you are only a bridge—and we shall pass over it.[13]

■ THE SECOND EMPIRE: FOREIGN POLICIES, 1852–1870

On balance it would seem that Napoleon III's foreign policy was more significant in its impact upon Europe than in what it did for France. For France, indeed, the effects were clearly mixed. As early as 1856 the Congress of Paris which closed the Crimean War showed that France had assumed a central role in European diplomacy. In 1860 France obtained Nice and Savoy from the kingdom of Piedmont, and during the reign there were substantial colonial gains. The conquest of Algeria was completed by 1857; in the same decade a French expedition was sent to Peking to obtain rights to treaty ports. The historic French interests in Syria and the Levant were reaffirmed, and settlements were made, or enlarged, on the African coast in Senegal, Dahomey, and Guinea. A new interest was aroused in Madagascar. Punitive expeditions were sent to Annam (1858) and Cochin China (1862) and a French protectorate set

---

12. The great cities, as always, were against Napoleon. Paris gave 138,000 ayes and 184,000 noes. Lyons, Toulouse, and Marseilles were also opposed.
13. LAVISSE, vol. VII, pp. 86–87, author's transl.

up in Cambodia (1863). These actions, laying the foundations for French control of Indo-China, were substantial achievements. Yet the grand outcome of Napoleon III's foreign policy was a shattering war, which destroyed his Empire and required France to turn over Alsace and Lorraine to Germany.

It has been said that few men have contributed more—unintentionally—to the making of modern Europe than Napoleon III. The sarcasm is less than fair. His Bordeaux speech of 1852 had insisted that the Empire meant peace. Napoleon III shares with Alexander I of Russia the honor of first proposing the need for general European disarmament. He was a strong advocate of the method of diplomacy by conference and offered his services as a mediator on more than one occasion. He was a keen advocate of the cause of nationality, and furthered this cause, wittingly or unwittingly, in the case of Rumania, Italy, and Germany. And he had also a vision of a federated Europe in which the various national units would be combined in some larger structure. These ideas were adumbrated in his *Napoleonic Ideas* of 1839, and were reflected in his subsequent actions. It is surely inadequate therefore to regard him simply as an incompetent who time and again was outwitted by craftier opponents and in the end brought disaster to France. What is striking about the foreign policy of Louis Napoleon is his failure to carry through with his original purposes, or to be quick enough in meeting the unanticipated outcomes of what he had begun.

The Roman expedition of 1849, in the very first year of his presidency, is a good example of this. Pius IX had been driven by revolutionary action from his states, and Austria had moved to help him. One of the last acts of the expiring French Constituent Assembly in March, 1849, had been to authorize credits for an expeditionary force to be sent to Italy to maintain Roman liberties against reactionary Austrian intervention. In a subsequent letter Louis Napoleon reiterated this purpose. Yet when the once-liberal Pius IX was restored by the French, he refused to have any dealings with reform. French troops stayed on as a garrison in the Papal States, defenders of the temporal power lest Austria come in, and Louis Napoleon's liberal reputation inevitably suffered.

In the Crimean War the emperor was able to reassert French traditional interests in the Levant and to make a grand display of military force. Three times as many Frenchmen served in the Crimea as British, though the losses incurred by these allies were about equal. Napoleon III was host at the Congress of Paris in 1856 which ended the war and at which some important rules of international law concerning blockade and contraband were laid down. The arrangements of 1856 also gave the two Rumanian provinces of Moldavia and Wallachia autonomy within the Ottoman Empire. Following this, Napoleon III was able in 1858 to push the establishment of parliamentary government in these principalities and by 1861 to persuade the powers to recognize Prince Alexander Cuza as the ruler over the unified territory of Rumania, which by

1878 would achieve full independence. In this sense he has a claim to be regarded as one of the founders of modern Rumania.

Napoleon III's relations with Italy raise very complex problems. As a young man in exile he had associated with the *Carbonari* in a rising of 1831 in Romagna. He was under pressure from the French Clericals to support the Roman Catholic Church. He was anxious to break the spell of the treaties of 1815, and he had continuing sympathies for Italian nationalism. But he could hardly work toward the goal of a powerful, closely united Italy. His dealings with Cavour and Austria are considered elsewhere.[14] In essence he was prepared to help Cavour, prime minister of Piedmont, to drive out Austria and unite northern Italy in the expectation that the outcome would be a federated Italy with an enlarged Piedmont in the north, a central Italian kingdom, a small papal territory, and a kingdom of Naples. At the price of military assistance France would get Nice and Savoy, and Napoleon's victories in the field would raise him to the rank of the great conquerors. Hence the secret arrangements made with Cavour at Plombières. The dream was only partly realized. France, in the end, did get Nice and Savoy, but the emperor's military reputation was hardly enhanced, the Clericals in France were unhappy, and the unification of Italy proceeded to an extent and at a speed far beyond what Napoleon had anticipated.

His other ventures were similarly compounded of cross-purposes and unexpected results. The Mexican affair arose almost fortuitously in 1861 when Benito Juárez, a revolutionary leader, seized power in Mexico. His repudiation of the public debts owed to foreign governments led England, France, and Spain to agree to send troops to the Mexican coast to protect their interests. In 1862 when the British and Spanish troops were withdrawn, Napoleon decided to send French troops to Mexico City and drive out Juárez. This done, Napoleon III now had dreams of a new sphere of influence in the western hemisphere. He persuaded the Austrian Archduke Maximilian, brother of the Emperor Francis Joseph, to accept the throne offered by the Mexican conservatives. But when the American Civil War came to an end in 1865, making it possible for the United States government to reassert the principles of the Monroe Doctrine, and when European problems became more urgent, Napoleon III was compelled to withdraw his troops. This was in February, 1867. Four months later Maximilian was shot, his wife went mad, and what had been a fiasco turned into a tragedy.

The Polish insurrection of 1863 was another occasion when Napoleon sought to do good and accomplished nothing. Sympathy for the Poles was strong in France. When Bismarck offered Prussian help to the tsar in putting down the revolt, Napoleon publicly protested, proposing instead that a Euro-

14. See pp. 116–128.

pean congress meet to deal not only with the Polish question, but with the entire European political structure. "The treaties of 1815," he declared grandiloquently, "have ceased to exist." Nothing came of this sweeping proposal; Russia alone put down the insurrection with great savagery, and Napoleon, the champion of nationality, was regarded by both Russia and Prussia as a dangerous meddler.

Diplomatic crises followed at lightning speed, for Bismarck was in the process of converting the old German Confederation of 1815 into the German Empire of 1871. To do this he maneuvered on the European scene with utter realism and dazzling virtuosity, moving step by step toward this anticipated goal. Napoleon, meanwhile, was torn by conflicting purposes. On the one hand, as an enemy of the treaties of 1815 and as a good Frenchman, he aspired to move the French frontier toward the Rhine. On the other hand, he wished to help the cause of European nationalities and to participate wherever possible in European congresses. The sequence of events shows him involved in both purposes. When the Schleswig-Holstein crisis developed in 1864, Napoleon proposed that the matter be referred to a congress, but he was unable to secure a congress or to prevent Bismarck's success. His hope, basically, was that difficulties between Prussia and Austria, complicated further by the dislike of the South German states for Prussia, would result ultimately in the appearance of a divided, tripartite Germany that would constitute the least possible threat to France. One is struck by the parallel here with what Napoleon had hoped for in Italy. Bismarck's ruthless moves, which are considered in detail elsewhere, were masterly in execution.[15] Napoleon, meanwhile, refused to be alarmed, for he was convinced that Bismarck was dividing, not uniting, Germany. In 1866 he proposed to Bismarck that France be allowed to annex Luxembourg or part of the Rhineland. A little later in the same year he suggested that he annex Belgium. Bismarck did not seem altogether unfavorable, but would promise nothing outright. Napoleon tried negotiating directly with the king of the Netherlands for the purchase of Luxembourg, but Bismarck strenuously objected and the plan was dropped. All Napoleon's diplomatic moves, whether animated by the desire to serve France or to serve the cause of European nationality, were used by Bismarck to whip up sentiment in Germany (most particularly in the South German states) against France.

■ THE SECOND EMPIRE: FINALE, 1870–1871

Foreign affairs brought the Second Empire to disaster. When a revolution in Spain left the throne empty and the new regime, searching in 1869 for a candidate, hit upon the young Leopold of Hohenzollern-Sigmaringen—a distant relative of the king of Prussia—France was inevitably concerned, as she

15. See pp. 144–157.

had been in every Spanish crisis during the nineteenth century. She could not now with equanimity contemplate Hohenzollerns in Spain as well as Prussia. Even in this tense period it is notable that the Ollivier government in January, 1870, asked Britain to approach Bismarck to see if there could be simultaneous disarmament on the part of France and Prussia. When the approach was made in February, Bismarck refused absolutely. He was able to keep the Spanish crisis alive after it had first died down; and, even when Prince Leopold had withdrawn his candidacy and all reason for hostility was at an end, he was able to profit by one last great French mistake. Both Guizot and Thiers stated that the French success in getting Leopold to withdraw his candidacy was the greatest diplomatic victory they had ever seen. But Ollivier, the French premier, and Gramont, the foreign minister, were not content. They sent the French ambassador, Benedetti, to see King William I of Prussia at Ems, asking him to refuse future support of such a candidacy. Definitely rejecting this undiplomatic request, the king dismissed Benedetti and reported the circumstances to Bismarck at Berlin in the famous Ems Telegram which he authorized Bismarck to "prepare" for the press. This Bismarck did with a vengeance. The resulting explosions of public opinion in Germany, and more particularly the feelings in the French Assembly, quickly brought on a war. France had no allies; she was far less ready than was believed; and the emperor himself was ill and in great pain. It was France who declared war upon Prussia in July, 1870; Ollivier, who had stated on June 30 that "not a cloud threatened the peace of Europe," now said that he entered the war "with a light heart." The minister of war assured Napoleon that the French army was "ready to the last gaiter button."

The Franco-Prussian War doomed the Second Empire. Bismarck had the military support of the South German states, now thoroughly alarmed at France, and the benevolent neutrality of Russia. France was isolated. Three German armies entered the country; Alsace and Lorraine were overrun in weeks; and Marshal Bazaine was besieged in the great fortress of Metz. The ailing Napoleon III, who had gone in person to take command, surrendered on September 2 at Sedan with an army of 81,000 men. Bazaine surrendered even more disastrously at Metz on October 27 with 173,000 men. Meanwhile the news of Sedan had reached Paris. On September 4 a group of republicans headed by Gambetta set up a provisional government of national defense and proclaimed the Republic, with General Trochu as president. When the Prussian armies soon besieged Paris, the 300,000 men of the National Guard were armed and the city turned into a vast entrenched camp. Gambetta escaped by balloon to Tours, where he sought to direct the national defense. In a spurt of energy the French won back Orléans from the enemy and held it for a month. Many Frenchmen carried on bravely, yet their courage was unavailing. After a four months' siege that brought the population to the point of starvation, Paris surrendered on January 28, 1871. On March 1 a newly elected national assembly voted to accept the Prussian terms, at the same time formally pronouncing the deposition of Napoleon III, now an unhappy prisoner in Germany. The definitive Treaty of Frankfurt was signed on May 10, 1871, and with it France entered a new era. Amid the disasters which had overcome the Second Empire, signalized most explicitly in the loss of Alsace and Lorraine, a German army of occupation, and an indemnity of five billion francs, it was not easy for Frenchmen to realize that Napoleon III, with all his faults and failures, had made notable contributions to the growth of France.

Reading List: Chapter 2

Artz, F. B., *France Under the Bourbon Restoration, 1814–1830* (1931), chs. 4–5. The state of society; the romantic revolt.

Brogan, D. W., "The French Restoration: 1814–1830," *History Today*, vol. VI (1956), no. 1.

Muret, C., *French Royalist Doctrines Since the Revolution* (1933), chs. 3, 5, 6. Chateaubriand, Benjamin Constant, Guizot.

Howarth, T. E. B., *Citizen King: The Life of Louis Philippe* (1961), pp. 139–60, 315–35.

Plamenatz, J., *The Revolutionary Movement in France, 1815–71* (1952), chs. 2–3. The Restoration and the July Monarchy.

Wright, G., "A Poet in Politics: Lamartine and the Revolution of 1848," *History Today*, vol. VIII (1958), no. 9.

Tocqueville, A. de, *Recollections* (1949), part I; part II, chs. 1–3, 9–10. Revolution of 1848 in France.

Gray, Alexander, *The Socialist Tradition: Moses To Lenin* (1946), ch. 9. Louis Blanc.

Thompson, J. M., *Louis Napoleon and the Second Empire* (1955), chs. 4–5. The President, 1848–1852; the Liberal, 1860–1869.

Guérard, A., *Napoleon III* (1943), ch. 9. "Saint-Simon on Horseback."

Gooch, G. P., *The Second Empire* (1960), ch. 17. The world of letters.

Williams, R. L., *Gaslight and Shadow: The World of Napoleon III, 1851–1870* (1957, paperback, 1962), chs. 4, 5, 7, 9. Offenbach, Sainte-Beuve, Pasteur, Courbet.

Chapter 3

The Struggle for Power
in Central Europe, 1848–1851

From Unrest to Revolution
The First Revolutionary Wave in Central Europe
Revolutionary Frustrations
Resurgence and Repression, 1849–1851
The Balance Sheet of Revolution

■ FROM UNREST TO REVOLUTION

The February Revolution of 1848 in France was the signal for a wave of revolutionary violence in central Europe which at first was strong enough to overthrow the solid, conservative regimes which for so long had prevailed. By midsummer the tide was at its flood, arousing, particularly in Germany, a widespread liberal enthusiasm for which the latter part of the century could offer no parallel. By autumn authority had begun to reassert itself. Then, at the year's end and in the early months of 1849, a second wave of revolution surged up. This, too, subsided so that, by the second midsummer, authority once again seized control and Europe was able to contemplate "the revolution that failed."

The disturbances in Austria, in Hungary, in Bohemia, in Prussia, in Lombardy, at Venice, in the Papal States, and elsewhere in Italy paralleled

SIGNIFICANT EVENTS

1847   United *Landtag* in Prussia (March–June)

1848   Constitutions in Naples, Tuscany, and Piedmont (January–March)

Revolution in Paris (February–June)

"March Days" in Vienna, Prague, Berlin, Budapest, and Milan

Constitutions authorized in Papal States, Austria, Hungary, Prussia (March)

Frankfurt Parliament (May, 1848–June, 1849)

Windischgraetz regains Prague (June), Vienna (October)

Servile dues abolished in Austrian lands (September)

"Fundamental Rights of the German People" (December)

1849   Kossuth declares Hungary independent (March)

Frederick William IV refuses headship of the new German state (April)

Hungarians surrender at Világos (August)

1850   Revival of the Diet of the Germanic Confederation (September)

Prussian "Humiliation" at Olmütz (November)

each other closely in time and in most cases were set off by news of the February uprisings in Paris—news which traveled for at least part of the way by means of the newly introduced electric telegraph. Yet quite clearly there was no concerted revolutionary plan. The simultaneous yet separate disturbances arose from similar causes and had in general similar aims. The degree of bloodshed and destruction was, on the whole, slight; even the savage "June days" in Paris give only a foretaste of the terrible excesses of the Commune of 1871. The uprisings were proletarian only to a minor degree; they were chiefly inspired by a bourgeois leadership that owed the genesis of its ideas more to France than to any other country. Yet the influence of France in the year 1848 must be counted as slight. Prussians, Czechs, Austrians, Hungarians, and Italians sought remedies for their own problems and in their own way. At the same time one cannot ignore the psychological significance of the first news coming from

THE KING OF PRUSSIA OFFERING HIS HELP TO HIS FELLOW GERMAN RULERS, 1848. This caricature from the satirical Munich journal, *Leuchtkugeln,* clearly sympathizes with the peasant who, although wearing the revolutionary cap of liberty, is cruelly muzzled and burdened by his rulers.

Paris, and one can well keep in mind the comment of that shrewd observer, Metternich. "When France catches cold," he once wrote, "Europe sneezes."

The revolutionary movements of 1848 made their simultaneous appearance over a very large area as a sequel to earlier disturbances that had no such closeness in time. Revolts that were essentially constitutional or nationalist in their aims had appeared sporadically during the three decades of conservative reaction: in Spain, Portugal, and Naples in 1820; in Piedmont, Moldavia, and Greece in 1821; in Russia in 1825; in France, Belgium, Poland, Parma, Modena, the Papal States, Brunswick, Saxony, and Hesse-Cassel in 1830–1831. In 1846 the peasants of Cracow had rebelled in order to better their conditions. The only result of this last revolt had been that Cracow, set up as a free city by the Congress of Vienna, had been quickly absorbed into the Austrian Empire. Troubles of a different sort had also arisen in Switzerland, a country more noted for its stability than for revolutionary unrest. In 1845 the nine Roman Catholic cantons had formed a special league, the *Sonderbund,* to defy the authority of the Protestant cantons. Though Austria at one time threatened to intervene on the Catholic side, the outcome had been a brief and almost bloodless civil war in which the Catholic cantons were easily defeated.

On the eve of 1848 liberal demands for political reform, interspersed with occasional protests against bad economic and social conditions, were widespread. These liberal demands were particularly apparent in Germany. In

Prussia a United Diet had been summoned in April, 1847, to consider the constitutional question, only to be dismissed in June. A group of German liberals drafted a constitutional program for Baden at Offenburg in September. Another group, meeting at Heppenheim in October, proposed a liberal revision of the constitution of the entire German Confederation.

Revolutionary leadership in country after country was to be that of liberals who were principally resentful of the absence of self-government and of genuine economic progress. They looked for some degree of parliamentary control and some guarantee of minimum human rights. Leadership was necessarily varied. It included liberal industrialists and professional men who wished fuller recognition of their new role in modern society. The attitude of these men is strikingly conveyed in a report submitted in 1844 to the Prussian ministry of the interior concerning the Rhine Province:

> The disgruntlement and dissatisfaction which are becoming evident in this province do not emanate from the lower classes, but from the so-called educated groups which . . . desire to put their ideas about freedom of the press and popular representation into practice at any cost. To this class belong mostly the lawyers, doctors, and merchants, who hope by the means which they advocate to achieve a greater importance, for no one believes that they have only the welfare of the country in mind, as they maintain. Yet they all belong more or less to the well-to-do classes of society, and they are very far from being in sympathy with communistic tendencies. Still, I can well believe that they would be prepared to make use of communism in order to create an unrest which they would exploit in their own entirely private interest.[1]

The atmosphere of crisis at the opening of the new year was made more intense by the ardent proponents of the new gospel of nationalism—men like Mazzini in Italy, Palacky in Bohemia, and Kossuth in Hungary. Economic causes also contributed to the unrest. Central European crop failures in 1845 had produced the "famine spring" of 1846. Blight destroyed the potato harvest of Ireland in 1845 and again in 1846. The serious business depression of 1847 reproduced in the industrial cities the miserable conditions of the countryside. Peasant disturbances in Austrian Galicia in 1846 gave the government much concern and were put down with the greatest ruthlessness, other peasants being hired to capture, and even massacre, the rebels. Food riots in Italy were widespread in 1847 because of harvest failures in the previous year, and the Sicilian risings of January, 1848, though they had the result of forcing King Ferdinand to promise a constitution, were partly set off by peasant unrest.

Occasionally leaders appeared, such as Louis Blanc in France, echoing the doctrines of Utopian Socialism, and even more radical figures, like the

---

1. Quoted in T. S. HAMEROW, *Restoration, Revolution and Reaction: Economics and Politics in Germany, 1815–1871* (Princeton, 1958), p. 60.

Rhineland tailor, Wilhelm Weitling, one of the earliest modern theorists of communism. In 1845 Friedrich Engels, the future collaborator of Karl Marx, had written his *Condition of the Working Classes in England,* based on the shocking evidence of parliamentary investigations. In it Engels prophesied that "the war of the poor against the rich now carried on in detail and indirectly will become direct and universal." In 1847 Marx and Engels formed a Communist League, and later in the year wrote their *Communist Manifesto,* which was published in February 1848. This famous document was to be, however, much more a concern of the future than it was actually of the revolutionary year 1848. Indeed, if the picture of widespread unrest in the 1840's has suggested an economic motivation arising from hunger and misery, such an explanation would be at best only partly true.

■ THE FIRST REVOLUTIONARY WAVE IN CENTRAL EUROPE

The Austria-Hungary where revolt broke out in 1848 was an extraordinary complex of nationalities. Germans, Czechs, Slovaks, Poles, Ruthenians, Magyars, Croats, Serbs, Slovenes, Rumanians, and Italians were linked together under the historic rule of the Hapsburg Monarchy. Although local diets existed in some areas, they were not genuinely representative bodies, and everywhere a German-dominated bureaucracy was imposed from Vienna. In Hungary, to be sure, there was a Diet, or parliament, which had been convoked in 1825 after an interval of thirteen years to meet the demands of the noble Hungarian landowners—the "magnates." This Diet of two houses met periodically, and, while generally conservative in tone, it contained some advocates of reform, most notably Stephen Széchenyi and Louis Kossuth. Count Széchenyi, who was responsible for surveying and improving much of the Danube, could be described as a conservative reformer, a nobleman who believed in breaking away from the Metternich system by means of peasant reforms and industrial innovations. He would still preserve the association with Austria. Louis Kossuth,[2] on the other hand, was an ardent Hungarian nationalist who insisted on political and democratic reforms, particularly in the Diet, and wished to see Hungary on terms of full equality with Austria, if not actually independent from it. Hungarian leaders had not the slightest hesitation in maintaining the vested interests of the Magyars (as the Hungarian-speaking majority was known) over the various minorities of Hungary.

The administration of the Hapsburg Empire was centered in Vienna, where the emperor asserted an absolute authority supposedly based upon divine

2. 1802–1894. Lawyer and journalist, an outstanding spokesman and leader of Hungarian nationalism, he was elected to the Hungarian parliament in 1847. His dominant role in the Revolution of 1848 was crowned by the declaration of Hungarian independence in April, 1849. Following the collapse of the independence movement, he lived a life of exile, refusing to accept the Compromise of 1867 and, like Mazzini, failing to see his dreams realized.

right. Yet the Emperor Ferdinand, who ruled from 1835 to 1848, suffered from serious physical incapacities and was equipped with mediocre intellectual abilities. A special Council of State was formed at the beginning of the reign with the emperor's uncle, the Archduke Ludwig, as president and Prince Metternich and Count Kolowrat as the other members. These two latter disliked each other so much that for years they had refused to communicate except by writing. In the Council of State they quarreled furiously and persistently, with Archduke Ludwig as inefficient arbiter. In Austria, where 140,000 government employees concerned themselves chiefly with keeping things as they were, the system was described by a contemporary as "pure negation." "It was a brazen tablet with these indestructible words on it: 'no concessions, no constitution, no innovation.' " For administrative purposes one chancellery at Vienna supervised the administration of the hereditary Austrian provinces, another looked after the affairs of Hungary, and a third directed the affairs of the eastern area known as Transylvania.

The economy was in bad shape. Agriculture dominated the scene, principally in the form of large noble estates where, especially in Bohemia and Hungary, a condition resembling serfdom prevailed. Compulsory labor service to the landlord (*Robot*) was widespread, as were heavy payments in money (*Zehnt*) or in kind. These were in addition to the land tax and the compulsory contributions to the Church. Some industrial development—textiles, paper manufacture, iron manufacture, glass and metal wares—and some railway building in the forties represented the slow beginnings of the new industrial age. By 1847 there were 469 steam engines operating in Austria in addition to 278 locomotives and 76 steamboats. Wages were miserably low, and government finances were precarious. Though taxes were regularly increased, the deficits were recurrent, with the result that by 1848 the financial administration was dangerously near the point of breakdown. A strict policy of repression, which, while directed toward both religion and education, was principally manifested in the press censorship and the usual activities of the police, tried to keep liberal ideas from finding free expression. Actually, the censorship was, like many things Austrian, ineffective in performance. Consequently in the decade of the forties a considerable agitation for western liberal ideas and constitutional change grew up, especially in Lower Austria, the nonmountainous area which included Vienna. Here an increasingly enlightened middle class and a small but radical city proletariat together reiterated their demands for reform.

The spark of revolt first appeared, not in Austria, but in Hungary. On March 3, hearing the news from Paris, Louis Kossuth made an impassioned speech in the Hungarian Diet at Pressburg. He denounced the tyrannous rule of Vienna and demanded a separate liberal, national program, if not actually independence, for Hungary. The news of this speech inspired public demonstrations in Vienna, where the Diet of Lower Austria had been summoned to meet on March 13. Businessmen and students, intent on presenting petitions to the Diet, clashed with the troops and in the ensuing panic the once seemingly indestructible Metternich, who had been at the center of Austrian affairs since 1809, determined to leave. Unwilling to face the reality of the revolution which he had long feared, he fled to England. The Emperor Ferdinand, tragically incapable of coping with any crisis, is reported to have spoken as follows: "I am the Emperor, and it is for me to decide; and so I yield everything. Tell the people I consent to all their demands." He then promised to guarantee freedom of speech and meeting, and to summon a constituent assembly for the Austrian lands.

A transformation seemed in the making. In Hungary the Diet quickly passed the March Laws providing for a democratically elected Hungarian parliament, abolition of serfdom, guarantees of the rights of man, and complete internal freedom from Austrian rule in Hungary. This was accepted by the emperor on April 11. Although he had promised a constituent assembly for Austria, Ferdinand did not wait for it to do its work. Instead, he proclaimed an Austrian constitution on April 25 setting up a parliamentary regime with a responsible ministry. This was later followed by the granting of universal manhood suffrage.

Meanwhile there had been trouble in Prague, the capital of Bohemia. This ancient kingdom had boasted a proud history of independence during the Middle Ages, until in 1547 the Bohemian crown lost its separate identity and became hereditary in the House of Hapsburg. Despite vigorous attempts to Catholicize and Germanize Bohemia, some sparks of national feeling had always persisted, to be fanned into vigorous flame by nationalist leaders in the early nineteenth century. In the 1848 crisis businessmen and students, with working class support, demonstrated in the streets, took possession of the royal palace, and quickly sent a delegation to Vienna. Under these circumstances it is not surprising that on April 8 the emperor issued a rescript promising a representative parliament for Bohemia and Moravia, political liberty, equality for the Slavic languages, and amelioration of the lot of the peasants. Flushed with victory, the Czechs summoned a Pan-Slav Congress to meet at Prague in June in order to further the unity of the Slavic peoples. It was to be divided into three sections: the Czechoslovak, the Polish-Ruthene, and the Yugoslav. Ironically enough, the only language common to the five hundred delegates was German. The Congress managed to draft a "vague, verbose, and ineffective document" extolling the virtues of the Slavs and proposing a universal congress of European nations to settle all outstanding problems. Its deliberations came to an end when street fighting broke out in Prague in June. Meanwhile the climax of this entire period of revolutionary success in the Hapsburg lands came on May 17, when the emperor and his family fled from the revolutionary atmosphere of Vienna to the comparative peace and security of Innsbruck, capital of the Tyrol.

March uprisings in Italy, where patriotic crowds quickly asserted independence from Austrian rule in both Milan and Venice, must briefly be noted here. On March 22 the kingdom of Piedmont, responding to an appeal from the Milanese, declared war on Austria and began the invasion of Lombardy. In a striking parallel to the events north of the Alps, Charles Albert of Piedmont on March 4 had granted a liberal constitution (the *Statuto*) to his people.

In Prussia the liberal elements had been bitterly disappointed at the failure of Frederick William IV to encourage the plans of the Constitutional Assembly of 1847. Unrest grew, and in March, 1848, the news from France provoked demonstrations in the streets of Berlin. These led the timid king to promise what he had previously refused—a representative constitution and freedom of the press. When in the course of further demonstrations street fighting broke out, many Berliners were killed by the police. Crowds carrying torches paraded the bodies in front of the royal palace on Unter den Linden. In the public funerals on the following day there were 183 coffins. The king, deeply moved, was obliged to salute the dead, after which, contrary to all Prussian tradition, he issued a proclamation that his kingdom would soon merge itself in a united Germany (*"Preussen geht in Deutschland auf "*). In May a Prussian constitutional assembly began its work. Meanwhile, similar uprisings and disturbances broke out in Baden, Württemberg, Bavaria, Saxony, and a number of the smaller states. As in Austria, the forces of revolution seemed to be on the point of triumph throughout the German Confederation.

Coincident with these revolutionary movements in the various states, a concerted effort was made at Frankfurt to remodel the creaking structure of the old German Confederation on genuinely liberal and national lines. Preliminary meetings of German liberals at Offenburg and Heppenheim in 1847 had already demanded such changes, but it took the spectacular news from Paris to bring matters to a head. Early in March a group of fifty-one German liberals meeting at the old university city of Heidelberg assumed the responsibility of arranging for a preliminary assembly (*Vorparlament*) of several hundred members from all over Germany to prepare for nation-wide elections. It met at the end of the month, sketched some rough outlines of a new German constitution, and arranged hastily for democratic elections to be held throughout Germany and Austria, on the basis of one seat for every fifty thousand voters. Following much discussion, it voted overwhelmingly to summon representatives from Schleswig, East Prussia, and West Prussia, none of which were members of the German Confederation of 1815.

The day of May 18, 1848, when 586 democratically elected deputies assembled in the old Church of St. Paul in Frankfurt-on-Main, might well have

MEETING OF THE GERMAN NATIONAL ASSEMBLY IN ST. PAUL'S CHURCH, FRANKFURT, 1848. This contemporary painting shows Heinrich von Gagern presiding over a most respectable bourgeois assembly. Note the presence of women in the galleries.

seemed a decisive turning point in German history. Inevitably there were wide divergences of opinion. On the right wing were a number of conservative monarchists and aristocrats, and on the extreme left was the small radical group of Jacobins seeking a republic. Yet the great majority was composed of substantial, able, middle-class citizens—some 200 lawyers, 140 business men, 100 professors and teachers, numerous physicians, judges, and public officials. Doubtless with some exaggeration, this body has been called "the most distinguished constituent body in history." A believer in constitutional government, Heinrich von Gagern from Hesse-Darmstadt, was chosen as president, and over its deliberations flew the black, red, gold flag of the *Burschenschaften*— the student societies which had carried this flag against Napoleon in the great War of Liberation of 1813.

By the opening of June, 1848, therefore, revolution seemed to have triumphed everywhere. In France a national assembly elected in April was at work on a new republican constitution. In Austria a constitution had been granted; in Hungary sweeping reforms had been effected; in Prussia a constituent assembly was at work; in Prague important concessions had been won for Bohemia; in Piedmont the king had granted a constitution to his people; in northern Italy revolt against Austria was in full swing; while even earlier the rulers of Tuscany, the Papal States, and Naples had likewise granted their people constitutions. At Frankfurt a sweeping transformation of the German Confederation seemed about to begin. A contemporary observer surely would have been justified in regarding these months as a period of tremendous achievement, for after a minimum of bloodshed the old rule of the despots was toppling everywhere. The spirit of these months is caught in the *Reminiscences* of a young German student Carl Schurz, who was to spend most of his life in the United States. He wrote of these revolutionary days thus:

> At last we closed our notebooks with a sigh and went away, impelled by a feeling that now we had something more important to do—to devote ourselves to the affairs of the Fatherland. And this we did by seeking again as quickly as possible the company of our friends, in order to discuss what had happened and what was to come. In these conversations, excited as they were, certain ideas and catchwords worked themselves to the surface. . . . First in line the convocation of a national parliament: then the demands for civil rights and liberties, free speech, free press, the right of free assembly, equality before the law, a freely elected representation of the people with legislative power, responsibility of ministers, self-government of the communes, the right of the people to carry arms, the formation of a civic guard with elective officers, and so on—in short, that which was called a constitutional form of government on a broad, democratic basis.[3]

The ideals of a liberal, bourgeois society could hardly have been better expressed.

■ REVOLUTIONARY FRUSTRATIONS

The summer and autumn of 1848 saw a sharp decline in revolutionary successes. Divisions between rival groups emerged, and the difficulty of persuading inexperienced men to agree upon common goals became more apparent. The Pan-Slavic Congress, for example, which assembled at Prague on June 2 with spokesmen of the three principal groups (Czechs and Slovaks; Poles and Ruthenians; Croats, Serbs, and Slovenes) in attendance, made fine statements about Slavic solidarity but could do little in the face of the practical difficulties arising from geographic separation, cultural differences, and political inexperience. The Austrian commander in Bohemia, Prince Windischgraetz, bombarded the city on June 17, recaptured it, set up a military dictatorship obedient to the emperor, and thus achieved the first breach in the revolutionary system.

At Vienna, meanwhile, a constituent assembly met in June. Out of its total of 383 members, 92 were peasants. It decided not to accept the constitution

3. *The Reminiscences of Carl Schurz* (1907), vol. I, p. 113.

offered by the emperor, but to proceed instead with a more democratic version. In September the assembly promulgated a decree emancipating the peasants from all feudal burdens. A speech of one of the peasant delegates against paying compensation for the abolition of servile dues illustrates the depth of feeling that existed:

> Yes, the nobleman is humane, for he encourages the tired robot-peasant with the whip, and if the peasant complains that his draft-animals are too weak to perform the prescribed labor, he is told: "Then harness yourself and your wife." . . . Three hundred steps from the manor-house he has humbly to take off his hat . . . and if the poor peasant wants to mount the stairs, he is told to stay in the courtyard, for he stinks. . . . And for such ill-treatment are we now to pay compensation? I say: No!! The whips which came down on our heads and tired bodies must suffice. Let these be the compensation of the masters.[4]

These agrarian reforms were in the great revolutionary tradition, yet other events during the summer indicated that the cause of the old monarchy was not lost.

Windischgraetz, as already noted, had won back control of Bohemia. In late July came the news of the Austrian victory over the Piedmontese and Lombard forces at Custozza. In August the emperor was sufficiently reassured to return from Innsbruck to Vienna. In September the government authorized the Croat General Jellačić, governor of Croatia, who had championed the cause of autonomy, to attack the Hungarian rebels, for which purpose he was made commander in chief of the anti-Hungarian forces. His first failure enabled the Hungarians to advance almost to Vienna, where further radical street demonstrations broke out in October and a howling mob took the life of the unpopular minister of war. These revolutionary victories were short-lived. The Austrian capital was actually bombarded by Windischgraetz and Jellačić, with the result that by the end of October order was restored. In November Prince Felix von Schwarzenberg,[5] brother-in-law of Windischgraetz, was appointed head of the government. The single-minded purpose of this ultra-conservative noble was to restore the authority of the Hapsburgs. The assembly sitting at Vienna was exiled to the provincial town of Kremsier—a rural setting safely away from the revolutionary dangers of the capital—where it became increasingly unimportant. Early in December Schwarzenberg persuaded the feeble-minded Emperor Ferdinand to abdicate in favor of his nephew, the

4. Quoted by L. B. NAMIER, *1848: The Revolution of the Intellectuals* (1946), p. 21.
5. 1800-1852. Nephew of the Austrian commander-in-chief against Napoleon, he served for six years as a soldier before being induced by Metternich to take up diplomacy. In office for only three years, he was responsible for calling in Russian troops to suppress the Hungarian revolution and, shortly before his death, for persuading Francis Joseph to suspend the last remnants of the Austrian constitution. The emperor always called him the greatest of his ministers.

eighteen-year-old Francis Joseph,[6] who was to occupy the apparently badly shaken throne for sixty-eight years, until his death in 1916.

In Prussia, similarly, royal authority soon reasserted itself. Frederick William IV had summoned a constituent assembly only under the fear of events. As the dangers receded, his courage increased until in November he was bold enough, like Schwarzenberg in Austria, to exile the assembly from Berlin. In December he unceremoniously dissolved it, announcing that the constitution upon which the members had been working would be completed and promulgated by himself. This constitution was soon to prove a bitter disappointment to all democratic hopes.

In Italy, likewise, the high aspirations of the nationalists soon subsided. Austrian victories forced Charles Albert to sign an armistice and retire from Lombardy. Pius IX, disappointing the hopes of the liberals in the Papal States, fled to the kingdom of Naples where he sought the assistance of the Catholic powers.

Only in Hungary, it would seem, did the prospects of the revolutionaries look bright. Here Kossuth and his followers vigorously repulsed the September attacks of Jellačić and his Croat forces. In order to support him the Austrian government on October 3 actually declared war on Hungary, and soon Windischgraetz's forces were able to seize Budapest. Later, however, Kossuth and his brilliant commander, Görgei, mobilized powerful resistance, so that at the opening of 1849 a Hungarian army was in the field vigorously defying the authority of the Hapsburg commanders.

At Frankfurt, meanwhile, the first proceedings of the parliament in May seemed businesslike and promising. A committee of thirty was chosen to draft a constitution, the old Diet of the German Confederation was suspended, and the liberal Archduke John of Austria was appointed "Imperial Regent," or temporary head of the government. This Frankfurt Parliament, therefore, combined the work of constitution-making with actual efforts to direct the affairs of the German Confederation.

In this latter respect an immediate issue arose—the first appearance on the European scene of that incredibly tangled business known as the Schleswig-Holstein affair. Schleswig and Holstein were two duchies not technically a part of Denmark, yet subject to the Danish king who was duke in each. The northern

6. 1830–1916. A great-great-grandson of Maria Theresa, he had Metternich for his tutor. As emperor, he associated himself first with Schwarzenberg's reactionary policies, but from 1852 to 1867 acted as his own minister-president. He reluctantly accepted constitutionalism in 1867, believing it basically impious and impossible. Escaping assassination in 1853, he lived to have his brother, Maximilian, shot in Mexico in 1867, his son, Rudolph, commit suicide in 1889, his wife assassinated in 1897, and his heir, Francis Ferdinand, assassinated in 1914. Though he managed to hold the Dual Monarchy together for sixty-eight years, distrust of ability has been called his greatest failing.

duchy, Schleswig, was part Danish-speaking and part German-speaking. The southern duchy, Holstein, was completely German-speaking and, moreover, a member of the German Confederation. In March, 1848, the new Danish ruler, Frederick VII, complicated the history of an already complicated year by seeking to unite the duchies to Denmark by means of a common liberal constitution. This led the German majorities in the local estates of both Schleswig and Holstein to ask for full independence, coupled with membership in the German Confederation. The Frankfurt Parliament, fearing what Denmark might do, authorized Prussia to send troops to the support of the duchies. This Prussia quickly did, thus becoming briefly involved in hostilities with Denmark. The Armistice of Malmö (August, 1848) required the withdrawal of both sides from the duchies and set them temporarily under a joint Prusso-Danish Commission. This was a blow to the prestige of the Frankfurt Parliament, which had sought to assert its authority over the duchies. Crowds at Frankfurt stormed the assembly in outraged protest, and two deputies lost their lives before order was restored. The Schleswig-Holstein affair was destined to a long history; at this point it served to administer a blow to the prestige of the Frankfurt Parliament.

The long debates at Frankfurt dragged on during the summer. One question was, what type of political structure should replace the old Confederation of 1815? The conservatives wished to keep the confederation weak, so that as much power as possible would remain with the states composing it. The republicans of the extreme left would have been happy to see a centralized republic. The moderates, naturally enough, sought a middle path which would result in a genuinely federal Germany with a hereditary monarchy at the head of it.

In view of the composition of the assembly, it is clear that economic considerations would play a considerable role in determining the outcome. In June, 1848, the chairman of the economic committee stated in striking terms his view of the close relations between political and economic progress:

> The liberated German nation is eager to reap the fruits of its political emancipation. It demands law and order, it demands the revival of industrial activity, it demands above all more remunerative work. It demands the political unity of Germany so that it can win for its country the eminent position in foreign commerce and in world trade to which it can rightly lay claim by virtue of its geographic position, its greatness, and the skill of its people, especially of its commercial and industrial classes. The divided states of Germany have until now been in no position to assert this claim against foreign nations, but the united states of Germany will know how to enforce it.[7]

Another major concern was the question as to what peoples should be included within the new Germany. Membership in the old Confederation had been eccentric, to say the least. It had included Luxembourg, which was subject

7. Quoted by HAMEROW, p. 132.

LINGUISTIC DIVISIONS in the HAPSBURG POSSESSIONS

Legend:
- Germans
- Magyars
- Italians
- Friulians
- Rumanians
- Ruthenians
- Poles
- Slovaks
- Slovenes
- Croats & Serbs
- Czechs & Moravians

MILES   0   50   100   150   200   250

The non-German peoples in the western half of the Empire actually outnumber the Germans, and the same is true of the corresponding non-Magyar groups in Hungary with respect to the Magyars. Substantial German minorities are scattered through Hungary, and a solid Magyar community exists to the east of the Rumanians in Transylvania. The Croats and Serbs of the southern provinces are closely akin to the neighboring peoples of the Ottoman Empire, as are the Poles and Ruthenians to their neighbors within the Russian Empire.

to the king of the Netherlands, and Holstein, ruled by the king of Denmark. It excluded the East and West Prussian provinces of the Prussian kingdom as well as the province of Posen, and it included such non-German parts of the Austrian lands as Bohemia, Moravia, and Carniola. On what ethnic, linguistic, or nationalist principles should the new German Confederation be erected? Should there be a greater Germany, extending from the Rhine to the Niemen? Should this greater Germany ride roughshod over the aspirations of the non-German minorities? Many Prussian patriots were eager to include the predominantly Polish-speaking province of Posen, on the assumption, doubtless, that the Polish peasantry would be good subjects for Germanization.

As reliable an estimate as any of the population of Posen in 1848 is that there were more than 800,000 Poles and certainly less than 500,000 Germans within its limits. Strong national feelings developed in Prussia, and, while Frederick William IV at first was persuaded to sign a cabinet order setting up a Polish National Committee for the Prussian province of Posen, it soon became clear that there was very little Prussian interest in supporting any Polish national revival, and, indeed, emphatic opposition to it. The decision finally reached at Frankfurt in July, by a vote of 342 to 31 (with 75 abstentions), was that a line of partition should be drawn in Posen which would put over one million inhabitants of the province within the new German state. This decision, which has been called a landmark in the German theory of the *Drang nach Osten* (the "drive to the east"), quite clearly would have meant that something like half a million Polish-speaking subjects would thereby have been included. It would also have meant that only about 300,000 Poles would remain in eastern Posen to form the nucleus of a hypothetical Polish state.

A similar problem was that of the Slavic peoples of Bohemia and Moravia. Despite the summoning of the Pan-Slav Congress at Prague, which might have served to remind Germans that the Slavs outnumbered them by two to one in the Austrian Empire, many Austrians doubtless felt that these Slavic areas were ripe for Germanization. When the great leader of the Czech national movement, Palacký,[8] was invited to take a seat in the Frankfurt Parliament he declined. His clear choice was for an Austrian federal structure in which Czech rights would be assured rather than for a German national state, as he made clear in a famous letter dated April 11:

> I am a Czech of Slav descent and with all the little I own and possess I have devoted myself wholly and forever to the service of my nation. That nation is

8. 1798–1876. An ardent Bohemian nationalist, editor of the *Journal of the Bohemian Museum*, his country's leading literary organ, and author of a still standard five-volume *History of the Bohemian People*, he refused to attend the Frankfurt Parliament in 1848, favoring instead a federation of Germans and Slavs under Hapsburg leadership. Sitting for years in the Bohemian *Landtag* and the Austrian upper house, and widely known as "the father of the nation," he was the greatest modern Bohemian before Thomas Masaryk.

small, it is true, but from time immemorial it has been an independent nation with its own character; its rulers have participated since old times in the federation of German princes, but the nation never regarded itself nor was it regarded by others throughout all the centuries as part of the German nation. . . . If anyone asks that the Czech nation should now unite with the German nation, beyond this heretofore existing federation between princes, this is a new demand which has no historical legal basis. . . .

You know that in southeast Europe, along the frontiers of the Russian empire, there live many nations widely different in origin, language, history, and habits—Slavs, Rumanians, Magyars, and Germans, not to speak of Greeks, Turks, and Albanians—none of whom is strong enough to be able by itself to resist successfully for all time the superior neighbor to the east; they could do it only if a close and firm tie bound them all together. The vital artery of this necessary union of nations is the Danube; the focus of its power must never be removed far from this river, if the union is to be effective at all and to remain so. Certainly, if the Austrian state had not existed for ages, we would be obliged in the interests of Europe and even of mankind to endeavor to create it as fast as possible. [9]

Thus there emerged at Frankfurt the conflict between *Grossdeutsch* and *Kleindeutsch*—the Great Germans and the Little Germans. Suspicion of Austria and fear of what the inclusion of non-German peoples, such as Czechs and Slovaks, Hungarians and Rumanians, might mean, led the majority of the Parliament to a compromise in October which stated that the new federation would include all German lands save any that should be linked with non-German areas. This was the *Kleindeutsch* solution, for clearly it would exclude Austria, unless she was willing to separate herself from the non-German lands. In this situation Austria recalled its representatives from Frankfurt and, for the time at least, the *Kleindeutsch* solution seemed to have prevailed. It would not suffice, however, to leave the picture in this form.

The debates at Frankfurt in the summer and autumn of 1848 convey quite clearly a strong sense of Germany's mission in eastern Europe. Speech after speech was made to this effect. Heinrich von Gagern, the first president of the assembly, recommended the exclusion of Austria from the new Germany so that she might concentrate on her task of eastward colonization. Wilhelm Jordan, an East Prussian who represented Berlin, declared that nationality was not the principle involved in these areas. Germany must rather seek to impose its civilization and to further its economic interests throughout these eastern borderlands. While German liberalism with a strong idealist tinge has often been taken as the chief mark of this critical year, it would be unhistorical to ignore the powerful element of aggressive nationalism that also was present.

During these same months the Frankfurt Parliament had succeeded in drafting a declaration of fundamental rights of the German people, proclaimed

9. Quoted in H. KOHN, *Pan-Slavism: Its History and Ideology* (1953), pp. 65–67.

in December. All Germans were to be citizens of the German Reich with equal rights in every state. No distinction of classes could exist before the law. Personal freedom was inviolable and none could be arrested save on a judicial warrant. Freedom of speech, writing, assembly, and petition was guaranteed. Every state was to have a constitution providing for popular representation and a responsible ministry. Ironically, these fundamental rights were proclaimed in December at the very time when the prospects of the new confederation were rapidly receding. Yet this document was to stand throughout the nineteenth century as a symbol to German liberals of what they had once striven to achieve.

■ RESURGENCE AND REPRESSION, 1849–1851

As the year 1849 opened, the evidences still were numerous of revolutionary success and revolutionary activity. The pledges of constitutional reforms throughout Germany and the Hapsburg lands had not as yet been withdrawn. In February, 1849, Italian revolutionaries led by Mazzini and Garibaldi proclaimed the Roman Republic. In March Piedmont re-entered the war against Austria. When Schwarzenberg felt strong enough to rescind the constitutional laws granted to Hungary in 1848, Kossuth responded in April, 1849, with a declaration of complete Hungarian independence. The new *Kleindeutsch* constitution for the German Confederation was completed and accepted by vote of the Frankfurt Parliament (in defiance of Austria's wishes) in March, 1849. All these could be taken as favorable omens for the cause of nationalism.

Yet the tide was beginning to run in the opposite direction. The success of Schwarzenberg in Vienna seemed to give heart to the counterrevolutionary forces. Frederick William IV of Prussia, having appointed two unquestionable reactionaries as his advisers, dissolved the constituent assembly on December 5. At the same time he himself decreed the outlines of a constitution and arranged for the election in February, 1849, of a second parliamentary body to discuss and revise his proposals. When this body quarreled with the king, he likewise dissolved it and undertook instead to make constitutional changes on his own. The net outcome was the Prussian constitution which, proclaimed in January, 1850, was to remain in effect until the First World War. Details of this basically undemocratic document are best postponed until the entire work of these revolutionary years is summed up.

Some small revolts and military mutinies occurred in April and May, 1849, in Baden, the Palatinate, and Saxony. These were quickly repressed by the local authorities with the aid of troops sent in by Prussia. This, if anything further were needed, could be clear evidence of the desire of Prussia to identify itself with the antirevolutionary forces.

Much more dramatic were the events in Italy. On March 23, after the Piedmontese army was overwhelmingly defeated by the Austrians at Novara,

Charles Albert abdicated on the field of battle. He died a few months later in Portuguese exile. In May, counterrevolutionary forces overthrew the new constitutions of Tuscany and Sicily. A similar fate was in store for the Roman Republic of Mazzini and Garibaldi. Pushed on by the clerical groups in France, and concerned that Austria would gain a favored position at Rome, Louis Napoleon sent French troops to besiege the city. After three months Rome fell, Garibaldi and Mazzini fled into exile, and Pius IX returned. In the stark words of a distinguished English historian,[10] France murdered the Roman Republic. The failure of Charles Albert likewise doomed the Venetian Republic.

Austria did not need to swing over to the side of reaction in 1849 because she had already done so. By the end of 1848 the Austrian government no longer made any pretense of being on the side of reform. After Windischgraetz had recaptured Vienna in November and arranged for Schwarzenberg to become principal minister, the pattern was evident. In March, 1849, Schwarzenberg dissolved the Austrian Diet sitting outside Vienna in the rural isolation of Kremsier and proclaimed a new constitution (largely the work of Count Stadion), emphasizing the complete unity, economic as well as political, of the Hapsburg lands. From this unity Lombardy-Venetia and the kingdom of Hungary were excluded. Thus it was abundantly clear that Austria, with its non-German dependencies intact, could not enter the new *Kleindeutsch* confederation currently proposed at Frankfurt.

The last and most stubborn resistance was offered by Hungary. In the March Laws of the preceding year, Austria had conceded virtual home rule to the kingdom with guarantees of freedom of the press, a responsible ministry, and a Hungarian national guard. Kossuth, as we have seen, had at last reached the point of declaring independence for Hungary. Further troubles had come from within, for the southern Slavs of Croatia had no desire to continue under Magyar rule. Hence the willingness of their leader, General Jellačić, to take the Austrian side against Kossuth's leadership. The decisive action, which spelled the doom of Hungarian liberties, came from that archreactionary, Nicholas I of Russia, who had become gravely concerned at the possibility of revolution spreading to his Polish province from Galicia. In May, 1849, therefore, he responded to the Austrian appeal for help by sending an army over the Carpathians into Hungary. By concerted action Jellačić recaptured Budapest, General Haynau won a victory at Temesvar in Transylvania, and the Russians forced the Hungarian commander-in-chief, Arthur von Görgei, to surrender in August at Vilagos. The Russian commander, Paskievich, sent his grim message to Nicholas I: "Hungary lies at the feet of your majesty," and Kossuth, having buried the historic crown of St. Stephen at the frontier town of Orsova, fled to exile in Turkey and later in America.

10. G. M. TREVELYAN, *Garibaldi's Defence of the Roman Republic* (1907), p. 109.

The Frankfurt Parliament completed its work of constitution-making, in the absence of Austrian representatives, in March, 1849. It provided for a federal state with a hereditary "Emperor of the Germans" who would have a suspensive veto over legislation. There was to be a legislature of two chambers, the lower elected by universal, secret, manhood suffrage. An elaborate statement of rights was provided, and the federal government would have complete control of military affairs, foreign policy, and questions of national finances. In late March, by a vote of 290 in favor and 248 abstentions, the imperial crown was offered to Frederick William IV of Prussia. The king's public reply was that he regarded himself as a divine right ruler who could accept a crown only if it was proffered by his brother monarchs: in private he described it as "a pig's crown" offered by the grace of "master bakers and butchers." On the news of his refusal, the majority of the governments withdrew their representatives from Frankfurt and the unhappy Frankfurt Parliament came to its inglorious end by withering away. A poor fragment transferred itself to Stuttgart, where the king of Württemberg in June ordered it dispersed.

This was not quite the end. Prussia was not happy to have Austria defy all attempts to challenge its leadership in the German Confederation. General von Radowitz, a principal adviser of Frederick William IV, drafted a plan in the summer of 1849 which he thought would ensure Prussian leadership. His idea was to create a large middle-European confederation in which the German states associated under Prussian leadership would comprise one part, and the entire Hapsburg possessions, German and non-German, would comprise the other. In May a draft of the first part, the "Prussian Union," was prepared and accepted by most of the German states. When, however, a truly national assembly was summoned to meet at Erfurt, only Prussia and some of the lesser states sent delegations. In October, 1850, these accepted the constitution proposed by Prussia.

By now, Schwarzenberg was firmly in control at Vienna and had ruthlessly re-established his authority in all parts of the Hapsburg realms. His purpose clearly was to re-establish the old Confederation of 1815 in which Austrian influence had been dominant. Hence, when Prussia indicated its intention of sending representatives to meet with the other states of the new Prussian Union, Austria mobilized its troops, obtained the backing of Tsar Nicholas I, and requested Prussian delegates to meet with Schwarzenberg in November at the town of Olmütz. Here, fearful of the consequences if she did otherwise, Prussia agreed to abandon the plans for a Prussian Union and to accept the revival of the old Germanic Confederation. As this meant the complete victory of Austria, it is easy to see why Prussian historians have referred to this last episode following the revolutionary crisis of 1848 as the "Humiliation of Olmütz."

■ THE BALANCE SHEET OF REVOLUTION

The Revolution of 1848 has often been pictured as a magnificent failure—a dramatic effort on the part of European liberals and nationalists to achieve goals that unhappily proved to be beyond their grasp. Like most generalizations, this is a mixture of truth and falsehood, yet certainly in the eyes of the men—and particularly the leaders—who had planned and fought in 1848 and 1849 the results were tragically disappointing. Certain outward signs would seem to underscore this conclusion.

Early in 1849 Austria had to all intents abandoned the constitution granted in the previous year. The conservative document which Schwarzenberg had proclaimed in March, 1849, was abolished by imperial patent in December, 1851. In August, 1851, the Diet of the German Confederation reconvened under the same terms of membership and procedure as those which had governed it from 1815 to 1848. Four months later the December coup d'état of Louis Napoleon rang the death knell of the Second Republic in France. The governments of the Italian states (save in Piedmont) were what they had been before revolution began.

The failures of 1848 are clear. In France, a workable republic in the great tradition of 1789 had been unable to survive. Attempts to remodel the German Confederation on truly national and liberal lines had likewise met defeat. The high hopes of liberals for genuinely constitutional regimes in the German states were disappointed. In Italy not only had unification made no headway; an atmosphere of reaction and repression was widespread throughout the peninsula. The national aspirations of the Poles, the Czechs, and the Slovaks had been sternly rebuffed. Last, whatever hopes the champions of the working classes may have had that sweeping measures would be undertaken to meet the new social problems of an industrial age were all disappointed.

Yet there are substantial advances to be recorded on the other side. The principle of universal manhood suffrage enunciated in France in 1848 was not repudiated under the succeeding regimes. The tradition of constitutionalism, democratic or otherwise, was very much alive. In two states the constitutions now granted remained in effect and served an important purpose in the years ahead. The *Statuto* issued in Piedmont by Charles Albert on March 4, 1848, was hardly a liberal document. It was less generous, even, than the French constitution of 1830 and enfranchised barely $2\frac{1}{2}$ percent of the population of the kingdom in the year when both France and Switzerland adopted the principle of universal manhood suffrage. Yet it served as the basis of the constitution for a united Italy. The Prussian constitution of 1850, which elevated the power of the king above that of the ministry and the parliament, lasted almost until the fall of the German Empire in 1918.

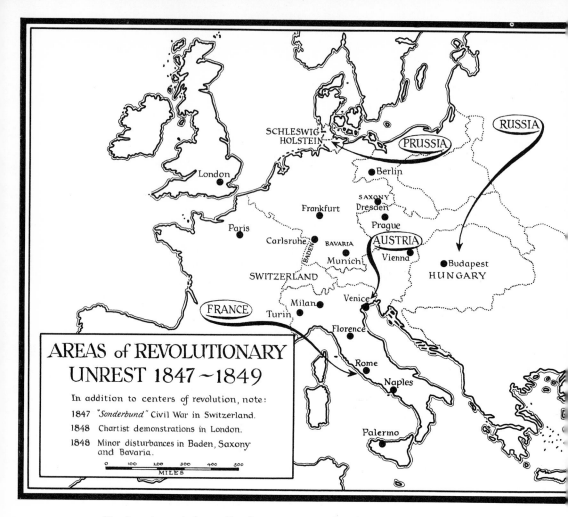

Note how the revolutionary disturbances concentrate largely in central Europe. A striking fact is that military intervention by four great powers outside their own territory did not precipitate a general war.

Other advances also deserve notice. The emancipation of the peasantry from servile dues, which had been proclaimed in Austrian Galicia in 1847 and in Austria proper and Hungary in 1848, remained in effect. In the expanding and overcrowded cities the revolutionary disturbances were marked by the presence of a proletarian element which was now larger than ever before. To be sure, the general pattern of urban economic life in central Europe was still that of handicraft industry, small shops, and gild enterprises. During the year of revolution many gatherings of master craftsmen sought to maintain their traditional powers by appealing strongly to the authorities for the prohibition of trade freedom. The journeymen and simple workers understandably would have favored less restriction. In the end they won little, and the economic life of Germany in the 1850's was not markedly different from what it had been in the 1840's. Yet the voice of the workers had been heard. They had helped to man the barricades, and their demands were to be reiterated with greater insistence and greater success in the years ahead. Even more significantly, the fires of nationalism were to burn more brightly after the Revolution than before.

It is noteworthy that even some countries taking no part in the Revolution made substantial gains in these years. In Belgium the property qualification for voting was reduced. The Netherlands revised its constitution in 1848 to reduce the power of the king and to increase the powers of the ministry and parliament. Denmark proclaimed a new constitution in 1848 in which the king shared legislative power with a bicameral parliament. Switzerland issued a new constitution in September, 1848, which created a federal union closely modeled on the United States of America. These changes are not to be explained merely on the basis of coincidence, for quite clearly the demand for constitutional reform, stimulated by the process of revolutionary events, was widespread.

The great wave of emigration from Europe to the New World has often been associated with the disillusionment of European liberals at the failures of 1848. The statistics suggest that the motivation was more economic and social than political. Emigration from Germany to America in the decade of the 1830's totaled 168,000. In the decade of the 1840's the figure rose to 500,000, with the greatest annual numbers in the "hunger years" of 1846, when there were 93,000 emigrants, and 1847, when there were above 100,000. The numbers actually dropped in 1848, 1849, and 1850 when a bitter persecution was affecting liberalism, and then picked up rapidly when hard times developed in 1851. In the decade of the 1850's more than a million Germans left, and of these over 90 percent came from the exhausted lands west of the Elbe. Though the economic motivation seems clear, one must recognize that the emigration included a number of liberals, the most notable, perhaps, being Carl Schurz, who made distinguished contributions to American life.

Certain final observations may be made and lessons suggested concerning these critical years. The years 1848 to 1850 mark the end of an age, and the instinct which has prompted many Germans to look back to "*Vormarz*" ("pre-March") as a time when liberalism, inspired by the ideology of the French Revolution, was building up its challenge to conservative authoritarianism is probably sound. That this German liberalism should have failed in its challenge had unhappy consequences for the political evolution of Germany throughout the nineteenth century. Yet the point is not merely that liberalism failed. The evidence likewise shows that, in addition to the force of German liberalism, there was also a powerful tide of German nationalism at work which exalted the idea of national destiny and cultural superiority—a superiority which should be exercised over the Slavic territories on the eastern borders of the Confederation.

A much more ruthless nationalism was in the making. The failures of 1848 led subsequent leaders to employ this new nationalism relentlessly for their purposes. After the first March Days it is instructive to see how generally the parliamentary bodies begin to lose the limelight, and how little control they had over the direction of affairs in the ensuing months. The political assemblies, it would seem, gain little credit for their work in these years. On the other hand one notes the powerful role of the big cities—Paris, Vienna, Berlin, Prague, Rome, and Milan. One witnesses the new role of the people, as in the great riots in the streets of Paris and Berlin, and the "Five Days" of Milan. One notes especially the role of armies under determined leaders. The Austrian victory at Novara doomed the cause of Charles Albert, even as the Russian victories in Hungary led to Görgei's surrender at Világos.

A new age followed the Revolution of 1848, as Bismarck was quick to realize. If the mistake of these years, as he said, was to believe that great decisions could be brought about by speeches and parliamentary majorities, the sequel would soon show that in an industrial era new techniques involving ruthless force were all too readily available. The period of *Realpolitik*—of realistic, iron-fisted politics and diplomacy—was beginning.

Reading List: Chapter 3

The New Cambridge Modern History, vol. X (1960), ch. 15. The Revolution of 1848.

Taylor, A. J. P., *The Hapsburg Monarchy, 1815–1918* (1947), ch. 5. The Revolution of 1848 broadly described.

May, A., *The Hapsburg Monarchy, 1867–1914* (1951), ch. 1. The realm of the Hapsburgs.

Ausubel, H. (ed.), *The Making of Modern Europe*, vol. II (1951), ch. 16. Articles by O. Odlozilik, "Storm Over the Danube," and H. Meinecke, "The Year 1848 in German History."

Hammen, O. J., "Economic and Social Factors in the Prussian Rhineland in 1848," *American Historical Review*, vol. LIV (1949), no. 4. Backgrounds.

Robertson, Priscilla, *The Revolutions of 1848: A Social History* (1952; paperback, 1960), ch. 21. "The Revolution of the Spirit."

Pascal, R., "The Frankfurt Parliament, 1848, and the Drang Nach Osten," *Journal of Modern History*," vol. XVIII, June, 1946. Describes an early form of German imperialism.

Kohn, H., *Pan-Slavism: Its History and Ideology* (1953; paperback, 1960), pp. 61–83. The Slavic Congress at Prague, 1848.

Rothfels, H., "1848: One Hundred Years After," *Journal of Modern History*, vol. XX, December, 1948.

Valentin, V., *1848: Chapters of German History* (1940), chs. 13, 16. Work of the Frankfurt Parliament; general results.

Hamerow, T. S., "History and the German Revolution of 1848," *American Historical Review*, vol. LX (1954), no. 1. The Revolution in the light of history.

Groot, Emil de, "Contemporary Public Opinion and the Revolutions of 1848," *History*, vol. XXXVIII (1953), nos. 131–32.

Chapter 4

Italy and Its Unification

Italy from 1815 to 1846
Reform, Revolt, and Reaction, 1846–1850
Italy and the French Alliance
1860: The Impact of Garibaldi
The Continuing Struggle: Venetia and Rome
An Imperfect Union

■ ITALY FROM 1815 TO 1846

Italy is surrounded by the Alps and the sea. Her natural limits are defined with as much exactitude as if she were an island. . . . Italy, isolated between her natural limits, is destined to form a great and powerful nation. Italy is one nation; unity of customs, language and literature must, within a period more or less distant, unite her inhabitants under one sole government. And Rome will, without the slightest doubt, be chosen by the Italians as their capital.[1]

The words which Napoleon wrote in exile at St. Helena present succinctly enough the program of Italian patriots in the great period of Italian history known to them as *Il Risorgimento*. But what is obvious is not necessarily easy to achieve. The soil of the peninsula required a prodigal expenditure of labor to secure the crops; other natural resources were few, and their development was

1. Quoted in J. A. R. MARRIOTT, *Makers of Modern Italy* (1938), p. 16.

106

SIGNIFICANT EVENTS

1820–1821, 1831	Carbonarist revolts
1846	Election of Pope Pius IX
1848	Year of revolutions
	Piedmontese constitution (March)
1852	Cavour prime minister of Piedmont
1859	Austro-French War
	Annexation of Lombardy to Piedmont
1860	Italian plebiscites and expedition of the Thousand
1864	Syllabus of Errors issued by the pope
1866	Seven Weeks War and annexation of Venetia
1870	Dogma of Papal Infallibility proclaimed
	Entry of Italian troops into Rome

handicapped by the very slow growth of modern communications. Most Italians were too poor to care about political unity, since nothing led them to believe that it would give them more bread. The various states had had long, and in some respects splendid, histories in separation, which they saw no particular reason to terminate. Moreover, the conservative influence of the Roman Catholic Church upon the minds of the many was especially strong in a country which, ever since the Dark Ages, had been accustomed to the rule of the pope over Rome itself and the States of the Church—a rule that made the very thought of national unity smack of impiety. But the pope was at least an Italian; how infinitely depressing to the reflective mind was the fact that, since the Italian wars of France and Spain began in 1494, most of Italy had always been at the mercy of secular foreign dynasties. Even reforms, such as those of the Milanese legist, Beccaria, had for the most part been imposed by foreigners

107

on passive subjects. For all these reasons Italian unity, as we shall see, proved to be incapable of achievement as late as the third quarter of the nineteenth century, unless powerful help could be obtained from outside—and the cost of that help largely determined the later fortunes of the new kingdom.

Although some sixty thousand Italian soldiers had been killed fighting for Napoleon in Spain and Russia, there was no concerted military action by Italians on their own behalf either in 1814 or when Murat, the Napoleonic king of Naples, raised the flag of independence against the Austrians during the Hundred Days. Nevertheless, the two decades of the French ascendancy had done great things for Italy. Ten independent rival states had been reduced to three dependent ones. In matters of law and order, public services, and facilities for industry and commerce, the watchword had been efficiency, even if it was an efficiency which served above all to swell the French exchequer. The result had been to spread abroad among significant elements in the upper classes new ideas about the rights of the individual and about the desirability of basing government upon some degree of popular support. A Corsican himself, Napoleon had been eager to breathe new life into a country upon which the hand of a long-dead past lay heavy; he had deliberately invoked the spirit of nationality there, and, although Napoleonic Italy fell to pieces almost as rapidly and quite as completely as his other creations, some Italians continued to feel with De Maistre that "nations are something in the world."

The Italy of 1815, which Metternich persisted in regarding as a mere geographical expression, consisted mainly of three kingdoms, one of which was Lombardy-Venetia, ruled by a viceroy on behalf of Metternich's master, the Hapsburg emperor. The second was the state based for many centuries upon Piedmont and Savoy, which had become the kingdom of Sardinia when that island was added to its possessions in 1720 and had newly acquired the seaport of Genoa. The third kingdom was that now officially known as the Two Sicilies, including the exhausted and barren lands of the southern half of the peninsula and the scarcely less poverty-stricken island which adjoins it. In between the two kingdoms of the north and the one to the south there lay two units of intermediate importance. The Papal States, ruled from Rome, included Romagna and the Marches on the northeast coast, linked by Umbria with the Patrimony of St. Peter on the west. The grand duchy of Tuscany, unlike its papal neighbor, had a tradition of enlightened government, and its capital, Florence, was still an important cultural center. The north of the peninsula also contained, as well as two minuscule territories, the self-contained small duchies of Parma, Modena, and Lucca. The mere enumeration gives a glimpse of the difficulties of Italian unification, since these states were not joined together in any formal way, as Germany, for example, was joined by the Bund.

Italians did, however, in several respects share a common lot. Nearly every region inherited a strong tradition of town life, a vast army of ecclesiastics (about 150,000 in the whole country), and a form of society in which only the few big cities possessed any sizable middle class of laymen interposed between the aristocracy and the poor. By 1815, too, each state was to some extent penetrated by the Carbonarist movement, which had been founded in the south as early as 1810 for the secret promotion of resistance to the Napoleonic regime. Based on the ritual of Masonic lodges, it appealed not only to patriotic feelings but to romanticism and the revolt of youth against the *status quo*—the kind of revolt to which the situation gave increasing stimulus.

Another common feature was the closeness of the ties which bound every one of the Italian states to the Austrian Empire and the policies of Metternich. As we have already seen, Lombardy, then the second most densely populated land in Europe, had been restored to Hapsburg rule, and the ancient Venetian state had been added to it in compensation for the lost Austrian Netherlands; military communications with Vienna were safeguarded by the Quadrilateral, four fortresses mutually supporting one another, of which the strongest was Mantua. Piedmont was an ally of Austria, and three of the four duchies had Hapsburg rulers, to one of whom the fourth (Lucca) was eventually ceded in 1847. The pope, busy restoring the rule of the cardinals, the Inquisition, and the Index, of necessity leaned heavily upon Austrian support. So did the restored Bourbon dynasty in the Two Sicilies. In Naples itself Ferdinand could, and did, rely partly upon the forty thousand professional beggars to help him keep down the liberals in the interest of mendicancy and superstition; but his island subjects treasured mutinous thoughts of their recent years of independence under the protection of the British fleet.

Nevertheless, for a generation Italy as a whole lay passive. It was only through their penetration of the armies that the *Carbonari* were able to achieve the temporary successes which so vexed the conservative powers of Europe in 1820–1821. Even so, the outbreak in Naples and its sequel in Piedmont were occasioned by an outside event, namely, the military revolt which had restored the constitution of 1812 in Spain. In 1831 again, the second main Carbonarist insurrection, which for a few weeks triumphed in the cities of the Papal States (except Rome itself) and in Parma and Modena, came about in consequence of the July Revolution in France, for there was a close link between French and Italian Carbonarists, and the new French government was believed to champion the principle of nonintervention. On both occasions Austrian forces, from their base in Lombardy-Venetia, put down the revolutions with the utmost ease, constitutionalists were punished, constitutions were canceled. In neither case were the sympathies of the middle class as a whole, much less those of the populace, seriously aroused; in neither case did the revolutionary program look beyond the benefits of the Napoleonic period to envisage a united Italy.

In the next half-generation (1831–1846), the important development was not the recurrence of sporadic outbreaks, which added to the roll of Italian martyrs who faced Austrian firing squads or languished in the Moravian prison-fortress of the Spielberg, but the change in the climate of opinion. Carbonarism, with its symbolism of the black charcoal kindling to a bright flame, its associations with Freemasonry, and its vague aspirations toward constitutionalism and Italian unity, slowly gave place to the stirrings of new ideas. In 1831 the exiled Carbonarist Mazzini[2] founded the society of Young Italy, his "brotherhood of Italians believing in a law of Progress and Duty," and pointed to a single republic of Italy as the aim. Mazzini, who was also the founder of Young Europe, regarded the nation-state as the instrument through which men of every nation could best make their contribution to the good of all mankind; but it was through a series of local plots—a mutiny in the Piedmontese army, an attempted invasion of Genoa from Switzerland, and a third forlorn hope, in which two Venetian nobles, the Bandiera brothers, perished in 1844—that Mazzini strove to rouse opinion in Italy and Europe. One result of their failure was to strengthen the case for a reformist movement existing side by side with that of revolution. This less violent cause was argued successively by three Piedmontese political writers—Gioberti, Balbo, and D'Azeglio. Gioberti, a priest, and Balbo, who had served his apprenticeship as an administrator under the Napoleonic Empire, both believed in an Italian federation on a monarchist basis. The former found the starting point in the temporal power of the pope, who was to preside over the federation of princes—a "neo-Guelph" program which made a very wide appeal. The latter looked to what the House of Savoy might undertake when the disintegration of the Turkish Empire directed Austrian attention elsewhere. Only D'Azeglio, who was among other things a historical novelist, faced up to the fact that the Hapsburgs would never surrender their position in Italy without a fight, and that the only possible leader against the Austrians was the head of the House of Savoy. In 1845, accordingly, he interviewed Charles Albert, who pledged himself to the Italian cause in passionate terms which were widely circulated—with D'Azeglio's cautious addendum, "These are his words, but God alone knows his heart."

■ REFORM, REVOLT, AND REACTION, 1846–1850

Change was precipitated by the election of a new pope, Pius IX, who had brought the books of the three liberal writers named above along with him to

2. 1805–1872. The son of a Genoese doctor with Jacobin leanings and a pious mother, he was imprisoned as a Carbonarist at twenty-five. He organized the unsuccessful revolts of 1834 and 1844, but apart from the revolutionary periods of 1848–1849 and 1859–1860 lived mainly in exile in England. A prolific propagandist and humanitarian idealist, he continued to oppose the monarchy, and died in English disguise at Pisa. Nietzsche considered that its singlemindedness made Mazzini's "the most enviable of all fine lives."

Rome for presentation to whoever might be elected. If a liberal pope was the one thing Metternich had never expected, it is clear that Pius IX in his turn had never expected the results to which his cautious, not to say halfhearted, liberalism would lead. The list of reforms was startling. It began with an amnesty combined with a loyalty oath. There followed a press law which put laymen in charge of the censorship; the formation of a ministerial cabinet, to be composed entirely of ecclesiastics; and the enrollment of a civic guard which would provide middle-class protection against extremism of all kinds. All this was the work of the twelve months following the election of Pius IX in July, 1846, but each change stimulated the demand for more and quicker changes, which reverberated through Italy. Indeed, one may reasonably date the Italian revolution of 1848 from the day in April, 1847, when the pope promised an unspecified share in legislation and financial authority to a Council of State, which was to be nominated by the existing provincial councils. Before the end of the year both Piedmont and Tuscany had modified their press law and police administration, and were being swept along by a tide of popular enthusiasm like the Roman toward the fulfillment of popular expectations. A formal link among the three states was even propounded in the shape of a customs union, to which Piedmont acceded in principle in November, 1847. In the same month nationalist feeling inside and outside the Papal States induced the Austrians to terminate the occupation since August of the papal town of Ferrara, where they normally held only the citadel.

Thus it came about that 1848 began with two serious Italian outbreaks, both of which antedated the revolutions in Paris and Vienna. In prosperous Milan the New Year was ushered in with a tobacco boycott, modeled on the Boston Tea Party; the Austrian garrison opposed it by methods which provoked street rioting, with consequent military action. By the middle of January a Mazzinist conspirator, Francesco Crispi, had roused Sicily to fight for its 1812 constitution. By the end of the month the rising had spread to the mainland and Ferdinand II had announced a constitution in Naples, which he vainly hoped might placate his Sicilian subjects as well. In February and March the rulers of Tuscany, Piedmont, and the Papal States followed suit. In each instance the system proposed was modeled closely upon the constitution of the July monarchy in France, and, except in the case of Rome, each Italian copy had been not merely contemplated but set up before the overthrow of Louis Philippe discredited that particular solution for difficulties which faced the whole of central Europe.

News of the March Days in Vienna reached Milan on the seventeenth; the imperial edict announcing the reforms was posted next morning, only to be defaced with the laconic inscription, "Too late." The authorities reluctantly conceded a civic guard, but its main function was to man the barricades, which made it a hopeless task for the Croat garrison to control the city from its central positions at the town hall and the cathedral. Its commander, the veteran field marshal, Count Joseph Radetzky, who, as a general staff officer, had helped to compass Napoleon's defeat at Leipzig, was not unduly perturbed. He withdrew his troops, first to form a ring around the insurgent city so as to starve or bombard it into submission; then, when he lost control of the perimeter, to the fortresses of the Quadrilateral, lying mainly in Venetia. What mattered at this juncture, however, was the news spreading throughout Italy that Italians had at last defeated Austrians.

Venice had risen independently under the inspiration of the news from Vienna. The nationalists already had a leader, a barrister of Jewish descent named Daniele Manin, whom they rescued from prison; and the cry arose for the revival of the Republic of St. Mark, extinguished only half a century before after a millennium of fame. The Austrians quickly lost every Italian stronghold except those of the Quadrilateral—an all-important exception—and the citadel of Ferrara. Among their lost strongholds were the duchies of Modena and Parma, whose rulers followed the Austrian troops into exile. Throughout the peninsula the events in Milan imparted a twofold impulse—toward the extension of constitutional liberties and to a combination against Austria.

Piedmont, by reason of its geographical proximity and military traditions, inevitably took the lead. On March 23, the day when Radetzky gave up Milan, Charles Albert proclaimed his intention of coming to the rescue of the people of Lombardy and Venetia. Tuscany, too, declared war; Naples dispatched a regular force northward, and for a time volunteers were forthcoming from every Italian state with the blessing of every government. The military operations proceeded slowly, but by the end of May Peschiera had fallen to Charles Albert, whom his troops acclaimed as king of Italy. Lombardy, Modena, and Parma had voted for union; Venetia was later to follow suit. Nevertheless, the sequel was a complete reversal of the situation when Radetzky, having obtained reinforcements, moved forward again from Verona in the Quadrilateral, and at the end of a three-day struggle (July 23–25) hurled the Italians back from the heights of Custozza. This event perhaps did more than any other to ensure the survival of the Austrian Empire; certainly it transformed the prospects of the Italians. Why did they fail?

A large part of the explanation lies in the quality of the military leadership on either side. Radetzky was certainly the most experienced, and quite possibly the ablest, soldier of the day; he was deservedly popular with his troops; and he had sufficient influence with the Austrian court to be able to play for time and secure a necessary minimum of additional troops. Charles Albert was a brave man but an indecisive ruler, nicknamed *Il Rey Tentenna* (King Wobbler), and he had no particular brilliance as a general in the field. His own army was fully up to average European standards in personnel and equipment, but the volunteers from other states, and especially the Lombards, were of very variable quality; and the king was always looking over his shoulder for fear of a republican rising in the rear. In these circumstances it is not surprising that the decisive battle was delayed until it suited Radetzky to renew the contest, or that the defeat at Custozza led to the surrender of Milan and the withdrawal of the Piedmontese army under an armistice.

Other factors besides military inferiority made Italian prospects begin to look very dim. One was the changed attitude of Pope Pius IX, who, at the end of April, 1848, in deference to the German Catholics, withdrew his official support from the war against Austria, and was rapidly losing sympathy with the constitutional system of government that he had himself established in Rome. A second factor was the defection of Naples from the common cause, which began with a counterrevolution in the capital in May, when the priest-led proletarians shouted, "Death to the nation"; but for the next twelve months the cruel energies of Ferdinand II were concentrated upon the destruction of the separatist movement in Sicily. Third, the conflict of purpose arising almost everywhere between moderates and democrats caused the political situation in Tuscany, for example, to change like a kaleidoscope in spite of the strong character of the moderate leader, Bettino Ricasoli.[3] For in 1848 even middle-class leaders lacked any clear picture of their political aims beyond liberation from despotic rule—and that was envisaged as a natural accompaniment of the expulsion of the Austrians from the peninsula, which had not in fact been achieved.

For a time, indeed, the revolutionary movement flared up again in Rome. On November 15 the pope's minister of the interior, Count Pellegrino Rossi, a former French ambassador and a moderate conservative of the school of Guizot, was assassinated, with the result that the pope fled to Gaeta in Neapolitan territory. This left his subjects free to revive the Roman Republic— a glorious, though brief, episode. On February 9 the republic was proclaimed by a constituent assembly that included Guiseppe Garibaldi,[4] who had already put his experience of guerrilla warfare to good use in the mountains of northern Lombardy and now asked nothing better than the chance to defend the

3. 1809–1880. A Florentine nobleman with strong agricultural interests, he pioneered Chianti wine. Pious and austere, he sought union with—but not under—Piedmont; he was prime minister of Italy for nine months after the death of Cavour and for a second short period in 1866–1867, but the "Iron Baron," as he was called, would not stoop to compromise for the sake of office.
4. 1807–1882. Son of a fisherman at Nice. After serving Young Italy at Genoa in 1834, he lived in exile and gained important military experience in South American wars. During a second exile he worked as a candlemaker on Staten Island, N.Y. (1850–1851). Leonine in appearance, immensely brave, disinterested, and ingenuous, his military feats made him a world hero; he accepted the monarchy with reluctance for the sake of the national cause, but remained politically uncontrollable by any king.

GARIBALDI IN 1860, WEARING A "PUNCIO." From a photograph taken immediately after the conquest of Naples. The loose grey sailor's trousers, red shirt, silk neckerchief, heavy sword, South American cloak (poncho), and black felt hat make up the romantic costume which Garibaldi invariably wore and which all Europe knew.

Eternal City. A month later Mazzini arrived in Rome, where he became the dominant figure in a ruling triumvirate which had its almost exact counterpart in neighboring Tuscany, whose grand duke had fled to join the pope. Such was the position toward the end of March when Charles Albert, employing a Polish general, was tempted a second time to try his fortunes against Radetzky, only to be defeated at Novara on the fourth day after the recommencement of hostilities. The new commander's blunders were perhaps the decisive factor, but the consequences were the abdication of Charles Albert and the humiliating surrender of his country; the restoration of the grand duke of Tuscany; and the dispatch of a French expeditionary force under Oudinot to anticipate the intervention of victorious Austria at Rome.

The French expedition proved to be the starting point of many troubles for France—and Italy. In his first advance at the end of April, Oudinot met with unexpected resistance, organized by Garibaldi, at the gates of the city; the pope's Neapolitan supporters were soon afterwards driven back across the frontier; and—but for the French threat—the forces in Rome might even have delayed the Austrian advance southward through the Papal States. But in June Oudinot received orders to set up a formal siege with the help of powerful artillery, and, when the issue was no longer in doubt, Garibaldi made his famous offer of "hunger, thirst, forced marches, battles, death" as the reward of those who chose to follow him across Italy into defiant exile. Only Venice, which had resumed its independence when the Piedmontese made their first surrender to the Austrian arms after Custozza, still survived as the free Republic of St. Mark under the virtual dictatorship of Daniele Manin. Linked to the mainland by a single railway bridge, Venice endured a long blockade, the fort protecting the far end of the bridge being held until the end of May and the city itself until two-thirds of it came under fire from the Austrian siege artillery, the first such ordeal in all its long history. The end came in late August.

In April, 1850, Pius IX re-entered Rome from Gaeta and resumed his throne under the embarrassing eyes of a French garrison, which stayed on as a diplomatic counterpoise to Austrian garrisons in the Romagna. As for the southern kingdom, by April, 1851, Gladstone was publishing his *Two Letters to the Earl of Aberdeen*, which brought the cruelties of the Neapolitan prisons to the notice of the civilized world and denounced the rule of Ferdinand II in a memorable phrase as "the negation of God erected into a system of government." The situation in Italy was very dark, and no new opportunities were visible over the European horizon. Yet, when they did appear, it would be found that important lessons had been learned from adversity.

The strength of the Austrian hold upon the country had been thoroughly tested, and it was clear that Italians could not force that grip to relax without help from outside. At the same time many episodes in the two defenses, of Rome and of Venice, had shown what heights of courage and endurance rank-and-file Italians could reach under good leadership. Manin, indeed, died in Paris in 1857, but their greatest leader, Garibaldi, returned from banishment after a few years to await a new opportunity at his farm on the islet of Caprera, off the coast of Sardinia. Meanwhile, he and many other Italians were slowly digesting a second lesson, namely, that Piedmont, where French was talked as much as Italian, was destined to provide the main basis for the next forward movement. Charles Albert's abdication on the morrow of his defeat at Novara and the accession of his son, Victor Emmanuel II, as brave and honest as he was vulgar and coarse, restored the personal fortunes of the royal house. At the same time the refusal of king and government to escape a war indemnity by agreeing to abandon the new constitution, when constitutions were falling like ninepins elsewhere, made the country once more the symbol of resistance to the will of Austria.

Moreover, the politics of the war years had brought a new influence to the front in Piedmont, that of the capitalist middle class. Reinforced by exiles from other Italian states, it was led by an enlightened aristocrat who modeled himself upon Sir Robert Peel—but in skillful opportunism far excelled his model.

Count Camillo Benso di Cavour[5] had been the editor of a newspaper, *Il Risorgimento*, heading the call for a constitution and for the war. When the war ended in disaster, he refused to despair of the other half of the program, but demanded further progress toward "a free church in a free state" and especially a regime of economic improvements, such as liberal capitalists in both Piedmont and Lombardy had long been demanding. In October, 1850, accordingly, Cavour entered the cabinet, of which d'Azeglio was the head, as minister of trade and agriculture; six months later he took over the portfolio of finance, embarking upon a policy of free trade and industrial expansion which was calculated to bring Piedmont within the orbit of the western powers.

■ ITALY AND THE FRENCH ALLIANCE

A century after the achievement of a united Italy it is all too easy to read back into the story of the unification an inevitability, ease, and consistency of effort which it did not possess. Because the Austrian Empire came to an un-lamented end in 1918, we tend to forget that Marshal Radetzky served what was in fact a great power to which Schwarzenberg appeared to give new cohesion by his policy of centralization. Because the papacy now finds the Vatican City a satisfactory (or at least tolerable) physical framework for its spiritual activities, it is hard to realize either the determination with which Pius IX clung to the temporal power or the complicated effects of the religious issue upon the minds and morals of the Italian people. Because the House of Savoy retained the throne of united Italy until 1946, it is easy to ignore the very real challenge to Piedmontese leadership during, and for many years after, the period of the unification. Because Italy has never again ceased to function as a unit—except during the bitter warfare of 1943–1944—the economic, cultural, and even linguistic, disunity of the not very distant past likewise tends to be forgotten.

By the time that Cavour became prime minister of Piedmont in November, 1852, the parliamentary system had become firmly established there and important steps had been taken toward economic and religious liberalism. The Siccardi laws had abolished the ecclesiastical courts and in other ways restricted the powers of the Church; commercial treaties had paved the way to free trade; railway building by the state and the start of a transatlantic steamship system had given a new stimulus to industry. In the seven years of the Great Ministry,

5. 1810–1861. Scion of a Piedmontese noble family, he was at first intended for a military career, but by 1840 was promoting the first railroad in the kingdom, in Savoy, and two years later was a founder of the Agricultural Society, where he preached the need for industrial development and free trade as well as scientific agriculture, in which he had made his own fortune. In politics a moderate who successfully established a coalition of the Center parties (the *Connubio*), he often resorted to Machiavellian subterfuges to carry through his policies both inside and outside the Chamber.

which now followed, Cavour's firm control of the Center parties enabled him to carry the new domestic policy, which had been largely of his contriving, to a pitch of success which made Piedmontese leadership attractive to the intellectual and entrepreneurial class in the other states. During the same period his foreign policy solved the Austrian problem, which loomed like a dark cloud over the affairs of all Italy. Moreover, it was essential for Cavour, unlike Bismarck, that his policy should be—or at least appear to be—based throughout on parliamentary votes and majorities. This meant that, in addition to all his other responsibilities, he had to play his part in the day-to-day activities of the Chamber of Deputies at Turin, where he figured as a genial debater but one whose early training as an engineer officer often enabled him to cut through a mass of verbiage with devastating effect.

As early as 1846 Cavour had created a sensation by an article, first published in Paris, in which he argued for an all-Italy network of railroads as an enterprise that would foster the national feeling even more than the commercial life of the peninsula. As prime minister he was responsible for the Mont Cenis tunnel scheme to link Piedmont with France. Though he did not live to see this great technical work finished, by the critical summer of 1859 the Piedmontese main lines were otherwise complete—and played an essential role in the switching of French forces from the right to the left flank before the battle of Magenta. The reorganization of the port of Genoa, which involved the transfer of the naval base to Spezia; expenditure on army reforms and new fortifications; the consequent raising of loans at home and abroad; and the steady pursuit of a free-trade policy in the wake of England—all these could be seen to be necessary steps in the creation of a greater Piedmont. The parliamentary combination of the Center, over which Cavour presided, also dealt successfully with the religious question. Having begun his ministry with an opportunist surrender to clericalist agitation against a bill for civil marriages, in 1855 he enacted a measure for the suppression of more than half the religious houses, especially those of the mendicant orders. The effect was to help the finances of the state and to assert its right to control all forms of property within its boundaries. No less important was the removal of the reproach that could be directed against a country of limited wealth, if it continued to support a proportion of ecclesiastics almost three times as large as sufficed for the neighboring dominions of the Catholic Austrian emperor.

By this time Cavour had also taken the first step in the diplomatic operations which were to remove the power of that mighty neighbor from the affairs of Italy. In the winter of 1854–1855, when the siege of Sebastopol[6] was in a condition of stalemate and Austria evaded every suggestion that she should play an active part alongside her allies, a Piedmontese force of 25,000 soldiers was

6. See p. 171.

Italy in 1815 is a mere "geograph-ical expression" under Austrian control. From 1849 onward her other main neighbor, France, plays a part, first at Rome and ten years later in Lombardy, which leads directly to the first stage of unifica-tion. In 1866 and 1870 the cause of united Italy benefits in turn from Prussian support, while the long seaboard gives importance to the benevolent interest shown through-out by Britain.

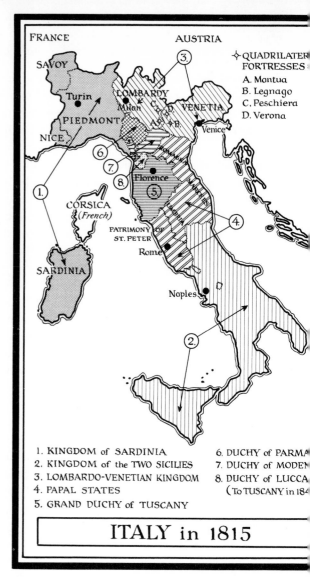

FRANCE   AUSTRIA

⟡ QUADRILATER
FORTRESSES
A. Mantua
B. Legnago
C. Peschiera
D. Verona

1. KINGDOM of SARDINIA
2. KINGDOM of the TWO SICILIES
3. LOMBARDO-VENETIAN KINGDOM
4. PAPAL STATES
5. GRAND DUCHY of TUSCANY

6. DUCHY of PARMA
7. DUCHY of MODEN
8. DUCHY of LUCCA
(To TUSCANY in 184

ITALY in 1815

provided in return for an English loan and—what was of priceless value—an agreement that the allies would bring the state of Italy before an eventual peace congress. In August the Piedmontese repulsed a Russian attack, thus silencing the doubters at home, who had been many, ending an unhappy record of military failures, and making Cavour's seat at the Congress of Paris next year secure and dignified. At the conference table the British foreign secretary, Lord Clarendon, discussed Italian misgovernment in terms of righteous indignation, whereas Cavour spoke after him with politic self-restraint. His object was to secure condemnation of Naples and the papacy and the isolation of Austria; he succeeded in both points, and failed only in an overoptimistic attempt to plead for practical support from Britain in a hypothetical war against Austria.

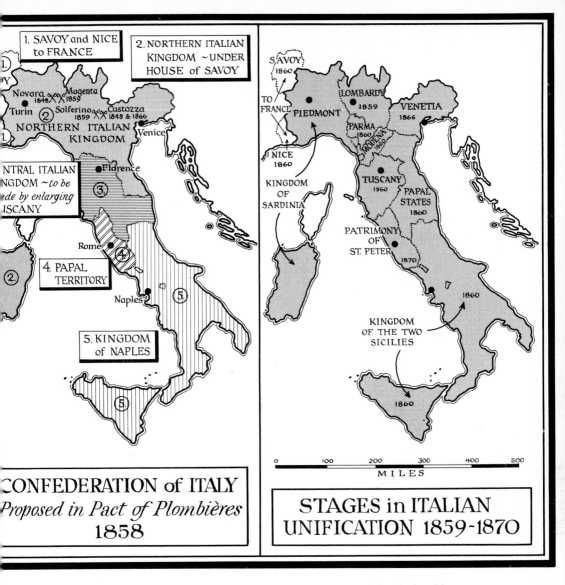

1. SAVOY and NICE to FRANCE

2. NORTHERN ITALIAN KINGDOM ~UNDER HOUSE of SAVOY

Novara 1849 × × 1859 Magenta
Turin ② Solferino 1859 × × Custozza 1848 & 1866
NORTHERN ITALIAN KINGDOM
Venice

①

NTRAL ITALIAN NGDOM ~to be de by enlarging JSCANY ③

Florence

Rome ④

4. PAPAL TERRITORY

Naples ⑤

5. KINGDOM of NAPLES

⑤

CONFEDERATION of ITALY
Proposed in Pact of Plombières
1858

SAVOY 1860
TO FRANCE
PIEDMONT
LOMBARDY 1859
VENETIA 1866
PARMA 1860
MODENA 1860
NICE 1860
KINGDOM OF SARDINIA
TUSCANY 1860
PAPAL STATES 1860
PATRIMONY OF ST. PETER 1870
1860
KINGDOM OF THE TWO SICILIES
1860
1860

0   100   200   300   400   500
MILES

STAGES in ITALIAN
UNIFICATION 1859-1870

Cavour returned home with increased prestige and a useful relationship to Napoleon III.

Two more years passed before the relationship could be turned into something more definitely profitable to the cause of Italian unity. During that period, however, the position of Piedmont had been further strengthened by an understanding with the National Society. This was a comprehensive patriotic organization, founded chiefly by Manin from his place of refuge in Paris, with "Unity, Independence, Victor Emmanuel King of Italy" as its slogan. The members condemned and opposed the futile republican plots of Mazzini, which had again cost valuable lives in Lombardy in 1853. They won Garibaldi to their side, thereby making more difficult such diversionary projects as that for the restoration of a Murat in Naples, with which Napoleon was briefly toying. Cavour dare not, as a responsible minister, offer public support to a subversive organization, since to do so might easily antagonize Napoleon, but if ever the emperor was brought to the point of action, a popular movement penetrating to all parts of the peninsula would render it easier for Cavour to control the final outcome of events.

It is ironical in the extreme that the situation Cavour desired was precipitated by an event of a kind which he would at all costs have sought to avoid —the attempt upon Napoleon's life by a Roman noble, a veteran of the 1849 siege and a Mazzinist, who sought to provoke revolution in Italy through revolution in France. Yet in fact the Orsini outrage in Paris in January, 1858, by which 8 persons were killed and about 150 injured, had the effect of rousing the emperor to a sense of urgency, partly perhaps through fear that the Italian situation might get altogether out of hand if he continued to ignore it, but chiefly through Orsini's dramatic appeal, not to save his own life (which was duly forfeited), but to serve his nation. "Deliver Italy," he pleaded, "and the blessings of twenty-five millions of Italians will follow you."

There followed the conspiratorial meeting of emperor and minister at Plombières in July, when Cavour was supposed to be on holiday in Switzerland. Unattended and unobserved, they drafted their agreement for an alliance to drive the Austrians out of Italy. The Kingdom of Lombardy-Venetia, together with the smaller duchies and the Romagna, would be annexed to Piedmont so as to form a Kingdom of Upper Italy. Together with a new Kingdom of Central Italy (Tuscany, Umbria, the Marches), the Kingdom of Naples (perhaps under a Murat), and a small Papal State consisting of Rome and its environs, it would form a fourfold Italian Confederation. This was to be modeled on the German Bund, with the pope as president. For the military operations France would provide 200,000 men to Piedmont's 100,000, claiming as her reward the cession of Savoy and probably Nice—this would constitute a breach of the 1815 settlement and a partial fulfillment of the traditional French demand for her "natural frontiers." Further, Napoleon's second heir, his disreputable cousin, Prince Jerome Napoleon, would marry the eldest daughter of the ancient Savoyard monarchy.

There is a sadly modern touch about the final provision of the treaty, which was that the occasion for this coolly planned war of aggression must be contrived by Piedmont in such a way that Napoleon could plausibly claim to be supporting her in a war of defense, with Austria figuring as the titular aggressor. At Plombières there had been a feverish study of the map, and a provisional choice of Massa-Carrara, a minuscule state which had been annexed in recent years by the Duchy of Modena. But Austria unwittingly helped the plan by a conscription decree for Lombardy-Venetia, fugitives from which

were enrolled in a volunteer corps on Piedmontese territory. After Piedmont
had called up its reserves in early March, there was pressure for a European
congress to prevent war, and Napoleon, for whom congresses had a strong
attraction, urged his ally to demobilize; he also knew that aggressive action by
France against Austria would probably provoke counteraction by Prussia on
the Rhine frontier. Piedmont had reluctantly decided to yield when Francis
Joseph on military advice issued an ultimatum, which presented his enemies
with the desired pretext and let loose the first of the three disastrous wars which
mark the long reign of that luckless emperor.

The Austrian war with France and Piedmont began when the Austrians
crossed the Ticino on April 29, but their inactivity gave time for 120,000
French to join forces with the 30,000 Piedmontese and after a month they retired into Lombardy. A confused battle at Magenta on June 4 was decided by
the arrival of an additional French army corps in the late afternoon. Milan and
the rest of Lombardy were freed. The Austrians withdrew to the Quadrilateral,
covering Venetia, but advanced again across the Mincio in order to renew the
contest before reinforcements reached the French, including a corps under
Prince Napoleon which had been landed at Leghorn to stake out a claim for the
throne of Tuscany. On June 24 the Austrians held the heights of Solferino and
San Martino, from which the French and Piedmontese armies respectively
drove them back in a day-long battle at heavy cost. At this juncture, when the
capture of Venice from the sea, the reduction of the Quadrilateral, the mastery
of all Italy, and even the shattering of the Austrian imperial power through the
secession of Hungary seemed to be within Napoleon's grasp, he made instead
the armistice of Villafranca.

The motives for Napoleon's sudden decision were complex. The Italian
people appeared to him to show not enough enthusiasm for fighting in the
war, and altogether too much for starting revolutions in central Italy, which
threatened to engulf the papacy and had greatly alarmed devout Catholics in
France. There were also non-Italian factors, ranging from a Prussian mobilization on the Rhine to his own nervous inability to accept past carnage and future
risks of failure. But in the context of the struggle for Italian liberation on which
he was embarked, the armistice, made without consulting Victor Emmanuel,
appeared an inexcusable jettisoning of good chances. After an angry scene with
his king, who had no alternative but to bow to French wishes, Cavour resigned
office.

By the preliminaries of Villafranca Piedmont gained Lombardy but not
Venetia or the Lombard fortress of Mantua, which was included in the Quadrilateral. Parma was tacitly conceded as well, but the rest of Italy was to be
returned to the *status quo*, with a view to the eventual promotion of a federation
under the pope, of which the Austrian emperor would be a member in respect

THE PLEBISCITE IN NAPLES, OCTOBER, 1860. The watcher at the left with a notebook is ready to take the names of those putting "no" ballots in the small, open ballot-box. Over a million voted to join the Kingdom of Italy; only ten thousand opposed.

of Venetia. But were the terms enforceable? While Napoleon hurried back to Paris, giving orders for his armies to follow him, and Cavour left for voluntary exile in Switzerland, the influence of the National Society made itself felt. Although from all Italy they had provided no more than 12,000 volunteers for the campaign against Austria, the patriots under Ricasoli had secured control of Tuscany in a bloodless revolution at the very outset of the war, and of Modena, Parma, and the Romagna soon after the battle of Magenta. With the help of Mazzini—who for once found himself acting in collusion with Cavour— these regions were all induced to vote for their absorption in Victor Emmanuel's kingdom and formed a military league. When peace was finally signed at Zurich in November, the problem was relegated to a congress which never met. Instead, Cavour returned to office in January, 1860, with a program of bartering Savoy and Nice for French acceptance of the *de facto* situation in central Italy, which was to be given a juridical basis by the holding of plebiscites. In March the popular vote brought an effective kingdom of Italy into existence, and in early April its first parliament met at Turin, though it lay under the shadow of a newly signed treaty for the abandonment by Italy of Savoy and Nice. There, too, plebiscites were held a few days later, in which even the patriotic fellow townsmen of Garibaldi were alleged to have voted almost unanimously—but in the opposite direction to the earlier plebiscites.

■ 1860: THE IMPACT OF GARIBALDI

The pope at least could hardly be expected to accept the principle of popular sovereignty, and he met the loss of the Romagna with a decision to form an army of his own, recruited from Belgium, Ireland, and other Catholic countries but placed under the command of a Frenchman, Lamoricière. This choice of an 1851 exile with Orleanist sympathies augured ill for Franco-Roman relations. But Napoleon's immediate interest was in seizing the chance to withdraw his own troops from Rome, since they no longer counterbalanced Austrian forces in other papal possessions and they hampered his dealings with liberal sympathizers at home and abroad. A convention for this purpose had actually been signed, when the sequence of events arising from the Franco-Austrian war of 1859 gave place to a new sequence, arising from Garibaldi's expedition against the kingdom of the Two Sicilies.

Ferdinand II had died in the first month of the war of 1859, but his son Francis II had resisted Cavour's farsighted efforts to turn him into a constitutional monarch and an ally—farsighted because the Piedmontese statesman knew that the assimilation of north and central Italy into his parliamentary and economic system would be a big enough task for the immediate future. His refusal had left the Mazzinians free to concentrate attention upon Sicily, with its age-old tradition of freedom movements. There was a tempting prospect that, if such a movement were to win an initial success, the island might hold out against the mainland until circumstances made it practicable for the forces of the north—or some outside power—to intervene. Francesco Crispi had been busy for some time organizing the islanders for resistance. Cavour, on his return to office in January, 1860, in appearance joined with the king in facilitating the provision of arms and other support. But the genuineness of his support is hard to judge, since he needed to be able to disavow participation in a plot against a friendly power and, what was more important, to reserve for himself complete freedom to follow alternative courses of action, if the plot were to fail. For failure seemed very probable: Mazzini was closely connected with the scheme, and he had failed so often before. Moreover, it was not until the last moment that Garibaldi, whose hatred of Cavour had been brought to fever pitch by the cession of his native city of Nice to the French against whom he had fought at Rome in 1849, consented to take the lead in the expedition with which his name is in retrospect indissolubly linked.

A force of 1072 men sailed from Genoa on May 6 in two small merchant ships to attack an island with a garrison of 23,000 troops on the spot, supported by another 100,000 on the mainland. Moreover, Mazzini had introduced a characteristic complication, which involved landing some sixty men for a feint operation against the Papal States, whose sole achievement was to postpone—

in effect by ten years—the departure of the French garrison then on the eve of leaving Rome. But the great gamble succeeded. Two Neapolitan warships just failed to prevent the landing, and at Calatafimi on May 15, the fourth day after their landing, the Garibaldini won at the point of the bayonet the initial success without which there would have been no others; in their leader's own words, uttered at the crisis of the fight, "Here we make Italy or die." A fortnight later he was battling his way into Palermo, while King Francis telegraphed five times a day for the papal blessing. Once the capital had been taken, the remaining posts of the Neapolitan army were quickly surrendered by commanders, many of them incompetent or cowardly, who were in any case operating with indifferent or positively untrustworthy troops among a rebellious population. When only the citadel of Messina still withstood him, Garibaldi resolved to cross the straits. The Thousand had received substantial reinforcements from north Italy, though Sicily itself contributed mainly guerrillas for local fighting, and it was with four thousand men that he arrived on the mainland on August 20 at daybreak. Apart from the first garrison at Reggio, the thirty thousand Neapolitan troops in Calabria offered virtually no resistance, and Garibaldi entered Naples itself by train in advance of his army on the nineteenth morning after he had landed. King Francis had fled to Gaeta, leaving Garibaldi in control of the kingdom as far as the River Volturno.

Cavour and Victor Emmanuel had meanwhile pursued a tortuous policy, which sought to evade responsibility for Garibaldi's actions, as long as they might fail, while supporting and directing them in secret, with a view to securing eventual control of whatever he might win. Hindsight enables us to see that the intervention of the powers at this time was unlikely, given the Russian hostility to Austria and British support for Garibaldi's venture counterbalancing the vacillations of Napoleon III. But Cavour and his king steered fearfully between the Scylla of action which might prove diplomatically disastrous and the Charybdis of inaction which might allow Mazzini to fill the vacuum. Cavour's duplicity cost him some supporters, including d'Azeglio, and, what is more important, the delay in annexing Sicily gave separatist leaders and political intriguers a hold on the island which they did not quickly lose. Yet he acted decisively enough at the final crisis: the day that Garibaldi entered Naples, Cavour directed an ultimatum to the papacy, demanding the disbandment of Lamoricière's new force.

It had been Garibaldi's intention to press on northward, so that Rome too might be added to the gifts of territory he was preparing to make—in his own way and time—to Victor Emmanuel, who was half in league with him. But Cavour persuaded Napoleon that he must act to prevent the situation from getting out of hand, and, without waiting for the pope's answer to his ultimatum, sent in the Piedmontese army, which scattered the papal force at Castelfidardo for a cost of forty killed. Though Victor Emmanuel's troops were then within three hours march of Rome, Cavour respected the French garrison and the presumed wishes of Napoleon, and only Umbria and the Marches were annexed on the usual plebiscitary conditions. In the following month the royal army continued southward until it linked up with the Garibaldians along the Volturno. Garibaldi's forces were now swollen to 24,000 men and had repulsed an attack by twice as many, but their victory had not dislodged the Bourbon army from Capua and Gaeta—the latter port, in fact, did not surrender until the following year. Nevertheless, Cavour's policy was crowned by the meeting between king and dictator—the title which Garibaldi had used at Crispi's suggestion since the Sicilian landing—at Teano on October 26. This ensured the incorporation of Naples and Sicily in the kingdom, as already approved by plebiscite, and finally disposed of any such alternative as the national constituent assembly proposed by Mazzini, whose influence in Naples was considerable.

In February, 1861, the first Italian parliament met in Turin. Garibaldi had withdrawn to Caprera, a hero of heroes, but one whose life was to close with twenty years of anticlimax. Cavour, his inveterate opponent, was perhaps more fortunate. He was still feeling his way as prime minister in dealing with a new legislative body more than twice the size of the old one when death came to him rather suddenly at the age of fifty-one, leaving the problems of Venetia and Rome to be solved by others.

■ THE CONTINUING STRUGGLE: VENETIA AND ROME

The kingdom that Cavour had created provided a very inferior base for further expansion. The electorate numbered about 150,000 in a population of nearly 22,000,000, which as yet was far from constituting a homogeneous society. The attitude to papal claims made a cleavage everywhere; each Piedmontese annexation was made at the cost of long-continued resentment among autonomists, federalists, and republicans, all feeling that their state had been stolen from them; and the sinister influence of the secret societies in Naples and Sicily was only one of many factors which cut off the south from any sympathetic understanding by the educated classes of the north. Instead, there was a ruthless imposition of centralized institutions under the Piedmontese constitution, which involved the acceptance of regional prefects, a different legal code, new currency, more exigent tax collectors, and even, in some cases, of carpetbag politicians by a public that neither expected nor desired a new way of life. The removal of internal customs barriers, too, operated chiefly to the advantage of Piedmontese business interests, which were the most efficient producers and largely monopolized the market. Even Piedmont lacked capital for the most urgent task of all, which was to open up backward regimes to new influences by building railroads—in 1860 the Two Sicilies had only a hundred miles of track, all of it on the mainland. The lines were doubled in length within eight years, but three out of the four principal companies were financed entirely from abroad.

The consequence of all this was that brigandage, endemic in Naples and Sicily, soon rose to the level of a guerrilla war, supported by ex-King Francis from papal territory across the frontier. The available evidence suggested that about eighty thousand rebels, who could rely upon passive support at least from the bulk of the peasantry, had been organized. There followed a little-advertised civil war, which cost more lives than all the other episodes of the *Risorgimento* put together. A regime under which any peasant found in possession of arms was liable to be shot inevitably provoked hideous reprisals, but by 1865 the national army, after deploying nearly one half of its total strength, had succeeded in driving resistance underground.

There remained the financial problem. Piedmont under Cavour had paid its way with difficulty. But his successors were less skillful administrators, and the economy of the new kingdom lacked the resilience of the Piedmontese, with its expanding machine industries. At the outset the rate of taxation per head was not heavy—about one half that which obtained, for instance, in France—but it had to be collected from pitifully small resources. In some districts the land tax was half the annual value of the land; income tax was exacted only upon the equivalent of fifty dollars a year; and Cavour's commercial treaties prevented any recourse to bigger customs duties. The result was that in the first eight years the new state spent as much as it could levy in taxes in fourteen years, so that it was forced to raise loans on increasingly disadvantageous terms, which brought it within measurable distance of bankruptcy. The worst crisis arose out of the new and inglorious war in 1866, which reduced Italian credit abroad to a desperately low level, while the costs to be met were three times as large as for the war of 1859. Although a much disputed Church Lands Act enriched the state at this juncture through the sale of monastic estates, resort was had to an oppressive tax on the grinding of corn and a currency inflation, which bore equally hard on small wage earners.

Against this background we must see the better known and more dramatic events of the decade. Of these the winning of Venetia through the Austro-Prussian War of 1866 is really a by-product of great-power relationships and may be dismissed briefly. In April, 1866, a treaty with Bismarck bound Italy to take part in such a war; in May the Italian government from a sense of honor refused to abandon the treaty when Austria offered Venetia, the intended reward of participation, as the reward of mere neutrality instead; and in June war was duly declared. The sequel was humiliating. The Italian generals attacked the Quadrilateral with about twice as many men as Austria could spare for its defense, but were beaten for the second time around the heights of Custozza. A sortie against the Austrian naval station at Lissa, in which Italy lost two of its ten ironclads, was another resounding defeat. Even Garibaldi, with 38,000 volunteers, made disappointingly slow progress through the Tyrol. In the circumstances Italy was bound to endorse whatever terms Bismarck might dictate; the Tyrol was perforce abandoned, but Venetia was handed over to the Italian kingdom, nominally through Napoleon III and on the basis of a favorable plebiscite. Thus a territory which Austria had valued more highly than Lombardy fell into the Italian lap like an overripe fruit, and gave as little satisfaction.

The main problem was that of Rome, a world symbol, the traditional Italian capital, or at the very lowest estimate a troublesome enclave within the new kingdom. The city itself had a population of only 184,000 (1861), but the Patrimony of St. Peter included the port of Civita Vecchia and a stretch of coast which separated Tuscany from Naples, together with a twenty to thirty mile hinterland containing Tivoli and three other towns. For Garibaldi and his followers—anticlericals, radicals, and enthusiasts—Rome was the objective of a crusade which had been wrongfully robbed of success in 1860. For many other Italians it was the obvious capital, which must be taken sooner or later, though the nuisance of Neapolitan plottings there, which was serious, needed to be balanced against the serious diplomatic risks involved in any premature action. For Napoleon the Roman question was a time bomb, which he would prefer to see laid and exploded by other hands. And for the pope Rome was the holy ground selected to fight a rear guard action of the medieval Church.

In 1862 Garibaldi took advantage of his position as a national hero, which made his person virtually sacrosanct, to assemble some thousands of volunteers in Sicily, with the watchword of "Rome or Death." In defiance of a royal proclamation, they crossed over into Calabria, where Garibaldi himself was slightly wounded in an abortive skirmish in the mountains near Aspromonte. The sequel was a French attempt to relieve the tension by a convention signed in 1864, in which Napoleon agreed to withdraw all French troops from Rome within two years in exchange for the Italian government's pledge of protection for the papal territory. At the same time the transference of the capital of Italy from Turin to some other city than Rome was to suggest to the world that the arrangements now arrived at were intended to last. But the suggestion was false. When the move from Turin to Florence duly took place, it marked for many Italians a further stage on the way to Rome; and the treaty deliberately left a loophole for intervention in Rome by the absence of any clear provision for what was to happen if an internal revolt made the continuance of papal rule in the city impracticable. In December of the same year the issue of the Syllabus, in which the pope formally condemned eighty "modern errors," including specifically liberalism, socialism, communism, and freedom of discussion, challenged the whole democratic position. It was safe to prophesy that the Romans, however docile and time-serving they might be at the moment, were bound some day to come again, as in 1849, into serious and open conflict with the Temporal Power in their midst.

The papal position did not seem in immediate danger. When the last of the French troops duly left the Eternal City, it had acquired a fair-sized garrison of papal Zouaves, supplemented by a body of French Catholics, known as the Légion d'Antibes; and whatever liberationists there were lacked effective unity because surviving Mazzinist influences in the city still called for a new republic. In October, 1867, Garibaldi with seven thousand men crossed the frontier from Tuscany, but found it impossible to seize Rome without either artillery to breach the walls or insurrectionaries in control of some key areas inside them. He was making for Tivoli instead when the papal garrison and a body of French troops newly dispatched from Toulon caught him at Mentana and mowed down his outnumbered men with the new *chassepot* rifle. Garibaldi was now what Mazzini had long since become—a spent force. The prestige of the pope, on the other hand, had been increased, and, as the Italian government had done less than nothing to hamper the abortive expedition, French forces remained at Civita Vecchia. When the Vatican Council assembled in December, 1869, the Italian government was for some time in fear that the proposed definition of Papal Infallibility might be extended to cover the temporal power, which it would then be incumbent upon all Catholics to defend.

However, the confirmation of the new dogma regarding the nature of the spiritual power coincided almost exactly with the outbreak of the Franco-Prussian War. Italy was more mindful of recent disappointments than of those eventful months, a little more than ten years before, when the help of Napoleon III alone made the unification of Italy a practical possibility. The government refused to support him in the war, though Garibaldi served with a force of volunteers; Mazzini tried to join the Prussian side. More important for Italians was the withdrawal of the French garrison from Civita Vecchia, which was completed in mid-August. For this time, events in the greater world moved swiftly in their favor. After Sedan and the fall of Napoleon III, the Convention of 1864 was a dead letter. Bismarck was favorable to an Italian move against Rome, which no Catholic power was at this juncture prepared to oppose; and the Italian government was able to dispatch fifty thousand men to confront a few thousand papal Zouaves. A four-hour bombardment on the morning of September 20 was made necessary by the pope's determination to prove to the diplomatic corps—who breakfasted meanwhile in the Vatican—that he yielded only to force. The wall having been breached, Italian troops took possession of the city, and a fortnight later a plebiscite endorsed what a show of force had accomplished. Next summer the king took up his residence at the Quirinal: the unification of Italy was at last completed.

■ AN IMPERFECT UNION

It was the end of a story illuminated by the heroic efforts of a number of individual Italians—Garibaldi; Mazzini; Cavour; Victor Emmanuel, who had not despaired of the Piedmontese constitution in the darkest hour; the Tuscan dictator, Ricasoli; and Crispi, the leader of the underground movement in Sicily. Except for Crispi, who dominated Italian politics toward the close of the century, they all followed Cavour to the grave without making any important further contribution, and in the hands of lesser men the history of united Italy proved to be a disappointing sequel to the long struggle. Since, however, the sense of disappointment is at least partly due to a misconception as to the character and results of that struggle, it may be profitable to make here a brief recapitulation and assessment.

In 1859, 1866, and 1870 the nationalist movement had owed its success primarily to the actions of stronger political forces outside Italy; even the expedition of the Thousand in 1860 could not have achieved what it did without the tacit support of outside powers. This consideration in turn drove Cavour and lesser men to gain their ends by devious means, so that the political tradition of the *Risorgimento* gave the new kingdom in some respects an uninspiring start. If the leaders had played their cards with less than complete honesty and straightforwardness, the backing given by the masses to the nationalist movement was never really wholehearted, except in plebiscites which served to register a *fait accompli*. It required all the energy of Ricasoli to hold the Tuscans to the idea of unity with Piedmont in the winter of 1859–1860. Garibaldi's conquest of Sicily yielded him only a few hundred Sicilian volunteers for the mainland campaign, in which the Neapolitans themselves remained largely passive. Garibaldi, again, had been disgusted by the absence of spontaneous support for his efforts in 1866, and the Roman population throughout the final decade offered no serious help in any of the various schemes for their liberation.

Moreover, under the immensely skillful guidance of Cavour the nationalist movement had become centered upon a Piedmontese leadership, involving the acceptance of the parliamentary regime as established there, of the Piedmontese economic and financial system, and, last but not least, of Cavour's program for "a free church in a free state." In 1870 the Piedmontese themselves had had only two decades in which to learn the art of self-government; the rest of the peninsula had had less, and the fact that each of the recently independent states began with a strong regional basis for its politics made it immensely hard for the cabinets and parliaments of united Italy to avoid dependence upon regional combinations. These were most readily based upon conciliation of local business interests, and corrupt capitalists came to be opposed in their turn, not by Mazzinian republicans, but by ruthless socialists and anarchists of the school of Bakunin.

Finally, there remained the implacable hostility of the papacy, to which the new government in Rome offered the most generous terms in vain. As early as March, 1871, it passed a Law of Guarantees, which provided the pontiff with sovereign honors, extraterritorial rights for the Vatican and Lateran palaces, and an annual grant equal to what had been assigned in his own last budget. The Italian priesthood would also be free in principle to practice its ministry unhampered by regulation or supervision on the part of the state. But Pius IX would have no relations with the "subalpine government"—he refused to call it Italian—which had usurped his temporal authority, and for nearly sixty years he and his successors continued to prefer the role of the "Prisoner in the Vatican," thereby weakening the position at home and abroad of what was in any case the weakest of the great powers.

Reading List: Chapter 4

Olschki, L., *The Genius of Italy* (1949), ch. 17. The *Risorgimento* in its larger setting.

Kohn, H., *Prophets and Peoples* (1946), ch. 3. Mazzini.

Salvemini, G., *Mazzini* (1956; paperback, 1957), pp. 56–91, 124–59. Extracts from his writings, with comments.

Whitridge, A., *Men in Crisis: The Revolutions of 1848* (1949), ch. 2. Mazzini and Garibaldi.

Mack Smith, D., *Garibaldi: A Great Life in Brief* (1956), chs. 4, 9, 10.

Hales, E. E. Y., "Mazzini," *History Today*, vol. VI (1956), no. 2.

Trevelyan, G. M., *Garibaldi's Defense of the Roman Republic* (1907), chs. 10–11. The siege of Rome.

———, *Garibaldi and the Thousand* (1909), chs. 13–17. The conquest of Sicily.

———, *Garibaldi and the Making of Italy* (1911), chs. 14–15. Garibaldi and Victor Emmanuel.

Thompson, J. M., *Louis Napoleon and the Second Empire* (1955), pp. 167–210. Napoleon III and Italy.

Binkley, R. C., *Realism and Nationalism, 1852–1871* (1935), ch. 10. "Confederation and Unity in Italy (1859–60)."

Woodward, E. L., *Three Studies in European Conservatism* (1929), pp. 276–339. Regime of Pius IX.

Chapter 5

The Unification of Germany and the European Balance, 1849–1871

Aftermath of the Revolution of 1848
The "Bach System" in the Hapsburg Empire, 1851–1859
Creation of the Dual Monarchy in Austria-Hungary, 1859–1867
The German Problem During the 1850's
Bismarck's First Approach to the German Problem
The Impact of Foreign Affairs: Poland and Schleswig-Holstein
Defeat of Austria and Formation of the North German Confederation
The Franco-Prussian War and the Creation of the German Empire

■ AFTERMATH OF THE REVOLUTION OF 1848

The failures of the revolutionary movements of 1848 and 1849 left enormous unsolved problems in a large area of central Europe—an area of critical importance. Out of an estimated total European population of 266,000,000, the inhabitants of the various German states, together with all those under the authority of the Hapsburgs, accounted for approximately one-quarter. Throughout this whole area strong demands for reform had made themselves heard. Broadly speaking, these demands had been of three kinds: one, to remodel the German Confederation of 1815 on genuinely constitutional lines; another, to reorganize the Hapsburg Empire so as to give some recognition to the national aspirations of its various ethnic groups; a third, to secure or strengthen liberal, parliamentary institutions in the various states making up this entire central European complex.

SIGNIFICANT EVENTS

1850	Reconvening of the Diet of the German Confederation (May)
1851–1859	Bach regime in Austria and Hungary
1854–1856	Crimean War
1859	Austro-Sardinian War
1861	Accession of William I in Prussia
1862	Bismarck minister-president in Prussia
1864	Danish War over Schleswig-Holstein
1866	Austro-Prussian War
1867	Dual Monarchy in Austria-Hungary; The North German Confederation
1870–1871	Franco-Prussian War
1871	Proclamation of German Empire (January)

Both for the Hapsburg lands and Germany proper, the significance of the two decades following 1848 is that new methods were employed to meet the problems which revolutionary methods had failed to solve. In an earlier chapter it has been seen how disappointing were the results of the 1848 revolution. By June, 1849, the last rump sessions of the Frankfurt Parliament, then meeting in Stuttgart, were dispersed. Early in 1850 Schwarzenberg, the new director of Austrian policy, had summoned the old Federal Diet to meet at Frankfurt in May. In the following November, by the Punctuation of Olmütz, he had rebuffed the tentative efforts of Prussia to assert a new leadership in Germany. Reaction, clearly, was in full swing. Although Schwarzenberg had announced in March, 1849, that a highly centralized, unitary constitution would be provided for the Hapsburg lands, it never materialized. Austria and Hungary were governed "provisionally" by an autocratic emperor, a prime minister re-

133

sponsible to no parliament, and by an increasingly elaborate, German-speaking bureaucracy.

Throughout Germany nationalism was a growing force. Yet in the general atmosphere of political reaction, the lesson of 1848 and 1849 seemed to be that this nationalism could not be realized through liberal channels. The failures of the liberal revolutionaries carried the clear indication that Germans would have to look elsewhere for leadership. Within the Hapsburg lands nationalism was a highly complex phenomenon. In various stages of development and in various areas, there existed a German-Austrian nationalism, a Magyar, a Czech, a Polish, a Croatian, and an Italian nationalism. Though the German-Austrian leadership had long assumed that it could exercise prime authority, the other groups were beginning to make ever-larger demands. For the government to surrender to these diversified demands would be fatal; to ignore them completely would be equally disastrous. The problem, obviously, was to establish some sort of middle path, and it was this problem which occupied the Hapsburgs for nearly two decades until, in 1867, a solution was found in the great constitutional compromise, the *Ausgleich*.

The European powers could not help being concerned in the working out of these problems. France had Rhineland and Italian interests; Russia had Polish and Balkan interests; Britain was concerned, less specifically but no less genuinely, with what her statesmen were accustomed to call "the European balance." If changes were to be made in the German Confederation or the Hapsburg Empire, it would be highly unlikely that the other great powers could remain indifferent. Thus the evolution of central European affairs in the two decades running from 1850 to 1871 was strongly influenced by the diplomatic consequences of various wars: the Crimean War of 1854–1856, the Austro-Sardinian War of 1859, the Danish War of 1864, the Seven Weeks' War between Prussia and Austria in 1866, and the Franco-Prussian War of 1870–1871. The first half of the century had experienced nothing comparable to this intricate association between war on the international scene and political transformations at home.

■ THE "BACH SYSTEM" IN THE HAPSBURG EMPIRE, 1851–1859

The Austrian Empire stood, during the decade of the 1850's, as a classic example of a country in which autocracy reasserted itself after a period of upheaval. The young emperor, Francis Joseph, was a convinced autocrat, never, throughout his long life, comprehending the modern world in which he lived and devoted only to maintaining the dynastic idea. The Hapsburg Empire would function, so he believed, if day in and day out he sat at his desk giving imperial assent to the necessary documents which his ministers brought him. The minister on whom he at first relied, Prince Schwarzenberg, was likewise a convinced believer in autocracy, dedicated to the exercise of force from above and skeptical even of his own aristocratic colleagues. Schwarzenberg rejected a scheme for a hereditary house of lords on the grounds that there were not a dozen Austrian noblemen fit to sit in it. No legislature was summoned in Austria as promised in the constitution of March, 1849, and in Hungary the constitution won by Kossuth was declared forfeit.

By June, 1849, power had come to lie chiefly in the hands of Alexander Bach.[1] Schwarzenberg, nominally head of the government until his sudden death in 1852, concerned himself, none too successfully, with foreign affairs. Bach took over the ministry of the interior from Stadion (who had gone mad) in June, 1849, and entrusted the ministry of justice to Schmerling, an able and vigorous administrator. Since all strings came into Bach's hands he seemed truly to exemplify the reaction.

The "Bach system" dominated the Hapsburg Empire until the minister's dismissal in 1859. It was essentially a return to absolutism, enforced by an elaborate bureaucracy and operating under a close system of centralization. The appropriate moment for the emperor and his advisers to make clear the new state of affairs came on St. Sylvester's Eve (December 31, 1851). The Sylvester Patent bluntly revoked Schwarzenberg's constitution of March, 1849, and in its place the emperor assumed sole political responsibility.

The heart of the Bach system lay in the vast imperial bureaucracy which extended downward so as to reach every village, and outward so as to encompass all of Hungary and its crown lands, now divided into five administrative parts. Local diets were abolished. The bureaucracy, directed from Vienna, was an effective means of Germanization; for while some provision was made for elementary education to be conducted and public notices to be issued in the local tongue, German was the only language to be used in the civil service and in the army. German, too, became standard in higher education; the ancient Polish University of Cracow, for example, was entirely Germanized in 1854, while in all secondary schools throughout the Empire German was obligatory as a subject and instruction was to be chiefly in that language. The bureaucracy itself was severely disciplined, the regulations going so far as to prescribe the type of clothing to be worn and even the cut of official beards. As there was no parliament, a new Council of State (*Reichsrat*), responsible only to the emperor, was supposed to direct the workings of the entire system. Actually, following the issuance of the Sylvester Patent, the emperor himself assumed ever-increasing authority.

1. 1813–1893. Born of a peasant family, he became a civil servant and a lawyer. Originally liberal in his ideas, he was one of the moving spirits in the March Revolution of 1848. In October he accepted a post in Schwarzenberg's counterrevolutionary government and from 1849 to 1859 was a key figure in the reaction, so powerful that his subordinates were nicknamed the Bach Hussars. Called a renegade by his opponents, he lived for over thirty years after his fall in obscure retirement.

Political reaction did not mean the absence of all progress. Steps were taken to provide lands for those peasants who had been freed in 1848 from their servile dues. Over 3,000,000 persons throughout the Empire received land and nearly 100,000 owners were compelled to cede it. In most cases, but not always, the peasant was required to pay a modest part of the cost of the land which he received. A new system of law courts, involving the use of the jury, was introduced. Railways became state owned, the postal service was reorganized, and efforts were made to stimulate economic life by means of chambers of trade and industry. Some improvements were made in the secondary schools and universities, and, as has been noted, in the primary schools it was decreed that some instruction should be given in the mother tongue. A concordat with the Roman Catholic Church, signed in August, 1855, restored many of the powers taken from the Church by Joseph II in the eighteenth century. It acquired full charge of all Catholic education, it was granted the right to conduct ecclesiastical courts, its property was declared sacred and inviolable, and the pope could communicate freely with his clergy. The obvious lack in all this program was any true recognition of national differences within the Empire, or any introduction of genuine representative institutions.

■ CREATION OF THE DUAL MONARCHY
IN AUSTRIA-HUNGARY, 1859–1867

The autocratic system built up by Bach and his colleagues soon proved to be unequal to the stresses of a warlike age or to the persistent demands of the national groups within the Empire. The first evidence of this appeared during the Crimean War. Austria quite clearly was a rival of Russia in the Balkans, and, when war came in March, 1854, and Russian troops began to occupy the principalities of Moldavia and Wallachia, Austria first called upon Russia to withdraw and then began to deploy her forces along the Turkish border. A military crisis was averted when Russia withdrew her troops from the principalities in August. Yet the Austrian occupation which followed was expensive, and, when in December Austria actually allied with England and France against Russia, the burden of the lengthy mobilization was very heavy.

So likewise in 1859, when the intrigues of Napoleon III and Cavour brought Austria to declare war on Piedmont, the Hapsburg Empire was again subjected to strain.[2] While Magenta and Solferino were not catastrophes, they were defeats which involved heavy Austrian casualties and the war ended with Francis Joseph agreeing to give up Lombardy. Actual danger of revolt arose in Hungary, where demands for the constitution of 1848 began to be heard.

2. The Austrian commander in Italy, who had assumed his post after the death of Radetzky in 1857, was spurred on to action by a telegram from Vienna reading: "Surely you can do as well as that old ass, Radetzky."

THE AFTERMATH OF BATTLE. During the Crimean War newspaper reporting in the modern sense began. Here the correspondent of *The Illustrated London News* walks alone over the battlefield of Inkerman—a poignant commentary on war itself.

Francis Joseph's first move on returning from Lombardy was to dismiss Bach (July, 1859), thereby indicating the termination of Bach's unique form of centralized autocracy, which had run since 1851. In the following year the emperor issued his October Diploma which, if honestly put into effect, would have created a truly federal system for the Hapsburg lands. The emperor was to exercise legislative power with the cooperation of the assemblies, or *Landtage*, in the various crown lands, and these would send delegates to the central imperial council which would now have substantial powers alongside those of the emperor. Hungary would get back its 1848 constitution which would function within the new federal framework.

It may be doubted how sincere these proposals were, or how well they would have worked, and certainly the sixty thousand copies of the October Diploma which were printed and circulated aroused little enthusiasm. Each national group expected more than it actually received, and the hopes of the liberals for a truly parliamentary regime were bitterly disappointed. In 1861 a further document, the February Patent, professed to interpret the October Diploma by stipulating the method of election to the diets of the various lands and to the new *Reichsrat*. Actually this document was a retreat from true federalism, since the election rules for a new two-chamber parliament were such that they would have given the German-speaking bourgeoisie a power out of all proportion to its numbers. Not true federalism, but Austrian preponderance throughout the Empire, would have been the outcome. Poles, Czechs, Slovenes, Croats, and Hungarians quickly voiced their protests.

The new Hungarian leader of this opposition was Francis Deák,[3] a worthy successor to Kossuth and an eloquent champion of the liberties for which Hungary had fought in 1848. This conservative member of the Magyar gentry had been trained as a lawyer and now sought, instead of independence, the guarantee of genuine liberal rights for Hungary.

During this time the fortunes of Austria were profoundly affected by the course of events in the German Confederation and more particularly in Prussia, where Otto von Bismarck had become minister-president in September, 1862. What Bismarck sought to do and what actually he achieved will be considered in detail shortly. Austria joined Prussia in 1864 in the brief war[4] with Denmark over Schleswig-Holstein, thereby falling into a trap which Bismarck deliberately set. The outcome was not friendship with Prussia but increasing hostility which resulted in the Seven Weeks' War of 1866. Austria's catastrophic defeat, her loss of Venetia to Italy, and her expulsion from the German Confederation, which Bismarck now transformed for his own purposes, meant that any plans for a truly federal solution of the Hapsburg problem were now outdated. Francis Deák's strong insistence upon Hungarian rights, vigorously backed by his colleague, Count Julius Andrássy, led to dualism as the solution rather than to either of the two other alternatives—a federal or a unitary state.

The arrangements were finally embodied in the Compromise (*Ausgleich*) of 1867. The Hapsburg Empire now became a Dual Monarchy (Austria-Hungary). Austria, with its seventeen provinces, made up one state, over which Francis Joseph ruled at Vienna with the title of emperor. Austria obtained an elected parliament, yet this was so constituted as to carry out the spirit of the February Patent and enable the Germans to dominate the Bohemian, Polish, Slovene, Ruthenian, and Italian minorities. In point of fact, the German-Austrians were themselves a minority when set against the total of the other groups. In Hungary, where Francis Joseph had the title of king and wore the thousand-year-old iron crown of St. Stephen, the Magyars also were actually a minority among the Croats, Serbs, Rumanians, Slovaks, and Germans. Yet the Magyars, by virtue of the restored constitutional arrangements of 1848, were able to dominate these other minorities and to be largely free from any control by Austria of their internal affairs.

Complicated provisions were made to enable the parliaments of the two halves to work together as parts of one greater political entity. Details of this

---

3. 1803–1876. A country squire, he entered the Hungarian parliament in 1833 and played a moderate role in the Revolution of 1848. Retiring in 1849, he helped to keep alive Hungarian patriotism during the Bach era. He submitted Hungarian national demands to Vienna in 1860 and, with Andrássy, negotiated the Compromise of 1867. A magnificent orator and confirmed bachelor, he was known as "the Sage of the Nation." Only briefly in office (1848), he refused all honors from the Crown, saying these were beyond its power to give.
4. See p. 146.

new political structure are best considered in connection with the history of Austria-Hungary in the half-century following 1867.[5] Broadly speaking the Compromise gave some kind of political and economic order to the large area sometimes known as "Danubia." It enabled the Dual Monarchy to limp along until the collapse of 1918 at the close of the First World War. Some credit for the working of the Compromise must be given to that utterly conservative, unimaginative, tragic, and yet dedicated figure, the Emperor Francis Joseph, who symbolized so much of the old Austria and for whom a genuine and widespread affection existed. Some credit must also be given to the powerful bureaucracy. Clearly, the non-German minorities, save for the Magyars, got a poor bargain. The Slavs were most acutely aware of this, and it is notable that the leaders quickly voiced their protests—Palacky for the Czechs, Goluchowski for the Poles, and Bishop Strossmayer for the Croats. To protest, however, is one matter; to bring about drastic, revolutionary change is another. The inadequacies of the Compromise contributed to the growing national tensions of the late nineteenth century. However effective it may have been in providing a way out of the immediate conflicts of the 1850's and the 1860's, the Compromise failed utterly in the larger purpose of keeping the various ethnic groups within the Dual Monarchy from moving slowly toward the ultimate goal of independence.

■ THE GERMAN PROBLEM DURING THE 1850'S

While the Dual Monarchy struggled with its complex problems, profoundly important changes were going on in the neighboring lands of the German Confederation. Here the failures of 1848 meant that the thirty-nine component states still bore the clumsy yoke put upon them by the arrangements of 1815. Liberalism had been discredited—so much so that in state after state the constitutions were being conservatively revised in order to cleanse them of what King Frederick William IV of Prussia vehemently described as "the democratic filth of the year of shame." Many liberals chose to emigrate, so that the total transatlantic flood surpassed that of the hunger years preceding 1848.

Head and shoulders above the other German states in size and power stood Prussia—a kingdom of twenty millions with a capital, Berlin, approaching the half-million mark. Particularly in the Rhineland provinces and in Silesia industry was making rapid growth; save in the Polish provinces, the country benefited from a good roads system and a rapidly developing railway network. Prussia was linked with most of the German states in the *Zollverein*—to the mutual advantage of all members—and two new additions, Hanover and Oldenburg, joined in 1853.

Although Prussia had its constitution and its *Landtag*, the nature of this

5. See pp. 417–423.

constitution was such as to give any political power which the king did not exercise to the nobility and the great landowners. Frederick William IV was a romantic reactionary—talented, eccentric, devoted to the past, and living in a world of capriciousness and conceit that ultimately turned into madness. His chief minister at this time, Joseph von Radowitz, was a deeply conservative Catholic convert who hoped that Protestant Prussia and Catholic Austria could work harmoniously together. In these circumstances it is hardly surprising that an air of negativism and conservatism settled upon the kingdom.

A certain spirit of German nationalism had existed before 1848 and had contributed substantially to the ferment of the great revolutionary year. This force continued to develop throughout the Confederation during the decade of the 1850's, but the development was now marked by the growing assertiveness of Prussia as the champion of the new national cause and the turning of much national sentiment from liberal to conservative leadership. The increase of national sentiment and the desire for strong military leadership was doubtless stimulated by the emergence of the Second Empire in France with its revival of Bonapartism, and even more by the example of Italy where, despite the failures of 1848, the struggle for unification went on. Heinrich von Treitschke, the great German historian, wrote of "this wonderful spectacle" of a nation, Italy, thus seeking its freedom. Other historians, among them Gustav Droysen and Heinrich von Sybel (later to write the classic account of the founding of the German Empire), proclaimed the doctrine that Prussia through her power would soon make German unity a reality rather than a dream.

In the summer of 1859 groups of North German liberals met to form an association working for German unification under Prussian leadership. The outcome was the *Nationalverein* (National Union), formally organized in September at Frankfurt. The date, it will be noted, coincides with the time when Piedmont, by winning Lombardy from Austria, had initiated the work of unification in Italy. The head of the *Nationalverein* was a distinguished liberal leader from Hanover, Rudolf von Bennigsen.[6] This union was the first political organization in Germany to transcend state borders and to seek to unite all liberals and democrats in a truly national party. It wished to see Germany become a unified, parliamentary state in which the component elements need not, however, lose their identity; it accepted Prussian leadership as axiomatic; and, with some divergences of opinion, it tended to believe in the exclusion of Austria. For ten years this association of businessmen, professional men, in-

6. 1824–1902. A Hanoverian, leader of the liberal opposition in its upper house, he founded the *Nationalverein* in 1859 to work for German unity on the model of the Italian National Society. In 1866 he became a Prussian subject. As leader of the National Liberals in the Reichstag he collaborated with Bismarck, 1871–1877; he resigned from the Reichstag in 1883 in protest against Bismarck's stern antisocialist measures. After his return to politics in 1887 he was awarded by William II the presidency of the province of Hanover.

tellectuals, and public servants worked steadily for the cause of national unity on a parliamentary basis. The *Nationalverein* was dissolved in 1868 when much of its work had been done, and when it was increasingly clear that German unity would be completed by a policy of force and at the point of the Prussian sword.

■ BISMARCK'S FIRST APPROACH TO THE GERMAN PROBLEM

The history of Prussia and of Germany in the second half of the nineteenth century is inseparably connected with the name of Otto von Bismarck. From 1862, when he became minister-president of Prussia, until 1890, when he resigned as imperial chancellor, he was uninterruptedly at the helm. It is hardly an exaggeration, therefore, to describe him as the outstanding figure in the history of Germany and of Europe in the second half of the nineteenth century. Of very moderate fortune, he belonged to the Junker nobility—the conservative, landowning class east of the Elbe River that for centuries had served the king by providing the administrative backbone of the Prussian bureaucracy and the officer class of the Prussian army. Born in the year of Waterloo, Bismarck was anything but a typical Junker—his mind was too subtle, his ambition too great, and his personality too complex. After some administrative training (and many adventures involving wine, women, and song) at the universities of Göttingen and Berlin, he served briefly in the Prussian administration. The explanation which he gave some years later for his early departure from government service is most revealing of him. "The Prussian official," he wrote candidly, "is like a member of an orchestra, but I want to play only the music which I myself like, or no music at all."[7] Bismarck had, in addition, one year of military service (1838–1839) in a fashionable regiment.

Some years spent in managing his estate were followed by membership in the United Diet which assembled at Berlin in 1847. Here Bismarck revealed himself in strong opposition to the liberal views, as he soon showed himself also to be to the revolutionary movements of 1848. These he regarded as a wave of illegal popular revolts seeking to destroy the historic rights of the monarchy. When Frederick William IV finally issued a constitution for his people, Bismarck was elected to the new Prussian *Landtag*, where he quickly aligned himself with the extreme right-wing groups.

Bismarck's role was not to be played out on the almost meaningless stage of the Prussian *Landtag*. Most significantly for his future policies, he spent the years between 1851 and 1859 as the Prussian envoy to the Diet of the German Confederation.

Though Bismarck was keenly aware of the need for German unity, he was not at first opposed to Austria, whom he regarded as a valued bulwark of

7. E. EYCK, *Bismarck and the German Empire* (1950), p. 14.

conservatism. His service at Frankfurt educated him in this respect. He was struck by the arrogance of the Austrian representatives and by the general weakness of the entire structure of the Confederation. Passages from dispatches to the Prussian prime minister, Manteuffel, vividly demonstrate the evolution of his views. In 1851, at the outset of his service, he wrote as follows: "I do not believe that the Federal Diet in its present form can be the last word in our politics; rather I see in it only a shell . . . that will drop off when the kernel is ripe." In 1853 he wrote: "Unless Austria renounces the policy of Schwarzenberg . . . sooner or later the federal wagon, pulled by the Prussian horse forward and by the Austrian horse backward, will go to pieces"; in 1856: "I will express my opinion that in no long time we shall have to fight Austria"; in 1858: "Your Excellency is aware that the Federal Diet and our disadvantageous position are Austria's best weapon"; and in 1859: "I believe we should take up the challenge."

Bismarck's opportunity came in 1858 when Frederick William IV, in whom signs of insanity had appeared, was replaced by his brother William, who held the title of prince regent. An unassuming man of mediocre abilities, William was nevertheless sincere and firm of purpose, a conservative of moderate outlook, seeking advisers less reactionary than Manteuffel and the crowd that intrigued on Manteuffel's behalf. The new cabinet, headed by the moderately liberal Prince Anton of Hohenzollern, soon came to be known as the "New Era Ministry." General von Roon, an able soldier, became minister of war and his friend, General von Moltke, chief of the general staff. In recognition of Bismarck's growing prestige, he was sent as ambassador to St. Petersburg, where during his three-year stay he learned the value and basic necessity of a Russo-Prussian understanding. The few months he then spent in 1862 as ambassador in Paris enabled him to confirm the impressions he had already gathered concerning the vaulting ambitions and the unfathomed weaknesses of Napoleon III. Bismarck's first reputation, however, was to be made on the Prussian rather than on the international scene; his opportunity came as the result of a political crisis of the first order in Berlin.

When Frederick William IV at last died in January, 1862, his brother became king as William I. Like all Hohenzollerns, he was a believer in divine right, yet his sense of duty and his reasonable outlook led him to accept the constitutional arrangements which had been in effect in Prussia since 1850. As for the larger German problem, William hoped that some day, probably not in his own lifetime, Prussian leadership would provide the answer.

The crisis which brought Bismarck back from Paris to assume the heavy duties of minister-president had been blowing up during the years of William's regency. It came to a head as the result of a dispute over the army and the budget. The Prussian system of conscription established in 1814 should have provided the country with 65,000 recruits annually to serve for three years, plus additional terms in the reserve and then in the *Landwehr* (a sort of home guard). Actually, only about 41,000 conscripts were taken annually. Von Roon wished to tighten up and expand the conscription system and to minimize the role of the *Landwehr*, which he regarded as an uncouth, undisciplined body with officers drawn largely from the bourgeoisie. His plans meant that, in time of war, Prussia would have a total available military strength of 756,000 men.

The Liberals, who were a growing force in the Prussian *Landtag*, disliked Roon's proposals and wished to reduce the term of service to two years; moreover, they resented the downgrading of the *Landwehr*. The opposition was strong enough to block Roon's original military measure, and so the bill was withdrawn and the government simply asked for an additional nine million thalers to be used for unspecified military purposes. In 1860 the *Landtag* agreed, and again in 1861 it voted, albeit reluctantly, an enlarged general appropriation. By 1862, however, the increase in the strength of the Liberals and Progressives in the May elections led to a deadlock. The legislature refused to approve unless the term of service was reduced to two years, the role of the *Landwehr* reestablished, and all details of the military budget made clear. The crisis was so acute that William I, like Cavour in 1859, actually contemplated suicide. Then, accepting the advice of his minister, he authorized Roon to summon Bismarck from Paris. The cryptic message contained five words: "*Periculum in mora. Dépêchez-vous*," ("Danger in delay. Hurry up!").

On September 24, 1862, Bismarck accepted the post of minister-president. Only the day before the lower house had rejected the government's budget proposals by a vote of 273 to 68. The Progressives, it was now clear, were strong enough to muster a heavy majority against him in the *Landtag*. In the immediate constitutional crisis which faced Bismarck as he took office, he boldly enunciated his basic attitude to government. This position was that in the case of a deadlock, i.e., a failure to vote the budget, the government must proceed with its duties, collect taxes, and spend money whether authorized or not. Within a week of assuming office Bismarck spoke to the Budget Commission in what has come to be one of the most famous of all his speeches:

> The position of Prussia in Germany will be determined not by its liberalism but by its power. Bavaria, Württemberg, and Baden may indulge themselves in liberalism but no one will assign to them the role of Prussia; Prussia must concentrate its strength and hold it for the favorable moment, a moment which has already been missed several times. . . . Not through speeches and majority decisions are the great questions of the day decided—that was the great mistake of 1848 and 1849—but by blood and iron.[8]

This contempt for majority decisions was soon translated into action. When the Diet protested Bismarck's behavior in carrying on the business of the

8. Quoted in K. S. PINSON, *Modern Germany* (1954), p. 128.

state without an authorized budget, he had it prorogued. Ordinances were issued restricting freedom of the press and limiting the field of activity of local government. When the new elections of October, 1863, produced an even larger opposition, Bismarck went stubbornly on his way, collecting taxes and ordering whatever expenditures he thought advisable. The protests were many—from industrialists, from jurists, and even from historians. King William is said to have looked down broodingly from the windows of his palace at the head of Unter den Linden into the courtyard below, picturing in his mind the guillotine that someday the mob would set up to dispose of him, a latter-day Louis XVI. Yet nothing happened to break the tension, and Bismarck went his way as minister-president until the dramatic impact of foreign crises turned public attention away from the troubles at home and made Bismarck a Prussian hero of the first magnitude to Liberals and Conservatives alike.

■ THE IMPACT OF FOREIGN AFFAIRS:
POLAND AND SCHLESWIG-HOLSTEIN

Bismarck's thesis upon assuming office was that he would assert Prussian leadership in the making of a new Germany. As this would inevitably mean a basic disagreement with Austria, it was clear to him that the use of force could hardly be avoided. Force, to be sure, has never been absent from European politics, and few statesmen of the nineteenth century could have taught Machiavelli, Richelieu, or Frederick the Great much about its carefully premeditated exercise. The novelty of the Bismarckian age lies in the frankness with which political leaders asserted the fundamental necessity of force, as in the case of the "blood and iron" speech of 1862, and in the intenser use of force made possible by the technology of the new industrial era. New states were in the making and the assertion of their national sovereignty took precedence over all else. Realpolitik—a word which first became current in a small pamphlet published in 1853 with the title Grundsätze der Realpolitik, or Foundations of Political Realism—gives the keynote of the age. The realism of men like Bismarck triumphed by a systematic disregard of sentiment, tradition, and ethical scruples; in their eyes such considerations were as strictly irrelevant to politics as they would be to a game of chess.

When Austria sent William I an invitation through the king of Saxony to attend a meeting of the German rulers at Frankfurt in the autumn of 1863 to consider a reform of the German Confederation, Bismarck managed only with the greatest difficulty to persuade his royal master not to do so. To go to Frankfurt would have meant accepting the continued fact of Austrian leadership. A Prussian memorandum sent to the conference stipulated that there must be a truly national parliament representative of the German people in which Prussia, equally with Austria, must have the right to veto war. Clearly, if

Austria still had any hopes that she might take the lead in a *Grossdeutsch* solution of the German problem, this memorandum—"the last nail in the coffin of Austrian greater-Germanism"—must have destroyed them.

The note of political realism is also seen in Bismarck's attitude toward the revolt which broke out in the Polish provinces of Russia in January, 1863. While Austria, Britain, and France all made representations to Tsar Alexander II on behalf of the Poles, Bismarck quickly sent Count Alvensleben to St. Petersburg where he signed the secret Alvensleben Convention (in April) offering Russia the support, if need be, of four Prussian army corps massed on the Polish borders. These, as it turned out, Russia did not need; Napoleon III's proposals for an international conference, which would discuss not merely Poland but all Europe's critical problems, fell to the ground; Russia broke off her friendly relations with France; and the way was open for Bismarck, now on cordial terms with Russia, to pursue his policy of *Realpolitik* in other directions.

The opportunity quickly came in the tangled problem of the two duchies of Schleswig and Holstein. These lands, linked in personal union with the king of Denmark, had been, it will be remembered, the source of a bitter dispute involving Denmark, Prussia, the German Confederation, and the great European powers in the years between 1848 and 1852.[9] The settlement reached by the London Conference of 1852 was that Denmark could not fully incorporate the duchies, as she had sought to do, but that both Holstein (which was German-speaking and a member of the German Confederation) and Schleswig (which was partly German- and partly Danish-speaking and not included in the German Confederation) should be recognized as united in personal union with Denmark under the Danish king. The other claimant, the duke of Augustenburg, was to be given a monetary indemnity. In 1863 the king of Denmark promulgated a law that would separate Schleswig from Holstein and incorporate it fully in the Danish kingdom. When he died in November, his successor, Christian IX, proclaimed a new constitution which carried out his predecessor's policy of incorporating Schleswig. This precipitated a crisis of the first order which Bismarck used with masterly skill.

The death of the king of Denmark raised once more the question of succession in the duchies and led the duke of Augustenburg to revive his claims. He was reputed to be a liberal and thus became the candidate of the liberal and national groups in Germany. Bismarck had no real sympathy with the claims of the duke of Augustenburg; and, while he professed to stand as a champion of the London Protocol of 1852, his real intention was to incorporate Schleswig and Holstein in Prussia, whenever it became possible, for ethnographic, geographic, strategic, and political reasons. For the time being, however, it was good, realistic power politics to support outwardly Augustenburg's claims. In

9. See pp. 93–94.

December the Diet of the German Confederation had ordered a "federal execution" against Denmark, sending Saxon and Hanoverian troops into Holstein on behalf of the Bund. Bismarck characteristically ignored this action and chose to work with Austria alone. In January, 1864, the two governments sent an ultimatum to Denmark demanding the restoration of the *status quo* within forty-eight hours—a striking example of the ultimatum technique destined to become so common in later European practice.

Counting upon European backing, Denmark refused, whereupon on February 1 Austrian and Prussian troops already in Holstein crossed the Eider River into Schleswig. Two points stand out concerning the war. One was the great success of the Prussian armies in their military actions, especially in winning the strong Danish fortress of Düppel—a vindication of Roon's work as minister of war and Moltke's as chief of staff. Blood and iron were indeed the determinants of victory. The second point was the complete inability of the other great powers to influence the eventual settlement. A conference was held at London but without reaching agreement, and Napoleon III's proposal of a plebiscite—in itself unexceptionable—fell by the wayside. Thus, the war ended in October by the formal Treaty of Vienna, according to the terms of which Schleswig, Holstein, and the small territory of Lauenburg were turned over jointly to Austria and Prussia.

This arrangement lasted for nearly a year. In his later accounts of these transactions, Bismarck insisted that he had no intention of coming to a definite settlement with Austria over the duchies, since the larger purpose of expelling Austria from the German Confederation was first in his mind. Hence, when the Treaty of Gastein (August, 1865) modified the original arrangement for joint occupation by providing that Austria should now administer Holstein and Prussia Schleswig, Bismarck could quite properly say that this merely "papered over the cracks," since an opportunity to challenge Austria's behavior could easily be found. The Augustenburg claims were now a thing of the past, and Austria had been maneuvered into abandoning the principle of working in the name of the Germanic Confederation. Bismarck was shrewd enough, too, to stipulate that Prussia should have the right to fortify the harbor of Kiel, which lay in Holstein and had already been set up as a Prussian naval base, as an alternative to Danzig.

In his first three years of office Bismarck had boldly seized the reins of power, won the friendship of Russia, outmaneuvered Napoleon III, fought a war, acquired territory, and placed Austrian leadership of the German Confederation in jeopardy. A glimpse of the contribution which *Realpolitik* made to all this can be obtained from the report of an interview with Bismarck, sent to the government of Hesse-Cassel by its representative at Berlin shortly after the Treaty of Gastein had been signed:

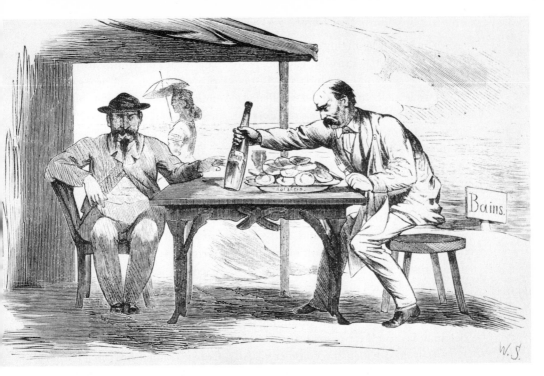

NAPOLEON III AND BISMARCK AT BIARRITZ, OCTOBER, 1865. This symbolic cartoon by the German artist, Scholz, shows a determined Bismarck taking possession of both the oysters and the Rhine wine.

Bismarck boasted with the candor peculiar to him of how from the beginning he had conducted the Schleswig affair in accordance with Prussian interests. He had posed conditions to the Danes which he knew they could not possibly have accepted. At the same time, he had by indirect means encouraged them to active resistance. Through his secret agents, he had put before them the certain prospect of English assistance, while he had assured himself in advance that France did not want to go to war and that therefore England too would keep her sword in the scabbard. At the London Conference, he had (*verba ipsissima*) hitched the Duke of Augustenburg as an ox before the plough to bring it ahead. As soon as the plough was in motion, he had again unhitched the ox. His own aim is the annexation of the duchies; the difficulty is to bring the King to do it. About Austria and the cleverness of its policy, Bismarck merely smiled.[10]

■ DEFEAT OF AUSTRIA AND FORMATION OF THE NORTH GERMAN CONFEDERATION

The force so effectively applied against Denmark was now to be turned upon Austria, always with the larger purpose of furthering Prussia's leadership in Germany. King William I had to be won over, for he, with his wife and the

10. Quoted in L. STEEFEL, *The Schleswig-Holstein Question* (1932), p. 256.

crown prince, was highly dubious about further military moves. By taunting the Liberals in the Prussian Chamber—referring to it contemptuously on one occasion as "a House of Phrases"—Bismarck provoked such an uproar that the king's resistance to them was stiffened. A much more tricky problem was Napoleon III, with his repeated proposals for European conferences, his constant suspicions of Prussian leadership in Germany, and his eagerness for Rhineland gains. Bismarck "accidentally" saw the French emperor at Biarritz (October, 1865) and, while he made no such precise bargain as Cavour had made with Napoleon in 1859 at Plombières,[11] gained the conviction that France would do nothing to help Austria in the event of a war with Prussia. Napoleon apparently had the impression that the war would be long, that it would exhaust both sides, and, if the German Confederation were broken up, that the outcome would result in a tripartite Germany—Austria composing one unit, Prussia and the North German states a second, and the South German states a third. Such an outcome he believed would benefit France, all the more so if in the resultant confusion he could push the French frontier further toward the Rhine, where the Bavarian Palatinate, Luxembourg, or possibly even Belgium, lay as glittering prizes.

Italy also had to be considered. At a Crown council held in February, 1866, Bismarck declared bluntly that war with Austria was inevitable and asked authority to conclude an alliance with Italy so that there could be an attack upon Austria simultaneously from the south. William I gave his approval, and so on April 8 (the precise date is important, for the Italians refused to be bound for more than three months) a most secret agreement was reached whereby Italy promised to join Prussia if a war came with Austria, her stipulated reward being Venetia. Since the constitution of the German Confederation explicitly forbade any member to ally with a foreign power against any other member, Bismarck's intention to destroy the existing Confederation stands out very plainly. Russian friendship could be counted upon ever since Prussia's offers of help at the time of the Polish revolt of 1863. England, so Bismarck felt, would not commit herself any more than she had done in the Schleswig-Holstein affair. As for the other member states of the Confederation, Bismarck was reasonably certain of their hostility and was prepared to accept it.

Few wars have been more deliberately provoked than the war of 1866 with Austria. On the day following the signature of the secret Italian treaty, the Prussian representative at the Diet at Frankfurt proposed a sweeping reform of the Confederation by establishing a truly German parliament based on a universal, equal, and secret franchise. This was tantamount to proposing the exclusion of Austria. He also made strong complaints against Austria's administration of Holstein, notably in encouraging the old claims of the duke of

11. See above, p. 120.

Augustenburg. When Austria sought to bring this latter issue before the Diet at Frankfurt, Bismarck claimed that Austria was violating the Convention of Gastein, and ordered Prussian troops into the duchy which Austria was administering. The rapid mobilization of troops on both sides made war practically inevitable. Austria, indeed, anticipating war in Italy (though William I had given his word of honor to Francis Joseph that no treaty between Prussia and Italy existed), foresaw the loss of Venetia, and therefore made a secret deal with Napoleon III whereby, in return for his promise of neutrality, he was to receive Venetia for subsequent transfer to Italy. If Austria won the war (vain hope!), she was to consult with Napoleon about any changes she might make in Germany. These, surely, were pipe dreams for both Austria and France.

On June 14, on Austria's motion, the Frankfurt Diet voted a federal execution against Prussia for its violation of Holstein's territory. Only a handful of states—some of the petty northern principalities and the three free cities of Hamburg, Bremen, and Lübeck—supported Prussia. Declaring the Confederation dissolved, Prussia on June 16 sent her troops into Saxony, Hanover, and Hesse-Cassel. The major campaign against Austria followed with lightning speed. In this Seven Weeks' War three campaigns were fought. In Germany the Prussians had little difficulty in disposing of the states that sided with Austria. After an initial setback, Prussian troops defeated the Hanoverians in a two-day encounter at Langensalza, quickly occupied Hesse, Nassau, and Frankfurt, and invaded Bavaria. South of the Alps, the Italians were defeated on land and sea, yet they performed the stipulated task of occupying substantial Austrian forces.

The most spectacular Prussian victories took place in Bohemia, where the Austrians had summoned the hapless Field Marshal Benedek. He was a lifelong student of the Italian terrain, but had been brought from Italy so that the Hapsburg Archduke Albert might replace him and win some easy victories in the south. Yet, despite Austrian blundering, chief credit goes to the Prussian strategy of battle. Helmuth von Moltke,[12] long an advocate of the use of railways, had carried out a trial mobilization during the crisis of 1859 and had gained further railway experience in the Danish War. While the Austrians moved their troops forward on only one principal line, Moltke used five, spreading his armies over the extraordinarily wide front of 270 miles. He could thus reach good strategical positions in advance of the enemy. The Prussians,

---

12. 1800–1891. The greatest military strategist of the later nineteenth century. He began military service in Denmark (1818) where his father lived, then served in the Prussian army from 1821 to 1888. He remodeled the Turkish army, 1835–1839, became Prussian chief of staff in 1857, and held the post for thirty-one years. He wrote a novel, translated Gibbon's *Decline and Fall* in eighteen months in order to get money to buy a horse, became an expert cartographer, and published classic works describing his travels in Turkey and Russia. His admiration for Mozart, Beethoven, and Schubert equaled his distaste for Wagner. His military treatises fill fifteen volumes. Nicknamed "the Silent," in the opinion of experts he never made a mistake in strategic planning or faced a military situation which placed any strain on his powers.

moreover, had the famous needle gun, a breech-loading, bolt-action rifle that, unlike the Austrian muzzle-loaders, could be reloaded by a soldier lying prone. Since each side disposed of something like 250,000 men, the overwhelming Austrian defeat on July 3, only seventeen days after war began, makes Sadowa (or Königgrätz) one of the great and decisive battles of modern times. Prussia had won not a Seven Weeks', but a Three Weeks', War.

The diplomatic maneuvering for peace involved more personal strain than the war itself. Bismarck was determined that, once Austria was expelled from the German Confederation, she should be leniently treated. Here he had to cope with the Prussian generals and King William, all wishing the traditional spoils of victory. Only by a long struggle and the threat of resignation was Bismarck able to make his will prevail.

The second problem was France. Failing in his proposal on the eve of hostilities that a congress be summoned, Napoleon III offered his mediation again on the very day after Sadowa, with a hint at the possibility of compensations for France. Other proposals followed. Bismarck's technique was to get Napoleon to agree to Prussian plans—the expulsion of Austria from Germany, a free hand for Prussia north of the River Main, and the forming of a new confederation that would leave out the South German states—by hinting at more drastic alternatives. Napoleon presumably regarded this as the creation of a tripartite and therefore weak Germany and was not troubled. Thiers, on the other hand, saw more clearly. "There are," he said starkly, "no mistakes left to commit."

Soon after the preliminaries of peace had been signed (July 26), Napoleon III sent his ambassador, Count Benedetti, to Bismarck. He brought the request that substantial Rhineland territories (the Bavarian Palatinate, part of Hesse, with Mainz or the Saar) be ceded to France. Bismarck indignantly refused, and saw to it that the story was published in a French newspaper, thereby arousing anti-French feeling in South Germany and helping him in his plans for treaties with these states. On instructions, Benedetti then submitted another written request, this time for France's annexation of Luxembourg or possibly Belgium in return for recognizing the complete unification of Germany. Bismarck again refused, but very astutely kept the documents secret, to be used with telling effect in 1870 when he wished to rouse German and other opinion against France. Thus, save for negotiating the transfer of Venetia from Austria to Italy, Napoleon III had failed in the 1866 crisis to play any appreciable role.

The arrangements with Austria which marked the end of the German Confederation of 1815 were embodied in the Treaty of Prague (August 23). This confirmed the preliminaries of Nikolsburg and added further details. Austria, now excluded from Germany, paid Prussia a moderate indemnity and gave up Venetia. North of the River Main Prussia was to annex the states of

Hanover, Nassau, Hesse-Cassel, Frankfurt, and the northern part of Hesse-Darmstadt. She was authorized to form a North German Confederation. South of the River Main the states of Baden, Württemberg, Bavaria, and Hesse-Darmstadt were authorized to form a separate confederation. Prussia treated them leniently. They paid her moderate indemnities, renewed the tariff union with Prussia which the war had ended, and each signed a secret treaty of mutual assistance with Prussia in the case of any threat to its territories.

Prussia's gains were spectacular. She had added 4,250,000 subjects; her lands now ran unbroken from the Rhineland to the River Niemen; and she had authority to form a North German Confederation from which Austria had been excluded. Though much was still to be done, it remains true that by the Treaty of Prague the German Empire was brought within sight of completion.

Bismarck now made his peace with the Prussian parliament in defiance of which he had ever since 1862 been arbitrarily levying taxes. The wars of 1864 and 1866 had immeasurably strengthened his position, and the wartime election, actually on the very day of the great victory at Sadowa, enlarged Bismarck's Conservative supporters at the expense of the Progressives. Hence in September he quickly introduced a Bill of Indemnity, retroactively legalizing government expenditures since 1862 in return for his admission that he had acted in violation of the constitution. The Bill passed by 230 votes to 75. An immediate sequel was a split resulting in the development of party alignments anticipating those under the Empire. Some of the extreme Conservatives, dubious about the imminent North German Confederation, were lukewarm in support of Bismarck; the others, the Free Conservatives, in general backed him. The former Liberals and Progressives likewise were split. A new party, the National Liberals, led by Bennigsen, supported Bismarck; the Progressives for the most part opposed him. Some Catholic deputies now began to form a Center group of moderate views; and in addition there appeared one Social Democrat and the inevitable small group of irreconcilables from the annexed territories.

Negotiations with the states north of the River Main lasted from August, 1866, to July, 1867, when, after acceptance by the various parliaments, twenty-two states were united in the North German Confederation. The president was the king of Prussia, whose people now comprised twenty-five millions out of the thirty millions making up the whole. He was served by a federal chancellor (Bismarck) responsible to him alone. A federal council (*Bundesrat*) was composed of delegations from the various states acting under instructions; Prussia had seventeen out of the total of forty-three votes, the next largest state had four. The lower house (*Reichstag*) was elected by secret, direct, universal manhood suffrage. Out of the total of 297 seats Prussia held 237. Thus the dominant role of Prussia is apparent. In this and many other respects the North German Confederation closely anticipated the German Empire of 1871.

UNIFICATION of GERMANY

Prussia in 1865.

Annexations of 1866.

Included in North German Confederation, 1867.

Allied in 1866 and included in German Empire, 1871.

Annexed as "IMPERIAL TERRITORY" 1871.

.... Boundary of North German Confederation - 1867~1871.

——— Boundary of German Empire, 1871.

0 40 80 120 160 200
MILES

The Schleswig-Holstein Affair

––– Boundary of German Confederation of 1815.

——— Boundary of German Empire, 1871.

ooooooo Linguistic Boundary.

0 20 40 60 80 100
MILES

The pressure of the new industrial forces was unmistakable. Hence economic union was provided for by the resurrection of the war-shattered *Zollverein*. A customs parliament, to which Bavaria, strongly suspicious of Prussian leadership, made temporary opposition, met in 1868 and undertook to regulate economic matters of joint concern. Full political union was quite clearly the next step. In the parliament of the North German Confederation, Bismarck spoke of the future as follows:

> If Germany attains its goal in the nineteenth century, I should regard that as a great achievement; if it were reached in ten or five years, it would be something quite extraordinary, an unexpected crowning gift from God.[13]

Actually, the work of unification was to be completed in less than four years.

■ THE FRANCO-PRUSSIAN WAR AND
  THE CREATION OF THE GERMAN EMPIRE

The last phase in the creation of the German Empire brought Bismarck into fateful contact with Napoleon III, still working for French gains in the Rhineland, seeking alliances with Italy and Austria that would offset the unexpected new power of Germany, and still hoping that France could serve as a chief arbiter of Europe's destinies. It may well be that Bismarck now felt war with France to be as inevitable as the war of 1866 had been with Austria; that he deliberately engineered it is less demonstrable than that he skillfully took advantage of every opportunity—including those which Napoleon III or his ministers recklessly threw in his way.

Twice during the Seven Weeks' War the French emperor had been rebuffed in his Rhineland ambitions. In 1867 he tried again. The duchy of Luxembourg, a possession of the king of the Netherlands, had been a member of the old Germanic Confederation, its capital garrisoned by the Prussians as a federal fortress. It was not included in the North German Confederation, and Napoleon III secretly arranged with the king of the Netherlands to buy it. Although Bismarck had promised not to oppose, he quickly let the news leak out to the German press, rightly anticipating an outburst of patriotic protest. Then he shrewdly made public his secret treaties of mutual assistance with the South German states. This was clear warning to France. The outcome was a meeting of the great powers in London (an echo of the older system of diplomacy by conference) at which France agreed to abandon the plan of purchase, Prussia withdrew its garrison, and Luxembourg became a neutral state with its independence collectively guaranteed by the great powers. Bismarck quite clearly had scored over Napoleon III.

The French emperor now tried to set up some countersystem. His ap-

13. Quoted in C. GRANT ROBERTSON, *Bismarck* (1918), p. 240.

proaches to the South German states were unavailing. Italy, from whom he might have expected some gratitude because of his part in helping to get her both Lombardy and Venetia, actually showed little warmth, since a French garrison at Rome still served as an obstacle to full Italian unity. Austria, so ruthlessly expelled from the German Confederation, might have seemed a better bet. Negotiations beginning in July, 1868, went on until October, 1869, and during them some approaches were also made to Victor Emmanuel. The outcome was an exchange of letters between Napoleon III on the one hand and Francis Joseph and Victor Emmanuel on the other, declaring their mutual affection and determination to aid each other if their power was threatened. In an age of Bismarckian *Realpolitik*, declarations of mutual affection would seem curiously inadequate safeguards—personal letters that in the crisis of 1870 would become truly meaningless.

In this growing atmosphere of tension Napoleon III took steps to strengthen his armies, enlarging the term of conscription, introducing a breech-loading rifle named after its inventor the *chassepot*, and experimenting with an elementary form of the machine gun, the *mitrailleuse*. Unhappily for the French, those responsible for army affairs placed far greater confidence in these measures than the future would warrant. It was under these circumstances that Bismarck more than once stated that war with France would be only a question of time. How and when the war actually would come he could not profess to know.

The precipitating crisis which led to war arose unexpectedly in Spain, where a revolution in 1868 left the throne empty. The provisional Spanish government, looking around for a possible king, hit upon Leopold of Hohenzollern, son of that Prince Karl Anton who had headed the New Era Ministry in Prussia in 1858, and a distant (Catholic) cousin of William I; in 1866 his younger brother Karl had been chosen as Prince of Rumania by referendum (in place of the deposed Alexander Cuza). Bismarck did not engineer this candidacy, which clearly would cause the utmost concern in France, but, having learned of it, as early as May, 1869, he sent secret agents to Spain, well equipped with funds to encourage its success. When a first Spanish offer was made to Leopold, he declined. Then on June 19, with the connivance of Bismarck, he was persuaded to change his mind, and William I was persuaded to give his approval. News of the arrangement, which was supposed to be kept secret, accidentally leaked out, with the result that the French foreign minister, the Duke de Gramont, made an inflammatory speech in the French Chamber referring in almost possessive tones to Spain as "a neighboring people" and in most hostile terms to the action of Prussia as threatening "to endanger the interests and the honor of France." If the arrangement persisted, Gramont declared ominously, "We shall know how to do our duty without wavering or weakness." He, much more than Napoleon III, who was now incapacitated by gallstones, was the reckless advocate of war.

The crisis seemed to be over when on July 12 Prince Karl Anton withdrew his son's candidacy, having been advised to do so by William I who in turn had been urgently approached by the French ambassador. Bismarck, away at his estate, had no hand in these proceedings. What caused the crisis to flare up again and what gave Bismarck his chance was an act of folly on the part of Gramont. Urgent instructions were sent to the French ambassador, Benedetti, at once to see King William, who was taking the waters at the resort town of Ems, and ask him to give assurances that the candidacy would never be renewed. Benedetti saw the king under rather informal circumstances, as he walked in the public gardens, and made his urgent request. The king, understandably irked at the unusual proceedings, told Benedetti he could make no such promise and walked on. The news was sent to Bismarck in a long telegram with the king's authority to prepare it for publication. Bismarck, who, back at Berlin in the company of Moltke and Roon, had been gloomily contemplating the failure of their hopes for scoring a decisive victory over France, now saw his chance. The Ems Telegram[14] was not falsified; it was, however, cut down and condensed so as to suggest that, after some insulting demands from Benedetti, William I had curtly rebuffed and dismissed him. In this form it went to the press.

The precise effect of the telegram on public opinion is hard to measure. It was played up by jingoistic newspapers and by reckless statesmen on both sides. Some Frenchmen, not necessarily disposed to war, felt that Prussia was forcing war upon them. Bismarck made no question of why he had handled the telegram as he did. On July 15 a belligerent French cabinet, led by the premier, Ollivier, and encouraged by Gramont, the foreign minister, and Leboeuf, the minister of war, asked the Chamber of Deputies for large war credits—tantamount to a declaration of war—and the vote was 245 to 10. The Empress Eugenie gave the war party her ardent backing, and the Emperor Napoleon was too ill to object. "I cannot rule unless I lead," he pathetically told an English friend, ". . . I have no choice but to advance at the head of a public opinion which I can neither stem nor check."[15] Four days later the official French declaration of war reached Berlin.

The Franco-Prussian War, an outline of which has been given earlier, destroyed the Second Empire in France and made possible the creation of a new Empire across the Rhine.[16] The South German states had already been made

14. See p. 79.
15. *Daily Telegraph*, London, July 25, 1870, quoted in *New Cambridge Modern History*, vol. X (1958), p. 600.
16. See pp. 79–80.

"THE PRUSSIAN HERCULES." This lithograph, published by Honoré Daumier in *Charivari* (1865) after Bismarck's first victories, expresses French doubts as to the enormous war burdens carried by the Prussian Hercules. By 1871 skepticism had disappeared.

aware of Napoleon's Rhineland intrigues and now came in on Prussia's side. When Paris was besieged in September, Bismarck set up his headquarters at Versailles and here, by a supreme irony, he undertook separate negotiations with Baden, Württemberg, Bavaria, and Hesse-Darmstadt for the creation of the German Empire. By the end of November they had been persuaded to agree, the greatest objector, Bavaria, being brought into line by the promise of a separate postal system, a separate peacetime army, and other concessions which in the long run were formal rather than substantial. The final problem was to persuade William I to accept an imperial crown, for, like Frederick William IV in 1849, his first and deepest devotion was to the crown of Prussia. He resented, too, the proposed title of "German Emperor" which to him seemed less possessive than "Emperor of Germany." Bismarck's solution was to get the impecunious Ludwig II of Bavaria, already showing signs of madness and devoted principally to his obsessive mania for castle building, to send a letter of invitation to William I—in return for which Ludwig was given a private grant of $45,000 a year out of the confiscated revenues of the ex-king of Hanover.

In a setting of royal and military splendor the German Empire was proclaimed in the Hall of Mirrors at Versailles, on January 18, 1871, ten days before Paris surrendered to the Prussian armies and four months before the definitive Peace of Frankfurt. "His Majesty was so offended at the course I had adopted," Bismarck wrote in his *Reminiscences*, "that, on descending from the raised dais of the princes, he ignored me as I stood alone on the free space before it, and passed me by in order to shake hands with the generals behind me." Writing to his wife, the unhappy William I declared that he very nearly abdicated and handed over everything to his son.

The constitution of the German Empire was formally proclaimed on April 17, 1871. It was essentially that of the North German Confederation enlarged by the inclusion of the four South German states and the "imperial territory" (*Reichsland*) of Alsace-Lorraine, taken from France in the Treaty of Frankfurt. In all there were four kingdoms (Prussia, Saxony, Bavaria, and Württemberg), three "free cities" (Hamburg, Bremen, and Lübeck), eighteen other states, and the one imperial territory. The overwhelming preponderance of Prussia, geographically, politically, and economically, was everywhere apparent. The great powers of William I as king and emperor, and the dual role of Bismarck, who added the new title of imperial chancellor to his former office of minister-president of Prussia, are all indicative of the Prussianization of Germany. Any hopes of a democratically organized German national state such as had been envisaged by the liberal patriots of 1848 had vanished. It will be seen later how the political machinery of the Empire was organized. For the moment it will suffice to say that the most powerful national state that Continental Europe had ever seen now came into being as the consequence of the most ruthless exercise of *Realpolitik* and military force.

Reading List: Chapter 5

Taylor, A. J. P., *The Hapsburg Monarchy 1815–1918* (1947), chs. 6–7. The system of Schwarzenberg and Bach; making of the Dual Monarchy.

The New Cambridge Modern History, vol. X (1960), ch. 20. Austria from 1848 to 1867.

Binkley, R. C., *Realism and Nationalism, 1852–1871* (1935), pp. 227–41; 274–79. Dualism in Austria-Hungary.

The New Cambridge Modern History, vol. X (1960), chs. 19, 22. Prussia, 1830–1866; Bismarck and German unity.

Eyck, E., *Bismarck and the German Empire* (1950), chs. 2–3.

Taylor, A. J. P., *Bismarck, the Man and the Statesman* (1955), chs. 4–5.

Valentin, V., *The German People* (1946), pp. 432–81. German unification.

Bismarck, O. von, *Bismarck, The Man and the Statesman* (Engl. tr., 1899), vol. II, chs. 20, 22, 23. The Austro-Prussian War, the Ems telegram, the creation of the German Empire, through Bismarck's eyes.

Howard, M., *The Franco-Prussian War: The German Invasion of France (1870-71)* (1961), chs. 1–2, 11. Backgrounds of the war; the peace.

Carsten, F. L., "Bismarck and the Prussian Liberals," *History Today*, vol. XI (1961), no. 11.

Chapter 6

Changing Russia, 1815–1871

The Reign of Alexander I
The Decembrist Conspiracy
Nicholas I: Orthodoxy, Autocracy, and Nationality
Foreign Policy: Russia and the Ottoman Empire
The Liberation of the Serfs by Alexander II
Concomitant Reforms
Problems of Polish and External Relations, 1855–1871
Conclusion

■ THE REIGN OF ALEXANDER I

The campaigns of 1813–1814, which marked the end of the great military ascendancy of the French in Europe, had brought the Cossacks for the first time into the west. Henceforth the potential military resources of the Russian Empire were to provide the big unknown factor in every European combination and conflict. The western powers accordingly developed a considerable interest in the affairs of their half-barbaric neighbor with the almost limitless resources in land and man power. But their knowledge never matched their interest. Diplomats reported sedulously on the life of the court; there were some threads of contact through trade and the arts; but the thoughts and feelings of the Russian people, scattered through thousands of villages to which no foreigner ever penetrated, were almost as unknown as if they had lived on another planet. Even the Tsar Alexander, whose autocratic power had made him the observed

158

SIGNIFICANT EVENTS

1825	Death of Alexander I
	Decembrist revolt against Nicholas I
1830–1831	Polish rebellion
1849	Repression of "conspiracy of ideas" of Dostoevsky, etc.
	The revolution in Hungary suppressed
1853–1856	Crimean War
1855	Nicholas I succeeded by Alexander II
1860	Foundation of Vladivostok
1861	Emancipation of the serfs
1864	First introduction of zemstvos
1871	Abrogation of Treaty of Paris

of all observers at the Congress of Vienna, presents an enigmatic figure to contemporaries and to historians.

Alexander I had ascended the Russian throne in 1801, when a palace conspiracy resulted in the death of his father, Tsar Paul, less than five years after the death of Catherine the Great. She had much preferred her grandson to her son, and, with the help of the Swiss liberal, La Harpe, had brought Alexander up to share many of the viewpoints of the Enlightened Despots. But the circumstances of his upbringing and of his accession—for Alexander had agreed to the deposition of his father though not to the murder—left him with a lifelong habit of dissimulation. They may also have had something to do with his religious susceptibilities, for Alexander saw his defeat of Napoleon in terms of Biblical prophecy. He was influenced by the aristocratic revivalist, Baroness Krüdener; and, as founder of the Holy Alliance, from 1815 onward regarded the activities of constitutional reformers as essentially anti-Christian. He traveled much, which meant that many acts of government were carried out by others in his name, but his ready charm hid so much of his real feelings that posterity is uncertain what reliance the emperor really placed upon any of his friends and advisers.

The early years of the reign had been an era of reform. Having relaxed the severities which made his father's rule intolerable, Alexander formed a private committee, or brain trust, of liberal advisers, which studied the reorganization of the senate—Peter the Great's "other self"—in terms of the separation of powers, and wrote for advice to Jefferson. Nothing came of this. A decree of 1803 authorized landowners to make voluntary agreements by which serfs could purchase their freedom and obtain land. Actually, less than 37,000 peasants so benefited during the entire reign. But it was at this time that Peter's system of administration by "colleges" finally gave place to a network of eight ministries, including a new ministry of education which succeeded in founding new universities at Kazan, Kharkov, and St. Petersburg. By the end of the reign, the number of students (trained almost exclusively for government service) had been quadrupled, and, at the other end of the scale, the number of parish schools—nearly all of them in towns—had grown from 69 to 418. But the villages still had nothing, and the secondary schools, which grew more slowly, were handicapped by a severe concentration upon classical studies, originating with the need to prepare for university courses conducted perforce by foreign professors in the Latin language.

Then came one of the several turning points at which Russian history failed to turn. The tsar's entourage at this time included Michael Speransky.[1] The son of a village priest, his brilliant career in the Ministry of the Interior demonstrated that he was well qualified to judge how far the forms of government of western Europe, such as the centralized system of Napoleonic France, were applicable to the peasant society of his native land. By 1809 he had been encouraged to frame a new "Autocratic Constitution," based on the proposition that "the actual form of government does not correspond to the state of public feeling, and the time has come to change this form and to found a new order of things." Speransky proposed that there should be an independent judicature, legislation through an indirectly elected Duma, and a council of state consisting of ministers and other high officials, which would be the general source of advice for the crown. He had some success. The council of state was promptly established, and functioned until 1905, though only as a nominated body to which

1. 1772–1839. Accompanied Alexander to his conference with Napoleon at Erfurt in 1808; but was dismissed in March 1812, perhaps to rally conservative opinion when war was imminent; served as governor-general of Siberia (1819–21) and as legal adviser to Nicholas I; he lost the reforming impulse of his youth, but his influence is traceable in the reforms of Alexander II and in the naming of the Duma of the Empire in 1905.

the tsar could refer legislative proposals if and when he wished. The ministries, raised to eleven in number, were also systematized in a manner which lasted down to 1917. For the rest, however, Speransky's proposals and their author rapidly lost the imperial favor, partly no doubt because of a temperamental incompatibility between the volatile tsar and the man whom Napoleon called "the only clear head" in Alexander's dominions. He lost his post as secretary to the new Council of State in 1812, and was out of favor for the rest of the reign.

Alexander's reign is, however, noted for the liberal institutions which this "Autocrat of All the Russias" bestowed on his non-Russian acquisitions. In the case of Finland (annexed in 1809), we can see Speransky's influence in the decision to treat with a duly elected diet, summoned by Alexander in his new capacity as grand duke of Finland, and to welcome its recommendations for the preservation of the fundamental laws and customs which had prevailed in the period of Swedish rule. The neighboring Baltic Provinces, which had now been under Russian rule for a century, are remarkable for the fact that here alone peasant unrest was allowed to lead to the abolition of serfdom, though the 400,000 ex-serfs received no allotment of land. There was also a noteworthy experiment in local autonomy for Bessarabia, which lasted for sixteen years after its annexation from Turkey in 1812. In the case of Poland, the notion of conceding autonomy under the Russian scepter dated back to the formation of the Third Coalition against Napoleon in 1804, when the Polish patriot, Prince Adam Czartoryski, had been Alexander's foreign minister. At the Congress of Vienna, where the tsar tried in vain to annex the whole of Poland, he did not waver in his determination to grant constitutional government to the major areas which he then acquired. This was provided in the treaty, and the constitution was duly promulgated in November, 1815. It placed the administration of the kingdom under a viceroy and council of state, but laws had to pass through a senate, nominated for life, and a lower chamber, elected by nobles and burghers; these were to assemble biennially. The Polish army was to be kept separate, and safeguards were provided for the language, local self-government, and civil rights. In 1818 the first Diet was opened by Alexander in person, with a eulogy of the regime and allusions to the possibility of its extension to other parts of his empire.

But the trend of the later years of the reign was in the opposite direction. From the time of the French invasion onward the strongest influence was that of Count Arakcheev,[2] a soldier and artillery expert who had been the personal friend of the Tsar Paul and the rival of Speransky for his successor's favor.

---

2. 1768–1836. Tsar Paul selected his motto, "Devoted, not servile"; he reformed the artillery before Austerlitz and led an army across the frozen Gulf of Finland in the successful campaign of 1809. On his model estate at Grouzino twenty-two serfs were done to death for the sole offense of failing to go to the rescue of his mistress, a coachman's wife whose wanton cruelties had provoked her murder.

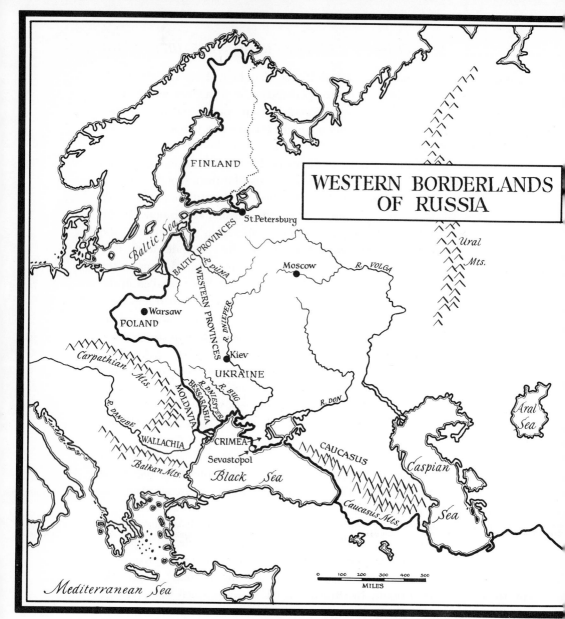

WESTERN BORDERLANDS
OF RUSSIA

These border areas, which included many recent annexations, were in general richer, more highly civilized, and far more densely populated than the lands inhabited by the "Great Russians" farther east.

After the war he became virtually prime minister, since it was through him that other ministers and the committee of ministers as a whole reported to the tsar. Arakcheev was a meticulous organizer and drillmaster, whose reputation is deeply stained by savage and illegal barbarities practiced upon his serfs, for which Nicholas later banished him from court. From 1816 onward this martinet was engaged in carrying out Alexander's bizarre project for combining good order with economy through the development of military colonies. The population of an entire district was absorbed into a model agricultural settlement, where men, women, and children lived in military uniforms and under military law, tilling the soil at the same time as they provided a supply of trained troops at minimum cost to the state. By 1825 there were 375,000 soldiers and their dependents condemned to this barrack-room servitude for life, and, although Nicholas I on his accession described it as "a most distressing picture," the system remained in use on a smaller scale for a further generation.

■ THE DECEMBRIST CONSPIRACY

Alexander's sudden death at Taganrog in the Crimea on December 1, 1825, occasioned a crisis which left a lasting mark on the history of Russia. His father had established the principle of primogeniture in the royal family, which meant that the childless Alexander was due to be followed by his brother Constantine, commander-in-chief in Poland. He had renounced his right to the throne in favor of the third, much younger, brother Nicholas, but the fact had not been published in advance, thus making the validity of the decision of a tsar who was now dead by no means unassailable. Assailed it was, because the guards regiments in St. Petersburg, where Nicholas was in charge, preferred the commander of the better paid Polish army and entertained rumors that he favored the abolition of serfdom. No such hopes could be entertained for the stern Nicholas. As a precautionary measure, Nicholas took an oath of allegiance to Constantine. Constantine, on the other hand, did not want the throne but, in annoyance over the awkward position in which he had been placed, would take no official step to renounce it. The interregnum gave insurrection its chance.

The reign of Alexander had been marked by the prominence of foreign advisers, such as Prince Czartoryski, and still more by the constitutional advantages gained by foreign elements in the Russian Empire. Moreover, its military triumphs had brought Russian officers into direct contact with the comparatively liberal institutions enjoyed by France and other western countries—countries whose institutions owed their survival or revival to the prowess of Russian arms. It was, indeed, in the army, with its twenty-five-year term of service, its recruitment through assignment of unruly serfs by their masters, and its savage discipline, that Russian institutions were to be seen at their worst. Among army officers, therefore, some organized protest against the existing order of society might appear to be not only justifiable but practicable—justified by ideas which had been penetrating Russia from the west with increasing vigor ever since the French Revolution, made practical by the presumed readiness of the rank and file to revolt.

In eighteenth-century Russia the Freemasonic movement had set the example in organizing upper-class societies with wide affiliations, more or less secret ritual, and vaguely philanthropic purposes. But after the war there were other patriotic models for Russians to follow, such as the German *Tugendbund*, Italian Carbonarism, and, nearer home, the *Hetairia Philike* of the Greeks. The first Russian society for the promotion of representative government was formed at St. Petersburg in 1816 by a score of army officers. By 1821 this had grown into two distinct societies. One was a welfare organization in the capital, which dissolved itself after its officer members in the Semenovsky Guards Regiment had failed to prevent a mutiny directed against illegal floggings by a new and unpopular colonel. The other originated as a southern branch under an ambitious young officer named Pavel Pestel, but was continued after 1821 as an independent body, with a strongly centralized republic as its aim and a military coup d'état as the first step toward its attainment. In 1822, when the Semenovsky regiment was allowed to return to St. Petersburg, its officers renewed their activities as a separate Northern Society, which refused to unite with Pestel's Southern Society because the Northerners expected their coup to prepare the way for a constituent assembly which might build a new Russia upon the existing monarchy. Provisional arrangements for simultaneous action to be taken in the spring of 1826 were discussed, but before then the interregnum had precipitated the tragic fate of the Decembrists.

On December 24, 1825, Nicholas in St. Petersburg learned simultaneously that Constantine refused officially to disclaim the throne and that both the southern army in the Ukraine and the guards regiments in the capital contained organized bodies of conspirators. In the excited situation of the moment, he did not dare to make any arrests, but gave orders for the oath of allegiance to be taken to him as tsar. This precipitated an ineffectual mutiny on the twenty-sixth in the Senate Square—ineffectual because it was only a part of the St. Petersburg garrison that refused the oath and because the leaders on the spot took no forward move, such as might have induced the civilian population to follow them. At nightfall four pieces of artillery under the direct orders of the new tsar opened fire at point-blank range and cleared the square at a cost of between seventy and eighty dead. Pestel and other leaders of the Southern Society had been arrested on the twenty-fifth, but a fortnight later some of them were able to get control of a single regiment, only to be overwhelmed at the first encounter. The sequel was a prolonged inquiry by a secret committee, which ruled that the rank-and-file soldiers had been misled and restricted the indictment to the most active conspirators, who were sentenced by a special tribunal under the guidance of Speransky. Pestel and four other leaders were hanged; more than a hundred were sent to penal settlements in Siberia.

Because the victims—and their wives, who in many cases accompanied them into exile—belonged to noble families and included a high proportion of young officers, their fate makes an appeal to the imagination like that of the

French aristocrats who faced the Revolutionary Tribunal a generation before. But the story of the Decembrists lived on for other and better reasons. They were the first upper-class opponents of the regime, and as such became a pattern for unselfish efforts against autocracy, maladministration, and serfdom itself, made by members of the intelligentsia and others who stood to gain nothing directly for themselves by a revolution which they risked everything to bring about. The close and detailed inquiry made into the motives of the Decembrists, which produced a large-scale document of popular grievances for the tsar and his ministers, showed clearly how much was amiss in Russian society. From then onward the government, however slow it might be to implement them, remained aware of the need for reforms. Last, the Tsar Nicholas, who had remarked bitterly on the evening of December 26, "Voilà un joli commencement de règne," was influenced to withdraw himself from direct contact with his people. As we shall see, a more effective, if not more brutal, police control distinguishes the thirty years of his reign; the secret societies, accordingly, were swept away, but not the need for them nor the ideals that they had stood for.

■ NICHOLAS I: ORTHODOXY, AUTOCRACY, AND NATIONALITY

Nicholas I was a far simpler character than his predecessor. Though the youngest brother, unlike Alexander, had never been trained for kingship, he was an ardent admirer of his father-in-law, Frederick William III of Prussia, and a hard worker who made the bureaucracy and the army work hard for him. Speransky was restored to favor, and in 1833 he completed both a fifty-one-volume *Collection of Laws* and a fifteen-volume *Code of Laws*, of which the latter gave a systematic presentation of every enactment still in use. Another key event was the establishment, as part of a comprehensive reorganization of the bureaucracy, of the Third Section of His Majesty's Own Chancery, a higher police authority designed to prevent any recurrence of Decembrist activities. It operated partly through a force of military gendarmery, divided into districts so as to cover the whole of Russia and commanded by upper-class officers. In addition, a large network of secret agents, including women and even school children, furnished reports on political and religious dissidents, foreigners living in Russia, and other categories of suspects. Since the director of the Third Section was the member of the committee of ministers who most readily obtained the ear of the tsar, and since he had charge of political prisoners, who might or might not have received any trial in open court, the result was the apotheosis of the police state.

The spirit of the police state was also demonstrated by the tsar in setting on foot from time to time inquiries by secret committees about possible reforms. The investigations were thus conducted so as to avoid raising undue expectations in the public mind, and ended usually in broad generalities that bolstered up the *status quo*. The one considerable exception was a decision which placed the state peasants—about one-sixth of the population, who lived and worked on land owned by the state—under a new Ministry of State Domains. This did a little to promote local self-government, equitable division of the land, and education. Even so, state peasants remained very much at the mercy of the state and its petty officials, though this was a much lighter burden than was borne by the serfs of private landowners, whose privileges Nicholas did not venture to assail. Prudence often dictated the tsar's course of action, but the underlying philosophy of the reign was that which his chief educational adviser, Count Uvarov, extolled as a synthesis of "the truly Russian conservative principles of Orthodoxy, autocracy, and nationality, our last anchor of salvation and the best guarantees of Russia's strength and greatness."

The only serious challenge came from the kingdom of Poland, where a link between Polish patriots and the Decembrists had been brought to light. It was in any case unlikely that Nicholas would view with more favor than Alexander had a people who, instead of accepting their constitutional status with gratitude, conducted an underground agitation in favor of complete independence or, at the very least, the incorporation of the Lithuanian provinces of Russia in the Polish kingdom of the tsar. However, in 1828 Nicholas was duly crowned king in Warsaw, and two years later he attended a session of the Diet, which closed a few weeks before the French Revolution of July. But by November he was preparing to use the Polish army against the revolutionaries in western Europe, and the police were on the track of the revolutionaries in Poland. Accordingly, on the evening of the twenty-ninth cadets and students attacked key points in Warsaw, rousing the populace and causing the Grand Duke Constantine, Russian commander-in-chief, to withdraw from the city. His subsequent hesitations encouraged the spread of the insurrection across the country, whereupon the Diet declared the Romanov dynasty to be deposed and the Lithuanian provinces incorporated in Poland. When the Russian troops, which for a time left the kingdom along with Constantine, returned under a sterner commander, the first encounter was a victory for the Poles. The attention of the Russians was also distracted to some extent by sympathetic outbreaks in Lithuania, and the armies were for a time immobilized by cholera, which carried off their commander-in-chief.

Nevertheless, by September the new commander, Paskievich,[3] was able to report to the tsar, "Warsaw is at your feet," a position from which unhappy Poland during the next eighty years stirred only once. Europe had done nothing to help her. In Lithuania the cause had found few adherents outside the upper

---

3. 1782–1856. A general at 29, he had won brilliant victories in the Persian and Turkish wars, and was again in chief command against the Hungarians in 1849; field-marshal of three armies (Prussian, Austrian, and Russian) and Prince of Warsaw.

classes. In Warsaw itself there were unresolved disputes between the noble leaders, such as Prince Czartoryski, and the liberal and radical elements, who insisted on independence for their country rather than mere autonomy. Elsewhere the peasants felt little enthusiasm for a nationalist rising which hesitated to offer any immediate program of improvement in their status. Part of the sequel was the banishment of 258 leaders, who formed the nucleus of an émigré Poland in Paris and elsewhere, prompt to fight in any revolutionary cause under the motto, *Ubi male, ibi patria* ("The oppressed of every nation are our compatriots"). The Polish constitution was replaced by a new Organic Statute which, while preserving in name the civil liberties of the people and a separate administration, was very differently interpreted in practice. Paskievich, as viceroy from 1832 to 1856, made it his business to assimilate the legal system, the economic life, the schools and university, and—as far as possible—the language and religion of the Poles to what he called "the administrative order of the empire as a whole." Poland suffered heavily. The University of Kiev at one time closed its doors; the Uniates, who had for centuries been allowed to combine eastern rites with the acceptance of papal authority, were driven back into the Orthodox Church; and a promised system of self-government in local affairs was not introduced until 1861—and was suppressed again within two years.

The maintenance of Orthodoxy, autocracy, and nationality was seen to require something more positive than the mere repression of subject peoples in the interests of a great Russia. There existed an official patriotism, which it was the business of government to inculcate. The reign was inaugurated with a new censorship law of 230 articles, which was slightly modified in 1828, but even then a censor himself suggested that the number of censorship officials exceeded the annual total of new books. Not only so, but Uvarov as minister of education made it his business to build "intellectual dams to hold up the flow of new ideas into Russia." Orders had already been given to exclude peasant children from any but elementary schools. Uvarov, while increasing the total numbers educated, reserved the German-type *gymnasium*, which prepared for the university, as far as possible for the sons of the nobility, and introduced (in 1835) a stricter regime in the universities themselves, placing the appointment of professors, the control of students' behavior, and the scope of the curriculum alike under ministerial supervision. It is therefore striking that this period of reaction witnessed the growth of a new romantic literature, a great ideological struggle between Westerners and Slavophiles, and the rise of a new class, for which the Russians themselves invented the name *intelligentsia*—the class that was eventually to take up the unfulfilled tasks of the Decembrists.

The men of letters, though their writings were not primarily political in content, created a pride in intellectual achievement which did much to create

PUSHKIN: SELF-PORTRAIT AND PAGE OF
MANUSCRIPT. Poet, dramatist, novelist,
and spokesman of Russian nationalism,
Pushkin is one of the great figures of early
nineteenth-century Russia.

the new class, and must therefore be mentioned first. With Pushkin, Lermontov, and Gogol, all of them scions of noble families, Russian literature began to enter into its great heritage. Alexander Pushkin (1799–1837) may be compared with Dante as the creator of a literary language for his country and with Horace for the perfection and charm of his lyrics. But the author of *Eugene Onegin* was also a novelist and a historian—all this in a life overshadowed by the censorship, punctuated by banishments from the capital, and terminated at a tragically early age in a duel with a raffish French émigré. The poet and novelist Michael Lermontov (1814–1841), a younger product of the romantic movement, passed even more rapidly across the stage, and he too met his death in a duel. Yet between them these two men made the early years of Nicholas I a golden age for Russian poetry. Prose came into its own a little later, with the work of Nicholas Gogol (1809–1852). A Ukrainian who first arrived in St. Petersburg at nineteen, he began with the romantic portrayal of Ukrainian life, then became the founder of the realist school, satirizing the corruption of the bureaucracy in his play, *The Inspector-General*, and implicitly condemning the whole social system based on serfdom in his picaresque novel, *Dead Souls*. Gogol directly prepared the way for the great realistic novelists, Turgenev, Tolstoy, and Dostoevsky. Turgenev's *Sportsman's Sketches*, a gentler attack upon serfdom, was published in 1852, but in that year its author was banished for writing a too-favorable obituary of Gogol. It is significant of the age that authority had likewise punished Lermontov for a too-angry comment on Pushkin's untimely death.

By 1840, with the help of German philosophy, the growing intelligentsia of Russia was dividing rapidly into two schools of thought. The Westerners welcomed the introduction of European cultural trends into Russia as a means to an end; the means might include radical and socialist ideas, such as were held for example by Alexander Herzen,[4] but the end was a Russian national development which was to have world significance. The Slavophiles, on the other hand, were enthusiasts for the Orthodox Church, the *mir*, or village commune, and a Russian national development of which the significance derived from its independence of the west. In their eyes the policy of Peter the Great marked a disastrous deviation from the true course of Russia's history. Both movements were intensely patriotic, but both considered the Russia of their own day to be grossly misgoverned. Though the Slavophiles could support the authorities in such activities as the persecution of Catholic Poland and did not want a western type of constitution, many were opposed to serfdom, some called for the restoration of the ancient national assembly of the Russians (the *Zemsky Sobor*), and the boldest spirits identified Nicholas's form of despotism as specifically one of the undesirable importations from the West, in this case from Prussia.

In 1847 Herzen left the country, and in the same year the government imposed penalties on the leaders of a secret society at Kiev, where a new university had taken the place of that in Lithuanian Vilna; its program called for the emancipation of the serfs and the autonomy of the Ukraine. The revolutions of 1848 produced a wave of repression in which Uvarov himself lost office because his treatment of the universities was deemed too soft. A group of Westerners in St. Petersburg, led by the co-author of a *Pocket Dictionary of Foreign Words*, held a dinner to honor the memory of the French socialist, Fourier, and were haled before a military court, which decided to emphasize the criminality of a "conspiracy of ideas." Fifteen death sentences were commuted only on the scaffold, when one victim had already been driven insane. The minor criminals included Dostoevsky, who had just begun to publish and was sent to spend ten years of his life in Siberia. Otherwise, the unrest in other countries had no counterpart in Russia, which suffered only the intensification of the *cordon sanitaire* against the West. In March, 1848, the tsar withdrew permission for teachers to travel abroad, and a subsequent remodeling of the universities gave an opportunity for banning the study of the constitutional law of European states. Between 1848 and the end of the reign, secondary and

---

4. 1812–1870. An illegitimate son who inherited wealth from his aristocratic father, he was twice in trouble with the authorities on minor charges, but left Russia in 1847 of his own accord. *Kolokol*, or *The Bell*, was published fortnightly from 1857 to 1865 and smuggled from England to Russia, where it had great influence on reforms. Championship of Polish claims in 1863 largely destroyed Herzen's popularity, and he was in any case too much of a humanitarian to sympathize with the growth of extremism in Russia.

university students declined in numbers, the latter being formally restricted to a total of three hundred per university, exclusive of medical students and holders of government scholarships.

■ FOREIGN POLICY: RUSSIA AND THE OTTOMAN EMPIRE

The foreign policy of Nicholas I, which was in principle moderate and pacific, ended in a military failure; this might never have occurred if Europe's interpretation of the foreign policy had not been colored by detestation of the domestic tyranny. At the end of the Turkish War of 1828–1829 a secret Russian conference determined that "the advantages of preserving the Ottoman empire exceed its disadvantages," and it now seems certain that the virtual protectorate over Turkey, which was conferred upon Russia by the treaty of Unkiar Skelessi in 1833, was regarded by the Russian government as a burden rather than an opportunity.[5] Russian expansion in the Near East, too, was less formidable than the British at least chose to believe. The Turkish had been preceded by a brief Persian War, the one yielding Erivan and naval control of the Caspian, the other the control of the Caucasus. But the Caucasus became the scene of a holy war on the part of the Muslim tribesmen under the romantic hero, Shamil, who did not finally surrender until 1859, while the advance into the Middle East culminated in 1839–1840 in a wholly unsuccessful expedition against the khan of Khiva. In 1841 the Straits Convention, concluded after the Russians offered to allow the special position they had acquired by the treaty of Unkiar Skelessi to lapse, marked the moment for a possible rapprochement with Britain.[6] Nicholas may have thought that the restoration of the so-called "ancient rule of the Ottoman Porte" gave him an absolute protection against a British entry into the Black Sea, though the British did not intend in all circumstances to concede this in practice. But France having been isolated, the way was now clear for the conversations which marked the tsar's visit to Windsor in 1844 as something more than a diplomatic courtesy. He returned home in the belief that a new system had been established: the *status quo* in Turkey was to be preserved as long as possible, but in the event of its collapse Russia and Britain would concert their measures before either of them consulted any other power.

Although Palmerston on his return to the Foreign Office in 1846 did not consider himself bound by the actions of his predecessor, Lord Aberdeen, Anglo-Russian relations stood the test of the 1848 revolutions fairly well. Joint action by Turks and Russians against the Rumanian nationalist movement in the principalities ended in the withdrawal of Russian (and Turkish) forces, as had been promised to Palmerston. Even the Russian intervention in Hungary was tacitly accepted, because the survival of Austria as a great power was deemed

5. See p. 31.
6. See pp. 31–32.

"TURKEY IN DANGER"—THREATS FROM THE RUSSIAN BEAR. This cartoon of April 9, 1853, from *Punch* illustrates the alarm in England over Russian threats to Turkey.

essential to the preservation of the European balance. It was only when Russia and Austria acted together to demand the surrender of Hungarian and Polish refugees by the Porte that the British government, with strong humanitarian support, sent the British fleet illegally into the Straits to oppose the threat—as they saw it—to Turkish sovereignty.

A similar misinterpretation, however, had far more serious consequences in 1853, after Russia had clashed with the French concerning rights of control at the holy places in Palestine, where Orthodox pilgrims outnumbered Catholics by a hundred to one. In four interviews with the British ambassador, the tsar sought to forestall disagreement on the whole eastern question by outlining a division of territory on the assumption that the Turkish bear was dying. Though the division proposed was not altogether remote from later realities, Britain brushed the offer aside. Instead, British and French fleets were sent to the Dardanelles to encourage Turkish resistance to the Russian claim, based on a treaty of 1774, to safeguard the rights of the Orthodox Church and its members in the Ottoman Empire. An invasion of the principalities having failed to produce Turkish compliance, the Russian fleet annihilated a Turkish squadron at Sinope in November, 1853, after which considerations of national honor rather than any major reason of state ranged Britain and France on the side of the Turks in the Crimean War.

The death of Nicholas I in March, 1855, saved him from witnessing the fall of Sebastopol after a heroic year-long defense, inspired by the engineer-general, Todleben, and immortalized in Tolstoy's *Sebastopol Sketches*. But the inglorious abandonment of the principalities to occupation by Austria, acting in agreement with Russia's enemies; the inability of Russia to contest the naval predominance of Britain and France in the Black and Baltic seas and even at remote Kamchatka; the failure to expel the invaders of the Crimea from Russian soil; and the gross mismanagement of transport and supply arrangements for the long journey to the scene of action, which rendered their Crimean losses twice as heavy as those of their opponents—these brought the reign to a catastrophic close. All that could be prophesied with certainty for Nicholas's successor was humiliation abroad and a day of reckoning at home.

Alexander II lives in history as the Tsar Liberator, but it is arguable that without the shock of Russia's suddenly reduced prestige he would have lacked the stimulus to earn that soubriquet. In any case, the ending of the war was a task which had precedence over all others, and it may therefore be considered first. The entry of the allied forces into the ruins of Sebastopol in September was a national disaster, offset to a small extent by the withdrawal of the Russian forces in good order to new positions about thirty miles to the northward, and more notably by the capture of Kars from the Turks. This event in late November secured the Caucasian front against British plans for the expulsion of the Russians from the eastern littoral of the Black Sea, and made it easier for Russia to yield to an ultimatum from Austria, which threatened her active participation if the war went on.

The peace congress at Paris involved Russia in only one direct loss of territory—a strip of Bessarabia, which was retroceded to Moldavia with the effect of removing Russian control of the left bank of the Danube estuary. But the neutralization of the Black Sea, which was the principal outcome of the war, was only the most serious and dramatic of a series of measures all of which were aimed at containing the westward thrust of Russia in Europe. The independence and integrity of the Turkish possessions were placed under the guarantee of the European Concert, to which any necessary rights of intervention on behalf of the Christian subjects of the Turk were also explicitly transferred. Moldavia and Wallachia, which had been occupied by Russian troops on three separate occasions in a period of thirty years, were likewise placed under the supervision of the great powers in general, from which situation the principality of Rumania quickly emerged as the protégé of Napoleon III. Even the demilitarization of the Aaland Islands in the Baltic was exacted as a countermeasure to hypothetical Russian intrigues against the integrity of Sweden-Norway, which had been made the most of in a vain effort to bring the dual monarchy of the north into the war.

The result was to make Russia a revisionist power, watching the diplomatic developments of the next fifteen years for the chance to breach the restraints of the Paris settlement, a chance which eventually came to hand. In the meantime some of the pent-up energy was to be used for expansion on other frontiers of her vast empire, a policy which, as we shall see later, yielded larger dividends. But the immediate need was to pursue an internal policy which would rally the people to the support of the throne before the prestige of the autocracy suffered further damage. Accordingly, the manifesto announcing that peace had been signed in Paris at the end of March, 1856, expressed a whole series of vague but pious hopes:

> With the help of Divine Providence, which has always protected Russia's welfare . . . may there develop in all spheres the urge towards enlightenment and every form of useful activity. May everybody, under the protection of laws equally just for all and giving equal protection to all, enjoy the fruits of his honest labor.[7]

■ THE LIBERATION OF THE SERFS BY ALEXANDER II

Unlike his father, Alexander II had been educated for the tsardom, but education could not give him his father's strength of purpose. It was characteristic of his good will that the surviving Decembrists were at once brought back from exile. It was characteristic of his intellectual limitations that from early childhood he took readily to military parades and reviews, but his interest in command was sufficient to cause him to meddle without ever having acquired a serious knowledge of strategy or tactics. As regards domestic reforms, too, the importance of what was achieved in his reign could not altogether conceal the fact that the autocrat on the throne lacked any clear and consistent intellectual grasp of the changes as a whole. The annual murders of landowners and bailiffs had risen steeply from eleven under Nicholas to seventeen in the first three years of his reign; he prudently preferred that reform should be started from above, not from below. Yet by the end of the epochal year 1861, Alexander Herzen from his vantage point in London was already announcing his loss of confidence in a ruler whom he had at first hailed with unbounded enthusiasm. If we compare the Tsar Liberator with the American president, who in the same period was engaged in freeing the slaves, some of the reasons for this disillusionment are at once apparent. Alexander's action was determined by considerations of expediency, not principle; he was working mainly with advisers whose instinctive attitude was one of conservatism and caution; and his object was to match a necessary minimum of concession to the expectant serfs with a maximum of compensation to the reluctantly yielding serf owners. Moreover, in America the liberated section of the population amounted to four million— one-eighth of the nation; in Russia it was more than twenty million or one-third of the nation.

The Edict of Emancipation signed by the tsar on March 3, 1861, and formally announced from the pulpits of St. Petersburg a fortnight later, comprised the contents of a 360-page volume, and was subject to numerous later emendations. The most important of these was a regulation of 1866, which

7. W. E. MOSSE, *Alexander II and the Modernization of Russia* (1958), p. 41.

converted the position of the state peasants to that of the ex-serfs, except that they received their land from the state on more advantageous terms. In brief analysis, the Edict had both legal, economic, and social aspects. The main legal change was the grant of personal freedom. The serf became a free citizen, whom the lord could not punish by flogging, draft into the army, or deport to Siberia; he had full control of his own affairs as regards family, property, or rights of litigation; and in theory he could move at will from place to place. For one class of serfs, those who were members of the lord's domestic household or who had been set to work for him in mines, factories, or other trading places, this legal change was decisive: for better or worse, they became landless proletarians.

But the typical serf had been bound to the soil; he was a person who labored at least half his time for the lord, cultivating his estate or perhaps working up its products for sale in manufactured form. At other times he cultivated the portion of land which the lord allocated for his own maintenance. To him, therefore, the most important aspect of the emancipation was its effect on the ownership and use of the land, a matter in which he was almost bound to be disappointed, since the peasant believed instinctively that the land had never ceased to be his even while he himself was treated as the lord's personal property. In practice, the tsar and his advisers, who had experienced great difficulty in getting the necessary minimum of support from the nobles for any form of emancipation, found it expedient to lean heavily to the side of the lord. The peasant was therefore required to pay either in money or (with his consent) in services for the portion of land which was allocated to him, maximum and minimum quantities being prescribed for each zone of the country separately. At a later stage, not compulsorily completed until 1883, the annual payments (calculated at 6 percent) were converted into a capital sum, the bulk of which was advanced to the lord by the government and repaid to the government by the peasants with interest over a period of forty-nine years. These repayments were eventually canceled as a result of the revolutionary disturbances in 1905.

The peasants would have resented paying in any case, and the lengthy period stipulated made matters worse. But there were three more specific grievances resulting from the measure. Except in the western provinces, where the government sought support from the peasantry against the more nationally minded Polish landlords, the land was assessed for redemption purposes at a price greatly in excess of the average land prices of the period. On the poor soil of the north, indeed, the excess was as much as 90 percent, which can only be accounted for as an attempt to compensate the lord for the loss of the serf as well as for the land, a compensation which the Edict had formally rejected from consideration. The second grievance concerned the Black Soil provinces of southern Russia, where crops were grown by modern methods for export and landlords were glad to be rid of inefficient serf labor. There the redemption charges were less inflated, but the landlords recouped themselves by reducing, sometimes by as much as one-quarter, the amount of land which the ex-serf was allowed to redeem. Last, with the growth of population, land hunger underlined the argument that emancipation ought to have freed all the land along with the peasants who had always tilled it.

The social change followed from the disappearance of the lord's authority. On the one hand, a new cantonal court was set up for a group of villages, in which village elders tried minor civil and criminal cases involving peasants only, using customary law and punishments which included flogging. Thus the peasant was still treated differently from other citizens. On the other hand, the administration of peasant land within each village was left to the village commune, or *mir*, which determined the crop cycle for the big open fields and, in most areas, redivided the arable strips from time to time in accordance with the varying sizes of the households. Consolidation of holdings appealed to the more enterprising, but the attitude of the *mir*—which Slavophiles supported as typically Russian and Westerners as typically socialist—was usually obstructive. The powers of the *mir* also made it difficult for the enterprising to break away from the village, because the redemption payments and other taxes must be provided for to its satisfaction before it would issue the identity card still indispensable for settlement elsewhere.

The general economic effects of the liberation of the serfs were, to begin with, unfavorable. Those branches of production which had depended on servile labor suffered a severe blow: the iron mines and metallurgical works of the Urals lost about one-fourth of their labor force, so that the output of pig iron was reduced temporarily by nearly one-third. There was likewise a temporary recession in the textile industries, intensified in the case of cotton by the world scarcity of the raw material during the later years of the American Civil War. But the long-term result was to give a great stimulus to industrial development, because it became easier for population to congregate in areas which could offer employment. When the cotton textile industry, which was Russia's largest, was freed from external limitations in 1865, the number of workers more than doubled within fifteen years. At the same time a great stimulus was given to the grain exports of south Russia, since free labor was available for the extension of the area brought under the plough: the quinquennial average of export quantities doubled between 1860 and 1870, and doubled again between 1870 and 1880. The growth of railways was in part the effect and in part the cause of the expanded market for grain, and was in any case stimulated by the supply of cheap labor, so that the one thousand miles of 1860 had grown to fourteen thousand miles by 1881.

Nevertheless, it would be wrong to conclude that, in a vast land of peasant agriculture, industrial growth was capable at this time of absorbing the huge supply of labor released by emancipation and swollen by a rapid growth of population. On the contrary, the tsar's achievement in forcing the nobles to let part of the land go to the ex-serfs soon seemed less important than the fact that the amount of land available was altogether inadequate. The position in 1878 was estimated by the Central Statistical Committee as follows: 13 percent of ex-serfs had plenty of land, 40–45 percent had enough, the rest could not be self-supporting agriculturists. "The rest" means a minimum of eight million people to be provided for. There are no comparable figures available for industry, but the province of Moscow was the chief industrial area at the date in question— and was then employing a total of 163,000 industrial workers from all sources of recruitment.

■ CONCOMITANT REFORMS

The Tsar Liberator made other reforms, which modernized the state and tended toward the closing of the gulf between classes. But these did not involve the same bitter controversy, because many of them were viewed by the upper class as a necessary consequence of the Edict of Emancipation and because they did not involve that class in any direct forfeiture of economic privileges. A reform of the judiciary, in particular, had been promised in 1856 and was urgently needed to fill the gap left by the disappearance of the lord's judicial authority over his serfs. Revolutionary changes were instituted both in personnel and in procedure. Elected justices of the peace were set up to deal with minor law cases, both civil and criminal. For major cases judges were to be appointed by the Crown from among qualified lawyers to preside over district courts. These new courts would hear counsel on both sides and for criminal charges they employed a jury; proceedings were in public; and a right of appeal was provided, first to a higher court and finally to the senate. In short, the judicial system was westernized, approximately on the French pattern, and separated in principle from the executive power. The result was an enormous improvement in the general conduct of trials and the growth of the legal profession, which became an influential element in the liberal middle class.

These reforms, announced in December, 1864, took more than a decade to spread across the empire, and were quickly subjected to important modifications. Thus trial by jury was not introduced in Poland, the western provinces, or the Caucasus, and was withdrawn for press cases (1862) and various categories of alleged crimes against the state (1872, 1878). Military courts remained in existence; officials could not be prosecuted without official permission; and an ambiguous clause in the 1864 edict provided that "executive power may take measures provided by the law to prevent crimes and illegal activities." This was interpreted to cover a wide range of police activities, from the summary flogging of rioters to the deportation of disaffected persons against whom no legal case could be made out. In other words, the effectiveness of the judicial reform was limited by the character of the autocratic state. Yet it marked a great step forward.

The new institutions of local self-government were likewise an important new departure, but even more than the judiciary they bore from the outset the marks of compromise with the spirit of the old regime. The feudal hierarchy gave place to a system based on zemstvos, "assemblies of the land." The decree of January, 1864, defined their structure and powers, and resulted in their establishment the following year in nineteen provinces, but it is worth noting at the outset that they still had not reached twenty-seven of the seventy provinces as late as 1914. A district zemstvo was elected by three separate groups—individual landed proprietors, urban property holders, and peasant communities—according to a highly complicated plan, representing a compromise between liberal and reactionary elements among the tsar's advisers. The result was a body in which rather more than two members in every five were landowners or government officials. A provincial zemstvo to deal with common interests was elected by the district zemstvos; members of either type of assembly held office for three years at a time, and operated through short annual assemblies and a small executive committee, whose president must be acceptable to the central government authorities.

Their functions, too, were narrowly restricted to the service of local economic needs. These included the promotion of agriculture and measures against famine; assistance to industry and commerce, especially as regards transport facilities; upkeep of public buildings, such as prisons; and work in the spheres of poor relief, public health, and education. The last items might suggest big possibilities, but there were two handicaps. The zemstvos had no legal executive powers, which made them dependent upon the cooperation of the provincial governor at the top and of local police and similar officials at lower levels. Furthermore, their powers of local taxation were strictly limited, and nearly half their funds were absorbed by compulsory payments for judicial and military costs incurred within their districts.

How small and slow was the advance toward true self-government may perhaps be measured by the fact that down to the end of the century the peasants were on an average paying twice as heavy taxes on their land as a noble paid on his, acre for acre. Indeed, the predominance of wealth was carried even further when town government was reorganized by a separate decree of 1870. This established dumas, or town councils, similar in status and functions to the district—or, in the case of the largest towns, the provincial—zemstvos, headed by a mayor who, like a zemstvo president, must be chosen in accordance with government wishes. The members of each duma were elected on the three-class principle used in the Prussian constitution of 1850, which meant that about 90 percent of local taxpayers, those who contributed one-third of the taxes from a multitude of small assessments, elected only one-third of the members. Nevertheless, even a partial introduction of local self-government had several important consequences. It gave the Russian people a faint glimmer of what democratic reform could achieve for them. In the course of time valuable progress was made in agricultural science, health improvements, and the spread of elementary education. The middle class was powerfully reinforced through the employment of doctors, teachers, and agricultural advisers; of the last-named, the zemstvos in 1877 employed one, in 1912 nearly five thousand. Above all, the actual members of a zemstvo, however small the scale of their operations, were gaining direct experience of self-government.

The early part of the reign of Alexander II was also marked by an intellectual liberation, parallel with the liberation of the serfs and in the long run perhaps equally significant, though here the change was much less simple and complete. Since the press had been allowed to discuss the peasant question in advance of the Edict of Emancipation, a natural sequel was a decree of April, 1865, which specifically allowed the newspapers to discuss government policy— a liberty which Nicholas would never have conceded. In principle, the system of censorship in advance of publication was now abolished, and any penalties to which a paper or book was liable subsequent to publication would be obtained by prosecution before the ordinary law courts. In practice, however, this decree, which remained in force for forty years, did not prevent a great deal of censorship by administrative action—the seizure of books, the banning of particular topics from the newspapers, and the imposition of fines not warranted by any law. All that can be said is that the new regime did bring about some alleviation, and that its restraints do not appear to have prevented the full flowering of the realist novel in the work of Turgenev, Tolstoy, and Dostoevsky, all of whom achieved fame in the 1860's.

Meanwhile, the way was being prepared for the educational achievements of the zemstvos (referred to above) by the actions of Golovnin, the intimate of the tsar's more radically minded younger brother Constantine,[8] who served as minister of education from December, 1861, to April, 1866. He freed primary education, what there was of it, from the stifling control of the Orthodox clergy. He gave a new impetus to secondary education by inquiring into the curricula of schools in other countries and as a consequence providing an equivalent for the German *Realschulen*, with the emphasis on modern studies. At the same time all forms of secondary education were made equally available to

8. 1827–1892. The Grand Duke Constantine Nikolayevich, admiral and minister of marine, had served for a time as president of the main committee preparing the Edict of Liberation, where he was provoked into saying that the Russian nobility were not worth spitting on. He tried unsuccessfully to conciliate the Poles, and throughout the reign exerted the strongest influence at court in the direction of reform.

THE BOLSHOI THEATER IN MOSCOW. Built in 1824, the theater still stands under its new name as a fine example of the neoclassical style so popular in Imperial Russia.

all classes of the population, subject to the payment of fees. He also produced a new statute for the universities, which restored their general autonomy and encouraged advanced studies, including scientific study abroad, so that even his dismissal did not prevent the period from 1863 to 1880 from being a brilliant era in the history of Russian higher education. Golovnin's downfall was a result of an attempt on the life of the tsar, which was the work of a radical student of noble birth, whose radicalism could be imputed to the educational changes. The tsar was greatly influenced in the direction of reaction by this event, so much so that the only important new reform achieved in the later years of the reign was the introduction of military conscription for all classes. This crowned the work of his minister of war, Miliutin, but, as it was a direct result of the Prussian victory over France in the war of 1870–1871, the whole subject of Alexander's military innovations may be left for consideration in a later chapter.

■ PROBLEMS OF POLISH AND EXTERNAL RELATIONS, 1855–1871

If the period 1855–1871 witnessed a transformation in Russian domestic policies, with which the modern history of the country really begins, Alexander II's impact on foreign policy in these years was dramatic only in Asia. In Europe he practised what might be described as a holding policy until the situation among the great powers was once again favorable to the advance of Russian interests in the Balkans. We may take first the Polish problem, which was a question of foreign policy because Napoleon III of France had used the revival of Polish claims as a threat to induce Alexander to bring the Crimean War to an immediate end. But it came to the fore mainly for domestic reasons, since every concession to his Russian subjects was bound to raise hopes in the breasts of Poles.

The death of the reactionary viceroy, Paskievich, a year after his master, Nicholas, made it easy for the new reign to begin with an amnesty and to continue with a program of conciliation in matters of religion and education. The time had also come to introduce some administrative reforms, which included the first elections for the local councils formally established thirty years before.[9] What Alexander did not intend, however, was to restore any kind of political autonomy which would enable the Poles to renew their dangerously disruptive demand for the incorporation of the western, or Lithuanian, provinces in a revived Polish kingdom. The consequence, nevertheless, was a series of nationalist demonstrations—in 1860, the celebration of the thirtieth anniversary of the revolt; in 1861, a sit-down strike in the Warsaw churches at services held to commemorate the anniversary of the death of their national hero, Kosciuszko; and in 1862, attempts on the lives of the newly appointed viceroy, the Grand Duke Constantine, and his chief Polish adviser, Wielopolski, a wealthy landowner and champion of the 1815 constitution, who together were trying to carry out a policy of gradual reform. To forestall the threatened rising, a levy of recruits was illegitimately employed as a means of calling up known revolutionaries, whereupon in January, 1863, the intended victims took to the woods in a movement which was more of a forlorn hope than a planned rebellion.

The insurgents were directed by two rival organizations, which were in firm agreement only on the utterly unrealistic demand for the western provinces. Having no more than ten thousand ill-trained men to pit against eighty thousand Russian regulars, they fought, not behind barricades in city streets, but in the woods and marshes of the countryside, where the apathy of the peasants was a conspicuous disadvantage to their cause. When the rising spread to the western provinces, the peasants there fought on the other side; in Poland itself they merely left the uneven struggle to members of the middle and lower middle classes, who were led by the nobility, including one or two veterans of the Crimean campaign, and even a Garibaldian. Since no help was forthcoming from the western powers or from supposed sympathizers among the Russians themselves, in spite of Herzen's eloquent appeals from London, a rebellion which lingered on for eighteen months achieved less than nothing in the end. The rule of Constantine and Wielopolski gave place to that of Count Berg, an admirer of Paskievich, while the western provinces were thoroughly subjugated

9. See p. 167.
9. See p. 167.

by Muraviev, "the hangman of Vilna," who rewarded the loyalty of the peasants by altering the conditions of the land settlement to the disadvantage of such of the Polish landowners as were neither hanged nor deported.

In Poland itself pacification had two aspects. In 1866 the kingdom became the "Vistula Region," administratively assimilated in all respects to the rest of the Russian Empire, with a Russian university at Warsaw, the Russian language introduced by stages as the medium of instruction in the schools, and a covert persecution of the Roman Catholic and Uniat Churches. But on the third anniversary of the Edict of Emancipation the peasantry of Poland were granted a far more generous land settlement than their Russian counterparts. The allotments were larger; redemption payments were replaced by a moderate tax payable on all land; and the new rural communes were dominated, not by the gentry, but by the peasants—and the Russian police. Polish nationalism survived the pressures, direct and indirect, as we shall see later; but it is noteworthy that the Tsar Liberator had continued to give with one hand when he drew back with the other.

A brief reference to the grand duchy of Finland may show how Alexander would have preferred to conduct his relations with the Poles. During the two preceding reigns there had been no further meeting of the Diet with which Alexander I had negotiated at the time of the annexation. A Russian governor-general ruled through a native senate or council of state, and a native Finn headed a state secretariat for Finnish affairs in St. Petersburg. What was more important, the laws and administrative system of the Swedish period survived and proved adequate for a small and quietly prosperous country with few problems. Even during the Crimean War the Anglo-French naval squadron's raids on the Finnish coast did not succeed in encouraging a separatist movement. For Alexander II, therefore, the three types of demand put forward by his Finnish subjects were all in principle acceptable. The Finnish-speaking majority (about 88 percent) wanted their language put on an equal footing with Swedish, which was a heritage from the centuries of Swedish rule and was spoken mainly by the upper class. Since the Swedish minority was always slightly suspect as likely to favor reunion with Sweden if an opportunity presented itself, it took only ten years (1856–1865) for the Finnish-speakers to secure equal status for their language in all public business. Nor had the tsar any reason to deprecate a program of economic reform—railroad building, scientific agriculture and especially forestry, and new banks—in a country whose exports, notably cotton textiles, directly benefited Russia. In these circumstances, the third Finnish demand, that their four estates should reassemble in the traditional Diet, could also safely be conceded. After some hesitation Alexander authorized elections for the Diet, which he opened in person in September, 1863, while Poland was still in arms against him. The Diet then continued to

Save for Manchuria, the arrows indicate thrusts largely of the 1850's and the 1860's. As a result of these developments contemporaries began to foresee a Russian threat to the Chinese and British-Indian Empires comparable to the existing threat to the Ottoman Empire in Europe. The Trans-Caspian Railway (1885–1888) and the Trans-Siberian Railway (1891–1904) belong to the period discussed in Chapter 14.

meet at regular intervals, and in 1869 the tsar confirmed a statute in which the Diet had declared that the fundamental laws of the grand duchy were unalterable without its consent.

The recovery of Russia's prestige in Europe may be said to begin with a negative success, when the powers for purely self-regarding reasons failed to embarrass her by championing Polish national claims in 1863. But she had to wait eight years longer before another combination of circumstances in her favor enabled her to abrogate the hated Treaty of Paris. Inactivity in the Balkans, however, meant that Russia was all the more active in her forward drive toward Asia, where resistance was weaker.

This followed two lines. The struggle for control of the region between the Black and the Caspian seas, where the allies had missed their chance during the Crimean War, was now carried to a successful conclusion. After 1859 Shamil lived on in honorable exile as a Russian nobleman, and in 1864 the surrender of the Circassians to the Russian arms was all the more important because it was followed by a mass migration across the frontier to join the Turks, to whom this fighting people rendered notorious service as the Bashi-Bazouks of the following decade. Thus the whole of the Caucasus was at last firmly held in Russian hands. Then, as one phase of Russian expansion to the southeast ended, a second began. The century-long expansion across central Siberia had had an almost spontaneous character, conducted at the expense of scattered nomadic

182

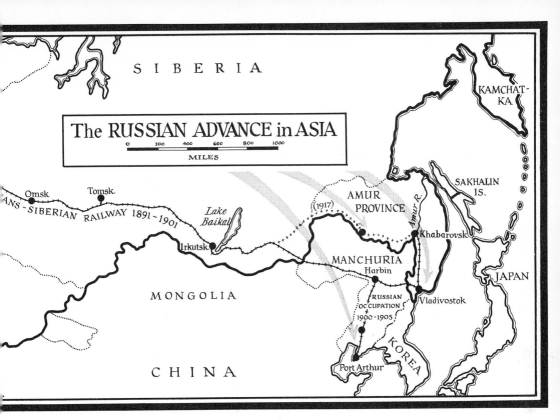

The RUSSIAN ADVANCE in ASIA

MILES
0   200   400   600   800   1000

SIBERIA

KAMCHAT-KA

Omsk   Tomsk
ANS-SIBERIAN RAILWAY 1891~1901

Lake Baikal

SAKHALIN IS.

(1917)   AMUR PROVINCE

Amur R.

Irkutsk

Khabarovsk

MANCHURIA
Harbin

JAPAN

MONGOLIA

RUSSIAN OCCUPATION
1900-1905

Vladivostok

KOREA

CHINA

Port Arthur

tribes and, apart from a limited resettlement of state peasants (which terminated in 1866), was hardly thought of in terms of agricultural exploitation. But by 1855 there had been a thrust southward from bases at Orenburg and Omsk, in which the Kazakhs had been conquered and the first contact made with the settled peoples of ancient civilization in the great river valleys of central Asia. Here Alexander II began a new policy, of which the Soviets are beneficiaries.

The conquest of the Uzbeks and Turcomans was necessitated, according to a circular addressed by Russia to the powers in November, 1864, by raids directed against Russian territory; it was also motivated by hopes of economic advantages which were not immediately fulfilled. Furthermore, considerations of prestige and rivalry with the British Empire in the shrinking no man's land which separated Asiatic Russia from India affected both the policy of St. Petersburg and the impulsive actions of the men on the spot. Hostilities began in the summer of 1864; in June, 1865, Tashkent was captured at the second attempt, and the city of Bokhara fell in May, 1868. By these operations Russia established protectorates over the khanates of Kokand and Bokhara and prepared the way for similar action against Khiva only five years later. Moreover, in 1869, the foundation of a Russian port on the east shore of the Caspian Sea foreshadowed a further advance across the Turcoman territory in the direction of Merv.

The government of Alexander II also elaborated a forward policy in the

183

Far East, which dated from the appointment of Muraviev-Amursky as governor-general of East Siberia in 1847. Before the outbreak of the Crimean War he had sent an expedition down to the mouth of the Amur River (from which he later received his title), and, after the Anglo-French naval attack at the other side of the Sea of Okhotsk on Kamchatka, he was encouraged to make a local treaty establishing big territorial claims along the Amur. The foundation of Vladivostok—Russian for "Rule over the East"—followed in 1860. In that year the Chinese government, as a sequel to its unsuccessful war against Britain and France, was obliged to recognize the sovereignty of Russia, not only inside the great southern bend of the Amur but along the entire coast line between Vladivostok and the mouth of the river. Commercial privileges were also conceded in Mongolia and Chinese Turkestan.

Against this background of Far Eastern expansion and rivalry, particularly with Britain, we may judge the at first sight surprising decision to sell Alaska. Russia's motives were various. The Monroe Doctrine prevented her from using Alaska as a basis for further expansion in that region. Alaskan furs—the only considerable trade—were not good enough for the European market, and their old market in China was now open to other powers. During the Crimean War Alaska had to be neutralized, after a fictitious transfer of the trading company to the American flag; and even when gold was discovered there in 1862, the Russian minister of finance looked forward complacently to a change which was "bound to increase the opportunities for disagreement between the United States and England." Regardless of possible future complications, it was a welcome change in the eyes of the then secretary of state, Seward, and the deal was approved by the United States Senate at a price of $7,200,000 within a month of the first Russian offer.

The few Russians who felt the sale of Alaska in 1867 as a blow to Russia's position among the powers were speedily consoled by the advantage accruing to her from the Franco-Prussian War. Three days after the capitulation of Metz, Russia informed the signatory powers of her intention to repudiate those clauses of the Treaty of Paris whereby the Black Sea had been neutralized. The need for some revision was not at issue, but even Bismarck, to whom Russian neutrality in the war then being brought to a successful climax had been most helpful, regarded the Russian mode of procedure with disfavor. The British, for their part, considered that the unilateral action of Russia threatened the foundations of international order and security. But the London Conference of January–March, 1871, can hardly be regarded as anything more than a face-saving device, since the Russians had not abated their demands in the meantime and obtained exactly what they wished. The fact that in the sequel they were very slow to rebuild their navy on the Black Sea indicates that a prestige victory had been their principal objective. It may also serve as a reminder that the lumbering Russian autocracy was more liable than most European governments of that age to see its best plans frustrated by administrative muddle and incompetence.

■ CONCLUSION

Nothing can rob Alexander II of his title to fame as the Tsar Liberator, for the abolition of serfdom is the event which begins the economic and social transformation of modern Russia. His other reforms, too, were important landmarks in the social evolution of the country, and, by 1871, as we have just seen, his foreign and imperial policy had gone some way toward recovering the prestige abroad and confidence at home which had been forfeited in the Crimean War. Nevertheless, a true summary of the situation at the end of the first decade of modernization must also emphasize the fact that Russia's basic problems, ranging from an equitable distribution of the land to the provision of sound administration and reasonable opportunities of social progress, were all of them far from solved. There was no general plan—or planner.

Since the tsar himself was a reformer from necessity rather than conviction, he was easily swayed in the opposite direction, not only by the attempt on his life (already mentioned), but by many more or less innocent demonstrations resulting from the popular mood of excitement and expectation. In 1861, Turgenev's *Fathers and Sons* had introduced the term "nihilism" for the attitude of mind which rejects all existing authority and rule, and the ensuing decade was marked by the spasmodic growth of ineffectual secret societies. As early as 1862 Alexander had three army officers shot for circulating subversive literature, such as *The Bell*, and soon the ministries of justice and the interior were restored to the hands of conservatives. Most important of all, from 1866 onward the minister of education was the reactionary Count Dmitry Tolstoy, who placed great emphasis upon classical studies in the *gymnasia* and upon Orthodox religious instruction at all levels. He also developed a system for penalizing political activity among university students by police measures, including expulsion, which circumvented the rights of autonomy conceded to the universities in 1863. In adopting this course he sowed the wind and reaped the whirlwind. Expelled students were to figure prominently in the more important revolutionary movement which was to characterize the final decade of the reign and, in a sense, pass judgment upon the whole of it.

Reading List: Chapter 6

The New Cambridge Modern History, vol. X (1960), ch. 14. Russia in Europe and Asia.

Young, I., "Alexander I, Emperor of Russia," *History Today*, vol. XI (1961), no. 5.

Curtiss, J. S., "The Army of Nicholas I: Its Role and Character," *American Historical Review*, vol. LXIII (1958), no. 4.

Wallace, D. Mackenzie, *Russia* (1877), chs. 6, 8 (village life); 11 (towns); 15, 16 (landed gentry); 25, 26 (St. Petersburg and Moscow); 29, 30 (serfdom). A famous contemporary account.

Shotwell, J. T. and Deák, F., *Turkey at the Straits* (1940), chs. 3–5. Russo-Turkish relations to 1856.

Mosse, W. E., *Alexander II and the Modernization of Russia* (1958, paperback, 1962), chs. 3–5. The reforms.

Blum, Jerome, *Lord and Peasant in Russia* (1961), chs. 25–27. Emancipation of the serfs.

Blinoff, M., *Life and Thought in Old Russia* (1961), pp. 172–201. Slavophiles and Westerners.

Carr, E. H., *Studies in Revolution* (1950), ch. 4. Alexander Herzen.

Woodcock, G., "Bakunin: The Destructive Urge," *History Today*, vol. XI (1961), no. 7.

Masaryk, T. G., *The Spirit of Russia* (Engl. tr., 1955), chs. 10, 12. Belinski and Herzen, by a distinguished Czech statesman.

Dulles, R. F., *The Road to Teheran* (1944), ch. 5. The sale of Alaska.

Chapter 7

Britain—The Epoch of Reform

Postwar Distress
Reforms of 1832–1850
The Politics of the Poor and the Growth of Free Trade
Foreign and Imperial Policy
The Second Era of Reform
Mid-Victorian Britain

■ POSTWAR DISTRESS

The United Kingdom of Great Britain and Ireland emerged from the Napoleonic Wars as the wealthiest of the powers, probably also the strongest and most self-confident, but not—in any except the most formal sense—a particularly united kingdom. The grievances of Ireland already cast a shadow which was to lengthen through the century. The prince regent, to whom the royal powers had been granted by parliament in view of his father's madness in 1811, was a self-indulgent fop, a patron of the arts, but qualified in no other respect whatever to win the loyalty or even the respect of his subjects. Lord Liverpool, as prime minister from 1812 to 1827, presided over a government in which the representative figure, down to the day of his death in August, 1822, was the foreign secretary, Lord Castlereagh, an aloof and chilly aristocrat who was popularly supposed to be hand in glove with the members of the so-called

188

SIGNIFICANT EVENTS

1815	Corn Law
1819	Peterloo Massacre
1832	Great Reform Act
1833–1835	Main Whig-Liberal reforms
1838	Publication of the People's Charter
1839	Durham Report
1846	Repeal of the Corn Laws
1854–1856	Crimean War
1857	Indian Mutiny
1867	Second Parliamentary Reform Act
	British North America Act
1869–1872	Main reforms of Gladstone's first government

Holy Alliance. Though he was not in fact an enemy of representative institutions at home or abroad, Castlereagh was the champion of order, and, like his colleagues, saw the evidences of social unrest as so many warnings that repression was the only alternative to revolution. Therefore no attempt was made to diagnose and prescribe for the sickness of the body politic, and the suffering majority was left with no remedy except the recourse to violence which in turn provoked the measures of repression.

These distresses, which were producing a greater disunity in British society than had been evident at any time since the Cromwellian civil war, were of several different kinds. Some belonged to the aftermath of war—the hardships of demobilization and the change-over in industry from war to peace, or the fall in money wages which necessarily accompanied the return from a depreciated paper currency to the gold standard, which was accomplished in

1819–1821. One or two, which naturally aroused the intensest indignation, were directly caused by government policy. Such was the Corn Law of 1815, which strove to preserve the wartime prosperity of agriculture by forbidding grain imports at a price below the starvation figure of eighty shillings a quarter, or ten shillings a bushel. Such, too, was the abolition of income tax in the following year, which redeemed a promise made to the middle class, when it was first levied during the war, but left a heavier burden of taxation to be borne by other classes.

For the most part, however, Britain was experiencing hardships that were caused or at least greatly intensified by the growth of the new industrial society —the first the world had ever seen—which was going on at an accelerating pace before, during, and after the long wars. There was technological unemployment, which confronted, for example, the hundreds of thousands of hand loom weavers as the power loom gradually offered a cheaper alternative to their work. There were depressions in smaller industries, often caused by foreign competition reviving with the return of peace to the Continent; and financial crises, such as recurred at intervals of a little more than a decade throughout the century. All these were more devastating in their effects on the worker now that he and his family were usually dependent on a single trade and lived exclusively on wages. As for living conditions, it is sufficient comment on the growth of industrial towns and slums to point out that, while the decennial censuses showed a rapidly mounting total population, in the first half of the new century the urban death rate also mounted.

Nevertheless, it is possible that less tangible causes of distress were among the most important. The change to factory employment was for many men a humiliating experience—an unskilled job which did not call for craftsmanship or initiative, monotony instead of variety, and work at fixed hours under the eye of a foreman instead of the old liberty to come and go. For women and children, too, the conditions of work might be harder and crueler than when the whole family worked in the fields, or, in any case, involved a novel strain. The change to an urban existence, the migration to the hurriedly constructed mean streets adjoining the place of employment, must in many cases have been altogether devastating. There were none of the amenities of country life. The ties with friends and relations would be largely broken. In place of the imperceptible gradations of the old class structure and the close proximity of rich and poor, which were characteristic of the villages they came from, the denizens of the new towns found themselves living in working-class quarters which, except for an occasional doctor or minister of religion, were drably uniform in their social complexion. It is easy to romanticize about aesthetic deprivations of which those concerned were utterly unaware, but eyes which no longer saw green fields, clear water, or even a smokeless sky missed one of the consolations from the past.

THE PETERSFIELD MASSACRE, MANCHESTER, 1819. This contemporary broadside suggests the popular shock at what came to be known as "Peterloo."

Discontent had found its first dramatic expression during the last few years of the war, when midnight rioters who called themselves Luddites smashed knitting frames in the East Midlands in the belief that machines caused their poverty. There was a recrudescence of Luddism in 1815–1816 and a series of small sporadic outbreaks in London, Derby, and Manchester. In August, 1819, again, St. Peter's Fields, Manchester, was the scene of an organized mass meeting to demand reform where the magistrates in a panic ordered a troop of hussars to charge, thereby causing eleven deaths and about five hundred injuries among the crowd. The following year witnessed a second cavalry charge against Scottish miners at Bonnymuir, and the betrayal of a plot to murder the entire cabinet at a London dinner table (the Cato Street conspiracy).

Yet Peterloo, as it was ironically nicknamed, is usually taken to mark the zenith of the era of repression. For one thing, it provided the occasion of the Six Acts, an English parallel to Metternich's Carlsbad Decrees which, though they stopped short of censorship, even imposed severe restrictions upon the right of public meeting. For another, a charge against defenseless civilians by troops which had last seen action at Waterloo lent itself readily to propaganda: the scene still lives for us in a cheap colored cartoon which was widely sold in London and elsewhere. The event is also famous for the fact that both the prince regent and the prime minister tendered their congratulations to the magistrates concerned. But what is most significant is the revulsion of feeling among the middle classes, evidenced in a formal protest by the Common Council of the City of London, as well as in student opinion at Cambridge, recorded by the future Lord Macaulay. Only four years had passed since the war, but already in Britain there were possibilities of sympathy and cooperation between classes, spanning the gulf which had opened up during the French Revolution between the have-nots and the haves.

When Canning succeeded Castlereagh both as foreign secretary and as leader of the House of Commons, an era of so-called liberal toryism began. Robert Peel,[1] who would have disdained the epithet "liberal," mitigated the rigors of the penal code and in 1829 transferred the idea of an unarmed police force from Dublin to London, hence their nickname of "bobbies." The liberal trade measures of Huskisson helped both the cost of living and the prospect of employment. In 1824–1825 a rather grudging toleration was given to trade unions, which however remained much longer under the ban in other parts of Europe. Even in the closing years of the decade, when Canning's followers proved unable to replace their dead master and the Duke of Wellington led the ministry with orthodox intentions, the rising spirit of the age caused the latter to concede full civil rights first to Protestant nonconformists and then to Roman Catholics. But it required a fortunate succession of circumstances—the death of George IV in June, 1830, the July Revolution in France, and the maladroit leadership of the Duke of Wellington, who treated his cabinet colleagues as his staff officers and was surprised when they resigned—to bring into office a new combination of Whigs and Liberal Tories, with a program of parliamentary reform. Its passage through parliament was bitterly contested, and in the end the king's power of creating new peers was invoked to terminate the opposition of the House of Lords. The underlying reality, however, to which the Continent could offer no parallel, was the fact that a reform which would directly benefit the middle class alone was promoted by a cabinet of noblemen and aristocrats, while the support for it in the country came from working-class as much as middle-class reform organizations.

■ REFORMS OF 1832–1850

The Great Reform Act, as it was enthusiastically called, had as its main feature the suppression of the separate representation of very small boroughs and the institution in all boroughs of a single uniform franchise, based on the occupation of premises worth ten pounds a year. Since the 143 suppressed seats were reallocated to the more populous towns and counties, one important effect was

1. 1788–1850. Son of a highly successful cotton-mill owner, the first Sir Robert Peel, he inherited the baronetcy in 1830. He was the first Oxford student to gain double first-class honors in classics and mathematics; a reforming home secretary in 1822–1827 and prime minister 1834–1835 and 1841–1846. A great financier and administrator, he is remembered especially as a political leader who clearly put country before party.

to give something like due weight in the national counsels to the new industrial areas of the north and Midlands and to the newer districts of London. The other important effect was to make the "ten-pound householder," who was likely to be a substantial shopkeeper or a respectable clerk, more closely linked to the capitalist than to the proletarian, the ultimate arbiter of his country's fate, for something like three-quarters of the seats were borough seats, where voters whose financial position was not much above the required minimum would be in the majority. What the Act did not do was to destroy aristocratic influence as distinct from control in elections; there was still no secret ballot, and in the county constituencies the Act had added to the existing franchise for freeholders a franchise for substantial tenant farmers, whose position could hardly be so substantial as to render them indifferent to their landlord's political opinions. Accordingly, the parliaments of the ensuing thirty-five years were still assemblies of relatively wealthy persons, with landowning interests well to the fore and a considerable proportion of members whose views were largely independent of party. Such persons gave their confidence to cabinets made up largely of peers and aristocrats; they would accept other leaders, such as Peel and Gladstone, who shared the education and way of life of the aristocracy; but brilliant adventurers like Disraeli, and tribunes of the people like Bright, were rare indeed. Even so, the cabinet and the houses, and the young queen herself, would have to be increasingly sensitive to middle-class opinion.

This middle-class opinion was usually something to be guessed at rather than measured, a climate rather than a set of facts; as reflected in the pages of Dickens or *Punch*, it often appears sentimental, wayward, or wrongheaded. But its instinctive hostility to mere tradition made it a vehicle for the very clear ideas on government which had been preached to the deaf ears of the preceding generation by Jeremy Bentham. He had died in the very week in which the Reform Bill became law, but John Stuart Mill and other philosophic radicals inspired by Bentham exercised an increasing influence on lawmaking. The fact-finding royal commission to justify new legislation and the body of salaried inspectors to enforce it, no less than the evaluation of any law or institution by asking whether it served "the greatest happiness of the greatest number," were Benthamite techniques which influenced public life throughout a long period, not least among people quite ignorant of their origins. A second strong influence was that exercised by evangelical Christianity, but, as this affected the heart rather than the intellect, it will be convenient to give examples of Benthamite reforms first.

The Municipal Reform Act of 1835 is important because it established a pattern of urban self-government for Britain which still applies, although it was originally devised to operate minimum services of street-cleaning, lighting, and police. The corrupt corporations, whose members were commonly chosen by cooption and retained their seats for life, gave place to councilors elected by all rate payers, each representing a section of the borough for a period of three years. The mayor, who was to act as chairman, and an addition of one-third to the membership, known as aldermen, were to be elected by the councilors; provision was made for a careful audit of accounts, and administration was through whole-time salaried officials, such as the chief constable for the new police force. A similar tidying-up process was attempted in the Church of England by the appointment of a permanent body of ecclesiastical commissioners to administer superfluous endowments—the see of Durham at this time had an annual revenue approaching twenty thousand pounds, Canterbury had thirty thousand pounds—and by an act which forbade any clergyman to hold more than two full-time posts at once. It is also possible to trace back to this period the beginnings of a slow process by which the state took over one of the most ancient and most neglected responsibilities of the church, namely, the provision of education for the poor, which was chiefly in the hands of two charities, the National Society, providing Church of England schools, and the British Society, which was nonsectarian. A token grant was first made in 1833; it grew, and in 1839 a small government department with salaried inspectors was set up to administer the grant.

The compulsory registration of births, marriages, and deaths was another valuable contribution to good order. The introduction in 1840, in face of bitter opposition, of the penny post based on prepayment and the simple new device of the adhesive postage stamp, is an example of an improvement which has served "the greatest happiness of the greatest number" in all parts of the civilized world. At the same time it would be misleading not to emphasize the fact that the influence of Benthamite ideas is nowhere clearer than in the new poor law of 1834, where the interests of efficiency as seen through the eyes of the middle class came into bitter conflict with working-class feelings and opinions.

The use of poor-rate subsidies in aid of wages, first introduced as a wartime expedient in Berkshire in 1795, was a method of averting starvation that had spread through half the counties of England. As a result, poor law expenditure had trebled in a generation. The new system was therefore run by a board of guardians, elected by the rate payers of a group of parishes, and the expenditure of each board was closely checked by government-appointed commissioners in London. In principle—though there were always exceptions, especially in periods of trade depression—no poor relief was to be given except in a special institution, the workhouse. Life there was to be made "less eligible" than life outside by discipline, segregation, toil, and privation, so that any kind of employment might seem preferable to unemployment and the private family unit be induced to carry the maximum burden of provision for widows and orphans and the incidence of sickness and old age. In spite of the heartrending appeal of Dickens's *Oliver Twist* and a huge popular agitation, shortly to be described, the system outlined above was not substantially modified until old-age pensions were introduced in Britain in 1908. The "workshop of the world," as Britain soon came to be called, believed in making its people work.

The rigors of the regime were mitigated to some extent at least by the strong influence of religion. In political life the leading representative of religious opinion in social matters was the Anglican Evangelical, Lord Ashley, who in 1851 inherited the Earldom of Shaftesbury.[2] But in a country where churchgoing, Bible reading, and Sunday school attendance linked up an earnest body of Anglicans, possessing considerable political influence, with the Methodists and other Protestant dissenters, who made up in numbers and energy what they lacked in political and social prestige, the religious element was important to humanitarian movements of widely varying character. Thus the foreign missionary societies, which had been very active since 1800 in most parts of the British Empire, were mainly responsible for the decision to free the slaves, for which £20,000,000 compensation was voted by a parliament from which the wider repercussions were, perhaps fortunately, hidden. In the British West Indies, with about 700,000 slaves, the resulting labor problem contributed to the rapid decline of the sugar plantations. In Cape Colony, where the 40,000 slaves were mainly field workers, the economic loss was much smaller; nevertheless, difficulties over the compensation payments to the Boer farmers helped to exacerbate relations and contributed to the Great Trek of 1836, in which all the later troubles of South Africa have their root.

As for factory legislation, where Britain set an example to the world in finding new remedies for evils which were only partly new, Ashley's motives were religiously based, as were those of his leading supporters. The achievement is spread over at least five main statutes passed between 1833 and 1850, the existence of grave abuses being established by royal commissions of enquiry, and the enforcement of remedial measures ensured by the other Benthamite device of the salaried inspector. The results were fourfold. The abolition of the labor of very young children in the textile factories and coal mines set a precedent for other industries. Women of all ages and boys under eighteen received legal protection as regards hours and places of employment. A beginning was made with the complicated task of enforcing measures to reduce industrial accidents. And in 1850, as the result of nearly twenty years' agitation in the factory districts, the hours of women and young persons were restricted to a specified

2. 1801–1885. Most famous English philanthropist and a leader of the strict Evangelicals, his compassion was first roused when a boy at Harrow School by the degrading sight of a pauper's funeral. He championed the oppressed, not only in the Factory and Coal Mines Acts for which he agitated, but in relation to the lunacy laws, the protection of "climbing boys," or child chimney sweeps, and the provision of special "Ragged Schools," better lodging houses, and better working-class housing.

period of twelve hours on the first five days of the week (including one and one-half hours for meals) and eight hours (with one-half hour break) on Saturdays, which indirectly secured the same sixty-hour week for all factory employees. Thus by mid-century the biggest British manufacturing industry had established its right to a regular Saturday half-holiday—something new and significant in human history.

Meanwhile the public health movement, where the interests of Benthamite efficiency and Christian humanitarianism were both involved, had made remarkably little progress, in spite of serious epidemics of cholera in 1831–1832 and 1847–1848. Boards of health set up in the 1832 emergency were allowed to lapse; few of the new town councils took on any sanitary responsibilities they could avoid; and, when a central board of health was established for a second time in 1848, its local boards covered only two million of the population and within ten years the second board was likewise defunct. *Punch* in this instance sided with the opposition—an interesting reminder of the fact that scientific ignorance and dislike of interference were the allies of the cheap building, house and room renting, shopowning, and water-supply vending interests, which found it more profitable to keep things as they were.

■ THE POLITICS OF THE POOR AND THE GROWTH OF FREE TRADE

In the field of public health, it was only an occasional bureaucrat like Edwin Chadwick, the secretary of the poor law commission and author of a revealing *Report on the Sanitary Condition of the Laboring Population* (1842), that knew the urgency of needs which the middle class found it convenient to ignore. But more generally the politics of the poor in this period show that the middle class was deliberately indifferent to their wants. In the winter in which it was preparing the reform bill, the Whig-Liberal government had repressed with severity the only large proletarian group which had played no conspicuous part in the disturbances of 1815–1820. The half-starved agricultural laborers of southeast England, having been roused by events across the Channel to demand a living wage, fired ricks and destroyed threshing machines but did not kill anyone; yet nine of them were hanged, and nearly two hundred transported for life. During the next eighteen months, as already noted, the help of the working-class political unions was essential to the passing of the reform bill.[3] But once its own position was secure, the middle class became once more a party of order.

The toleration—it was nothing more—which had been conceded to the basic activities of trade unions by the legislation of 1824–1825 enabled Robert Owen,[4] the factory-owner, philanthropist, and visionary, to organize a Grand National Consolidated Trades Union; the workers had been refused the vote,

3. See pp. 192–193.
4. See pp. 43–44.

THE

Freemen

AND

ELECTORS

OF ROCHESTER,

Are respectfully informed that

LORD CHARLES WELLESLEY,

Son of the Duke of

WELLINGTON

Dictator of England!

And sworn foe of Civil and Religious Liberty,

WILL ARRIVE IN THIS CITY,

At 10 this Morning.

All the Friends of Military Government—Tory Policy--and Abuses in Church and State, are invited to lend their assistance in securing his Election.
Rochester, Dec. 12th, 1834.

but if they held together their right to control industrial life could not be gainsaid. This was a bold proposition, but before Owen's supporters had got as far as planning the general strike, which would enable them to take over industry, the movement petered out in local strike actions. Although at its height in the early months of 1834 the GNCTU had half a million supporters, this first mass movement in British trade union history is nowadays remembered chiefly for the savage sentences of transportation imposed on six farm laborers of Tolpuddle, Dorset, technically on a charge of administering illegal oaths as defined in an act of 1797, practically because they stood for a type of organization which offered the one hope of betterment to the most ill-used section of the proletariat. In the same year the passing of the new poor law enforced the lesson in town and country alike, by giving the maximum incentive to strikebreaking and whatever else might accrue to the employer from the pressure to be exerted upon the unemployed, who constituted the "reserve army of labor."

Out of the universal hatred for the poor law came the strength of the working-class support for the political movement known as Chartism. For a decade (1838–1848) the workers demonstrated by petitions to parliament, by public meetings, marches, and strikes in favor of a six-clause charter which would provide manhood suffrage, secret voting, equal constituencies, annual elections, and the democratization of the membership of parliament by abolishing financial qualifications and reintroducing salaries for members. Though such a reform of parliament was naturally envisaged as a panacea for all the evils of industrialism and poverty, the new poor law—already held up in some districts by mob violence—would have been the first evil to be swept away in the triumph of democracy.

But democracy did not triumph. In 1839 a petition bearing 1,200,000 names was refused consideration by parliament, and, when the Welsh coal miners resorted to direct action, a handful of soldiers dispersed them with a loss of twenty-four lives. In 1842 a second petition with 3,300,000 names was similarly rejected, whereupon the Chartist leaders linked their cause with a series of industrial strikes. The strikes failed, but the government had been seriously alarmed—at one time Manchester was held by 2,000 soldiers with six pieces of artillery—and numerous Chartists were sent to prison for incitement to violence. Here the story would have ended had not the European revolutions of 1848 encouraged the presentation of a third petition. This time the signatures were fewer; the reception by parliament colder, if possible, than before; and neither in London nor in the provinces were there any disturbances to correspond with the precautions that had been taken to meet the supposed emergency.

Suffrage demands having receded for nearly twenty years, we must look in two other directions to trace the advance of the working-class movement. Among the skilled workers, in trades with a long tradition of solidarity and strong apprenticeship regulations to restrict numbers, trade unionism had survived Owen's fiasco of 1834. In the early 1840's the total membership has been estimated at less than 100,000, and in 1844 it was the opinion of Engels, the friend of Marx, that they remained "powerless against all great forces." But the fact that in 1844 the new Miners' Association of Great Britain and Ireland was in a position to pay £1,000 a year for legal advice is a reminder that the decade, which was retrospectively named the "Hungry Forties," saw the turn of the tide toward prosperity. In 1851 the formation of the Amalgamated Society of Engineers, with 11,000 members subscribing at the rate of a shilling a week, marks the emergence of a new model for trade unions in skilled crafts, with the emphasis on accumulation of funds, respectability encouraged by insurance benefits, and a preference for shrewd bargaining rather than wildcat striking. These truly Victorian qualities were likewise exemplified in the movement for consumers' cooperative shops, which began in Rochdale, Lancashire, in 1844. By 1851 there were about 130 such organizations, with perhaps 100 member-customers apiece, saving the retailer's profit for themselves by running their own little concern. Here, too, some return to prosperity was the essential basis for the advance.

In contrast with all this, free trade was a policy organized by the middle class, though it brought enormous incidental benefits to the British workers. In relation to the landed nobility and gentry, on the other hand, its triumph in 1846 marked the moment of acceptance of the principle that Britain as the workshop of the world need no longer regard the cultivation of her own soil as a matter of paramount importance. The fact that British agriculture nevertheless continued to flourish until the later 1870's does not alter the significance of the class conflict over the Corn Laws.

The resumption of Pitt's commercial policy, based on Adam Smith but interrupted by the long French wars, was the subject of a London merchants' petition to parliament in 1820, and was the object pursued by William Huskisson, who had been a secretary to the treasury under Pitt, when he was president of the board of trade in 1823–1827. He succeeded in reducing a great many duties to the advantage of the poorer consumer, with 20 percent as a maximum for the tariff on manufactures. By a series of reciprocity treaties he made it easier for foreign shipping to trade in approved commodities with British ports, including the ports of the colonial empire, to which he gave a large measure of commercial freedom. But the British governing class was not yet educated to accept major fiscal changes, which came when Peel's government of 1841–1846 followed a long series of unbalanced Whig-Liberal budgets. Peel reintroduced the income tax as a temporary precaution, but based his policy on the belief that a low tariff would stimulate imports to such an extent that adequate revenue would still be forthcoming. In 1842 he made 5, 12, and 20 percent the upper limits of taxation on raw materials, semimanufactured goods, and manufactures respectively. Reviewing the situation after three years, he felt justified in making some additional reductions, but renewed the income tax for a further period. Thus his successors in office were encouraged to make complete free trade their aim in the knowledge that, if the yield from indirect taxation flagged, they had a readily variable form of direct taxation on which to fall back.

Peel was also faced by the problem of the Corn Law of 1815, which Huskisson had replaced by a sliding scale to discourage speculators. The result had been to make Huskisson unpopular with the landed interest without his earning any appreciable thanks from those who believed the price of bread was still kept artificially high. From 1839 onward the problem was made more urgent and more formidable by the establishment and growth of a propaganda organization, the Anti-Corn Law League. Its basis, significantly, was in Manchester; its money came from the middle class, its membership from middle and working class alike. They were united to do battle against aristocratic privilege and on behalf of cheap bread, though the middle-class manufacturer in fact saw it also as a question of markets which would be opened in grain-producing countries and of wages which might be expected to fall with the cost of living. The leaders of the League, Richard Cobden and John Bright, were two Lancashire manufacturers of high principles and great talents; their entry into parliament added stature to their cause and to their class.

Nevertheless, the repeal of the Corn Laws could scarcely have been accomplished in a house where the majority of members had been elected to maintain them if the wet summer of 1845 had not brought it about that a deficient grain harvest in Britain coincided with the first ravages of the potato blight in Ireland. Repeal could not save the population of the overcrowded and

GLADSTONE IN 1859. A fine portrait suggesting the power of the rapidly rising Liberal leader.

poverty-stricken island, where the majority depended on subsistence agriculture and a single crop. Even so, Peel could not conscientiously do otherwise than try, so the measure was forced through with the help of Whig-Liberal votes at the cost of a split in the Tory party, which went out of office in the summer of 1846 and did not recover power until 1874. When Peel died unexpectedly in 1850, a London journalist saw people in working-class streets weep at their doors because he had sacrificed his career to end an injustice.

The middle class having won this further triumph in alliance with the workers against the aristocracy, the establishment of complete free trade could not be long delayed. The Navigation Acts, which aimed at preserving the carrying trade of Britain and the Empire from foreign competition, came to an end generally in 1849, and in 1854 even the coastal traffic was thrown open to foreign shipping. By the latter date Gladstone, who was in many respects the heir of Peel, had produced the first of a series of brilliantly executed budgets which removed the remaining duties so that ultimately no taxes on foreign imports survived except purely for purposes of revenue. The last of these budgets was in 1866, but we may take the Great Exhibition of 1851 as marking the moment when British trade advertised its readiness to face with confidence the competition of the world. It was also a moment when, as foreign visitors observed, something approaching a harmony of classes had been achieved among the fortunate British—their less fortunate Irish neighbors being conveniently forgotten. The further belief that the success of the Great Exhibition somehow symbolized a universal peace which would be the accompaniment of universal free trade was quickly shown to be a delusion; a pause to consider external relations will indicate how that delusion originated.

■ FOREIGN AND IMPERIAL POLICY

The forty years' peace, which in 1851 was nearing its end, was for Britain a period of great general prestige, a few dramatic successes, and quiet imperial growth. If Castlereagh had been wrongly suspected of truckling to the conservative powers, his successor Canning had championed the independence of Spanish Americans and Greeks, while leaving neither friend nor enemy in any doubt that with him British national interests had first place. Palmerston,[5] whose tenure of the foreign office spans nearly sixteen years in the period 1830–1851, was the heir of Canning, but was continuing his policy in more favorable circumstances, for the three eastern powers were now less closely united than in the days of the congress system. France under Louis Philippe alternately followed in the wake of Britain or rued her failure to do so, and the revolutions of 1848 gave Britain all the prestige of an unshaken throne and a demonstrably loyal people.

Palmerston's first success was also his greatest, when the independence, constitutional monarchy, and neutralization of Belgium were firmly established by skillful diplomacy to the entire satisfaction of her British neighbor across the Channel. By the Straits Convention of July, 1841, too, he reaffirmed the "ancient rule of the Ottoman Porte," supposedly upset by Russia eight years before, which forbade the passage of foreign warships to and from the Black Sea as long as the Turks were at peace. An unjust but advantageous war against China, the Opium War of 1839–1842, had a small-scale parallel in Europe, when in 1850 the claims of the Portuguese moneylender and British citizen, Don Pacifico, were enforced by naval blockade against the Greeks. An overhasty gesture of congratulation to Louis Napoleon, however, on the occasion of his coup d'état of December, 1851, gave Queen Victoria a chance to rid herself temporarily of a foreign minister who would not make a proper pretense of consulting the royal wishes. Even so, Palmerston did not exaggerate when he invited a successor next year to observe "what a power of prestige England possesses abroad."

Retrospectively, however, the forty years' peace appears to have left a more enduring mark on British history through unplanned imperial developments carrying little prestige. In India, indeed, the peace was far from unbroken, for even after the overthrow of the last Mahratta princes in 1819, Sind and the Punjab remained to be conquered in the following thirty years, leaving yet other unsolved problems in the Indian borderlands of Afghanistan and

5. 1784–1865. He was the most popular British statesman of the mid-nineteenth century, holding minor office as secretary-at-war, 1809–1828; foreign secretary, 1830–1834, 1835–1841, 1846–1851; home secretary, 1852–1855, when he became prime minister as the man who could win the Crimean War. He died in office at the age of eighty, with a half-finished dispatch before him on his table.

Burma. Elsewhere, however, annexations were for the most part peaceful, as in the case of New Zealand, where the treaty of Waitangi recorded the transfer of sovereignty from the Maori chiefs in February, 1840, just in time to balk the French. But it was the flow of immigrants from the United Kingdom which staked out claims that would outlast Britain's naval and financial ascendancy. The movement to Canada received official encouragement while memories of American attacks in the war of 1812 were still fresh, and there was likewise a political motive behind the first British settlement of Cape Colony in South Africa in 1820. Moreover, from the publication of Gibbon Wakefield's *Letter from Sydney* in 1829, important attempts at systematic colonization were made both in Australia and later in New Zealand. These were helped in the former case by the agitation against peopling the colonies with convicts, which led to the abolition of this practice by stages between 1840 and 1866. We must, however, attribute mainly to private motives—dissatisfaction with their old home and hopes regarding the new one—a total outward flow from the United Kingdom of 225,000, 655,000, and 1,545,000 persons respectively in the three decades from 1821 to 1851. Even when allowance is made for the superior attraction of the United States—which at mid-century contained 1,365,000 persons who were born in the United Kingdom, the majority of them Irish—the figures for the Empire are big; and for Australia the discovery of gold in February, 1851, brought an inflow which more than doubled its population within the decade.

In 1815 and for many years afterwards the British Empire, to which victory had brought such valuable additions as the Cape of Good Hope, Ceylon, Malta, Mauritius, and Trinidad, was lightly regarded by its proprietors. The positions of importance for control of the seas were unlikely to be threatened in any foreseeable future; the prizing of colonies for economic reasons seemed to be part of a dying mercantilist way of thought; and the political relationship with bodies of white settlers was deemed in view of the American experience to be too evanescent to deserve the attention of a cabinet faced with urgent problems nearer home. The one exception, as we have seen, was the question of slavery, where religious and humanitarian interests exacted a prompt solution from the Reformed Parliament in 1833. But in 1837 a small rising in Lower Canada touched off an even smaller rising in Upper Canada. Both were suppressed within a few weeks in actions involving at most a few hundred participants on either side, but sufficient alarm was caused in London for Lord Durham,[6] a radical nobleman of great energy, common sense, and courage, to be sent to

6. 1792–1840. A wealthy radical of ancient family, son-in-law of Lord Grey, he helped to prepare the Great Reform Bill, but left the cabinet, unregretted by fellow members, in 1833. He resigned the governor-generalship and left Canada after five months because the cabinet refused to support deportation of rebel leaders to Bermuda; one of his advisers was Gibbon Wakefield.

investigate the neglected problems of the relationship between governor and colonial assembly. Such was the origin of the great Durham Report, published when its author had already returned from Canada under a cloud. From the principle of responsible government, that the executive must be politically answerable to the legislative power, which was first enunciated in his report, its practice followed in due course. Responsible government was formally authorized in Nova Scotia in November, 1846, and, more dramatically, in the reunited provinces of Canada in 1849, when Durham's son-in-law, Lord Elgin, refused to disallow a Rebellion Losses Bill, in which ministers responsible to the Canadian parliament leaned to the side of the disaffected French. In 1850 the Australian colonies were empowered to draft their own constitutions on the same basis, and thereafter responsible government was available to each British colony of settlement as soon as it felt capable of shouldering the burdens, as well as the privileges, involved in full control of its own internal affairs.

Small colonies were unlikely to wish to challenge the mother country's control of their external affairs. Looking ahead to the end of our period, however, we may notice that the British North America Act, which in nearly every respect followed a draft made overseas, created in 1867 a federal union of Canada. The former provinces of Quebec and Ontario, together with New Brunswick and Nova Scotia, made provision for the eventual inclusion of other provinces from coast to coast. The union was occasioned by considerations of external policy, namely, the fear of the reunited, and for a short time militant, southern neighbor. Only four years later, the Washington Treaty, which removed the threat of war by referring the *Alabama* claims to arbitration and opened inshore Canadian fisheries to the Americans, provided the first occasion when a colonial representative (the prime minister of Canada) took part in the framing of British external relations.

The years from 1850 to 1871 had witnessed the climax of Victorian prosperity, but Britain had not played a part commensurate with her inherent strength in the great international developments of the age. It is true that in 1856 she emerged as a victor from the Crimean War, her only involvement against a great power in the century after Waterloo. The siege of Sebastopol had some heroic aspects—the charge of the Light Brigade "into the jaws of death" at Balaclava, the repulse of the Russian infantry in the fog against odds of two to one at Inkerman—and Florence Nightingale's intervention in the hospitals at Scutari is perhaps the greatest single event in the history of the emancipation of modern woman. But almost every important aspect of the campaign from siege tactics to logistics was disastrously mismanaged, so much so that the sufferings of the army in the Crimean winter as reported by the first war correspondents created a wave of popular indignation which overturned the cabinet responsible for the conduct of the operations. Positive results, however, were few. By the end of the war, Britain's French allies were already preparing to divert their friendship to the Russians; Turkey, having finally forfeited the principalities, did not cease to be the "sick bear" of Europe; and the only solid advantage gained was the neutralization of the Black Sea, which lasted for no more than fifteen years.

Moreover, the Crimean War was followed almost immediately by the nerve-racking episode of the Indian Mutiny, which was to some extent occasioned by the withdrawal of troops to the theater of war on the Black Sea and the spread of reports that, in the Crimea no less than in Afghanistan and the Punjab, British armies had shown that they were no longer invincible. The Indian Mutiny, however, affected only one of three Sepoy armies and a handful of native princes. Having first flared up at Meerut in May, 1857, it passed its danger point as early as September, when Delhi was recaptured; by that time reinforcements from Britain were preparing to march across Bengal to the relief of Lucknow and the suppression of the last embers of revolt in central India. Accordingly, the blow to British prestige was not very heavy. The opportunity was taken to abolish the East India Company (which had finally ceased to be a trading organization a quarter of a century earlier), and British administration under the direct authority of the cabinet and parliament in London became more watchful, more efficient, and more paternalistic. Nevertheless, memories of the grim events of the mutiny undoubtedly deepened the cleft between the white man and the native, and gave Indian nationalists of a later generation the legend of a "first war of Indian independence."

A direct consequence of the Crimean War was the rise of Palmerston to the office of prime minister, which he retained with one short interval until his death in 1865. Yet he played an effective part in relation to only one of the great issues which were being fought out in this decade, and his immediate successors were at least equally passive. Palmerston and his colleagues gave full moral support to the cause of Italian unification, though it was Napoleon III who, by throwing the sword of France into the scales against Austria, made that unification practicable. But, in the case of German unification, British opinion was divided as to the merits of the end, while virtually though ineffectively united in deprecating the means which Bismarck employed. In 1864 the invasion of Schleswig-Holstein produced no reaction more helpful to the cause of the Danes than a demand for a European conference to consider the situation, which achieved nothing for their benefit. The second and third stages of the Bismarckian operation followed after Palmerston's death: Austria was decisively defeated in the Seven Weeks' War of 1866, while the British government was suspiciously watching for France to take sides; in 1870, again, suspicion of France evaporated too late for Britain to do anything to mitigate a disaster which made the new Germany the master of the Continent. But the foreign policy of Gladstone, who had come into power in 1868, for the time being suited the recently democratized British electorate. If he did not save France, her ruler was after all a Napoleon, and Gladstone's prompt appeals to both sides to respect the neutrality treaty of 1839 were believed to have saved Belgium. If he failed for want of an ally to make Russia respect the Black Sea clauses of the Treaty of Paris, he induced the London conference to denounce any unilateral abrogation, and in the same year at the Treaty of Washington, mentioned above, pinned his faith to arbitration methods such as during the twentieth century have won wide approval.

The event outside Britain which both divided its sympathies and influenced its future most decisively was the American Civil War. The affairs of the *Trent* and the *Alabama* showed Palmerston's government at its clumsiest, for prejudice largely blinded its members both to the aims and to the prospects of the North. The very opposite was true of the instinctive opinions of the workers, above all in industrial Lancashire, where the blockade of southern ports by northern warships, which stopped the supply of raw cotton, was the cause of mass unemployment and serious suffering. Nevertheless the workers, many of whom corresponded with relatives and friends settled in the northern states, believed that the war was about slavery and that it directly or indirectly concerned the rights of free men everywhere. The eventual triumph of the North therefore pointed the contrast between the policy of the governing class and the experts, which had failed, and the policy favored by the unenfranchised masses, which had been vindicated.

■ THE SECOND ERA OF REFORM

Palmerston's death prepared the way for a classic period in British political life, when for fifteen years the rivalry between Gladstone and Disraeli gave the strife of parties the glamour it so often lacks. The years up to 1871, with which this chapter closes, are also the period of a great transition from the rule of a middle class to that of an increasingly artisan electorate, for whose favor parliamentary candidates, still drawn mainly from the higher social levels, had periodically to contend. The electoral reform itself was chiefly the work of Disraeli,[7] the changes in institutions and attitudes which immediately followed were the work of Gladstone.[8] But if we look beyond parliament to the

7. 1804–1881. A baptized Jew of modest middle-class origins, he became the most important leader of the Tory Party after the split over Corn Law repeal (which he bitterly opposed) in 1846. A successful novelist, a brilliant debater, and a bold innovator in Tory policies, he was chancellor of the exchequer in Derby's three minority Tory governments, he became prime minister in 1868, and headed a Tory majority government in 1874–1880.
8. 1809–1898. Son of a Liverpool merchant of Scottish descent, he became the representative leader of the Liberal Party, though he began his career as a Tory minister and a follower of Peel. He was free trade chancellor of the exchequer, 1852–1855 and 1859–1866, and four times prime minister, his later ministries being devoted chiefly to Irish problems which proved insoluble.

meetings and demonstrations in London and the big provincial towns, which showed what twenty years of prosperity had done to make the artisan class at once respectable and formidable, the most significant leader is clearly John Bright. Cobden, who had shared with him the championship of free trade, peace abroad, and the abolition of class privilege at home, died in the same year as Palmerston, whereas from 1857 Bright continued for a whole generation to serve as a member of parliament for Birmingham, a city of small hardware manufactures in which the gap between employer and employee was so small as to be almost meaningless.

As compared with the Great Reform Act of 1832, Disraeli's Representation of the People Act was the far less systematized result of pressures and counterpressures, with much calculation of what was the most the party would accept in the House of Commons and what was the least that would satisfy the people outside. In the end, a Liberal bill, which was rejected as too far-reaching in 1866, was followed by a Tory bill, which became law in August, 1867, at the end of a session devoted largely to the piecemeal insertion of democratic amendments. The effect was almost to double the electorate in England and Wales by giving a vote to every urban householder, irrespective of the value of his house; to urban lodgers, provided the lodgings were worth ten pounds a year unfurnished; and to rural occupants of property worth twelve pounds a year. Coupled with a redistribution of seats taken from the smallest boroughs, the Act gave further recognition to the importance of industrial towns in an increasingly industrialized England, and it was in such towns that the artisan vote henceforth predominated. Although no immediate change took place in the type of representative chosen, there was a noticeable change in party programs and a tendency for a wider electorate to desert one party for the other in accordance with the supposed needs of the hour—the so-called "swing of the pendulum."

At the very first election under the new system, the new voters declined to show the expected gratitude to Disraeli, who had enfranchised them, preferring the large promises of other reforms to follow which were presented to them by Gladstone. From December, 1868, accordingly, Gladstone was given the same chance as had fallen to an earlier generation of Liberals in the 1830's, when a similar backlog of reforms awaited their turn. One such reform, indeed, which had figured among the six points of the charter, might seem to us to be a necessary concomitant of the law to enfranchise employees who were still very much at the mercy of employers. Yet it was not until 1872 that the House of Lords was induced to pass the Ballot Act, which set up the modern system of carefully protected anonymous voting. This made it very difficult for employers to exercise undue influence, because the effectiveness of bribery or intimidation upon individuals could no longer be ascertained. But Gladstone was prompt to embark upon several far-reaching schemes of reorganization in the public service, of which the effects on the voter were important but indirect.

The army now underwent the thorough overhaul which had been im-pending since the revelations of inefficiency made during the Crimean War. Under the influence of Prussia's military successes, changes were made in the supreme command, in the recruitment of officers and men, and in the geo-graphical basis of the army. The reactionary commander-in-chief, a cousin of Queen Victoria, was subordinated to the secretary of state for war, and the royal prerogative was used to end the traditional system by which officers bought their promotions as far as a colonelcy. The men they commanded were at the same time encouraged to regard army life as something more than the last resort of the unemployed and the unfortunate by making the term of service six years (instead of twelve) with six in the reserve, by giving each infantry regiment of the line a county or other area of recruitment, where the training barracks would be situated, and by the abolition of flogging. Troops were brought home from the self-governing colonies, which were invited to provide for their own defense, and the necessary garrisons in India and elsewhere re-plenished by the "linked-battalion" system, trained men from the home battalion of a regiment being sent out in drafts to its second battalion abroad. Though there was still no proper general staff organization, in most other respects the British army, re-equipped with its first good breech-loading rifle, was now restored to full efficiency—and, to Gladstone's great satisfaction, its cost had actually been reduced.

Equally important in the long run was the administrative change which gave Britain its modern civil service. In 1855 a civil service commission had been set up to conduct examinations as part of the system of recruitment, but it was in 1870 that the examination became strictly competitive, open to all candidates of British birth, and giving access to all higher posts in the service, except for the foreign office and posts for which a particular professional quali-fication was needed. One result was to give a tremendous fillip to university studies, to which the examination at its highest level related. Another was to reduce the power of snobbery in English society by practically destroying what had been a valuable type of patronage—the ability to secure a government post for a favored individual through knowing someone in the government. But the most important result was the creation of an elite corps of intelligent and in-dustrious administrators, whose careers were unaffected by vicissitudes of party, a corps which was always capable of expansion as the sphere of government activity expanded. A third type of reorganization speaks for itself. The proposal to remodel two systems of law (common law and equity) into one, and at the same time to unify the seven existing courts into one Supreme Court of Judica-ture, had been ventilated by a royal commission before Gladstone took office, and was essentially an interparty measure, though the Liberals take the credit for the enactment in 1873 of changes which put an end to agelong scandals of litigation denounced by Dickens.

In an epoch of large reforms there were inevitably some failures. Gladstone himself had declared at the outset that his mission was to pacify Ireland, where he handled a very difficult situation with only partial and temporary success. Ever since the famine, the Irish people had continued to vote against British rule by the most effective means at their disposal—the emigrant ship— and from their new homes in the United States sent money to encourage acts of violence by an underground movement known as the Fenian Brotherhood. Since the end of the American Civil War, the Fenians had struck sensational blows across Niagara Falls, and in England at Chester, Manchester, and at a London prison—things known to every newspaper reader, which probably helped Gladstone to pass his two measures. The first of these, in 1869, disestablished the Anglican state church in Ireland, where it had no moral justification for its legal privileges among a predominantly Roman Catholic population. The other, in 1870, was a land act, which tried to help oppressed tenant farmers by giving them a legal right to compensation for any improvements made by them to their holding during their period of tenure and to damages for eviction, unless they were evicted for nonpayment of rent. But the act did not do what was needed most, namely, give protection against rack renting, that is, the arbitrary increase of rent to as high a figure as the market would bear.

Two other partial failures, unlike the case of Ireland, show the limits of Gladstone's sympathies. In establishing the Local Government Board to supervise the affairs of town councils, public health authorities, and poor relief, he allowed the restrictive policy of the poor law to be a dominant influence, thus effectively restraining the growth of local self-government. In the same way his trade union legislation, passed at a time when the new-model unions were becoming nation-wide in scope, coupled the first clear legal statement that trade unions were in the full sense lawful associations and entitled to the protection of the law with an equally clear reminder of the penalties to which unions were liable under the Act of 1825 if strike action involved intimidation, molestation, or obstruction.

Last, Gladstone made himself responsible, though without enthusiasm, for an educational reform which can be variously regarded as a necessary concomitant, like the Ballot Act, of household suffrage in the towns; as a remarkable example of the overpowering strength of financial and religious considerations in mid-Victorian England; and as a rather depressing case of class legislation. In any event, while the result was to bring English education nearer to the

The map shows the close concentration of industry in small and therefore densely populated areas adjacent to the coalfields. Note the nearness of iron deposits to coal and the accessibility of seaports for overseas trade. Southern and eastern England (except in the neighborhood of London and Bristol), the northern parts of Scotland, much of Wales, and almost the whole of Ireland retain the characteristics of an older rural society.

Iron
Glasgow
Cottons
Coal
Ships
Coal
Ships
Newcastle
Woolens
Londonderry
Linen
Belfast
Ships
Iron
Iron
Cottons and
Woolens
Leeds
Hull
Ships
Bradford
Coal
Ships
Manchester
Iron
Liverpool
Sheffield
Cutlery
Dublin
Machinery
Nottingham
Pottery
Stafford
Woolens
Birmingham
Hardware
Coal
Iron
Ships
Cardiff
Woolens
London
Bristol
Southampton
Ships
Tin
Granite
Copper
Plymouth
Ships

BRITAIN AT MID-CENTURY
WORKSHOP of the WORLD

0   50   100   150   200   250

MILES

level reached by the leading countries of the Continent, it was still allowed to lag behind them, with results which were plainly disastrous. The voluntary schools, to which reference has been made, had expanded as a result of rival religious enthusiasms until at least half the children of the nation were receiving some sort of education. But what of the other half of the children? To minimize expense, the government decided to leave the voluntary schools in possession wherever an increased grant would enable them to accommodate every child, subject only to provision for exemption from religious instruction, if the school belonged to a denomination different from that of the parents. Where the building of new schools was unavoidable, however, they were to be placed under the charge of a board elected by rate payers for the purpose, and the religious instruction given in those schools would be nondenominational.

Thus the elementary education system remained a patchwork, with the emphasis, not on the national need and opportunity, but on the perfunctory discharge of an unavoidable quasi-charitable obligation to the poor. Middle-class children continued to begin their education in private schools, from which they proceeded to grammar schools and public boarding schools; the state did nothing to help the children of the poor to proceed beyond the three R's, which were sufficient preparation for the labor market on which they would be thrown at thirteen or, if they passed through the courses quickly enough, at ten years of age. But Gladstone's government did, characteristically, ease the path of higher education where the barrier was not financial, for the tests which had restricted membership of Oxford and Cambridge universities to students belonging to the Church of England were at last abolished. This was the more important because, even with the inclusion of struggling newer institutions in London, Manchester, and Durham, England and Wales (though not Scotland) had a smaller provision of universities in proportion to population and wealth than any other important country in western Europe.

■ MID-VICTORIAN BRITAIN

The Britain over which Queen Victoria had now ruled for a full generation was a land of contrasts. To the French critic, Taine, who had been a frequent visitor throughout the 1860's, it excelled France in its political constitution, religion, and in "the greatness of the acquired wealth, combined with the increased power of producing and amassing." But he found it inferior, not merely in climate but in things which were under human control—the distribution of wealth, and the domestic and social life. Though Taine could not readily guess it, he was examining Britain near its apogee, when the possibilities of progress for the island people still appeared to be unlimited and no effective economic rival had crossed the horizon. The unevenness of the Victorian achievement in its most characteristic period therefore deserves a brief assessment.

In two decades the population of Great Britain had risen from 21,000,000 to 26,000,000, an increase which gave cause for satisfaction as long as a blind eye was turned to the fact that Ireland, on the other hand, alone among the countries of Europe, had had a shrinking population since the time of the famine. By 1871 the British birth rate was just reaching its recorded maximum, while the slowly declining death rate compared favorably with that of France, Prussia, or Belgium. The ten-hour day, which the textile workers had achieved in 1850, was now beginning to give place in many skilled industries to one of nine hours. Money wages had risen by nearly 40 percent for an average job and by nearly 50 percent for the average worker, the difference being accounted for by the decline in the proportion of workers in the poorer jobs, such as farm labor. Prices had fallen slightly during the two decades and the quality of the goods, for example, food products, clothing, and houses, had on the whole improved. The foundation of the first cooperative wholesale society to serve cooperative stores in the north of England was an event of 1863 which, like the foundation of the Trades Union Congress a few years later, showed that a large element among the workers could now stand firmly on its own feet.

There is, however, a less rosy side to the picture. The so-called golden age of English farming, the period since the repeal of the Corn Laws in which prices were still remunerative and rising industrial wages encouraged mass consumption, had brought very little advance to the farm laborer; in 1871 trade unionism made a fresh start among them, but by the end of the decade it was to subside into disaster. Even worse was the plight of the unskilled, the underemployed, and the unemployable at the base of the industrial pyramid in London, Glasgow, and other large cities. Though no calculation of their numbers had yet been attempted, the work of individual philanthropists, like Shaftesbury and Barnardo, of city missions, and of the Charity Organization Society lit up a few dark corners well enough to show that there were many more; the 30 percent below the poverty line in the London of the eighties quite possibly represents an improvement upon conditions in 1871.

In another sense, too, mid-Victorian Britain was a land of contrasts. The Royal Navy patrolled and controlled all the chief sea routes of the world, but Britain's wealth and strength did not, on the whole, make her a bellicose or disturbing force in the eyes of other powers. In spite of Palmerston's moments of braggadocio, British foreign policy always took account of commercial interests, which engendered a love of peace. The efforts to preach the gospel of free trade, which reached their climax in the Cobden-Chevalier treaty with France, were not designed to secure a British manufacturing monopoly but to achieve a lasting international harmony. Nevertheless, this was also a period when the British outlook on the world scene was complacent to a degree, and for reasons, which often created antagonism.

Britain's enormous relative prosperity resulted in part, it was true, from the fact that other nations dissipated their energies to a far greater extent in internal and external conflicts. But she prospered more particularly because of a well-established technological lead, as the next chapter will show, and because she had convenient access to what were then the essential raw materials of industry, among them coal. In addition, Britain had evolved through a process of trial and error commercial policies which accorded with her commercial interests. The element of temporary good fortune in all this was all too frequently ignored and an unworthy emphasis laid upon British piety, capacity for hard work, and other virtues associated with their island race. Hence she maintained a sense of separateness from the whole outside world and superiority to it—an attitude which was to prove a serious obstacle to Britain's foreign relations long after the strength derived from her industrial leadership had begun to decline.

Reading List: Chapter 7

Somervell, D. C., *English Thought in the Nineteenth Century* (1928), pp. 1–59. Background to the 1815–1832 period.

Hammond, J. L., and B., *The Bleak Age* (rev. ed., 1947), chs. 7, 10, 12. The new poor law, chartism, public health agitation.

The New Cambridge Modern History, vol. X (1960), ch. 13. Britain and the Empire from 1830 to 1870.

Trevelyan, G. M., *Illustrated English Social History*, vol. IV, *The Nineteenth Century* (1952), chs. 1–3.

Kitson Clark, G. S. R., "The Repeal of the Corn Laws and the Politics of the Forties," *Economic History Review*, 2nd series, vol. IV (1951), no. 1.

Briggs, Asa, "Cobden and Bright," *History Today*, vol. VII (1957), no. 8.

———, *Victorian People* (1954), ch. 2. "The Crystal Palace and the Men of 1851."

Taylor, A. J., "Progress and Poverty in Britain Between 1780 and 1850," *History*, vol. XLV (1960), no. 153.

Woodward, E. L., *The Age of Reform, 1815–1870* (2nd ed., 1962), Bk. I, ch. 3. Chartism and factory legislation. Bk. II, ch. 3. The Eastern question and the Crimean War.

Strachey, L., *Queen Victoria* (1921), chs. 4–6. Her married life.

Hammond, J. L., and Foot, M. R. D., *Gladstone and Liberalism* (1953), chs. 7–8. Gladstone in the 1860's.

Briggs, Asa, *The Age of Improvement* (1958), chs. 9–10. "Victorianism"; setting of the Reform Act of 1867.

Chapter 8

The Industrial Revolution
in Europe to 1871

Conditions in 1815
Economic Development, 1815–1850
Economic Development, 1850–1871
Armaments
Social Consequences of Technological Change
The Life of the Masses

■ CONDITIONS IN 1815

Two generations separate Waterloo from Sedan, the England of the Regency and the Luddites from that of Gladstonian Liberalism and the first board schools, the Europe of Metternich and Talleyrand from that of Bismarck and Gambetta. After a period of seeming inertia, a series of great political upheavals brought Europe by 1871 to a condition of equilibrium which was not seriously disturbed again until 1914. The political events of the 1850's and 1860's are therefore seen readily as milestones of history. But the technological changes of the same half century have often been regarded virtually as an aspect of the history of Britain, "the workshop of the world," and their place in the development of Europe as a whole treated as a matter of minor importance, with the excuse that the industrial growth of the period after 1871 is after all far more widespread and dramatic. The present chapter seeks to redress the

214

SIGNIFICANT EVENTS

1816	Davy safety lamp
1822, 1830	Power loom and self-acting mule perfected by Roberts
1825	Stockton-Darlington railway opened
1829	Stephensons' *Rocket*
1838	Steamer crossings of Atlantic in both directions established
	Electric telegraph installed on railway
1839	Daguerre's photographic process
1840	Liebig's *Chemistry in Relation to Agriculture*
1845	Heilmann's comb for manufacture of yarn
1851	Dover-Calais cable established
1856	Bessemer steel
	Perkin's first aniline dye
1861	Solvay's soda-making process
1866	Nobel's dynamite
	Siemens-Martin open-hearth steel
1869	Suez Canal opened

balance by tracing the progress which had been made since 1815 on the Continent as well as in Britain, progress without which the 50 percent growth of population in this period would have imposed an intolerable strain, progress which laid an indispensable foundation for later achievements, and which was of the utmost importance for the better known political changes of its own era.

If we take our stand once more at the year 1815, we see that this material progress is also remarkable because of its unpromising start. For more than two decades the normal course of economic development had been affected by virtually incessant warfare—a serious drain on manpower and other resources, a distraction to inventors forced to work for temporary military purposes, and a hindrance to trade. This had to be diverted from its normal channels to narrower and temporary ones, so as to circumvent the rival blockades of Napoleon and his enemies. Even in Britain, where the war had given a big though intermittent stimulus to the transoceanic trades, which were closed to her enemies, the position in 1815 seemed to underline the ominous warnings given by Malthus.[1] During the decade following the first census (1801), her population had grown by one-seventh, so it was not unreasonable to look forward to a future dominated by pressure of population against subsistence, to be relieved chiefly by what Malthus had called positive checks—

> unwholesome occupations, severe labor and exposure to the seasons, extreme poverty, bad nursing of children, large taxes, excesses of all kinds, the whole train of common diseases and epidemics, wars, plague, and famine.

Of Europe's 200,000,000 inhabitants, at least three-quarters still obtained their living directly from the soil. The proportion was highest in the great plains of central and eastern Europe, which lacked large-scale industries and big commercial centers, and lowest—apart from Belgium—in England. Nevertheless, the rapid advance of the enclosure movement during the war and the well-established leadership of landlords interested in scientific farming gave Britain at this time a clear superiority in agricultural techniques. The use of ploughs and other implements of all-iron construction, resort to the seed drill and horse hoe, the substitution of root crops and clover for fallowing, and selective breeding of cattle were all well-established practices in England and the Scottish lowlands. In France, on the other hand, the wide diffusion of land ownership, which had been one of the most immediate and most lasting results of the Revolution of 1789, placed the two obstacles of peasant conservatism and peasant poverty in the way of agricultural progress. The cultivation of the sugar beet had been introduced by Napoleon to counter British blockade measures; in general, his prefects had pressed for more efficient cropping—but that is roughly all. Outside France the same period had seen the decline of serfdom as a result either of French influence or—as in the case of Prussia—of the desire to build up the national resistance to France. In Germany improvements may be dated from the publication in 1798–1800 of the *Introduction to the Knowledge of English Agriculture* by Albrecht Thaer, a Hanoverian who became a professor at Berlin. But in 1815 even the Junkers of Brandenburg and East Prussia lacked the capital to make use of the new knowledge, and they alone had the consolidated farms to which it could be applied. Though the planting of sugar beet had made some progress in Germany, as in France, the only respect in which

---

1. 1766–1834. A clergyman and professor, who published the first edition of his *Essay on the Principle of Population* in 1798 and an enlarged version in 1805. His assertion that population tends to increase faster than the means of subsistence has never been effectively challenged, though the spread of the practice of birth-control has made the danger less immediate than he supposed. Malthus's views helped to make economics the "dismal science," and were cited as proof for the theory that wages could not permanently rise above subsistence level.

Germany was definitely ahead of French agricultural practice was in the more widespread cultivation and consumption of the potato: by 1831 it was used, for instance, in more than half the distilleries of Prussia.

As regards industry, the dominant fact is of course the lead which Britain had gained over France during a long succession of wars. The French had lost nearly all their colonies and other trade connections overseas. At the moment when the cotton manufacture surged ahead of other textiles to make the fortunes of the English, the French were cut off from supplies of raw material. Internal conditions had also proved unfavorable to the growth of French industry. The great chemist, Lavoisier, was executed during the Reign of Terror; Leblanc, who invented the first process for manufacturing soda from common salt, was driven to commit suicide in 1806; a couple of years earlier, Lebon, the pioneer of gaslighting, had been murdered by robbers in the Champs Elysées. The work of Jacquard, whom Napoleon brought to Paris from Lyons to develop his loom—an early example of automation—is one of the few clear cases in which any lasting stimulus was given to an economic development in France during the period of maximum French ascendancy in Europe. It is true that coke smelting of iron was introduced at Le Creusot in 1810, and a little steam spinning was begun in Alsace. But it was only in Belgium, during the period when it formed part of the French Empire, that coal mining, iron founding, machine making, and the use of steam power were being developed— chiefly by an English expatriate—on a scale comparable to what was being done on the other side of the Channel.

Britain by 1815 had wrested from France a leadership which she was to keep until the last quarter of the century. But the degree of industrialization in Britain seemed great chiefly by comparison. In the field of textiles, cotton spinning was the factory industry par excellence, and yet even here more than half the mills were turned by water power and the weaving of the spun yarn into cotton cloth, now the principal British export, was still done mainly by hand looms without benefit of any kind of power. In iron the general adoption of the coke-smelting and puddling processes, for which Britain possessed suitably located coal supplies of adequate quality, had put her far ahead of her former rivals, Russia and Sweden. Britain had also developed two forward-looking skills—the making of machine tools, such as Maudslay's all-metal lathe with slide rest, and interchangeable-part manufacture, the economies of which had been organized to meet the Royal Navy's needs for pulley blocks during the war. Nevertheless, in 1815 the population of Britain was still two-thirds rural; many even of her export industries depended, as the potteries did, upon cheap raw materials, cheap labor, and artisan skill for their success; wood was as yet pre- ferred to iron for many structural purposes, including shipbuilding; and much

BUILDING THE MONT CENIS TUNNEL. Constructed between 1857 and 1871, and nearly eight miles long, this first of the great European mountain tunnels illustrates the cooperative work of French and Italian engineers.

less steam power was used than water and wind power, to say nothing of the man power and animal power expended as from time immemorial in field labor and transport.

The physical and commercial conditions affecting transportation in Europe are closely interrelated. The development of canals and hard-surfaced turnpike roads in Britain toward the end of the eighteenth century had been occasioned by the growth of commercial interests, but an added incentive was given by the total absence of internal customs barriers. Similarly, the canals, and more especially the roads of the Continent, benefited from the economic as well as the military needs of the Napoleonic Empire: fourteen imperial highways radiated from Paris, routes through the Alps were reconstructed, and the great St. Quentin canal was built to link Belgium with Paris and Le Havre. In 1815, accordingly, Europe was in a position to improve its internal communications, in so far as the return to legitimist principles and petty sovereignties might permit, and every such improvement would provide a much-needed stimulus to commerce. Sea-borne trade would in any case cease to be virtually a British monopoly, as it had been during the war, when London built its first extensive system of docks. The steamboat, which had made its first appearance on the Clyde and the Hudson, was ready to attempt the shorter sea passages. In due time the possibility of speedier communication between Europe and the outer world would provide the greatest commercial stimulus of all.

■ ECONOMIC DEVELOPMENT, 1815–1850

Economic history in general, and technological history in particular, seldom fit neatly into the history of political units, such as nation-states, or of political periods as defined by reigns, constitutions, or even wars. Broadly speaking, however, the character of the industrial development of modern Europe may be seen to change at mid-century. Before then the story was mainly one of British technical supremacy and the slow diffusion over the Continent of practices which had been begun and had first proved their worth on the other side of the English Channel. The Great Exhibition of 1851 marked the climax of this. Then followed two decades in which an immensely prosperous Britain nevertheless began to be overtaken by her Continental rivals in the spheres of inventiveness and organization, the first step in the process by which in much later decades they were eventually to overtake her in prosperity. Meanwhile, the commercial and financial preponderance of Britain produced the trend toward world free trade, which was characteristic of the 1850's and 1860's— before the growing international economic rivalries became really acute.

Even in Britain, which had experienced no invasion, no occupation, and no final defeat, the first years of peace were years of trade depression and social distress. They were marked by a revival of the machine-wrecking movement known as Luddism and culminated in the Peterloo massacre at Manchester in August, 1819—two months after a professional magistrate had reported, there in the very center of the cotton industry, that "the distresses of the laboring classes are great beyond all expression."[2] But in the following decade Huskisson's efforts to stimulate trade by tariff reforms were accompanied by big technical advances in each of the four main branches of economic activity in which the British of the preceding generation had successfully established a lead. The cotton industry obtained its first fully satisfactory power loom and the self-acting mule for spinning, perfected by Richard Roberts in 1822 and 1830, respectively; these confirmed Lancashire in its position in the making both of textiles and of textile machinery. The iron industry, which had also suffered a depression with the fall in munitions requirements in 1815, received a fillip through Neilson's invention of the hot blast, which enabled coal to be substituted for coke, with big resultant economies in smelting. Yet the total output of coal approximately doubled in the twenty years after the invention was made in 1829. Progress in agriculture is harder to determine, but the introduction of the threshing machine, a cause of grave distress to the ill-used farm laborer of southeast England in 1830, helped to achieve a noteworthy economy. For the amount of

2. See p. 191.

wheat grown almost kept pace with the rise of population during this period, while the quantity of labor employed remained roughly constant.

More important than any of these changes, however, was the great invention which was to transform both the speed and the cost of inland transportation. The spread of the macadamized road made the 1820's the golden age of the English mailcoach, even though its average speed of ten miles per hour was available only for a restricted number of passengers, plus the letters and other light packages for which the system had originally been designed. Canals were still increasing, though less in England than on the north European plain; they reduced the cost of conveyance for heavy goods by at least 50 percent but were very slow. On estuaries, lakes, and short sea crossings, such as the Strait of Dover, the paddle-wheel steamer was beginning to be important; in 1822 an English firm constructed the first steamship of iron, for service on the Seine. But the key event was the introduction to the railway, a device which had been employed for centuries to facilitate the transport of coal, of the locomotive steam engine. The fact that the iron wheel would not slip unduly in contact with an iron rail had been demonstrated as early as 1804, but the two characteristic features—a multitubular boiler and a device for turning the exhaust steam into the chimney—first became effective in the Stephensons' *Rocket* of 1829. Though George Stephenson had already made use of locomotive engines on the Stockton-Darlington coal railway in 1825, it is the opening of the Liverpool and Manchester railway in 1830, and its successful conveyance of passengers in large numbers and at speeds of more than thirty miles per hour, which marks the start of the railway age.

By 1850 the British main-line railways had either been built or were being built, whereas on the Continent only Belgium, being well supplied with iron and keenly interested in transit traffic, had an effective network in existence— her Malines railway of 1835 in fact preceded any of the British main lines. The effect of Britain's leadership in this great development was to give direct stimulus to the British iron and machine-making industries through work for British and foreign railways, and an indirect stimulus to most other industries by cutting transport costs for raw materials and finished products alike. In 1840 one-third of the foreign trade of the world was British; Peel's tariff reductions of 1842 and 1845 and his repeal of the Corn Laws in 1846 made it still easier for foreign countries to sell to Britain—and therefore to buy from her. Of British inventions during these two decades James Nasmyth's steam hammer was perhaps the most significant, as an outstanding example of the general development of machine tools, both powerful and accurate, by such men as Sir Joseph Whitworth, the first machine-tool manufacturer, who had twenty-three devices at the Exhibition in 1851. Between 1830 and 1848 the output of iron in Great Britain trebled; it went into buildings, bridges, and armaments; to an increasing extent into ships and their equipment, including the new screw-propeller; and into the innumerable kinds of tools which enabled the hand labor of the coal miner and the agriculturist, for instance, to keep pace with the other needs of an Age of Iron. The supply of foodstuffs might, indeed, have failed but for two other advances made at this period. Field drains were one of many new products now made by machinery, which meant improved yields from increased areas of arable land; and, with the manufacture of superphosphate, Britain also pioneered the large-scale use of artificial fertilizers.

In the meantime the possibilities for transferring British techniques to the Continent had increased. Although the statutory ban on the movement of artisans and machinery into foreign countries had never been wholly effective, even during the Napoleonic Wars, the repeal of the laws, as regards migration of artisans in 1824 and as regards export of machinery in 1843, made such movement easier. Thus in 1825 there were believed to be fifteen thousand British workers employed in France. The repeal of the Corn Laws in 1846 and of the Navigation Laws in 1849 virtually completed a process which by encouraging imports to Britain, also encouraged exports from Britain. As the peoples of the Continent thus became familiar with the new machine-made goods, they soon sought to make them for themselves, initially with the help of British engines and machinery. In addition to factory equipment of all kinds, Britain was a great supplier of railway material to the awakening Continent. Carriages, rails, and locomotives were all made in England, with considerable economies resulting from experience and large-scale production, and British entrepreneurs were prepared to supply a large part of the skilled labor force needed to build the actual railway lines.

But we must not exaggerate. Even in their chosen field of textiles, British inventors did not have it all their own way. Ring spinning, which was to predominate in the later part of the century, had already been invented in New England, and a satisfactory mechanical comb, for which the worsted industry had been seeking since Cartwright made his first attempt in 1790, was mainly developed by Frenchmen in Alsace. The French also were the first to introduce the turbine, though its main importance came when hydroelectricity began to be generated on a big scale toward 1900. By 1849 the then little-known Prussian firm of Krupp was beginning to experiment with the use of cast steel in armaments manufacture, but the basic German achievement so far was in chemistry, the serious application of which to agriculture dates from Liebig's treatise of 1840.

An economic survey of Europe in 1851 would perhaps have treated industrial inventiveness as a chance phenomenon in the light of the remarkable American exhibits such as the McCormick harvester, which occasioned great surprise when shown in that year at the Crystal Palace. But there were three

THE "GREAT TRANSEPT" OF THE CRYSTAL PALACE, LONDON, ON OPENING DAY, MAY, 1851. On the dais Queen Victoria receives the Commissioners for the Exhibition.

kinds of progress receiving ready acknowledgment. One was progress in agriculture. The Junkers of eastern Germany were spreading information among themselves by the organization of shows, societies, and colleges, with the result that their technical practice was on a level with the English, but their bookkeeping and—if Bismarck's activities in 1839–1847 are a fair specimen—their energy were superior. In France, too, each decade is believed to have brought an extension of the tilled area and an improvement in the uses to which it was put, partly because a society of free men, owning the land they worked, tended ultimately toward improvement, even if the rate at which new ideas spread was often painfully slow. More specifically, there was the incentive given by transport improvements—first, the completion of the Napoleonic highroads and a big program of canal works; then, under a law of 1836, the construction of by-roads opening up the remoter countryside; and finally, during the 1840's, the appearance of the first important railways, linking the peasant as never before with his best market in the large town.

Second, from the first day of 1834 onward a large part of central Europe had received an important economic stimulus from the German *Zollverein*. A fifteen-year struggle had resulted from the exacerbation of petty rivalries, as the Prussian tariff of 1818 was seen to threaten the jealously guarded rights of her small neighbors. The upshot was the establishment of a free-trade area with a population equal to that of the United Kingdom, a market for which traders had long waited. In retrospect this was a memorable moment:

> Long trains of wagons stood on the highroads, which till then had been cut up by tax barriers. At the stroke of midnight every turnpike was thrown open, and amid cheers the wagons hastened over the boundaries, which they could thenceforward cross in perfect freedom. Everyone felt that a great object had been attained.[3]

The horse-drawn wagons struggling along uneven highroads began to give place to railways—the first short stretch completed in 1835—which had grown to more than 3,500 miles by mid-century. The increased ease of exchange between the food-producing areas of the east and the manufacturing districts of the Rhineland and Saxony stimulated improvements of technique in both regions, and the attraction of the larger internal market in general encouraged the smaller states to specialize. For political reasons Germans later on tended to look back and attribute all this to the *Zollverein*, though other factors certainly helped, and some manufacturers even claimed that the low external tariff precluded them from deriving reasonable advantages from the *Zollverein* market. This view on behalf of infant industries in need of temporary protection was argued by Friedrich List, who had spent an observant period of exile in the United States, in his *National System of Political Economy*, published in 1841. But his protectionist arguments did not win wide acceptance until a later generation. With the firm establishment and maintenance of a low-tariff customs union, Germany began to emerge as an economic force in modern Europe.

Third, we may notice the growing industrialization of France. At mid-century, Belgium, with its big resources in coal and iron, well-established engineering works (from which much machinery was sent into Germany and other parts of the Continent), and a total of more than 400,000 industrial workers in a population not greatly exceeding 4,000,000, was the only country on the Continent of which the development was comparable with that of Britain. But the smallness of Belgium set a limit to the significance of the Belgian achievement, whereas the changes in France influenced the whole Continent. The Industrial Revolution had come to France in the later years of the restored Bourbon monarchy and gathered impetus all through the reign of Louis Philippe, when, for nearly two decades, government by the middle class for the middle class prevailed. When the revolutions of 1848 made a temporary interruption, France had as many steam engines as the rest of the Continent combined, most of which served the highly flourishing textile industries, and Paris with its 400,000 workers had become the world's largest manufacturing city, though

3. Recollections of Gustav Fischer, published in a German economic annual in 1865, quoted by W. O. HENDERSON, *The Zollverein* (1939), p. 94.

dependent on domestic rather than factory employment. France excelled, as one might expect, in industries involving an element of taste, as was the case with many of her glass, porcelain, and paper manufactures; she also had important inventions in matchmaking, galvanization, and daguerrotype photography.

The economic growth of France suffered, however, from one marked deficiency. In railway development she lagged surprisingly far behind, a circumstance which seems to have been due partly to financial intrigues in the Chambers, even worse than those which vexed the committee rooms of the House of Commons in England; partly to strict conditions imposed on private enterprise by the government engineers; and partly to the fact that she had relatively little heavy industry to stimulate the demand for rail transport. The first locomotive in France ran over a line linking the St. Etienne coalfield with Lyons in 1832, but when a suburban railway for Paris was being authorized three years later Thiers still saw fit to describe it as a toy which would "never carry a passenger or a package." Although a general plan for seven main lines to radiate from Paris was approved in 1842, France emerged from the banking and financial crisis of the revolutionary years 1848–1850 with a total of about two thousand miles of railway actually in operation—about one-third of the length of those which then served the neighboring island.

■ ECONOMIC DEVELOPMENT, 1850–1871

At first sight the two eventful decades which stretch from the Great Exhibition of 1851, with the hopes that it inspired for an era of world peace and world free trade, to the inauguration of the German Empire at Versailles in 1871 were highly propitious to British industry and commerce. When the electric cable linked London with Paris in 1851 and New York in 1866, the world market which was then firmly established was certainly a market centering on London, for Britain was concerned in only one of the five European wars of the period, and the American Civil War diverted into other fields the energies which had built up the only mercantile marine which was a serious rival. Moreover, two big new developments in transport gave an enormous fillip to the British shipyards. One was the substitution of iron for wood as a shipbuilding material, which became general in the 1860's; the other was the long-delayed triumph of the steamship, which resulted partly from the opening of the Suez Canal (not navigable by sail) in 1869, and also from the spread at about the same date of the more economical compound engine, which left enough space for profit-earning cargo. Not only so, but steamships presented Britain with a most profitable market for coal, mined in coastal areas and a readily salable return cargo for ships from any country. In 1870 one half of all the coal mined anywhere in the world was mined in Britain. There was also a well-established market for British textile machinery, locomotives, and engineering products of

DEPARTURE OF THE "GREAT WESTERN" FROM BRISTOL FOR NEW YORK IN 1838. This voyage marks the inauguration of the first regular transatlantic service by big steamship. The crossing took two weeks.

all kinds, the result of her pioneer past. These might be expected to cushion her against the shock as foreign countries developed their own manufactures of the simpler products, such as cotton cloth or replacements of rails for the permanent way.

Such circumstances did in fact make these decades uniquely prosperous, for even with a rapidly rising population the value of British exports went up by 140 percent per capita. But by 1871 it was clear that the introduction of cheap steel, which was the biggest technical advance of the age, would tend to reduce the competitive advantages of British technology. In 1856, with the needs of British ordnance for the Crimean War as the incentive, Henry Bessemer invented his converter, in which a blast of air blown through the molten pig iron was found to be capable of burning out the carbon, and which for the first time made it possible to produce steel in quantity. The result was that, while Britain's iron output nearly trebled between 1850 and 1870, her output of steel grew three times as fast. It is significant, however, that the first big improvements to the Bessemer process were made only a couple of years later in Sweden, and that within another decade an alternative method, which was more economical and more exact, had been developed with French collaboration by Wilhelm von Siemens, a German naturalized in Britain. This open-hearth process eventually replaced Bessemer's even in Britain. Moreover, Britain possessed only limited quantities of the nonphosphoric iron ores to which alone these new processes were applicable; pending further changes, she became largely dependent on Spanish and Swedish ore. Meanwhile France had at last made the difficult change from charcoal smelting to coke smelting—difficult not only because she lacked coal but because much of the iron ore lay in tempting proximity to woodland areas—and by 1869 was producing a million tons of wrought iron and steel. This was only one-fifth of British production, but it still exceeded the German.

Steel rails, many times more durable than those of iron, came into widespread use in the 1870's, by which time the railway network in Europe had been enormously extended. Under the Second Empire the French largely replaced the British, whose investments in this respect went farther afield, as the chief European railway promoters. Since their own main lines were substantially completed by 1860, the schemes of the following decade included that which linked France with Italy by the Mont Cenis tunnel through the Alps. French capital, made available through the Crédit Mobilier, and French engineers, trained in the Ecole Polytechnique, also played a leading role in constructing the main lines, not only of Italy but throughout the Austrian Empire, in Switzerland, Spain, and even Russia, where a total length of 1000 miles was fully quadrupled between 1860 and 1870. Germany during the same period, but independently of France, increased her railway network from 3600 to 12,000 miles, and its efficiency was amply demonstrated in the wars of 1866 and 1870–1871. In Europe as a whole the increase was from 14,000 to 65,000 miles, with important consequences for every aspect of civil life.

This was the quarter century in which the concentration of landownership reached its maximum, and the high-quality farming made possible by heavy capital expenditure spread rapidly from England to the Continent. Imports of guano and the discovery of potassium salt deposits assisted the provision of crop fertilizers; cattle breeding, reforestation, and rotation of crops were placed on a more scientific basis; in Germany, especially, there was a rapid increase in the use of machinery. For a time disease, which played havoc with the French silkworm industry in the 1850's, the French vineyards in the 1860's, and the cattle farming of England in 1868, seemed to be the only hazard which European agriculture had still to face. But this was before the flood of American wheat came in. Pending the development of the American Middle West, the Black Earth belt of southern Russia provided the reserve resources which enabled a mounting population to be fed: in the three decades up to 1870 Russian agricultural exports trebled. The railways, which were largely instrumental in causing urban areas to grow, brought to them not only the grain but also meat and dairy produce from farms within striking distance of a town. By facilitating the conveyance of heavy materials where carriage by water remained impracticable—canals were still being built, particularly as links between important rivers—the railways also had much to do with the increased amenities of town life in the way of better building construction and better drainage, more comfortable furniture, and more adequate supplies of winter fuel.

It may be convenient at this point to set the growth of the railways side by side with that of the mercantile marine. Taken together, they illustrate the economic development of the three western powers, including the slow progress of steam shipping, already noted.

GROWTH OF TRANSPORT, 1850–1870

LENGTH OF RAILWAYS (miles)		QUANTITY OF SHIPPING (thousands of tons)	
1850	1870	1850	1870
Britain 6,562	15,312	3,565 (168 steam)	5,691 (1,113 steam)
France 1,875	10,937	688 (14 steam)	1,072 (154 steam)
Germany 3,750[4]	12,187[4]		982 (82 steam)

The stimulus of the railways also interacted with the movement toward free trade, which is characteristic of the period that has the Cobden-Chevalier treaty at its mid-point, to bring about the extension of the use of steam power far beyond the textile, iron, and other metalworking industries which had been its main users hitherto. France, for example, used five times as much steam power in 1870 as in 1850. In Britain its uses extended to steam ploughing, steam printing with the rotary press introduced from Philadelphia, and steam rolling for road surfaces. With the big improvement in the quality of lubricants, the growing acceptance of the American system of manufacture with interchangeable parts (neglected in Britain after the end of the French Wars), and the greater precision of machine tools—in 1856 Whitworth was able to measure to a millionth of an inch—there seemed no obvious limit to the possibilities of replacing hand work by machine work and man power by steam power.

Already one minor use of the steam engine was for the generation of electricity by means of the dynamo, which had been employed in England as early as 1857 to supply arc lamps for lighthouses. So far the main importance of electricity had been its use in the electric telegraph, which was predominantly an English invention. But as the time drew near when it would have wide importance as a source of light, heat, and power, the main impetus to research in applied electricity was given by brilliant students of other nationalities, such as the German brothers, Wilhelm and Ernst von Siemens. Other examples of the same trend are the first development of ferroconcrete for building and the first unrewarding attempts to make practical use of the newly recognized metal, aluminum, both of which were pioneered by subjects of Napoleon III. Still more significant was the first introduction of synthetic dyes, which resulted from the discovery of aniline purple, derived from coal tar, by the eighteen-year-old London student, W. H. Perkin, in 1856. Other synthetic dyes were discovered in the next few years by English, French, and German scientists alike,

4. Area of 1871.

and in 1869 Perkin made his second great discovery, a substitute for madder (the plant source of scarlet), though the Germans anticipated his patent by one day. From then onward, however, the Germans proceeded steadily to make this trade virtually their monopoly. Again, there was a very important Belgian contribution in the invention of the ammonia-soda process by Ernest Solvay, first patented in 1861, which halved the cost of the alkali required in textile, glass, and soap manufactures. Belgium, as we have previously noticed, was the first Continental power to become thoroughly industrialized. Sweden, on the other hand, had waited till mid-century before the increasing demand for timber helped to revive its ancient industrial prosperity. But it was a Swede, Alfred Nobel, whose invention of dynamite in the 1860's, began a new era in the use of explosives in ore mining and building construction.

■ ARMAMENTS

The technical revolution which occurred between 1815 and 1871 had a marked effect on the art of war, where every government knew that conservatism might spell disaster. This was even true of navies, in spite of Britain's strong disinclination to innovate, since the old had served her so well and cost her so much. Thus it was left to the Frenchman, Henri Joseph Paixhans, to preach the superior efficacy of a fleet of iron warships, steam driven, and armed with heavy, shell-firing guns, and it was not until after the siege of Sebastopol that his preachings were accepted. In the 1860's the armored iron-clad was developed in Britain and France, with rifled guns firing an elongated cylindrical shell of modern pattern; the British, however, reverted to muzzle-loading in 1865–1881 after some unsatisfactory experiments with breech-loaders. Since there were no battles fought by major fleets in Europe, both Sinope and Lissa being single-squadron affairs, it was left to the Americans to introduce the gun turret which figures in the *Monitor*, though the floating mine and the self-propelled torpedo, respectively, were first produced by the Russians to defend Kronstadt during the Crimean War and by a Scotsman in Austrian service in 1864.

In land warfare technical advances had a greater practical importance, since the major powers were not unevenly matched and the cost of improvements did not yet make it impossible for smaller powers to seek to strengthen their position. To some extent these advances grew directly out of contemporary progress in the arts of peace. Thus the railway between France and Piedmont was completed, except for the tunnel at the Mont Cenis, six months before the war of 1859, in which the railway was used, not only to carry much of the French army into Italy, but also to transfer its main strength to the left flank on the eve of the battle of Magenta. In 1866 the Prussians were able to mobilize along five lines of railway, in 1870 they got 380,000 men into the forward zone in eighteen days—and on both occasions speed played a decisive part in victory. The electric telegraph, too, was used from the Crimean War onward to keep governments in touch with armies, and by 1870 the Prussian army was provided with at least seven field telegraph detachments. The increased strength of building materials, from wrought iron to reinforced concrete and steel, was also reflected in the increased strength of fortresses, such as the fifteen forts built to defend Paris in the 1840's, those at Kronstadt in the sea approaches to St. Petersburg, which was modernized by Todleben after it had done service against the Anglo-French squadron in 1854, or the Austrian improvements in the Quadrilateral.

On land as on sea the mobile artillery, which fortifications were designed to resist, made corresponding progress. The rifling of cannon to ensure greater accuracy of flight, and breech-loading for improved rate of fire, had been the subject of experiment for centuries, and both the Piedmontese and the Prussian armies were trying them out in combination before the outbreak of hostilities in Europe in 1848. At the siege of Sebastopol the British found it necessary to improvise rifling, but from then onward methods were developed of strengthening the metal of the gun barrel, and it became the general practice to rifle it. But breech-loading made slower progress in field artillery, as in naval use. Throughout the 1860's Krupps were supplying it in the guns they sold to the Prussian state or exported, for instance to Russia, but in the war of 1870 the French were still using bronze muzzle-loaders against these cast-steel breech-loaders, which proved the decisive factor in the great artillery battle of Sedan. Yet what was newest and potentially of most importance was the experimental use of the machine gun, the very name of which links the new technology with war. The earliest was the Gatling gun, which was one of the many inventive devices introduced to overpower the less industrialized South in the American Civil War. A much larger version provided the French with their secret weapon in preparation for the war of 1870. Designed to fire up to 125 shots a minute from a position beyond range of ordinary rifle fire, the *mitrailleuse* failed partly because of inexpert handling and partly because it was wrongly placed in forward positions where it could easily be picked off by the Prussian artillery.

Since cavalry could not be mechanized, *l'arme blanche* lost most of its significance as successive improvements in hand firearms enabled a disciplined body of infantry to halt the bravest charge. Those improvements began with the introduction of the percussion cap just after 1815 and the redesigning of the bullet and cartridge case, completed by mid-century in France. This made breech-loading possible and the use of rifling easier than before. The British army began to manufacture rifles on the American system, the interchangeable parts having been on show at the Exhibition in 1851, but did not introduce a breech-loading mechanism until its value had been clearly shown in the

Austro-Prussian War of 1866. That war was won to a great extent by the needle gun, a breech-loading rifle with which the Prussian army had been re-equipped completely by 1858. Though the firing pin, or "needle," easily went wrong and the range was short, Austrian regiments preparing to discharge their muzzle-loaders offered a standing target to the Prussian taking aim from prone positions behind cover. By 1870, however, the French had a new breech-loading rifle, the *chassepot*, which outranged the needle gun by several hundred yards. It had served their turn against the Garibaldians at Mentana, but neither Bazaine nor MacMahon proved capable of maneuvering with sufficient speed to reap the advantage before the Prussian artillery could intervene. One result of the Franco-Prussian War was to give a great impetus to the adoption of conscription, since it was a conscript army that had triumphed, and the quality of new infantry weapons—such as the British Martini-Henry rifle of 1872—therefore became of greater importance than ever.

■ SOCIAL CONSEQUENCES OF TECHNOLOGICAL CHANGE

The munitions of war thus briefly described differed from all the other products of the Industrial Revolution in the mode of their distribution, which was clearly a function of government. Everything else was being distributed through a price mechanism, with which fluctuations in demand between boom and depression periods are clearly associated. The fact that no desperate general conflict developed between the have-nots and the haves suggests that the increase of production at least kept pace with the increase in population. However, to be able to judge the value to human society of the change in material provision between 1815 and 1871 we need to go further, and must consider how the distribution of goods was effected as among the different classes of European society.

There seems to be no reason to doubt that ruling families and the territorial nobility and aristocracy prospered everywhere. The pressure of population increased the value of their estates, because it paid to develop the land more intensively for maximum food production. Wherever industry grew up or towns expanded, rent rolls were increased and immense profits accrued from mining royalties. Many of the largest English country seats, for example, date from this period, and their surviving contents bear witness to a profuse and often tasteless luxury. The great industrial entrepreneurs, whose profits far exceeded the amount that could be ploughed back into the business, and the bankers and other financial middlemen who largely dictated the direction of industrial growth, likewise tended to spend lavishly to demonstrate their solidity and solvency. George Hudson, the English railway king, a few years before his downfall was the owner of three country mansions and one of the most sumptuous town houses in London. It is even suggested that heavy Victorian furniture, typically in mahogany, enjoyed its popularity because its costliness conferred status in an age when ancient lineage was no longer the one thing needful in good society. Paris, too, under the Second Empire catered to a lavishly spending international plutocracy such as Europe had never seen before.

"Middle class" is a term that escapes positive definition, but it is here used to include all grades of society between the one described above and the wage earner or his self-employed counterpart. This class increased more rapidly than the population as a whole: officials, lawyers, accountants, commercial travelers, shopkeepers, and the army of clerks and assistants proliferated as the range and complexity of large-scale industry increased. This class would also include the labor-employing tenant farmer of England and the Continental peasant of equal status, who shared in some degree in the prosperity which the big landowner derived from the demand for food. But for the most part its activities were not directly productive. In status and spending power, members of the middle class were normally superior to the workers, while some of the professional members might in these respects approach the level of the aristocracy. Almost by definition the whole of this class lived at something above the subsistence level. They enjoyed a rising standard of diet and domestic comfort, and along with this they had a variable margin for expenditure on education and cultural interests, which might range from the purchase of a fine private library or valuable pictures to the acquisition of a secondhand cottage piano or a subscription to a newspaper.

At the outset of the industrial changes the burden of saving had fallen most heavily upon the entrepreneur and his family; his standard of life was often prevented from rising because it was only through personal savings that he could finance expansion. But legal changes were made, notably the *société en commandite*, which spread across Europe from Napoleonic France, and the British limited liability company, introduced by degrees in the 1840's and 1850's, to enable persons to invest savings without accepting the financial responsibilities of partnership. This took the burden of saving off the shoulders of the factory owner, who could allow his standard of living to rise to suit his taste, which was often luxurious. It also led to the growth of the *rentier* class, people whose income came from ownership of investments, sending their money wherever interest rates were highest—from France to Spain and Russia, from Britain to America, India, and the colonies. This created an important additional spending power for a section of the European middle class.

Despite such enlargement of the middle class, the greater part of the population in every country consisted of many stratified categories of workers. Dependent upon manual skills or other bodily effort to secure their livelihood, they varied greatly in every other respect as between occupations, districts, and states. Until 1848 there was virtual serfdom in the Austrian Empire, until 1861 full serfdom in Russia, and a decade later the emancipation of the peasant from the economic burdens of the old feudal order had only just been completed in Prussia and was far from complete in Bavaria. Again, the ban on trade unionism, which was lifted in Britain in 1824, lasted until 1846 in Sweden, 1864 in France, and 1866 in Belgium. Nevertheless, it is possible to draw a broad distinction between the artisan and small peasant proprietor or tenant, whose land was fully viable, and the mass of laborers and occupants of farm fragments, who were, and commonly knew themselves to be, at the broad base of the social pyramid. In Victorian England the dividing line was often provided by the concept of respectability—people who kept up appearances of godliness and cleanliness could usually also keep up their pride and courage by looking at others who were recognizably their inferiors.

The growth of population and industry undoubtedly lifted many peasant farmers from the rut of subsistence agriculture to a place in a money economy, so that by 1870 urban manufactures of furniture and clothing were raising the standard of rural life in most areas, even if aesthetic traditions suffered. The position of the industrial craftsman does not lend itself so easily to generalization. On the one hand, the decline of the gilds and of compulsory apprenticeship left the field open to rigorous competition, including the competition of factory products, against which the hand loom weavers (for example) fought a long and losing battle in country after country. On the other hand, such statistics as are available show that the wages of skilled operatives in British factories tended to increase in value, while hours declined and the physical circumstances of their work improved—though the gain might all be lost in the event of a trade depression. In the 1860's, to take the most favorable decade, when real wages for all workers rose on an average by about 15 percent in Britain and about 18 percent in France, it is safe to suppose that skilled workers starting from a relatively high level still made important gains. Further evidence of well-being is provided by the growth of the consumers' cooperative movement in Britain—by 1863 it was strong enough to form its own wholesale society to serve the various shops—and by its beginnings among German artisans through the credit societies organized by Franz Hermann Schulze-Delitzsch. The English trade unions of skilled workers based on the new model of the Amalgamated Society of Engineers, which was formed in 1851, with their high subscription rates and insurance benefits, are a further indication of the existence of an aristocracy of labor.

The benefits provided by such unions commonly included assistance for bona fide emigrants, a reminder of the important part which the New World played in raising the living standards of the Old. By removing trade competitors from the labor market, the lure of the New World helped in raising wage rates.

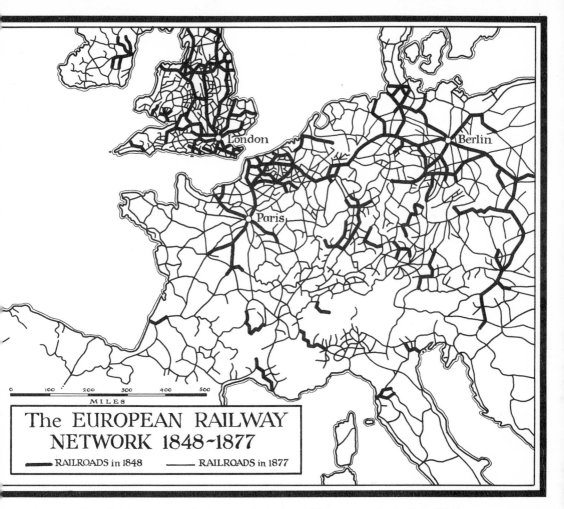

The dramatic mid-century growth of railways is clearly shown. The concentration in Great Britain, northeastern France, Belgium, the Rhineland, Saxony, and northern Italy emphasizes the areas of industrial growth. By 1871 one railway tunnel, the Mont Cenis, has pierced the Alps.

By enabling countless thousands of immigrants to reach a wholly superior standard of living, America tended to incite new wage demands in the homeland. By remittances, which became a considerable factor in impoverished families of Ireland and Italy, the generosity of those who had emigrated increased the purchasing power of those they had left behind.

■ THE LIFE OF THE MASSES

But what benefits had the Industrial Revolution so far conferred upon the proletarian masses—the farm laborers, the domestic servants (who formed the two largest occupational groups in Britain), and the host of unskilled or at least unqualified workers, often of both sexes and nearly all ages, who abounded in the bottom ranks of every industry? Statistically, no answer is obtainable, since money wage rates, their purchasing power, the chances of finding work for all members of a family, and above all the incidence of unemployment varied from year to year and from region to region. There were also important groups which suffered special hardship—the hand loom weavers, who in almost every corner of Europe fought a disastrously long battle against the intrusion of the power loom, and the farm hands in all areas remote from urban industrial influences, even in Great Britain, who were unable to escape from a condition of abject poverty sanctioned by tradition and forced upon them by their isolation and ignorance. The probability is that in the years just after the Napoleonic Wars the average of proletarian earnings fell back toward subsistence level, while between 1830 and 1850 there was some recovery in Britain, owing to increased productivity, but little gain on the Continent. The 1860's, however, were a decade in which, after a period of rapidly rising prices, the purchasing power of wages increased all round, though for the unskilled worker the gain was smaller than the overall figures for Britain and France already quoted. More-over, from 1845 onward the great industrial developments, such as the building of the railways, had undoubtedly decreased the proportion of the population in the less fortunate category of unskilled workers which we are now considering.

In 1848 John Stuart Mill wrote:

> It is questionable if all the mechanical inventions yet made have lightened the day's toil of any human being. They have enabled a greater population to live the same life of drudgery and imprisonment, and an increased number of manu-facturers and others to make fortunes. They have increased the comforts of the middle classes.[5]

Mill allowed these words to stand in successive editions for a quarter of a century, during which wages on the whole rose more than prices, so that by 1870 the increase of comfort—in spite of Mill's assertion—had spread far beyond the middle classes. It is also necessary to qualify in other respects his picture of mechanical inventions as merely enabling more people to live "the same life of drudgery and imprisonment." A truer picture blends light and shade.

In the first place, mechanical inventions were causing more people to live in towns—by 1870 the proportion in Britain was more than one-half urban, in Germany rather more than one-third urban, and in France one-third. This meant exposure to conditions of overcrowding, which brought with it a high rate of infant mortality, typhus, and epidemics of cholera. But such concentra-tion of the population also made remedial action possible. By 1870 some English

5. J. S. MILL, *Principles of Political Economy* (1848), Book IV, ch. 6, p. 2.

towns already had medical officers of health and local housing acts, and the urban death rate had begun to fall; though Continental towns on the whole still had a worse record, they were preparing to follow the British example.

Second, the new working conditions—the congregation of labor in factories, in iron foundries and engineering workshops, and in coal mines— involved notorious evils, such as the exploitation of woman and child labor, a high accident rate, and hours of work rendered more arduous by the discipline of the machine and the overseer. On the other hand, there is plenty of evidence to show that women who spun in their homes and children who were set to scare birds as soon as they could walk, seamen and soldiers, and self-employed craftsmen, had all been exposed in their several ways to similar hardships for centuries. What was most significant was the new possibility of effective remedial action. The Factory Acts of 1833 and 1844, the Coal Mines Act of 1842, and the Ten Hours Acts of 1847 and 1850 were landmarks in history, because these measures, which enormously improved conditions in Britain, provided a pattern for the industrial development of other countries. A French law of 1841 gave much the same protection to factory children as in Britain, except that the efforts made to enforce it did not have the backing of an inspectorate. Prussia had a child-labor law as early as 1839, and inspectors were appointed in 1853, though in Germany, as in France (and America), the biggest improvements came after 1870.

Last, there is the broader issue—to be considered further in the next chapter—of the impact of the industrial changes upon popular culture and enlightenment. Friedrich Engels' *Condition of the Working Class in England*, Louis Blanc's *Histoire de dix ans*, and the speeches of a multitude of social reformers have exposed the cultural desolation of the new industrial areas—few churches, no libraries, no access to unspoiled natural surroundings, and a rigid segregation from the society of other classes. But from William Cobbett onward the reformers tend always to idealize what must usually have been the petty narrowness and sterility of life as lived in the preindustrial village. In the new surroundings numbers gave courage, which led to the growth of trade unions, cooperative societies, and friendly societies, with benefits that gradually penetrated further and further into the proletarian mass. By mid-century associations for mutual improvement, often under church auspices, public libraries, and cheap newspapers were beginning to give a new color to urban life. By 1870, when universal elementary education made its very belated appearance in England, the more advanced systems of Prussia and most of the west European countries had made a superior quality of education one of the features of urban society which was to be of enormous importance for further advance in politics and in culture.

Reading List: Chapter 8

Heaton, H., "The Industrial Revolution," *Encyclopaedia of the Social Sciences*, vol. VIII.

Knowles, L. C. A., *Economic Development in the Nineteenth Century—France, Germany, Russia, and the United States* (1932), pp. 134–47, 211–14 (France); 165–69, 216–18 (Germany); 255–66 (the *Zollverein*).

The New Cambridge Modern History, vol. X (1960), ch. 2. Economic change and growth.

Ashton, T. S., *The Industrial Revolution, 1760–1830* (1948), ch. 6. The course of economic change.

Chambers, J. D., *The Workshop of the World* (1961), ch. 2. Industrial progress in Britain.

Young, G. M. (ed.), *Early Victorian England* (2 vols., 1934), ch. 1. "Work and Wages" (Chapter by J. H. Clapham).

Hammond, J. L., and B., *Lord Shaftesbury* (1923), chs. 2–4. The first Factory Act in Great Britain.

Klemm, F., *History of Western Technology* (1959), part VI. Industrial progress through Continental eyes.

Gallagher, J., and Robinson, R., "The Imperialism of Free Trade," *Economic History Review*, 2nd series, vol. VI (1953–1954), no. 1.

Mumford, L., *The Culture of Cities* (1936), ch. 3. "The Insensate Industrial Town."

———, *Technics and Civilization* (1934), chs. 4–5. A sociological approach to the Industrial Revolution.

Chapter 9

Movements of
Thought and Culture, 1815–1871

A Retrospective Glance: Reaction and Romanticism
The First Great Scientific Advances
Mid-Century Transition to Realism in the Arts
Darwinism, Science, and Life
Science and the Study of Society
Religion, Science, and Social Issues

▓ A RETROSPECTIVE GLANCE: REACTION AND ROMANTICISM

A study of the activities of men living in organized societies leads one to ask many questions which go beyond the conventional topics of politics, economics, diplomacy, and war, for man is not only a doer of deeds, the master (or victim) of events. He is also an artist, tireless in his efforts at aesthetic expression, communicating his thoughts and his emotions to his fellows in every medium: in imaginative literature, in the drama, in painting, in sculpture, in architecture, and in music. Horace called poets the first instructors, and Shelley called them "the unacknowledged legislators of the world." Man is also the observer, the persistent questioner, seeking order and meaning in the phenomena of nature, and determined to extend his control over the world about him thereby to better his physical environment. He is likewise a creature influenced by his sensitiveness to human suffering and injustice, so that again and

238

SIGNIFICANT EVENTS

1817	Ricardo: *Principles of Political Economy*
1819	Géricault: "Raft of the Medusa"
1820	Lamartine: *Meditations*
1830	Berlioz: *Fantastic Symphony*
1830–1833	Lyell: *Principles of Geology*
1833	Ranke's historical seminar founded at Berlin
1847	Helmholtz's law on the conservation of energy
1848	Marx and Engels: *Communist Manifesto*
1857	Flaubert: *Madame Bovary*
1859	Darwin: *Origin of Species*
1862	Hugo: *Les Misérables*
1863	Manet: "Déjeuner sur l'Herbe"
1866	Dostoevsky: *Crime and Punishment*
1869–1876	Wagner: *Ring* cycle

again there have appeared powerful advocates of new political and economic systems. And even as man has been concerned with these matters, so also has he sought to uncover his mysterious past and to probe those deepest realms where religion and philosophy have long occupied themselves with the meaning of life, the nature of reality, and the destiny of man.

The extraordinary richness of European artistic and intellectual life in the nineteenth century demonstrates the vigor with which all these interests were now being pursued. Ideas put forward in many fields were gradually popularized so that they came to be understood and accepted by a steadily widening audience. Thus some examination of these fields will give clues to the attitudes and intellectual interests of a growing public and illustrate developments in social history. Closest attention must be given to the central decades of the nineteenth century, for these constitute the critical period; a later chapter will pursue the subject to the outbreak of the First World War. As a beginning, however, a quick retrospective glance will recall some of the ideas prevalent in the early decades, and give us the necessary point of departure.

Some aspects of what has been called "the revolt against the eighteenth century" have already been suggested.[1] Since the outcome of the Age of Reason had been bloody revolution, those responsible for stemming that revolution quite naturally mistrusted the period of its origins. In contrast to the rationalism, the religious disbelief, the cult of progress, and the assumption of human perfectibility which had marked the eighteenth century, the tendency in the period succeeding the Napoleonic age was to seek a principle of life based less upon reason than upon authority. Custom and tradition would bulwark the cult of stability by which men could live. Organized society, as Edmund Burke had taught, must be regarded not as the mechanical product of man's logical faculties, but rather as the natural, organic product of historical growth. "The roots of the present lie deep in the past," as the English historian, Bishop Stubbs, declared, and the complex layers of human society are what they are because of an altogether natural development. To Metternich, the established order was the natural, and therefore the legitimate, condition of society. Even those early nineteenth-century champions of national unification who sought change argued that the struggle to create a nation-state was to be justified by virtue of the historic forces which had caused people to be what they were.

Much of this outlook can be associated with the term "romanticism," which implies a revolt against the classical traditions of the eighteenth century. Yet the romantic revival is a phenomenon whose protean manifestations are much easier to observe than to define. Some romantics, of whom Shelley, Byron, and Heine are examples, were liberal, revolutionary spirits. Others, like Scott and Wordsworth, were highly conservative in their views of society and politics. Many of the German romantics were converts to Roman Catholicism, a religion to which they were attracted because in addition to being based on authority it seemed to them the embodiment of colorful mystery and medieval splendor. Certainly the romantic fondness for that which was intuitive, emotional, and traditional gave strength to this pervasive cult of authority.

Georg Friedrich Hegel,[2] the great German Idealist philosopher of the romantic age, saw history as the unfolding of God's plan for men. History, he asserted, is not a matter of the crude sequence of events; it is an unceasing *dialectical process*. Any age is governed and made what it is by a dominant idea— the *Zeitgeist*, or spirit of the age. This dominant idea can be said to constitute a

1. See pp. 6–7; 20–25.

2. 1770–1831. On taking his degree, he was reported to be especially deficient in philosophy. He lectured to very small classes at Jena but later held the leading chair of philosophy at Berlin University, of which in 1830 he became rector, teaching that "only the real is rational and only the rational is real." World history falls into three periods, the Oriental, the Classical, and the Germanic, as one people after another embodies the Universal Spirit.

thesis. In time a challenge comes to the established order in the form of a new concept, the *antithesis.* To resolve the conflict of these two there follows a sort of blending and union of opposites, a step forward which is the *synthesis.* The synthesis is at the same time a new thesis which will in turn provoke a new challenge, and so the historical process by which freedom (as Hegel specifically saw it) develops is continuous and endless. These ideas of Hegel, which gave comfort to many liberals, were embodied in his Berlin lectures later published as *The Philosophy of History.* Yet Hegel also argued in his *Philosophy of Right* (1820) that, although the individual seeks to act as a free man, he can only attain this freedom as a member of a strong state. Significantly enough, Hegel took this "strong state" to be his own Prussia.

The romantic revival, especially in literature, is often thought of as a manifold series of protests against the age of reason. It is easy to set the emotional content of Wordsworth's *Prelude* against the cold brilliance of Pope's *Essay on Man.* Admirers of romanticism elevated the heart as against the brain. "A poet," Chateaubriand had written in his *Genius of Christianity,* "by means of a few verses lives to the remotest posterity, immortalizes his age, and transmits to future times those whom he deigns to celebrate in his compositions; the man of science, scarcely known during his lifetime, is forgotten the day after his death." These admirers of romanticism set the richly colored *Waverley Novels* of Sir Walter Scott, or Victor Hugo's *Les Misérables,* against the altogether different eighteenth-century products of Fielding or Smollett. They were stirred by the historical plays of Friedrich von Schiller, as they were by August Wilhelm von Schlegel's translations of Shakespeare, Cervantes, and Dante, and by Friedrich von Schlegel's appeal for a return to the religion and romanticism of the Middle Ages. They set the quiet landscapes of Constable and the dramatic tableaux of Delacroix and Géricault against the classic portraits of Gainsborough and the perfectly ordered canvases of the French neoclassicist, David. They set the new music of Beethoven, Schubert, Berlioz, von Weber, Mendelssohn, and Chopin against the measured grace of Mozart and Haydn. They set the artificially romantic architecture of the Gothic revival against the conventional neoclassical forms of the late eighteenth century. They set the new historical school of jurisprudence, which regarded law as the historical outgrowth and embodiment of the customs of a people, against the classical concept of law as a formulation based on reason and logic. They contrasted the Catholic revival in France and Germany (marked in one small concrete sense by the completion of Cologne Cathedral after six hundred years of building) with the skepticism and godlessness of the age of reason. Yet in the end romanticism, with its strong cult of individualism, escapes precise definition, and, while there was much in romantic thought which buttressed the conservative reaction, there was much also that helped to lead Europe into a new age.

Many other currents of thought were apparent. Romantic writers had been interested in the past because of its color and glamour. Yet in the very hey-day of this romantic period, the modern, scientific approach to historical studies became established. One example of this was the beginning of widespread, large-scale publication of treaties, charters, medieval chronicles, and other source materials with the aid of which historians could reconstruct the past. Leopold von Ranke founded his historical seminar at the University of Berlin in 1833 with the express purpose of training young scholars in the technical handling of historical evidence so that they could tell, in Ranke's famous phrase, "what actually happened."

Other students of society, the classical economists, professed to find mechanical laws at work in the field of economics. Thomas Malthus, for ex-ample, whose *Essay on the Principle of Population* had appeared in 1798, pointed to the ominous evidence of a rapidly increasing population held in check only by the inevitable failures of the food supply and by accompanying misery. David Ricardo propounded his iron law of wages and his marginal theory of rent. There were liberal and utilitarian political theorists, such as Jeremy Bentham and John Stuart Mill, who conceived it to be the duty of government to rid society of its most flagrant abuses by establishing the necessary minimum of factory legislation, poor law reform, and the like, and then stand back. The utilitarians, putting forth their principle of "the greatest happiness of the greatest number" as a guide for governments, held that, having removed the most obvious and glaring obstacles to happiness, governments should thence-forth act merely as passive policemen. Even in early nineteenth-century Britain, where the Great Reform Bill of 1832, the first factory acts, and a number of con-comitant reforms had been won, the sphere of government activity was still generally held to be severely limited.

The theoretical role of the Utopian Socialists has already been con-sidered.[3] They were stimulating, if eccentric and at times even unbalanced, critics—dreamers and visionaries with a sure knack for singling out injustices and abuses for which less radical minds had found no remedy. Occasionally, as in the case of Robert Owen at New Lanark, it was possible to transform ideals and dreams into some kind of reality. Yet for the most part it remained true that the pressure of social and economic change was creating more prob-lems for society than the theorists could even dream of solving.

In another great field, that of emergent national sentiment, a transforma-tion was at work. The eighteenth-century "cosmopolitan nationalism" of the German writer, Johann Gottfried von Herder, was based on the view that dif-ferent national groups were branches of one common tree of humanity. This benign doctrine could hardly survive the harsh antagonisms of the Napoleonic age or the authoritarian reaction which followed. The new nationalism which

3. See pp. 41–45.

began to stir among the Italians, the Germans, the Poles, the Czechs, the Croats, the Serbs, and the Greeks, took on a more aggressive complexion. Joseph Mazzini founded his Young Italy society while an exile at Marseilles in 1831—an important date in the history of a nationalism which was frankly revolutionary in nature. The ferment in Italy and elsewhere grew steadily in the ensuing years. It is true that this nationalism was often deeply literary in inspiration; it was stimulated by poets, such as the Russian Pushkin and the Polish Mickiewicz, by historians, such as the Czech Palacký, by philologists, such as the Greek Koraës, and by novelists, such as the Italian Manzoni. Even so, and however great its romantic inspiration, nationalism was moving steadily in the direction of a realistic program of action.

■ THE FIRST GREAT SCIENTIFIC ADVANCES

All students of science are familiar with the giant names of men such as Boyle and Newton in the seventeenth century, of Buffon, Priestley, and Lavoisier in the eighteenth century, and of Darwin, the towering figure of the mid-nineteenth century. At this point, we must turn briefly to observe the pattern of scientific knowledge in the years preceding Darwin's great theoretical formulation of 1859.

The years between 1830 and 1870 can be regarded as a mid-period, preceded by a great formative age during which the character, methods, and problems of modern science had been established. This mid-period was to be followed by the modern age, in which science has won its unquestioned ascendancy. The impressive advance in all fields of scientific investigation during the nineteenth century gave science a larger place in education, especially in the universities. Elaborate research laboratories, which coordinated the work of many investigators, took the place of the modest establishments of individual scientists, such as Lavoisier and Faraday. These research laboratories almost of necessity required government patronage and support. Germany, Great Britain, and France were clearly in the lead, though occasional notable contributions came from Italy and Russia. Scientific associations, as distinct from the scientific academies which Europe had known since the seventeenth century, were a new development. The earliest of these was the German Scientific Association founded in 1822, soon followed by the British Association for the Advancement of Science, which held its first meeting at York in 1831.

In this period science was able to make key generalizations in several basic fields. Building upon the work of its predecessors, it produced four controlling concepts: first, the idea of atomicity; second, the idea of space as a continuity, pervaded by fields of physical activity; third, the idea of the conservation of energy; and fourth, the idea of evolution.

In briefest summary, these notions may be clarified as follows. With respect

MICHAEL FARADAY LECTURING AT THE ROYAL INSTITUTION, LONDON. This modern relief shows Faraday lecturing and demonstrating to an audience which includes Tyndall, Huxley, Darwin, and Kelvin.

to the atom, the English chemist and Quaker, John Dalton, established the essential basis of the theory in 1804 when he proposed the view that the ratio of the weights of two elements in their simplest compounds measured the weights of their respective atoms. From the Italian scientist, Count Avogadro, came the further concept of these atoms combining in what were called molecules. Such ideas in chemistry were transferred to the realm of biology when the Dutch scholar, Matthias Schleiden in 1838, and the German, Theodor Schwann in 1839, propounded the cellular theory in botany and zoology.

The theory of continuity in space involved the concept of ether as a space-filling substance, through which it was assumed that waves of light pass. Two Frenchmen, Augustin Fresnel and Jean Foucault, separately propounded this theory of light waves undulating in a mysterious something which scientists chose to call ether. From this came steady progress in the highly rewarding field of spectrum analysis, where the study of light contributed to the knowledge of chemistry. A parallel development likewise occurred with respect to magnetism and electricity. Michael Faraday demonstrated in 1831 that electrical currents could be induced in one circuit when a magnet was brought near; from this grew the concept of the magnetic field which another Englishman, James Clerk Maxwell, brought to fuller development in the 1870's.

The third concept, that of conservation of energy, arose in connection with studies of the relationship of heat to work. As early as 1824 a Frenchman, Sadi Carnot, had raised some of the problems connected with the change of work into heat and vice versa. A German, Hermann von Helmholtz, read a scientific paper in 1847 which stated the great law of the conservation of energy—that nature possesses a store of force which cannot in any way be increased or diminished. This was followed five years later by the statement of William Thomson (later Lord Kelvin) of the complementary law of the dissipation of energy—that, while the total remains constant, useful energy is diminished by the continual degeneration into nonuseful heat. Popularization of such ideas came in 1863 with John Tyndall's volume, *Heat a Mode of Motion*.

The fourth concept, that of evolution, will be considered later in this chapter. Here one can simply note that some sense of nature as an evolutionary process had been inherited from Buffon and other great naturalists of the eighteenth century; that Jean Baptiste Lamarck's *Natural History of the Invertebrate Animals*, appearing between 1815 and 1822, called attention to the importance of variation in animal species; and that Charles Lyell's *Principles of Geology* (1830–1833) insisted upon the enormous antiquity of the earth and upon the significance of the fossil remains found in various layers of the earth's surface.

Science was thus clearly advancing on a broad front. By mid-century the European world was being profoundly affected by rapid changes of all kinds: the onward rush of the Industrial Revolution, the struggles for national freedom and unification, the demands for political rights and for social justice. Amid these changes it is important to consider how deeply new knowledge was penetrating into society. This is no easy matter to determine, yet it is safe to say that, though democracy was not yet in the saddle, the intellectual enlightenment of the middle classes had made some significant progress.

A new reading public encouraged the growth of a literature which sought the wide dissemination of ideas. In England Charles Knight's *Penny Cyclopedia*, whose name speaks for itself, commenced publication in 1833. Henry Bohn began in 1847 to publish his inexpensive Standard, Scientific, Classical, and Antiquarian Libraries, which eventually included six hundred titles. A modest start was made in the provision of free public libraries in Britain. Reading rooms were among the more flourishing activities of the Mechanics' Institutes, which had been founded a generation earlier in many of the manufacturing towns but had served the needs of the lower middle class rather than of the manual workers, because the latter still lacked for the most part any solid foundation of elementary education on which to build. Nevertheless, there were many enterprising and ambitious workers, as the attendance at the Great Exhibition in 1851 clearly showed. It is noteworthy that Thomas Huxley, a distinguished scientist in his own right and one of Darwin's most militant advocates, considered his lectures on science, for audiences of workingmen, to be one of his most necessary and valuable duties.

My workingmen stick by me wonderfully [he wrote to his wife in his genial and effervescent way in March 1861], the house being fuller than ever last night. By next Friday evening they will all be convinced that they are monkeys. . . . Said lecture, let me tell you was very good. Lyell came and was rather astonished at the magnitude and attentiveness of the audience.[4]

The desire for culture could be met in other ways. In addition to the art museums, in which by long tradition European monarchs had displayed their historic treasures to the public, other collections devoted to science and technology began to take shape. In the period now being considered such museums were in existence in Paris, London, Manchester, and Edinburgh, and many others were soon to follow.

■ MID-CENTURY TRANSITION TO REALISM IN THE ARTS

The mid-nineteenth century saw important new trends in the field of literature and the arts. General opinion would probably rank the great scientific generalizations concerning the world of nature as the major intellectual achievement of this time, and along with them the efforts to apply scientific techniques to the study of history, society, and religion. But the literary and artistic developments were almost equally challenging in their implications. Before considering the spectacular new impact of science we shall, therefore, glance briefly at these other fields.

To characterize this general change in taste and expression as a shift from romanticism to realism is, of course, greatly to oversimplify. Yet much can be learned from examining the problem first in this way. The transition from the imaginative and often remote world of romantic writers, such as Scott or Hugo, to the contemporary, harsh, and often psychologically tormented world of realistic literature could not be altogether sudden or total. The exaggerations and sentimentality found in the novels of Charles Dickens (1812–1870) would justify a romantic label, yet his photographic and poignant depiction of English workhouses, of prison hulks, run-down schools, and London slums puts him quite clearly in the category of realists. Victor Hugo, a giant of romanticism, spares little of realistic impact in many of the great scenes of Les Misérables. Gustave Flaubert's study of the progressive degradation of a country doctor's wife in Madame Bovary (1857) makes this novel one of the landmarks in the history of realistic literature, together with Honoré de Balzac's huge panorama of French society begun in the 1830's and known collectively as The Human Comedy. Ivan Turgenev's Sportsman's Sketches (1852), which critically discussed serfdom in Russia, his Fathers and Sons (1862), and Feodor Dostoevsky's Crime and Punishment (1866) similarly are monuments of the realistic movement in literature—a movement which could be followed to the close of the century in

4. LEONARD HUXLEY, The Life and Letters of Thomas Henry Huxley (1916), vol. I, p. 205.

the English novels of Thomas Hardy, the plays of the Norwegian author, Henrik Ibsen, or the novels of the Frenchman, Emile Zola.

The change is also to be followed in painting and—to some extent—in music. The romantic art of the earlier years was in many respects inappropriate for the new age, though almost inevitably romantic painting and *objets d'art*, often in a cheap and vulgarized form, persisted in the drawing-room decorations of Victorian England and in their Continental counterparts. Sir Edwin Landseer's dogs and deer, Franz Winterhalter's exquisitely pretty court ladies, and the sentimentally inspired landscapes of many an anonymous artist seem to have had an overpowering effect on both the aristocratic and middle class. Much of this taste persisted, as in the long-lasting vogue of the thoroughly mediocre, yet enormously popular, French painter, Adolphe Bouguereau.

Artistic fashion in mid-nineteenth century England, under the Second Empire in France, and in the newly emerging Germany, involved large elements of eclecticism. The Gothic revival, as it found expression in Sir Charles Barry's rebuilding of the Houses of Parliament in London between 1840 and 1860, conveys the effect of romantic grandeur. Few, however, would nowadays surrender themselves to the charms of that extraordinary hodgepodge of sculpture, mosaics, giltwork, bronze, and marble making up the huge Albert Memorial, begun in 1864, which was erected as a national memorial to Queen Victoria's husband. And many would question the propriety of employing, under the stimulus of John Ruskin, the style of Venetian Gothic for the railway stations, the railway hotels, and the town halls of the new industrial cities. Techniques of mass production, as much as dubious taste, doubtless can be held responsible for the clutter of ornament, the bric-a-brac, the rich carpets and hangings, and the heavily carved walnut and mahogany furniture of this solid and substantial gaslit age. Art, in short, closely reflected much of the social direction of the times.

Though the words are often used with varying connotations, the realistic trend can clearly be seen in the development of painting in France. The breach with the romantic tradition of Delacroix and Géricault came in the 1850's. Gustave Courbet's concern as an artist was to paint relentlessly what he saw, and so he offered his vivid depiction of people such as wrestlers and bathers. Honoré Daumier, brilliant as a cartoonist, could catch equally well in his paintings a Paris street or the interior of a third-class railway coach, thereby making his work a penetrating social document. This attempt to paint without illusions or fancies led to one of France's greatest contributions to nineteenth-century painting, the impressionist school, a conscious revolt against the canons of academic taste. To paint properly, so it was held by the impressionists, one had to understand the nature of light, to know what it is that one actually sees, and to substitute the immediate impression for the permanent fact. In so doing the artist is in one sense not far from the scientist, for it is the multitude of tiny colors which makes it possible for nature to convey to us our broad impression of a scene. Claude Monet made his canvases a glowing mosaic of tiny colors—impressions—which he put together to convey an almost scientific truth, as one feels in his fascinating combination of blue and white, smoke and steam, light and shadow, which made up his representation of the Saint-Lazare railway station in Paris. The "Déjeuner sur l'Herbe" of Edouard Manet,[5] another violator of tradition, was rejected by the Salon of 1863. In his defense he wrote: "There is only one thing true: to paint from the first what one sees. When that is done, it is done. Everything else is nonsense. Art is the servant of facts." Whether we call it impressionism or realism, the subtle play of light and color appears in another form in the enchanting ballet dancers, the jockeys, and the common folk of Edgar Degas' canvases.

Music could escape only with difficulty from its romantic heritage. Gounod, Verdi, Rossini, and Tschaikovsky stuck largely to the romantic tradition, though Rimsky-Korsakov, with his themes drawn from Russian folk music, was closer to the realistic current. Richard Wagner,[6] turning to the Norse Eddas and the German *Niebelungenlied* to make the libretti for the *Ring* cycle of operas, dramatized for his German hearers the romantic elements of their past. Wagner chose the opera as his medium of expression because he believed that through it all aspects of theater—drama, dancing, painting, architecture, orchestration, and song—could be brought together in a single vast synthesis which he called a *Gesamtkunstwerk*. The similarities between what Wagner sought to do and what the scientists were attempting in their search for unity in nature have often been remarked. He has been called a law unto himself and it remained for Claude Debussy of a later generation truly to launch the movement of impressionism in music.

■ DARWINISM, SCIENCE, AND LIFE

Probably not even the Copernican hypothesis of the sixteenth century created as much of a furore or affected so profoundly the general view of man on this earth as the publication by a mild-mannered, noncontroversial scientist in 1859 of a book entitled *The Origin of Species by Means of Natural Selection.*

5. 1832–1883. An artist of inherited wealth, who was always able to live comfortably, he was indebted to Hals, Rembrandt, Tintoretto, Velasquez, and Goya, and in the 1860's led the impressionist revolt against the academicians when his paintings were repeatedly rejected and derided at the annual Salons. He depicted "a world of movement seen through half-closed eyes" on the principle that color does not exist as a definite quantity but is the result of light playing upon form.
6. 1813–1883. The most spectacular name in nineteenth-century music, who transformed the opera into a new music drama based on libretti of his own composition, *leitmotivs*, and new harmonic schemes. He won the devoted admiration of the mad King Ludwig II of Bavaria. A revolutionary participant at Dresden in 1849, he later displayed dictatorial and antisemitic enthusiasms and with his romantic admiration for the heroic age of German mythology anticipated many of the traits of the later Nazis.

Charles Darwin's theories, so momentous in their impact, came at a time when the scientific view of life was being enlarged in several directions. A brief glance at some of these other views is offered first.

In organic chemistry, for the first example, the studies of Justus von Liebig at the University of Giessen, leading to the artificial production of organic chemical fertilizers, had furthered the view of life as a process of chemical change, a view confirmed by the discovery of the high phosphorus content of the brain and the important nitrogen element in muscular tissue. In bacteriology and medicine there were likewise important contributions at this time to the understanding of life. Louis Pasteur's studies of fermentation, first undertaken at Lille in 1856, led to the knowledge of micro-organisms later termed "microbes," and enabled Joseph Lister in 1868 to initiate antiseptic surgery at Glasgow. Contemporaneously Rudolph Virchow was working in his Pathological Institute in Berlin, where in 1858 he published his great work on cellular pathology.

Materialism as a philosophic creed had some vigorous exponents in Germany. Ludwig Feuerbach, "the philosopher par excellence of emancipated and self-contained humanity," had begun as a Hegelian. He turned, however, to interpreting religion from a purely psychological point of view. His *Essence of Christianity* (1841), for example, had declared that religions are produced by man and exist only to satisfy his needs. "Do you want to improve the people?"

DARWIN, AGE THIRTY-FIVE, WITH HIS SON.
A striking example (1842) of the daguerrotype, the first demonstrations of which
were made three years earlier to the French
Academy of Sciences.

he asked. "Then instead of preaching against sin, give them better food. Man is (*ist*) what he eats (*isst*)." Ludwig Büchner, whose work, *Force and Matter* (1855), has been called the Bible of German materialism, was dismissed from the University of Tübingen because of the public uproar caused by his views. "Man," he wrote, "is not a work of God but a product of nature." None of this can compare, however, in spectacular importance, to the work of Darwin, for in touching on the doctrine of evolution he, albeit unwillingly, committed himself to the great battle over man's historic place and purpose in the cosmos.

Charles Darwin (1809–1882), son of a country doctor in Shropshire and grandson of the famous pottery maker, Josiah Wedgwood, ranks with Copernicus, Newton, and Einstein as a central figure in one of the great revolutions in scientific outlook. His father's plans to make him a doctor by study at Edinburgh or a clergyman by study at Cambridge both fell to the ground. Darwin, who graduated from Cambridge tenth in the list of men who did not seek honors, quickly found his vocation in the field of biology. "I have steadily endeavored," he once explained, "to keep my mind free so as to give up any hypothesis, however much beloved (and I cannot resist forming one on every subject), as soon as facts are shown to be opposed to it." He was a gentle and uncombative figure, living quietly in the country just outside London and, although he was happy with a family of ten children, he once doubted whether a man of science should have children, or even a wife. Conventional in his religious practices, he complained that reading philosophy caused him indigestion. Once, studying a portrait of himself, he objected mildly that it made him look like "a very venerable, acute, melancholy, old dog."

The lucky chance of an appointment as naturalist aboard H.M.S. *Beagle*, sent by the British government to survey the coasts of South America, gave him his start. Between 1831 and 1836 he was able to observe the amazing complexity of animal and plant life, the variety of geological formations, the links between living species and ancient fossils, and the variations of species which occurred as he moved from one environment to another. On the trip he read Lyell's *Principles of Geology*, and began to question the stability of various living species and to ponder the reasons for variation. "Science," he wrote later in his autobiography, "consists in grouping facts so that general laws or conclusions may be drawn from them." The voyage of the *Beagle* (of which Darwin's account was published in 1839) provided him with a rich variety of evidence and a stimulus to further speculation. His problem was to account for the extraordinary complexity of living species on some other basis than the theory of divine creation at a given point in time.

The concept of evolution has a long history, in one sense going back to the Greeks. Buffon's great eighteenth-century compilations on natural history had, in his phrase, placed man in the category of the animals. Darwin's own grandfather had suggested an evolutionary hypothesis to account for the variety of human life. The French naturalist, Jean Baptiste de Lamarck, who died in 1829, had proposed the thesis that all animals and plants have evolved from the same remote, simple ancestry. His *explanation* of this evolution was found in what he called the "tendency" of living things to growth and elaboration (which Darwin labeled nonsense and really no explanation at all); in the effects upon various organs of constant use or disuse; and in the assumption that acquired characteristics could be passed on to offspring. Lamarck was widely attacked and built up no school. A fellow naturalist of Darwin's, on the other hand, Alfred Russel Wallace, in the 1850's made observations in the East Indies which led him to think along the same lines as Darwin.

Darwin's search for an acceptable theory was stimulated by his reading of Malthus' famous *Essay on the Principle of Population*, for here it was demonstrated that the overfertility of man comes up against the blindly operating forces of a harsh environment in the face of which only the fittest can survive. Between 1842 and 1844 Darwin had completed a manuscript sketch of his theory which he described as "gleams of light," but he deferred its publication because of the need for much more substantial evidence. In 1858, when shown a manuscript from Alfred Russel Wallace, which closely corresponded to his own views, he agreed that his should be made public. Thus, on the historic date, July 1, 1858, the papers of Darwin and Wallace, jointly entitled "On the Tendency of Species to Form Varieties; and on the Perpetuation of Varieties and Species by Means of Selection," were read to a meeting of the Linnean Society in London. More than a year later, in November, 1859, Darwin's book, *On the Origin of*

Species by Means of Natural Selection, was published by John Murray and the whole edition of 1250 copies was exhausted on the day of issue.

Unlike Darwin's previous writing, the book occasioned a storm of controversy, the height of it coming at a meeting of the British Association at Oxford in 1860. Here the Bishop of Oxford, Samuel Wilberforce ("Soapy Sam" to the undergraduates), met on the same platform with Darwin's scientific friend and defender, Thomas Huxley,[7] and sneeringly asked the scientist whether he claimed descent from the apes on his grandfather's or grandmother's side. Huxley dramatically gave his famous answer:

> A man has no reason to be ashamed of having an ape for his grandfather. If there were an ancestor whom I should feel a shame in recalling, it would be a *man*, a man of restless and versatile intellect, who . . . plunges into scientific questions with which he has no real acquaintance, only to obscure them by an aimless rhetoric, and distract the attention of his hearers from the real point at issue by eloquent digressions and skilled appeals to religious prejudice.[8]

While it is important to be aware of this highly emotional conflict which Darwin's views engendered, the basic question centers on what he had to put forward as an argument. The *Origin of Species* is an elaborate explanation rather than a proof. It brings forth a large mass of evidence which it presents with unquestioned literary skill. The points of Darwin's theory are, in essence, these.

First, all groups of organisms, instead of precisely reproducing their kind, tend to vary. Many of these variations are hereditary. Some groups are better fitted to survive than others—the giraffe with the longer neck, for example, who reaches higher on the tree for his food, has the advantage over his shorter fellow. Second, nature "selects" by offering to living things an environment with which some can cope and others cannot. In consequence of this, there occurs, third, a struggle for existence. Fourth, out of this struggle comes the survival of the fittest, and with it the steadily increasing variety of living forms. Darwin had to presuppose an immensely long period of time, for which the evidence of geology gave him strong support. He likewise had to recognize many gaps in the evidence, yet despite these he had no doubts of the general truth of what he wrote.

The picture he presented was almost benign in its simplicity:

> The affinities of all beings of the same class have sometimes been represented by a great tree. I believe this simile largely speaks the truth. The green and bud-

---

7. 1825–1895. A distinguished scientist who described his unusually brief elementary schooling as "two years of pandemonium." He was for a time a naval surgeon, whose interest in biology was stimulated by a voyage to the Australian Barrier Reef, then taught at the Royal College of Mines and became a convert to Darwinism, lecturing widely to public audiences. Secretary to the Royal Society, he was a member of ten royal commissions of inquiry and a vigorous advocate of enlarged public education.

8. HUXLEY, *The Life and Letters of Thomas Henry Huxley,* vol. I, p. 199.

ding twigs may represent existing species; and those produced during former years may represent the long succession of extinct species. . . . Of the many twigs which flourished when the tree was a mere bush, only two or three, now grown into great branches, yet survive and bear the other branches; so with the species which lived during long past geological periods, very few have left living and modified descendants. From the first growth of the tree, many a limb and branch has decayed and dropped off; and these fallen branches of various sizes may represent those whole orders, families, and genera which have now no living representatives, and which are known to us only in a fossil stage. . . . As buds give rise by growth to fresh buds, and these, if vigorous, branch out and overtop on all sides many a feebler branch, so by generation I believe it has been with the great Tree of Life, which fills with its dead and broken branches the crust of the earth, and covers the surface with its ever-branching and beautiful ramifications.[9]

This, in simple summary, was the theory destined to cause such enormous commotion—less in the world of science, as it happened, than in the world of social and religious thought.

■ SCIENCE AND THE STUDY OF SOCIETY

Darwin's theories were to produce violent disagreements, of which the platform exchanges between Huxley and Bishop Wilberforce at Oxford in 1860 were only a mild and minor sample. Before turning to this great battle, we must note some new views of man in society which, like Darwin's interpretation of the world of nature, sought to discover a sweeping and systematic pattern of development beneath the apparently confusing operation of blind natural forces. Auguste Comte (1798–1857), a Frenchman, Herbert Spencer (1820–1903), an Englishman, and Karl Marx (1818–1883), a German, serve this purpose.

The writings of Auguste Comte, an examiner in mathematics at the Polytechnic Institute in Paris and an early follower of the Utopian Socialism of Saint-Simon, illustrate the tendency to vast and inclusive generalizations. As early as 1822 he had made a sketch of his positivist philosophy, but a nervous breakdown, an attempted suicide by throwing himself into the Seine, and confinement to institutions kept him from issuing his *Course of Positive Philosophy* until the years 1830–1842. His *System of Positive Polity* appeared between 1851 and 1854. In Comte's view of human behavior, man has historically passed through three states: the *theological*, in which life is marked by belief in the dominance of supernatural powers; the *metaphysical*, in which explanations are found in the supposed operation of abstract concepts, such as natural rights or popular sovereignty; and the *positive*, in which the observation of actual facts, divorced from theory and preconceptions, will enable the study of political, economic, and social life to proceed by the same methods as those of science.

9. C. DARWIN, *The Origin of Species*, ch. 4.

There should be, indeed, a science of society for which in 1839 Comte devised the term "sociology." Comte believed that this science of society was part of a larger whole, for all sciences he held to be branches from a single trunk. Comte then went beyond the simple study of society to build up a kind of religion of humanity, in which the select few who can grasp the true laws of sociology should employ this knowledge for the regeneration of the whole world. In so doing these leaders and experts must be ruthless in the employment of force. One of the most striking features of the Comtean system is that, though it inspired a fanatical devotion in his immediate followers and though Comte can quite properly be called the father of sociology, as a system it fell sadly short of the hopes which the author had put in it.

Herbert Spencer, the son of a Derby schoolmaster, the inheritor of Quaker and Methodist traditions, and for eleven years an engineer on the London and Birmingham railway, turned out to be one of the most prolific philosophic writers and most confident masters of sweeping generalizations to appear during the nineteenth century. He had no use for conventional religion or for the study of history, which, he said, offered him only "the indebtedness of antagonism," and he prided himself on looking at life quietly and directly through his own eyes. What have been called his magnificent powers of intellectual digestion led him to adopt the view that all aspects of man's social activities could be brought together and explained in one enormous synthesis. (This synthesizing tendency once led Spencer even to devise a synthetic salmon fly to be used for all purposes in fishing.) What he sought in his studies was an evolutionary social science which would be based on a belief in progress—a belief that could be elevated into the supreme law of the universe. Either society had its laws, Spencer declared again and again in his works, or it did not. Without law there could be no certainty or system. If there were laws governing society, then they must be sure, inflexible, and without exception. Man's freedom, he declared in his *Social Statics* (1850), will eventually produce an equilibrium if allowed to operate unchecked. But it should not be manipulated. Governments must not undertake by state action to coddle human beings, for, as Spencer wrote elsewhere: "The ultimate result of shielding men from folly is to fill the world with fools." Seeking some law comparable to the classic formulations of physics, Spencer found his clue in what he asserted to be an evolutionary law of progress: "from the homogeneous to the heterogeneous."

In 1860, close on the heels of Darwin's great work, Spencer terminated what he called the miscellaneous period of his life by publishing the elaborate prospectus of his *Synthetic Philosophy*. This outlined his ideas and plans for a comprehensive survey of the world as a whole. He followed this prospectus with volume after volume (*First Principles, Principles of Biology, Principles of Psychology, Principles of Sociology, Principles of Ethics*), working away until, by 1896, the vast ten-volume undertaking was completed. All human activities are to be understood in the spirit of natural science which Spencer took to be "continuous disclosures of the established order of the universe." His monumental synthesis, so arduously put together and today so largely unread, remains a giant effort to explain society as an evolving organism.

Other writers, among whom John Stuart Mill (1806–1873) was one of the most prominent, attempted, like Comte, to undertake a scientific study of human society and thereby to further the course of human progress. These names, however, were to be overshadowed by that of a German theorist who sought not merely to understand or to improve society, but rather to associate his doctrines with what he prophesied would be the inevitable revolutionary downfall of the entire bourgeois capitalist order.

Karl Marx (1818–1883) was the son of a middle-class Jewish lawyer of Trier in the Rhineland, who in 1824 was converted to Christianity. At the universities of Bonn and Berlin, Marx studied the philosophy of Hegel, who regarded history as a process, and of Ludwig Feuerbach, who interpreted the universe in materialistic terms. As editor of a democratic Rhineland journal, Marx was led into the study of economics; he observed the beginnings of German industrialism, and, on moving to Paris in 1843 and later to Brussels, began to absorb revolutionary ideas. Thus he quickly became a deep sympathizer with the problems of a working class to which he did not belong. In 1844 Marx struck up what was to be a lifelong friendship with another German, Friedrich Engels,[10] newly come from England where he had observed at close hand, and also studied in the parliamentary reports, the shocking conditions of the English factory workers. Engels' volume, *The Condition of the Working Class in England* (1844), provided Marx, as the voyage of the *Beagle* had done for Darwin, with a most useful fund of evidence on which to build his subsequent theories. Together Marx and Engels reorganized the Communist League which held meetings in London. For it they jointly wrote the *Communist Manifesto*, a brief but powerful statement of revolutionary socialist doctrine, published in January, 1848. Marx took part in the subsequent revolutionary movements in the Rhineland, and following their failure went to London in 1849. Here, until his death in 1883, he lived the life of a political exile, intermittently poverty-stricken, and going daily to the British Museum to work on the successive volumes of his huge *Das Kapital*. He engaged in controversy with the anarchists,

---

10. 1820–1895. The conservatively educated son of a wealthy German cotton spinner, he was influenced while in England on family business in the 1840's by the Owenite and Chartist movements. He collaborated closely with Marx after 1844, gave him money, delivered the oration at his grave, comparing him to Darwin, and completed *Das Kapital*. He was responsible for some of the best known Marxian phraseology: "the revolutionary dictatorship of the proletariat"; "the state is nothing more than a machine for the oppression of one class by another"; "the state is not abolished, it withers away." He was also a respected authority on military science.

whose theories were not his, but met few, if any, workmen, and, in the phrase of Sir Alexander Gray, spent his years "chewing his intellectual cud with his back firmly planted towards the window." Few notable lives have seemed to be less concerned with action; few have more profoundly influenced the actions of later generations.

The ideas persuasively and dramatically put forward in the *Communist Manifesto*, and more elaborately in the three volumes of Marx's *Das Kapital*, break away from the early Utopian Socialist notion of a gradual transformation of society ("utopian" is the word Marx himself scornfully applied to such views) to the prophecy of a revolutionary, "proletarian" destruction of the entire capitalist system. The word, prophecy, should be stressed, for Marx did not so much advocate as forecast what he was convinced would, in the nature of things, inevitably come about.

Marx begins with a theory of history, which is that of *economic determinism*. By inverting Hegel's notion of the "spirit of the age"—that ideas work themselves out in the concrete processes of history—Marx turned to the notion of the primacy of material forces. All history is determined by economic forces; the ultimate cause of all important events, therefore, will be found "in the changes in modes of production and exchange, in the consequent division of society into distinct classes, and in the struggles of these classes against one another." It follows as a second major point that the *class struggle* has been a standard phenomenon throughout history, and that this in our age has taken the form of the capitalist exploitation of the workingman. According to Marx the truly evil figure of our day is the bourgeois—the employer of labor consistently taking advantage of the proletarian worker, who is the true creator of value. From this follows Marx's third point, his theory of *surplus value*. The laborer in the course of his work invariably produces more value than is turned over to him in his subsistence wage. The capitalist, even if we recognize that he is entitled to payment for his managerial and risk-taking activities, filches from the worker an additional and unjustifiable sum (surplus value) which constitutes his profit.

The next point involves Marx's theory of revolution. The process by which the capitalist takes from the worker in order to increase his own wealth produces in the end a concentration of wealth in a few hands and a society so topheavy that it will inevitably collapse of its own weight. Economic crises will increase in intensity. The capitalists, Marx insists, are "digging their own graves." When the point of collapse comes, the proletarians must seize power by force, and in a transitional period marked by the *dictatorship of the proletariat* liquidate whatever is left of the bourgeoisie. The final outcome will be the *classless society*, where, in Engels' phrase, the state will "wither away." This phenomenon, which would not be immediately apparent to those acquainted with the nature of the powerful and monolithic Soviet state today, is based on the assumption that the traditional *political* structure by which one class has exercised power over another no longer will have any reason to exist. Society will be organized on the basis of self-regulating associations of workers, operating on the principle of production for use and not for profit.

A few points deserve emphasis. Unlike the Utopian Socialists, who proclaimed what *ought* to be done, Marx in the first place professed to know what *will be*. The *Communist Manifesto* therefore is more than an appeal; it is a prophecy. "The proletarians have nothing to lose but their chains. They have a world to win. Workers of the world unite!" Marx believed that what he taught was founded in the logic of history; for this reason he called his movement scientific, and that is why it made so great an appeal to workers seeking assurance. In the second place, Marxian socialism is revolutionary. Violence is built into the communist argument; without it the liquidation of the bourgeoisie is not possible. In the third place it is international, finding the lines of division and combat not vertically, between states, but horizontally, between classes. And thus, like Darwinism, Marxism sees the elements of conflict and struggle as inescapable in human history.

Though Marxism was clearly international in scope and though Marx was among the founders of the First International Workingmen's Association in 1864, one of the most striking phenomena of this period was the emergence of separate socialist parties within various European countries with Marxian teachings as their basis. Even the fact that some of Marx's fundamental assumptions went astray—the poor, for example, did not seem in general to be growing poorer nor the rich in general richer; revolution did not come first in the most highly developed countries; and "revisionist" parties inconsiderately undertook to remodel Marx's teaching in such a way as to lead him to say "I am not a Marxist"—all this did not prevent Marxism from having a growing attraction for the world's dispossessed. Furthermore, it has permanently influenced the historian's view of history, even as Darwin has influenced the scientist's view of the physical world. Whatever the final truth of his arguments, it is generally agreed that Marx must rank as one of the most profoundly original and most influential figures of the nineteenth century.

■ RELIGION, SCIENCE, AND SOCIAL ISSUES

The steady growth of scientific knowledge, the advance of worldly prosperity, and the challenge of new social problems in the life of an industrial society meant that the position of religion in European life was certain to be affected. In the early years of the nineteenth century, following the godlessness of the revolutionary era, there had been a distinct return to religion, evident in the vigor of French Catholicism during the romantic era, the High Church Oxford Movement in England, and the revival of fervor in both Catholic and Protestant circles in Germany. Liberal Catholicism in France under the banner of Lamennais, Montalembert, and Lacordaire sought to counteract the indifference to religion prevalent in the educated classes and to build a new edifice of faith. Their purpose was to cause religion to play a larger role in public life.

This liberalism, however, was not long-lived, either in France or elsewhere. In general the churches took the side of the established powers, defended the cause of orthodoxy, and held to intellectual positions and to a social outlook that paid little regard to the vast changes operating in European life. One exception seemed notable in 1846 when the College of Cardinals elected a new pope, Pius IX, whose reputation was that of a liberal. Italian patriots, who were touched by the reforms launched in the Papal States, envisaged "Pio Nono" as the head of a federally united Italy, but were quickly disillusioned by the revolutionary events of 1848 and 1849 which caused Pius IX to shed whatever elements of liberalism he had first demonstrated. During the ensuing years the Roman Catholic Church quickly reasserted its authority wherever it could, re-establishing the temporal power of the papacy in Italy, winning an important position in France during the Second Empire, and consolidating its historic rights by concordats or agreements with various countries: with Spain (1851 and 1859), with Austria (1855), with Württemberg (1857), and with Baden (1859).

Though liberal Catholicism began to reassert itself in France, Germany, and Austria, the official trends were otherwise. Pius IX proclaimed the Dogma of the Immaculate Conception in 1854, making the belief, long held by the Church, that "the Virgin Mary was, in the first instant of her conception . . . preserved untouched by any taint of original sin," an article of faith. In 1863 the German Catholic theologian, Dr. Döllinger, organized a meeting of one hundred liberal Catholic leaders at Malines, in Belgium, to discuss the attitude of the Roman Catholic Church toward modern social problems and modern science, and to consider the prospect of reuniting Anglicans, Lutherans, and Greek Orthodox believers with the Roman communion. After four days Pius IX suppressed the conference. In December, 1864, in the encyclical *Quanta Cura*, Pius IX appended the Syllabus of Errors, censuring the evils of pantheism, naturalism, indifferentism, socialism, communism, freemasonry and similar beliefs, and declaring it to be an error that "the pope may and must reconcile himself with and adapt himself to Progress, Liberalism, and Modern Civilization." Still again, in 1870, at the time when the temporal power of the papacy clearly was coming to an end, the Vatican Council, which had been summoned in the previous year from all parts of Christendom, proclaimed the dogma of Papal Infallibility that—

the Roman pontiff, when he speaks ex cathedra, that is, when he, in the exercise of his office as Shepherd and teacher of all Christians, by virtue of his supreme Apostolic authority, decides that a doctrine concerning faith or morals is to be held by the entire Church . . . possesses, in consequence of the divine aid promised him in St. Peter, that infallibility with which the Divine Savior wished to have His Church furnished for the definition of doctrine concerning faith or morals. . . .[11]

While some prelates had at first opposed the issuing of the dogma, all ultimately gave their assent. Opposition, nevertheless, quickly arose among the Old Catholics in Germany, led by Dr. Döllinger, of Munich. Austria at once annulled its concordat, and in Prussia Bismarck's *Kulturkampf*, or war with the Church, soon was in full swing.[12] Anticlericalism became a growing force in France, with the result that the Third Republic, now painfully coming to birth, moved in a direction which ultimately meant the termination of the historic privileges that Catholicism had long enjoyed. These, to be sure, were matters of the future. During the decade of the 1860's the position of the Church in French life was not significantly changed.

Clearly enough, Darwinian science was having its influence upon other fields. New views of man's place in the universe and new secular dogmas—the creeds of liberalism, nationalism, and socialism—all concerned in one way or another with the destiny of man, were taking shape. The scientific study of historical documents and new developments in archaeology, papyrology, and Assyriology resulted, in the field of religion, in biblical texts being now submitted to the same kind of technical evaluation that was being applied to other documents. Thus the "higher criticism" challenged the literal interpretation of the Bible as the inspired word of God and repudiated the Genesis account of creation. As early as 1835, the German scholar, David Friedrich Strauss, had written a *Life of Jesus* in purely historical terms, and Ernest Renan, who declared that history is the true philosophy of the nineteenth century, wrote a French *Life* in 1863 similar in nature. J. R. Seeley's *Ecce Homo* (1866) described Jesus as "a young man of promise, popular with those who knew him"—a statement which outraged conservative religious sensibilities.[13]

Efforts to stem this first tide of modernism had little success. A Frenchman, Louis Veuillot, published a small book in 1866, *The Liberal Illusion*. He denounced all religious compromise with liberalism, declaring that "the liberty that is man's due is liberty to attain his supernatural end, which is union with Christ." Liberal Catholicism he called an illusion; the church should be supreme

11. *Catholic Encyclopedia*, vol. XV, p. 308.
12. See pp. 313–314.
13. R. C. BINKLEY, *Realism and Nationalism, 1852–1871* (1935), p. 52. For further discussion, see ch. 16, pp. 458–462.

over the state; and "when the Sovereign Pontiff has proclaimed a pastoral decision, no one has the right to add or suppress the smallest vowel. . . ."[14]

The materialistic trends were running strongly, as Friedrich Lange's *History of Materialism*, published in 1867, rather sadly admitted. Arthur Schopenhauer's *World as Will and Idea*, appearing almost unnoticed in 1819, achieved a considerable popularity when it was reissued a generation later. The universe, it argued, is ethically barren, the only intelligence is that of animals, the only reality is blind, struggling will; if man is to escape at all it must be through art, the only knowledge not subject to the will.

Thus, as post-1870 Europe moved into what has aptly been called "a generation of materialism," it brought with it the confusions and conflicts of the preceding decades. These conflicts of science and religion had not been resolved.

Reading List: Chapter 9

Brinton, C., *Ideas and Men, The Story of Western Thought* (1950), ch. 12. A survey of European thought in the nineteenth century.

The New Cambridge Modern History, vol. X (1960), chs. 3–7. The scientific movement and its influence; religion and politics; education and the press; art and architecture; imaginative literature.

Randall, H. J., *The Creative Centuries* (1947), ch. 40. The intellectual revolution of the nineteenth century.

Hearnshaw, F. J. C. (ed.), *Social and Political Ideas . . . of the Age of Reaction and Reconstruction, 1815–65* (1949). See chapters on Chateaubriand, Hegel, Mill, and Comte.

Bowle, J., *Politics and Opinion in the Nineteenth Century, An Historical Introduction* (1954), Bk. I, ch. 9; Bk. II, ch. 1. Tocqueville and Mill; the impact of Darwinism.

Darwin, C., *Autobiography*, ed. by N. Barlow (1958), pp. 71–82, 116–26. Voyage of the *Beagle;* publication of the *Origin of Species*.

Hearnshaw, F. J. C., *Social and Political Ideas . . . of the Victorian Age* (1950). See chapters on Carlyle, Spencer, Bagehot, and Marx.

Marx, K., and Engels, F., *Manifesto of the Communist Party* (many editions).

Berlin, I., *Karl Marx* (1939; paperback, 1959), chs. 1, 6, 7, 9.

Cranston, M., "J. S. Mill as a Political Philosopher," *History Today*, vol. VIII (1958), no. 1.

Burrow, J. W., "Herbert Spencer, The Philosopher of Evolution," *History Today*, vol. VIII (1958), no. 10.

Chambers, F. P., *The History of Taste* (1932), ch. 9. "Nineteenth Century Revivals."

Leichentritt, H., *Music, History, and Ideas* (1938), ch. 10. The romantic movement.

14. Quotations from E. N. JOHNSON, *An Introduction to the History of the Western Tradition* (1959), vol. II, pp. 536–37.

P A R T   I I

THE UNCERTAIN

BALANCE

1871–1914

*"The grandeur of history lies in the perpetual
conflict of nations, and it is simply foolish
to desire the suppression of their rivalry.
Mankind has ever found it to be so. . . .
When a nation's existence is at stake there is no
outside Power whose impartiality can be trusted."*

HEINRICH VON TREITSCHKE, *Lectures on Politics,*
delivered at the University of Berlin in the
1880's and 1890's.

Prologue:
The Forty Years' Peace, 1871–1914

■ POLITICAL TRENDS

The historian who uses the year 1871 as the vantage point from which to look ahead at the fateful decades preceding the outbreak of the First World War is in a position to link the course of events that lay in the future with the developments of what was then the recent past. Whatever novelty he may find, it is clear that these closing decades were not a totally new age, for however decisive the climactic years 1870 and 1871 may have been in ending one chapter of European history and beginning another, the connections with the earlier period were close. The Italy of 1870, for example, which consolidated its national unity by absorbing what was left of the Papal States, was in effect reaching a goal toward which Italian patriots had struggled for two generations. The fall of the Second Empire in France made possible the reassertion of a republicanism, which had first been realized as early as 1792 and again in 1848. If Bismarck's German Empire, as it has been said, lay in the logic of history, it was a history which he had undertaken to direct since 1862.

In no field is this continuity more evident than in that of political evolution. Here one of the main developments of the preceding period had been the emergence of a number of new states out of the supposedly stable arrangements of 1815: Greece and Belgium by 1830; then, a generation later, a united Italy; then, in 1871, the German Empire. Serbia, having gained its autonomy from the Turk in 1817, and Rumania, in 1856, were by 1871 approaching the complete independence which came just seven years afterwards. A concomitant development was to be the steady freeing of almost the entire Balkan area from Turkish rule. Greece, Serbia, and Rumania were all enlarged, while by 1914

Bulgaria, Montenegro, and Albania had been recognized as fully independent. At the other end of Europe, and by much less drastic means, the personal union linking Sweden and Norway ended in 1905.

The European states, during this age of growing industrialism, were showing more marks of resemblance than of difference, and this in spite of the strident nationalism which was so unhappy a mark of the pre-1914 years. In number, if one excludes the minuscule territories of Monaco, Andorra, Lichtenstein, and San Marino, by 1914 they totaled twenty-three. Six of these were reckoned as great powers, all with populations of over thirty-five millions, and all six entering into major groupings which dominated the European balance of power. Spain, with something less than twenty millions, and the Ottoman Empire, with something above twenty millions (most of them in Asia), counted as intermediate states. The pattern was still overwhelmingly monarchical, for in this period the Swiss Republic had been joined by only two others: France in 1870 and Portugal in 1910.

To the general observer, the great states, and doubtless even most of lesser rank, would have seemed in little danger of revolutionary transformation or overthrow. The German Empire, after so many years of national frustration, stood as the very embodiment of strength. Great Britain saw her empire steadily enlarging at a time when she could still claim to be the world's banker and its leading industrial power. France, as the sequel to a veritable kaleidoscope of political regimes, had established the Third Republic, destined to last for sixty-five years. The constitution of the Dual Monarchy, drawn up in 1867, encountered no truly explosive challenge until 1918. The grave weaknesses underlying the Italian parliamentary system were to some degree obscured by a substantial material growth; and imperial Russia was held by many, after the great constitutional decree of 1905, to have weathered its worst storms.

A most significant development of the first part of the century had been the rise of parliamentary regimes based on some degree of popular franchise. In 1815 these regimes were the exception; by 1871 they were the rule. The principle that governments should be subject to the control of an elected legislature was no doubt more important than the actual fact of universal manhood suffrage, which was established in one country after another in the closing years of the century. Universal suffrage in itself, however, could prove deceptive. Though France had won it as early as 1848, it did not impede the dictatorial functioning of the Second Empire; nor did the voting provisions of the Prussian constitution of 1850, or those in the constitution of the German Empire of 1871, basically impede the operation of autocracy. Switzerland alone, asserting the principle of universal manhood suffrage in her constitution of 1848, had at this early date established the essentials of a democratic regime which the constitutional revisions of 1874 served only to strengthen. On the other hand, in Great

Britain the assertion of the power of the House of Commons over the government long anticipated the wide extension of the franchise to the workingman which came about in 1884. The following table, therefore, showing the dates at which universal manhood suffrage was achieved in various countries, is chiefly important as indicating a significant trend developing during the span of one generation, and must in other respects be interpreted in the light of many qualifications:

ESTABLISHMENT OF UNIVERSAL MANHOOD SUFFRAGE

COUNTRY	DATE	COUNTRY	DATE
France	1848, 1852	Norway	1898
	1870	Austria	1907
Switzerland	1848, 1874	Ottoman Empire	1908
German Empire	1871	Sweden	1909
Great Britain	1884	Portugal	1910
Spain	1890	Italy	1912
Belgium	1893	Denmark	1915
Netherlands	1896		

NOTE: In some cases statements as to universal manhood suffrage are only an approximation which is qualified by continuing limitations on voting. The statistics are compiled from a variety of sources.

Woman suffrage, it can be noted, was established in Norway in 1907 and in Finland, still a part of the Russian Empire, in 1906.

Many obstacles continued to impede the operation of a popular franchise. Italy, with nearly three-quarters of its population illiterate in 1871, demonstrates one problem. The German Empire, where the Reichstag stood as the foremost example of "a parliament without parliamentary government," showed what little effect elections could have upon governmental policy. In Denmark, Sweden, and the Netherlands the royal veto continued to be a powerful force. The parliamentary regimes of Spain and Portugal were clearly ineffective, as were the arrangements made by the Turkish constitutional reforms of 1908. In Turkey political power lay in the hands of a military clique, while the constitution was associated with too inexperienced an electorate to be effective. Similarly, the entrance of Russia in 1906 into the world of parliamentary states, even though a momentous beginning, did not basically alter the workings of historic Russian autocracy. With all these qualifications, however, the existence of parliamentary regimes of which the backing had to be sought in the event of war, and to which it would then be necessary to turn for the voting of military credits, was becoming the established rule.

A few further points in the general workings of the European political system deserve notice. With the exception of Great Britain and Belgium, the standard political pattern in European countries was that of a multiplicity of parties—quite generally a half-dozen or so major groupings along with a changing variety of unstable smaller groups. Among the many reasons for this can be suggested the effect of the widely copied French mode of election known as the "second ballot." Any number of candidates could compete in the first round of voting, following which, if none secured a majority, a second vote was taken a week or two later on those with the highest totals. The temptation, therefore, was for a large number of parties to take their chances on the first round. Another most significant feature of these years was the arrival of socialism as a political force and the appearance of socialist parties of one sort or another in nearly every European country. The trade unions, too, undertook political activities of varying degrees and with varying success.

At least one disturbing development was observable in the political life of late nineteenth-century Europe. While the public and statesmen in general were disposed to accept parliamentary regimes as an inescapable fact of life, this acceptance was not unqualified or invariable. Critics as different as Carlyle and Nietzsche questioned the political wisdom embodied in electorates and elected assemblies. Bismarck manipulated the press with the utmost cynicism to influence public opinion. Leaders of ultranationalist groups used highly charged emotional arguments for the purpose of urging their followers to accept a leadership which was often dictatorial in nature. "We do not wish to upset the Republic," the French neoroyalist leader, Léon Daudet, was to write, "we want to cut its throat. We are not a political party; we are a conspiracy." The principle of democratic leadership was further threatened by revolutionary Marxian theorists who, having defined the capitalist state as "an instrument of class domination," set out to destroy it. Lenin's classic *What Is to Be Done?* (1901–1902) advanced the theory of the small, highly trained body of professional revolutionaries whose business it would be to direct the attack. Equally emphatically, the anarchist and syndicalist groups preached doctrines of violence that quite clearly were intended to destroy rather than to capture the existing machinery of the parliamentary state. Yet they remained minorities—forces in opposition rather than leaders of a dominant trend.

■ THE COURSE OF ECONOMIC AND SOCIAL DEVELOPMENT

The economic developments of the late nineteenth century, enormously productive in most respects, helped, nevertheless, to create or enlarge many troublesome social problems. Basically, the period was marked by a most substantial economic advance. Neither the heavy stream of emigration nor the sporadic outbreak of epidemics in western Europe had had any significant effect upon the European population which, as the accompanying simple chart indi-

cates, grew from an estimated figure of 200,000,000 in 1815 to around
300,000,000 in 1871 and to 450,000,000 in 1914, the annual rate of growth for
the second period eventually becoming about double that of the first.

GROWTH OF EUROPEAN POPULATION, 1770-1920, IN MILLIONS

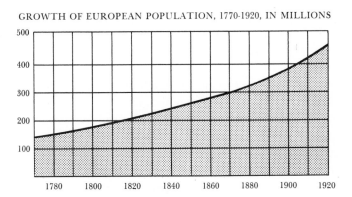

Adapted from A. M. Carr-Saunders, *World Population* (1936), p. 20.

The industrialism which had first made its mark upon England and
Belgium had by 1871 spread to France and Germany and was beginning to
spread elsewhere. By then the population of Great Britain had become more
than one-half urban and that of Germany and France in the neighborhood of
one-third. In the following years Germany was to pull far ahead of France so
that, while Germany's rural population remained nearly stationary, by 1914
her urban population showed a threefold increase. The European rail network
had grown from near nothing in 1830 to 65,000 miles in 1871, constituting one-
sixth (and that the most important sixth) of the ultimate total. The development of the steamship meant that the golden age of sail was coming to a close.

During the late nineteenth century the industrial position of two powers,
Great Britain and Germany, was outstanding. Since Britain's leadership was
traditional, the new role of the German Empire assumed all the more importance. Most striking was the speed and extent of this German advance,
illustrated concisely by the simple fact that, while Britain's annual production
of pig iron grew between 1871 and 1913 from 6,500,000 tons to 10,000,000 tons,
the comparable German growth was from 1,200,000 to 15,000,000 tons. In
another respect, the location of the rapidly growing German railway network,
admirably suited to handle a very large share of the European carrying trade,
proved a source of strength, as did Germany's growing financial resources. By
1914 she had managed to link the economies of various European states, already
tied to the economy of Great Britain, closely to herself. The British Isles were
Germany's best European customer, and Germany herself became the best

customer of Russia, Austria-Hungary, Italy, Switzerland, Belgium, Holland, and Norway, and the third best customer of France. The significance of the growing share of the world market steadily being appropriated by Russia, Japan, and the United States doubtless was not fully realized. Yet in 1913 Russia's production of pig iron was half that of France, and her production of steel was two-thirds. Russia's railway mileage, taking into account the more than six thousand miles of the Trans-Siberian Railway, exceeded that of Germany.

Another phenomenon of major significance was the steady growth of overseas commerce and, as an aspect of this, the strong economic motivation of the new imperialism. The enormous sums needed for investment abroad underscored the role of the international banker and demonstrated the ever-enlarging place of investment capital alongside the industrial capital of the preceding age.

The countries of western Europe, despite the general return to high tariffs, all imported more goods than they exported, making up the balance in various ways—by the profits from the European shipping which crisscrossed the seven seas, by the provision of insurance services, by interest on money loaned abroad, and by the profits on the huge amounts of capital which were regularly exported. The almost universal acceptance of the gold standard, by which currencies such as pounds, dollars, marks, francs, and pesos were all defined as the equivalent of so many grains of fine gold, meant that national currencies were readily interchangeable. They were also, in contrast to those of our own day, remarkably stable, so that businessmen could engage, if they wished, in complicated trade negotiations involving the currencies and products of several countries. In 1913 the imports and exports of seven European states (Great Britain, Germany, France, Belgium, the Netherlands, Switzerland, and Denmark) constituted one half of total world trade.

So sweeping an economic advance in Europe was bound to have profound social consequences. There can be little question of the rise in material well-being, whether measured by the upward trend of real wages, the general decline in rates of infant mortality, the prolongation of life, the widespread improvements in health, the lessening of working hours and the work week, the rise of the school-leaving age, or by the ever-widening consumption of luxury goods. The pattern, to be sure, was variable; in some countries improvement was slow, in others the general expectation of life, for example, increased at the rate of two years a decade. With respect to the figures of mortality the generalization can be made that in the hundred years from 1850 to 1950 western civilization has added a full generation to the average length of human life.

By 1914 "all Europe was being sent to school." Technical and university education made great strides; merely as illustrations one notes that two Portuguese universities, Lisbon and Oporto, were founded in the same year (1911), and that between 1881 and 1909 Great Britain saw the appearance of no less than six: Wales, Birmingham, Liverpool, Leeds, Sheffield, and Bristol. The extension of literacy, together with the increasing importance of the ballot, made it tempting to use the new mass media, chiefly the popular press, for propagandist purposes. In times of diplomatic crises, the calculated use of the newspapers to whip up popular sentiment became in some countries almost a standard procedure.

The steadily enlarging area of social legislation was one of the most obvious phenomena of the new age. The first factory acts in England had been sponsored by high-minded legislators in the face of substantial opposition from vested industrial interests. By 1914, save for Russia and the Balkans, every European country had reasonably well-developed codes of factory and labor legislation. Even in Russia some beginnings had been made and some rudimentary forms of trade-union activity had become possible. The opposition of writers such as Bentham and James Mill early in the century to the extension of state activities had been swept away in the face of what were accepted as the necessities of an industrial society. The most vivid evidence of this enlargement of public services came in the field of local government which assumed a steadily larger role in such varied matters as sanitation, transportation, the furnishing of gas, water, and electricity, public markets, slaughterhouses, labor exchanges, museums, parks, libraries, and schools.

The use of taxation, not simply as a device to secure ever-larger revenues, but as a deliberately intended instrument of social change is well illustrated in the "Lloyd George budgets" in the England of 1909 and subsequent years. A French observer shrewdly commented in 1920 upon this striking phenomenon, so typical of the transformation coming over European society:

> In the twenty years I have been here [in England] I have witnessed an English Revolution more profound than the French Revolution itself. The governing class have been almost entirely deprived of political power and to a very large extent of their property and estates; and this has been accomplished almost imperceptibly and without the loss of a single life.[1]

■ THE INTERNATIONAL ANARCHY

The picture of international politics observable during the latter part of the nineteenth century differs in marked respects from that of the preceding period. The wars fought before 1871 had been relatively few, moderate in size, and short in duration. They were not basically aggressive in the traditional

1. The French ambassador, Paul Cambon, to Winston Churchill, quoted in *The New Cambridge Modern History*, vol. XII (1960), p. 58.

sense. Most of them had served the cause of national independence or unification, as in the case of the subject peoples of the Ottoman Empire, or the Italians
seeking unity in the face of Austrian opposition. Bismarck's three brief wars had
been deliberately employed by him for a similar purpose. Alliances, such as they
were, had been organized for specific objectives and were seldom permanent,
falling apart when the immediate goal had been attained.

The developments after 1871 were very different. Until the catastrophe of
1914, no great wars, to be sure, devastated Europe. Statesmen—and none more
insistently than Bismarck—professed that the maintenance of peace was their
major concern. Yet states were becoming more heavily industrialized, and consequently, in the military sense, far more powerful. New nationalist philosophies
seemed to set a unique value upon the particular destiny of one state as against
another. Competition for overseas markets and for new sources of raw materials
became more acute. Thus Europe witnessed the growth of an increasingly tense
and ominous atmosphere.

Though major wars did not come, it was clear that plans for them were
developing on an ever-larger scale. The weapons of war grew steadily more
complex, more costly, and more destructive. In all European countries save
Great Britain military conscription became standard. This meant the existence
of huge reserves of militarily trained civilian man power, ready at the declaration of general mobilization to assemble at their depots, put on their uniforms,
and almost overnight raise the total armed strength of any one of the major
powers from a figure reckoned in the hundreds of thousands to one reckoned in
millions. Great Britain, relying chiefly on her naval strength, had actually a
total expenditure (military and naval) planned for 1914 which would be
greater than that of her principal rival, Germany.

A complex system of alliances based upon more or less secret treaties was
the principal mark of the new diplomacy. Although these alliances, according
to the literal wording of the engagements, were usually defensive in nature, it
seems undeniable that they tended to encourage a more aggressive attitude on
the part of countries possessing unfulfilled aspirations or nursing old grievances.
In the beginning stage of these alliances the dominant figure unquestionably
was Bismarck. Following his retirement in 1890, Germany continued by virtue
of her central position, her rapidly growing economic power, and her victorious
armies to be the most formidable military machine in the world, and thus the
alliance system still had Germany in a sense as the central point.

After 1871 Bismarck again and again declared the German Empire to be
a "saturated" power; his policy was to ensure that the arrangements of 1871
were not to be altered, more especially by any action of the French. Hence the
famous Dual Alliance of 1879, in which Germany and Austria-Hungary promised to come to each other's help if attacked, can quite properly be called a

turning point in the history of recent times. Unlike preceding alliances, which usually were transitory, the Dual Alliance lasted until 1918 and soon became the progenitor of a complex system which aligned the six great powers into two almost equally balanced and opposing groups of three.

No more than a suggestion of what followed can be given here. The Dual Alliance became the Triple Alliance when Italy, aroused at the French seizure of Tunis, asked in 1882 to be included. Bismarck's other great purpose was to reassure himself about Russia. He had been the "honest broker" at the Berlin Congress in 1878, where Russia's powerful moves against the Ottoman Empire had been rebuffed, to the advantage of both Austria (who got Bosnia-Herzegovina to administer) and Great Britain (who got Cyprus on the same basis). In order to keep Russia from turning to France, Bismarck managed in 1881 to revive his earlier and very informal league of the three eastern emperors established in 1872 and turn it into a signed treaty arrangement. By this each of the three promised "benevolent neutrality" if one of them became involved in war with a fourth power. When, in lieu of this, Bismarck made his Reinsurance Treaty with Russia in 1887, which (with two significant exceptions) promised benevolent neutrality in the event of either of them being at war, he could hope to have strengthened the prospects of peace. Yet there were large elements which might actually encourage, rather than avert, conflict. It was unlikely in the extreme that France would permanently accept the role of isolation into which Bismarck had maneuvered her. The network of alliances that Bismarck had created could easily become an entangling web, and in fact the observation of Caprivi, his successor, that the Bismarckian system was too complicated, is confirmed by the verdict of history.

Bismarck's system was soon transformed, and this development gives the dominant characteristic to the period which follows 1890. The Franco-Russian Alliance, which began with the first friendly declarations of 1891 and was fully established by the final ratifications of January, 1894, had the explicit promise of large-scale military support in the event of a German attack upon either signatory. It marked the beginnings of a system counter to that of the Triple Alliance. Though the terms were most secret, the existence of the Alliance was publicly admitted in 1895, and an argument could be made that the two sets of commitments for a time actually preserved the peace of Europe. When the atmosphere did alter, the change was due largely to overseas expansion and rivalries. How significant such changes were can be demonstrated by the circumstances of Great Britain's departure from her "splendid isolation." In 1902 Britain signed an agreement with Japan pledging mutual support if either's interests in the Far East were threatened. In 1904 Britain's Entente Cordiale with France was based on the recognition of special French interests in Morocco and special British interests in Egypt. Britain's 1907 agreement with Russia was correspondingly based on the recognition of mutual spheres of influence in Persia. No clearer evidence, surely, could be given to show the impact of colonial and imperial problems upon the European alliance system.

The succession of crises large and small, beginning with the Franco-British clash at Fashoda on the White Nile in 1898, contributed to the steadily heightening tensions of these years. It gave strength to those who sought ever-larger armaments and intensified the nationalist ardors of one country after another. Thus, despite the efforts of well-intentioned men in all fields and the laborious construction of some rudimentary machinery for international peace, such as the work done at the Hague Conferences of 1899 and 1907, the ominous signs continued to mount. Competitive naval building programs, ever-larger military budgets, and the extension of the terms of conscription became typical. The phrase, "international anarchy," coined by one student to describe it, conveys some sense of the nature of this troubled period. The lamentable truth is clear that the efforts of men to create a world based on mutual trust and good will were woefully inadequate to cope with the tensions and antagonisms which faced them.

■ CULTURAL CHANGES

An intellectual tradition which is not escapist will necessarily reflect the complex quality of its setting. Thus, in the late nineteenth century, almost every aspect of learning and the arts revealed something of the vitality possessed by the European industrial civilization. To summarize or to give an advance view of these aspects is not easy, for in any creative activity the thing done is far more meaningful, surely, than the comment made about it.

One is struck both by the amazing variety of technological and scientific advances in this period and by the profound consequences of a few. The internal combustion engine, responsible for a veritable revolution in transportation, was a product of these years. The airplane, in time to be responsible for still another revolution in transportation, made its appearance as the period closed. In pure science, as distinct from technology, the revolutionary concepts and new knowledge about the structure of the atom brought men to the threshold of the coming age of atomic power, even as in physics Einstein's theory of relativity destroyed the seeming stability of the Newtonian concepts of time and space. Biological knowledge, especially in the field of genetics, showed how complex were the forces underlying what had come to be the generally accepted hypothesis of evolution.

The study of man in society continued to be influenced by the techniques and assumptions of the scientists. The historians, for example, with their specialized institutes and cooperative enterprises, their ever-larger accumulation of factual data, and their insistence upon scientific method in the interpretation of such data, vied with the newer schools of economists, political scientists, and sociologists, all equally determined to be scientific in their methods and to set as their goals the discovery of laws. Marx himself had declared socialism to be scientific—the outcome of material forces—and many noncommunist students of society soon revealed in their writings the influence of this Marxian principle of economic determinism. The study of man in society, moreover, could no longer be the exclusive preserve of the historian and the political scientist. Anthropology, social psychology, and scientific archeology were but a few of the various new disciplines that came to be employed.

Literature and art did not fail to reflect their setting. Even such a phenomenon as the dilettantism and aestheticism of the 1890's showed by its very protest against the prevailing temper of the times how powerful these forces of materialism and industrialism were. Though some might escape from Philistinism to the distant world of Japanese art, and others to the fragile lyricism of the French symbolist poets, yet the great march of the scientific and industrial age continued. Concern with the problems of society was more characteristic than any attempt to escape from them. Novels and plays dealing with social issues abounded, and a new literature of social criticism, reminiscent in many respects of the work of the eighteenth-century *philosophes*, took shape.

In the fine arts broad characterization is not easy. The generation of post-impressionist painters, especially in the France of the 1890's, cannot neatly be put into one category. Yet their very restlessness and experimentalism, their bold advocacy of unusual schools, such as those of cubism or futurism, suggest again the reactions of the artist to a world which was changing at breath-taking speed. This uncertainty and experimentalism, and this constant pressure of change, are striking features of an age which now we may see was clearly coming to its end, even though many still hoped that they would be able to cling to the past as they had known it.

In conclusion, what is said here of the realm of culture could doubtless be applied to other aspects of European life. Many men were disposed to accept the European world which they knew as the rich embodiment of long traditions and the realization of historic aspirations. Others were prepared to undertake radical transformations of the existing scheme of things. Whether they did this to gratify their own selfish ambitions or to further what they conceived to be the age-old quest for social justice, the outcome in either case was an atmosphere of tension and uncertainty.

Chapter 10

The Triumph
of Machine Industry, 1870–1914

Introduction
Increase in Industrial Production
Transport and Communications
The Growth of World Trade
Urbanization and Emigration
European Agriculture
The Growth of Armaments
The Role of Government

■ INTRODUCTION

In contrast to the preceding decade, the period between the Peace of Frankfurt and the outbreak of the First World War was for Europe as a whole a period of relative political calm. Economically, however, it was a period of very rapid development, in which an inner "Europe of steam" became established, stretching from Scotland to north Italy and from Rouen to Warsaw. That central area, too, was ringed by other concentric regions—from the rest of Europe to the rest of the world—which were all to some extent influenced by the technological advances and commercial impulses of the center. The only possible rival to Europe in this sense was the United States of America, but down to 1914 her colossal economic development made relatively little impact on the outside world. The United States of America was still a debtor nation; even in Latin America, British, French, and German investments were nearly three

SIGNIFICANT EVENTS

1871	Mont Cenis Alpine railway tunnel opened
1873	First Russian oil wells sunk near Baku
1876	Invention of the telephone
1877	First shipment of frozen mutton
1878	Thomas Gilchrist basic process for making steel
1882–1884	Germs of tuberculosis, diphtheria, and cholera discovered
1884	Parsons' compound steam turbine
	Hiram Maxim's machine gun
1897	Manufacture of Diesel engine begun in Germany
1901	First transatlantic message by wireless telegraphy
1903	First successful airplane flight
1906	Discovery of vitamins
1909	Model-T Ford motorcar in production

times as large as those of Wall Street. Great industrial complexes, once characteristic only of Britain (and Belgium), now exploited the newest techniques in north Italy, Sweden, and Switzerland, as well as among Britain's closer neighbors. Their commercial strength, in turn, was made possible by concomitant developments in transport and communications, which enabled food and raw materials to be exchanged for manufactures, on terms highly favorable to the producer of the last-named commodities, with an ease never known before. But the rising standard of living during this period, though associated especially with urbanization, was also characteristic of many rural areas, where subsistence agriculture was wholeheartedly abandoned in favor of farming both grain and animal products by new techniques for an ever-expanding market. Typical of these more fortunate agriculturists were the emigrants, who went out in great numbers at this time to break virgin soil in America and Australasia.

"OVER LONDON BY RAIL," an engraving by Gustave Doré. The engraving hardly exaggerates the appalling living conditions caused in some areas by the huge growth of London's population.

Finally, this chapter will attempt to show some of the ways in which government action, at national or local levels, sought to direct this tremendous surge of economic vigor. It was in this period that the modern social services made a tentative start and authority set out in earnest to render town life healthy and agreeable for the masses. At the same time tariff laws, control of capital investment, and programs of territorial annexation were all used by European states to exert pressure in the international field, each hoping to gain for its own nationals advantages over all foreign rivals. Armaments therefore were not allowed to lag behind in the general advance of technology.

■ INCREASE IN INDUSTRIAL PRODUCTION

If we examine the last third of a century before the outbreak of the First World War, the advances made by the European economy in general are seen to be enormous. While population rose from about 300,000,000 to 450,000,000 —an increase of 50 percent—industrial production rose by 260 percent, and even the production of grain in face of the competition of other continents by 35 percent. Some of this growth was due to the better organization of human effort—increased subdivision of labor and regional specialization. Much of it, too, was attributable to improvement of transport and communications, which facilitated world trade and enabled Europeans to concentrate largely upon the most productive activities, so as to exchange their products on very advantageous terms for food and raw materials produced more economically in other continents. This was in part a result of technological advance, but it will be more convenient to postpone consideration of means of conveyance until we have marked the impact of new discoveries—new machines, new processes, new materials, and new sources of power—upon the output of commodities in general.

Since steel in place of iron was the characteristic structural material of the period, from the mild steel of ordinary rivets to the high-speed steel alloys used in machine tools, such as the turret lathe, we may take first the growth in steel output. This became very rapid after the so-called basic process for using phosphoric iron ores had been established by the English amateur chemists, Gilchrist and Thomas, in 1878 to the notable profit of the German Empire, which had so recently annexed Lorraine where phosphoric ore was plentiful. The French were correspondingly handicapped throughout this period by the loss of that province, as well as by the comparative poverty of their coal resources, which they nevertheless struggled hard to develop. Since coal was the fuel used in most metallurgical processes, in addition to its use in the provision of steam power, statistics of steel and coal output may be examined side by side.

PRODUCTION OF STEEL

(Thousands of tons)[1]

	BRITAIN	FRANCE	GERMANY	U.S.A.	ALL COUNTRIES
1870	240	90	140	40	550
1913	8,500	5,100	20,500	34,400	81,600

COAL OUTPUT

(Thousands of metric tons)

	BRITAIN	FRANCE	GERMANY	U.S.A.	ALL COUNTRIES
1871	117,400	12,900	29,300	42,500	230,000
1913	292,000	40,800	190,100	571,100	1,504,100

In both cases the trends were the same: an enormous overall increase; the growth of United States output, so that by 1913 in both steel and coal it exceeded that of her three west European rivals taken together; and the growth of German steel output, which by 1913 was virtually two and one-half times as big as the British. The growth in the use of other metals—copper, lead, zinc, aluminum—was also significant, and, in the case of gold and silver, a new

1. S. B. CLOUGH, *The Economic Development of Western Civilization* (1959), pp. 377, 385.

cyanide process, which facilitated the separation of very small proportions of precious metals, was an important factor in stimulating business through an increase in the available circulating medium.

Mining profited directly from the progress of the explosives industry, which had made its first important advances beyond gunpowder when the Swede, Alfred Nobel, invented dynamite in 1867; this prepared the way for innumerable other blasting explosives and the propellants and detonators used in modern firearms and artillery. Other branches of applied chemistry served exclusively the arts of peace, at least until the Germans began the manufacture of poison gas in 1915. The development of aniline dyes commonly attracted most attention, both because the inability to make satisfactory artificial dyes had long constituted a bottleneck in the textile industry and because it was an English invention of 1856 (Perkin's aniline mauve) from which German enterprise, based on elaborate laboratory investigation, built up one of its most remarkable triumphs. By 1914 Britain was importing 80 percent of its dyestuffs, mainly from Germany. Other chemicals, which formed the basis of the soap and glass manufactures as well as of artificial fertilizers for agriculture, were likewise a German specialty. By 1913 Germany produced nearly as much salt and nearly twice as much sulphuric acid as Britain, a quantity of nitrates rivaled only by Chile, and, from the deposits at Stassfurt, what was virtually the world supply of potassium. Examples of direct consumer benefits from the achievements of industrial chemistry are found in the making of paper from wood pulp, which brought much wealth to Sweden; in the improvement of photographic processes; in the progressive cheapening of safety matches; and in the production of synthetic medicines, perfumes, and flavorings from coal tar. The importance of the discovery of radium, on the other hand, was only in course of realization by 1914.

Thus the increased productivity in this period resulted in part from a more sophisticated use of materials and, in addition, from a greater resourcefulness in obtaining them—the coal hewn in ever-deeper mines or the supply of natural rubber extended by the transfer of the tree from the wild forest to the plantation. It was also the result of improvements in machinery. In textiles, for instance, there was the automatic loom, a Massachusetts invention of 1895, and the spread of power weaving among carpet makers. The clothing industry, the potteries, furniture making, lumbering, and metalworking were all brought more and more under the spell of labor-saving devices of increasing intricacy, until the use of the conveyor belt for the model-T Ford motorcar foreshadowed the day when not merely man power but man's directive work also would become a decreasingly significant cost factor in industrial output.

Meanwhile the limitations of human and animal muscle were more and more transcended. Steam power spread into new regions, such as Russia, where the decade 1890–1900, for example, witnessed a trebling of the steam power employed per metallurgical worker. At the same time it gained in efficiency, with a series of improvements to compound engines. But the future lay with wholly new devices. In 1884 Parsons developed the water turbine, which required a big head of water, into the steam turbine, a more efficient version of the steam engine. Nearly ten years before this the first efficient gas engine had been designed for industrial use in Germany; special gaseous fuels were developed, and gas engines were employed in increasing numbers up to the First World War. Two other types of internal combustion engine, however, soon attracted more attention—the Diesel engine, run on heavy oil, and the gasoline engine, having occasional industrial uses but designed from the first as the means of propulsion for some form of carriage. Industry, on the other hand, needed to replace the steam engine with some form of power which could be readily applied to individual machines, without the workshop's becoming cluttered up by overhead shafting. At the same time it had to be a form of power which could be economically provided and distributed over a considerable area from a single central source of supply and, if possible, clean and relatively noiseless in operation.

Hence the rapidly growing importance, toward the end of this period, of the electrical industry. Its development in a sense spans the entire nineteenth century, but, for fifty years after Faraday's momentous demonstration of electromagnetic induction in 1831, the generation of electric current on any large scale was an experimental project, and it was not until the incandescent lamp was invented that the demand for current became commercially significant. Though some of the earliest incandescent lamps illuminated the House of Commons in London in 1881, the Germans soon took the lead as suppliers of equipment in Europe. Coal-operated power stations began to appear in large towns, and by 1900 the first important hydroelectric installations were at work at Niagara Falls and at Schaffhausen in Switzerland. By 1914 electricity was beginning to oust gas as a source of light and heat in the newer European homes; the electric tram, too, had become well established, and the electric railway was much more than a novelty. As the methods of long-distance transmission of electric power improved, a great decentralization of industry became possible. The use of hydroelectricity, in particular, took away the monopoly of the coal-bearing regions of Europe. By 1914 Italy, which has very little coal, disposed of nearly 1,000,000 h.p. of electricity obtained from her waterfalls; Switzerland and France came close behind, followed by Sweden and Norway.

Electrification was one of the contributory factors in a marked change in the distribution of industry among the powers, which may conveniently be represented by a table. Since the total of world manufacture was at least quadrupled during the period, clearly the growth in Russia, Sweden, and even

TRAMCARS ON THE FIRST ELECTRIC STREET RAILWAY IN EUROPE, FRANKFURT-AM-MAIN, 1884. First introduced in Germany, electric tramcars were in use in the United States (Richmond) by 1888 and in Britain (Leeds) in 1891.

Italy was quantitatively considerable, quite apart from the relative advance in comparison with Britain, France, or Belgium. These countries were in fact entering upon a period of rapid change comparable in many ways to Britain's Industrial Revolution of a century before.

WORLD MANUFACTURE[2]

percentage shares of total

	BRITAIN	GERMANY	FRANCE	RUSSIA	BELGIUM	ITALY	SWEDEN	UNITED STATES
1870	31.8	13.2	10.3	3.7	2.9	2.4	0.4	23.3
1913	14.0	15.7	6.4	5.5	2.1	2.7	1.0	35.8

The economic development of united Italy first gained some impetus in the early 1880's, when coal imports rose to 300,000 tons a year; by 1914 they had reached 12,000,000 tons. The government subsidized heavy industry to help armament production. Even so, the silk industry, in which the Italians were traditionally expert, alone had international importance as long as Italy depended upon imported fuel. Even the electrification of the railroads made slow progress up to 1914 for fear of giving too much control to foreign capital. So the fellow countrymen of Volta and Marconi remained hopelessly divided between

2. League of Nations: Economic, Financial and Transit Departments: *Industrialization and Foreign Trade* (League of Nations, 1945), p. 13.

a half-prosperous north and a wholly poverty-stricken south with an average national income per head in 1911–1913 less than half of that enjoyed by their neighbors in France. Only the triangle bounded by Milan, Turin, and Genoa belonged in effect to the "inner Europe" of industrial growth.

Sweden, like Italy, had a traditional industrial skill—her metalworking—which had first been eclipsed by Britain about 1800. She also had the same initial handicap as Italy, though the Swedish coal output (in Scania) was small rather than nonexistent. But Sweden benefited directly from the new chemical processes which added wood pulp and paper to the original export trade in timber. She benefited even more strikingly from the introduction of the basic process in steelmaking, which enabled her to develop a huge export of phosphoric iron ore from barren Lapland: total iron ore exports by 1913 were a hundred times what they had been in the 1880's. The Swedes also expanded their iron industry, first into an engineering industry which supplied the home market with sawmill equipment, steam engines, and agricultural machinery, and then into an export trade in advanced machinery, including electrical equipment. Finally, in the last decade before the First World War, "white coal" became a very important factor in Swedish industry, both for electrometallurgical and for electrochemical manufactures.

The economic development of Russia was very uneven. The textile processes were effectively mechanized between 1866, when there were 42 cotton mills, and 1897, when there were 722 such mills employing 325,000 workers. The iron and steel industries moved rather more slowly: as late as 1900, 43 percent of pig iron was obtained with wood fuel; 10 percent of furnaces operated on the obsolete cold-blast principle; and one-third of the steel was made in Bessemer rather than the more efficient open-hearth furnaces. The petroleum industry, centered on the rich oil fields round Baku and Grozny, was the great exception: by 1901 Russia had a peak output of nearly 12,000,000 tons, which made her at that date the largest oil producer in the world. The overall picture, as we approach 1914, is of a vast empire which lagged far behind its smaller neighbors (and the United States) in the use of the mechanical prime movers which create modern industry. Both Englishmen and Americans had at their disposal fifteen times as much horsepower in relation to population, and Germans eight times as much, as the Russians had. But the power available in Russia had increased by 50 percent in the first decade of the new century, and in the metallurgical industries of the southern part of the country more than one-third of that power was derived from electricity.

■ TRANSPORT AND COMMUNICATIONS

A rise in the productivity of industry in any European country, and especially in those that were too small for much expansion of the domestic market, was very largely dependent upon the rapid growth of facilities for moving heavy goods, including vast quantities of food and raw materials, between regions and countries and continents. To some extent it was a matter of developing with a greater sense of urgency devices which were already familiar. The digging of the Suez Canal in 1869, for instance, was followed in 1894 by that of the Kiel Canal, linking the Baltic with the North Sea; the Dutch, too, in 1876 built a new ship canal for by-passing the shallows of the Zuider Zee. The big French canal system was standardized in depth and in the length of locks, and the Germans similarly improved the canal connections with their main river highways, the Rhine and the Elbe. In France, which had by far the biggest network of actual canals in western Europe—though Germany had a greater length of navigable rivers—the use made of inland waterways doubled between 1886 and 1913.

Railways, however, kept the predominant position which the main lines were establishing for themselves in 1870. The needs of commerce and travel caused branch lines to be added to main lines and single-track main lines to be doubled. All told, the growth of railways in western Europe amounts to a trebling in forty years, except for Britain, which added only one half to its already fairly adequate provision. In what had been the more backward countries in the Europe of 1870 the rate of increase was proportionately higher: the length of the Swedish railways, for instance, was multiplied by eight in this period, and of the Russian by five. If we except Russia, with its great rivers, huge distances, and late start in railway building, the railways of Europe carried at least four times as much as the inland waterways, with wheeled traffic along macadamized roads serving mainly as a feeder to both systems. From 1900 onward there was a beginning of electrification, at first applied mainly to local rail services; up to 1914 this made less progress than the gasoline-engined motorcar, which was reducing the macadam road to dust and obsolescence.

However, the biggest single factor in lowering the cost of heavy long-distance transportation during this period was the long-delayed turnover from the use of timber-built sailing ships, with their restricted size, low average speed, and dependence on seasonal conditions of wind and weather, to the modern steamship. This was a change of twofold importance for Britain. The use of steamships gave her a big advantage in freight costs, because bunker coal was cheaply obtainable in Britain as an ever-ready return cargo to any part of the world. At the same time, British engineering experience, in combination with a plentiful supply of iron and steel, enabled her to gain a lead such as her shipbuilding industry had never had before. In the early 1890's four-fifths of all new construction for the mercantile marines of the whole world was in British hands; in 1913 her share was still more than three-fifths. As for the change in the character of British shipbuilding, by 1898–1899 Bessemer could record that

98.8 percent of ships launched were made of steel, and by 1913 only 4 percent of ships launched were for sailing. Thus the sailing ships, so comely and so cheap to run, slowly vanished from the seas, even though as late as 1910 they still composed nearly half of the total tonnage owned, for instance, by the thrifty French.

By the outbreak of the First World War the basis of international trade was provided by a steamer fleet of 45,400,000 gross tons at the disposal of the leading carrying nations. In addition, the introduction of quadruple-expansion engines, the designing of specialized cargo ships, such as oil tankers, and the improved distribution of coaling facilities in both hemispheres had created conditions in which a steamship on the average did four times as much work in the year as a sailing ship. Taking all methods of propulsion together, significant proportions of world tonnage were owned in 1914 by the following powers: by the United Kingdom, 39.2 percent; by Germany, 11.1 percent; by the United States, 10.9 percent (of which nearly one half was employed in the Great Lakes); by Norway, 5.1 percent; and by France, 4.7 percent.

The growth of a world economy, directed largely from Europe and to the initial advantage largely of Europeans, required an adequate network of communications as well as transportation. The submarine telegraph, indeed, to some extent preceded the spread of steam freighters over the ocean routes, for Britain was effectively linked with the United States in 1866 and with Australia in 1871. The development of the telephone (from 1876 onward) and of wireless telegraphy, which sent its first message across the Atlantic in 1901, completed the process of creating a world market, in which the movement of commodities and the level of prices could respond almost instantaneously to changes of conditions in distant regions. In several other ways new technological devices made communication easier. The typewriter became available in 1874 to transform the character of business records and correspondence. For newspapers the rotary press, printing from continuous rolls and folding the cut sheets ready for the vendors, and the use of half-tone blocks and photogravure for illustration, gave a cheapness and a lightness which appealed to millions of new readers, so that people and events were made to interact upon each other for better or worse. Most startling of all was the effect of cinematography, which grew out of photography in the last years of this period, since it could display the life of a strange nation or civilization to big audiences, largely made up of people to whom a foreign language or the difficulty of imagining a faraway, strange environment had been insuperable obstacles.

To many ordinary citizens, however, the group of inventions which seemed to matter most were those which transformed the mobility of the individual. This was of course one aspect of the use of steamship and railway, which modified the conventional idea of a long or impracticable journey, just as the airplane has done in more recent days. The suburban railway, followed by the underground railway, was also an important factor in enabling ordinary people—as distinct from "carriage folk"—to live beyond walking distance from their place of work. Horse-drawn omnibuses, in spite of their name, were too slow and expensive to serve the needs of the masses; and streetcars on rails had only a limited vogue until overhead electric power replaced horse or steam traction in the 1890's. Equally characteristic of the closing years of the nineteenth century was the vogue of the safety bicycle, for which Dunlop provided the pneumatic tire in 1888. Finally, as we approach 1914, there is the early automobile; in Europe, though it was still largely a rich man's toy, large towns such as London and Paris were already introducing motor omnibuses.

■ THE GROWTH OF WORLD TRADE

The enormous technical advances of the age both stimulated and were stimulated by the growth of world trade. Up to the outbreak of the First World War the world, still led by Europe, was moving rapidly, if unevenly, in the direction of a world economy, as the following table shows.

WORLD TRADE[3]

Total of exports and imports in million pounds

	1874–1875	1885	1895	1905	1913
United Kingdom	656	584	657	914	1,186
Germany	300	290	353	719	1,021
France	296	287	287	380	607
Russia	148	157	128	170	303
Rest of Europe	576	759	880	1,404	2,010
Europe total	1,976	2,077	2,305	3,587	5,127
United States	200	268	333	584	868
Rest of America	207	265	316	484	866
Asia	212	285	374	629	956
Australasia	84	120	104	125	202
Africa	61	70	123	215	335
World total	2,740	3,085	3,555	5,624	8,354

When allowance is made for the long fall in prices (to 1896) and the subsequent recovery, these figures show that the volume of world trade trebled dur-

3. *Encyclopaedia Britannica* (1947), vol. XXII, p. 350. Except in 1874–1875, the United Kingdom totals of exports and (in 1913 only) the totals of imports are reduced to allow for re-exports. Separate figures for Russia are included because of their intrinsic interest, although they were not normally the fourth largest in Europe.

ing the first thirty years of this period and continued to grow at a still more rapid pace up to the war. It may safely be said that there had been no economic expansion comparable to this in the whole of earlier history. Inside Europe, indeed, its most striking feature was the speed with which Germany was overhauling Britain and the concomitant advance of lesser powers, such as the Netherlands, Belgium, Italy, and Sweden, whose trade over the whole period can be seen to have grown at least twice as fast as Britain's. But, from a world point of view, what is most significant is the predominance of Europe in this tremendous advance. In 1874–1875, 72 percent of the total trade was hers; in 1913 the percentage was still as high as 61.

It is true that the other main areas of the world improved their relative positions. Thus America's share rose from 15 to 21 percent during the period, almost exactly one half of that share being the trade of the United States both at the beginning and the end. The share of Asia rose from 8 to 11 percent, largely because the trade of Japan multiplied itself fifteen times. The African share also rose from 2 to 4 percent, leaving only Australasia in a relatively stationary position. But in order to estimate the true bearing of this change upon the economic position and strength of Europe, it is necessary to take into account the part played by international investment, in which, in 1913, certain European powers had an as yet unchallenged lead.

LONG-TERM FOREIGN INVESTMENTS[4]

(in million pounds)

	BRITAIN	FRANCE	GERMANY	NETHERLANDS	UNITED STATES
1880	1400	700	300	100	———
1914	4000	1750	1400	400	600

The rapidity of growth shown by the table is in any case remarkable, as is also the modest extent to which the United States participated. Her share in 1880 amounted to nothing, and even in 1914 was only 50 percent bigger than that of a smaller European power such as the Netherlands. The full impact of Europe upon the rest of the world, however, can only be measured by distinguishing the destinations of the investments, so far as these are known. European powers might be expected to invest first and foremost in their own continent. The greater part of both French and German lending went there. France for political reasons interested herself especially in the development of Russia, which both at the turn of the century and in 1914 was receiving almost exactly 25 percent of the available French surplus, while Germany showed a similar, though less strongly marked, preference for investment in Austria-

4. *Chambers's Encyclopaedia* (1955) vol. V, p. 791. The analyses of the investments in the following paragraphs are based on figures in the work by H. Feis, *Europe the World's Banker 1870–1914* (1930), p. 34.

Hungary. Britain, however, by 1914 had ceased to lend on a large scale in any European country except Russia, and even there the British stake was only one-quarter the size of the French.

Britain, which up to the outbreak of the war was still the world's great lender, concentrated her attention increasingly upon the outer continents. One half of all British overseas investment was within the British Empire, chiefly in Canada, Australasia, the Indian subcontinent, and South Africa, and in that order. Another 20 percent was placed in the United States—a sum exceeding the whole of United States foreign investment, which was directed almost entirely to Canada and Latin America. Britain placed a further 20 percent in Latin America, while Japan, Egypt, China, and the Ottoman Empire each received an important share of her available surplus. As for the other powers, the Dutch invested very largely in their colonies, the French to the extent of 9 percent, and the Germans much less. Both the French and the Germans placed about 15 percent of their investments in Latin America, while the United States and Canada received about 30 percent of the German and 7 percent of the French total. The Ottoman Empire was the only major area where the actual amount of French and of German capital exceeded the British.

What conclusions should be drawn from these facts? In the first place, they are a reminder that less progressive countries could only be developed with the help of these transfers of capital, which enabled them to buy the instruments of development, such as the railways to carry their produce to the world market. Second, the growth of world trade which normally followed was directly related to the investments, since it was by the sale of their products that the debtor states paid the interest on the loans received. A third consideration of importance is the extent to which the ability to lend depended upon the willingness of the small-income groups in western Europe to save. In France, for example, where there was comparatively little large-scale industry, the thrifty peasant family was the unit directly concerned. But a big part was also played by banks and other credit institutions, which made a handsome and in some cases extravagant profit on the issue of foreign bonds, and were responsible for selecting those issues for which they believed they could find buyers. The great German banks, in particular, borrowed money from foreign sources to supplement the rather small proportion of savings—a maximum of one-fifth as compared with two-fifths in France—which their own nationals were disposed to send abroad.

Last, it is clear that banks and private investors alike were influenced in the choices they made primarily by the two factors of rate of profit and degree of risk. They expected their money to earn more abroad than at home, but they also faced greater uncertainties regarding climatic and other natural hazards, the careless or deliberate misuse by borrowers of funds obtained from distant sources, and the possibility of revolution and repudiation. In so far as this led to governmental control of investment, it will be considered later in the chapter. Here we may conclude by noticing that for millions of Europeans—there were 1,600,000 separate French holdings in Russian securities alone—a personal link existed with the affairs of other countries, additional to, and greatly strengthening, the ties which were automatically created by the vast growth of world trade and the consequent subdivision of labor among nations—which corresponded to the way in which labor was already subdivided among persons.

■ URBANIZATION AND EMIGRATION

In the late nineteenth century western European man was becoming preponderantly a city-dweller. Urbanization was the leading social result of the big increase in manufacturing industry, based chiefly on steam power, and of the accompanying increase in transportation facilities, which made it practicable to feed big concentrations of population in areas remote from agriculture or other primary food production. The transformation was most striking in Germany, where the total population was increased by three-fifths during the period; about 90 percent of this increase (22 out of 25 millions) was urban, which means that the actual number of town-dwellers was practically quadrupled. But the phenomenon was remarkable throughout the "Europe of steam" and even as far afield as the western provinces of Russia.

POPULATION LIVING IN COMMUNITIES OF 2000 AND UPWARD

(Approximate percentages)

	ENGLAND AND WALES	FRANCE	GERMANY
1871	62	33	36
1911	78	44	60

To anyone judging by conditions in the large European towns of the past, from London to Naples, such a concentration of population might appear to be a major catastrophe, since similar conglomerations had only been able to exist by draining away young and healthy immigrants from the countryside. Even after the advances in public health at the time of the start of the Industrial Revolution, industrial towns retained an obstinately high death rate. But the last quarter of the nineteenth century was on the whole propitious to the growth of many advantages in town life. An instructed and increasingly democratic public opinion influenced the organs of local government, even where—as in Germany, for instance—these were bureaucratic in form. Scientific knowledge was newly available as regards the main health problems. The physical means for constructing urban complexes with efficient services were now to hand. The scientists led the way. Pasteur's pioneer work on bacteria was concerned with such varied problems as the silkworm disease which ravaged France in the late

1850's, the treatment of hydrophobia, and the nature of the fermentation process in yeast. From it came Lister's development of the use of antisepsis, and the identification by Virchow and Koch of the bacilli causing tuberculosis, diphtheria, typhoid, and cholera. The effectiveness, however, of the measures taken to control these scourges depended on the availability of the techniques for equipping large concentrations of population with sufficient quantities of pure water and an efficient system of drainage. The completion of the London main drainage system in 1875, for example, or of the 96-mile aqueduct to bring the Lake District water into Manchester, are illustrations of innumerable constructional achievements made possible by advances in building materials and design.

Town life was becoming not only healthier but more agreeable. Gas lamps, and even electric lights, indoors and in the streets; roadways and sidewalks that were properly paved and drained; working-class houses, still ranged in monotonous rows but at least built with some regard to the admission of sun and air and the exclusion of damp—all these were improvements which spread fast across Europe. Such changes did not commonly occur in country villages. Moreover, where population was closely concentrated, it was relatively easy to provide other amenities which might appeal to the masses. Neatly arranged parks and recreation grounds, public libraries, art galleries, museums, and other improved educational facilities are examples which spring readily to mind, and all of these undoubtedly had their strong supporters. It would be realistic also to include the professional football teams, which originated in the factory towns of northern England; the department stores, first seen in Paris; the concert halls and suburban beer gardens of Germany; and, by 1914, the novel attraction of the cinema.

Urbanization also led eventually to the revival of town planning, which had fallen almost entirely into abeyance during the half-century or so of most widespread laissez-faire tendencies. In some Continental cities the demolition of fortifications gave a chance to plan, as at Cologne and Vienna, or special powers were used to site public buildings advantageously, following the example of Haussmann's activities in Paris under the Second Empire. Germany in 1875 gave legal powers to a majority of the property owners in a given district to carry through desired improvements, and in the same year Disraeli enabled municipal authorities in Britain to demolish and rebuild slum property. There followed the building of housing estates and eventually of garden cities, in keeping with the English idea that a yard or garden was essential to full satisfaction and privacy, and of improved blocks of flats occupying less crowded sites, such as the *Arbeiterkolonien* provided by the Krupps for the workers of Essen. In 1914 it was still the case that, the larger the city or conurbation, the greater its attractions for industry and commerce and all who live by them. Moreover, the demand for improvements of all kinds grew with the increasing weight of the highly organized urban electorates, so that in the twentieth century, as in ancient Greece, politics were firmly based on the *polis*.

The movement to the cities had its counterpart in migration overseas. The new facilities in transport and communication—including all the novel circumstances, such as cheap newspapers and cheap overseas postal services, which spread information about conditions elsewhere—carried population not merely to new cities but to new continents. Men aspired to a higher standard of living and better opportunities for themselves and their families. In the homeland this usually meant industrial employment and city-dwelling. Overseas, in the first generation at least, it could mean work on virgin soil without any serious burden of rent. One obvious exception to this was emigration brought about by news of gold rushes and pioneering for metals in general; another, the absorption of a mass of unskilled industrial labor in steel works, railroad construction, and similar activities in America, where boundless opportunities made it difficult to retain native American workers in such humble activities for long.

The scale of movement was prodigious. In 1871–1875 the oceans were crossed by an annual average of about 380,000 presumed emigrants. With two brief setbacks, the figure rose until, in 1901–1905, it exceeded 1,000,000, and in the prosperous last three years before the outbreak of the First World War the average stood at 1,650,000. To this must be added the flow of emigration overland from Russia to Siberia—about 2,000,000 in the period 1871–1900 and 3,500,000 in the following 14 years. The statistics are not precise, for we lack information as to the number of emigrants who returned eventually to make fresh homes in Europe, either because they had gone abroad only temporarily to make money or because they failed to establish themselves satisfactorily in a new country. Nor do the statistics shed any light on motives, except that the general correspondence between periods of prosperity in Europe and periods of increased emigration from Europe suggests that hope played a larger part than desperation. It was the first time in the world's history that individuals in large numbers had been free to migrate, if they so wished; the first time that people had had definite knowledge of new countries offering boundless prospects of wealth and advancement; the first time that technological progress, by means of the railway and the steamship, had made so long a journey fully practicable.

The statistics show two things quite clearly. One is the change in the country of origin of the typical transatlantic migrant. In 1871–1875 the point of departure for more than 50 percent was the British Isles and for nearly 20 percent more was Germany; by 1896–1900 those percentages had shrunk respectively to 25 and 5. The place of the Anglo-Saxons had been taken by Italians above all, but also to a notable extent by other Latin peoples and by Austro-Hungarian and Russian subjects, such as Poles and persecuted Jews. The other clear indication concerns the overwhelming popularity of the United States as a destination for emigrants. In the entire recorded period,

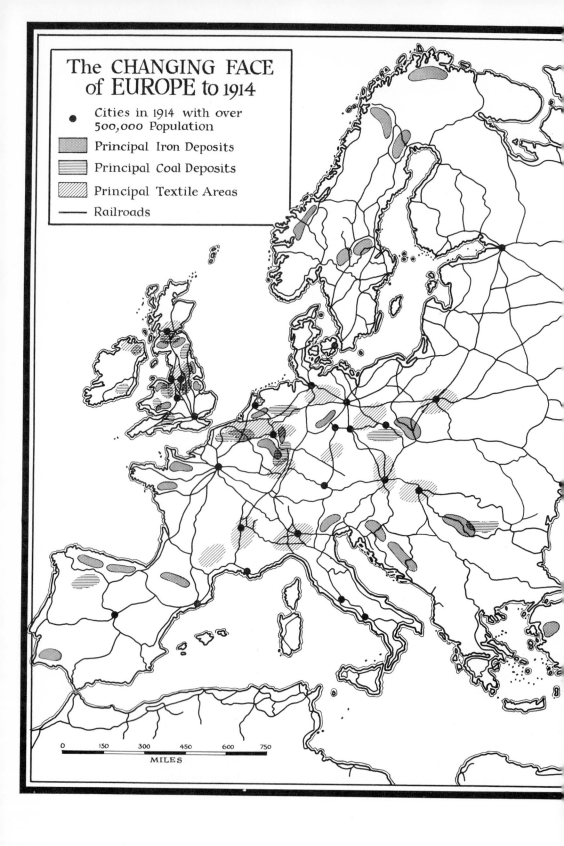

The CHANGING FACE
of EUROPE to 1914

• Cities in 1914 with over
   500,000 Population

   Principal Iron Deposits

   Principal Coal Deposits

   Principal Textile Areas

— Railroads

0   150   300   450   600   750
            MILES

which runs from 1856 to 1932, out of 59,000,000 persons who crossed the oceans from Europe, 54,000,000 landed in the Americas, and of these the proportion directly entering the United States was 80 per cent or more up to 1875 and never less than 60 percent at any time up to 1914. Canada, Argentina, and Brazil shared the rest of the American intake in fairly equal proportions; the remaining 5,000,000 included nearly 3,000,000 going to Australia and considerably less than 1,000,000 to South Africa and to New Zealand.

The prime importance of this to the history of Europe is of course the spread of a European stock into new regions, which effectively transplanted European cultures and for a time strengthened the position of the powers of Europe to some extent as the colonizing powers of that day. But the economic effects were also important. On the one hand, there was the relief to over-population in such countries as Italy and Ireland, and the direct help given by remittances to dependents and through the spending power of those who came home to retire in familiar surroundings. Then we must notice the addition to the raw material supplies for European industry, which came from mines, sheep farms, and plantations. Finally, the rising standard of life in the industrial re-gions of Europe was helped by the availability of Canadian and Australian wheat, Argentine and American beef, New Zealand lamb and dairy produce, which the new techniques of cooling and freezing made it possible to send in, wherever tariff conditions permitted. Moreover, by 1914, Siberia, though lack-ing in capital and in transportation facilities, was growing twice the amount of grain needed for its total population of 10,000,000. As for the United States, for a whole generation its Middle-Western states figured as the biggest granary of all; after the turn of the century, when Americans began to need their harvest for home consumption, American industrial progress, to which a series of brilliant immigrant inventors made big contributions, provided a challenge which European industrialists ignored at their peril.

■ EUROPEAN AGRICULTURE

Workers in industry and trade commonly produce goods to twice the value of those produced by the same amount of work in agriculture, which enables urbanized industrial communities to afford more—and more varied—food. In this circumstance and in the growth of urban population lay a great stimulus to expansion in agriculture. Therefore in Europe itself the exploita-tion of the soil became generally more intense and other continents could employ immigrant populations to grow food for export. The technical achieve-

Although iron deposits are widespread, and ore is moved in increasing quantities from Spain and northern Sweden, the nearness of iron ore to the coalfields gives particular importance to the industrial areas of the English Midlands, Lorraine, the Rhineland, and Upper Silesia. Only the principal railways are shown.

ment involved was truly remarkable, for not only was a hugely increased population fed, but even the rural dietary never fell below the needed minimum; witness the fact that, with the help of better transport conditions, famine disappeared at last from the west European scene. As for the urban population, such factors as average length of life and stature suggest that its dietary was notably improved in quality as well as in quantity.

One important change in agricultural methods was the spread of the use of machinery driven by mules and horses, steam engines, and eventually the gasoline engine, from America, where the shortage of labor had stimulated invention, to the age-old fields of conservative-minded Europe. In Britain the use of some machines characterized the "high farming" which reached its zenith just after 1870; in Germany the large Junker estates of the east were excellently equipped before the end of the century; and in the last decade or so before the First World War the French peasant was belatedly adopting mowing machines, reapers, and binders. In Russia, too, twenty years after the serfs were freed, the estate farms of the nobility employed machinery on a considerable scale to compensate for the scarcity of labor.

Second, there was a great increase in the use of artificial fertilizers, which were still almost a novelty in the middle of the nineteenth century. By 1913 the world was using annually about 600,000 tons of nitrates, 1,348,000 tons of potash, and 16,251,000 tons of superphosphates. The fertility of the soil was also being improved by increasingly efficient drainage, better knowledge of crop rotation, and better practices which were gradually replacing the immemorial traditions of communal strip-system tillage.

Last, productivity was enhanced by better seed selection (as with the Marquis wheat of the Canadian prairie); by selective breeding of cattle, sheep, and even pigs; and by the attention paid to special field crops of roots and vegetables.

Quite apart from the inflow of food to Europe from other continents, an important differentiation of function grew up within the European food-producing regions. Near industrial districts farmers tended to specialize in the production of meat, including pig meat and poultry, eggs, and dairy produce, and garden stuff, all of which could be sold advantageously to townspeople in search of a more varied and healthier diet. Of this tendency, Denmark, with its bacon and eggs, is the best example, since ready access to the British and German industrial markets in this case enabled a whole nation of agriculturists to organize a very profitable type of specialization. In other areas, on the other hand, grain was grown in large quantities to compete with transoceanic wheat. Thus the prosperity of South Russia was for a time firmly based on exports via the Black Sea or by railway into Germany, though between 1890 and 1913 the increased home demand reduced the percentage of the wheat crop exported from 46 to 15 percent. A more stable situation was that of the Danube lands, where Hungary was second only to Russia in the quantity exported; in the early years of the new century, Russia and the Danubian region between them were responsible for two-fifths of the wheat export trade of the whole world.

To sum up, the period 1870–1914 was catastrophic for the agricultural population of one country only, the United Kingdom, where free-trade imports were allowed to destroy arable farming for the sake of a cheaper food supply for the people of the towns. In other countries tariffs were used to maintain the profitability of agriculture. Barring such disasters as the phylloxera (green fly), which ravaged the French vineyards in the 1870's, efficient farmers prospered, and even the wages of farm laborers rose with proximity to industrial centers. In Germany, indeed, while the proportion employed in agriculture (and forestry) declined from 47 to 34 percent in a population which increased by more than 50 percent, agricultural output nevertheless grew faster than population. But extremes of poverty and physical misery remained in the special conditions of such regions as southern Italy and Sicily and other Mediterranean lands, where a backward peasantry clustered upon thin soil at the mercy of avaricious land-lords and its own conservative prejudices. In Russia, too, it was only after the upheavals of 1905 that the peasant was free to shake off the control of the *mir*[5] and develop the land as he pleased; up to that time the number of two-horse farms—to use an easy standard—was actually declining.

■ THE GROWTH OF ARMAMENTS

One of the arguments commonly advanced for maintaining the profit-ability of agriculture in the different states of Europe was the military value of a plentiful rural population. The countryman, robust, calm, and inured to physical hardship, was still thought of as a tremendous asset on the battlefield. But in fact machinery was now as predominant in war as in peace. Since the earliest days of the Industrial Revolution, machine industry had, indeed, owed its growth in part to the needs of arms manufacture. Wilkinson's cannon-borer, which played a vital part in the evolution of the first effective steam engines; the system of manufacture with interchangeable parts, invented for military and naval purposes; and Bessemer's steel converter, occasioned by the Crimean War, are famous early examples. In the same way, after 1870 there was a close interaction between industrial progress and the progress of the arts of war, with the latter engaging the attention of a high proportion of resourceful inventors and entrepreneurs.

The big armament firms were in many cases international in character: they sold their wares impartially to both sides in a dispute or, to their greater profit, sold new offensive weapons to one party and the corresponding means of defense to the other. But the power and influence exerted by such firms as Krupp, Schneider, and Armstrong-Whitworth—to take examples from Ger-

5. See p. 175.

many, France, and Britain, respectively—were a symptom or a stimulus rather than the originating cause of a very dangerous trend of events. Basically, it was the rivalry between nations, including the struggle for colonies and markets, which made a mounting expenditure on arms tolerable and even popular. Thus at every stage of invention each power felt the urge, if not to get ahead, at least to keep abreast, of its neighbors. This climate of opinion made for a rapid growth in the technology of destruction, the means by which states prepared to destroy lives and property in the pursuit of their supposed national interests. A table will show the justification for calling the result an arms race:

GROWTH OF ARMAMENTS[6]

Cost in dollars per head of population, with figures in brackets showing percentage of national income, if known

	BRITAIN	FRANCE	GERMANY	RUSSIA	AUSTRIA-HUNGARY	ITALY
1870	3.74 (2.0)	3.03	1.33	1.34	1.16	1.44
1890	4.03 (2.3)	4.87	2.95	1.32	1.56	2.63
1910	7.56 (3.6)	6.70	4.17	1.91	1.77	3.50
1914	8.53 (3.4)	7.33 (4.8)	8.52 (4.6)	2.58 (6.3)	3.48 (6.1)	3.81 (3.5)

Every great power and the wealthier and more exposed of the smaller powers, like Belgium, spent much money in the elaboration of fortresses at key positions, such as Metz, Liège, and Verdun. The use of ferroconcrete and specially hardened steel alloys made it possible to give very heavy protection to both men and guns, the latter being mounted in steel cupolas which could be raised, revolved, and lowered out of sight again by machinery. Despite this, the fire power of siege artillery had ended the day of impregnable fortresses, as the Japanese demonstrated when their eleven-inch howitzers reduced Port Arthur to rubble in 1904. In the case of capital ships, too, vast sums were expended in search of an impregnability which proved illusory. The armor plating, first of the ironclad and later of the dreadnought, and even the powerful turbine engines of the latter, did not prevent the capital ship from presenting a vulnerable target not only to the gunnery of its peers, when turret fired against turret, but to the torpedo boat and its similarly armed successor, the destroyer. From 1901 onward the development of the heavy-oil engine and storage batteries gave enough mobility to the submarine for it to present the battleship with a further challenge.

The art of war might be expected to have benefited proportionately from the fact that this was an age of rapid transport improvements. This was only partly the case. The mobilization of armies depended, indeed, on the increasingly elaborate network of rail communications, which in many frontier areas were financed by governments for this very purpose. Warships, too, were driven by coal-burning, and in a very few cases oil-burning, engines; mention has

6. QUINCY WRIGHT, *A Study of War* (2 vols., 1942), vol. I, pp. 670–671.

just been made of the turbines which gave the dreadnoughts a far higher speed than any earlier type of battleship. But it is remarkable that up to 1914 all armies depended on horse-drawn transport as soon as they left their railhead; the value of the automobile or even the motorcycle went almost unrecognized, even for reconnaissance. As for the possibilities of air warfare, though the Germans had taken a serious interest in the development for military uses of the lighter-than-air Zeppelin, the airplane itself was still thought of in terms of reconnoitering rather than bombing.

One factor that swelled the cost of military material was the steady improvement in explosives and the means for their discharge. The self-propelled torpedo, running at high speed under water and therefore all the more deadly on impact, has already been mentioned. The naval mine was a weapon of almost equal efficiency, at least when laid for the protection of harbor mouths and narrow coastal waters. But in both land and sea warfare the increased weight, accuracy, and rate of fire of the artillery were expected to be the determining factor in the wars of the future. Germany and Austria-Hungary, like Japan, had trains of huge siege howitzers. Britain designed the first dreadnought as an "all-big-gun" ship, a mobile battery of ten 12-inch guns, each of which could hurl a projectile weighing 850 pounds on to a 10-mile distant adversary. The French, for their part, had developed the first completely successful quick-firer, the "75", using both shrapnel and high explosive, to match against the heavy ordnance for which Krupp enjoyed a world-wide reputation.

If cannon, even in Germany, were in limited supply and not easy to move, infantrymen had always hitherto been an economical instrument of war. Conscription now made infantry available to each of the main Continental powers in very large numbers. Even in the relatively peaceful decade of the 1890's both France and Germany kept nearly half a million men under arms, spending roughly equal amounts of money on their equipment. Russia normally had more men called up than France or Germany, Austria-Hungary, fewer; in both cases their standard of equipment was much inferior. As for the use to be made of this mass of infantry, which in time of war would be expanded to millions, the bayonet still played a large part in their training, just as the lance did with the obsolescent cavalry arm. The function of the infantry was, however, greatly modified by three inventions.

One of these resulted from the progress of the explosives industry, which was furnishing the artilleryman with increasingly powerful forms of high explosive. To the infantryman it gave smokeless powder, beginning with the French "Poudre B" in 1886, which meant that rifle fire, like cannon fire, ceased to betray its point of origin or to spread the fog of war. In the same decade the introduction of the magazine rifle, beginning in Germany, enormously increased the rate of fire of a perhaps invisible opponent. It was, however, the third invention, that of the machine gun, which above all gave the advantage to the defense. Rudimentary types of machine gun had been used in the American Civil War and by the French in 1870, and the direct ancestor of the modern version was put on the market by Hiram Maxim in 1884. Its weight of about one hundred pounds was a drawback, but once in position it fired at a rate of two to four hundred rounds a minute, in the face of which an unsupported direct advance by infantry was virtually impossible.

Nevertheless, the doctrine of the offensive and its irresistible momentum was still taught in every army. Up to 1914, not even the Germans had foreseen the destiny of the machine-made soldier of the machine age—to dig entrenchments, using some of the skills of the miner; to guard them with the barbed wire, which was a characteristic mass product of the metalworker; and to establish the superiority of defensive tactics by discharging a hail of bullets from a machine gun—itself a fine product of the principle of interchangeable manufacture—which made individual heroism seem almost irrelevant. Only the Polish banker, Ivan Bloch, dimly foresaw some of the consequences:

> When you must dig a trench before you can make any advance, your progress is necessarily slow. . . . It is very doubtful whether any decisive victory can be gained. Every great state would . . . be in the position of a besieged city. . . . How long do you think your social fabric will remain stable under such circumstances?[7]

■ THE ROLE OF GOVERNMENT

Living in an age when the stability of the social fabric is the perennial concern of every government and its teams of planners, it is hard for us to realize how small a directing role the state played in most aspects of the transformation of European society during this period of the recent past. War and preparation for war were its concern, as has just been shown, but for the purposes of peace the state provided at the most a kind of framework of obligations and basic policies, within which the individual was at liberty to employ his capital or his skill for what purposes he pleased.

Britain had led the way in establishing on humanitarian grounds some control of the conditions under which industry was conducted. Some forty years of factory legislation had by the 1870's ended the employment of children, except as "half-timers"—a category that survived in the cotton mills until the war of 1914–1918; had excluded women from mining; had required the fencing of machinery; and had brought the standard factory day down to nine and one-half hours. A second parallel line of advance had been the development of local institutions of self-government, which the European towns had possessed since the Middle Ages, so as to mitigate the unhealthy and uncomfortable conditions

7. I. S. BLOCH, *The Future of War*, trans. R. C. Long (1903), vol. VI, pp. xvi, xli.

of town life for the new industrial populations. Here, too, Germany, Belgium, and other countries improved upon sanitary and housing legislation, which the authorities of such English towns as Liverpool and Birmingham had acted upon and experimented with earlier. Bismarck's insurance schemes,[8] however, gave a comprehensive protection, except against unemployment, for which the contemporary British worker had no counterpart but the tender mercies of the poor law and the first narrowly drawn Employer's Liability Act of 1880. The German system was imitated in most European countries as regards full protection for workers against industrial accidents, and in half a dozen as regards compulsory contributory insurance for sickness and old age. Provision for unemployment, however, never got beyond small-scale municipal schemes, such as were devised in Switzerland and in Belgium, until Part II of Lloyd George's Insurance Act of 1911 provided it for shipbuilding and certain other British industries which suffered notoriously from seasonal and cyclical fluctuations.

The triumph of machine industry also provided conditions that were conducive to the growth of self-help on the part of the workers. Their manner of employment brought them together in large numbers, accustomed them to orderly and disciplined cooperation in what they were set to do, and made elementary education almost a necessity. Hence the successful pressure for the legalization of trade unions and socialist parties, wherever their formation was still illegal. In France restrictions on trade unionism were finally withdrawn in 1884, in Germany in 1890, while in Russia the first limited concessions were made in 1906. As for Marxian socialism, the German Social Democratic Party was formed out of earlier socialist parties in 1875 and its membership in the Reichstag only increased in face of Bismarck's persecution. Belgium and France were quick to follow suit, and by 1889 a Socialist International (the Second International) had been instituted as a league of national parties, including the British and the Russian: the former did not get representation in parliament until 1892, the latter at that date still had no parliament in which to get it. By 1914 socialism, as well as trade unionism, was an aggressive force in all the industrialized countries, and there had been a parallel growth in cooperative and friendly societies. These latter served mainly the industrial worker, though their aims—the encouragement of thrift and economy in purchasing—were so congenial to the middle class as to ensure their full toleration.

For European society was distinctively middle class in its orientation, one in which the main function of the state was to provide a satisfactory framework of law within which the capitalist and entrepreneur could operate freely, to the presumed advantage of all. To some extent the framework was international— the acceptance of the gold standard throughout the civilized world (except in China and Ethiopia); the growth of international patent law under a protective

8. See pp. 319–320.

convention signed in 1883; agreements facilitating the general use of canals and other international waterways; the Universal Postal Union, formed in 1874; and the numerous extradition treaties signed in the 1870's. All these in their different ways fulfilled the needs of a middle-class industrial society. Domestic legislation and administrative action likewise were much concerned with trade conditions—company law, banking, credit facilities, and trademarks.

Last, a new trend deserves notice which invaded both the national and the international sphere, having originated in Germany during the period of trade depression after 1873. This was the cartel, a syndicate of producers which aimed at maintaining profits by the reduction of competition, either through division of the market among members, through some system of price-fixing, or through amalgamation to form a single monopoly. German law favored the system, unlike the position in Britain, France, and America, where cartels were contested in the law courts as conspiracies in restraint of trade.[9] The four hundred German cartels therefore had no exact counterpart elsewhere. But some monopolies, starting with the Nobel dynamite trust of 1886, were successfully established in Britain and other countries, and there were some very important international cartels, such as the shipping rings which effectively controlled ocean fares and freight rates.

If the first German cartels were occasioned by the industrial collapse of the middle seventies, it is reasonable to expect some bigger economic changes as the result of the much longer period of general trade depression and falling prices, which continued without any major respite until 1896. Its prime effect was to cause the states of Continental Europe to safeguard their agriculture against the influx of cheap American wheat by returning to a heavy protective tariff. But alleged British dumping of cheap surplus manufactures during bad years was regarded, especially in Germany, as an important justification for the turnover to high industrial tariffs, which characterizes the years from 1879, when Bismarck first made friends with the protectionists, to the enactment of the Méline tariff in France in 1892. Austria, Italy, and Russia followed the German lead; the United States was ahead of Germany, and did not begin to moderate her tariff until 1913. By that date several powers were beginning to be influenced by the determined British rejection of tariff reform, as preached by Joseph Chamberlain, a rejection which seemed to have been justified by her entry during the first decade of the new century into a period of renewed prosperity under free-trade auspices. But then came the war.

If Bright and Cobden were not wholly mistaken when they saw in tariff rivalries a potent cause of war, the same may be said of two other interrelated movements, namely, colonialism and the export of capital. The former was obviously under government control; there was also a less readily defined element of government direction in the latter, which we will briefly consider first.

9. See p. 328.

Governments might actually veto stock exchange dealings in particular foreign shares or take other formal action, as when Bismarck unintentionally helped on the *rapprochement* between Russia and France by forbidding the Reichsbank to accept Russian securities as collateral for loans. Much more usual, however, was the exercise of government influence behind the scenes in advising banks and other major financial concerns as to the desirability or otherwise of supporting foreign ventures. Interference was no doubt at its smallest in Britain, where so much of the overseas investment went to the Empire and where the city magnates prided themselves on their independent judgment. Yet the Liberal foreign secretary, Grey, is on record as explaining to the House of Commons (on July 10, 1914) that his government felt it to be its duty to support British capital in "applying for concessions to which there is no valid political objection," a statement from which the converse proposition can safely be inferred.

Where, as in Morocco and for a time in Persia, rival national groups of investors were officially encouraged, the result could be something resembling a cold war. Occasionally, as in the case of the Baghdad Railway agreement of 1914,[10] the upshot of a long-drawn-out conflict for ascendancy in a particular foreign country was an arrangement to share the prospective spoil. More often, as with the French in Tunisia and the British in the Transvaal, financial led on to political and military commitments. There were even foreign loans for directly military purposes, as when the confidence shown by both British and American investors helped Japan to wage her war against Russia in 1904–1905. The best example, however, is the troubled history of the Balkan states, which could not develop without foreign loans and could obtain no loans without political implications, causing every issue to be jealously watched by rival governments. Foreign investors paid largely for the arms used by both sides in the Balkan Wars of 1912–1913, and no sooner was peace restored than the Russian and French foreign ministers became concerned with the flotation of a new Serbian loan on the Paris money market, a loan without which the Serbian army could not have faced the risk of war again in 1914.

It is true that the foreign investor, even when his government encouraged a loan which was earmarked for strategic railways or actual armaments, was usually chary of lending his money for purposes of military aggression as distinct from defense, because he feared to lose it in a gamble. Nevertheless, a potent cause of war is indicated in the measured terms in which the historian of this little-explored subject sums up his conclusions: "The official circles of lending countries gradually came to envisage the foreign investments of their citizens, not as private financial transactions, but as one of the instruments through which national destiny was achieved."[11]

National destiny was still more manifest, of course, in the rivalry en-

---

10. See pp. 424; 490–491.
11. H. FEIS, *Europe The World's Banker 1870–1914* (1930), p. xvi.

This shows a vanished world of great empires in which Europe reigned supreme. The almost complete political control of Africa and of large parts of Asia is associated with the further phenomenon of economic imperialism.

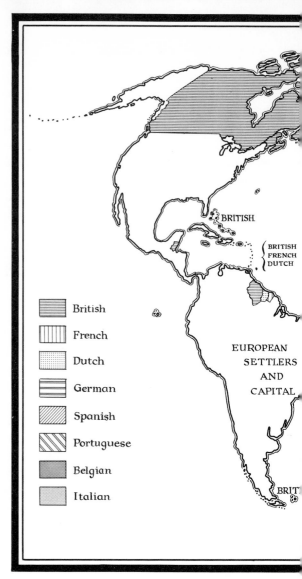

British

French

Dutch

German

Spanish

Portuguese

Belgian

Italian

BRITISH

BRITISH
FRENCH
DUTCH

EUROPEAN
SETTLERS
AND
CAPITAL

BRIT

gendered by the struggle for colonial territory, which reached its height at the Fashoda crisis in 1898, and again when Germany challenged France at Agadir in 1911. The situation, when war finally broke out among the powers three summers later, may be seen from the map above and the table on page 301. These colonial empires, as we now see, represented largely the pursuit of an illusion, for they were founded in the belief that a permanent relationship could be established, one that might benefit both parties but would certainly benefit the colonizing power. Perhaps the civilizing mission was not altogether illusory, but the search for uncontested markets, for politically safe and highly profitable fields of investment, for minerals, industrial raw materials, and foodstuffs, for places of white settlement, and for a supply of spirited if primitive native soldiery—all these have recoiled upon the heads of the colonizers.

300

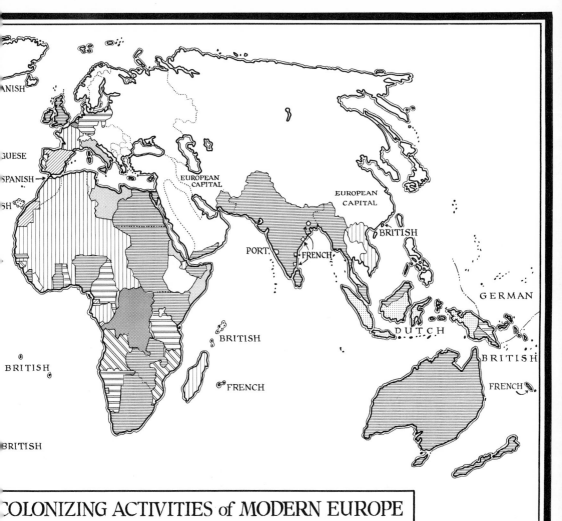

COLONIZING ACTIVITIES of MODERN EUROPE

WORLD COLONIAL EMPIRES, 1914

	AREA in thousand square miles	POPULATION in thousands
Britain	12,044	391,583
France	4,110	62,350
Germany	1,231	13,075
Belgium	910	15,000
Portugal	804	9,680
Netherlands	763	37,410
Italy	591	1,396
Total	20,453	530,494

301

The strength of the purely economic motives varied greatly from country to country and from decade to decade. In general, however, the economic results were smaller than expected. Even Britain, which not only had the biggest share of colonial territory, but had great advantages in shipping, capital, and experienced man power available for its development, never reached the stage at which more than one-quarter of her trade was with her colonies. Germany, relatively a newcomer to the tasks of empire building, was still awaiting results in 1914, at which date none of her African colonies except Togoland was self-supporting and total trade with all her colonies amounted to 0.5 percent of German foreign commerce. The French, with the second largest empire, brought the colonial trade up to 11.22 percent (average of 1901–1905) and ten years later could muster 800,000 natives from their colonies for war. Three of the four lesser colonial powers had continuing military expenditure and some loss of prestige from military reverses to set against the trade profit, which was highest in the case of the Netherlands East Indies. Finally, we may note the special circumstances of the Congo Free State, which was despotically exploited by its owner, King Leopold II of the Belgians, for over thirty years. By 1905 he was taking rubber, ivory, and other commodities out of the country to a value of $11,000,000, while the total imports amounted to only $4,000,000, but in November, 1908, the outraged opinion of the civilized world forced him to cede the state to Belgium.

Nevertheless, the newspaper-reading and map-conscious public of the industrial powers valued colonial acquisitions for future, as well as supposed immediate, profits, and were not disposed to doubt the worth of land, however barren, that was gained in dramatic competition against rival nations. The following chapters will show something of that drama.

Reading List: Chapter 10

Hayes, C. J. H., *A Generation of Materialism, 1871–1900* (1941), ch. 3. The mechanizing of work and thought.

The New Cambridge Modern History, vol. XI (1962), chs. 2–3. Economic conditions; science and technology.

Rostow, W., *Stages of Economic Growth* (1960; paperback, 1961), chs. 2, 7. A "non-Marxist" interpretation of modern industrial evolution.

Bowden, W., Karpovich, M., and Usher, A. P., *An Economic History of Europe Since 1750* (3rd ed., 1952), chs. 15, 19, 32. Technology; iron and steel; use of power.

Ashworth, W., *Short History of the International Economy* (1952), ch. 6. The emergence of an international economy before 1914.

Clapham, J. H., *The Economic Development of France and Germany* (4th ed., 1936; paperback, 1963), chs. 8–12.

Knowles, L. C. A., *Economic Development in the Nineteenth Century—France, Germany, Russia, and the United States* (1932), pp. 209–28. Transportation in France, Germany, and Russia.

Heaton, H., *Economic History of Europe* (rev. ed., 1948), chs. 17–23. The late nineteenth century in a wider setting.

Straub, H., *History of Civil Engineering* (1952), ch. 8. Nineteenth-century developments.

Birnie, A., *An Economic History of Europe, 1760–1939* (rev. ed., 1957), ch. 14. Social insurance.

Fuller, J. F. C., *The Conduct of War, 1789–1961* (1961), ch. 5. The influence of the Industrial Revolution on the conduct of war.

Lipson, E., *Growth of English Society* (1950), chs. 12–14. Nineteenth-century Britain.

Chapter 11

The German Power in Europe

The Political Structure of Imperial Germany
The Party System
Political Developments Under Bismarck
Economic Growth and Its Consequences, 1871–1890
Germany and the European Balance, 1871–1890
Transition to a New Age
Economic and Social Growth Under William II
Imperial Germany and the World Stage

■ THE POLITICAL STRUCTURE OF IMPERIAL GERMANY

Between 1871 and 1914 Imperial Germany rose to a position in Europe, if not of complete preponderance, then certainly of spectacular power. For the first time since the Middle Ages, when the Hohenstaufens had given some semblance of unity to the German-speaking lands, a new Germany appeared in 1871, politically unified, economically strong, crowned with victory, and claiming a leading place among the major powers.

While the Empire was created on the federal principle, the term was clearly imprecise, since one state, Prussia, with three-fifths of the population, was everywhere dominant. By adding the four South German states and his new conquest of Alsace-Lorraine to the North German Confederation of 1867, Bismarck now created an Empire made up of four kingdoms (Prussia, Saxony, Bavaria, Württemberg), eleven duchies and grand duchies, seven lesser princi-

SIGNIFICANT EVENTS

1873 Falk Laws in Prussia, lasting until 1879
1875 Gotha Program of Social Democratic Party
1878 Berlin Congress: Bismarck's Anti-Socialist Law
1879 New protective tariff: Dual Alliance with Austria
1882 Triple Alliance with Austria and Italy
1883–1889 Bismarck's program of social legislation
1884–1885 Establishment of German Colonial Empire
1890 Resignation of Bismarck
1898–1912 German Navy Laws
1912 Haldane Mission to Germany

palities, three free cities (Hamburg, Bremen, Lübeck), and the "imperial territory" of Alsace-Lorraine. All these comprised a single economic community. Politically, each state retained its own constitution (save for Alsace-Lorraine) and its system of local government; special privileges were granted to Hamburg and Bremen as free ports; and certain concessions involving the ownership of railways, exemption from some excise taxes, special postal reorganization, and special military arrangements were granted to the South German states with whom special treaties had been made. Thus, the unity achieved in 1871 was not that of a truly national state. Prussia had not merged itself in Germany as Frederick William IV once had promised. The Prussian monarchy, the Prussian bureaucracy, the Prussian army, and above all the Prussian minister-president, Bismarck, in his new role as imperial chancellor, exercised the decisive power.

Federal authority found expression in a bicameral legislature. This legislature had very broad legislative powers with respect to customs and excise duties, defense, citizenship, consular service, protection of foreign commerce, administration of posts and telegraphs (except in Bavaria and Württemberg), and regulation of railroads, weights, measures, coinage, banking, copyrights, and patents. It could regulate the press and labor associations and it controlled the whole domain of civil and criminal law. Administrative powers, as distinct from legislative, were left largely in state hands. The lower house, the Reichstag, was elected for five years by universal, direct manhood suffrage beginning at the age of twenty-five. Payment of members was not authorized until 1906. Bismarck had consistently opposed this. In 1885, when Socialist members were paid by their own party, he initiated and won an action in the courts forcing them to turn the money over to the treasury. Out of a total of 397 seats (never reapportioned during the entire history of the Empire), Prussia held 236. The next largest number went to Bavaria, with 48, then came Saxony with 23, Württemberg with 17, and Baden with 14. The Reichstag gave assent to all laws, to treaties which involved matters falling within the domain of legislation, and to new budgets; thus ostensibly it had a substantial veto power. There were, however, serious flaws. The Reichstag had no effective control of foreign affairs or of ministerial action, and the principal revenue laws which provided income from customs and excise dues were permanent. All states were required to make annual contributions from their own revenues, thereby relieving the chancellor from many fiscal fights in the Reichstag. There was no annual submission of a complete budget. The power of control over the purse, the subject of long political struggles in other countries, was not truly in the hands of the Reichstag.

The upper house, the Bundesrat, was not unlike the old Germanic Diet which had met at Frankfurt. It had originally 58 seats (with 3 given later to Alsace-Lorraine). Prussia had a delegation of 17, Bavaria had 6, Saxony and Württemberg had 4 apiece. Each group, nominated by its government, voted as a unit and under instructions. Since only 14 votes were required to defeat a constitutional amendment, Prussia, with her 17 votes, in this respect had an effective veto. Furthermore, as the Bundesrat had concurrent legislative power with the Reichstag, the joint action of a few of the largest states was sufficient to determine the fate of any proposal. The Bundesrat could, and in fact usually did, initiate legislation. Thus the Bundesrat, in which the sovereignty of the Empire legally resided, and which combined some of the qualities of a supreme court, a meeting of ambassadors, a cabinet, and an upper house, seriously undercut the parliamentary authority of the Reichstag.

The heart of the constitution, however, lay in the powers of the emperor and his principal agent, the imperial chancellor. The former had great power

BISMARCK IN MIDDLE AGE. This photograph shows Bismarck at the height of his power, before he became the venerable figure who imposed his will upon the German Empire.

as commander-in-chief of the Prussian army and as "war lord" (*Kriegesherr*) of united Germany. He was technically responsible for the appointment of all federal officials, above all for the federal chancellor, who was responsible to him alone. These powers of the emperor were vigorously supplemented by his great authority as king of Prussia, for here, under the conservative constitution of 1850, his authority was still that of an absolute, divine-right ruler. The imperial chancellor, responsible solely to the emperor, was the only federal minister. There was no imperial cabinet, so that the heads of the departments of state whom he appointed were little more than administrative officials. The chancellor presided over the Bundesrat and had a special bench prominently reserved for him in the Reichstag from which he could address its sessions. Thus he took the initiative in introducing legislation, in steering it through the two houses, and in directing all matters of foreign policy. Both Bismarck and his immediate successor, Count von Caprivi, combined the office of imperial chancellor with that of minister-president in Prussia. Though Caprivi resigned the post of minister-president after two years, his successors down to 1918 once more combined the two offices.

In essence, therefore, at a time when genuine parliamentary democracy was rapidly evolving in Europe, imperial Germany displayed the outward façade of a parliamentary regime behind which operated an autocratic system dominated by the historic traditions of the Prussian monarchy. Some state governments, to be sure, were genuinely liberal, and it would be unfair to a great many Germans to say that under the Empire they were deprived of the possibility of bona fide political activity. Yet this activity went only so far, and, while Bismarck was willing to associate the rising and prosperous middle class politically with the military aristocracy of Prussia under the leadership of the Hohenzollern autocracy, he remained completely unsympathetic to the political aspirations of the working classes. "Every great community," he declared in 1892, "in which the careful and restraining influence of the propertied classes is lost will always develop a pace that will cause the ship of state to founder. . . ."

■ THE PARTY SYSTEM

After 1871 Germany, like France, witnessed the growth of a large number of political parties. In the election of 1912 there were fourteen. Unlike France, however, these parties rarely combined into major blocs so as to create workable parliamentary majorities, and even had they done so their effectiveness would still have been gravely limited. Before 1866 the broad pattern in Prussia had been that of a division between the Conservatives, who supported Bismarck, and the much larger number of Progressives, who opposed him. During the short life of the North German Confederation a split occurred, for some of the extreme Conservatives were dubious about Bismarck's new creation, while an offshoot, the Free Conservatives, ardently supported him. The Progressives still opposed Bismarck, and a new group, the largely non-Prussian National Liberals, supported him. These four passed over into the Empire where, with some changes in policy and in competition with new parties, they continued throughout the entire history of the imperial period.

The Conservatives remained a Junker, divine-right party, drawing their strength from the great farming areas of East and West Prussia, Pomerania, Mecklenburg, and Brandenburg. For this reason they were strongly agrarian in their interests, opposed at first to protection, and changing over only when the competition of foreign grain in the late 1870's threatened their interests. Devoutly Lutheran in their sympathies, with the newspaper *Kreuzzeitung* as their mouthpiece, and with much backing in army circles, the Conservatives were a pillar of the Prussian monarchy. The Free Conservatives (*Reichspartei*), who split off from the original grouping, were more German and less Prussian. They drew their strength from the large landowners of Silesia and some of the great Rhineland industrialists. With their slogan, "The Fatherland above the Party," they gave Bismarck some of his strongest support in the first years of the Empire. Eventually, they tended to coalesce once more with the Conservatives.

In point of numbers the National Liberals, with 150 deputies in 1871, were then the strongest group in the Reichstag. They were the successors of Bennigsen's *Nationalverein* of the 1860's[1] which at that time was working for German unity, and therefore could be described as the only truly national party of the Empire. They had no particular program in 1871 save that in general they gave Bismarck their strong support in working for unity and economic strength. They drew much support from bourgeois and professional groups. Strongly anticlerical, the National Liberals supported Bismarck in his

1. See pp. 140; 151.

contest with the Roman Catholic Church. Steadily becoming more national and less liberal, drawing support from the great industrialists such as Krupp, Thyssen, and Ballin, and advocating a high industrial tariff, the party dwindled so that in the election of 1912 with 45 seats it had fallen to one-third of its original strength.

REICHSTAG ELECTIONS, 1871–1890[2]

PARTY	NUMBER OF DEPUTIES							
	1871	1874	1877	1878	1881	1884	1887	1890
Conservatives	54	22	40	59	50	78	80	73
Free Conservatives	38	36	38	57	28	28	41	20
National Liberals	150	155	128	99	47	51	99	42
Progressives	47	50	52	39	115	74	32	76
Center	58	91	93	94	100	99	98	106
Social Democrats	2	9	12	9	12	24	11	35
Irreconcilables and others	33	34	34	40	45	43	35	40
Anti-Semites	—	—	—	—	—	—	1	5
Total	382	397	397	397	397	397	397	397

The Progressives—a sort of left wing of the National Liberals—rose from 47 seats in 1871 to a high of 115 seats ten years later, then gradually sank to 42 in 1912. They were advocates of genuine parliamentary government, free trade, and antimilitarism, and in general stood as spokesmen of the enlightened middle classes. A prominent figure in the Progressive Party during its later period was Friedrich Naumann, a brilliant advocate of social reform and democracy, who pointed out the startling contrast between the tremendous political power exercised by the conservative agrarian interests in Germany and the limited political role of the workers and business groups. He was, however, more of a prophet than an effective political leader, and a good deal of the Progressive following moved over into the ranks of the Social Democrats.

The German Catholics, roughly one-third of the total population, were represented by the Center Party, a remarkably stable group which rose from 58 deputies in 1871 to 106 in 1890 and subsequently kept close to that figure. Its principal support came from Bavaria, where the peasant interest was strong, and from the thriving industrial centers of the Rhineland. The growth of the Center Party reflected the increasing concern of the Roman Catholic Church with social issues, more especially when Leo XIII succeeded Pius IX in 1878. The Center's principal leader in the Reichstag was Ludwig Windthorst, an

2. See p. 329 for subsequent elections. Based on PINSON, *Modern Germany*, pp. 572–573.

astute parliamentarian from Hanover who cleverly championed the cause of constitutional government in order to gain his ends and on many occasions held the balance of power in the Reichstag. Bismarck despised Windthorst and mistrusted the Center, which, however, he was unable to destroy. "Hate," Bismarck once said, "is just as great an incentive to life as love. My life is preserved and made pleasant by two things—my wife and Windthorst. One exists for love, the other for hate."[3] The Center successfully survived Bismarck's attacks and remained a moderate, middle-of-the-road party, leaning in the direction of states' rights, encouraging measures of social reform, and yet, with its basic belief in an orderly and inherently conservative society, generally tending to support the policies of the government.

The ruthless measures which Bismarck used to create the Empire produced a small group of Irreconcilables—certainly not a party in the true sense—comprising the sixteen or so representatives from the Polish-speaking areas, the few Guelphs from Hanover, the solitary Dane from Schleswig, and, beginning with 1874, the fifteen deputies from Alsace-Lorraine. These were a permanent reminder not only of the force that had been invoked in the days of unification but of the subsequent harsh measures against non-German groups that the government continued to employ.

The party destined ultimately to become the largest in the German Empire, and indeed one of the most efficiently organized socialist parties in Europe, the Social Democrats, had an inauspicious origin. German socialism, in the sense of a systematically organized protest against capitalist society, had made a hesitant appearance during the Revolution of 1848, when voices such as that of the Rhineland tailor, Wilhelm Weitling, were heard, if with little effect. Though the *Communist Manifesto* of Marx and Engels appeared in 1848, its true importance belongs to the years that follow, and even more on the international than on the German scene. Not until the 1850's, when the German textile and iron industries began to develop significantly in the Prussian Rhine Provinces, in Saxony, Bavaria, and Baden, did a working-class movement begin to develop. This movement, at first leaderless and uncoordinated, found an unexpected champion in a brilliant young Jewish intellectual and journalist from Breslau, Ferdinand Lassalle.[4] Flamboyant in dress and manners, passionately romantic in his private affairs (he died at the age of thirty-nine in a duel), a friend of the poet Heine, Lassalle would seem a most unlikely candidate for the leadership of the German workingmen. Yet he had been sufficient of a leader to

3. Quoted in PINSON, *Modern Germany*, p. 190.
4. 1825–1864. Son of a prosperous silk merchant, he made a name for himself by prosecuting the case of Countess Hatzfeldt against her husband before thirty-six tribunals and for eight years of litigation, winning a settlement which had the further result of providing Lassalle with an annuity for life. His founding of the German Workingmen's Association in 1863 gives him a pioneer place in the history of German socialism.

have been jailed for six months in 1849 for revolutionary activities, and on going to Berlin in 1857 he quickly made a name for himself as a radical journalist and working-class champion.

Lassalle's two principal theoretical convictions were that the modern industrialist operated under the "iron law of wages," which kept the working-man living on the very margin of subsistence, and that if the workers were to break away from this state of affairs they must organize so as to win political power through universal suffrage. They could then set up their own producers' associations and bring an end to the capitalistic exploitation of labor. When an association of workers at Leipzig asked Lassalle to formulate his ideas, he expressed them in a famous *Open Letter* (1863), followed in the same year by his organization of the German Workingmen's Association—the first concrete step in the history of the socialist movement in Germany. On Lassalle's death his associate, J. B. von Schweitzer, carried on his work. Though Marx, who in this same year 1864 organized his International Workingmen's Association in London, had the most contemptuous view of Lassalle as a theorist, he wrote a few years later to Schweitzer as follows: "After a slumber of fifteen years Lassalle aroused once more the labor movement in Germany, and this remains his immortal achievement."

Lassalle did not live to see his Workingmen's Association take part in politics, and, indeed, its progress was very slow. The subsequent growth of the Social Democratic Party was chiefly influenced by two South Germans, August Bebel,[5] trained as a woodworker, and Wilhelm Liebknecht, a journalist. Both followers of Marx, they organized in 1869 the Social Democratic Labor Party at Eisenach, and in 1871 these Social Democrats were able to elect two deputies to the Reichstag and in 1874, nine. In 1875 the Social Democrats and Lassalleans came together and devised the Gotha Program—a combination of basic Marxian anticapitalist theory and the more moderate Lassallean aims of immediate political and social reforms (a secret ballot, payment of deputies, a progressive income tax, workers' cooperatives, and so forth). Though Marx described this Gotha Program as "petty bourgeois" and "contemptible," it provided, nevertheless, both a theoretical and practical basis upon which the party continued to thrive.

Over twelve million Germans voted in the election of 1912—the last election before the war—and, of these, approximately one-third supported the Social Democrats. The truest commentary upon the Bismarckian system is that

5. 1840–1913. Son of a Prussian noncommissioned officer and trained as a woodworker, he was elected to the parliament of the North German Confederation in 1866 and subsequently to the Reichstag. He opposed the annexation of Alsace-Lorraine and Bismarck's repressive policies. During several terms of imprisonment, he enlarged his scanty formal education. His book, *Woman and Socialism*, ran to fifty-two editions, and even his opponents recognized him as the most brilliant speaker in the Reichstag.

in 1912, despite all changes, power still remained essentially where he had put it: in the hands of the Prussian monarchy and of a privileged ruling caste.

■ POLITICAL DEVELOPMENTS UNDER BISMARCK

In his new office as imperial chancellor, Bismarck was concerned with maintaining and strengthening the Germany which he had created, and simultaneously with keeping the peace abroad in a Europe from which he felt that the main centers of danger had been removed. Devoted to the emperor, as William I was to him, Bismarck exercised for eighteen years a power to which possibly only that of Richelieu could be compared. Determined to maintain the authority of the monarchy and the Junker class, Bismarck nevertheless found that the extreme Conservatives, dubious in many respects about political trends in the German Empire, could not be his principal support. Neither could he count upon the clerical Center nor upon the Progressives, with their genuine dedication to the cause of parliamentary government. Between 1871 and 1878, therefore, he leaned upon the National Liberals, with their 150 seats in the Reichstag and their corresponding strength in the Prussian Landtag. This alliance with Bennigsen and his group was, to be sure, a marriage of convenience in which Bismarck, skillfully introducing a program that appealed to liberal sentiments in the Germany of his day, never for a moment abandoned his traditionally conservative monarchical beliefs.

The legislation of this National Liberal period first concerned itself with administrative problems in the new Empire. A code of criminal law was adopted in 1871, followed by uniform rules of legal procedure. Though the principle of a general civil code was established in 1873, the work was not completed until 1896 and the code did not come into effect until 1900. As a sop earlier promised to Saxony, a supreme court was set up at Leipzig. A common imperial currency, in which the mark replaced the thaler, was issued in 1871 and the metric system adopted. An Imperial Bank was established in 1876 and the banking laws were revised. A federal postal system was set up. A code of commercial law was drafted and new provisions made for patents and trademarks. Efforts to create an imperial railway system aroused objections from some of the states which already had their own state railway systems. Nevertheless, an Imperial Railway Office was created in 1873 to standardize rates. Within Prussia many private lines were transferred to the state. By 1910 there were nearly 35,000 miles of railways in Germany, of which 23,350 miles were owned by Prussia and 10,675 by Bavaria and other larger states. It remained for the Weimar Republic in 1919 to nationalize the entire German railway system. A press act in 1874 abolished censorship along with the old system of financial deposits required as a guarantee from publishers.

Military reforms likewise were made. A special fund, including 120 million marks from the French indemnity, was set aside for war emergencies. In 1871 the Prussian system of conscription was applied to the whole Empire, with a peacetime army fixed at 400,000 men. Only Bavaria, Saxony, and Württemberg retained their independent military establishments, and these in time of war fell under the power of the emperor as war lord. In 1874, overcoming the opposition of the Center, the Progressives, and the Social Democrats, Bismarck obtained the *Septennat*, that is, the fixing of the military appropriation for a period of seven years. Recognizing the powerful role of the Prussian army in German life, Bismarck encouraged the army chiefs in two momentous policies. One was to reduce as far as possible the jurisdiction and powers of the minister of war, turning these over to the officers of the general staff. The other was to withhold commissions from candidates with "dangerous" ideas and thus strengthen the officer corps in its traditional role as a bulwark of royal power. Both policies, while successful, were ominous for the future.

During these years of National Liberal support, Bismarck became involved in a serious conflict with the Roman Catholic Church. The first half of the nineteenth century, despite the eventual collapse of the temporal power of the papacy in 1870, had been a period of marked vigor and growth. Country after country witnessed a new vigor in preaching and proselytizing, the growth of seminaries, and a wider Church activity in education. Pius IX, taking sharp issue with many of the trends in the new age of science, had proclaimed the dogma of the Immaculate Conception in 1854; ten years later in his Syllabus of Errors he attacked the materialistic trends of the times. In 1870 the Vatican Council proclaimed the dogma of Papal Infallibility—that the pope, when speaking officially from his throne in questions of faith and morals, is possessed of unchallengeable authority. Most of the German bishops at the Vatican Council had initially opposed the issuance of the dogma, but submitted eventually. Some German priests and their flocks, following the lead of the Bavarian theologian, Dr. Döllinger, refused to submit and became known as the Old Catholics.

Bismarck's direct support of these Old Catholics (he provided their leaders with positions and income) was inspired far more by political than by religious considerations. In association with the National Liberals he maintained the supremacy of the secular state; the newly formed Center Party he regarded as a monstrosity—a political party with a religious basis. And he feared that such a party would command support in areas where unrest already existed: in the Polish provinces and in Alsace-Lorraine. Bismarck, furthermore, associated his misgivings as to the German Catholics with his fears of clericalism in France, a force, so he thought, capable of stirring up a strong national revival there. "It is not precisely the Catholics with whom Bismarck is angry," the French ambassador at Berlin wrote in 1873, "but the alliance that France might make with them." In the light of the growing strength of anticlericalism in France, these fears were surely unnecessary.

The campaign against the Catholic Church, to which a zealous supporter of Bismarck in the Prussian Landtag gave the name of *Kulturkampf,* or "a struggle for civilization," was carried on largely but not exclusively in Prussia. During 1871–1872 various Prussian enactments placed all schools under state supervision and forbade members of religious orders to teach. Dr. Falk, a strong anticlerical, became Prussian minister of education, and the May Laws of 1873 moved directly into the realm of Catholic administration. The authority of bishops over their clergy was reduced, withdrawal from the Church was facilitated, and candidates for the priesthood had to be German-born and German-educated. In 1874 civil marriage in Prussia was made compulsory. In the case of resistance, government grants to churches were suspended. All religious orders, except those caring for the sick, were dissolved. Federal legislation, meanwhile, introduced compulsory civil marriage, banned political sermons (police officers attending with notebooks), and exiled the Jesuit Order.

By 1877 eight archbishops and bishops had been removed in Prussia, leaving only four in office. Jail terms had been inflicted on the archbishops of Cologne and Posen and on the bishop of Trier, as well as on hundreds of lesser clergy. In 1876 over 1400 Prussian parishes were vacant. Yet in the Reichstag elections of 1874 the Center Party's representation was almost doubled, rising from 58 to 91 seats. In 1874 an attempt was made to assassinate the chancellor. By 1878 Bismarck, pressed by other matters, had come to realize the lack of success of these anti-Catholic policies. The accession of Leo XIII in that same year made the work of compromise much easier. Thus the Falk Laws were gradually dropped and in 1879 Falk himself was dismissed. Between 1880 and 1887 most of the rights of German Catholics were restored, and the Center became a moderate, loyal party, still not attractive to Bismarck, yet drawing support from all parts of the realm.

The major development of 1878 was the swing of the National Liberals away from Bismarck and the turning of the Conservatives to his support. The former were resentful of the few ministerial appointments he would concede them, and as traditional free-traders they disliked Bismarck's new tariff proposals. The Conservatives made gains in the elections of 1878 at the expense of the National Liberals, even though these had actually split and produced a right wing which supported Bismarck's tariff policies. Others joined the Progressives to form a German Independent Party—a movement of liberal views which steadily dwindled.[6]

Catholic support was also needed. Early in 1879 Bismarck swallowed his distaste of the Center Party and negotiated with Windthorst, thereby assuring

6. See chart p. 309.

himself of backing for the tariff in return for relaxing the anticlerical laws. Thus the passing of the tariff law in July, 1879, by a vote of 217 to 117 coincided with Germany's entry into a period of spectacular growth and prosperity.

Confident of his strong position, Bismarck now turned his fire on the socialists. The Social Democratic Party had increased its representation in the Reichstag from two in 1871 to nine in 1874 and twelve in 1877, when it polled nearly half a million votes. This was a process concerning which Bismarck had the deepest misgivings. Two attempts upon the life of William I in 1878 by radical fanatics prompted him to action. He called for new elections in 1878, the result being a Conservative gain. In October a stringent antisocialist law was passed. Socialists were forbidden to hold meetings, and the government was empowered to suppress all labor and socialist political organizations, together with their newspapers, periodicals, and printing presses. Professional agitators were to be expelled and martial law was authorized in restless areas. This powerful act was renewed periodically until 1890. An immediate result was a wave of arrests and a drop in the Social Democratic vote in the election of 1881. The party, however, did not yield; its organization was transferred to Switzerland and its literature smuggled in from abroad.

Bismarck's hope was that by a policy of paternal legislation he could scotch the socialist movement.[7] Yet, despite all he could do, the statistics from 1884 onward show a steady upward growth of the party which he sought to destroy, as the following table will indicate.

GROWTH OF THE SOCIAL DEMOCRATIC PARTY IN GERMANY, 1871–1890

ELECTION YEAR	POPULAR VOTE WITH % OF TOTAL	DEPUTIES TO REICHSTAG
1871	124,000 (3.0)	2
1874	352,000 (6.7)	9
1877	493,000 (8.9)	12
1878	437,000 (7.5)	9
1881	312,000 (5.9)	12
1884	550,000 (9.5)	24
1887	763,000 (10.1)	11
1890	1,427,000 (19.6)	35

In the year of Bismarck's departure from office in 1890, the Social Democrats won nearly 20 percent of the votes and over 11 percent of the seats in the Reichstag election. Had there been any reapportionment of seats to take account of the rapid growth in the industrial areas, the gains of the Social Democrats undoubtedly would have been larger. Yet the constitution being what it was, the winning of seats alone could not in any case have affected Bismarck's political power, which remained strong until the end.

7. See pp. 319–320.

THE KRUPP STEEL WORKS AT ESSEN, IN THE RUHR. Though the photograph is of a later date, this huge industrial complex is evidence of the steadily growing industrial might of Imperial Germany.

■ ECONOMIC GROWTH AND ITS CONSEQUENCES, 1871–1890

The spectacular economic growth of Germany, beginning under Bismarck and continuing uninterruptedly until the coming of war in 1914, is one of the major phenomena of recent European history.[8] All was not steady progress, for the boom of 1873–1874 in railway construction and heavy industry was quickly followed by a bad depression, the effects of which were felt until 1879. A number of points stand out in this Bismarckian period. One was the relatively late date at which industrialization occurred, making it possible for Germany to take advantage of progress in technology and avoid many of the pitfalls and difficulties encountered by countries such as Britain. Closely related to this was the conscious use made by German industry of the remarkable abilities of its scientists. Still another significant factor was the acquisition of the coal mines and the iron ore of Lorraine. The new Thomas Gilchrist open-hearth process for smelting these ores with a high phosphoric content came into use in the 1880's; this meant that the Lorraine ore could now be combined with the great coalfields of the Ruhr to make possible huge steel enterprises such as the Krupp works at Essen. The highly developed textile industry of Alsace, and the Alsatian potash deposits exploited after 1890, likewise contributed to Germany's industrial power. Between 1870 and 1890 German annual coal production (including lignite) increased from 37,900,000 tons to 89,100,000 tons. Pig iron output in-

8. For comparison of the German with other European economies, see ch. 10.

creased from 1,200,000 tons to 4,000,000 tons. Steel production grew from 130,000 tons in 1870 to 2,100,000 tons in 1890.

Agriculture likewise flourished, encouraged in part by important advances made in industrial chemistry, for example, in the extraction of sugar from beet roots, and also in part by the tariff of 1879 on grain, and by a policy of subsidies and loans to farmers. Yet the trend basically was away from agriculture and toward industry. The following population percentages show that between 1871 and 1900 the balance shifted from a preponderance of rural to a preponderance of urban population.

CHANGE FROM RURAL TO URBAN POPULATION IN GERMANY[9]

DATE	PER CENT RURAL (living in communities of less than 2000)	PER CENT URBAN
1871	63.9	36.1
1880	58.6	41.4
1890	57.5	42.5
1900	45.6	54.4
1910	40.0	60.0

A further significant aspect of German economic life is its impact upon colonial development. Bismarck was not himself interested at first in the acquisition of overseas territories and it is literally true that the Germany whose fortunes he directed in 1871 had not a single overseas possession. His interest, indeed, did not extend even to any kind of European expansion; on one occasion he crudely declared himself unwilling to get involved in a war in southeastern Europe "because of a few stinking Wallachians." Germany, in his opinion, was a satiated power. Though these views on further German expansion in Europe never changed, his views on the colonial question underwent a dramatic reversal, clearly reflecting the pressure of new economic forces.

The drive for colonies was in its beginning the work of merchants, missionaries, and publicists, including certain strongly nationalist historians, such as Heinrich von Treitschke[10] who used his professorial chair at Berlin as a kind of patriotic pulpit. Much earlier, in 1841, Friedrich List, in his *National System of Political Economy*, had maintained that colonialism was an essential part of a German national program. The obvious success of merchants from various European countries in making profits in Africa and elsewhere aroused the

9. From PINSON, *Modern Germany*, p. 221.
10. 1834–1896. A Saxon by birth, he became one of the most ardent champions of the Prussian state and German nationalism. His career was crowned by appointment to the University of Berlin where his lectures commanded national attention. Beginning as a liberal, he ultimately propounded a theory of power in which the state was all-important. A strong supporter of Bismarck, he attacked universal suffrage, Jews, Catholics, and socialists. His *History of Germany in the Nineteenth Century* (going only to 1847) became one of the most widely read historical works in Germany.

interest of commercial houses in the old Hanseatic towns. Moreover, the continued heavy flow of emigration from Germany, which in one year alone reached 230,000, gave many patriotic Germans great concern.

When the French declared a protectorate over Tunisia in 1881 and the British intervened in Egypt in 1882, it was hard for Germany not to consider some similar action. In Africa, German merchants from the old Hanseatic towns had been making modest ventures since the 1830's, and German foreign missionary societies, of which at least eight had been founded before 1870, were also vigorously at work. Some German activity was present in the South Seas. The German Colonial League was founded in 1882, followed two years later by the Company for German Colonization, which had the very practical object of raising money to finance colonies in East Africa.

Bismarck approached the colonial question with evident reluctance. He told a group of businessmen in 1876 that he was unwilling "to embark upon colonization without adequate preparation and a definite impulse from the nation itself." By 1882 this moment seemed to be drawing near, for in that year Bismarck was ready to promise the Bremen merchant, F. A. Lüderitz, that the government would support his efforts to acquire colonial rights in what was to be German South-West Africa.

By 1884 a German colonial empire was under way. In April the flag was first raised at Lüderitz Bay in South-West Africa. In July a protectorate was proclaimed further north over the coast of Togoland and the Cameroons. In February, 1885, Germany declared a protectorate in the East African territory, where a hard-driving colonial adventurer, Karl Peters, had already signed treaties with the native chiefs. In this same year the German East Africa Company was chartered. Almost simultaneously in the Pacific, footholds were secured in German New Guinea (1885), in the near-by Bismarck Archipelago (1884), and in the Marshall Islands (1885). Though some subsequent additions were to be made, by 1890 by far the greater part of Germany's colonial empire had been acquired. The final additions under William II included some further Pacific islands (1899), the port of Kiao-Chow on the Chinese mainland (1898), and a strip of territory ceded from the French Congo (1911). These gave Germany by 1914 an empire of more than 1,000,000 square miles with a native population of some 12,000,000 and a white population of about 25,000, mostly officials, soldiers, and police.

The value of these new possessions was, to say the least, uncertain. Clearly, the colonies provided no place for German emigration. Moreover, the economic return derived from the colonies was far less than the costs of conquest and maintenance. None of the principal African colonies ever balanced its budget, the deficits being made up by the German taxpayers. Germany's colonial trade in 1914 was about one-half of 1 percent of her total commerce. Yet the enthusiasm for colonies persisted. Bismarck had set Germany on the path of overseas empire, a path which was to have profoundly significant consequences.

The problems of the German workingman were dramatized and made more urgent by the rapid rate of industrial expansion at home and by the growth of new imperial commitments abroad. Bismarck never ceased to mistrust and oppose those measures which would put political power in the hands of the common man. His view of the social problem in Germany was that by a policy of paternalism he could head off the growing socialist movement, thereby removing a threatening source of political opposition. He would, so he felt, be able to give the German workers everything they could expect to win through their own political efforts. The tariff of 1879 he looked upon as a shield which would further the progress not only of German industry but also of German agriculture. Concerning the industrial worker, he spoke in May, 1884, as follows:

> Give the workingman the right to work as long as he is healthy, assure him care when he is sick, assure him maintenance when he is old. If you do that and do not fear the sacrifice, or cry out at state socialism, if the state will show a little more Christian solicitude for the workingman, then I believe that the gentlemen of the Social-Democratic program will sound their bird calls in vain . . . yes, I acknowledge unconditionally a right to work, and I will stand up for it as long as I am in this place.[11]

Impressive measures were introduced to benefit the workingman. The first proposals in 1881 for insurance against industrial accidents were defeated through Centrist opposition in the Reichstag—an illustration of the obstructive power this body occasionally could employ. The Sickness Insurance Act, successfully enacted in 1883, provided protection for workers and their families out of funds to which employers contributed two-thirds and workers the rest. In 1884 accident insurance was provided out of funds to which the employers alone contributed. In 1887 the hours of labor for women and children in industry were limited, a maximum working day was set for certain industries, and Sunday was stipulated as a day of rest. In 1889 a scheme of old-age pensions, beginning at the age of sixty-five, was authorized out of a pension fund to be built up by contributions from employers, employees, and the state.

Germany under Bismarck was therefore the first country to establish what in many respects was a model system of protection against the hazards of life in the new industrialized age. While these measures failed utterly to stop the growth of the Social Democratic movement, they unquestionably provided Germany with a stable and economically prosperous labor force at a time of

11. GRANT ROBERTSON, *Bismarck*, p. 382.

great economic expansion. What was equally significant, they heightened the impact of this newly united nation upon the complex scene of international politics.

■ GERMANY AND THE EUROPEAN BALANCE, 1871–1890[12]

The essential starting point for Bismarck's foreign policy after 1871 was that Germany was a "saturated power," whose unswerving purpose must be to guarantee her own security by maintaining things as they were. The leader who had indulged in a decade of war now stood as an angel of peace. This peace could be endangered from either side. In the west, France had accepted the Peace of Frankfurt, but could hardly be expected to regard it as morally binding. It was Bismarck's aim, therefore, to isolate France, while at the same time encouraging her in her colonial ventures so as to divert her from the idea of a war of revenge in Europe. "The hostility of France," Bismarck wrote in December, 1872, "compels us to desire that she may remain weak." In the east, the danger was that Balkan problems would rouse the animosities of the Ottoman Empire's nearest neighbors, Russia and Austria-Hungary. Bismarck therefore sought to keep these two powers from coming to blows and to maintain a friendship with both.

Bismarck's offers of assistance to Russia during the Polish troubles of 1863 now stood him in good stead, as did his leniency to Austria after her defeat in 1866. In 1872 the Emperor Francis Joseph and Tsar Alexander II visited Berlin, the outcome being an informal, verbal agreement to keep the peace. Though it was followed in 1873 by a similar visit from the king of Italy and even by some written communications, the understanding remained shadowy. Certainly tensions were present. When two years later a war scare blew up as a result of what the German general staff considered to be a threatening increase in the size of the French army, it was hard to determine whether French belligerency or an eagerness on the part of some quarters in Germany to take advantage of it was the greater danger. In any event, partly due to Anglo-Russian mediation, the scare blew over.

A more serious crisis soon followed in the Balkans, testing whether Bismarck's skill was sufficient to keep the peace among the major powers. In July, 1875, the provinces of Bosnia and Herzegovina, lying close to the Hungarian border, rose against Turkish rule, and their action was quickly followed by an uprising in Bulgaria and the launching of an unsuccessful attack upon the Turks by Serbia and Montenegro. In 1877 Russia declared war on Turkey and carried it on so successfully that by March, 1878, she was able to dictate the Treaty of San Stefano of which, by-passing its details, one may say simply that

12. Much that is said in this section should be related to the discussion in ch. 17 on the background of the First World War.

it would have virtually driven Turkey from Europe and given Russia a dominant role in the Balkans. Since both Britain and Austria were gravely concerned at this, the danger was that sooner or later they would be at war with Russia. Bismarck, who had once declared the Balkans "not worth the bones of one Pomeranian grenadier," now offered his mediation in the role of honest broker.

The outcome was the Berlin Congress of 1878 at which Bismarck, whether honest broker or not, presided over a compromise settlement, most of the terms of which had been worked out privately in advance. The result of a compromise is often to leave the parties dissatisfied. The arrangements allowed Turkey to regain some considerable part of the Balkans, forced Russia to renounce the dream of a greater Bulgaria existing under her tutelage, and gave Austria the right to occupy and administer Bosnia-Herzegovina. With so many conflicting interests, future troubles were certain to develop.

In such circumstances Bismarck's policy clearly was to seek closer relations with Austria. A little more than a year after the Berlin Congress, Germany and Austria signed the famous Dual Alliance (October, 1879). Each promised to come to the aid of the other if attacked by Russia or by another power supported by Russia. The treaty, which was at first kept secret (though William I confidentially informed Tsar Alexander II of it), was periodically renewed down to 1914. It was the cornerstone of the Bismarckian diplomatic system—the first in the series of alliances and counteralliances which henceforth divided the great powers into two rival camps.

Despite all difficulties, Bismarck still counted upon the old friendship with Russia. Hence in 1881 he was able to do what had not been possible in the verbal agreement of 1872—to establish the Three Emperors' League (*Dreikaiserbund*) on the basis of a written treaty. Austria, Russia, and Germany now agreed that if one of them was at war with a fourth power, the other two would observe a benevolent neutrality. Though renewed in 1884, the fundamental Balkan antagonisms of Russia and Austria cast a shadow upon this agreement from its very beginning. Meanwhile Italy, incensed at France's occupation of Tunisia in 1881, made overtures to Bismarck and was referred by him to Vienna. In 1882 the Dual Alliance of 1879 was converted into a Triple Alliance, Italy being promised support by Germany and Austria if attacked by France, and Germany being promised Italian support if similarly attacked. When Austria signed an alliance with Serbia in 1881 and with Rumania in 1883, the elaborate network of agreements was such as to bring France's isolation into spectacular prominence. Bismarck's diplomacy could quite properly be described as at its zenith. The European center of gravity in international politics can often be ascertained by noting the capital at which great international conferences are held. Thus it came about that the Berlin Congress of 1878 was followed by another Berlin Conference in 1884–1885 at which fourteen nations met to iron out some of the tangled problems arising from the partition of Africa. Bismarck's dominant role was apparent.

A Bulgarian crisis beginning in 1885 dramatically revealed the basic antagonisms between Austria and Russia.[13] Since Austria now supported a greater Bulgaria and Russia did not, Bismarck's concern was to see that their opposing policies did not lead to war. He did not hesitate to warn Austria that she could not count on Germany's help in the event of a war with Russia. This does not mean that Bismarck was deliberately pro-Russian, and Tsar Alexander III publicly blamed him for pursuing a double-faced policy in the Balkans. Bismarck's real fear was that, if Russia kept on seeking for allies, she would almost certainly turn to France.

When the continuing antagonism between Austria and Russia made it clear in 1887 that the Three Emperors' League could not be renewed, Bismarck sought by more complex means to keep the peace. He gave his support to two Mediterranean Agreements by the first of which, in February, Britain, Italy, Austria, and Spain had agreed to maintain the *status quo* in the Mediterranean and the Black Sea. The second, signed in December, committed Britain, Italy, and Austria to support Turkey if threatened by Russia. Midway between these two, Bismarck accepted Russia's proposal of a Reinsurance Treaty, by which each of the two signatories promised benevolent neutrality if the other found itself at war with a third great power. Germany recognized Russia's preponderant influence in the Balkans. In strictly legal terms, the treaty, which was most secret, was not incompatible with the Dual Alliance, and thus Bismarck, while still committed to help Austria if she were *attacked* by Russia, had managed "to keep open the wire to St. Petersburg." Only a virtuoso, however, could keep up so delicately balanced a relationship, and it is hardly surprising that after Bismarck's fall the treaty was allowed to lapse.

In sum, Bismarck had been remarkably successful in building up a complex network of alliances to guarantee German security, and successful also in preventing the creation of any rival system. Yet to praise him unreservedly is to ignore the amount of resentment and suspicion which his policies bred. The close alliance with Austria, publicly revealed by Bismarck in 1888, was basically unacceptable to Russia, while France, unhappy in her isolation, stood ready to build up a system counter to that of Bismarck. Even before his fall in 1890, France and Russia were drawing together. Russian landlords were bitter toward Germany because of the increased tariff on agricultural imports, and the French were beginning to sell munitions to Russia, to make loans, and to invest money in other ways. To a very considerable degree the Bismarckian system of alliances, however brilliantly executed, contained within itself the seeds of its own undoing.

13. See pp. 400–401.

"DROPPING THE PILOT," from *Punch*, March 29, 1890. Perhaps the most famous of all *Punch* cartoons, this drawing by Tenniel, the illustrator of *Alice in Wonderland*, perfectly catches the human implications of the German political crisis.

■ TRANSITION TO A NEW AGE

Between 1888 and 1890 Germany moved from one age to another. In March, 1888, the old emperor, William I, with whom Bismarck had worked for more than a quarter of a century, died in his ninetieth year. The reign of his son, who took the title of Frederick III, was a tragic interlude of three months, for the emperor on his accession was already dying of cancer of the throat. Frederick's son and successor, William II, destined to reign from 1888 until 1918, was only twenty-nine. A fluent talker, romantic, headstrong, arrogant, theatrical, and at times almost unbalanced, William concealed a certain nervousness and insecurity beneath the splendid externals of the emperorship. Though he was an autocrat and a militarist who never hesitated to voice his contempt for the "muttonheads" who made up the Reichstag, his versatile intelligence led him to find pleasure in the new world of business and finance, and, indeed, to declare a deep sympathy for the lot of the working classes.

On March 18, 1890, the seventy-five-year-old Bismarck, who had forecast long years of future service for himself, resigned. His breach with the emperor, who at first professed deep devotion to Bismarck, arose from a number of concrete disagreements as to their respective spheres of authority. Yet the fundamental incompatibility was that of two men, the one long used to the exercise of power, the other determined to seize it. Bismarck returned to his estate at Friedrichsruh, where for eight more years he lived in bitter retirement, giving interviews and using certain newspapers as a mouthpiece for his criticisms of the new order. *Punch's* most famous cartoon, "Dropping the Pilot," caught to perfection this end of one age and the beginning of another.

Shortly after Bismarck's departure William II called for the nation's loyal cooperation and stressed the "new course" which Germany was now to follow. In foreign affairs the change, as will be seen subsequently, was all too clear.[14] In domestic matters, however, the emperor could hardly divorce himself from the policies which Bismarck had established. Bismarck, to be sure, had shown considerable subtlety in handling political parties, while William II felt himself above any such necessity. He boasted that he never looked at the newspapers, and in 1908 declared that he had never read the imperial constitution. "There is only one master in the Reich, and that is I," he announced in one of his typically inflated speeches, "and I shall tolerate no other." His leadership, however, was capricious and bombastic rather than strong. The four chancellors who served him in the years down to the coming of the World War in 1914 were none of them dominant men, and so in a political sense Germany floundered. In 1909 one of Germany's most brilliant industrialists, Walter Rathenau, described the situation as follows:

> How can we justify the fact that Germany is ruled in a more absolute fashion than almost any other civilized country? . . . It will be difficult to show—especially to foreigners who are asked to respect us—why by his constitution the German is allowed so much less influence in affairs of state than the Swiss, the Italian, or the Rumanian. The Continental barometer stands today at "self-government" and we cannot very long continue to have a special climate of our own.[15]

However erratically and unpredictably, the emperor took over some of the leadership exercised by Bismarck. There was also some growth of power on the part of the ministers, for example, in the case of Tirpitz at the Admiralty. Foreign policy showed itself subject to pressures from various propaganda leagues, to the influence of the general staff, and to the sinister power of Holstein, permanent counsellor of the Foreign Office from 1878 to 1906, a strong Anglophobe and a highhanded intriguer. Sir Edward Grey complains, in his *Twenty-Five Years*, that it was impossible through the normal channels of diplomacy to reach the men who really directed Germany policy.

The new course in domestic matters began with a considerable departure from Bismarckian policies. Caprivi, the Prussian soldier whom William II appointed to the chancellorship in 1890, showed an unexpected spirit of moderation and conciliation. The antisocialist laws on which Bismarck had counted were not renewed; a lighter hand was imposed upon Alsace-Lorraine and the Polish provinces; arbitration courts were set up for industrial disputes, and the working hours of women and children in industry were still further reduced. Following a lowering of the tariff, a series of commercial treaties was made with neighboring countries. This brought the Junkers and other landowners into

14. See pp. 330–333.
15. H. KESSLER, *Walter Rathenau* (1930), pp. 123–24.

opposition and led in 1893 to the forming of what was to become a very powerful pressure group, the Farmers' Union (*Bund der Landwirte*). The Social Democrats, meanwhile, now freed from the restrictions imposed on them in 1878, made impressive gains in the elections of 1893. The kaiser, who had boldly declared, "My course is right and I shall follow it," quickly reversed himself and in 1894 dismissed Caprivi and brought this liberal, or perhaps better pseudoliberal, period to an end.

Henceforth the prevalent tone was one of reaction. Prince Hohenlohe, an elderly Bavarian aristocrat, held the chancellorship for six years. His successor, Count, later Prince, von Bülow (1900–1909),[16] who in contrast to Bismarck, the Iron Chancellor, has come to be known as the Silken Chancellor, was truthfully and perhaps too charitably described as a man of expedients. Under pressure from the Farmers' Union and the Central Union of German Industrialists, in 1902 he substantially increased the tariff both on grain and manufactures. A new, repressive policy was undertaken against the minorities in the Polish provinces and Alsace-Lorraine. Some further social legislation did not arrest the steady growth of the Social Democrats who in the elections of 1907 polled 3,300,000 votes and won 43 seats. Yet the failure to redistrict Germany meant that the Conservatives with only 1,500,000 votes gained 84 seats. What might have been a significant development was the creation of the "Bülow bloc" in the Reichstag—a combination of Conservatives, National Liberals, and Progressives after the election of 1907. Bülow was unable, however, to hold this together for more than two years and thus in 1909 he resigned.

Bethmann-Hollweg, Bülow's successor, was a serious, unimaginative, Prussian civil servant, notable chiefly for his failure to curb those forces leading to a crisis in German foreign policy. The increasing demands for political reform at home met little response. The Social Democrats, to be sure, polled 4,250,000 votes and won 110 seats in the elections of 1912, thereby becoming the largest party in the Reichstag. In any true political sense this was an empty victory. In the previous year a constitution of sorts had been granted to Alsace-Lorraine; three delegates were now sent to the Bundesrat, in addition to the fifteen deputies sent since 1874 to the Reichstag, and there was to be an elected bicameral legislature to administer local affairs. For the Reich as a whole, further substantial extensions were made in the insurance provisions for the German workers. Yet against this should be set the passage of the Army Bill of 1913, which raised the peacetime forces from 544,000 to 870,000 and levied a special

---

16. 1849–1929. He served in the Franco-Prussian War, then in the diplomatic service, becoming ambassador to Italy. As chancellor he tried to model himself on Bismarck, saying that the state should follow its own interests disregarding ethical considerations. Witty, cultivated, and urbane, he has been called too much of a diplomat to be a great statesman, and, although he disapproved of Tirpitz's naval program, was unable to curb it. His successor, Bethmann-Hollweg, charged Bülow with having bequeathed him an impossible diplomatic situation.

national defense tax of a billion marks to support it. In this era of prosperity and power the ominous words of Rathenau, written in 1913, again deserve quotation:

> I see shadows rising wherever I turn. I see them in the evening when I walk through the noisy streets of Berlin; when I perceive the insolence of our wealth gone mad; when I listen to and discern the emptiness of big-sounding words. . . . An age is not without care just because the lieutenant beams and the attaché is full of hope.[17]

■ ECONOMIC AND SOCIAL GROWTH UNDER WILLIAM II

To summarize the economic and social growth of Germany under William II is to extend, with some new emphases, the description of the Empire under Bismarck. By 1914 Germany had a population of 65,000,000—second only to Russia among the European states. Berlin had a population of over 2,000,000; five cities had passed the 500,000 mark (Hamburg, Munich, Leipzig, Cologne, Breslau); two others, Frankfurt-am-Main and Essen, closely approached it. The contrast with France, where, after the 3,500,000 figure for Paris, only two other cities (Marseilles and Lyons) were anywhere near the 500,000 mark, is striking.

Germany pressed hard on the heels of Great Britain as an economic power, and in some respects had even surpassed her. Germany's annual steel production, for example, had risen from about 2,000,000 metric tons in 1890 to 17,300,000 tons in 1913, this being far ahead of Britain's 8,500,000 or France's 5,100,000. Steel meant power, whether in the manufacture of the tools of industry or of the weapons of war. The great Krupp factories at Essen—the world's greatest munitions plant, with a practical monopoly of supplies for the Prussian army and with salesmen all over the globe—by 1912 employed 68,300 workers. Fritz Thyssen carried on at Mulheim in the Ruhr the great steelworks established by his father in 1871. Germany's coal output from the Ruhr, the Saar, and the Upper Silesian basins had tripled since 1890; the coal figure for 1913 was 190,000,000 tons, and, if to this is added 89,000,000 tons of lignite, the total came very close to Britain's 1913 output of 292,000,000 tons of coal. The German railway network of 38,000 miles in 1910 was second only to that of Russia among the European powers. Germany's 1913 share of world manufacture was 15.7 percent; Britain's was 14 percent. Her long-term foreign investments in 1913 were nearly five times what they were in 1880. And by 1913 one-third of the world's output of electrical products was in German hands.

German foreign trade made impressive growth. Exports, rising from about $865,000,000 in 1890 to $2,524,000,000 in 1913, had nearly trebled; annual imports grew from $1,070,000,000 to $2,693,000,000 over the same period. The

17. Quoted in PINSON, *Modern Germany*, p. 291.

deficit in the trade balance was easily covered by shipping revenues and by the interest on German investments abroad; these investments by 1914 totaled nearly $5,000,000,000. The German merchant marine had grown spectacularly; by 1912 it had 3,000,000 tons of shipping, second only to Great Britain which with its 12,000,000 tons was far in the lead. Yet the three great German shipping companies—the Hamburg-America Line, the North German Lloyd, and the Hansa—were thriving concerns of great economic power, and the German ship-building yards at Hamburg, Bremen, and Stettin were world-famous.

In some economic respects German progress was unique. To a degree that other countries could not approach, Germany skillfully combined its industrial resources with the scientific skills of its universities, technical schools, and commercial institutes. Illiteracy in Germany by 1914 was four-tenths of 1 percent; university attendance had risen from 13,000 in 1870 to 60,000 in 1914. The work of great chemists, such as Liebig, profoundly stimulated the chemical industry which quickly made use of it. In 1900 the six leading chemical firms in Germany employed over 650 trained scientists, while at the same time the entire British chemical industry employed only between 30 and 40.

Well provided with chemical deposits, Germany quickly led in the production of bulk products, such as potash, sulphuric acid, ammonia, and potassium salts, for manufacturing purposes, for agriculture (artificial fertilizers), and for munitions. Research in coal-tar derivatives resulted in the production of synthetic dyes—a field in which German leadership was unchallenged and in which the famous I. G. Farben Works grew to dominate the entire industry. Other equally famous fields were those of pharmaceutical products and photographic supplies.

The support of German scientists was equally apparent in the electrical industries. An engineer and inventor, Werner von Siemens, who as early as 1847 had organized the firm of Siemens and Halske for telegraphic construction, invented the electric dynamo in 1866 and went on to make his firm one of the giant industries of Germany. Its rival was the A. E. G. (*Allgemeine Elektrizitäts Gesellschaft*), growing out of the German Edison Company. In competition they dominated the huge expansion in the field of telegraphs, telephones, electric lighting, electric trains, electric trams, wireless, and the general use of electric power in industry. The creation of this industry has truly been called the greatest single economic achievement of modern Germany.

An unusually close connection existed between banks and industry. Some twenty-five important business banks had grown up by 1914, concerning themselves principally with the promotion of industry and trade. Outstanding were the famous four "D-Banks": the Darmstädter Bank (1853), the Diskontogesellschaft (1856), the Deutsche Bank (1870), and the Dresdner Bank (1872). These helped to float companies, provided long-term credits, had their representatives on numerous boards of directors, encouraged the forming of cartels, and sub-sidized foreign trade.

A striking feature of Germany's industrial growth was the cartel.[18] While Americans became accustomed to antitrust laws and the British courts held that agreements "in restraint of trade" were not legally enforceable, German busi-nesses in increasing numbers began to form close associations to regulate the amount of production, prices, and marketing methods. Such cartels could be either horizontal (a group of firms producing similar goods), or vertical (a group of firms engaged in different stages of production from the raw material to the finished product).

Cartels grew up for a variety of reasons: bad economic conditions; need for large amounts of capital in new industries; possession of a monopoly, such as potash; and tariff protection beginning in 1879, which made it tempting for manufacturers to combine in order to make high profits at home while simul-taneously winning markets abroad by dumping goods at an agreed low price. A few cartels existed before the tariff of 1879; many then quickly followed, so that by 1905 the Cartel Commission listed 366 such industrial combinations. These had the protection of the law, their agreements being recognized as private contracts. The most striking feature was the enormous size and power of a few great cartels: the Rhenish-Westphalian Coal Syndicate made up of eighty-seven mining enterprises, the Steel Works Association, the I. G. Farben Industries, and the great electrical combine, the A. E. G. Closely aided by the big banks, and in turn exercising much influence in the Free Conservative Party and the right wing of the National Liberals, these associations of big business added significant strength to the Empire.

Agriculture fell far behind industry in this picture of economic growth, for, as has been noted, by 1910 the population was 60 percent urban. Germany ceased to be a food-exporting, and became a food-importing, country. Yet there was no such catastrophic decline as in England. Some protection for grain growers came from the tariff of 1879 but not enough, and it was only under the higher tariff of the 1890's that grain prices began to rise, as they con-tinued to do until 1914. With the aid of government subsidies and loans, pro-duction of wheat, rye, pigs, and potatoes showed a steady increase. Substantial side industries, such as distilleries and the production of beet sugar, prospered. Though most of the benefits went to the large landowners, it is also true that landbanks and farmers' cooperatives helped to improve conditions for the small farmer. German forestry, thriving and scientific, led the world in its techniques.

How did the average worker progress under these conditions? He had the vote, though it is clear that the political mechanism of the Empire rendered it to a large degree ineffective. He had the benefits of the elaborate system of social

18. See p. 298.

legislation initiated by Bismarck and enlarged by his successors. He had the benefits of an elaborate system of free public education and of distinguished universities and technical schools. The governments of the newly growing cities, too, were frequently models of administrative efficiency, though it is true that the slum areas of the Ruhr and even of Berlin created serious problems in health and housing.

The German worker, for his part, despite the opposition of some industrialists, showed a steadily increasing tendency to trade-union membership. The legal right of labor to organize was established under the North German Confederation in 1869. The "free" or socialist trade unions grew most rapidly, reaching a membership of 2,500,000 by 1913, to which should be added close to 500,000 in the Catholic and other trade unions. Strikes and lockouts grew; big disturbances arose among the Ruhr coal miners in 1872 and 1889, the steel workers in 1905, the Hamburg dock workers in 1897, and the Saxon textile workers in 1903. Between 1902 and 1906 strikes averaged more than two thousand a year.

The attitude of the Social Democratic Party to the German Empire is a matter of some significance. The Gotha Program of 1875 had fused the Lassallean and Marxian wings into a compromise creed recognizing labor as the source of all wealth, calling for "the extinction of every form of exploitation," and demanding the democratization of the state. Despite Bismarck's persecution, the Social Democratic Party grew steadily in the 1880's and the 1890's. At the Erfurt Congress of 1891 the party, under the influence of Karl Kautsky, adopted a more strictly Marxian program based on the theory of the class struggle, of revolution, and of the destruction of capitalism through joint action of the working classes the world over. Still led by August Bebel in the Reichstag until his death in 1905, the Social Democratic Party gained increasing strength until, in the elections of 1912, it won one out of every three votes of that year and captured 110 seats.

GROWTH OF THE SOCIAL DEMOCRATIC PARTY IN GERMANY, 1890–1912[19]

PARTY	1890	1893	1898	1903	1907	1912
Conservatives and Free Conservatives	93	100	79	75	84	57
National Liberals	42	53	46	51	54	45
Left Liberals	76	48	49	39	49	42
Center	106	96	102	100	105	91
Social Democrats	35	44	56	81	43	110
Irreconcilables	38	35	34	32	29	33
Anti-Semites	5	16	13	11	16	13
Others	2	5	18	8	17	6

19. Based on PINSON, *Modern Germany*, p. 573.

Quite clearly, nevertheless, a great many Germans who had voted for a party which had declared itself revolutionary in aim were not themselves revolutionary.

During the 1890's a movement led by Eduard Bernstein, and calling itself revisionism, grew up in German socialism. Bernstein argued that many of Marx's assumptions and prophecies simply were not true. The poor were not getting poorer, and the capitalist class showed few signs of digging its own grave. Socialists, therefore, should not count on the revolutionary chaos supposedly to follow the imminent collapse of the capitalist system. They should, instead, work through the parliamentary system toward a cooperative scheme of production. "I strongly believe," Bernstein wrote, "in the socialist movement, in the march forward of the working classes, who step by step must work out their emancipation by changing society from the domain of a commercial landholding oligarchy to a real democracy which in all its interests is guided by the interests of those who work and create." With some 4,250,000 German voters subscribing in whatever limited degree to the tenets of the Social Democratic Party in 1912, it is quite clear that, despite growing prosperity, the magnificent externals of Imperial Germany harbored some ominous centers of opposition.

■ IMPERIAL GERMANY AND THE WORLD STAGE

When William II spoke in 1890 about the new course of German policy it was, above all, the stage of world politics to which he referred. As Bülow put it in a Reichstag speech of 1897, "We do not desire to put anyone else in the shade, but we want our place in the sun." Powerful pressures were working at home to encourage these demands. German nationalism, stimulated by the spectacular successes in the wars, became strident. This was particularly true of the University of Berlin, where, from 1874 until his death in 1896, Heinrich von Treitschke gave his lectures on politics to crowded classrooms. "War," he declared, "must be taken as part of the divinely appointed order. It is both justifiable and moral, and the idea of a perpetual peace is not only impossible but immoral as well." Other eminent historians spoke similarly, notably Heinrich von Sybel and Gustav Droysen, leading Lord Acton, the English scholar, to characterize them in 1886 as "a garrison of distinguished historians that prepared the Prussian supremacy together with their own, and now hold Berlin like a fortress."

Militarism became a creed and a gospel. The most striking example of all this came much later in Friedrich von Bernhardi's *Germany and the Next War* which, published in 1911, had two years later reached a sixth edition. He defined war as "the highest expression of the strength and life of truly cultured peoples." It "gives a biologically just decision, since its decisions rest on the nature of things." There must be a final reckoning with France, for Germany

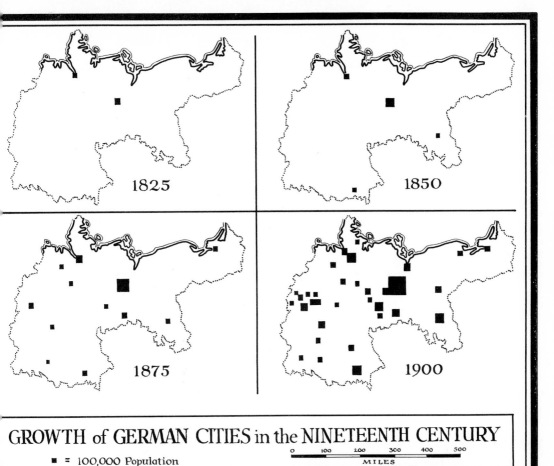

GROWTH of GERMAN CITIES in the NINETEENTH CENTURY

■ = 100,000 Population

```
0      100     200     300     400     500
|———————|———————|———————|———————|———————|
              MILES
```

Berlin's central position on the international railway network and its role as capital of the German Empire help to make it the greatest industrial and commercial city on the Continent. By 1910 the urban population of Germany is 60 percent of the whole.

faces the alternative of "world power or destruction." Bülow's *Imperial Germany*, written in 1912, contains the passage: "In the struggle between nations, one is the hammer and the other the anvil."

As Germany developed in the colonial field, a number of organizations arose with the purpose of encouraging her world ambitions. A Colonial League was founded in 1882; a Navy League in 1898, which ten years later had over a million members; and in 1893 the Pan-German League took formal shape. This last, though not large in numbers, was particularly violent in its expansionist tendencies and obtained substantial financial backing from some of the leaders of German heavy industry.

The Pan-German League echoed the theories of earlier writers, such as the German orientalist, Paul de Lagarde, who had demanded a German-dominated central Europe. Its first president was the African explorer, Karl Peters, soon to be replaced by Ernst Hasse, a Leipzig professor of limited intelligence and tireless determination, who urged the incorporation of Belgium, Luxembourg, the Netherlands, Bohemia, Moravia, and French and Russian frontier districts in a Greater Germany. "We want territory," he wrote, "even though it be inhabited by foreign peoples." Strongly anti-British, the Pan-German League declared itself ready to combat all forces that checked German national development. There were, to be sure, corresponding movements in other countries. Some Germans looked askance at these developments—the great historian, Theodor Mommsen, for example, referred to the Pan-Germanists as "patriotic idiots"—yet the movement could count on substantial support from government, business, army, press, and university circles.

Along with the leaders of Pan-Germanism were others: those, for example, like the composer Richard Wagner, who engaged in a grandiose glorification of Germany's mythical past; or the disciples of the renegade Englishman, Houston Stewart Chamberlain, who, in his *Foundations of the Nineteenth Century* (1899), dramatized the vicious doctrine of Aryan supremacy; or the anti-Semitic writers led by Adolph Stöcker who, in 1878, had organized his Christian Social movement; these were further influenced by the political anti-Semitism in Austria led by Georg von Schönerer and Karl Lueger.

When Bülow created a separate colonial office under a former banker, Bernhard Dernburg, in 1907 the new colonial era may be said to have begun. Improved methods of administration, much activity in the way of speeches, propaganda, railway building, subsidies to planters, and tours of inspection, and the founding of the Colonial School at Hamburg were all evidence of Germany's determination to take her colonial role seriously and to build up her possessions in the hopes of equaling those of the other great imperial powers. In 1907 Gustav Stresemann, later to play so important a role in the Weimar Republic, referred to the colonies as "a piece of the German soul."

Tensions inspired by rivalries in Africa and the Far East were accompanied by a new concern over the Ottoman Empire, once again seeming to live up to its reputation as the "Sick Man of Europe." German policy toward Abdul Hamid II was one of friendship. William II visited him in 1889 and again in 1898, and on the latter occasion going on to declare at Damascus that 300,000,000 Moslems could be assured that he would ever be their friend. Military and economic connections with Turkey grew close, so that by 1903 German business interests had railway concessions all the way to Baghdad and the Berlin to Baghdad railway became a realizable possibility.

A new naval tradition began to arise alongside the old Prussian military tradition. (The kaiser, it is said, insisted on attending a performance of Wagner's *Flying Dutchman* in full-dress admiral's uniform.) Admiral von Tirpitz, at the navy department since 1897, was the chief instigator of a great program of naval expansion. This led to the succession of navy laws—1898, 1900, 1906, 1908, and 1912—which, following Britain's introduction of the *Dreadnought* in 1906, resulted in a prolonged building race with Britain. Germany rose from seventh to second place among the world's naval powers; she spurned the proposals for disarmament made at The Hague in 1907; and she would not encourage the efforts made by Lord Haldane in his 1912 mission to Germany to find some end to the mutually destructive naval race.

This tense and strident atmosphere provides the background for the long series of crises, large and small, which could be said to begin with the kaiser's telegram of congratulations in 1896 to President Kruger of the South African Republic at the time of his resistance to the Jameson Raid which William II assumed to be British inspired. Such tensions continued until the assassination of the heir to the Austrian throne at Sarajevo in 1914. These are properly a part of a history of the coming of the First World War.[20] The essential points are that the efforts first made in the 1890's to reach good relations with Great Britain failed; that William II's abandonment of the wire to St. Petersburg (despite his continuing personal friendship with his cousin "Nicky") led inevitably to the Franco-Russian Alliance; that Italy's role in the Triple Alliance grew progressively weaker; and that by the close of 1905 Germany was almost completely isolated. This meant in simple terms that Germany must now rely almost completely upon the Dual Alliance with Austria. During the Bosnian crisis of 1908, when Russia's friendship with Serbia made a war with Austria likely, Bülow wrote to the Austrian foreign minister as follows: "I shall therefore regard the decision to which you ultimately come as that demanded by the circumstances." The crisis blew over, yet the German commitment to Austria is striking. Bülow resigned in 1909, and his successor, Bethmann-Hollweg, well-intentioned though he may have been, was unable to do anything to change the situation whereby Europe, armed to the teeth and divided into two hostile camps, was increasingly at the mercy of a situation where one last crisis would lead to war.

Reading List: Chapter 11

Pinson, K. S., *Modern Germany: Its History and Civilization* (1954), chs. 10–12. Political, social, and economic developments, 1870–1914.

The New Cambridge Modern History, vol. XI (1962), ch. 10. The German Empire.

Bruce, Maurice, *The Shaping of the Modern World* (1958), ch. 2. The correlation between political and economic factors.

20. See ch. 17, pp. 478–489.

Gooch, G. P., *Germany* (1925), chs. 4–5. Economic and cultural developments.

Bismarck, O. von, *The Kaiser Versus Bismarck* (1921), chs. 8, 10. Dismissal; William II.

Craig, G., *The Politics of the Prussian Army, 1640–1945* (1956), chs. 6–7. "The State within the State"; the Schlieffen Plan.

Townsend, Mary E., *The Rise and Fall of Germany's Colonial Empire* (1930), chs. 2–3, 9. Beginnings of colonialism; the "New Era."

Hallgarten, G. W. F., "Heinrich von Treitschke," *History*, vol. XXXVI (1951), no. 128.

O'Boyle, L., "Liberal Political Leadership in Germany, 1867–1884," *Journal of Modern History*, vol. XXVIII (1956), no. 4.

Bülow, Prince von, *Imperial Germany* (1914), pp. 3–50. Germany as a world power.

Earle, E. M. (ed.), *Makers of Modern Strategy* (1948), ch. 8. Moltke and Schlieffen.

Koehl, R. L., "Colonialism Inside Germany, 1886–1918," *Journal of Modern History*, vol. XXV (1953), no. 3. The attempt to plant German settlers in Posen and West Prussia.

Chapter 12

Republican France, 1870–1914

The Aftermath of Defeat
Establishing the Republican Constitution
Parties and Politics
Stresses and Strains in the Third Republic
Problems of Church and State
Socialism and the Social Problem
France Overseas
"La Douce France"

■ THE AFTERMATH OF DEFEAT

The immediate occasion of the establishment of the Third Republic, destined to a life of nearly seventy years, was military defeat; more basically the Republic was the outcome of political aspirations which had existed and of struggles which had gone on intermittently since 1789. On September 4, 1870, following the disastrous surrender at Sedan and the capture of Napoleon III, a noisy Paris crowd invaded the parliamentary chamber where the deputies, led by Léon Gambetta, agreed to the proclamation of a republican regime. It was to be announced, significantly enough, at the Hôtel de Ville, so that Paris, as on so many earlier occasions in French history, might play the central and decisive role. Very quickly a provisional government, nominally headed by the military governor of Paris but actually dominated by Gambetta, was organized.

SIGNIFICANT EVENTS

1870   Proclamation of the Republic and Provisional Government (September)

1871   Paris Commune (March–May); Treaty of Frankfurt (May)

1875   Organic Laws establishing the Constitution of 1875 (January–July)

1879   Election of Grévy as president

1881   Occupation of Tunis

1890   "Rallying" of Catholics to the Republic

1894–1906   The Dreyfus Affair

1901–1905   Separation of church and state

1904   Entente Cordiale with Britain

1913   Three years' Conscription Law

The immediate aim of the provisional government was to transform defeat into victory. This purpose, despite heroic efforts and some unexpected military successes, it failed to realize, and in January, 1871, the siege of Paris ended in near starvation and surrender. One of the provisions in the armistice was that immediate steps should be taken to elect a national assembly. Though some of the ardent republicans still wished to carry on a last ditch struggle, the general desire by now was to end the war. Thus the February 8 election produced a legislature with about four hundred royalists, two hundred republicans, and a mere thirty Bonapartists. Since it was the republican leaders who had been most eager to continue the war, the monarchist majority in this hasty election was quite clearly a mandate for peace.

This National Assembly was to govern France until 1875. Meeting at

Bordeaux, it quickly elected the elder statesman, Adolphe Thiers, as chief of the executive power of the French Republic, it being understood that this title would not prejudice any future form of constitution that might be devised. Thiers, who initially made his name as historian of the first Napoleonic Empire, had been a notable figure under the Orleans monarchy and an equally notable critic of the Second Empire. This small, shrewd former protégé of Talleyrand had cleverly refused to join the provisional government of September and remained uncompromised by its failures. In the February elections he had exercised his right to have his name put forward in more than one constituency, with the astonishing result that he was chosen in no less than twenty-six departments, while only nine chose Gambetta. Now he conceived his first major purpose to be to secure an acceptable peace, and to this end he made the Pact of Bordeaux, by which various political groups put aside their party differences in the interest of national preservation.

In what the French long referred to as *l'année terrible*, peace had to be made quickly with the German Empire, so dramatically proclaimed in the Hall of Mirrors at Versailles on January 18. Order, furthermore, had to be secured at home. The Treaty of Frankfurt (May 10) stipulated, as has been shown,[1] the loss of Alsace and the greater part of Lorraine, a five-billion-franc indemnity payable within three years, and an army of occupation in the northeastern departments. The terms meant the loss of famous cities, such as Strasbourg and Metz, of more than a million and a half people, rich iron deposits, many textile factories, and large forest and agricultural areas.

The immediate impact of such terms was obscured by the tragic phenomenon known as the Paris Commune. Social unrest was nothing new; it had grown with the progress of industrialism, and it was intensified by the particular hardships in Paris during the siege. As far as the uprising had an ostensible purpose, it sought to set up a revolutionary communal government in Paris and to encourage other French cities to do likewise. In this sense it seemed an echo of the revolutionary Paris Commune of 1792. It may have reflected, too, something of the radical demands of violent agitators, such as Auguste Blanqui, who had, so the saying went, "been on the barricades" since 1827. The uprising has assumed a place in socialist and communist mythology, hardly justified by the evidence, as the first great proletarian uprising of modern times. In actuality it was the product of many less radical forces, among them anger at the loss of the war, the state of near starvation in Paris, fear of the royalist majority shown in the February elections, and public dislike of some of the new government's measures. Among these were the attempt to take away the cannon from the National Guard which it mistrusted, the termination of its pay, and the ending of the moratorium on rents and debt payments which had been in effect. The

1. See p. 80.

well-to-do, who began to desert Paris before the siege, continued to do so after it was over. Most of the people who remained wished to keep up the fight, and it is significant that, of the forty-three deputies elected by the capital in February, all but six favored continuing the war.

In its inception the Commune was not the sinister, destructive force that its opponents have often made it out to be. It had the support of scores of thousands of average citizens, artisans, and skilled craftsmen—patriots who were honestly trying to save the Republic which had been so precariously launched in the preceding September and to bring about a better day for the average man. An effort was made to set up an orderly government and to legislate for the improvement of working hours and conditions of labor. One of the curiosities of the Paris uprising, indeed, was that the Bank of France, with its large stores of gold, remained unmolested and was able even to further its business by advancing loans to both sides. The Commune was briefly paralleled by the appearance of communal uprisings in other industrial cities—Lyons, Marseilles, Saint-Etienne, Toulouse, Narbonne—which, however, were quickly repressed.

Ruthless measures against Paris were quickly ordered from his headquarters at Versailles by Thiers. He later declared himself to have followed the model of Windischgraetz at Vienna in 1848 in having first withdrawn from the capital in order to launch the armed forces that would recapture it. He moved sternly to put down the revolt, instructing Marshal MacMahon to undertake "a second siege of Paris." Mobilizing large military forces, drawn in part from the military prisoners whom the Germans now obligingly released, MacMahon began his task in April. In the suburb of Courbevoie the army of Versailles shot every prisoner which it took. After heavy bombardments, the attackers entered the city through a breach in its walls. During the terrible Week of Blood (May 21–28), Paris was conquered street by street by troops acting with almost unbelievable ruthlessness; men, women, and children died in indiscriminate shooting; in reprisal for the summary execution of their captured leaders, the Communards put to death hostages, including the archbishop of Paris; and famous buildings, such as the Tuileries, the Courts of Justice, and the old Hôtel de Ville, went up in flames. For five nights burning buildings illuminated the skies and it was by pure chance that such monuments as the Louvre, Notre-Dame, and the Saint-Chapelle, were saved. The last of the Communards were rounded up in the Père Lachaise cemetery where, against the *Mur des Fédérés*, to which the socialists have since faithfully made their annual pilgrimage, the final remnant of a hundred and fifty were shot. The casualties were appalling, for an estimated twenty thousand persons died either in combat or by summary execution, among them hundreds of women and children. Deaths among the assaulting troops have been put at one thousand. Subsequent arrests have been soberly estimated at over fifty thousand, and more than twenty courts kept steadily at work, some of them until 1876, disposing of the cases. In the end, over thirteen thousand were given prison sentences, more than half of them involving deportation to the prison colony of New Caledonia in the Pacific.

The Commune shocked Europe and left behind a legacy of mistrust and bitterness in France. It marked the end of the National Guard—that popular force born of the Revolution of 1789, which had played an important role both then and in 1830 and in 1848. It discredited the cause of socialism and trade unionism for at least a decade, if not for a generation. And yet, by removing some of the most violent elements of opposition—in however bloody a fashion—the government of Thiers was enabled to proceed with the complex and uncertain task of organizing the new regime.

Thiers had not wished to press the issue of the precise form of government that France was to assume, knowing well the conflicting emotions that would be aroused in an assembly where the monarchists were in a majority. Yet some clarification was made, for the so-called Rivet Law of August, 1871, declared explicitly: "The head of the executive power shall take the title of *President of the French Republic*," and affirmed the principle of parliamentary sovereignty. The most pressing need, however, was to settle accounts with Germany. Thiers managed to pay off the war indemnity by floating two loans, one of June, 1871, and the other of July, 1872, to which the thrifty French quickly subscribed many times over. By September, 1873, the last German uniform was gone from France.

Another measure was that of army reforms. France had long operated under a complex system in which the ranks of a long-service professional army were filled out by a loosely enforced system of conscription first authorized in 1818. To meet the challenge of the German system of three years' service, France in 1872 made all men liable to five years active service followed by the usual reserve duty. A comprehensive plan of exemptions was provided for those fortunate enough to draw certain numbers, or to belong to the exempted categories—students, priests, seminarists. Volunteers who could find fifteen hundred francs could have their service limited to one year. On this basis France eventually built up a standing army of half a million men and a capable officer corps, which by the mid-eighties was judged by ardent nationalists to be fit for a war of revenge against Germany.

The first provisional government, known to some as the "Republic of M. Thiers," lasted for over two years. He had followed a cautious conservatism in financial matters, rejecting proposals for an income tax and beginning to counter the free-trade policies of the 1860's by a return to protectionism. Whatever his original royalism, Thiers was convinced by 1873 that a republic was "the government that divides us least"—a lukewarm statement, to be sure, and less than satisfactory to the many radical republicans who won by-election after by-election and looked to the great orator and patriot, Léon Gambetta, as their leader.[2]

The royalists, whose majority in the National Assembly was dwindling, feared for their part what Thiers' policies might lead to, and at last withdrew their support. In May, 1873, therefore, the seventy-four-year-old Thiers resigned his presidency. The successor chosen by the Assembly was Marshal MacMahon—a professional soldier, a royalist, and presumably safe. Strangely enough it was under MacMahon rather than under Thiers that the Third Republic came definitely into being.

■ ESTABLISHING THE REPUBLICAN CONSTITUTION

The constitution of the Third Republic did not take final shape until 1875, when several "organic laws," voted by the National Assembly, together provided the major elements of France's new political structure. The situation was complicated and lent itself to complex proposals and maneuvers. The Republic had been provisionally announced on September 4, 1870; then the elections held in the following February had shown a surprising two-to-one royalist majority. Thiers had been immediately elected by the new National Assembly as chief of the executive power in the new provisional government, where he succeeded in persuading his colleagues to postpone the constitutional issue until some kind of order was re-established in France.

This constitutional issue, however, could not wholly be ignored. If, as the election appeared to indicate, France was still monarchist, could an acceptable candidate for the throne be found? The elections had produced about two hundred deputies who called themselves Legitimists, supporting the claims of Henry, Count of Chambord, grandson of the last Bourbon king, Charles X. There were also two hundred Orleanists, whose candidate was the Count of Paris, grandson of Louis Philippe. Had these two groups been able to agree on a compromise candidate, say, the childless Count of Chambord, with the succession passing afterwards to the Orleanists, their combined numbers would originally have been twice those of their Republican opponents. They were, indeed, prepared to do so, but they would have to act quickly, for the temper of France was changing, and the by-elections of July, 1871, gave the Republicans 100 out of 118 contested seats. The Count of Chambord cooked his own goose. He issued a dramatic manifesto saying that he would accept a con-

2. 1838–1882. This Italian grocer's son and lawyer first made a name for himself by denouncing the Second Empire. He escaped from Paris by balloon during the siege of 1870 and became a key figure in the provisional government. A magnificent orator and strong anticlerical, he helped to create the Third Republic, held various ministries, yet only once, and in his last year, headed a French cabinet.

stitutional regime but that, come what may, his flag must be the historic white standard of the Bourbons. As a lineal descendant of the great Henry IV, he claimed the right to demand not only this symbol but also the allegiance of all Frenchmen. To the Republicans, for whom the tricolor had become a sacred symbol, and likewise to the Orleanists, this was impossible. Thiers declared acidly that Chambord deserved the title of the French Washington, for it was he who had founded the Republic. In the course of 1872 Thiers made it even clearer that to him a republic must be the inevitable outcome. "The Republic exists," he declared in his November message to the Assembly, "it is the legal government of this country; to wish for anything else would be tantamount to revolution—the most formidable of all revolutions." In 1873 the Count of Chambord reinforced his contribution to the outcome; he ended what seemed like a possible compromise agreement with the Orleanists by proclaiming once more his unshakable devotion to the white flag of the Bourbons. The best that the royalists could now do was to vote Marshal MacMahon, who had replaced Thiers as president, a term of seven years, hoping that somehow he would keep the throne in readiness for some future occupant.

A parliamentary regime had come into existence in France in the months before the war with Prussia. Now, with much hesitancy and uncertainty, the institutions of the Third Republic took definite shape. There was no sealing of a charter; there was no formal proclamation of the Republic. "We are entering the Republic backwards," Gambetta's newspaper declared. The main constitutional provisions were worked out piecemeal. The Wallon amendment of January, 1875, prescribing the manner of election and term of office of the president, included almost casually the phrase, "the President of the Republic," and this amendment was carried by a majority of one. Two organic laws dealing with the powers of the president and of the upper and lower house, and another dealing specifically with the Senate, were passed by June. Subsequent legislation enlarged and modified the original terms, and thus, despite the untidiness of the procedure, the Republic, which had existed provisionally since 1870, now received its permanent definition.

The president was elected for a term of seven years by an absolute majority of the two chambers sitting jointly. He had the power to supervise the execution of laws, to appoint civil and military officers, to grant pardons, and to share in the conduct of diplomacy. He likewise had power to convene special sessions of parliament and to adjourn parliament. Yet every act of the president had to be countersigned by a minister. The lower house, the Chamber of Deputies, was chosen for four years by universal, direct, secret, manhood suffrage beginning at the age of twenty-one; the number of members, initially 533, was to increase with the growth of population. This was the principal lawmaking body.

Theoretically the president could dissolve it at any time, with the approval of the Senate, thus necessitating a general election. The attempt, as will subsequently be seen, was made only once. The Senate, whose three hundred members were to be at least forty years old, was chosen indirectly by a system of electoral colleges for a period of nine years, one-third being renewed every three years. (The original provision that seventy-five senators be named by the Assembly for life was dropped in 1884.) It had coordinate powers of legislation with the lower house, save that it could not originate financial measures. Members of both houses were to be paid.

Since the duties of the president were in a large degree ceremonial, political leadership fell necessarily to that figure, the premier, who could organize a cabinet, and command a majority in the Chamber of Deputies, his tenure of office being determined by his ability to command such a majority. He thus resembled his British counterpart, being subject to a vote of confidence at any time, though unlike the British prime minister he lacked the power to call for a dissolution of parliament when the occasion seemed to require it.

It is striking, in view of the precedent set by the French Declaration of the Rights of Man issued in 1789 which had been followed hitherto, that no formal bill of rights was issued in 1875. In 1881 laws were passed guaranteeing freedom of the press and of speech. The provisions for departmental and municipal government and for the judiciary remained essentially what they had been before—the permanent legacy of the great structural reforms of the revolutionary and Napoleonic age. Though the eighty-seven departments each had an elected general council, substantial powers were retained by the prefects, nominated from Paris. Similarly, one must stress the great importance in France of the *fonctionnaires*, those permanent officials or civil servants, the legacy of Richelieu, Colbert, and Napoleon I, who carried the administrative burden of the Third Republic. Carefully selected and rigorously trained for a lifetime career, they were not infrequently unsympathetic to some of the aims of the Third Republic. The administrative pyramid was crowned by the *Conseil d'Etat*, a quasi-judicial body nominated by the president with one of its duties to give advice on new legislation. It represented one pole of the French political system—professional, judicial, and permanent—even as the turbulent political arena of the Chamber of Deputies represented the other.

When the constitutional arrangements of 1875 came into effect, about ten million Frenchmen could vote. More than half of these lived by agriculture and more than a third owned the land which they farmed. Industrial wage earners numbered about three millions, and the business and middle class about three quarters of a million. It remained true, therefore, that France, if only by a small margin, was still a rural democracy.

■ PARTIES AND POLITICS

How was the new political machinery to operate? It was not clear in 1875 that the government must necessarily be responsible to the majority in the Chamber. Without question the president had considerable legal powers if only he could exercise them. A trial of strength soon followed.

When the National Assembly, which had been in existence since February, 1871, was finally dissolved in December, 1875, new elections quickly were held. The result was a substantial Republican majority in the Chamber of Deputies and a strongly conservative majority in the Senate. On May 16, 1877, a day to become memorable in French parliamentary history, President MacMahon— no lover of parliamentary democracy—invoked his legal rights as president, forced the cabinet to resign, appointed a monarchist (the Duke de Broglie) as premier, and obtained the Senate's consent to the dissolution of the Chamber of Deputies. A strenuous campaign, with Gambetta as the eloquent champion of the Republican cause, gave the Republicans 321 seats and the Right 208—a substantial victory for the opponents of MacMahon. A striking phenomenon was the temporary resurgence of Bonapartism. Its spokesmen won 104, or exactly half, of the anti-Republican seats; royalists of various allegiances held an equal number. When the Senate elections of January, 1879, likewise brought a Republican majority of 50 in the upper house, President MacMahon accepted the inevitable and resigned, two years before his term was up.

The presidency was now assumed by Jules Grévy, an elderly lawyer of modest origins whose republicanism went back to 1848. Thus, with the elimination of the Duke de Broglie and of MacMahon (who had the title of Duke of Magenta), what was sometimes cynically known as "the Republic of the Dukes" came to an end and political power was truly in the hands of Republicans. Symbolism having the importance which it does in public life, it should not pass unnoticed that at this time the great revolutionary hymn, the *Marseillaise*, was made the official national anthem of France, and that July 14, the anniversary of the fall of the Bastille, became the chief national festival. All this, to be sure, is not to say that the Third Republic was at the end of its troubles. In many respects it might seem that they were only beginning.

French political parties are the outcome of political groupings, for and against the Republic, that began in the legislative sessions of the years following 1789. These parties never crystallized into two well-organized entities like the Liberals and Conservatives in Britain or the Democrats and Republicans in the United States, but followed instead the general Continental pattern of multiplicity. To be sure, it might plausibly be argued that such groups fell roughly into the two broad divisions of parties of the right and parties of the left, but, even so, the divisive elements must be emphasized. In Britain and America long political experience in self-government and no doubt other factors have produced a willingness to compromise—to vote for a party with which one broadly agrees, despite differences on specific issues. No such willingness is observable in France, where political groupings have grown out of long, historic disagreements, have developed against a background of conflicting social forces, and have been intensified by the economic pressures of the new industrial age. Differences arising from these divergent historic traditions, from incompatible religious allegiances, from regionalism, and from conflicting class interests have combined with what is said to be the stubborn individualism of the Frenchman to produce a veritable spectrum of parties.

The elements of flux and change make it impossible for party developments under the Third Republic to be narrated accurately or in summary form. Deputies in the French Chamber sat in a semicircle facing the podium of the presiding officer. In 1876 it is possible to make a rough listing of five principal groups: the Monarchists on the right (themselves divided into Legitimists, Orleanists, and Bonapartists); the moderate Republicans of the center recently converted from monarchism, with leaders such as Thiers; the more bourgeois Republicans of the center left led by Grévy and Jules Ferry; the Radical Republicans who followed Gambetta; and on the extreme left a small group of intransigeant Radicals.

Many changes took place. The Republicans of the left and the followers of Gambetta came together in an affiliation with various names (Opportunists, Moderates, Progressists, and finally the Republican Federation) which from 1878 to 1898 really controlled France. From 1900 to 1905 a new party, the Radical Socialists, with the assistance of the Democratic Republicans and the Socialists formed a Republican Bloc which, as will shortly be observed, carried out a strongly anticlerical program and managed to make its influence felt until 1910. In the elections of 1914 at least ten major parties were listed, though these for practical purposes could be grouped into three associations of the right, the moderate center, and the left.

The royalist groups, steadily dwindling in number, were often labeled simply Right, or Conservative. Another conservative association of big business, Catholic, and landed interests in 1903 created the Republican Federation. It accepted the Republic in a fashion, but was strongly clerical, antisocialist, and antireformist. An electoral league of more moderate conservatives was eventually formed with the title of the Democratic Alliance. It carried on something of the tradition of Thiers.

From the ardent Republican supporters of Gambetta, first organized in what was called the Republican Union, eventually developed the Radical and Radical Socialist Party, the strongest and best organized group in the Chamber. It was anticlerical and reformist, strongly rooted in the individualist traditions of the French bourgeoisie, and derived its inspiration, as Gambetta did, from the legacy of the great French Revolution. It combined members of the professional and white-collar classes with prosperous artisans and peasants. Thus the word, "socialist," as applied to the party is a misnomer, and the word, "radical," would not have the meaning it holds today. These Radicals and Radical Socialists provided some of the greatest names of the Third Republic.

French socialists, proscribed after the Commune of 1871, did not become politically active until the 1880's. Seventeen were elected in 1889 and fifty in 1893. A socialist, Millerand, was included in the Waldeck-Rousseau cabinet of 1899. The United Socialist Party was formed in 1905, and in the elections of 1914 won 102 seats. The Communist Party in France did not emerge until 1920.

The preceding description does not do full justice to the excessive individualism of French politics, for again and again splinter parties were created by dissident minorities. The typical French politician, it is said, regarded as ideal a party that consisted of himself and just enough voters to get him elected. It is clear that under such circumstances most governments of necessity would be coalitions (blocs), running all the risks inherent in such uncertain alliances. Since one party never commanded an absolute majority, it could hope to stay in office only by seeking the support of its neighbors to the right or the left, in accordance with the prevailing temper of the times. Thus, from 1875 to 1912 there were forty-five cabinets, having an average lifespan of less than ten months apiece. Two circumstances helped to mitigate the effects of this evident instability and lack of continuity. One was the great power and the unquestioned permanence of the official class—the *fonctionnaires*. The other was the reappearance in cabinet after cabinet of many of the same individuals. Ministries changed more frequently than ministers. The fall of a government often meant simply the shedding of one wing from a coalition and the addition of an opposite wing, with the central groups remaining the same. In this way a prominent figure, such as Aristide Briand or Raymond Poincaré, could appear in one ministry after another.

A tabulation of the election results of 1914 will indicate the complexity of the French political picture. Such a summary is given on the following page. The trend, clearly, was to the left, though it is to be stressed that the nomenclature of French parties and indeed the voting habits of many Frenchmen suggest a degree of radicalism much greater than was actually the case.

What is also striking is the overwhelmingly bourgeois character of the Third Republic. The brief ministry of the Duke de Broglie in 1877 is the last in French history to be headed by a nobleman. MacMahon, who made no play of his former imperial title of Duke of Magenta, was the only holder of a title to be president of France. Aristocratic families counted for very little in the French parliament, and the peasant and proletarian class contributed even less.

FRENCH ELECTIONS OF 1914[3]

	PARTY	SEATS
Right (75)	"Right" (Royalist)	16
	Action Libérale Populaire (Catholic)	23
	Republican Federation (Big Business)	36
Moderates (176)	Democratic Left	34
	Republicans of the Left	54
	Radical Left	65
	Independent Left	23
Left (297)	Radicals and Radical Socialists	172
	Socialist-Republicans	23
	United Socialists	102
Other (54)	"Not Inscribed" (Usually voting with the Right)	46
	Independent	8
		602

Gambetta, a product of the petty bourgeoisie, whose father was a small shop-keeper in a provincial town, symbolized the new age. Lawyers, professors, business and professional men, civil servants—all were part of the middle and petty bourgeoisie that gave the Third Republic its distinctive character.

Finally, one must note the continuing uncertainties facing the Republic. Though by 1878 comfortable Republican majorities had been won in both houses, strong antagonisms still existed, so much so that the phrase, "the two Frances," is often used to describe them. Many were uncertain in their allegiance to the Third Republic; some were frankly hostile. Part of this opposition was open, part concealed. In the stormy last two decades of the nineteenth century, when political crises racked the Republic, the parties of the right in general took the offensive. The parties of the left, while defending the Republic, tended on the whole to be opportunist, seeking to further their own advantage. After 1899 these parties were strong enough to combine in a militant reform program. When the deep conflict of the Dreyfus case ended in 1906, it seemed that the Republic at last was on an even keel. Yet the incompatibilities remained, to be revealed in the tragic consequences of the catastrophe which came over France in 1940.

■ STRESSES AND STRAINS IN THE THIRD REPUBLIC

The Republic so laboriously established soon found itself subject to some alarming stresses and strains. In the elections of 1885 the parties of the right made a sharp increase, winning 201 seats as against the 80 they had obtained in

3. Based on the statistics, slightly modified, in LAVISSE, vol. VIII, p. 288.

1881. Although the Republican groups had 383 seats, they clearly were exposed to a much greater challenge than before.

A republic born amid so many confusions and disagreements was sure to have its critics and opponents. Some of the opposition, naturally enough, came from the Bonapartists, Legitimists, and Orleanists in the traditionally royalist salons of the Faubourg Saint-Germain who never ceased to look backward. Some of the opposition came from Roman Catholic sources, for the clericals, with much reason, were concerned with what the anticlerical elements in the Third Republic might do to their historic vested interests. Some of the opposition was now viciously anti-Semitic, claiming that banking and other financial circles where Jewish influence was strong were undermining France. Largely because of emigration arising from unrest in the Russian Empire, the Jewish population of France rose from an estimated 80,000 in 1880 to nearly 200,000 in 1900. Edouard Drumont wrote a sensational book, *La France juive*, to this effect in 1886, and in 1892 began publishing a vicious and similarly sensational newspaper, *La Libre parole*. He found many followers.

Another kind of criticism and unrest was fomented by an extreme variety of jingoistic nationalism—certainly not unique to France—which grew up in these years. Much of it was antirepublican. In 1875 appeared the first volume of Hippolyte Taine's *Origins of Contemporary France*, a brilliant work which, while not fanatically nationalist, launched an eloquent attack on the entire revolutionary tradition to which the Third Republic was heir. In his preface Taine sharply denounced the theory of democracy on the principle that ten million ignorances do not make knowledge. Naturally enough, royalists and Catholics welcomed the work, while republicans denounced it. Of a different sort was the nationalism of Paul Déroulède, never a major figure, yet a patriotic poet and essayist who was bitterly shocked at the humiliation France had experienced in 1871. He organized the League of Patriots in 1882 to work for a war of revenge against Germany and the restoration of the two lost provinces. It was he who declared in 1883, "I have found my man; his name is Boulanger." Later, at the time of the Dreyfus Case, Déroulède tried to persuade a French general to lead an attack on the Elysée Palace. Still another example was the novelist, Maurice Barrès, who as a young man read Taine and Nietzsche and who later wrote novels, most notably *The Uprooted* (1897), exalting what he called "the national egotism." The extreme nationalism generated in these years was of minor proportions, yet it lasted through the entire history of the Third Republic. Its immediate effect was to help in mobilizing a certain segment of opinion in support of some highly dangerous causes.

One of these causes emerged in the person of General Boulanger and the movement known as *Boulangisme.* A popular soldier, who had been wounded in Italy in 1859 and again in the Franco-Prussian War, Boulanger had also served in Algeria, Tunisia, and Indo-China. In 1886 he became minister of war in the Freycinet cabinet. Some of his first steps, such as improving the living conditions of the ordinary soldier, reducing exemptions from military service for privileged groups (notably the clergy), and proposing the reduction of the conscription term from five years to three, gave him an immediate popularity. This was at a time when an economic depression had been intensified by the ravages of the phylloxera pest in the vineyards, when small socialist groups newly appearing were quarreling bitterly with one another, and when the poor caliber of many of the newly elected deputies was notorious. At first Boulanger had the backing not of the royalists but of the Radical Republicans, and for a time there were at least fifty deputies in the Chamber who could be called Boulangists. When this handsome, bearded figure rode through the streets of Paris on a black charger, the crowds hailed him as a new hero who could give strength to a government which sorely needed it and as the hoped for Man of Destiny could win back Alsace and Lorraine from Germany in a war of revenge.

Small happenings can produce crises, and, when in April, 1887, the German authorities in Alsace arrested a French police official, Schnaebele, in what seemed a most highhanded manner, a tense situation developed. Bismarck, for his own reasons, drew back, yet popular opinion held that it was Boulanger who had outfaced him. Thus, when conservative forces brought about Boulanger's resignation in May, popular emotion burst out in his support. When Boulanger sought to leave Paris, immense crowds gathered at the Gare de Lyon and three thousand people stood or lay on the tracks seeking to prevent his departure. In 1888 he was dismissed from the army. He now demanded a revision of the constitution and won backing from the Orleanist and Bonapartist groups. His attack on the regime was given substance when it was discovered that the son-in-law of President Grévy, living in the Elysée Palace, had organized a lucrative business which involved selling the decoration of the Legion of Honor for large sums. Although Grévy was not implicated, the scandal forced him to resign and seemed still further to discredit the Republic.

With wildly enthusiastic popular backing, Boulanger now launched a political campaign, demanding the election of a new constituent assembly. He was chosen in six by-elections in the departments as well as winning by a big majority in Paris. A new cabinet finally had the courage to issue a warrant for his arrest on the grounds of conspiracy against the state. The outcome was anticlimactic. Rather than precipitate the expected crisis as Louis Napoleon had done in 1851, Boulanger fled abroad. Quickly condemned *in absentia* by the Senate to deportation, two years later he committed suicide at Brussels on the grave of his mistress. Though *Boulangisme* had failed, it clearly revealed the lurking elements of disloyalty to the Republic, and an enthusiasm among small and irresponsible groups on the right for a war of *revanche* against Germany. A more positive result was that it led those who genuinely believed in the Republic to rally more sincerely to it.

This *Ralliement*, or rallying to the Republic, manifested itself particularly in Catholic circles. The Roman Catholic Church had consistently been in opposition to the Republic, which had attacked the religious orders, expelled the Jesuits, and placed heavy restrictions upon church schools. The Radical Republicans were militantly anticlerical. Since the accession of Pope Leo XIII in 1878, however, the hostile attitude which had existed under Pius IX had been gradually reversed. Thus, in 1890, Leo encouraged Cardinal Lavigerie, the French primate of Africa, to propose a toast to the Third Republic at a banquet in Algiers. Two years later Leo XIII addressed an encyclical letter to all French Catholics ordering them to cease from their attacks and to accept the constituted authorities of France, working for what reforms they could through constitutional channels. The *Ralliement* had made notable progress.

Yet troubles were by no means over. In 1889 came the Panama scandals. Eight years earlier Ferdinand de Lesseps, the brilliant builder of the Suez Canal, had organized, along with Eiffel and other French engineers, a company to build in Panama a canal of seventy-four kilometers with no locks or tunnels. Though French investors had put up large sums, the work went very slowly and inefficiently with the result that by 1889 the company collapsed. It soon came out that at least a hundred deputies, some senators, and even ministers had accepted substantial bribes in order to assist and favor the companies involved. In 1893 Lesseps and certain associates were found guilty, as were a number of government figures. Though the sentences were ultimately set aside under the statute of limitations, the reputation of French politicians in general had been

THE DREYFUS CASE: "J'ACCUSE!" Zola's famous letter to the President of the French Republic denouncing the miscarriage of justice in the Dreyfus case appeared on the front page of the newspaper, *L'Aurore,* on January 13, 1898.

badly besmirched and the fact that the two principal intermediaries between the company and parliament were Jewish further stirred up the anti-Semitism aroused by the publicist, Edouard Drumont. All this led directly to the famous Dreyfus Case, which for more than a decade was to make sensational news in France and throughout the world.

In 1894 Captain Alfred Dreyfus, a well-to-do Jewish officer on the French general staff, was declared guilty by a court martial of selling military documents to agents of a foreign government. He was therefore stripped publicly of his rank and sentenced to penal servitude for life on Devil's Island, a lonely spot off the coast of French Guiana with a high mortality rate. In 1896 the new head of the secret intelligence service, Colonel Picquart, became convinced that a shocking injustice had been done to Dreyfus by means of forged evidence at which responsible officers had connived, and that the real traitor was a Major Esterhazy, a dissipated French officer of remote Hungarian ancestry. Thereupon Picquart was quickly transferred by his superiors to Tunisia. When, however, other similar evidence emerged, the military authorities were forced to bring Esterhazy to trial (1898); nevertheless, he was quickly acquitted and officially congratulated.

By this time there was sufficient indication of forged evidence and high-handed procedures to arouse many distinguished political and literary figures. Prominent among these "Dreyfusards" was the novelist, Emile Zola, who in

1898 published his famous open letter, *J'Accuse*, to the president of the Republic, denouncing by name members of the general staff. Zola was quickly sentenced to a year's imprisonment which he avoided by escaping to England. The "anti-Dreyfusards" included royalists, high army officers, extreme nationalists, and advocates of anti-Semitism—all eager to use this supposed evidence of incompetence and corruption to discredit the regime. There were also those who were willing to accept the condemnation of an innocent man if it were necessary for what seemed to be the deepest interests of the state.

In 1898 a high officer in the intelligence service first admitted to having forged a series of documents that were in question and then committed suicide. The death of President Faure in 1899 and the election of Emile Loubet to succeed him helped Dreyfus, for Loubet, unlike his predecessor, was sympathetic to reopening the case. Thus Dreyfus, after four years of solitary confinement, was brought back for retrial by court martial at Rennes in September, 1899. The unusual verdict (that Dreyfus was guilty but with "extenuating circumstances") and the sentence (ten years' imprisonment with a recommendation of pardon) indicated the stubborn unwillingness of army circles to remedy what by now could clearly be seen to be an outrageous perversion of justice. Not until 1906 was it possible for the Court of Cassation, the highest civilian tribunal, to clear Dreyfus completely and for the president to order his restoration to the army and decorate him with the Legion of Honor. Not until 1906, consequently, had the Republic been able fully to vindicate itself against opponents who were prepared to use the most reckless and unsavory means to discredit it. The affair, on the other hand, dealt a substantial blow to the *Ralliement*, for it was clear that despite the policy of Leo XIII many French clericals were still deeply hostile to the Republic.

It is notable that in the course of the affair various republican groups were at last able to come together and form the *Bloc des gauches*, or Republican Bloc, which also took in the Socialists who by now were members of the Chambers. This bloc, militantly opposed to the royalists and the clericals, made possible the new Waldeck-Rousseau ministry of 1899 and for the first time in the history of the Third Republic saw a socialist, Millerand, a member of the cabinet. He was, indeed, the first socialist to enter any European cabinet. This bloc was quick to introduce some dramatic changes, chiefly affecting the historic position of the Roman Catholic Church in France.

Only the briefest mention can be made here of France's establishment of a seemingly secure place in the European system of alliances. The completion of the defensive alliance with Russia in 1894 and the understanding (Entente Cordiale) with Great Britain in 1904 were products of the effort to find some counterpart to the threatening alliance system stemming from Bismarck's Dual Alliance with Austria in 1879. So likewise the action of parliament standardizing the three-year conscription term of service in 1913 showed that the Republic was concerned with this same problem of security in the face of mounting dangers.

■ PROBLEMS OF CHURCH AND STATE

Ever since 1801 and throughout all changes of regime, France had lived in general acceptance of the Napoleonic Concordat which gave government support and an official and privileged status to the Roman Catholic Church, as it also in a modest degree supported the Protestant and Jewish faiths. While most Frenchmen were Catholics, they were likewise jealous of their political rights; moreover, a long tradition of Gallicanism existed whereby the Catholic Church in France was in many respects subject to the authority of the state. Thus, with the increasingly secular trends of the nineteenth century, the conflict between the clericals, defending and even seeking to enlarge the political position of the Church, and the anticlericals, whose hostility was evident, steadily developed.

The matter was particularly acute in the realm of education where traditionally the Catholic teaching orders had played a large part. The Falloux Law of 1850, passed at a time when clerical influence was very strong, had notably extended the activity of the Church's role in the field of education.[4] In 1879 Jules Ferry[5] entered the first cabinet of Grévy's presidency as minister of public instruction. The bill which by 1882 he eventually succeeded in making into law was a direct blow at clericalism, which Ferry, along with Gambetta, had long since pointed out as the enemy. Primary education was made free, compulsory and secular, that is, without religious instruction. Church schools could, to be sure, still serve those who wished to attend them. During the crises associated with Boulanger and Dreyfus, the close link between clerical groups and the forces hostile to the Republic became unhappily evident, and in time led the Radicals and Socialists to make sweeping criticisms of the position of the Church in France. Though Waldeck-Rousseau, head of the government from 1899 to 1902, was not as militant as many of his followers, under the impetus provided by the formation of the Republican Bloc, a heavy attack was launched on the Roman Catholic Church.

In 1901 the Law of Association was passed. The numerous religious orders in France comprised altogether more than 3,000 different communities, with nearly 200,000 members. Their property was estimated to be worth a billion francs, and a great many of these congregations, as they were called, were still engaged, despite the Ferry laws, in teaching. The act of 1901 provided that there

4. See p. 68.
5. 1832–1893. Lawyer and journalist, critic and opponent of the Second Empire. Prominent in the provisional government of 1870 and the administration of Paris during the siege, he was one of the founders of the Third Republic, served as minister of education and of foreign affairs, and was twice premier (1880–81 and 1883–85). He was responsible for the law of 1882 making primary education free, non-clerical, and obligatory. A vigorous leader, he stimulated the imperial revival of the 1880's in which France acquired Tunis, Tonkin, and Madagascar.

should be general freedom of association for native religious societies provided that they would obtain authorization from the government and submit to continuous regulation. No member of an unauthorized society could be permitted to teach. Since the elections of 1902 strengthened the Republican Bloc, the government continued to act vigorously. Nearly fifteen hundred congregations were disbanded, many of their members leaving France, and three thousand unauthorized schools were closed. An act of 1904 forbade any further teachings by religious orders, and all such orders were to be suppressed within ten years. Thus, only those engaged in hospital work, such as the Sisters of Charity, and those engaged in missionary activity, would ultimately be permitted to remain.

In 1903 the statesmanlike Leo XIII was succeeded by Pius X, a more uncompromising figure who in many respects resumed the militant policies of Pius IX. He quarreled with the French government over the appointment of bishops, and protested when President Loubet visited the king of Italy, calling the visit offensive to the Holy See. The Rouvier ministry which took office in 1905 assigned to Aristide Briand, a young Socialist destined to a long and distinguished career, the responsibility of guiding through parliament the sweeping act for the final separation of church and state. By December, 1905, this was done, and the Concordat of over a hundred years came to an end. Complete separation was obtained by proclaiming full liberty of worship with no connection, financial or otherwise, between state and church. This, it will be noted, applied equally to Protestant pastors and Jewish rabbis, both groups which previously enjoyed state support. All church property was to be handed over to new "associations for the purpose of worship" (*associations cultuelles*), which would be legally empowered to administer it and maintain services. In a sense all church buildings were now public monuments. Pensions and some indemnities were provided for aged clergy; the clergy now generally assumed the normal burdens of taxes and of military service.

With these measures the fires of the anticlerical conflict subsided. Though Pius X issued an encyclical *Vehementer* against the laws, the continuing majorities given in the election of 1906 to the Republican Bloc indicated that the country as a whole registered its approval. Indeed, for the first time since 1877, the parties of the left won an absolute majority in the lower chamber. By 1914 4,500,000 children attended state primary schools and only about 1,000,000 were found in church schools. In the tradition of Jules Ferry, public education had become overwhelmingly patriotic, standardized, and secular.

■ SOCIALISM AND THE SOCIAL PROBLEM

Though socialism as a movement of theory has a long history in France reaching back to some of the thinkers of the Enlightenment, as an organized movement it is of comparatively recent development. Writers such as Saint-Simon and Fourier contributed notably to the literature of debate, and Louis Blanc in 1848 brought socialism momentarily to have an impact upon government. Yet it remained for a German, Karl Marx, to sweep aside the arguments of these utopians and proclaim his doctrine of "scientific," Marxian socialism— a fighting creed that found exponents in country after country. Proletarian elements with some of these militantly revolutionary views were present in the Paris risings of 1848. The Commune of 1871 was assumed by some to have carried on this doctrine of a people's uprising aiming at the destruction of the old order. Yet the excesses associated with the Paris Commune, its ultimate failure, and the savagery involved in its suppression all combined to drive socialism out of active French public life for a decade.

The ultimate organization of French socialism is marked by a vast medley of personalities and groups. Very slowly in the late seventies and early eighties Marxian socialism found its way into France. Jules Guesde, a Paris journalist driven into exile for his share in the Commune and one of the greatest figures in the history of French socialism, was instrumental in organizing at Marseilles in 1879 the Socialist Workers of France which included both revolutionary (Marxian) and moderate (Possibilist) elements. The succeeding years saw much bickering and divergence in socialist circles, so much so that by the last years of the nineteenth century at least five main groups had developed: Guesde's Workers' Party, which was Marxian; the Revolutionary Socialist Party founded by Edouard Vaillant in 1881, stressing trade unionism; the moderate Federation of Socialist Workers founded in 1882; the Revolutionary Socialist Workers Party, preaching class war; and the Independent Socialists, prepared to act through parliamentary channels and including some names very prominent in French political life, notably Jean Jaurès,[6] Millerand, and Briand. In the elections of 1893 the various socialist groups managed to win 50 seats; by 1906 the number was 59; in 1910 it was 76; and in 1914 it was 125.

Efforts to bring the various socialist parties together met great difficulties. An attempt at fusion in 1898 was followed three years later by a split into two groups. Guesde's left-wing followers formed the Socialist Party of France, while the moderates called themselves the French Socialist Party. Their leader Jaurès, though disagreeing in many matters with Guesde, in 1905 managed to reunite the two wings so as to form the United Socialist Party—a union which lasted until 1914. The party was professedly revolutionary in its aim, but less so

---

6. 1859–1914. One of the great figures in modern socialism, he was a teacher of philosophy who was elected to the Chamber in 1885. Powerfully influenced by Marx, he also believed in a distinctively French socialism. He founded the paper, *Humanité*, and wrote six of the twelve volumes of the *Socialist History of France*. In 1914 he advocated a general strike of German and French workers to prevent war, and was assassinated by a French ultra-Nationalist. He was one of the greatest orators of the Third Republic.

in practice. Its manifesto of 1905 declared "fundamental and irreducible opposition to the whole bourgeois class and to the state which is the instrument of that class." Yet in 1914 it stated: "We wish to secure, to seize, the maximum of political and social reforms that are obtainable under the present social system."

An important development in France was the growth of a workers' movement committed less to parliamentary than to direct action. The right of French workmen to form associations or unions, long forbidden, came to be tolerated under the Second Empire and was fully established by law in 1884. The General Confederation of Labor—a broad association of unions—was organized in 1895. This trade-union movement, or syndicalism (from the French *syndicat*), did not work closely with parliamentary groups as was the case in England, but stressed instead the policy of direct action by means of strikes and violence outside parliamentary channels. Direct action stressed the importance of every strike, boycott, and local gain in wages, no matter how small, carried out by an active minority. It led ultimately to the concept of the general strike which, hopefully, could bring a government to its knees in a few days. The Amiens Charter of the General Confederation of Labor (1906) put forward this view, refused to collaborate officially with any political parties, and declared itself in favor of the general strike.

Such views found eloquent expression in Georges Sorel's *Reflections on Violence* (1908), a classic work preaching the doctrine of the general strike which, whether or not actually realizable, had that quality of myth necessary to arouse the emotions and *élan* of the working class. The leaders of such a social war would of necessity constitute a social elite. In point of fact industrial unrest grew steadily after 1906. Strikes and disturbances were frequent, and in 1909 the government met the threat of a general strike by a wave of arrests, the calling out of troops, and the dismissal of postal workers and other civil servants who had struck. Again, in 1910, a strike of railway workers was met by mobilization orders and the calling out of troops. Despite such disturbances the French labor movement was more impressive potentially than actually; union membership grew from 140,000 in 1890 to 1,029,000 in 1911; yet even this figure was only one-fifth of the number of eligible workers, and these were a small minority of the total population.

While no carefully planned and comprehensive system, such as that which Bismarck introduced for the protection of the German workingman, was introduced in France, a substantial body of social legislation and governmental provisions of various kinds grew up under the Third Republic. The lot of the factory worker could not be ignored. A law of 1874 provided for the state inspection of industrial establishments and between 1880 and 1900 the doctrine of state intervention to protect the workers was firmly established. The great act of 1892 belatedly limited the employment of women, forbade that of children under thirteen, regulated the working conditions of miners, and set a maximum working day of ten hours with one obligatory day of rest per week. Free medical attention was guaranteed to workmen and their families in 1893, and a workmen's compensation act for injuries sustained while at work was passed in 1898. Though a Labor Office was created in 1900, and in 1906 a Ministry of Labor was set up, adequate finances were rarely available to supervise and enforce the new legislation. While no general scheme was adopted, social insurance was applied to many separate industries and groups. Similarly, the establishment of a Ministry of Agriculture in 1881 followed by a variety of agencies to meet special agricultural problems showed the government's concern for this major area of French economic life. Even so, France lagged behind other industrial countries in almost every social service.

■ FRANCE OVERSEAS

Still another important development was that of France's overseas empire, which, at the opening of the twentieth century, added an impressive sixty million people to the forty millions of what was called "Metropolitan France." The immediate sequel to the Franco-Prussian War had been a limitation of overseas commitments in order to conserve and build up France's shaken strength at home. Thus in 1874 French forces evacuated Tonkin, in Indo-China. Nevertheless, a change soon came, associated especially with the name of Jules Ferry. In 1881, having secured the backing of parliament, he outmaneuvered the Italians by making the Treaty of Bardo with the bey of Tunis, which converted this historic land into a French protectorate. Tonkin was won back in 1883. While Radical opposition persisted, the work of expansion went on—in Madagascar, in the Congo Basin, and in the Far East. Conflicts and disagreements with other European powers inevitably arose, first with England over Egypt, the Sudan, and the Niger Valley, then with Germany over Morocco. Yet by 1914 France could contemplate overseas territories with a population of sixty millions as compared with the five millions of 1871—an empire second only to the British in numbers and area.

The Empire was world-wide. Surviving from the eighteenth century were the aristocratic West Indian colonies of Martinique and Guadeloupe, French Guiana in South America, Réunion in the Indian Ocean, and the five trading posts on the coast of India. These all sent deputies and senators to France. In North Africa, Algeria, occupied by progressive stages since 1830, had a substantial French population of one million alongside nine million natives. Its fertile northern parts—Mediterranean rather than African—were divided into three departments directed from Paris by the Ministry of the Interior. Morocco, acquired in 1912, was, like Tunis, a protectorate. The two retained their native rulers who were "advised" by French residents and "protected" by French troops. The connection with France, therefore, was maintained through the Ministry of Foreign Affairs. Indo-China was a complex of various units, part colony and part protectorate, vastly profitable to French investors. Other distant areas, such as some of the Pacific islands, Madagascar, West and Equatorial Africa, and Somaliland, were administered conventionally as colonies.

Traditionally the Empire had been one in which Frenchmen governed natives. France had joined in a declaration at the Congress of Vienna in 1815 against the slave trade; she had made this trade illegal in French possessions in 1818; and in 1848 one of the first acts of the provisional republican government had been to abolish slavery entirely. Yet the lot of native peoples improved only slowly. The policy of assimilation meant very roughly that the peoples of the Empire were expected ultimately to become Frenchmen; more precisely it meant that France was ready to share her civilization and her institutions with that small minority of natives capable of benefiting from them. Thus members of colored races could sit in the Chamber of Deputies and even reach cabinet rank. A negro such as Félix Eboué could develop the remarkable talents and insight shown in his memoranda on native problems and rise to high administrative rank. Though the hand of the soldier, the bureaucrat, and the merchant was often brought down with marked severity, it was also true that a great African administrator, such as Marshal Lyautey,[7] could speak quite sincerely of his deep affection for his charges and insist upon the prime responsibility of France for the preservation of native cultures. Nevertheless, the French continued to regard the Empire as a vast reservoir of man power and as a closed economic system within which the special advantages would be reserved for the mother country. The colonies, which in many cases were highly profitable areas for French investors, had to accept the domestic tariff on their goods entering France, but could impose no tariff in return.

Toward the end of the century a new policy of association began to make itself heard. This would still encourage a small native elite to become thoroughly French in training and life, but at the same time it would pay marked respect to native culture and especially to tribal organization and usages within the larger framework of the French imperial system. Under this policy of association the ultimate goal would seem to be that of self-governing peoples free within a French commonwealth. At a time when imperial rivalries were becoming intensified by the system of alliances and the armaments race, any goal of full

7. 1854–1934. One of the great administrators of the modern French Empire, he first served in Indo-China and Madagascar, where he showed remarkable skill in handling native problems; he then won fame by pacifying Morocco (1912–1924) after it became a protectorate, and was made marshal of France (1921) for these services. Elected to the French Academy, and described as "a Royalist who gave an Empire to a Republic," he advocated a colonial policy based upon a deep sympathy for native institutions and a conviction of the destiny of France.

independence would be unthinkable. Thus France, understandably enough, developed strategic Mediterranean and African naval bases, such as Oran, Bizerta, Dakar, and Djibouti, as well as Camranh Bay in Indo-China. And large masses of native troops supplemented the forces which France had under arms during the First World War.

Overseas commitments helped to bring France more closely into the European alliance system and contributed to the series of crises which by 1914 resulted in war. Though the Entente Cordiale of 1904, by which France recognized Britain's protectorate over Egypt in return for Britain's recognition of her free hand to take whatever action she considered necessary in Morocco, was not an alliance in the strict sense of the word, it inevitably drew the two countries together. It was quickly followed by the First Morocco Crisis (1905), when William II of Germany, landing at Tangier in a visit to the sultan of Morocco, was pushed by his advisers into a declaration that Germany would claim equal rights in Morocco with other powers. Something in the nature of a panic ensued in Paris, and the French foreign minister, Delcassé, repudiated by the cabinet, resigned. At the subsequent Algeciras Conference (1906) France and Britain found substantial European backing for the 1904 thesis that France had special interests in Morocco, and thus Germany in the end suffered a diplomatic defeat. Consequently the tense atmosphere continued, and, when the French, who had some police responsibilities in Morocco, actually sent troops to Fez in 1911 to restore order, the Germans sent a gunboat to the port of Agadir. This Second Moroccan Crisis was likewise resolved—France obtaining her protectorate and Germany receiving as compensation part of the French Congo—yet war, if not rendered inevitable, was appreciably nearer.

Such an atmosphere of growing imperial commitments and recurrent European crises inevitably raised the question of the strength of the French armed forces. The law of 1905, reducing active military service from three to two years but allowing practically no exemptions, came at the time of the First Moroccan Crisis. By 1913, when with the Balkan Wars the atmosphere again seemed critical, a campaign led by the members of the right and bitterly opposed by the Socialists and some of the Radicals resulted in re-establishing the three-year term.

■ "LA DOUCE FRANCE"

Few countries have had more experience of the buffetings of fortune than France. For centuries a leader in European politics and culture, France brought to the nineteenth century her great revolutionary legacy of human rights and national faith to which aspiring peoples in other parts of Europe turned for their inspiration and consolation. Polish, Russian, Italian, German, and Balkan exiles made Paris their headquarters. With this legacy, and with the splendid improvements which Napoleon III made in his capital, Paris became, as it was said, every man's second home. To be sure, the pre-eminence of France was in time challenged by powerful new rivals, most notably by imperial Germany. A population, which in 1821 numbered 30,500,000, had grown by 1876 to 36,900,000. Yet by 1911 it had increased only to 39,600,000. At a time when the population of other countries was increasing rapidly, that of France had almost ceased to enlarge. Otherwise expressed, in 1800 France's population was about one-fifth that of Europe; in 1911 it had become one-tenth.

The externals of life in general provided a decent level of economic security and even modest comfort for the average thrifty Frenchman. A rich countryside, painstakingly tilled by hard-working peasants, furnished the healthy staples of living. When the ravages of the phylloxera had been overcome in the 1890's, France resumed her role as a great vinegrower and exporter of wine. The government helped in many directions through bounties, agricultural schools, cooperative societies, and mutual-loan banks. Méline, of whom it was said, "His heart beats only for cereals," sponsored the 1892 tariff which increased agricultural duties about 25 percent and gave protection to the silk and other industries. He headed a cabinet in 1896–1898 which put the interests of the farmer as one of its primary concerns. By 1914 France was self-sufficient in foodstuffs, exported luxury vegetables and fruits, and ranked second only to Russia as a European grain grower.

French industrial growth was likewise impressive. Despite the loss of the great iron deposits of Lorraine, others remained and were developed. France became the greatest exporter of iron ore in the world and also produced large quantities of bauxite, antimony, and potash, while from the overseas possessions came lead, tin, zinc, nickel, cobalt, chrome, manganese, graphite, and phosphates. A thriving export trade in silks, worsteds, cottons, laces, china, gloves, perfumes, and wines gave France its world-wide reputation as the incomparable producer of luxury goods. In addition, the invisible export of capital took place on a large scale, so that ultimately France stood second to England as Europe's banker. In 1914 her foreign investments totaled 45,000,000,000 francs.

Certain economic and social weaknesses existed. Good coal was scarce, and the main coalfields lay near the dangerously exposed northeast frontier. France had no petroleum. Population growth was at a standstill. In part due to the rise in real income, the consumption of spirits at the expense of wine increased, and with it alcoholism became a disturbing problem. The movement from a predominantly rural to an urban economy was very slow; in 1914 only 44 percent of the population lived in towns of over 2,000, and only 25 percent in towns of over 20,000 inhabitants. In the countryside the petty proprietor was the typical figure, and here antiquated farming methods, though undergoing some modern-

A COMPARISON OF THE GROWTH OF RURAL AND URBAN
POPULATION IN GERMANY AND FRANCE

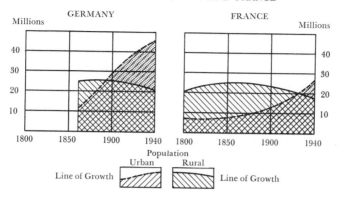

Adapted from C. Morazé, *The French and the Republic* (Ithaca, 1958), p. 36.

Excess of urban over rural population is shown by dark shading. Note that the point at which urban population exceeds rural population is much later in France than in Germany. Note also that the German population advance over the French is due almost entirely to urban growth.

ization, were widely employed. In the urban areas, despite the growth of new industries and the substantial increase in iron and steel production, small industry remained typical. As late as 1931, 60 percent of France's industrial population worked for firms employing less than twenty persons. Compared to Great Britain or Germany, France was relatively unready for the rapid mass production necessitated by large-scale modern war.

The class structure of France reflected the great changes brought about by the French Revolution. Save in a social sense, the French aristocracy counted for little; this class played very little role in politics or in the Church; only in some government departments, in the diplomatic corps, and in the army did an aristocratic caste continue, and even here the transformation was at work. In 1914 the British commander-in-chief in France felt obliged to warn Lord Kitchener that he could not expect to find French general officers drawn as exclusively from an upper social group as was the case in England. One would assume the widespread peasant influence to be conservative; it was so only to a degree, for, ever since the French Revolution, certain rural districts showed a strong pattern of radicalism. This radicalism, to be sure, had marked differences from that in the newly developing "red suburbs" of the industrial cities. By 1914 one could count an urban proletariat of perhaps five millions, and a skilled artisan and craftsman class of two or three millions, numerically far fewer than their rural counterparts. A bourgeoisie of varying levels of wealth and education dominated the world of politics, industry, the arts and letters, crowded into the relatively few universities, and provided a handsome market for the endless production of books, journals, and reviews of all kinds. It was this bourgeoisie, far more than any other class, that made France what it was.

In the religious sense France no longer counted as one of the great Catholic countries. Though nine out of ten Frenchmen were nominally Roman Catholics, it may be doubted whether more than a third were practicing Catholics, and anticlericalism remained a characteristic and powerful force in French life. The million or so active members of the Protestant minority exercised an influence quite out of proportion to their numbers.

The complex attractions of French life drew an endless stream of foreigners to France, as they had come ever since the days of Louis XIV. The new splendors of Paris—"*la ville lumière*"—in the age of gas and electricity, France's authoritative role in gastronomy and fashion, and the lavish variety of pleasure which the great city afforded, gave the capital a unique importance. Paris was confirmed in its position as the arbiter of fashion, though it is curious that it was a Lincolnshire boy, Charles Worth, apprenticed to the London drapers' firm of Swan and Edgar, who won the highest fame in Paris under the Second Empire and established the great dressmaking firm that still bears his name. France remained a leader in the fields of the arts and sciences—fields so rich and complex as to defy any summary here.[8] In painting, where none could touch her, in music, in the theater, in all fields of university study, France drew her pupils from every corner of the globe.

No estimate of French life under the Third Republic could ignore the strong sense of national patriotism, and along with it a powerful sense of complacency arising from an adequate, if not generous, standard of living which encouraged Frenchmen to cultivate their garden, literally or metaphorically, within the limits of a fairly narrow parochialism. The "typical" Frenchman— very hard to identify, but certainly not the *boulevardier* of Paris—is often said to be marked by peasant caution, thrift, and a strong sense of family. Frenchmen have set great store upon what they call civilization, always very Gallic in flavor, and frequently have been indifferent to some of the material blessings of the machine age. They seem to have felt little necessity to enlarge their horizons by accepting foreign ideas and foreign ways of life. The defeat of 1871 and the loss of Alsace-Lorraine accentuated a kind of militant patriotism which at times led small groups to follow fanatical leaders of the type of Déroulède or Boulanger. More than once Frenchmen have been swept off their feet by the appeal of glory or a sense of mission. In the phrase of André Maurois, France by 1914

8. See pp. 446–469.

had about one-tenth of Europe's population at the time when, in a diplomatic sense, she had assumed one-half of Europe's responsibilities. And, as the 1914 war would show, Frenchmen have revealed an astonishing capacity to serve their country—"la douce France"—in conditions of almost intolerable hardship.

Reading List: Chapter 12

Wright, G., *France in Modern Times, 1760 to the Present* (1960), chs. 18–23. Covers 1870–1914.

Maurois, A., *History of France* (Engl. tr., 1957; paperback, 1960), pp. 455–503. Covers 1870–1914.

The New Cambridge Modern History, vol. XI (1962), ch. 11. The French Republic, 1871–1890.

Thomson, D., *Democracy in France: The Third and Fourth Republics* (3rd ed., 1958), chs. 2, 3. "The Social Bases"; "The Democratic Instrument."

Morazé, C., *The French and the Republic* (1958), pp. 17–90. "Political Psychoanalysis of France."

Mason, E. S., *The Paris Commune* (1930), chs. 4–5. Detailed account of the uprising of 1871.

Roberts, John, "The Myth of the Commune," *History Today*, vol. VII (1957), no. 5.

Earle, E. M. (ed.), *Modern France: Problems of the Third and Fourth Republic* (1951), chs. 1, 5, 6, 16. Useful essays on aspects of French public life.

Roberts, John, "The Dreyfus Case," *History Today*, vol. IV (1954), no. 6.

Scott, J. A., *Republican Ideas and the Liberal Tradition in France, 1870–1914* (1951), pp. 126–56. Clemenceau and the Radical Party.

Jackson, J. Hampden, *Clemenceau and the Third Republic* (1948), chs. 6–7.

Cameron, R. S., "Economic Growth and Stagnation in France, 1815–1914," *Journal of Modern History*, vol. XXX (1958), no. 1.

Chapter 13

Britain and Her Empire

Introduction
Limits of Victorian Reform Programs
The Problem of Ireland
Imperialism and the Empire
The South African War and Its Consequences
The Liberal Revival
The Years of Increasing Strain
Foreign Policy and Imperial Defense

■ INTRODUCTION

In the later Victorian period, Britain and the British Empire appeared to be an immensely stable force as compared with the volatile French Republic and the German Empire, impressive but new. In fact, however, this was a period of transition. For reasons outlined in an earlier chapter, Britain was ceasing to dominate the world economy; accepting the role of an industry state, she allowed her agriculture steadily to dwindle, but was not rewarded by the retention of the unchallenged industrial supremacy for which she hoped. Instead, Britain became involved in the power struggle and the competitive annexation of colonial territories, which by the turn of the century had made her foreign policy likewise transitional. She found herself between the traditional isolationism (ironically known in the 1890's as "splendid" isolation) and the alliances which have determined her twentieth-century position for better

364

SIGNIFICANT EVENTS

1872	Disraeli's Crystal Palace speech on Empire
1874–1880	Disraeli's second government
1884	Third Parliamentary Reform Act
1886, 1893, 1912	Irish Home Rule Bills introduced in Parliament
1887	Queen Victoria's Golden Jubilee
	First Colonial Conference
1897	Diamond Jubilee
1899–1902	South African War
1901	Commonwealth of Australia established
1901–1910	Reign of Edward VII
1905–1915	Liberal governments under Campbell-Bannerman and Asquith
1906	Labor Party established
	Trade Disputes Act
1911	Parliament Act
	National Insurance Act

or worse in peace and war. A transition took place, too, in intraimperial relations. In 1871 both the Dominion of Canada and the smaller self-governing colonies in Australasia and South Africa were held within the orbit of the United Kingdom by its overwhelming superiority in wealth, population, and political experience, an automatic relationship about which neither side showed particular concern. Canada had, however, developed a national tariff policy and by 1897, to the disappointment of many people in the home country, the self-governing colonies as a whole were opposed to ideas involving closer political federation. The centrifugal tendencies which date from the Durham Report and the repeal of the Navigation Acts were not to be reversed.

Corresponding changes were visible in Britain's domestic affairs. The decline of agriculture coincided with a decline in the centuries-old authority of the great families and the landed interest, though it was not so much the captains of industry who began to step into their place as the financiers, for in the late Victorian age joint stock companies and company promoters wielded enormous influence. At the same time there were new stirrings among the workers. For nearly a quarter of a century (1873–1896), an almost continuous reduction of trade occurred, with falling prices and mounting unemployment. The category of skilled workers who kept their jobs prospered, since the drop in wages lagged considerably behind prices, but the sufferings of the unskilled were often severe. Accordingly, the dock strike of 1889 marks the beginning of a new workers' movement, which was destined eventually to place the less skilled in the position of economic security which the more skilled workers already to some extent occupied—and with an altogether greater political influence.

The opening years of the new century were marked by bitter strife. The Conservative Party, after a period of great success, was fatally weakened by a premature attempt to end the era of free trade. The Liberal Party, which had been split over the issue of home rule for Ireland, now revived. Impelled partly by the emergence of an as yet small Labor Party further to the left, it gave Britain the first installment of its modern social services, raised the taxes to pay for them, and in 1911 destroyed the power of the House of Lords to resist. When war came, the transition to the welfare state had been made more urgent because prices were rising more rapidly than wages, but on the very eve of war two great political conflicts—over Irish home rule and votes for women—had for the time being taken possession of the stage. Perhaps, after all, the main transition was from the humdrum Victorian virtues and solid achievement to the heroism and wastefulness of an age of violence.

■ LIMITS OF VICTORIAN REFORM PROGRAMS

Gladstone's first Liberal government, as we have seen, passed a whole series of remarkable reforms through parliament. But by 1872 Disraeli was able to compare its once-formidable members to a range of exhausted volcanoes, and, when the next general election came in 1874, they paid the price of their success, because every reform had disturbed some established interest and created some enemies. Disraeli therefore obtained a majority, the first the Conservatives had had since the repeal of the Corn Laws in 1846. At the age of seventy he lacked the physical energy of Gladstone, and was primarily interested in a program of imperial development which appealed strongly to the important aristocratic element among his followers. Nevertheless, the diagnosis of the evils attendant upon the growth of an industrial civilization, which he had made in his novel *Sybil* a generation earlier, now bore fruit in a series of reforms which did much to change the basis of town life for the better.

The Public Health Act of 1875 codified and systematized health regulations which had been introduced piecemeal in particular areas. It required every borough to appoint a qualified medical officer; made the provision of pure water and proper drainage, and measures for coping with epidemics, a regular local obligation; and enabled the central government (through the Local Government Board, established by Gladstone) to insist upon minimum sanitary standards being maintained even in the remotest rural areas. A second measure in the same year, requiring local authorities to appoint public analysts and to support their findings, took a long step toward the suppression of the adulteration of food and drugs, which was then a notorious evil. A third measure gave local authorities the power to buy and clear slum areas, and to build suitable housing for the population displaced, though it required a further act in 1890 before there was any widespread activity in slum clearance. Since at the same time the trade unions were given the freedom of strike action which they had sought in vain from Gladstone, it is not unreasonable to describe 1875 as a "year of wonders." After this, Disraeli turned his attention elsewhere, but in 1878 his home secretary, Cross, added a Factories and Workshops Act, which consolidated some forty existing laws and extended their application to workshops employing less than fifty persons.

Later governments made elementary education compulsory and free, raised the minimum age for part-time factory employment belatedly to eleven, and in 1897 established the principle of workmen's compensation—that is to say, that the cost of accidents to employees must be carried by the industry in which they occurred. Generally speaking, however, the defeat of Disraeli's government in the election of 1880 ushered in a period of a quarter of a century in which the attention of governments and parliaments was turned elsewhere. Gladstone's second Liberal government completed the framework of political democracy by giving the franchise to county areas in 1884 on the identical terms on which it had been given to the boroughs in 1867, by reducing the possibility of corrupting voters, and by reorganizing the constituencies so that votes might be roughly equal in value. The parties then vied with each other in giving local self-government to the county areas—county councils, district councils, and parish councils—and elaborating the provisions made in 1835 for self-government in the towns. What they did not do was to take any important step beyond those indicated, with a view to extending such positive provision for social welfare as Disraeli had made in 1875.

The next major reform was, in fact, the Education Act of 1902, carried by Arthur (later Lord) Balfour[1] in the year when he succeeded his uncle, Lord Salisbury, as Conservative prime minister. This was the first law which made

---

1. 1848–1930. He was private secretary to his uncle at the Congress of Berlin; author, in 1879, of a famous *Defense of Philosophic Doubt;* prime minister, 1902–1905, but was forced to resign the Conservative leadership in 1911. He was in office again in 1915–1922 and 1925–1929, and was responsible for the definition of dominion status in the Statute of Westminster.

the provision of free secondary education possible, except as a mere appendage to the top end of an elementary school or possibly as technical instruction. But free secondary schooling grew at first quite slowly, for the most part by grants enabling the cleverest elementary school pupils to occupy places at existing secondary schools where fees were paid. In the eyes of the public the main interest attached to other provisions in the law, particularly those that enabled local taxation to be used to help the religious voluntary schools, which already had help—but not enough—from the national taxes. It was Balfour's chief object to ensure the survival of Church of England elementary schools which he believed to serve the interests of the Conservative Party. Conversely, it was the chief object of the Protestant nonconformists, who were numerous in the Liberal opposition, first, to prevent the bill from passing, and, failing that, to obstruct its execution. Even in 1902 sectarian animosities were still a great factor in English—and still more in Welsh—life.

■ THE PROBLEM OF IRELAND

Sectarian animosity, which was always a lamentable characteristic of Victorian Britain, was among the factors which made the Irish question intractable, and that intractability in turn does more than anything else to explain the stultification of domestic reform in the 1880's and 1890's. During Disraeli's great ministry, the remedies which Gladstone had applied in Ireland could be seen to be mere palliatives. Neither the disestablishment of the Protestant Church nor compensation to evicted tenants[2] did anything to prevent the birth in 1870 of a demand for home rule, vainly laid before parliament in courteous speeches by Isaac Butt in 1874 and following years. Then in 1880 a younger man, taking over the leadership, began to drill the Irish M.P.'s in the arts of parliamentary obstruction. This was Charles Stewart Parnell,[3] commonly regarded as the strongest and most resourceful internal enemy that confronted the modern British Empire until the days of Mahatma Gandhi. But even Parnell might have achieved little had not the fall in agricultural prices reduced the Irish peasantry to a desperation which found expression in the formation of a Land League with him as president.

Gladstone's second government therefore found itself engaged in a double conflict, against an obstructive group in the House of Commons, led by a master of parliamentary tactics, and against an unscrupulous peasant organization,

2. See p. 208.

3. 1846–1891. Son of a Protestant Irish landowner and the daughter of an American admiral; educated at Cambridge; as Irish leader, aloof from his followers, he exercised a magnetic influence upon them; his association with Mrs. O'Shea, by whom he had several children, began about 1880 and had been tolerated by Captain O'Shea in view of an expected inheritance; his early death was due to overexhaustion in the pursuit of the party feud in Ireland.

AN IRISH EVICTION. Note the presence of government officials and armed troops, the miserably small thatched cottage, and the battering ram used to make the building uninhabitable.

waging an illegal war against the landowners in Ireland. His second Land Act in 1881 tried to deprive both these bodies of their main justification by giving the Irish tenant rights that were conveniently summarized as the three F's—a fair rent, determined by an independent tribunal; fixity of tenure, for a minimum period of fifteen years; and free sale by the tenant of his rights in the holding. But peasant opposition, which ranged from boycotting—so called because a prominent early victim was a landlord's agent named Captain Charles Boycott—to cattle maiming and murder, failed to subside. The government therefore used its special powers under a Coercion Act to arrest Parnell and other Irish leaders. After six months the situation in Ireland was even worse, so Parnell was released on the understanding that he would use his influence to prevent further crime. But the sequel was the murder in Phoenix Park, Dublin, in broad daylight of the chief secretary (the cabinet minister responsible for Irish affairs) and the head of the Irish civil service. Although Parnell had had no chance to prevent their assassination, it made further negotiations with him difficult for the Liberals. He therefore made a bid for the support of the Conservatives, and at the next election used his influence to help them win in those British constituencies which had large populations of immigrant Irish workers.

The consequence was that in January, 1886, the election results left the Irish Party holding the balance of power. Without their support in parliament Gladstone could not form his third government. The price for that support was an undertaking to give Ireland home rule. Accordingly, he brought forward a bill to set up a bicameral legislature in Dublin, which would deal with all purely domestic questions, but not with external relations of any kind; the constitutionality of its actions was to be determined by a court of appeal in London. But Gladstone was deserted by the great Whig landowners, by an influential group of Radicals headed by Joseph Chamberlain,[4] and even by the veteran, John Bright. The defeat of the bill by a margin of only thirty votes lost what was probably the best chance of effecting a reconciliation with Ireland while Britain was still able to negotiate from a position of strength.

Although a general election, the second in twelve months, gave the Conservatives a majority, Gladstone at the age of seventy-seven still hoped to educate British opinion in favor of the measure. But Parnell was an unaccountable ally. In February, 1889, he was on the crest of the wave, when it was proved at a judicial inquiry that letters, which *The Times* had published over his signature as evidence of his complicity in the Phoenix Park murders, were barefaced forgeries which the paper had purchased in an irresponsible way from a needy journalist. But next year he was cited as co-respondent by an injured husband who had long been complaisant to the affair, and, when Gladstone urged the necessity of his retirement from the Irish leadership because of the scandal that this had created among British Liberals—to say nothing of many Irish Catholics—Parnell preferred to see his following break in half sooner than resign. He died only a few months later, but the damage was done, and at the next general election, in 1892, Gladstone was returned with a majority of no more than forty. The second Home Rule Bill, which included one new provision, for a small number of Irish representatives to sit and vote on imperial questions at Westminster, duly passed through the Commons, only to be rejected in the House of Lords by a majority of ten to one. Gladstone then finally retired.

For the next one and a half decades, Ireland ceased to interest the British electorate. The Liberal Party, which had been its champion, was in effect broken. It lingered on in office for another year (1894–1895), accomplishing almost nothing under Lord Rosebery, while its once-predestined leader, Chamberlain, attached his fortunes firmly to the Conservative, or Unionist, Party. The cause of social reform, neglected by despondent Liberals, was not likely to be taken up by Lord Salisbury. Instead, the country as a whole—or at least its more articulate elements—became caught up in the complex of motives and achievements we call imperialism, which was fast approaching its climax.

---

4. 1836–1914. Having made £120,000 as a screw manufacturer by the age of thirty-eight, he became radical republican mayor of Birmingham in 1873, president of Board of Trade, 1880–1885; opposed Home Rule as "tantamount to a proposal for separation"; had a following of seventy-eight Liberal Unionist MP's, and in 1895 joined Salisbury as colonial secretary, with an active development policy. He resigned in 1903 to conduct a Tariff Reform campaign, and was permanently incapacitated by a stroke after the election of 1906.

■ IMPERIALISM AND THE EMPIRE

In 1871 Britain was unquestionably the chief colonial power, with Russia and France for her nearest rivals. In relation to the colonies of settlement, the policy of allowing full internal self-government (including control of tariffs) was now firmly established. The suppression of the Indian Mutiny had tied the subcontinent, with a population ten times that of Britain, in a closer formal relationship than before as a direct possession of the Crown. As for the Crown colonies in general, the new additions since 1815 were not insignificant. Singapore, the Falkland Islands, Aden, Hong Kong, and Lagos were all in British hands by 1860, small areas of high value for naval bases or entrepôt markets. But it was not until Disraeli's ministry of 1874–1880 that the Empire as it was and as it might be became a subject of political controversy and widespread popular interest. After 1880 Gladstone and his followers struggled in vain against the prevailing climate of opinion, which was one of the reasons why his Irish home rule proposals were inacceptable to the British electorate. In the 1890's, which is the period when the name "imperialism" first came into vogue, the temper and attitude it described became for a time completely dominant.

This could not all have sprung from Disraeli's announcement in his Crystal Palace speech of 1872 that "the preservation of our Empire" was one of the three great objects of Conservative policy, although his genius at once invested that object with new glamour. Nor should overmuch weight be attached to the writings—Dilke's *Greater Britain* (1868), Seeley's *Expansion of England* (1883), Froude's *Oceana* (1886), and all that Kipling laid before a wider public, from *Departmental Ditties* (1886) to *Take Up the White Man's Burden* (1899). For politicians and writers alike owed their success to certain general trends in contemporary society.

One was the growing sense of political rivalry among the great powers. Kept in check by the genius of Bismarck, this no longer found expression in territorial struggles on the European mainland, in which Britain could afford to be disinterested, but in the struggle for colonies elsewhere. The periodic excitements over the Eastern question illustrate this, for when the British music-hall song proclaimed to eager audiences, "The Rooshians shall not have Constantinople," it was the supposed consequences for the Mediterranean sea routes and British possessions in Asia rather than the Balkan imbroglio itself that aroused feeling in Britain. In all this, economic interests underlay the surface clashes of politics. Markets which could not be closed by an unfriendly tariff, chances for the investment of capital with maximum profit for minimum risk, and new sources of raw materials were all important objectives for Britain now that her position as workshop of the world was being successfully challenged by rival firms. And below the economic considerations, again, it is possible to discern the psychological or emotional factors. As Britain became step by step more democratic, rule over backward peoples offered an increasingly satisfactory alternative way of life to the products of the exclusive public schools and the ancient universities—numerically insignificant but highly influential as leaders and molders of public opinion. For the same slow advance of democracy, it must be remembered, was creating a huge, semiliterate public, just sufficiently educated to sense the monotony and subjection of their daily round. This public was easily led by election speeches, romantic novels and short stories, and above all by newspapers of the type of the *Daily Mail* to experience a vicarious satisfaction as fellow countrymen of empire builders, a psychological condition which found notorious expression in the "mafficking," or riotous celebrations, at the news of the relief of Mafeking in 1900.

Disraeli's contributions must now be briefly enumerated. By his purchase from the khedive of Egypt of his holding (seven-sixteenths) in the Suez Canal Company in 1875, he set Britain's course toward the control of the country through which the Canal ran. In the following year, by making the Queen *Kaisar-i-Hind* (Empress of India), he gave new color to a connection which meant so much to Britain in prosaic terms of trade above all, but also in terms of military weight in the affairs of Asia. By allowing his representatives to adopt a forward policy in South Africa, he was responsible for the conquest of the Zulus and for the annexation to the British Empire of the territory of their intended victims, the Transvaal Boers. By his diplomatic intervention against Russia to safeguard Constantinople for the Turks, he obtained Turkish consent to the occupation of Cyprus.

The sum total is not very large, but Gladstone in the next five years proved unable to reverse the trend. Though he gave back independence to the Boers (except for the power of making treaties), he had become involved in hostilities against them, and a small British defeat at Majuba Hill had grave repercussions later on. In Egypt the claims of European creditors against the khedive, much too large to be settled from the Suez Canal money, had been coordinated under French pressure in a special fund, the *Caisse de la Dette publique*, for the purpose of administering Egyptian finances. The result was a revolt by army officers under a native leader, Arabi Pasha, against economies enforced by the Frenchman and Englishman in charge of the *caisse*. The French having at the last moment refused to act, it was left to Gladstone's government to restore order by the bombardment of Alexandria, a night march against Arabi, and the occupation of Cairo. Sir Evelyn Baring, later Lord Cromer, was then put in charge of a wholesale modernization of every department of the Egyptian government, from irrigation works to army training; although his subordinates were only advisers to native ministers and he himself no more than agent and consul-general, the presence of British forces made the advice mandatory.

Gladstone refused to accept even temporary responsibility for the Egyptian empire in the Sudan, and sacrificed General Gordon at Khartoum to his determination to evacuate that whole area; yet, when he left office in the summer of 1885, Britain had become involved in the affairs of Egypt on a temporary footing which lasted in one form or another until 1956.

Gladstone's governments were also responsible for the authorization of two of the four chartered companies, organizations which enabled private money and enterprise to be harnessed to the task of political negotiation and commercial development of uncivilized regions where the British government hesitated to act yet wished to forestall other powers. These were the British North Borneo Company (1881) and the Royal Niger Company (1886), of which the latter in fourteen years succeeded in staking out the British claim to its most populous African acquisition, Nigeria. The British East Africa Company and the British South Africa Company, formed in 1888 and 1889 respectively, performed a similar function in relation to Kenya and Uganda and the two Rhodesias.

The main activities of these companies, however, belong to the period after the failure of the first Irish Home Rule Bill, when liberalism was mainly in eclipse and the mood of the country was fairly represented by the realist diplomacy of Lord Salisbury and the aggressive annexationist planning of Cecil Rhodes,[5] clergyman's son, diamond millionaire, and colonial premier. At the cost of a small war against the Matabele, fought mainly by the South Africa Company's armed police force, he occupied the region of the two Rhodesias and planned to organize an all-British route for a railway between Cairo and the Cape. Meanwhile Lord Salisbury, in the year 1890 alone, made treaties with France, Germany, and Portugal, clearing the way for British advances by bargains with the two former powers and a virtual ultimatum to the Portuguese, when they tried to claim a hinterland for their ancient African possessions stretching right across the continent in Britain's path. But the Boers, newly enriched by finding gold on the Rand and nursing grievances as old as the Great Trek of 1836, interposed a more serious obstacle on the right flank of the British advance northward. Since Johannesburg was full of discontented gold miners, who resented the combination of heavy taxes with the denial of civil rights, Rhodes decided to stage a rising by these *Uitlanders*. His henchman, Dr. Jameson, would bring in the South Africa Company's police to restore order, and the Rand—where Rhodes had invested heavily—would pass smoothly

5. 1853–1902. He went to South Africa in 1870 and made his first fortune at Kimberley; he was active in Bechuanaland in 1884 and in Matabeleland from 1888, formed De Beers Consolidated Mines (1888) and acquired interests in the Rand gold fields, was chairman of the British South Africa Company (1889), and prime minister of Cape Colony (1890). After the Jameson Raid fiasco he was mainly concerned with the development of Rhodesia and the elaboration of his will, which created the Rhodes Scholarships for Britons, Americans, and Germans.

LONDON, THE HEART OF AN EMPIRE. The air photograph gives impressive evidence of England's long traditions. Against the Houses of Parliament, begun in 1840, lies Westminster Hall begun by William Rufus in 1097. Westminster Abbey can be seen, and above it to left-center the Treasury and Foreign Office, obscuring Downing Street. Whitehall, where Charles I was executed, leads to Trafalgar Square, off the picture to the left. The Thames, with its bridges, gives London its incomparable setting.

under British control. But the Jameson Raid, as the incursion into Boer territory by the armed police is called, proved a fiasco: the *Uitlanders* refused to rise for the sake of British rule, and Jameson's forces were quickly surrounded and taken prisoner. At the same time a telegram from the German emperor, William II, to the Boer president, Kruger, implied that the Boers could have counted on German support if necessary.

Nevertheless, at the time of Queen Victoria's Diamond Jubilee in 1897 the Empire might seem to have gathered an irresistible momentum. The accessions of territory in south, west, and east Africa had their counterpart in the Far East, where the Malay States in the hinterland of Singapore had been brought into a dependent relationship, and in the islands of the Pacific, where big claims had been staked out in New Guinea and North Borneo. An unchallenged and seemingly unchallengeable navy lay off Spithead, and the Jubilee review, which inspired Kipling's "Recessional" hymn, showed "the captains and the kings" the unpalatable truth that their colonies were held on sufferance only, because Britain could cut off access at any moment. At that time, also, an Anglo-Egyptian expedition under an engineer general, Kitchener, was assembling at a Nile railhead, whence in the following year it launched an attack across the desert to avenge Gordon, occupy the Sudan, and force the withdrawal of a French party advancing over the watershed from the Congo. At Fashoda the French in effect acknowledged the superior strength and cohesion of a British Empire which in a quarter of a century (1875–1900) was able to engulf nearly five million square miles of territory with more than ninety million inhabitants. Though Jameson and his fellow freebooters had been turned over to Britain for trial and were sentenced to short terms of imprisonment, the colonial secretary, Joseph Chamberlain, and his high commissioner in South Africa, Milner, fairly represented the general view of the British public when they refused to allow the aged Boer president to prevaricate and procrastinate longer on the issue of conceding the franchise to the *Uitlanders.*

■ THE SOUTH AFRICAN WAR AND ITS CONSEQUENCES

The South African War began with a series of disasters such as Britain had not experienced since the bitter and tragic, but far less humiliating, days of the Indian Mutiny. The Boers declared war while the British were still belatedly fetching in reinforcements; laid siege to Kimberley, Mafeking, and Ladysmith; and in a single "Black Week" inflicted three defeats on the troops dispatched in haste to relieve them. The British then mustered large armies under the capable command of Field-Marshal Lord Roberts, with Kitchener as his chief of staff. The Boers, outflanked, outnumbered, and sometimes outgeneralled, were compelled to raise their sieges and retreat across the veldt until the capitals, both of the Transvaal and of its smaller ally, the Orange Free State, were occupied and their governments put to flight. The Boer states were then formally annexed and Roberts went home, the last of many bearers of good news from her Empire to be received by Victoria.

But the war, already expensive in men, money, and prestige, was still not over. For another year and a half Boer commandos, small bodies of horsemen living off the country and apt to melt, whenever they were cornered, into the farming population from which they sprang, kept up the fight in the conquered territory and even made raids into Cape Colony, where they had sympathizers. Eventually Kitchener found it necessary to partition the veldt with barbed-wire fences, which were protected by blockhouses containing guns and search-lights. Even this was not enough: the Boer farms had also to be depopulated and burned to deprive the commandos of hiding places, which meant the transfer of their inhabitants en masse to camps, where insanitary conditions—for which Boer ignorance was mainly responsible—produced a horrifying death rate, especially among women and children. Though these concentration camps bore no resemblance to the German camps of the 1930's and early 1940's, an English Liberal leader denounced their use as "methods of barbarism," and foreigners who had envied the British Empire its greatness were not slow to point out to what depths it had sunk in enforcing its will against two small and weak peoples. When the war ended at the treaty of Vereeniging in May, 1902, the world was in no mood to recognize the generosity of the settlement. The commandos laid down their arms and accepted the sovereignty of the British Crown; in return the defeated side was given promises of self-government and an immediate gift of three million pounds to restart their farms.

The disappointments of the war brought to an end the period of crude imperialist sentiment, at least as a force in the politics of the United Kingdom. The Conservatives had won a "khaki election" in 1900, but when the next electoral test came in January, 1906, the war worked to their disadvantage because of the memories of repeated failure, the experience of world hostility, and the absence of any very satisfying fruits of victory. What Milner and a devoted body of young imperialists had done to reconstruct the war-stricken areas of South Africa was completely lost to view in an outcry against "Chinese slavery" —the indentured labor he had brought across the Indian Ocean to restart the gold mines of the Rand.

The events of the Boer War were also significant in relation to other aspects of the imperial idea. The success of the partly federal institutions of the Dominion of Canada, and the strength of federalism as exemplified in the United States and the German Empire, had stimulated the growth of a movement to federate the British Empire. From 1884 to 1893 propaganda was conducted by an Imperial Federation League for a representative Council of Empire to be set up in London. Joseph Chamberlain was a powerful advocate. The colonial conferences, of which the first had been held on the occasion of the 1887 Jubilee, seemed to provide a nucleus around which some federal organ might be established. At the 1897 conference Chamberlain had initiated a discussion on closer relations, arguing for a "great Council of the Empire" and claiming that a federal council must be the ultimate ideal. He was strongly opposed by the prime minister of Canada, the French-Canadian Sir Wilfrid Laurier, with the result that general approval was expressed for the political *status quo*. But the political link might perhaps be strengthened through new economic ties. The British government therefore welcomed a Canadian offer of tariff preferences available to the mother country as a possible first step toward an imperial *Zollverein,* and took the risk of denouncing long-standing trade treaties with two of her most important foreign customers, Germany and Belgium, in order to make acceptance feasible.

When the next colonial conference assembled, however, in the summer after the close of the South African War, Chamberlain's proposed Council of the Empire was not even discussed. Although Canada, as well as Australia and New Zealand, had furnished contingents for the war, Laurier was anxious not to involve Canada in any general scheme of defense organization, much less of political cohesion, and, although the Australian colonies had now (1901) been federated into a single Commonwealth of Australia, Canadian opinion still carried the most weight.

Three consequences of the negative results of Chamberlain's political efforts may now be traced. First, after much further discussion, the Colonial Conference of 1907 agreed upon a rudimentary constitution for future meetings. They were to be summoned quadrennially, composed of prime ministers, and based on the principle of one vote to each government; known henceforth as imperial conferences, the increase of dignity did not signify any change in their purely advisory functions. Second, Chamberlain himself was encouraged, by the emphasis which had been laid upon the idea of tariff reciprocity at the conferences, to devote his last political campaign to a call for tariff reform in Britain. But at the election of 1906 the electorate clearly affirmed its unwillingness to lose the traditional benefits of free trade for any benefits accruing from an imperial *Zollverein*. Third, from the fact that the results of the Boer War had left the colonies with less than no desire to combine for purposes of defense, it came about that, in the course of a prolonged search for measures to promote military efficiency, there was brought into existence in 1904 the Committee of Imperial Defense. This, too, was an advisory body, of which the United Kingdom prime minister was its chairman and only permanent member; other ministers, representatives from dominions and colonies who happened to be available, and any number of military and other experts could be summoned as the needs of any particular meeting might require.

The starting point of the work of the new committee was to be the ascertainment of "the great first principles governing our imperial defense." For the Boer War had given an immense jolt to Britain's habitual complacency regarding her foreign relations. It seemed as though only her naval supremacy had prevented the intervention of a European coalition against her in South Africa. In 1900, Germany, whom Chamberlain and others had regarded as Britain's natural friend, doubled the provisions of a big program of naval expansion passed only two years before, and she proved unhelpful when an agreement was made with her for holding Russia in check in Manchuria. That function was discharged instead by the rising power of Japan, with whom Britain signed her first peacetime alliance for several generations in January, 1902—an alliance, however, which concerned only the affairs of the Far East.

The vital change was the decision, taken by the Conservative government in 1903–1904 and ably supported by the new king, Edward VII, to court no more rebuffs from Germany and achieve a friendly understanding with France instead. Painstaking negotiations terminated existing friction in many colonial areas; bartered the recognition of Britain's special interests in Egypt for a similar recognition of prospective French interests in Morocco; and in secret clauses equated special interests with contingent rights of annexation. At the time when the Conservatives went out of office, the value of this entente was being tested by the Germans, with results that belong primarily to the history of Continental rivalries.[6]

■ THE LIBERAL REVIVAL

The solid Conservative majority, which Lord Salisbury handed over to his nephew and successor, Arthur Balfour, in 1902, steadily lost its hold in the country from the end of the war onward, though it was not until December, 1905, that Balfour resigned in advance of an election in which his party suffered the biggest electoral defeat since 1832. The new government under Campbell-Bannerman, who was replaced by Asquith a few weeks before his death in 1908, comprised an unusually able group of ministers—the youthful Winston Churchill[7] was no more than an undersecretary at first, so great was the competition for places—and was supported by an unusually earnest body of followers, in which Protestant nonconformists, sworn to avenge the Education Act, were uniquely numerous and members of the old governing class a declining force. Lloyd George,[8] who did such great things at the Board of Trade that he was promoted to Asquith's place at the Exchequer in 1908, is probably the most representative figure in what we may call the last era of liberalism. Then politics was conducted on a basis of universal and unqualified respect for the verdict of the ballot box, the forms of the constitution, and the liberties of the individual, including his right to the peaceful enjoyment of private property subject to the requirements of lawful taxation. That era, lasting until 1911, was productive of some valuable reforms.

It must be realized, however, that from the very beginning there were

6. See pp. 481–489.
7. 1874–   . Son of Lord Randolph Churchill and his American wife, he was cavalry officer, war correspondent, and from 1900 M.P. He joined the Liberals in 1905, and from colonial undersecretary rose to head successively the Board of Trade, Home Office, and (1911–1915) the Admiralty. He was blamed for the Dardanelles failure and put out of office, 1915–1917, served under Lloyd George, 1917–1922, and as Conservative chancellor of the exchequer under Baldwin, 1924–1929. He opposed concessions in India; returned to the Admiralty on outbreak of war, and was prime minister, 1940–1945, and again in 1951–1955.
8. 1863–1945. Brought up by a shoemaker uncle in North Wales, he became a solicitor, and entered parliament in 1890 as a Welsh antiimperialist. He did important work as president of Board of Trade, 1905–1908, and chancellor of exchequer, 1908–1915. His energetic leadership at the Ministry of Munitions and War Office, plus intrigue, enabled him to replace Asquith as prime minister in December, 1916; he never returned to office after 1922, though invited to join Churchill's war cabinet in 1940.

strong unliberal pressures making themselves felt. The period of prolonged unemployment in the last decades of the nineteenth century had given rise to
significant new political movements. One of these was the middle-class, intellectual pressure group of the Fabian Society, so-called from its policy of gradualism. This body had already enjoyed a good deal of success in introducing
socialist reforms through the activities of municipalities and the new county
councils, and was now working for the abolition of the existing poor law and the
introduction of a national minimum, a standard of living below which no one
should be allowed to fall. Another was the Independent Labor Party, which
had been formed in 1893 under the leadership of an ex-coal miner member of
parliament, Keir Hardie, with a generally socialist program and a particular
aim of sponsoring parliamentary candidatures by workingmen who, if elected,
would act as independent representatives of their class rather than as humble
left-wing allies of the Liberals. The I.L.P. had no more than two or three representatives at a time in parliament, but in 1900, with the help of the Fabians, it
had organized a Labor Representation Committee, which, by disavowing any
definitely socialist program, was able to get much-needed financial help from
the trade-union movement. The L.R.C. won twenty-nine seats in 1906, and
thereupon adopted the name and nature of a formal Labor Party, to which
fourteen other coalminer M.P.'s adhered in 1909, leaving only a remnant of
about a dozen "Lib-Labs" still outside.

   This important new political force emerged in 1906 not so much as a result
of new organization but because working-class attention was newly engrossed in
politics. Since 1889 the world of the workers was being transformed gradually by
the permeation of trade unionism into the thinking and acting of the masses.
The London dock strike of that year, in which an amorphous body of extremely
poor casual laborers was successfully organized by two engineers, Burns and
Mann, to win a minimum wage of sixpence an hour, was a landmark in social
development. Farm laborers, railway workers, and sailors are examples of submerged elements which took heart from the example of the dockers; and the
existing unions of skilled workers, such as the engineers, who had done much
to help them, also benefited from a wave of expansion. Though progress was not
of course uninterrupted or uniform, by 1900 trade unionism had a stronger hold
upon the workers, including women workers, than it had ever had before.
Therefore the impact of an unexpected legal decision, the Taff Vale Judgment,
which directly imperiled the funds of any striking trade union by declaring that
a union could be sued as a corporation to claim damages for the civil losses
which a strike inevitably caused, was simply enormous. From 1901 to 1906
trade unionists protested in vain. Hence the strong support given to Labor
Representation Committee candidates at the election, and the speedy enactment by the new Liberal government of a Trade Disputes Bill; this measure,

using terms selected by the new Labor Party, reversed the effect of the judgment and gave trade unions complete immunity from civil actions arising out of any trade dispute.

Thus the Liberal government was induced by outside pressure, while redressing an undoubted wrong, to create for trade unions a position of illiberal privilege. The employers retorted by securing a second legal decision, the Osborne Judgment, which precluded the unions from using their funds to support political candidatures or objects of any kind. This caused the Liberals in 1911 to introduce payment of members of parliament, which had long been part of their program. Two years later a Trades Union Act authorized the unions to divert funds to political uses as before, subject to the right of any member to "contract out" from the proportion of his subscription which was to be used in this way.

Before we pass on to consider the last years before 1914, when liberalism was succumbing to outside pressures of many different kinds, some attention must be paid to the string of measures by which the party laid the foundations of the modern welfare state. It was their great achievement that they tackled the problem of the poor, to whom the rich Victorian age had offered only the gospel of self-help, the very limited benefits of religious charities, and the rigors of the poor law system. The last was not overthrown, in spite of great efforts by the Fabians, Sidney and Beatrice Webb. On the other hand the government tackled one after another and in each case with some success the great problems of underprivileged childhood, defenseless old age, sickness, the unemployed, and the unsatisfactorily employed.

Three measures known collectively as the Children's Charter introduced juvenile courts for delinquency and struck at the roots of that and other evils by providing free medical inspection and, in cases of proved hardship, free meals in the schools. Old-age pensions were made available, subject to a means test, at a level which was just sufficient to enable over-seventies to live in frugal independence where relatives or friends could offer houseroom. A national health insurance scheme, Lloyd George's masterpiece, paid for medical treatment, drugs, and support during sickness by a compulsory weekly levy on employees and employers, together with a (smaller) subsidy from the state—to go to all manual workers and to persons earning not more than three pounds a week. The same great Act of 1911 made a tentative start with unemployment insurance on a similar basis to provide temporary payments in a few industries, such as building and engineering, which were liable to periodical fluctuations of activity. As for the unsatisfactorily employed, Winston Churchill marked his rise to cabinet rank by the introduction of Labor Exchanges to make vacant jobs readily known, and of the first Trade Boards, a device for fixing and enforcing a minimum standard of wages and conditions in the so-called sweated trades, such as domestic tailoring, where the workers, mostly women, were too abjectly poor to be able to help themselves.

Such were the fruits of English liberalism in its last—and some would think its greatest—phase. Its climax was a struggle over the constitutional authority of the House of Lords, which since the Irish home rule controversy had become an overwhelmingly one-party organization, giving almost automatic support to Conservative governments and opposition to the Liberals. In view of the big Liberal majority in 1906, however, the Lords played a cautious game, accepting with little demur both the Trade Disputes Act and the earlier of the social reforms enumerated above, and rejecting only such measures as an Education Bill (to meet the wishes of the Nonconformists) and a Licensing Bill (to meet the wishes of enemies of the drink trade), to which the general public was indifferent or even hostile. By 1909, however, the rising costs of social reform and the heavy burden of naval expansion provided Lloyd George with a chance, which he seized with relish, to pass through the Commons a deliberately provocative "People's Budget." It included such measures as a new supertax on large incomes, a rise in the existing income tax and death duties, and a complicated system of land value duties, to be paid on unearned increment and latent values as soon as a complete valuation could be made of the entire surface of the country. The Land Tax foreshadowed socialism, though in a distant future, and Lloyd George's gift for invective, much publicized by cheap newspapers, drove the Lords into the folly of rejecting his budget. By convention and by logic this was an unconstitutional action for a nonrepresentative body to take, and, when a general election in January, 1910, showed that the budget expressed the will of the people, the Lords withdrew their opposition.

It was now too late. The Liberals themselves might have been content with a compromise, but their majority had now been reduced so that they could no longer govern without Labor and Irish Nationalist support. The death of Edward VII in May created a lull in the party conflict, but in December another election produced identically the same strength of parties. In 1911, accordingly, the political conflict reached a height of bitterness without parallel since the Reform Bill crisis of 1832. Fortified by the verdict of two elections, the Liberal government advised the new king, George V, that it was his constitutional duty to enable them to impose a permanent reduction in the powers of the upper house. In the end, the royal promise in writing to the effect that any necessary number of new peerages would be created if the Conservative majority among existing peers required to be outvoted on this issue, induced all but a few diehards to abstain from voting against a constitutional change which they bitterly resented. So the Parliament Bill duly became law.

By the Parliament Act the Lords lost all vestiges of financial authority. Any measure which the Speaker of the House of Commons certified to be a finance measure was in future to become law without their consent. At the same time their authority and function as a revisory body and independent judge of the propriety of legislation in general was severely circumscribed. The rejection or inacceptable amendment of a bill during its passage through the House of Lords lost all validity if the House of Commons passed the bill through all its stages in their house on three separate occasions stretching over a period of not less than two years. As the Parliament Act also reduced the maximum interval between elections from seven to five years, the result was to give each newly elected House of Commons a period of three years during which it could override the veto of the Lords; after that period the Lords could hold up a measure until the next general election. A second Parliament Act was not required for forty years.

■ THE YEARS OF INCREASING STRAIN

The struggle against the House of Lords was only the first of a series of conflicts, in which Liberal ideas of toleration, gradualism, and respect for ballot-box decisions seemed to be submerged by a rising tide of violence. One such conflict, which now appears to belong to a very distant past, was the campaign which the so-called militant suffragettes conducted when peaceful methods brought votes for women no nearer than they had been in Gladstone's day, although the experience of Finland and New Zealand had shown that the admission of women voters imperiled no established interest except possibly male vanity. From 1906 onward disorderly conduct at public meetings, as well as independent demonstrations of various kinds, were used to induce the Liberal government to take the women's cause seriously. Their response proving slow, the suffragettes began to use physical force against individuals and both public and private property. Finally, in January, 1913, they believed themselves to have been tricked, when an amendment to a Franchise Bill, which would have produced a free vote on the issue in parliament, was unexpectedly ruled out of order. The result was a brutalizing struggle, which lasted until the outbreak of war in 1914 without any settlement of the issue coming into sight. One woman deliberately sacrificed her life under the hooves of the horses at the Derby. There were numerous cases of arson and, when the women who had perpetrated such offenses were sent to prison, they resorted to hunger-striking, which meant that they had to be forcibly fed, in some cases at the risk of their lives. The impression made was all the greater because, with a few notable exceptions, the militant suffragettes were recruited from what were then the leisured classes.

The workers during these years faced a grimmer problem—not the winning of new rights, but the holding on to such position in society as they had already achieved. For, while the Liberals were introducing new services, some

BURSLEM, A STAFFORDSHIRE POTTERY TOWN. The present-day photograph shows the intermingling of industrial and living areas—an outcome of the unregulated conditions of the Industrial Revolution.

of them on a contributory basis, the turn in the trend of price levels, which began in 1896, was producing a situation in which the utmost efforts of organized labor could no longer save them from a gradual decline in their standard of living. By 1910 prices had risen so much in fourteen years that, in spite of some wage increases, average rates of real wages were down by 4 percent: the working-class home was able to afford less meat, less sugar, less beer and spirits, and no more bread than it had had in 1896. Hence a swing away from the Labor Party, whose representation in parliament declined slightly at the 1910 elections, toward the practice of direct action through determined leadership in the trade-union movement. The program was that of syndicalism, aiming at the complete control of industry by the workers. This came to Britain both from the American I.W.W. and from the French *Confédération Générale du Travail*, but derived much of its driving force through the return from Australia just at this time of Tom Mann, a future organizer of the British Communist Party.

The result was a series of major strikes in 1911–1912 of a more formidable complexion than modern Britain had previously experienced. In the course of a single, abnormally hot summer the sailors stopped work at the ports, followed by dockers, who were followed in turn by other transport workers. These episodes led to a general railway strike, which coincided with a crisis in Anglo-German relations and was called off after a couple of days, partly for that reason. Then in March, 1912, the coal miners, influenced by a once-famous syndicalist pamphlet, *The Miners' Next Step*, downed picks a million strong—a force unprecedented in British industrial history—and induced the government, which in 1908 had conceded them a legal eight-hour day, to turn their demand for a reasonable minimum wage into an act of parliament. A few months later there was a further dock strike in London, at which the strike leader prayed publicly, "God strike Lord Devonport dead!" Despite this, the noble chairman of the Port of London Authority survived and won.

What had been achieved? In the first place, real wages were brought back to the level of 1906, though not of 1900. In the second, syndicalist influence had led to the creation of a new model union, of which the National Union of Railwaymen was the first example, where the basis of recruitment was the entire industry rather than a single craft. In the third place, the future power of the workers was foreshadowed, not merely or perhaps chiefly by the rise in trade-union membership to a total which approached 4,000,000, but by the creation of a so-called Triple Alliance. This united 1,350,000 miners, railwaymen, and transport workers in an organization "whose object was plainly and simply to arrange for concerted strikes."[9] However, the clash of wills and of rival economic forces was fated to give place at this point to the clash of arms.

Yet by July, 1914, neither the suffragettes nor the trade unionists were so prepared to resort to the arbitrament of force in domestic issues as were the protagonists on either side in Ireland. There the Conservatives had applied many remedies—light railways, agricultural education, help for congested districts, new forms of local self-government, and big land purchase schemes, which even included a government subsidy of 12 percent to encourage the peasants to buy— but as measures of lasting pacification their effects had been negligible. Instead, the first moment at which the British government once more became dependent on Irish support in parliament was the moment at which the introduction of a Third Home Rule Bill became mandatory. It differed from the second bill chiefly in providing safeguards for the mainly Protestant province of Ulster through the system of election to the senate or upper house. But this was not enough for the Ulstermen, with their British and largely industrial sympathies and interests; and the certainty that the bill would become law over the Lords' veto in 1914 caused the Conservative Party in Britain to encourage Ulster to resist any inclusion of that province, if need be by force of arms.

The result was the drilling and illegal arming of the Ulster Volunteers, to which the Irish Nationalists replied by similar measures. Then in March, 1914, a number of Regular Army officers stationed at the Curragh seriously embarrassed the government, besides setting a singularly bad example of seditious conduct, by indicating that they would rather be dismissed than obey orders to act against the Ulstermen. From March to July attempts were made to find a

9. G. D. H. COLE and R. POSTGATE, *The British Common People, 1746–1946* (2nd ed., 1947), p. 416.

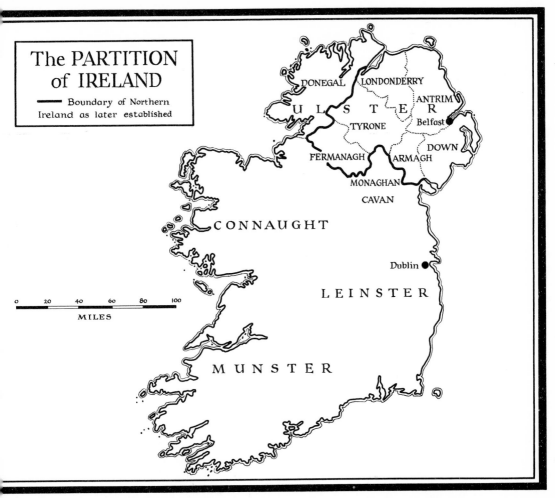

The PARTITION of IRELAND

— Boundary of Northern Ireland as later established

DONEGAL LONDONDERRY
ANTRIM
U L S T E R
TYRONE Belfast
DOWN
FERMANAGH ARMAGH
MONAGHAN
CAVAN

CONNAUGHT

Dublin

LEINSTER

MUNSTER

0 20 40 60 80 100
MILES

Among the four ancient provinces of Ireland (indicated in large type) Ulster had the largest and densest population. Of its ten counties two (Cavan and Monaghan) were inhabited mainly by Catholics and were included in the Home Rule area. Two others (Tyrone and Fermanagh) having a small Catholic majority were disputed between the two sides.

compromise, but each of many proposals for allowing Ulster to opt out of home rule broke down on the question of the exact area to be exempted and the period for which partition was to be definitely established. The Germans, who as late as July 26, 1914, were impartially supplying guns to both sides, had some reason to think that the enactment of home rule would be the signal for civil war. In the event, the bill became law in September and was suspended for the duration of hostilities with the acquiescence of both sides.

■ FOREIGN POLICY AND IMPERIAL DEFENSE

To some extent the atmosphere of violence in domestic matters may reflect the violence of successive crises in foreign affairs.[10] The entente with

10. For a further discussion, see pp. 478–489.

France had stood the first test in 1905–1906, culminating in the Algeciras Conference, on the eve of which the foreign secretary, Sir Edward Grey, had felt obliged to authorize secret military conversations between the two staffs. In 1907 negotiations about existing points of friction and an agreement for spheres of interest in Persia brought about a second entente with Russia, and the resulting Triple Entente had an appearance of greater strength by reason of the Franco-Russian Alliance, though it in fact did very little to help Russia in the Balkan imbroglio of 1908–1909.

It was otherwise in the 1911 crisis, when the Germans sent the *Panther* to the Moroccan Atlantic port of Agadir and sought to strike a hard bargain for the final abandonment of Morocco to the French. For Lloyd George, with the prime minister's approval, then publicly asserted that Britain's interest might cause her to intervene:

> If a situation were to be forced upon us, in which peace could only be preserved by surrender of the great and beneficent position Britain has won by centuries of heroism and achievement, by allowing Britain to be treated, when her interests were vitally affected, as if she were of no account in the Cabinet of Nations, then I say emphatically that peace at that price would be a humiliation intolerable for a great country like ours to endure.[11]

British intervention was not in fact required, and, when the outbreak of war in the Balkans brought on a fresh crisis only twelve months later, it was the conference of ambassadors, sitting under Grey's chairmanship in London, which staved off a general conflict by a policy of skillful compromise. The British peacemakers on that occasion, in their anxiety to settle the affairs of the Balkans in a spirit of fair play, leaned often to the side of the Triple Alliance. But all in vain. When the murders at Sarajevo reopened the Balkan question the next year, no appeals to fair play were allowed to prevent Europe from completing its journey along the road to Armageddon.

Thus the Liberal governments had been obliged to divert some of their attention to a policy of military and naval development; the latter, as we have seen, also cost much money. The inadequacy of the British army had been common knowledge since the first of the Boer War disasters, but it was left to the Liberal secretary for war, Haldane, to carry through a rational reorganization. He created a general staff, an elaborate mobilization plan, and a large new reserve body of partly trained volunteers, the Territorial Army, which in the event of war would be quickly available for home defense. On this basis he was able to develop the small Regular Army for the task of providing a highly trained and fully equipped expeditionary force, which the navy could put ashore on the Continent at very little notice. All this was satisfactorily achieved,

11. *War Memoirs of David Lloyd George* (2 vol. ed., 1938), I, 26.

and in 1914 the army was actually costing one million pounds a year less than before Haldane took office.

The Royal Navy, in contrast, depended for its value in the existing world situation, not upon small-scale efficiency with relation to a single main object, but upon expansion to meet world-wide obligations. The Anglo-Japanese alliance had, indeed, relieved pressure upon British resources in the east. In 1904–1905 Japan defeated Russia, and the alliance was subsequently renewed on a basis that provided for joint action against any attack on the Far Eastern possessions of either power, including India. But Britain had an island base to defend from invasion by the much larger conscript armies of Continental powers; an absolute dependence upon open sea lanes for her food supply in time of war; and a reasonable expectation that her ability to win a major war would depend upon her sea power's being great enough to blockade the coasts of the enemy and deny him access to the trade routes of the world. The traditional solution of the problem was to maintain a 10 percent superiority over the two next largest navies. Since 1900, however, the rapid growth of the German navy had made this standard in any case less easy to maintain, and in October, 1905, Admiral Fisher, anticipating the technical progress which other powers would shortly make, had laid down the *Dreadnought*, the first all-big-gun, turbine-engined capital ship. On her completion in the record time of a year and four days, the new Liberal government was faced with the problem of the obsolescence of all earlier capital ships, in which the British navy had a vast preponderance.

The ensuing naval race against Germany was the aspect of foreign policy of which the newspaper-reading public was most clearly aware. The Germans responded quickly to the challenge of the *Dreadnought:* by 1908 they had laid down four ships of this type, to which the British government intended to reply with six new constructions, but public opinion for once drove the estimates up with the cry, "We want eight, and we won't wait." To build twice as fast as the Germans, whose overall industrial capacity now exceeded that of Britain, was not permanently practicable. Failing an agreement for a naval holiday, which the kaiser spurned, the British government decided to maintain a 60 percent lead in capital ships for a possible conflict with the Germans in the North Sea and a lead of roughly 100 percent in the cruisers, which were required to control the trade routes of the world.

In retrospect, the link between foreign policy, defense, and the Empire appears closer than it did to contemporary observers. The Liberals left their mark upon imperial affairs chiefly through Campbell-Bannerman's effort to heal the wounds of South Africa. He conceded full colonial self-government to the Transvaal and, a little later, to the Orange Free State; no act of parliament was required, but the consent of the cabinet was conceded to the prime minister's personal convictions. The consequence was that, a few months after his death, the two ex-Boer colonies, under Boer premiers, began negotiations with Cape Colony and Natal, from which emerged the agreement to form a single strong dominion on terms approved by parliament in 1909. For nearly two generations the Union of South Africa stood as seemingly incontestable evidence of the wisdom of showing generosity to the defeated. In India, too, an attempt was made to allay the growing discontent with foreign rule by granting a modest installment of self-government. The legislative councils of the various provinces were placed for the first time upon a partly elective basis, and the more powerful executive councils, including the Viceroy's Council at the center, were to a small extent diluted by native appointments. Despite these reforms unrest continued, even when the new king-emperor at his splendid Coronation Durbar in 1911 reunited Bengal—where a great furore had been caused by its partition for administrative reasons a few years earlier—and announced that the seat of Indian government would be brought back to the traditional Mogul capital at Delhi.

Finally, the attempt was made to build up imperial defenses. On the one hand, colonial ministers were encouraged, when available, to attend meetings of the new Committee of Imperial Defense, which tended increasingly to think in terms of imperial responsibilities: from 1909 onward the effective head of the British Army was styled Chief of the *Imperial* General Staff. On the other hand, the Colonial Conference of 1907 made arrangements for a special subsidiary Defense Conference to be held for purposes of consultation in 1909, and in 1911 the Imperial Conference itself devoted part of its time to a proposal by the prime minister of New Zealand for the institution of an "imperial parliament of defense." Nothing came of this proposal, since the desire of the dominions for complete autonomy was matched by the desire of the United Kingdom government to keep control of the wider issues of policy in its own experienced hands. When the war came there was neither an imperial army nor an imperial navy in the full sense of the word, but there were Dominion warships put at disposal of the mother country, a reservoir of Dominion soldiers, organized originally for home defense, and—what mattered most—a general will to cooperate in defense of common values.

Reading List: Chapter 13

The New Cambridge Modern History, vol. XI (1962), ch. 14. Great Britain and her Empire.

Maurois, A., *Disraeli* (1928), part III. His prime ministership.

Monypenny, W. F., and Buckle, G. E., *Life of Disraeli* (rev. ed., 2 vols., 1929), Bk. V, chs. 10–12. Domestic and foreign policy of Disraeli's main government.

Young, G. M., *Victorian England: The Portrait of an Age* (2nd ed., 1953), sec. XXX. Imperialism.

Plumb, J. H., "Cecil Rhodes," *History Today*, vol. III (1953), no. 9.

James, R. R., "Radical Joe [Joseph Chamberlain]," *History Today*, vol. VII (1957), no. 9.

Goodwin, Michael (ed.), *Nineteenth Century Opinion* (1951), pp. 19-82. Growth of social conscience as seen in review articles of 1877-1900.

Cole, G. D. H., and Postgate, R., *The British Common People, 1746-1938* (1939), chs. 37-40. Growth of the labor movement.

Cole, Margaret, *The Story of Fabian Socialism* (1961), part I. Early days of the movement.

Somervell, D. C., *British Politics Since 1900* (1950), chs. 3-4. The reforms and the approach of war.

Halévy, E., *History of the English People in the Nineteenth Century*, vol. VI (1950; also paperback, 1963), Bk. I, Pt. 2, ch. 1 and ch. 2, sec. iii.

Woodward, E. L., *Great Britain and the German Navy* (1935), pp. 1-18. Summary of the problem of naval rivalry, 1898-1912.

Chapter 14

Russia at the Parting of the Ways

Introduction
Alexander II: The Last Decade
The Reign of Alexander III
Nicholas II and the Russo-Japanese War
The Growth of Opposition
Revolution and Reaction, 1905–1907
The Stolypin Regime and Its Development to 1914

■ INTRODUCTION

When the age of imperialist expansion began, Russia resembled Britain in the advantages she enjoyed from her peripheral position. Command of the sea encouraged Britain to exploit an insular situation so as to build and rebuild a great transoceanic empire, which mattered more to her than the mutual relations of the merely European powers. In the same way Russia had all Asia at her back door, encouraging her, like Britain, to look at frontiers other than those of Europe. What the steamship was doing for the British Empire, the railway could do for the Russian, though—as we shall see—the Russians were slow to develop the railways and the necessary flow of immigrants into Siberia and, in the struggle for an economic empire in the Far East, met with a reverse such as British fortunes had not experienced since 1783. Both Britain and Russia also had important relations with France and with Germany. Through their re-

390

SIGNIFICANT EVENTS

1877–1878	Russo-Turkish War
1881	Assassination of Alexander II
	Accession of Alexander III
1889	Introduction of land captains
1891–1894	Formation of alliance with France
1891	Trans-Siberian Railway begun
1892–1903	Witte minister of finance
1894	Accession of Nicholas II
1898	Lease of Liaotung Peninsula, including Port Arthur
1904	Outbreak of Russo-Japanese War (February)
1905	Bloody Sunday (January)
	Treaty of Portsmouth, N. H. (August)
	Manifesto establishing constitutional monarchy (October)
1906	First Duma (May–July)
1907	Second Duma (March–June)
1907–1912	Third Duma
	Stolypin's land reform

spective ties with France—the Franco-Russian Alliance and the Entente Cordiale—they were eventually brought together in the Triple Entente of 1907. But up to, and even after, that date Germany exercised a much stronger influence upon her nearer neighbor than she did upon Britain, since the seemingly stable hierarchic structure of imperial Germany provided the model on which the tsardom would have liked to base itself.

Nevertheless, any comparison is fallacious, since Russia with a population at the first comprehensive census (1897) of 117,000,000, had problems of different dimensions from those which faced other powers. The Edict of Emancipation had whetted a huge unsatisfied appetite for land for peasant use, which became all the more acute as the fall in world grain prices made a tiny holding almost valueless in terms of its purchasing power. In the 1880's, too, Russia experienced the start of industrial development—railway building, the sinking of oil wells, the use of improved textile machinery, the growth of coal and iron production —involving difficult questions of labor relations. To cope with all this was in any case beyond the capacity of an autocratic government with a horde of venal officials. But to effect an intelligent reform of that government was hopelessly impracticable, because the mass of the population was illiterate, widely scattered, and largely indifferent, while the potential leaders of a reform movement were divided among themselves and disregarded by the autocracy because their following was small. Moreover, the mass was not even united firmly by ties of nationality, as were the British, the French, or the Germans, for, of the 117,000,000 Russian subjects referred to above, only 55,000,000 were Great Russians, that is, people for whom Russian was their mother tongue. The other elements included 22,000,000 Ukrainians (then known as Little Russians), nearly 10,000,000 Poles, nearly 6,000,000 White Russians (Byelo-Russians), fourteen other groups of a million or more, and thirty-one smaller minorities.

■ ALEXANDER II: THE LAST DECADE

By 1871 the Tsar Liberator had long lost all appetite for liberation, at least at home. Significantly enough, however, the one sphere of continuing reform was the army, whose organization, training, discipline, and weapons had been undergoing a series of changes in the light of the disastrous experiences of the Crimean War. This process did not reach its climax until 1874, when conscription was introduced on the German model. For the first time in Russian history, military service was imposed in principle on all classes alike; the army ceased to be a penal institution, and its peasant recruits were even taught to read and write. Thus the army became to some extent a democratizing influence in Russia, though the immediate effect was to encourage the tsar to make use of his new army, long before the reforms could produce much additional military efficiency, in a war of liberation in the Balkans.

The forward policy was in line with a new doctrine which was becoming popular in reactionary circles. This was the Pan-Slav movement, which had much in common with the vaguer aspirations of the Slavophiles. It laid less emphasis, however, on the superiority of the Orthodox Church and Russian culture, and much more on the idea, already widespread among Slavs under Austrian or Hungarian rule, of a historic struggle between Slavdom and the West. Its Russian exponents taught that it was the duty of Russia as the great Slav power to form a Slav federation under her leadership. If this was to include all Slavs, then she must be prepared to fight the Germans for control of the Danube valley. Or perhaps—in view of Polish ingratitude—she should confine her attention to Orthodox Slavs, in which case it might be sufficient to fight the Turks. Accordingly, Pan-Slav volunteers were recruited in Russia to help the

Serbs in their brief campaign of July–October, 1876, when the latter gave ineffectual help to the insurrection against Turkish rule in Bosnia-Herzegovina. The Serbian failure made the Pan-Slavs all the more determined to intervene on behalf of the Bulgarian insurrectionaries, over whom the Turks had enjoyed a bloodier triumph, for as one Pan-Slav propagandist put it, "Bulgaria is much more important for us and for the future of Slavdom than Serbia." Since they had the backing of the tsarevich, the future Alexander III, and of General Ignatiev, then ambassador at Constantinople, the Pan-Slavs bear part of the responsibility for the Russo-Turkish war which followed in April, 1877.

The Russians advanced quickly on both sides of the Black Sea, as far as the Shipka Pass in the Balkan Mountains and the town of Kars in Armenia. But Kars held out until November, while the Turkish stronghold of Plevna outflanked any further advance via the Shipka Pass against Constantinople. The Rumanian army was called in; the Russian Guards regiments, which had been kept out of the Crimean War, were summoned to the Balkans. Three assaults on Plevna were repulsed, however, and not until December did Todleben starve it into surrender. The sequel was a quickly renewed advance on Constantinople and the occupation of the north shore of the Sea of Marmara, whose waters were controlled by the British Navy. At home there was strong Pan-Slav pressure for an attack which would hoist the cross on San Sofia. But the army was deemed inadequate to the purpose, and the Black Sea fleet had not yet been rebuilt. Instead, Russia made the treaty of San Stefano in March, 1878, so as to secure the creation of a big Bulgarian satellite, which would include the whole of Macedonia except Salonica and part of Thrace, with other advances on the Caucasian frontier. However, as a result of secret negotiations with Britain, which were ratified in July of the same year at the Congress of Berlin, she bartered the reduction of Bulgaria for British acceptance of her Caucasian gains, namely the port of Batum and the fortresses of Kars and Ardahan.

The main consequence was the collapse of Pan-Slavism, for the new Bulgaria proved to be a most disappointing and refractory satellite. It was true that the war had also gratified national pride through the reannexation of southern Bessarabia, which had been Russian territory from 1812 to 1856; this was now exchanged by the Rumanians under compulsion for inferior territory taken from the Turks in the northern Dobrudja. But Austria-Hungary had to be allowed by Russia to compensate herself by occupying Bosnia-Herzegovina; in addition, the forced exchange cost Russia the good will of her Rumanian allies. Nor could it be pretended that a war which had achieved so little in the character of a crusade had achieved compensatory economic advantages. French capital was brought in to build the Bulgarian railways, for, as even the Pan-Slav journalist, Katkov, acknowledged, Russia herself had no capital to spare. Russia was not strong enough to withstand the opposition of Britain and

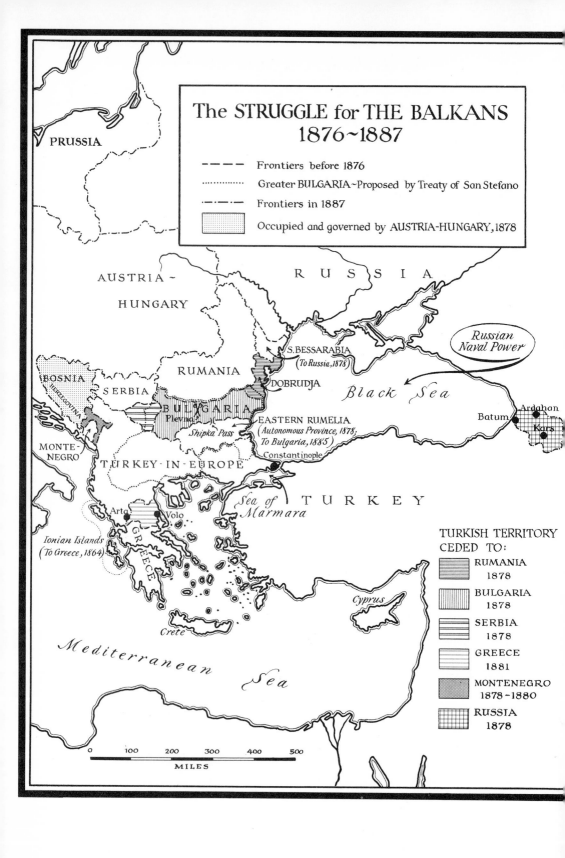

The STRUGGLE for THE BALKANS 1876~1887

- – – – – Frontiers before 1876
- ⋯⋯⋯⋯⋯ Greater BULGARIA~Proposed by Treaty of San Stefano
- –·–·–·– Frontiers in 1887
- ▦ Occupied and governed by AUSTRIA-HUNGARY, 1878

PRUSSIA

AUSTRIA ~
HUNGARY

R U S S I A

*Russian
Naval Power*

BOSNIA

HERZEGOVINA

SERBIA

RUMANIA

S. BESSARABIA
(To Russia, 1878)

DOBRUDJA

Black Sea

BULGARIA

Plevna

Shipka Pass

EASTERN RUMELIA
(Autonomous Province, 1878;
To Bulgaria, 1885)

MONTE-
NEGRO

TURKEY·IN·EUROPE

Constantinople

Batum

Ardahan

Kars

*Sea of
Marmara*

T U R K E Y

Arta

Volo

GREECE

*Ionian Islands
(To Greece, 1864)*

Cyprus

Crete

Mediterranean Sea

TURKISH TERRITORY
CEDED TO:

RUMANIA
1878

BULGARIA
1878

SERBIA
1878

GREECE
1881

MONTENEGRO
1878~1880

RUSSIA
1878

0   100   200   300   400   500
MILES

Austria, who had enjoyed tacit support at the Congress of Berlin from the seemingly disinterested Germans. The failure to make a due return for the benevolent neutrality of Russia in the wars of the preceding decade might be remembered to Germany's disadvantage at a later day. But Russia's first decision was to cut her losses and help to re-form the League of the Three Emperors, so that she might be able better to withstand the pressure of Britain, always anxious about the security of her vast Indian possessions.

Although Russia's economic interests in central Asia were scarcely more important at this time than in the Balkans, the closing decade of the reign of Alexander II brought the program of expansion there virtually to its completion. It was, indeed, a program only in the sense that the central government sent generals, troops, and administrators on missions of pacification in existing frontier regions, and did not effectively discourage them from advancing beyond the frontier to pacify troublemakers who were always to be located in the regions beyond. Thus by 1873 the khanates of Khiva and Bokhara had been made into Russian protectorates, although in the case of the former explicit assurances that this would not be done had been given in London only a couple of months before the expedition was launched. Two years later a revolt in the third Uzbek khanate, Kokand, which was already a protectorate, led to its annexation. While acting as military governor there, General Skobelev made the only definitely known Russian plans for the invasion of India, in the belief that a successful rebellion could be promoted by the entry upon the scene of a Russian force of only fifty thousand men. But after he had figured as one of the Russian heroes of the siege of Plevna, Skobelev's next assignment was to penetrate the Turcoman territories lying between the Caspian Sea and the frontiers of Afghanistan. Severe fighting and a lost campaign preceded his capture of the main Turcoman stronghold, where he massacred the civil population, in January, 1881, two months before the death of Alexander II. The completion of the conquest in the next reign, when the Russian flag was planted at Merv and Penjdeh and the Trans-Caspian Railway was built across the steppes, proved to be quite easy. But, although the Russians discovered that the high mountains supposedly separating their conquests from Herat in Afghanistan do not exist, neither of the two last tsars countenanced any serious scheme for the invasion of India.

After six failures, in March, 1881, an elaborately organized plot of which about one hundred people had advance knowledge succeeded in taking the life of Tsar Alexander II. This appears at first sight to provide a strange and inconsequent denouement to the reign of the liberator who had also done much to restore Russia's prestige in the eyes of the world. But reforms which were all of them compromises, raising great hopes in the minds of the beneficiaries and great fears in the minds of those who lost their position of complete privilege, did not possess for either side the character of a final settlement. In some matters, such as the control of education, the tsar had come to side openly with the reactionaries. Even without this, his policies had created an atmosphere of social ferment which conduced to a sudden outburst of revolutionary activity.

As early as 1862–1863 a shadowy movement had existed briefly among some of the intelligentsia, which, under the name of "Land and Liberty," planned big changes which were to follow the success of the Polish revolt. It was sponsored by the great anarchist, Bakunin, and by Alexander Herzen, both of whom died in exile. A less fortunate intimate of Bakunin was Russia's first professional revolutionary, Serge Nechaev,[1] who was extradited from Switzerland in 1872 and died after ten years of solitary confinement, a devotee of terrorism. More important was the fact that Herzen, Bakunin, Nechaev, and—in the world of literary journalism—the representative "penitent noble," Mikhailovsky, all espoused the view that Russia, thanks to the strong cooperative traditions of the *mir*, was capable of achieving a socialist society directly, without passing through any intermediate phase of capitalism. Hence the movement known as Populism or, in Lenin's contemptuous words, "peasant socialism," which an earnest and numerous body of students in 1873 endeavored to forward by going to the people. The peasants could make nothing of the socialist gospel they preached, and in many cases helped the authorities to repress them. A second attempt followed in 1876, when groups of students, including many young women, adopted a more effective policy of practicing a trade among the people they wished to influence. The sequel was two mass trials—of 50 and 193 revolutionaries respectively—at which long and spirited defenses were offered, and a wave of violent actions broke out against the authorities.

By this time the movement had been brought under the control of a new and more radical secret society, named Land and Liberty after the earlier abortive venture of 1862. The leaders now aimed, not at mere propaganda, but at a peasant uprising, which was to be based on a nation-wide organization, and the use of all appropriate methods, including terrorist strokes against their opponents and work among the urban no less than the rural population. But terrorism provoked stern countermeasures by the authorities, with the result that Land and Liberty was split between two successor organizations. One of these was content to continue with propaganda among the peasants and achieved nothing in Russia, though its prophets in exile provided the nucleus of the Russian Marxist theorists.[2] The other successor group, known as "The People's Will," decided that the most important immediate object was the

1. 1847–1882. Son of a sign-painter, he became a schoolteacher and student at St. Petersburg. His brutal murder of a fellow revolutionary provided a theme for Dostoevsky's *The Devils;* his later revolutionary directives, smuggled out of prison, rejected a proposal for his own rescue because it would delay the assassination of the tsar.

2. See pp. 456–457.

murder of the tsar, believing that this would cause the entire regime to capitulate.

In 1879 some of its members mined a heavily guarded railway line; in 1880 they blew up a part of the Winter Palace. After these two narrow escapes the tsar entrusted General Loris-Melikov and a Supreme Commission with the double task of suppressing revolutionary activity and removing its causes. Under the first head Loris-Melikov abolished the Third Section, so as to place all police work under the minister of the interior, whose office he shortly assumed. Under the second he made plans to have legislative proposals examined by representatives of the zemstvos and larger town councils before the Council of State in turn expressed its advisory opinion to the tsar. But the People's Will got its stroke in first. On the day in March, 1881, when he had given his assent to Loris-Melikov's plans, two bombs were thrown at Alexander as he drove back to the palace from a military parade in St. Petersburg. The second dismembered him, and he died within the hour; five indefatigable plotters, one of them a general's daughter, died with equal bravery on the gallows.

■ THE REIGN OF ALEXANDER III

As soon as life had left his father's body, Alexander III gave his first quick orders and departed to his own palace at high speed under escort of a troop of cavalry. The last era of effective Romanov despotism had begun. Unlike his predecessor, he was a strong man, simpleminded, consistent, a virtuous husband and father, well suited to make the old system work—in so far at least as that system could be restored and put in working order. Serfdom was, of course, a closed issue, and both Slavophilism and Pan-Slavism were giving place to the cruder cult of Pan-Russianism. But in the main it proved quite possible to return to the ideas of Orthodoxy, autocracy, and nationality. The steady maintenance of the new course was, moreover, greatly furthered by the influence of Constantine Pobedonostsev, who had been the new tsar's tutor and from 1880 to 1905 held office as chief procurator of the Holy Synod. Pobedonostsev drew the picture of a Russian peasantry which not only welcomed autocratic government in principle, but applauded it most readily in practice when its measures were directed to the suppression of every alien religion and nationality. He was ably abetted by Katkov, as editor of the ultranationalist and highly influential *Moscow Gazette*.

The involvement of a Jewess in the murder of Alexander II gave rise in the same year to more than a hundred anti-Jewish mob outbreaks, or "pogroms"—a Russian word for violent destruction—and these were followed by a series of anti-Semitic regulations imposed by the government. Rules dating from the end of the previous century had prescribed that the Jews should reside only in the western provinces outside Russia proper; these rules were now more strictly enforced, together with specific provisions against their making new homes in rural areas, even in the western provinces. The number of Jewish students in secondary schools and universities was also severely restricted, and they were entirely excluded from participation in the affairs of zemstvos or town dumas—hence, a large-scale exodus of Jews, especially to America, which did much to build up hatred and contempt for the tsarist tyranny.

Otherwise there was little to suggest to the outside world anything but an attitude of docility among Russian subjects. The revolutionary movement, having achieved no favorable public reaction by killing the tsar, subsided almost of itself. In the new reign there was only one memorable regicide plot, and that is memorable chiefly because the unsuccessful assassins who paid the death penalty included the elder brother of Lenin. Populism virtually disappeared, and, while it was at this time (1883) that the first Russian social-democratic organization came into existence among exiles in Switzerland, the first industrial strikes in the same decade owed nothing to Marxist political groups and were in any case easily suppressed.

Anti-Semitism was paralleled by harsh treatment of other religious and national dissidents. The Roman Catholic and Protestant faiths suffered minor persecution, along with the Polish and Baltic languages with which they were associated. Dissenters from the Orthodox Church, numbering about one-seventh of the entire Russian population, suffered more severely from the attentions of Orthodox missionaries, who had the help of the police in their ministrations, the worst treated being the Dukhobors, who were pacifists; to convert from the Orthodox faith was a legal offense, punishable by imprisonment or exile to Siberia.

Two other types of reactionary measures also affected the general population. One was the repression of intellectual life through new censorship rules, which made it almost impossible for opposition newspapers and periodicals to remain in circulation, and through educational restrictions, designed to reduce even more effectively the numbers of persons capable of entertaining dangerous thoughts. In accordance with a plan first formulated by Dmitry Tolstoy in the preceding reign, the universities lost the autonomy they had enjoyed, in theory at least, since 1863 and were placed under the control of the Ministry of Education. Admission to the *gymnasia*, from which university students were recruited, was likewise restricted by raising fees and by officially recommending the exclusion of the children of the poor, who "should not be led to break away from the milieu to which they belong."[3] Finally, a good deal of public money was spent in increasing the number of church schools and bringing other elementary schools under church influence.

3. Minister of Education's Circular of June 18, 1887, quoted by M. T. FLORINSKY, *Russia: A History and Interpretation* (1947), vol. II, p. 1115.

CONVICTED NIHILISTS LEAVING FOR SIBERIA. From *The Illustrated London News,* June 4, 1887. Four years later George Kennan's *Siberia and the Exile System* denounced this tsarist system of "exile by administrative process."

The other major change was the attempt to set the clock back by reducing the modest installment of freedom and local self-government which the Tsar Liberator had accorded to the rural population. Since such a policy appeared rash even to many members of the upper classes, it was pursued with some circumspection. On the financial side, where the position of the peasant was known to be desperate, ameliorative measures were taken, such as the scaling down of all redemption payments, formation of a State Peasant Bank to help land purchases, and abolition of the poll tax, to which only peasants were liable. But the state recouped itself to some extent by imposing redemption payments on the entire class of ex-state peasants, who had hitherto escaped them. On the side of legal status, however, the changes made in the reign, which began with the abandonment of Loris-Melikov's modest constitutional proposals, were all for the worse. All withdrawals from the village were made subject to the approval of the village assembly. A new upper-class official, the land captain, was introduced to supervise the affairs of that assembly and to take over the functions of a rural justice of the peace. Last, the share of the peasantry in zemstvo institutions was drastically reduced—their representatives were to be nominated by the governor from a list made up of one person chosen by each village, and in any case were to number only 30 percent of any zemstvo assembly. At the same time the activities of zemstvos and of town dumas, where the franchise was likewise restricted, were all made more dependent than before upon the approval of provincial governors.

The rural policy of the reign may be summed up, not unfairly, in the story of the famine of 1891. Crop failure still brought starvation to thousands, and thousands more died in the cholera epidemic which followed. There was no movement of revolt, but the government was impelled grudgingly to relax its rules sufficiently for the zemstvos to share in the relief work. This in turn gave new color to the faded Populist vision of a peasant revolution.

The reign of Alexander III also marked the dawn of the era of industrialization in Russia. In 1881–1894 imports of raw cotton were almost doubled; in 1889–1902 railway mileage likewise was almost doubled; and in the single decade of 1885–1895 production both of pig iron and of oil was trebled. The number of industrial workers rose correspondingly to a total of more than two million, employed to an increasing extent in very large industrial units. Though some restriction was attempted on the use of female and child labor, living conditions in all the industrial towns were monstrously bad, and wage rates in centers like Moscow, which was surrounded by an overpopulated rural region, were quite appalling. Nevertheless, a ban was imposed on the formation of trade unions and striking was a legally punishable offense. For all this the reckoning lay in the future. At the time, state intervention was chiefly directed by the very able finance minister, Witte,[4] toward the encouragement of industrial development by raising the tariff barrier, by struggling to place Russia on the gold standard (reached in 1897), by planning the railway network, and above all by bringing in foreign capital. The government itself borrowed in order to buy arms and build strategic railways, such as the Trans-Caspian and the Trans-Siberian, and it gave every facility to foreign investors. In 1888–1900 no less than 250 foreign companies were founded on Russian soil, and by 1914 about one-fourth of all the industrial capital of the country came from foreign sources.

The need for capital from abroad eventually influenced Russia's foreign policy, in which a decisive step was taken by the end of the reign. Though Alexander's aims were those of an ardent Pan-Russian, eager to contest with Austria the hegemony of the Balkans, up to 1887 the mainstay of his policy was the revived League of the Three Emperors. When Russia became involved in a further frontier quarrel with Britain over Russian encroachments in Afghanistan, German pressure secured a promise from the sultan that the British fleet would not be allowed to attack Russia through the Straits. But the failure of the Russian attempt to control her Bulgarian satellite through the first prince of Bulgaria, the tsar's youthful cousin Alexander of Battenberg, was a disappointment which became all the more bitter when, in 1885, the country was peace-

4. 1849–1915. A Baltic German, educated at Odessa University, he first made his name in railroad administration. He became finance minister 1892–1903; lost favor because he opposed the Far Eastern policy, but was made a count, for his services in negotiating the Treaty of Portsmouth in 1905, and prime minister, 1905–1906. A supporter of autocracy but intensely ambitious, he was distrusted by Nicholas, with some reason, as Witte's own posthumous *Memoirs* show.

fully united with Eastern Rumelia in defiance of the decisions made at the Congress of Berlin. Though the Russians were able to drive Alexander from his throne, they were not able to assert effective control over his former subjects or over his eventual successor, Prince Ferdinand of Saxe-Coburg, who was not recognized by Russia until 1896. Under the influence of Katkov, the tsar attributed the Bulgarian imbroglio primarily to the actions of Austria. The League of the Three Emperors therefore came to an end, but was replaced for three years by Bismarck's famous Reinsurance Treaty. The failure to renew it in 1890 was the consequence of a German decision, taken very rapidly after the fall of Bismarck, the effect of which was to precipitate the formation of the Dual Alliance between Russia and France.

Clearly, no alliance could be less congenial to Tsar Alexander III than one with France, but it was partly for that very reason that the Germans played fast and loose with his support. In 1887, however, Russo-German tension over Bulgaria had coincided with Franco-German tension over the affairs of Alsace, and Katkov (who died in July) was able to show the direction in which a shared hatred should lead. Then the financial interest began to weigh, as Bismarck—by one of his few imprudences—closed the Berlin money market to the Russians as a temporary measure which would quickly bring them to heel. It had the very opposite effect, for a loan launched tentatively in France was enthusiastically oversubscribed; this proved to be the first of many, with high interest rates as the main inducement on one side, and the need for heavy constructional works (such as railways) on the other. Russia also made significant arms purchases, beginning with Lebel army rifles in 1888.

The tsar slowly accepted an alliance arrangement which lay in the logic of history. In August, 1891, just after the French fleet had been welcomed at Kronstadt and the tsar had shown in public his agreement that Paris was well worth a salute to the "Marseillaise," a political convention was duly signed. A year later this was supplemented by a Franco-Russian military agreement for specific military support against Germany. But the military document bore only the signatures of the respective chiefs of staff, and it was not until January, 1894, that the Russian foreign minister made the final ratification. The death of Alexander from nephritis, a few months in advance of his fiftieth birthday, followed before the end of the year.

■ NICHOLAS II AND THE RUSSO-JAPANESE WAR

The reign of Nicholas II has something of the quality of a great tragic drama. The tsar himself has often been compared with Louis XVI of France, whose character and fate he shared—a model family man, of simple tastes, not interested in ideas or innovations, acting according to the desires of his strong-willed wife or under the influence of the last minister who had spoken with him, and altogether blind to the realities of a situation which would have justified him in echoing the complaint of Hamlet—

> The time is out of joint; O cursed spite,
> That ever I was born to set it right!

Like Louis XVI, he had an unpopular foreign wife, a German princess who had been brought up in England at the court of her grandmother, Queen Victoria. Converted to Orthodoxy as a condition of the marriage, which took place just after the accession, Alexandra had all the zeal of a convert for her new faith and regarded autocratic rule as her husband's sacred duty. In addition, all her later life was overshadowed by the fact that her fifth child and first son was afflicted with hemophilia. When it was found that the pitiful and dangerous bleedings could be brought under control by the mesmeric influence of a highly disreputable fakir or wandering religious teacher, Gregory Rasputin,[5] what was in any case a narrowly reactionary court came to be dominated by an ignorant and degraded peasant, to whom the tsar was as loyal as he was disloyal to his properly accredited advisers.

Such were the influences that surrounded a ruler under whom Russia was to be put to the severe test of fighting two disastrous wars. Defeat at the hands of Japan in 1904–1905 brought about a revolutionary situation inside Russia, which the monarchy just, and only just, surmounted. Defeat at the hands of Germany in the first two and one-half years of the First World War brought about a second, more overwhelmingly revolutionary situation, which the House of Romanov did not surmount. Finally, in July, 1918, the dethroned monarch, his wife, daughters, and almost helpless son were brutally done to death in a cellar, bereft of everything but dignity.

In the early years of the reign it is possible, indeed, to observe the ominous rumblings of the coming storm. When he had been on the throne for less than three months, the new tsar emphasized his refusal to come to terms with moderate liberal opinion by publicly dismissing as senseless dreams the reports then current to the effect that zemstvo representatives were to be given some share in the central government. On the contrary, in 1901 what they could do in local affairs was circumscribed by new limitations imposed upon local taxation. With the growth of industry continuing throughout the first decade of the reign, there was some official limitation of working hours and provision of compensation for accidents. But there was also a provision made for police-controlled

---

5. 1871–1916. Gregory Efimovich earned the name of Rasputin ("debauchee") before leaving his native village in western Siberia by his doctrine of salvation through sin. Since the tsar and tsarina refused to believe any reports of his debaucheries, though they were practiced in St. Petersburg society, by 1914 he could overthrow any minister. He opposed the war as endangering the principle of autocracy, and was poisoned, shot, and battered to death by Prince Yusupov and others in December, 1916.

TSAR NICHOLAS II OF RUSSIA AND THE TSARINA ALEXANDRA IN COURT ROBES. The robes, worn for the Easter Eve celebration in the Kremlin (1895 or 1896), suggest the Byzantine and non-western influences still persisting in Russia.

dummy labor organizations and deportation of genuine strike leaders by administrative action. Most significant of all, in 1899 the constitution of Finland was in effect suspended in accordance with Alexander III's intentions, and in 1903 anti-Semitism, which had long been active below the surface of Russian life, erupted as in 1881 in a formidable two-day pogrom at Kishiniev, the capital of Bessarabia. The intensely reactionary Pobedonostsev served Nicholas II as he had served his father, and the finance minister, Witte, was likewise a firm believer in autocracy as long as it believed firmly in itself.

The preference of the autocrat, however, was not for dull problems of domestic discord but for a policy of adventure in the Far East. Soon after his appointment as finance minister, Witte had reported to Alexander III that the Trans-Siberian Railway would eventually replace the Suez Canal as the main link between Europe and the China trade. Nicholas, whose limited past experience had included a world tour, saw in this situation immense possibilities of Russian aggrandizement. In the first year of his reign the Japanese defeated the Chinese Empire, which was only saved from dismemberment at the Treaty of Shimonoseki by the joint intervention of Russia, France, and Germany. The immediate sequel was the foundation of a Russo-Chinese bank (floated on French capital) and provision for a Chinese Eastern Railway, running across Manchuria from the Trans-Siberian Railway direct to Vladivostok. In the railway zone the privileges of what was in effect an organ of the Russian state, thinly disguised as a railway company, included the right to maintain an armed police force. The fact that all this was coupled with a secret Sino-Russian alliance did not prevent Russia, when the Germans leased a naval base at Kiaochow, from exacting in 1898 a similar lease of Port Arthur, together with the commercial port of Dairen and the hinterland of the Liaotung Peninsula. Other Chinese territory was claimed as compensation by France and Britain, leaving Japan with little except the recognition by Russia of her special economic interests in Korea; and even here a huge timber concession on the northern border organized by an adventurer named Bezobrazov, who enjoyed close personal and financial relations with the tsar, was expressly designed to achieve further Russian penetration.

In theory, the Russians were committed to preserving the territorial integrity of China and the Open Door for trade, as proposed by the American secretary of state in September, 1899. In practice, the next year saw their military occupation spread from the railroad zone to the whole of Manchuria. Though this was to meet an emergency, three years later most of Manchuria was still occupied and a new Russian viceroyalty of the Far East had just been announced, to be held directly under the tsar by a close associate of Bezobrazov. Such were the circumstances in which the Japanese, after several vain attempts to negotiate an effective settlement with Russia, made the alliance with Britain. This gave them a five-year period in which they could plan a war against Russia, knowing that Britain would enable them to fight undisturbed, because she was pledged to go to war against any second power that became involved. Meanwhile, Russian contempt for the "little apes" encouraged Plehve, who replaced Witte as the tsar's principal official adviser in 1903, in his belief that Russia not only needed a small successful war but could stage such a war in the Far East without any special difficulty. He believed this, although the Japanese at the outset would have about twice as many soldiers in the theater of war and the Trans-Siberian Railway still had a considerable gap in its single track along the rocky shore of Lake Baikal.

The contest began with a Japanese torpedo boat attack at Port Arthur, which preceded the declaration of war and proved to be only the first of a series of small-scale naval actions in which the Japanese won command of the sea from their approximately equal opponents. By July what was left of the Russian Pacific squadron was bottled up in Port Arthur, where it was destroyed by the Japanese siege guns. Meanwhile, the Japanese landed their armies in Korea (which preserved a benevolent neutrality), defeated the Russians in early May at the battle of the Yalu River—a momentous turning point in the affairs of Asia—and made good their passage to the Liaotung Peninsula on the Russian flank. Having driven one Russian army back northward along the line of the

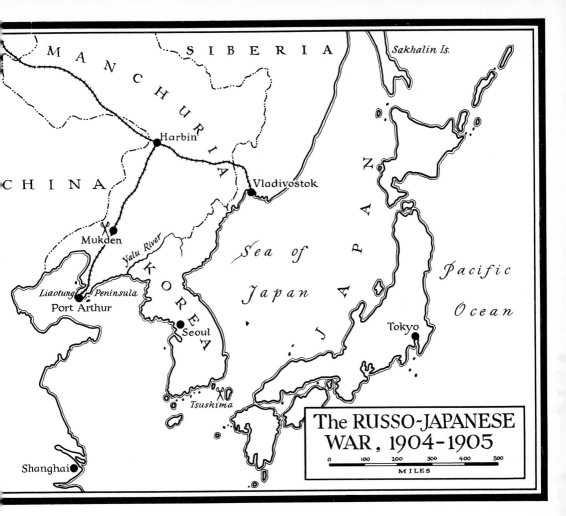

The RUSSO-JAPANESE
WAR, 1904-1905

| 0 | 100 | 200 | 300 | 400 | 500 |

MILES

This map shows only the local setting of the struggle. The Japanese had virtually uninterrupted sea communications via the 120-mile-wide Korean Strait; the Russians were dependent upon the single-track Trans-Siberian Railway, which in 1904 had a gap of 100 miles at Lake Baikal.

railway toward Mukden, the Japanese were able to concentrate on Port Arthur, which capitulated after a four-months' siege in December. In February, 1905, the Japanese armies won a further big battle at Mukden. Despite these reverses, the Russians, who were now being reinforced steadily over the Trans-Siberian Railway and whose resources were by no means exhausted, held their ground north of Mukden and needed only a single strategic success to achieve a stalemate against their smaller adversary. Hence the importance, as well as the dramatic interest, attaching to the long voyage of the Russian Baltic fleet, which was hastily fitted out and left its home bases in October, 1904. The news of the fall of Port Arthur led the Russians to delay for three months off Madagascar while awaiting reinforcements. In May all eight battleships were destroyed by Admiral Togo in the most decisive of modern naval battles, fought as the fleet tried to pass through the Strait of Tsushima into the Sea of Japan to join forces with the remaining Russian naval units at Vladivostok.

Witte was restored to power as the negotiator of the Treaty of Portsmouth (New Hampshire), in which Russia sacrificed a little less than she had feared. No war indemnity was exacted, though the Japanese gained an equivalent in public works and properties in the Liaotung Peninsula and along the South Manchurian Railroad, where the Russians surrendered all claims. In addition, they ceded the southern half of the island of Sakhalin, and acknowledged that in Korea the "paramount political, military, and economic interests" were those of Japan, while undertaking to renounce any exclusive claims for Russian interests in Manchuria, which was to be equally independent of the Japanese. Each side had spent about $1,000,000,000 and lost nearly 250,000 men in killed and wounded, but what one had gained and the other had lost in terms of prestige was enormous, incalculable, and fraught with wide consequences.

■ THE GROWTH OF OPPOSITION

The immediate consequence of the defeat of Russian arms abroad was to give at least a temporary victory to revolutionary forces at home. The year of the Portsmouth treaty was also the year of the Constitutional Manifesto, published by the tsar under extreme pressure in October, a fact which will warrant an examination of the growth of an opposition which was about to become briefly but significantly effective. For military failure merely brought to kindling point a smoldering discontent affecting nearly all the main aspects of Russian life.

The passage of time had increased rather than diminished the land hunger among the peasants, the average household allotment in European Russia having sunk from thirty-five acres in 1877 to twenty-eight acres in 1905. In industry there had been a tendency for earnings to increase during the first period of expansion, but in 1899–1903 there was a slump in which the gains were lost, resulting in July, 1903, in a general strike which brought out a quarter of a million men in South Russia. The liberals in the zemstvos had been rebuffed at the very beginning of the reign, as we have seen, and were further humiliated by persistent rumors that Witte intended to abolish local self-government as being incompatible with autocracy. There was also grave unrest among university students, who were forbidden any form of corporate activity under the rules imposed since 1884. In 1899 they went on strike, but the government restored discipline by providing that students expelled or suspended from university attendance would be drafted automatically into the army. Last, the economic and social bases of opposition were supplemented by bitter national antagonisms. Not for nothing had Russia been called "that great graveyard of nationalities." Poland, Georgia, Finland, the Baltic Provinces, and the Ukraine all had claims based on past history and pride in their own religions, languages, and literatures, which—as the Jews knew by long and sad experience—were liable to cut across purely economic and social interests for better and for worse.

At least three types of leadership had been trying to organize this amorphous mass of discontent for the benefit of their own political program. The least important for the time being was the Marxist body, which had been founded by the ex-Populist, Plekhanov, in 1883, and became active in the St. Petersburg region in 1895. Its leaders were Lenin and a slightly younger man, Julius Martov, who was descended from a line of rabbinical scholars; their joint organization was formally established as the Social Democratic Labor Party three years later. Lenin was then already in exile, and eight of the nine delegates who formed the party were likewise promptly arrested. Nothing of practical importance had therefore been achieved when the party held its second conference in 1903, adjourning from Brussels to London, where a split developed between a minority group (hence called Mensheviks) under Martov and a majority group (Bolsheviks), which was headed by Lenin. The former held that the first postrevolutionary stage should be a democratic republic, the latter that Russia should pass immediately to the dictatorship of the proletariat. This difference of program corresponded to a difference of method, Martov favoring the creation of a large party, democratically controlled by its members, Lenin, a restricted body of dedicated revolutionaries under authoritarian control. Lenin's organization was fated ultimately to shake the world, but in the first years of the new century neither Mensheviks nor Bolsheviks left any great mark upon Russian society.

The same could not be said, however, of the Social Revolutionaries, a party formed in 1900 from the Populist group, which had revived with the revival of general unrest in the preceding decade. The Social Revolutionaries believed that the fall of the monarchy would lead directly to socialism, so that full cooperation with the liberal middle class was a correct technique to employ. They believed, as the Populists had done, in the full participation of the peasants in the revolutionary process, making possible the socialization of the land under the supervision of the commune. They believed in general in the virtues of decentralized control and the abolition of bureaucracy, whereas the Marxists favored a bureaucratic centralism. Finally, they believed more wholeheartedly than the Marxists in backing up their propaganda with the regular practice of terrorism.

It is characteristic of the appeal that the Social Revolutionaries made to youth that their first shot was fired by a twice-expelled student who fatally wounded the minister of education. In 1902 they shot the minister of the interior; in 1904 his successor, Plehve, was blown up as he rode in his carriage under close police guard; in February, 1905, the tsar's uncle, commander of the Moscow garrison, was assassinated in the Kremlin in broad daylight. These are only a few dramatic examples of a campaign which compassed the deaths of obscure functionaries as well as the supposed leaders of repression; it was intensified year by year until 1907, when the terror claimed 2500 victims—about seven murders a day.

Nevertheless, at the dawn of the revolutionary year, 1905, the future of Russia appeared to lie with yet a third force to which popular discontent had lent strength. The government's attacks upon the zemstvos, which were intensified by Plehve, caused their leaders, such as the historian Paul Miliukov,[6] then recently dismissed as a troublemaker from a post at Moscow University, to agitate by private conferences and a smuggled journal on behalf of the view that social reform required the establishment of representative government in Russia. This agitation came to a head at a conference in Kharkov in September, 1903, at which a Union of Liberation was formed, linking the zemstvo constitutionalists with other liberal intellectuals. Next autumn the zemstvos demanded a constituent assembly as their maximum, a legislative assembly as their minimum, program, but all they got was the elaboration of an existing project for the enlargement of the council of state—from which the tsar himself struck out a proposal to include elected representatives of the zemstvos and other bodies.

■ REVOLUTION AND REACTION, 1905–1907

Three weeks after the surrender of Port Arthur to the Japanese, the internal conflict likewise came to a head in St. Petersburg. On Bloody Sunday Father Gapon, a priestly demagogue who received his pay but not necessarily his instructions from the police, organized a march of working-class petitioners to the Winter Palace, some of whom carried sacred icons and portraits of the tsar. They were shot down in hundreds—even the official estimate was 130 dead —by the soldiers who barred their way. As a result the image of the tsar as the beneficent Little Father was shattered, the strike movement already in progress became more vehement, and the liberals gained fresh courage. The government thereupon announced the intention to institute a rather vaguely defined program of reform, which included a consultative assembly to be elected by the people in a manner unspecified, and in April full toleration was conceded to the religious dissenters.

But while the country was kept waiting for details of the official proposals, the Union of Liberation and various other groups representative of the zemstvos and of professional organizations, under the leadership of Miliukov, began to press for a constituent assembly based on manhood suffrage. Their voice

6. 1859–1943. Son of an architect, he became an important historian and teacher at Moscow University; he formed the Constitutional Democratic Party and was its leader until 1917, when he became foreign minister. His ideas, and perhaps also his personality, were too rigidly western to be popular.

seemed the more likely to be heard because news of military disasters continued to foment unrest: there was an eleven-day mutiny in the heavy cruiser *Potemkin*, belonging to the Black Sea squadron, and countless unpublicized agrarian disturbances against which the big landowners were for the moment helpless. Finally, in early August, just before the humiliating Treaty of Portsmouth was signed, the government announced an electoral procedure which would give great weight to the hypothetically loyal mass of peasants (though through a system of indirect voting) and give no vote at all to the bulk of the urban industrial population.

The result was a general strike, which the government was for a time powerless to combat. It began in Moscow, spread from the railways to the telegraph and telephone services, and eventually engulfed the whole of industry, the public offices, and even the *corps de ballet*. When Witte, returning from Portsmouth, New Hampshire, with the laurels of a peacemaker, was called in to advise the tsar, the only means of communication with the Peterhof Palace, eighteen miles from St. Petersburg, was by boat. The middle-class demand for a constituent assembly based on manhood suffrage had been endorsed by a widely based Peasant Union at a secret conference in Moscow at the beginning of August. In October the demands of the St. Petersburg workers, through their Soviet, or council of delegates, in which the guiding influence was that of the Mensheviks and a certain Leon Trotsky, were more radical: a democratic republic to be proclaimed forthwith under the protection of a workers' militia. Witte therefore advised the tsar that one possibility was to appoint a military dictator—a post which his second cousin, the Grand Duke Nicholas, then in command of the St. Petersburg garrison, refused to accept. The only other possibility, in Witte's view, was to concede the constitution which he was prepared to draft and operate.

In writing to his mother, the widow of the last successful Autocrat of All the Russias, Nicholas excuses his decision in the following terms:

> Witte put it quite clearly to me that he would accept the Presidency of the Council of Ministers only on the condition that his program was agreed to. . . . We discussed it for two days and in the end, invoking God's help I signed. . . . In my telegram I could not explain all the circumstances which brought me to this terrible decision which nevertheless I took quite consciously. . . . There was no other way out than to cross oneself and give what everyone was asking for.[7]

The October Manifesto, which the tsar promulgated with such evident reluctance, announced as an immutable rule that every law must be approved by the State Duma; promised the extension of the franchise for the Duma election to the classes excluded by the arrangement made two months earlier; and invested every citizen with certain elementary rights, such as freedom of speech

7. Quoted by R. PARES, *The Fall of the Russian Monarchy* (1939), p. 90.

and association and protection from arbitrary arrest or imprisonment without trial. The absolute autocracy was thus at an end. Whatever his subsequent vacillations, the tsar had taken a long and irretraceable step in the direction of parliamentary government and liberty for the individual as practiced in the West.

Witte now took office as president of the Council of Ministers, a term which implied the introduction for the first time in Russian history of a cabinet system. Pobedonostsev vacated the position he had occupied so long on the steps of the throne, and Miliukov and other liberals were given a chance of office. They declined because they distrusted Witte, who had to choose bureaucrats of the old regime instead, to the lasting misfortune of the liberal cause. At the same time the mounting urgency of the agrarian claims was recognized by an immediate announcement that all redemption payments would be finally terminated in the course of a twelvemonth. Witte also cut his losses in Finland, where the Social Democrats had organized an effective general strike. The Finnish constitution was not only restored but remodeled, with universal suffrage for both sexes at the age of twenty-four.

Witte's policy was designed to ride out the storm. In the closing months of 1905 the countryside was ablaze with agrarian outbreaks, in which over two thousand manor houses were destroyed; the Trans-Siberian railroad was in the hands of rebellious troops returning from the war; and St. Petersburg and other large cities were being organized for some further revolutionary stroke by their Soviets. But by December a showdown appeared practicable. The members of the St. Petersburg Soviet were arrested, whereupon the leadership among the extremists passed to the Soviet of Soldiers at Moscow; they resorted to an armed rising, but were crushed by a Guards regiment and artillery within a week. A start was then made upon the more formidable task of suppressing the movement toward complete expropriation of big landowners, which the Peasant Union had called for at its second conference in November, and the nationalist movements which were challenging the reduced power of Russia in all her border provinces.

In the early months of 1906, however, the revolution was a spent force, and the introduction of quasi-parliamentary government could now take place in an atmosphere almost of anticlimax. The elections to the first State Duma were held as promised, under a revised law which allowed almost universal indirect suffrage and gave the urban population its due. The result was an assembly in which the Constitutional Democratic Party (or Cadets), as the liberals were now called, occupied fully one-third of the seats and were the predominant force. But before the Duma was inaugurated on April 26, 1906, its powers—and hopes—had been enormously reduced.

The State Council, remodeled to consist, as to one half, of Crown nominees and the other half of representatives of public bodies, was to have concomitant powers of legislation. A series of Fundamental Laws was announced, which reserved to the Crown the control of the Orthodox Church, the declaration of war and peace, the right to dissolve the Duma and to make emergency regulations when it was not in session, and sole authority over the ministers. Since these Fundamental Laws were to be immutable except on the initiative of the Crown, the hope of establishing responsible government had suddenly vanished. Moreover, the author of the constitution had ceased to preside over its destinies. After Witte had negotiated a record loan from France (supported by Britain), the tsar could feel more independent, and Witte himself, having disappointed everybody's expectations—including probably his own—was glad to give place to Goremykin. This new minister was an elderly bureaucrat in whose eyes representative institutions were nonsense. At his side there loomed a more formidable figure, Peter Stolypin,[8] a landowner who had won renown as a provincial governor by his resolute handling of outbreaks among the peasantry.

The situation remained tense for a considerable period. The First Duma sat for two and a half months, virtually united in its opposition to the Goremykin ministry, whose resignation it repeatedly demanded. For a moment the tsar contemplated a transfer of power to Miliukov, which might have changed the course of Russian history, but instead he decided to dissolve the Duma in July, with provision for its successor to assemble in the following February. By then Stolypin, promoted to the headship of the government, had transformed the situation on two fronts. He used an emergency provision in the constitution both to inaugurate a new stage in the land reform (which will be discussed later) and to institute a system of field courts-martial for crushing the terrorists. For some time there continued to be more assassinations than executions, and Stolypin's own daughter was crippled for life in a bomb outrage at his summer residence, in which the Social Revolutionaries killed thirty-one innocent victims. But before the close of 1907 capital sentences freely imposed by summary courts and punitive expeditions directed against disaffected nationalities had restored order throughout the vast empire.

By the same date order had been restored also in the central institutions of government. The Second Duma sat hardly longer than the first. The Constitutional Democrats were outnumbered by the sixty-five Social Democrats and thirty-four Social Revolutionaries, whose parties had boycotted the previous election. When it was clear that approval for Stolypin's land reform, which stole the thunder of the Left, would not be forthcoming, a pretext was found for a

8. 1862–1911. He was a landowner of the western provinces, where other landowners were Polish, and governor of Saratov on the Volga, where the Social Revolutionaries organized big agrarian disturbances. A resourceful speaker and resolute administrator, he was opposed by both extremes in the Duma and at the time of his assassination was awaiting dismissal by the tsar, who resented his authority.

sudden dissolution. Then came the decisive stroke—the issue of a new electoral law in defiance of the constitutional rights of the Duma as stated in the immutable rule of the October Manifesto. Its effect was to minimize the representation of the peasants, the professional classes, and the smaller nationalities, and to maximize that of the country gentry, the largest urban property owners, and any Great Russian minority. To illustrate the last point, the Poles had their total representation cut from thirty-six to fourteen, of whom Warsaw would return only two—one for the Polish, and one for the Russian, inhabitants of the Polish capital.

■ THE STOLYPIN REGIME AND ITS DEVELOPMENT TO 1914

Stolypin had triumphed. When the Third Duma assembled in November, 1907, out of a total of 442 members, approximately 150 belonged to parties of the right and about the same number were Octobrists (moderates who thought that the October Manifesto went far enough toward reform). There were only 53 Cadets; the Social Democrats, most of whose members in the Second Duma had been given heavy prison sentences at the end of its session, were now reduced to 14; the Social Revolutionaries had boycotted the election. This Duma lasted its full term of five years, and the Duma which followed it in 1912 was even more conservative. Stolypin, too, had conservative successors when his five years in office ended with his assassination by a quondam police spy. The tsar had been about to dismiss him through envy of his masterful successes.

As regards the land, Stolypin adopted a policy which was both realistic and ruthless. It was realistic because it recognized that a large body of reasonably satisfied peasant proprietors would be a conservative influence more durable than that of any nobles; it was also ruthless because it unhesitatingly allowed the weakest to go to the wall. The Third Duma eventually confirmed his land decrees which he had expounded in trenchant terms to its recalcitrant predecessor:

> The government has placed its bet, not on the needy and the drunken, but on the sturdy and the strong—on the sturdy individual proprietor who is called upon to play a part in the reconstruction of our tsardom on strong monarchical foundations.[9]

The war and the Revolution supervened so quickly that Stolypin's work can be judged only as one of the great might-have-beens of history. In ten years, however, the proportion of peasant households in European Russia which possessed hereditary rights of ownership in lieu of communal tenure and joint family ownership, with all their hampering restrictions upon the enterprise of the individual, had risen from 20 to over 50 percent. In the same period not

9. Speech of May, 1917, quoted by A. E. MAZOUR, *Russia Past and Present* (1951), p. 378.

much more than 10 percent of land allotted had been consolidated into enclosed farms, but there was also a great deal of land where partial consolidation
had made a compulsory rotation of crops unnecessary.

The increase of efficiency in Russian agriculture, however, did nothing to
help the ever-growing number of landless peasants, except in so far as it stimulated an industrial development which might eventually absorb the superfluous
supply of labor. But Stolypin did his best to open up two additional resources to
the more enterprising of the land-hungry peasants. He greatly encouraged the
Peasant Bank, which could advance the entire purchase price of land to an
individual peasant for repayment through a long-term mortgage. This stimulated the sale of imperial and state property, and more especially the property
of nobles, so that total peasant holdings were increased in ten years by 6 percent.
Even so, the general position in European Russia in 1914—more than half a
century after the liberation—was that the peasants held only two-fifths of all
land, though the fraction would be appreciably higher if forest and waste could
be excluded from the calculation. The other resource available was the opening
up of Siberia. A resettlement bureau had been established as early as 1896 to
plant groups of peasants along the line of the advancing railroad, but it was only
under Stolypin that a large-scale movement was seriously encouraged. In 1908
no fewer than 759,000 made the long journey, but thereafter the number was
never quite so high again and a significant proportion found the life so rigorous
that they returned to European Russia. Altogether Siberia between 1896 and
1914 absorbed 3,500,000 colonists, whereas the natural growth in the rural
population from which they came was about 30,000,000.

The trend of Stolypin's agrarian policy was in the right direction, though
it remains an open question whether, if there had been no war in 1914, the
system of peasant proprietorship at which he aimed could finally have triumphed in what was after all a slow-moving rural society. Though the dearth of
land continued, there were not wanting changes to encourage the peasant. By
1906 his status was much more nearly that of a free and equal citizen: local
officialdom and the land captains had lost most of their power over his movements and actions, and his representatives in the zemstvo had ceased to be
chosen for him by the governor. There was a remarkably rapid growth in cooperative societies, especially for the supply of credit. Some progress was made
with the provision of nation-wide rural elementary education, promised by a
law of 1908. By 1911 about one-quarter of the seven to fourteen age group were
attending school, and the schools were losing their narrowly religious character.
Perhaps it is significant that in the last years before the war, while industrial
strikes were once more on the increase, the number of local agrarian disturbances definitely declined.

The Social Democratic leaders, Menshevik and Bolshevik alike, had been driven underground by 1908, as we have seen. Stolypin and his immediate successors did their best to exterminate trade unions (which were in theory tolerated by a law of March, 1906) by measures forbidding them to organize public meetings and banning strikes as disturbances of the social order. In 1912 the minister of the interior was able to dismiss the outcry against the misuse of troops at the Lena goldfield in Siberia, where two hundred strikers were killed, with the bland observation, "It has always been so—it always will be so." In fact, up to the year 1914 the strikes were primarily an economic phenomenon in no way endangering the stability of the regime. Even at the end of a quarter of a century of industrial expansion, the level of real wages was still so close to mere subsistence that striking was considered as a natural reaction on the part of the workers and had few political overtones.

Instead, the most urgent problem in the Stolypin era, apart from the land, was that of the non-Russian nationalities, to which the upheavals of 1905 had seemed to present the opportunity for release. But Stolypin was himself an avowed believer in "a great Russia," and his supporters in the Third Duma included representatives of the ultranationalist Union of the Russian People and its later offshoot and rival, the Union of Michael the Archangel. These organizations, which were responsible for pogroms and even for the murder of left-wing politicians, had the backing of the tsar and subventions from public funds. Though Jews were eligible for the franchise and for membership in the Duma, all their existing disabilities were retained. In general, the reduction of the representation of minor nationalities, already noted as a feature of the new electoral system of 1907, corresponded to a return to their former subject status. Thus a law of 1910 overruled the restored constitution of Finland in all matters which the Russian legislative authorities might deem to be of imperial interest. Attacks were made upon the Ukrainian language, similar to those which had long been in use as a means of holding in check the national aspirations of the Poles. Finally, in 1911, when zemstvo institutions were belatedly introduced into the western provinces, the predominance of the Russian minority among their inhabitants was secured by holding elections in nationally grouped colleges and expressly requiring that a majority of zemstvo members and employees be Russian.

Up to the outbreak of war in 1914, the direction that Russian internal development would finally take was very uncertain. The quasi-constitutional regime had one big achievement to its credit—Stolypin's land reform—and some smaller ones, such as the elementary education law, which justified the existence of the Duma. In the words of Miliukov, it had succeeded "in making itself an indispensable factor in the national life." Since capitalist industry, which had been the harbinger of political democracy in other countries, was now advancing rapidly in Russia, the Duma might be expected to gather strength. But the forces of reaction were still very powerful, both in repressing subject nationalities and in maintaining, even within the charmed circle of Great Russians, high barriers of social and economic privilege. This situation was made all the more perilous by the blind obscurantism of the court. As for the insurrectionary forces, which in 1905 seemed ready to overthrow the monarchy, they had been driven underground and in the eyes of most contemporaries had ceased to count. Nevertheless, the last word is with Lenin, who remarked in 1913 from his place of exile that a war between Russia and Austria-Hungary would be "a very useful thing for revolution."

Reading List: Chapter 14

The New Cambridge Modern History, vol. XI (1962), ch. 13. Russia from 1860 to 1906.

Vernadsky, G., *A History of Russia* (4th ed., 1954; paperback, 1961), chs. 10–12.

Kennan, G., *Siberia and the Exile System* (1958), a reprint of the 1891 edition, chs. 2–5. Firsthand reports by an American visitor of 1885.

Shotwell, J. T., and Deák, F., *Turkey at the Straits* (1940), chs. 6–8. Russia and Turkey from 1856 to 1912.

Maynard, J., *Russia in Flux* (1948), ch. 2. The peasant in the nineteenth century.

Kohn, H. (ed.), *The Mind of Modern Russia* (1955), ch. 10. Danilevsky and Pan-Slavism.

Tompkins, S. R., *The Russian Intelligentsia: Makers of the Revolutionary State* (1957), chs. 3, 4, 9. Nihilism, Populism, beginnings of Marxism.

Dallin, D., *The Rise of Russia in Asia* (1949), chs. 2–3. Russia, Japan, and the Far East, 1890–1905.

Wilson, Edmund, *To the Finland Station* (1940; paperback, 1953), Part III, chs. 1–4. Early years of Lenin and Trotsky.

Haimson, L. H., *The Russian Marxists and the Origins of Bolshevism* (1955), chs. 7–11. Lenin and Plekhanov.

Wolfe, Bertram D., *Three Who Made a Revolution: A Biographical History* (1948; paperback, 1955), chs. 9, 12–14. Lenin's early revolutionary plans.

Halpern, A. J., "Revolution in Russia, 1905 and 1917," *History Today*, vol. IV (1954), no. 2.

Chapter 15

Austria-Hungary,
Italy, and the Lesser Powers

Intermediate Status of Austria-Hungary and Italy
Lands of the Dual Monarchy
Turkey and the Balkans
The Kingdom of Italy
The Iberian Peninsula
Stabler Small Powers North of the Alps
Conclusion

■ INTERMEDIATE STATUS OF AUSTRIA-HUNGARY AND ITALY

One of the most interesting aspects of the forty years' peace, as the period 1871–1911 is sometimes called, is the great opportunity for self-development which it gave to the lesser powers, whose varying fortunes are now to be examined. With this category it is appropriate to group the last two of the six great powers, which in the theory and practice of contemporaries constituted the Concert of Europe. Austria-Hungary and Italy were peers of the other four in population; both Vienna and Rome were unquestionably among the principal centers of European civilization; and, whereas the Hapsburg lands and the Hapsburg emperor had already been dominant factors in power politics for several centuries, the new Kingdom of Italy was only too eager to assert its claims to equal consideration. But in point of fact neither country had the strength needed at this time to sustain the role of a great power. Conflicts between nationalities reduced the Dual Monarchy to a condition so precarious

416

SIGNIFICANT EVENTS

1867	Establishment of the *Ausgleich* in Austria-Hungary and of two-chamber parliament in Sweden
1876–1909	Reign of Abdul Hamid II in Turkey
1885	Unification of Bulgaria and Eastern Rumelia
1893	Manhood suffrage (with plural voting) introduced in Belgium
1896	Italian army defeated at Adowa: fall of Crispi
1898	Spanish-American War
1901	Responsible government restored in Denmark
1905	Haakon VII became king of Norway
1907	Manhood suffrage introduced in Austria
1908	Young Turk revolution (July)
1910	Republican revolution in Portugal

that one of its own statesmen declared it to be ready to step into the place of the dying Ottoman Empire as "the sick man of Europe." As for Austria's south-western neighbor and former dependent, d'Azeglio said: "We have made Italy, we have now to make Italians"—an uphill task which involved the new state in strenuous but largely ineffective efforts at self-assertion.

In the diversity of European life lie much of its charm and a large part of its value. But in a survey of what was happening in its various regions, the points of resemblance deserve to be noticed as well as the differences in opportunities and in the effective response to opportunity.

■ LANDS OF THE DUAL MONARCHY

The Austro-Hungarian monarchy, though composed of two states, formed a single unit from the standpoint of international law because of certain common institutions provided in the *Ausgleich*, or Compromise, of 1867. The

417

main link was the monarchy, and it affected the whole working of the scheme that Francis Joseph remained politically active almost to the end of a very long reign (1848–1916). He, as sovereign, appointed common ministers of foreign affairs, defense, and finance. They could not be simultaneously members of the separate government in Austria or Hungary, and a Crown council, to which the emperor-king occasionally summoned them along with his two prime ministers, had no basis in the constitution. On the contrary, the sixty-man delegation which each parliament appointed annually to vote on the common budget and any other common measures, though it met in the same place (each capital, alternately) and at the same time as the other delegation, held no common deliberations whatever. But the system made it possible to maintain a common foreign policy, based from 1879 on the German alliance, which suited Hungary almost as completely as Austria; a common army, over which the emperor-king successfully asserted his rights of control; and a common financial system, which included a customs union—an institution of the highest signifi-cance, but one that the Hungarians were entitled to abolish if they chose. From 1878 onward the occupied Turkish provinces of Bosnia-Herzegovina were added to the responsibilities of the common finance minister, for the character-istic reason that the Hungarians refused either to take an additional Slav population under their own charge or to see such a population added to the charge of the Austrians.

Although the Compromise was both complex and cumbrous, creaking more and more as time went on, it lasted for a full half-century. It was not, however, a machine which could easily be adapted to changing needs, as the balance of power in the Hapsburg lands was modified. As a force in interna-tional affairs the Dual Monarchy was from the outset weakened by the need to play off German-Austrian against Magyar interests; with the growth of Slavdom its international position became progressively feebler. This becomes all the clearer when the two halves of the monarchy are considered separately.

In Austria the city of Vienna, with its glittering aristocratic society, its artistic and intellectual achievements—it was the home of Freud as well as of Schnitzler and Johann Strauss—its highly developed bureaucracy, and its swarm of luxury trades, provided a fine center for that half of the Dual Mon-archy which was officially defined as "the kingdoms and countries represented in the Reichsrat." The emperor ruled as a constitutional monarch, through ministers responsible to the lower house of the bicameral legislature. But the elections were organized on a system of classes, which gave the peasants and qualified townspeople about three-eighths each, while the remaining quarter of the total representation went to the great landed proprietors. The upper house, too, was heavily weighted on the side of large property, and the emperor through his ministers had a power of emergency legislation valid as long as the legislature was not in session. When it is added that the emperor had effective control over all the proceedings of the seventeen provincial diets, it is clear that this was a constitutional system which could easily lead to an utter impasse. That it did not do so was due to the skill with which the imperial government manipulated the rivalries of the different nationalities.

At the very outset, in 1871, the emperor wished to broaden the basis of support by receiving the crown of Bohemia at Prague, thus taking into partnership the most industrialized people in his dominions. Since both Germans and Magyars objected to the admission of the Czechs as a third partner, the chance was let slip. For social reasons, it was easy to make a more lasting *rapprochement* with the big Polish landowners of Galicia. But the main supporters of the Empire were the German-speaking Liberals, who had affinities with the party on which Bismarck was then relying further north: they organized the class-franchise system described above, and encouraged the influx of Jews to Vienna, where mounting prejudice held them responsible for the financial collapse of 1873. In spite of trade depression the general record of the Liberals was good, in matters ranging from religious toleration and freedom of the press to the principle at least of universal elementary education. But when they opposed the occupation of Bosnia-Herzegovina, it was tempting to Francis Joseph to turn to a fresh parliamentary combination, made between the Conservatives, natural champions of imperial prerogative, and one or another of the Slav peoples.

An able and experienced parliamentarian, Count Taaffe,[1] then ruled for fourteen years. His greatest success was that he induced the Czechs to end a boycott of the Reichsrat, which they had imposed since 1871, and to support the Conservative cause there, in return for a series of concessions to their wishes as regards language, education, and administration in the Bohemian province. But the nationalist appetite grew; in particular, the Young Czech Party, of which Professor T. G. Masaryk[2] was already the leading light, adopted an obstructive attitude in the Reichsrat, which caused an Old Czech moderate to enquire with prophetic insight:

> What will you do with your country, which is too small to stand alone? Will you give it to Germany or to Russia, for you have no other choice if you abandon the union with Austria?[3]

1. 1833–1895. A nobleman of Irish lineage, he was, though three years his junior, Francis Joseph's friend since childhood. Prime minister of Austria, 1868–1870, and 1879–1893, he ruled by combining Catholic, Czech, and Socialist parties in parliament against the German Liberals.
2. 1850–1937. Son of a Slovak coachman on the imperial estates, he became professor of philosophy and sociology at Prague, and was in the Austrian parliament 1881–1893 and 1912–1914. He exposed bogus Czech manuscripts and fraudulent anti-Semitism as well as forgeries used by Austria against Serbs, and worked abroad in 1914–1918 to secure independence for Czechoslovakia, of which he was made president (1918–1935) and honored as a true philosopher-king.
3. Prince Charles Schwarzenberg, quoted by A. J. May, *The Hapsburg Monarchy, 1867–1914* (1951), p. 199.

Prague was for a time placed under martial law, and as the party vendettas in the Reichsrat became more and more unruly, resort was often had to emergency decrees. Nevertheless, the issue on which Taaffe eventually fell from power was one in which he had the support of the Young Czechs as well as of several of the German-language groups—a proposal for extending the franchise to all literate men, which was bitterly opposed by the Conservatives and other bodies which believed that their prospects would suffer.

The decade of the 1890's saw the rapid growth of the Christian Socialist Party, based on Vienna, where support for the small man, social reform, civic improvements, the Catholic Church, and an enlightened attitude toward every group except the Jews and the capitalists were popularized by the self-made lawyer, later burgomaster, Karl Lueger. The growth of industry was also helping the growth of their rivals, the Social Democrats: they, too, were primarily interested in social reform. Meanwhile, interracial politics had reached such a pitch of fury that a connoisseur was able to collect 1763 abusive epithets from the Reichsrat debates. Then came the Russian upheaval of 1905 and the institution of the Duma, encouraging Francis Joseph to adopt the view that, since all else had failed, the asperities of nationalism might possibly be softened by the introduction of full democracy. In 1907 a new franchise system gave what was virtually manhood suffrage, except that voting was by national groups, and the wealthier and more educated nationalities received rather more than their share of seats. The result was the return of thirty parties in all, but the national extremists got little representation. Instead, the Christian Socialists emerged as the largest party, while the Social Democrats, with 87 seats, were now more numerous in the Reichsrat than in any other parliament in Europe.

Among the reasons for the emperor's action in 1907 was the situation in the Kingdom of Hungary, where the threat to introduce manhood suffrage—which would put an immediate end to the ascendancy of the Magyar ruling class, and of the Magyars in general—was brought into play by Francis Joseph at this time in order to cow the Magyar nationalists at the head of the government. To explain this it is necessary to go back to the settlement of 1867, which was much more illiberal in Hungary than in Austria, for the lower house of the Hungarian parliament, on which the ministers depended, was oligarchic in character. Only one adult male in four had the vote, for which there were more than fifty different qualifications; there was no secret ballot; and all candidates must be able to speak Magyar, which was the only language used in parliamentary debate and in government. The solitary exception to this basis of Magyarization is significant: the Croats, having served the unity of the Empire so faithfully in 1848, had rights of local self-government, and their Diet sent forty members to the Hungarian lower house to discuss matters of interest to the entire kingdom. For many years the only redress available to the smaller nationalities was emigration, for their representatives were not only effectively excluded from parliament, but an attempt to appeal to Francis Joseph as their king resulted in a prosecution. In education, in the press, and even in family and place names, the policy of Magyarization was ruthlessly pursued, and laws which proclaimed racial equality were systematically ignored.

The Magyars themselves, however, became divided between those who considered the benefits received from the *Ausgleich* to be sufficient warrant for its continuance, and a new Independence Party under Kossuth's son, Francis, which sought to abolish every common institution except the actual person of the sovereign. Kossuth's followers made an issue of the language of command used in the army: if Magyar were placed on a level with German in this respect, the way would be cleared for making it an independent army of Hungary and at the same time they would be imposing the Magyar language upon the minor nationalities, from which the majority of the army contingents came. It was against this proposal that Francis Joseph brought forward the threat of manhood suffrage, by which the Magyars would have been swamped. It remained, however, only a threat, as the Magyars gave way over the army for the time being, and, in the years immediately preceding the First World War, Count Tisza kept the followers of Kossuth at bay, while making very little concession to any nationality except the Croats, to whom he restored certain rights that had been for a time suspended.

In both halves of the monarchy the absence of customs barriers contributed undoubtedly to their economic progress in this period. Though the total population was still more than half agricultural, Bohemia became an important industrial region. In Austria coal output increased by 370 percent, and the

DISTRIBUTION OF POPULATION IN 1910[4]

in thousands

AUSTRIA (by language)		HUNGARY (by language)	BOSNIA-HERZEGOVINA (by religion)
Germans	9,950	2,037	
Magyars	11	10,050	
Slavs: Czechs	6,436		
Slovaks		1,968	
Poles	4,968		
Ruthenes	3,519	472	
Slovenes	1,253		
Croats ⎫		1,833	442
Serbs ⎭	783	1,106	825
Italians	768		
Rumanians	275	2,950	
Others	608	469	631
Total	28,571	20,885	1,898

4. *Chambers's Encyclopaedia* (London, 1955) vol. I, p. 837.

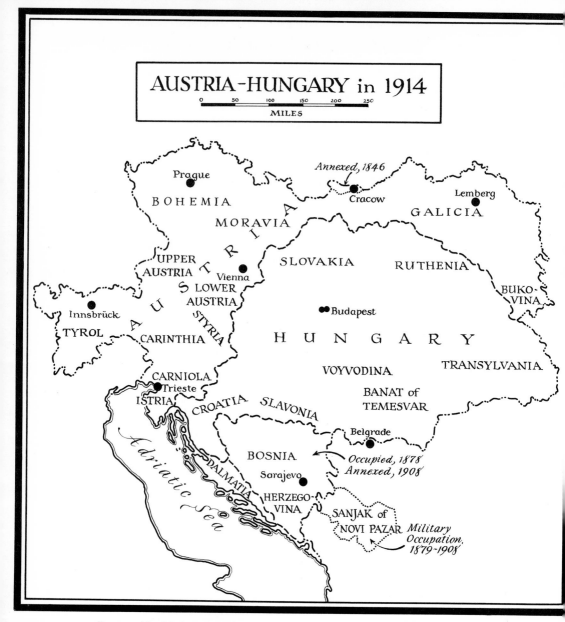

AUSTRIA-HUNGARY in 1914

0   50   100   150   200   250
MILES

Prague

BOHEMIA

MORAVIA

Annexed, 1846

Cracow

Lemberg

GALICIA

UPPER AUSTRIA

Vienna

LOWER AUSTRIA

Innsbrück

TYROL

CARINTHIA

STYRIA

SLOVAKIA

RUTHENIA

BUKO-VINA

Budapest

H U N G A R Y

TRANSYLVANIA

CARNIOLA

Trieste

ISTRIA

CROATIA

SLAVONIA

VOYVODINA

BANAT of TEMESVAR

Belgrade

Adriatic Sea

DALMATIA

BOSNIA

Sarajevo

HERZEGO-VINA

Occupied, 1878
Annexed, 1908

SANJAK of NOVI PAZAR *Military Occupation, 1879-1908*

Compare this with the linguistic map of the same areas given on page 95. Two significant features are the intermingling of nationalities within the country as shown by the intermixture of languages, and the fact that nowhere do the political frontiers of the Dual Monarchy coincide with the linguistic frontiers.

petroleum resources were developed in Galicia. Hungary, with wheat crops which trebled in the last thirty years of the century, was one of the main granaries of Europe, and the extension of the Austro-Hungarian railways from 4,000 to 27,000 miles under the *Ausgleich* suggests that an economic unity was to some extent achieved. But even the economic—to say nothing of the political and social—development of the lands of the Dual Monarchy was retarded by the unsolved problem of the Third Force, the Slavs.

A glance at the table suggests that, when the last peoples were added in 1908, the Slav problem had become insoluble. This must be considered in a later chapter. In the meantime it may be remarked that the hackneyed epithet, "ramshackle empire," is almost an understatement for the condition of weakness to which the unresolved tensions of half a century had reduced the Hapsburg lands.

■ TURKEY AND THE BALKANS

The history of the Ottoman Empire in the reign of Abdul Hamid II (1876–1909) resembles that of the Dual Monarchy, as seen in retrospect at least, in that its lands in Europe and Asia alike were ready to dissolve into other national units, so that the main task of the existing government was to postpone the day of reckoning. Moreover, in the case of their remaining Slav territories, the Turks feared the emergence of the selfsame "Third Force" as did the rulers of Austria-Hungary. The main difference lay in the fact that the dismemberment of Turkey had already proceeded far. In 1878 the Congress of Berlin secured formal acknowledgment by the sultan of the complete independence of Serbia, Rumania, and Montenegro, as well as the concession of complete autonomy to Bulgaria; the Congress also recognized Russia's conquest of a part of Armenia and agreed that Bosnia-Herzegovina should be occupied by Austria-Hungary, and Cyprus by Britain. There was also an important difference in the constitutional position; for the Turkish constitution of 1876, once it had served its purpose of preventing intervention in the internal affairs of Turkey by the powers assembled at the Congress of Berlin, was promptly suspended, and it was as an oriental despot that Abdul Hamid earned his soubriquet of "the Damned."

In the 1880's Abdul Hamid accepted the coup by which self-governing Eastern Rumelia was joined to the new Bulgaria. In addition Tunisia fell to France and Egypt in effect to Britain, while nearer home a considerable area in Thessaly and Epirus was ceded to Greece, which had made no direct gains at the Congress of Berlin. Thenceforth in the two following decades, down to the summer of 1908, the process of disintegration was held in check. In 1895 the Turks were able to stamp out the Armenian nationalist movement in blood without any effective protest by the powers. Only two years later, when the Turks defeated the Greeks in a three-weeks war provoked by Greek claims in Crete, they were allowed to win back part of Thessaly. In Crete, indeed, the powers set up a system of full self-government, but the great Greek island was left under Turkish suzerainty, which was continued in spite of a further rising in favor of union with Greece in 1905.

The most important development of these years was the growth of German influence in Turkey, advertised to the world by visits from the Emperor William II immediately after his accession in 1888 and again on a grander scale ten years later, when he made it clear to the world that the Armenian atrocities had no adverse effect on his friendship with the sultan and his high regard for all Islamic peoples. German traders were quick to build upon the good will generated by Bismarck at the Congress of Berlin, where Germany in the Turkish view figured as the only disinterested peacemaker among the powers. As early as 1883 the Germans had stepped into the shoes of the French as military advisers, when Colmar von der Goltz became the trusted organizer of the Turkish general staff. In 1888 Constantinople had at last been linked up with the other European capitals by rail, and within five years German enterprise carried the line onward from the other side of the Straits to Ankara. By the turn of the century, accordingly, the Deutsche Bank, which had financed the Anatolian Railway and other German business activities in Turkey, had its eyes upon two further prospects—the reopening of the great medieval overland trade route between Constantinople and the Middle East, and the exploitation of mineral deposits, such as the petroleum of Mesopotamia, whose value was unknown to medieval entrepreneurs. Hence the project for the so-called Berlin-Baghdad Railway, for which a definitive convention was signed in 1903. In fact the new line was to run from Konia, where the existing Anatolian Railway terminated in Asia Minor, through Baghdad to Basra on the Persian Gulf, a distance of 1415 miles. The reference to Berlin in the conventional title is also a little misleading, since part of the capital came from French investors and part of the expected benefits were military advantages accruing to the sultan. In granting the concessionaires such lavish inducements as free land, tax exemption, and guaranteed minimum receipts, Abdul Hamid was looking forward to the day when the increased mobility of his army would double its value, whether for driving the British out of Egypt or for suppressing domestic insurrection.

But, while the railway was still hardly more than a pawn in the diplomatic game, Abdul Hamid's prospects were decisively changed by an event occurring in the no man's land or everyman's land of Macedonia, which had been restored from the "Big Bulgaria" to his rule in 1878. Here Bulgars, Greeks, Serbs, Albanians, and even some isolated pockets of Rumanians continued to dispute the claim to the eventual succession in terms of race, language, and religion, with the help of local organizations known as *comitadjis*, whose activities would have been indistinguishable from mere brigandage, did they not, in the words of Samuel Butler:

> Prove their doctrine orthodox
> By apostolic blows and knocks.

In 1898 Russia and Austria attempted to pacify the region by an agreement to maintain the *status quo*. In 1901 the kidnapping of an American woman missionary, whom the *comitadjis* released for a payment of $80,000, advertised the fact that peace still did not reign in Macedonia. The same two powers made a further agreement at Mürzsteg, under which they joined with Britain, France, and Italy in staffing and supervising a gendarmery to assist the Turkish army in maintaining order. Germany significantly abstained. In the summer of 1908, however, the Turkish army corps stationed in Macedonia rose under the auspices of a Committee of Union and Progress to support the aims of the Young Turks. This latter was a movement, organized in 1891 in Geneva and later in Paris, which united army officers, doctors, journalists, and other educated elements in Turkish society to support a policy of westernization. The wily sultan capitulated at once to the mere threat of force, restoring the parliamentary constitution of 1876, proclaiming equality for all races in his dominions, and professing to have disbanded his force of forty thousand spies. For a short time even the peoples of Macedonia exchanged fraternal embraces instead of bullets.

What the Young Turks really aimed at was a rejuvenation of the Ottoman Empire, with equal rights for all *loyal* subjects. The western powers, on the other hand, believed what they wished to believe, namely, that a liberal Turkey was now coming into existence. Turkey's small neighbors in the Balkans were less credulous, but for them too the summer of 1908 marked the beginning of a new situation, one in which their significance for the rest of Europe reached an unexpected climax. This was in contrast with the period of the long peace, in which their development had on the whole been slow. But before these countries are considered separately, it will be convenient to recall that the emancipation of each of them formed part of a long and complicated struggle. This is set out in the table (page 426), which includes for the sake of completeness the results of the Balkan Wars of 1912–1913. These are reserved for discussion in Chapter 17 because they are very closely connected with the outbreak of the First World War.

Serbia and its western neighbor, the little principality of Montenegro, had enjoyed their freedom longest: indeed, the Montenegrins—the Serbs who lived on the "black mountain"—thanks to their inaccessibility and a long-standing friendship with Russia, had never been brought completely under the Turkish yoke. But neither of these two countries had any substantial trade or other important contacts with the outer world, to which they were known chiefly through the feuds of the rival Serb dynasties, the Karageorgevici and the Obrenovici. In 1903 the pro-Austrian Obrenovic king, his consort, and two of the consort's brothers were the victims of a cold-blooded murder plot engineered by army officers. Serbia, where war or violence disturbed the course of every reign, gained an added reputation for barbarism. Under her new king, Peter I, she joined Montenegro in dependence upon Russia, while Austria-Hungary for a time ruined the only Serbian export by a ban on its pigs.

Bulgaria resembled Serbia in the absence of an aristocracy or even a substantial middle class; indeed, in her case the Turkish officials had remained as late as the 1870's. Again like Serbia, the country had little town life, but agriculture provided the Bulgars with comparatively important exports of grain. Moreover, Bulgaria had produced an effective political leader in Stefan Stambulov, an innkeeper's son and sometime Russian nihilist, who established the Saxe-Coburg dynasty on its very precarious throne and earned the soubriquet of "the Bismarck of the Balkans."

Rumania differed in several respects from the poor peasant states that have just been described. For one thing, she had a different approach to power politics, because she looked to Hungarian Transylvania rather than to Turkish Macedonia for the field in which she hoped someday to assert her major national claims. For another thing, Rumania was the fortunate possessor, not only

RE-EMERGENCE OF BALKAN NATIONS

	MONTENEGRO	SERBIA	GREECE	RUMANIA (PRINCIPALITIES)	BULGARIA	BOSNIA-HERZEGOVINA	ALBANIA
1800	never fully subjugated	subject to Turks					
1804		in revolt					
1817		autonomous					
1821			in revolt	in revolt			
1830			independent	occupied by Russia			
1856				autonomous			
1861				united			
1876					in revolt	in revolt	
1878	independent	independent		independent	autonomous	occupied by Austria-Hungary	
1881			enlarged				
1885					enlarged		
1908					independent	annexed by Austria-Hungary	
1913	enlarged	enlarged	enlarged	slightly enlarged	slightly enlarged		independent

of a fertile grain-exporting region, but of an important industrial resource in its petroleum wells, with the result that her total trade exceeded that of the rest of the Balkan countries combined. The capital, Bucharest, was the only large city between Budapest in Hungary and Constantinople, a token of the considerable prosperity which Rumania enjoyed under her Hohenzollern dynasty.[5] The Belgian-type constitution, which had been established since the 1860's, was more stable than the democratic parliamentary institutions of Serbia and Bulgaria. Power rested chiefly with a class of large landowners, who were in origin Greek and in culture Francophile. In 1864 there had been a parcelling out of land among the peasants, but the smallness of the parcels made them still dependent upon wages earned on the big estates. In 1907, partly as a result of events across the frontier in Russia, Rumania experienced a large-scale agrarian rising, which it took a force of 140,000 soldiers to repress. The country was also notorious for anti-Jewish pogroms, in spite of an undertaking to practice complete religious toleration exacted at the Congress of Berlin; the causes included a big influx of Jews from Russia and their alleged prominence as middlemen in the exploitation of peasant agriculturists.

Greece, as befitted the ancient homeland of democracy, was furnished with a single-chamber parliament, elected by manhood suffrage. Greece also had a middle class with a long history of maritime and mercantile enterprise, capable of conducting politics along western lines under the sagacious Danish King George I, who was elected to the vacant throne in 1863 and held it for nearly half a century. But in fact the Greek parliamentarians were as venal as they were verbose, exacting their full price from the government of the day for providing the absolute majority, without which the constitution allowed no law to pass, or the quorum of one half the total membership, without which no political business could be conducted at all. The one outstanding figure, the lawyer and insurgent leader, Eleutherios Venizelos,[6] was at this time concerned only with the previously mentioned insurrections in his Cretan homeland.

■ THE KINGDOM OF ITALY

The Kingdom of Italy had strong connections with both the regions that have so far been surveyed in this chapter. Austria-Hungary, a fellow member with her in the Triple Alliance, was also sovereign over territory in the Trentino, Trieste, and the Istrian Peninsula, which it was the prime object of Italian ambition to reunite with what was claimed to be their motherland. The Ottoman Empire was likewise an area to which the Italians looked for imperial

5. See p. 154.
6. 1864–1936. A lawyer and Liberal politician in Crete, he was prominent in the 1896 rising; he first came into power in Greece in 1909, organized the Balkan League, and supported the Allied cause both before and after Greek intervention in World War I. He presented Greek claims at the peace conference of 1919 with great skill, and was eight times prime minister.

gains—at first vainly, in Tunisia; later, with more success, in Tripoli. Her foreign policy exemplified the status of Italy as technically a great power, but what is of primary concern here is the limiting factor of Italian domestic politics and achievements.

It is tempting to offer the explanation that Italy had no great statesmen to replace the prematurely deceased Cavour or to suggest that quick unification meant slow amalgamation. In reality, the fundamental difficulty was the lack of helpful natural resources—no coal, thin and exhausted soil, lack of good harbors, and mountain barriers impeding the growth of railways—a situation which would have reduced any national government to mean shifts, because its authority could not be based upon a genuine growth in wealth and power. In addition, it must be borne in mind that the Church, in most Roman Catholic countries an influence to reconcile men to authority, was for many years an implacable enemy to the Italian state. The papacy forbade Catholics to take part in political life, while in 1875 the state expelled no fewer than thirty bishops from their sees for refusing to accept the royal authority. Relations became rather easier after the death of Pius IX (1878), but Rome was still a capital city where a rival court with an ancient world-wide prestige treated the king as a usurper.

The newly completed kingdom was ruled at first by the parties of the right, but they made themselves trebly unpopular by retaining the narrow franchise of the original Piedmontese constitution, deprecating educational reform on the score of expense, and introducing what was believed to be the most burdensome tax regime in the whole of Europe—there was even a tax on flour—with the praiseworthy object of balancing the budget. From 1876 onward they gave place to the men of the left, who abolished the hated flour tax, provided elementary schools—though at the end of the century nearly half the population was still illiterate—and increased the electorate from 500,000 to 3,000,000. They continued, however, with a very expensive military and naval program, commensurate with Italy's ambitions as a great power rather than her actual economic resources. They also had a high tariff, with which they tried to safeguard industry and at the same time help to balance the budget; this raised the cost of living to the further detriment of the poor. But for a long time the left kept itself in office with the help of a system known as *trasformismo*, or transformism: party lines were deliberately obscured, awkward critics being induced by cash and other favors to give the ministry their support. The leading ministers, Depretis and then Crispi,[7] were both Sicilians, and their methods of

7. 1819–1901. A Mazzinian who became pro-dictator of Sicily during Garibaldi's expedition, he was not a party man, but, as head of government, aimed at moral unity, harshly repressing disturbances in his native Sicily and building up colonies. At Adowa the Italian commander fought the Abyssinians, against his better judgment, at Crispi's orders.

controlling the electorate descended from bribery to direct intimidation through the southern secret societies of the Mafia and the Camorra. When Crispi fell from power as the person responsible for the colonial disaster at Adowa in 1896, his place was taken by Giolitti,[8] a Piedmontese lawyer with some genuine liberal enthusiasms: in 1912 he introduced manhood suffrage. Alarmed by the growth of radical movements far to the left of the government, the pope now gave Catholics full permission to use the vote on behalf of "the higher interests of society, which must at all costs be protected." But in practice the devious methods of control which had served his predecessors continued under Giolitti right up to the First World War.

The great economic developments which were taking place benefited the north of Italy, not the south, and the northern factory owner and entrepreneur much more than his employees. In the 1880's the completion of the railway network and the establishment of a subsidized mercantile marine promoted the growth of heavy industry, which was necessarily based on imported raw materials. By 1905 the north was also profiting in a new way by the exploitation of hydroelectric power, in which Italy became the leader among the countries of Europe. Agriculture, too, became better organized through the work of agricultural schools and cooperative purchasing societies, and the introduction of drainage schemes and health measures. Again, however, it was the more enterprising north which chiefly profited. Moreover, the total crop raised was never more than two-thirds of the French crop, although the Italian population unlike the French was still rapidly increasing. In 1893 and 1894 the Sicilian farm laborers, feeling that they were worse off than before liberation, rose in revolt, only to be crushed by the former hero of the liberation, Crispi.

In the absence of any effective direction by parliament, the Italians sought remedies elsewhere for the ills against which the country was vainly struggling. Imperialists, indeed, aimed at colonial expansion, which began with posts on the Red Sea coast at Assab and Massawa, grew to include both Eritrea and a long stretch of the Somali coast, but failed disastrously to reach its main objective in Ethiopia. The colonies, with their meager resources and unendurable climate, did almost nothing to relieve the pressure of surplus population, which was therefore forced to give up the attempt to live under the Italian flag. The rate of emigration increased in every decade, until in 1910 it stood at 1.165 percent, the highest rate in the whole of Europe. In such circumstances it was hardly surprising that a virulent, self-pitying form of nationalism grew up outside parliament, a nationalism which claimed that Italy, unless she asserted herself violently, would continue to be treated as "the proletarian among

---

8. 1842–1928. Prime minister in 1892–1894 (when he fell through a bank scandal), 1903–1905, 1906–1909, 1911–1914, and 1920–1921, he opposed participation by Italy in the First World War, and ended up as a discreet opponent of fascism.

nations." Last, the lack of any positive social policy caused bitter resentment to grow up among the industrial masses in the north, where Bakunin's ideas spread from Switzerland. This culminated at the end of the century in an insurrection in Milan, which cost nearly one hundred lives, and in the assassination of King Humbert. Giolitti adopted a more sympathetic attitude to workers than his predecessors, and, although syndicalist projects for transferring the ownership of industry to the workers by direct action had a considerable vogue in north Italy, where there was an effective general strike in 1904, a decade later a manhood suffrage law led to the establishment of a parliamentary Socialist Party of seventy-two members.

■ THE IBERIAN PENINSULA

Spain and Portugal were quasiconstitutional monarchies whose history in many respects resembled that of Italy in this period—a history made up of inconsequent episodes, grave disappointments, and relatively small accessions of prestige abroad or social betterment at home. One difference lies in the fact that Spain, with a population at the end of the nineteenth century of only 18,000,000 to Italy's 32,000,000, was not tempted to rival the Italian effort to figure as a great power. As for Portugal, its population of 5,400,000 was actually exceeded by that of one of the Balkan states (Rumania). Another important difference lies in the contrast between the Italian attempts to build a new colonial empire and the Spanish and Portuguese attempts to prevent the dismantling of their ancient colonial heritages. Third, whereas the House of Savoy did not lose its hold upon the Italian people until the catastrophe of the Second World War, Spain experimented with a republic in 1873–1874; Portugal abandoned monarchy permanently in 1910, and in both countries republicanism was an important factor throughout the period.

As regards the Spanish monarchy, it will be recalled that the search for a new king to replace the dethroned Isabella came first in the chain of events which led directly to the outbreak of the Franco-Prussian War. While that war still raged, the second son of Victor Emmanuel, the first king of united Italy, had arrived in Spain to fill the vacancy; but his principal supporter died by the hand of an assassin on the day of his arrival, and, after experimenting with six governments in two years, Amadeo abdicated to avoid a similar fate. The republic which followed was attacked by each of the four dominant forces in the country —supporters of Isabella's son, supporters of a rival Bourbon line (the Carlists), the leaders of the Church, and the higher officers of the army—with the result that Isabella's son became king in 1874 as Alfonso XII. He was succeeded in 1886 by his posthumously born son of the same name, who in later life proved to be the most adept politician in his realm and kept his seat on an often-tottering throne until 1931. A bicameral legislature was established by the new constitution of 1876, members of the lower house being elected by taxpayers at first, then on the basis of manhood suffrage, and for a time by manhood suffrage with compulsory voting. Whatever the system was, it made no difference, as the respectable and not wholly distinguishable parties of Conservatives and Liberals alternated in office. On one occasion a government newspaper, by excess of zeal, printed the results of the elections before they had been held.

The interest in Spanish affairs accordingly lay elsewhere than in the debates of parliament. Catalonia was demanding a high tariff to shelter the industrial development which was growing up there and to a less extent on the northwest coast among the Basques and in Madrid. The traditional separatism of Barcelona and its hinterland therefore became an increasingly dangerous factor. But the biggest problem was presented by Spain's overseas empire, which for many years had faithfully reproduced the discords and inefficiencies of Spanish government at home. Cuba, followed by Puerto Rico, had staged a series of insurrections since 1869. A new one began in 1895 and was imitated in the Philippines, whereupon the Spanish generals in Cuba applied drastic measures of repression. A combination of idealism, imperialism, and newspaper sensationalism urged on the United States to consider the propriety of intervening, and a Spanish decree offering the Cubans self-government came too late to stay the tide of events. The still unexplained explosion, which destroyed the U.S. battleship *Maine* in Havana harbor, destroyed the transoceanic empire of Spain. Her large but ill-trained army and her obsolete fleet were completely defeated within ten weeks, and the Philippines and Puerto Rico were transferred to American sovereignty and Cuba to American guardianship.

At the present day it appears in retrospect that Spain lost relatively little through the sacrifice of overseas possessions which she lacked the strength to govern and develop. On the other hand, she gained much in the long run through the writers and thinkers, known as the "generation of 1898," who reacted to the disaster by preaching the need for internal reconstruction on a modern European pattern. One result was a serious attempt to limit the numbers of religious houses, which tended to increase as a consequence of persecution in France. The immediate prospect, however, was darkened by the combination between Catalan separatism and extremist socialism. As far back as the years of the republic, Bakunin's teachings had 300,000 adherents among the oppressed peasantry on the great estates of southern Spain, peasants who in the following decades moved into Barcelona in large numbers with the hope of finding industrial employment; from 1888 onward Barcelona was a center of syndicalism. Thus the love of decentralization, a passion for individual freedom, and the aspiration to wrest industrial control from the hands of the employer provided the elements of a powerful separatist movement, which fought even against a socialist movement with national aims based on Madrid.

A peasant revolt broke out in southern Spain in 1892, and was followed by a long series of anarchist bomb outrages, which culminated in an attack on the king during the procession on his wedding day in 1906. In the same year the various separatist parties coalesced in a single *Solidaritat Catalane*. But violence begat violence, the most hated of the repressive measures being one which empowered military courts to try all offenses against the armed forces. In 1909 matters came to a head as the result of a defense crisis. The French activities in Morocco had given Spain the prospect of developing a sphere of influence in the hinterland of her ancient coastal possessions there, which made it urgently necessary to defend the port of Melilla against attacks by tribesmen. When reinforcements were called up in Barcelona, the conscripts were easily persuaded that they were being sent out to protect Jesuit mining interests, and the result was the "tragic week," in which 22 churches and 34 convents were burned down and 175 workers killed by troops in the streets. In the end, martial law had to be proclaimed throughout the country, and the leaders whom the government executed in reprisals included Ferrer Guardia, the famous organizer of antireligious, secularist schools. Thus in 1914 Spain was still too deeply divided for the proper practice of parliamentary government. No compromise seemed possible between the allied forces of the monarchy, Church, army, and big business and those which were ranged behind the banners of anarchism, syndicalism, separatism, and anticlericalism.

The story of Portugal bears a strong resemblance to that of her larger neighbor. After Carlos I succeeded Louis I in 1889, the king himself, being both absolutist and egotistic in temperament, contributed far more directly than the politic Alfonso XIII of Spain to the ultimate downfall of the monarchy. But there was the same kind of two-chambered legislature—though in Portugal there was no approach to manhood suffrage—in which two not very dissimilar parties maintained a political system known as "rotativism," agreeing to successive tenure of office. The republicans, meanwhile, gathered strength outside the charmed circle of the constitution. In 1891 the example of the new republic in Brazil encouraged them to rise in Oporto, which gave the government an excuse for outlawing the party, and a few years later sixty-six opponents of the regime were got rid of in one fell swoop under a new law for banishing alleged anarchists without trial to Timor in the East Indies.

Portugal, too, had problems arising out of her imperial possessions, though her policy was a more positive one than the Spanish, based on the idea of joining Angola and Mozambique in Africa, so as to establish a solid belt of Portuguese territory from east to west—a project known as "the rose-colored map." The claim to do this was based on rights of prior discovery, of exploration (hurriedly arranged in 1877), and even of effective occupation. But in 1890 Britain threatened to sever relations with her oldest ally unless she agreed, without any resort to arbitration, to acknowledge the validity of British claims to advance northward across the disputed area. Portugal was left, however, with African territory twenty times as extensive as the homeland, and this she succeeded in retaining intact, thanks to British abandonment in 1899 of a tentative arrangement with Germany made the year before, by which Portugal might have been induced to pledge colonies to both powers in return for a much-needed loan to the bankrupt Portuguese treasury. Yet her situation remained precarious.[9]

Colonial disappointments strengthened the republican movement, and gave an opening to João Franco to form a new party which was to have a firmer colonial policy. In 1906 Franco was put in power by the king as a dictator who would follow a different path and in fact ruled in direct defiance of all constitutional rights. Within two years the king and his eldest son were assassinated in the streets of Lisbon. The second son, Manoel, dismissed Franco but found no alternative support; he therefore capitulated to the republicans in October, 1910, having reigned for only two and a half years. A new constitution was then set up, with a wide extension of the franchise, disestablishment of the Church, enactment of the right to strike, and a clause requiring the armed forces to be "essentially obedient." In the next sixteen years Portugal had forty-three governments, but three attempts to restore Manoel to the throne all failed.

■ STABLER SMALL POWERS NORTH OF THE ALPS

Europe north of the Alps contained six lesser sovereign powers—Switzerland, Belgium, the Netherlands, Denmark, Sweden, and Norway. In population Belgium came first, with 6,700,000 inhabitants in 1900—not much more than one-third the population of Spain, but about 30 percent larger than either

9. See p. 491.

Portugal, Sweden, or the Netherlands. Switzerland, Denmark, and Norway followed in that order, with 8,000,000 inhabitants in all.

Danish sovereignty extended over Iceland, Greenland, the Faeroes, and the Virgin Islands; self-government was restored to the Icelanders in 1874, and the other possessions did not add substantially to Denmark's wealth or political responsibilities. In respect to valuable overseas possessions Belgium and the Netherlands bore a closer resemblance to the Latin states of southern Europe. Leopold II,[10] the second King of the Belgians, devoted much of his attention during a very long reign (1865–1909) to acquiring a vast territory in tropical Africa, where the slave trade had to be attacked at its source and no great power was willing to see the establishment of a strong rival. Leopold became personal sovereign of the Congo Free State and made a vast fortune in ivory and rubber. But at the turn of the century he incurred the obloquy of the civilized world on account of the barbarities—including the mutilation of reluctant native workers —practiced by his concessionaires, and in 1908 he consented to hand over this very rich possession as a Belgian colony. The Netherlands East Indies, on the other hand, were only a single element, though the most important one, in a widespread maritime empire which had been established by Dutch enterprise in past centuries. The commercial wealth and many of the manufactures of Amsterdam and Rotterdam were sustained by the flow of imports from the Far East. Possession was not challenged by any European power, but the system of forced cultivation in Java was successfully denounced by a former official who wrote under the pseudonym of *Multa Tuli* ("long-suffering"). In the later years of this period the only serious trouble was in North Sumatra, where one of the sultans continued in arms against the Dutch from 1873 down to 1910. Sweden, Switzerland, and Norway each had a flourishing overseas trade but no overseas possessions.

What all these countries of Europe had in common was a constitution which worked, in the sense that it commanded popular support and was not only theoretically adaptable but in actual practice adapted to meet the changing needs of society. All except Switzerland were monarchical in form, and during this period one tiny monarchy became more distinctly independent, when the Grand Duchy of Luxemburg passed from the Netherlands crown to the House of Nassau because it could not under its existing law be inherited by a woman. In Switzerland the executive power was accorded to a federal council of seven members, one of whom was president for the year, and a cantonal council protected the sovereign rights of the twenty-two separate cantons. The essence of

10. 1835–1909. An able diplomat and unscrupulous monopolist, he caused Stanley to open up the Congo territory explored by him, secured recognition for the International Association of the Congo, and in 1885 proclaimed himself as sovereign of the Congo Free State. He was also keenly concerned with the improvement of the Belgian fortresses and army, to the great benefit of his nephew and successor, Albert I.

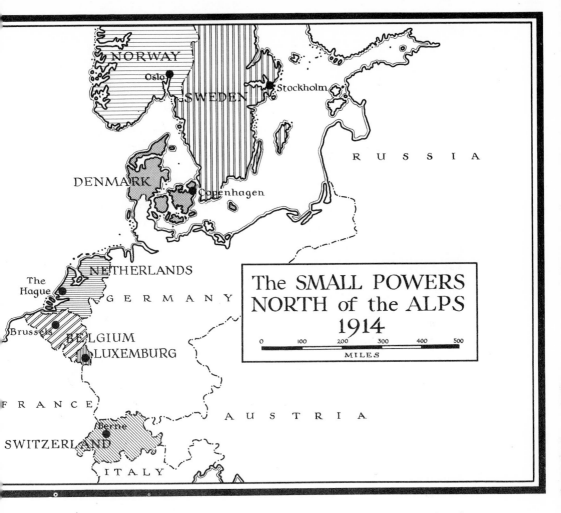

The development of four of these countries is helped by good access to sea communications, that of Belgium by its early and complete railway network, and that of Switzerland by the Alpine tunnels and mountain railways constructed towards the end of the nineteenth century.

each constitution was a strongly established system of representative government and legally protected liberties for the individual citizen.

By 1870 each of these countries had an influential middle class—even Switzerland acknowledged its "railway king"—who concerned themselves primarily with the economic development of the country and its government in their own interests; but that class invariably included a strong liberal element, which aimed at democracy by installments. In consequence the period is marked by educational reforms, which often put these small countries ahead of their larger neighbors in what they provided for the masses, and by extensions of the franchise. Norway achieved manhood suffrage in 1898; Belgium appeared to have reached the same goal five years earlier, but there the propertied classes

had extra votes amounting to three-eighths of the total that could be cast. By 1914 successive changes had brought all the other countries within sight at least of manhood suffrage, and Norway had just extended the vote to women on the same terms as men. Meanwhile Switzerland, which still had some cantons small enough to practice direct democracy as among the ancient Greeks, extended popular control beyond the election of the federal legislature by providing powers of referendum and initiative which enabled the voters themselves to vote upon or to propose new laws.

The common factor which lay behind the political and social progress of all these countries was their economic development. Belgium was the most heavily industrialized region of the Continent, the Netherlands one of the main arteries of its commerce, and Sweden (as we have seen) enjoyed a belated Industrial Revolution, enabling her to profit from the mistakes of others. Denmark, too, earned a special position when she resolutely met the threat of cheap Russian and American grain, which in the 1870's bade fair to ruin her economy, by a highly skillful adaptation of her agriculture to provide pork, bacon, eggs, and dairy products for the markets of her industrial neighbors. Switzerland already had some textile and machinery industries, to which the railways gave a stimulus, while they also brought foreign holiday makers to supplement the once-meager livelihood of the Alpine valleys. As for Norway, the profits of a huge carrying trade were supplemented by the development of Antarctic whaling, of which Norwegians had a virtual monopoly. Her industries, too, like those of other well-watered mountainous terrains which lack coal-bearing strata, began to be transformed by hydroelectric installations.

The contribution of these small peoples to European culture in its widest sense was surprisingly great. Since this will be more fully illustrated in the next chapter, it will be sufficient here to name single examples. To Switzerland, with its special position of internationally guaranteed neutrality, the world owes the institution of the Red Cross, for it was the Swiss banker and philanthropist, Henri Dunant, by chance an eyewitness of the carnage at Solferino, who first roused the conscience of the world to the sufferings of the wounded as potentially a world-wide problem. It was likewise a Swiss committee which organized the first Geneva Convention, signed in 1864, and the International Committee of the Red Cross has always been composed exclusively of Swiss citizens. The fact that the Netherlands as a sequel to the Hague Conferences became the seat of the Court of International Justice is also not wholly fortuitous, if we may trust the opening speech made by the Russian who presided over the Conference of 1899:

> In the quiet surroundings of The Hague—in the midst of a nation which constitutes a most significant factor of universal civilization, we have under our eyes a striking example of what may be done for the welfare of peoples by valor, patriotism and sustained energy. It is upon the historic ground of the Netherlands that the greatest problems of the political life of States have been discussed; it is here, as one may say, that the cradle of the science of International Law has stood.[11]

If Sweden has had no tradition to match with Grotius, it was by the beneficence of a Swedish industrialist that the Nobel world prizes came into use in the first year of the new century to mark, as they still do, the triumphant progress of the sciences, the achievements of literature, and the attempts of such men as Dunant to plot the paths of peace. The Norwegian achievement which was best known to contemporaries was undoubtedly the supremacy that country achieved in the much publicized field of polar exploration—the voyage of the *Fram*, the penetration through the Northwest Passage, Roald Amundsen's arrival at the South Pole. Denmark, on the other hand, was thought of as the pioneer of the Folk High School movement and the leading exponent of methods of agricultural cooperative marketing, which by 1914 were being imitated all over the world. Belgium's distinction was perhaps the slightest of the six, though the city of Ghent in the first year of the new century originated its own unem-

11. Speech of Baron de Staal, Russian ambassador to Britain, quoted by J. B. SCOTT, *The Hague Peace Conferences of 1899 and 1907*, 2 vols., (1909), vol. I, p. 49.

ployment insurance system, based on the idea of supplementing grants paid by trade unions, and at the same time declared war on infant mortality by founding the first school for mothers. Both ideas were widely imitated in other countries and produced important results.

In the absence of any severe pressure from greater powers, the history of each of these smaller countries turned on issues of domestic policy. Since what happened in one of them was usually paralleled in another, an example taken from each in turn may be enough to illustrate the general course of events. Switzerland, indeed, was so well insulated by her rigorous neutrality on the one hand, and the very wide powers of the separate cantons (roughly comparable to American state powers) on the other, that major issues were few. She was, how-ever, affected at the beginning of this period by a struggle of the same character as the *Kulturkampf* in Germany. One of the Catholic cantons asserted the right of local communities to choose their own priest; certain bishops who enforced acceptance of Papal Infallibility were driven from their sees; and the Swiss government for a time had no diplomatic relations with the papacy, which was a serious situation in a country where two-fifths of the people were Catholic. One consequence was the recognition of a Swiss equivalent to the Old Catholic Church, which still retains about 25,000 adherents. More important was a revision of the constitution in 1874, which made civil marriage obligatory and gave the federal government control over the development of new Catholic institutions; there was also a more general increase in federal authority over the separate cantons.

Developments in the two kingdoms of the Low Countries were to some extent parallel. In both countries the middle-class parties in power contended bitterly over religious instruction in the schools, through which they sought to establish a hold upon the minds of the rising generation which would justify the expenditure of public money upon the education of the poor. But in so Catholic a country as Belgium, the Liberal agitation in favor of secular schools was almost bound to fail, and the result was to put the Catholic Party into office for a whole generation (1884–1914), with a program which made elementary education religious but not compulsory. Though an outburst of strikes and threats of violence forced the Catholic Party to make the qualified grant of manhood suffrage in 1893 (already mentioned), the growth of social reform was slow. The Socialist Party gained less than one-quarter of the seats in the Chamber, and in 1910 a careful British sociological study of Belgium established as one of its conclusions that "there is little doubt that the proportion of workmen who are adequately fed is much smaller than in Britain."[12]

On the whole the most significant controversy in Belgium was over language. The Flemings of the northern provinces, amounting to rather more

12. B. SEEBOHM ROWNTREE, *Land and Labour: Lessons from Belgium* (1910), p. 528.

than half the total population, pressed the French-speaking Walloons of the south, who included most members of the upper classes, to give due recognition to their tongue, which closely resembled Dutch. It was not until 1873, after two Flemish speakers had been tried and executed for a murder they did not commit by a court whose proceedings they could not follow, that Flemish was made available in trial cases. In 1898 Flemish was officially recognized as the second language of the country, and in 1914 primary schools in Flemish areas were allowed to make it the exclusive language of instruction. But by that time a movement which had been concerned with the revival and imitation of the notable Flemish literature of the Middle Ages had developed overtones of political separatism, which the German invaders in both world wars were prompt to exploit.

In the Kingdom of the Netherlands, where modern industrialism was a later growth than in Belgium, the suffrage movement made correspondingly slower progress, and social reform proceeded no more rapidly. In 1903 troops were employed to break a big railway strike, and a law was passed restricting the right to strike in vital services. Ten years later the Social Democratic Party had grown to be the second largest of the separate political parties, but its chance of getting into power remained very slender as long as no more than 14 percent of population had the vote. The principal subject of parliamentary controversy, which was not finally settled until a special article was written into the constitution in 1917, concerned religious education. Education as a whole was taken more seriously than in Belgium. A tradition of learning existed dating back to the golden age of Dutch commerce and civilization in the seventeenth century, when there were already four universities in the Dutch to one in the Spanish Netherlands; the modern kingdom was one of the first European countries to have a separate education department and systematic plans of development. Since the population was two-thirds Calvinist and one-third Catholic, the Liberal solution of providing nondenominational state schools seemed appropriate. It was opposed, however, both by strong Calvinists and by a Catholic Party which received an impetus from the Vatican Council. In 1888, after some extension of the franchise, the two clerical parties formed a coalition, which overthrew the Liberals and instituted a system of equal subsidies for denominational and nondenominational state schools. But the coalition, which was in power again from 1901 to 1913, continued to press for the solution finally adopted. This gave formal equality to both types of school, with the result that private schools belonging to religious denominations have since predominated, at the secondary as well as the primary level.

In the three Scandinavian kingdoms the almost universal acceptance of the Lutheran State Church obviated any serious dispute over religious education. As compared with the Low Countries, social cleavages were also in general

less sharp, as evidenced in the readier acceptance of the growth of a labor movement and the more rapid provision of humanitarian reforms by the middle-class
parties which were in power. Instead, the most significant political conflicts
centered upon the working of the constitution. Denmark's was a product of the
revolutionary era of 1848–1849, but it had been modified in the era of disillusionment after Denmark lost Schleswig-Holstein in the war of 1864. The modification concerned the upper house of the Danish legislature, which came to
represent almost exclusively the larger property owners of the country. They saw
eye to eye with King Christian IX about the desirability of spending more
money on the army and on static defenses, whereas to the general public the
lesson of the war seemed to be that its geographical position had placed Denmark at the mercy of the new German Empire so that there was no point in
throwing good money after bad. Since the constitution placed the two houses
on an equal footing, the king was able to keep in office a series of ministries
which had the confidence of the upper house only, and the necessary financial
support was obtained from provisional budgets rather in the manner of Bismarck's earlier dealings with the Prussian Diet. But the fortification of Copenhagen brought no spectacular results to mollify public opinion as Moltke's
victories did in Prussia, and, after a period of compromise, King Christian
finally accepted the principle of ministerial responsibility to the lower house five
years before his long reign ended in 1906. In 1915 a new constitution made all
men (and women above a certain age) electors for, and eligible to, both houses.

Though Sweden and Norway had been united since 1814 in a common
monarchy, their constitutions, dating respectively from 1809 and 1814, were
otherwise almost entirely separate. The Swedish system, which was founded to a
great extent upon the idea of the separation of powers, left a good deal of
authority in the hands of the king, even after a two-chamber legislature had
replaced the ancient and cumbrous Estates of the Realm in 1867. Given the
circumstance that the great period of industrial growth in Sweden coincided
with the long reign of Bernadotte's very able grandson, Oscar II (1872–1907),
it is not surprising to find that the last steps toward political democracy were not
taken until the twentieth century. Although Sweden possessed in Hjalmar
Branting[13] perhaps the foremost socialist leader of his generation, a six-week
general strike in 1909 proved a disastrous failure for the whole labor movement.
Manhood suffrage, indeed, was established in the same year, but it was coupled
with a scheme for proportional representation in both chambers designed to
prevent the establishment of a definite governing party majority in the lower

13. 1860–1925. Son of a professor and trained as an astronomer, he became leader of the Socialist
Party in 1889 and in 1896–1902 was its sole representative in the legislature. From 1914 onward his
was the largest, though not the majority, party, and he was premier in 1920 and 1921–1925. He
championed the independence of Norway, the Allied cause during the First World War, and the
League of Nations.

one. At last, in February, 1914, a Liberal government, which was concentrating public expenditure upon social reform, was turned out of office by the new king, Gustav V, when the peasants organized a demonstration in favor of increased provision for defense, the policy which had his personal support. The sequel was a right-wing ministry under the elder Hammarskjöld, which won the ensuing election, but the effect on Sweden of a war fought by other peoples "to make the world safe for democracy" included a thoroughgoing democratization of its political institutions in the autumn of 1918.

In Norway the later years of the nineteenth century witnessed a remarkable intertwining of liberalism with nationalism. In 1884 by a cumbrous and rather unfair resort to impeachment, the principle was firmly established that the king's ministers in Norway were directly responsible to the majority in its single-chamber legislature. Manhood suffrage was introduced fourteen years later, again without any obstacle interposed by the Crown, which under the Norwegian constitution possessed only a suspensive veto. But the Norwegians still nursed other grievances, particularly that, as the joint foreign minister was always for practical reasons a citizen of the larger country, the consular service was under Swedish control; this to some extent hurt the interests of the very large Norwegian mercantile marine as well as the national pride. The Conservatives were compelled to join the Liberals on this issue by patriotic pressure, and, when King Oscar II in 1905 refused to accept forthwith a Norwegian bill for introducing a separate consular service, the Norwegian ministry resigned and the legislature unanimously resolved that the common monarchy had ceased to function. The Swedes accepted a 2000 to 1 majority in a plebiscite of the Norwegian electorate as evidence of the general will, and exacted no more than the dismantling of some Norwegian fortifications recently established in the frontier zone, which was now formally demilitarized. King Oscar then abdicated from the throne of Norway, which after a second plebiscite was accepted by a grandson of the king of Denmark, who was also the son-in-law of the English King Edward VII. Haakon VII was fated to reign for more than fifty years (including five of German usurpation) over Europe's smallest and most democratic monarchy; it was also the last to be established on any permanent footing.

■ CONCLUSION

The separation of the Norwegian Crown, which affected the balance established in northern Europe at the time of the Congress of Vienna, took place as smoothly as it did, and without recourse to arms, because, in the year of the Tangier crisis and the battle of Tsushima, the great powers did not wish it otherwise. This suggests the general reflection that the lesser powers, as we have called them, were able for the most part to develop peacefully within their established frontiers because it suited the strong at this time to respect the sovereign rights of the weak. What happened when the pressure changed is most vividly illustrated by comparing the map in 1908 and in 1918 in the two cases of Austria-Hungary and the Ottoman Empire. But it is a truth of wider scope that the invasion of Belgium in 1914 began an age in which, although their numbers notably increased, the position of lesser powers in a rapidly changing world lost its former security. Thus retrospect largely justifies the view held by contemporaries that the phenomena just described belonged to an age of improvement. In spite of disappointments and setbacks, in more than half of the countries now under consideration the generation of men who were growing old in the first years of the new century could reasonably believe that their lifetime had seen in public affairs a course of change which was broadly identifiable as progress.

Contemporaries were, however, inclined to attach undue importance to constitutions and parliaments as evidences of liberal achievement. Hindsight enables us to see that there were two overruling considerations. One was that extreme poverty, as in the Iberian Peninsula, southern Italy, and in many parts of the Balkans, easily converted parliamentary government into a dangerous farce, which served to conceal the facts of exploitation until a chance spark touched off an explosion. The other was that liberalism was not a panacea for the troubles of nationalism. In Austria, for example, representative government could never satisfy the minor nationalities, any more than the Turkish parliamentary constitution of 1876, even if the parliament had not been suspended for thirty years, could have satisfied the appetites which launched the Balkan Wars of 1912–1913.

Reading List: Chapter 15

The New Cambridge Modern History, vol. XI (1962), ch. 12. Austria-Hungary, Turkey, and the Balkans.

The Cambridge Modern History, vol. XII (1910), chs. 9–11. Convenient though old-fashioned accounts of the Low Countries, Spain, Portugal, and Scandinavia.

May, A. J., *The Hapsburg Monarchy* (1951), chs. 16, 19. Magyar culture; Austria on the eve of war.

Ramsaur, E. E., Jr., *The Young Turks: Prelude to the Revolution of 1908* (1957), ch. 4. Analysis of the movement.

Lengyel, E., *The Danube* (1939), part III. A vivid picture of the Balkans.

Croce, B., *History of Italy, 1871–1915* (1929), ch. 1. Reflections on Italian politics by a great modern philosopher.

Sprigge, C. J. S., *The Development of Modern Italy* (1943), chs. 2–4. Italy from 1871 to 1914.

Halperin, S. W., "Italian Anticlericalism, 1871–1914," *Journal of Modern History*, vol. XIX (1947), no. 1.

Livermore, H., *History of Spain* (1958; paperback, 1960), pp. 361–414.

Kohn, H., *Nationalism and Liberty: The Swiss Example* (1956), chs. 18–21.

Barnouw, A., *Making of Modern Holland* (1944), ch. 11. "The Age of Wilhelmina."

Derry, T. K., *Short History of Norway* (1957), chs. 7–10.

Chapter 16

European Cultural
Influences at Their Zenith

A Generation of Materialism
Changing Concepts in Physical Science
Man and Nature
Man and Society
Socialist Interpretations of Society
Religion in the New Age of Science
Literature and the Arts
Crosscurrents

◼ A GENERATION OF MATERIALISM

In the intellectual history of the period from 1871 to 1914 one point is clear. The scientific achievements, the cultural trends, and the general outlook of these years in Europe were all closely knit with what had gone before. It may well be that in a political sense the competitive policies of the national states, many of them newly formed, gave to these closing decades of the nineteenth century a distinctive quality which set them apart. Culturally, however, the links with the preceding generation were very close.

Darwin's *Origin of Species*, the appearance of which in 1859 had inaugurated a new scientific era, contained some propositions which in many respects were tentative and incomplete. The succeeding decades saw his hypotheses challenged, enlarged, modified, substantiated by new evidence, and

444

SIGNIFICANT EVENTS

1871	Mendeleev: Periodic Table of the Elements
1873	Clerk Maxwell, *Treatise on Electricity and Magnetism*
1874	Wundt, *Foundations of Physiological Psychology*
1875	Tolstoy, *Anna Karenina*
1879	Ibsen, *A Doll's House*
1884	Fabian Society organized
1885	Pasteur: Inoculation for hydrophobia
1885–1886	Nietzsche, *Thus Spake Zarathustra*
1886–1890	Harnack, *History of Christian Dogma*
1891	Leo XIII: Encyclical *Rerum Novarum*
1898	Pierre and Marie Curie: Discovery of radium
1899	Lenin, *Development of Capitalism in Russia*
1900	Freud, *Interpretation of Dreams*
1901	Planck: Quantum theory
1905	Einstein: Special theory of relativity
1907	Bergson, *Creative Evolution*

brought nearer to general acceptance. The bold efforts of Auguste Comte in the 1840's to establish his science of society had been followed by Herbert Spencer's first outlines of a synthetic philosophy. Until his death in 1903 Spencer was endlessly occupied with the outlines of an evolutionary system in almost every branch of human thought. Marx's *Communist Manifesto* of 1848 was followed by a steady enlargement of his ideas, which in time meant challenge, elaboration, and revision. The current of realism, so manifest in the literature of the mid-century, led to a steadily enlarging interest in social problems and psychological analysis, even as, to take one very different example, the impressionist and postimpressionist schools of French painting grew out of the efforts of earlier artists to express the reality which they saw about them. And, finally, the momentous forward steps taken at the close of the century toward understanding the intricate structure and behavior of the atom grew out of closely linked scientific investigations that went back a hundred years to Dalton and Lavoisier.

The decades under consideration were a time when factories were crowded with workers, when new modes of transportation enabled them to move about more freely, when literacy was becoming, if not universal, at least more general, and when the power of the ballot was being put into the hand of the common man. Knowledge was more widely diffused, and many fields of intellectual interest which had been the exclusive preserve of an elite were now open to a much larger public. How much of a dilution or vulgarization of ideas occurred in this process the historian would be hard put to determine. It is clear, however, that the debate on various social issues reached a larger audience than ever before, and that in times of crisis it became possible for newspapers with mass circulation to influence public opinion in various ways, both good and bad.

The historian of ideas may well have difficulty in determining what is cause and what is effect. The steady growth of membership in labor unions or socialist parties is much more easily attributable to economic circumstances than to eloquent arguments concerning the nature of social justice and injustice. Even so, it seems evident that a new gospel—that of Marxism, for example, or of modern nationalism—can frequently make skillful use of words to rally supporters to a new cause. Ideas may be studied as contributory forces in the actual working out of events. They may also be studied as a means of enlarging our understanding, after the event, of what actually was going on. In either case one may notice the interconnections and, as in the case of this so-called "generation of materialism," establish the particular quality of the times.

■ CHANGING CONCEPTS IN PHYSICAL SCIENCE

The continued impressive advances in the physical sciences were built upon the substantial theoretical achievements of the earlier decades. Since steam and electricity held promise of becoming man's most useful servants, the scientists pushed hard to understand more fully the theoretical principles underlying their operation. The association between research in the university laboratory and the actual functioning of industry had its origins in these years.

In physics important formulations had already been made concerning thermodynamics. There also developed the kinetic theory of gases and the wave theory of light and heat. In chemistry, to what was already known about the atom and the molecule, a new pattern of regularity was made clear when the Russian scientist, Dmitri Mendeleev, in 1869, formulated his periodic law and soon after drew up his periodic table of the elements. According to this table every element was grouped according to its atomic weight and its combining properties. Mendeleev listed the known elements and was able to predict those points in his table where sooner or later new elements could assume their proper places. Thus gallium was discovered in 1871, germanium in 1886, and helium in 1895. By 1900 about seventy-five elements were known and it was recognized that others existed but had not yet been isolated and identified. Physical nature was clearly demonstrating a greater unity and symmetry.

The study of electricity likewise underwent dramatic development. In the first half of the century an elementary form of the electric cell or battery had been devised by the Italian, Alessandro Volta, in 1800; Hans Christian Oersted, a Dane, and André Marie Ampère, a Frenchman, had soon recognized that the electric current flowing from a battery through a wire would deflect a magnetic needle lying parallel to it. The Englishman, Michael Faraday, had already used this interaction of electric and magnetic fields to produce mechanical motion, and as early as 1831 had, to all intents and purposes, devised the electric motor which produces mechanical power, and had also envisaged the corresponding machine, the dynamo, in which mechanical power is used to create electricity. The further progress during the period now under consideration is more properly an aspect of technology than of science.[1] The appearance of central power-generating stations was a phenomenon of the 1880's; growth, however, was slow and the widespread use of electricity, except for lighting, did not come about until after 1900.

Advances in the study of electricity led to even more striking advances in knowledge of the structure of matter. Clerk Maxwell had pursued his electromagnetic studies on the basis of the wave theory, treating the phenomena of electricity as akin to those of optics. Visible light rays he came to regard as a selection from an immense range of electromagnetic wave phenomena. In 1888 a German scholar, Heinrich Hertz, used oscillating discharges to produce electromagnetic waves in space—the "Herzian waves," which later were the basis of Guglielmo Marconi's invention of wireless telegraphy. In 1895 another German, Wilhelm von Röntgen, discovered at a very short wave length the Röntgen rays, or X-rays, that were to have such profound scientific applications. Then a French scholar, Henri Becquerel, observed in 1896 the radioactivity of numerous uranium compounds, and by 1900 Pierre and Marie Curie[2] found that pitchblende, a mineral containing uranium, could be used to produce radium, a new element of unique qualities. Though many tons of the

1. See ch. 10, p. 279.
2. Pierre (1859–1906), professor of physics at the Sorbonne, married Marie (1867–1934), a Polish student compelled because of revolutionary connections to leave Warsaw. They jointly shared a Nobel prize for physics with Becquerel. After her husband was killed in a street accident, Marie was promoted to his chair and herself won a Nobel prize for chemistry. The curiegram, the unit of measurement for radium emanation, was named for her.

mineral were required to yield a small fraction of a grain of radium salt, an epochal advance had been made.

Further progress was to lead directly into what has been called the fourth great scientific revolution of modern times, the development of atomic physics. The seventeenth century had seen the emergence of Newtonian physics; the close of the eighteenth saw Lavoisier propound the concept of chemical elements, from which Dalton went on to his atomic theory; and the mid-nineteenth century had learned of Darwin's evolutionary biology. Now, in the century's closing years, Sir Joseph Thomson, working in Cambridge at experiments which involved passing electricity through gases, concluded in 1897 that electricity was made of particles or corpuscles, and that these corpuscles, later termed "electrons," were also a component part of atoms. Thus the atom could no longer be regarded as the smallest part of matter. Even more significantly, electricity (a form of energy) and matter were explicable in interchangeable terms.

Later advances, chiefly made by Sir Ernest Rutherford, dealt with the structure of the atom, at first believed to be like a solar system in miniature with the electrons moving in predictable orbits. Delicate experiments showed, however, that the motions of the electrons were not predictable and regular, but more like those of individuals in a crowd, with regard to which certain general statements only are feasible. The *quantum theory* of Max Planck (1901) held that energy was not released in a continuous stream but in successive bursts (quanta). Not until 1927 was a further refinement to come with Werner Heisenberg's *principle of indeterminacy*, which in essence held that the more accurately the position of a particle within an atom could be specified, the less accurately its velocity could be predicted. One may generalize, therefore, about the behavior of large numbers of subatomic particles, but, in the light of Heisenberg's principle, scientists have realized the futility of trying to make exact analysis of all aspects of atomic and molecular behavior. Atomic studies further demonstrated that it was possible for elements, such as radium and uranium, to disintegrate and release hitherto inconceivably powerful amounts of energy. This is what Sir Arthur Eddington calls the greatest change in our idea of matter since the time of Democritus. Though much of this development lay in the future, the foundations had been established. A still further refinement was the discovery that the protons and neutrons of a given element might form slightly different structures, enabling the atoms of this element to exist in two different forms with different atomic weights. These variant forms came to be known as isotopes.

Arising out of these new concepts came a momentous challenge to the older Newtonian view of the universe as a three-dimensional structure in which motion, space, and time were absolutes and in which every part was in a fixed, mathematically ascertainable relation to every other part. In 1905 a young

German-Jewish mathematician and physicist, Albert Einstein,[3] then working in the Swiss patent office at Berne while pursuing his studies in science, published in an article the outlines of his "special theory of relativity," as momentous in its consequences as Newton's *Principia* or Darwin's *Origin of Species*. This theory in essence was based on the principle that the circumstances under which an observation is made influence that which is observed. In the physical universe, where motion is everywhere, man has no fixed platform from which to measure, no yardstick of absolute length, no absolute system of time. The only absolute is the speed of light. Since every part of the universe is constantly changing its position in relation to every other, no system of calculation involving the three dimensions of length, breadth, and depth is acceptable unless one makes time the fourth dimension, and this within a new time-space concept known as a continuum. Einstein did not so much overthrow Newtonian physics, which remains one of man's greatest intellectual achievements, as submit it to a subtle and all-pervasive process of modification.

> Even matter, the concept of which underlies classical dynamics, has now vanished. The essential idea of a substance, as something extended in space and persistent in time, is now meaningless, since neither space nor time is either absolute or real. A substance has become a mere series of events, connected in some unknown and perhaps casual way, taking place in space-time.[4]

■ MAN AND NATURE

Darwin's basic theory of evolution had been given to the world in 1859. The second phrase in the title of his work, *The Origin of Species by Means of Natural Selection*, shows what stress Darwin chose to put upon nature's selection of variations which he held, with Lamarck, to come largely as the result of the inheritance of acquired characteristics. Some of the German advocates of the theory, notably Haeckel, came out so strongly in support of this view that they were, in a sense, "more Darwinian than Darwin." In the years following 1871 the scientific, as distinct from the religious, opposition to Darwin's views centered on this matter of inheriting acquired characteristics.

The advances subsequently made on Darwin's original hypothesis were concerned with the nature of variations and the machinery and scope of heredity. A professor from the University of Freiburg, August Weismann, raised serious obstacles to Darwin's views on the inheritance of acquired characteristics, by distinguishing between ordinary body cells, which are subject to

3. 1879–1955. After posts at Zurich and Prague, he became in 1913 director of the Kaiser-Wilhelm Physical Institute at Berlin, and Nobel prizewinner in 1921. He left Germany under threat of Hitler in 1932, then made his home at the Institute for Advanced Study at Princeton. A fervent Zionist and pacifist, he wrote to President Roosevelt in 1939 assuring him that the proposals to produce atomic power by splitting the atom were scientifically feasible.
4. Sir WILLIAM CECIL DAMPIER, *A History of Science* (1952), p. 409.

modification, and the reproductive or germ cells, which transmit protoplasm or vital material from one generation to another and which are not subject to modification. Under this view, modifications or variations in the body cells could not be transmitted to offspring. Thus this left only natural selection as a possible means of evolutionary change. Not until the end of the century, when a Dutch scholar, Hugo De Vries, resurrected some neglected publications of an Austrian monk, Gregor Mendel, was a deeper understanding of the workings of inheritance made possible. Mendel had experimented in the 1860's with crossing numerous varieties of garden peas and had elaborately recorded the changing outcomes. He concluded that there existed certain determinants which by cross-breeding transmit dominant or recessive traits to the descendants in definite mathematical patterns. Proceeding from this, De Vries noticed the sudden origin of new varieties of plants by the new patterning of hereditary materials. Such changes he called mutations, which nature could then accept or reject according to their adaptability to life. Still further elaborations involved the concept of chromosomes, or threadlike bodies existing within the nuclei of reproductive cells and containing hereditary factors known as genes. As the cells divide and go on from one generation to another, the chromosomes with their genes make new combinations and produce old or new hereditary traits.

Such refinements and elaborations, along with a steadily accumulating volume of biological evidence, left scientists with no grounds to dispute the basic phenomena of evolution. The most important development within the field of biology, consequently, might well be taken to be the rejection of the Lamarckian view, which held that acquired characteristics had the controlling importance in evolution, replacing this with the combination of Mendelian principles of heredity and the older Darwinian theory of natural selection.

These basic generalizations about biological phenomena were paralleled by a much greater knowledge of specific subjects. Louis Pasteur, for example, continued his study of bacteria, and, acting on the evidence that animals inoculated with the weakened virus of a disease were rendered immune to it, developed vaccines against anthrax in cattle and hydrophobia, or rabies, in humans. Robert Koch's Institute for Infectious Diseases in Berlin, the Pasteur Institute in Paris, Rudolf Virchow's Institute of Pathology in Berlin, and Joseph Lister's Institute of Preventive Medicine in London isolated the germs of tuberculosis, cholera, malaria, leprosy, pneumonia, tetanus, typhoid, influenza, and the bubonic plague.

Important progress was made in psychology, which removed the study of the human mind and human behavior from the realm of the metaphysicians and theologians and brought it into the realm of the scientists. In this respect the founder of modern psychological studies unquestionably was Wilhelm Wundt. His *Foundations of Physiological Psychology* (1874) made the connections between the physical mechanism on the one hand and thought and behavior on the other. It was in his laboratory at Leipzig that cats, dogs, rabbits, and mice were first employed in the study of all kinds of behavior patterns. Wundt had many disciples. One of the best known experiments was that of the Russian scientist, Ivan Pavlov. By presenting food to dogs, he caused their mouths to water; at the same time he rang a bell. Eventually he found that he could produce a similar result, or conditioned reflex, simply by ringing a bell. Objective techniques for mental measurement were first developed by Alfred Binet at the Sorbonne around 1900. The Austrian physician, Sigmund Freud,[5] moved into another realm, that of psychiatry, when he began his remarkable studies of organic disturbances for which no organic cause was apparent, going on to explore the subconscious level of the human mind, and eventually sorting out the human personality on the three levels of the *id* (unconscious), the *ego*, and the *superego*. Freud laid great stress on unconscious driving forces, and employed the therapy that believes that if the individual can uncover and understand his neuroses he is well on the way to curing them. Like Pavlov a distinguished scientist, Freud brought into prominence the role of automatic responses and of subconscious motivations, and thus his influence was felt in fields not strictly those of medicine, where much of the behavior of men came to be explained in other than rational terms.

In still another scientific realm, that of anthropology, the late nineteenth century literally uncovered evidence of the great antiquity of man who, perhaps half a million years ago, had existed in a form more animal-like and brutal than the *homo sapiens*, which includes all present races. Comparative anthropology led to the study of primitive peoples in various environments and shed much light on their social customs. Such anthropological studies made it clear that man could not be understood by looking at him simply as an actor moving upon the stage of history. An elaborate range of disciplines became necessary to understand the full complexity of his development and his nature.

The last volume of a major historical enterprise, brought to completion through the efforts of many scholars in the year 1910, well summarizes and characterizes these views as to the interrelationship of many fields of knowledge:

> Perhaps the most striking feature of the more recent discoveries has been their cumulative effect. A new branch of Physics at once bears chemical fruit, while knowledge gained in Physical Chemistry is applied alike by physicists, chemists, and physiologists. Archaeology throws light on Anthropology, and Anthropology on the Comparative History of Religion. Academic study of the problems of

---

5. 1856-1939. Turned from science to medicine through reading Goethe, he began with studies of hysteria and later substituted the technique of free association for hypnosis in the exploration and treatment of neuroses, thereby elaborating his psychoanalytic method. Elected to the British Royal Society in 1936, he fled from Vienna, where he had lived for seventy-eight years, to London when Hitler invaded Austria. He was a pioneer and genius in studying the subconscious levels of the mind.

heredity has immediate bearings on Agriculture and Sociology, while the mechanical arts are lying in wait for the results of research in the laboratory, and in using extend them. We understand at last that knowledge is one. . . .[6]

■ MAN AND SOCIETY

Studies of man's position in the world of nature were closely linked with the problems of man in society. Darwin's *Descent of Man* (1871) had been preceded by Thomas Huxley's *Man's Place in Nature* (1863), putting *homo sapiens* with the order of primates. Ernst Haeckel's *Evolution of Man* (1874), the work of Darwin's most vigorous advocate in Germany, saw no need for any explanations for human evolution which went beyond the physical facts of nature. Haeckel, a convinced materialist, who held the chair of zoology at Jena from 1862 until his death in 1919, published his *Riddle of the Universe* in 1899, preaching the doctrines of the essential unity of organic and inorganic nature, declaring psychology to be a branch of physiology, and denying the immortality of the soul, freedom of the will, and the existence of a personal God.

Much attention was given to evidences as to the long history of human growth. A French excise officer, Boucher de Perthes, had begun as early as 1841 to collect curiously shaped flints in the Somme valley and six years later made his first published reports on what he called "Celtic antiquities." Sir Charles Lyell's *Antiquity of Man* (1863) assembled the archeological and geological evidence for man's long presence on the earth, and thus began the modern study of anthropology. Sir John Lubbock's *Prehistoric Times* (1865), building on an earlier division of the ages of man into the three periods of stone, bronze, and iron, invented the terms Paleolithic and Neolithic for the two main divisions of the Stone Age. His *Origin of Civilization* (1870) saw human society as a slow, evolutionary product.

The social scientists were quite evidently influenced by such views. The Polish sociologist, Ludwik Gumplowicz, for example, in a series of works beginning with his *Race and State* (1875), described life as a ceaseless struggle in which only the strongest survive—a struggle first between primitive racial groups, then between states, and lastly between classes within states.

> Out of frictions and struggles [he wrote], out of separations and unions of opposing elements, finally came forth as new adaptation products the higher sociopsychical phenomena, the higher cultural forms, the new civilizations, the new state and national unities. . . .[7]

The study of society proceeded to a considerable extent along the positive, factual line which Comte had preached, with a strong stress on evolutionary concepts. The three volumes of Herbert Spencer's *Principles of Sociology*, which

6. *The Cambridge Modern History* (1910), XII, p. 791.
7. Quoted in J. H. RANDALL, *Making of the Modern Mind* (1926), p. 492.

appeared between 1877 and 1896, were a part of the huge *Synthetic Philosophy* planned in 1860, the purpose of which has already been sketched.[8] In it reappear the inevitable Darwinian phrases concerning evolution, the struggle for existence, and the survival of the fittest. The idea of evolution, to Spencer, could not be separated from the idea of progress. "The ultimate development of the ideal man is logically certain," Spencer had written much earlier in his *Social Statics*, "as certain as any conclusion in which we place the most implicit faith; for instance that all men will die." With a somewhat different emphasis, Walter Bagehot, a shrewd observer of English political life, sketched an essay, *Physics and Politics* (1872), assuming many similarities between natural science and social science and undertaking to describe the evolution of political communities in Darwinian terms. His treatment of tradition, the "cake of custom," revolt, innovation, and imitation makes his volume an important introduction to modern social psychology. Like Spencer, Bagehot uses such terms as "natural selection" and "evolution" to explain the growth of political communities. "In every particular state of the world," Bagehot confidently asserted, "those nations which are strongest tend to prevail over the others; and in certain marked peculiarities the strongest tend to be the best."

The positivist, determinist influence can also be seen in the brilliant historical and literary works of Hippolyte Taine. Culture this French scholar held to be the product of physical forces working in history. Taine thus came out with his famous formulation that an artist, a work of art, and even a national literature are, individually or jointly, the product of three inexorable forces. The first of these is *race*—the hereditary element and, in Taine's view, the master element. The next is *milieu*—the environment. The third force, *moment*, is better described as momentum, the accumulated pressure of the past converging on a given moment in history. Taine's semifatalistic views, and his profound antipathy to the French Revolution and its legacy, gave him no ground for anything save the deepest pessimism. "Man," he concluded, "is a fierce and lustful gorilla."

The attempts at the scientific study of man in society involved many techniques. The German scholar, Georg von Mayr, pioneered in the use of statistics, which he regarded as the way to truth. Sir Francis Galton, a cousin of Darwin, by elaborate studies of the lives and families of distinguished Englishmen, contributed to the founding of the science of eugenics. The French sociologist, Emile Durkheim, focused his technical studies on particular problems, such as the effects upon society of the division of labor and the factors involved in suicides. Another French scholar, Pierre LePlay, made elaborate scientific studies of the family and its interrelations with the life of the community. A prosperous Liverpool shipowner, Charles Booth, devoted much time

8. See pp. 254–255.

and money to the statistical investigation of social problems, the grand outcome being the eighteen volumes of his *Life and Labor of the People in London* (1891–1903). In this work numerous varicolored maps show, street by street, the actual degrees of poverty of the city-dwellers as part of a larger purpose of demonstrating "the numerical relation which poverty, misery and depravity bear to regular earnings and comparative comfort, and to describe the general conditions under which each class lives."

The actual writing of history likewise reflected much of the new attitude found in the world of science. The historical seminar, so marked a feature of the German universities since the days of Leopold von Ranke, came to have its counterparts in the universities of other lands. The large-scale publication of documentary sources, begun in the second quarter of the century, went on apace, and with it grew the highly technical, elaborately documented, objective historical monograph. Scholars undertook the joint production of multivolumed historical works with each chapter written by a specialist, of which the twelve volumes of *The Cambridge Modern History*, begun in 1902, or the twelve volumes of the *Histoire générale*, begun in 1893, are the outstanding examples. Such works illustrate the ever-enlarging trend to make the study of man's history more thorough and more scientific.

■ SOCIALIST INTERPRETATIONS OF SOCIETY

Socialist ideas, which had developed so powerfully around mid-century, underwent both elaboration and modification in the ensuing decades. In Germany, with the program of the Social Democratic Party under the Empire, Marxism had become a political force. As we have seen,[9] the Lassalleans and Social Democrats had come together in 1875 to draft the Gotha Program which combined Marxian revolutionary goals with a list of immediate political and social reforms. Then once again, in 1895, the official Social Democratic Party policy tended to swing back to the orthodox Marxian doctrine of class struggle and the violent destruction of capital through revolutionary means. The French Socialist Party likewise committed itself in 1905 to a program of revolutionary action. Even more striking were the theories of syndicalism, which called for widespread, united violence (i.e., the general strike) on the part of the working class as the means to its goal.[10]

Important developments of theory should be noted in Russia. The new generation of the 1860's with its conscience-stricken intellectuals reacted against the earlier outlook of the romantics and professed to see no solution for its country's troubles along parliamentary lines. Chernyshevski's novel, *What Is to be Done?* (1884) earned him a sentence of twenty-four years in Siberia and be-

9. See p. 311.
10. See p. 356.

came a revolutionary classic. In Turgenev's *Fathers and Sons* (1862) appeared the great portrait of the nihilist hero, Bazarov, who refuses "to talk nonsense about art, parliamentarism, trial by jury—while all the time it is a question of getting bread to eat," and who is convinced that there is "no single institution in our present mode of life that does not call for complete and unqualified destruction." This nihilism, or total disbelief in the existing institutions of society, was paralleled by the actual movement of terrorism—not so much a creed as a crude program of ruthless action—striking down any official, the higher in rank the better, who exercised political authority. Populism was a faith that the future of Russia lay with the peasant and that therefore it was a deep obligation of the intelligentsia to go to the people on whose labor the wealth of the aristocracy had been built, to share their problems, and to become identified with them. These were the teachings of such men as Peter Lavrov and Nicholas Mikhailovsky. Thousands of idealists, young and old, were impelled in the 1870's to act in this way, even at the cost of imprisonment. Populist sentiment led ultimately to the founding of the Social Revolutionary Party in 1901, an agrarian, revolutionary group which, as it turned out, was to be less significant in Russia than in other large peasant areas of eastern Europe.

Anarchism was another development which could be regarded as an extreme form of the views taken by Proudhon in his attacks on the capitalist state. It could also be said to have some faint connection with the greatly diluted views of John Stuart Mill's essay, *On Liberty*, or of Spencer in his *Man Versus the State*, both suspicious of too much state power. As distinct from these, anarchism was clearly a revolutionary doctrine. Michael Bakunin (1814–1876) was a young Russian army officer of noble birth who turned to the life of a restless, uprooted intellectual, and in the course of his wanderings was briefly involved, along with Richard Wagner, in the revolutionary disturbances at Dresden in 1849. Turned over to the Russian police and condemned to death, he was imprisoned for seven years and then sent to Siberia, whence he managed to escape, via Japan, to England. In 1868 Bakunin formed his Social Democratic Alliance and used this as a means to enter the International which Marx had organized. Here he carried on a violent and unsuccessful struggle with Marx for its control. His writings took the form of violent attacks on all organized society. "We object," Bakunin wrote in *God and the State* (1882), "to all legislation, all authority, and all influence, privileged, patented, official, and legal, even when it has proceeded from universal suffrage, convinced that it must always turn to the profit of a dominating and exploiting minority. . . ." Bakunin's huge, bearded figure, his incessant demands for mass insurrection and destruction of the state, and his creed of atheism, anarchism, assassination, and unrestrained social upheaval have made him the principal nineteenth-century symbol of revolutionary violence in its most extreme form.

By contrast, another conscience-stricken intellectual, the Russian noble-man, Prince Peter Kropotkin (1842–1921), offered far milder proposals. Having made a name as a geographer, anthropologist, and geologist, he began in the 1870's to associate himself with the anarchist section of the First International. After two years of Russian imprisonment, he escaped in 1876, was later expelled from Switzerland, jailed for three years in France, and then settled happily in England where this singularly gentle figure, "with his benevolent beard billow-ing in the breezes of Brighton," became one of the most beloved of political exiles.[11] Regarding the state as the archexploiter, Kropotkin believed that not only private property but the state itself must go. On the analogy of the evi-dence, which he offered in his *Mutual Aid* (1902) to show that cooperation is as significant as conflict in biological evolution, Kropotkin argued that autono-mous groups of workers could successfully replace the rigidly disciplined political state. People, he somewhat naively held, could live happily together as oblivious to the cost of what they consume as would be the visitors whose only concern was to admire the paintings in a public art gallery.

Though anarchism had some success in associating itself with the cult of violent revolutionary activity among extreme groups in Spain and Italy, the major trend of revolutionary doctrine was associated with the theories of Karl Marx. In Russia the name of George Plekhanov (1857–1918) first stood out. Renouncing the ideas of populism which had first attracted him while a student at St. Petersburg, Plekhanov turned to Marxism, translating the *Communist Manifesto* into Russian for the first time (1882) and strongly influencing the young Nicolai Lenin's views on the revolutionary significance of the urban proletariat of their country. This father of Russian Marxism was thus Lenin's teacher, and the views expressed by Lenin in his *Development of Capitalism in Russia* (1899) could have been those of Plekhanov himself. Lenin characterized the transformation of Russia in the 1890's as follows:

> The Russia of the wooden plow and the flail, of the water mill and hand loom, rapidly began to be transformed into the Russia of the steel plow and the threshing machine, of steam-driven flour mills and looms. . . . The development of capital-ism in Russia rouses the worker to think . . . transforms a petty, fragmentary, and senseless revolt into an organized class struggle for the liberation of all the toiling people.[12]

Plekhanov had been one of the founders in 1898[13] of the Social Democratic Labor Party, an essentially proletarian movement based on the urban workers

---

11. The word-picture is that of Sir ALEXANDER GRAY, in *The Socialist Tradition from Moses to Lenin* (1946), p. 363.
12. Quoted in D. SHUB, *Lenin* (1948), p. 36.
13. See p. 407.

and a rival to the agrarian Social Revolutionary Party. The breach between Plekhanov and Lenin came in 1903 when Lenin, an advocate of revolutionary violence spearheaded by a trained corps of leaders, headed the Bolshevik (majority) wing as against Plekhanov's gradualist and moderate Menshevik (minority) wing. In this division lay the first beginnings of the Bolshevik revolution of 1917.

While the socialist movements on the Continent were marked by a growing trend to revolutionary violence, the corresponding theory and practice in Great Britain tended very strongly toward moderation. The early Christian Socialism of the 1850's, led by clergymen such as Frederick Denison Maurice and Charles Kingsley (author of *Alton Locke, Westward Ho!* and *The Water Babies*), had held that socialism was, in truth, Christianity applied to the problem of social reform. It had some significance in calling attention to public responsibility for the injustices of an uncontrolled industrial society, yet failed to gather momentum. John Stuart Mill's declarations of sympathy with the Utopian Socialists of the Continent did not bring him much support, or even occasion much comment. Though Marx spent thirty years in London, his influence in Great Britain was not direct or widespread. Henry M. Hyndman was a journalist who had studied Marx's *Das Kapital* and, indeed, discussed its problems with the author. He organized what was never more than a very small Social Democratic Federation of English radicals, including the artist and writer, William Morris. In 1883 Hyndman published his *Historic Basis of Socialism*, espousing Marxian ideas, but he still failed to command a large following or build up an effective party.

What was to be the truly significant and effective movement of English socialism originated in 1884 when the Fabian Society was founded with the purpose of "reconstructing society in accordance with the highest moral possibilities." Its membership soon included George Bernard Shaw, Sidney Webb, and Graham Wallas. In 1889 the society published its *Fabian Essays in Socialism*, followed soon by the cheaply printed *Fabian Tracts*. Advocating, like the Roman general Fabius Cunctator, a policy of patient waiting, the English Fabians were also prepared to strike hard when the time came. They planned to educate the public and concurrently to encourage municipal reform and to stimulate necessary action by political leaders on the national level. To the revolutionary creed of Marx they would oppose the principle of "the inevitability of gradualness." The Fabians encouraged the political activity of the trade unions and cooperated with them in founding the British Labor Party (1900–1906).[14] Thus socialist theory in England had in general become closely related to a program of political action which found its expression in the established parliamentary channels.

14. See p. 379.

■ RELIGION IN THE NEW AGE OF SCIENCE

The growth of theories of evolution was only one of many indications of the way in which modern science seemed to be in conflict with religious thought. As more and more emphasis was put on the search for natural causes in the physical world, it is not surprising that the need to subject traditional religious beliefs to the test of scientific critical analysis was asserted. The attack on religion had been mounted once before by the deists and skeptics of the eighteenth century; now it developed over a broader area and with new weapons.

Literal accounts in Genesis of the creation of man at a specific time could not be easily reconciled with the visible new evidence of man's antiquity. The assertion of belief in miracles, in the Virgin Birth, and in the Resurrection were unacceptable to many men of science. In the less vital field of dates the disputes also raged. In 1650 James Usher, Archbishop of Armagh, had published an elaborate work on biblical chronology which fixed the creation of man precisely in the year 4004 B.C., and his chronology had in some way come to be inserted in the margins of reference editions of the Authorized (King James) Version of the Bible. A contemporary of Usher, Dr. John Lightfoot, a distinguished Hebrew scholar of Cambridge University, had gone so far as to fix the creation of man "on the twenty-third of October, 4004 B.C., at nine o'clock in the morning." Thus, while clearly no part of the biblical record, Usher's chronology was associated by scientific zealots with a pattern of belief which flew in the face of geological evidence and evolutionary theories.

Sources of dispute were various. The dogma of Papal Infallibility proclaimed at the Vatican Council in 1870, though limited to ex cathedra pronouncements on matters of faith and morals, was taken in many circles to be an assertion of unlimited authority in other matters of belief. Conventional religion came under fire likewise from the socialists. Marxian argument was based primarily on a theory of materialism, that all history is determined by economic forces, and Marx repeatedly made it clear that he wished, as he once wrote, "to set the conscience free from religious superstition." A large literature critical of orthodox religion began to appear. J. W. Draper's *History of the Conflict Between Science and Religion* (1873), written by an American professor of science, made its attack chiefly upon the Roman Catholic Church in the light of what had been done at the Vatican Council of 1870. A. D. White's *History of the Warfare of Science with Theology in Christendom* (1896) was a two-volume expansion of an original popular lecture and booklet. W. E. H. Lecky's earlier *History of the Rise and Influence of the Spirit of Rationalism* (1866) was in the same key. In England many scientists took an unsympathetic view of conventional religion. Few managed to be as militantly vituperative as Thomas Huxley. "Extinguished theologians," he wrote in one of his *Essays*, "lie about the cradle of every science as the strangled snakes beside that of Hercules."[15]

In the first years of these controversies the various churches, Protestant and Catholic alike, held firmly to their established positions. The Anglican Church, for example, was not slow to express its repugnance toward the new trends. When Bishop Colenso of Natal, in the course of translating the Bible into Zulu, also published his doubts as to the trustworthiness of the first five books of the Bible as a historical record, he was deposed (illegally) by the bishop of Capetown. The nonconformist churches, too, were generally hostile, and it was only gradually that they began to relinquish their original position. Even after most of them did so, a strong element of fundamentalism, basing itself on the literal truth of the inspired word of the Bible, remained.

The older, conventional religious views of man's place in the universe, however, were influenced not only by Darwin's theories of evolution, but equally as much by the growth of biblical studies in the light of what came to be known as the "higher criticism." As historians began to develop highly technical means for enlarging their knowledge of the past, for example in the comparative study of religions, it was natural that the scriptural texts should come under scrutiny. Critical studies were undertaken of the literary methods and sources used by the authors of the books of the Old and New Testament, and in so doing the tendency was to regard the Bible as an historical document to be evaluated very much as any other historical document would be.

Such an approach conflicted with that of the fundamentalists to whom the inspired word of the Bible could be subject to no such criticisms. In time both sides tended to recede from their extreme positions. The opening of the Vatican archives in 1881 made possible a scholarly study of the papacy. Liberal Protestantism found a steadily larger foothold. Its most distinguished champion, Adolf Harnack, held the chair of church history at Berlin from 1889 to 1924. His monumental *History of Christian Dogma* (1886–1890) held that the primitive teaching of Jesus became distorted by the philosophical interests of the Greek world when Christianity ceased to be predominantly Jewish. Liberals, therefore, tried to recover the teaching of Jesus before it had been thus transformed. Harnack's liberal Protestantism could thus be reduced essentially to an affirmation of the fatherhood of God and the brotherhood of men.

One may note also changes in Judaism. Though most of the Jews in eastern Europe remained orthodox, under the impact of modernism changes occurred in western Europe and America. Here the new influences of modernism and liberalism led to the growth of a reformed Judaism with less emphasis on its ritual and its exclusive beliefs.

15. Quoted in C. GILLISPIE, *Genesis and Geology* (1951), p. 3.

POPE LEO XIII. A striking portrait of one of the outstanding figures of the late-nineteenth century, whose pontificate extended from 1878 to 1903.

The Roman Catholic Church had stood firm under Pius IX in its opposition to the secular trends of the modern world to such an extent that it clearly was in danger of losing substantial parts of its following. Liberal Catholicism in England, France, Germany, and Austria had raised its voice of protest or warning at the Vatican Council in 1870, though in the end it had submitted. Difficulties from other quarters were quick to appear. Bismarck's *Kulturkampf* was clearly political and nationalist in its inspiration, yet it represented a danger to the Catholic Church, as did the even more hostile and, in the end, much more successful policies of the anticlericals in France.

A notable strengthening of the Roman Catholic position became apparent soon after Pope Leo XIII succeeded Pius IX in 1878. Elected at the age of sixty-eight, he was expected to hold the papal throne only for a short time and as a transitional figure. His pontificate actually lasted a quarter of a century and was of such weight as to justify his being regarded as one of the greatest of modern popes. Although Leo took a strong stand against the more aggressive aspects of modernism in religion, making the philosophy of St. Thomas Aquinas the cornerstone of priestly studies, founding an academy for this purpose in Rome, and directing the preparation of a new edition of St. Thomas' writings, he was also aware of the importance of modern biblical scholarship. He declared that the Roman Catholic Church did not repudiate the discoveries of modern scientific research. He made the Vatican Library and Archives available to scholars and founded the Vatican Observatory, which he equipped at his own expense with the most modern instruments.

Concerning the great social issues of his times, Leo XIII made frequent pronouncements. One of his first moves was to denounce nihilism, communism, and socialism. Freemasonry, which in Italy was strongly radical and political in tone, he also attacked. Yet he was deeply sympathetic to the working classes, and in his most famous encyclical, *Rerum Novarum* (Of New Things), issued in 1891, he dealt with modern social problems. Private property is a natural right, but should be fairly distributed. The Church must be concerned with the well-being of its members, since labor is not a commodity and "it is shameful and inhuman to treat men like chattels to make money by." Both employers and employees should accept their Christian responsibilities. There should be legislation to assure families a living wage, to limit working hours, and to protect working conditions of women and children. In agriculture the farmers' cooperative movement should be encouraged and in industry collective bargaining should be recognized. It is not surprising, therefore, that Leo has won the title of "the workingman's pope."

Leo XIII also directed the attention of Catholics to political matters. In Italy, where the government in 1870 had taken from the papacy the last (save for the Vatican) of its temporal possessions, he maintained his predecessor's instructions to Catholics against voting at elections, though this was commonly disregarded. Elsewhere he encouraged Catholics to take part in politics, with the consequence that, in Germany, Belgium, Austria-Hungary, Switzerland, and the Netherlands, Catholic parties of moderate outlook began to concern themselves with social reform. Catholic trade unions, especially in Germany, where Archbishop von Ketteler of Mainz was active in their encouragement, also developed.

Leo XIII did much to bring the Roman Catholic Church into closer harmony with modern times and to encourage the substantial work which Catholic scholars undertook in every field of science; yet there were limits beyond which the Church could not go. Modernism in religious matters assumed that the great advances achieved by research in the natural sciences, in historical studies, in textual criticism, anthropology, and comparative religion made necessary some reinterpretation and restatement of traditional Christian teachings. Were this view to prevail, the historic dogmas of the Church would clearly be threatened. Hence in 1899 Leo XIII warned the French clergy against the dangers of modernism, and, though he expressed himself as being deeply concerned to end the schisms and divisions of Christianity, he was resolute in insisting upon complete acceptance of Roman Catholic dogmas and papal supremacy as a condition of reunion. His successor, Pius X, in 1907 formally condemned modernism as a heresy and in the following year excommunicated the brilliant French Catholic priest and scholar, Alfred Loisy, some of whose works had already been placed in the Index of Prohibited Books. Thus the accommodation of the Roman Catholic Church to modern trends was substantial and at the same time explicitly limited.

■ LITERATURE AND THE ARTS

The continuing upward surge in material prosperity in a world of ever-growing political rivalries was accompanied by vigorous developments in literature and the arts. These, inevitably, reflected the particular atmosphere of the times. Especially in the novel and the drama the great artists were concerned with social issues and with psychological probings of the human mind.

The novel is perhaps the best illustration of the influence of the times. In France Emile Zola continued until his death in 1902 his complex sociological depictions of French family patterns. In England Thomas Hardy made characters, such as the heroine of *Tess of the D'Urbervilles*, tragically and inescapably the victims of fate. The most striking developments came from Russia. During the 1860's western Europe had discovered to its surprise that Russia, with no long native tradition of literary sophistication, was the home of novelists and dramatists of astonishing psychological subtlety. The great works of Ivan Turgenev and Fedor Dostoevsky had then become known, and, while the former (whom both Dostoevsky and Tolstoy grew to detest) settled abroad where he was better liked, Dostoevsky went on to write his somber novels, *The Possessed* (1871) and *The Brothers Karamazov* (1880). These books had a great influence on French, German, English, and Scandinavian writers. Leo Tolstoy's[16] *War and Peace*, completed in 1866, combined a vast panorama of Russian life in the Napoleonic age with a profound depiction of men moving amid the fateful dictates of the gods.

The realistic psychological drama likewise emerged. Audiences that had gone to the theater to be amused, thrilled, or patriotically aroused now were presented with an astonishingly skillful technique of character analysis. By 1904 Anton Chekhov had written his *Seagull*, his *Uncle Vanya*, and his *Cherry Orchard*. In England George Bernard Shaw offered his audiences the brilliant list of *Plays Pleasant and Unpleasant*, and Oscar Wilde his sparkling satires upon society. The dramas of Hermann Sudermann and Gerhard Hauptmann in Germany

---

16. 1828-1910. One of the most dramatic figures of the nineteenth century, and of noble family and dissolute youth, he was a soldier during the Crimean War, and became a world-famous novelist while managing his huge Volga estates. He turned to the life of a peasant-recluse (1879) in opposition to the conventionally organized church, state, and society, believing man's religion to be within him.

explored the problems of the times, most memorably in Hauptmann's *The Weavers* (1892), a play based on the life of the Silesian workers. A most striking illustration came from Norway, where in a single decade Henrik Ibsen's *Doll's House*, his *Ghosts*, his *Wild Duck*, and *Rosmersholm* appeared; they have been called the most vigorous revelation of the mind of a nation in recent times. The tormented plays of the Swedish author, August Strindberg, resemble and perhaps match those of his brilliant Norwegian colleague.

The poets could hardly be expected to manifest this active psychological and sociological concern. One of the chief movements in late nineteenth-century poetry was that of the French symbolists. This group, of whom Stéphane Mallarmé, Paul Verlaine, and Arthur Rimbaud were the principal figures, put as their esthetic goal "the sense of the ineffable." The purpose of their fragile and music haunted verse was to communicate the most intimate and transitory types of human experience, and thus they sought for a subtle delicacy of metaphor and attuned their ears to the faintest of musical tones. In England Walter Pater and Oscar Wilde were champions of a similar estheticism. Wrote Pater in 1873:

> Every moment some form grows perfect in hand or face; some tone on the hills or the sea is choicer than the rest; some mood of passion or insight or intellectual excitement is irresistibly real and attractive to us—for that moment only. Not the fruit of experience, but experience itself is the end. . . . How shall we pass most swiftly from point to point, and be present always at the focus where the greatest number of vital forces unite in their purest energy? . . . For art comes to you, proposing frankly to give nothing but the highest quality to your moments as they pass, and simply for those moments' sake.[17]

In painting it is difficult to establish a close relation between the most significant movements in art and the dominant social trends of the time. The postimpressionism of the 1880's in France, heralded by the paintings of Paul Cézanne and Vincent Van Gogh, deliberately used the impressionist techniques in the handling of light, but moved on to a new sense of form. Cézanne wrote, "I wished to make out of Impressionism something solid and durable like the art of the museums." He thus turned away from the purely atmospheric effects of the impressionists to obtain the sensations of depth and mass. This he did by using changes of color to indicate the different planes of his modeling, and by simplifying and distorting the shape of objects when he wished to convey the actual impression they had made on him. Other painters, notably Paul Gauguin and Van Gogh, used colors and forms even more boldly, never departing from nature, but suffusing what they saw with a profound sense of what they themselves felt. Other painters, among them Henri Matisse, Raoul Dufy, Georges Rouault, and Georges Braque—the "wild beasts," or Fauvists, as they were

17. *The Renaissance* (1928 ed.), pp. 220–21, 223.

widely called—pushed on with experiments in strong color and distortion fertile enough to leave a large progeny to the twentieth century.

Music in the late nineteenth century saw no great transformation like the Wagnerian revolution of the earlier period. Tchaikovsky continued along the lines laid down by Brahms, while Richard Strauss (*Till Eulenspiegel*, 1895) in his symphonic poems developed further the principles of Liszt and Wagner. Nationalism produced Edvard Grieg in Norway, Jan Sibelius in Finland, Anton Dvořák in Bohemia, and Nicolai Rimsky-Korsakov in Russia. With César Franck and Gabriel Fauré, France gained her freedom from the Wagnerian yoke.

The really important trend for the future, however, lay in the breakdown of traditional harmony and tonality. Claude Debussy in his revolt from the conventional, with his system based on the medieval modes and on the whole-tone scale, produced a new type of composition comparable to what the impressionists did in painting. Arnold Schönberg, who began as an exponent of Wagnerism, came to eschew tonality altogether, and developed his famous twelve-tone music, the most violent of the new experiments. Finally, Igor Stravinsky, the Proteus of the first half of the twentieth century, had, by 1913, written his three great ballets, *The Firebird*, *Petrouchka*, and *The Rites of Spring*.

Architecture in the late nineteenth century sheds a curious light upon the times. Material progress and urbanization meant a furious tempo of building, yet architecture in the sense of creative achievement has rarely been so unproductive. City planning, in which the eighteenth century had made some highly intelligent experiments, was hardly undertaken again until toward the end of the nineteenth. Judgment at its most sympathetic has described this age as "full of interesting suggestions but on the whole barren"; at its most critical, "a time of darkness when inventiveness lay stagnant." The wealth which was poured into new buildings demanded traditional correctness rather than innovation; the advance of architectural scholarship made it easy for the experts to furnish demonstrably accurate reproductions; and a rapid tour of the massive structures housing the new parliaments, in Belgium, Germany, Austria, Hungary, and Scandinavia, would show a preponderance of the classical or Renaissance style with an occasional excursion into the Gothic.

The main advances were in the realm of technique. The use of iron and steel, of cement, and reinforced concrete underlay all significant progress. With these the much larger employment of glass surfaces became possible. The wide-arching roofs of the new railroad stations and bridges of growing size were some of the first examples of the new developments. The Eiffel Tower, 984 feet high, built for the Paris World's Fair in 1889 to demonstrate the capabilities of wrought iron, was a great landmark, literally and metaphorically. A few years earlier, in 1885, William LeBaron Jenney had constructed the Home Insurance

Building in Chicago with a steel skeleton—the progenitor of the modern sky-scraper. Finally, Walter Gropius, whose genius as a modern architect is general-ly associated with the most recent period, exhibited at Cologne in 1914 a flat-roofed factory of glass, brick, and steel with exposed staircases, which embodied the essential features of functional contemporary design. Thus the industrial and technical progress of the late nineteenth century was at length opening up new vistas for man's creative activity in this field of the arts.

■ CROSSCURRENTS

The growth of scientific knowledge, the steadily enlarging sphere of rational thought, and the rich proliferation of the arts suggest the picture of a progressive, orderly world in which man could grow in self-expression and be-come fully the master of his own destiny. Much, indeed, in the outlook of the late nineteenth century recalls the reasoned outlook of the eighteenth-century thinkers of the Enlightenment. Again and again in England, for example, the note of Victorian optimism was heard.

The spread of education and the extension of knowledge to an ever-widen-ing public would seem to confirm this optimism. As late as the 1860's the vast majority of Europeans had been unable to read and write. While, to be sure, the incidence of illiteracy grew less as one left the eastern and southern parts of the Continent, the general situation was bad enough. Illiteracy, moreover, was everywhere the mark of a particular segment of society. When it is said that the illiteracy figure for Italy in 1871 was 72 percent, this would mean that in a rough sense the whole lowest level of society in most parts of the peninsula would be unable to write or to understand the printed word. In Denmark a system of state elementary schooling, authorized in 1814, had been improved in 1856. State primary schools were authorized in Norway in 1860. In the German states generally education was compulsory though not gratuitous. Prussian schools had long been held up as models by foreign observers. In 1831 a French visitor, Victor Cousin, called Prussia "that classic land of barracks and schools, of schools which civilise the people and of barracks which defend them."[18] Without itemizing the details, one may say simply that, between 1868 and 1882, com-pulsory elementary schooling of one sort or another, sometimes limited to only a few years, had become a reality in France, Britain, Austria-Hungary, Ger-many, Switzerland, Italy, Belgium, the Netherlands, and Scandinavia.

The continuing spread of books and, even more, the growth of a popular press widened the public area of knowledge. Between 1866 and 1900 the number of European newspapers increased from about 6,000 to 12,000. Greatly improved printing machinery, the relaxation of press censorship, the cheapening of prices, and the growth of literacy all worked in the same direction. In 1860

18. Quoted in *The New Cambridge Modern History*, vol. X (1960), p. 109.

A New London Morning Paper

Will appear shortly. It will be owned by Mr. C. ARTHUR PEARSON, and will be called

The Daily Express.

Its price will be a **Ha'penny.** It will differ in many respects from all other daily papers, and will possess an absolutely unrivalled organisation for the collecting of news.

Special Correspondents have been appointed in every part of the world. No event can occur in even the most remote corner of the earth without

The Daily Express

being placed in immediate possession of its fullest details.

Particularly will this be the case as regards all parts of the British Empire.

The Daily Express

Has its Own Correspondent in every town over which the British flag waves, and one of its great aims will be to bring the far-distant parts of our mighty Possessions into closer touch with the Mother Country.

* * *

The Daily Express

Has despatched Seven Special Correspondents to South Africa. They will follow closely and report fully every detail of the War.

* * *

It would be unwise to speak in advance of the Special Features of

The Daily Express.

They have been planned with the utmost care, and will prove themselves to be varied, and of unique interest.

* * *

The demand for

The Daily Express

promises to be immense. *Will you let me reserve you a copy?* If so, please fill in and return the form overleaf.

PROSPECTUS FOR "THE DAILY EXPRESS," 1900. Details in this prospectus bring out the aims of popular journalism in the new democratic age.

the largest daily circulation of a newspaper in England was that of the London *Times*, with about 50,000 copies. In Paris the *Petit Journal* reached a daily circulation of about 650,000 in 1878. By 1900 the London *Daily Mail* was near the million mark, as were the *Petit Parisien* and *Petit Journal* in Paris, and the *Lokal-Anzeiger* in Berlin. It would be important to question, as it still would be today, whether these enormous circulation figures could be taken as a reassuring guarantee of public education and enlightenment. Bismarck's "reptile fund," which he employed to influence the press in support of policies which he favored, is the best-known example of a practice common among many European governments.

Robert Lowe, an English member of Parliament, had pointed out the dangers of extending the franchise to those who were inexperienced in its use. "We must," he said, after the passage of the Second Reform Bill in 1867, which doubled the number of British voters, "induce our masters to learn their letters." The same bill caused Thomas Carlyle, ever-mistrustful of the crowd, to write his infuriated article, *Shooting Niagara: and After?* in which he protested against the counting of heads being taken to be "the Divine Court of Appeal on every question and interest of mankind." Disraeli's success with the voters Carlyle described as "leading them by the nose, like helpless mesmerized somnambulant cattle."

In this period, then, when an increasingly literate public was steadily winning a larger control of political power, there is ample evidence of forces at work which appealed as much to the cruder emotions of men as to their reason. Nationalism took on a particularly strident tone, with aggressive demands for territory and power. War, in the pseudoscientific jargon of some of its advocates, was described as a biological necessity. The scientific study of anthropology, with its differentiation of racial types, caused certain political leaders to boast of the physical superiority of their people over others. Even linguistic and literary studies could be used for the purpose of encouraging an unhealthy form of national self-glorification.

The doctrine of racial superiority came to have highly explosive consequences. The terms "Nordic," "Alpine," and "Mediterranean," while useful and meaningful if employed by anthropologists to describe certain European physical types, became highly dangerous when employed by politicians to construct a doctrine of "Nordic supremacy." The term "Aryan," equally useful and meaningful when applied to a group of common Indo-European languages, lost all scientific significance when used as a designation of race. An eccentric Frenchman, Count Joseph de Gobineau, composed his huge *Essay on the Inequality of Human Races* (1853–1855), which singled out the white races as the only true creators of culture, and among them hailed especially what he chose to designate as the Aryans. Taken up enthusiastically by some Germans (including Richard Wagner, who greeted him as a master prophet), Gobineau was one of the chief sources of inspiration for Houston Stewart Chamberlain's *Foundations of the Nineteenth Century* (1899). This work by a renegade Englishman used the terms "Aryan," "Nordic," "Teutonic," and "German" to describe the people whom Chamberlain considered the master race, the inheritors of a splendid past, and the only hope of the world. Chamberlain married Wagner's daughter and became the honored friend of Emperor William II.

Pan-Germanism and Pan-Slavism were also concepts which offered a certain pseudoscientific justification to the economic and political considerations which basically inspired them. The scheme to link together all German-speaking peoples, while advocated by those who sought wider markets in central and eastern Europe, was bolstered also by a good deal of jargon concerning the common qualities and destiny of the German "race." A parallel development grew up in Russia. In 1871 a pseudoscientist, N. Danilevsky, published his *Russia and Europe* in which, influenced by current biological concepts, he wrote of the Slavs as a distinct and superior biological type, among whom the Russians were clearly the most powerful. Arguing that Russia should take the lead in creating a vast Slavic federation with Constantinople as its capital, he became the principal exponent of a Pan-Slavism which, while basically economic and political, sought further justification from the ethnographers and anthropologists.

Anti-Semitism as a phenomenon of the later nineteenth century had some association with these doctrines of race. Hostility to Jewish minorities and actual persecution had existed ever since the Middle Ages, surging up from time to time in waves of savage violence. It grew up in Germany and Austria again in the 1870's at a time of economic depression. In Prussia a Lutheran army chaplain and court preacher, Adolph Stöcker, won political support from many conservatives for his vituperative attacks on the Jews, whom he labeled a non-German and nonassimilable class:

> The Jews are a nation within the nation, a state within the state, a race in the midst of another race. All other immigrants are finally assimilated in the nation where they live, but not the Jews. Their unbroken Semitism and their rigid ritual system and enmity to Christianity stand in direct contrast to the German spirit.[19]

Though there was much protest in liberal circles, anti-Semitism continued in Germany throughout all this period.

Other countries experienced the same phenomenon. In Russia anti-Semitism was an integral part of governmental policy, forcing the Jews to live in what was virtually the huge ghetto of the western provinces. Police measures permitted, and in some instances seem actually to have incited, the terrible pogroms of the 1880's when hundreds of Jewish men, women, and children were slaughtered and thousands reduced to beggary. In Austria-Hungary anti-Semitism was deliberately used by political figures, such as Dr. Georg von Schönerer, who built up a national party upon it, and by Dr. Karl Lueger, who was elected burgomaster of Vienna in 1895 on an anti-Semitic program. The Dreyfus Case in France, described elsewhere,[20] gave international prominence to the same phenomenon of anti-Semitism, of which Edouard Drumont was the principal and most fanatical French advocate.

Other trends existed which ran counter to the prevalent belief in a rational order in which democracy was in the ascendant and material progress a rule of life. A brilliant group of dissenters was not slow in making itself heard. Chief among these must be put Friedrich Nietzsche,[21] a German writer deeply influenced by Schopenhauer's *World as Will and Idea* and "a destructive genius of the first order." Nietzsche, who became a friend of Wagner, joined with the composer in a mutual contempt for what they both regarded as the German lack of a true culture. Nietzsche set himself in opposition to the economic, political, and intellectual ideals of the nineteenth century. As against the inherited Greek values of the good, the beautiful, and the true, Nietzsche declared

---

19. Quoted in C. J. H. HAYES, *A Generation of Materialism, 1871–1900* (1941), p. 261.
20. See pp. 351–352.
21. 1844–1900. Village pastor's son and brilliant Greek scholar, he became professor of classical philology at Basel before taking his degree. Deeply influenced by Schopenhauer and Wagner, he regarded Wagnerian opera as the true successor to Greek tragedy. Having made a reputation by his philosophical writings, he went through a period of mental crisis further affected by illness contracted during his service in the Franco-Prussian War. He underwent complete mental breakdown in 1889. His teachings sought a new class of masters uncorrupted by Christian morality, and visualized a pan-European society that would be destructive of all national cultures.

that man was dominated only by "the will to power." He condemned what he called Judaeo-Christian morality for perverting this will to power and substituting for it the "slave morality" of humility, patience, and sacrifice. A transvaluation of values was needed to establish the new creed. Nietzsche opposed parliamentary government and the power of the press, "because they are the means whereby cattle become masters." Modern democracy is "the historic form of the decay of the state." Nietzsche proclaimed the doctrine of the Superman (*Uebermensch*)—the "blond beast" whose guide is this instinctive will to power. "God hath died," he wrote in *Thus Spake Zarathustra:* "now do *we* desire the superman to live."

In *The Will to Power* Nietzsche wrote as follows concerning universal suffrage:

> It is necessary for *higher* men to declare war upon the masses! In all directions mediocre people are joining hands in order to make themselves masters. Everything that pampers, that softens, and that brings the "people" or "woman" to the front, operates in favor of universal suffrage—that is to say, the dominion of *inferior* men.

It would be difficult to find any thinker comparable in ruthless destructive force to Nietzsche. Of quite another type, and yet illustrative also of the challenging conflicts in European thought at the close of the century, was a French philosopher who lectured in exquisitely polished language to crowded and fashionable audiences at the Collège de France. Henri Bergson (1859–1941) challenged the Platonic view which linked the finite being with eternal reality and instead substituted for static existence the concepts of motion and change. The Bergsonian revolution required the thinker to abandon universal systems and devote himself only to particular problems. The true nature of things will be learned intuitively. His *Creative Evolution* (1907) denies the wisdom of building up a theory of existence by assembling the scattered fragments of available evidence. Instead he offers the concept of an *élan vital*, a vital urge by which man ever strives to realize himself.

One of the most vivid impressions derived from any such brief glance at the patterns of the European outlook is that of their complexity and variety. One finds an inherited and deep respect for the dignity of man, a continuing concern to explore the mysteries of nature, an acute regard for the unsolved problem of social justice, and a fairly confident belief in human progress. On the other hand one is impressed by the existence of a vigorous minority of dissent. The answers are not uniform, so that a striking outcome of this "century of hope" is the repeated note of scientific, religious, and philosophic uncertainty which had emerged by its close. In the political relations between states, as the next chapter will make clear, this note of uncertainty was even more striking and more ominous.

Reading List: Chapter 16

The New Cambridge Modern History, vol. XI (1962), chs. 4–7. Social and political thought, literature, art and architecture, education.

Brinton, C., *Ideas and Men, The Story of Western Thought* (1950), ch. 13. Late nineteenth-century thought.

Hayes, C. J. H., *A Generation of Materialism, 1871–1900* (1941), chs. 4–5. Religion and the arts; emergence of the masses.

Wagner, Donald, *Social Reformers* (1935), chs. 24–26, 28. Useful passages from Bakunin, Georges Sorel, Lenin, and Leo XIII.

Bowle, John, *Politics and Opinion in the Nineteenth Century. An Historical Introduction* (1954), Bk. II, ch. 8, Schopenhauer and Nietzsche; ch. 9, Catholic attitudes; ch. 10, Georges Sorel.

Markham, S. F., *A History of Socialism* (1931), ch. 6. Socialism and anarchism in Russia.

Nietzsche, F., *Living Thoughts*, ed. by T. Mann (1939), pp. 70–127. Critiques of European culture.

Tolstoy, L., *Living Thoughts*, ed. by S. Zweig (1939), pp. 52–81. Criticisms of his age.

Priestley, J. B., *Literature and Western Man* (1960), part IV, "The Broken Web." Deals interestingly with European literature of the late nineteenth century.

Kohn, H., *Pan-Slavism* (1953; paperback, 1960), ch. 2. "Pan-Slavism and Russian Messianism, 1860–1905."

Freud, S., *Living Thoughts*, ed. by R. Waelder (1941), pp. 93–116. On dreams.

Harris, D., "European Liberalism in the Nineteenth Century," *American Historical Review*, vol. LX (1955), no. 3. A valuable interpretation.

Chapter 17

The Road to War

Introduction
The Heritage of Bismarck
Alliances and Regroupings, 1890–1907
Conflicts and Compromises, 1908–1913
Underlying Causes of War
1914: Events Leading to War
Conclusion

■ INTRODUCTION

In the present chapter we shall trace the course of events which led to the outbreak of the First World War, and try to show what their underlying forces and the motives and impulses at work were. Though this is a subject to which many volumes of official documents and the labors of many historians have been devoted, it is impossible to arrive at finality. For many years after the Peace of Versailles, the matter was studied primarily with a view to proving or disproving the validity of the so-called war-guilt clauses arraigning Germany and her allies, which were a burning issue in the evaluation of that treaty. No general agreement on the reapportionment of the guilt ever resulted. More recently, however, a generation which itself fears to stumble unawares into a third world war has been disposed to lay greater emphasis on the absence of any

472

SIGNIFICANT EVENTS

1879	Dual Alliance between Germany and Austria-Hungary
1882	Triple Alliance of Germany, Austria-Hungary, and Italy
1891–1894	Formation of Franco-Russian Alliance
1902	Anglo-Japanese Alliance
	Rapprochement between Italy and France
1904	Entente Cordiale between Britain and France
1907	Anglo-Russian Agreement, creating the Triple Entente
1908	Annexation of Bosnia-Herzegovina by Austria-Hungary
1909	Racconigi Agreement between Russia and Italy
1911	Agadir crisis and final Moroccan settlement
1912–1913	Balkan Wars
1914	Sarajevo assassinations
	Outbreak of First World War

deliberate planning by the leaders of any of the countries concerned to bring about a general war in 1914, but again there is no unanimity.

The subject is as complex as it is interesting. With the end of the Franco-Prussian War, Europe passed into a period in which the pacific influence of the Concert of Europe had lost most of its former effectiveness, though for the first two decades the precariousness of the balance on which peace rested was concealed from most eyes by the consummate skill with which Bismarck manipulated alliances so as to preserve the situation he had created to suit German interests. The next fifteen years, on the other hand, were a period of movement, marked by great clashes of interest outside Europe, in both Africa and Asia, and inside Europe by the gradual establishment of a combination of powers to challenge the predominance of Germany. By 1907 there seemed to be a definite pat-

H.M.S. "DREADNOUGHT." Authorized in 1905, *Dreadnought* was completed in December, 1906. With a length of 490 feet, a displacement of 17,900 tons, and with ten twelve-inch guns disposed in five turrets, it was the first British battleship to steam at 21 knots, the first large warship to have turbines, and the most powerful naval vessel afloat.

tern of opposition between Triple Alliance and Triple Entente, but in fact neither Italy nor Britain was firmly attached to its respective partners—though for very different reasons—and the groupings were still oriented toward purposes of defense rather than offense. Thereafter a succession of crises, each with difficulty surmounted and each rendering the peaceful solution of the next critical situation less feasible, ranged the powers more firmly in two camps, promoted the growth of armaments at a dangerously accelerated pace, and made offense appear to some to be the best form of defense. The assassination of the heir presumptive to the Austro-Hungarian thrones at Sarajevo in June, 1914, then provided the occasion of the war, partly because the actors on the political scene at that juncture had their full share of human shortsightedness, recklessness, and folly, but chiefly because a whole generation of men had done so little to stop the worsening of international relations while there was still time.

In 1914 an age of liberal progress gave place to an age of violence, of which the end is not yet in sight. The causation of so great a turning point in history deserves relatively full treatment. We shall therefore place it in the context of the alliance system which grew up between 1871 and 1907, even at the cost of some recapitulation of what has been said in describing the separate development of the different national policies. The diplomatic events of 1907–1914 must then be traced in detail up to the moment when Princip fired in a narrow Bosnian street a shot that eventually rang round the world. At that point in the discussion it may be logical to consider the general factors in the society of the time which enormously increased the possibility that a given diplomatic situation would build up into the outbreak of a widespread war. Last, some space must be given to the moves and countermoves during the final crisis, by which the powers in their different ways all sought to avoid such a war, provided its avoidance could be contrived without detriment to their various interests.

■ THE HERITAGE OF BISMARCK

Bismarck's conception of diplomacy had been based on a system of groups—"Try to be *à trois* in a world governed by five powers." At the outset this appeared to be almost too easy, since a weakened and distracted France stood face to face with three empires, to each of which a weak republic was an unattractive partner. The meetings of the three emperors in Berlin in September, 1872, and the Russo-German and Russo-Austrian conventions of the following summer, which together were taken as establishing a *Dreikaiserbund* (League of Three Emperors), therefore represented a condition of monarchical solidarity which might prove stable as long as no major issues arose. Then came the war scare of 1875, when Russia ranged herself with Britain against a hypothetical second German attack on France. That scare had scarcely subsided before a new crisis over the Eastern question placed Germany in a position where she could only retain the support of Austria-Hungary at the cost of the alienation of Russia, or vice versa. One reason why Germany then made the momentous choice of Austria-Hungary as her partner in the treaty of October, 1879, was that this choice did not exclude the possibility of a further link with Britain, as the choice of Russia—Britain's rival in the Middle East—would certainly do. Though the treaty was kept secret until 1888, remained subject to periodic renewal, and concerned itself only with defense against a Russian attack, it was a constant major factor in European affairs down to the catastrophe which befell the Central Powers in 1918.

Although the Bismarckian system never obtained a firm hold on Britain, in other respects its development in the early 1880's surpassed expectation. For six years (1881–1887) the obligations of the second *Dreikaiserbund* (which was a formal treaty) bound Russia on a reciprocal basis to a policy of benevolent neutrality if either of the other empires were at war, and in principle achieved a reconciliation between the respective Balkan interests of Germany's two partners. At the same time Germany's control over the diplomatic situation was strengthened by the fact that her main ally, Austria-Hungary, established treaty relations with Serbia, which two years later were extended to Rumania by an agreement to which Germany also adhered. Meanwhile, in 1882 the Triple Alliance had brought Italy, the latest and least of the great powers, from a position of isolation to one in which she was linked with Germany and Austria-Hungary in the event of a war against the two other powers or an attack on

All the major European powers found themselves involved in Mediterranean rivalries, including those not actually the possessors of territory. Imperial Germany in 1905 and in 1911 challenged the French claims to Morocco, and on the eve of 1914 had a powerful influence in Turkey. Imperial Russia, traditionally seeking control of the Straits, deeply resented Austria-Hungary's annexation of Bosnia in 1908.

Italy by France—and with Germany in the event of a French attack on that country.

All this was put to the test in the complex crisis of 1887, when the danger of Russian intervention to restore Bulgaria to satellite status coincided with a second threat to peace, namely, the danger of ill-considered French moves to placate chauvinist propagandists, such as Boulanger. Bismarck rose to the height of the occasion. On the one hand, he sponsored two Mediterranean Agreements. By the first of these Britain became linked in succession with Italy, Austria, and Spain for the preservation of the *status quo* in the Mediterranean area, including the Black Sea. By the second agreement the same powers less Spain offered their specific support for the maintenance of Turkish rights over Bulgaria and over the Straits. Thus Turkey, in the event of any forward move by Russia, would have the support of Britain, Italy, and Austria, whereas Russia at best would have only the support of France. On the other hand, in June of the same year, sandwiched between the two Mediterranean Agreements, came Bismarck's famous—though long most secret—Reinsurance Treaty. This replaced the *Dreikaiserbund*, which Russia had refused to renew, by a neutrality pact, applicable except in the event of a German attack on France, or a Russian on Austria, in which case the German-Austrian alliance of 1879 would take effect, as its publication shortly made clear. The price paid by Germany was to promise support for Russian claims upon Turkey which other powers (as has been

476

Map legend:

GROWTH of
MEDITERRANEAN RIVALRIES
in the NINETEENTH CENTURY

FRENCH
BRITISH
ITALIAN
AUSTRIAN-HUNGARIAN
RUSSIAN
SPANISH

shown) were being organized to resist. This was not a high price, in Bismarck's view, for an arrangement which removed the risk of an alliance between Russia and France. The reinsurance system was allowed to lapse three months after the removal of Bismarck from office by William II in March, 1890.

At first sight, the rule of Bismarck over imperial Germany might be acquitted of any responsibility for the European catastrophe of 1914, since his arrangements appear basically defensive. In this light, should we not attribute it to the dominant influence of Germany as a satiated power that the Russo-Turkish War of 1877–1878 proved to be the only important interruption to the peace of Europe throughout two decades? This, surely, could be regarded as the logical consequence of Bismarck's skill in weaving a whole network of defensive treaties, which gave the maximum of security to the maximum number of powers and reduced to a minimum the number of powers outside the network, thus achieving a proportionate reduction in the chances of aggression. But there are darker aspects to the huge influence which Bismarck wielded. His principal objective, after all, was the isolation of France, an isolation which did not render the cession of Alsace-Lorraine any more acceptable—and this was a wrong to France for which Bismarck was ultimately responsible, since he was aware of its unwisdom and could probably have prevented it. Although Bismarck from time to time distracted French attention toward colonial compensations, the regime he established for the imperial territory of Alsace-Lorraine, which waited forty years for a constitution, helped to keep alive the French hatred of Germany over the treatment of lands which had been a part of France.

The Bismarckian regime was also responsible for bringing into regular diplomatic use two instruments, which in less skilled hands later proved very dangerous to the peace of Europe. One was his reliance upon secret treaties of alliance as a part of the regular organization of international affairs, notwithstanding the absence of any specific danger. Even his alliance with Austria-Hungary, a peacetime agreement of general scope which was renewed quinquennially for nearly forty years, was never published in its entirety until after the war. In the case of the *Dreikaiserbund* treaty of 1881, Bismarck wrote out the documents with his own hand and placed the relevant diplomatic correspondence in a special category of secret papers, with the result that the world never even suspected its existence before 1918. Germany's rivals followed suit, so that from 1879 onward the effects of the alliances in a given situation were never wholly calculable. At the same time Europe was left in no doubt that, however pacific the aims of Bismarck's diplomacy, its functioning was based upon the possession of overwhelming force. His own words ring down the years to 1914, from the speech in which he urged an increase of the army by forty thousand men to meet the critical situation of 1887:

> The difficulty of our position is not to keep peace with Austria and Russia, but between Russia and Austria. . . . With words I can do nothing. Words are not soldiers, nor are speeches battalions. . . . The possibility of a French attack, which today is not imminent, will recur as soon as France thinks she is stronger than we are, either by alliances or being better armed.[1]

■ ALLIANCES AND REGROUPINGS, 1890–1907

The years from 1890 to 1907, viewed from the standpoint of the present study, form a kind of interlude between the age of Bismarck and the immediate prewar period—recognizable as such at least in retrospect—in which the European powers drift into, rather than deliberately take up, new and potentially dangerous positions of rivalry. Three considerable wars took place outside Europe—in the Spanish colonial empire, in South Africa, and in the Far East—each of which had important effects on its European participant; but in Europe itself there was no armed conflict more serious than a one-month contest between Greeks and Turks. On the contrary, in 1899 and 1907 Europe was the scene of two conferences which aimed at some agreed measure of international disarmament and did at least set up the first tentative international court of arbitration at The Hague. Moreover, there were also two occasions in this period when the Continental powers found themselves virtually united in a different sense—by common opposition to the insular power of Britain. In 1895

1. Speech in the Reichstag, January 11, 1887.

Russia, Germany, and France formed a league of three, to which Britain was not a party, in order to exploit the situation in the Far East following upon the defeat of the Chinese Empire by Japan; and in the early phases of the Boer War of 1899–1902 there was a virtual unanimity of public opinion on the Continent, championing Boer against Briton, though governments did not allow its practical expression to go beyond exploratory conversations, in which Russia apparently took the lead and Germany declined to follow.

Yet we may distinguish in this period the development of several changes of lasting importance. The first was the change in the position of Russia. Difficulties for which Bismarck was partly responsible had caused the first of many Russian loans to be floated on the French money market in 1888; two years later his successors broke with the policy of the Reinsurance Treaty, thus giving the French a chance to escape from the position of isolation in which they had fretted for two decades. In January, 1894, almost two and a half years after the signature of a vague political convention, imperial Russia became linked with republican France by the terms of a military pact. Its existence was made known by the French in 1895 and the tsar two years later, though nothing was disclosed about the actual terms which were duly honored in 1914. The German General Staff, who left nothing to chance, accordingly based their plans upon the hypothesis that war against Russia and war against France was a single problem, to be solved by directing the full weight of the German army's initial stroke against France. In 1899, too, when the dissolution of the Hapsburg monarchy from internal causes seemed imminent, the Russo-French alliance was extended to cover the maintenance of the balance of power as well as the preservation of peace: they would act together as allies if Austro-Hungarian territory were to be reapportioned.

It is true that in 1905, under the stress of defeat abroad and revolutionary upheavals at home, the Tsar Nicholas put his signature to the abortive Treaty of Björkö, by which the German emperor hoped to draw Russia back into the German camp. But even the tsar soon had second thoughts about the advisability of granting such a treaty "until we know how France will look at it," and his advisers were quite unwilling to sacrifice the existing relationship with France, which produced the largest of a long series of urgently needed loans to meet the difficulties of 1906. Thus the treaty, which was designed to take effect at the termination of the Russo-Japanese War, then in its final stage, came to nothing. Although the royal houses and governing classes of Germany and Russia continued to have important interests in common, which limited the effectiveness of the alliance between Russia and France, from 1907 onward the latter relationship was strengthened rather than weakened.

Second, these years witnessed a progressive deterioration in Anglo-German relations. Toward the end of the Bismarckian era, the Mediterranean

Agreements had provided a definite link, and neither the British addiction to a policy of splendid isolation, nor Bismarck's resentment at the inconsistencies and uncertainties resulting from the fact that British ministers were answerable to parliament, had prevented a generally harmonious relationship developing over a much longer period. Most Britons of the governing class would have subscribed to the view that, if changing circumstances caused splendid isolation to be abandoned, it was to the Triple Alliance that Britain must inevitably turn. But when such events as the Venezuelan boundary controversy with America, the Fashoda crisis with France, and the Black Week of Boer victories in 1899 showed that the circumstances had indeed changed, the result was a turning away from, instead of toward, a pact with Germany. Personal factors played an important part—the impetuosity of the kaiser in prompting the dispatch of the telegram of support to Kruger at the time of the ill-starred Jameson Raid in January, 1896; the anti-British sentiments of Holstein,[2] at work behind the scenes in the German Foreign Office; and the duplicity which was second nature to Bülow, who noted in British politicians "a certain blind confidence. They find difficulty in believing in really evil intentions in others." A further comment from the same pen on the same occasion—a visit to Britain in attendance on the kaiser at the end of November, 1899—describes the attitude of German public opinion at this juncture:

> In general, there is no question that the feeling in Britain is much less anti-German than the feeling in Germany is anti-British. For that reason those Englishmen who . . . know from personal observation the acuteness and depth of Germany's unfortunate dislike of Britain are the most dangerous to us. If the British public clearly realized the anti-British feeling which dominates Germany just now, a great revulsion would occur in its conception of the relations between Britain and Germany.[3]

Between 1898 and 1901 Joseph Chamberlain was allowed by Lord Salisbury on three occasions to make overtures for an Anglo-German alliance. Each time they led to nothing because of the German belief that they could afford to wait until a friendless Britain accepted their terms, however onerous, for want of any alternative partner. Only one localized agreement was signed and came for a short period into force—an arrangement made in 1900 to maintain the *status quo* in the Yangtze Valley, which broke down as soon as the Germans made it clear that Britain could not look to them for any help

---

2. 1837–1909. A diplomat who had served, and been ill-used by, Bismarck, from 1890 to 1906—and again in 1908–1909—he determined the foreign policy of successive chancellors, playing off Russia against Britain and treating the latter with hostility. He resigned because Bülow would not run the risk of war in the attempt to break up the Entente after the fall of Delcassé. A good duellist, stock-exchange speculator, and wire-puller, he only met William II once and proposed that he be certified insane.

3. Prince VON BÜLOW, trans. F. A. VOIGT, *Memoirs 1897–1903* (1931), p. 332.

against Russian domination in Manchuria. Since this was the period in which the first two German Navy Laws came into effect, offering what appeared to most Englishmen to be a wanton threat to the security of their island base and its imperial communications, the moment was fast approaching when public opinion would be one factor in favor of finding other friends—the alternative solution so rashly disregarded by the Germans.

In January, 1902, the British relieved the pressure against their interests in the Far East by signing the Anglo-Japanese alliance. Two years later the formation of the Entente Cordiale with France made a reorientation of Britain's attitude toward the rival groups in Europe for the first time appear possible. Since the British had secured French support for their established interests in Egypt in exchange for supporting French interests not yet clearly established in Morocco,[4] the Germans were entitled—though not necessarily well advised—to send the kaiser to Tangier to challenge those interests. The immediate result was the dismissal of Delcassé,[5] the prime architect of the Entente, as a foreign minister who had dangerously provoked the Germans. But the British, the weakness of whose army had been exposed in the Boer War, now made the first tentative arrangements for military help which might in a given case be supplied to France. Parliamentary approval would be the all-important prerequisite for any action; yet the gesture, made in January, 1906, and for the next six years known only to a small inner circle of the newly formed Liberal cabinet, influenced in some degree the whole sequence of events down to 1914. In the same month, too, the Algeciras Conference met at Germany's behest, and to her surprise all the powers except Austria-Hungary united to give France a privileged position in Morocco, from which she might eventually gain what she wanted there.

At the time of the Algeciras Conference, the defeat of Russia by Japan had removed the main source of contention from Anglo-Russian relations, since the Russians had been forced to abandon their forward policy in the Far East. But there was certainly no common front against Germany, as Sir Edward Grey[6] was well aware. "The door is being kept open by us for a *rapprochement* with Russia," he observed in February, 1906. "An entente between Russia, France

4. See pp. 377–378.
5. 1852–1923. A follower of Gambetta, of humble origins, he was minister for foreign affairs from June, 1898, to June, 1905. In the year of the French debacle at Fashoda, he already aimed at the Entente with Britain, and by 1903 he was planning the extension of the as yet uncompleted arrangements to Russo-British relations. He returned to the government in 1911, was ambassador in St. Petersburg in 1913–1914, and foreign minister again in 1914–1915.
6. 1862–1933. Collaterally related to Grey of the Reform Bill, and British foreign secretary for a record continuous period, Grey had been undersecretary in 1892–1895. He belonged to the so-called imperialist wing of the Liberal Party, but the mainspring of his policy was cooperation with France and Russia for the amelioration of German militarism. He retired in December, 1916, and, in spite of failing eyesight, wrote an effective defense of his diplomatic purposes in his *Twenty-Five Years* (1925).

and ourselves would be absolutely secure. If it is necessary to check Germany it could then be done." There were friendly informal discussions at the Conference, and in April, 1906—for the first time since the Crimean War—British finance shared in the flotation of a big French loan, which (as we have seen) served to put the tsardom on its feet again after the year of revolution. A year later the outstanding subjects of dispute, all of them in the Middle East, were settled by an open convention, designed to protect the neutrality of Tibet, the security of British India vis-à-vis Afghanistan, and a peaceful division of Persia into spheres of influence. The convention was not aimed against Germany, and the very term "Triple Entente" was disapproved of in official circles in Britain, for the restored Russian autocracy was very unpopular with Liberals. But when the next expansion of the German navy was announced in the dreadnought-building program of November, 1907, the British relationship with Russia was clearly relevant to the worsening situation. In the words of the civil service head of the foreign office:

> It was impossible to ignore the fact that, owing to the unnecessarily large increase in the German naval programme a deep distrust in England of Germany's future intentions had been created. . . . In seven or eight years' time a critical situation might arise, in which Russia, if strong in Europe, might be the arbiter of peace. . . . For this reason it was absolutely necessary that England and Russia should maintain towards each other the same cordial and friendly relations as now exist between England and France.[7]

The growth of what was potentially a rival structure was accompanied by changes in the Triple Alliance and its subordinate connections. Italy, which had always opted out of any obligation to enter a war of the Alliance against Britain, weakened it further in 1902 by an important treaty with France. In return for support of Italian ambitions in North Africa, she undertook to remain neutral if France went to war either in self-defense or "as the result of direct provocation." In the following years the restoration of the Karageorgevic dynasty in Belgrade began the process by which Serbia, too, transferred its loyalty away from Austria-Hungary, which foolishly attempted certain tariff reprisals dignified by the name of the "Pig War."

The Ottoman Empire, on the other hand, was moving steadily into the German camp, largely as a result of economic ties. In October, 1898, William II had paid his second visit to Constantinople, and the Baghdad railway scheme was launched soon after. In terms of economic as well as military strength, Germany still had an ascendancy on the Continent, to which her central geographical position lent additional weight. Germans complained of a policy

---

7. Sir Charles Hardinge, when reporting remarks made by him to the Russian foreign minister Izvolsky during King Edward VII's visit to the tsar at Reval, June 12, 1908 (*British Documents on the Origins of the War*, Vol. V, 1928, No. 195).

RUSSIAN PREWAR MANEUVERS. The Russian Minister of War, General Sukhomlinov, and his aides embody the ancient spirit of military pomp which the First World War was so ruthlessly to destroy.

of encirclement, with Edward VII as its Machiavellian contriver. What they were really experiencing was an evening up of the balance of power, which for nearly forty years had been weighted in Germany's favor.

■ CONFLICTS AND COMPROMISES, 1908–1913

The development of international relations in Europe moved very quickly between the signature of the Anglo-Russian convention of August, 1907, and the assassination of the Archduke Francis Ferdinand at Sarajevo in June, 1914. The result has been well summarized in the remark that the Triple Alliance and Triple Entente, which at first stood side by side, by 1914 stood face to face.

The Eastern question, which had never completely slept, came to life again early in 1908, when the Austrians projected a scheme to build a railway through the small Turkish province, the Sanjak of Novi Pazar. This would complete a through route to Salonika, but the immediate object was to emphasize the separation of Serbia from Montenegro and the sea, for which purpose Austria-Hungary had been empowered to maintain a garrison in this strip of Turkish territory ever since the Congress of Berlin. Though objections were naturally raised by the Russians, who produced a railway scheme of their own, the Young Turk revolution then created a new situation, which the Austro-

Hungarian and Russian foreign ministers, Aehrenthal[8] and Izvolsky,[9] planned to exploit in common. Austria-Hungary was to annex Bosnia-Herzegovina, a move which had been authorized by the *Dreikaiserbund* only three years after the occupation had begun, and which now appeared urgent because the Young Turks showed signs of attempting to recover the occupied provinces. Russia in return was to secure the opening of the Straits to her warships, control being of paramount importance to her as she now depended on the Black Sea trade for economic stability. The scheme broke down within a month, because Aehrenthal proclaimed the annexation of the provinces (less the Sanjak) as an immediate sequel to a Bulgarian proclamation of complete independence. This was before the Straits project, to which Germany and Italy offered no serious objection, had been laid before the British, who were courting the favor of the Young Turks and said that Turkish consent must first be obtained.

In these circumstances Russia had British and French support for nothing more than a demand that the Austro-Hungarian action in Bosnia should be referred for consideration to a European conference. Aehrenthal refused this, but offered acceptable financial compensation to the Turks, who also received indirect payment from the Russians for recognizing the abolition of their nominal suzerainty over Bulgaria. The debacle of her war against Japan and the revolutionary disturbances of 1905 were too close for Russia to enter upon another war. Therefore in March, 1909, Izvolsky gave way before a stiff German note. Russia accepted the annexation herself, and took no action when her protégé, Serbia, was forced to swallow her indignation over the definitive loss of the territory she had hoped some day to acquire; Serbia's acquiescence had to be accompanied by the demobilization of her army. One lasting result of the crisis was that Britain, though deploring the hasty surrender of the Russian case for an international conference, began to take the initially rather unpopular tie with Russia more seriously. Another was the imputation to the rulers of Austria-Hungary of a readiness to act highhandedly, which Germany did nothing to keep in check; on the contrary, the kaiser openly boasted of supporting the Austrian cause "like a knight in shining armor." Most important of all, however, was the stimulus given to the rivalries which culminated in the Balkan Wars. Izvolsky, who was later to hail the war of 1914 as "my war,"

8. 1854–1912. An aristocrat with a long career in the diplomatic service, he had favored the Mürzsteg Agreement and, on becoming foreign minister in 1906, aimed at friendly relations with Russia. He carried through the annexation of Bosnia-Herzegovina (for which he was made a count) in face of Russian opposition, but maintained a peace policy, which caused the resignation of Conrad von Hötzendorff a few months before his resignation and death. His successor complained of "a thick atmosphere of bad faith."

9. 1856–1919. He rose in the diplomatic service through the influence of the dowager empress, was foreign minister 1906–1910, when he strove to strengthen the alliance with France and helped to create the Triple Entente; he was unsuccessful, however, in his bargaining with Aehrenthal, and was transferred to the Paris embassy, from where he continued to influence policy down to 1917. King Edward VII thought him to be the cleverest diplomatist in Russia.

busily plotted his revenge on Aehrenthal, and before his demotion to the Paris embassy in 1910 he had made the Treaty of Racconigi; this secured Italian support for his Straits program in return for Russian support if Italy were to attack Turkish possessions on the North African coast.

Izvolsky's successor as foreign minister, Sazonov, began his term of office by negotiating the Potsdam Agreement with the Germans, who accepted the Russian sphere of influence in north Persia in return for the acceptance of German claims in the matter of the Baghdad railway. Since the British had been striving for the principle that this was a matter in which all three members of the Triple Entente should stand together in their dealings with Germany, it is clear that mutual confidence was still often lacking. The words in which Sazonov at this time refers to the working of the Anglo-Russian Convention of 1907 speak for themselves:

> The English, engaged in the pursuit of political aims of vital importance in Europe, may, in case of necessity, be prepared to sacrifice certain interests in Asia in order to keep a Convention alive which is of such importance to them. This is a circumstance which we can, of course, exploit for ourselves, as, for instance, in Persian affairs.[10]

While the Anglo-Russian relationship remained an uncertain factor even after the events of 1908–1909, the relation between England and France emerged from the further test which the Germans deliberately imposed upon it in 1911 stronger than it had been in 1906, to say nothing of the original position in 1904. For in the second Moroccan crisis the British believed their own naval interests to be at stake; spoke for the first time in terms of the national honor; and, as a consequence of the Haldane reforms in the army, were able to co-operate with French military planning in a manner which was something more than a gesture. This is at first sight surprising, since in 1908 a Moroccan dispute concerning German consular privileges—the so-called "affair of the Casablanca deserters"—had been successfully referred to arbitration; and in the following year a Franco-German agreement was signed which promised equality of economic opportunity to the Germans in return for their recognition of the special French political interests in Morocco. By 1911 the internal situation had again deteriorated, with the result that a French military expedition marched inland to restore order in Fez. But the acute crisis, which began in early July and lasted for four months, is not attributable to the necessities of the situation; it was deliberately occasioned by the new and uncompromising German foreign minister, Kiderlen-Wächter, who wished to hold the French to ransom for as much colonial territory as they could be induced to give.

By sending a gunboat, the *Panther*, to protect the alleged interests of

10. Letter to Russian minister in Teheran, October 8, 1910, cited by s. b. fay, *The Origins of the World War* (rev. ed., 1931), vol. I, p. 222.

German merchants at what was then the open Atlantic roadstead of Agadir, Kiderlen-Wächter caused the British to develop apprehensions regarding a possible German naval base, an outcome which he certainly never intended. By first leaving it to the French to make an offer, and then demanding the whole of the French Congo as compensation for Morocco, he increased British suspicions that the real objective was strategic. And by excluding Britain from the discussions conducted with French representatives in Berlin, Kiderlen-Wächter caused Lloyd George (as we have seen) to denounce emphatically a policy of peace at any price. These were not mere empty words, for on the day before the chancellor of the exchequer spoke, unofficial conversations were held between general staff representatives in Paris "to determine the new conditions for the participation of an English army in the operations of the French armies in the northeast in case of a war with Germany."[11] Contact had been maintained between the two staffs since 1906, but Haldane's expeditionary force was not constructed until 1910, so that 1911, when the Germans fomented a crisis, was the first year when plans for Anglo-French military cooperation could have much serious content. In all the circumstances, the 100,000 square miles of jungle which Germany now gained from the French Congo as her final compensation for disinteresting herself in the fate of Morocco were worth very little in comparison with the concomitant strengthening of the Entente Cordiale.

Moreover, the final abandonment of Morocco to France started a kind of chain reaction which led on toward the catastrophe of 1914. It quickly resulted in the establishment of a formal French protectorate, with what was in effect a small subprotectorate on the north coast for Spain. The Italians, wishing to counterbalance French gains at the other end of the North African coast line, decided that the time was ripe in the autumn of 1911 for an aggression against the Turkish Empire—a further upsetting of the *status quo*, for which Italian diplomacy had secured the assent rather than the approval of the other powers. Such was the genesis of the twelve-months war for Tripoli; during its first month discussions began for a treaty of alliance between Serbia and Bulgaria, and in its last month the alliance, expanded to include Greece and Montenegro, sought to emulate the Italian success by launching its own war against the Turks.

The Balkan Wars began with a triumphant surge of nationalist enthusiasm. At Kumanovo the Serbs avenged on the same field of battle the biggest disaster in their earlier history; two great victories brought the Bulgarians up to the last line of defense before Constantinople; Salonika fell to the Greeks; and at the end of the second campaign the crescent flag flew over no major city except the capital. In a sense the grand alliance against the Turk was a Russian

11. *Les Armées françaises dans la Grande Guerre* (French General Staff History), quoted by FAY, vol. I, p. 291.

creation, but Austria-Hungary and Italy claimed an equal interest in the resulting redistribution of territory, which might well have proved the occasion of a general war. That it did not do so was the remarkable achievement of the conference of ambassadors of the great powers in London, which supervised the peacemaking of the combatants and in the end resorted to an ultimatum to enforce the acceptance of the Treaty of London (May, 1913). The success of the British foreign secretary, Grey, in restraining Russia's championship of Serbian claims, was matched by the work of the German chancellor, Bethmann-Hollweg, in restraining Austria-Hungary, even when a second Balkan War, rashly provoked by her protégé, Bulgaria, resulted in quick and complete defeat for the Bulgarians at the hands of their former allies and the Rumanians and the Turks.

Grey, writing retrospectively, saw in the conference of ambassadors a device which proved so effective that its continuance or revival might have saved the situation in the following year:

> We had been a means of keeping all the six Powers in direct and friendly touch. The mere fact that we were in existence, and that we should have to be broken up before peace was broken, was in itself an appreciable barrier against war. We were a means of gaining time. When we ceased to meet, the present danger to the peace of Europe was over . . . the things that had threatened the relations between the Great Powers in 1912–1913 we had deprived of their dangerous features.[12]

But, given the existence of two clearly defined rival groups in Europe, each compromise in a sense made the next compromise harder, because the compromise had been achieved by some reasoned refusal to back up one's own side at all costs. The proceedings of the London Conference left the Austrians in a mood of disappointment regarding the Germans, and the Russians in the same mood with regard to the British: further disappointment might break up the relationship.

The Balkan settlement, moreover, contained in itself the seeds of future conflict. Defeated Turkey turned to Germany. She brought in a German military mission under Liman von Sanders to reorganize her army, a stroke which necessitated the negotiation of a further compromise, the Russians agreeing to tolerate the presence of Sanders on condition that he held no executive command in the Turkish capital. Defeated Bulgaria would be only too glad to help to kindle another war to recoup her losses in Macedonia. Of the Balkan victors, none was entirely satisfied with its gains; all had experienced the excitement of a successful campaign; and one at least was left to nurse a major grievance. Serbia, though vastly increased in size and population and there-

---

12. Viscount GREY OF FALLODON, *Twenty-Five Years, 1892–1916* (1925), vol. I, p. 262.

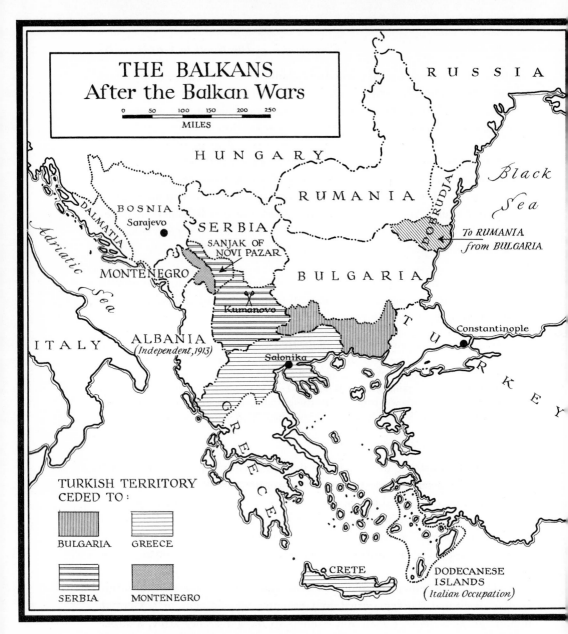

THE BALKANS
After the Balkan Wars

0   50   100   150   200   250
MILES

R U S S I A

H U N G A R Y

R U M A N I A

Black Sea

DALMATIA

BOSNIA
Sarajevo

S E R B I A

SANJAK OF
NOVI PAZAR

MONTENEGRO

Adriatic Sea

DOBRUDJA

*To RUMANIA
from BULGARIA*

B U L G A R I A

Kumanovo

I T A L Y

ALBANIA
(*Independent, 1913*)

Salonika

Constantinople

T U R K E Y

G R E E C E

TURKISH TERRITORY
CEDED TO:

BULGARIA   GREECE

SERBIA   MONTENEGRO

CRETE

DODECANESE
ISLANDS
(*Italian Occupation*)

Every state except Rumania has made major gains from Turkey, who retains only a toehold in Europe.
Albania, newly created, bars Serbia's way to the Adriatic.

fore more formidable than before, had been deprived of the Adriatic coast line,
which she had conquered in arms, by Austrian policy. With the support of
Italy and the concurrence of Germany, the new kingdom of Albania had been
brought into existence, to be ruled uneasily from March to September, 1914, by
a German prince, William of Wied. Given that this was the second great
territorial disappointment suffered by the Serbs in less than five years, it becomes

tempting to conclude that, if the Sarajevo assassination had not come when it did, some such event would sooner or later have had to be invented.

■ UNDERLYING CAUSES OF WAR

The crisis of July, 1914, proved fatal to the old Europe, not because of the supreme complexity of the existing situation—complex as we shall undoubtedly find it to be—but because of the underlying causes making for an almost inevitable explosion. So, before we trace the crowded events which finally set the armies of a whole continent in motion, it will be helpful to attempt to summarize the dangerous trends. But in judging the statesmanship of those who held the fortunes of whole generations in their hands, it is always to be borne in mind that hindsight is easier than foresight.

The first and perhaps the most obvious danger was the growing strength of nationalist sentiments and ambitions, the fulfillment of which in some cases clearly involved the destruction of the old order. The South-Slav or Yugoslav movement, for example, could not aspire to rebuild the medieval empire of the Serbs except by compassing the disruption of Austria-Hungary. In 1913 the population of Serbia had been increased from 3,000,000 to 4,500,000, yet three-fifths of the South Slavs remained under Hapsburg rule. The selfsame Dual Monarchy contained an almost equally numerous and restive northern Slav element, with a strong industrial and cultural base in Bohemia, of which no part had as yet aspired to independence. Rumania and Italy, too, had irredentist claims against Austria-Hungary, which were no longer wholly stifled by their obligations as allies. In addition, one submerged nation with quite recent great-power traditions, namely Poland, was biding its time to challenge all three of the east European empires in a struggle for independence; as regards Russia at least, the hostility of the Poles was matched by that of the Finns, Ukrainians, and a dozen other border populations. Though the German Empire was more homogeneous than the other two, in Alsace-Lorraine it contained a minority whose separatist passions were ceaselessly stimulated by a neighboring great power. For forty years Frenchmen in Paris had kept the statues representing the former French cities of Strasbourg and Metz draped in black, while every French child lived over again the personal tragedies of the cession as he read Daudet's story of *La Dernière Classe*.

The strength of national feeling among a mass of persons who were subjects of an alien power gave encouragement to an aggressor by holding out prospects of internal subversion; it might also make war attractive as a defensive measure —to crush subversive influences inside and outside the frontier. But it must not be forgotten that dominant nationalities, too, were often actuated by national feeling in their more assertive policies. Pan-Germans and Pan-Slavs; Frenchmen dreaming of *La Révanche* and Germans toasting *Der Tag;* the British reading their Kipling and congratulating themselves on their freedom from

> Such boastings as the Gentiles use,
> Or lesser breeds without the Law—[13]

all shared in a national pride, compounded in varying degrees of a sense of political, industrial, social, cultural, and even religious achievement which was believed to distinguish their nation from the others. Though we cannot measure it, the positive patriotism of the masses was very likely greater at this time than at any earlier period in the history of civilization, because the continuous progress of the past forty years had all been expressed in terms of national achievement—*our* wonderful parliamentary system, *our* glorious literature, *our* rapidly rising standard of living, and even *our* missionaries converting the heathen. Neither Christian brotherhood nor the unity preached by socialist doctrine could be effectively opposed to the nationalist sentiment on which the rulers of the great powers would rely to obtain mass support in the event of a major war.

It was nationalism that lent glamour to economic imperialism, that outward spread of European sovereignty and influence which had been motivated by the needs of industrial development. The migration of population, which, except for the fortunate British and Russians (and for the French in Algeria), meant normally a change of allegiance, created little rivalry. From the 1870's onward the struggle in Africa and Asia, and even among the islands of the Pacific, had been primarily for tropical possessions, where production of foodstuffs, minerals, and other industrial raw materials could be profitably organized with the help of European administration, capital, and technical skill; European exports would of course find a correspondingly attractive market there. Where annexation was impracticable, as in the Chinese Empire or Asiatic Turkey, the establishment of spheres of influence served much the same purpose, though the fact that there was no formal transfer of sovereignty made each such transaction more precarious.

The manipulation of railway and banking concessions and consequent trading advantages lent itself to many forms of ambiguous compromise. Russian claims in Manchuria are one good illustration. Another is provided by the tortuous story of the Baghdad railway: it was a source of diplomatic troubles throughout the first decade of the twentieth century; it set Britain and Russia, as well as Britain and Germany, at cross-purposes; and it was not definitely settled until too late. In June, 1914, an Anglo-German Convention was initialed, but the outbreak of hostilities prevented formal signature; this agreement

---

13. Rudyard Kipling, "Recessional" (begun on the day of Queen Victoria's Diamond Jubilee and published in *The Times*, London, July 17, 1897).

balanced German rights in the eventual railway link between Europe, Baghdad, and Basra against British rights on the Persian Gulf and in the exploitation of the Persian and Mesopotamian oil fields.

On the whole, it is true to say that economic imperialism lacked the decisive effect which Marxists attribute to it, because the possibilities of compromise were very considerable. If Germans were wont to complain that the British Empire had stolen a march on their fatherland and robbed them of a place in the sun, they were well aware that spheres of influence could still be found to reward the best organized and most alert among the trading powers— which was certainly Germany. Moreover, the existing colonial empires were not necessarily definitive. In 1911 Germany's gains in French Equatorial Africa gave her a common frontier with the Belgian Congo, some part of which Britain had been willing that she should buy, subject to a right of way for a British Cape to Cairo railway and a Baghdad railway agreement such as was in fact achieved in 1914. In 1914, too, an Anglo-German agreement was initialed on the subject of the Portuguese colonies in Africa. This would have given Germany more favorable rights of purchase, as compared with Britain, than had been accorded by a previous abortive treaty in 1898, though there was to be publication also of the Anglo-Portuguese alliance, as confirmed in 1899, to encourage the Portuguese to retain their colonies as long as they might find it financially practicable.

Mention has been made already of the influences which the system of secret alliances exercised toward generalizing what might otherwise have been a local conflict. But perhaps the most baneful influence of the alliances was through the emphasis which they caused to be placed on military preparedness. An unarmed power was unworthy of being accepted as an ally—a dangerous position to be in. The leader of an alliance must be proportionately well armed —here lay a direct incentive to an armaments race. To counteract an alliance contingent plans must be made; thus Schlieffen prepared the German army to meet the Franco-Russian threat by striking a lightning blow against France, even if she were not immediately involved in Russia's war. Similarly, Haldane between 1906 and 1911 built up the British Expeditionary Force on the hypothesis that it might be required for service on the Continent in support of the French—and it can scarcely be questioned that the very existence of such a force and the staff talks about its hypothetical use made eventual British intervention for better or worse more probable.

It might logically be supposed that the adoption of short-service conscription on the German model, by which all Europe except Britain expressed its reluctant admiration of what Moltke's army had achieved in 1870, would have signally reduced the popular appeal of any policy which was likely to lead to war. It did not have this effect, military service being generally accepted without demur, even in small neutral countries like Switzerland and Norway, as an obligation of citizenship. On the contrary, because a man had been trained for war, he was inclined to regard war as a part of life. It is significant that the French, the most democratic of the great powers concerned, accepted in 1913 a three-year period of service with virtually no exemptions, as the only means of holding their own against the mounting German population. In the same year the Germans added 131,000 men to their army, but at the beginning of their mobilization in 1914 they had no more men serving with the colors than the French had.

Conscription may even have enhanced the readiness of the taxpayer to meet the bill for arms, since to some extent it might be his own equipment and his direct protection that were involved. Between 1880 and 1914 German expenditure on arms was quintupled, that of Russia and Britain trebled; in terms of a percentage of national income, Austria-Hungary spent as readily as Russia, and France as Germany. The dreadnought battleship was only the most conspicuous among many new devices for both offensive and defensive warfare, as harder alloy steel was matched with more powerful explosives and the first attempts were made to adapt to military uses the petrol engine, which was later to transform warfare on land and in the air. Armaments manufacturers undoubtedly prospered, and were ready to stimulate sales by fomenting war scares and by promoting competition between rival customers. Their profit was certainly derived from exploiting an ugly side of human nature. Yet it is, surely, a distorted view of economic processes to make the existence of private arms manufacture the chief evil of what is vaguely called militarism. Governments would otherwise have produced the arms they needed in their own nationalized ordnance factories and shipyards. Indeed, such government establishments had already met a part of the demand.

There was, however, a big danger involved in the militarism (and navalism) of the officer caste. The link between the landed aristocracy and military command, dating back to feudalism, was strong everywhere in Europe, but strongest in Germany, where the expansion of the army in 1913–1914 was limited by the fear of diluting the officer caste with too large a middle-class element. The imitation of this feature of the German system was therefore combined with the introduction everywhere of a general staff based on the German practice, which permeated the entire army with a common body of doctrine and with trained minds ready to apply it to every situation of war. Their inevitably conservative outlook in domestic politics tended automatically to exclude from military and naval circles the influence of liberal and cosmopolitan ideas which made war appear outmoded. Instead, they would echo (as Foch did) the aphorism of von der Goltz: "Modern wars have become the nations' way of doing business." The privilege of birth gained undue attention for them from their

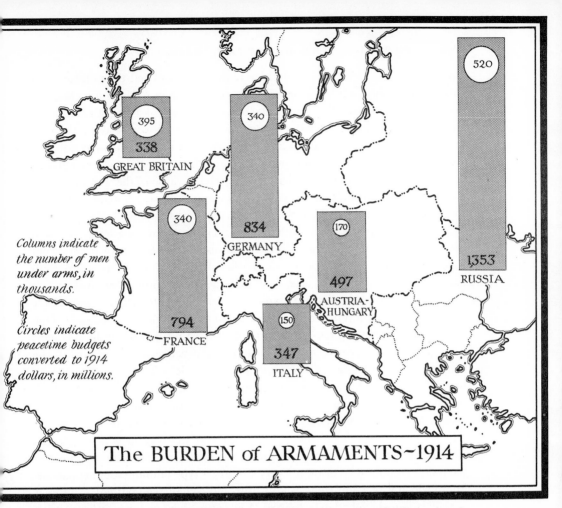

Columns indicate the number of men under arms, in thousands.

Circles indicate peacetime budgets converted to 1914 dollars, in millions.

395
338
GREAT BRITAIN

340
834
GERMANY

340
794
FRANCE

520
1,353
RUSSIA

170
497
AUSTRIA-HUNGARY

150
347
ITALY

The BURDEN of ARMAMENTS~1914

The figures include both naval and military expenditures and manpower. Great Britain was the only power to spend more (almost double) upon its navy than upon its army. Russia could maintain very large forces at a relatively low per capita cost, while the British volunteer army was paid at a much higher rate than were Continental soldiers. Derived from B. Schmitt, *Triple Alliance and Triple Entente* (1934), pp. 117–120.

rulers, to whom they preached the inevitability of war, since it enhanced the importance of the warrior, and the desirability of large-scale preparations. In any time of crisis their influence was positively pernicious, since easy access to the ear of the sovereign—the kaiser had a separate military cabinet, and even in England a well-connected general might canvass for court support, as Haig did with George V—gave great weight to their eager admonitions to forestall the potential enemy by acting first.

This was particularly important because carefully prepared mobilization schemes represented the acme of military science. Magazines and depots had been sited, railway networks elaborated, and timetables prepared with a view to deploying the maximum of men in the minimum of time in a frontier area from which they could strike a decisive blow. Once they left the railhead their overall speed, even while unopposed, was no faster than infantry marched and horses hauled. To mobilize a day too soon would be to risk being stigmatized as the aggressor, but to mobilize a day too late would be to risk losing the war. In 1914, as we shall see, the military caste, which in more than one country effectively overruled the civilians, cannot escape the reproach of warmongering.

In the last analysis, however, the underlying cause of the war was surely the psychological condition of civilized European man, which made him ready to sacrifice so much for the rather modest incentives that we have described. War has always provided an outlet for mass emotions, ranging from sadism to pity, from greed to generosity, from the lowest manifestations of the herd instinct to the loftiest aspirations of self-sacrifice. But since it is also associated with frustration, hardship, pain, loss, fear, and the uncertainty of survival, it was natural to suppose that civilized man was growing out of the habit of war. Three things, as it seems in retrospect, chiefly conditioned him to its continuance. One was the misleading impression made by those past wars of which he was most fully aware. The three wars which Prussia fought between 1864 and 1871, the campaign of Garibaldi and the Thousand, the little wars in Africa and Asia, were all of them short, inexpensive, adventurous, and not particularly lethal. By comparison the large-scale, murderous campaigns of the American Civil War or of the Russo-Japanese struggle in the Far East had made little impression on the European mind. Another big factor was the way in which universal elementary education, the popular press, the novel, and even the teachings of the pulpit combined to instill in every country a type of unquestioning patriotism to which war might come as a surprise and a challenge, but not as a threat to civilization which had to be resisted. A literature denouncing war, based upon the contrast between expectation and experience, came into vogue only after the Great War.

The third psychological factor is the one which most easily escapes our attention. The tortuous diplomacy of the powers, the motives with which they entered the war, and the various aims and hopes which encouraged them to continue fighting have all been explored by historians in great detail. In August, 1914, however, men answered the call to the colors under two emotional pressures. One was an automatic response to the call of "King and country," the command of the emperor who was also the War Lord or the Little Father, or simply the appeal of *La Patrie* with all its autochthonous virtues and blessings. The other was the sense of a wrong to be righted: for Austrians an assassination; for Serbs an overbearing ultimatum; for Russians a series of past humiliations, patiently borne; for Germans, the plot of encirclement; for Frenchmen, the German annexation of Alsace-Lorraine and the menace of a second unprovoked invasion; and for the British, a direct breach of treaty obligation, supported by a vaguer notion that naval competition was

THE AUSTRO-HUNGARIAN DECLARATION OF WAR ON SERBIA, JULY 28, 1914. This is the message, written in French and preserved in the State Archives at Vienna, that precipitated the First World War. The passage struck out at the lower left alleges that the Serbians had already opened fire. The last sentence reads: "Austria-Hungary consequently considers herself henceforward in a state of war with Serbia." At the bottom is the annotation, in German: "Sent on 28 July, 1914, 10:55."

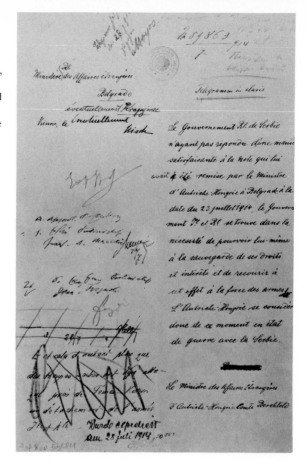

somehow unfair. These were the things which moved men's minds: as we shall now see, they were related to—but by no means identical with—the sequence of events from which the declarations of war were derived.

▪ 1914: EVENTS LEADING TO WAR

Shortly before noon on Sunday, June 28, 1914, the Archduke Franz Ferdinand, heir presumptive to the Hapsburg throne, and his morganatic wife died at Sarajevo in Bosnia from two shots fired at point-blank range into a stationary car by the nineteen-year-old Gavril Princip. The assassin and his accomplices, one of whom had thrown a bomb earlier that day, were Bosnian students; they had prepared their plot across the frontier in Belgrade, where they were in league with a Serbian secret society, the Black Hand, which had even provided them with shooting practice. Because Sarajevo was the capital of the recently annexed province, the well-advertised visit of the archduke was an act of provocation in the eyes of all Pan-Serbs, and the fact that he favored a reorganization of the Hapsburg lands on a federal basis made it likely that, if he lived to reign, the prospects for an independent Yugoslavia would be further reduced. Some members of the Serbian government knew of the plot, and made an attempt to stop the assassins before they crossed the frontier into Bosnia; but they gave no specific warning to the Austro-Hungarian authorities, whose failure to take adequate police precautions on such an occasion is, nevertheless, hard to explain.

Since no civilized country could condone the crime, and since the circumstantial evidence for supposing that Serbia had played a part in it was strong, the general expectation in Europe was that the government of Austria-Hungary would seize its chance to impose humiliating and weakening conditions, to which Serbia would be obliged to submit. However, no overt action was taken for nearly four weeks, partly because time was consumed in inconclusive police inquiries, through which the Austro-Hungarian government tried to prove the complicity of the Serbian government in the plot (which was of course firmly denied), and partly, perhaps, because there was a practical advantage to be gained by first getting in the harvest. But the main consideration was the imminence of a state visit to St. Petersburg by the heads of the French government, which made it desirable to delay the Austrian move until the evening of July 23, lest the leaders of the Franco-Russian Alliance should be presented with an easy opportunity to concert their countermeasures. As it was, President Poincaré and the Russian foreign minister, Sazonov, probably reached a verbal understanding that, if necessary, France would accept Russia's going to war in defense of Serbian independence as requiring action under their treaty; but they may well have been tempted to share the view of the uninstructed public, that the long interval bespoke diminished tension.

On the contrary, as early as July 5, the Germans had taken the most decisive of the steps that led to general war. The fire-eating chief of the Austro-Hungarian general staff, Conrad von Hötzendorf, favored war against Serbia, though the opportunity in his opinion was less auspicious than in 1909 or 1912. His view was accepted by Berchtold, the foreign minister, and all others present at a Crown Council except the Hungarian prime minister, Tisza, but action depended on German approval. On July 5 a special mission, bearing a letter and memorandum from Francis Joseph, both couched in general terms, was received at Potsdam by the German emperor, who conferred briefly with the chancellor but with no military or naval representative. The kaiser said that, if the Austro-Hungarian government had decided that military action against Serbia was necessary, he would be sorry to see them miss "the present moment which was so favorable."[14] Bethmann-Hollweg, in a separate message, added that his imperial master "cannot interfere in the dispute now going on between Austria-Hungary and that country, as it is a matter not within his competence," but would "faithfully stand by Austria-Hungary."[15] By giving the Dual

---

14. Report from the Austro-Hungarian ambassador to Berchtold, cited by FAY, vol. II, p. 204.
15. *Outbreak of the World War: German Documents Collected by Karl Kautsky*, ed. M. MONTGELAS and W. SCHÜCKING (1924), No. 15.

Monarchy carte blanche to start a small war, the German government brought about a situation leading directly to the big war, which they did not want but failed to prevent.

In Austria-Hungary Tisza was now converted to the war party, which decided that, if they drove the Serbs to resistance rather than submission, they would be acting in accordance with German wishes and would strengthen their own position within the Triple Alliance. On July 23 at 6:00 P.M. Berchtold issued a forty-eight-hour ultimatum. This demanded a public repudiation of propaganda against Austria-Hungary and specific measures of collaboration in its suppression. The Serbians, who in the absence of unequivocal backing from the Russians were not eager to fight a great power while they were still recuperating from the strain of the Balkan Wars, accepted most of the demands and suggested some form of arbitration for the others. But the Austrian minister in Belgrade, on receiving this reply, severed relations and left for home within half an hour. The Austrian army, however, was not ready to undertake any major operations before the end of the second week in August, so Berchtold contented himself with a single bombardment of Belgrade on July 29, the day after Austria-Hungary had declared war; this, so far as the Serbian quarrel was concerned, had the intended effect of closing the door to mediation.

The German emperor, on learning the extent to which the Serbs had capitulated to the Austrian ultimatum, declared that, in the light of Austria's "brilliant performance" and "great moral victory,"[16] there was no longer any occasion for war. But he reckoned without the warmongers, such as the members of his own general staff, who seem to have prompted Berchtold's declaration of war referred to above. That event, on the twenty-eighth, convinced the Russians that they must mobilize in support of the Serbs, yet even a partial mobilization —against Austria-Hungary and not against Germany—would inevitably result in a war of great powers, unless some form of pacification could be found without delay. This seemed for a moment possible, because on the twenty-seventh the British foreign secretary had caused the German ambassador in London to warn his government, "In case of war we would have England against us,"[17] thus giving Bethmann-Hollweg good reason to call for an Austrian "halt in Belgrade"—with no mobilization against Russia—if England could impose corresponding restraint upon the Russians.

By July 30 the moment had passed. While Bethmann-Hollweg's pacific proposals to the Austrians were counteracted by bellicose messages from Moltke to his fellow chief of staff, the Russian generals with Sazonov's support finally convinced the vacillating tsar that general mobilization was essential, both because a partial mobilization could not be enlarged without confusion and also because the less efficient power was desperately anxious to keep one move ahead

16. *Ibid.*, No. 271.
17. *Ibid.*, No. 258.

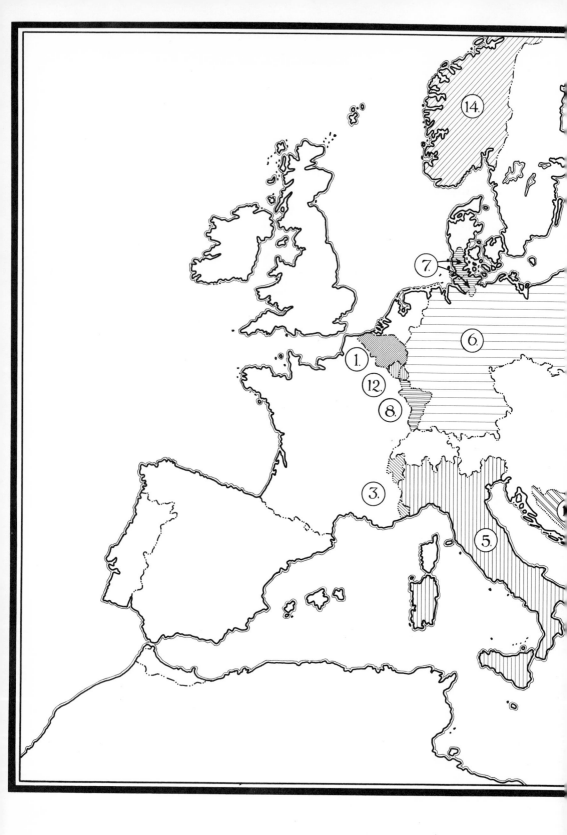

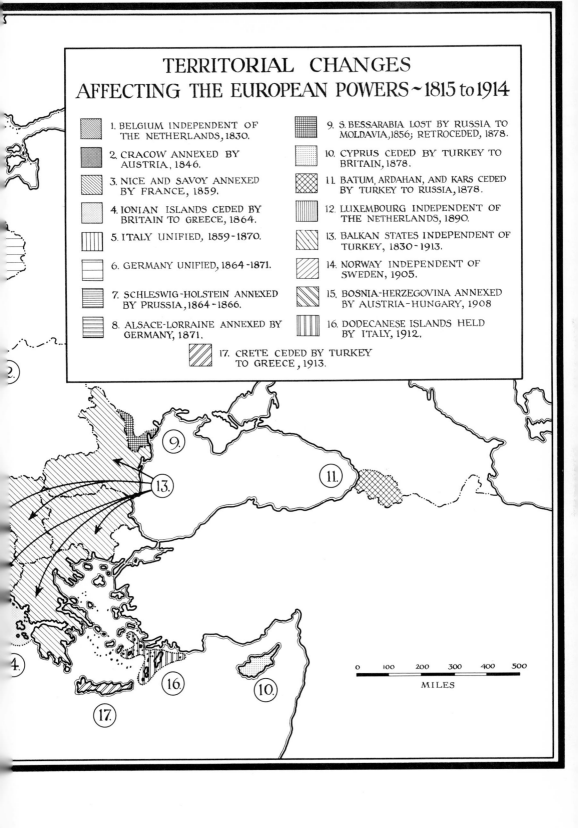

TERRITORIAL CHANGES
AFFECTING THE EUROPEAN POWERS ~ 1815 to 1914

1. BELGIUM INDEPENDENT OF THE NETHERLANDS, 1830.

2. CRACOW ANNEXED BY AUSTRIA, 1846.

3. NICE AND SAVOY ANNEXED BY FRANCE, 1859.

4. IONIAN ISLANDS CEDED BY BRITAIN TO GREECE, 1864.

5. ITALY UNIFIED, 1859-1870.

6. GERMANY UNIFIED, 1864-1871.

7. SCHLESWIG-HOLSTEIN ANNEXED BY PRUSSIA, 1864-1866.

8. ALSACE-LORRAINE ANNEXED BY GERMANY, 1871.

9. S. BESSARABIA LOST BY RUSSIA TO MOLDAVIA, 1856; RETROCEDED, 1878.

10. CYPRUS CEDED BY TURKEY TO BRITAIN, 1878.

11. BATUM, ARDAHAN, AND KARS CEDED BY TURKEY TO RUSSIA, 1878.

12. LUXEMBOURG INDEPENDENT OF THE NETHERLANDS, 1890.

13. BALKAN STATES INDEPENDENT OF TURKEY, 1830-1913.

14. NORWAY INDEPENDENT OF SWEDEN, 1905.

15. BOSNIA-HERZEGOVINA ANNEXED BY AUSTRIA-HUNGARY, 1908

16. DODECANESE ISLANDS HELD BY ITALY, 1912.

17. CRETE CEDED BY TURKEY TO GREECE, 1913.

MILES

0 100 200 300 400 500

of the more efficient Germany, whose mobilization appeared imminent. Austria-Hungary had decided already on a full mobilization, though the Russians did not know it; German mobilization followed Russian; and the French kept pace with the Germans. Thus Russia, from weakness rather than strength, incurred a terrible responsibility. The effect of her decision was to give more control over events to her military advisers, for in Russia, as in every Continental government, the business of mobilizing was their concern. Moreover, it was the accepted dogma that mobilization meant war.

Nevertheless, in so great an emergency, dogmas did not necessarily determine men's actions. The Russians, whose military preparations were timed for completion in 1917, not 1914, had mobilized in order to demonstrate support for Serbia, not in order to launch a general war, and a period of several weeks was to intervene before their forces became seriously engaged. In that time much might happen to improve the prospects of agreement, and their French allies would have been equally willing to hold up mobilization as soon as a diplomatic opportunity presented itself. But it was otherwise with the Germans, for whom strategy at this stage dictated policy.

The execution of the Schlieffen Plan, the sovereign German recipe for winning a two-front war, demanded the unfaltering development of the planned procedure from the first day of mobilization onward. France must be attacked, and the attack must come through Belgium. No further attempt was made to temporize or to localize the conflict; if France had been willing to stay neutral, the pledge was to be the impossible one of handing over the fortresses of Toul and Verdun to German custody. Even the twelve-hour ultimatum to Belgium, which the German minister in Brussels presented on the evening of August 2, had been drafted by the chief of staff on July 26, complete with specific references to threatening advances by the French. This aspect of events enables the only historian who has written on the basis of the full documentation of these crowded weeks to reach his emphatic conclusion:

> . . . the final, definite responsibility for the outbreak of the war lies with the German plan of mobilization, while the primary responsibility . . . rests on the actions of the Central Powers, who thought they could frighten the other Powers by their strength and thus "localize the conflict," but made a thorough miscalculation.[18]

18. L. ALBERTINI, trans. and ed., I. M. MASSEY, *The Origins of the War of 1914* (1952–1957), vol. II, p. 581. This important work by the former editor of the *Corriera della Sera* is based on all types of material made available in the principal European languages up to the death of the author, two years before the original Italian version was published in 1943. It supersedes in some respects the views advanced by S. B. FAY in his *Origins of the World War* (1930), pleading that "the verdict of the Versailles Treaty that Germany and her allies were responsible for the War . . . is historically unsound." In his apportionment of the responsibility, Fay attached much weight to the culpability of Russia's action in mobilizing first, and tended to ignore the fact that, if the German war leaders had so desired, they could still have allowed mobilization to be combined with mediation.

The Schlieffen Plan, which was responsible for so much, was responsible also for the prompt entry of Britain into the war. Grey, as has been pointed out, used the possibility of British intervention to give weight to his claims to act as a mediating influence. But his hands were tied by the generally pacific views of the Liberal majority in parliament, which were also represented in the cabinet; by the widespread distrust of tsarist Russia; and by the fact that the military and naval obligations arising from the Entente had never been publicly recognized. Indeed, it was not until August 2 that the promise of Conservative support emboldened the cabinet to concede a guarantee of the French Channel coast, as a natural consequence of the arrangement by which the French Navy had for several years past been concentrated in the Mediterranean, so that British ships might be withdrawn from there to face the Germans in the North Sea.

Then came the news of the German ultimatum to Belgium and its brave rejection. Grey made eloquent use of this in his speech in parliament the following afternoon, when he won almost unanimous support by an appeal addressed alternately to the sense of moral obligation and of political interest. The inexpediency of allowing an aggrandizement of Germany at the cost of France, which might terminate in a Continental dictatorship, would quite possibly not have been recognized by the majority of Grey's hearers until too late. But Germany's wanton disregard for the Belgian treaty of 1839, involving the rights of a small neighbor which were also the interests of Britain, provided a clear-cut issue which everybody could understand. At midday on August 4 the British government gave the Germans twelve hours in which to withdraw from Belgian soil, as required for "the observance of a treaty to which Germany is as much a party as ourselves."[19] Whatever the broader issues, for most British people, including the peoples of the self-governing dominions, the war began as a "war for Belgium."

■ CONCLUSION

If the underlying causes are weighed together with the events which actually precipitated the outbreak of the First World War, it becomes clear that none of the original participants is altogether free from war guilt. Even the most innocent power had some selfish and aggressive aims which it desired to pursue, did not renounce the possibility of war in pursuit of those aims, and was to that extent a consenting party in what happened. Yet with occasional exceptions, of which the retrocession of Alsace-Lorraine is the most obvious, neither statesmen nor nations entertained any clear-cut objective in 1914 which was achieved in 1918. For the decisive factors had little to do with the causation of the war, were

19. Sir Edward Grey to Sir E. Goschen, British Ambassador in Berlin, August 4, 1914 (*British Documents on the Origins of the War*, vol. XI, 1926, No. 594).

certainly unforeseen, and were largely unforeseeable—the long duration of the struggle, which Kitchener was the only expert to prophesy; its unparalleled cost in blood and treasure; the overthrow of the autocratic empires on both sides in the conflict; and the role of the United States in the denouement of what began as a distinctively European tragedy. Indeed, the mustering of the armies on the traditional battlegrounds of the north European plain, while it linked August, 1914, with the diplomatic history of all the years since 1871, leads on to the whole series of events in Europe and the world at large which constitute the tangled theme of the final volume of this work—*Europe and the World Since 1914*.

Here it is unnecessary to do more than point out that, for Europe as a whole, 1914 is a turning point far more significant than 1815 or 1648 or any other cardinal event in its earlier history. In spite of the recent defeat of Russia by Japan, the Europe of William II and Francis Joseph, of Asquith and Poincaré, had never been more self-confident or less aware of any challenge to its leadership of the civilized world. Perhaps Sir Edward Grey, gazing reflectively from the windows of the British Foreign Office as darkness fell after his famous speech in parliament (referred to above), came closest to an appreciation of the true position. "The lamps are going out all over Europe," he said; "we shall not see them lit again in our life-time." But even the detached and philosophic Grey could hardly have imagined that, when the lamps of political wisdom, intellectual and artistic progress, economic growth, and moral stability were at last rekindled, they would be found to shine less brightly in the ancient centers of European civilization than in countries and continents that had been believed for centuries to look to Europe for enlightenment.

In two world wars, ten years of mortal conflict, the old Europe compassed its own destruction. Perhaps a new Europe will arise Phoenix-like from the ashes. In any case, the outbreak of war in 1914 will always be viewed in retrospect as a considerable dividing line in human annals, with which the history of nineteenth-century Europe comes inevitably to its close.

Reading List: Chapter 17

Schmitt, B. E., *Triple Alliance and Triple Entente* (1934), chs. 1–3. Brief, useful survey.

The New Cambridge Modern History, vol. XI (1962), chs. 20–21. International relations, 1870–98. *Ibid.* vol. XII (1961), chs. 11–12. Covers the period 1898–1914.

Fay, S. B., *The Origins of the World War* (2 vols., 1930), vol. I, ch. 1; vol. II, ch. 12. Evaluation of causes.

Manhart, G. B., *Alliance and Entente, 1871–1914* (1931). Very convenient brief collection of documents.

Schmitt, B. E., "July 1914: Thirty Years After," in H. Ausubel (ed.), *The Making of Modern Europe* (vol. II, 1951), pp. 833–54. A re-examination of the literature.

Tuchman, B. W., *The Guns of August* (1962), chs. 1–5. Prewar military planning, vividly criticized.

Grey, E. (Viscount Grey of Fallodon), *Twenty-Five Years, 1892–1916* (2 vols., 1925), chs. 16–18. A famous account of the 1914 crisis.

Sazonov, S., *Fateful Years 1909–1916* (1928), ch. 8. The 1914 crisis described by the Russian foreign minister.

Taylor, A. J. P., *The Struggle for Mastery in Europe* (1954), chs. 21–22.

Angell, N., *The Great Illusion* (1910, frequently reprinted), chs. 1–3. The most famous attack on the thesis that war pays.

Cairns, John C., "International Politics and the Military Mind: the Case of the French Republic, 1911–1914," *Journal of Modern History*, vol. XXV (1953), no. 3. French military policies on the eve of war.

Schmitt, B. E., "The Origins of the War of 1914," *Journal of Modern History*, vol. XXIV (1952), no. 1. A review of Albertini's "masterly work."

BIBLIOGRAPHY

Bibliography

General

BIBLIOGRAPHIES

The American Historical Association's Guide to Historical Literature (1961). A complete revision of the work first published in 1931.

Historical Association (London), *Modern European History, 1789–1945. A Select Bibliography* (1960).

Burston, W. H., and Green, C. W. (eds.), *Handbook for History Teachers* (1962). Contains extensive critical lists of books, compiled by university specialists.

Ragatz, L. J., *A Bibliography for the Study of European History, 1815–1939* (1942–1945).

Bullock, A., and Taylor, A. J. P., *A Select List of Books on European History, 1815–1914* (rev. ed., 1957).

R. R. Bowker Company, *Paperbound Books in Print* (1963). Issued quarterly.

REFERENCE WORKS

Encyclopaedia Britannica (11th ed., 1910; 14th ed., 1929; subsequent revised editions). Some historical subjects are treated more fully in the 11th than in later editions.

Chambers's Encyclopaedia (new ed., 1950; rev. ed., 1959). Every article is a post-1945 treatment of its subject.

Encyclopaedia of the Social Sciences (15 vols., 1930–1935). Excellent articles on general subjects; often on a historical basis.

Langer, W. L. (ed.), *An Encyclopaedia of World History* (3rd ed., 1956).

Webster's Biographical Dictionary (rev. ed., 1951). Comprehensive and convenient for quick reference.

The Concise Dictionary of National Biography (2 vols., 1961). The first volume contains lives of British subjects to 1901, the second to 1950. These are very carefully scaled down from the full accounts in the original dictionary and its supplements.

ATLASES, ETCETERA

Shepherd, W. R., *Historical Atlas* (8th ed., 1956).

Sellman, R. R., *A Student's Atlas of Modern History* (1952).

Palmer, R. R., *Atlas of World History* (1957).

Muir, R., and Philip, G., *Philip's Historical Atlas, Ancient, Medieval, and Modern* (8th ed., 1952).

Fox, E. W., and Deighton, H. S., *Atlas of European History* (1957).

The Cambridge Modern History Atlas Volume (2nd ed., 1924).

Robertson, C. G., and Bartholomew, J., *Historical Atlas of Modern Europe, 1789–1922* (2nd ed., 1924).

Webster's Geographical Dictionary (1949). Contains useful historical data under major place names.

COLLECTIONS OF SOURCE MATERIAL

Stearns, R. P. (ed.), *Pageant of Europe: Sources and Selections from the Renaissance to the Present Day* (rev. ed., 1961).

Baumer, F. le Van (ed.), *Main Currents of Western Thought* (1952).

Weber, E., *The Western Tradition, From the Ancient World to the Atomic Age* (1959).

Columbia College (eds.), *Introduction to Contemporary Civilization in the West: A Source Book* (2 vols., 3rd ed. rev., 1960).

Knowles, G. H., and Snyder, R. K. (eds.), *Readings in Western Civilization* (1951).

Snyder, L. S. (ed.), *Fifty Major Documents of the Nineteenth Century* (1955). A convenient short paperback collection.

Cook, A. N. (ed.), *Readings in Modern and Contemporary History* (1937).

Scott, J. F., and Baltzly, A. (eds.), *Readings in European History Since 1814* (1934).

Laffan, R. G. D. (ed.), *Select Documents of European History* (3 vols., 1930–1931).

Young, G. M., and Handcock, W. D. (eds.), *English Historical Documents, 1833–1874*, vol. XII, pt. I (1956), of general series. Material on the Victorian social and political transformations.

Cole, G. D. H., and Fison, A. W. (eds.), *Documents of British Working Class History, 1789–1875* (1951).

MULTIVOLUME HISTORIES OF EUROPE

The Rise of Modern Europe, ed., Langer, W. L. (to be completed in 20 vols., 1935–   ). Three volumes so far deal with the period between 1814 and 1900. Also paperback.

The Cambridge Modern History (12 vols., atlas volume, and index volume, 1902–1912). Out of date, but comprehensive and still in parts extremely useful.

The New Cambridge Modern History (to be completed in 12 vols., companion volume, and atlas volume, 1957–   ). An entirely new work, on a rather smaller scale, which is much less political in outlook.

The European Inheritance, eds., Barker, E., Clark, G., and Vaucher, P. (3 vols., 1954). Volume III contains a survey of Europe, 1815–1914, by G. Bruun.

European Civilization, Its Origin and Development, ed. Eyre, E. (7 vols., 1934–1939).

Peuples et civilisations, histoire générale, ed., Halphen, A., and Sagnac, P. (1926 ff.). Vols. XV–XIX go from 1815 to 1918.

Propyläean Weltgeschichte, ed., Mann, Golo. Vol. VIII (1960) of this unusually well-illustrated history, completely revised by an international group of scholars, deals with the nineteenth century.

WORKS DEALING WITH SPECIAL ASPECTS OF EUROPEAN HISTORY

Geographical

East, W. G., *An Historical Geography of Europe* (4th ed., 1950).
Pounds, N. J. G., *An Historical and Political Geography of Europe* (1949).
Whittlesey, D. S., *Environmental Foundations of European History* (1949).
Fitzgerald, W., *The New Europe: An Introduction to its Political Geography* (1945).
Valkenburg, S., and Huntington, E., *Europe* (1935).

Economic

Heaton, H., *Economic History of Europe* (rev. ed., 1948). A standard textbook of uniformly high quality.
Clough, S. B., and Cole, C. W., *Economic History of Europe* (1946).
Ogg, F. A., and Sharp, R. W., *Economic Development of Europe* (rev. ed., 1949).
Gras, N. S. B., *History of Agriculture in Europe and America* (1925).
Bowden, W., Karpovich, M., and Usher, A. P., *An Economic History of Europe Since 1750* (1937).

Diplomatic

Taylor, A. J. P., *The Struggle for Mastery in Europe, 1848–1918* (1954). A detailed narrative of international relations; important general description of source material in various languages.
Mowat, R. B., *History of European Diplomacy, 1815–1914* (1922). A still useful outline.
Albrecht-Carrié, R., *A Diplomatic History of Europe Since the Congress of Vienna* (1958).
Ward, A. W., and Gooch, G. P. (eds.), *The Cambridge History of British Foreign Policy 1783–1919* (3 vols., 1923). The second volume begins in 1815, the third in 1866; the third volume is the least authoritative, as it was published before many documents were available.

Military and Naval

Vagts, A., *A History of Militarism* (rev. ed., 1959).
Fuller, J. F. C., *A Military History of the Western World* (3 vols., 1954–1956). The third volume deals with the modern period.
Wright, Q., *A Study of War* (2 vols., 1942). A remarkable attempt at statistical analysis.
Stevens, W. O., and Westcott, A. F., *A History of Sea Power* (1942).
Earle, E. M. (ed.), *Makers of Modern Strategy* (rev. ed., 1952). Very useful essays.
Ropp, T. W., *War in the Modern World* (1959; paperback, 1962). A scholarly analysis.
Fuller, J. F. C., *The Conduct of War, 1789–1961* (1961).
Nef, John U., *War and Human Progress* (1950). An essay on the rise of industrial civilization.

Scientific and Technological

Singer, C., *A Short History of Scientific Ideas to 1900* (1959; paperback, 1962).
Derry, T. K., and Williams, T. I., *A Short History of Technology* (1960).
Forbes, R. J., *Man the Maker: A History of Technology and Engineering* (1952).
Giedion, S., *Mechanization Takes Command: A Contribution to Anonymous History* (1948).
Habakkuk, H. J., *American and British Technology in the Nineteenth Century: The Search for Labour-Saving Inventions* (1962).

Sociological, Intellectual, and Legal

Coon, C. S., *The Races of Europe* (1939).
Huntington, E., *Civilization and Climate* (rev. ed., 1924).
Brinton, C., *Ideas and Men, the Story of Western Thought* (1950).
Randall, J. H., *Making of the Modern Mind* (rev. ed., 1940).
Friedell, E., *A Cultural History of the Modern Age* (3 vols., 1930–1932).
Butler, D., *The Study of Political Behaviour* (1959).
Sabine, G. H., *A History of Political Theory* (3rd ed., 1951).
Watkins, F. W., *The Political Theory of the West* (1948).
Brierly, J. L., *The Law of Nations* (5th ed., 1955).
Oppenheim, L. F. L., *International Law* (2 vols., 8th ed., 1955–1957).

Artistic, Literary, and Musical

Gardner, H., *Art Through the Ages* (4th ed., 1959). A standard work.
Gombrich, E. H. F., *The Story of Art* (4th ed., rev., 1952). Useful.
Hauser, A., *The Social History of Art* (2 vols., 1951; paperback, 1957–1958).
Read, Herbert, *A Concise History of Modern Painting* (1959; paperback, 1962).
Fletcher, B., *A History of Architecture on the Comparative Method* (17th ed., rev. and reset, 1961). A famous, lavishly illustrated work.
Pevsner, N., *An Outline of European Architecture* (5th ed., 1957; paperback, 1953).
Priestley, J. B., *Literature and Western Man* (1960).
Cohen, J. M., *A History of Western Literature* (rev. ed., 1961).
Sachs, C., *A Short History of World Music* (3rd ed., 1956).
Westrup, J. A., *An Introduction to Musical History* (1955).
Lang, P. H., *Music in Western Civilization* (1941).

Religious

Latourette, K. S., *Christianity in a Revolutionary Age: A History of Christianity in the Nineteenth and Twentieth Centuries* (vols. I–IV, 1959–1962). The first two volumes deal respectively with the history in the nineteenth century of the Roman Catholic Church, and of the Protestant and Eastern Orthodox churches.
Wand, J. W. C., *A History of the Modern Church* (1951).
Hughes, P., *A Popular History of the Catholic Church* (1949; paperback, 1962).
Parkes, J. W., *History of the Jewish People* (1962).
Sachar, H. M., *The Course of Modern Jewish History* (1958). A history since 1789, with emphasis on sociological and psychological factors.

By Chapters

CHAPTER 1   The Years of Uncertainty, 1815–1848

THE CONGRESS OF VIENNA AND THE POSTWAR ALLIANCE

Webster, C. K., *The Congress of Vienna, 1814–1815* (rev. ed., 1934). A brief summary by the leading authority.

Nicolson, H., *The Congress of Vienna* (1946; paperback, 1961). Carries the story to 1822.

Phillips, W. A., *The Confederation of Europe* (enlarged ed., 1920). The pioneering study.

Schenk, H. G., *The Aftermath of the Napoleonic Wars. The Concert of Europe, an Experiment* (1947). Places the diplomatic problem in the larger cultural setting.

Kissinger, H., *A World Restored: Metternich, Castlereagh, and the Problems of Peace, 1812–1822* (1957). A scholarly interpretation by a distinguished student of contemporary power politics.

Gulick, E. V., *Europe's Classical Balance of Power* (1955). A study of the congress system.

Cecil, A., *Metternich, 1773–1859: A Study of His Period and Personality* (2nd ed., 1943).

Du Coudray, H., *Metternich* (1935). This and the preceding item are two well-balanced biographies.

Sweet, P. R., *Friedrich von Gentz, Defender of the Old Order* (1941). Deals with one of Metternich's close collaborators.

THE EASTERN QUESTION, 1815–1841

Crawley, C. W., *The Question of Greek Independence* (1930). Scholarly.

Woodhouse, C. M., *The Greek War of Independence* (1952). A convenient brief summary.

Webster, C. K., *The Foreign Policy of Palmerston, 1830–1841* (2 vols., 1951). Based on detailed archival research.

Marriott, J. A. R., *The Eastern Question: An Historical Study in European Diplomacy* (4th ed., 1940). A standard work.

POLITICAL IDEAS AND PRINCIPLES

Artz, F. B., *Reaction and Revolution, 1814–1832* (1934 and frequent reissues). One of the best treatments of this period, with stress on ideas.

Bowle, J., *Politics and Opinion in the Nineteenth Century: An Historical Introduction* (1954). Excellent.

Woodward, E. L., *Three Studies in European Conservatism* (1929). Deals with Metternich, Guizot, and the Catholic Church.

Ruggiero, G. de, *History of European Liberalism* (1927; paperback, 1959). A philosophical analysis.

Hayes, C. J. H., *The Historical Evolution of Modern Nationalism* (1931; reprinted, 1955). A pioneering work.

Gray, A., *The Socialist Tradition: Moses to Lenin* (1946). Extremely readable. Generally critical in tone.

Cole, G. D. H., *A History of Socialist Thought* (5 vols., 1953–1960). The first three volumes deal with the forerunners and the nineteenth-century movements.

Brinton, C., *The Political Ideas of the English Romanticists* (1926).

Barzun, J., *Romanticism and the Modern Ego* (1943). The relation of the romantic outlook to European life.

CHAPTER 2   Four Regimes in France, 1814–1870

UP-TO-DATE GENERAL HISTORIES

Seignobos, C., *History of the French People* (1953). By a distinguished French scholar.
Maurois, A., *History of France* (Eng. tr., 1957; paperback, 1960). A very readable summary.
Bury, J. P. T., *France, 1814–1940: A History* (1949; paperback, 1962). The most satisfactory single volume for this period.
Cobban, A., *A History of Modern France* (2 vols., 2nd ed., 1961, paperback). The first volume begins at 1715, the second covers 1799–1871, with an epilogue on the Third Republic.
Guérard, A., *France: A Modern History* (1959). Brief, readable.
Brogan, D. W., *The French Nation from Napoleon to Pétain, 1814–1940* (1957). A brilliant, allusive essay.
Wright, G., *France in Modern Times, 1760 to the Present* (1960). The emphasis is on the more recent period.

THE RESTORATION AND THE ORLEANS MONARCHY

Artz, F. B., *France Under the Bourbon Restoration, 1814–1830* (1931). The most useful general survey.
Allison, J. M. S., *Thiers and the French Monarchy, 1797–1848* (1926). A substantial study.
Plamenatz, J., *The Revolutionary Movement in France, 1815–1871* (1952). Includes the Revolution of 1789 and stresses the great influence of Rousseau and Proudhon.
Leys, M. R. D., *Between Two Empires, A History of French Politicians and People, 1815–1848* (1955).
Evans, D. O., *Social Romanticism in France, 1830–1848* (1951). A study of the relation between romanticism and revolutionary thought.

THE SECOND REPUBLIC AND THE SECOND EMPIRE

Simpson, F. A., *The Rise of Louis Napoleon* (3rd ed., 1950). Brilliantly written.
———, *Louis Napoleon and the Recovery of France* (new ed., 1952). Goes to 1856.
McKay, D. C., *The National Workshops: A Study in the French Revolution of 1848* (1923). A carefully documented monograph.
Thompson, J. M., *Louis Napoleon and the Second Empire* (1955). A well-rounded study.
Guérard, A., *Napoleon III* (1943). Stresses his social contributions; weak on foreign policy.
Gooch, G. P., *The Second Empire* (1960). A very substantial appraisal.
Williams, R. L., *Gaslight and Shadow: The World of Napoleon III, 1851–1870* (1957; paperback, 1962). An interesting social study, using the biographical approach.
Pinkney, D. S., *Napoleon III and the Reconstruction of Paris* (1958). A scholarly account of the work of Haussmann and Napoleon III.
Soltau, R., *French Political Thought in the Nineteenth Century* (1931). Useful for this period.
Zelden, T., *The Political System of Napoleon III* (1958). A documented study of Napoleon III's techniques of government.

CHAPTER 3   The Struggle for Power in Central Europe, 1848–1851

GERMANY BEFORE 1848

Dill, Marshall, Jr., *Germany, A Modern History* (1961). A detailed study of all aspects of German life, concentrating on the period after 1790.

Pinson, K. S., *Modern Germany: Its History and Civilization* (1954). Contains valuable analyses of political, social and economic developments since the time of the French Revolution.

Flenley, R., *Modern German History* (1953). From the Reformation to the present.

Taylor, A. J. P., *The Course of German History: A Survey of the Development of Germany Since 1815* (1946; paperback, 1962). Stimulating and highly critical.

Passant, E. J., *et al.*, *A Short History of Germany, 1815–1945* (1959; paperback, 1962). A factual survey made for the British Admiralty during the Second World War. Excellent maps and charts.

Valentin, V., *The German People* (1946). A very readable survey by a German scholar.

Hamerow, T. S., *Restoration, Revolution, Reaction: Economics and Politics in Germany, 1815–1871* (1958). Emphasizes the part played by the artisan and the peasant.

THE AUSTRIAN EMPIRE BEFORE 1848

Taylor, A. J. P., *The Hapsburg Monarchy, 1809–1918* (2nd ed., 1949). A scholarly work.

Kann, Robert A., *A Study in Austrian Intellectual History* (1960). Contains a stimulating essay on the Metternich system.

Jászi, Oscar, *Dissolution of the Hapsburg Monarchy* (1929; paperback, 1961). Has a valuable analysis of the Hapsburg problem.

THE REVOLUTIONS OF 1848 AND THEIR CONSEQUENCES

Fejtö, F. (ed.), *The Opening of an Era: 1848—An Historical Symposium* (1949). Useful essays.

Whitridge, A., *Men in Crisis: The Revolutions of 1848* (1949). Biographical in approach.

Robertson, Priscilla, *The Revolutions of 1848: A Social History* (1952; paperback, 1960). An interesting narrative.

Valentin, V., *1848: Chapters in German History* (1940). A learned study.

Namier, L. B., *1848: The Revolution of the Intellectuals* (1946). Questions the liberalism of the German intellectuals.

Rath, R. J., *The Viennese Revolution of 1848* (1957). An outstanding monograph.

Bruun, G., *Revolution and Reaction, 1848–1852, A Mid-Century Watershed* (1958, paper). Valuable brief outline, with documents.

CHAPTER 4 Italy and Its Unification

UP-TO-DATE GENERAL HISTORY

Salvatorelli, L., *A Concise History of Italy from Prehistoric Times* (1940).

Mack Smith, D., *Italy: A Modern History* (1959). Covers domestic more fully than foreign or colonial policy, with 1861 as starting point.

Whyte, A. J., *The Revolution of Modern Italy, 1715–1920* (1950).

Olschki, L., *The Genius of Italy* (1949). A valuable work of interpretation.

NARRATIVE OF THE UNIFICATION

Albrecht-Carrié, R., *Italy from Napoleon to Mussolini* (1949; paperback, 1950). Political and diplomatic.

Greenfield, K. R., *Economics and Liberalism in the Risorgimento: A Study of Nationalism in Lombardy, 1814–1848* (1934). Brings out the economic pressures for unification.

Marriott, J. A. R., *The Makers of Modern Italy* (1931). Old but useful.

King, Bolton, *History of Italian Unity* (2 vols., 2nd ed., 1912). Still a standard history.

Thayer, W. R., *The Life and Times of Cavour* (2 vols., 1911). Many documents.

THE REACTION AFTER 1815 AND THE REVOLUTIONS OF 1848

Berkeley, G. F. H. and J., *Italy in the Making, 1815–1848* (3 vols., 1932–1940).
Trevelyan, G. M., *Daniel Manin and the Venetian Revolution of 1848* (1923). All Trevelyan's
   volumes are classics in the liberal tradition.
———, *Garibaldi's Defence of the Roman Republic* (1907; frequent reissues).
Salvemini, G., *Mazzini* (1956; paperback, 1957). By a distinguished Italian liberal.
Griffith, G. O., *Mazzini, Prophet of Modern Europe* (1932). One of the best brief lives.

THE EVENTS OF 1859–1860

Whyte, A. J., *The Political Life and Letters of Cavour, 1848–1861* (1930). Standard.
Mack Smith, D., *Cavour and Garibaldi in 1860* (1954). Critical of Cavour.
Hancock, W. K., *Ricasoli and the Risorgimento in Tuscany* (1926).
Trevelyan, G. M., *Garibaldi and the Thousand* (1909; frequent reissues).
———, *Garibaldi and the Making of Italy* (1911; frequent reissues).
Mack Smith, D., *Garibaldi: A Great Life in Brief* (1956).

THE ROMAN CATHOLIC PROBLEM

Hales, E. E. Y., *Pio Nono* (1954; paperback, 1962).
Halperin, S. W., *The Separation of Church and State in Italian Thought from Cavour to Mussolini* (1937).

CHAPTER 5   The Unification of Germany and the European Balance,
            1849–1871

For general histories of Germany and Austria, see pp. 512–513.

EVENTS AND POLICIES OF THE PERIOD AS A WHOLE

Eyck, E., *Bismarck and the German Empire* (1950). Sober.
Taylor, A. J. P., *Bismarck, the Man and the Statesman* (1955). Vigorously critical.
Mosse, W. E., *The European Powers and the German Question, 1848–1871* (1958). An im-
   portant documentary study.
Darmstaedter, F., *Bismarck and the Creation of the Second Reich* (1948).
Marriott, J. A. R., and Robertson, C. G., *The Evolution of Prussia: The Making of an
   Empire* (1915). Old but still useful.

PARTICULAR ASPECTS

Craig, G. A., *The Politics of the Prussian Army, 1640–1945* (1955). A study of the powerful
   role of the military.
Anderson, E. N., *The Social and Political Conflict in Prussia, 1858–1864* (1954). A specialized
   monograph.
Friedjung, H., *The Struggle for Supremacy in Germany, 1859–1866* (abridged ed., 1935).
   A classic study.
Steefel, L. D., *The Schleswig-Holstein Question* (1932). The standard work, heavily docu-
   mented.
Lord, R. H., *The Origins of the War of 1870: New Documents From the German Archives*
   (1924). Long a standard work. Its conclusions are modified by the monograph of
   Bonnin.
Howard, M., *The Franco-Prussian War: The German Invasion of France, 1870–71* (1961).
   An up-to-date account of the war in all its main aspects.

Oncken, H., *Napoleon III and the Rhine: The Origins of the War of 1870-71* (1928). An abridgment of a long German work, highly critical of French intrigues.

Bonnin, G., *Bismarck and the Hohenzollern Candidature for the Spanish Throne* (1958). Employs documents not available to Lord, and emphasizes Bismarck's dominant role.

Whitton, F. E., *Moltke* (1921). Still the best biography in English.

CHAPTER 6   Changing Russia, 1815–1871

GENERAL HISTORIES

Florinsky, M. T., *Russia: A History and an Interpretation* (2 vols., 1947). The second volume gives the most satisfactory account in English of the period 1802–1917.

Walsh, Warren B., *Russia and the Soviet Union* (1958). One-quarter of the volume is devoted to the nineteenth century.

Pares, B., *A History of Russia* (rev. ed., 1953). By a distinguished scholar.

Vernadsky, G., *A History of Russia* (4th ed., 1954; paperback, 1961). Standard.

Sumner, B. H., *A Short History of Russia* (2nd ed., 1948; paperback, 1962). Uses a topical rather than a chronological approach, working backward from the present.

Charques, R. D., *A Short History of Russia* (1956; paperback, 1958). Very short and clear.

THE PERIOD 1815–1855

Strakhovsky, L. I., *Alexander I of Russia* (1949). A convenient biography.

Mazour, A. G., *The First Russian Revolution, 1825: The Decembrist Movement* (1937). An important, scholarly monograph.

Zetlin, M., *The Decembrists* (1958). A vivid, biographical account, first published in Russian in 1928.

Grunwald, C. de, *Tsar Nicholas I* (1955).

Riasanovsky, N. V., *Nicholas I and Official Nationality in Russia, 1825–1855* (1959). The attempt of Nicholas I to preserve Russia from Western influences.

Simmons, E. J., *Pushkin* (1937). A standard biography.

THE PERIOD 1855–1871

Seton-Watson, H., *The Decline of Imperial Russia, 1855–1914* (1952; paperback, 1956). A clear, scholarly, and thoughtful account.

Mosse, W. E., *Alexander II and the Modernization of Russia* (1958; paperback, 1962). The best brief account.

Graham, S., *Tsar of Freedom: Alexander II* (1935). Older, but still useful.

SOCIAL AND ECONOMIC ASPECTS

Yarmolinsky, A., *Road to Revolution: A Century of Russian Radicalism* (1959; paperback, 1962). Ends at 1881.

Malia, Martin, *Alexander Herzen and the Birth of Russian Socialism, 1812–1855* (1961). A scholarly monograph.

Hare, Richard, *Pioneers of Russian Social Thought* (1951). Deals with the first half of the nineteenth century.

Lampert, E., *Studies in Rebellion* (1956). Belinsky, Bakunin, Herzen.

Kohn, H. (ed.), *The Mind of Modern Russia* (1955). Well-chosen extracts from Russian writers, with introductory essays.

Mavor, J., *Economic History of Russia* (2nd rev. ed., 2 vols., 1926). A standard work.

Blum, J., *Lord and Peasant in Russia* (1961). An elaborate historical study.

Robinson, G. T., *Rural Russia Under the Old Regime* (new ed., 1949). An authoritative monograph.

Wallace, D. Mackenzie, *Russia* (1877). Though revised in later editions this is essentially based on six years' residence in the Russia of the 1870's.

Riasanovsky, N. V., *Russia and the West in the Teachings of the Slavophils* (1952). A study of the anti-Western movement in Russia.

THE POLISH REVOLTS

Leslie, R. F., *Polish Politics and the Revolution of 1830* (1956). A detailed study of the social background and a critical account of the conspiratorial activities of the period.

Halecki, O., *History of Poland* (1942). By a distinguished Polish scholar.

Frankel, H., *Poland, the Struggle for Power, 1772–1939* (1946). A survey of Poland's place in Europe.

CHAPTER 7   Britain—The Epoch of Reform

GENERAL

Trevelyan, G. M., *History of England* (rev. ed., 1937). A beautifully written, slightly old-fashioned narrative.

Feiling, K., *A History of England* (1950). A detailed factual survey.

Smith, Goldwin, *A History of England* (2nd ed., 1957).

Carrington, C. E., *The British Overseas* (1950). A sympathetic and vigorous account of the growth of the Empire and Commonwealth.

Trevelyan, G. M., *English Social History* (1942). A one-volume panorama of social life at different periods from the fourteenth to the late nineteenth century.

POLITICAL DEVELOPMENT, 1815–1871

Woodward, E. L., *The Age of Reform, 1815–1870* (2nd ed., 1962). A volume in the Oxford History of England series.

Halévy, E., *History of the English People in the Nineteenth Century* (vols. 1–4, 2nd ed., 1949–1950; 6 vols. paperback, 1961). Vol. I is a detailed analysis of British institutions in 1815; Vols. II and III give the history of 1815–1841 very fully; Vol. IV continues in detail to about 1850 and ends with an outline sketch to 1895 by another hand. There are two further volumes beyond this period.

Briggs, Asa, *The Age of Improvement, 1783–1867* (1959). Includes a study of public opinion.

Trevelyan, G. M., *British History in the Nineteenth Century and After (1782–1919)* (2nd ed., 1937).

Marriott, J. A. R., *England Since Waterloo* (1913). Political and military.

SOCIAL AND ECONOMIC HISTORY

Roberts, David, *Victorian Origins of the British Welfare State* (1960). The achievements of the early Victorian administrators.

Clapham, J. H., *An Economic History of Modern Britain* (3 vols., 1926–1938). The classic account of the period 1820–1914, with epilogue.

Court, W. H. B., *A Concise Economic History of Britain from 1750 to Recent Times* (1954).

Chambers, J. D., *The Workshop of the World* (1961). A short economic history for 1820–1880.

Cole, G. D. H., and Postgate, R., *The British People, 1746–1946* (rev. ed., 1956; paperback, 1961).

Hovell, M., *The Chartist Movement* (1925). Still the standard work on its subject.
Thomas, M. W., *The Early Factory Legislation* (1948).
White, R. J., *Waterloo to Peterloo* (1957). Social disturbances in Britain.
Woodham-Smith, C. B., *The Great Hunger. Ireland, 1845–1849* (1962). The Irish famine.

THOUGHT AND OPINION

Young, G. M., *Victorian England: The Portrait of an Age* (2nd ed., 1953; paperback, 1954).
Brinton, Crane, *English Political Thought in the Nineteenth Century* (2nd ed., 1949; paperback, 1962). A good introduction.

FOREIGN POLICY

Seton-Watson, R. W., *Britain in Europe, 1789–1914* (1937).

CHAPTER 8   The Industrial Revolution in Europe to 1871

For works dealing with Great Britain, see p. 516.

CONTINENTAL EUROPE

Bowden, W., Karpovich, M., and Usher, A. P., *An Economic History of Europe Since 1750* (3rd ed., 1952). Makes a convenient division at 1870.
Knowles, L. C. A., *Economic Development in the Nineteenth Century—France, Germany, Russia, and the United States* (1932).
Clapham, J. H., *The Economic Development of France and Germany, 1815–1914* (4th ed., 1936; paperback, 1963). Still a standard work.
Henderson, W. O., *The Industrial Revolution on the Continent: Germany, France, Russia, 1800–1914* (1961). A mine of facts.

SINGLE COUNTRIES AND THEIR ECONOMIC INFLUENCE

Dunham, A. L., *The Industrial Revolution in France, 1815–1848* (1955).
Henderson, W. O., *The Zollverein* (1939). An elaborate monograph.
———, *Britain and Industrial Europe, 1750–1870* (1954).
Cameron, R. E., *France and the Economic Development of Europe, 1800–1914* (1961). Much information on French capital exports and railway building.
Clough, S. B., *France, A History of National Economics, 1789–1939* (1939).
Heckscher, E. F., *An Economic History of Sweden* (1954).

CHAPTER 9   Movements of Thought and Culture, 1815–1871

For general histories see the references on pp. 509–510.

NINETEENTH-CENTURY THOUGHT

Merz, J. T., *History of European Thought in the Nineteenth Century* (4 vols., 2nd ed., 1912–1928). Still the fundamental work, with stress on science and philosophy.
Mead, G. H., *Movements of Thought in the Nineteenth Century* (1936). Undergraduate lectures.
Johnson, E. N., *An Introduction to the History of the Western Tradition* (vol. 2, 1959). A large part deals with the nineteenth century.
Randall, H. J., *The Creative Centuries* (1947). Has some useful chapters on the nineteenth century.

Routh, H. V., *Towards the Twentieth Century: Essays on the Spiritual History of the Nineteenth* (1937). A distinguished work.

Barzun, J., *Darwin, Marx, Wagner* (1941; paperback, 1958). Relates these to the intellectual climate of the age.

POLITICAL AND ECONOMIC THOUGHT

Hearnshaw, F. J. C. (ed.), *Social and Political Ideas of Some Representative Thinkers of the Age of Reaction and Reconstruction, 1815–1865* (1949). Essays on English and Continental writers.

Viereck, P., *Metapolitics: From the Romantics to Hitler* (1941; paperback, 1961).

Halévy, E., *The Growth of Philosophic Radicalism* (1950; paperback, 1955).

Marvin, F. S., *Comte the Founder of Sociology* (1937).

Muret, C., *French Royalist Doctrines Since the Revolution* (1933).

Bober, M., *Karl Marx's Interpretation of History* (rev. ed., 1948).

PHILOSOPHY AND RELIGION

Hook, S., *From Hegel to Marx* (1936). Useful.

Moore, E. C., *An Outline of the History of Christian Thought Since Kant* (new ed., 1947). An important summary.

SCIENCE

Wightman, B., *The Growth of Scientific Ideas* (1950). The best general history for the nineteenth century, especially on physics.

Gillispie, C. C., *Genesis and Geology* (1951; paperback, 1959). The background of Darwinism.

Irvine, W. I., *Apes, Angels, and Victorians* (1955). The reception of Darwinism.

Himmelfarb, G., *Darwin and the Darwinian Revolution* (1959). Substantial.

O'Brien, John A., *Evolution and Religion* (1932).

Dubos, R. J., *Louis Pasteur, Free Lance of Science* (1950).

LITERATURE AND THE ARTS

Brandes, G., *Main Currents of Nineteenth Century Literature* (Engl. tr., 6 vols., 1906). Still a mine of information on the first half of the century.

Croce, B., *European Literature in the Nineteenth Century* (Engl. tr., 1925).

Sloane, Joseph C., *French Painting . . . From 1848 to 1870* (1951).

Raynal, M. *The Nineteenth Century . . . Goya to Gauguin* (1951). Beautifully illustrated.

Hitchcock, H. R., *Architecture: Nineteenth and Twentieth Centuries* (1958).

Leichentritt, H., *Music, History, and Ideas* (1938).

Einstein, Alfred, *Music in the Romantic Era* (1947).

Barzun, J., *Berlioz and the Romantic Century* (1950; paperback, 1956).

MISCELLANEOUS

Gooch, G. P., *History and Historians in the Nineteenth Century* (1913; paperback, 1959). A valuable contribution to intellectual history.

Butterfield, H., *Man on His Past* (1955; paperback, 1960). Deals largely with nineteenth-century historical scholarship.

Kohn-Bramstedt, E., *Aristocracy and the Middle Classes in Germany* (1937). A sociological study of literature and society.

Barnard, Howard C., *A Short History of English Education From 1760 to 1944* (1947). Useful.

CHAPTER 10 The Triumph of Machine Industry, 1870–1914

For main works covering the whole century see p. 517.

THE LATE NINETEENTH CENTURY

Ashworth, W., *A Short History of the International Economy, 1850–1950* (1952).
Rostow, W. W., *Stages of Economic Growth* (1960; paperback, 1960). A "non-communist manifesto."
Stolper, G., *The German Economy, 1870–1940* (1940).

SPECIAL ASPECTS

Hobson, J. A., *Imperialism, A Study* (3rd rev. ed., 1938). A vigorous critique of imperialism.
Feis, H., *Europe: The World's Banker, 1870–1914* (1930). Has much on the financing of imperialism.
Burn, D. L., *The Economic History of Steel-Making, 1867–1939: A Study in Competition* (1940).
Pratt, E. A., *The Rise of Rail-Power in War and Conquest 1833–1914* (1915).
Ropp, T., *War in the Modern World* (1959: paperback, 1962).
Schumpeter, J. A., *Capitalism, Socialism, and Democracy* (3rd ed., 1950).
Ropke, W., *German Commercial Policy* (1934).
Kuczinski, J., *Labour Conditions in Western Europe, 1820 to 1935* (1937).

CHAPTER 11 The German Power in Europe

For general histories of Germany see pp. 512–513.

GENERAL DEVELOPMENT AFTER 1870

Rosenberg, A., *The Birth of the German Republic, 1871–1918* (1931). A distinguished study.
Dawson, W. H., *The German Empire and the Unity Movement* (2 vols., 1919). Old, but still useful on social problems.
Bruck, W. F., *Social and Economic History of Germany from William II to Hitler, 1888–1938* (1938).
Anderson, E., *Hammer and Anvil: the Story of the German Working Class Movement* (1945).
Dorpalen, A., *Heinrich von Treitschke* (1957). A case study of German nationalism.
Townsend, Mary E., *The Rise and Fall of Germany's Colonial Empire* (1930). A standard monograph.

DIPLOMACY OF THE BISMARCKIAN ERA

Langer, W. L., *European Alliances and Alignments, 1871–1890* (2nd ed., 1950). In general a defence of Bismarckian policy. The changes in the second edition are bibliographical.
Pribram, A. F., *The Secret Treaties of Austria-Hungary* (2 vols., 1920–1921). The first significant revelation of prewar secret diplomacy.
Medlicott, W. N., *The Congress of Berlin and After* (1938).
———, *Bismarck, Gladstone, and the Concert of Europe* (1956). These two books trace in detail the diplomatic developments of 1878–1882.

THE PERIOD FROM 1890 TO 1914

Hammann, Otto, *The World Policy of Germany, 1890–1912* (1927). A German defense of Bismarckian policies.

Nichols, J. A., *Germany After Bismarck: the Caprivi Era, 1890–1894* (1958). A full account.

Gooch, G. P., *Germany* (1925). Contains five chapters describing the development of the country up to 1914.

Schorske, Carl W., *German Social Democracy, 1905–1907* (1955). A substantial account.

CHAPTER 12   Republican France, 1870–1914

For general histories of France see p. 512.

THE PERIOD AFTER 1870

Brogan, D. W., *The Development of Modern France, 1870–1939* (1940). A detailed history, based on a wide knowledge and sympathetic understanding.

Thomson, D., *Democracy in France: The Third and Fourth Republics* (3rd ed., 1958). An important study of institutions.

Bainville, J., *The French Republic, 1870–1935* (1936).

Hale, R. W., *Democratic France* (1941). A sympathetic history of the Third Republic.

SPECIAL TOPICS

Jellinek, F., *The Paris Commune of 1871* (1937). Now more useful than the older (1931) study of E. S. Mason.

Joughin, J. T., *The Paris Commune and French Politics, 1871–1880* (2 vols., 1955). A study of changing attitudes toward the *Communards* resulting in the general amnesty of 1880.

Jackson, J. Hampden, *Clemenceau and the Third Republic* (1948). An admirable brief biography.

Bodley, J. E. C., *France* (rev. ed., 1899). A study in depth by a resident British journalist of the France he knew.

Chapman, G., *The Dreyfus Case: a Reassessment* (1955). Scholarly and up-to-date.

Priestley, H. I., *France Overseas, a Study of Modern Imperialism* (1938). Covers all parts of the French Empire from 1815 to 1936.

Earle, E. M. (ed.), *Modern France: Problems of the Third and Fourth Republics* (1951). Valuable essays by a group of specialists.

Morazé, C., *The French and the Republic* (1958). A political and economic analysis.

Scott, J. A., *Republican Ideas and the Liberal Tradition in France, 1870–1914* (1951). A doctoral dissertation.

Shapiro, D., *The Right in France, 1890–1919: Three Studies* (1962).

Jackson, J. Hampden, *Jean Jaurès* (1944). A useful biography.

Power, T. F., *Jules Ferry and the Renaissance of French Imperialism* (1944).

CHAPTER 13   Britain and Her Empire

For works covering the whole century see p. 516.

GENERAL HISTORY FROM 1870 TO 1914

Ensor, R. C. K., *England 1870–1914* (1936), in the Oxford History of England series.

Halévy, E., *History of the English People in the Nineteenth Century* (vols. V and VI, 2nd ed., 1949–1950; paperback, 1961). Covers the period from 1895 to 1914 in great detail, with valuable footnote references.

Spender, J. A., *Great Britain, Empire and Commonwealth, 1886–1935* (1936). By a great Liberal journalist, drawing on his own political experience.

Gretton, R. H., *A Modern History of the English People, 1880–1922* (1930). History built up from newspapers.

Marriott, J. A. R., *Modern England, 1885–1945* (4th ed., 1948).

Benians, E. A., Butler, J. R. M., and Carrington, C. E. (eds.), *The Cambridge History of the British Empire*, vol. III, *The Empire-Commonwealth, 1870–1919* (1959).

SPECIAL TOPICS

Hammond, J. L., *Gladstone and the Irish Nation* (1938).

Dangerfield, G., *The Strange Death of Liberal England* (1936; paperback, 1961).

Ashworth, W., *An Economic History of England, 1870–1939* (1960).

Grey, E. (Viscount Grey of Fallodon), *Twenty-Five Years, 1892–1916* (2 vols., 1925).

Johnson, F. A., *Defence by Committee: the British Committee of Imperial Defence* (1960). A careful study of planning to meet the risk of war.

Kruger, Rayne, *Good Bye Dolly Gray: The Story of the Boer War* (1960). A highly readable account by a South African.

Fremantle, A., *This Little Band of Prophets* (1960; paperback, 1960). A good account of Fabian Socialism.

CHAPTER 14 Russia at the Parting of the Ways

For general works see p. 515.

GENERAL HISTORIES COVERING THE PERIOD 1871–1914

Pares, B., *The Fall of the Russian Monarchy* (1939; paperback, 1961). A standard account, based partly on the author's experiences.

Charques, R., *The Twilight of Imperial Russia* (1959). A study of the reign of Nicholas II.

COLONIAL AND FOREIGN POLICY

Sumner, B. H., *Russia and the Balkans, 1870–1880* (1937).

———, *Tsardom and Imperialism in the Far East and the Middle East* (1942).

Dallin, D. J., *The Rise of Russia in Asia* (1949).

Treadgold, D. W., *The Great Siberian Migration: Government and Peasant in Resettlement from Emancipation to the First World War* (1957). An important monograph, extolling the work of Stolypin.

SUBJECT NATIONALITIES

Greenberg, L. S., *The Jews in Russia* (1944).

Wuorinen, J. H., *Nationalism in Modern Finland* (1931).

Jackson, J. H., *Finland* (2nd ed., 1940).

———, *Estonia* (1941).

REVOLUTIONARY MOVEMENTS

Venturi, F., *Roots of Revolution* (1960). Populist and socialist movements.

Billington, J. H., *Mikhailovsky and Russian Populism* (1958). A study of Populist thinking.

Wolfe, Bertram D., *Three Who Made a Revolution: a Biographical History* (1948; paperback, 1955). An account of the earlier activities of Lenin, Trotsky, and Stalin.

Wilson, Edmund, *To The Finland Station* (1940; paperback, 1953). The derivation of the Russian revolution from earlier radical movements.

Berdyaev, N., *The Origin of Russian Communism* (1937; paperback, 1960). Classical Marxism and Russian communism.

Footman, D., *Red Prelude* (1945). The assassination of Alexander II.

INTELLECTUAL BACKGROUND

Maynard, J., *Russia in Flux: Before October* (1941; paperback, 1963). An interesting, discursive history which traces currents of thought.

Masaryk, T. G., *The Spirit of Russia: Studies in History, Literature, and Philosophy* (2 vols., 1919). By one of the founders of Czechoslovakia who was also a profound student of Russian culture.

Tompkins, S. R., *The Russian Intelligentsia: Makers of the Revolutionary State* (1957). A short study, with useful quotations.

Bruford, W. H., *Chekhov and His Russia* (1948). A vivid reconstruction of the old Russia.

Fischer, George, *Russian Liberalism: From Gentry to Intelligentsia* (1958). Traces the growth of an enlightened class in Russia.

CHAPTER 15   Austria-Hungary, Italy, and the Lesser Powers

AUSTRIA-HUNGARY

See in addition the references on p. 513.

May, A. J., *The Hapsburg Monarchy, 1867–1914* (1951). A scholarly study.

Kann, R. A., *The Multi-National Empire: Nationalism and National Reform in the Hapsburg Monarchy, 1848–1918* (2 vols., 1950). A very detailed treatment.

Namier, L. B., *Vanished Supremacies: Essays on European History, 1812–1918* (1958). Contains a short but authoritative account of the political structure resulting from the *Ausgleich*, dated 1919.

Seton-Watson, R. W., *A History of the Czechs and Slovaks* (1943). By a distinguished authority.

Thomson, S. Harrison, *Czechoslovakia in European History* (1943). A valuable treatment of the Czechs and Slovaks, principally before their independence.

TURKEY AND THE BALKANS

Miller, W., *The Ottoman Empire and its Successors, 1807–1927* (new ed., 1936). A standard work.

Ramsaur, E. E., Jr., *The Young Turks: Prelude to the Revolution of 1908* (1957). Growth of the revolutionary movement in Turkey.

Wolf, J. B., *The Diplomatic History of the Baghdad Railroad* (1936).

Seton-Watson, R. W., *The Rise of Nationality in the Balkans* (1917).

Forster, E. S., *A Short History of Modern Greece, 1821–1956* (3rd ed., 1958).

Temperley, H. W. V., *History of Serbia* (1917). A standard work.

Seton-Watson, R. W., *A History of the Roumanians* (1936). Standard.

Black, C. E., *The Establishment of Constitutional Government in Bulgaria* (1943).

ITALY

See, in addition to the references on p. 513:

Croce, Benedetto, *History of Italy, 1871–1915* (1929). A study by a philosopher-historian.

Salomone, A. W., *Italian Democracy in the Making* (1945).

SPAIN AND PORTUGAL

Madariaga, S. de, *Spain, A Modern History* (1958; paperback, 1960). Deals mainly with the twentieth century.

Altamira, R., *History of Spain from the Beginning to the Present Day* (1949).

Bertrand, L., and Petrie, C., *The History of Spain* (rev. ed., 1952).

Trend, J. B., *The Origins of Modern Spain* (1934).

Livermore, H. W., *A History of Portugal* (1947).
Nowell, C. E., *History of Portugal* (1953).
Atkinson, W. C., *A History of Spain and Portugal* (1960). A reflective survey rather than a narrative of facts.

SWITZERLAND

Bonjour, E., Offler, H. S., and Potter, G. R., *A Short History of Switzerland* (1952).
Oechsli, W., *History of Switzerland, 1499–1914* (1922).

THE LOW COUNTRIES

Meeüs, A. de, *History of the Belgians* (1962).
Cammaerts, E., *The Keystone of Europe: History of the Belgian Dynasty, 1830–1939* (1939).
Vlekke, B. H. M., *Evolution of the Dutch Nation* (1951).
Vandenbosch, A., *Dutch Foreign Policy Since 1815: A Study in Small Power Politics* (The Hague, 1959). A clear account of major events.
Putnam, Ruth, *Luxemburg and Her Neighbors* (2nd ed., 1919).

SCANDINAVIA AND FINLAND

Lindgren, R. E., *Norway-Sweden: Union, Disunion, and Scandinavian Integration* (1959). Relations between Sweden and Norway since 1815.
Lindberg, F., *Scandinavia in Great Power Politics, 1905–1908* (Stockholm, 1958).
Andersson, I., *A History of Sweden* (1956).
Danstrup, J., *A History of Denmark* (Copenhagen, 1949).
Birch, J. H. S., *Denmark in History* (1938).
Larsen, K., *A History of Norway* (1948).
Derry, T. K., *A Short History of Norway* (1957).
Gjerset, Knut, *History of Iceland* (1924).
Jutikkala, E., *History of Finland* (1962).

CHAPTER 16   European Cultural Influences at Their Zenith

GENERAL WORKS

In addition to the references on pp. 509–510, see:

Hayes, C. J. H., *A Generation of Materialism, 1871–1900* (1941). Though highly critical of many aspects of this age, a valuable and stimulating work.
Masur, G., *Prophets of Yesterday: Studies in European Culture, 1890–1914* (1961). Important analysis of key figures.

POLITICAL AND SOCIAL THOUGHT

Hearnshaw, F. J. C. (ed.), *Social and Political Ideas of Some Representative Thinkers of the Victorian Age* (1950). Useful essays by various authorities.
Brinton, C., *Nietzsche* (1941). Very readable.
Gay, Peter, *The Dilemma of Democratic Socialism: Edward Bernstein's Challenge to Marx* (1952). A study of revisionism.
Humphrey, R., *Georges Sorel: Prophet Without Honor* (1951). The theory of direct action.
Joll, James, *The Second International, 1889–1914* (1955).

SCIENCE

Barnett, L. K., *The Universe and Dr. Einstein* (1960; paperback, 1963).
Russell, B., *The ABC of Relativity* (1925; paperback, 1959).

Jeans, J., *The Growth of Physical Science* (2nd ed., 1951; paperback, 1963). By a distinguished physicist.

Shryock, R., *The Development of Modern Medicine* (1947).

Wittels, F., *Freud and His Times* (new ed., 1948; paperback, 1958).

Nelson, Benjamin (ed.), *Freud and the Twentieth Century* (1947). An interesting series of essays.

LITERATURE AND THE ARTS

The Cambridge History of English Literature, vol. XIV (1917, reissued 1932). Some chapters deal with the later part of the century.

Mirsky, D. S., *Modern Russian Literature* (1925). Brief but useful.

Slonim, Marc, *From Chekhov to the Revolution. Russian Literature, 1900–1917* (1962; paperback, 1962).

Simmons, E. J., *Leo Tolstoy* (1946; paperback, 1960).

Koht, H., *Life of Ibsen* (Engl. tr., 2 vols., 1931). By a distinguished Norwegian historian.

Miliukov, P., *Outlines of Russian Culture*, ed. M. Karpovich (1942; paperback, 1960), vols. II, III. Literature, music, architecture, and painting.

Craven, Thomas, *Modern Art: The Men, The Movements, The Meaning* (1934). A readable introduction.

Hunter, Sam, *Modern French Painting, 1855–1956* (1956; paperback, 1959).

Hamilton, G. H., *Manet and His Critics* (1954).

Schapiro, M., *Paul Cézanne* (1952).

Barr, A. H., *Matisse, His Art and His Public* (1951).

Hitchcock, H. R., *Architecture: Nineteenth and Twentieth Centuries* (1958).

CHAPTER 17   The Road to War

FORMATION OF RIVAL GROUPS IN EUROPE

See, in addition to the works listed on pp. 519–520:

Langer, W. L., *The Diplomacy of Imperialism, 1890–1902* (new ed., 1951). A continuation of the earlier volume.

Brandenburg, E., *From Bismarck to the World War, 1890–1914* (1927). A well-balanced German work.

Schmitt, B. E., *Triple Alliance and Triple Entente* (1934). A brief, useful summary.

Fay, S. B., *The Origins of the World War* (2nd ed., 2 vols., 1930). The first volume deals with the 1871-1914 period.

Sontag, R. J., *European Diplomatic History, 1871–1932* (1933). A useful, clear outline.

Dickinson, G. L., *The International Anarchy, 1904–1914* (1926). A classic protest against the old diplomacy.

Gooch, G. P., *Before the War: Studies in Statecraft and Diplomacy* (2 vols., 1936–1938). Useful, judicious essays.

Mansergh, N., *The Coming of the First World War: A Study in the European Balance, 1878–1914* (1949). A brief British evaluation of war origins.

Pribram, A. F., *England and the International Policy of the European Great Powers* (2nd ed., 1931).

Schmitt, B. E., *The Annexation of Bosnia* (1937). A model contribution.

Helmreich, E. C., *The Diplomacy of the Balkan Wars, 1912–1913* (1938). A very learned monograph.

Woodward, E. L., *Great Britain and the German Navy* (1935). A valuable study.
Anderson, E. N., *The First Moroccan Crisis* (1930). Deals with the period 1898 to 1906.
Barlow, I. C., *The Agadir Crisis* (1940). Useful.

ASPECTS OF THE UNDERLYING CAUSES

Moon, P. T., *Imperialism and World Politics* (1926). Old but still useful.
Lenin, V. I., *Imperialism, the Highest Stage of Capitalism* (new ed., 1937; paperback, 1939). The communist attack on imperialism.
Marder, A. J., *The Anatomy of British Sea-Power, 1880–1905* (1940). A detailed analysis.
Nickerson, H., *The Armed Horde* (1940). A good study of the development of modern war.
Fuller, J. F. C., *War and Western Civilization, 1832–1932* (1932). By a distinguished military critic.

THE CRISIS OF 1914

Albertini, L., *The Origins of the War of 1914* (Engl. tr., 3 vols., 1953–1957). The most detailed study of war origins. Vol. I deals with backgrounds.
Schmitt, B. E., *The Coming of the War* (2 vols., 1930). Covers the same ground as Fay's second volume, but is more critical of German policy.
Seton-Watson, R. W., *Sarajevo. A Study in the Origins of the Great War* (1926). By a leading Balkan expert.
Renouvin, P., *The Immediate Origins of the War* (1928). The outstanding French work on this period, moderately revisionist in tone.

COMPARATIVE
CHRONOLOGICAL TABLES

Comparative Chronological Tables

	DIPLOMATIC, MILITARY AND POLITICAL	SOCIAL AND ECONOMIC	RELATING TO OTHER CONTINENTS
1814	Congress of Vienna meets		
1815	Final overthrow of Napoleon		Slave trade condemned by Vienna Treaty
1816		Anti-machinery riots in Britain	Argentina independent
1817	Serbia independent	Wartburg Festival	
1818	Congress of Aix-la-Chapelle		
1819		Carlsbad Decrees Peterloo Massacre, Manchester	Singapore founded
1820	Revolutionary outbreaks Congress of Troppau		First British settlers in South Africa
1821	Congress of Laibach Greek war of Independence		Peru and Mexico independent Liberia founded as Negro state
1822	Congress of Verona		Brazil independent
1823			
1824		Trade unions legalized in Britain	British conquest of Burma begins
1825		Decembrist Revolt in Russia	
1826			
1827	Battle of Navarino		
1828	Russo-Turkish War		
1829	Greek independence secured		Persian Armenia annexed by Russia
1830	Revolutions in France and Belgium	Great cholera epidemic spreading from London	French begin conquest of Algeria
1831	Suppression of Polish revolt		
1832	Great Reform Bill in England	Mazzini founds "Young Italy" Baedeker's first guidebook	
1833	Treaty of Unkiar-Skelessi	First effective factory act in Britain	Slavery abolished in British Empire
1834	*Zollverein* treaties take effect in Germany	Mazzini founds "Young Europe" at Berne	
1835			
1836			
1837	Reign of Queen Victoria begins	Froebel's first kindergarten	
1838		Chartism in England	
1839	Belgium neutralized by Treaty of London		British occupy Aden Opium War in China
1840		Cunard Line founded	British occupy Hong Kong New Zealand colonized
1841	Straits Convention		
1842			Opening of Chinese ports by Treaty of Nanking

The following tables summarize a mass of historical data, some of it additional to what is in the text, arranged so that each type of material may be visualized either in chronological sequence (vertical columns) or as part of a contemporaneous series (horizontal columns). Titles of books and other printed matter are distinguished by italics, works of art are in quotation marks, and asterisks have been used to distinguish scientific from technological advances. Unless otherwise stated, the date is that of commencement. The selection of single events, and still more that of particular works of art, to illustrate the varied achievements of a crowded century is necessarily arbitrary, but the intention is to remind the reader of things that were important for Europe as a whole rather than for the history of a single people.

	SCIENCE AND TECHNOLOGY	LITERATURE AND OTHER ARTS	RELIGION, PHILOSOPHY, POLITICAL AND ECONOMIC THOUGHT
1814	Steam-printing of *The Times* Gas lighting of London streets	Scott, *Waverley*	Restoration of Jesuit Order
1815	Davy's safety-lamp	Grimm's *Fairy Tales* completed Goya, "Disasters of War"	
1816		Rossini, *Barber of Seville*	
1817		Keats, *Poems* Constable, "Flatford Mill"	Ricardo, *Principles of Political Economy*
1818	*Berzelius, Table of Atomic Weights		
1819		Shelley, *Masque of Anarchy* Géricault, "Raft of the Medusa"	Schopenhauer, *World as Will and Idea*
1820		Lamartine, *Meditations* Thorwaldsen, "Lion of Lucerne"	
1821			Hegel, *Philosophy of Law*
1822	Roberts' improved power loom	Schubert, *Unfinished Symphony*	
1823	Soda-production in Liverpool by Leblanc process	Beethoven, *Ninth Symphony*	
1824	*Sadi Carnot's theory of heat	Delacroix, "Massacre of Scios"	Ranke, *Critique of the Newer Historians*
1825	First German technical high school Stockton-Darlington Railway	Pushkin, *Boris Godunov*	Saint-Simon, *New Christianity*
1826	*Lobachevski's non-Euclidean geometry	Mendelssohn, *Midsummer Night's Dream Overture*	
1827	Fourneyron's water-turbine	Heine, *Buch der Lieder*	Guizot, *History of Civilization in Europe*
1828			Rise of Liberal Catholicism
1829	Stephensons' *Rocket*	Balzac, *La Comédie humaine*	Catholic emancipation in Britain
1830	*Lyell, *Principles of Geology*, Vol. I	Victor Hugo, *Hernani* Berlioz, *Symphonie fantastique*	Comte, *Course of Positive Philosophy*, Vol. I
1831	*Faraday, electro-magnetic induction	Daumier's caricatures first published	
1832	*Liebig's paper on benzaldehyde	Goethe, *Faust*, Part II	
1833	Gauss and Weber's electromagnetic telegraph		Beginning of Oxford Movement
1834	Jacobi's electric motor	Mickiewicz, *Sir Thaddeus* Ranke, *History of the Popes*, Vol. I	
1835			Strauss, *Leben Jesu*
1836	Dreyse's needle gun	Dickens, *Pickwick Papers*	
1837		Carlyle, *French Revolution*	
1838	Screw-propeller Electric telegraph in use on railway		
1839	Steam-hammer Daguerrotype photography	Stendhal, *La Chartreuse de Parme*	Louis Blanc, *Organization of Labor*
1840	*Liebig, *Chemistry in Relation to Agriculture*		Proudhon, *What is Property?*
1841			
1842			

	DIPLOMATIC, MILITARY AND POLITICAL	SOCIAL AND ECONOMIC	RELATING TO OTHER CONTINENTS
1843			
1844		Consumers' Cooperative Movement (Britain) Folk high schools (Denmark)	
1845		Irish potato famine	
1846		Repeal of Corn Laws in England	
1847	*Sonderbund* War in Switzerland		
1848	Year of Revolutions Austrian War against Piedmont	Marx and Engels, *Communist Manifesto* National Workshops, Paris End of servile dues in Austria	California gold rush Slavery abolished in French colonies
1849	Russian intervention in Hungary	End of British Navigation Acts	British conquest of India completed
1850	Prussian "Humiliation" at Olmütz	First free libraries in England and Germany Ten Hours Act (Britain)	
1851		Great Exhibition (Crystal Palace)	Australian gold rush
1852	Schleswig-Holstein settlement by Treaty of London Beginning of Second Empire in France		
1853			
1854	Crimean War		
1855		First department store (Paris)	Livingstone reaches Victoria Falls
1856	Congress of Paris		
1857			Indian Mutiny Anglo-French War against China
1858	Rumania promised independence by great powers		
1859	Austro-Sardinian War		
1860	Kingdom of Italy established	Anglo-French commercial treaty	Vladivostok founded
1861		Serfdom abolished in Russia	
1862	Bismarck minister-president in Prussia		First French annexations in Cochin China
1863	Second Polish Revolt		
1864	Schleswig-Holstein War	Red Cross established First International Workingmen's Association	
1865			
1866	Seven Weeks' War		
1867	North-German Confederation		Dominion of Canada established Diamonds found in South Africa
1868	First Gladstone ministry in England		
1869		Social Democratic Workingmen's Party founded in Germany	Suez Canal opened
1870	Franco-Prussian War		
1871	Paris Commune German Empire established France becomes a republic		

	SCIENCE AND TECHNOLOGY	LITERATURE AND OTHER ARTS	RELIGION, PHILOSOPHY, POLITICAL AND ECONOMIC THOUGHT
1843	Superphosphates manufactured in England		Kierkegaard, *Either/Or*
1844	Morse telegraph between New York and Baltimore	Dumas, *Three Musketeers*	
1845			
1846			
1847	*Helmholtz, theory of conservation of energy	Thackeray, *Vanity Fair*	
1848		Macaulay, *History of England*, Vols. I & II	Mill, *Principles of Political Economy*
1849	Krupp's first steel gun		
1850		Tennyson, *In Memoriam* Courbet, "Stone Breakers"	
1851			
1852			Gobineau, *Inequality of Human Races*
1853		Hugo, *Les Châtiments*	
1854	First railway route through the Alps (Semmering Pass)	Mommsen, *History of Rome*, Vol. I	
1855	Zurich Polytechnic founded	De Tocqueville, *L'Ancien Régime*	
1856	First aniline dye Bessemer Steel		
1857	*Pasteur's discovery of nature of fermentation	Flaubert, *Madame Bovary*	
1858	*Virchow's cellular pathology	Offenbach, *Orpheus in Hades*	
1859	*Darwin, *Origin of Species* *Bunsen and Kirchhoff, spectrum analysis	Gounod, *Faust*	Mill, *On Liberty*
1860		Eliot, *Mill on the Floss*	
1861	Solvay's soda-making process		
1862	Steel rails	Hugo, *Les Misérables* Turgenev, *Fathers and Sons*	Anarchism preached by Bakunin
1863		Manet, "Déjeuner sur l'herbe"	Renan, *Vie de Jésus*
1864	Siemens-Martin steel-making process		Pius IX, Syllabus of Errors
1865	*Mendel's law of heredity Lister's antiseptic surgery		
1866	Invention of dynamite Transatlantic cable completed	Dostoevsky, *Crime and Punishment*	
1867	Siemens' dynamos Ferro-concrete in use (Monier)		Marx, *Das Kapital*, Vol. I
1868		Brahms, *German Requiem*	
1869		Tolstoy, *War and Peace* Wagner, *The Ring* cycle	
1870			First Vatican Council Dogma of Papal Infallibility
1871	*Mendeleev's Periodic Table of Elements	Zola begins *Les Rougon-Macquart* Verdi, *Aïda*	Darwin, *Descent of Man*

	DIPLOMATIC, MILITARY AND POLITICAL	SOCIAL AND ECONOMIC	RELATING TO OTHER CONTINENTS
1872		Conscription introduced in France	
1873	Three Emperors' League		
1874			
1875	"War Scare" between France and Germany French republican constitution completed	Universal Postal Union	Britain purchases Suez Canal shares
1876			
1877	Russo-Turkish War		First rubber plantations, Ceylon First shipments of frozen meat to Europe
1878	Congress of Berlin	Salvation Army founded	
1879	Dual Alliance	Reversion to high tariffs (German)	Zulu War
1880	Gladstone's second ministry		
1881	Three Emperors' League revived		French occupy Tunis
1882	Triple Alliance		British intervention in Egypt
1883		Bismarck's State Socialism	
1884		Trade unions finally legalized in France	German colonies founded Berlin Conference on Africa
1885	Serbo-Bulgarian War		Canadian-Pacific Railway completed
1886			Gold discovered in Transvaal
1887	Mediterranean Agreements Reinsurance Treaty		
1888			
1889		Second International Workingmen's Association	Foundation of Rhodesia
1890	Dismissal of Bismarck	First labor celebration of May Day	Main treaties in partition of Africa
1891	Russo-French Political Convention		
1892		Méline customs tariff in France	Antislavery measures ratified by 19 powers
1893		Independent Labor Party in Britain	
1894	Dreyfus Case Russo-French Military Convention		
1895		Spread of syndicalist ideas Founding of London School of Economics	Joint action of France, Germany, and Russia in Far East
1896		Olympic Games revived	Italian defeat at Adowa
1897	International occupation of Crete	First Zionist Congress in Basel	
1898	First German Navy Law		British conquest of Sudan
1899	First Hague Conference		South African War
1900			International expedition to Peking (Boxer rising)

	SCIENCE AND TECHNOLOGY	LITERATURE AND OTHER ARTS	RELIGION, PHILOSOPHY, POLITICAL AND ECONOMIC THOUGHT
872	*Voyage of the *Challenger*		
873	*Clerk Maxwell, *Electricity and Magnetism* Baku oil industry	Rimbaud, *Une Saison en Enfer*	Spencer, *Study of Sociology* *Kulturkampf* in Germany
874	*Wundt, *Foundations of Physiological Psychology*		
875			
1876	Sulphuric acid made by contact process Otto's gas engine	Taine, *Origines de la France contemporaine*	
1877		Rodin first exhibits at Paris Salon	
1878	*Pasteur's lecture on the germ theory at the Academy of Medicine Steel making by basic process		
1879	Siemens' electric railway (Berlin)	Ibsen, *A Doll's House* Treitschke, *German History*	
1880		Dostoevsky, *Brothers Karamazov*	
1881	*Schott and Abbé's optical glass (Jena)	Maupassant, *La Maison Tellier*	
1882	*Tuberculosis bacillus isolated by Koch	Wagner, *Parsifal*	
1883	Maxim's machine-gun		Nietzsche, *Thus Spake Zarathustra*
1884	Parsons' steam-turbine		
1885	"Safety" bicycle		
1886	Aluminum made by electrolytic process	Kipling, *Departmental Ditties*	Nietzsche, *Beyond Good and Evil*
1887	Daimler's automobile	Strindberg, *The Father*	
1888	*Hertz's work on electromagnetic waves Dunlop's pneumatic tire	Van Gogh, "Sunflowers"	
1889	Eiffel Tower built	Mahler, *Symphony No. 1*	*Fabian Essays in Socialism*
1890	Bridge over Firth of Forth	Hamsun, *Hunger*	
1891	Trans-Siberian Railway begun	Hardy, *Tess of the D'Urbervilles* Gauguin, "Women of Tahiti"	Leo XIII, Encyclical, *Rerum Novarum*
1892		Hauptmann, *The Weavers*	
1893	*Voyage of the *Fram* (Nansen)	Tchaikovsky, *Pathetic Symphony*	
1894	Kiel Canal opened	*The Yellow Book*	
1895	First cinema (Paris)	Conrad, *Almayer's Folly*	
1896	*Research leading to discovery of vitamins *Röntgen's discovery of X-rays	Chekhov, *The Seagull*	Herzl, *Der Judenstaat*
1897	Diesel engine in use	Cézanne, "Lake of Annecy"	
1898	*Radium discovered by the Curies		
1899	*Freud, *Interpretation of Dreams*		Lenin, *Development of Capitalism in Russia*
1900	*Planck's Quantum Theory First Zeppelin flight		

	DIPLOMATIC, MILITARY AND POLITICAL	SOCIAL AND ECONOMIC	RELATING TO OTHER CONTINENTS
1901	End of reign of Queen Victoria	Nobel Prizes first awarded	Australian colonies federated
1902	Anglo-Japanese Alliance		
1903		Split of Bolshevik and Menshevik Russian socialist groups	
1904	Anglo-French Entente	First unemployment insurance (Ghent)	Russo-Japanese War
1905	Separation of Norway and Sweden	Proletarian risings in Russia	
1906	Algeciras Conference First Duma meets in Russia	Liberal social reforms in Britain	
1907	Triple Entente Second Hague Conference		
1908	Bosnian Crisis Young Turk Revolt		
1909			Political concessions in India
1910	Overthrow of Monarchy in Portugal		Union of South Africa
1911	Agadir Crisis		Italian conquest of Tripoli
1912	Balkan Wars		
1913			
1914	Outbreak of First World War		Panama Canal opened

	SCIENCE AND TECHNOLOGY	LITERATURE AND OTHER ARTS	RELIGION, PHILOSOPHY, POLITICAL AND ECONOMIC THOUGHT
1901	Marconi's transatlantic wireless telegraphy	Thomas Mann, *Buddenbrooks*	
1902		Debussy, *Pelléas et Mélisande*	
1903	Wright brothers' airplane flight		
1904	Completion of Trans-Siberian Railway	Shaw, *John Bull's Other Island*	
1905	*Einstein's Theory of Relativity	Wells, *Kipps*	Separation of Church and State in France
1906	The *Dreadnought*		
1907		Picasso, "Demoiselles d'Avignon"	Bergson, *Creative Evolution*
1908		Bennett, *Old Wives' Tale*	Sorel, *Reflections on Violence*
1909	Blériot's cross-channel flight		
1910		Stravinsky, *The Firebird*	Russell and Whitehead, *Principia Mathematica*
1911	*Rutherford's nuclear model of the atom	R. Strauss, *Der Rosenkavalier*	
1912			
1913	Haber-Bosch ammonia manufacture	D. H. Lawrence, *Sons and Lovers* Proust, *A la recherche du temps perdu,* Vol. I	
1914		Matisse, "Les Poissons rouges"	

INDEX

INDEX

Aaland Islands, 172
Abd-el-Kadir (1807?–1883), 62
Abdul Hamid II, of Turkey (1842–1918), 332, 423–425
Aberdeen, Lord (1784–1860), 170
Acton, Lord (1834–1902), 330
Adams, John Quincy (1767–1848), 28
Additional Act, France, 8
Adowa, Battle (1896), 428, 429
Adrianople, Treaty (1829), 29
Aehrenthal, Count von (1854–1912), 484–485
Africa, Partition of, 318, 357, 358, 372–375
Agadir crisis, 300, 359, 486
Agriculture, improvements in, 32, 174, 216, 219, 221, 222, 226, 275, 291–293, 328, 360, 413
Airplanes, 272, 284, 295
Aix-la-Chapelle, Congress (1818), 26
Alaska, sale of, 184
Albert, Alexandre (1815–1895), 65
Albert, Archduke (1817–1895), 149
Albert I, of Belgium (1875–1934), 434
Albert, Prince Consort of Britain (1819–1861), 247
Alexander I, of Bulgaria (1857–1893), 400, 401
Alexander I, of Russia (1777–1825), 9, 18, 20, 28, 76, 158–163
Alexander II, of Russia (1818–1881), 172–185, 320, 321, 392–397
Alexander III, of Russia (1845–1894), 322, 393, 397–401
Alexandra, Tsarina (1872–1918), 402, 403
Alfonso XII, of Spain (1857–1885), 430
Alfonso XIII, of Spain (1886–1941), 430, 432
Algeciras Conference (1906), 359, 481
Algeria, 62, 69, 70, 75, 490
Alsace-Lorraine, 79, 80, 157, 306, 313, 316, 324, 325, 338, 349, 362, 401, 477, 489, 494, 501
Alvensleben, Gustav von (1803–1881), 145
Amadeo, of Spain (1845–1890), 430
Amundsen, Roald (1872–1928), 437

Anarchism, 45, 255, 266, 455–456
Andrássy, Count (1823–1890), 138
Anglo-Japanese Alliance (1902), 271, 377, 387, 404, 481
Anti-Semitism, 329, 348, 351, 397–398, 414, 427, 467–468
Anton, see Karl Anton
Arabi Pasha (1841?–1911), 372
Arago, François (1786–1853), 65
Arakcheev, Alexis (1769–1834), 25, 161–163
Architecture, 11–12, 247, 464–465
Armaments, 228–230, 270, 293–296, 492–493
Armenia, 423, 424
Armies (see also Conscription, Mobilization): 142–143, 207, 295, 313, 325, 386, 492
Armstrong-Whitworth, of Elswick, 293
Artois, Count of, see Charles X
Arts, developments in the, 11–13, 238–242, 246–248, 462–464
Ashley, see Shaftesbury
Aspromonte, Battle (1862), 127
Asquith, Henry (1852–1928), 378
Auber, Daniel François (1782–1871), 55
Augustenburg, Christian, Duke of (1814–1869), 145
Augustenburg, Frederick, Duke of (1829–1880), 145–147, 149
Ausgleich, Compromise of 1867, 134, 136–139, 417–418, 421, 422
Australasia, 275
Australia, 202, 203, 291, 365, 377
Austria (see also Austria-Hungary): population, 6; to 1848, 5, 18, 20, 24–29, 84; to 1867, 68, 86–88, 90–102, 104, 116, 117; to 1914, 418–420
Austria-Hungary (see also Ausgleich): population, 421; parties, 419–420; foreign policy, 320–322, 333, 483–485, 488, 495–500; other aspects, 138, 139, 416–423, 489
Austro-Franco-Sardinian War (1859), 73, 120–122, 136
Austro-Prussian War (1866), 126–127, 149–151, 204

539

Bach, Alexander (1813–1893), 134, 135, 137
"Bach System," 134–136, 137
Baden, 25, 85, 151, 306, 310
Bagehot, Walter (1826–1877), 453
Baghdad Railway, 299, 322, 424, 482, 485, 490–491
Bakunin, Michael (1814–1876), 130, 396, 430, 431, 455
Balaclava, Battle (1854), 203
Balbo, Cesare (1789–1853), 110
Balfour, Arthur (1848–1930), 367, 378
Balkan States, 28–30, 320–322, 393, 423–427
Balkan Wars (1912–1913), 299, 359, 425, 442, 486–489, 497
Ballin, Albert (1857–1918), 309
Baltic Provinces of Russia, 161, 406
Balzac, Honoré de (1799–1850), 246
Bandiera, Attilio (1811?–1844), 110
Bandiera, Emilio (1819–1844), 110
Barcelona, see Catalan separatism
Bardo, Treaty (1881), 357
Baring, see Cromer
Barnardo, Dr. (1845–1905), 211
Barrès, Maurice (1862–1923), 349
Barrot, Odilon (1791–1873), 68
Barry, Charles (1795–1860), 247
Bavaria, 25, 36, 89, 149, 151, 156, 231, 306, 310, 313
Bazaine, Marshal (1811–1888), 79, 230
Beauharnais, Hortense de (1783–1837), 63, 70
Bebel, August (1840–1913), 311, 329
Becker, Nikolaus (1809–1845), 46
Becquerel, Henri (1852–1908), 447
Beethoven, Ludwig van (1770–1827), 12, 241
Belgian colonial empire, 301–302, 434
Belgium: population, 23, 433; parties, 438–439; industries, 5, 216, 223, 280; other aspects, 20, 23, 30, 61, 103, 148, 150, 297, 434–439, 500, 501
Benedek, Ludwig von (1804–1881), 149
Benedetti, Count (1817–1900), 79, 150
Bennigsen, Rudolf von (1824–1902), 140, 151, 308, 312
Bentham, Jeremy (1748–1832), 38–40, 193, 242, 269
Béranger, Jean de (1780–1857), 63
Berchtold, Count (1863–1942), 496, 497
Berg, Count (1793–1874), 180
Bergson, Henri (1859–1941), 469
Berlin: city, 5, 89, 317, 326, 331; Congress (1878), 321, 393, 395, 423, 424, 427, 483; Conference (1884–1885), 321
Berlin-Baghdad Railway, see Baghdad Railway
Berlioz, Louis (1803–1869), 55, 241
Bernadotte, see Charles XIV
Bernhardi, Friedrich von (1849–1930), 330
Bernstein, Eduard (1850–1932), 330
Berri, Duke de (1778–1820), 26, 53
Bertrand, Henri (1773–1844), 63

Bessarabia, 18, 28, 172, 393, 403
Bessemer, Henry (1813–1898), 225
Bethmann-Hollweg, Theobald von (1856–1921), 325, 333, 487, 496, 497
Bezobrazov, Alexander (1855–?), 404
Biarritz, meeting at, 147, 148
Binet, Alfred (1857–1911), 451
Bismarck, Otto von (1815–1898), 77, 78, 104, 128, 141–157, 222, 270, 304–325, 466
Bismarckian diplomacy, 15, 475–478
Björkö, Treaty (1905), 479
"Black Week," 375, 480
Blanc, Louis (1811–1882), 44, 60, 64–66, 85, 235, 355
Blanqui, Auguste (1805–1881), 60, 338
Bloch, Ivan (1836–1902), 296
"Bloody Sunday" (1905), 408
Boer War, see South African War
Bohemia, 88, 91–92, 96, 419, 421, 489
Bohn, Henry George (1796–1884), 245
Bolsheviks, 407, 413, 457
Bonald, Vicomte de (1754–1840), 53
Bonaparte, Louis (1778–1846), 63
Bonaparte, Napoleon, see Napoleon
Bonapartism, 52, 63–64, 67–72
Bonnymuir, 191
Booth, Charles (1840–1916), 453
Bopp, Franz (1791–1867), 12
Bosnia-Herzegovina, 320, 321, 333, 393, 418, 419, 421, 423, 495, 496
Boucher de Perthes, Jacques (1788–1868), 452
Bouguereau, Adolphe (1825–1905), 247
Boulanger, General (1837–1891), 349–350, 353, 362, 476
Bourgeoisie, see Middle classes
Boycott, Charles (1832–1897), 369
Brahms, Johannes (1833–1897), 464
Branting, Hjalmar (1860–1925), 440
Braque, Georges (b. 1882), 463
Briand, Aristide (1862–1932), 346, 354, 355
Bright, John (1811–1889), 193, 199, 206, 298
Britain, see Great Britain
British colonial empire, 20, 195, 201–203, 301–302, 365, 501
Broglie, Duc de (1785–1870), 51, 73
Broglie, Duc de (1821–1901), 344
Buchner, Ludwig (1824–1899), 250
Bulgaria, 320–322, 393, 400–401, 423–427, 476, 484, 486–489
Bülow, Prince von (1849–1929), 325, 330–332, 333, 480
Buonarroti, Philippe (1761–1837), 59
Burns, John (1858–1943), 379
Butt, Isaac (1813–1879), 368
Byelo-Russians, 392
Byron, Lord (1788–1824), 29, 240

Cables, submarine, 224
"Cadets," see Constitutional Democrats

Cadiz, Francis, Duke of (1822–1902), 61
Calatafimi, Battle (1860), 124
Cambon, Paul (1843–1924), 269
Campbell-Bannerman, Sir Henry (1836–1908), 378, 387
Canada, 202–203, 291, 292, 365, 376, 377
Canals, 4, 218, 220, 222, 226, 282
Canning, George (1770–1827), 27–29, 192, 201
Caprivi, Count (1831–1899), 307, 324, 325
Carbonari, 37, 47, 63, 77, 109, 110, 164
Carlists, 430
Carlos I, of Portugal (1863–1908), 432
Carlsbad Decrees (1819), 24, 191
Carlyle, Thomas (1795–1881), 266, 466
Carnot, Sadi (1796–1832), 244
Carol I, of Rumania (1839–1914), 154
Cartels, 298, 328
Castelfidardo, Battle (1860), 124–125
Castlereagh, Lord (1769–1822), 4, 10, 27, 188
Catalan separatism, 431–432
Catholic Party: Belgium, 438; Netherlands, 439
Cato Street Conspiracy (1820), 191
Caucasus, 29, 170, 172, 176, 182, 393
Cavaignac, Godefroy (1801–1845), 57
Cavaignac, General (1802–1857), 67
Cavour, Count (1810–1861), 7, 14, 116–126, 129, 428
Center Party (Germany), 151, 309–310, 312–315, 329
Cézanne, Paul (1839–1906), 463
Chadwick, Edwin (1800–1890), 196
Chamberlain, Houston Stewart (1855–1927), 332, 467
Chamberlain, Joseph (1836–1914), 298, 370, 376–377, 480
Chambord, Count of (1820–1883), 341–342
Charles X, of France (1757–1836), 23, 53–56, 62, 196
Charles XIV, of Sweden (1763?–1844), 24, 440
Charles Albert, of Sardinia (1798–1849), 89, 93, 99
Charter of 1814, 8, 52, 56–57
Chartered companies, 373
Chartism, 197–198, 255
Chassepot, 154, 230
Chateaubriand, Vicomte de (1768–1848), 12, 55, 241
Chaumont, Treaty (1814), 9
Chekhov, Anton (1860–1904), 462
Chemical industry, 227–228, 278, 327
Chernyshevski, Nikolai (1828?–1889), 454
Chevalier, Michel (1806–1879), 43
China, 75, 201, 286, 403–406, 490
Chopin, Frédéric (1810–1849), 241
Christian IX, of Denmark (1818–1906), 440
Christian Socialist Movement (Britain), 457

Christian Socialist Party (Austria), 420
Churchill, Winston Spencer (b. 1874), 378, 380
Civil War (U.S.), 77, 175, 208, 224, 228, 229, 296, 494
Coal, 208, 212, 217, 219, 224, 277, 326, 421
Cobbett, William (1763–1835), 235
Cobden, Richard (1804–1865), 199, 206, 211, 298
Cobden–Chevalier Treaty (1860), 211, 227
Colenso, Bishop (1814–1883), 459
Coleridge, Samuel (1772–1834), 12, 22
Colonial Conferences, British (*see also* Imperial Conferences), 376, 377, 388
Colonialism, *see* Imperialism
Commerce, *see* Trade
Committee of Imperial Defense, Britain, 377, 388
Commune, Paris (1871), 83, 338–340, 355
Communism, 85, 86, 255–257, 346, 383, 456–457, 461
Compagnonnages, 34
Compromise, Austro-Hungarian, *see Ausgleich*
Comte, Auguste (1798–1857), 253–254, 445, 452
Concert of Europe (*see also* Congress System, Quadruple Alliance), 172, 416, 473
Congress Poland, 25
Congress System, 26–28
Conrad von Hötzendorf, Franz (1852–1925), 484, 496
Conscription: 270, 272, 295, 491–492; France, 340, 352, 359; Prussia, 142–143, 230, 313; Russia, 179
Conservatism, 20–25
Conservative Party: Austria, 419–420; Britain (*see also* Tory), 366–368, 370, 371, 378, 384, 501; France, 345; Germany, 151, 308, 309, 312–314, 325, 329
Constable, John (1776–1837), 241
Constant, Benjamin (1767–1830), 39, 40
Constantine, Grand Duke (1779–1831), 163, 166
Constantine, Grand Duke (1827–1892), 178, 180
Constantinople, 28, 371, 372, 393, 424, 467, 482
Constitutional Democratic Party (Russia), 410–412
Constitutionalism (*see also* Liberalism), 7, 39, 101, 269
Convention, Franco-Italian (1864), 127, 128
Cooperative movement, 44, 198, 211, 232, 297, 437, 461
Corn Law of 1815, 190, 199–200, 220, 366
Cotton, *see* Textile industries
Courbet, Gustave (1819–1877), 247
Cousin, Victor (1792–1867), 465
Cracow, 84, 135

Crete, 423, 427
Crimean War (1854-1856), 75, 76, 117-118, 136, 137, 171-172, 181, 203-204, 225, 228
Crispi, Francesco (1819-1901), 111, 123, 125, 129, 428, 429
Croats, 92, 93, 99, 112, 420, 421
Cromer, Lord (1841-1917), 372
Cross, Richard (1823-1914), 367
Cuba, 431
Curie, Madame Marie (1867-1934), 447
Curie, Pierre (1859-1906), 447
Custozza, Battles: (1848), 92, 112, 113; (1866), 127
Cuza, Alexander, Prince of Rumania (1820-1873), 76, 154
Cyprus, 271, 372, 423
Czartoryski, Prince (1770-1861), 8, 161
Czechs, see Bohemia

Daguerrotype, 224, 250
Dalton, John (1766-1844), 244, 446, 448
Danilevsky, Nicolai (1822-1885), 467
Danish colonial empire, 434
Darwin, Charles (1809-1882), 243, 245, 248-253, 257, 449
Daudet, Alphonse (1840-1897), 489
Daudet, Léon (1867-1942), 266
Daumier, Honoré (1808-1879), 51, 58, 156, 247, 348
David, Jacques (1748-1825), 53, 241
Deák, Francis (1803-1876), 138
Debussy, Claude (1862-1918), 248, 464
Decembrist Conspiracy (1825), 164-166, 167
Degas, Edgar (1834-1917), 248
Delacroix, Ferdinand (1798-1863), 55, 241
Delcassé, Théophile (1852-1923), 359, 481
Denmark, 93, 145-146, 292, 434-437, 439-441
Depretis, Agostino (1813-1887), 428
Dernburg, Bernhard (1865-1937), 332
Déroulède, Paul (1846-1914), 349, 362
Devonport, Lord (1856-1934), 384
De Vries, Hugo (1848-1935), 450
Dickens, Charles (1812-1870), 193, 195, 207, 246
Diesel engine, 279
Dilke, Charles (1843-1911), 371
Disarmament projects, 76, 333
Disraeli, Benjamin (1804-1881), 193, 205, 206, 288, 366-368, 466
Dobrudja, 393
Döllinger, Dr. (1799-1890), 258, 259, 313
Dominions, British self-governing, 365, 377, 388, 501
Dostoevsky, Fedor (1821-1881), 169, 178, 246, 396, 462
Drang nach Osten, 96
Draper, John (1811-1882), 458
Dreadnought battleships, 294, 295, 333, 387, 492

Dreikaiserbund, see Three Emperors' League
Dreyfus, Alfred (1859-1935), 351-352
Dreyfus Case, 347, 349, 351-353, 468
Droysen, Gustav (1808-1884), 140, 330
Drumont, Edouard (1844-1917), 348, 351, 468
Dual Alliance (1879), 270, 321, 322, 333, 352, 418, 475-478
Dual Monarchy, see Austria-Hungary
Dufy, Raoul (1877-1953), 463
Dukhobors, 398
Duma: town, 177, 309; state, 160, 409-412, 414, 420
Dumas, Alexandre (1802-1870), 55
Dunant, Henri (1828-1910), 437
Dunlop, John (1840-1921), 284
Düppel, Battle (1864), 146
Durham, Lord (1792-1840), 202-203
Durham Report (1839), 203, 365
Durkheim, Emile (1858-1917), 453
Dvořák, Anton (1841-1904), 464
Dyes, see Chemical industry

Eastern Rumelia, self-governing Turkish province (1878-1885), 393, 401
Eboué, Félix (1884-1944), 358
Economic imperialism, 299-300, 490-491
Eddington, Arthur (1882-1944), 448
Education: 5, 235, 268-269, 438, 465; Austria-Hungary, 419; Britain, 194, 208-210, 245, 367-368; France, 57, 68, 73, 353, 354; Germany, 24, 327; Italy, 428; Russia, 160, 167, 169, 178-179, 185, 398, 413
Edward VII, of Britain (1841-1910), 377, 381, 441, 483
Egypt, 61, 271, 318, 372-373, 423, 481
Eiffel, Alexandre (1832-1923), 350, 464
Einstein, Albert (1879-1955), 250, 272, 449
Electricity (see also Hydroelectricity): 221, 227, 229, 244, 279, 280, 326, 447
Elgin, Lord (1811-1863), 203
Emancipation Edict (1861), 173-176, 181, 391
Emigration overseas, 103, 139, 202, 232-233, 266, 275, 289-291, 420, 429, 490
Ems Telegram, 79, 155
Encirclement, German fear, 482-483, 494
Engels, Friedrich (1820-1895), 86, 235, 255, 256
England, see Great Britain
Entente Cordiale: (1834), 61; (1904), 271, 352, 359, 378, 385-386, 481
Esterhazy, Major (1847-1923), 351
Eugénie, Empress (1826-1920), 70, 155
Europe: population, 6, 215, 216, 267, 276; armaments, 493; investments, 285; manufactures, 280; number of states, 264; trade, 284; transport, 227; universal manhood suffrage in, 265
European expansion, see Imperialism

Evolution, 250–253, 444, 448–453, 459

Fabian Society, 379, 380, 457
Factory legislation: 269, 296; Britain, 195–196, 235, 367; France, 60, 235, 356–357; Prussia, 235; Russia, 400
Falk, Adalbert (1827–1900), 314
Falloux Law (1850), 68, 73, 353
Faraday, Michael (1791–1867), 243–244, 279
Fashoda crisis, 272, 300, 375, 480
Faure, Félix (1841–1899), 352
Fauré, Gabriel (1845–1924), 464
Favre, Jules (1809–1880), 75
Ferdinand I, of Austria (1793–1875), 87, 88, 92
Ferdinand I, of Bulgaria (1861–1948), 401
Ferdinand I, of Two Sicilies (1751–1825), 24, 27
Ferdinand II, of Two Sicilies (1810–1859), 112, 113, 115
Ferdinand VII, of Spain (1784–1833), 8, 23, 27, 54
Ferry, Jules (1832–1893), 75, 345, 354, 357
Fertilizers, 226, 249, 278, 292, 327
Feuerbach, Ludwig (1804–1872), 249
Finland, 18, 25, 161, 181–182, 382, 406, 410, 414, 489
First World War, 429, 472, 483, 501
Fisher, Admiral (1841–1920), 387
"Five Days," Milan (1848), 104, 111
Flaubert, Gustave (1821–1880), 246
Flemings, 439
Foch, Marshal (1851–1929), 492
Foucault, Jean (1819–1868), 244
Fourier, Charles (1772–1837), 14, 43, 59, 169
France: population, 6, 55, 59, 357, 360, 362; to 1848, 21, 23, 27, 29, 31, 34, 50–64; to 1871, 64–80, 224, 232; to 1914, 336–363; Third Republic, constitution, 342–343; parties, 53, 56–58, 344–347; economic life, 279, 280, 283, 360; foreign policy, 349, 352–353, 359, 476, 479, 481, 484–486, 496, 500
Francis I, of Austria (1768–1835), 7
Francis II, of Two Sicilies (1836–1894), 123, 124, 126
Francis Ferdinand, Archduke (1863–1914), 93, 495
Francis Joseph, of Austria (1830–1916), 93, 121, 134, 137–139, 149, 154, 320, 418–421, 496
Franck, César (1822–1890), 464
Franco, João (1855–1929), 433
Franco-Prussian War, 79–80, 155, 204, 357
Franco-Russian Alliance (1891, 1894), 271, 333, 352, 401, 479, 485, 496
Frankfurt: Parliament (1848–1849), 89–91, 93–98, 100, 133; Treaty (1871), 80, 320, 338
Frayssinous, Denis de (1765–1841), 53

Frederick III, German Emperor (1831–1888), 323
Frederick VII, of Denmark (1808–1863), 94
Frederick William III, of Prussia (1770–1840), 25, 78, 165
Frederick William IV, of Prussia (1795–1861), 89, 93, 98, 100, 139–142
Free Trade (see also Tariff systems), 35, 72, 192, 199, 211, 219, 220, 223, 293, 377
Freemasonry, 109, 110, 163, 461
French colonial empire, 17, 75–76, 301–302, 353, 357–359
French Revolution of 1789, 6, 13, 41, 45, 63, 103, 163, 346, 361, 453
Fresnel, Augustin (1788–1827), 244
Freud, Sigmund (1856–1939), 418, 451
Freycinet, Charles de (1828–1923), 349
Froude, James (1818–1894), 371

Gagern, Heinrich von (1799–1880), 97
Galicia, 18, 85, 99, 102, 419, 421
Gallicanism, 53, 62, 353
Galton, Francis (1822–1911), 453
Gambetta, Léon (1838–1882), 75, 80, 336, 338, 341, 342, 344, 345, 347, 353
Gandhi, Mahatma (1869–1948), 368
Gapon, Father (1870?–1906), 408
Garibaldi, Guiseppe (1807–1882), 68, 113–115, 119, 123–125, 127–129
Gastein, Treaty (1865), 146, 149
Gauguin, Paul (1848–1903), 463
General strikes, 197, 356, 406, 409, 430, 454
Geneva Convention (1864), 437
Gentz, Friedrich von (1764–1832), 7, 21
George I, of Greece (1845–1913), 427
George IV, of Britain (1762–1830), 188
George V, of Britain (1865–1936), 381, 493
Georgia, 406
Géricault, Théodore (1791–1824), 12, 55, 241
German colonial empire, 301–302, 317–319
German Confederation (see also Germany), 8, 20
German Customs Union, see Zollverein
Germany: population, 326; to 1848, 24, 30, 35–37; to 1871, 78, 85, 89–91, 93–98, 100, 101, 139–157; to 1914, 304–334; Imperial constitution, 305–307; parties, 308–311, 329; economic life, 278–280, 283, 326–328; foreign policy, 320–322, 333, 475–488, 496–501
Gilchrist, Percy (1851–1935), 277
Gilds, 35, 102, 232
Gioberti, Vincenzo (1801–1852), 110
Giolitti, Giovanni (1842–1928), 429, 430
Gladstone, William (1809–1898), 115, 193, 200, 205–210, 366–373
Gobineau, Joseph de (1816–1882), 467
Goethe, Johann von (1749–1832), 11
Gogh, Vincent van (1853–1890), 463

Gogol, Nikolai (1809–1852), 168
Gold standard, 189, 277–278, 297, 400
Golovnin, Alexander (1821–1886), 178, 179
Goltz, Colmar von der (1843–1916), 492
Gordon, General (1833–1885), 373, 375
Goremykin, Ivan (1839–1917), 411
Görgei, Arthur von (1818–1916), 93, 99
Gotha Program (1875), 311, 329, 454
Gothic Revival, 12, 22, 54, 55, 241, 247
Gounod, Charles (1818–1893), 248
Gourgaud, Baron (1783–1852), 63
Goya, Francisco (1746–1828), 12
Gramont, Antoine de (1819–1880), 79, 154, 155
Great Britain: population, 6, 190, 211; to 1871, internal affairs, 23, 33, 188–212; parties, 200, 205; economic life, 215–222, 224–227, 230–235; foreign policy, 26–27, 29–30, 61, 77, 170–172, 201–205; to 1914, internal affairs, 364–388; parties, 366, 379; economic life, 274–288, 297–302; foreign policy, 322, 371, 377–378, 386–387, 480–482, 485–487, 497, 501
Great Reform Act (1832), 192–193
Great Russians, 392, 414, 415
Greco-Turkish War (1897), 478
Greece, 27–30, 201, 423–427, 486
Greek Church, see Orthodox Eastern Church
Gregory XVI, Pope (1765–1846), 63
Grévy, Jules (1807–1891), 344, 345, 350, 353
Grey, Lord (1764–1845), 481
Grey, Sir Edward (1862–1933), 324, 386, 481, 487, 501, 502
Grieg, Edvard (1843–1907), 464
Grimm, Jacob (1785–1863), 12
Grimm, Wilhelm (1786–1859), 12
Grossdeutsch, German program, 97, 145
Grundtvig, Bishop (1783–1872), 47
Guarantees, Law of (1871), 130
Guardia, Ferrer, Francisco (1859–1909), 432
Guesde, Jules (1845–1922), 355
Guizot, François (1787–1874), 51, 57, 58, 63, 64, 73, 79
Gumplowicz, Ludwik (1838–1909), 452
Gustav V, of Sweden (1858–1950), 441

Haakon VII, of Norway (1872–1957), 441
Haeckel, Ernst (1834–1919), 449, 452
Hague Conferences (1899, 1907), 272, 333, 437, 478
Haig, Field Marshal (1861–1928), 493
Haldane, Lord (1856–1928), 333, 386, 491
Hammarskjöld, Hjalmar (1862–1953), 441
Hand loom weavers, 35, 190, 232
Hanover, 25, 30, 35, 139, 140, 149, 151
Hapsburg Empire, see Austria
Hardie, Keir (1856–1915), 379
Hardinge, Charles (1858–1944), 482
Hardy, Thomas (1840–1928), 247, 462

Harnack, Adolf von (1851–1930), 459
Hasse, Ernst (1846–1908), 332
Hauptmann, Gerhard (1862–1946), 462
Haussmann, Baron (1809–1891), 70, 72, 288
Haynau, General (1786–1853), 99
Hegel, Friedrich (1770–1831), 21, 240–241, 256
Heilmann, Josué (1796–1848), 215, 221
Heine, Heinrich (1797–1856), 20, 240, 310
Heisenberg, Werner (b. 1901), 448
Helmholtz, Hermann von (1821–1894), 245
Hertz, Heinrich (1857–1894), 447
Herzen, Alexander (1812–1870), 169, 173, 180, 396
Hesse-Cassel, 30, 35, 146, 149, 151
Hesse-Darmstadt, 25, 36, 90, 151
Hetairia Philike, 28, 164
Historical studies, 13, 47, 242, 259, 272, 451, 454, 459
Hohenlohe, Prince (1819–1901), 325
Holstein, Friedrich von (1837–1909), 324, 480
Holy Alliance, 9, 20, 26, 28, 159
Hudson, George (1800–1871), 230
Hugo, Victor (1802–1885), 55, 57, 60, 63, 71, 73, 241, 246
Humbert I, of Italy (1844–1900), 430
"Hundred Days" (1815), 50, 108
Hungary (see also Austria-Hungary): to 1867, 5, 86–88, 90, 92, 93, 102, 136–139; to 1914, 292, 420–422, 496
Huskisson, William (1770–1830), 192, 199, 219
Huxley, Thomas (1825–1895), 245, 252, 452, 458
Hydroelectricity, 279, 281, 429, 437
Hyndman, Henry (1842–1921), 457

Ibrahim Pasha (1789–1848), 31
Ibsen, Henrik (1828–1906), 247, 463
Ignatiev, General (1832–1908), 393
Illiteracy, 5, 392, 465
Imperial Conferences, British, 377, 388
Imperialism (see also Economic imperialism): 268, 298–302, 317–319, 358, 370, 371–375
Impressionism, 247–248, 463
Independent Labor Party (Britain), 379
India, 201, 204, 372, 388, 395
Indian Mutiny (1857), 204, 371, 375
Indo-China, 76, 357
Industrial Revolution, 13, 14, 32, 42, 72, 214–235, 274–287
Ingres, Jean (1780–1867), 55
Inkerman, Battle (1854), 203
Insurance, Social, 297, 319, 325, 357, 380, 438
Intelligentsia, 167
International, Second, 297
"International anarchy," 272

International Exhibitions: 1851, 72, 200, 219, 220–222, 224, 229, 245; 1859, 72; 1889, 464
International investment, 231, 274, 284–287, 298–299, 326, 360, 400
International Justice, Court of, 437
International Workingmen's Association (First International), 14, 311, 455
Ireland, 85, 199–200, 208, 211, 368–370, 384–385
Iron industry (see also Steel): 175, 217, 219, 220, 224–225, 267–268, 291
Isabella II, of Spain (1830–1904), 61, 430
Italian colonial empire, 429
Italo-Turkish War (1911–1912), 486
Italy: to 1848, 4, 18, 24, 27, 30, 37, 61, 106–111; to 1871, 68, 73, 77, 89, 91, 111–136, 154; to 1914, internal affairs, 416–417, 427–430; economic life, 279–281; population, 430; foreign policy, 321, 322, 333, 475, 482, 489
Izvolski, Alexander (1856–1919), 484–485

Jacquard, Joseph (1752–1834), 217
Jameson, Dr. (1853–1917), 373, 375
Jameson Raid, 333, 373–374, 480
Japan, 294, 377, 403–406
Jaurès, Jean (1859–1914), 355
Jefferson, Thomas (1743–1826), 21, 160
Jellačić, General (1801–1859), 92, 93, 99
Jesuit Order, 53, 62, 314, 350, 432
Jewish religion and people, 62, 353, 354, 398, 407, 414, 419, 427, 459, 467–469
John, Archduke of Austria (1782–1859), 93
Jordan, Wilhelm (1819–1904), 97
Juárez, Benito (1806–1872), 77
Jubilees of Queen Victoria (1887, 1897), 374, 376
July Revolution (1830), 54–56, 109, 192
"June Days," Paris (1848), 67, 82
Junkers, 216, 222, 292, 308, 312, 324

Karamzin, Nikolai (1766–1826), 47
Karl, Prince, see Carol
Karl Anton, Prince (1811–1885), 142, 154, 155
Katkov, Michael (1818–1887), 393, 397, 401
Kautsky, Karl (1854–1938), 329
Kelvin, Lord (1824–1907), 245
Ketteler, Wilhelm von (1811–1877), 461
Kiderlen-Wächter, Alfred von (1852–1912), 485–486
Kiel Canal, 282
Kipling, Rudyard (1865–1936), 371, 374, 490
Kitchener, Lord (1850–1916), 361, 375, 502
Kleindeutsch, German program, 97–99
Knight, Charles (1791–1873), 245
Koch, Robert (1843–1910), 288, 450
Kollàr, Jan (1793–1852), 47
Kolowrat, Count (1778–1861), 87

Königgrätz, Battle (1866), 150
Koraës, Adamantios (1748–1833), 47, 243
Korea, 404–406
Kossuth, Francis (1841–1914), 421
Kossuth, Lajos (1802–1894), 85–87, 93, 98, 99
Kotzebue, August von (1761–1819), 26
Kropotkin, Peter (1842–1921), 456
Krüdener, Baroness (1764–1824), 159
Kruger, Paul (1825–1904), 333, 374, 480
Krupps, Essen, 35, 221, 229, 288, 293, 295, 309, 315, 326
Kulturkampf, 259, 313–315, 438
Kumanovo, Battle (1912), 486

Labor Party (Britain), 366, 379, 383, 457
Labor Unions, see Trade Unions
Lacordaire, Jean (1802–1861), 62, 258
Lafayette, Marquis de (1757–1834), 55–57
Laffitte, Jacques (1767–1844), 57
Laibach, Congress (1821), 27
Laissez-faire, 39, 40
Lamarck, Jean (1744–1829), 245, 251, 449
Lamartine, Alphonse de (1790–1869), 55, 57, 63, 65, 66
Lamennais, Robert de (1782–1854), 62–63, 258
Lamoricière, General (1806–1865), 123, 124
"Land and Liberty," 396
Land captains, 399, 413
Landseer, Edwin (1802–1873), 247
Lange, Friedrich (1828–1875), 260
Langensalza, Battle (1866), 149
Las Cases, Comte (1766–1842), 63
Lassalle, Ferdinand (1825–1864), 310–311
Latin America, 28, 274, 284, 286, 291, 431
Lauenburg, 146
Laurier, Wilfrid (1841–1919), 376, 377
Lavigerie, Cardinal (1825–1892), 350
League of Three, Far Eastern intervention (Dreibund), 403, 479
Leboeuf, Edmond (1809–1888), 155
Lecky, William (1838–1903), 458
Ledru-Rollin, Alexandre (1807–1874), 65, 67
Legion of Honor, 52, 350, 352
Legitimacy, 18
Lelewel, Ignaz (1786–1861), 47
Lenin, Nicolai (1870–1924), 266, 396, 407, 415, 456, 457
Leo XIII, Pope (1810–1903), 309, 314, 350, 352, 354, 460–461
Leopardi, Giacomo (1790–1837), 47
Leopold I, of Belgium (1790–1865), 30
Leopold II, of Belgium (1835–1909), 302, 434
Leopold of Hohenzollern-Sigmaringen, Prince (1835–1905), 78, 79, 154
Le Play, Pierre (1806–1882), 453
Lermontov, Mikhail (1814–1841), 168
Lesseps, Ferdinand de (1805–1894), 43, 350
Liberal Catholicism, 62–63, 73, 258, 259

Liberal Empire, France, 73–75
Liberal Party: Austria, 419; Belgium, 438; Britain, 192, 196, 199, 200, 205–207, 242, 366, 367, 369, 370, 378–382, 386, 387, 481, 482; France, 53–54, 74; Germany (see also National Liberals, Progressives), 85, 89, 91, 93, 98, 103, 139, 140, 143, 145, 148, 329; Netherlands, 439; Norway, 441; Russia, 408, 410; Sweden, 441
Liberalism: to 1871, 7, 13, 38–41, 59, 74, 84–85, 91, 97–98, 101, 116, 140, 157, 192, 206; to 1914, 307, 308, 345, 366, 408, 419, 435
Libraries, 245, 288
Liebig, Justus von (1803–1874), 221, 249
Liebknecht, Wilhelm (1826–1900), 311
Liman von Sanders, Otto (1855–1929), 487
Lissa, Battle (1866), 127, 228
List, Friedrich (1789–1846), 223, 317
Lister, Joseph (1827–1912), 249, 288, 450
Liszt, Franz von (1811–1886), 43, 464
Literature, 12–13, 47–48, 168, 241, 246–247, 273, 462–463
Lithuania, 166, 180
Liverpool, Lord (1770–1828), 23, 188
Lloyd George, David (1863–1945), 269, 297, 378, 380, 381, 386
Loisy, Alfred (1857–1940), 462
Lombardy, 4, 18, 24, 108, 109
London: 191, 211, 276, 374, 454; Treaties (1827), 29, (1839), 30, 501, (1840), 61, (1913), 487; Conferences (1852), 145, 147, (1867), 153, (1871), 184
Lönnrot, Elias (1802–1884), 47
Loris-Melikov, Count (1825?–1888), 397, 399
Loubet, Emile (1838–1929), 352, 354
Louis I, of Portugal (1838–1889), 432
Louis XVIII, of France (1755–1824), 4, 23, 52–54
Louis Napoleon, see Napoleon III
Lowe, Robert (1811–1892), 466
Lubbock, John (1834–1913), 452
Lucca, 24, 108, 109
Luddites, 191, 219
Lüderitz, Adolf (1834–1886), 318
Ludwig I, of Bavaria (1786–1868), 30, 47
Ludwig II, of Bavaria (1845–1886), 156, 248
Lueger, Karl (1844–1910), 332, 420, 468
Luxembourg, 78, 94, 148, 150, 153, 434
Lyautey, Marshal (1854–1934), 358
Lyell, Charles (1797–1875), 245, 246, 251, 452

Macaulay, Lord (1800–1859), 192
McCormick harvester, 221
Macedonia, 393, 424–426, 487
MacMahon, Marshal (1808–1893), 230, 339, 341, 342, 344
Mafeking, Siege (1899–1900), 372, 375

Magenta, Battle (1859), 117, 121, 122, 136, 228
Magyars, see Hungary
Maistre, Joseph de (1753–1821), 21, 53, 108
Majuba Hill, Battle (1881), 372
Mallarmé, Stéphane (1842–1898), 463
Malmö, Armistice (1848), 94
Malthus, Thomas (1766–1834), 40, 216, 242, 251
Manchuria, 403–406, 481, 490
Manet, Edouard (1832–1883), 248
Manin, Daniele (1804–1857), 112, 115, 119
Mann, Tom (1856–1941), 379, 383
Manoel II, of Portugal (1889–1932), 433
Manteuffel, Otto von (1805–1882), 142
Manzoni, Alessandro (1785–1873), 47, 243
"March Days," 87–89
March Laws, Hungary, 88, 99
Marconi, Guglielmo (1874–1937), 281, 447
Marie, Pierre Thomas (1795–1870), 65
Martov, Julius (1873–1923), 407
Marx, Karl (1818–1883), 14, 45, 86, 253, 255, 273, 311, 455, 458
Marxism, 256–257, 266, 273, 454, 456, 457
Masaryk, Thomas (1850–1937), 419
Materialism, 249, 250, 260, 273, 458
Matisse, Henri (1869–1954), 463
Maudslay, Henry (1771–1831), 217
Maxim, Hiram (1840–1916), 296
Maximilian, Archduke (1832–1867), 77, 93
Maxwell, Clerk (1831–1879), 447
Mayr, Georg von (1841–1925), 453
Mazzini, Giuseppe (1805–1872), 47, 68, 85, 110, 114, 119, 122–125, 128, 243
Mechanics' Institutes, Britain, 245
Mediterranean Agreements (1887), 322, 476, 479
Mehemet Ali (1769–1849), 29, 31, 61
Méline, Félix (1838–1925), 360
Mendel, Gregor (1822–1884), 450
Mendeleev, Dmitri (1834–1907), 446
Mendelssohn, Felix (1809–1847), 241
Mensheviks, 407, 413, 457
Mentana, Battle (1867), 128, 230
Metternich, Prince (1773–1859), 7, 10, 14, 24, 26, 28, 30, 31, 84 87, 88, 93, 108, 109, 111, 240
"Metternich System," 24, 86
Metz, Siege (1870), 79
Mexico, 77
Michelet, Jules (1798–1874), 47
Mickiewicz, Adam (1798–1855), 47, 243
Middle classes, 7, 14, 39, 83, 102, 231, 297
Mikhailovsky, Nicholas (1842–1904), 396
Miliukov, Paul (1859–1943), 408, 411, 414
Miliutin, Dmitri (1816–1912), 179
Mill, James (1773–1836), 269
Mill, John Stuart (1806–1873), 40, 193, 234, 242, 255, 455, 457

Millerand, Alexandre (1859–1943), 352, 355
Milner, Alfred (1854–1925), 375, 376
Mobilization, 228, 270, 294, 386, 493–494, 497, 500
Modena, 24, 30, 108, 109, 112, 120, 122
Moldavia, 28, 29, 76, 136, 170, 172
Moltke, Count Helmuth von (1800–1891), 142, 146, 149, 155
Moltke, Helmuth von (1848–1916), 497
Mommsen, Theodor (1817–1903), 332
Monet, Claude (1840–1926), 248
Monroe, President (1758–1831), 28
Monroe Doctrine, 28, 77, 184
Montalembert, Comte de (1810–1870), 62, 73, 258
Montenegro, 320, 423–427
Montholon, Comte de (1783–1853), 63
Montpensier, Duc de (1824–1890), 62
Morny, Duc de (1811–1865), 70
Morocco, 271, 299, 357, 359, 386, 432, 481, 485–486
Morris, William (1834–1896), 457
Moscow, 400, 410
Motorcars, 272, 278, 279, 282, 284
Mukden, Battle (1905), 405
Müller, Adam (1779–1829), 21
Murat, Joachim (1767?–1815), 108
Murat, Lucien (1803–1878), 120
Muraviev, Michael (1796?–1866), 181
Muraviev-Amursky, Nicolai (1809?–1881), 184
Mürzsteg Agreement (1903), 425, 484
Museums, 246, 288
Music, 241, 248, 464

Naples: city, 113, 115, 124, 125; kingdom, see Two Sicilies
Napoleon I (1769–1821), 4, 6, 9, 50–52, 63, 68, 106, 108, 161
Napoleon II, see Reichstadt
Napoleon III (1808–1873), 14, 55, 63, 64, 67–80
Napoleon, Prince (1822–1891), 120, 121
Nasmyth, James (1808–1890), 220
National Guard, France, 56, 79, 338, 340
National Liberal Party (Germany), 140, 308–309, 312–314, 325, 329
National Society, Italy, 119, 122
National Workshops, France, 60, 65–66
Nationalism: to 1871, 14, 41, 45–48, 85, 96–98, 101, 103–104, 110, 140, 242–243; to 1914, 264, 397, 406, 414, 421, 426, 466–467, 489–490
Nationalverein, Germany, 140–141, 308
Naumann, Friedrich (1860–1919), 309
Navarino, Battle (1827), 29
Navies, 211, 228, 333, 374, 377, 387, 390, 404–406, 481, 501
Navigation Acts, 200, 221, 365

Nechaev, Serge (1847–1882), 396
Needle gun, 150, 230
Neilson, James (1792–1865), 219
Neo-classicism, 11, 22, 241
Neo-Gothic, see Gothic Revival
Netherlands, 4, 30, 103, 153, 434–439
Netherlands colonial empire, 301, 302, 434
New Zealand, 202, 291, 377, 382, 388
Newspapers, 73, 203, 269, 446, 465–466
Ney, Marshal (1769–1815), 52
Nice, 75, 120, 122
Nicholas I, of Russia (1796–1855), 31, 71, 99, 100, 163–171
Nicholas II, of Russia (1868–1918), 333, 401–404, 408–415, 479
Nicholas, Grand Duke (1856–1929), 409
Nietzsche, Friedrich (1844–1900), 110, 266, 468–469
Nightingale, Florence (1820–1910), 203
Nihilism, 185, 399, 426, 455, 461
Nikolsburg, see Prague
Nobel, Alfred (1833–1896), 228, 278, 437
Nobel prizes, 437, 447
North German Confederation (1867–1871), 151, 153, 157, 308
Norway, 8, 24, 279, 283, 434–437, 439–441, 492
Novara, Battle (1849), 98, 114

October Diploma (1860), 137
October Manifesto (1905), 406, 409, 412
Oil, 281, 400, 424, 427, 491
Old Catholics, 259, 313, 438
Ollivier, Emile (1825–1913), 74, 75, 79, 155
Olmütz, 100, 133
O'Meara, Barry (1786–1836), 63
Orléans, campaign for, 79
Orsini, Felice (1819–1858), 73, 120
Orthodox Eastern Church, 166, 167, 171, 181, 392, 397, 398, 402, 411
Oscar II, of Sweden (1829–1907), 440, 441
Otto I, of Greece (1815–1867), 30
Ottoman Empire: to 1871, 28, 31, 61, 76, 170–172, 182; to 1914, 265, 286, 320–322, 332, 423–425, 482–489; population, 264; constitution of 1876, 423, 425, 442
Oudinot, General (1791–1863), 114
Owen, Robert (1771–1858), 14, 43, 196, 197, 242

Pacifico, Don (1784–1854), 201
Painting, 12, 55, 241, 247, 273, 362, 463
Paixhans, General (1783–1854), 228
Palacký, Frantisek (1798–1876), 47, 85, 96, 243
Palmerston, Lord (1784–1865), 14, 30, 31, 61, 170, 171, 201, 204–205
Panama canal project, 350
Pan-Germanism, 331–332, 467, 489

Pan-Russianism, 397, 400
Pan-Slav Congress (1848), 88, 91, 96
Pan-Slavism, 392–393, 397, 467, 489
Papal Infallibility, dogma of, 128, 258–259, 313, 438, 458
Papal States, 24, 30, 68, 73, 76, 107, 109, 111, 114, 120, 122–125, 127, 128
Paris, Comte de (1838–1894), 65, 341
Paris: city, 5, 50, 65–67, 71, 72, 360, 362, 464; siege (1870–1871), 80, 223, 229; Commune (1871), 338–340, 346; Treaty (1815), 17; Congress (1856), 75, 76, 172–173, 184
Parliament Act (1911), 381–382
Parma, 24, 30, 108, 109, 112, 121, 122
Parnell, Charles (1846–1891), 368–370
Parsons, Charles (1854–1931), 279
Parties, political, *see* names of parties and sub-entry under names of major powers
Paskievich, Field Marshal (1782–1856), 99, 166, 167, 180
Pasteur, Louis (1822–1895), 249, 287, 450
Pater, Walter (1839–1894), 463
Patrimony of St. Peter, 108, 127
Pavlov, Ivan (1849–1936), 451
Peasants: to 1871, 7, 14, 92, 102, 175, 232; to 1914, 292, 360, 399, 409, 413, 426, 431
Peel, Sir Robert (1788–1850), 192, 193, 199, 200
Perkin, William (1838–1907), 227, 228, 278
Persia, 170, 386, 482
Persigny, Duc de (1808–1872), 70
Pestel, Pavel (1793–1826), 164
Peter I, of Serbia (1844–1921), 426
"Peterloo Massacre," 33, 191, 219
Peters, Karl (1856–1918), 318, 332
Petition of London Merchants, 40, 199
Petroleum, *see* Oil
Philosophic studies, 21, 240–241, 249–260, 452–461
Phoenix Park murders, 369, 370
Picquart, Georges (1854–1914), 351
Piedmont, 6, 17, 20, 24, 27, 75, 108, 111–116
"Pig War" (1905–1907), 426, 482
Pius VII, Pope (1742–1823), 10
Pius IX, Pope (1792–1878), 68, 76, 93, 110, 111, 113, 115, 116, 127–128, 130, 258, 313, 428, 460
Pius X, Pope (1835–1914), 354, 462
Planck, Max (1858–1947), 448
Plehve, Wenzel von (1846–1904), 404, 407, 408
Plekhanov, George (1857–1918), 407, 456
Plevna, Siege (1877), 393
Plombières, negotiations at, 77, 120
Pobedonostsev, Konstantin (1827–1907), 397, 403, 410
Poincaré, Raymond (1860–1934), 346, 496
Poles (*see also* Cracow, Galicia, Posen): to 1871, 4, 18, 20, 61, 77–78, 84, 96, 99, 139,
161, 174, 176; to 1914, 324, 325, 392, 406, 412, 489
Polignac, Prince de (1780–1847), 51, 54
Polish Revolts: (1830–1831), 31, 166–167; (1863), 77, 145, 180–181, 182, 396
Populism, 396, 398, 400, 407, 455
Port Arthur, Siege (1904), 294, 404, 405, 408
Portsmouth, Treaty (1905), 406, 409
Portugal, 27, 37, 373, 432–433; population, 430
Portuguese colonial empire, 301, 433, 491
Posen, 20, 96
Positivism, 253–254, 452
Potsdam Agreement (1910), 485
Potteries, 217, 383
Prague: city, 88, 91; Treaty (1866), 150
Prince Regent, *see* George IV
Princip, Gavril (1893?–1918), 474, 495
Principalities, The, *see* Moldavia *and* Wallachia
Progressive Party (Germany), 143, 151, 308–309, 312–314, 325
Proletariat: to 1871, 7, 14, 37, 83, 87, 102, 234–235; to 1914, 265, 297, 346, 355, 400, 409, 414
Proudhon, Pierre (1809–1865), 44, 455
Prussia: population, 6, 139, 151; to 1848, 5, 20, 35; to 1871, 84, 85, 89, 93, 94, 96–98, 100, 101, 139–157; to 1914, 304–305, 308
Prussian Tariff Act (1818), 35, 222
"Prussian Union" (1850), 100
Public Health, 6, 196, 234, 287–288, 366–367
Punch, 171, 193, 196, 296–297, 323

Quadrilateral, 109, 112, 121, 126, 229
Quadruple Alliance (1815), 10, 20, 26, 53
Quinet, Edgar (1803–1875), 46
Quintuple Alliance (1818), 26

Racconigi, Treaty (1909), 485
Race doctrines, 332, 467
Radetzky, Count (1766–1858), 112–114, 116, 136
Radical and Radical Socialist Party (France), 345, 347
Radowitz, General von (1797–1853), 100, 140
Railways (*see also* Baghdad and Trans-Siberian Railways): 221, 226, 227, 233, 267, 282; Austrian, 87, 422; Balkan, 483; Belgian, 220; British, 220; French, 59, 66, 222, 224, 226; German, 139, 223, 226, 267, 312; Italian, 117, 126, 429; Russian, 175, 268, 390, 400
Ralliement, of supporters of French Republic, 350
Ranke, Leopold von (1795–1886), 242, 454
Raspail, François (1794–1878), 67
Rasputin, Gregory (1871–1916), 402

Rathenau, Walther (1867–1922), 324
Realism, 246–248, 445
Realpolitik, 15, 104, 144–146, 154, 157
Red Cross, 437
Reform Bill crisis, Britain, 192, 381
Reichstadt, Duc de (1811–1832), 70
Reinsurance Treaty (1887), 271, 322, 401, 476–477
Religion, 257–260, 458–462
Renan, Ernest (1823–1892), 259
Republicanism, 65, 113, 263–264, 340, 409, 430, 433
Revolutions of 1848, 41, 64–68, 82–104, 170–171, 198, 223
Rhineland, 20, 35, 78, 85, 139, 150, 153, 310
Rhodes, Cecil (1853–1902), 373
Ricardo, David (1772–1823), 40, 242
Ricasoli, Baron (1809–1880), 113, 122, 129
Richelieu, Duc de (1766–1822), 51
Rights of Man, 4, 6, 8, 38, 39, 44, 97, 343
Rimbaud, Arthur (1854–1891), 463
Rimsky-Korsakov, Nikolai (1844–1908), 248
Rivet Law (1871), 340
Roads, 218, 220, 222, 282
Roberts, Lord (1832–1914), 375
Robot, see Servile dues
Rocket, 220
Romagna, *see* Papal States
Roman Catholic Church, 21, 62–63, 107, 128, 258–259, 313, 353–354, 460–462
Romanticism, 11, 240–242
Rome, 68, 98, 99, 113–115, 124, 127–129
Röntgen, Wilhelm von (1845–1923), 447
Roon, Albrecht von (1803–1879), 142, 143, 146, 155
Rosebery, Lord (1847–1929), 370
Rossi, Count (1787–1848), 113
Rossini, Gioacchino (1792–1868), 55, 248
Rotteck, Karl von (1775–1840), 39
Rouault, Georges (1871–1958), 463
Rouvier, Pierre (1842–1911), 354
Rudolph, Austrian Crown Prince (1858–1889), 93
Rumania, 76–77, 172, 321, 393, 423–427, 475, 487, 489
Ruskin, John (1819–1900), 247
Russell, Lord John (1792–1878), 40
Russia (*see also* Siberia): population, 6, 391, 392; to 1848, 5, 18, 25, 27, 31, 158–170; to 1871, 77, 170–185; to 1914, 390–415; industry, 280–281, 400; constitution and parties, 407–411; foreign policy, 390–393, 400–406, 479, 483–485, 487, 496–500
Russian Asiatic empire, 170, 183–184, 395
Russo-Japanese War (1904–1905), 299, 404–406, 479, 494
Russo-Turkish Wars: (1828–1829), 166, 170; (1877–1878), 393
Rutherford, Ernest (1871–1937), 448

Sadowa, *see* Königgrätz
Sainte-Beuve, Charles (1804–1869), 55, 72
St. Petersburg, 5, 164, 229, 408–410
Saint-Simon, Comte de (1760–1825), 42, 59, 72, 253, 355
Salisbury, Lord (1830–1903), 367, 370, 373, 480
San Stefano, Treaty (1878), 320, 393
Sand, Karl (1795–1820), 26
Sanjak of Novi Pazar, 483, 484
Sarajevo assassination, 333, 386, 474, 489, 495
Sardinia, Kingdom of (*see also* Piedmont): 17, 108
Savoy, 17, 75, 120, 122
Saxe-Weimar, 25
Saxony, 20, 30, 35, 98, 149, 306, 310, 312, 313
Say, Jean (1767–1832), 40
Sazonov, Sergei (1866–1927), 485, 496, 497
Schlegel, Friedrich (1772–1829), 241
Schlegel, Wilhelm (1767–1845), 241
Schleiden, Matthias (1804–1881), 244
Schleswig-Holstein, 78, 89, 93–94, 145–149, 310, 440
Schlieffen, Count Alfred von (1833–1913), 491
Schlieffen Plan, 491, 500, 501
Schmerling, Anton von (1805–1893), 135
Schneckenburger, Max (1819–1849), 47
Schneiders, Le Creusot, 293
Schnitzler, Arthur (1862–1931), 418
Schönberg, Arnold (1874–1951), 464
Schönerer, Georg von (1842–1921), 332, 468
Schopenhauer, Arthur (1788–1860), 260, 468
Schubert, Franz (1797–1828), 241
Schulze-Delitzsch, Hermann (1808–1883), 232
Schurz, Carl (1829–1906), 91, 103
Schwann, Theodor (1810–1882), 244
Schwarzenberg, Prince (1800–1852), 92, 93, 98–100, 116, 133–135
Schweitzer, Johann (1834–1875), 311
Scientific studies, 15, 243–246, 248–260, 446–454
Scott, Walter (1771–1832), 12, 21, 240, 241
Sedan, Battle (1870), 79, 229, 336
Seeley, John (1834–1895), 259, 371
Septennat, 331
Serbia: to 1900, 28, 29, 299, 320, 321, 333, 393, 423–424, 475; to 1914, 425–427, 482, 484, 486–489, 495; population, 489
Serfdom: incidence, 5, 161, 163, 231, 246; abolition, 25, 88, 169, 173–176, 216
Servile dues, 5, 92, 102, 136
Seward, William (1801–1872), 184
Shaftesbury, Lord (1801–1885), 195
Shamil, Imam (1797–1871), 170, 182
Shaw, Bernard (1856–1950), 457, 462
Shelley, Percy Bysshe (1792–1822), 238, 240
Shimonoseki, Treaty (1895), 403
Shipbuilding, 220, 282–283
Sibelius, Jan (1865–1957), 464

Siberia, 164, 169, 174, 182–184, 289, 291, 390, 398, 413, 414

Sicily (see also Two Sicilies): 85, 109, 111, 124, 429

Siemens, Ernst Werner (1816–1892), 227, 327

Siemens, Wilhelm (1823–1883), 225, 227

Siemens-Martin process, 215, 225

Silesia, 35, 37, 139

Simon, Jules (1814–1896), 75

Sinope, Battle (1853), 171, 228

Sismondi, Jean Charles (1773–1842), 42

Skobelev, General (1843–1882), 395

Slavery, 173, 358

Slavophiles, 167, 169, 175, 392, 397

Social Democratic or Socialist Party: Austria, 420; Belgium, 297, 438; Britain (see also Independent Labor Party), 457; France, 65–67, 297, 345–347, 352, 354–356; Germany, 14, 151, 297, 309–311, 313, 315, 319, 325, 329–330, 454; Italy, 430; Netherlands, 439; Russia (see also Social Revolutionary Party), 398, 407, 410–413, 456–457; Sweden, 440

Social Revolutionary Party (Russia), 407, 455

Socialism, see Communism, Social Democratic or Socialist Party, Utopian Socialists

Solferino, Battle (1859), 121, 136, 437

Solvay, Ernest (1838–1922), 228

Sonderbund, 84

Sorel, Georges (1847–1922), 356

Soult, Marshal (1769–1851), 58

South Africa, 202, 291, 299, 365, 372–376, 387–388

South African War (1899–1902), 375–376, 479

Southey, Robert (1774–1843), 21

Soviet, 409, 410

Spain: to 1871, 8, 23, 27, 28, 37, 38, 61, 77, 79, 154; to 1914, 322, 430–432, 486; population, 264, 430

Spanish-American War (1898), 431

Spanish colonial empire, 431, 432

Spencer, Herbert (1820–1903), 253, 254–255, 445, 452–453, 455

Speransky, Michael (1772–1839), 160, 161, 164, 165

"Splendid Isolation," 271, 364

Stadion, Count (1806–1853), 135

Staël, Germaine de (1766–1817), 12

Stambulov, Stefan (1855–1895), 426

Stanley, Henry (1841–1904), 434

State peasants, Russia, 166, 174, 183, 399

Steam power, 5, 32, 87, 217, 218, 223, 227, 274, 279

Steamships, 72, 220, 224–225, 227, 282–283

Steel, 225–226, 268, 277, 281, 283, 294, 316–317, 326

Stephenson, George (1781–1848), 220

Stephenson, Robert (1803–1859), 220

Stöcker, Adolph (1835–1900), 332, 468

Stolypin, Peter (1862–1911), 411–414

Straits (Bosphorus and Dardanelles), 31, 61, 170, 393, 400, 484, 485

Straits Convention (1841), 31, 61, 170, 201

Strauss, David Friedrich (1808–1874), 259

Strauss, Johann (1825–1899), 418

Strauss, Richard (1864–1949), 464

Stravinsky, Igor (b. 1882), 464

Stresemann, Gustav (1878–1929), 332

Strindberg, August (1849–1912), 463

Stubbs, William (1825–1901), 240

Sudan, 373, 375

Sudermann, Hermann (1857–1928), 462

Suez Canal, 224, 282, 350, 372, 403

Suffrage, universal manhood, 264–265

Sukhomlinov, General (1848–1926), 483

Sweden: to 1871, 24, 172, 181, 228; to 1914, 278, 279–281, 434, 437, 439–441; population, 434

Switzerland: to 1871, 20, 23, 84, 101, 103; to 1871, 279–280, 297, 434–438, 492

Sybel, Heinrich von (1817–1895), 140, 330

Syllabus of Errors, Papal, 127, 258, 313

Sylvester Patent (1851), 135

Syndicalism, 266, 356, 383, 384, 430, 431–432, 454

Synthetic philosophy, 254, 445, 453

Széchenyi, Count (1791–1860), 86

Taaffe, Count (1833–1895), 419, 420

Taine, Hippolyte (1828–1893), 210, 348, 453

Talleyrand, Prince (1754–1838), 6, 51, 56, 338

Tangier crisis, 359

Tariff systems (see also Zollverein): 35–36, 72, 298, 315, 319, 324, 340, 358, 377, 418

Tchaikovsky, Peter (1840–1893), 248, 464

Telegraph, 83, 227, 283

Telephone, 283

Temesvar, Battle (1849), 99

Textile industries (see also Hand loom weavers): 33–34, 175, 217, 219, 221, 278, 316, 360, 400

Thaer, Albrecht (1752–1828), 216

Thiers, Adolphe (1797–1877), 51, 55, 57, 58, 61, 64, 65, 67, 73, 74, 79, 150, 224, 338–342, 345

Third Section, Russian Chancery, 165, 397

Thomas, Sidney Gilchrist (1850–1885), 277

Thomson, Joseph (1856–1940), 448

Thomson, William, see Kelvin

Three Emperors' League, 321, 322, 395, 400, 401, 475, 478, 484

Thyssen, August (1842–1926), 309

Thyssen, Fritz (1873–1951), 326

Tirpitz, Admiral von (1849–1930), 325, 332

Tisza, Count (1861–1918), 421, 496, 497

Tocqueville, Alexis de (1805–1859), 34, 57

Todleben, General (1818–1884), 171, 229, 393

Togo, Admiral (1847–1934), 405
Tolstoy, Count Dmitri (1823–1889), 185, 398
Tolstoy, Count Leo (1828–1910), 171, 178, 462
Tory Party (Britain), 192, 200, 205–206
Town planning, 288, 464
Towns, see Urbanization
Trade, 5, 218, 227, 267–268, 282, 284–285, 298, 302, 318–319, 360, 366, 434
Trade unions, 73, 192, 196–198, 208, 211, 232, 266, 297, 329, 356, 366, 367, 379, 380, 383–384, 414, 446, 461
Transport, see Motorcars, Railways, Roads, Steamships
Trans-Siberian Railway, 400, 403–405, 410
Treitschke, Heinrich von (1834–1896), 6, 140, 261, 317, 330
Triple Alliance (1882), 271, 321, 333, 386, 427, 474, 475, 480, 482, 483
Triple Entente (1907), 271, 386, 474, 482–485
Tripoli, 428, 486
Trochu, General (1815–1896), 79, 80
Troppau, Congress (1820), 26, 27
Trotsky, Leon (1877–1940), 409
Tsushima, Battle (1905), 405–406
Tunisia, 299, 318, 357, 423, 428
Turbines, 279, 294, 295
Turgenev, Ivan (1818–1883), 168, 178, 185, 246, 455, 462
Turkey, see Ottoman Empire
Tuscany, 24, 108, 111–114
Two Sicilies, Kingdom of the, 24, 27, 108, 109, 111–115, 118, 120, 123–126
Tyndall, John (1820–1893), 245

Uitlanders, 373–375
Ukraine, 392, 406, 414, 489
Ulster, 384, 385
Ultramontanism, 53, 62, 63
"Ultras," France, 23, 50, 53, 54, 56
Uniates, Greek Catholics, 167, 181
United Diet, Prussian Landtag of 1847, 85, 141
United Netherlands, 20, 23
United States (see also Civil War): to 1865, 28, 77, 202, 203, 221, 229; to 1914, 233, 235, 274, 280, 283, 285, 286, 289, 291, 298, 299, 344, 383, 398, 431, 465, 480, 502
Unkiar-Skelessi, Treaty (1833), 31, 170
Urbanization, 5–6, 206, 234, 267, 287–289, 317, 360–361
Utopian Socialists, 41–45, 242, 253, 255, 256, 355, 457
Uvarov, Count (1786–1855), 166, 167

Vaillant, Edouard (1840–1915), 355
Vatican Council (1869–1870), 128, 258, 313, 439, 458
Venetia, 4, 18, 24, 108, 109, 112, 115, 121, 126–127, 148, 150

Venizelos, Eleutherios (1864–1936), 427
Verdi, Guiseppe (1813–1901), 248
Vereeniging, Treaty (1902), 376
Verlaine, Paul (1844–1896), 463
Verona, Congress (1822), 27
Veuillot, Louis (1813–1883), 259
Victor Emmanuel I, of Sardinia (1759–1824), 6
Victor Emmanuel II, of Italy (1820–1878), 115, 119, 121–125, 129, 154
Victoria, of Britain (1819–1901), 61, 201, 402
Vienna: Congress (1814–1815), 9, 16–20, 24, 358; Conference (1820), 24; Treaty (1864), 146
Vigny, Alfred de (1797–1863), 55
Vilagos, Capitulation (1849), 99
Villafranca, Armistice (1859), 121
Villèle, Comte de (1773–1854), 54
Virchow, Rudolph (1821–1902), 249, 288, 450
Vladivostok, 184, 403
Volturno, Battle (1860), 125
Vorparlament, Frankfurt (1848), 89

Wages and purchasing power of workers, 232, 234, 268, 292, 297
Wagner, Richard (1813–1883), 248, 332, 455, 464, 467, 468
Wakefield, Gibbon (1796–1862), 202
Waldeck-Rousseau, Pierre (1846–1904), 352, 353
Walewski, Count (1810–1868), 70
Wallace, Alfred (1823–1913), 251
Wallachia, 29, 76, 136, 170, 172
Wallas, Graham (1858–1932), 457
Wallon Amendment (1875), 342
Waterloo, Battle (1815), 52, 64
Webb, Beatrice (1858–1943), 380
Webb, Sidney (1859–1947), 380, 457
Weber, Karl Maria von (1786–1826), 241
Weismann, August (1834–1914), 449
Weitling, Wilhelm (1808–1871), 310
Welfare state, 366
Wellington, Duke of (1769–1852), 27, 29, 192
Western provinces (see also Lithuania): 174, 176, 180, 397
"Westerners," Russia, 167, 169, 175
Whig Party (Britain), 192, 196, 199, 200, 370
White, Andrew (1832–1918), 458
White Russians, see Byelo-Russians
"White Terror," France (1815), 52
Whitworth, Joseph (1803–1887), 220, 227
Wied, Prince William of (b. 1876), 488
Wielcpolski, Count (1803–1877), 180
Wilberforce, Samuel (1805–1873), 252
Wilde, Oscar (1856–1900), 462, 463
William I, German Emperor (1797–1888), 79, 142–144, 147, 150, 154–157, 312, 315, 321, 324

William II, German Emperor (1859–1941),
    323, 324, 326, 330, 332, 333, 359, 374, 424,
    478, 482, 484, 496, 497
William I, of Netherlands (1772–1843), 23
Windischgraetz, Prince (1787–1862), 91–93,
    99
Windthorst, Ludwig (1812–1891), 309–310,
    314
Winterhalter, Franz (1805?–1873), 70, 247
Wireless telegraphy, 283
Witte, Count (1849–1915), 400, 403, 406,
    409, 411
Woman suffrage, 265, 366, 382, 436
Wordsworth, William (1770–1850), 12, 21,
    240, 241
Working classes, *see* Peasants, Proletariat

Worth, Charles (1825–1895), 362
Wundt, Wilhelm (1832–1920), 450, 451
Württemberg, 25, 36, 151, 306, 313

Yalu River, Battle (1904), 404
Yangtze Agreement (1900), 480
Young Italy, 47, 110, 243
Young Turks, 425, 483, 484
Ypsilanti, Prince Alexander (1792–1828), 28
Yugoslav (South Slav) movement, 421, 423,
    489, 495

Zemstvos, 177, 398, 399, 400, 402, 406, 408,
    413, 414
Zola, Emile (1840–1902), 247, 351–352, 462
Zollverein, 36, 139, 151, 153, 222–223

Illustration Acknowledgments

PAGE

18   Haus, -Hof-und Staatsarchiv, Vienna

22   From *Vues de l'Église Sainte Geneviève de Paris,* Paris, 1826
From C. von Lorcke, *Karl Friedrich Schinkel,* Rembrandt-Verlag, Berlin, 1939. Photographs, courtesy Avery Library, Columbia University

39   Photo Bulloz

58   Courtesy, The Museum of Modern Art, New York

59   *Charivari,* January 17, 1834. New York Public Library, Prints Division

71   From Edmund Texier, *Tableau de Paris,* Vol. 1, Paris, 1852. New York Public Library

84   From J. Grand Cartaret, *Les Moeurs et la Caricature en Allemagne,* Paris, 1885. New York Public Library

90   Courtesy, Historisches Museum, Frankfurt am Main

114   Radio Times Hulton Picture Library, London

122   *Illustrated London News,* November 10, 1860. New York Public Library

137   *Illustrated London News,* February 3, 1855. New York Public Library

147   *Kladderadatsch,* October 22, 1865. New York Public Library

156   Scribner Art File

168   Slavonic Division, New York Public Library

171   Copyright, *Punch,* London. New York Public Library

179   Sovfoto

191   Copyright, British Museum

197   From the collection of ephemeral printing at the University Press, Oxford, by permission

200   Radio Times Hulton Picture Library

218   *L'Illustration,* September 16, 1871

222   Copyright, British Museum

225   The Science Museum, London

244   Imperial Chemical House, London

249   German Information Center

250   Courtesy, George Darwin, London

276   From W. Jerrold Blanchard and G. Doré, *London. A Pilgrimage.* 1872. New York Public Library, Prints Division

280   The Bettmann Archive

307   The Bettmann Archive

316   Brown Brothers

323   Copyright, *Punch,* London. New York Public Library

348   Yale University Library

351   Bibliothèque Nationale

369   National Library of Ireland

374   Aerofilms and Aero Pictorial Limited

383   *The Times,* London

399   New York Public Library

403   Ullstein Photo Library

432   Radio Times Hulton Picture Library

436   American Red Cross, Greater New York
New York Public Library

460   United Press International Photo

466   *The Daily Express,* London, and University Press, Oxford

474   Radio Times Hulton Picture Library

483   Imperial War Museum, London

495   Haus,-Hof-und Staatsarchiv, Vienna

EUROPE AND THE WORLD SINCE 1914

Ernest John Knapton   Wheaton College, Norton, Massachusetts

Thomas Kingston Derry   Visiting Professor of History, Wheaton College

CHARLES   SCRIBNER'S   SONS   NEW   YORK

EUROPE

AND THE WORLD

SINCE 1914

ACKNOWLEDGMENTS

The two stanzas from "A Shropshire Lad" quoted on page 2 are from the Authorized
Edition of *The Collected Poems of A. E. Housman*. Copyright 1939, 1940, © 1959 by Holt,
Rinehart and Winston, Inc. Reprinted by permission of Holt, Rinehart and Winston, Inc.

The figures for the chart on page 86 were taken from Heinrich E. Friedlaender & Jacob
Oser, *Economic History of Modern Europe,* © 1953. Used with the permission of Prentice-Hall,
Inc., Englewood Cliffs, New Jersey.

The illustrations on the title page are as follows:

THE GREAT STACK, SHEFFIELD, 1909, an etching by Joseph Pennell, reproduced from the
Collections of the Library of Congress.

Astronaut Edward H. White II is shown floating in space during the third orbit of the
Gemini-Titan 4 flight, June, 1965. From National Aeronautics and Space Administration.

PREFACE

The present work surveys the half-century which runs from the outbreak of war in 1914 to the close of 1964. It follows the same general pattern as the two earlier volumes, *Europe: 1450–1815,* and *Europe: 1815–1914,* allocating substantial space to economic, social, and cultural developments. Because of the shorter time-span involved in this volume, key events can be presented in greater and more illuminating detail. It has been necessary to find some space for examining the rapid flow of changes in Asia and Africa, to say nothing of the new role of the United States, without which the study of Europe is no longer intelligible. Tracing the fortunes of the principal European powers remains, however, as the central theme.

Maps, illustrations, and bibliographies have been planned to meet the same needs as in the previous volumes. The reader should nevertheless note that books on near-contemporary history must often reflect the temper of the times when they are written. Since the period covered in this volume is relatively brief, the authors have not included the kind of chronological tables found in the earlier volumes; they hope, however, that the list of events found at the beginning of each chapter will effectively serve the students' purposes.

Much of the preliminary work was undertaken when the authors were serving together as members of the Department of History at Wheaton College; it is therefore appropriate to begin by thanking the authorities of the College for their help and encouragement. The authors are also grateful to Miss Hilda Harris, Librarian of Wheaton College, and her staff for help with many problems. They thank Mrs. Lea M. Landers and Mrs. Rosemary Currie for their expert stenographic assistance. Valuable suggestions on many points of detail have been given by members of the College faculty, especially by Professors Willard F. Enteman, Paul C. Helmreich, Bojan H. Jennings, J. Arthur Martin, and Frank W. Ramseyer. Once again the authors are indebted to the college department and staff of Charles Scribner's Sons for their patient advice and scrupulous attention to all details, as well as to Professor Goldwin Smith, college consultant to the publishers, for his thoughtful comment and assistance. They are also indebted to Professor Blair C. Currie of Hobart College for preparing the very useful graphs dealing with economic growth in Communist China, and to Mr. Leonard Darwin who has most skillfully converted the authors' instructions and sketches into the maps which, it is hoped, will serve as a useful supplement to the text.

Last but by no means least, on the occasion of the completion of our long task, we should like to pay tribute to the sustaining encouragement and exemplary patience of our wives.

E. J. K.

November, 1965 T. K. D.

CONTENTS

		Page
LIST OF ILLUSTRATIONS		xi
LIST OF MAPS		xiii

Part I   The Dominance of War, 1914–1945

PROLOGUE: UNRESOLVED CONFLICTS   2

CHAPTER 1   THE FIRST WORLD WAR   14

The Long Four Years
1914: The First Onslaught
1915: Stalemate Established
1916: Stalemate Unbroken
1917–1918: Germany in the Ascendant
1918, July–November: The Collapse of the Central Powers
Europe at the Termination of Hostilities

CHAPTER 2   THE RUSSIAN REVOLUTION, 1917–1921   40

Russia and the War, 1914–1917
The Failure of the Liberals
The Transfer of Power
The Communists and the Civil War
The Communists and the World
How Communism Survived
Communism: Theory and Practice

CHAPTER 3   THE RESETTLEMENT OF CONTINENTAL EUROPE   64

The Background of the Peace Treaties
The Negotiations at Paris
The Treaty with Germany
The Lesser Treaties
The League, Mandates, and Minorities
The Uncertain Voice of Democracy
The Green Revolution
The Further Search for Security

CHAPTER 4   CONSERVATIVE BRITAIN   94

"A Land of Just and Old Renown"
Britain During Four Years of War
Postwar Britain and the Irish Problem

The Changing Pattern of Party Politics
Economic Change
Empire into Commonwealth
Britain and the World

CHAPTER 5   EUROPE AND THE WORLD EAST OF SUEZ   118
The Emergent Nations of the Middle East
The New Turkey
The New Arab States: Saudi Arabia and Egypt
Iran
Middle Eastern Mandates: Syria and Lebanon
Middle Eastern Mandates: Palestine and Transjordan
Middle Eastern Mandates: Iraq
British Problems of Empire
French and Dutch Imperialism in the Interwar Years
The Far East: China and Japan
A Continent in Ferment

CHAPTER 6   EUROPE AND THE WORLD ECONOMY   144
The Dethronement of Western Europe
War and the European Economy
The Years of Recovery, 1924–1929
The World Economic Crisis
Economic Nationalism in the Ascendant, 1933–1939

CHAPTER 7   THE RISE OF THE DICTATORSHIPS   168
Democracy and Dictatorship: The Challenge
Fascist Italy: Background
Fascist Italy: The Take-over
The Reorganization of Fascist Italy: The Corporative State
Other Dictatorships of the 1920's
Dictatorship During the 1930's
Efforts for a Democratic Germany
Problems of the Weimar Republic
Hitler and National Socialism
Dictatorship in Hitler's Third Reich

CHAPTER 8   THE DEVELOPMENT OF THE U.S.S.R.   202
The Russian Enigma
The New Economic Policy
The Constitution of 1924
The Mantle of Lenin
The Five-Year Plans
The New Soviet Society
The New Constitution of 1936, the Party, and the Purges
Russia and the World

CHAPTER 9   DEMOCRACY ON THE DEFENSIVE   228
The Challenge of Dictatorship
The Italian Invasion of Ethiopia
The Remilitarization of the Rhineland
Fencing for Position: Europe and the War in Spain

The Absorption of Austria in Germany
The Dismemberment of Czechoslovakia
War for Poland?
Responsibility for the Outbreak of War

CHAPTER 10   THE SECOND WORLD WAR   256

The Emergence of Total War
The First Blitzkrieg and the German Breakthrough to the Atlantic
The British at Bay
The German Invasion of Russia
The Japanese Conquests in East Asia
Mounting the Counterattack of the Western Allies
The Destruction of Hitler's Europe
The Counterattack on Japan

Part II   A World in Ferment, 1945–1964

PROLOGUE: WORLD ORDER OR WORLD DISORDER   292

CHAPTER 11   THE TRANSFORMATION OF WESTERN EUROPE, 1945–1950   296

Transition from War to Peace
Germany, 1945–1950
Postwar Britain
Reconstruction in France
Italy and the Lesser Democracies
The Twilight of Colonialism
First Steps Toward European Cooperation

CHAPTER 12   THE U.S.S.R. AND SATELLITE POWERS   322

The Breach Between East and West
Postwar Russia
The New Communist States of Eastern Europe
Cold War from Behind the Iron Curtain
The Succession to Stalin
Russia and the World

CHAPTER 13   THE NEW ASIA AND THE NEW AFRICA   350

National Aspirations: Retrospect and Prospect
India and Pakistan in the New Age
Japan: From Defeat to Recovery
Conflict in China and Korea
The New Nationalism in Southeast Asia
The Middle East: Israel, Turkey, and Iran
The Middle East: The Arab States
African Independence
Continuing Stresses in Asia and Africa

CHAPTER 14   THE CULTURAL REVOLUTION   378

The "Two Cultures": Developments in Contemporary Society
The World of Nature
The World of Man

Religious and Philosophical Trends
Contemporary Trends in the Arts
Technology and Culture

CHAPTER 15   UNITY AND DISUNITY, 1949–1960   400
A World Divided, or a World United?
The Role of the United Nations
Regional Efforts to Establish Political and Military Order
Plans for Economic Integration
Disarmament and the Problem of Atomic Weapons
Tensions Between Eastern and Western Europe

EPILOGUE: NEW PERSPECTIVES IN WESTERN HISTORY   422
               BIBLIOGRAPHY   439
               INDEX   461

LIST OF ILLUSTRATIONS

American and Canadian Troops Behind a British Tank   26
Lenin Speaking at Petrograd in 1917   46
The Big Four at Versailles   69
The General Strike of 1926   104
Foreign Investment in Saudi Arabia   126
Inflation, German Style   151
Children of the She-Wolf   174
"Guernica"   187
Hitler Making a Speech   196
Moscow University   219
Signatories of the Munich Agreement, 1938   246
The Yalta Conference, February, 1945   298
Government in the Soviet Union   329
The New Africa at the United Nations   373
UNESCO Headquarters in Paris   380
Franco-German Reconciliation   403

LIST OF MAPS

Europe in 1914	16–17
The First World War	30–31
The European Peace Settlement, 1919–1921	74
The European Alliance System, 1919–1927	88
The Middle East After the First World War	125
Territorial Changes in Europe, 1935–1939	235
Hitler's Domination of Europe, 1933–1945	250–251
World War II in Europe: Blitzkrieg in the West, May–June, 1940	263
The Liberation of North Africa, 1942–1943	276–277
The Liberation of Western Europe, 1943–1945	280
The War in Eastern Europe, 1941–1945	282–283
The Second World War in Asia	288
Treaties of 1947 with Italy, Finland, Hungary, Rumania and Bulgaria	301
Postwar Arrangements for Germany and Poland	303
Postwar Europe Divided	320
The Soviet Union: Economic Resources	326–327
Expansion of the Soviet Union to the West since 1940	335
Disposition of the Former Japanese Empire, 1951	356
Southeast Asia, 1963	362–363
Mutual Assistance Agreements and Regional Alliances, 1960	412–413
European Economic Rival Blocs	416
Growth of Independence in Tropical Africa	428
Middle East Oil Production, 1958	431

P A R T   I

THE DOMINANCE

OF WAR

1 9 1 4 – 1 9 4 5

"Our nineteenth century science taught us

how to mobilize the forces of nature,

but it did not strengthen our social conscience correspondingly,

and the result is that all these forces have been collected

into a horrible engine of destruction

which moves . . . like some blind destiny

treading over our civilization."

GENERAL JAN CHRISTIAAN SMUTS, MAY 14, 1917

Prologue: Unresolved Conflicts

On the idle hill of summer,
  Sleepy with the flow of streams,
Far I hear the steady drummer
  Drumming like a noise in dreams.

Far and near and low and louder
  On the roads of earth go by,
Dear to friend and food for powder,
  Soldiers marching, all to die.

From A. E. Housman,
A Shropshire Lad (1896)

The span of time with which this volume deals was introduced by the most devastating war Europe had ever known. This conflict brought the nineteenth century to a close and ushered in our troubled era. Dominated by a second world war the period ends with man in possession of new weapons of appalling destructiveness, still uncertain whether the control of war is humanly possible. Since the First World War is our starting point, we should begin with some brief examination of its causes.[1]

The explosion of 1914 must be associated logically with the assumption made by the leaders of all great states that war is the *ultima ratio*—the last resort when vital interests which cannot be safeguarded in any other way are at stake. Every one of the six major European powers had some reason to be concerned about threats to the status quo which would menace its security. Russia and Austria were rivals in the Balkans; France and Britain suspected hostile aims in the Middle East; France, moreover, was deeply outraged at the German treatment of Alsace and Lorraine; and Italy was furious when France moved

1. A fuller treatment is given in the authors' *Europe: 1815–1914,* ch. 17.

into Tunisia before she herself could act. German railway building in the Ottoman Empire and her training of its modern army aroused deep suspicion on the part of both France and Britain, to say nothing of Russia.

Closely related to these conflicting national attitudes was the growth of an elaborate network of alliances. The first and most basic of such arrangements was the Dual Alliance of 1879, by which Austria-Hungary and Germany each promised to support the other if attacked by Russia. It remained in effect until 1918. Italy joined these two in a Triple Alliance in 1882 by agreeing to give aid if Germany were attacked by France, while Austria and Germany gave a corresponding promise to Italy. Bismarck's efforts to retain a link with Russia, first through the Three Emperors' League of 1881 and later through the Reinsurance Treaty of 1887, in the end proved unavailing. In 1890, just three months after Bismarck's dismissal, the young Emperor William II brought such arrangements to a close.

The elements of a countersystem emerged in 1894, when France completed four years of negotiation with Russia by signing a military pact stipulating full Russian military support to France if she were attacked by Germany. If Russia were attacked by Germany, either alone or in combination with Austria, France would come similarly to her help. Though Great Britain would establish no such close European links, she did in 1902 undertake an alliance with Japan recognizing the independence of China and Japan's special interests in Korea. The treaty provided under certain circumstances for joint support in the case of war in the Far East.

Britain's European commitments took shape in the last decade of peace. The Entente Cordiale of 1904 with France was not an alliance in any formal sense, but primarily a French recognition of the British occupation of Egypt in return for Britain recognizing France's special interests in Morocco. Similarly, the Anglo-Russian Entente of 1907 recognized separate spheres of interest for Russia and Britain in Persia. Yet in each case there were subsequent military or naval "conversations" between the signatories—very elaborate in the case of France and England—relating to the hypothetical disposition of armed forces in the event of war. Thus, on the eve of 1914, a Triple Alliance of Germany, Austria-Hungary, and Italy faced a Triple Entente of France, Britain, and Russia. Italy, to be sure, had become a most uncertain member of the Triple Alliance. She had taken some steps toward reducing her grievances with France and at the same time she had aspirations to gain those parts of "unredeemed Italy" still in Austrian hands.

Ever enlarging preparations for war also marked this age. All Continental countries employed conscription, by means of which the major powers could within a few days of general mobilization add millions of trained reservists to their standing armies. France in 1913 authorized a three-year period of service with practically no exemptions. Though her population was much smaller than Germany's, in 1914 she put under arms about four million men—only a million less than did Germany. Railways on the Continent were built with strategic objectives in mind. The general staffs, knowing their probable enemies, made enormously complex plans. The most famous of these, Germany's Schlieffen Plan, was based on the assumption of a two-front war with Russia and France. Hence, a lightning move of huge infantry masses through Belgium would bypass the French fixed defenses located further south and deliver the knockout blow within a few weeks. Then the German forces could turn east to deal with what inevitably would be the much slower mobilization of Russia.

Britain's military conversations with France were predicated on sending a moderate-sized British Expeditionary Force across the Channel to take up positions beside the French armies. Nevertheless, there was no explicit commitment to act. Britain's chief reliance for her own defense, as always, was upon her navy, for which her imperial interests were held to require a strength equal to that of any two potential enemies. When the Reichstag, conscious of Germany's new colonial aspirations, passed its first navy law in 1898 authorizing the construction of a bigger fleet, a determined Anglo-German naval rivalry began to take shape. It was marked most dramatically by Britain's launching of the *Dreadnought* in 1906, the first battleship to be equipped entirely with heavy guns. By 1914 Britain had twenty-nine similar ships afloat and thirteen more under construction, while Germany had eighteen battleships in operation and nine more in the shipyards. The challenge to Britain was obvious.

Such competitive armament programs were accompanied by vigorous appeals to patriotism and national interest. It can hardly be doubted that imperial rivalries contributed to national self-glorification and to the growth of armaments, as well as to other forms of economic rivalry. Yet imperialism as a precipitant of the war can perhaps be overstressed. War came in 1914 as the result of a European crisis, and as a sequel to other crises more or less in the same region. It was fought preponderantly upon European battlefields and, unlike the Second World War, only incidentally in non-European areas.

Nationality problems, more than imperialism, helped to augment European tensions. This was particularly true of the Balkans. Yet when we speak of the ambitions of the nation-states and the impact of these nationality problems, we mean much more than inflamed words, demonstrations in the streets, or conspirators secretly plotting assassinations. We mean also the considered policies of statesmen who in defense of the national interest would be prepared to use large-scale force. Austrian ministers were prepared to use force when they contemplated punitive action against Serbia in 1914, as were some Russian leaders at the time of the Bosnian crisis of 1908.

The assassination of the heir to the Austro-Hungarian throne at Sarajevo, the capital of Bosnia, on June 28, 1914, set off what amounted to a chain re-action. This was the last of a series, any one of which might conceivably have caused an explosion. The First Morocco Crisis of 1905 had come about when the French maneuvered to secure a protectorate over that country. Eventually the storm blew over. It was soon followed, however, by the crisis of 1908, when Austria proclaimed the annexation of Bosnia and Herzegovina. Though out-raged Russian leaders made clear their warm sympathy for Serbia, Russia's unpreparedness caused her in the end to acquiesce.

Once again, in 1911, when the French tried to set up a protectorate in Morocco, the Germans moved menacingly, sending a gunboat, the *Panther,* to Agadir. War was averted when in November Germany conceded France a free hand in Morocco in return for being granted part of the French Congo. Still one more crisis came with the Balkan Wars of 1912 and 1913, when the great powers were deeply concerned about the attack on Turkey by Bulgaria, Serbia, and Greece. Though negotiations in London ended the First Balkan War, they could not prevent the outbreak of a second, when Bulgaria was defeated by her former allies, assisted by the Rumanians and the Turks. These recurrent crises in every case threatened, or seemed to threaten, the vital interests of great states.

When the Archduke Franz Ferdinand and his wife were killed at Sarajevo by the bullets of a young Bosnian-Serb nationalist, a critical situation arose which no amount of maneuvering was able to dispel. Impetuous promises of support, quickly given to Austria by the Kaiser and the German chancellor, though later qualified by exhortations to caution, were followed within a month by a most drastic Austrian ultimatum to Serbia containing a forty-eight-hour time limit. Since Serbia did not accept all its terms, Austria on July 28 declared war on her. This was the decisive act from which all else followed. The Russians declared general mobilization on July 30, the easily influenced Nicholas II having previously issued and then recalled the fateful order a day earlier.

Germany declared war on Russia on August 1. Two days later she de-clared war on France, simultaneously launching her invasion of neutral Bel-gium, as required by the Schlieffen Plan though forbidden by the treaty of 1839 that was still valid. Belgium chose to resist. Great Britain, who had sought the role of mediator and had been unable to give any firm commitment to France, regarded the invasion of Belgium as a threat to her vital interests as well as an outrage to her sense of moral responsibility. Since Germany disre-garded a British demand that she withdraw from Belgium, at midnight on August 4 Britain declared war. In the space of a single week the five major European powers, along with Serbia and Belgium, were committed to what turned out to be four years of deadly conflict. Italy for reasons of "sacred egoism" entered the war in 1915 on the Franco-British side. The conflict clearly was no chance event, no tragic accident that the wit of man somehow ought to have been able to avoid. Forces deep at work in the nineteenth century had bequeathed to the twentieth this grim outcome.

An imaginary observer looking down upon the European world of the twentieth century in the manner of the Ironic Spirit in Thomas Hardy's *Dynasts* might be disposed to reduce what he saw to the following summary. First, he would see four years of enormously destructive war. Second, he would see two troubled decades of "peace," in which democracy after democracy was replaced by new forms of dictatorship, and in which the central landmark was a world economic crisis, beginning in 1929 and growing to staggering dimensions. Third, he would see erupting a second world war, more truly global than the first, more than a year longer in duration, and many times more terrifying in the destructive power of its new weapons. Fourth, he would witness a confused period of reconstruction and intermittent conflict, one of its outstanding features being the state of "Cold War" between the Soviet Union and the United States. He would note a dramatic transformation in the former colonial world and the beginnings of a population explosion of incalculable consequence.

The undeniable certainty in the contemporary world is that of tremendously accelerated change in almost every aspect of human affairs. Three points stand out with respect to such change. The first is that modern societies have demonstrated the capacity to generate and to accumulate reserves of *power* on a scale greater than ever before. Nuclear weapons now mean the existence of a power capable of destroying all life on this planet—a power almost impossible for the average person to imagine. Yet modern societies have not found the means either to abolish the wars that put this power into deadly operation, or to harness it safely for constructive ends. The second consideration is that change is proceeding so rapidly that men can easily fail to grasp the accelerated speed of the years. The third is that a remarkable shift has occurred in the centers of power. The leadership of western Europe in the old sense is gone. The United States and the Soviet Union constitute the world's two chief power centers, both with advanced forms of nuclear weapons and long-distance delivery systems. The peoples of Asia and Africa are assuming a role—or at all events claiming a position—in a way that would have been impossible fifty years ago. In terms of population, three of the five largest states in the world— China, India, and Indonesia—are to be found in Asia.

The political changes in the contemporary world have been striking. Though the nineteenth century dealt major blows to the vested rights of a traditional governing class, it did not truly establish the rule of democracy. After 1918, to be sure, absolute monarchy was a thing of the past. Elected parliamentary regimes, some of them still limited monarchies, were the rule. Yet soon there were other types: the slowly crystallizing dictatorship of the Communist Party in Russia; Mussolini's Italian Fascism; the dictatorships, more or less benign, in many parts of eastern Europe; and, finally, the hideous dictatorship of Hitler's Germany. The parliamentary states which maintained more effective continuity with their nineteenth-century antecedents—Great Britain, France, Belgium, the Netherlands, Switzerland, and the Scandinavian countries—all witnessed the rise of socialist or communist parties within them, some satisfied with a cautious rate of change, others eager to achieve the complete overthrow of capitalistic society.

The Second World War, which destroyed the dictatorships of Hitler and Mussolini, was not an overwhelming victory for democracy. It closed with the Communist Party still exercising an iron grip upon the people of Russia. Many states were drawn into the orbit of the Soviets. If one of the dubious outcomes of the First World War had been "the Balkanization of Europe," then surely the descent of the Iron Curtain, which not only split Europe but in addition divided one major nation, Germany, into two states, was a tragic outcome of the Second.

European economic life following the First World War also showed many changes, for a striking shift occurred in the relative importance of certain countries. Britain's former unquestioned leadership as the world's banker and the workshop of the world was gone. France had suffered a grave blow in the loss of young manpower and the serious damage to some of her most important economic regions in the northeast. Postwar Italy was so weak economically that she contributed by this fact alone to the triumph of Mussolini. In Russia the famine of 1921–1922 was greatly aggravated by the economic collapse which had preceded it. Even so, Russia's recovery was in the end to be spectacular. Germany, exhausted by the burden of the war and then subject to a devastating inflation, soon showed a greater resilience than either Britain or France.

Before 1914 half of the world's trade had consisted of the imports and exports of seven European countries: Great Britain, Germany, France, Belgium, the Netherlands, Switzerland, and Denmark. In the interwar decades the new role of the United States, Japan, and eventually the Soviet Union made this no longer true. Moreover, as the European dictatorships assumed larger importance, their success seemed to show that the old rules of economics had been superseded. Neomercantilism—a conscious state control of economic life— began to assert itself, to some degree in the western European countries but most dramatically in Russia. Here state ownership and operation of all means of production and distribution was a Communist specific. To expand production Josef Stalin announced in October, 1928, the beginning of his first Five-

Year Plan, quickly followed by another, and then by still another. Mussolini's Italy and Hitler's Germany adopted a somewhat similar pattern of state control. In Germany, perhaps more than in Italy, such programs were linked with the deliberate assumption that someday the outcome must be war. This meant, therefore, that the German economy became a *Wehrwirtschaft,* an economy whose overriding purpose was to see that the country was ready in all respects for the supreme test of battle.

The concept of the welfare state grew in importance during the twentieth century. Inherent in it was the responsibility of the national government to oversee and guarantee, if not actually to provide for, the well-being of all its citizens, in a phrase made famous in Great Britain, "from the cradle to the grave." No state, it is clear, attained such final goals; many made demonstrable progress toward them. In every case, the drive for improved living standards and the emphasis upon public welfare continued.

Many new problems arose concerning the relations between states. The two great wars which form the chief landmarks in our period involved the entire resources, human and material, of the participants. In a shattering repudiation of the nineteenth-century efforts to establish peaceful procedures for handling international disputes, such wars set up force as the supreme arbiter. The consequence was that the League of Nations established in 1919 ultimately met disaster, and even the United Nations of 1945, the creation of a much more sophisticated generation, has aroused considerable doubts as to its genuine efficacy. If this indeed is to be described as "The Era of Violence,"[2] the justification for such a phrase comes in large degree from the way in which issues arising between states actually had been handled.

The period abounds in contrasts. On the one hand it witnessed many praiseworthy attempts to reduce, and someday end, the necessity for war. Various efforts were made at disarmament, the one real success—and that only for a few years—being the Washington Treaty of 1922. The Locarno Treaties of 1925 were the outstanding example of the effort to remove a historic source of conflict by guaranteeing the Franco-German frontier. The 1928 Pact of Paris tried to mobilize the moral sentiment of the world with a solemn pledge to renounce aggressive war. Attempts to strengthen the League Covenant by getting nations to agree in advance that certain types of dispute would automatically be subject to arbitration had, unhappily, little practical success.

The efforts to guarantee peace by alliance fall into a different and more dubious category. After the First World War France secured treaties of mutual assistance with Belgium, Poland, Czechoslovakia, Rumania, Yugoslavia, and

---

2. Such is the title given to the concluding volume of *The New Cambridge Modern History,* covering the years between 1898 and 1945.

ultimately Russia, hoping by such means to guarantee the security which she most emphatically did not see in the League of Nations. Poland aligned herself with Czechoslovakia, Rumania, and Yugoslavia. Hitler and Mussolini formed in 1936 the Rome-Berlin Axis. And in the least pacific classification of all, surely, must be put the Russo-German Pact of Non-Aggression, signed on the very eve of the Second World War for no other purpose than to facilitate schemes of aggression against other powers pending the final clash between themselves. If after 1945 doubts existed as to the efficacy of the United Nations, the older method of close military alliance still remained. The North Atlantic Treaty Organization was a response to the political insecurity of the post-1945 period. Yet it occasioned a rival defense organization, the Warsaw Pact established in 1956 by the Soviet Union and its satellite countries. All this was to some observers too reminiscent of the rival alliances in the pre-1914 years to be accepted as any sure guarantee of peace.

Though clear-cut generalizations as to the new pattern of relations between states are difficult, a few may be ventured. One such generalization points to the political decline of Europe. The world leadership which the Continent had exercised in the nineteenth century began to falter during the First World War and collapsed during the Second. No western European power in 1945 could match the military power or the economic resources of the United States or the Soviet Union, and this latter can be described as being in Europe but not of it. If China seemed destined someday to play a comparable role in the Far East, she could only be described in these years as a sleeping giant.

One hopeful sign in international affairs was the reduction of national differences because of the pressure of economic forces. The association of Belgium, the Netherlands, and Luxembourg—"Benelux"—for their own economic advantage was soon followed by other combinations: the European Coal and Steel Community (1951); Euratom, or the association of states for the peaceful use of atomic energy (1957); and the Common Market organized by France, West Germany, Italy, and the Benelux countries in 1957. Here were examples of economic necessity counteracting some of the traditional rivalries of political life.

The change in the relationships between the European powers and what was once loosely known as "the colonial world" will almost certainly count in the long run as the most significant feature of the twentieth century. During the 1880's and the 1890's imperialism had thrived as never before. Yet imperial policy in general meant that in many areas the European powers were content to impose "colonial rule" and, as in the case of France, to hold out to only a small native élite the opportunity to acquire the language, the education, and the culture of their imperial masters. The First World War proved to be a remarkable solvent of such policies. The cry of national self-determination, sounding so clearly in Europe, had its echoes in Asia and to a lesser degree in Africa. The Second World War led to the almost complete liquidation of colonial empires. This remarkable process took place chiefly in the fifteen years from 1945 to 1960. Britain made the transition with the least friction. The French, who sought by various schemes to create a "French Union" and then a "French Community" in which native peoples would be independent yet "members of the Community," were more reluctant.

The above are little more than illustrations of a vast tide that swept the peoples of Asia and Africa toward a new freedom. One way to demonstrate the remarkable alteration that has come about is to observe the changing membership roll of the United Nations. Of the original 50 members, 4 were African (counting Egypt among them) and 9 were Asian—together about one-quarter of the total. At the end of 1964, out of a list of 115 members, 35 states were African and 26 states were Asiatic, together making over one-half of the complete membership. Only the merest vestiges of Europe's former colonial possessions remained. Nevertheless, the ominous shadows of a new Russian imperialism and of an even newer Red Chinese imperialism had emerged.

The total effect of scientific advances in the last fifty years must be regarded as monumental. This remains true even though it would be difficult to single out any scientific work of the same epochal character as Newton's *Principia* of 1687, Darwin's *Origin of Species* in 1859, or Einstein's paper, "The Special Theory of Relativity," published in 1905. The steady investigation of atomic structure which was to lead eventually to the splitting of the atom meant the development of atomic power for military purposes on an almost unbelievable scale. This power could also be used for peaceful purposes. Though grasped only with difficulty by the layman, biology has seen enormous advances. What kind of future, one could ask, lies in store for a society that would be able consciously to plan, determine, and direct the process of its own physical evolution?

Technological advance has given our own age its unique significance. Only two generations separate the present from a world that knew little, if anything, of the automobile and the airplane, that had not yet brought the telephone and electric light into common use, or enjoyed the experiences of moving pictures, radio, and television. Only within two generations have new drugs such as cortisone, insulin, and the antibiotics won their astonishing victories over disease. Chemical advances in other fields, notably in the development of new fabrics and new construction materials and in agriculture, revolutionize other aspects of modern life. All of this means continuing advances for many parts of the globe in population, longevity, health, wealth, and literacy.

Certainly this twentieth century has eagerly investigated—perhaps as never before—the problems of man in society. The present generation has carried on the work begun as the century opened. It has pursued Freud's psychoanalytical studies, the philosophic questioning of Nietzsche and Bergson, and the quest for modernism and ecumenicism in religion. Experimentalism and revolt in literature, music, painting, sculpture, and architecture have continued to be the marks of our own age, encouraged no doubt by the political and economic upheavals of a war-torn world. The modern rebuilding of England's Coventry Cathedral and of the Dutch Rotterdam, or the erection of the Hansa Quarter in West Berlin, have been an outcome of war's destruction.

This truly has been an age of conflict. Yet one of the paradoxes of our world today is the rich creativity of the human spirit and the dedication of millions to the service and enlightenment of their fellows at a time when political and social conflict has rarely been more intense.

Chapter 1

The First World War

The Long Four Years
1914: The First Onslaught
1915: Stalemate Established
1916: Stalemate Unbroken
1917–1918: Germany in the Ascendant
1918, July-November: The Collapse of the Central Powers
Europe at the Termination of Hostilities

■ THE LONG FOUR YEARS

One of the most startling features of the First World War was its long duration. Since the time of the great conflicts with Napoleonic France, only the American Civil War of 1861–1865 came within a few months of equaling it. In August, 1914, the British secretary of state for war, Lord Kitchener, who had fought two three-year campaigns in Africa, was virtually alone in forecasting a struggle of similar length in Europe. The general expectation was that it would be over in six months. That length of time had sufficed to bring about the capitulation of France to Germany in the war of 1870–1871, and the campaigns in Europe in 1859, 1864, and 1866 had been still shorter; even the Crimean War of 1854–1856 had involved only a single twelve-month period of continuous fighting. Moreover, it was confidently supposed in 1914 that the economic strain of war fought by mass armies with elaborate and highly de-

SIGNIFICANT EVENTS

1914   German victory over Russians at Tannenberg (August)
Schlieffen Plan foiled at the Marne (September)
Turkey joined Central Powers (November)

1915   First Gallipoli landings (April)
Italy joined Allies (May)
Germans captured Warsaw (August)

1916   German attack on Verdun (February–July)
Battle of Jutland (May)
Successful Russian offensive against Austria–Hungary (June–
September)
British attack on the Somme (July–October)

1917   Unrestricted German submarine warfare begun (February)
Russian revolutions (March, November)
United States declared war on Germany (April)
Failure of French offensive under Nivelle (April)
Italians defeated at Caporetto (October)
Armistice between Central Powers and Russia (December)

1918   Five German attacks on western front (March–July)
Commencement of main Allied counteroffensive under Foch
(August)
Armistice with Germany (November)

structible material would quickly drive the weaker side into bankruptcy, to say nothing of the possibility of a moral collapse in a population exposed to food scarcity and other shortages. Both sides therefore initiated an offensive strategy designed to produce quick results. The German attack on France, unlike the initial Russian and French offensives, came very near to success. When it failed the German high command, no less than the comparatively amateur strategists of other countries, was taken by surprise and had to resort to improvisations.

The long duration of the war was most significant also because it intensified the disastrous aftereffects. These will be examined in the study of the postwar era. Here we note in passing that Europe, especially western Europe, lacked the boundless natural resources, the intake of new population, and the psychological resilience which had enabled the United States two generations earlier to recover so rapidly from the ravages of her four years of civil war. The

Dates show subsequent entrance of
European powers into the war.
Among non-European powers
Japan declared war on Germany on
August 23, 1914, and the United
States on April 6, 1917. China broke
off diplomatic relations with
Germany in March, 1917, and sent
labor forces to Europe.

losses resulting from the prolongation of the war were felt all the more acutely later because of the high morale with which both sides had carried on the conflict. No feature of the war is more impressive than the powers of endurance shown by the German people, on the home front as well as on the battlefield, living year after year under siege conditions and shouldering the main burden for each of Germany's allies. On the other side, what could be more remarkable than the support which the United Kingdom war effort received from Canada and Australasia, whose inhabitants could never have been constrained to fight if they had not freely chosen to come to the help of the mother country? Indeed, every one of the combatant powers was served with devotion by large numbers of men and women who, though they might not have used that term, believed

16

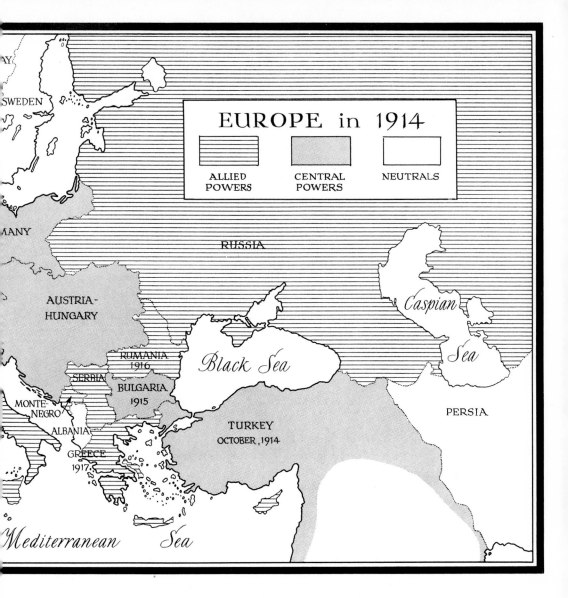

EUROPE in 1914

ALLIED POWERS   CENTRAL POWERS   NEUTRALS

SWEDEN

RUSSIA

AUSTRIA-HUNGARY

Caspian

Sea

RUMANIA 1916

SERBIA

BULGARIA 1915

Black Sea

MONTE-NEGRO

ALBANIA

PERSIA

TURKEY
OCTOBER, 1914

GREECE 1917

Mediterranean   Sea

implicitly in the righteousness of their cause. Time tarnished the ideals, and when the long-postponed end came, the victors suffered a disillusionment only less disheartening than the fate of the vanquished.

The diplomatic developments of forty years had divided Europe into two camps, fairly evenly matched in military and economic resources. Therefore, once the Germans had failed in their carefully planned design to knock the French out before the slow-moving Russians could bring their strength to bear, the issue had to be decided either by a long and costly process of attrition or by the introduction of a new weight into the balance. Since the high command on both sides was inflexible and unadaptable, little serious attempt was made either to shift the center of the struggle to new theaters by turning the European war into a world-wide war or to force a decision by means of new developments in military technology. Instead, the years 1915, 1916, and 1917 were mainly years of mere attrition. In the air, indeed, progress was fairly rapid from the primitive biplanes which reconnoitered ahead of the armies in the early days to the faster and more maneuverable aircraft, equipped with machine guns and small bombs, or elaborate photographic apparatus, which by 1916 operated far behind the enemy lines. The winter of 1918–1919 would have seen the first large-scale bombing of industrial objectives. But in ground warfare, while the trench line condemned the cavalry arm to obsolescence, nothing more original than howitzers and field guns of existing types (though used in unprecedented quantities) was available to open the way for infantry advancing with rifle, bayonet, and hand grenade. The defense in its turn relied heavily upon machine guns, which in 1914, however, were available only in small quantities even to the principal armies, and on barbed wire.

While each side struggled furiously to maximize its output of such well-proven armaments, the introduction of new weapons—poison gas by the Germans, the tank by the British—was allowed to take place piecemeal and almost casually, with correspondingly meager results. A model tank was under construction by March, 1915, thanks to the enterprise of Winston Churchill; forty-nine were mustered for action in September, 1916, of which fifteen rendered service in the field. Yet not until fourteen long months later were tanks first used in formations and in adequate numbers at Cambrai, where they scored a resounding success. Even key inventions for combating the submarine menace, such as the hydrophone and the depth charge, were manufactured belatedly in 1917 to meet a need which had been apparent two years before.

Accordingly, in default of decisive advantages in the technological field, the military balance between the opposing sides continued until it was upset eventually by the revolutions occurring in the sphere of politics. In March, 1917, a series of cataclysms began in Russia, a by-product of which was a relaxation of military pressure, a flood of desertions, then an armistice, and finally a treaty of peace on the eastern front. This meant that for the campaign of 1918 the Germans would be able to concentrate their full military strength against France and Britain, who had so far withstood with difficulty only half of it. But by a strange fatality of judgment, in February, 1917, the Germans had embarked upon the policy of unrestricted submarine warfare which had the predictable result of bringing the enormous new resources of an outraged America to the service of the flagging alliance. This was the second revolution, the outcome of which was that the Germans lost the race against time by a narrow margin and then collapsed quickly, though not as quickly as the rest of the Central Powers whom German fortitude had so long sustained. Thus the

war of 1914–1918 was like a three-act play with a dramatic start and a powerful denouement, separated by a second act of inordinate length which, as we
shall see, weighed with tragic heaviness on all the players.

■ 1914: THE FIRST ONSLAUGHT

The short war, which the peoples of Europe in August, 1914, believed
themselves to be engaged upon, was remarkably popular. Antiwar influences,
whether of stock-exchange investors or international socialists or Christian and
other humanitarian idealists, seemed to vanish overnight. In each of the main
countries concerned, the cause for which men were required to fight made a
strong emotional appeal; the actions of opponents appeared to have made war
inevitable; and although there were no clearly defined war aims, there was a
general expectation that victory—victory soon and certain—would mean both
the redress of old grievances, new national gains and opportunities, and the
establishment of a vaguely better Europe. The mobilization for which all the
general staffs had prepared with infinite care was carried through in every case
without any serious breakdown. The French, for example, who had mobilized
with such difficulty in 1870, this time contrived to move 3,781,000 men forward
in seven thousand trains within sixteen days.

The high speed of mobilization was related to an almost mystical belief in
the virtue of taking the offensive. This view had been preached especially by
the younger generation of French generals but was the accepted doctrine at this
time of all the European general staffs. The fire-eating Austrian chief of staff,
Conrad von Hötzendorf, launched a very early attack to chastise the Serbians;
before Christmas the Austrians retired across the Danube, having lost more
than half the troops engaged. Meanwhile, their main force collided with the
Russians on the frontier between Austrian and Russian Poland, adopted an
aggressive strategy which was beyond its strength, and by early October had
been driven completely out of eastern Galicia. The result was a permanent
lowering of morale among the subject nationalities who formed more than half
the numerical strength of the armies of the Dual Monarchy.

Even more disastrous was the great offensive which the French commander in chief, Joseph Joffre,[1] had resolved to launch against the Germans in
Lorraine on either side of the fortress of Metz, "whatever the circumstances." [2]
The circumstances proved to be a great German superiority in the number of
howitzers, in the use made of machine guns and barbed-wire defenses, and in

1. 1852–1931. Designated commander in chief in 1911, he was the author of the disastrous Plan 17,
but his imperturbability made possible the great French recovery at the Marne. His popularity diminished with the unsuccessful offensives of 1915, and it was claimed that he had neglected the defenses of Verdun. Though superseded in December, 1916, he became the first marshal of France to
be appointed under the Third Republic.
2. Such was the stipulation in the French official *Plan 17: Directions for the Concentration.*

their general preparedness. The French object was to paralyze any German advance elsewhere by dislocating their rearward communications on the left bank of the Rhine; the result was a defeat which cost France 300,000 men—a quarter of all the troops engaged—and left her permanently weakened, with a memory of unavailing heroism.

The German Schlieffen Plan was the only one of these projects for seizing the initiative which came near to complete success. Essentially, it consisted of an enveloping and wheeling movement by the right wing of the German armies ranged against the French. Reaching the region of Paris at high speed and in great strength, it was intended to drive the French left wing and center eastward, so that in the last stage of a six-week operation the French would be caught in a pincer movement with the help of the much weaker German left wing advancing from Lorraine. The result would be a second, and much greater, Sedan. Throughout August, 1914, the fate of Europe hung upon the execution of this great design. A slight delay was caused by the resistance of the Belgian fortresses of Liège and Namur, which had to be reduced by heavy siege howitzers. A force also had to be detached to protect the German flank against the risk of a sortie by the Belgian field army, which had fallen back on Antwerp. A second delaying factor was the arrival of the British Expeditionary Force on the left flank of the French. By Continental standards their numbers were unimpressive—about seventy thousand at the outset, equivalent to half the French losses in the first four days' fighting—but they were a highly trained professional force who fought stubborn delaying actions at Mons on August 23 and a little farther back at Le Cateau. They were taking part in a retreat, however, in conformity with the movements of the much-harassed French armies, which on this flank were outnumbered by the Germans two to one. The British commander, a former cavalry officer named Sir John French, judged the situation to be so desperate that at the end of the first week he would have withdrawn his troops from the line to re-form, thereby endangering the whole fate of the alliance, if he had not received counterorders from Kitchener in person.

The German chief of staff, nephew and namesake of the great Helmuth von Moltke, felt sufficiently sure of the situation to leave full discretion to his army commanders in the west while detaching two army corps from their resources as a reserve for the badly threatened eastern front. The German right flank, however, failed by a small margin to move sufficiently fast and sufficiently far. It passed in front of Paris instead of behind the city, as the Plan required, and failed to outflank the French. Helped by the garrison of Paris, the Allies rallied, took the exposed right wing of the Germans in the rear, and fought their way into a gap which opened between two German armies at the crossing of the Marne. Moltke, through an officer dispatched from his headquarters far in the rear at Luxembourg, authorized the exposed right wing to retreat.

This thirty-mile retreat, beginning on September 9, proved to be a major turning point in the war. Moltke was replaced a few days later by Erich von Falkenhayn, the Prussian minister for war, who tried to revivify the Plan by a further effort to outflank the Allies towards the sea. The surrender of Antwerp put additional troops at his disposal, and these joined with an ardent body of volunteers in a vain attempt to break through the British forces at Ypres in early November. Thereafter the location of the trench line, at first hastily improvised and then elaborated season by season, did not until the spring of 1918 vary by more than a few miles.

Meanwhile, almost equally decisive events had taken place on the eastern front, where the Russians, possessed by the universal spirit of the offensive, had mobilized faster than expected and by August 20 had crossed the East Prussian frontier on both sides of the Masurian Lakes. To meet the emergency the sixty-seven-year-old General Paul von Hindenburg,[3] a veteran of Bismarck's wars, was brought from retirement; joining him as chief of staff was a brilliant young major general who had been the hero of the hour in the capture of Liège. This Erich Ludendorff,[4] using a plan already prepared by the head of the operations department, encircled his opponent in the south in a battle to which he gave the historic name of Tannenberg; 200,000 Russian prisoners were taken, and the opposing commander shot himself. The Germans then turned northward and routed the other Russian army beside the Masurian Lakes with a further loss of 125,000 men.

In contrast to these overwhelming defeats, the Russians, as has already been noticed, gave a much better account of themselves when matched against the polyglot forces of the Dual Monarchy, one-half of whom felt no interest in winning the war for their German-Austrian and Magyar masters. In early September the battle for Lemberg, the Galician capital, cost the Austrians at least as many casualties as Tannenberg had cost the Russians, who in any case had much greater reserves of manpower. In consequence of this diversion the German armies failed in two attempts on Warsaw, and not until February could they even complete the expulsion of the Russians from German soil in the bitterly fought "winter battle of Masuria." Accordingly, at the close of the

3. 1847–1934. An officer's son, he had served with distinction at Sadowa and assisted Schlieffen on the general staff. He supplied stability, a power of reflection, and moral force to the victorious partnership with Ludendorff, of which he was also the dignified popular figurehead. In 1915 and 1916 he commanded all German forces on the eastern front; from August, 1916, to the end of the war as chief of the general staff he was responsible for all military, and many political, decisions. He emerged from retirement in 1925 to become president of the Republic in the conservative interest.

4. 1865–1937. He had seventeen years of general-staff experience before the war, but made his name in action when he stormed Liège at the head of an infantry brigade whose general had been killed. A soldier of genius, tireless and resourceful, he served through the war as Hindenburg's quartermaster general (chief of staff), the intellectual driving force behind their common strategy. On September 29, 1918, he demanded that the government undertake immediate armistice negotiations, and was removed from his post a fortnight later, becoming a reactionary politician under the Republic and an early associate of Hitler.

year Falkenhayn reluctantly decided to give first priority in 1915 to the eastern front.

Although the German armies, when spring came, were firmly established on enemy territory on both fronts, the Central Powers were nevertheless placed under siege conditions which, if maintained long enough, must prove fatal to their cause. In early November they had been joined by Turkey, who had signed a secret alliance with Germany three months before, and had finally been induced to commence hostilities against Russia as a result of the presence in Turkish waters of two German warships which had eluded the British Mediterranean fleet in the first days of the war. Though the Turkish decision did nothing to open world trade to Germany and Austria-Hungary, it did make Russia's supply position in some respects more precarious than their own. Now Russia was shut off from contact with the industrial resources of her allies by the closing of the Black Sea route as well as that through the Baltic. The oceans, however, were all under Allied control, in the sense that no ship could reach any European port except by leave of the British and French navies, which had successfully established their blockade immediately on the outbreak of war. A number of British fighting ships were lost through mines, submarines, and hit-and-run raids. Two British cruisers were sunk at Coronel, off the west coast of South America, when they met the German Pacific Squadron, which in turn was annihilated soon after by another British force at the Falkland Islands. The one serious loophole in the Allied blockade was that caused by neutral traders. Only by the widest interpretation of the term "contraband" was it possible to starve Germany of imports from America; only by the most rigorous blacklisting of pro-German firms was it possible to stem the flow of Dutch and Scandinavian importations destined for unacknowledged German consumers.

All this pressure took time to organize, but in some other respects the fact that the Central Powers were under siege was at once obvious. Britain and her allies bought freely in all the world markets. They carried their forces unhindered over the seas: the 33,000 Canadians who landed in England early in October were the largest military unit that had ever crossed the Atlantic. Conversely, the position of German colonial possessions was hopeless. The North Pacific Islands and Kiaochow fell to the Japanese, who had entered the war in 1914 in pursuit of their Pacific interests; the rest, apart from a brilliantly fought struggle in Tanganyika, quickly fell to the forces of the British Empire.

■ 1915: STALEMATE ESTABLISHED

Throughout 1915 and 1916 the basic feature of the war was the continuous unrelenting siege of the Central Powers by the Allies and its disappointing results. The situation was not much affected by the adherence of Italy to the

Allies in May, 1915, as a result of the secret Treaty of London of the previous month which promised Italy substantial acquisitions at the expense of Austria and Turkey. The Italian armies, fighting to gain some of the coveted Austrian territory beyond their northeastern frontier, battered in vain against the mountainous defenses of the Isonzo River line, barring the way to Trieste.

The entry of the remaining Balkan states into the war likewise made relatively little difference. Toward the end of 1915 the Bulgarians joined the Central Powers in order to have their revenge on Serbia, which was caught between two fires and duly overrun, together with its ally, Montenegro. One consequence was the landing of an Allied force at Salonika to help the Serbs, who had treaty relations with the Greeks. This force, however, remained immobile, while Greece preserved a status of quasi-neutrality under King Constantine, a brother-in-law of the German emperor. Rumania, like Italy, deserted her former allies, Germany and Austria-Hungary, in the hope of large gains of Austrian territory. Her foolish mistake was to wait until the autumn of 1916 to do so, with the result that three-quarters of the country, including the chief grain-growing areas and the oil fields, were overrun before the end of the year.

The German efforts in the west during 1915 were limited in scope as a result of the decision to relieve Austria-Hungary, whose military value German officers were by now assessing in a mordant phrase, "We're shackled to a corpse." Though standing chiefly on the defensive in the west, Falkenhayn, the commander in chief, launched a second attack in April against the British in the Ypres salient with the help of cloud-gas emitted from cylinders—a device which was not specifically banned by the Hague Convention of 1899 against the use of asphyxiating-gas shells. Ypres was held, nevertheless, and in the later months of the year both the French and the British, whose armies had now expanded to about one-third the size of the French, passed to the offensive. Their attacks failed to gain more than three miles at any point, and in every important case the attackers seem to have lost more lives than the defenders. The British suffered from a serious lack of artillery and an inadequate commander in chief; the former weakness was remedied by an intenser industrial effort, the latter only in part through the replacement of Sir John French at the end of the year by Sir Douglas Haig[5]. But even with adequate artillery preparation the range prevented effective demolition of the veritable maze of defenses which the industrious Germans proved adept at preparing.

5. 1861–1928. A Scottish cavalry officer who had played a large part in carrying out Haldane's army reforms and had married a lady of Edward VII's court. A much more intelligent and purposeful commander than French, under whom he had served, he was taciturn and seemingly insensitive and was distrusted by Lloyd George, especially after the huge losses incurred in 1917. In August, 1918, however, he was the first leader to see the possibility of finishing the war that autumn, and his leadership of the British forces in the last phase was highly successful.

Their troops were the first to dig several lines of support trenches, protected by huge barbed-wire entanglements and carefully sited machine gun posts, with deep dugouts to shelter troops not required to man the parapets. Moreover, the artillery preparation advertised the intention to attack, enabling the enemy to bring up his reserves.

The eastern front was too large for any continuous defense line to be established. There the Central Powers enjoyed a spectacular triumph under Falkenhayn's personal supervision. During May they broke through the Russians, who were already short of arms and munitions, in the Galician territory which the latter had overrun in the previous campaign. Some ground had already been gained by Hindenburg, who was advancing into the huge salient of Russian Poland from its northern extremity. Warsaw fell in August, and by the end of 1915 the eastern front ran due south in a straight line from Riga.

A striking prospect which emerged in 1915 was that of opening new fronts in the Near East. Since Russia had almost unlimited men and territory, the disastrous Galician campaign of 1915 would have meant little if her allies had succeeded in their attempt to establish a supply route and a flank support by knocking Turkey out of the war. Furthermore, Churchill, Lloyd George, and other unorthodox strategists cherished the hope of launching a campaign through the Balkans against Austria-Hungary, so as to prepare the way for the final overthrow of the Central Powers by other means than costly frontal assaults in France. These "easterners," as they are sometimes called, were opposed by most professional soldiers, especially the French, on the ground that the Germans could never be decisively defeated except by breaching their main front, for which reserves must always be husbanded.

Such were the origins of the ill-fated Gallipoli campaign, which arose out of the attempt from February to March, 1915, to force a way through from the Aegean Sea to Constantinople by warships alone. Although the Turkish batteries at the Narrows were silenced, four capital ships struck an undiscovered minefield, causing a hasty decision to replace the naval venture by a landing to clear the path to Constantinople. A force, which included British regulars from India, the Australian and New Zealand Army Corps (the ANZACS), and two French divisions, had already been assembled in the Near East to follow in the wake of the navy. Instead, they were put ashore on beaches where the Turks under an able German commander had had due notice of their coming. Two main landings were made on the west side of the Gallipoli Peninsula, in April and in August. On neither occasion did the heroic efforts of the rank and file—the record of some senior officers does not merit the same tribute—succeed in conquering the ridge only a few miles inland, from which they had hoped to sweep down to the shore of the Dardanelles. At the end of the year a skillfully conducted operation brought the survivors away from the beaches without any final disaster. A total of 250,000 casualties had been incurred to no purpose, British prestige had suffered a severe blow, Russia remained isolated, and the lesson seemed to be that the issue of the war could be determined only by costly head-on attacks on the western front.

■ 1916: STALEMATE UNBROKEN

In 1916, accordingly, each side made a supreme effort to end the deadlock in the west. Falkenhayn, who realized the enormous difficulty of achieving a breakthrough, decided instead to wear France down by a series of attacks in an area which was too precious to be relinquished. The great fortress of Verdun was selected, because it was already half-encircled and therefore easier to attack than to defend, and because its historic importance gave it a symbolic value that would compel the French to risk almost any losses to save it. By the fifth day the Germans, with a three-to-one superiority of men at the point of attack, had pierced the outer French defenses and captured an armored fort which they justly termed "the north eastern pillar of the defenses of Verdun." Nevertheless, the French under General Philippe Pétain[6] contrived somehow to hold out; the second and last line of forts was still manned, though at tremendous cost, when the Crown Prince's army was forced to relax its pressure in July. A British historian who fought side by side with the French during the war makes an impressive comment:

> The amazing toughness and self-sacrifice of the French resistance before Verdun is perhaps the most wonderful of "toutes les gloires de la France," just because it ran so counter to the ordinary stream of national temperament.[7]

On July 1 the British had come to the rescue in the long-planned battle of the Somme, in Flanders, where 140,000 infantrymen, the volunteers who had responded to Kitchener's call to arms in 1914, were launched after incomplete artillery preparation against the all-too-complete German positions. Of this flower of British youth an unprecedented proportion—60 percent of the officers, 40 percent of other ranks—fell in a single day. Despite such appalling losses, Haig was encouraged by the French, who had successfully attacked simultaneously on a shorter front south of the British, to continue an operation which undoubtedly relieved the pressure on Verdun. By the end of September, with the help of the first small surprise attack from tanks, an advance averaging four miles had been achieved along a thirty-mile front. In August Falken-

6. 1856–1951. A military hero because of his defense of Verdun, he became in 1918 a marshal of France. In 1939 he was French ambassador to Spain, being recalled to Paris as vice-premier during the crisis of June, 1940. He quickly succeeded Reynaud as premier, negotiating the armistice with Germany and subsequently becoming "chief of state" in the government at Vichy which accepted collaboration with Hitler as inescapable. He was taken to Germany in 1944, returning voluntarily a year later to stand trial for treason. At the age of 89 he was stripped of his honors and given a death sentence, commuted by General de Gaulle to life imprisonment.

7. C. R. M. F. CRUTTWELL, *A History of the Great War 1914–1918* (2nd ed., 1936), p. 254.

AMERICAN AND CANADIAN TROOPS BEHIND A BRITISH TANK. Used ineffectively and on a small scale in 1916, tanks, which were so designated originally to confuse the Germans, had become by 1918 a powerful weapon for exploiting a break in enemy defenses.

hayn was replaced by Hindenburg, and early in 1917 the Germans abandoned the very difficult position which had been left them at the end of the battle, deliberately withdrawing to the newly constructed Hindenburg Line some twenty-five miles farther back.

In the absence of any definite victory on the western front, the Allies longed for a spectacular success at sea. The pressure of the British naval blockade had been steadily sustained, while the first German attempt to reply by a submarine blockade, which involved the sinking of defenseless merchant vessels and even passenger liners without warning, was suspended towards the end of 1915 in face of mounting American hostility. Admiral Sir John Jellicoe's Grand Fleet, however, was Britain's supreme weapon, and nearly two years passed before the German High Seas Fleet could be brought within range of it.

The Battle of Jutland was fought in the afternoon and misty evening of the last day of May, 1916, when Jellicoe was able to deploy twenty-four dreadnoughts against sixteen of the enemy. The British suffered serious losses in the initial action between squadrons of battle cruisers, and achieved no decisive results in the gun duel of the great battleships, which they twice interrupted in order to evade the heavy risks of a torpedo attack. However, when night fell victory seemed to be within their grasp, because they had put themselves in superior strength between the enemy and their bases; but by bold maneuvering the Germans made good their escape in the darkness. All told, the British losses in men and tonnage at Jutland were twice as grave as the German. Unaware that it would take the British twelve months to re-equip with better shell—the battle had shown the existing pattern to be seriously ineffective at long range—the Germans were reluctant deliberately to provoke any sequel to an encounter from which they had been glad to escape under cover of night. Nevertheless, as late as April, 1918, they sallied in strength into the North Sea with a view to preying on the convoy passing between Britain and west Norway. Thus the British command of the sea had been tested but not decisively challenged.

Meanwhile the Russian armies in 1916 staged a remarkable recovery. When an appeal for Russia to create a diversion came both from the French at Verdun and from the Italians, who were being pressed back from the direction of the Trentino as well as Trieste, Nicholas authorized Alexei Brusilov, his one general of genius, to take the offensive in the region just north of the Rumanian border. By dispersing his reserves and foregoing any preliminary concentration of artillery, Brusilov made it impossible for the Austrians to know where his attacks were coming. The result was a deep Russian penetration of the front and the capture of nearly half a million prisoners. Fifteen German divisions had to be diverted from the western front to the east, where a supreme German control was now established over all forces of the Central Powers. The Russian losses, including those by desertion in the following winter, were tremendous and formed an important contributory cause of the Russian Revolution. Even so, the Brusilov offensive had reduced the prestige of the Dual Monarchy to a level at which its survival was also becoming virtually impossible.

The Russians had made a considerable impact, too, upon their third enemy neighbor, the Turks, in a campaign conducted from Transcaucasia. They captured the fortress of Erzerum and the port of Trebizond, entered Mesopotamia, and in small numbers outflanked the Ottoman Empire from Persia. Mesopotamia had also been entered from the sea by a British expedition based on India, which advanced up the Tigris from Basra and got within sixteen miles of Baghdad. A superior force of Turks then barred the way; General Sir Charles Townshend fell back to Kut-el-Amara; and there he surrendered after a five-months siege in April, 1916. The fact that British forces kept a secure hold on Egypt, which was proclaimed a protectorate in November, 1914, and on the Suez Canal hardly compensated for a surrender which was said to be without parallel in British military annals since Cornwallis came out of Yorktown in 1781.

In all the circumstances it is not surprising that at the close of 1916 proposals for a negotiated peace, to which President Woodrow Wilson as head of the only important neutral power had for some time lent his authority, began to be heard above the seemingly ineffectual clash of arms. The death of Francis Joseph in November had brought to the throne the young Emperor Karl, who believed that a quick peace might still save the Hapsburg dynasty. Every belligerent country had some members of the governing class of the type of Lord Lansdowne, foreign secretary in the British Conservative government which had made the Entente in 1904. These saw clearly that, whichever side won, a prolongation of the struggle would mean the ruin of the old social order. And undeniably a feeling of war weariness now grew among the masses, who were beginning to pay less attention to patriotic propaganda and more to the evidence of huge losses and small gains. On December 12 the Central Powers put out a note, expressing their willingness to negotiate but carefully avoiding any mention of terms; a few days later Wilson formally proposed that "soundings be taken." The Allies replied by stating a series of war aims which were not very different in principle from those ultimately achieved.

The peace overtures were denied any effective hearing by rulers who feared to show weakness. Both sides then turned their attention to planning the decisive effort which would crown three years of endurance with final victory. In Britain Lloyd George became firmly established as a "win-the-war" prime minister in place of Herbert Asquith; in France the Briand cabinet was reconstructed with the same object; and in Germany Ludendorff came to exercise more political authority than Bethmann-Hollweg or any of his successors in the chancellorship down to the last weeks of the imperial regime.

■ 1917–1918: GERMANY IN THE ASCENDANT

On February 1, 1917, the German government under the influence of Ludendorff and the naval staff declared an all-out submarine offensive against every vessel, whether belligerent or neutral, attempting to ply to or from any harbor of the United Kingdom or her European allies. It was assumed that the decision would probably bring the United States into the war, but the six-months period needed to force Britain to surrender would be much too short for the Americans to influence the result. Taken by itself, the second half of the proposition was not unreasonable. The United States declared war on April 6, when the effects of the sinking of American ships were reinforced by the British interception of a secret German offer to Mexico of an alliance to take back Texas, Arizona, and New Mexico from the Union. Ships of the United States Navy were immediately available to serve the Allied cause, and the problem of financing purchases of munitions in America vanished overnight. Wilson, who had been re-elected the previous November as a peace president, had done virtually nothing to expand the army or its equipment from its modest peacetime status. Consequently, the landing of a single American infantry division in France on June 25, 1917, represented a pledge of great moment for the future rather than any immediate relief in the actual military situation.

The knockout blow at sea was narrowly averted. Not only did the submarine sinkings reach such dimensions that they could not be published but, to begin with, the Germans realized their expectation that two-fifths of the neutral shipping could be scared into inactivity. The submarines were five times as numerous as they had been during their campaign of 1915; mine barrages proved ineffective except in such narrow waters as the Strait of Dover; and the destroyers which provided the chief antisubmarine weapon were handicapped by the fact that two-fifths of them were always in attendance on the battleships of the Grand Fleet. In the month of April, 1917, the tonnage lost was 881,000, Britain was down to a six-weeks supply of grain, and although the reduction of inessential imports, the expansion of home agriculture, and rationing of food would probably have made it possible in the event to hold out longer, November 1 was named in official circles as the limit of British endurance.

However, the ancient practice of convoy, which proved to be the essential method of defense, was tardily adopted at the insistence of Lloyd George and against the weight of British expert naval opinion. Experience showed that a large group of merchant ships sailing in formation, with a carefully planned escort of destroyers and smaller antisubmarine vessels, offered a less rewarding target to the enemy than the same number of ships making their individual courses across the ocean. At the same time improved methods of offense were found by technical experiments, which produced hydrophones for locating submarines, depth charges and improved types of mines and nets for their destruction. Finally, the whole challenge of the U-boat was progressively reduced as gigantic shipbuilding programs got under way in British, and still more in American, shipyards. In the last quarter of 1917 the losses were half what they had been from April to June, and in 1918—by which time the building program was in full swing—the monthly average of losses fell again by nearly one-third.

In retrospect, the submarine crisis of 1917 is seen to be matched in significance by the fall of the Russian monarchy in March and by the rapid dissolution of the eastern front, looming up with the downfall of the tsardom. The contemporary picture, however, was quite different, for the parliamentary regime of Prince Lvov and Alexander Kerensky was not only welcomed as democratic, particularly in the United States, but was for some months believed to be potentially a more effective ally than its predecessor. The breakdown of Russian military discipline was not immediately assessed at its full value, even by the Central Powers, who preferred to play a waiting game and avoid close contact. Indeed, at the beginning of July the Germans once more

The map shows the principal pattern of the war as it had been established, largely as a result of trench warfare, by 1917. The Eastern Front had more flexibility than the Western, and for a short time in 1914 the Russians were in East Prussia and across the Carpathians in Hungary. The insert map shows the operation of the German Schlieffen Plan in 1914.

Atlantic

Ocean

GREAT BRITAIN

IRELAND

NETHE LANDS

BEL

FRANCE

PORTUGAL

SPAIN

THE FIRST WORLD WAR

transferred troops from the western to the eastern front to meet the threat of Brusilov's last Galician offensive, which in point of fact rapidly flickered out. Under these circumstances a great Allied offensive, planned during the winter, could still be expected to yield fruitful results.

When the French government was reconstructed as a result of the disappointments of 1916, Joffre was replaced as commander in chief by Robert Nivelle, a young general who had distinguished himself in the counterattacks at Verdun. Nivelle was a brilliant talker, who captivated Lloyd George with the result that the British armies were placed at his disposal for the great breakthrough which he planned for April. His technique was simple: a tremendous weight of artillery fire; a carefully timed creeping barrage; behind it,

30

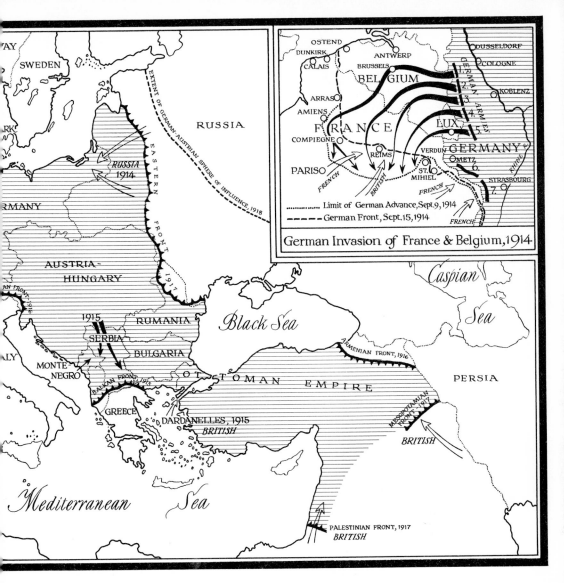

German Invasion of France & Belgium, 1914

.... Limit of German Advance, Sept.9, 1914
— — — German Front, Sept.15, 1914

a force of 1,200,000 men to burst through the German line in the first twenty-four hours—"and then the pursuit."

Nivelle's plans were first upset by the very skillful German withdrawal in February to the Hindenburg Line, twenty-five miles shorter than the old line at the Somme, and therefore requiring about thirteen fewer divisions for its defense. Unhindered during their withdrawal, the Germans had systematically devastated the area to be taken over by their opponents. Then the whole operation had gone on without French opposition because Nivelle believed such a voluntary retreat to be a psychological impossibility. The British attack in front of Arras, in which the Canadians secured the commanding height of Vimy Ridge, though the most successful battle the British had yet fought, did

31

not distract German attention as much as was hoped from the French blow which was to follow. Lastly, on the eve of the great offensive Nivelle's plans were captured and the weather broke. Consequently, the first day's advance on April 16, 1917, was shorter than that of the British at Arras, there was no breakthrough, and the battle which dragged on for almost four weeks involved nearly 200,000 French casualties.

The sequel was mutiny, which in one way or another affected about one-half of the sorely tried armies of France. Nivelle's successor, Pétain, restored order in about a month, partly by concessions and partly by the passing of death sentences upon 432 ringleaders, of whom 55 were actually shot. But for the rest of 1917 it was essential to distract the enemy, who remained in ignorance of the mutiny, from mounting any major attack against the French sector of the line. The British, who now had nearly as many soldiers on the western front as the French, were therefore obliged to prolong their offensive operations as much as possible.

Fate dealt unkindly with Haig's big autumn attack at Ypres, which was intended to win control of the submarine bases at Zeebrugge and Ostend. A ten-day bombardment destroyed the surface drainage of the battlefield, as the Belgians had said it would, thereby increasing the delaying effects of the abnormally wet weather. Moreover, the Germans had perfected a system of elastic defense, based on small concrete machine-gun posts or "pillboxes." Conditions were so appalling that toward the end of the hundred-days struggle British soldiers, slowly pressing forward to the capture of Passchendaele, were often literally drowned in the all-engulfing mud. Even the dramatic stroke at Cambrai, later in November, when 381 tanks were for the first time used without any artillery preparation to overrun the enemy trenches in a massive surprise, could not erase the sense of horror and futility. Lloyd George thereupon determined to hold back his last supply of fit men in Britain, so that Haig, whom he distrusted but dared not dismiss, should be unable to waste them.

The situation of the Allied armies at the close of the campaigns of 1917 was in many respects gloomy. At the height of the struggle on the western front in October, both French and British troops had been diverted to Italy, where the eleven drawn battles on the Isonzo front had been followed by a complete breakthrough at Caporetto by a mixed German and Austrian force under German command. Though more than half of their huge losses were by desertion, the Italians were able to rally in front of Venice just before help arrived. One consequence of the emergency was a meeting at Rapallo, which very belatedly set up a Supreme War Council to co-ordinate military policy and allot troops accordingly. Even the splendor of the progress made against the Asiatic empire of the Turks was clouded by the fact that it involved a heavy expenditure of manpower in what was still a distant theater. Baghdad had been captured in March, which meant that most of Mesopotamia (Iraq) was securely in British hands. Shortly before Christmas the other prong of the British advance, based on Egypt and aided by the revolt in the Arabian Desert which brought fame to the name of T. E. Lawrence, enabled General Sir Edmund Allenby to place Jerusalem in Christian hands for the first time since the Crusades.

The submarine menace, it is true, had been brought under control, and a regular flow of American troop convoys to France had now begun, promising certain relief if the Allies could hold out for one more year. But this was a very big "if." In early September the German capture of Riga was followed by the complete disintegration of the Russian armies and the regrouping of German strength in the west, until only some forty inferior divisions were left to enforce German terms upon a helpless Russia. The Bolshevik revolution of early November, which aimed at making peace and was for the time being incapable of waging war, was followed next month by the armistice of Brest Litovsk.[8] This meant that the large-scale transfer of veteran German forces to the west was no longer likely to be reversed.

Accordingly, on March 21, 1918, Ludendorff launched the first of five tremendous attacks. His object was to break through to Amiens and pin the British back against the Channel ports. Their Fifth Army was overrun, and in the absence of available reserves the position became desperate. By the seventh day, however, the German attack had exhausted its momentum without reaching its objective, as the British, putting every man in the line, just held out in front of Amiens. Elsewhere French reinforcements prevented a fatal gap from opening between French and British armies. These were at last placed under the supreme command of a single French general, Ferdinand Foch.[9] The new commander in chief was generously allowed by the American authorities to make piecemeal use of their troops in France, which did not yet form a separate army. Yet a second attack, which was directed against the British farther north a fortnight later, began with a spectacular rout of a Portuguese division and pressed so close to Calais that the usually taciturn Haig in an Order of the Day to his tired troops was moved to speak of the plain duty of each one to fight on to the end, "with our backs to the wall." The imperturbable Foch, believing that Haig would somehow hold out, husbanded his reserves, and

8. See pp. 50–51.

9. 1851–1929. Grandson of one of Napoleon I's officers and a devout Catholic, he was also a firm friend of Clemenceau, who in 1907 made him head of the *École de Guerre,* where he taught "Victory = Will." As an army commander he played a key part at the Marne, and helped to establish good inter-Allied relations. Superseded along with Joffre, he became chief of the general staff under Pétain from May, 1917, until his appointment to the supreme command, made definitive on April 14, 1918. A leading theorist of the art of war, he was almost certainly the ablest strategist among the Allied commanders. A significant example of his writing is the article, "Morale," in the *Encyclopaedia Britannica* (14th edition).

after a week the attack again died away, leaving the Germans again in possession of no more than a big bulge in the line.

Ludendorff then turned against the French farther south, with results that brought his armies in early June back to the River Marne, and within fifty-six miles of Paris. A fourth attack to some extent consolidated the position there, following which the Germans decided that another big thrust southward across the Marne was needed to exhaust the French reserves before striking their *coup de grace* against the British at the Channel ports. In mid-July six divisions stormed the four-hundred-foot heights on the far bank, but the attack was held by French and American troops, organized for defense in depth. Once more the Germans had created a formidable dent in the Allied line, to be met this time by an immediate and successful counterattack. On July 18 an Allied offensive was launched in which the Germans soon lost a hundred thousand men and all the ground they had recently gained. It was the beginning of the end.

■ 1918, JULY–NOVEMBER: THE COLLAPSE OF THE CENTRAL POWERS

In less than four months the German armies passed from victory to surrender; Bulgaria, Turkey, and Austria-Hungary, once the Germans were on the defensive, proved even quicker to give up the struggle. The Germans at last knew that they had shot their bolt. They had no fresh resources of manpower on which to draw, whereas their opponents could count on the steady growth of the American forces in Europe, which numbered a little over two million by the date of the armistice. The meager supplies acquired by the Germans in the Ukraine did not counterbalance the long-term effects of the Allied naval blockade, which after the entry of the United States into the war had become more stringent in relation to neutral sources of supply. Indeed, the overrunning of Allied supply dumps in the great German victories of 1918 had actually had a depressing effect, inasmuch as it revealed to the soldiers the superiority of the rations enjoyed by their opponents. Technically, too, the Germans were at a disadvantage. They had not equipped themselves with tanks, which were proving increasingly effective; after starting the war with a fleet of lighter-than-air Zeppelins, to which the Allies had no equivalent, they were by 1918 outnumbered in heavier-than-air machines by the British, without counting French or American aircraft; and in general they had only about one-half the manufacturing capacity of the other side.

Foch, it has been well said, conducted the movements of the Allied armies in this last stage of the war as with a conductor's baton, his object being to achieve the harmony of successive coordinated thrusts at different sectors of the German line. On August 8 the first main attack, with more than four hundred tanks and a fresh Canadian corps as its spearhead, drove the Germans back through a maze of defenses in the region of the Somme. The evidences of declining morale caused Ludendorff in retrospect to call this "the black day of the German army." A Crown Council was held on August 14 which accepted military advice that the war could no longer be won, though a gradual withdrawal might be expected to keep German troops firmly established on French soil while negotiations were in progress. But negotiations were delayed by the political authorities throughout the rest of August and September, while the Allied armies were busy making the contemplated withdrawal less gradual. A whole series of British and French advances drove the Germans back to the Hindenburg Line, and by mid-September the initial victory of Pershing's American forces at Saint-Mihiel, where they took twice as many prisoners as the casualties they incurred, gave further signs of an irresistible turn of the tide.

The first of Germany's associates to collapse was Bulgaria. Since the autumn of 1915 an Allied force had been assembled at Salonika, but apart from helping to push Greece into the war on the Allied side in June, 1917, it had achieved virtually nothing. This army in a fortnight's fighting drove the Bulgarians out of the war. Thereupon the Rumanians, who had made peace in May, seized their chance to rejoin the winning side. The Turkish armies, too, were rapidly disintegrating. A heavy defeat at Megiddo and the ensuing large-scale air bombing of troops on the retreat—the first example of its kind— drove them back beyond Damascus. As for the Austro-Italian front, in mid-September the Emperor Karl addressed an urgent peace note to the Allies, to which they did not trouble to reply. By the time of the Bulgarian surrender (September 29), the threat to Hungary added the Magyars to the long list of nationalities that wished to dissolve the Dual Monarchy in order to salvage their separate interests.

On September 26, Foch began a series of attacks in the center of the German line, and the British at the end of a week's fighting made a way through the third and last of the Hindenburg systems of defense. The situation as seen by Ludendorff was now sufficiently desperate for him to demand of the kaiser on September 29 that a new government should be formed to apply for an immediate armistice. On October 3 Prince Max of Baden took office, with the support of a majority in the Reichstag which definitely sought the termination of hostilities.

Nevertheless, another month passed in diplomatic exchanges, during which a series of pincer movements steadily drove back the Germans, before the armistice at last came into force, at eleven o'clock on the morning of November 11. The Americans were then fighting their way across the Meuse, the British had just re-entered Mons, and the historic symbol of Sedan had been secured for the French. Even so, the four-year siege of Germany ended without any penetration into German territory, while the defeated German armies, in the subsequently stated opinion of both Foch and Haig, were still capable of making good a fighting withdrawal behind the Rhine.

The above considerations are important, not merely to any fair assessment of the valor and endurance of the German soldier, but also to the interpretation of the terms of armistice.[10] The defeat was, however, overwhelming in three other respects. The cumulative effects of the naval blockade meant on the one hand an acute shortage in oil and other essential military supplies, and on the other hand a condition of near starvation in the civilian population, for neither of which was any remedy in sight. Second, and partly in consequence of the blockade, morale had at last collapsed behind the lines. A mutiny in the fleet, when ordered out upon a last great diversionary operation, spread rapidly from Kiel to create a series of antiwar and antimonarchist demonstrations in most of the chief towns of Germany during the week before the armistice. Third, it was clear that Germany would at best have been left to fight on alone. A separate armistice had been negotiated by the Turks on the last day of October. Four days later, when the Italians were rapidly overrunning the Austrian territory opened to their armies by the decisive victory of Vittorio Veneto, the conclusion of an armistice with them was the last act of the general staff of the expiring Hapsburg monarchy. An independent republic had already been proclaimed in Prague, the capital of Bohemia, and the Hungarian minister for war had instructed Magyar units to lay down their arms.

■ EUROPE AT THE TERMINATION OF HOSTILITIES

The terms of the armistice granted to Germany had their basis in the recognition by both sides of the dominant position attained by the United States. It followed automatically from the late date at which a country of such tremendous resources in men and material had entered the conflict that the rest of the victors, in comparison with America, appeared almost as exhausted as the vanquished. The Allies therefore could not avoid the fact that the Germans in the first place sought an armistice on the basis of the Fourteen Points which Wilson had proclaimed as his war aims in the different circumstances of the previous January. But in committing themselves to a more or less generous eventual settlement, the Allies at the same time made sure that Germany should lie immediately at their mercy. The German armies were to be withdrawn beyond the Rhine and certain of its bridgeheads, and they were to surrender specified quantities of war material, including artillery and machine guns. Sixteen of their capital ships were to be interned and all submarines handed over. Even though captured merchant shipping was to be restored by the Germans, the Allied naval blockade would be continued.

10. See below and p. 67.

The casualties on both sides had been enormous. Two and three-quarter million Germans, more than a million subjects of the Dual Monarchy, a third of a million Turks, and nearly a hundred thousand Bulgars had died in the war to escape the fate of the vanquished, and in the hope, which had so narrowly escaped fulfilment, of imposing that fate upon their enemies. On the side of the victors the Russian losses, which had been the heaviest, may have exceeded the German. France had lost nearly a million and a half, including deaths among her African troops. The British Empire lost nearly a million men, Italy nearly two-thirds of a million, and the United States 126,000 men.[11] Many civilians met death by direct action, such as the German torpedoing of passenger ships. Many more died through indirect action, for example through the privations inflicted on the aged, the women, and the children by the Allied naval blockade. Millions died through the ravages of disease, principally in the world-wide influenza epidemic of 1918–1919, which the war had made people less capable of resisting. It seems likely that the inclusion of these totals would more than treble the entire death roll connected with the war. It has also to be borne in mind that the ten millions who died on the field of battle represented mainly the group whose loss mattered most—the physically and mentally fit in the best years of their manhood.

The material losses proved comparatively easy to replace, for the battle zones of northern France and Belgium and parts of Poland were the only big industrial areas to have suffered serious devastation. It was not difficult to make good the destruction of merchant shipping, while the development of air transport was directly stimulated by the rapid production of aircraft for military use in the later years of the war. Most serious perhaps was the continuing effect on Europe's trade with other continents of the wartime diversion of the economy to serve mainly military objects.

Was there also an imponderable loss in the things of the spirit? Did the war cause Europe to vacate at an artificially enhanced speed the position of world leadership which had been hers through temporary natural advantages in recent centuries? The fact that what was universally identified as "the Great War" was not followed by a great peace, but by an interwar period sometimes dismissed, in Foch's prophetic phrase, as no more than "the twenty years armistice," suggests that European man in the 1920's and 1930's somehow failed to rise to the height of his opportunities. The cease-fire which was greeted with such relief on both sides of the battle line may have marked the onset of an exhaustion which was more than physical.

11. The estimates of the United States War Department are not always on a strictly comparable basis. Only the figures for the British Empire are official. The German "Lists of Honor" add up to nearly twice their official total of just over 2,000,000. J. E. EDMONDS, *Short History of World War I* (1951), p. 426.

Reading List: Chapter 1

The New Cambridge Modern History, vol. XII (1960), ch. 13. World War I in outline.

Ritter, G., *The Schlieffen Plan* (Engl. tr., 1958), part I, sec. 2. Its political implications.

Tuchman, B. W., *The Guns of August* (1962, also paperback), ch. 14. The battle of the frontiers.

Barnett, C., *The Swordbearers* (1963), part IV. The personality of Ludendorff.

Terraine, J., "Lloyd George's Expedients," *History Today,* vol. XI (1961), no. 5, and vol. XII (1963), no. 5. The civilians and the generals.

Koehl, R. L., "A Prelude to Hitler's Greater Germany," *American Historical Review,* vol. LIX (1954), no. 1. German expansionist aims.

Taylor, A. J. P., *The Struggle for Mastery in Europe, 1848–1918* (1954), ch. 22. Diplomacy during the war.

———, *The Habsburg Monarchy, 1809–1918* (rev. ed., 1948, also paperback), ch. 18. The end of the Hapsburgs.

Chapter 2

The Russian Revolution, 1917–1921

Russia and the War, 1914–1917
The Failure of the Liberals
The Transfer of Power
The Communists and the Civil War
The Communists and the World
How Communism Survived
Communism: Theory and Practice

■ RUSSIA AND THE WAR, 1914–1917

The Russian Revolution, from which such vast consequences flowed and still flow for Russia and for the world, was in part a consequence of centuries of political, economic, and social repression of the masses, only half-heartedly relieved by belated policies of reform. In part, too, the Revolution resulted from the workings of the Marxist-Leninist system of ideas, tenaciously held by a disciplined body of extremists. It was also influenced at each decisive phase by the interplay between leader and led, between the will of the extraordinary new rulers whom the emergency brought to power and the psychology of the bewildered and almost desperate multitude of ordinary human beings. But the all-important starting point of the train of dramatic events now to be described was the third year of a war in which the people of Russia had been exposed to greater strains than those of any other major combatant power.

SIGNIFICANT EVENTS

1917   Strikes leading to republican revolution in Petrograd (March)
        Kerensky prime minister in succession to Prince Lvov (July)
        Bolshevik revolution in Petrograd; decrees on peace and land
            approved by Soviet Congress (November)

1918   Constituent Assembly (January)
        Peace of Brest Litovsk (March)
        Clash with Czechs on Trans-Siberian Railway (May)
        Ex-tsar and family murdered at Ekaterinburg (July)
        Establishment of Kolchak as "Supreme Ruler" at Omsk
            (November)

1918–1920   Russian Civil War

1919   First Congress of Third (Communist) International (March)
        Denikin's closest approach to Moscow and Yudenich's threat to
            Petrograd (October)

1920   Russo-Polish War (May–October)
        Congress of Peoples of the East, Baku (September)

1921   Kronstadt mutiny; announcement of New Economic Policy
            (March)
        Treaty of Riga, fixing Russo-Polish border (March)

Russian armies had experienced more defeats than victories, and from 1915 onwards a large area of territory all along the western frontier lay in enemy hands. This military failure was made all the more unacceptable to the people by the "scorched earth" policy carried out as the armies retreated, farms being destroyed wholesale by order of the Russian high command. Moreover, after a few months of war the supply of rifles, shells, and other munitions could not be kept up because of Russia's industrial backwardness and the acute difficulties of importation via Vladivostok or Archangel, the only routes which the Central Powers were unable to close. Every campaign, whether lost or won, therefore involved disproportionately heavy casualties: in 1916, the year of Brusilov's great onslaught on Austria-Hungary, Russia lost two million men in killed and wounded and a further one-third of a million taken prisoner.

The patriotic enthusiasm, which was certainly widespread at the outbreak of hostilities, might have lasted longer if there had been any war aims which appealed greatly to the Russian peasant-soldier. There were not. The intended annexation of Constantinople and the region of the Straits, to which Britain and France gave their consent early in 1915, might perhaps have been popular. However, the secret agreement for this object was not made public until December of the following year, when the general situation was too bad for the announcement in the Duma to have any marked effect, even upon the upper- and middle-class society which that parliamentary body chiefly represented.

During the war the rift between Duma and government had widened. After the deportation of its five antiwar members (the Bolshevik group) to Siberia the Duma hoped that its whole-hearted support of the war effort would result in the appointment of ministers who enjoyed its confidence. On the contrary, the ministry continued to be headed by an elderly bureaucrat. Moreover, after August, 1915, when the tsar in person became the nominal commander in chief, his absence from Petrograd (as the capital was now named) enhanced the influence of the tsarina and her sinister confidant, the debauched "holy man," Grigori Rasputin. Both were more interested in bolstering up the autocratic powers of the tsar than in winning the war, and in 1916 they placed at the head of the ministry a person who was widely believed to be pro-German. His dismissal as the result of a dramatic protest in the Duma by the Liberal leader, Paul Miliukov, was followed by the death of Rasputin at the hands of infuriated noblemen.

The Revolution broke out, however, not because of political grievances felt by the few but because of economic hardships borne by the many. Rather more than one-third of Russia's manpower was serving in the army, and the peasants left behind on the farms prospered by providing the army with its food supply. But in a country whose industries were notoriously underdeveloped, the effort to supply even a part of the army's needs of equipment and munitions reduced to almost nothing the quantity of consumer goods available for the civil population. If the peasants could not buy from the towns, they would eat their crops rather than sell them, and their need for ready money had in any case been reduced by a wartime ban on the sale of liquor. In the winter of 1916–1917 food prices were four times as high as before the war. Moreover, even at inflated prices the townsman was no longer sure of any supply since the needs of the army virtually monopolized what was left of Russia's very inadequate railroad facilities.

On March 10, 1917, the third day of unorganized street demonstrations in Petrograd calling for bread and better wages, the tsarina reported to her husband:

This is a hooligan movement, young people run and shout that there is no bread, simply to create excitement, along with workers who prevent others from working. If the weather were very cold they would all probably stay at home. But all this will pass and become calm, if only the Duma will behave itself.[1]

On March 12, however, these demonstrations became a successful rebellion, as the soldiers, many of them recently recruited, began to pass over almost spontaneously into the ranks of the demonstrators. By nightfall the commander of the Petrograd garrison, who supposedly had under his control 160,000 troops— two for every five workers in the city—regarded himself as powerless. Reinforcements sent to the capital likewise melted away on contact with the rebels, and after Moscow had accepted the Revolution (on the afternoon of the fourteenth) without a fight, it was too late for the military supporters of the monarchy to act. Next day the tsar, whose train had been held up to prevent his return to the capital, renounced the throne for himself and his ailing son. His younger brother, the Grand Duke Michael, likewise declined the honor, when the president of the Duma admitted that he could not guarantee that his life would be safe if he accepted. In this way the Romanov dynasty came unceremoniously to an end.[2]

■ THE FAILURE OF THE LIBERALS

For the next eight months of 1917 the power vacuum, which had been so suddenly and unexpectedly created, was filled nominally by a provisional government, chosen by a committee of the Duma which had remained unofficially in session. Its formation received the approval of the Petrograd Soviet of Workers' and Soldiers' Deputies, which had sprung up in prompt imitation of events during the attempted revolution of 1905, on condition that the new government made clear its intention of summoning a constituent assembly. It received the unqualified recognition of the United States and of Russia's allies in the war. The head of the new government, Prince Lvov, was an aristocrat who had earned great popularity by organizing war relief and war work through the existing units of local self-government known as zemstvos. The foreign minister, Paul Miliukov, and most of the other original members were former stalwarts of the Liberal opposition, while the views of the Petrograd Soviet found expression through the new minister of justice, a thirty-six-year-

1. Quoted from the Russian by W. H. CHAMBERLIN, *The Russian Revolution, 1917–1921* (1935), vol. I, p. 73.
2. Since Russia did not adopt the Gregorian calendar until February 1, 1918, its dates were thirteen days behind those of the West. The events described above are therefore known as the "February Revolution" and the second revolution, which followed on November 7, as the "October Revolution."

old barrister named Alexander Kerensky,[3] whose advanced views and rhetorical utterances had won him a higher standing among the masses than in the Duma.

Though slow to summon the Constituent Assembly, which they expected under war conditions would prove dangerously radical, the Provisional Government stood for broad principles of political democracy and liberty of the individual. As regards economic policy, indeed, their outlook was originally very circumspect, but ministers who represented socialist parties were brought into the government in May and were eventually in the majority, while in July Kerensky replaced Lvov as prime minister. Yet in November this government was overturned by violence, and few blows were struck in its defense. How are we to account for the rapid collapse of a regime which was much more democratic than anything that Russia had ever known before and more advanced in social sympathies than its contemporaries in Britain, France, or the United States?

The answer lies partly in the unsatisfactory basis of its authority. The Provisional Government represented in some sense the Duma, but it had been called into existence by the popular movement which had overthrown the tsardom. That popular movement had also called into existence its rival, the Petrograd Soviet of Workers' and Soldiers' Deputies. Set up while the struggle was still in progress in the streets, the Soviet had an even weaker formal basis, though in theory it contained one deputy to represent each group of two thousand workers or soldiers. But its executive committee had the advantage of direct contact with some three thousand representatives of the revolutionary people of the capital. Moreover, the Petrograd Soviet persuaded the Provisional Government to agree that the revolutionary garrison of the city should not be removed elsewhere, and the Soviet then established elective committees of soldiers in every regiment to supervise discipline and control stores of arms. In this way the authority of the Provisional Government was widely undermined by a system of dual power in which the Petrograd Soviet steadily gained the advantage.

The spread of soviets of workers, soldiers, and peasants in varying proportions across the country was extremely rapid. As early as June a Congress of Soviets assembled from all parts of Russia and appointed an executive committee to serve until its next meeting. By the end of August there were said to be a total of six hundred soviets, representative of 23,000,000 electors. In the

---

3. 1881–   . The role of this eloquent defense lawyer has been compared to that of the "silver-tongued Lamartine" in the French Revolution of 1848. He had concealed his membership in the non-Marxian Social Revolutionary Party, which boycotted the fourth Duma, to which he was elected. After his escape from Russia in 1918, he became an American citizen and active publicist, explaining where the Revolution went wrong.

very first days of the Revolution the extremist sailors of the Kronstadt naval base adjoining the capital had coined the slogan, "All Power to the Soviets!" This lost none of its force as the membership of soviets, which changed immediately with every change of opinion among those who sent them, began to show a general trend toward the Left.

Nevertheless, the Provisional Government deliberately refused to give the people the things they wanted most. Its immediate actions included, indeed, the concession of equal political and personal rights to all citizens, among them the Jews. It restored the constitutional liberties of Finland and encouraged the other subject nationalities to expect the formation of a federation of free peoples under Russian auspices. But the soldiers wanted peace; the peasants, the land; the urban population, food. The official interim policy regarding the war was one of continued loyalty to Russia's allies. With respect to the land, which was the only aspect of the Revolution of any interest to the peasants, the government urged delay and careful inquiries preparatory to a great final reform. Locally, however, peasant soviets were anticipating such a reform by piecemeal expropriation of big estates. The food supply of the towns could not be assured in any case until the land question was settled and was made more difficult by a mushroom growth of factory committees and so-called trade unions, which caused many employers to close down their factories in despair.

During the summer months, while the liberal policies of the government still had the support of the Social Revolutionaries, who were by far the largest political party in the country, the situation in the capital grew steadily more tense. At the beginning of July the oratory of Kerensky, now minister of war, galvanized the troops into launching a new offensive.[4] Though a disastrous failure, it helped to precipitate a severe outburst of street-fighting in Petrograd, in which the government triumphed temporarily over the extremists of the Left. As a last resort, the government in September decided to risk appealing to a nation-wide constituent assembly, which they had long postponed as dangerous. They now hoped that the millions of illiterate peasants would prove to be a moderating influence. But what they hoped, others feared. When the elections did come in November, Kerensky, the Provisional Government, and all moderate programs had been ousted by a personality, a party, and a program of historic vigor and incisiveness.

At the first onset of revolution in March, 1917, the Bolshevik group of the Social Democratic Party had been an insignificant force. Its austere doctrines had kept the membership small; its opposition to the war caused its leaders to be in Siberian prisons or in exile. Among these exiles Josef Stalin was one who owed his return to a general amnesty granted by the Provisional

4. See pp. 29–30.

LENIN SPEAKING AT PETROGRAD IN 1917.
This dramatic photograph suggests the
oratorical power which along with a profound grasp of mass psychology made
Lenin so effective a revolutionary leader.

Government; Nicolai Lenin[5] was enabled by the enemy to pass through Germany from Switzerland in the justified expectation that he would help to disrupt the Russian war effort; Leon Trotsky had the Atlantic to cross; Vyacheslav Molotov, who restarted the suppressed newspaper, *Pravda,* was almost the only leader to be immediately available. Lenin, arriving in the capital on April 16, was welcomed at the Finland Station by an immense crowd, at a time when his actual party supporters numbered no more than 16,000 in the city and only 80,000 in the whole of Russia. At the first Congress of Soviets in June the Bolsheviks were still a minority urban party of 20 percent. As late as August the membership was only 200,000, including 41,000 in the capital. Yet in November they were able to sweep away the Provisional Government and to replace it by a regime of their own devising.

One factor in this second revolution was certainly the force of a carefully worked-out doctrine regarding the revolutionary process. The Bolsheviks saw history through the eyes of Karl Marx as a class struggle from which the proletariat was predestined to emerge victorious. It would then consolidate its victory in a ruthless dictatorship of the proletariat as a necessary preliminary to the communist millennium. It was true that the socialist revolution accord-

5. 1870–1924. Born V. I. Ulyanov, the son of a school inspector, he was strongly influenced by his eldest brother's execution for an assassination plot against the tsar in 1891, the year in which he himself qualified as a barrister. He married N. K. Krupskaya, "his nearest helpmate," while exiled to Siberia, where he first wrote under the pseudonym of N. Lenin. He became leader of the Bolshevik section of the Social Democratic Party, formed in 1903, and had lived abroad since 1907, clarifying Bolshevik aims and methods in relation to the changing situation. Gorky's *Life* assigns him his place in history as "a man who prevented people from leading their accustomed lives as no one before him was able to do."

ing to Marxist theory was due to occur first in the most industrialized states, which clearly did not include Russia. But the writings of Lenin had set such revolution in the context of imperialist war as the last and ultimately fatal stage of capitalist development. From this he was able to draw two practical conclusions—that Russia should withdraw completely from the existing "imperialist" war, and that she should prepare to support any future war of colonial or other subject peoples rising against the imperialist powers.

A second factor in the November Revolution was the unusual force of the leading personalities who based their policy on these doctrines. Lenin was one of the most remarkable combinations of theorist and man of action, of idealism and ruthless realism, that has yet come forward to govern human destinies. His absolute certainty regarding ends enabled him to be infinitely adaptable regarding the means to be employed in a quickly changing situation. In Trotsky[6] he had a second in command who coupled intellectual brilliance and audacity with gifts of oratory and magnetic command both of colleagues and crowds. The Georgian, Stalin,[7] who was regarded as an expert on nationalities, at this time ranked only as one among half a dozen of the most prominent supporters of Lenin and Trotsky, all of them tested—and perhaps twisted—by long years of unsuccessful conspiracy and ideological disappointment.

The story of the second revolution, however, involves also a third element: the chances of an immensely confused and rapidly changing situation in which fortune favored the bold. From April to July, 1917, the Bolshevik leaders were making their way as a minority movement inside the Petrograd Soviet, extolling its value as the only working-class institution available, and preaching that the middle-class phase of the revolution both could and should be immediately superseded. However, the upshot of the July rising in Petrograd, already mentioned, was the proscription of the Bolshevik leaders as German agents in disguise. Lenin fled to Finland to escape arrest, Trotsky was for a time imprisoned. But in an ensuing struggle against right-wing extremists Kerensky called upon the Bolsheviks for help in organizing the masses, as a sequel to which they at last secured a majority in the Petrograd and Moscow Soviets. This result showed Lenin that the time for action had come. Since the

6. 1879–1940. Born L. D. Bronstein, he was the son of middle-class Jews. Having been exiled as a revolutionary to Siberia, he escaped to England with a passport forged in the name of Trotsky. He was a leader of the St. Petersburg Soviet in 1905, and after a second escape from Siberia he edited Social Democratic papers in Vienna, Zurich, Paris, and finally New York. He joined the Bolshevik Party in July, 1917, and, as long as Lenin lived, carried more weight than any senior member. He was murdered, after eleven years of exile, in Mexico.

7. 1879–1953. Born J. V. Djugashvili, son of a peasant shoemaker in Georgia, he was educated in a seminary for the priesthood. A Bolshevik agitator with eight arrests, seven deportations, and six escapes on his record, he had been since 1913 in banishment in North Siberia. His choice of a revolutionary pseudonym (Stalin means Man of Steel) seems apt in view of his overthrow of all rivals after the death of Lenin.

second Congress of Soviets was now impending, whatever was done in Petrograd could be expected to get wider support.

Because Lenin was still in hiding, the operations were in the charge of Trotsky as the elected chairman of the Petrograd Soviet and of its Military Revolutionary Committee. The Committee threw down the gauntlet by proposing to countersign all orders issued to the garrison. Since one effect of this requirement was to postpone impending departures to the front, the garrison sided with the Soviet, and the bombardment of the seat of government at the Winter Palace by the Bolshevik-controlled ship *Aurora* was hardly needed as an act of war. On the morning of November 6, Kerensky began the trial of strength by sending officer-cadets of the Petrograd Military School, who were his most reliable troops, to close down Bolshevik newspapers. Only twenty-four hours later he fled the city under the protection of the American flag, with plans for a return in strength which never took place. His colleagues were taken prisoner on the night of November 7–8, still in ineffectual session at the Winter Palace. As Trotsky truly observed, "The weakness of the government exceeded all expectations."

■ THE TRANSFER OF POWER

The revolutionaries announced their success in a proclamation addressed "To the Citizens of Russia":

> The Provisional Government is overthrown. State power has passed into the hands of the organ of the Petrograd Soviet of Workers' and Soldiers' Deputies—the Military Revolutionary Committee, which stands at the head of the Petrograd proletariat and garrison.

> The cause for which the people fought—immediate proposal of a democratic peace, abolition of landlords' property rights in land, workers' control over production, the creation of a Soviet Government—this cause is assured. Long live the Revolution of the working soldiers and peasants![8]

The wording clearly shows that what had so far been achieved was no more than a coup in the capital city. In Moscow, to the surprise of Lenin, the revolutionaries lost 238 lives in a week of street-fighting before the Kremlin finally capitulated. Out of a total of seventy-four principal provincial cities or administrative centers, one-third did not formally accept the change until the early months of the following year. But the army promptly endorsed the action of the Petrograd garrison, and the commander in chief surrendered his power to the emissary of the new authorities in Petrograd without a fight. His reward

8. Translation in CHAMBERLIN, *Russian Revolution*, vol. I, p. 315. A facsimile of the original, which he "helped to distribute from a motor truck just after the surrender of the Winter Palace," is given by the American journalist and former Harvard student John Reed in *Ten Days that Shook the World* (1919), ch. 4.

was to be lynched by a mob of soldiers. Other more fortunate generals made good their escape to the outlying regions. Thus Lenin and his associates were given a breathing space in which to organize the possession of power.

Lenin's constitutional position was that of president of the Council of People's Commissars, a group of fifteen prominent Bolsheviks, including Trotsky as commissar for foreign affairs and Stalin as commissar for affairs of nationalities. This list was laid before the second Congress of Soviets, which began its dramatic meetings only a few hours before the surrender of the Provisional Government. The Bolsheviks had a small majority in the Congress; the other parties, except for the Left Social Revolutionaries, absented themselves in a vain effort to gather some support for Kerensky. Their absence ensured a smooth passage, not only for the confirmation of the list, but for the two decrees by which Lenin secured a growing measure of popular support for the commissars.

The first of these, the Decree of Peace, took the form of a proclamation to peoples and governments, proposing the signature of an immediate peace without annexations or indemnities. Lenin, as will appear later, was optimistic regarding the effectiveness of his appeals to peoples, if not to governments. The immediate object was to win over to his side the great mass of Russian soldiers, their dependents, and every one else who wished Russia to leave the war. Lenin and the Bolsheviks had consistently opposed Russian participation; they now reaped their due reward from a thoroughly war-weary and disillusioned people. The second decree, the Decree on Land, on the other hand, reveals Lenin as a skillful opportunist, temporarily abandoning his socialist doctrine of land use in order to "let the peasants decide all questions, let them organize their own life." The large estates were to be handed over without payment of compensation to the peasants, who were vaguely instructed to provide small holdings for all comers, periodically reapportioned in the interests of equality.

Although the entire bourgeois civil service went on strike, the Council of People's Commissars worked at high speed to consolidate its position, promulgating 193 decrees in the first fifty-three days. The industrial population was given wide powers of workers' control through factory committees and trade unions; social insurance was to be instituted entirely at the cost of employers; and a twenty-three-clause law to reduce hours of labor "becomes effective by telegraph." Banks were nationalized and payments of interest and dividends discontinued. The position of the bourgeoisie was further attacked by the separation of church and state, the reorganization of the law courts so as to serve "the revolutionary conscience and the revolutionary conceptions of right," and the introduction of a special police force, the Cheka, to oppose the counter-revolution. At the same time world opinion was challenged by the repudiation of secret treaties and all government debts; the principle of self-determination was acclaimed for use within the Russian Empire and elsewhere; and attention was even given to such formal breaches with the past as the abolition of the old calendar and of all ranks and titles except that of citizen.

These actions produced the desired result. In December the more radical majority among the Social Revolutionaries joined the government, and the support of this Left Social Revolutionary Party helped the Bolsheviks to win much-needed majorities in peasant soviets. On a national level, indeed, Bolshevism was still a minority movement, as was clearly shown when the long-awaited Constituent Assembly met in January. Though the complete election results were never made known, the Social Revolutionaries (Left and Right) and smaller groups of moderate Socialists had about 62 percent of votes cast and the middle-class parties had 13 percent, leaving for the Bolsheviks only one vote in four. The last-named therefore withdrew from the Assembly, which was closed down by its military guards after one day. That day's deliberations had merely followed the pattern of decisions the Bolsheviks had already taken, and no repercussions came after Lenin's highhanded dismissal of the only genuinely democratic representative body Russia has ever known.

It was very different when Lenin proceeded to put through the other measure which he believed to be essential to his party's continuance in power, the termination at all costs of Russia's part in the war. That the cost would be high was evident from the military situation, for Russia's armies had steadily melted away, and she no longer held any enemy territory which could be used for bargaining. In addition, the bargaining power of the enemy was unintentionally enhanced by the encouragement given to national aspirations in the border territories, Stalin having declared on behalf of the Council of Commissars that the "equality and sovereignty of all the peoples of Russia" gave them the right to secede and form separate states. Thus the independence of Finland was duly acknowledged in December, 1917, the immediate sequel being a civil war of Reds and Whites. The Russians backed the Reds, who lost, so that within six months the country re-emerged as a German satellite.

A much graver problem was presented by a nationalist movement in the Ukraine, where a virtually independent republic was proclaimed in November under a journalist, Simon Petliura. A civil war followed, as in Finland, but it led at first to an opposite result, for by the end of February, 1918, the Russians had placed the Ukrainian Communists in power.

Meanwhile, in December, an armistice had been signed with the Central Powers at Brest Litovsk, in Poland, where Trotsky soon arrived to conduct negotiations for a definitive peace. Since his opponents had all the advantages in military strength, his object was to gain time by arguing about the principle of self-determination and appealing for the sympathy of peoples and armies over the heads of governments and commanders. When the representatives of

the Central Powers proved adamant in their determination to take the territories that lay within their grasp, Trotsky split the Bolshevik government and
the Party by proposing that, rather than recognize any annexations, Russia
should resort to a temporary formula of "No war—no peace." Lenin was for
the moment outvoted, but when the enemies whom they no longer recognized
as such began an unresisted advance along the entire front, at the same time
making their terms more onerous, the attitude changed. Trotsky and the rest
of the opposition gave way to Lenin's threat of resignation unless a formal
peace was at once secured. The latter was right in thinking that the territorial
settlement would not last, though he expected its abandonment to be the result
of revolution affecting both sides rather than of the military triumph of the
Allies. What he realized most clearly, however, was the need to buy what he
called a "breathing space," in which to consolidate the revolution at the center
of the Russian state. For this purpose he was prepared to pay any immediate
price in territory at the periphery.

The terms, as finally accepted in the Brest Litovsk Treaty of March 3,
1918, were exceedingly severe. Russia lost a quarter of her territory, containing
44 percent of the population, one-third of the crops, three-quarters of the coal
and iron, and more than half of all industrial undertakings. The surrender of
Bessarabia to the Rumanians was added a few days later, and the Turks eventually settled for the frontiers of 1829. It is significant that Lenin now moved
the capital back into the interior from Petrograd, with its European orientation and dangerous proximity to the new frontier, to Moscow, the heart of old
Russia. The Bolsheviks, henceforth to be known as Communists, accordingly
transferred their main center of authority to the Kremlin, where it remained;
their new official name had been adopted at the same Party Congress which
with many misgivings finally approved the Treaty of Brest Litovsk.

■ THE COMMUNISTS AND THE CIVIL WAR

The respite gained by the Treaty of Brest Litovsk was very short, far too
short for peace to bring the transfer of revolutionary energies from destruction
to construction for which Lenin was hoping. The people in the towns still went
hungry; the people in the country were engrossed in the struggle for land. In
the local soviets the Communists were busy ousting the other socialist parties
from positions of authority. An uncertain situation favored the growth of counterrevolutionary forces.

In the winter of 1917–1918, when the fate of the Ukraine was in the balance, a "Volunteer Army" had been formed there by counterrevolutionary
officers, which with Cossack help disputed Bolshevik control of the territories
of the Don and the Kuban. But its survival in these southeastern regions was
due chiefly to the proximity of the Germans, who had easily overrun the

Ukraine. The Allies, too, had begun to intervene at the extremities of Russian territory: in March some British marines were sent to protect military stores at Arctic Murmansk from falling into German hands, and in April Japanese and a few British marines landed temporarily for the same purpose at the munition-filled Pacific port of Vladivostok.

Eager to salvage what they could from the destruction of their eastern front against Germany, the Allies also negotiated a friendly agreement by which the Czechoslovak Corps or "Czech Legion," formed chiefly from prisoners of war who had been willing to fight on the Russian side for the overthrow of the Dual Monarchy, should be allowed to transfer their services to the western front. The plan was for them to go by the Trans-Siberian Railway to Vladivostok and then circle the globe. On May 14, however, a casual brawl between the Czechs and some passing Hungarian prisoners at a railroad junction in the Urals fired Communist suspicion that these 35,000 men had counterrevolutionary sympathies. In the fighting which followed, the Legion, part of which was already in Vladivostok, quickly seized the towns along the railway east of the Urals, and by August American, Japanese, British, and even French troops from Indochina had joined the Czechs at Vladivostok. One consequence was the establishment of a conservative regime in Siberia. But the most serious immediate threat to the survival of the Communist government was in the region of the Volga, where anti-Communist elements among the Social Revolutionaries in alliance with the Czechs revived the Constituent Assembly and set up a People's Army on a democratic basis; in early August this Army had penetrated as far as Kazan on the Volga, due east of Moscow.

The Communists now stood alone, without "fellow-travellers." They bore sole responsibility for the cold-blooded killing of the ex-tsar and his family, which was done on July 16, 1918, to avoid any chance of their liberation by the advance of White forces. They were also responsible for the reign of terror which the Cheka, or secret police, organized as a sequel to the wounding of Lenin by a Social Revolutionary. They had made the decisive moves towards the complete nationalization of economic life, including state control of labor in town and country alike, in a desperate attempt to arrest the further advance of the "bony hand of hunger." But all this would mean nothing if they could not stop the military advance of their enemies on Moscow. The key event, therefore, was the building up of the Red Army by Trotsky.

The Revolution had at first relied for its defense upon the Red Guard, a workers' militia which was about 20,000 strong at the time of the seizure of power by the Communists in Petrograd. Though recruitment for a Red Army began in January, 1918, only about 100,000 men of uncertain value were under arms when Trotsky took over the post of war commissar in March. His abundant energy and clear vision quickly introduced the principles of conscription, respect for discipline, reliance on proved military techniques (even though it meant the employment of former tsarist officers), and centralized control. This he exercised in person from an armored train. Even so, he resorted at first to such extreme measures as the literal decimation of a regiment of Petrograd workers who fled from action, and the use of commissars to shoot commanders who retreated. In September, 1918, the Red Army saved the capital from immediate danger by the recapture of Kazan.

A second phase of the Civil War opened in mid-November. A dictatorship under Admiral Alexander Kolchak[9] replaced the Constituent Assembly which had been revived by the anti-Communist Social Revolutionaries at Omsk, east of the Urals in Siberia. Since the Allies were now free to take sides against the Communists without any fear of driving them into the arms of the Germans, intervention might be expected to become more formidable. Moreover, both the Baltic and the Black seas were available to the Allies for naval pressure and the landing of men or supplies.

Except in munitions, Allied help to the counterrevolutionaries never amounted to much: the British, for example, supplied Kolchak with 100,000 tons of material, but their total casualties in northern Russia, where Allied troops did most fighting, were less than a thousand men. In March, 1919, when there were 118,000 foreign soldiers in Siberia, the front was held exclusively by Russians. No soldier wanted to go on fighting once the general war had ended, least of all in a cause which many of them viewed with grave political suspicion. The Whites for their part did their best to justify those suspicions by their open support of a reactionary land policy, terrorist outrages which fully matched those of their opponents, and a general lack of self-discipline. The Red Army, on the other hand, was welded by Trotsky into an increasingly effective amalgam of enthusiastic rank-and-file recruits, including a high proportion of Communist Party members, and a corps of officers in which graduates of the new military schools were actually outnumbered by men who had served the old empire. When hard pressed, as it often was, the Red Army moreover had the advantage of operating upon interior lines, while its opponents, as we shall see, were never capable of synchronizing their efforts sufficiently to strike a knock-out blow.

The possible area of conflict was now widened, since the Ukraine and the Baltic Provinces were being vacated by the defeated Germans, and the Communists after denouncing the Treaty of Brest Litovsk were free to regain what territory they could. This confused situation for the most part helped the Com-

9. 1875–1920. He made his name as an Arctic explorer and by conspicuous gallantry in the defense of Port Arthur during the Russo-Japanese War; from 1916 to 1917 he was rear admiral commanding the Black Sea Fleet. He was chosen "Supreme Ruler of Russia" after a coup by army officers with Allied support at Omsk, to serve until a national assembly could be convened; after trial by his Communist captors he was shot in February, 1920.

munists, except in Estonia where they faced a strong White Russian leader, Nikolai Yudenich, as well as the Estonian nationalists, supported by the British navy. At this juncture, however, the main White Russian advance came from Siberia, directed by Kolchak himself against Moscow. Much of the ground lost in the previous autumn was regained: the Urals were crossed, the Volga towns threatened, and on Kolchak's northern flank it seemed possible that contact might be established with an Allied force operating south of Archangel. But he failed to co-ordinate his advance with that of his strongest supporter, Anton Denikin, in the south. In consequence the Reds were able by a supreme effort to press him back in the direction of Siberia shortly before Denikin was ready to launch his big southern offensive. In January, 1920, after abdicating in favor of Denikin, Kolchak was handed over by the Czechs, who had long since lost interest in the Allied intervention, to be put to death by the advancing Red Armies.

Meanwhile, a more formidable White offensive by three armies had been directed against Moscow from the south. In mid-October it reached within 250 miles of Moscow, while Yudenich, whom Britain had supplied with tanks, advanced simultaneously from Estonia into the suburbs of Petrograd, where Trotsky commanded the defense in person. Yudenich's thrust failed by a narrow margin, and further Red successes then compelled Denikin to withdraw from all the territory he had gained, including the Ukraine and even the lands of the Don Cossacks.

The Civil War now rapidly subsided. The White regime in the extreme north had not long survived the departure of the Allies in September, 1919, and in Siberia the only opposition remaining was in the region of Vladivostok, which the Japanese held for their own purposes until 1922. The British had also abandoned an attempt to support independent southern regimes at the Baku oil fields and in Georgia. A last flare-up resulted, however, from the intervention of the new Polish Republic. In the early months of 1920 it offered help to Simon Petliura, the Ukrainian nationalist leader, whose success would serve to weaken the new Communist Russia by the creation of a large new border state under Polish influence.

The consequence was the Russo-Polish War, which passed quickly through three contrasting phases. In the first, the Poles advanced into the Ukraine and captured Kiev. In the second, they were driven back and pursued to the outskirts of Warsaw as the result of a surge of nationalist enthusiasm among the Russians, which brought such commanding figures as Brusilov to the support of the Reds. In the third phase, however, the Poles with French backing were able to outnumber and outmaneuver the Russians, who by October were glad to cease hostilities, although the result was the very disadvantageous Treaty of Riga.[10] Meanwhile Denikin's successor, Baron Peter

10. See p. 77.

Wrangel, had emerged from the Crimea into the southern Ukraine and attempted to raise a new revolt among the Cossacks. His only solid achievement was the benefit accruing to the Poles by distracting their Communist foes. On the third anniversary of the Communist Revolution its armies stormed their way into the Crimea. Here the last of the White forces and accompanying refugees—a total of nearly 150,000 persons—were evacuated to Constantinople and lifelong exile.

■ THE COMMUNISTS AND THE WORLD

The Civil War was tremendously important because it settled whether communism was to survive in Russia. The Communists themselves envisaged it as part of a wider struggle, which was to bring about the triumph of communism, not merely in Russia but in the more advanced industrial states of Europe and subsequently throughout the world; indeed, the fear of such a struggle was one reason for the Allied intervention, the failure of which has just been traced. To complete the picture, however, it will be necessary to consider the external relations developed by Lenin from his first seizure of power in November, 1917, and the way in which the world reacted to them.

During the last twelve months of the World War, Communist policy looked beyond the achievement of peace for Russia to the disruption of the war effort in every country concerned by convincing the masses that they were fighting only for the imperialist interests of the capitalist class. Revolutionary proclamations were therefore addressed across the lines to the soldiers of the Central Powers, and money was voted as early as December, 1917, for the conduct of propaganda in foreign countries. A still more dramatic step was the decision to publish the repudiated secret treaties from the tsarist archives as "documentary evidence of the plans which the financiers and industrialists, together with their parliamentary and diplomatic agents, were secretly scheming."[11] Words fell on deaf ears, but in October, 1918, when the victories of the Allied armies and the pressure of their naval blockade had brought Germany to the verge of capitulation, Lenin was hoping to give active help to the German workers both in food from Russia's meager stocks and in men from a projected Red Army of three million. Before the end of the year the head of the propaganda organization, Karl Radek, had arrived secretly in Berlin, and numerous other agents, including former prisoners of war, had been dispatched to prepare the triumph of the Communist Party in both Germany and the former Austria-Hungary.

Lenin, however, was a realist tactician as well as a visionary strategist. While his long-term object was world revolution, it might nevertheless be desirable to safeguard the revolution in Russia by making some temporary bar-

---

11. Trotsky in *Izvestiia,* November 23, 1917, quoted by J. BUNYAN and H. H. FISHER, *The Bolshevik Revolution, 1917–1918* (1934), p. 244.

gain with the capitalist powers. In December, 1918, accordingly, he pleaded with Wilson for the admission of Russian representatives to the forthcoming peace conference, only to be rebuffed by the French. Instead, Wilson and Lloyd George proposed a separate conference, to be held on Prinkipo Island near Constantinople, at which both Reds and Whites should meet the Allies, compose their own differences, and settle the relations between the new Russia and the world. Since the Whites refused the invitation point-blank, nothing came of the proposal, except in so far as Allied reluctance to abandon intervention or relax the rigorous economic blockade of Red Russia caused the latter to resort more readily to the weapon of subversion.

In March, 1919, delegates from nineteen Communist parties, of which only the Russian was a strong nation-wide body, assembled in Moscow to inaugurate the Third or Communist International. Two Communist risings in Germany, a country which Lenin regarded as most ripe for the triumph of the proletariat, had been quickly suppressed and the three main leaders killed without trial. But in April Munich and much of Bavaria passed under Communist control for several weeks, and a similar regime under Bela Kun in Hungary lasted until August. The Hungarians cherished hopes of Russian support in regaining lost territory, and the Russian Communists tried hard to join hands with them by reconquering the much-disputed Ukraine and re-entering Bessarabia. They did not succeed, but it was significant that the suppression of the Hungarian revolution was entrusted by the Allies to the Rumanians and Czechoslovaks, its enemies on nationalist grounds, rather than to the large French army available in the Balkans. The latter might easily become infected by communism, to which it had proved susceptible earlier in the year, when it had been stationed in support of the Ukrainian nationalists at Odessa. For 1919 was a year of discontent and unsettlement among victors as well as vanquished, with soldiers mutinying to speed up demobilization in all armies, including the British, and civilian populations half-disposed to try to improve conditions by the resort to force which war had made familiar. In Italy, for instance, the first Fascist bands were already being formed to combat the disorders on which communism throve.

At the second meeting of the new Third International in the summer of 1920, for which delegates from thirty-nine countries on every continent were brought together in the throne room of the Kremlin, two resolutions were adopted under Lenin's guidance which shaped the pattern of Communist influence. One of these imposed a list of twenty-one conditions, designed to make the world Communist movement as centralized and disciplined as the party which had triumphed in Russia. Some moderate Marxists, such as the British Socialist leader, Ramsay MacDonald, were excluded by name; other moderates, it was hoped, would be repelled by specific demands for subversive activity in national armies and the creation of an illegal organization to function side by side with any legally tolerated Communist Party. The other main resolution directed the attention of every national group of dedicated Communists to the duty of fomenting revolution among dependent colonial peoples. As the chief victims of capitalist imperialism, they must be roused to rebel, and each such rebellion, by reducing the prosperity of the exploiting state, would make the rising of the industrial workers there more likely.

The Russians themselves were prompt to set the example. A month after the International had dispersed from Moscow, they summoned a "First Congress of Peoples of the East." This brought a handful of Hindus and Chinese and hundreds of Turks, Persians, and Armenians to mix with Russia's own "free" Asiatic subjects at Baku on the shore of the Caspian, where Europe stretches farthest towards the heart of Asia. The immediate results were negligible; even a Communist regime which had just been established in a part of Persia collapsed the following year. Nevertheless, Grigori Zinoviev, who was one of Lenin's oldest and closest associates, brought the whole audience to its feet with a prophetic peroration, in which he declared: "The real revolution will blaze up only when the eight hundred million people who live in Asia unite with us, when the African continent unites, when we see that hundreds of millions of people are in movement."[12]

For the moment, however, Communist Russia was chiefly concerned to limit its commitments. Finland had been virtually abandoned to anti-Red nationalists after imperial Germany intervened in their bitterly contested civil war in 1918. The first formal peace treaty was signed with Estonia in February, 1920; the independence of Latvia and Lithuania, because they were more distant, was more readily conceded in the course of the summer. By the Treaty of Riga with Poland, ratified in March, 1921, shortly after the Congress of the East, Russia surrendered, along with her hopes of communizing the Poles, a considerable area in the much-contested White Russia and Ukraine. These lands lay to the east of the line of Polish nationality as propounded at the Paris Peace Conference by a committee under the British Conservative minister, Lord Curzon. Some four million White Russians and Ukrainians remained under Polish rule until 1939.

Even in central Asia the Red Army stopped short at the reconquest of Mohammedan Khiva and Bokhara, when excuses could easily have been found to advance to the overthrow of their coreligionists and sympathizers in Afghanistan. In fact, the desert spaces of Outer Mongolia, where one of Kolchak's officers had established a temporary base, was the only region of Asia outside the tsarist realm to be brought within the Communist orbit. Nearer home, for

12. "The First Congress of the Peoples of the East": Stenographic Report, quoted by CHAMBERLIN, *Russian Revolution*, vol. II, p. 392.

a period of about twelve months the independence of Georgia, which the Allies had recognized in January, 1920, was accepted by the Russian government, subject to the legalization of the native Communist Party, although the Red Army moved in eventually to crush the national resistance as the tsars had done.

The Civil War left Russia too weak for aggression. To some extent this was the result of external pressure. The Allied blockade had been formally lifted in January, 1920, but Russia's neighbors, including even the small border states, held back from normal dealings until the Anglo-Soviet trade treaty of March, 1921, signified the tacit approval of the great powers. For the most part, however, it was the Civil War and the accompanying practice of War Communism which had reduced the economic life of the country to a level at which the survival of the regime—let alone any expansion—seemed most unlikely and the force of its propaganda was practically nil.

■ HOW COMMUNISM SURVIVED

From May, 1918, until the autumn of 1920 the Russians lived in conditions of civil war, superimposed upon conditions resulting from the three preceding years of international war. The term "War Communism," commonly applied to the economic policy of this period, therefore refers both to the necessarily stringent arrangements for eking out diminished resources of every kind, from food to manpower, and to the intensification of inevitable hardship by the decision to treat the emergency as an opportunity to proceed to the most rigorous measures of socialization. Before this period Lenin had recognized some need to compromise and move slowly, because such representative middle-class types as factory managers, successful peasant-farmers, and even retail shopkeepers had a technical efficiency which he could not afford to lose. By this time, however, the class war became a purpose to be pursued almost for its own sake, and fanaticism appeared as a virtue.

The general principle underlying the long succession of decrees issued by the Council of Commissars was to make the centralized state organization responsible for all agriculture, industry, and transport. Since most forms of private property, from factories and big houses to contents of private libraries and personal jewelry, were confiscated and money lost all value, a rationing system which, for example, gave the heavy manual worker three times as much food as the professional man, was a very satisfactory weapon of class warfare. Where War Communism failed completely, however, was in organizing production.

Industry, which was already badly run down when the Communists took over, especially the transportation of raw materials and stocks, continued to decline. By 1920 the output of small concerns was 43 percent, and that of large concerns 18 percent, of the prewar figure; in terms of purchasing power, the meager wages earned by the Russian worker in 1913 had shrunk by nearly two-thirds; and his output in relation to the wages paid him had shrunk by fully three-quarters. One consequence was a mass of illegal barter trade, both in concealed private valuables and in goods stolen from factories, to procure food; another was that something like one-half of the industrial labor force removed itself to country districts. Support for the Revolution was in any case most meager in the countryside, a fact which received official recognition in July, 1918, when the first Communist constitution gave the town soviets five times as much weight in national elections as their population warranted. Rural resistance to the system of requisitioning, by which the state exacted food for the towns and the armies in exchange for a very scanty supply of manufactures or worthless paper money, was continuous and fierce. Nor did it subside when attempts were made to proceed to the final stage, in which the state would itself determine the cropping plan and allocate the labor supply accordingly.

What had been barely endurable in the critical phase of the Civil War became completely unendurable as soon as the crisis had passed. Previously the industrial worker had feared the return of the factory owner and the factory police; the peasant had feared the return of his landlord; and the active Communist had feared the firing squad. These dangers had lessened, and thus even Trotsky was unable to breathe new life into industry by converting the forces no longer needed to fight the Whites into "revolutionary armies of labor." The overwhelming desire was to get home, and though some much-needed work of reconstruction (particularly for transport) was accomplished, all Trotsky's efforts were impeded by ill will toward the bureaucracy, whose projects were viewed by the soldiers as mere obstacles to demobilization. Another modest contribution to industrial needs was made by volunteer spare-time work known as "Saturdaying," done by the more ardent members of the Communist Party, but in general it found more admirers than imitators.

In the winter of 1920–1921 opposition developed on a wide front. A short-lived proposal arose within the Communist Party for transferring the management of industry to the trade unions. Serious peasant risings broke out in the Ukraine, in western Siberia, and in the province of Tambov southeast of Moscow. The most dangerous threat to the regime came from an utterly unexpected quarter, however, when a strike of factory workers due to the chronic shortages of food in Petrograd touched off a mutiny in the garrison at Kronstadt. The mutineers, many of them peasant recruits for the navy from the Ukraine, called for a "Third Revolution, which will strike the last chains from the working masses." When the fortress was captured after a severe struggle by a night attack across the ice, the firing squads of the Cheka obliterated the demand for this Third Revolution; nevertheless, the Second Revolution had been forced to enter upon a new phase through the abolition of War Communism.

At a Party Congress held in early March, 1921, while the struggle for Kronstadt was in progress, Lenin announced a new economic policy. This substituted a graduated tax in kind for the hated requisitioning of the peasant's total surplus of grain: he was now free to sell his surplus on the open market. In other commodities and manufactures, too, Lenin restored a limited freedom to private trade and small-scale industry within the framework of the state monopoly of foreign trade, large-scale industry, and transportation. Lenin himself compared the change of tactics to the decision of the Japanese in 1905 to reach the same goal by trench warfare, when they had failed to capture Port Arthur by storm. It will be the concern of a later chapter to trace the stages by which the Communists finally subjugated all the forces of private enterprise in Russia. In 1921 they were glad to call in the "Nepmen," or capitalists of the New Economic Policy, to redress a truly desperate economic situation. The scanty urban bread ration had recently been cut by one-third, industries were closing down for want of fuel, and the long years of social upheaval had produced a general attitude of disillusioned apathy which militated against a new start. To the outside world it seemed a hopeful possibility that the Communist Revolution, having failed to spread abroad, was now about to die out at home. To all except a hard core of Communist enthusiasts the "indestructible union of the workers and peasants," acclaimed by the commissars, was a concept which had so far brought more suffering than joy.

■ COMMUNISM: THEORY AND PRACTICE

The vast series of events described in this chapter grew directly out of the circumstances of the war, which loaded the ill-organized government of Russia with burdens too heavy for it to bear. Its collapse in the so-called "February Revolution" was followed by a period of confusion, during which a provisional government attempted to prepare the way for a liberal parliamentary regime while continuing to support Russia's allies in the war. This, too, collapsed after only eight months in consequence of the "October Revolution," when power was seized by an extremist group of Social Democrats called Bolsheviks, led by Lenin and Trotsky. At the only nation-wide democratic election ever held in Russia they obtained no more than one vote in four. Even so, they hung on to power during the winter of 1917–1918 by promising peace at any price to the soldiers, land without compensation or control to the peasants, and full self-determination to Russia's subject nationalities.

It is doubtful whether even the Bolshevik leaders, much less the many and various forces which were ranged against the new regime, expected it to survive. The opposition included the Central Powers which imposed harsh peace terms at Brest Litovsk in March, 1918; the Allies, bitterly resentful of Russia's withdrawal from the war and fearful that Bolshevik ideas might spread; and the parties of resistance inside the country to whom the Allies gave both direct and indirect support. These parties of resistance ranged through the whole gamut, beginning with members of the nobility and the officer caste, and including middle-class liberals and constitutionalists, a large proportion of the well-to-do peasants represented by the Social Revolutionary Party, and the Menshevik, or less extreme, section of Social Democrats. Under such circumstances, the fact that the Bolshevik regime was still in existence at the end of an immensely bitter three-year struggle is one of the great surprises in history.

Hardly less surprising was the contrast between theory and practice in the affairs of the new state. In theory the Union of Soviet Socialist Republics—the title formally adopted in 1924—was a federation, in which the subjection of minor nationalities characteristic of the tsarist empire had given way to free association. In practice, however, at the end of the Civil War a powerful central authority was systematically reimposed except where the border peoples had proved strong enough to wrench themselves free. In theory, too, the basic institution was the "soviet" or local council, spontaneously formed by workers, soldiers, or peasants and joining together in National Congresses of Soviets. But the elected Soviets and their congresses—though they still cause "Soviet" to be used as a synonym for Russian "Communist"—in practice carried very little weight in comparison with the single Marxist Party. Recruited in effect by co-option, the Party was so constructed as to culminate in a five-man Political Bureau headed by Lenin and Trotsky. At each lower level the all-powerful Party likewise entered into and determined the action of every organ of the state.

A third example of these contrasts is still more striking. In March, 1918, a few months before banning their last rivals, the Bolsheviks formally adopted the name of Communist for their type of Marxist Socialist party, on the ground that Bolshevik (Majority) Social Democrat, the term in use since 1903, was scientifically inaccurate. In proposing the change, Lenin argued as follows:

> In the process of revolutionary development the old conception of democracy, bourgeois democracy, has been left behind. . . . In undertaking socialist reforms, we should clearly indicate the object toward which these reforms are directed. That object is to create a Communistic Society . . . and realize the principle: *from each according to his ability and to each according to his needs.* That is why the name "Communist Party" is the only scientifically correct name.[13]

13. Lenin's Statement at the Seventh Communist Party Congress, March 8, 1918, quoted by BUNYAN and FISHER, *The Bolshevik Revolution,* p. 544.

Here again the practice of the U.S.S.R. down to the present day has borne little direct relation to a noble ideal, which makes the satisfaction of human need the sole concern in distributing the product of labor. Yet, although communism in the strict theoretical sense of the word gave way to the harsh necessities of shaping and defending a workers' state, far-reaching ideas of social rights have emerged to influence friend and foe alike. Since the French Revolution of 1789 set ideas of political and national rights marching across the world, no movement of equal importance has arisen to stir and divide mankind. For better or worse, the year 1917 was one of the main turning points in history.

Reading List: Chapter 2

Reed, J., *Ten Days that Shook the World* (1926, also paperback), chs. 4–5. Events of November 7th and 8th, 1917, in Petrograd, described by an American eyewitness.

Lockhart, R. H. B., "The Unanimous Revolution," *Foreign Affairs*, vol. XXXV (1957), no. 3.

The New Cambridge Modern History, vol. XII (1960), ch. 14. The revolutions in 1917.

Woodward, D., "Lenin's Journey, April, 1917," *History Today*, vol. VIII (1958), no. 5. The return to Russia.

Bailey, S. D., "Brest-Litovsk: A Study in Soviet Diplomacy," *History Today*, vol. VI (1956), no. 8.

Reshetar, J. S., *The Ukrainian Revolution, 1917–1920* (1952), ch. 7. Why Ukrainian nationalism failed.

Footman, D., "The Civil War," *History Today*, vol. IV (1954), no. 3, vol. VI (1956), nos. 2, 12.

Chapter 3

The Resettlement of Continental Europe

The Background of the Peace Treaties
The Negotiations at Paris
The Treaty with Germany
The Lesser Treaties
The League, Mandates, and Minorities
The Uncertain Voice of Democracy
The Green Revolution
The Further Search for Security

■ THE BACKGROUND OF THE PEACE TREATIES

The peace treaties of 1919 were intended to establish order and security in a continent torn by four years of war. In this sense the historic settlement can be regarded as another in the long list of periodic rearrangements of the European map—Westphalia (1648), Utrecht (1713), Vienna (1815)—coming at the close of an age of general conflict. Much, however, was unique in this latest attempt. The 1914–1918 war was the first in which the power of the Industrial Revolution was widely deployed, the first truly to mobilize the entire resources of nation after nation, the first to occasion such widespread destruction, the first in which mass propaganda aroused such profound emotions. Treaty arrangements had to be sought while many confused struggles still went

SIGNIFICANT EVENTS

1918   President Wilson's Fourteen Points (January)
           Treaty of Brest Litovsk between Germany and Russia (March)

1919   Paris Peace Conference (January–June)
           Treaty of Versailles; First minority treaty with Poland (June)
           Treaty of St. Germain with Austria (September)
           Treaty of Neuilly with Bulgaria (November)

1920   League of Nations officially in existence (January)
           Treaty of the Trianon with Hungary (June)
           Treaty of Sèvres with Turkey (August)

1921   Franco-Polish treaty of military alliance (February)
           Treaty of Riga between Russia and Poland (March)
           Little Entente between Czechoslovakia, Yugoslavia, and Rumania (June)

1921–1922   Washington Disarmament Conference (November–February)

1922   Treaty of Rapallo between Germany and Russia (April)

1923   Occupation of the Ruhr by France and Belgium (January–September)
           Treaty of Lausanne with Turkey (July)

1924   Treaty of alliance between France and Czechoslovakia (January)

1925   Locarno Treaties (October)

1926   Germany admitted to the League of Nations (September)

1927   Geneva Naval Disarmament Conference (June–August)

1928   Pact of Paris (August)

on in eastern Europe and a vast social revolution of incalculable portent raged in the murky distances of Russia.

The proceedings were burdened by a complex network of prior negotiations and secret treaties. Italy had joined the Allied Powers in May, 1915, with the promise, embodied in the Treaty of London, that she would get the South Tyrol, Trieste, Istria, northern Dalmatia, the Dodecanese Islands off the Turkish coast (occupied since 1912), a sphere of influence in Anatolia, and a possible extension of her African colonies. Rumania had been promised Bukowina, Transylvania, and the Banat of Temesvar in August, 1916. Britain had promised independence within certain limits to the Arab peoples then subject to the Ottoman Empire (the McMahon Pledge of October, 1915). Spheres of influence had been arranged for France and Britain, with Palestine to be under an international regime (the Sykes-Picot Agreement of May, 1916). Support for a Jewish "national home" in Palestine had been pledged by the British in the Balfour Declaration of November, 1917. Lloyd George shortly afterward obtained the assent of Georges Clemenceau to having both Palestine and the oil fields of Mosul in the British sphere of influence.

Russia's breach of her old commitments to the Allied Powers and the continuing storms of revolution kept her from any part in the peace negotiations. Japan had made her "Twenty-One Demands" on China in January, 1915; they included a sphere of influence in the Shantung Peninsula, where the Germans had held Kiaochow, and special rights in southern Manchuria. A large part of these claims China was compelled, albeit reluctantly, to recognize, and Japan vigorously reasserted them at the peace conference.

Many war aims, in addition to those embodied in such secret commitments, were proclaimed by champions of the new cause of national self-determination. The entrance of Italy and Rumania into the war highlighted the prospect of actually dismembering the Austro-Hungarian monarchy—a prospect nowhere in sight in 1914. Revolution in 1917 spelled doom to the centuries-old Russian Empire. In April of that year the British government announced its adherence to the principle of an independent and reunited Poland. During the last year of the war, as the fabric of the old empires began to collapse, former subject peoples one after another won their independence. The Ukrainian People's Republic was proclaimed as early as November, 1917; in the next month Finland followed. Latvian independence was announced in January, 1918; that of Estonia and Lithuania came in February. The independence of a united Poland was declared at Warsaw in October, 1918; during the same month Yugoslavia and Czechoslovakia took similar steps, followed quickly in November by action on the part of the separate states of Austria and Hungary.

Several dramatic public pronouncements, in contrast to the secret wartime agreements, had been made by President Wilson of the United States,[1] most notably in the Fourteen Points of his address to Congress in January, 1918. These in part were general formulations broadly expressed: "open covenants of peace openly arrived at"; "freedom of navigation upon the seas"; "the removal, as far as possible, of economic barriers"; reduction of armaments "to the lowest point consistent with domestic safety"; an adjustment of colonial

1. 1856–1924. President of Princeton University, governor of New Jersey, and from 1913 to 1921 president of the United States. His "Fourteen Points" marked him as the champion of an equitable peace, recognizing the rights of nationalities. Yet his role at the Paris Peace Conference attracted as much criticism as praise, perhaps because he seemed unaware of the "realities" of international politics. His principal achievement was to insist upon the formation of the League of Nations which was to a very considerable extent his memorial.

claims taking into account the interest of the populations concerned; and the formation of "a general association of nations." Wilson also dealt with specific territorial questions, though again with frequent imprecision: the evacuation of all Russian territory; the restoration of Belgium; the return of Alsace-Lorraine to France; readjustment of the frontiers of Italy along clearly recognizable lines of nationality; and autonomous development for the peoples of Austria-Hungary, "whose place among the nations we wish to see safeguarded and assured." Rumania, Serbia, and Montenegro were to be evacuated; Turkish portions of the Ottoman Empire were to be recognized as sovereign, while other parts were to be assured "an absolutely unmolested opportunity of autonomous development." The Dardanelles should be opened to the ships and commerce of all nations and an independent Poland set up "including the territories inhabited by indisputably Polish populations, which should be assured a free and secure access to the sea."

Reinforced by later declarations and accepted cautiously and with reservations by Britain and France, the Fourteen Points were taken by the German government to be the general basis of peace when it applied on October 4, 1918, for an armistice. Two significant reservations were made by the Allies when on November 5 they sent Germany their reply. They stipulated (1) that they would reserve complete discretion concerning freedom of the seas, and (2) that compensation was to be made by Germany for all damage done to civilian populations of the Allies and to their property. No mention had been made of reparations or indemnities in the Fourteen Points—only that occupied territories should be restored. The November 5 memorandum, however, took the word "restored" to mean that reparation would be required of Germany for the civilian losses which she had occasioned.

■ THE NEGOTIATIONS AT PARIS

The great conference whose work primarily was to prepare the German peace treaty opened in plenary session at Paris on January 18, 1919—a little more than two months after the armistice. Thirty-two "Allied and Associated" states, those at war with the Central Powers, attended. Only seven plenary sessions were held during the five months of the proceedings, and at only one of these did any substantial discussion—on the Covenant of the League of Nations—take place. It is surely significant that the plenary conference received the full text of the German treaty from the drafters only one day before members of the German delegation themselves received it. As was true at the Vienna Congress a century before, and perhaps inescapably, effective leadership lay in the hands of the major powers.

The real work at Paris was carried on by a continuation of the Supreme War Council (Britain, France, the United States, and Italy) with the addition of Japan; and as each of these states had two principal representatives, the group became known as the Council of Ten. Since Japan limited her interests to the Far East, and since Lloyd George, Clemenceau,[2] Wilson, and Vittorio Orlando carried the weight of the negotiations, the "Big Four" played the major role. Indeed, since the Italian Orlando was so frequently isolated and since he at one point returned home in protest, the "Big Three" in the last analysis dominated the Paris meetings. The five principal foreign ministers, who were present as deputies to their respective leaders, constituted a separate Council of Five which sought to give expert attention to the complex problems of Austria, Hungary, Bulgaria, and Turkey.

President Wilson came to Paris as the eloquent spokesman of a New World country with vast resources, many high ideals, and few traditional diplomatic commitments. He was so deeply impressed by the crowds who hailed him tumultuously on his brief preliminary European tour that this gave some substance to the charge he was developing a Messianic complex. His critics—and they grew in number—found him austere, unfamiliar with European realities, academic in his approach, and capable of shifting unpredictably from the loftiest idealism to a most unexpected and disconcerting willingness to compromise and bargain. Lloyd George was a superb politician, quick to grasp the essentials of European problems although he often initially knew very little about them. He can rightly be described as an opportunist, seeking the best possible European peace that would at the same time safeguard all vital British interests. The seventy-eight-year-old Clemenceau impressed one observer as being less like the tiger whose name had been applied to him as a war leader than a tired old walrus. Yet he was the ever alert champion of his country's interests, and the ever suspicious guardian against the German menace which he had first seen explode in the war of 1870. "He had one illusion—France," wrote John Maynard Keynes, "and one disillusion—mankind, including Frenchmen and his colleagues not least."[3] A weak Germany was to Clemenceau the best guarantee of both French and European security.

The various foreign offices had done what they could in advance of the meetings to prepare studies of problems bound to arise. Large bodies of experts attended. Lobbyists, as they would be called today, worked hard for many special interests. Altogether, seventeen principal and over forty other commissions were established. Though some effort was made to restrict the

2. 1841–1929. A visitor to the United States immediately after the Civil War, he first served in the French National Assembly in 1871. For many years a champion of the extreme Left, he became during the First World War a brilliant wartime leader. An ardent champion of French nationalism and a determined opponent of leniency to Germany, his autobiographical work, *Grandeurs and Miseries of Victory,* suggests something of the skepticism of his outlook.

3. *The Economic Consequences of the Peace* (1919), p. 32.

THE BIG FOUR AT VERSAILLES. Lloyd George, Orlando, Clemenceau, and Wilson display a genial affability in public rarely present during their private discussions.

discussions at Paris to the treatment of Germany and, as Wilson insisted, the formation of the League of Nations, any discussion of Germany's frontiers automatically involved the vital interests of her neighbors. Italy, moreover, categorically refused to sign a German treaty unless her own claims against Austria and Yugoslavia were met. Complex discussions, therefore, were inevitable. In addition to the work of peacemaking, the leading statesmen were required to act in some sense as a cabinet of Europe, dealing with the continuance of the German blockade, the possibility of negotiating with the Communist regime in Russia, the distribution of food supplies, and the action to be taken in face of the highly disturbing eruption of at least half a dozen European civil wars and minor conflicts. Wilson, too, had to be absent from February 15 to March 14—a most critical period—to face the hostile Republican majorities in the newly elected American Congress.

The Paris Peace Conference opened at a time when wartime bitterness still prevailed, when disruptive strikes weakened the economy in England and Italy, when revolutionaries were attempting to seize power in Berlin, in Bavaria, and in Hungary, and when Russia, torn by revolution, loomed up as a vast enigma. During the first winter of peace, starvation threatened large parts of Europe and a world-wide influenza epidemic killed, almost unbelievably, about twice as many people as the war itself had destroyed. The proceedings at Paris went on amid the rivalries and even the personal antipathies of statesmen. The defeated powers were not represented and were not allowed to present their case. The proposal to open discussions with Russian delegations at Prinkipo, an island in the Sea of Marmara, failed. Too much was attempted with too little preparation, and in too short a time, by men whose energies were sapped by wordy disagreements and by long hours spent in stuffy and overheated rooms. Thus, cynical nicknames such as "the lost peace" and "the peace that passeth all understanding" were all too easily applied to the settlement which they ultimately produced.

The topics of discussion at Paris frequently overlapped. Wilson had put the Covenant of the League of Nations high on his agenda; it had received the attention of able men both in France and Britain; and so, by the time of his departure for the United States in February, a draft was submitted for discussion to the third plenary session. It was adopted by the fifth plenary session on April 28, 1919. France felt that her own security and stability would be best safeguarded if, in addition to Alsace-Lorraine, she could control the Rhineland. As the best available safeguard against future German aggression, France proposed that a neutral buffer state be detached from Germany and set up on the west bank of the Rhine. She also sought the coal-rich Saar valley in compensation for her coal mines that Germany had destroyed. She sought also to establish as strong a Poland as possible along Germany's eastern frontier. In all these matters compromise proved inevitable.

The wartime secret treaties caused much trouble. Italy's chief concern was to rectify her borders with Austria and the new Yugoslav state so as to complete the unfulfilled aspirations of 1871. She also desired the Adriatic port of Fiume. Here differences became so acute that the resentful Italian leaders for a time left the conference, returning in the end to accept compromises, most of which were inserted in the Austrian rather than in the German treaty. Japan's claims to the former German possessions of Tsingtao and the Shantung Peninsula in north China likewise provoked a violent storm, as this area was indisputably Chinese.

Disagreement also arose over the questions of war guilt and reparations. Despite the pre-armistice understanding that Germany was to provide compensation for all damage done to the civilian population of the Allies and to their property, the cry was quickly raised, especially in France, that payment of the full cost of the war—which would be astronomical—should be required. When this claim was dropped, Lloyd George successfully demanded that war pensions (later defined as "all pensions to military and naval victims of war . . . and allowances to families and dependents of mobilized persons") be included among civilian damages. A special commission on war responsibility was set up which after a mere six weeks' investigation made its finding, on the basis of such evidence as was then available, that "the war was premeditated by the Central Powers together with their allies, Turkey and Bulgaria." At the sixth plenary session on May 6, 1919, the draft of the peace treaty was approved.

A delegation from the new German Republic meanwhile had arrived at Versailles, where it waited for over a week, carefully isolated in its hotel behind barbed wire. On May 7 the two-hundred-page treaty draft was formally submitted to the Germans.

> We have no illusions [declared the head of the German delegation on that tense occasion] as to the extent of our defeat and the measure of our impotence. We know that the power of German arms is broken, and we are aware of the fury of hate which greets us. We are asked to assume the sole guilt of the war. Such a confession from my lips would be a lie. We have no intention of absolving Germany from all responsibility for the war. . . . But we expressly contend that Germany, whose people was convinced that it was fighting a defensive war, should not be saddled with the whole responsibility.[4]

The Germans were given two weeks, later extended to three, for their reply. On May 29 they submitted 443 pages of "observations," a document more than twice the size of the treaty itself. The Allies accepted a few minor points— a plebiscite, for example, was promised in Upper Silesia and by districts in Schleswig—but insisted that if the terms as drafted were not accepted by June 23, they would advance into Germany with thirty-nine divisions. A cabinet crisis in Germany led to the forming of a new government and this, at five o'clock on the very afternoon of the time limit, indicated its readiness to sign. Consequently on June 28, 1919, five years to the day since the assassination at Sarajevo, a new German delegation appeared in the Hall of Mirrors at Versailles and signed the 440 articles of the historic Treaty of Versailles. Philip Scheidemann, who retired as provisional chancellor rather than be responsible, had earlier declared that the hand must wither which signed such a treaty.

■ THE TREATY WITH GERMANY

Part I of the Versailles Treaty constituted the Covenant of the League of Nations which Wilson had fought hard to include. His further expectation, however, that the United States Senate would be obliged to ratify the Covenant along with the rest of the Treaty, was to be sharply disappointed, since Republican leadership in the Senate chose rather to turn down the entire document. The United States remained technically at war until July, 1921, and a separate American treaty, excluding the League Covenant, was signed in

4. Quoted in G. P. GOOCH, *Germany* (1925), p. 214. Article 231 states collective responsibility, but not "sole guilt." See p. 73.

August of that year. China, too, objecting to the cession of the Shantung Peninsula to Japan, refused to sign.

The territorial provisions required Germany to cede the small areas of Eupen and Malmédy to Belgium, and to return the "lost provinces" of Alsace and Lorraine to France.[5] Northern Schleswig, after a favorable plebiscite, went to Denmark, and a slight border area near Troppau went to Czechoslovakia. Treaty stipulations subjected Upper Silesia to a plebiscite in 1921, when the smaller, but economically much more valuable, portion went to Poland. This new country obtained the greater part of West Prussia (the Polish Corridor) as an outlet to the sea, and the greater part of the province of Posen. Plebiscites held in the southern areas of East Prussia confirmed that these should remain as parts of the new Germany. At the extreme eastern limit of East Prussia, Memel was placed at the disposition of the Allies; it later was to become Lithuania's principal outlet to the sea. Danzig, at the mouth of the Vistula River, being indisputably German in population, was denied to Poland and set up as a free city under the League of Nations.

France's claims upon the Saar were met by a compromise. As compensation for German destruction of French coal mines, she received full and absolute possession of the Saar mines for fifteen years. The Saar itself for this period would be administered by the League, after which a plebiscite would determine its future status. Germany further agreed to recognize the independence of Austria, "which shall be inalienable, except with the consent of the Council of the League of Nations." She confirmed her abrogation of the Treaty of Brest Litovsk with Russia (March, 1918), and renounced ownership of every inch of her overseas territories, which were to become mandates under the League. This meant the loss of a million square miles of colonial possessions, and in Europe the loss of some 10 percent of her population and 13 percent of her natural resources and industrial output.

The military provisions were introduced with the statement: "In order to render possible the initiation of a general limitation of the armaments of all nations, Germany undertakes strictly to observe the military, naval, and air clauses which follow." Later, however, when the defeated powers realized that disarmament was a reality for them alone, their protests were loud. The military provisions required Germany to reduce her army to 100,000 men recruited by voluntary enlistment for a term of twelve years. Officers were to serve for twenty-five years. This small, professional army, having no tanks, airplanes, or heavy artillery, would constitute a sort of police force and would end, it was hoped, all prospect of a nation in arms. Actually, it was in time to provide the professional cadres, or skeleton forces, around which the huge armies of Hitler's Germany were assembled. The German general staff was to be dissolved, the

5. See map, p. 74.

fortifications of Helgoland destroyed, and the navy restricted to six warships of not more than ten thousand tons, six light cruisers, and twelve destroyers. No submarines were to be permitted. All German territory west of the Rhine and in addition a thirty-mile zone east of the river were to be totally and permanently demilitarized.

The question of war responsibility was embodied in the famous Article 231 introducing the financial provisions of the Treaty:

> The Allied and Associated Governments affirm and Germany accepts the responsibility of Germany and her allies for causing all the loss and damage to which the Allied and Associated Governments and their nationals have been subjected as a consequence of the war imposed upon them by the aggression of Germany and her allies.

Argument has raged ever since over this "war guilt clause," drafted largely by a young American expert, John Foster Dulles. Quite clearly, the commission which had been set up at Paris to determine war responsibility could not in a few weeks and in the absence of major documentary evidence produce any historically sound verdict. The imposition of this clause to some degree represented the desire of Lloyd George and Clemenceau to saddle a moral guilt upon Germany, since it had proved impossible to ask her to reimburse the victors for the full costs of the war. The article in another sense has been claimed to be simply a lawyer's clause—a kind of rhetorical flourish or "whereas" preceding the paragraphs in which actual reparations were levied in respect to damage done to civilians and their property. One thing is certain: to the Germans this was the most outrageous and intolerable clause of the Treaty, a clause that gave weapons to the opponents of the Weimar Republic which had accepted it, and a clause that Hitler exploited most skillfully during his rise to power.

The total sum of Germany's reparations bill was not fixed. Germany was to pay the equivalent of five billion dollars by May, 1921, to deliver specified quantities of coal, timber, other building materials, livestock, rolling stock, and shipping, and to bear the cost of the armies of occupation. By this date a Reparations Commission was to determine the full monetary amount that Germany was to pay and to arrange for its transfer to the recipients within a period of thirty years.

Under the heading of "Guarantees," Allied occupation troops were to hold the Rhineland and bridgeheads east of the Rhine for fifteen years. Withdrawals were to take place at regular intervals beginning in five years. The kaiser was to be brought to trial "for a supreme offence against international morality." About one hundred other persons who were charged with war atrocities were also named for trial. As it turned out, the Netherlands government refused to deny the kaiser his right to asylum, and only a dozen Germans

THE EUROPEAN PEACE SETTLEMENT, 1919-1921

Atlantic Ocean

North Sea

NORWAY

SWEDEN

FINLAND

U.S.S.R.

ESTONIA

GREAT BRITAIN

DENMARK

LATVIA

SCHLESWIG

MEMEL

LITHUANIA

DANZIG

EAST PRUSSIA

NETHERLANDS

POSNAN

POLAND

BELGIUM

EUPEN MALMEDY

GERMANY

UPPER SILESIA

LUX.

SAAR

TESCHEN

SILESIA

LORRAINE

CZECHOSLOVAKIA

ALSACE

FRANCE

SWITZ.

AUSTRIA

SOPRON

HUNGARY

KLAGENFURT

TRANSYLVANIA

TYROL

BESSARABIA

TRIESTE

CROATIA

RUMANIA

ZARA (IT.)

BANAT

DALMATIA

YUGOSLAVIA

Black Sea

MONTE NEGRO

SERBIA

BULGARIA

SPAIN

CORSICA

ITALY

DOBRUDJA

ALBANIA

THRACE

SARDINIA

GREECE

TURKEY

Mediterranean Sea

SMYRNA

SICILY

DODECANESE ISLANDS (IT.)

CRETE

1914

	FRANCE
	GERMANY
	AUSTRIA-HUNGARY
	ITALY
	BELGIUM
	DENMARK
	RUSSIA
	RUMANIA
	BULGARIA
	SERBIA
	MONTENEGRO
	GREECE
	TURKEY
	PLEBISCITE AREAS

actually were tried, not by the Allies, but—as a concession—by the German Supreme Court at Leipzig. The meager results were convictions and light sentences for just six of the accused.

Since France had not been able to have her way in the Rhineland, she had been given by Wilson and Lloyd George a mutual pledge of military assistance in the event of German aggression. A formal document to this effect was appended to the Versailles Treaty. When the United States failed to ratify her treaty, the British treaty, which was dependent upon it, went by the board and France remained without the promised guarantee.

■ THE LESSER TREATIES

Negotiations concerning the fate of the other defeated powers were carried on at Paris concurrently with the making of the German treaty. The Treaty of St. Germain with Austria was signed in September, 1919. The territorial losses were heavy. Austria ceded Trieste, Istria, and the South Tyrol to Italy, so that the Italian flag now stood at the Brenner Pass. While the southern part of this last acquisition, Trentino, was purely Italian, the northern part, the upper Adige, contained some 230,000 German-speaking inhabitants. Bohemia, Moravia, Austrian Silesia, and parts of Lower Austria went to Czechoslovakia; Bukowina went to Rumania; Austrian Galicia, reserved to the Allied and Associated Powers by the Treaty, eventually went to the new Poland.

These changes meant that in addition to the huge loss of her non-German-speaking peoples, Austria gave up nearly four million German-speaking subjects to her neighbors. The total prewar population subject to Austria had been nearly 30,000,000. It was now 6,500,000, of whom one-third lived in the capital city of Vienna. Austria's area was reduced from 115,000 to 32,000 square miles. The army was limited to 30,000 men. Reparations, preceded by

A comparison of the frontiers established by the peace treaties (heavy black lines) with the various shadings will show the losses of territories, for example from Germany to France and Poland. The dotted areas indicate continued disputes and friction. The plebiscite areas were disposed of as follows:

Eupen and Malmédy: after nominal plebiscite to Belgium.
Northern Schleswig: partitioned, after plebiscite in two zones, between Denmark and Germany.
Southern part of East Prussia: after plebiscite to remain German.
Upper Silesia: partitioned, after plebiscite, between Germany and Poland.
Teschen: partitioned, without plebiscite, between Poland and Czechoslovakia.
Sopron: by plebiscite to Hungary.
Klagenfurt: by plebiscite to Austria.

Eastern Thrace and the area around Smyrna, allotted to Greece, were reacquired by Turkey in 1923.

a war guilt clause, which interestingly enough caused few repercussions, were to be paid over a period of thirty years. Actually, Austria paid only for ten years. *Anschluss,* or union with Germany, was forbidden except with the consent of the League of Nations.

The Treaty of Neuilly, signed with Bulgaria in November, 1919, returned the country to its prewar situation, with some minor losses. Small border areas in the west went to Yugoslavia and a larger area, western Thrace, to Greece. This latter transfer deprived Bulgaria of her outlet to the Aegean. Disarmament and reparations were also stipulated.

The Treaty of Trianon with Hungary was completed in June, 1920. A brief Communist regime set up in March, 1919, had left the new Hungarian state quite powerless. The leader, Bela Kun, a prisoner of war returned from Russia, attacked private property in a variety of measures. Among them were decrees limiting individual clothing to a maximum of two suits, two shirts, two pairs of shoes, and two pairs of socks. Private bathrooms were to be made publicly available on Saturday nights. A special corps of released criminals was organized and sent into peasant districts which opposed the regime. Bela Kun fled when the Rumanians occupied the capital. By the Treaty the Hungarians lost almost three-quarters of their prewar territory and two-thirds of their population, the numbers falling from twenty-one to eight million; nearly three million Hungarians were included among the losses. Slovakia and Sub-Carpathian Ruthenia were made part of the new Czechoslovak state; Bosnia, Croatia-Slavonia, and part of the Banat went to Yugoslavia; Transylvania and the rest of the Banat went to Rumania. Even defeated Austria received part of the common Austro-Hungarian frontier area—the Burgenland. Reparations and disarmament clauses were included. Little wonder that for years Budapest was covered with posters on which the words *Nem! Nem! Soha!* (No! No! Never!) expressed the Hungarian view of the Treaty.

The arrangements with Turkey involved much confusion. By the Treaty of Sèvres (August, 1920) the Turks renounced all claims to non-Turkish territory, thus accepting the existence of the new Arab states. In addition to these, Syria was to become a French mandate; Palestine and Iraq were to be British mandates. Armenia was to be independent. Greece was temporarily to administer Smyrna, in Asia Minor, with its hinterland. Having received western Thrace from Bulgaria, Greece was now to receive eastern Thrace from Turkey so that her new frontier pushed close to Constantinople. By separate agreements Italy had promised that the Dodecanese Islands, including ultimately Rhodes, were to go to Greece—a promise that was not kept. The Straits, leading into the Black Sea and historically the source of long conflict, were to be set up as an international zone governed by a six-power commission under the League of Nations.

The settlement quickly became a dead letter, for the simple reason that a new nationalist Turkish movement led by Mustafa Kemal Pasha refused to accept it.[6] Obtaining military assistance from Soviet Russia, Kemal drove the Greeks from Anatolia with great savagery. Tensions mounted until the Allies, deciding that maintenance of the Treaty of Sèvres was not worth an open war, began new negotiations in Switzerland. By the Treaty of Lausanne (July, 1923), Turkey again gave up all claims to the non-Turkish territories where the Arabs had won their freedom. On the other hand, she scored a great victory against Greece, keeping Anatolia, two of the Aegean Islands, and eastern Thrace. Italy retained the Dodecanese Islands and Britain kept Cyprus. A new regime for the Straits was now essential. The solution was to leave them Turkish, but demilitarized. They were to be open to ships of all nations in times of peace, and even in time of war if Turkey remained neutral. These arrangements—a substantial restriction upon Turkey's power—stayed in effect until the Montreux Convention of 1936, when Turkey was allowed to refortify the Straits.

These various treaties had done much to remake the map of Europe in closer accord with the principle of nationality than ever before. In the east the Treaty of Riga (March, 1921) brought to an end the Russo-Polish War and established the common border of these two countries far to the east of the famous "Curzon Line." This Line had been defined on the basis of ethnic data by a committee under Lord Curzon during the Peace Conference at Paris in 1919. The frontier of 1921, which gave Poland a total population of twenty-seven million, put over four million White Russians and Ukrainians within the Polish state. In 1921, too, the Poles seized Vilna from Lithuania, an act of force reluctantly accepted by the Allies two years later.

Other acts of force were evident in the relations between Italy and Yugoslavia. Though Italy did very well around the Adriatic in the peace settlement, especially in gaining Trieste, she bitterly opposed the Yugoslav plea that Fiume, whose status had been left uncertain, was the country's only remaining practicable port. The Italian poet D'Annunzio precipitated a crisis in September, 1919, by seizing Fiume for Italy. Long disputes followed, the outcome of which was that at Rapallo in November, 1920, Italy was given the entire Istrian Peninsula with its largely Slavic population, and Fiume, like Danzig, was declared a free city. In March, 1922, Italian Fascists again seized Fiume—an arbitrary move completely without legality which Yugoslavia in 1924 was induced at long last to countenance.

The unhappy general deterioration of conditions in the two decades following the peace has led many to put the blame for it upon the 1919–1920 settlement. The treaties were criticized as being too hastily drawn, wrong in

6. See pp. 120–122.

imposing what the Germans chose to call "sole war guilt" on the defeated powers, and impossibly harsh in the matter of reparations. It was said to be unwise to create so many small states by a process trenchantly described as "the Balkanization of Europe," and unrealistic to expect truncated units such as Austria and Hungary to prosper. Russia, so it was argued, should somehow have been brought into the discussions, and the German Republic should not have been kept out of the League. The peacemakers were charged with leaving numerous national minorities without adequate safeguards inside the new states. They failed to make the League of Nations strong enough for its essential purposes. Within Germany and Hungary, far more than in Austria, protest against the peace settlement soon developed. By 1932 the German universities had produced no fewer than 287 doctoral theses dealing with the Treaty of Versailles.

On the other hand, it is all too easy for the critics of the treaties of 1919 to confuse what is ideal with what was then possible. Whatever their defects, the new frontiers of the European states more nearly satisfied national aspirations than had been the case ever before. Plans were soon launched for the protection of minorities through special treaty arrangements. It was something, too, that the concept of general disarmament was stated in the treaties. The many defects, of which Wilson and others were fully aware, might reasonably be reduced by degrees through the work of the League of Nations and the many commissions for which provision was made. Yet Marshal Foch prophesied that the settlement would produce in Europe only a "twenty years' armistice." He was, unhappily, an astute prophet.

■ THE LEAGUE, MANDATES, AND MINORITIES

The League of Nations arose out of long efforts to find some better means than armed force for solving disputes between states. During the war men in various countries had turned their attention to the problem. Wilson had listed "a general association of nations" as the last of his Fourteen Points. At Paris a special commission put the draft into final shape. General Jan Christiaan Smuts of South Africa—a philosopher-statesman of unique quality—later described the Covenant of the League as "one of the great creative documents of human history."

The League of Nations closely foreshadowed in structure the United Nations, which developed, indeed, as the logical sequel to it. The General Assembly was to meet at stated intervals and deal "with any matter within the sphere of action of the League or affecting the peace of the world." Each member was to have only one vote. Since decisions had to be unanimous, the General Assembly could hardly be an efficient means for vigorous action. It would provide, rather, a forum for public discussion—a service which, especially in giving small powers an opportunity to present their views, should not be underrated.

The League Council was to consist of five permanent members (the United States, Great Britain, France, Italy, and Japan) and four elected non-permanent members. The United States, fearful of infringements upon its sovereignty, though assured by Article XXI that nothing in the Covenant would affect the validity of the Monroe Doctrine, never joined. Both Germany and the Soviet Union later acquired permanent seats; and the nonpermanent membership on the Council eventually rose to nine. The Council was authorized, in precisely the same language used for the Assembly, "to deal at its meetings with any matter within the sphere of action of the League or affecting the peace of the world." The League was to have a permanent Secretariat and a Secretary-General; its headquarters were to be in Geneva; and associated closely with it were to be the International Labor Organization and the Permanent Court of International Justice.

What active part was the League intended to play? The French had tried hard to create an organization that would be essentially an alliance of the five victorious Powers, armed with military force and intended to guarantee security. "They can christen it the Society of Nations to please Mr. Wilson," wrote a French newspaper. "That will hurt no one." The Americans and the British, with their Anglo-Saxon concept of the reign of law, saw it otherwise. The League as constituted was neither a military alliance nor a super state, but an association of sovereign members pledged to work together for certain limited purposes mentioned in the Preamble: ". . . to promote international co-operation and to achieve international peace and security." It was in this sense more properly an outgrowth of the old Concert of Europe than a new attempt at a world parliament.

The League's purposes are shown in the salient articles of the Covenant. Article VIII committed members to seek the reduction of armaments "to the lowest point consistent with national safety," for which purpose the Council was to formulate plans and a Permanent Commission was to be set up. Article X, which committed members to a mutual guarantee of territorial integrity and political independence, has been called the legal cornerstone of the entire security edifice. Article XI provided for conciliation in the event of a war or threat of war. Articles XII and XIII provided for the well-established methods of arbitration and judicial settlement when disputes arose "likely to lead to a rupture." Article XVI, which turned out to be a sticking point for the United States, reads in its salient passages as follows:

Should any Member of the League resort to war in disregard of its Covenants under Articles 12, 13, or 15, it shall *ipso facto* be deemed to have committed an act of war against all other Members of the League, which hereby undertake immediately to subject it to the severance of all trade or financial relations. . . . It shall be the duty of the Council in such case to recommend to the several Governments concerned what effective military, naval, or air force the Members of the League shall severally contribute.

Two words in this article deserve comment. "Immediately" implied that the imposition by all members of economic sanctions was to be automatic; and "recommend" was a clear indication of the limitation set upon the Council's military authority.

The League, therefore, was intended in summary to provide the machinery whereby nations could maintain regular and effective contact with one another; it involved a mutual guarantee of territorial integrity; it provided for arbitration and judicial settlement; and, failing these, it contemplated economic sanctions against an aggressor plus such further measures as the Council should "recommend." Sixty-three states were at one time or another members. Germany joined in 1926 and withdrew in 1934, the year in which the Soviet Union entered. Six states in all, including Japan, Italy, and Brazil, chose to withdraw. The Soviet Union, in consequence of its attack upon Finland in 1939, was the only member ever to be expelled. While the League never was joined by its principal sponsor, the United States, and rarely had more than the lukewarm support of the other major powers that were members, it provided a welcome forum for statesmen of the lesser countries. Some distinguished leaders, such as Eduard Beneš,[7] a president of Czechoslovakia, Eleutherios Venizelos, a prime minister of Greece, and Fridtjof Nansen[8] of Norway, played honorable roles.

The International Labor Organization, authorized in Part XIII of the Versailles Treaty, was declared in a preamble to have the purpose of furthering social justice by improving the conditions of labor. Usually avoiding the political storms to which the League was subject, it included in its membership some states (the United States after 1934, for example) which did not join the

7. 1884–1948. Born of poor parents, he became professor of sociology at the University of Prague. He strongly supported the Czechoslovak nationalist movement headed by Masaryk and was one of the creators of his country's independence. Foreign minister from 1918 to 1935, he was principal architect of the Little Entente. President from 1935 to 1938, he resigned after Munich. President again from 1945 to 1948, he lived long enough to see his country become a Soviet satellite.
8. 1861–1930. Trained as a naturalist, he soon became equally distinguished as a polar explorer, a writer, a humanitarian, and a statesman. He had championed the independence of Norway from Sweden in 1905 and subsequently held several diplomatic posts. He won the Nobel Peace Prize in 1922 for his humanitarian work in Russia where he had been responsible for the repatriation of nearly half a million prisoners of war and for large-scale famine relief. From the beginning he was a member of the Norwegian delegation to the League of Nations and was responsible for the resettlement and care of the Greeks who were driven out of Anatolia by the Turks after the First World War.

League, and others which remained in the I.L.O. after withdrawing from the League. So significant, indeed, was its economic contribution that it remained active during the Second World War and continued after 1946 as one of the specialized agencies of the United Nations.

The Permanent Court of International Justice, authorized in Article XIV of the League Covenant, was a kind of extension of the Permanent Court of Arbitration set up by the Hague Peace Conference of 1899. Fifteen paid judges were to be elected by the League Council and Assembly for nine-year terms and were to sit regularly at The Hague. States were not bound to submit their disputes to the Permanent Court, or World Court, as it came to be known, though they could in any given treaty include a clause accepting the jurisdiction of the Court in case of conflict. They could, further, accept the Optional Clause (Article 36 of the Statute of the Permanent Court), agreeing in advance to accept its jurisdiction in specified cases. Forty states in all subscribed to this Optional Clause and eventually fifty had participated in the work of the Court. Yet only thirty-two judgments and twenty-seven advisory opinions were rendered between 1922 and 1942; machinery was lacking to enforce its decisions, and in questions of major importance few states were prepared to commit their national interests to a court of fifteen judges, no matter how eminent or how seemingly disinterested they might be.

An entirely novel development of the peace settlement was the creation of mandates, provided for in Article XXII of the League Covenant. These were intended to solve the problem of the former German colonies and those non-Turkish parts of the former Ottoman Empire not yet ready for independence. The inhabitants of such areas were to be regarded as a sacred trust to be directed by "advanced nations who by reason of their resources, their experience, or their geographical position can best undertake this responsibility." The goal should be, in some cases, complete independence, in others, the obtaining of as high a degree of political, economic, and social justice and well-being as was possible. A Mandates Commission at Geneva was to receive annual reports and exercise general direction and supervision.

Mandates were divided into three classes. The "A Mandates" were made up of the former possessions of the Ottoman Empire, all candidates for eventual independence. Syria and the Lebanon were allotted to France; Palestine, Transjordan, and Mesopotamia (Iraq) to Britain. The "B Mandates" were the former German possessions in central and east Africa. Togoland and the Cameroons were divided between Britain and France; the greater part of Tanganyika, or German East Africa, went to Britain, and the remainder (Ruanda-Urundi) to Belgium. The "C Mandates," which could best be administered by the mandatory power "as integral portions of its territory," comprised German Southwest Africa, administered by the Union of South Africa; German Samoa, by New Zealand; German New Guinea and former German islands south of the equator, by Australia; the Carolines, the Marianas, and the Marshalls, by Japan.

The mandates system was a new beginning in the evolution of colonial peoples. Inevitably there were troubles. Syria and Palestine placed difficult burdens on the mandatory powers. The race-conscious Union of South Africa was soon under fire for the ruthless administration of its mandate. And Japan violated her responsibilities in the later 1920's by secretly fortifying some of her Pacific island acquisitions and refusing the Mandates Commission access to them.

A further problem of the peace arrangements was that of Europe's minorities, that is to say, people of one language, religion, or nationality living under the rule of another. These, in the Europe of 1914, were in the neighborhood of one hundred million, and while the treaties of 1919 redrew frontiers so as to make them correspond more closely than ever before to national groupings, no amount of ingenuity could solve the problem completely. Estimates of the total of these minorities after the treaties of 1919 vary from twenty-five to thirty million—in either case a very substantial reduction of the prewar figure. Yet they seemed there to stay. The only case in which a population transfer was formally carried out was that of the Greco-Turkish agreement of 1923, by which some 400,000 Turks in Greek territory in the Balkans were exchanged for 1,300,000 Greeks still living precariously in Asia Minor.

How complex the problem was may be seen from the tabulation on page 83 which gives the total population of thirteen countries having minority treaties, roughly around 1930, and indicates only the largest (and not the whole range) of the minority groups in each. Safeguards were put into the other peace treaties, and in addition special minority agreements were signed by the five principal powers or by the League with those countries where important minority problems existed. Interestingly enough, Italy, and even defeated Germany, were not asked to make formal commitments to treat their minorities well, nor—as history was to show—did they do so.

A Permanent Minorities Commission of the League was to receive the annual reports of the states concerned and to advise the Council, which set up special subcommittees to hear petitions. In two decades nearly a thousand were received, of which more than half were found "acceptable." Yet the effectiveness of such procedures could be questioned. Some good was done by the pressure of public opinion, and certainly Europe's minorities as a whole had better treatment than ever before. Yet the discontents remained, and even grew. Poland, for example, announced in 1934 that she would no longer recognize the jurisdiction of the League Council in minority questions. Moreover, it is a matter of record that Hitler, building up the supposed sufferings of the German minorities in Czechoslovakia and Poland to a point far beyond what

POSTWAR MINORITY GROUPS[9]

COUNTRY	TOTAL POPULATION	PRINCIPAL MINORITIES	
Estonia	1,100,000 (1931)	Russians	92,000
Latvia	1,900,000 (1930)	Russians	233,000
		Jews	93,000
Lithuania	2,200,000 (1931)	Poles	73,000
		Germans	71,000
Poland	32,700,000 (1931)	Ukrainians	4,200,000
		Jews	2,700,000
		Germans	1,700,000
		White Russians	1,500,000
		Lithuanians	300,000
Czechoslovakia	14,700,000 (1930)	Germans	3,300,000
		Hungarians	719,000
		Ukrainians	569,000
		Jews	357,000
Austria	6,700,000 (1934)	Jews	191,000
		Yugoslavs	85,000
		Czechoslovaks	52,000
Hungary	8,600,000 (1931)	Germans	479,000
		Jews	444,000
		Czechoslovaks	105,000
Rumania	17,800,000 (1930)	Hungarians	1,400,000
		Germans	740,000
		Jews	725,000
		Ukrainians	578,000
		Russians	415,000
		Bulgarians	361,000
Greece	6,200,000 (1928)	Turks	103,000
		Bulgarians	82,000
		Jews	70,000
Bulgaria	5,500,000 (1926)	Turks	578,000
		Rumanians	69,000
Yugoslavia	13,900,000 (1931)	Germans	499,000
		Hungarians	468,000
		Albanians	342,000
		Rumanians	229,000
		Czechoslovaks	176,000
Turkey	13,600,000 (1927)	Kurds	1,800,000
		Greeks	120,000
Iraq	3,100,000 (1930)	various non-Moslems	700,000

9. Derived from H. Kohn, "Minorities," *Encyclopaedia Britannica* (1963 issue), vol. XV, p. 570.

the evidence justified, made dramatic use of these alleged wrongs in his inflammatory appeals to the German people on the eve of the Second World War.

■ THE UNCERTAIN VOICE OF DEMOCRACY

National self-determination on a democratic basis had emerged as one of the great war aims of the Allies, and certainly such claims on behalf of nationality had received a substantial recognition in the peace treaties. The change was striking. The German, Russian, Austro-Hungarian, and Ottoman empires were gone. Germany, Austria, Hungary, and the new succession states emerging from the ruins of the Hapsburg empire had acquired what appeared to be democratic regimes. Republicanism, too, was increasing. Europe in 1914 consisted of twenty-two independent states, including only three republics; in 1919, however, twelve states out of twenty-eight were republican.

The older democratic countries quickly restored many political freedoms suspended during the war. Woman suffrage scored widespread victories, and in other ways women's rights were more widely recognized. Article VII of the League Covenant, for example, required all positions in the League to be open equally to men and women. New social rights were also stressed. Here the most striking example undoubtedly was the second part of the German republican constitution of 1919, which provided for a comprehensive scheme of social security and elaborate guarantees of social welfare, including the stipulation of an eight-hour day for all workers.

Exceptions to this trend were not hard to find. In Russia the forms of parliamentary government envisaged by the moderate revolutionaries of March, 1917, were soon swept away by the arbitrary dictatorship of Lenin's single-party Communist state. The presence of ostensibly parliamentary regimes in Spain and Portugal hardly concealed the overwhelming political power of the army and of small privileged groups, or the staggering degree of peasant poverty and general backwardness. The Balkan states, deficient in political experience and all too familiar with the techniques of violence, could not long avoid the triumph of dictatorial regimes.

Only brief mention is made here of the very early trends toward dictatorship in this postwar world.[10] The pattern of dictatorship, though often veiled, soon began to appear. As early as March, 1920, for example, the Hungarian assembly chose Admiral Nicholas Horthy as regent, and from then on the old privileged aristocratic class was back in the saddle. Benito Mussolini's twenty-year Italian dictatorship began with the March on Rome in October, 1922. In the following year General Miguel Primo de Rivera began a dictatorship which dominated Spain until the fall of the monarchy in 1931. The demo-

10. For a fuller discussion see ch. 7.

cratic Polish constitution of 1921 failed to prevent the trend to dictatorship which became clear in 1926 under Marshal Josef Pilsudski's premiership. In the Baltic area, Lithuania turned to a more or less mild dictatorship in 1926. Austria, though organized as a republic with a very democratic constitution, began to show a similar trend by 1930. Attempts to overthrow the German Republic by sudden risings such as the "Kapp Putsch" of 1920 date almost from its beginning. It is clear that strong forces opposed to democracy were at work, and these, coupled with the growth of bad economic conditions after 1928, helped to make Germany tragically receptive to the dictatorial ambitions of Adolf Hitler. Thus doubt was cast on the high hopes widely held that the sacrifices in the First World War would make the world safe for democracy.

■ THE GREEN REVOLUTION

A striking aspect of social change in eastern Europe was the Green Revolution. This can be defined as the widespread attack upon the system of large landed estates which, despite the various reform programs of the nineteenth century, continued to exist in that belt of territory running from Finland to the Balkans. Here a privileged system of landholding had flourished for centuries. Two hundred Baltic German families, for example, owned more than half the farming land of Estonia. Over half of Latvia was covered by only 1,300 estates. In the extreme case of Hungary more than a third of the arable land was in estates exceeding three thousand acres, while three Hungarian landowners between them held title to half a million acres of land.

The war, the confusions which followed it, and the reformist or revolutionary tendencies in the postwar legislatures stimulated widespread agrarian programs. Efforts to break up the great landed estates usually involved expropriation, that is, the payment of some compensation to former owners rather than outright confiscation. Owners were guaranteed possession of some part of their old estates. Even so, valuations were usually set low, and payments to former owners were slow or incomplete. On the other hand, peasants were helped by government loans and by an easy schedule of repayments. Russian land reform was a special case, for Lenin's policy of "all land to the peasants" had resulted in the liquidation of the old landowning class and the redistribution of land on a local basis. Yet the trend was clearly to state ownership rather than to peasant ownership, and led to the experiment of collective farms operated by large-scale methods.

The results of the Green Revolution in eastern Europe were in general somewhat mixed. A substantial transfer of land did occur. Little, one must admit, was done in Germany's provinces east of the Elbe; little was done in Austria, and even less in Hungary. In Poland, where several laws were enacted in the 1920's, some 800,000 peasant families actually were enabled over the course of two decades to acquire land. These peasant gains were largely in the Corridor, in Posen, and in Polish Silesia, where former German owners usually were the losers. This transfer, however, fell far short of solving Poland's problem, since in sum, only 6 percent of Polish land was turned over to peasants. Hungary saw only about one-tenth of the land redistributed, and this chiefly to needy veterans.

Other countries showed more creditable progress. Czechoslovakia, where a substantial equalization of holdings was achieved, saw a total of 1.9 million acres, which was more than half the area of the big arable estates, transferred by 1929 to peasant purchasers. Rumania, stimulated by the agrarian leader Juliu Maniu, worked vigorously at the problem. By 1927 nine million acres had been made into peasant holdings and only 10 percent of the country remained in estates of more than 250 acres. The Baltic States, as could have been prophesied, very quickly rid themselves of the old Baltic German landlords. Greece actually redistributed the largest percentage of its land to the peasants, as the following table shows:

PERCENTAGES OF FARM LAND REDISTRIBUTED
IN EASTERN AND SOUTHEAST EUROPE DURING THE 1920's[11]

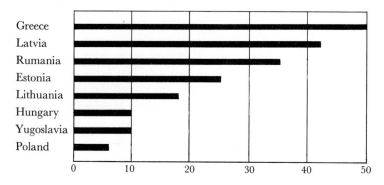

Where the Green Revolution did operate, the powers of the old feudal caste were either destroyed or weakened, and those of the peasantry correspondingly increased. Since the process was dominated more by political and social than by economic motives, the results in the economic sense were not always good. The new peasant owners had little capital, their small-scale methods were generally antiquated, and they tended to concentrate upon production for local needs rather than to grow exportable crops. Thus the reforms for many years actually had a deterring effect upon agricultural enterprises; and, particularly in the case of wheat, industrial Europe looked abroad for the greatest part of its grain supply. Agrarian reform, clearly, had some unexpected and indeed unwelcome consequences.

11. From H. E. FRIEDLANDER and J. OSER, *Economic History of Modern Europe* (1935), p. 385.

■ THE FURTHER SEARCH FOR SECURITY

The years following the peace treaties were filled with a variety of efforts to establish a greater degree of security. One of these was a return to the old technique of alliances, where the most striking example was that of France. Profoundly mistrustful of Germany and unwilling to depend upon the League, disappointed in her expectation of a military guarantee from Britain and the United States, France signed a military convention with Belgium in September, 1920, promising mutual help in the case of a German attack. France sent a military mission to help Poland during her war with Russia in 1920, one of its members being the young Charles de Gaulle. In the following February France signed with Poland a guarantee of mutual help in the case of a German attack. Thus Poland began to assume something of the place in French military and diplomatic calculations that Russia had occupied before 1914.

A similar policy was pursued by Czechoslovakia, who in 1920 signed with Yugoslavia a treaty of mutual guarantee against an attack by Hungary, and in the following year a similar treaty with Rumania. Yugoslavia and Rumania completed the "Little Entente" in June, 1921, by a defensive agreement directed against both Hungary and Bulgaria. Eventually France established close links with this network, signing defensive treaties with Czechoslovakia in 1924, with Rumania in June, 1926, and with Yugoslavia in November, 1926. It is clear that this new system aligned France with the powers who were chiefly concerned with maintaining the new status quo in Europe and against those powers interested in modifying it. One of these latter was Italy, whose diplomatic interests now seemed to put her on the side of Germany and Austria, her recent wartime opponents.

Another means of guaranteeing European security from the French viewpoint would be to see that Germany lived up to her obligations under the reparations agreements. The Reparations Commission in April, 1921, had set the total figure for Germany at 132 billion gold marks. The new coalition government of Germany established in May under the Centrist leader, Dr. Karl Joseph Wirth, with Walter Rathenau as minister of reconstruction, announced the policy of "fulfilment." This meant in essence that Germany, by faithfully attempting to carry out the Allied financial demands, would in the end demonstrate how impossible they were. Rathenau was assassinated in June, 1922, by some youthful nationalists. The imperial government had left a heavy debt structure and an inadequate tax system which the Republic did not correct, and mounting inflation gravely aggravated the economic problems. Continued failure to meet payments, even payments in goods, led the Reparations Commission to declare in the following January that Germany was in default. This caused France in association with Belgium to invoke her

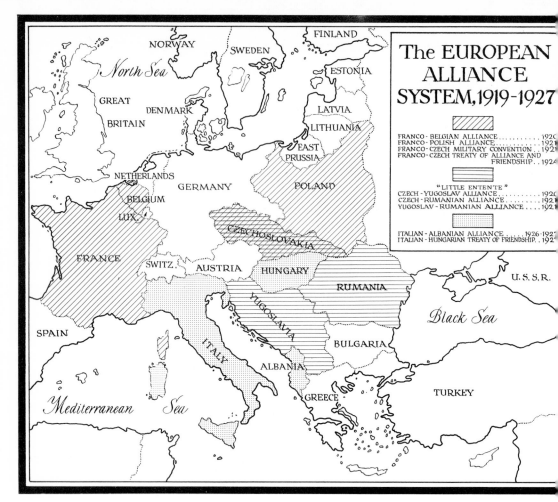

The EUROPEAN ALLIANCE SYSTEM, 1919-1927

FRANCO-BELGIAN ALLIANCE..........1920
FRANCO-POLISH ALLIANCE..........1921
FRANCO-CZECH MILITARY CONVENTION..1921
FRANCO-CZECH TREATY OF ALLIANCE AND
FRIENDSHIP..1924

"LITTLE ENTENTE"
CZECH-YUGOSLAV ALLIANCE..........1920
CZECH-RUMANIAN ALLIANCE..........1921
YUGOSLAV-RUMANIAN ALLIANCE....1921

ITALIAN-ALBANIAN ALLIANCE....1926-1927
ITALIAN-HUNGARIAN TREATY OF FRIENDSHIP..1927

Note the key position of Czechoslovakia in these alliances. In addition Poland made a Treaty of Alliance with Rumania (1921), and France made Treaties of Friendship with Rumania (1926) and Yugoslavia (1927).

rights under the Versailles Treaty and to send troops into the great industrial area of the Ruhr. Her declared purpose was to give the Germans "the will to pay." At the same time French intrigues promoted a revival of the separatist movement in the Rhineland.

The German response to the Ruhr occupation consisted of strikes, passive resistance, and the printing of still larger quantities of paper money. A disastrous inflation resulted. By September, 1923, German passive resistance fortunately had ended, and later in the following year, with pledges of economic assistance to Germany from Britain and the United States, the withdrawal of French troops was begun. A new *Rentenmark* was issued, and tax and budgetary reforms were undertaken by the German government. The

Dawes Plan of April, 1924, for reparations provided what seemed like a moderate and workable scheme of payments for Germany. With the aid of a gold loan to stabilize her currency, followed by other foreign loans, the Plan was expected to tide her through the next five years. The Locarno Treaties of 1925 (see pages 90–91) promoted mutual confidence. Thus, in the outcome, an era of good feeling seemed to be emerging from the worst years of tension.

Attempts at disarmament were made in this same period. A Permanent Advisory Commission was set up by the League in 1920 and a Temporary Mixed Commission in 1921. Very little was achieved by either. A naval conference was summoned in Washington in November, 1921, on the initiative of the United States. The five participants, by virtue of limiting themselves to the problem of capital ships, were able to agree to the ratio of 5 for Great Britain and the United States, 3 for Japan, and 1.67 for France and Italy. Seventy ships built or being built, amounting to a total of 1.6 million tons, were to be scrapped by Great Britain, France, and Japan. No new capital ship was to be built for ten years; none could be replaced until twenty years old. Figures were also set for the total tonnage of aircraft carriers for each of the five powers. This Washington Treaty of February, 1922—the only really firm disarmament achievement of these postwar years—stands in sharp contrast to the subsequent failure to reach any disarmament agreement whatever with respect to land forces. The Washington agreement about capital ships was extended at London in 1930 to cover cruisers, destroyers, and submarines, but only by the United States, Britain, and Japan. The extension had so many qualifications, provisos, and escape clauses that it had little practical effect. Quite clearly, the interests and fears of the major powers were such that the direct approach to disarmament held out little hope of success.

Did the League of Nations in the immediate postwar years make any significant contributions to international order? Its role was made less central by the existence, first, of the Allied Supreme Council and, later, the Conference of Ambassadors set up in Paris to deal with matters arising from the treaties. The League did, nevertheless, arrange a settlement (1920–1922) between Finland and Sweden concerning the Aaland Islands in the Baltic; Finland was given sovereignty and the rights of the Swedish fishermen were guaranteed. It tried, albeit unsuccessfully, to induce the Poles to return to Lithuania the city of Vilna, which they seized in 1920. It drafted the Memel Statute in 1924 granting autonomy to the German inhabitants of this area acquired by Lithuania. It tried, with limited success, to negotiate a settlement between Italy and Greece of a dispute arising from the murder of an Italian general during boundary determinations in Albania and from the subsequent Italian bombardment and seizure of Corfu (1923–1924). It worked out the boundaries for Upper Silesia after the plebiscites of 1921, and helped to define a number of other central European boundaries. In the Mosul frontier dispute (1924–1925) between Britain and Iraq on the one hand and Turkey on the other, the League was able to arbitrate successfully. It also played an important role in the financial rehabilitation of Austria and Hungary. Supervisory and administrative duties were carried out with respect to mandates, minorities, and the special problems of the Saar Basin and the Free City of Danzig. It dealt with humanitarian problems such as the slave trade. In view of all this work, an observer of the 1920's might indeed have felt confident that the League was steadily growing in responsibility and effectiveness.

Thoughtful men were concerned, nevertheless, with additional means to strengthen the machinery of peace. In 1923 a Draft Treaty of Mutual Assistance was prepared under the sponsorship of the League for the purpose of defining aggression and making specific arrangements for dealing with an aggressor. Objections of Great Britain and the Dominions, based on the difficulty of reconciling these new obligations with the existing relationships of members of the British Commonwealth, caused the treaty to be rejected by the League Assembly in 1923. This rejection led directly to the Geneva Protocol of 1924—a proposed amendment to the Covenant whereby members were to agree to refrain from any act which might constitute aggression and to refer all justiciable disputes to the World Court. The League Council in doubtful cases would define the aggressor and apply sanctions. This amendment, it was hoped, would close a noteworthy "gap in the Covenant." Though sponsored by the British Labor prime minister, Ramsay MacDonald, the Protocol failed of acceptance by the League Assembly in 1925, when it became clear that neither the newly victorious Conservative government in Britain nor the Dominions would support it.

The Locarno Treaties of 1925, emerging out of this mixed atmosphere of progress and disappointment, were regarded by many European statesmen as the high point of a new era of good will. They are inseparably connected with the names of Austen Chamberlain,[12] foreign minister in the British Conservative government taking office in November, 1924, Aristide Briand,[13] who be-

12. 1863–1937. Eldest son of the Liberal-Unionist, Joseph Chamberlain, he was chancellor of the exchequer, 1903–1906 and 1919–1921, secretary of state for India, 1915–1917, and a member of Lloyd George's war cabinet. As foreign secretary in 1925 he worked with Briand and Stresemann to put into effect the Locarno Treaties. He received the Order of the Garter and with his French and German colleagues the Nobel Peace Prize for 1926.

13. 1862–1937. A French Socialist and eleven times premier, he served as foreign minister almost uninterruptedly from 1925 to 1932. He championed a policy of reconciliation with Germany, with whom he signed the Locarno Treaties and whose admission to the League of Nations he sponsored. He was chiefly responsible, along with the United States secretary of state, Frank B. Kellogg, for the Pact of Paris (1928), renouncing aggressive war. He was awarded the Nobel Peace Prize, along with Stresemann and Austen Chamberlain, in 1926.

came French foreign minister in April, 1925, and Gustav Stresemann,[14] briefly chancellor of Germany in the autumn of 1924 and foreign minister continuously from August, 1924, until his death in 1929. All three prided themselves on being "good Europeans," convinced of the need to bring about a permanent improvement in the relations between France and Germany. The latter country had, indeed, proposed a mutual guarantee pact for the Rhineland area in February, 1923, but with the troubles of that year the scheme had made no progress. By February, 1925, the skies were much clearer, so that the German government again put forward the idea of some kind of Rhineland pact. Negotiations of the three powers were concluded in October on a most cordial basis at the Swiss resort of Locarno.

The outcome was a cluster of treaties known collectively as the Locarno Pact. The most important was a treaty of mutual guarantee of common frontiers signed by Germany, France, and Belgium and having Great Britain and Italy as the guarantors. These frontiers were to be inviolable, the demilitarization of the Rhineland was reaffirmed, disputes between the signatories would be settled by arbitration, and Britain and Italy were bound to come immediately to the help of the party attacked if the undertaking were violated. A German-French and a German-Belgian Arbitration Convention pledged the use of peaceful methods to solve disputes. At the same time German-Polish and German-Czechoslovak Arbitration Treaties were signed, significantly, however, with no guarantee of frontiers. To complete the agreements, France and Poland signed a Treaty of Mutual Assistance promising "immediate aid and assistance" if either were to suffer from a German "unprovoked recourse to arms." A similar treaty was signed between France and Czechoslovakia.

These treaties had an enthusiastic reception in the West, one evidence being the cordial welcome given by Briand and his colleagues to Germany on her admission to the League in September, 1926, with a permanent seat on the Council. Their lurking inadequacies—which caused Winston Churchill to refer later to "the pale sunlight of Locarno"—were not so immediately apparent. Germany alone remained disarmed. The absence of any "Eastern Locarno," since hardly a German would accept the eastern frontiers as definitive, demonstrated an evident and major weakness. Yet statesmen can hardly be blamed if, when confronted with enormously complex problems, they undertake to find a solution for only one part of them.

14. 1878–1929. After the First World War he founded and led the German People's Party, a successor to the National Liberals. In the Reichstag he voted against the ratification of the Treaty of Versailles. Chancellor briefly in 1923, he made his reputation chiefly as foreign minister between 1923 and 1929. Though he has been charged with negotiating secretly to have German forces trained in the Soviet Union and to obtain an eastern alliance, his principal reputation comes from working with Austen Chamberlain and Briand for a general betterment of relations with the powers across the Rhine, and for this work he shared with them a Nobel Prize in 1926.

When the Pact of Paris was signed in 1928 the pale sunlight of Locarno seemed to shine a little more brightly. Early in 1927, Foreign Minister Briand had proposed informally in a statement to the American press that France and the United States, with their long historic friendship, should celebrate the tenth anniversary of America's entry into the First World War by jointly agreeing to outlaw war between themselves. The subsequent "outlawry of war" campaign in the United States led Frank B. Kellogg, the secretary of state, to propose that the treaty be multilateral. The result was that in August, 1928, fifteen invited nations, not yet including the Soviet Union, signed at Paris the General Treaty for the Renunciation of War, known less formally as the Pact of Paris, or the Kellogg-Briand Pact. Forty-nine other states were immediately invited to adhere, and by 1933 the total of ratifications numbered sixty-five, including that of the Soviet Union.

The terms of the Pact were of striking simplicity:

I   The High Contracting Parties solemnly declare in the names of their respective peoples that they condemn recourse to war for the solution of international controversies, and renounce it as an instrument of national policy in their relations with one another.

II   The High Contracting Parties agree that the settlement or solution of all disputes or conflicts of whatever nature or of whatever origin they may be, which may arise among them, shall never be sought except by pacific means.

Critics could point out that war was not defined in the treaty. They could soon note that nation after nation reserved the right of self-defense, and that France specifically reserved its freedom to act under previous treaty commitments, which in some eventualities contemplated war. Both the United States and Japan quickly made it clear that certain areas of special interest existed outside their actual borders and that here they might be justified, under certain threats, in employing military force. The limitations in the treaty were many, yet as in the case of the Locarno Pact widespread opinion hailed it as the harbinger of a better age.

Contemplating the distance which Europe had traveled between 1919 and 1929, one might indeed be excused for thinking that the Continent had good reason to pride itself upon its achievements. The general gains seemed remarkable. A new Europe had been created in which far more people were in charge of their own destinies than ever before. Some measure of prosperity had succeeded to the years of inflation and crisis. The machinery of international cooperation had grown both in scale and ramifications and, apparently, in effectiveness. Such gains were in sharp contrast to the deterioration soon to be evident in the second decade following the First World War.

Reading List: Chapter 3

The New Cambridge Modern History, vol. XII (1960), ch. 16. The peace settlement of Versailles.

Keynes, J. M., *The Economic Consequences of the Peace* (1920), ch. 3. Includes a mordant description of the Big Four of the peace conference.

Seymour, C., "Woodrow Wilson in Perspective," *Foreign Affairs,* vol. XXXIV (1956), no. 2.

Curry, G., "Woodrow Wilson, Jan Smuts, and the Versailles Settlement," *American Historical Review,* vol. LXVI (1961), no. 4.

De Conde, A., *A History of American Foreign Policy* (1963), ch. 19. War and peace-making.

Toynbee, A. J., *The World After the Peace Conference* (1925), chs. 3–5. Situation and prospects.

Brogan, D. W., *The French Nation from Napoleon to Pétain, 1814–1940* (1957, also paper-back), ch. 5. The interwar period.

Chapter 4

Conservative Britain

"A Land of Just and Old Renown"
Britain During Four Years of War
Postwar Britain and the Irish Problem
The Changing Pattern of Party Politics
Economic Change
Empire into Commonwealth
Britain and the World

■ "A LAND OF JUST AND OLD RENOWN"

Britain in 1914 entered upon a struggle which tried her much more severely than had any earlier war. Emerging triumphant, she was confirmed in her addiction to a slow and empirical approach to new problems. Having played the leading part in the defeat of Germany, as it seemed to the British they had, could they not face the future confidently in reliance upon well-tried methods? Viewed in retrospect, the answer to the question is clearly, No. Both the economic stability of the United Kingdom and its imperial leadership were threatened by forces which existed before the war began and which became more dangerous for every year that it continued. In all probability the decline could not have been permanently held in check by any degree of political wisdom which the British people might have shown. But it is most likely that the decline would have been slower and less painful if more radical measures had been adopted. At home and abroad, Britain faced a new age

94

SIGNIFICANT EVENTS

1916–1922	Lloyd George's coalition government
1918	Representation of the People Act
1922	Irish Free State established
1924	First Labor government
1926	General strike
1931	Financial crisis and fall of second Labor government
	Statute of Westminster
1932	Ottawa Conference
1936	Abdication of King Edward VIII
1937	Baldwin succeeded as prime minister by Chamberlain

with conservative policies, seeking to preserve as much as possible of the past rather than to come to terms effectively with the future.

This failure in self-adaptation needs to be traced in some detail because of its threefold importance for the later stages of this history. First, the relative decline of Britain meant that during a period of rapid political change in Europe her particular type of state, based on tradition, compromise, and an easy acceptance of the differences between classes, was decreasingly influential as a model to other communities. Second, the island kingdom began to lose its capacity for holding together a world empire of widely differing cultures. Third, a weaker Britain was less able to check the deterioration of relations among the Continental powers, which caused the shadow of a second world war to fall so quickly over the European scene. The chief aspects of British history between 1914 and 1939 must therefore be reviewed, each of which has its bearing upon wider issues.

■ BRITAIN DURING FOUR YEARS OF WAR

Since none of the many wars waged by Britain during the nineteenth century had caused any serious interruption to peacetime activities, it was quite natural that the slogan in 1914 was "Business as usual." Second only to the navy in importance would be the value to the Triple Entente of Britain's industrial strength and accumulated wealth; the British contribution to the forces on land would be well trained and well equipped but numerically not very considerable. Only Kitchener foresaw a long and wasting contest, and even he did not anticipate the situation which arose in 1917, when there came to be more Britons than Frenchmen fighting on the soil of France. Nor was it realized in advance that so much of the manufacturing capacity of the country would have to be diverted to munitions, or that the pressure of the German submarine blockade would reduce the country to siege conditions. Under such circumstances the maintenance of the normal export trades would lose its importance except in so far as these contributed directly to the food supply or, as in the case of coal exports, to the war effort of Britain's allies.

The introduction of conscription in 1916 and of food-rationing in 1918 brought the British nearer to what a later generation meant by "total war." So did the loss of life, which was twice as heavy as in the Second World War, in spite of the fact that there was no seriously destructive bombing of Britain from the air. To contemporaries, indeed, it seemed that the old form of society had disintegrated. The rich suffered to some extent from wartime shortages—particularly of servants—while a large section of the poorer classes, ranging from munition workers to farm laborers, were for the first time able to command relatively high wages. It is equally noteworthy that the failure to curb profits produced a rapid increase in the number of *nouveau riche* families, and that the armed services continued to be run on the basis that only the wellborn and well educated should become officers without any period of probation in the ranks. It might fairly be claimed that, at the date of the armistice, men and women of all classes had been in some measure shaken out of their conventional concepts and traditions, but that the old framework of British society was still capable of repair—if that was all that was meant by "reconstruction." For this task, indeed, a special government department had been appointed a full year before the end of hostilities.

In the field of party politics the demands of war leadership had quickly terminated the period of Liberal rule which dated from 1905. In May, 1915, the principal Conservative leaders were invited to serve in a coalition government under the Liberal prime minister, Asquith, and a year and a half later their dissatisfaction with his conduct of the coalition resulted in his replacement at the head of affairs by the more dynamic figure of Lloyd George. Although he had made his name as a Liberal of much more radical views than Asquith, Lloyd George was above all an opportunist. Having been brought into power by Conservative support, he found Conservative ministers to be on the whole his most valuable colleagues in the new government; indeed, none of the remaining Liberals were included in the inner war cabinet of half a dozen members, which was the main instrument through which the new prime minister gave fresh impetus to the war effort. Immensely popular with the masses, a splendid emotional orator, and a genius in the art of getting things done, by the time of the armistice Lloyd George was almost universally acclaimed in Britain as "the man who won the war." He seized the chance to fight an immediate election, in which his supporters, both Conservative and Liberal, won an overwhelming victory over those Liberals who had remained loyal to Asquith and over the still small Labor Party, which was handicapped by the fact that some of its ablest members had been notorious opponents of the war.

The general election of 1918 was the first to be based on full manhood suffrage. The Representation of the People Act in that year had detached the right to vote from its former association with the occupation of a house or of lodgings of a given value. Every male person over twenty-one could now vote after six months' residence in any constituency; this meant an increase of nearly 50 percent in the number of voters. In addition, the right to vote was for the first time conferred on women, subject to an age limit of thirty and certain minor restrictions. This franchise meant a further increase equal to the whole of the prewar electorate. Earlier in the same year the government had anticipated the demands of the postwar world in a second way, by an educational reform which abolished school exemptions below the age of fourteen and erected the first ladder enabling clever children from poor homes to make their way from state primary schools through state secondary schools to the university. Otherwise, the war period had been too crowded with other urgent business for any regular reform program. The government's conciliatory attitude in all matters of labor relations had, however, been one factor in the growth of trade unions, which in five years virtually doubled their membership. The prime minister was himself a son of the people. He had been foremost in using the election slogan of "Homes for Heroes" to suggest that the returning soldiers deserved to have their housing and other social needs met. Thus it might be expected that an era of fundamental social progress was about to begin.

■ POSTWAR BRITAIN AND THE IRISH PROBLEM

One important matter in 1919, the order of demobilization, enabled the people in arms to assert their will successfully against that of their rulers. The government had planned to demobilize in the order that suited the requirements of industry, but a number of small mutinies forced them to adopt instead the democratic principle of "First in, first out." The result was not the industrial dislocation which had been feared. Instead, the combination of general optimism about the future with pressing specific needs—chiefly the backlog of home and export orders which would not be fulfilled in wartime—created a boom in trade lasting for nearly two years after the armistice. It was accepted that the problems of peacemaking must inevitably engross the attention of Lloyd George and many of his colleagues during much of this period. Domestic problems were deliberately shelved, therefore, until the ex-soldiers had forgotten possibilities of reform through direct action. In the key industry of coal mining, for example, when an elaborate official inquiry unexpectedly recommended by a majority of one that existing difficulties should be met by nationalization, its report was ignored for exactly thirty years. One problem, postponed at the outbreak of the war, could not be shelved, and it in consequence provided the main test for Lloyd George's government. This was home rule for Ireland.

The Home Rule Act to re-establish an Irish parliament for all except the predominantly Protestant northeastern region of the Catholic island had been passed in August, 1914, together with a measure postponing its operation until the war was over. The Irish Nationalists under the leadership of John Redmond regarded the cause of Catholic Belgium, oppressed by the great power of Germany, with much sympathy, and volunteered for the army in large numbers. But radical views persisted, with the result that at Easter, 1916, a rebellion organized in Dublin by the extremists of Sinn Fein, a party name meaning "Ourselves Alone," took the government by surprise. Some five hundred casualties were incurred by British troops in the street fighting; three thousand rebels were arrested, and fifteen were executed after trial by court-martial. The brief episode seemed to many British people to be a stab in the back; perhaps to most Irish people it gave the independence movement new value and urgency, now that it was sanctified by the blood of its martyrs. In 1917 Eamon De Valera,[1] who had been saved from execution because he was an American by birth, became president of Sinn Fein. Under the new democratic franchise Ireland at the 1918 election voted overwhelmingly in favor of the Sinn Feiners. These Sinn Fein M.P.'s had pledged themselves in advance to ignore the British parliament at Westminster. They consequently formed their own parliament in Dublin, which proclaimed a republic, established a

1. Born in 1882 in New York, the son of a Spaniard and an Irishwoman, he was sentenced to life imprisonment after the Easter Week rebellion, was amnestied and reimprisoned, and finally escaped. As president of the "Irish Republic" in 1919, he raised $6,000,000 in America; he became head of the Irish Free State government in 1932, and was mainly responsible for the secession of the Irish Republic from the Commonwealth in 1949.

cabinet under De Valera, and was in nominal control of the main underground movement known as the Irish Republican Army.

To British politicians an Irish republic was anathema, yet to take the large-scale military measures which might have crushed the movement at this juncture was unthinkable. A new war against a kindred people was repugnant to the whole outlook of a country busy with demobilization and the return to all its peacetime activities. Such a war would, in addition, involve a grave affront to American opinion. The result was a series of half-hearted measures for suppressing the gunmen of the I.R.A. These were carried out by a British irregular force, nicknamed the Black and Tans, because of the color of their improvised uniforms, which earned a very grim reputation for reprisals against property and persons, for shooting of prisoners, for looting, and even for acts of purely wanton violence. It is important not to exaggerate: the special force was not set up until the summer of 1920, when the tale of Irish outrages had been mounting for a year and a half, and the inhumanities of the Black and Tans were matched by those of their opponents. Even so, liberal opinion in England, which was kept informed by newspaper correspondents, was indignant and ashamed at the evidence of deeds of vengeance perpetrated with the approval, or at the very least the connivance, of a powerful British government.

Ministers tried to meet the situation by passing a fourth Home Rule Bill in December, 1920. This Bill provided single-chamber parliaments at Dublin and Belfast, with additional small-scale representation for both parts of Ireland at Westminster, and an All-Ireland Council. From all this a united Ireland might later be developed. Irish Nationalists continued to demand instead an independent republic extending over the whole island, but Ulster's acceptance of the law led to the opening of the first parliament of Northern Ireland by George V in June, 1921. Risking his life at the hands of the Nationalist gunmen, the king made a dramatic appeal "to all Irishmen to forgive and to forget, and to join in making for the land which they love a new era of peace, contentment and goodwill." His action helped notably in breaking the stalemate: a truce was agreed to in Ireland, and representatives of the Nationalists went to London to negotiate with members of the British cabinet. Though De Valera himself was not prepared to accept anything short of complete independence, other Irish leaders were willing to compromise, even though it meant that Northern Ireland might continue to be joined to Britain as provided by the recent act. After prolonged discussions, Lloyd George used a threat of immediate "terrible war" to get the agreement signed without reference to the illegal Irish parliament, the Dail Eireann. A month later, in January, 1922, the Dail ratified it by a majority of only seven votes, whereupon De Valera, supported by the I.R.A., launched a further guerrilla struggle against the new Irish government. He was defeated in the end, but not until eleven thousand of his supporters had been placed in internment camps and seventy-seven executed by their fellow countrymen—about three times as many as the number of military executions authorized by the British in the struggle of 1920–1921.

Under the treaty southern Ireland became the Irish Free State, self-governing in its internal affairs to exactly the same extent as the Dominion of Canada. It was linked to Great Britain in the same way through the oath of allegiance to the Crown, which was to be taken by all members of the Dail, and through the exercise of the royal powers by a governor-general appointed on behalf of the Crown. An option, quickly acted upon, entitled Northern Ireland to remain separate.

For nearly a decade southern Ireland enjoyed a period of repose and recovery such as she had not known for many generations. The treaty was a personal triumph for Lloyd George, who had the advantage of judging the situation from the point of view of a fellow Celt. His chief helpers, however, had been Conservative colleagues who had formerly been the most implacable enemies of the Irish claims. The British had once more shown their genius for compromise, or at least a readiness to accept the inevitable graciously and make the best of things. Nevertheless, Lloyd George's Irish settlement was one of the reasons why the rank and file of the Conservatives decided to jettison him, thereby provoking the renewal of the long-dormant struggle of parties.

■ THE CHANGING PATTERN OF PARTY POLITICS

The coalition government which Lloyd George had formed in December, 1916, had a total life of nearly six years. During its course the man who won the war was to prove increasingly unable to win the peace. By 1921 the post-war trade boom had ended, and a policy of financial retrenchment was adopted on the ground that reductions in taxation would stimulate investment. The check to government spending meant the curtailment of the educational re-forms and of certain services provided under the national health insurance scheme of 1911. The occasion was also seized to pass a Safeguarding of Indus-tries Act; this modest installment of protection was enough to impair relations between the Conservative majority and the Liberal free-trade minority within the ranks of coalition supporters in parliament. Considerable uneasiness, too, was caused by the almost public sale of titles and decorations in order to raise money for party funds, a proceeding which culminated in the offer of a peerage to a South African financier whose malpractices had been recently exposed in the law courts. After a protest from the king, a new system was adopted requir-ing the prime minister's nominations to be examined by persons of independ-ent status. Though a sensible arrangement, it did not reflect favorably upon the ethical standards of the premier whose actions had made it necessary. Accordingly, when the Irish crisis was followed by the Chanak crisis with Turkey,[2] the rank and file of the Conservatives seized the opportunity to put an end to the coalition: they thought of Lloyd George as leading them into dangerous adventures abroad and uncertain courses at home.

Although several of the most prominent Conservatives stood by Lloyd George, he was driven out of office, and a purely Conservative government— the first for seventeen years—was formed under Andrew Bonar Law, the Conservative Party leader from 1911 to 1921. The government was confirmed in power by the test of a general election, but when Bonar Law's health collapsed within a few months he gave place to the then little-known Stanley Baldwin,[3] a wealthy ironmaster who had played an important part in the movement against Lloyd George. Believing that the most urgent need of the economy was a return to full-blooded protection, Baldwin dissolved parliament at the end of 1923, but failed to carry the country with him. After the election the Conservatives were still the most numerous party in the House; nevertheless, the Labor Party had only sixty-seven fewer and the balance was held by a reunited Liberal Party under Asquith and Lloyd George. Since the Labor and Liberal votes taken together gave a clear majority against protection, Baldwin's government was bound to be driven from office. Many antisocialists in alarm urged Asquith to arrange a Conservative-Liberal coalition in order to keep Labor out. But the Liberals were as much opposed in principle to protection as they were to socialism; Asquith therefore decided to support the formation of a Labor government and its continuance for as long as it could avoid a direct conflict with Liberal principles.

At the next election in October, 1924, the Liberals lost nearly three-quarters of their seats, no doubt because antisocialist votes were diverted to the Conservatives. In spite of this setback, for a few years their fortunes seemed to be reviving. The quarrel between Asquith and Lloyd George, which broke out afresh when the latter took the side of the trade unions over the general strike of 1926, was terminated by the older man's retirement. Lloyd George then prepared a great comeback. He published a series of Liberal plans for economic recovery and used a large political fund which had been at his personal disposal since the end of the coalition to place five hundred Liberal candidates in the field at the next opportunity. Despite his efforts, the electors in 1929 returned only fifty-nine of them—an increase of seventeen seats. As

2. See p. 121.
3. Born in 1867, he was a cousin of Rudyard Kipling, with Methodist ancestry on both sides and a great capacity for understanding, and appealing to, the common man; Lloyd George, Lord Beaverbrook, Churchill, and King Edward VIII were all at different times defeated by his calculated simplicity. He became chancellor of the exchequer under Bonar Law and lord president of the council under MacDonald (1931–1935). Having retired in May, 1937, with an earldom, he was later reviled as a scapegoat for the inadequacies of British policy vis-à-vis unemployment and, still more, the rise of Hitler; he died in 1947.

an effective organization the Liberal Party had now shot its bolt. After giving lukewarm support to a second Labor government, the Liberals split over the question of adhesion to the so-called National government which replaced it two years later, and again over the introduction of a full protective tariff in 1932.

The increasing importance of the Labor Party dates back as far as to 1918. It is associated with the marked decline of the Liberal Party during the later interwar years, a party on which Labor when in office still depended for support. The prewar Labor Party had been no more than an association between the trade unions and certain rather small socialist societies; in the last year of the war, however, the decision was taken to remodel it on the pattern of the other British party organizations, with local branches and individual supporters. At the same time a cautiously socialist program was adopted, which might appeal to large sections of the middle class as well as to the workers. The general objective as defined in the constitution was:

> to secure for the producers by hand and by brain the full fruits of their industry, and the most equitable distribution thereof that may be possible, upon the basis of the common ownership of the means of production and the best obtainable system of popular administration and control of each industry and service.

Though Labor became the second largest party in 1918, it did not reach a respectable size until 1922, when records of wartime pacifism ceased to handicap some of its leaders. Although strikes and general industrial unrest clearly favored its growth at this time, the situation which brought it suddenly into office was unexpected.

The achievements of Labor ministers, both in 1924 and again in 1929–1931, reflected both the strength and the weakness of their leader, James Ramsay MacDonald.[4] His fine presence, wide culture, and talent for rhetoric gave him an unchallenged ascendancy among his supporters and made it difficult for opponents to identify him with "Red ruin." He shone in the conduct of foreign affairs, improving relations with France, attending the League of Nations Assembly in person, and attempting to alleviate Europe's worst wound by giving official recognition to the Soviet Russian government. In home affairs, however, he deferred all too readily to Liberal susceptibilities, and the 1924 ministry produced only a housing act. This trebled the subsidy for building approved houses under municipal ownership which had been brought

---

4. 1866–1937. The illegitimate child of a Scottish peasant girl, he was leader of the Labor Party, 1911–1914, and 1922–1931. Author of books on socialism, and widely traveled, he was known to his associates as "Gentleman Mac," and his secession from the Labor movement in 1931 aroused great bitterness. He carried little weight in the National government; yet, after resigning the premiership in failing health, he continued as lord president of the council until a few months before his death in November, 1937.

in by the Conservative minister of health, Neville Chamberlain,[5] the previous year. But MacDonald, who was very thin-skinned, readily dissolved parliament when his government was criticized for failing to prosecute a Communist editor for sedition. This third election in three years gave Baldwin a strong majority.

Apart from raising great expectations which were doomed to disappointment, the first Labor government had made little contribution to the problems of industrial conditions—wages, hours, and the incidence of unemployment—in which the Labor movement as a whole was chiefly interested. The big strikes, which had been frequent in the years immediately before the war, had begun again in 1919. In 1921 a coal strike had very nearly occasioned a sympathetic strike by the railwaymen and other transport workers. Under the Baldwin government matters came to a head when declining profits caused the coal owners to demand more from their workers, to which they replied that the inefficiency of the management called for nationalization and that the workers would yield nothing—"Not a penny off the pay, not a minute on the day." Baldwin arranged a nine-month subsidy for miners' wages, while a commission again inquired ineffectively into the needs of the industry. Meanwhile, the government made plans to maintain order and distribute food supplies in the event of a wider conflict. It was probably not a coincidence, therefore, that twelve well-known Communists were sentenced to imprisonment at this juncture under an Incitement to Mutiny Act dating from 1797. If the trade-union movement as a whole was disposed to use its economic power to force legislation on behalf of the miners, the authorities by May, 1926, felt that they were well prepared to meet what they regarded as a serious challenge to Britain's parliamentary constitution.

Such was the background to the nine days' general strike of 1926. It was general only in the sense of a general response in those "first-line" industries—transport, printing, building, iron and steel, heavy chemicals—upon which the trade-union leaders called for action. The middle classes, rallying almost unanimously to the side of the government and to the cry of "The constitution in danger," helped to run skeleton transport services, so that food supplies were maintained. If the strike leaders had persisted and had called out their "second-line" industries as well, a revolutionary situation might have developed. Since, however, they were not aiming at revolution but only at a mammoth demon-

5. 1869–1940. The younger son of Joseph Chamberlain and long overshadowed by his brother Austen, the author of the Locarno Treaties. A Birmingham businessman, he was a great success as minister of health, 1923 and 1924–1929, but his services to working-class housing, etc., made less impression on the public mind than his ill-concealed contempt for Labor politicians. As chancellor of the exchequer, 1931–1937, he was mainly responsible for the tariff. As prime minister, 1937–1940, he preserved peace by postponing as long as possible the decision that Hitler and Mussolini could never be trusted. He remained in office as lord president of the council under Churchill until a week before his death in November, 1940.

THE GENERAL STRIKE OF 1926. A London police escort accompanies a food truck as part of the government's determination to maintain essential services.

stration of working-class solidarity to get support for the miners, they now tried to arrange a compromise, which the miners refused to accept. Then, fearing that the situation might get out of hand, they surrendered to the government. The miners held out until November, when hunger and cold drove them back to work on the owners' terms. The sequel was a big drop in trade-union membership, to which hard times also contributed, and a more significant decline in the incidence of strikes. For better and worse, the aggressive mood of the industrial workers, first evident about 1911, subsided for many years into an angry silence, while the employing classes became correspondingly less apprehensive.

The general unemployment problem remained acute. In each year of the 1920's an increasing number of children left school to join the ranks of the unemployed; young people were marrying and setting up house on no income but the "dole"; and older men, who had been out of work too long, became not merely unemployed but unemployable. In coal mining and other hard-hit regions whole towns fell into decay, with disused workplaces, derelict shops, and shabby proletarian homes declining into slums. An acute and sympathetic observer, looking back to the last years of this decade, writes as follows:

> I remember the shock of astonishment it gave me . . . to find . . . decent young miners and cotton-workers gazing at their destiny with the same sort of dumb amazement as an animal in a trap. They simply could not understand what was happening to them. They had been brought up to work, and behold! it seemed as

though they were never going to have the chance of working again. In their circumstances it was inevitable, at first, that they should be haunted by a feeling of personal degradation. That was the attitude towards unemployment in those days: it was a disaster which happened to *you* as an individual and for which *you* were to blame.[6]

The second Labor government was in some respects a repetition of the first. It came into office when the election of 1929—the first in which women voted on the same basis of universal adult suffrage as men—produced no overall majority. Labor was, however, for the first time the largest single party in the House of Commons. Since the government depended upon the support, or at least the toleration, of the Liberals, it was not in a position to make bold socialist reforms, even if the handicaps imposed by the slump in world trade[7] could somehow have been surmounted. Moreover, MacDonald, who was still the universally accepted leader, shone chiefly in the conduct of foreign affairs. He worked steadily for the pacific settlement of international disputes, resumed relations with Russia which the Conservatives had broken off in 1927, and sedulously cultivated the friendship of the United States. But in the face of mounting unemployment his government could find no positive remedies, and the palliatives which he applied to make the lot of the unemployed a little easier involved a heavy increase in expenditure, only partly covered by an increase in taxation imposed on the higher-income groups.

The result was a crisis, of which the details are still not wholly clear. The effect was certainly to postpone the advent of the Labor Party to power as distinct from office for another fourteen eventful years. The crisis was precipitated by the publication in 1931 of an alarming report from a committee on national expenditure, which the government itself had appointed, forecasting a deficit of 120 million pounds in the public accounts and proposing that half of this sum should be raised by economies at the expense of the unemployed. Two results followed. At a time when investors all over the world were in a condition approaching panic, the news stimulated withdrawals of gold from the Bank of England, which help from the Federal Reserve Bank in New York and from the Bank of France was unable to hold in check. Meanwhile, the cabinet was divided as to the propriety of placating nervous foreigners by balancing the British budget at the expense of the already hard-pressed unemployed. Since the division in the cabinet was almost exactly even, it was expected that the Labor government would be displaced by a Conservative-Liberal coalition, leaving the Laborites with good chances of recovering their position at the next election. Instead, the king made an arrangement with the leaders of all three parties, by which MacDonald continued to head a small National government, composed of himself and three other right-wing Labor

6. G. ORWELL, *The Road to Wigan Pier* (1937), p. 85.
7. See pp. 157–163.

representatives, four Conservatives, and two Liberals. The main body of Labor members then passed into opposition.

The maneuver did not succeed in its immediate object of restoring confidence in British finances, for within a month the gold standard was abandoned, the value of the pound in terms of dollars falling temporarily by about 30 percent. The final shock to foreign investors had been administered by the refusal of twelve thousand seamen of the Royal Navy stationed at Invergordon, Scotland, to accept their share of the national economy measures, which fell three times as heavily on a rank-and-file seaman as on a lieutenant commander. In general, however, the proposed economies were successfully imposed, not only on the unemployed but on all persons in public employment. There was a corresponding increase in direct and indirect taxation, designed to touch all pockets. The lasting result, whether intended or not, was the complete discomfiture of MacDonald's left-wing colleagues, who represented the program of social transformation upon which the Labor Party was founded. For what had been announced as a temporary measure to save the pound long outlived its failure to save it.

An election in October, 1931, where appeals to patriotism were skillfully blended with warnings that national bankruptcy would almost automatically follow a Labor Party victory, gave the National government a majority of ten to one. The opportunity was too good to be lost: the Conservatives' thirty-year-old policy of protection could at last be put into effect, MacDonald being kept as titular head of the government so as to preserve its "national" character. In 1935 Baldwin, who had been the power behind the scenes for so long, became prime minister again, and in the election which shortly followed won a majority which kept the National government, under his leadership and later that of Neville Chamberlain, secure in office and secure in its Conservative tenets until the party game was again interrupted by war.

It is not unreasonable to call the period 1922–1940, even though he resigned before its close, the Age of Baldwin. He was the main Conservative leader at a time when both the other parties passed into eclipse. In addition, having already ousted Lloyd George, from 1931 onward he was mainly responsible for the exclusion from office of the dynamic Winston Churchill. After serving as chancellor of the exchequer in Baldwin's government of 1924–1929, Churchill had separated himself from the main body of the party by his hostility to reforms in India, and was not encouraged to return. All this was partly a cause and partly an effect of a fundamental apathy toward international affairs which was characteristic of Baldwin. Though this was to cost him dear in the end, in the early 1930's a good many people shared or at the very least tolerated a point of view which they later denounced as disastrous.

Public attention was to a very great extent diverted from the foreign situation to Britain's economic difficulties. For these Baldwin prescribed a protective tariff coupled with financial orthodoxy, and added a special contribution of his own in his resolute and high-principled opposition to anything that savored of class war. State pensions for widows and orphans, the reorganization of local government, and the central administration of poor relief—even with its intensely unpopular "means test" to restrict state support to the genuinely necessitous—were features of Conservative legislation which prepared the way for the modern welfare state. The unemployed and their families were better off under Baldwin and Chamberlain than the families of unskilled laborers in full employment had been on the eve of the First World War. Seen in retrospect, conditions in England, and still more in South Wales and part of Scotland, were very wretched. But it is significant that Sir Oswald Mosley's British Fascist movement of the 1930's, in comparison with its counterparts in other European countries, had only a negligible membership, in spite of the economic stresses to which the British economy was particularly exposed.

■ ECONOMIC CHANGE

Modern statistical studies have enabled historians to trace far back into the nineteenth century the onset of the changes which converted the "workshop of the world" into one competing against other workshops of the world under increasingly disadvantageous conditions. For the present purpose it is more important to realize that when the First World War had resulted in the defeat of Britain's chief European industrial rival and in considerable acquisitions to an empire consolidated by victory, the British were encouraged to view the future with unreasoning optimism. Even when the short postwar trade boom gave place to depression, it seemed plausible to blame the rise of unemployment upon the unsettled world conditions.

As a trading nation keenly interested in a return to normality, Britain took the lead in promoting the settlement of the difficult problems of war debts and reparations.[8] As regards war debts, Baldwin in January, 1923, accepted terms of settlement less favorable than those which Washington granted to less prompt debtors later on.[9] Then, in 1924, the MacDonald government played a leading part in the negotiation of the Dawes Plan which, helped by the flow of foreign capital to Germany, prevented German reparations payments from disturbing the European economy for the remainder of the decade. Next year, when Churchill had become chancellor of the exchequer under Baldwin, Britain proclaimed her belief in the possibility of a return to the old order. Once again she showed her reliance upon the strength and stability of the City of

8. See pp. 148–151; 156–157.
9. See p. 161.

London as the controlling factor in world trade by restoring the gold standard at the prewar rate of exchange.

To do this successfully, British export industries needed to be capable of selling their wares on the world market in competition with countries whose wares were cheapened by the fact that a foreign purchaser could buy their currency at a depreciated rate because they had not returned to gold at the old level. France, for example, stabilized the franc late in December, 1926, at one-fifth of its prewar value. The failure of Britain's attempt to maintain the gold standard, which had to be abandoned after six years, underlines the fact that her economy was declining in relation to others even in the later 1920's when Europe as a whole seemed to be on the highroad to recovery. By 1928 the real value of French, Italian, and Swedish exports was greater than before the war, while those of Britain had declined by about 20 percent.

COMPARATIVE TABLE OF EXPORTS, IMPORTS, AND UNEMPLOYMENT[10]

	1913	1921	1922	1923	1924	1925	1926	1927	1928	1929	1930
Exports, by volume (1924=100)	131.4				100	99.3	88.9	102.3	104.7	108.3	88.7
Imports, by volume (1924=100)	94.2				100	103.9	108.6	111.2	107.8	114	111.4
Number of unemployed (in thousands, as of December)[11]		2,038	1,464	1,229	1,263	1,243	1,432	1,194	1,334	1,344	2,500

The figures for unemployment in the above table give us the most important single fact in the social history of Britain between the wars. The geographical distribution of the unemployed made clearer every year the contrast between the old industrial areas of northern England, South Wales, and around Glasgow and Belfast, with their inactive coal mines, textile factories, shipyards, and steel works, and the new industrial areas, mostly in London and southern England, which flourished on the manufacture of the less durable consumer goods. The prosperous areas never succeeded in restoring the health of the economy as a whole or in absorbing the mass of unemployed because their trade was mainly in the home market. They were not in a position to export on the scale that the industrial north had formerly achieved. Thus the gap between the volume of exports and that of imports continued to widen.

10. C. L. MOWAT, *Britain Between the Wars* (1955), p. 261.
11. No exact records of unemployment are available before the extension of the insurance system by the act of 1920, but the percentage of unemployed may be approximately estimated at 2 percent in 1913 as compared with 15 percent in 1931.

Two factors prevented the situation from becoming completely cata-strophic. Throughout this period the foodstuffs and raw materials which Britain needed to buy from abroad commanded lower prices on the world market than the manufactures which Britain sold there. Moreover, in making her necessary purchases Britain could still rely in part on the earnings of the British mercantile marine, payments for insurance and other financial services provided in Britain, and the interest on her overseas investments. Since the terms of trade could not be expected to remain permanently in Britain's favor, and since new overseas investments were being made on a smaller scale than before the war, the peril was advancing rather than receding. But as production and importation both continued to increase, the return on capital and the purchasing power of wages were satisfactory in the short run both to employer and employee.

In retrospect, the resignation with which the British year after year accepted the continuance of large-scale unemployment seems astonishing. Each of the two Labor governments ordered a full public inquiry and Lloyd George conducted an informal investigation on behalf of the Liberal Party, the published results of which were widely read. The general diagnosis emphasized the period of the war when Britain had for a time been almost out of business, a situation which had encouraged her customers either to supply themselves or to look to the United States or Japan as suppliers. Attention was also directed to the greatly reduced demand after the war for British coal, partly because newer coal mines were worked more efficiently in other countries and partly because petroleum and hydroelectricity were replacing it as a source of power. For a time, also, there was the special competition of German coal exported as reparations to France and then resold.

Slowly the awareness grew that the handicaps imposed by Britain's past triumphs included not merely a mass of semiobsolete industrial equipment but the hardly less obsolete furniture of people's minds. Employers rivaled trade unionists in their addiction to old methods; labor-saving machinery was seldom adopted with enthusiasm; and a tendency existed to blame the fickleness of the foreign customer rather than the unimaginative conservatism of the British producer when regular markets were slowly lost. Yet no serious attempt was made to reconstruct the export industries on a sounder basis. Just before the general collapse began in 1929, a German technical study showed that 42 percent of British exports were of those types of goods for which world demand was expanding least rapidly, and only 4 percent of types in which the expansion was most rapid.

Then came the great depression, spreading from the United States to central Europe and from central Europe to Britain.[12] The contraction of world

12. See pp. 157–163.

trade, which caused unemployment in Britain to soar to three million, brought about the final abandonment not only of the gold standard in 1931 but of free trade in 1932. The cry for a tariff had been raised by Joseph Chamberlain in 1903, and some special duties had been imposed from time to time during and immediately after the war and again, under a Safeguarding of Industries Act, in 1925. Joseph's younger son, Neville, as chancellor of the exchequer brought back a general tariff in 1932 and tried also to use it according to his father's intention as a cement of empire.

The general level of duties was fixed by the new law at 10 percent, with the exception of wheat, meat, and most industrial raw materials. An advisory committee soon raised this level to 20 percent, and in the end only about a quarter of imports came in free. The effect was most striking in the steel industry, which increased its output by 40 percent under a system which facilitated reorganization and modernization at home and profitable agreements abroad with a European cartel. In general it is not easy to determine how much of the recovery which Britain experienced from 1933 onward was due to the tariff and government manipulations such as import quotas and marketing schemes, or to the reduction in the price of the pound. The main impulse to change came from the cheapening of imports as world prices fell, which meant that wage-earners in steady employment were better off. One result was a housing boom, which achieved a good deal of what a public-works program achieved, for instance, in the United States. Some help came also from the beginning of rearmament. Even so, nearly two million were unemployed at the outbreak of the Second World War.

One definite disappointment attaching to the tariff was the very limited practical results of the Imperial Economic Conference, held at Ottawa in the summer of 1932. Britain signed seven agreements with the different Dominions, the Irish Free State excepted, by which she gave increased preferences to their foodstuffs and other products. But the preferences she received in return were of relatively slight value.[13] Enough was done to cause the free-trade members of the National government to resign; in the long run, however, it was more significant that Chamberlain himself and his imperially minded colleagues returned home in a state of disillusionment as regards the economic bonds of empire, doubting the possibility of a British *Zollverein* such as the late-Victorians had sometimes foreseen.

■ EMPIRE INTO COMMONWEALTH

The Ottawa Conference of 1932 was one of a series of events which marked the progressive weakening of Britain's function as the provider of the centripetal force holding together a great and varied collection of peoples and

13. See p. 164.

nations. The war had seemed to mark an increase of cohesion. Not only had every part contributed to the war effort—on the western front, on the Gallipoli beaches, in Mesopotamia, in Africa, or on the high seas—but Lloyd George in 1917 and 1918 had presided for considerable periods over an imperial war cabinet, in which the direction of the war effort was shared between a little group of United Kingdom ministers and the premiers of the self-governing Dominions. Emerging from the war with the lion's share, if only as mandates, of German colonies and Turkish-Asiatic territories, the British Empire might well appear to be stronger than ever before in its long history.

The general trend, however, was in the other direction. India became impatient at the delay in implementing the historic promise made in August, 1917, that there would be:

> increasing association of Indians in every branch of the administration, and the gradual development of self-governing institutions with a view to the progressive realization of responsible government in India as an integral part of the British Empire.[14]

A particularly dangerous situation developed in the Punjab. There Moslems sympathized with the defeated sultan of Turkey, and, after several Europeans had been murdered by mobs, a British general, in the mistaken belief that his orders were defied by the mob, perpetrated the massacre of Amritsar. By shooting down some 1,400 persons, of whom 379 were killed, General Dyer may have saved the province, but his action made it unlikely that the reforms which were duly instituted only a few months later[15] could reconcile the Indians permanently to the British connection. Egypt, which had been formally proclaimed a British protectorate on the outbreak of war against the Ottoman Empire in 1914, had risen in rebellion even earlier, and quickly secured the status of an independent monarchy, bound to Britain by defense arrangements.

Still more significant was the promptness with which the Dominions asserted a claim to individual participation in the peacemaking, followed by individual membership in the League of Nations. The war had made these countries increasingly aware of their stature as separate nations, and in 1923 Canada carried this to its logical conclusion by requiring that a fisheries treaty with the United States, which concerned only Canadian interests, should be signed by a Canadian delegate alone. Moreover, their sacrifices in the war made the Dominions sensitive regarding any commitment to British policy which might involve them in another war. At the time of the 1922 Chanak crisis[16] only New Zealand was willing to give automatic support if Lloyd

14. A statement made by E. S. Montagu, secretary of state for India, in the House of Commons, August 20, 1917.
15. See p. 113.
16. See p. 121.

George's policy should lead to a renewal of hostilities against the Turks, and in December, 1925, the Dominions abstained from the Locarno negotiations and accepted no responsibility for the execution of the resulting settlement.

The Imperial Conference of 1926, therefore, found it necessary to attempt a definition of the new relationship between Britain and her Dominions. In Balfour, an elder statesman, a conservative, and a philosopher, it found the very man to turn informal practice into formal principle and to win the consent of the Conference for a carefully balanced formula:

> Great Britain and the Dominions are autonomous communities within the British Empire, equal in status, in no way subordinate one to another in any aspect of their domestic or external affairs, though united by a common allegiance to the Crown, and freely associated as members of the British Commonwealth of Nations.

Five years later this definition was included in the preamble of the Statute of Westminster, enacted by the parliament of the United Kingdom in order to make equality effective in the sphere of legislation. By this law the United Kingdom agreed to divest its laws of any surviving effect in relation to any Dominion except in so far as the Dominion itself might request it, but provision was made to preserve the federal system in Canada and Australia, which depended on British statutes of 1867 and 1900. So far as law was concerned, all that remained was a paragraph asserting that "it would be in accord with the established constitutional position" for each parliament in future to give its assent to any change in the royal titles or in the succession to the throne.

What were the realities, however, which survived the abolition of legal pretenses regarding the superior powers of the United Kingdom parliament? One was certainly the strong appeal of the personality of George V, dignified, dutiful, and shrewd, whose position gained authority from the fact that governors-general of Dominions were now to be regarded as his direct representatives. Some slight centralizing influence may be attributed to the existence in Britain of a supreme appeal court (the Judicial Committee of the Privy Council) which continued to serve each Dominion unless and until the Dominion determined otherwise. In tranquil times, however, the value of London as a financial center was more important, and in times of international tension the value of the British navy was more important as a security against isolation or attack. From the viewpoint of the United Kingdom, one underlying assumption probably weighed the most. This was the belief that generosity would be answered by generosity, that by meeting halfway every demand for evidence of their freedom, Britain would forestall the temptation for any Dominion to go the whole way to untrammeled independence. For a long time at least, equality of status would not mean equality of function: the facts of history, geography, and economics would enable Britain to replace authority by influence.

The Union of South Africa and the Irish Free State, however, were inspired by recollections of recent and bitter struggles against Britain to push legal freedom to its logical limits. Even before the Statute of Westminster became law, South African politicians were canvassing the right to secede, and by 1934 they had made technical provision to enable South Africa to remain neutral if Britain went to war. This was the more remarkable in view of the restraining influence exercised by General Jan Christiaan Smuts,[17] the only political leader in any of the British Dominions who was an important figure on the world stage. In the Irish Free State a critical situation began to develop as early as 1932. The intransigeant republican De Valera, having triumphed at a general election, virtually abolished the powers and position of the governor-general, ended the oath of allegiance, and began a quarrel, eventually settled by compromise, about the repayment of moneys advanced for land purchase in Ireland from British sources. Finally, in 1937 De Valera seized a propitious moment to do away entirely with the constitution established by treaty only sixteen years before, replacing it with one which received the approval of only an indecisive popular vote. There was to be a new state called Eire, headed by a republican president but accepting the use of the Crown where necessary in the conduct of external relations. Perhaps the United Kingdom gained a little indirect compensation from De Valera's uncompromising attitude, for it at least made certain that Northern Ireland would refuse any proposal for union with her southern neighbor.

If the history of Ireland in this period showed that the fullest constitutional liberty may not suffice to hold an independence movement in check, that of India showed that a carefully controlled series of concessions may not prove any more successful. Before the end of 1919 the British had carried out their wartime promises by introducing dyarchy, a system under which each provincial governor had certain departments run by his officials as before, while others such as education, public health, or agriculture were handed over to Indian ministers responsible to the elected provincial council. The range of transferred subjects was to be extended as the Indians became accustomed to this degree of responsibility, and some useful experience was in fact obtained. The general tendency, however, was for Indians to concentrate attention upon the number of subjects which were not transferred to their charge. They could, consequently, deprecate the fact that in the central government of India the

17. 1870–1950. He was born in Cape Colony and educated at Cambridge (England) and became a prominent Transvaal leader in the South African War, 1899–1902. He commanded in operations against Southwest and East Africa, 1914–1916, represented South Africa in the imperial war cabinet, 1917 and 1918, and helped to found the League of Nations. He was South African prime minister, 1919–1924 and 1939–1950, and brought South Africa into the Second World War, throughout which he figured as one of Churchill's closest advisers. He received the rank of field marshal and the Order of Merit.

legislative assembly, elected on a very narrow franchise, had no final control of legislation or finance or of the supreme executive. This executive was the viceroy's council, made up of departmental heads. Unrest which had become formidable during the war therefore continued, under the skillful leadership of Mahatma Gandhi,[18] a Hindu ascetic whose campaign of civil disobedience (nonpayment of taxes) was the first serious defiance of British authority since the suppression of the mutiny in 1857–1858. Though there was a lull in the mid-1920's, when Gandhi was in prison and disillusioned by the acts of violence which his followers had perpetrated, it was clear that India urgently needed some further installment of self-government. However, if Britain was to fail in this greatest and most complex of her imperial tasks, it would not be for want of trying. A parliamentary commission under the chairmanship of John Simon, a distinguished Liberal lawyer, prepared an elaborate report, which among much else declared dyarchy to be unworkable. Two Round Table Conferences were held in London, the second of which in 1931 was attended by Gandhi in person. Yet from all of this no lasting settlement emerged.

It was not to be expected that to establish self-government in a subcontinent which had the second-largest population in the world would be a simple task. There were at least three special complications. Gandhi was a visionary, as obstinate as he was heroic, who never shared the British enthusiasm for workable compromises. His weapons were the Eastern ones of campaigns of nonviolence which resulted in violence, and of fasts unto death to which authority succumbed rather than risk his self-martyrdom. The Indian princes, on the other hand, were the exact opposite—despots whose thrones, fabulous wealth, and dubious way of life could not survive the withdrawal of the British support guaranteed to them by their century-old treaties of subsidiary alliance. Their policy was to delay and obstruct for obvious personal reasons whatever changes would imperil their own security. In the third place, the subcontinent possessed the biggest and most intractable minority problem in the world—the eighty million Moslems whose relations with the Hindu majority were compounded of mutual fear and suspicion. Churchill, who was strongly opposed to any further reforms in India, waxed eloquent upon this theme, reminding the British parliament that in India there were "mobs of neighbors . . . who, when held and dominated by these . . . passions will tear each other to pieces, men, women, and children, with their fingers."

18. 1869–1948. Son of a Hindu merchant who served as prime minister of one of India's small native states, he studied at London University and was admitted to the bar. In South Africa, 1893–1914, he became champion of the oppressed Indian community there. Returning to India, he was twice president of the Indian National Congress, first championing home rule through nonviolent noncooperation and, later, independence. He denounced the British government after the Amritsar massacre as "satanic," and was frequently imprisoned. When independence came in 1947, he was hailed by the viceroy, Earl Mountbatten, as "the architect of India's freedom." He was assassinated in 1948 by a Hindu extremist. Gandhi has listed the principal influences upon his thought as the *Bhagavad-Gita*, the New Testament, and the writings of Ruskin and Tolstoy.

In 1935 a Government of India Act, passed after long debate, proved to be the last in the long and not ignoble series of statutes by which Britain, negotiating from a position of strength, gave new institutions to her dependencies large and small. Her action was a considered response to need rather than a hasty surrender to clamor. Elections were to be based on communal representation, so as to protect both the Moslems and other, smaller minorities, such as the "untouchables" (the outcast Hindus) and the Christians. Within a federal system the provinces were to enjoy wide powers of self-government, though provision was still made for intervention in emergency by the governor of the province, who would be responsible through the viceroy to the United Kingdom parliament. This part of the constitution was after some demur accepted by the Hindu Congress Party, which by 1937 controlled ministers and legislatures in seven of eleven chief provinces. But the larger design of a federation of all India, with an upper house to represent the princes, was resisted by public, and especially by princely, opinion. Consequently, in September, 1939, India still lacked any central representative authority which might have acted with greater moral force than the viceroy-in-council to commit the Indian Empire to the impending world conflict.

■ BRITAIN AND THE WORLD

The foreign policy of Britain in the 1920's was primarily concerned with the restoration of normal conditions of trade through a return to prewar conditions of confidence among nations. The establishment of the League of Nations, for instance, was welcomed by realists as well as idealists in the hope that it would co-ordinate efforts towards the preservation of the peace of the world without calling for any large-scale action on the part of Britain. The limitation of capital ships by the Washington agreements, too, had loyal support from Britain as a means of avoiding an arms race, even though it went along with the abandonment of the Japanese alliance. The French advance into the Ruhr and the Italian bombardment of Corfu, however, were strongly deprecated by the British because they involved a return to the arbitrament of force. The Locarno agreements, because of their exactly opposite effect, were regarded as the greatest diplomatic triumph of the decade. If MacDonald in his two minority Labor governments went furthest in supporting formal obligations to abandon the use of force in world affairs (the Geneva Protocol in 1924 and the General Act for the Pacific Settlement of International Disputes in 1931), it was the Conservatives who authorized their advisers from the armed forces to work on the assumption that they would receive ten years' warning of the approach of another major war. That warning was not given until 1934, when Hitler had been in power for a year.

The new decade had begun auspiciously enough with the final preparations for a long-delayed general disarmament conference under the aegis of the

League of Nations, and the Labor government's foreign secretary, Arthur Henderson, was elected to its presidency shortly before the government fell. He proved to be both an earnest and a tactful president, but the conference met too late: in September, 1931, the Japanese had launched a major campaign in Manchuria in deliberate defiance of world opinion, and in January, 1933, Germany acquired in Hitler a new chancellor, whose withdrawal from the League of Nations and soon after from the disarmament conference indicated that the tactics which had profited Japan were to be practised nearer home. The world was entering upon another "prewar" period, a fact to which the National government in Britain turned a blind eye, failing to grapple effectively with an increasingly serious situation either by skillful diplomacy or by high-speed rearmament. By their inaction MacDonald and Baldwin prepared the way for Chamberlain's debacle at Munich five years later.

It is easy to be wise after the event and tempting to belittle the difficulties which hampered British judgment of the situation: at the time appeasement of the aggressors looked less like cowardice and more like common sense. The Japanese attack on China in September, 1931, exactly coincided with the crisis over the gold standard in Britain, and in the following years it was of obvious importance to avoid inflicting any unnecessary strain upon the economy. For any positive action, too, Britain needed the support of allies, but France was politically unstable, Italy as likely as not to side against the democracies, and the United States firmly attached to her neutrality. Moreover, in spite of MacDonald's efforts, there was no real rapprochement with Soviet Russia, even when she joined the League of Nations in 1934. As for public opinion, the Peace Ballot of 1935, in which eleven million persons participated, and the sustained attacks of the Labor opposition upon all measures of rearmament showed the extent to which support for the League served as an emotional substitute for any admission that Britain herself must act. Lastly, for a considerable part of 1936—a year when the power of Germany was rapidly mounting—the decision of the new king, Edward VIII, to marry a divorcee against the advice of his ministers and his consequent abdication distracted the attention of the whole of the politically minded public. Those events also endangered the unity of the Commonwealth, since every member-state had to be brought into agreement over the change of sovereign, and their outcome had the important side effect of enhancing the prestige of Baldwin, the minister who was responsible for the foreign policy of drift.

In essence the failures of British policy were numerous and disconcerting to all who valued Britain as a steadying influence in world affairs. The sequence of events will be considered in detail in its European context. Italy was not prevented from conquering Abyssinia. A deal was made with Germany in the naval treaty of 1935 which condoned, while it also sought to limit, her breaches of the limits set in the 1919 peace settlement. In the following year no action was taken to expel the small German military forces which had re-entered the Rhineland, although this time it was the voluntarily accepted Locarno Treaty which was being defied. Then, in a struggle which the whole world watched with breathless interest, German and Italian military aid won the Spanish Civil War for the antidemocratic forces through violations of non-intervention agreements which were largely sponsored by Britain. Austria and Czechoslovakia in turn had been swallowed up in Greater Germany, while Britain watched as though hypnotized.

These many diplomatic failures corresponded to the slow pace of British rearmament, which began with a modest enlargement of the air force in 1934 and became an official policy in the following year, when Baldwin blandly admitted that the government had been mistaken as to the rate of growth of the German *Luftwaffe*. But it was not until early in 1938 that air-force expansion was increased to the capacity of the industry and the first mission sent to buy airplanes in the United States. Though the navy had less distance to catch up, it began to make some provision against German commerce-raiders in 1935, the year of the Anglo-German naval treaty. The army remained very much undermechanized, with no provision for a Continental expeditionary force, and was re-equipped chiefly for purposes of antiaircraft defense. The story may be summed up in financial terms. In 1934 Germany was spending nearly three times as much on armaments as Britain. Four years later, after Britain had experienced a whole series of ominous reverses, Germany was spending nearly five times as much. Truly these were for the British, who were so soon to be confronted with the most mortal perils of all their long history, "the years that the locust hath eaten."

Reading List: Chapter 4

Gretton, R. H., *A Modern History of the English People, 1880–1922* (single-volume ed., 1930), book III, ch. 9. British attitudes in 1919.

Clapham, J. H., *An Economic History of Modern Britain,* vol. III (1938). Epilogue. Reviews developments from 1914 to 1929.

Somervell, D. C., "Stanley Baldwin," *History Today,* vol. II (1952), no. 4.

Raymond, J. (ed.), *The Baldwin Age* (1960). Article on the Labor Party, entitled "Confusion on the Left."

Mowat, C. L., *Britain Between the Wars, 1918–1940* (1955), ch. 9. Social conditions in the 1930's.

Marwick, A., "Middle Opinion in the Thirties: Planning, Progress, and Political Agreement," *English Historical Review,* vol. LXXIX (1964), no. 310.

Watt, D. C., "The Anglo-German Naval Agreement of 1935: An Interim Judgment," *Journal of Modern History,* vol. XXVIII (1956), no. 2.

Medlicott, W. N., "Neville Chamberlain," *History Today,* vol. II (1952), no. 5.

Carrington, C. E., *The British Overseas* (1950), ch. 17. Commonwealth, 1917–1939.

Chapter 5

Europe and the World
East of Suez

The Emergent Nations of the Middle East
The New Turkey
The New Arab States: Saudi Arabia and Egypt
Iran
Middle Eastern Mandates: Syria and Lebanon
Middle Eastern Mandates: Palestine and Transjordan
Middle Eastern Mandates: Iraq
British Problems of Empire
French and Dutch Imperialism in the Interwar Years
The Far East: China and Japan
A Continent in Ferment

■ THE EMERGENT NATIONS OF THE MIDDLE EAST

Enormous changes occurred east of Suez in the years following the First World War. These developments, some already suggested in the brief survey of events within the British Empire,[1] caused Europe's role to come under attack. As some older Asiatic states sought to modernize and transform themselves and as new states appeared, a basic shift in world power began to develop. So momentous a shift is too new for full evaluation; here we are concerned with the immediate problems which confronted the European powers and by which their fortunes were quickly affected.

The term Middle East has now quite generally replaced the historic ex-

1. See pp. 110–115.

SIGNIFICANT EVENTS

1915   McMahon Pledge concerning a future Arab state (October)
1916   Sykes-Picot Agreement on Syria (May)
1917   Balfour Declaration on Palestine (November)
1920   San Remo Conference. Authorization for British and French
        mandates (April)
        Treaty of Sèvres with Turkey (August)
1922   Egyptian independence recognized by Britain (February)
1923   Treaty of Lausanne with Turkey (July)
        Turkish Republic proclaimed (October)
1925   Riza Khan becomes shah of Iran (October)
1927   Ibn Saud proclaimed ruler of Hejaz and Nejd (February)
1930   Anglo-Iraqi treaty recognizes independence of Iraq (June)
1931   Japan begins occupation of Manchuria (September)
1935   Government of India Act (August)
1936   Montreux Convention restores Turkish control of Straits (July)
        Anglo-Egyptian treaty of alliance (August)
1937   Japan begins large-scale invasion of China at Shanghai (July)
1939   British White Paper on Palestine (May)

pression Near East. Some authorities, in defiance of geographic actualities, would extend the western boundary of the Middle East to the Atlantic coast of Morocco. The eastern boundary, in this view, would include West Pakistan, presumably on account of the dominant Moslem faith and the considerable use of the Arabic language. The view adopted here is more restricted, beginning with Cyprus and Turkey, including Egypt and the Sudan, and adding to these the Levantine states (Syria, the Lebanon, Palestine, and Transjordan). It includes also the various states of the Arabian Peninsula (Saudi Arabia, Yemen, Oman, and the sheikdoms along the Persian Gulf) and concludes with Iraq and the non-Arab, yet preponderantly Moslem, state of Iran. The total population around 1925 would, by rough estimate, exceed sixty million.

Largely undeveloped, these areas included, nevertheless, some of the world's richest deposits of oil. They constituted an important crossroad of world communications, and ever since the days of the Crusades they have been the occasion of rivalries among the major European powers.

■ THE NEW TURKEY

Among the countries of the Middle East, Turkey can be assigned a unique place. Its decline, following a long and imposing history, led to the title, "The Sick Man of Europe," given to it in the nineteenth century. A widespread attitude of European hostility was most vigorously expressed by Mr. Gladstone, who proclaimed so often that the knell of Turkish tyranny had sounded. Yet this empire played an important role on the side of the Central Powers in the First World War and subsequently maintained a European toehold across the Straits.[2] During the war the Ottoman Empire had been marked by the Allies as a subject for partition. Britain and France looked forward to special spheres of influence while also making promises to the Arabs. These reached their climax in the Anglo-French declaration of November 7, 1918, announcing "the complete and final liberation of the people who have for so long been repressed by the Turks."

The partition of Turkey was announced to the world in 1920 by the Treaty of Sèvres.[3] Only a tiny remnant of Turkey in Europe was to remain. The lands making up Anatolia were to form the greater part of the new Turkey flanked by an independent Armenia and Kurdistan. Even here the Greeks were given a five-year occupancy of the port of Smyrna and some of the Anatolian hinterland, with a view to their final incorporation in the Greek state. In addition, they had obtained the right to occupy most of Turkey's islands in the Aegean. Four months before, the Allied Conference at San Remo in April, 1920, had formally arranged for France to take over the Syrian-Lebanese mandate and Britain the two mandates of Palestine-Jordan and Iraq.

This drastic partition of Turkey was realized only in part. Even before the Treaty of Sèvres was signed, a vigorous Turkish nationalist movement was on foot, led by one of the most remarkable figures of the postwar era, Mustafa Kemal Pasha.[4] A military officer who had taken part in the 1908 Young Turk revolt, Kemal had fought at Gallipoli and in Syria during the recently concluded war. As early as 1919 he and a group of associates, aroused by the de-

---

2. See pp. 24–25; 32–33.
3. For details of the treaty see pp. 76–77.
4. 1880–1938. A professional soldier who joined in the Young Turk revolution of 1908, he became a general in the First World War. By 1921 he had become the leader of the movement to repudiate the Treaty of Sèvres, which he regarded as intolerable. His biography between 1921 and 1938 is identical with the history of modern Turkey whose modernization he, more than any other individual, was responsible for achieving.

cision at the Peace Conference to put Greek troops in Smyrna, had defied the sultan, organized a congress, and called for a new, independent, undivided, and strongly modern Turkey. They were successful in the postwar elections, with the result that when the Turkish parliament met in January, 1920, the Kemalites forced the adoption of the National Pact—virtually a declaration of independence aimed at creating a new state. When Kemal summoned a parliament in April to meet at Angora, as the capital city of Ankara then was called, this National Assembly chose him as its president.

Kemal's immediate purpose was to resist the terms of the Treaty of Sèvres with respect to Anatolia and the Straits. His first efforts were directed against Greek armies advancing from Smyrna and threatening Angora itself. The tide was turned in September, 1921, with a Turkish victory in the little-known but momentous fourteen-day Battle of the Sakkaria. Just a year later Kemal's victorious forces entered Smyrna, destroying the city by fire, imposing heavy loss of life upon the civilian population, and forcing the remaining Greeks to flee. The Turks also won diplomatic successes. Early in 1921 the Italians agreed to evacuate the zone intended for them in Anatolia in return for economic concessions. At the same time Soviet Russia recognized Turkey's possession of Kars and Ardahan in Armenia in exchange for the oil port of Batum. Later in the year France, like Italy, agreed to evacuate its prospective sphere of influence in Anatolia. Kemal had done well.

The year 1922 was critical for the relations between Kemal and the Allies. When the British government landed a small force at Chanak for the defence of the Straits according to the terms of the Treaty of Sèvres, it found that it could expect little support from France, Italy, or even its own Dominions. Rather than engage in open hostilities alone, Britain signed an armistice with the Turks at Mudania in October, 1922—the preliminary step to a substantial revision of the original peace terms. At the same time Kemal made equally spectacular domestic moves. The Turkish National Assembly proclaimed the abolition of the sultanate in November, 1922. This was to all intents the finale of the Ottoman Empire. Kemal was then elected president by the National Assembly, and his close associate, Ismet Pasha, became premier. The first and most critical stage of the Turkish revolution had succeeded.

A definite settlement with Turkey had not yet been reached. Negotiations were undertaken in Switzerland, the outcome being the Treaty of Lausanne of July, 1923. By it Turkey willingly renounced, as it had already done in the National Pact, all claims to the non-Turkish lands, principally in Arabia, lost after the First World War. Her gains in respect to the terms originally imposed were, however, notable. In the lower Balkans she recovered eastern Thrace, thereby becoming once again a European power with effective occupancy of the whole northern shore of the Straits. She regained from Greece two Aegean islands close to the mouth of the Dardanelles. Since the Greek forces had already been driven from Anatolia, a separate convention now arranged for the mutual transfer of 400,000 Turks living in Greece and 1,300,000 Greeks living in Turkey. Worked out under the supervision of the League, this transfer raised many complex problems, and its successful completion under the direction of the Norwegian explorer and humanitarian, Dr. Fridtjof Nansen, is an early landmark in the history of such enterprises. Turkey was to pay no reparations. The historic capitulations, by which foreign countries had been allowed to have their own courts and special legal privileges on Turkish soil, were abolished. In contrast to these terms, the retention of the Dodecanese Islands, including Rhodes, by the Italians and the retention of Cyprus by the British seemed from the Turkish point of view an acceptable bargain. Changes with respect to the control of the Straits were also notable. The area once intended for international administration became unquestionably Turkish, though, as has been noted in connection with the peace treaties, Turkey was not allowed to fortify the zone—a restriction which remained until 1936.[5]

The completion of the Treaty of Lausanne in July and the proclamation of the Turkish Republic in November made it possible for President Kemal to push ahead with a spectacular series of domestic reforms. The abolition of the sultanate in 1922 was followed in 1924 by the abolition of the Ottoman caliphate, which meant that the former ruling House of Osman no longer could claim the spiritual leadership of all Islam. By a series of subsequent enactments Turkey increasingly became a secular state.

A new constitution was completed in 1924, providing for a National Assembly elected by universal suffrage for a four-year term. A president was also elected for four years by the assembly; he appointed a premier governing through a cabinet chosen from the elected deputies. The state-supported school system was unified and modernized. Islam ceased to be the state religion in 1928, and all religious orders were suppressed. Divorce was legalized and civil marriage became compulsory. In 1926 the old Koranic laws were replaced by new civil, criminal, and commercial codes. In 1928 the complex Turkish script gave way to the Latin alphabet, and in 1930 place-names were revised. Constantinople became Istanbul, Angora became Ankara, and Smyrna became Izmir. Other changes were those forbidding men to wear the fez, discouraging women from wearing the veil, and requiring surnames in the Western style—Kemal, for example, became Kemal Ataturk. In economic matters the principle of *étatisme,* or state control, stood high: protective tariffs were introduced, and government monopolies were created for tobacco, alcohol, salt, matches, explosives, and sugar, as well as for railroads and municipal public services. Peasants were safeguarded in the possession of their farms, and various kinds

5. See p. 123.

of social insurance, health services, and agricultural cooperatives set up. In a country long subject to the heavy hand of tradition and authority, these were sweeping changes indeed.

All these reforms were dominated by the great figure of Kemal Ataturk, who after 1930 tolerated no party save his own—the People's Party of the Republic. When Kemal died in 1938 his trusted collaborator, Ismet Inönü, assumed the presidency of a regime that was undoubtedly totalitarian in many respects, yet was unmarked by the large-scale jailings, confiscations, police control, and banishments which were so common a feature of the European dictatorships. The regime was clearly acceptable to the great majority of the Turkish people.

Turkey's foreign relations prospered. She made nonaggression and trade pacts with most of her neighbors. A dispute with Great Britain over the boundaries of the Mosul oil fields lying near the common borders of Turkey and the British mandate of Iraq was settled with the assistance of the League of Nations in 1926. Relations with Greece, with whom a nonaggression pact was signed in 1933, were correct, if cool, as were those with Soviet Russia. In 1932 Turkey became a member of the League of Nations. In 1934 she joined with Greece, Rumania, and Yugoslavia in the Balkan Pact, guaranteeing the mutual security of their frontiers.

Turkey, concerned by Italy's warlike acts in Ethiopia, asked in 1936 for permission to refortify the Straits. Following an international conference, she was allowed to do so and to take over the rights of supervision. In time of war, if Turkey was neutral, she would be required to prevent the passage of belligerent warships. This Montreux Convention is a good example of the growing prestige enjoyed by Turkey. In 1939 both Great Britain and France made mutual assistance pacts with her should war come in the Middle East. With a population in 1927 of 13.6 million, an efficient army, and some growing importance as an industrial power (Turkey was the world's largest producer of chrome), the new republic quite clearly had moved into the middle rank of European powers.

■ THE NEW ARAB STATES: SAUDI ARABIA AND EGYPT

Arab hopes for independence had been fostered during the war by Allied promises, most notably those contained in the correspondence of 1915 between the British high commissioner in Egypt, Sir Henry McMahon, and Sherif Husein of Mecca. Britain later made agreements with France and Italy, as well as promises to Zionist leaders about a Jewish national home, not easy to reconcile with this so-called "McMahon Pledge." The French, indeed, later pleaded ignorance of it. Essentially McMahon promised that England would support the independence of the Arabs in the large area bounded on the north by the 37th Parallel, in the east by the Iranian border down to the Persian Gulf, and in the south by the Arab Gulf states.[6] When Husein asked that the Red Sea and the Mediterranean coast be the western boundaries of such a pledge, McMahon in his reply excluded the whole coastal belt "lying to the west of the districts of Damascus, Homs, Hama, and Aleppo," which would be subject to the claims and interests of Britain's ally, France. This took coastal Syria and the Lebanon from the Arab sphere, though the Arabs remained confident that Palestine was not similarly excluded.

The peace settlement of 1919 frustrated the Arab hopes of unity. The subsequent Allied Conference of San Remo (April, 1920) authorized the establishment of French mandates in Syria and the Lebanon, and British mandates in Palestine, Transjordan, and Iraq, thereby cutting sharply into Arab ambitions and arousing a profound sense of resentment. The only Arab state actually recognized by the Treaty of Sèvres in 1920 was the Kingdom of the Hejaz —a vaguely delimited area of western Arabia important because it contained the two Moslem holy cities of Mecca and Medina. It was ruled by Husein, spokesman of Arab nationalism and champion of the Hashemite Moslems. He thus stood out at the close of the war as the principal leader of the Arab world. Yet this leadership was quickly and in the end decisively challenged by a spectacular rival.

The successful challenger to Husein's leadership was that remarkable figure, Abdul-Aziz ibn-Saud,[7] a leader of the fanatical branch of the Sunni Moslems known as the Wahabi. At the beginning of the twentieth century these had won control of the area of central Arabia known as the Nejd, later adding to it the territories of the Hasa, Qatif, and Jubail touching the Persian Gulf.[8] Ibn Saud had a standing army of fifty thousand men, and held authority over twice that many followers organized in some seventy military agricultural colonies known as "Brethren." Technically neutral during the war, Ibn Saud was induced by British subsidies to maintain a benevolent attitude toward the Arab revolt. In 1919 he attacked Husein, whose territories of the Hejaz bordered upon the Nejd, and occupied some border areas. The ensuing uneasy truce was broken in 1924 when Ibn Saud actually invaded the Hejaz. By 1926

---

6. See map on facing page.
7. 1880–1953. A member of a former ruling family in the Nejd, he was in exile from 1890 to 1901, returning to recapture its capital with only fifteen men. In the three subsequent decades he won the position of outstanding Arab leader, bitterly opposing the Hashemite leader, Husein. He based his strength on the skillful control of colonies of Arab warriors. He won Mecca from the Hashemites in 1923, took the title of king of the Hejaz and the Nejd in 1927, and that of king of Saudi Arabia in 1932. Oil concessions granted after 1936 to foreign oil companies, chiefly American, brought him enormous wealth. During the Second World War he was a strong supporter of the British cause, and President Roosevelt went out of his way to visit him on his return from the Crimea Conference in 1945.
8. See map on facing page.

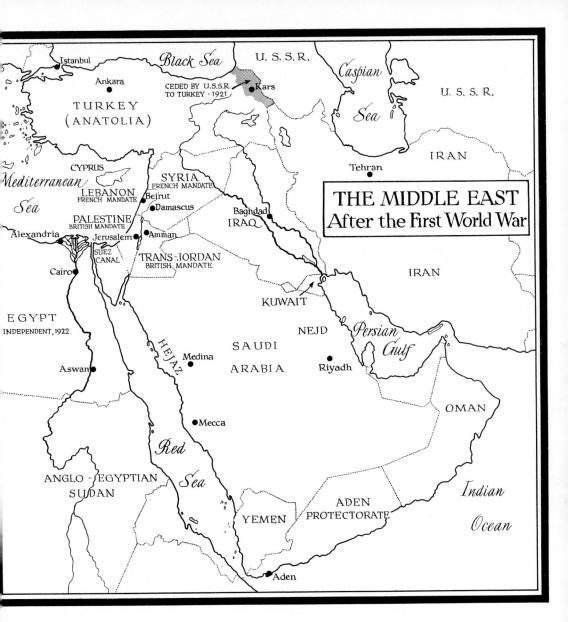

THE MIDDLE EAST
After the First World War

Istanbul
Ankara
TURKEY
(ANATOLIA)
Black Sea
U. S. S. R.
CEDED BY U.S.S.R. TO TURKEY - 1921
Kars
Caspian
Sea
U. S. S. R.
IRAN
Tehran

CYPRUS
Mediterranean
Sea
LEBANON
FRENCH MANDATE
Beirut
Damascus
SYRIA
FRENCH MANDATE
Baghdad
IRAQ
PALESTINE
BRITISH MANDATE
Alexandria
Jerusalem
Amman
SUEZ
CANAL
Cairo
TRANS-JORDAN
BRITISH MANDATE
IRAN

EGYPT
INDEPENDENT, 1922

KUWAIT

HEJAZ
Medina
Aswan
NEJD
SAUDI
ARABIA
Riyadh
Persian
Gulf

OMAN

Mecca

Red
Sea

ANGLO - EGYPTIAN
SUDAN

Indian
Ocean

YEMEN
ADEN
PROTECTORATE

Aden

Note that Turkey is restricted to the Zone of the Straits, Anatolia, and part of Armenia. Frontiers within the Arabian Peninsula cannot be accurately indicated.

Husein was forced to abdicate and Ibn Saud was proclaimed king of the Hejaz in his place, receiving in May, 1927, the formal recognition of the British. When in September, 1932, his lands were renamed Saudi Arabia, Ibn Saud's name was attached to four-fifths of the Arabian Peninsula with an area of 870, 000 square miles and a population of some six million. It included the holy cities of Mecca and Medina and, though not known at the time, had oil reserves now estimated to be second only to those of the fantastically rich sheik-

FOREIGN INVESTMENT IN SAUDI ARABIA. A maze of oil pipes seen beside the Ras Tanura refinery of the Arabian American Oil Company.

dom of Kuwait. Ibn Saud had become the most powerful figure in the Middle East.

The discovery in 1932 of oil in Ibn Saud's territories led two years later to the granting of vast concessions to the Arabian-American Oil Company. From four million barrels produced in Saudi Arabia in 1938, the figure soared to 200 million barrels (not far behind the 255 million of Iran) in 1950. This spectacular output provided enormous revenues, ultimately some $250 million per year, for Ibn Saud and gave the United States a vital interest in the Middle East.

Ibn Saud's major role in Arabia affected his relations both with his neighbors and with the great powers. Britain, in addition to her colony of Aden, had *de facto* protectorates over several small sheikdoms. She also was committed to administering the mandates of Palestine, Transjordan, and Iraq. On the whole, Ibn Saud's policy came to be that of the "good neighbor," even with respect to his ancient rivals, the ruler of the Yemen and the two rulers of Iraq and Transjordan. Both of these latter were sons of King Husein and were on terms of close association with Britain. In the end, though parts of the Moslem world were shocked at the conquest of Mecca and Medina by Ibn Saud's fanatical Wahabi sect, a good deal of Arab harmony was secured.

The position of Egypt, where the British had been in military occupation since 1882, underwent significant changes. Great Britain announced a formal protectorate in December, 1914, replacing the pro-Turkish khedive, or ruler, by his nephew and making Egypt an important center for Allied Middle Eastern operations. At the close of the First World War, the tide of Egyptian nationalism was running strong—witness the growth of the nationalist party known as the Wafd. The British chose the path of compromise, carrying on negotiations until February, 1922, when they announced their recognition of King Fuad as ruler of an independent Egypt. At the same time they reserved rights of intervention for themselves in pursuit of four interests: (1) the security of imperial communications, i.e., the right to garrison the Suez Canal;[9] (2) the defense of Egypt against foreign attack; (3) the protection of foreign interests and minorities; and (4) continuation of the dependent status of the Sudan with respect to both Egypt and Britain. The nationalist Wafd Party—the strongest political power in Egypt—bitterly opposed these continuing rights. In 1924 the British commander in chief of the Egyptian army and governor-general of the Sudan was assassinated. After much tension, though the Wafd Party continued its opposition, conditions temporarily improved.

The next major landmark came in the Anglo-Egyptian treaty of alliance signed in August, 1936, after the Italian attack on Ethiopia. Egypt was recognized as fully independent, so that the military occupation was to end. Great Britain retained the right to maintain forces in the Suez Canal Zone for twenty years, after which the situation was to be reviewed. In the event of war Britain was to have the full use of airports, anchorages, and Egyptian transport facilities. There was to be a joint and equal administration of the Sudan (a continuation of the old "condominium") and it was agreed to end the regime of capitulations in Egypt—a pledge actually carried out in 1937.

Egypt's entrance into the League of Nations in 1937 was the outward sign of its independent status. Its population was estimated in 1927 at over seventeen million of which 90 percent were peasants. The density of population—1,054 persons per habitable square mile—was one of the highest in the world. The economy was based largely upon agriculture, and especially cotton-growing. For this, large-scale irrigation projects were essential and foreign capital and engineering skill had to be sought. These considerations, together with Egypt's strategic location in the Middle East, made it certain that her role would be important.

■ IRAN

Another independent state, Iran, formerly Persia, provided a good illustration of the pressure of imperial interests in a new age. Its position on the wild upland Iranian Plateau bordering both Russia and India gave it political

---

9. This, by the International Suez Canal Convention of 1888, was always to be open "in time of war as in time of peace to every vessel of commerce or of war, without distinction of flag."

and strategic importance. The first oil concession had been granted to William D'Arcy, an Australian, in 1901, although oil was not actually discovered until 1908. Such prospects, however, made the great powers eager to obtain special concessions for their exploitation. Consequently Great Britain and Russia had agreed in 1907 to establish their own spheres of influence in the south and north respectively, with a buffer area in between. The Anglo-Persian Oil Company quickly undertook heavy investments in order to develop the oil resources. During the First World War German agents led by Consul Wassmuss—the counterpart to Lawrence of Arabia—had some success in stirring up Persian tribes against the British. At the end of the war Britain seemed in a very strong position, with some temptation to bring all Persia, by then estimated to have a population of twelve million, within her sphere of influence. A treaty of August, 1919, between Britain and Persia provided for the restoration of order largely through military and financial missions. A strong upsurge of nationalism, however, led the Persian parliament to refuse to ratify the agreement.

The sequel was the rise of a new Iranian leader, Riza Khan, a soldier-adventurer whose role resembled that of Kemal in Turkey. By a military coup in February, 1921, he became commander in chief and minister of war, thereby dominating the new government at Tehran. Soviet Russia, meanwhile, sought to woo Iran with kindness, managing in 1921 to obtain a treaty of friendship in which the Russians renounced their old insistence upon concessions and extra-territorial privileges. Riza Khan assumed the title of prime minister in 1923, driving the weak-willed shah from the country. When in October, 1925, the Iranian parliament formally deposed the absentee ruler and proclaimed Riza as Shah of Iran, a new dynasty was established and a new era had begun.

Riza's reforms were perhaps more striking in their externals than in their actual effect. The new constitution proclaimed that the official religion of Iran was Islam, and that the shah must profess and propagate this faith. The truly significant matters were the assertion of Iranian nationalism and the increasing autocracy of the ruler. The Anglo-Iranian Oil Company was forced to re-negotiate its concession in 1933 on much less favorable terms than before. As in Turkey, the old foreign capitulations were abolished. Efforts were made to emancipate women. The army was modernized, the judicial system over-hauled, and some schools, roads, and railways were built. The government undertook to regulate economic life; oil and opium production, for example, were to be government monopolies. The Trans-Iranian Railway, running from the Caspian Sea through Tehran to the Persian Gulf, was begun in 1927 and completed in 1939. In 1934 a university with six faculties was established at the capital.

In foreign matters Iran sought peace and friendship with her neighbors.

Thus she signed in 1937 the Middle Eastern pact of nonaggression with Turkey, Iraq, and Afghanistan. In general Iran stood aloof from the complex problems of the Arab countries. Her relations with Soviet Russia have been described as correct but not cordial. The Soviets, for example, complained that the oil concessions which Iran was prepared to grant to British and American interests ran counter to promises in the Russo-Persian Treaty of 1921. Britain and Iran managed to keep on generally friendly terms, largely since both benefited from the operations of the Anglo-Iranian Oil Company. Germany supplied experts and goods, helping with hospital and railway building as well as encouraging agriculture and industry. Toward Germany, especially after Hitler came into power, Iran was well disposed for economic reasons, with the result that by 1939 some 41 percent of Iran's foreign trade was with Germany. Nevertheless, Iran's first move on the outbreak of war in 1939 was to proclaim her neutrality.

■ MIDDLE EASTERN MANDATES: SYRIA AND LEBANON

The Middle Eastern mandates set up in the first years of peace seemed to create almost as many problems as they solved. This new experiment was intended basically to provide order and assist progress in those Arab parts of the old Ottoman Empire not yet ready for full independence. Somewhat paradoxically, however, one of the most backward areas, the Hejaz, was given such full independence. Another purpose of the mandates was to further the various secret arrangements made by the Allies during the war, so that to a great many Arabs the pursuit of such aims marked the frustration of their hopes.

The French mandate over Syria and Lebanon was a case in point. The term Syria had generally been used in the past to indicate the entire eastern Mediterranean littoral, including Palestine. The Anglo-French declaration of November, 1918, had assured the people of Syria, though with no specific promise of independence, that they had the right to establish their own fortunes through "national governments and administrations that shall derive their authority from the free exercise of the initiative and choice of the indigenous populations." Moreover, late in 1915, when the British were seeking to raise an Arab revolt against the Turks, Sir Henry McMahon had pledged his country's support to the independence of the Arabs in the large area reaching northward from Arabia, with some exclusions, to the 37th Parallel.[10] Yet by the Sykes-Picot Agreement of May, 1916, concluded in great secrecy between France and Britain, France had been conceded the administration of the whole Syrian area and more, south of the 37th Parallel. She was, in addition, to have a zone of influence still further south. This would extend along the coast almost as far as Haifa, with a boundary running inland in a northeasterly di-

10. See pp. 123–124.

rection so as to include the Mosul area on the Tigris. South of it was to be a corresponding British zone of influence. It had initially been stated that both the French and British areas would form a kind of confederation of Arab states. The actual outcome, since the French refused to recognize Britain's specific promise to Husein, was very different, and extremely frustrating to Arab hopes.

The King-Crane Commission—an inquiry consisting of two Americans sent to Syria by the Peace Conference in 1919—reported that the whole area should be treated as a single unit. According to the Commission the opposition to France was overwhelming. A congress of Syrian notables meeting at Damascus in March, 1920, offered the crown of a joint Syrian-Palestinian kingdom to Emir Faisal, son of Sherif Husein. Though Faisal accepted, the San Remo Conference in the following month assigned the mandate for Syria-Lebanon to France, with Mesopotamia and Palestine as a mandate to Britain. The actual act of mandate was signed in London more than two years later, in July, 1922.

These arrangements were to cause even more trouble to the French than to the British. The former had a long interest in the Levant, where French missionaries, teachers, soldiers, and merchants had all made their influence felt during the nineteenth century. Yet the new fact was that of Syrian nationalism, strengthened by the preponderantly Moslem faith of the area and wholly out of sympathy with any French claim to a civilizing mission. Only in Lebanon, which the French soon established as a separate entity, did some pro-French sentiment exist. Here the majority was not Moslem but Christian, half of the latter belonging to the Maronite sect.

The first French move was to send General Henri Gouraud as high commissioner and to oust Faisal forcibly from Damascus in July, 1920. Endless troubles followed, which the French met by rigorous military rule. After Gouraud came Maxime Weygand, then Maurice Sarrail, with ever increasing numbers of French troops and always with a characteristically French insistence upon centralized administration. Syria, to be sure, was split into four units, but only the better to ensure French control from above. Sarrail's ruthlessness led to a full-fledged revolt in 1925 among the Druse tribesmen. His savage measures of repression, which included a three-day bombardment of Damascus in 1925 and another in 1926, in each case with an estimated loss of a thousand civilian lives, led to the recall of Sarrail and the subsequent censure of France by the Mandates Commission of the League of Nations.

Gradually the bitterest tensions subsided. Greater Lebanon was officially declared a separate republic, though not independent of France, in May, 1926; an assembly was permitted in 1928 to draft a constitution for it, which after some modification the high commissioner promulgated in 1933. Meanwhile,

Syria was proclaimed a republic in 1930 with a new constitution effective in 1932. Yet the mandate continued. When a more liberal French government, the Popular Front, took office in 1936, it tried to reach an accommodation with the Syrian nationalists. These wished a Franco-Syrian treaty relationship to take the place of the mandatory regime. In response France signed treaties of alliance with both Syria and Lebanon, promising that they would be guaranteed admission to the League of Nations as independent states three years after ratification of the treaties. France stipulated, somewhat as Britain had done in Egypt, that she be allowed to retain certain special privileges for twenty-five years. Despite such promises, the less liberal French governments which soon succeeded the Popular Front failed to ratify the treaties, with the consequence that the mandates continued until the coming of the war in 1939. Not surprisingly, the interwar period closed with a new upsurge of anti-French discontent.

■ MIDDLE EASTERN MANDATES: PALESTINE AND TRANSJORDAN

Palestine created even greater problems for the European powers. Both Arab and Jew—fellow users of the Semitic tongue—could claim a long history of settlement in Palestine; and the city of Jerusalem counted within its boundaries holy places that were sacred either to Jew, Moslem, or Christian. In this tiny land of some 750,000 people—a population comparable to that of a large American city—the Jews in 1922 numbered about 11 percent.[11] Yet this small area generated world-wide concern, in part because of its strategic location, but even more because of the phenomenon of Zionism. Ever since the destruction of the Temple at Jerusalem by the Roman Emperor Titus in 70 A.D., the Jews of the Diaspora, or Dispersion, had clung to the vision of some future reestablishment of their national identity as a people. Zionism during the nineteenth century manifested itself in actual hopes and plans for the creation of a Jewish state in the ancient homeland. Late in the century, when anti-Semitism had become a political force in Europe, a few Jewish pioneer agricultural colonies were settled in Palestine. In 1896 Theodore Herzl, an Austrian Jew, published his epochal work, *The Jewish State,* detailing a scheme for an autonomous Jewish commonwealth in Palestine under the suzerainty of the sultan. In the following year the first international Zionist congress met at Basel.

During the First World War the prospect of the collapse of the Ottoman Empire led Zionist leaders, especially in Britain, to enlarge their plans. In spite of substantial British commitments to the Arabs, the foreign secretary, Arthur Balfour, in November, 1917, addressed his famous letter to Lord Rothschild, one of the leaders of the Jewish community. The declaration, submitted to and approved by the British cabinet, read as follows:

11. Arabs, 589,000; Jews, 84,000; Christians, 79,000.

His Majesty's Government view with favour the establishment in Palestine of a national home for the Jewish people, and will use their best endeavours to facilitate the achievement of this object, it being clearly understood that nothing shall be done which may prejudice the civil and religious rights of existing non-Jewish communities in Palestine or the rights and political status enjoyed by Jews in any other country.

The consideration that the word "home" was used, rather than "state," that this home was to be "in" Palestine, and that the rights of "non-Jewish communities" (Christian and Arab) were to be respected, could not keep Zionist leaders from taking this Balfour Declaration as a powerful reinforcement of their aspirations. The British scientist, Dr. Chaim Weizmann,[12] president of the World Zionist Organization, attended the Paris Peace Conference in 1919, pressing demands for a Jewish state of Palestine within the larger framework of the Arab world.

The immediate outcome, from the Jewish point of view, was disappointing. No specific settlement was made at Paris. At San Remo in 1920, as has been shown, the Allies allocated Palestine and Iraq to Great Britain as mandates—a decision approved by the League of Nations in 1922, when Transjordan was also recognized as a separate British mandate. Thereupon Britain, still deeply committed to her imperial interests throughout the Middle East, undertook these new and difficult duties, which she performed with an ever growing sense of frustration in Palestine until the official termination of the mandate in May, 1948.

Palestine, in view of the population figures of 1922, could in one sense be described as a mandate over Arabs, yet important commitments had been made to the Jews. The British high commissioner quickly promulgated a constitution providing for an appointed executive council and for a legislature to be in part elected. Deeply resentful at these arrangements and suspicious of the pledges concerning a Jewish national home, the Arabs refused to participate. They were not placated by the 1922 pledge of Winston Churchill, then colonial secretary, that his country's policy did not contemplate "a wholly Jewish Palestine." Active opposition remained, however, at a low ebb until 1929, when disturbances involving loss of life began to break out. In 1930 the British announced a ban on further Jewish immigration, which had been averaging about 12,000 per year. This ban was relaxed in 1932 only to the extent of allowing Jews with a capital equal to $2,500 to come in on a limited

---

12. 1874–1952. Born in Russian Poland, he became a distinguished research chemist, teaching in Switzerland and Great Britain. His important war work on acetone brought him in contact with many national figures, and as an outstanding Zionist he had a large share in pressing for the Balfour Declaration of 1917. He was president of the World Zionist Organization from 1920 to 1930 and again from 1935 to 1946. In 1929 he was selected as chairman of the Jewish Agency for Palestine. He became the first president of the new state of Israel in 1948 and was re-elected in 1951, shortly before his death.

monthly quota. The number of immigrants, nevertheless, soon rose to an average of about 34,000 annually. This rise was clearly associated with the beginnings of the Jewish persecution in National Socialist Germany.

The real problem in Palestine was that of increasing conflict between the interests of the Arabs and the Jews. The hard-working Jewish settlers, with their advanced technical skills, were engaged in industrial enterprises and land reclamation projects with which the Arabs could not hope to compete. Arab land was owned by absentee landlords. The Jews bought the land and then proceeded to push out the Arab tenant farmers. Proposals by the British in 1936 to extend the area of self-government were opposed by the Jews as giving too much power to the Arabs, and by the Arabs as still leaving too much authority to the high commissioner.

The report (1937) of the Peel Commission, which had been sent out by the British government, proposed the partition of Palestine into an Arab and a Jewish state, with a neutral area containing Bethlehem and Jerusalem remaining under British control. This led only to further protests and disturbances—in effect an Arab rebellion which required the British to send nearly 20,000 troops to maintain order. The outcome was a proposal in 1938 that in place of partition some kind of economic federalism be attempted. Little real progress actually was being made, though under the pressure of Hitler's violent anti-Semitism Jewish immigration into Palestine, both legal and illegal, was increasing.[13] In the fifteen years from 1922 to 1937 the Arab portion of the total population, although it grew by figures almost equal to the Jewish growth,

PALESTINE POPULATION[14]

DATE	MOSLEM	JEWISH	OTHER	TOTAL
1922	589,000 (79%)	84,000 (11%)	79,000 (10%)	752,000
1927	680,000 (74%)	150,000 (16%)	87,000 (10%)	917,000
1932	771,000 (73%)	181,000 (17%)	100,000 (10%)	1,052,000
1937	883,000 (63%)	396,000 (28%)	122,000 (9%)	1,402,000
1940	948,000 (61%)	464,000 (30%)	133,000 (9%)	1,545,000
1945	1,042,000 (62%)	500,000 (30%)	145,000 (8%)	1,687,000
1962	171,000 (8%)	1,985,000 (89%)	76,000 (3%)	2,232,000

JEWISH IMMIGRATION INTO PALESTINE

1919–1923— 35,000	1940–1948—110,000
1924–1931— 82,000	1948–1951—600,000
1932–1939—225,000	

13. See the accompanying chart.
14. Adapted from G. LENCZOWSKI, *The Middle East in World Affairs* (2nd ed., 1956), p. 547.

had dropped from 79 to 63 percent and the Jewish portion had increased from 11 to 28 percent.

A round table conference summoned in London early in 1939 met with failure. Consequently in May of that year the British government was led to issue its famous White Paper—the last official British proposal for reconciling the conflicting interests in Palestine. It began by stating that the whole of Palestine west of the River Jordan was excluded from the McMahon Pledge of 1915 to Sherif Husein. Britain would emphatically back a Jewish national home, but not a Jewish state, since "His Majesty's Government believes that the framers of the Mandate in which the Balfour Declaration was embodied could not have intended that Palestine should be converted into a Jewish state against the will of the Arab population of the country." The White Paper proposed the creation within ten years of a Palestinian state, linked to Britain by a special treaty and safeguarding the "essential interests" of both Jews and Arabs. During the next five years Jewish immigration into Palestine was to be limited to 75,000, after which immigration would cease, "unless the Arabs of Palestine are prepared to acquiesce." This would have meant a Palestine still having a clear Arab majority. Profoundly shocked, the Jewish leaders unconditionally rejected these proposals, as did the Arabs. The Second World War, indeed, was soon to demonstrate that the Arabs were in many cases willing subjects for the propaganda of the Axis powers.

Transjordan, lying directly to the east of the River Jordan, was an area where British imperial interests were closely involved, for this Arab territory lay in the very center of the land route from the Mediterranean to the Persian Gulf. The Turkish-built railway line running southward from Aleppo and Damascus to Medina passed through Amman, the Transjordanian capital. Arab hopes had originally been that this area would be part of the great Arab state to be set up, following the war, under Emir Faisal with its capital at Damascus.[15] This plan fell through when the French took over the Syrian mandate. The British, anxious to re-establish their influence among the Arabs —and particularly among the Hashemite Moslems, the rivals of Ibn Saud— pushed for the creation of a Transjordanian Arab state, separate from Palestine though technically within the British mandate.

All this was accomplished by 1922. In the previous year another son of Sherif Husein, the Emir Abdullah, had adopted the title of Emir of Transjordan. In 1923 the British recognized the independent authority of his government, though still of course asserting a supervisory influence as the mandatory power.

The history of Transjordan in these years, unlike that of Palestine, was relatively uneventful. The British regularly provided subsidies. They approved

15. See p. 130.

of the policy which forbade Jews even to buy land in Transjordan. The Arab Legion, first organized in 1921 and trained by British officers, though small was highly efficient. Under the command of "Glubb Pasha"—Brigadier John Bagot Glubb,[16] a professional soldier with a profound knowledge of the history and culture of this area—it became for a time a useful adjunct to British policy. The great rivalry with Ibn Saud lasted until 1927 when the Treaty of Jidda established a *modus vivendi* giving Transjordan possession of the port of Akaba and thereby access to the Red Sea. The Anglo-Jordan treaty of 1928 gave Abdullah's government greater legislative and administrative power, though subject ultimately to the British resident, who was in turn responsible to the high commissioner in Palestine. Yet the country remained backward and remote, one striking illustration being the fact that the Transjordan section of the railway once linking Damascus and Medina lost both its northern and southern extremities, becoming almost literally a railway that started nowhere and ended nowhere. The rivalry with Palestine, moreover, was continuous, bitter, and unresolved.

■ MIDDLE EASTERN MANDATES: IRAQ

Iraq, historically more familiar under the name of Mesopotamia, with its capital at Baghdad, had in 1920 a population of something less than 3,000,000, of whom more than 2,500,000 were Moslems. Like Transjordan it lay in a region of British imperial interests, where at the war's close in 1918 the British were in full occupation. With the French they had promised to set up "national governments and administrations" in the parts of the Arab world now freed from Turkish control, a promise which specifically included Mesopotamia. Local resentment grew at the continued British occupation; and following the San Remo declaration of 1920 that Iraq was to be a mandate, insurrections occurred. Eventually the British managed to form a native Arab government with Emir Faisal, frustrated in his hopes of a great Syrian kingdom, as ruler. In a referendum of August, 1921, he received 96 percent of the votes cast—a phenomenon which the English observer Gertrude Bell described as "politics running on wheels greased with extremely well-melted grease."[17]

Something of the flavor of an older imperialism persisted. An Anglo-Iraqi treaty of October, 1922, gave Britain continuing privileges for twenty years and authorized the retention of key British officials. In 1924 an Organic Law provided Iraq with a constitution "which established a pseudo democracy for the

16. Born in 1897. He was a professional British soldier who organized a native police force in Iraq in 1920. When transferred to Transjordan in 1930 he established the desert patrol known as the Arab Legion, the most efficient Arab fighting force in the Middle East. A powerful and somewhat enigmatic behind-the-scenes figure, he was dismissed in 1956 when Arab critics began to refer to him as "Emperor of Jordan."

17. Quoted in LENCZOWSKI, *The Middle East in World Affairs*, p. 233.

upper stratum of elderly politicians."[18] Yet this westernization contributed to the growth of Iraqi nationalism. The result was that in June, 1930, a new Anglo-Iraqi treaty was signed proclaiming Iraq's complete independence and the termination of the mandate. Britain was promised a twenty-five-year alliance with pledges of close cooperation in foreign policy, and with the right to have air bases and transit facilities. In October, 1932, Iraq was admitted to the League—the first of the mandated territories thus to be accepted.

Oil concessions had been granted in 1925 to the Iraq Petroleum Company in which French, British, American, and Dutch companies all held equal shares. Oil production in 1935 was some thirty million barrels. Pipelines running across Jordan and Syria were eventually constructed, with Mediterranean outlets at Haifa and Tripoli. Cotton and winter wheat were added as supplementary products to Iraq's great economic asset of oil, yet political uncertainty continued. When Faisal I died in 1933, he was succeeded by his son Ghazi, whose major interests seemed to be automobiles and motorcycles. Ghazi's accidental death in 1939 was an almost certain guarantee of still further confusion, for his son and successor had not yet reached the age of four, and no strong leader was in sight. Independence in itself was no guarantee of security.

■ BRITISH PROBLEMS OF EMPIRE

The subcontinent of India gave Britain some of its most serious problems. Since these have already been discussed in relation to the general evolution of the Commonwealth,[19] only those matters need be touched upon here which furnish illuminating parallels and contrasts to the problems of other imperial powers in the areas east of Suez. The total emancipation from British rule, long desired and persistently sought by the Indian nationalists, largely through the techniques of passive resistance, still remained in the 1930's unachieved. Despite unrest in India and elsewhere, the British Empire and Commonwealth stood unquestionably as the greatest of the world's imperial structures. In addition to India and the Dominions, now known as the Commonwealth countries, the roster was world-wide. It included British Guiana and the partly derelict West Indies. In Africa lay the populous basin of the lower Niger together with other West African territories, the two Rhodesias, Kenya, Uganda, and colonies and protectorates along the eastern side of the continent, as well as the condominium of the Anglo-Egyptian Sudan. To these were added Malaya, Singapore, and Hong Kong; important islands in the Pacific; and in the Mediterranean, Gibraltar, Malta, and Cyprus. Britain, furthermore, had her several mandates. Shortly before his death in 1930, Lord Balfour made the following note:

18. *Ibid.,* p. 243.
19. See pp. 110-115.

Whence comes the cohesion of the British Empire?
> 1. Patriotism. Loyalty. Custom.
> 2. Religion. Race. Pride in various manifestations. Habit. Language. *Mere* law is the weakest of all bonds.[20]

Too complex for simple characterization, Britain's possessions were to be a source of both strength and weakness to her in the world conflict which erupted in 1939. Perhaps the surest generalization to be made is that changing conditions both in the European and the non-European world were leading more and more Englishmen to realize that the old forms of imperial control were no longer either possible or desirable.

At the time in the mid-thirties when India's problems were becoming acute, Afghanistan, on the northwest frontier, also showed some spirit of nationalism. Here, as early as 1907, Russia had recognized Great Britain's special position. A wave of nationalist sentiment in 1919 led to a bitter frontier war, terminated in 1921 by Britain's recognition of complete Afghan independence. The attempts of King Amanullah to modernize his country led, however, to his overthrow in 1929. Then a capable army officer, Mohammed Nadir Khan, won the title of shah. Though Nadir was assassinated, his son tried to carry on the progressive reforms which had been initiated. In 1937 Afghanistan joined Turkey, Iraq, and Iran in signing a mutual pact of nonaggression.

■ FRENCH AND DUTCH IMPERIALISM IN THE INTERWAR YEARS

Like those of Great Britain, French imperial possessions were the source of both satisfaction and concern to the parent country in the years following the First World War. In a world of power politics it was reassuring for the French to be able to count the more than sixty million living overseas beside the forty million inhabitants of France. During the First World War native troops had been drawn in large numbers from French Africa, and substantial labor forces had been recruited similarly from the Far East. France had pointed with pride to the small native elite in her colonies which she welcomed into the administrative and cultural framework of French life. The "ancient colonies" of the Western Hemisphere, as well as Cochin China and the five establishments on the coast of India, were directly represented in the French parliament. Algeria also sent its deputies to Paris, though these were chosen almost exclusively by the French and not by the native elements.

Yet serious problems existed, and in the world east of Suez France encountered some ominous portents which by mid-century were to bring her empire to an end. The difficulties of the French mandates in Syria and Lebanon have already been outlined.[21] The five Indian establishments, with a

20. Quoted in a letter to *The Times* (London), December 14, 1936.
21. See pp. 129–131.

total population of less than 300,000, were too small to create any major crisis. The real troubles developed in Annam, Tonkin, Cambodia, Laos, and Cochin China, the five states making up French Indochina. Here surely the worst features of European imperialism were in evidence. This fertile land with its more than 20,000,000 inhabitants ranked with Burma and Siam as one of the world's great rice-exporting areas. Yet the economy was badly exploited. Huge profits went to the French possessors, who paid miserably low wages to native labor. The collapse of world prices in the 1930's brought on a severe economic depression which French tariff policy intensified. It is a curious fact that, although the French developed a school of Far Eastern languages and archeology at Hanoi, they failed signally to train the French members of their highly centralized civil service in the use of native tongues.

A consequence of this situation was the growth of a native movement of protest, particularly in Annam. Much of this was influenced by Chinese revolutionary activity at Canton, and some Communist teachings began to take hold. Even before this postwar unrest, the University of Hanoi, soon after its founding by the French in 1907, had been closed for nine years (1908–1917) because it was regarded as a hotbed of nationalist agitation. Severe repressive measures by the French in the 1920's failed to stem the nationalist movement. By 1925 a revolutionary party was in existence, and during 1930 and 1931 the troubles spread northward to Tonkin, leading the French to take stern measures there too. The introduction of local advisory councils in which the French, although numbering only about twenty-five thousand in a total population of over twenty million, always seemed to be in a majority did little to improve the situation.

The Netherlands Empire in Asia, third in world rank after the British and the French, demonstrated many of the same problems. Stretching for nearly 3,000 miles east and west, and with a total population in 1925 of 51 million, the Netherlands Indies had only about 210,000 European residents. The economic value of the area for the Dutch had steadily grown, the major agricultural products being tea, quinine, rubber, vanilla, tobacco, cacao, and sugar, along with tin, bauxite, and oil. In 1938 half the world's tin and practically the whole of the world's rubber were produced by the combined French, British, and Dutch possessions in Southeast Asia.

Somewhat less ruthless than the French, the Dutch nevertheless exercised a firm paternalism in government. Some Indonesians were trained in Dutch universities and eventually a native university was established at Bandung. The Dutch spoke much of ethical policy, using the phrase, *een Eereschulde* (a debt of honor), to describe the fulfilment of their obligations to the natives. "Ethical policy" has been skeptically described as a kind of eleventh-hour repentance for the exploitation of the natives by Dutch private interests during the nineteenth century. In 1917 the Dutch authorized a *Volksrad,* or People's Council, at first advisory in nature, but later granted some legislative power subject to the veto of the governor-general. Even so, the *Volksrad* was half-appointed and half-elected, with Europeans always in a majority. Native discontent was predictable. A nationalist association called "High Endeavor" had been founded as early as 1908. Three years later a popular revolutionary party was established, holding national congresses, organizing strikes, and demanding independence. During the 1920's Communist groups, closely in touch with Moscow, developed. Serious revolts broke out in Java in 1926–1927, resulting in the arrest and internment of hundreds of leaders. Among them was Dr. Achmed Sukarno, founder of the National Indonesian Party, who had based many of his ideas upon the program of Mahatma Gandhi in India.

■ THE FAR EAST: CHINA AND JAPAN

Other changes in the Far East affecting Europe came in connection with the momentous developments within China and Japan. The Chinese Revolution of 1911–1912 had overthrown the decadent Manchu imperial dynasty and established a republic, with Sun Yat-sen as provisional president. His Chinese Nationalist Party, the Kuomintang, came into existence at Canton. It was liberal in nature and therefore opposed by the conservative Yüan Shih-kai at Peking, who soon succeeded Sun Yat-sen as president. Great political confusions followed, with rival capitals being established and numerous ambitious war lords seeking personal aggrandizement. Under such conditions, too, the influence and special privileges of foreign powers in or adjacent to China actually seemed to increase. France had her sphere of influence in the south at Kwangchowan; Germany, to the north in Shantung province; Britain, at Hong Kong and in the Yangtse Valley; Russia, in North Manchuria and Outer Mongolia; Japan, in South Manchuria.

China, huge yet weak, found herself threatened by the rising power of Japan. Successful in a remarkable program of modernization, Japan won substantial gains in three successive wars, neatly spaced at ten-year intervals. The first, in 1894, forced China to yield Formosa; the second, in 1904, gave Japan Port Arthur in Manchuria, and a favored position in the whole province; she also got the southern half of the island of Sakhalin—all at the expense of Russia. In the third war, that of 1914–1918, Japan declared war on Germany in order to secure control over the Shantung Peninsula on the Chinese mainland, with a view to its "eventual" restoration to China. In addition Japan captured from Germany and later administered supposedly as mandates the Mariana, Marshall, and Caroline Islands. Actually they were, at least after 1926, valuable strategic additions to her Pacific empire.

Though the Peking government, professing to speak for all China, had declared war on Germany in 1917, it was in no condition to win benefits for itself. Two years earlier, in May, 1915, Japan had made the notorious Twenty-One Demands upon China, claiming control of Shantung, southern Manchuria, and Inner Mongolia, with Japanese advisers in all key posts. China was compelled reluctantly to agree to most of the demands. The United States and Japan by the Lansing-Ishii Agreement of 1917 reaffirmed the famous Open Door Policy in China, providing equal commercial opportunities for all powers. The United States concurrently recognized Japan's special, though not "paramount," interests in China. Thus, at the end of the First World War, Chinese nationalism had won at best a very partial victory; the country was divided, and the threat from Japan was clearly growing.

The Washington Conference of 1921–1922 had as one of its outcomes the Nine-Power Treaty, in which the signatories reaffirmed the Open Door Policy. Japan and China, moreover, signed a special agreement providing that Shantung was to be returned to China. This was done in December, 1923. Yet it would have been unrealistic to take this evidence to mean that Japan's ambitions with respect to China were subsiding.

A major component of the continuing crisis was China's inability to grapple successfully with her own problems. Yuan Shih-kai had died in 1916. In the immediate postwar years the central government of China enjoyed little effective authority and was challenged in one province after another by self-seeking war lords. Dr. Sun Yat-sen died in 1925, having ruled weakly at Canton. In his last two years he had increasingly relied on the support of the Soviet Union, which provided technicians, material, and some degree of actual leadership. Sun's intended successor, Chiang Kai-shek, whose first military training had been in Japan, had as his immediate purpose to assert his authority against the war lords of northern China. In 1928, having seized Hankow and Nanking, he entered Peking. He had clearly moved to the right wing of his party and now opposed the Chinese Communists. In the course of this change he broke off diplomatic relations with Moscow.

To many it seemed that Chiang had now become the master of the new China, all the more so since in 1928 he issued an Organic Law creating a new Nationalist government. The first, military stage of Sun Yat-sen's program was at an end, now to be followed by a period of political tutelage under the Nationalist Party, the Kuomintang. This tutelage was intended to continue until the third, completely democratic, stage could be achieved. During the early 1930's China made extraordinarily rapid economic progress, yet the civil war against the Communists in south China continued, while other parts of China refused to recognize Chiang's government.

In these circumstances the great new fact was the dramatic increase of Japanese pressures upon China. Japan's special interests in Manchuria, thwarted in 1894–1895, dated back to the Russo-Japanese War of 1904, as a result of which she had obtained the ports of Dairen and Port Arthur. By 1931 her investments in Manchuria amounted to a billion dollars, with a practical monopoly of banking and control of the South Manchurian Railway running from Dairen to Changchun. In the leased territory of Kwantung, containing both Port Arthur and Dairen, Japan exercised practically full sovereignty. And all this in a Manchuria which received a large immigration from China proper, and which, with a population of thirty million and an area equal to that of France and Germany combined, was claimed as an integral part of the Chinese Republic!

Japan's resort to open, unabashed force can well be regarded as the first significant breach in the system of collective security so painfully sought by some of Europe's statesmen in the years following the Treaty of Versailles. The explosion of a bomb on the Japanese-operated South Manchurian Railway in September, 1931, provided the incident which the Japanese employed as a pretext for launching a full-scale military occupation of Manchuria. This was followed by Japan's creation of the new state of Manchukuo, under the ostensible rule of the last Manchu emperor—now a Japanese puppet—Henry Pu Yi. When the League of Nations sent an investigating commission under Lord Lytton, and as a result of its report condemned Japan as an aggressor, Japan resigned from the League. Yet none of its members would contemplate further action against Japan beyond refusing diplomatic recognition as proposed by the United States secretary of state, Henry Stimson. In 1933 Japan pushed her advance from Manchuria southward into Jehol Province as far as the Great Wall of China. By 1935 she had advanced beyond the Great Wall and occupied the Hopei and Chahar provinces of the Chinese Republic. Whatever Japan's claim to special rights in Manchuria, this advance into China proper could hardly be considered anything but flagrant aggression. The Chinese were compelled, nevertheless, in December, 1935, to agree to the establishment of a semi-independent regime in these provinces, including the historic city of Peking, now renamed Peiping.

An exchange of shots between Chinese and Japanese sentries at the Marco Polo Bridge in Peiping on the night of July 7, 1937, was the spark which set off the greatest explosion of all. Japan then launched an all-out, full-scale war, ludicrously misnamed by her the "China Incident," the result of which was the seizure, first of Shanghai after a bloody four-months' battle running from August to December, 1937, then the cities of Nanking, Chenchow, Sinyang, Hankow, and Canton. In little over a year the Chinese had lost two million soldiers killed or wounded; some sixty million civilians had been uprooted in huge areas of "scorched earth"; and the Chiang Kai-shek regime had been driven out of the main cities and coastal areas of China, to improvise a new capital far in the interior at Chungking. Now unquestionably the leader of the Chinese Nationalists, Chiang received credits and other aid from the United States, Britain, and France. He also succeeded in incorporating into his forces the Chinese Red Army, under the name of the Eighth Route Army. Thus Nationalists and Communists were joined in an uneasy association against the Japanese. Though the complete conquest of China still eluded the invader, on the eve of the Second World War Japan's aggressive policies had in all externals been spectacularly successful.

■ A CONTINENT IN FERMENT

Events in Asia were moving during these interwar years at as fast a pace as in Europe. In the course of the nineteenth century the great powers had developed large Asiatic interests; these were intensified by the pressures of the Industrial Revolution and had been displayed to the world under the colors of the New Imperialism. The elaborate secret agreements made during the First World War and, to some extent, the treaty arrangements at its close were intended to further Europe's interests in a world made up of what it had long treated as subject peoples. Yet new forces were at work in these ancient lands.

Nationalism was the driving force beginning to affect the destinies of Asia. Factors which one may describe as political, economic, religious, and cultural were all associated under this larger concept. Nationalism was the hallmark of the new Turkey; it was seen in Egypt; it brought apparently insoluble problems to Britain and France as they sought to administer their mandates; it launched Iran upon its new course. In British India, in the Netherlands Indies, in French Indochina, and in China itself a new generation announced its complete unwillingness to accept the traditional order. Ever enlarging national aspirations were the mark of the new Japan.

In contrast to many of these policies of stubborn imperialism, the United States, having taken over the Philippines from Spain in 1898 and having undertaken to develop the islands for self-government, finally passed the Tydings-McDuffie Act in 1934 providing for a transitional period of ten years, the outcome of which was to be full independence. What was possible for America might not be so easy for a European imperial power to concede. Yet in many areas forces were unleashed far beyond the capacity of Europe to contain. These forces radically transformed the spirit of the Asiatic world and indirectly they affected the pattern of the European alliances. Japan eventually aligned herself with Fascist Italy and National Socialist Germany—the "Axis" powers. The Arab states shrewdly maneuvered for the support of whichever state would further their own selfish interests, giving not a little support in the end to Germany during the Second World War. As an already complex European world moved toward this disastrous outcome, the countries of Africa and Asia added still further complexities.

Reading List: Chapter 5

Barraclough, G., *An Introduction to Contemporary History* (1964), ch. 6. "The Revolt Against the West." An interesting survey of Africa and Asia.

Hudson, G. F., *The Far East in World Politics* (1937), chs. 10–13. The general interwar situation.

Latourette, K. S., *A Short History of the Far East* (3rd ed., 1957), ch. 16.

McAleavy, H., "China under the War-Lords," *History Today,* vol. XII (1962), nos. 4–5.

Storry, R., "Fascism in Japan: The Army Mutiny of February 1936," *History Today,* vol. VI (1956), no. 11.

Badeau, J. S., *East and West of Suez* (Headline Book No. 39, Foreign Policy Association, 1943). Still valuable as a brief introduction to the area.

Chapter 6

Europe and the World Economy

The Dethronement of Western Europe
War and the European Economy
The Years of Recovery, 1924–1929
The World Economic Crisis
Economic Nationalism in the Ascendant, 1933–1939

■ THE DETHRONEMENT OF WESTERN EUROPE

This chapter will examine the working of economic forces which have profoundly affected the modern world. These are technical questions, involving a departure from the usual historical narrative, and yet essential to its full understanding. Such matters as debt-funding, the gold standard, inflation, and currency stabilization have become the province of the historian as well as of the economist, for they are involved in the growth and conflict of political policies shaping the fate of nations.

Europe in 1914 stood at the center of a world economy which had had its dim beginnings four centuries earlier in the Portuguese and Spanish expeditions of discovery, conquest, and exploitation. Thanks to the steamship, the railway, the submarine cable, and all the other technical devices for facilitating the exchange of goods and services, this world economy was becoming more

SIGNIFICANT EVENTS

1919	Transatlantic flight by Alcock and Brown
1921	Emergency Quota Act restricting immigration to the United States
1923	French occupation of Ruhr; great German inflation
1924	Dawes Plan for payment of reparations
1929	Stock Exchange collapse in the United States
1933	World Economic Conference, London
1936	German four-year plan for autarky
1939	Atomic fission achieved by Hahn and Strassmann

effective every year. London, Berlin, and Paris were leading financial centers, where business concerns from every continent did their large-scale borrowing, banking, and insuring. The widespread acceptance of the gold standard made it easy to negotiate multilateral trade transactions involving the sale and purchase of goods or services in many different countries. When the First World War began, some people, especially readers of Norman Angell's *Great Illusion,* believed that because of the financial repercussions it could not last for more than a few months. It is doubtful whether anybody seriously entertained the view that the war, even if its length should somehow exceed all anticipations, could possibly sound the death knell of that European economic leadership which was believed to benefit as surely as it dominated the whole civilized world.

For reasons shortly to be explored, the war effort of the rival alliances

145

brought about a dislocation of economic life which was both more intense and more widespread than that caused by any previous international struggle. By 1918, the physical destruction it had involved seemed to contemporaries to be almost irreparable. Nevertheless, recovery in that respect was rapid, and by 1925 the financial problems arising out of the peace settlement appeared also to be in course of solution. For a few years it looked as though the kind of relationships which had made up the flourishing economic life of the late nineteenth-century world could be revived: a convalescent Europe was at least potentially a rival to the new economic ascendancy of the United States. Then in October, 1929, the New York Stock Exchange crisis inaugurated a second period of economic dislocation no less drastic in some respects than the war itself. For nearly four years the prospect steadily darkened, and when a rather slow and partial recovery did begin, its basis was not the re-establishment of multilateral trade relationships within a world economy but programs which aimed at national self-sufficiency. Where that was impossible, bilateral and regional agreements on a restricted scale were undertaken.

The result was an economically disunited world, an unbalanced world, and a world in which Europe had lost its key position. The unpalatable truth was to some extent disguised by an improvement in business conditions and an accompanying fall in unemployment which Europe experienced in the later 1930's. These, however, were partly due to heavy expenditure on armaments and stockpiling for war in what was rapidly developing into a second prewar era. When the new war did break out in Europe in 1939, one way in which the situation differed from that of 1914 was that many Europeans this time could to their dismay foresee the permanent effect which a second long-continued dislocation of trade would have upon an already damaged European economy.

■ WAR AND THE EUROPEAN ECONOMY

Any closely matched, long continued struggle wears down both combatants to the point of absolute exhaustion. Between 1914 and 1918 only the repeated raising of age limits, the lowering of minimum physical standards, and the combing-out of all except key workers from civilian occupations provided the necessary supply of cannon fodder. The general needs of industry and commerce were steadily subordinated to the insatiable demand for munitions of all kinds and to food requirements, both military and civil. Every consideration of financial orthodoxy gave place to the need to raise loans to support the war effort. Even though the Allied countries could use the sea routes to buy in America and elsewhere the foodstuffs, raw materials, and armaments essential for winning the war, a condition of exhaustion nevertheless existed which—except in the case of the United States—was nearly as complete on the side of the winners as on that of the losers. It was therefore very difficult for even the wisest of men to see at the time which consequences of the war were only temporary and which were permanent.

Out of sixty-five million men mobilized for war, about one in five had been killed or permanently disabled. The disabled constituted a gradually diminishing burden which was readily borne by their communities. The death toll had a qualitative as well as a quantitative importance, since in modern war the bravest and most vigorous types of men and, above all, the young officers of an army tended to fall first. Even so, by 1928 the total population of Europe had risen by thirty-six million since 1913—a gain of 7 percent. Still more rapid was the progress in making good material damage. At the date of the armistice it was doubted whether the belt of French and Belgian territory which had been blasted by heavy artillery for more than four years could ever recover, and the British at the height of the German U-boat campaign in 1917 had felt that their mercantile marine, though supported by the American and such neutral shipping as dared to ply to Britain, was nothing but a wasting asset. Despite these fears, the shipping at the disposal of the Allies reached a bigger tonnage in 1918 than in 1914, and the ravaged territory was likewise restored so rapidly by a great national effort on the part of the French and Belgians that full industrial activity was restored within a year or two.

National organization for war to some extent facilitated reorganization afterwards for peace. To combat shortages of food, raw materials, industrial requirements, and manpower, the extent of state intervention in every aspect of economic life had increased enormously. In Germany, the Jewish industrialist Walther Rathenau[1], a director of sixty-eight businesses, was given control of raw materials in the first month of the war and ended it with such dictatorial powers over his fellow magnates that he may justly be acclaimed as the father of modern economic planning. Britain to begin with had a much smaller proportion of men in the fighting forces and had less need to husband materials than had the blockaded Germans. But her armies had grown, and Lloyd George both as minister of munitions and still more as prime minister had given great authority to new government departments, which were often staffed by experts from private business. Where there were divergent Allied interests, as in the case of shipping, well-administered inter-Allied plans and controls were likewise brought into existence. Although at the end of the war a

---

1. 1867–1922. He was the son of the founder of the electrical firm, Allgemeine Elektricitäts-Gesell-schaft, of which he became a director (1899) and president (1915). In 1914–1915, as director of the Division of War Raw Materials in the Prussian ministry of war, he formed compulsory cartels, organized block-purchasing from neutrals, and developed synthetic substitutes for imported fertilizers and foodstuffs. He became minister of reconstruction, 1921, and as foreign minister, 1922, signed the Treaty of Rapallo with Russia; he was murdered by anti-Semitic reactionaries belonging to the *Freikorps*.

complete return to private enterprise was vociferously demanded in various countries, controls continued to be widely used to restart the economies, not least the economy of the devastated areas.

Moreover, the expenditure which wartime governments had lavished on such technical developments contributing to victory meant that in some respects postwar Europe was prepared for rapid advances. This was conspicuously true of transport. The first regular air route for passengers and mail was established between London and Paris in the winter of 1918–1919; the Atlantic was successfully flown by Alcock and Brown in the following summer; and Germany, compelled to destroy seventeen thousand military airplanes under the terms of the peace treaty, quickly developed the first internal intercity network of flights in Europe. The war had also quickened the tempo of the mechanization of land transport, not only because of the eventual triumphs of the tank but also because of the increasing use of armored cars, trucks, and motor ambulances. War had prepared the way for changes in factories and workshops because employers had been influenced by the example of the munitions industry, where intricate machinery had been installed to facilitate the employment of unskilled labor. Again, the wartime search for more powerful explosives and more lethal poison gases, coupled with the urgent demand for substitute materials and artificial fertilizers, had strengthened the chemical industry among victors and vanquished alike.

The peace treaties left a more important burden in the shape of reparations payments to be made by the Central Powers. The German total was by far the largest and was not fixed until 1921. In addition, the Allies had unfunded debts which were owed partly to Britain but chiefly to their rich and all-powerful associate, the United States of America. It suited the Allied governments to regard the two sets of transactions as interrelated: if the Germans could not pay the Allies then neither could the Allies pay the Americans, who were expected to regard any such failure as a part of the losses incurred in the common enterprise of war. The Americans, on the other hand, were well aware that nearly one-third of the total debt of more than ten billion dollars had been incurred for the quite different purpose of postwar reconstruction, and that all of it was borrowed unconditionally like an ordinary commercial loan. Moreover, from the time of the armistice negotiations onward some powerful business interests wished to disentangle the United States from any joint politico-economic responsibility for the affairs of war-torn Europe. On November 8, 1918, Herbert Hoover[2] as United States food administrator was

2. 1874–1964. A mining engineer with world-wide interests, he was chairman of the commission for relief in Belgium, 1914–1919, and later of the American Relief Administration which fed millions of Russians after the famine of 1921, and the European Children's Fund. He was also United States food administrator, 1917–1919, secretary of commerce, 1921–1928, and thirty-first President, 1929–1933.

authorized to reply as follows to Allied proposals for the continuance of joint control over food imports to both sides of the armistice line:

> This government will not agree to any program that even looks like inter-Allied control of our resources after peace. After peace, over one-half of the whole export food supplies of the world will come from the United States, and for the buyers of these supplies to sit in majority in dictation to us as to prices and distribution is wholly inconceivable. The same applies to raw materials. Our only hope of securing justice in distribution, proper appreciation abroad of the effort we make to assist foreign nations, and proper return for the service we will perform will revolve around complete independence of commitment to joint action on our part.[3]

American charity in the immediate postwar years knew no limit. Five million tons of foodstuffs were distributed to twenty-three countries in the first eight desperate months, Hoover's American Relief Administration combated the great Russian famine of 1921, and by June, 1922, a nongovernmental European Children's Fund had fed eight million and clothed two million of the destitute and orphaned. At the same time, however, the United States government was disentangling itself as fast as possible from most of the commitments arising out of its wartime relationships and the treaties of peace.

A British suggestion for an all-round renunciation of war-debt claims and the reduction of reparations, put forward in the Balfour Note to the French government in August, 1922, proved wholly unacceptable to American opinion. The same note announced as an alternative Britain's intention of limiting her claims to debt repayments from her allies to whatever sum, in addition to receipts from reparations, might be needed for meeting her own debt payments to the United States. The consequences were doubly unsatisfactory. The British, anxious at all costs to bring back normal economic relations, funded their debt to America—a total of 978 million pounds—as early as January, 1923. The terms of their funding, or final settlement, reduced the rate of interest on the debt from 5 to 3.5 percent. The French and Italians, on the other hand, were rewarded for a long refusal to pay by interest rates of 1.6 and 0.4 percent respectively. For almost a decade the British attempted to carry this burden with very little to help them in the way of claims that they in turn could make upon their former allies or upon the Germans. At the same time the United States refused to link reparations (for which she had made no claim) with war debts. This confirmed the French in the belief that their best course would be to concentrate on squeezing the maximum of reparations from the defeated Germans.

The moral case for reparations was much stronger than the economic. Eastern France and Belgium had been overrun and fought over for four years; German territory had virtually escaped the horrors of war, and the armistice

3. F. M. SURFACE and R. L. BLAND, *American Food in the World War and Reconstruction Period* (1931), p. 23.

terms brought Allied occupying forces no farther than the bridgeheads on the east bank of the Rhine. Yet it was the Germans and their allies who, in the general opinion of the rest of the world, had provoked the ruinous conflict. "Reparation for damages" had therefore figured in the armistice conditions, and at the time of the peacemaking, few on the Allied side doubted the moral justification for including war pensions and separation allowances as part of the "damage done to the civilian population of the Allies and to their property." These, indeed, had been specified for reparations in an inter-Allied note of November 5, 1918. The failure to fix a final total at the peace conference, again, was a tactical rather than a moral error, though it was hotly denounced to deaf ears by the rising English economist John Maynard Keynes. In any case, the Germans replied pretty effectively by paying no more in the first two years of peace than would cover costs of the control commissions and armies of occupation. In May, 1921, the Germans finally agreed to pay thirty-three billion dollars (plus the Belgian war debt) on the basis of a detailed schedule, with an Allied occupation of the Ruhr to follow as the penalty for any default. When the Germans defaulted in less than two years and French and Belgian troops entered the Ruhr as a way of exacting penalties under the Treaty of Versailles, the British strongly opposed their action, not so much for any moral obliquity as for its economic rashness.

The war debts, as the Allied debtors were ever ready to point out, proved difficult to pay. Any genuine payment would have to be made either in gold, of which they had too little, or by fresh borrowings from private sources, not easy to arrange in disturbed postwar conditions, or through their being allowed to export more than they imported, however damaging this might be to the trade of the creditor power. Each of these considerations applied even more cogently in the case of German reparations. The Germans had been able to make some initial payments in kind, including ships, coal, and building materials for the devastated areas. But at this time they had little gold, were too bad a risk for foreign lending, and had great difficulty in reconstructing their export trades, which in many cases could only flourish at the expense of the exports of Britain or another of the Allies. Besides, the new Weimar Republic had inherited a huge national debt and grossly inadequate revenues. These hard facts would still have existed even if the Germans had wanted to pay reparations, whereas to make quite sure of not paying, their capitalists sent more than one billion dollars out of the country. They then counted on the depreciation of the mark to enable them to declare a very profitable kind of bankruptcy.

The occupation of the Ruhr, besides its political consequences in embittering Franco-German and even Franco-British relations, encouraged the German government to acquiesce in a prodigious currency inflation. This, as in-

INFLATION, GERMAN STYLE. Marks, numerically worth billions, are being baled as waste paper in a Berlin junk shop. Runaway inflation has taken from them all value save this.

tended by some at least of the controlling interests, made nonsense of the entire economy. As compared with prewar levels, prices in this period of acute strain throughout central and eastern Europe were multiplied by currency inflations to a fantastic extent. In Austria they were multiplied 14,000 times, in Hungary, 23,000 times, in Poland, 2.5 million times, and in Russia, 4 billion times. In Germany the figures rose to 750 billion times. By the autumn of 1923 a stalemate had been achieved: the French found that the use of force in the Ruhr brought no worthwhile economic results; the Germans found that the passive resistance by which they had opposed the French was bringing their whole country to the verge of ruin.

On the international plane the sequel was the acceptance of the Dawes Plan (1924), under which the Stresemann government undertook to begin to pay reparations without any settlement of the vexed question of the sum ultimately involved. The size of the annual payments was to rise gradually over a five-year period, the first payment being scarcely larger than an international loan which was raised simultaneously to help to stabilize the German currency and economy. On these terms the French and Belgians evacuated the Ruhr, after which agreed payments were rendered regularly for five years, and international economic disputes arising out of the war receded into the background. On the domestic plane, however, although a new Reichsmark stabilized the currency, the disappearance, as a result of the preceding currency inflation, of middle-class savings and every form of wealth not based on owner-ship of land and goods or of capital sent abroad left Germany with a rootless, discontented middle class. This group some day would find a chance to reas-sert itself against its supposed enemies at home and abroad.

Unfortunately, too, in other respects Europe emerged from the immediate aftermath of war to find the road to prosperity seriously impeded. By 1914 Europe had experienced a full generation of high-tariff systems operated by all the great powers with the single exception of Britain. The total effect had been in some measure to restrict the flow of trade between country and country. This did not matter very much, however, since Europe was then the unquestioned center of world trade. Some of the areas enclosed by a tariff wall—Austria-Hungary or the Russian Empire, for example—were sufficiently large and variegated to form vigorous self-contained economic units. But it was very un-fortunate for Europe that under the terms of the peace settlement of 1919–1920 the triumph of political nationalism carried with it the triumph of economic nationalism. The new and smaller states emerging from the ruins of the Dual Monarchy or from the clutch of the great Slav despotism piled up tariffs against the outside world with a view to fostering native industries. In some cases the exclusion of foreign goods served no economic purpose except to im-poverish a hated neighbor such as the new republic of Austria, which was vir-tually surrounded by countries resentful of a past history of subjection. About twelve thousand miles of new customs barriers were in course of erection at a time when war destruction, currency crises, and the related problems of war debts and inflation made these additional handicaps to the free flow of goods plainly inopportune.

The trend to tariffs was not confined to the succession states. The United States tariff legislation of 1921 and 1922 set an example that was widely ob-served, while Britain's Safeguarding of Industries Act showed a breach in her long-honored free trade policy. President Wilson, when he demanded a reduc-tion of tariff barriers as one of his Fourteen Points, had envisaged the growth of a world economy far more conducive to international cooperation and world peace.

In a period of inevitable postwar confusion it took long to realize that in two respects the economic life of Europe would never return to what prewar society regarded as normal. It was true that since about 1900 the United States had ceased to play the role mainly of a primary producer and had begun to enter the world market as a more efficient rival of European manufacturers. But the fact that she was still, on balance, a debtor country had made it easy to belittle or even to ignore the effect of her industrial growth on Europe's long-term prospects. The war, however, provided a period of four or more years in which Europe's customers were more or less completely cut off from their accustomed suppliers and there was no means of knowing when these customary supplies could be resumed. Given the stage of development which the world economy had reached by 1914, the results were inevitable. The United States and Japan expanded their manufacturing capacity to supply themselves and the economically least advanced countries with what they lacked. Another category of countries—in South America and among the British Dominions, for instance—expanded fast enough to become largely self-sufficient, even if they could not export manufactures on any significant scale. At the same time merchant fleets were increased, particularly that of the United States, in order to serve new export trades. New customers also provided American capital with an important field of investment where rivalry did not become very formidable even when the war was ended. In the years 1920–1927 new British overseas investment was made at less than half the rate of 1905–1913.

Such warning signs were not immediately convincing. By 1925 Europe as a whole was producing as much food and raw materials as she did just before the war, her output of manufactures had been approximately restored, and more than half the trade of the world passed again through European hands. In this year of the Locarno agreements it seemed to observers who could recall the immediate postwar situation that Europe was now on the highroad to lasting recovery. But even at that date other statistical facts were recognizably discouraging. Whereas world production of food and raw materials had risen by something like 25 percent and production of manufactures by about 20 percent, Europe's share in the increased world trade implied by these figures had declined by fully 10 percent.[4] Moreover, quite apart from any question of an economic contest between Europe and other continents, Europe by 1925 was confronted with a new socioeconomic policy of restrictive immigration, originating in the United States but very likely to be imitated by British Dominions, the South American states, and any other areas to which white immigrants might be attracted. This meant that Europe could no longer count on emigration to relieve the pressure of its population upon the means of subsistence.

For several generations the Atlantic Ocean had provided the path for the greatest *Völkerwanderung* of modern history, as millions of Europeans, in moods which ranged from glowing ambition and idealism to passive acceptance of fate, took the plunge into the melting pot of nations. From professor to peasant they were all people who knew that they could find an alternative to what Europe had to offer. In 1913 2,000,000 Europeans moved overseas, mainly to the United States; in 1918–1919 800,000 moved to the United States alone. Then came a year-to-year quota act, by which Congress restricted immigration

4. MAURICE CROUZET in *L'Epoque contemporaine*, 1957 (*Histoire générale des civilisations*, t. VII), p. 58, gives comparative figures of 63 percent in 1913 and 52.5 percent for 1925.

to a quota of 3 percent of fellow nationals recorded as resident at the United States census of 1910. In 1924 this act was replaced by more stringent legislation, reducing the quota to only 2 percent and basing the allotment upon the census of 1890, when the generally wealthier countries of northern Europe had been far more plentifully represented in the American population than the countries of the south and southeast. It was for the latter that the safety valve of emigration was most vitally necessary: yet in the 1930's, when the total of European immigration into the United States was 350,000, Italy was the only country in southern Europe entitled to send in more than 500 immigrants per annum. As for alternatives, Brazil and the Argentine accepted about 2,240,000 immigrants in the 1920's. Half of these returned home, however, and the selective, government-assisted immigration schemes operated by the British Dominions were aimed primarily at the recruitment of the agricultural population.

The tide of political refugees which had flowed across much of Europe in the early postwar years was one of the reasons for the drastic change in American policy. This tide subsided in the course of time. Kindred problems, nevertheless, remained and were not easily solved. The European scene continued to be darkened by the obvious waste and misery of unemployment, as seen in the older industrial districts of Britain and Northern Ireland, and by the less obvious phenomenon of underemployment, which was characteristic of almost all the peasant lands of Europe, from the new Irish Free State to the immemorial olive groves of Greece.

■ THE YEARS OF RECOVERY, 1924–1929

The period from 1924 to 1929—more exactly, from the entry into force of the Dawes Plan for reparations in July, 1924, to the New York Stock Exchange collapse of October, 1929—was in general a period of economic recovery. Its feeling of optimism and reassurance is not easy to recapture because those of a later generation can see it only as an interlude between the frustrations of the peace settlement and the frenzies of a second era leading to war. To contemporaries the statistics of world economic activity in these five years were clearly encouraging. The production of foodstuffs and raw materials increased by 11 percent and that of manufactured goods by 26 percent. With the help of a shipping fleet which was 60 percent larger than before the war, world trade expanded by 19 percent by 1924 and regained to a large extent its multilateral character. For Europe these were years of opportunity, in which it still seemed possible for her to win back something of her old position as the center and principal beneficiary of a self-regulating international system for the exploitation of natural resources.

Accordingly, a determined effort was made to restore the gold standard.

First, in 1924, came Sweden, a wartime neutral; then, in 1925, Britain boldly adopted the prewar rate of exchange; and in the later years of the decade Belgium, Italy, France, and other countries followed. The French franc and the Belgian franc, however, were re-established at one-fifth of their former gold value, and the Italian lira at one-fourth. In the case of Britain, most economists hold that the exchange rate was set too high in relation to other national currencies. For the others, in terms of national income, the effort was duly rewarded. Whereas by 1925 the income level in major component countries (eastern Europe excepted) was about the same as before the war, by 1929 it had on an average risen by 30 percent.

Moreover, this was a time when the technical means for exploiting the resources of nature were notably on the increase. The gasoline-driven internal-combustion engine, with its high power-to-weight ratio, was transforming transportation on the roads and establishing itself for the first time also in the skies. It speeded up the whole tempo of life, just as the coming of the railroad had done a century before. Radio and the expansion of long-distance telephone services had a similar if smaller impact. Electric power, too, which could now be transmitted cheaply and efficiently over long distances from any convenient generating area, could serve any number of separate machines in a single workshop or factory without the formidable network of belts and pulleys needed for the use of steam power. Such technical facilities served as a direct incentive to rationalization—a new word used to describe the attempt to streamline processes and plan all the tasks of business organization and production. These innovations had originated in the United States under the guise of Frederick Winslow Taylor's "scientific management."

In the long run, the most significant new trend in these years was the establishment of the professional scientist as a key figure in the economy. The experience of the war had fully justified German practice in this respect, and now every industrial nation relied upon its university-trained chemists to provide synthetic substances from plastics to artificial rubber and textiles as a constant stimulus to industry. The agriculture of the world likewise benefited from the new fertilizers invented by chemists and the improved strains of cattle and plants produced by the biologists. The fundamental researches of the physicists were to lead eventually to new sources of power of unparalleled destructive (or constructive) strength—but not within the hopeful confines of the 1920's.

One prominent feature of the period was the amount of building work done: in 1925 one-seventh of the industrial population of Europe is said to have been employed in this way. Apart from the restoration of war damage comparatively little building had been undertaken during the period of political uncertainty just after the war. Now, however, capital was readily expended on new industrial plants; bigger and brighter shops were everywhere in demand; and ambitious and successful persons, as in earlier societies, built homes to increase their comfort and emphasize their success. A characteristic feature of the new age was the large-scale use of public money in different forms to make possible the rehousing of the masses. Most famous were the working-class housing blocks of socialist Vienna, but local authorities in Britain put up 1,000,000 "council houses," and the German authorities constructed 1,500,000 dwellings of equivalent types. There was also much building of social-service structures, ranging from new schools and hospitals to public halls and swimming pools.

The last of these items suggests another prominent feature of the period, namely the enhanced demand for comforts and luxury goods or services of a type which before the war had enjoyed only a restricted middle-class market. Wages had risen, and a reduction in the average size of family was accompanied by a big increase in the number of women in employment: hence the ability of industrial workers to buy much more than the bare necessities of life. Sales of ready-made clothes and furniture therefore expanded; bicycles, cosmetics, and the more expensive types of children's toys brightened family life at a much humbler level than formerly; foodstuffs were bought packaged and ready to serve, regardless of the economies formerly secured by home preparation and home cooking. Lastly, Europe experienced the growth of cinemas, the huge sales of radios, and the expansion of the holiday industry. Such growth showed that the workers, instead of assuming that the good things of life were reserved by providence for their betters, were beginning to demand a share in every new amenity. The mass market had come, and entertainers were not the least efficient among capitalists in redesigning their wares when necessary in order to suit mass requirements.

The contrast with the early 1920's was most striking in Germany, so recently laid low by military defeat. Its industrial output rose to 22 percent above prewar figures and a marked expansion in provisions for social welfare was in progress alongside the modernization of much industrial equipment on American lines. The fact that these results depended upon loans from the United States (and smaller loans from British and other European sources), for which the Germans paid an average of 2 percent above normal rates of interest, roused few qualms; the boundless prosperity of the United States at this juncture suggested that her readiness to lend overseas would continue indefinitely. By 1929 Germany's financial situation seemed so satisfactory that the vexed matter of reparations payments was at last put on a long-term basis. A committee of experts headed by the American Owen D. Young negotiated a scheme for a series of payments to be completed by 1988. The Germans were to pay a principal sum of nine billion dollars instead of thirty-three billion dollars as fixed in 1921, and they were to pay through a new bank of international settlements in Switzerland, thus avoiding any further Allied supervision. The new scheme was acceptable to all the more reasonable elements in a country where exports had increased every year since 1924 and had never totaled less than five times as much as was paid in reparations. The payments, moreover, were covered one and a half times over by foreign loans.

In Europe as a whole recovery was far from uniform. Britain, as was shown in Chapter 4, experienced no real revival in her heavy industry and traditional cotton exports. Coal mining continued to be ill-rewarded in Britain and other countries, in part at least because of the attractiveness of the substitute fuels now becoming available. Serious political disquiet arose also in many parts of Europe because of the low level of wheat prices, attributable to the fact that the huge expansion of agriculture in other continents during the war was not followed by any contraction when European agricultural output recovered. The tendency to overproduction was enhanced by the spread of improved methods of tillage. These low food prices, which bore hard on peasant producers, did, however, leave the consumers, the urban population, with a bigger margin for other purchases. On the whole, contemporary opinion believed the principal menace to continued prosperity to lie only in the continued growth of tariffs and trade prohibitions. Two conferences were accordingly organized in 1927 by the League of Nations at Geneva, with the result that the rise in tariffs was temporarily checked and a convention for a ban on prohibitions of trade came within two votes of ratification. This activity proved, however, to be the highwater mark of international economic confidence and cooperation.

■ THE WORLD ECONOMIC CRISIS

It is possible to look at the great depresssion of 1929 as a slump following a boom, an oft-repeated phenomenon which many economists were expecting, and then to wonder why it should have loomed so large on the stage of world politics. One reason is certainly the fact that its dimensions, measured in terms of duration in time, extension in space across the world, and intensity of effect upon the life of civilized man, give this depression a magnitude quite without parallel in earlier economic history. Another aspect, now too readily forgotten, was the loss of prestige to the whole capitalist system when it was seen that the United States had not after all solved the problem of perpetual prosperity and that only the despised Russian Soviet economy appeared immune to the resulting shock. In the eyes of many of the thirty million or more of unemployed spread over the world, the self-regulating system might well seem a proven failure—the kind of situation for which Marx and Lenin had waited in vain. But the most important aspect of the whole crisis was that which showed itself when a shaken but reconstructed capitalist society emerged again from the depression. The old basis of international economic co-operation having vanished, it left in its place the rival economic nationalisms which soon paved the way to universal war.

Warning signals of approaching trouble appeared even before the New York stock market crash. A fall in world prices of foodstuffs and raw materials was, to be sure, already apparent in 1928; this meant a reduction in the purchasing power of their producers and a consequent reduction in the sales and profits of manufacturing industry. No fewer than four European capitals— Rome, Brussels, Vienna, and London—had experienced small-scale banking or stock exchange crises in the first three quarters of 1929, that is to say, before any serious break occurred on Wall Street. But it was the scale of the crisis in the United States which gave it a world significance. Stock values having approximately doubled between December, 1928, and September, 1929, from late October they lost an average of 40 percent in less than a month; then, after rallying in the first half of 1930, they plunged again until the average loss on leading industrial stocks reached 75 percent. In three and a half years of depression five thousand banks in the United States closed their doors and the number of unemployed reached a total variously calculated at between twelve and fifteen million. Even the smaller total would have been sufficient to shake world confidence.

The first effect of the crisis in the United States upon the fate of Europe was to intensify a movement which had already begun. In 1928 the stock exchange boom had caused Americans to place in domestic speculation sums which might otherwise have been invested in Germany or elsewhere in Europe, and for the same reason to recall some short-term money already sent. The immediate consequence of the crisis on Wall Street was to send American money abroad again; then in the second half of 1930 nervousness spread from the domestic to the foreign investment area, with the result that the flow of capital into Europe dried up entirely.

The second effect was to intensify another movement already under way, namely the fall in the prices of primary products. Canadian wheat, for example, lost half its value between 1929 and 1931, Australasia sold larger quantities of its wool and other staples for a 45 percent smaller reward, and Brazilian coffee shares lost two-thirds of their value. This loss was further stimulated by the decline in purchasing power of the industrial populations, and can best be measured in the United States, where the overall drop in agricultural prices between June, 1929, and December, 1932, totaled 57 percent. Not so easily measurable but about equally important was the extent to which agriculturists resorted to subsistence agriculture, ceasing to buy either equipment or consumer goods from urban sources to which it no longer paid them to sell.

The third effect, to which the revival of subsistence agriculture contributed, was the shrinkage of industrial production. A factory or workshop
unit, unlike a farm, cannot to any appreciable extent consume its own products if outside demand for them disappears. This was in a sense the central
phenomenon of the crisis, since it affected most seriously the heavily industrialized countries, such as the United States, Germany, Britain, France, and
the Low Countries, which at that time provided among them more than three-
quarters of the industrial production of the world. It was undoubtedly the
main social phenomenon, since the industrial areas of these countries held the
great mass of the unemployed, whose numbers were trebled in three years.
Perhaps even more striking was the phenomenon of sheer disorganization, since
the overall diminution of output by 38 percent compares with a figure of only
30 percent for the fall of production among the European powers under the
strain of the First World War.

The depression was prolonged by a financial crisis, which derived partly
from the sequence of events already described, but partly also from the unsatisfactory way in which the gold standard had been worked since its revival
halfway through the decade of the 1920's. There had been no return to a circulating gold currency; instead, the metal was made available only in bars of
a given weight, enabling a large payment to be based if necessary on something
more demonstrably valuable than a national paper currency. As the world
supply of gold increased quite slowly, the efficient working of the system depended upon a sedulous avoidance of the accumulation of gold in any one
financial center. Formerly, a debt on London was easily paid in other ways
because the British free trade system offered so many alternatives. But New
York and Paris, which jointly with London now financed the trade of the
world, were much more closely concerned with domestic interests. The result
was that gold tended to accumulate in those two capitals instead of remaining
widely diffused in support of the many other national currencies tied to gold.

The withdrawal of American money from Europe had already made the
European financial situation very vulnerable, when early in 1931 French and
Italian funds were withdrawn from Austria in protest against a proposal for
an Austro-German customs union. The sequel was a declaration of insolvency
by the largest Austrian bank, the *Kreditanstalt*. No sooner had its liabilities been
covered than a run started on various German banks, so that a moratorium
had to be declared on all short-term credits advanced to Germany. This moratorium added to the domestic difficulties which, as related in Chapter 4, were
causing pressure to be directed against the British pound. When the pound
sterling, too, gave way, in September, 1931, the financial ties of the whole
world were fatally strained. Some countries followed Britain in abandoning
the gold standard but linked their currency to sterling. A second group let their

THE CONTRACTING SPIRAL OF WORLD TRADE [5]
Month by month January 1929 - October 1934
(In millions of U.S. (gold) $)

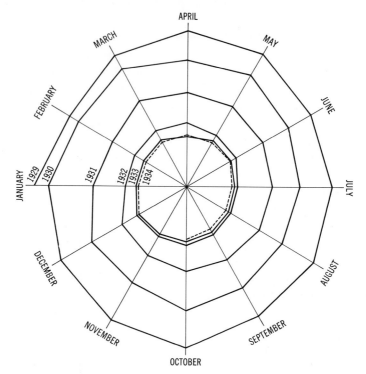

currency find its own level. A third group—the United States, France, Germany, the Low Countries, Italy, and Poland—remained for a short time longer on the gold standard at existing rates, with results that were catastrophic for their external commerce, since few foreigners could afford to pay prices based on gold. An inevitable consequence was the postponement of the vitally needed recovery of world trade.

From the European point of view it was this drastic decline of world trade and its very slow recovery which mattered most, since it augured ill for the survival of the world economy of which Europeans were the greatest beneficiaries. A contracting spiral, plotted by the economic intelligence service of the League of Nations, shows that as late as October, 1934, the machinery was continuing to run down. Even in the period of recovery which was then beginning, world trade lagged far behind world production. By 1937 the output of

5. Based on a chart by the Economic Intelligence Service of the League of Nations.

manufactures, raw materials, and foodstuffs exceeded the 1929 totals by 20, 16, and 8 percent respectively. Only in the case of raw materials, however, was the volume of trade greater than in 1929, and even there the percentage gain was no more than 8, in other words exactly half as much as the increase in production. World trade in foodstuffs stood at 6.5 percent below the 1929 total, and in manufactures it was still 13 percent below.

The reason for this disparity between the eventual recovery in general economic activity and the recovery in world trade becomes apparent as soon as we consider the measures adopted to combat the depression as it deepened between 1929 and 1933. These were broadly speaking of three kinds. In the first place numerous attempts were made to restore profit to agriculture or industry by cutting costs. Production was to be restricted, or in some other way prices were to be maintained, or technological advances were to be so applied that profit margins would be increased. Thus the Germans, whose coal output sank even lower in relation to its 1913 level than did the British, based a remarkable recovery in part upon the thorough exploitation of the innumerable chemical by-products. These attempts, however, did little or nothing to stimulate purchasing power, without which the economic system could not be revived. Such limited success as appeared was gained by the more efficient countries chiefly at the expense of the less efficient.

In the second place, a concerted international effort was made to rid the world of the various types of financial encumbrance which were seen to be clogging the wheels of trade. These included reparations, intergovernmental debts, and variable rates of exchange. In July, 1931, President Hoover proposed a one-year moratorium on debts and reparations. It had not quite expired when a meeting at Lausanne in July, 1932, agreed to slash reparations by more than 90 percent. The final figure is almost irrelevant since Hitler came into power only six months later and he contemptuously ignored the matter. The continuance of the Hoover moratorium for a further six months produced no agreement regarding war debts, which the Allies proposed should be reduced in relation to their own intended action over reparations. Britain, Italy, and four smaller powers made one more full debt payment in December, 1932, and a second token payment in June, 1933; after that, all except Finland defaulted permanently.

The problem of currency stabilization, too, was eventually left to settle itself because the retreat from the gold standard, which was headed by Britain in September, 1931, created a twofold difficulty. Those countries which retained the gold standard, such as France and for nearly two years the United States, were opposed to any agreement which would deprive their hoarded bullion of its world significance. At the same time the majority, namely the countries which were dependent on an inflated and variable paper currency, favored only such terms of stabilization as would not damage their export trades, because it was easier for foreigners to finance payments in currencies further depreciated than their own. The breaking point came, significantly enough, at a World Economic Conference in London in the summer of 1933. Here President Roosevelt, who had recently taken the United States off the gold standard, let it be known that his intention was to relate the value of the dollar to domestic needs rather than to give any lead in the direction of a new international currency standard. The devaluation of the United States dollar by approximately two-fifths in terms of its gold content followed in January, 1934; this action was designed to raise wholesale commodity prices at home and in the export market.

Meanwhile, the World Economic Conference had witnessed the tacit abandonment of any serious attempt at international control of the measures by which every country strove to better its own trading position regardless of the needs of others. The economics of siege, more grandly described as the pursuit of autarky (self-sufficiency), had quickly replaced the movement towards a tariff truce which the League Assembly had been discussing in the fateful autumn of 1929. The Hawley-Smoot Tariff instituted by the United States in June, 1930, with its record average height of 53.2 percent, is said by American historians to have resulted in the establishment of retaliatory tariffs by twenty-five countries within two years, though after 1934 it was modified by a long series of reciprocal trade agreements. The powerful example set by the United States Congress was of course only one factor in producing tariff rates which, over most of continental Europe, were already 60 to 100 percent higher in 1931 than in 1929, and were followed next year by the institution of a British tariff, initially (but only briefly) of 10 percent.

Foreign trade was also regulated in other ways. Governments obtained powers in this time of emergency to fix quotas—no more than a given quantity of a given commodity was to be imported from a given source in a given period of time. This principle was applied by the French to eleven hundred commodities which might otherwise have jumped the tariff wall. Alternatively, nations used the device of restricting foreign exchange, so that purchases could only be made from a foreign country in strict proportion to what was being sold to it; the result was that bilateral replaced multilateral trade. Finally, currency was manipulated to encourage exports rather than imports of food and manufactures. This manipulation might help unemployment at home, but in the larger sense it entirely disregarded the existence of a world crisis.

All these restrictions upon the free flow of world trade were widely established when the World Economic Conference assembled in London in June, 1933. Its disbandment in the following month without reaching any important conclusions would be in any case significant. The fact that no further general

attempt to solve world economic problems on an international basis was made
before war came makes it clear in retrospect that this was the end of an era.

■ ECONOMIC NATIONALISM IN THE ASCENDANT, 1933–1939

   To form a balanced impression of the economic position of Europe in
these years is difficult. Emphasis has already been laid upon the failure to
revive the world economy: two further illustrations of deterioration are provided by the stagnation of foreign investment, which was so complete that between 1935 and 1939 America's stock of gold increased by 8 billion dollars,
and by the decline in the total of world shipping from 70 million tons in 1929
to 65 million tons in 1939. On the other hand, the concentration of attention
upon the domestic or regional field had certain valuable consequences. One
was the modernizing of British agriculture through the stimulus of government
controlled marketing schemes. Another was the trend towards mass production
and automation, which was fostered by the post-depression belief in many industrial countries that the alternative was to rationalize or perish. Still another consequence was that to some extent the challenge of adversity itself inspired an effective response, as when Hitler partly solved his unemployment
problem by constructing the great *Autobahnen* or when desolate British shipyards sprang to life to build the world's largest liners, *Queen Mary* and *Queen
Elizabeth*.

   The most spectacular technical advances were still being made in the
field of communications. The world of 1939 had developed a piston-type
monoplane which would fly at 450 m.p.h. and reach an altitude of 57,000 feet;
it had more recently invented the helicopter; and it was bringing into commercial use a German twelve-engined flying boat with room for 170 passengers. In both France and Britain the number of automobile owners doubled
during the 1930's, and diesel-electric locomotive engines were being brought
into operation to retain a share of traffic on the iron road. This was also the
period in which radio transmission was perfected by the introduction of fre-
quency modulation (1933), in which the first public television service was
established in Berlin (1934–1935), and in which Watson Watt's researches
(1935–1939) resulted in the British invention of radar for direction finding in
war and peace.

   The advances made in agriculture and manufacturing industry had
greatest effect on the general standard of life. By 1939 even the small-sized
fields of Britain found employment for 55,000 tractors, and both seed and
stock were being improved by large-scale scientific research to the ultimate
benefit of the consumer. As for manufacture, this was the age of the invention
of nylon and polythene, of new metal alloys of unequaled durability and
strength cheaply prepared in the electric furnace, and of the first sulfanilamide

drugs and antibiotics such as penicillin (1929) for the treatment of pneumonia and other killing diseases. Yet the advance which mattered most to the future of humanity was none of these. In 1932 Chadwick in Cambridge (England) discovered the neutron, and in January, 1939, Hahn and Strassmann in Germany by bombarding uranium with neutrons succeeded in the first splitting or fission of the atom.

In marked contrast to the world-wide interrelationships on which the epoch-making advances of science were largely dependent, the economy of the globe had fallen back to what was at best a regional basis. Thus the Imperial Economic Conference at Ottawa in 1932 advertised a British intention of doing whatever might still be possible to build up trade within the Empire. Some advantages certainly resulted, for instance to the coffee-growers of Kenya. In general, however, each proposal for freer trade was shown to involve a detrimental effect either upon the struggling industry of some Dominion (usually Canada) or upon the struggling agriculture of the mother country. New imperial preferences were therefore based after much hard bargaining not upon a lowering of trade barriers inside the British Empire, so as to create possibilities for an effective customs union, but upon the raising of additional trade barriers against the outside world. The United Kingdom transferred about 10 percent of her import trade from foreign countries to the main countries of the Commonwealth and Empire, while the latter transferred an average of no more than 2 to 3 percent of their import trade to Britain in return. The share of the United Kingdom in the export trade of the world nevertheless continued to decline from 10.75 percent in 1929 to 9.8 percent in 1937. The other colonial empires of the world had always been protectionist in character, but in each of them the attempt to build up intra-imperial trade was a feature of this period. For France, indeed, which retained the gold standard until 1936, the high prices of her exports meant that "the empire was the principal market which remained open."[6]

Germany having no empire to turn to, its Nazi leaders combined political with economic advantage by building up an elaborate series of bilateral clearing agreements which stretched throughout southeastern Europe. German manufactures were in effect exchanged for foodstuffs and raw materials on terms which were often weighted in Germany's favor, since the smaller partner could never afford to risk a breakdown in the relationship once begun. The exchanges also conferred important economic benefits on the small powers concerned, whose governments did not at the time resent, generally speaking, the fact that they were also being drawn into the political orbit of the new Germany. The figures speak for themselves:

6. CROUZET, *L'Epoque contemporaine*, p. 145.

GERMAN PERCENTILE SHARE IN TRADE OF SOUTHEASTERN EUROPE[7]

	1929		1933		1937	
	IMPORTS	EXPORTS	IMPORTS	EXPORTS	IMPORTS	EXPORTS
Hungary	22.0	11.7	19.7	11.2	25.9	24.0
Rumania	24.1	27.6	18.6	10.6	28.9	22.3
Yugoslavia	15.6	8.5	13.2	13.9	32.4	21.7
Bulgaria	22.2	29.9	38.2	36.0	54.8	43.1
Greece	9.4	23.2	10.1	17.1	27.2	31.0
Turkey	15.3	13.3	25.3	18.9	42.1	36.5

Thus for Germany as for the imperial powers the pursuit of national self-sufficiency involved regional aspirations and commitments abroad to bolster up a predominantly industrialized economy at home. The depression had made self-sufficiency at least equally attractive to the agrarian economies of South America, Asia, and eastern Europe, whose peoples bought machinery, raised tariff walls, and achieved a rapid increase in their industrial production. By 1937 Lithuania and Chile, for example, had more than doubled their textile output since 1929. In consequence, the pursuit of autarky did not solve the fundamental economic problems of Europe. France in 1937 had an industrial production 17 percent below the level of 1928 and, after hoarding 20 percent of the world's supply of gold, found it expedient to allow a 40 percent depreciation in the franc, which became reattached to the pound sterling. Britain in 1937 still had a higher unemployment figure than in 1929. Although her costs of food and raw material imports had made it possible to raise the standard of living and carry out vast rehousing schemes, the unfavorable balance of trade, cessation of overseas investment, and slow decline in the value of the pound meant that the country as a whole was gradually becoming poorer. In Germany by 1936 the Nazi government had embarked upon a four-year production plan with complete self-sufficiency as its object, and the vigor already shown in the direction of labor and capital made success likely. Even so, the price which the Germans were paying for their strictly controlled economy included a decline of 6 percent in the level of real wages.

From 1937 onwards an armaments boom gave a febrile vigor to each of the big national economies. Even that of the United States, for which the New Deal had spelled new life, benefited to some extent from the stimulus given to airplane development in Europe. Stockpiling helped to sustain the prices of primary products; unemployment was held generally at bay, and in Germany it dwindled to nothing. In Britain, where rearmament was slow to get under way, the most prosperous industries nevertheless were those concerned with naval construction, engineering, and aviation. In some respects the concentra-

7. C. A. MACARTNEY and A. W. PALMER, *Independent Eastern Europe* (1962), p. 315.

tion upon armaments itself emphasized the weaknesses in the position of Europe as a whole—its lack of the oil which was now one of the main sinews of war and of the nonferrous metals essential for airplane building. Quite clearly, the accumulation of arms for purposes of mutual destruction would do less than nothing to redress the economic balance of the continents.

That balance was by this time gravely upset. Since the 1920's Europe's share in world trade had sunk from 52.5 to 39.5 percent. Her share in world production had also sunk: in the key material of steel, the proportion made in Europe had declined by 10 percent since before the war, coal output was stationary in face of a big world increase, and silk and wool are examples of a positive decline.

In summary, during the quarter-century which has been passed under rapid review in this chapter, the peoples of Europe considered as a single economic group had undergone a series of new experiences. Between 1914 and 1918 they had been subjected to a heavier strain than in any earlier war, with the result that capitalist bourgeois society had been shaken everywhere and in Russia completely shattered. Inflation and rising taxation had subsequently prevented the middle classes from recovering their old sense of security based on unchanging values. The heavy incidence of unemployment in Britain and elsewhere gave the workers a feeling of helplessness in face of economic disaster. This situation in turn prepared the way for the acceptance of economic planning, to which every government in some degree resorted and where Soviet Russia, long disregarded, led the way.[8]

Only by slow degrees the nations of Europe, deeply concerned about the division of the total economic product between countries and classes, came to realize that the product itself—their share, as it were, of the world cake—had ceased to be the lion's share. No amount of skill on the part of European statesmen in the interwar period could have called back the day that was past. True as this is, if Europe's attention had been less wholly absorbed in the political rivalries described in our next chapters, the Continent might have been better prepared for the economic stringencies of the morrow. Instead, political rivalry found convenient expression in an intensified economic nationalism and the desire for autarky. Such policies did little to promote the well-being of the total European economy and much to stimulate the rise and bellicose attitude of the dictators who were to work its ruin.

---

8. For the economic development of the U.S.S.R., which was to a great extent isolated from the world economy, see pp. 204–207; 213–220.

Reading List: Chapter 6

Bogart, E. L., *Economic History of Europe, 1760–1939* (1942), chs. 15, 17, 18, 20, 23.

Heaton, H., *Economic History of Europe* (rev. ed., 1948), chs. 28–29. The two interwar decades separately and succinctly examined.

Clough, S. B., *The Economic Development of Western Civilization* (1959), chs. 18–19.

Spender, J. A., *Great Britain, Empire and Commonwealth, 1886–1935* (1936), chs. 65–67. A review of world economic developments by an English Liberal of long political experience.

The New Cambridge Modern History, vol. XII (1960), ch. 2. The economic world map, 1900–1945.

Chapter 7

The Rise of the Dictatorships

Democracy and Dictatorship: The Challenge
Fascist Italy: Background
Fascist Italy: The Take-over
The Reorganization of Fascist Italy: The Corporative State
Other Dictatorships of the 1920's
Dictatorship During the 1930's
Efforts for a Democratic Germany
Problems of the Weimar Republic
Hitler and National Socialism
Dictatorship in Hitler's Third Reich

■ DEMOCRACY AND DICTATORSHIP: THE CHALLENGE

The rapid spread of dictatorial regimes in Europe following the First World War marked the repudiation of many earlier predictions and hopes. A common generalization made during the nineteenth century had been that this was the age pre-eminently of parliamentary democracy. Country after country had adopted a constitutional regime and widened its voting franchise so that by 1914 autocracy had lost most of its ancient prestige. Four years later, the 1914 prophecy of the Rumanian statesman Take Ionescu that the war would be followed by a cascade of thrones was spectacularly fulfilled, for the outcome proved fatal to the dynasties in Germany, Russia, Austria-Hungary, and Turkey.

168

SIGNIFICANT EVENTS

1919   Founding of the National Socialist Party in Munich (January)
1922   Mussolini's March on Rome (October)
1923   Primo de Rivera begins dictatorship in Spain (September)
1926   Pilsudski's coup in Poland (May)
1929   King Alexander suspends constitution of Yugoslavia (January)
1932   Dollfuss becomes chancellor in Austria (May)
1933   Hitler becomes chancellor in Germany (January)
1934   Attempted Nazi Putsch in Austria; murder of Dollfuss (July)
1935   Italy invades Ethiopia (October)
1936   Schuschnigg virtual dictator in Austria (May)
       Franco launches civil war in Spain (July)
1937   Violently anti-Semitic government in Rumania (December)
1938   German occupation of Austria (March)
       Munich Agreement over Czechoslovakia (September)
1939   German annexation of Czechoslovakia completed (March)
       Franco wins civil war in Spain (March)
       German–Soviet Pact of Nonaggression (August)

Very soon various forms of dictatorship began to replace some of the newly founded democracies. Even before these latter had fully revealed their weaknesses, one of the older parliamentary states, Italy, accepted in 1922 a leader, Benito Mussolini, whose policies repudiated the entire democratic parliamentary tradition. The same repudiation, though usually less spectacular, was soon witnessed in many other states. How is this phenomenon to be explained? Political inexperience and overenthusiasm followed by disillusionment may provide part of the answer. Severe economic difficulties, unavoidable at the end of a savagely destructive world war, may provide another reason. Fear of Communism could well be a third. It is also significant that nearly all Continental countries operated under a multiparty system. This required governments to be coalitions, which could more easily be overthrown than when a government, under the two-party system, was supported by a clear majority of the electorate. Thus, when the European public saw democratically elected governments collapsing in rapid succession, the temptation to seek an authoritarian, one-party regime could become very strong.

Such tendencies were reinforced by certain heavy pressures in modern political society. Nineteenth-century nationalism had taught that some overriding purposes exist which states should pursue at almost any cost. To attain national goals, to defend hard-won gains, or to end continuing injustices, the surrender of domestic political liberties might seem to the average man a worthwhile bargain. Finally, some currents of nineteenth-century thought had brought democratic institutions under vigorous attack. Writers such as Nietzsche, condemning the "herd morality" of popular government, or Georges Sorel, urging "direct action," or Bergson, with his *élan vital,* or Treitschke and Bernhardi, accepting doctrines of force and glorifying the inevitability of war— all had their following. It would be unwise to see the rise of dictatorships as the manifestation of any precise purpose, or to make the explanations of them too rigidly intellectual and consistent. The upsurge of emotion and the operation of chance no doubt played their part. Many men, while not forsaking all belief in parliamentary regimes, seemed disposed to give temporary allegiance to the rule of a strong man—all the more so if they saw evidences of success in the programs of similar strong rulers elsewhere.

■ FASCIST ITALY: BACKGROUND

Italy, the first example of a major country turning from conventional parliamentary life to a dictatorship, differed in many respects from the democracies of the West. The united Italy that emerged in 1871 after the troops of Victor Emmanuel II had occupied Rome lacked true unity. While industrialism, as seen in the thriving cities of Turin and Milan and the great port of Genoa, had made substantial progress in the north, southern Italy was still largely a backward peasant land, with more than half its population illiterate. For Italy as a whole the figures for illiteracy were: 69 percent in 1872, 48 percent in 1901, 38 percent in 1911, and 27 percent in 1921. One might question, indeed, whether political democracy had ever truly existed. The prominent prewar leaders all governed by a uniquely Italian process of parliamentary manipulation known as *trasformismo.* This was the art of maintaining a majority by bribes and other opportunist devices which brought enough support from opponents to pass measures deemed essential.

The outcome of the First World War gave most Italians little comfort. Some 5,500,000 men had been mobilized; 650,000 were dead; huge numbers, variously estimated at from 150,000 to 500,000, were in hiding as deserters, many of them living as bandits. The Italian economy was badly disrupted, while the gains by the peace treaties were widely regarded as inadequate. Italy failed to acquire any mandates under the League of Nations. Unemployment, inflation, and a notably insecure economy all magnified the discontent.

Many Italian radicals, affected by this atmosphere and disillusioned with their own parties, began to look to the example of Communism in Russia. The elections of 1919 saw 157 Socialists in a legislature of over 500. In January, 1921, by a secession from the Socialist Party, an Italian Communist Party was formed. This, however, was able to win only 16 seats in the general election of that year. Another phenomenon was the rise of a Catholic Popular Party, the *Popolari*, organized on democratic principles and led by a brilliant young Sicilian priest, Don Luigi Sturzo, who took advantage of a Vatican statement in 1919 permitting Catholics to join in the political life of Italy. The Popular Party won 107 seats in these 1921 elections, championing the cause of land reform for the peasants. It was in conflict, however, with the Socialists, as these were with the older Liberals and Democrats in the Chamber of Deputies. The result was that workable coalitions were impossible to maintain, and that leaders such as Francesco Nitti, who headed short-lived governments in 1919–1921, and Giovanni Giolitti found that the old techniques of manipulation and compromise were ineffective. War veterans, bitter at the seemingly small outcome of their sacrifices, industrialists concerned about their investments, and ardent nationalists mesmerized by the spell of hotheads such as the poet Gabriele D'Annunzio, who had seized Fiume at the sword's point for Italy,[1] were all receptive to advocates of a new political system.

For over twenty years Benito Mussolini was to provide Italy with the mixed blessings of one of the earliest and longest of the European dictatorships. This "Sawdust Caesar" was born in 1883 in the district of Romagna, one of the most radical areas of Italy, the son of a Socialist blacksmith married to a former schoolmistress. Young Mussolini fled Italy for Switzerland (1902–1904) to escape his military service. In this haven of exiled radicals he picked up many "restaurant socialist" ideas, among them the direct-action views of the French Syndicalist Georges Sorel. Returning to Italy, he followed the career of journalist; in 1912 he became editor of the Milanese journal *Avanti*, the leading Socialist paper in Italy. During the war he saw action on the Isonzo front where he was wounded by the accidental explosion of a mortar; like Hitler, he never rose above noncommissioned rank. The war and its outcome intensified his contempt for the democratic process and led him to espouse a program soon to be known as Fascism.

1. See p. 77.

This term, Fascism, was derived from the Latin *fasces* or bundle of rods bound around an axe and carried by the *lictors*, the attendants of the ancient Roman magistrates, as symbols of their authority. The first Fascist action groups (*fasci d'azione*) were organized by Mussolini in 1915 to help his propaganda in favor of Italian intervention in the war. They were reformed in the spring of 1919 to combat the threat of communism and to give Italy the disciplined strength which the parliamentary regime had signally failed to provide. The black shirt, the Fascist dagger, and the Roman salute became the symbols of these groups who paraded through the streets of Italian towns. A National Congress in Rome officially proclaimed the National Fascist Party (*Partito Nazionale Fascista*) in November, 1921, though the general elections of the previous May had failed to produce more than three dozen Fascist deputies in a legislature of over five hundred.

Fascism was inspired by no systematic program. Some writers, such as the philosopher Giovanni Gentile and Alfredo Rocco, a publicist later made rector of the University of Rome, eventually sought to give an historically based justification for Fascism, emphasizing the restless energy of man, stressing will rather than reason, glorifying war, and going so far as to speak as Mussolini did of Fascism's "superb aimlessness." The doctrine was principally a call to action, attacking the weaknesses of liberalism, democracy, and socialism. It offered inspired catchwords such as "audacity," "heroism," "sacrifice," "education to combat," "obedience," and "conquest." The three commands stenciled along with Mussolini's crude portrait on walls all over Italy were "Credere! Obeddire! Combattere!" (Believe! Obey! Fight!) Few nations have been led to such great adventures and disasters on so meager an intellectual diet.

A few passages from Mussolini's own statements will indicate how he sought to give intellectual respectability to Fascist doctrines:

> Anti-individualistic, the Fascist conception of life stresses the importance of the State and accepts the individual only in so far as his interests coincide with those of the State, which stands for the conscience and the universal will of man as a historic entity.
>
> · · · · ·
>
> Fascism discards pacifism as a cloak for cowardly, supine renunciation in contradiction to self-sacrifice. War alone keys up all human energies to their maximum tension and sets [the] seal of nobility on those people who have the courage to face it.
>
> · · · · ·
>
> Fascism denies that numbers, as such, can be the determining factors in human society. . . . It asserts the irremediable and fertile and beneficent inequality of men who cannot be leveled by any such mechanical and extrinsic device as universal suffrage.[2]

2. Quoted from w. c. LANGSAM, *Documents and Readings in the History of Europe Since 1918* (1951), pp. 498, 499, 501.

■ FASCIST ITALY: THE TAKE-OVER

By May, 1921, when the Fascists elected a mere thirty-five members to
the Chamber, they had nevertheless become a movement of national proportions with a quarter of a million members and a reputation for street demonstrations, brawling, and even murder. The following year saw the domestic
crises become worse. The Socialists called a general strike in August which the
government seemed helpless to end; Fascists attacked the various strike headquarters, broke up labor demonstrations, and took it upon themselves to see
that public utilities functioned. Under these conditions the general strike
failed. When a succession of weak governments proved utterly unable to control events, Mussolini was confident enough to announce in October plans for
a march on Rome, with the purpose of taking over the government. He had
reason to feel that King Victor Emmanuel III would be receptive. While fifty
thousand armed Fascists were converging on Rome, Mussolini unheroically
chose to remain in Milan where, if plans fell through, he could quickly move
into Switzerland. Only when the king brought about the government's resignation by refusing to declare martial law, and then informed the Fascist spokesmen in Rome that he would invite their leader to form a ministry, did Mussolini come. While hordes of rain-drenched Fascists paraded through the streets
of Rome on October 28, 1922, Mussolini, like a privileged guest, arrived by
sleeping car from Milan—the heroic man of action, well rested, outfitted in
borrowed morning clothes, top hat, and white spats—ready to receive his appointment from the king. The threat of force sufficed; authority was legally
bestowed upon the new leader; and the truly revolutionary acts were yet to
come.

The political transformation of Italy was achieved at a deceptively slow
pace. The first cabinet had only four Fascists among its fourteen ministers, with
Mussolini holding the portfolios of foreign and home affairs and the prime
ministership. Late in November, the Chamber voted him full powers to last
until December, 1923. Fascist prefects and subprefects were quickly appointed
in the provinces, and a Fascist Grand Council was set up as a major link between party and state.

Much more ominous was the Electoral Law of November, 1923, which
ingeniously provided that the party gaining the largest number of votes in a
national election, provided that this was one-quarter of the total, should have
two-thirds of the seats in the Chamber. It was passed with the assistance of
Liberal and other moderate votes. The law hardly seems to have been needed,
for in the April, 1924, election 4.7 million votes were cast for the new government's supporters and only 2.25 million for its opponents. The next step showed
increasing ruthlessness. An outspoken Socialist deputy, Giacomo Matteotti,

CHILDREN OF THE SHE-WOLF. Members of the new Fascist corps, "Figli della Lupa," carrying miniature rifles, parade past Mussolini in 1935 on the twentieth anniversary of Italy's entry into the First World War.

was found murdered in June, 1924. Though Mussolini professed to deplore this act, he would not investigate it or punish its perpetrators, and later evidence shows that he himself was actually implicated. Further repressive measures led some members of the Chamber to "secede" in protest—a gesture which made Mussolini's power all the stronger.

Throughout 1925 and 1926 the dictatorial regime grew more flagrant. By 1926 parties were officially dissolved, non-Fascists were removed from government posts, labor was placed under severe restrictions, and the press was rigidly controlled. Instead of elected mayors, Fascist appointees known as *podestas* took office in the larger towns. An elaborate Fascist youth organization covering the years from eight to twenty-one and heavily military in character was organized in 1926 and soon had over three million members.

The Electoral Reform Act of May, 1928, and the new regulation of the Fascist Grand Council in December, 1928, gave definitive form to the unitary, monolithic, Fascist regime. The franchise was now restricted to men over twenty-one who were members of the new syndicates (to be described in the next section) or who were large taxpayers. The electorate was thereby cut from almost ten million to three. From a list of one thousand candidates drawn up by members of the various syndicates, four hundred were selected by the central authorities to constitute the Fascist Chamber of Deputies. Then the names were submitted *in toto* for what amounted to automatic acceptance by the electorate. Selection of deputies was one of the tasks of the Fascist Grand Council, whose members were appointed and removed by the king at the recommendation of Mussolini. The Grand Council was defined as "the supreme organ which coordinates and integrates all the activities of the Regime. . . ." In this Grand Council Mussolini held eight portfolios.

Mussolini, with the title of *Il Duce* (the Leader), was by 1928 supreme both as party chief and prime minister. He was surrounded by a party militia. The statutes of the Fascist Party, which by 1934 numbered about 1,500,000 members, stipulated that the following oath be taken by all:

> In the name of God and of Italy I swear to carry out without discussion the orders of the Duce and to serve the Cause of the Fascist Revolution with all my might and if necessary with my life.

■ THE REORGANIZATION OF FASCIST ITALY:
THE CORPORATIVE STATE

The domestic policies which gave Mussolini his great, and it would seem now largely undeserved, contemporary reputation were associated with syndicalism and the corporative state. Syndicalism, largely a French development, had sought to organize workers in militant occupational associations so that by means of the general strike they could exercise decisive political power. Acting in an altogether different sense, Pope Leo XIII in his famous encyclical, *Rerum Novarum* of 1891, had urged workers and employers to combine in associations for their mutual good. The arrangements made by Mussolini in Italy have some relation to both trends, though he had not the slightest intention of letting either workers or employers become masters of their own destinies. He organized Italian economic life on a functional, rather than a geographic, basis, and directed it from above. This "corporative state" would affect the make-up of the Italian parliament, for the usual territorial method of representation would give place to representation of occupational groups—farmers, transport workers, professional men, and the like. The old Chamber of Deputies was replaced in 1938 by the splendid-sounding "Chamber of Fasces and Corporations"—as it turned out, a hollow sham and total deception. Even so, Mussolini's reorganization of the political life of Italy on the basis of economic realities struck many as a remarkable forward step.

The Syndicalist Law of 1926 set up syndicates for workers in industry, agriculture, commerce, sea and air transport, land transport, and finance; six corresponding syndicates were organized for employers; and a thirteenth was set up for intellectuals. These could draw up collective labor contracts; they were to submit their disputes to a new system of labor courts; strikes and lockouts were consequently forbidden. The system was elaborated in the Labor Charter of 1927, in which the term "Corporative State" was proclaimed and the promise made of accident, unemployment, and health insurance for all workers. The syndicates designated lists of candidates for the new Chamber of Deputies, and final selections were made from the lists by the Fascist Grand Council. A National Council of Corporations was set up in 1930—an unwieldy body of more than a hundred representatives of employers and employees to advise on economic affairs.

The climax came with the February, 1934, Law on Corporations, setting up an elaborate scheme of twenty-two corporations or syndicates in the fields of agriculture, industry, and public services. This elaborate structure was crowned in 1938 by the formation of a new Chamber of Fasces and Corporations which, though announced as a parliament based on representation by function, was in operation an utterly powerless body. The system of corporations emphasized the strong position of the employers, enlarged the scope of the bureaucracy, and gave additional authority to the personal dictatorship of Mussolini. In the scathing words of Gaetano Salvemini, one of Fascism's first eminent victims and one of its most brilliant and severest critics, the corporate structure of Italian life was no more than "an elaborate piece of imposing humbug."

A showman like Mussolini could, nonetheless, dress his program in an attractive garb. He decreed in 1925 the *Dopolavoro*, or "After Work" Society, providing healthful recreation and leisure for workers at government expense. He initiated an elaborate program of public buildings, eliminated malaria in the marshy lands around Rome, drove beggars from the streets, reduced the exploitation of tourists, and boasted of making trains run on time. His scheme of old age, disability, and health insurance echoed earlier schemes in Germany and Britain. The "Battle of Wheat," in which land reclamation and the manufacture of fertilizers played a big part, by 1932 achieved self-sufficiency. And it was all to Mussolini's advantage to be photographed at harvest time, shirtless and sun-tanned, contributing, if only for an hour, to getting in the crop.

The problem of the state and the Roman Catholic Church afforded Mussolini an apparently resounding victory. With the final seizure of papal territory in 1870, relations between the temporal and spiritual power had reached an impasse. Italians had been instructed by the papacy not to vote in parliamentary elections. In practice they did vote, and many working accommodations had been made. For example, in 1905 the pope declared that under certain circumstances bishops could authorize their flocks to take part in elections. The ban on political activity had been fully lifted in 1919. The situation was aided by the election in February, 1922, of Pope Pius XI, a pontiff who, though distrusting political Catholicism of the kind seen in the Catholic Popular Party, had recently been nuncio to Poland where he had had first-hand experience of Bolshevism. He consequently was prepared to recognize the Fascist state as a bulwark against it. Mussolini, to be sure, was hardly a sympathetic character for such negotiations. His early radicalism had been militantly anticlerical; and one of his youthful indiscretions had been to write a lurid novel entitled *The Cardinal's Mistress.* Despite such handicaps, the negotiations undertaken in 1926 led in three years to a spectacular success.

The Lateran Treaty, signed with great pomp on February 11, 1929, recognized Roman Catholicism as "the only state religion" and granted the pope full sovereignty over the one-mile-square Vatican City, with all diplomatic rights. The Holy See recognized the Kingdom of Italy as the legitimate ruler of all other Italian territory. By an accompanying Concordat the Roman Catholic Church was assured full jurisdiction in ecclesiastical matters. The pope was to appoint bishops and archbishops, having first communicated the names to the Italian government in order to be sure that the latter had no objections of a political nature. Priests were to take an oath of allegiance to the state, which would enforce canon law and pay clerical salaries; Church views on marriage were to prevail, the civil ceremony being made optional; and the teaching of Christian doctrine "in the form admitted by Catholic tradition" was to be compulsory in all elementary and secondary schools. Finally, in a financial settlement the state agreed to pay the equivalent of ninety million dollars to the papacy in full compensation for the loss of its temporal possessions in 1870.

Thus the Fascist regime appeared to have solved the baffling "Roman Question." When, however, Mussolini began to align himself more closely with the intolerant dictatorship of Hitler, the breach widened, and in his last years Pius XI was engaged in indignant controversy with the Fascists. His successor, Pius XII, elected in 1939, continued this policy of evident mistrust, though not of downright opposition.

Mussolini's foreign policy, based first on a vigorous program of rearmament, claimed to be a revival of the grandeur of the ancient Roman Empire. If only the Mediterranean could become an Italian lake—"Mare Nostrum"— and if only Italy could win overseas possessions in Africa and make gains in the Balkans or the Middle East, then a glorious future would be in store. Military, naval, and air preparations went on apace. Italy's determination to play a larger role led her in the 1930's to weaken her connections with Britain and

France and to align herself with Nazi Germany. The Rome-Berlin Axis came into being in October, 1936, with an agreement between Italy and Germany linking together their two foreign policies.

The widely admired Italian dictatorship appears in retrospect shot through with weaknesses. The strutting, vulgar figure of Mussolini, the generally low level of ability in the men who served him, the corruption of the governing cliques, and the apathy of the public, especially the peasants, were disguised by the outward appearances of vigor. Uniforms, parades, fine public buildings, new roads—these were among the splendid externals of Mussolini's "Balcony Empire" which under the fiery test of war proved to be so shoddy.

■ OTHER DICTATORSHIPS OF THE 1920'S

What Mussolini did with such seeming success in Italy was attempted by dictatorial regimes elsewhere. The remarkable career of Mustafa Kemal Pasha in Turkey has already been sketched.[3] Other dictatorships arising during the first decade of peace must now be summarized.

Hungary, where revolution broke out in October, 1918, proclaimed a republic in November, three days after the abdication of the Hapsburg Emperor Charles. A provisional government was set up under a liberal aristocrat, Count Michael Károlyi. He was almost immediately challenged by the professional revolutionary Bela Kun, who was eventually driven out in August, 1919, with the assistance of Rumanian troops. Hungarian counterrevolutionaries, unwilling to restore the provisional republic, proclaimed a regency for the absent monarchy, and eventually turned to Admiral Nicholas Horthy. A constituent assembly of 1920 elected him lifetime regent for the Kingdom of Hungary. To have an admiral without a navy as regent for life in a kingdom without a king suggests something of the unreality of Hungarian politics.

For ten years the premier was the very conservative Count Stephen Bethlen; he opposed the liberalism of Károlyi, terminated the latter's program of land distribution to the peasants, reintroduced open voting in village elections, and in general successfully preserved the ancient privileges of the aristocracy. He was popular because of his constant demands for revision of the Treaty of Trianon.[4] However, his failure to deal successfully with the depression in Hungary forced his resignation in 1931, following which his successors kept up the pattern of illiberal rule. Julius Gömbös, for example, was a fascist and an anti-Semite who courted Hitler and aligned Hungary very closely with National Socialist Germany. Continuing economic difficulties, however, held Hungary back from any of the outwardly spectacular achievements that shed so much false glamor on Fascist Italy.

3. See pp. 120–123.
4. See p. 76.

Greece, similarly, saw dictatorship make a fairly early appearance. During the war, King Constantine I displayed strong sympathies for Germany, while Eleutherios Venizelos, Greece's leading statesman, was equally strong for the Allied side.[5] In June, 1917, the king abdicated and Venizelos obtained a declaration of war upon Germany, Turkey, and Bulgaria. Hopes for substantial gains at the expense of Turkey were shattered when Greece was expelled from Anatolia by Mustafa Kemal in 1922.[6] The monarchy fell into such disfavor that Constantine (who had been restored after the death of his second son, King Alexander, in 1920) abdicated a second time; then in December, 1923, King George II, Constantine's son and recent successor, was forced to flee. Greece in the following year was proclaimed a republic.

This Greek Republic lasted for eleven years. Though the new constitution guaranteed universal suffrage, and though part of this period can be called the era of Venizelos, the elder statesman met many severe challenges and, in the end, disaster. Military power counted, for example, in the years 1925–1926 when General Theodore Pangalos defied the constitution and made himself dictator. It took another general, Georgios Kondyles, to defeat Pangalos and promulgate a truly republican constitution. Royalist sentiment began to reemerge, with the result that in March, 1933, an acknowledged Royalist became premier. The Republican Venizelos, who during these years had resumed the premiership, fought to keep alive his liberal principles, and headed an uprising in 1935. It failed, and in the following year the great Greek patriot, sentenced to banishment, died in exile at Paris.

Similar confusions were seen in Spain and Portugal. The stormy history of nineteenth-century Spain had been tempered by the adoption of the constitution of 1876, with provision for a bicameral legislature in which the lower house was chosen by manhood suffrage. Economic difficulties after the First World War stimulated the growth of many left-wing groups. Unrest was intensified by the failure of the government to cope with native revolts in the Riff, a part of Spanish Morocco. Further troubles arose from the demands in Catalonia for home rule. Not surprisingly, therefore, in September, 1923, King Alfonso XIII gave his approval to a military coup led by General Primo de Rivera at Barcelona. Alfonso agreed to dissolve the Cortes, or parliament, suspend jury trial, and maintain a severe censorship. The king's views were hardly to be doubted. On a visit to Italy in November, 1923, Alfonso spoke to General

---

5. 1864–1936. A native of Crete, he took part in the insurrection of 1896 against Turkish rule, and subsequently worked for union with Greece, not achieved until 1913. He was premier of Greece, 1910–1915, and again, 1917–1920, 1924, 1928–1932, and in 1933. He favored the Allies during the First World War, and played a prominent role at the Paris Peace Conference and in the League of Nations. The greatest statesman of modern Greece, the failure of Venizelos to avert the return of the monarchy by an armed uprising in 1935 was followed by his exile and, within a year, his death.
6. See p. 121.

Italo Balbo as follows: "I admire Fascism. You are happy here in being so near the end of your labors. We are just beginning."

Though technically the dictatorship ended in December, 1925, when Primo de Rivera resumed the system of cabinet government, actually there were no elections and the dictatorship continued. When ill health forced Primo de Rivera's resignation in 1930, another general, Dámaso Berenguer, attempted a policy of conciliation and restored the democratic constitution. The Republicans, however, saw their chance, and in April, 1931, Alfonso XIII was forced into exile. Despite this, the Republican regime, which took shape during the year, was unable permanently to consolidate itself.

Portugal, where the monarchy had fallen in 1910, had a republican regime which was seldom free from military threats. By a coup in 1926 General Carmona seized power, with a young professor of economics from the University of Coimbra, Antonio de Oliveira Salazar, as minister of finance.[7] By 1932 Salazar had become prime minister and, in essence, dictator, although this retiring, studious, devout, and personally unambitious leader, who undoubtedly bettered the economic condition of his country, had little in common with the strutting dictators in other parts of Europe. His was a government of technicians: a lawyer became minister of justice; a diplomat, minister of foreign affairs; an engineer, minister of public works; and a soldier, minister of war. The essence of Salazar's policy is contained in his statement: "The people have less need of being sovereign than of being governed."

The Balkans provided several examples of dictatorial regimes obstructing the growth of parliamentary institutions. The tiny peasant state of Albania, for example, was set up by the powers at the close of the First Balkan War in 1913 as a kingdom. It struggled with grave economic problems in the immediate postwar years, while efforts to create a democratic republic had little effect. Late in 1924 Ahmed Zogu, a member of the cabinet since 1921, returned after a brief exile, and in January, 1925, the Albanian National Assembly proclaimed a republic with him as its president. Working for a policy of friendship with Italy and doing what he could to remedy Albania's appalling backwardness, he assumed in 1928 the title of King Zog I, and with it the typical attributes of dictatorship.

A very much larger Balkan state, Yugoslavia, represented the fusion of the Southern Slavs—Serbs, Croats, and Slovenes—into the Greater Serbia of which many had dreamed in prewar years. Here domestic rivalries were in-

---

7. Born in 1889, he became a distinguished professor of economics at the University of Coimbra. His devout Catholicism committed him to the social program of Pope Leo XIII. First elected to parliament in 1921, he subsequently held several ministerial posts, in which he successfully reorganized Portuguese finances. Made premier in 1932, he reorganized the constitution in 1933 along dictatorial and corporative lines. The only attempt to create a democratic opposition (1945) was ended by intimidation.

tense. After the assassination of the great Croat leader Stefan Radich by a Montenegrin deputy during a parliamentary sitting in 1928, normal constitutional government proved impossible. King Alexander I, head of the dynasty which had ruled prewar Serbia, met the problem by a decree of January, 1929, suppressing all political parties, dissolving parliament, imposing a severe censorship, and arresting the principal Croat leaders. Though the end of the dictatorship was proclaimed in September, 1931, only a semblance of parliamentary government reappeared.

Rumania, similarly, met heavy going. There a parliamentary regime directed a country that had made huge territorial gains in the 1914–1918 war. Leaders such as Ion Bratianu and Juliu Maniu were able, experienced men, western-educated in the best liberal parliamentary tradition. Some of Rumania's problems came with the great depression; others arose from the widespread corruption among political cliques and from the failures of the monarchy. The infant Michael I, grandson of the popular Ferdinand I (1914–1927), held the throne under a regency from 1927 until 1930, when his dissipated father returned from exile with the title of Carol II. Without ability himself, Carol ruled through a kind of cabinet dictatorship. This was a period of extreme political instability when no strong dictator emerged, but when fascist organizations, most notably the strongly anti-Semitic Iron Guard, developed.

Bulgaria, where savage political strife was continuous, saw no clear-cut fascist regime appear in the 1920's. The great peasant leader Alexander Stambolisky was assassinated in 1923 by nationalist fanatics. Not until the mid-thirties, however, did a group of army officers succeed in establishing a forceful, fascist-type dictatorship, which King Boris supported.

The little state of Austria, a mere remnant of the vast Hapsburg realms, emerged from the war years as a federal, parliamentary republic of 6.5 million souls as against the prewar population of 51 million for the entire Hapsburg Empire. *Anschluss,* or union with Germany, was forbidden by the Treaty of St. Germain. An odd coalition of Christian Socialists (Catholics) and Social Democrats (Marxists) first attempted to share the responsibilities of government. The Christian Socialists were soon in the ascendant under the leadership of Ignaz Seipel, a Catholic priest who was twice chancellor of the Republic. The Social Democrats became the leading party of opposition. Seipel drew support from nationalist groups and from organizations such as the *Heimwehr,* a sort of private army organized by a reactionary nobleman, Prince Stahremberg, whose strutting ambitions were combined with a lack of perspicacity leading him to favor Mussolini (a professed champion of Austrian independence) rather than Hitler. While no ostensibly fascist party took the helm in Austria, the Christian Socialist leadership displayed many of the marks of a dictatorship. When Seipel retired from public life in 1929, *Anschluss* soon became a critical issue, although a proposal in 1931 for a customs union provoked such a loud outcry from France, Italy, and Czechoslovakia that the scheme was dropped.

Poland offered still another variant of the dictatorial pattern. The difficulties of this newly reconstituted state—large in population, poorly bounded, divided into many ethnic groups, torn by political factions, and coveted by hostile neighbors—were little short of appalling. The constitution adopted in March, 1921, within weeks of the close of the Russo-Polish War, set up a parliamentary republic which made determined efforts to face the problems of reconstruction. Complex rivalries arising from a multiplicity of parties elected by an elaborate system of proportional representation made the operation of the constitution almost impossible. In May, 1926, the Polish hero Josef Pilsudski, whose whole life had been one of conspiracy against the Russians and who had headed various provisional regimes between 1919 and 1923, led three regiments upon Warsaw in a military coup which made him a virtual dictator. He actually refused the office of president, which went to a friend, Ignacy Moscicki, but accepted the premiership in October, holding this until 1930. Despite his official resignation, Pilsudski's regime actually lasted until his death in 1935. It had mixed elements, and Pilsudski could properly be described as a most reluctant dictator, who held parliamentary elections, refused to form a single party, and instead accepted the support of loose blocs of sympathizers. Unquestionably he was a strong man, accustomed to the use of force. After 1930, when Pilsudski, "the Jupiter of the Belvedere Palace," began to move into the background, Poland was governed much more as a thoroughgoing dictatorship with a camarilla of army officers in command.

The new Baltic States became the scene of a mild version of dictatorship. Between 1920 and 1922 Estonia, Latvia, and Lithuania, preponderantly agrarian countries and dangerously close to Soviet Russia, adopted constitutions based on universal suffrage. All had their problems, compounded of economic difficulties, political inexperience, minority demands, and communist and fascist agitation. As early as December, 1926, ardent nationalists in Lithuania put their leader into the presidency, and by 1928 they succeeded in promulgating an authoritarian constitution. Similar trends were observable in the other Baltic States, though it was not until the 1930's that these dictatorships became truly effective.

■ DICTATORSHIP DURING THE 1930's

The trend to dictatorship became even more marked during the decade of the 1930's, stimulated by the world economic crisis which, beginning in 1929, lasted for the greater part of four years. Certain ominous aspects such as the much wider use of uniforms and military formations and the growth of vicious secret-police methods and general brutality were apparent. Economic life was elaborately regulated. Propaganda, especially through the new medium of the radio, became at the same time more blatant and more effective. In one country after another the polarization of the two extremes—a fascist Right and a communist Left—meant actual violence in the streets and, as an almost inevitable sequel, a growing contempt for parliamentary institutions. Perhaps most ominous of all was the widespread pattern of rearmament, indicating the ever growing threat of war. Armed conflict, indeed, became more than a threat. The Spanish Civil War, which ran from 1936 to 1939, saw approximately one million people perish or pass into lifelong exile.

The Balkans were characteristically unsettled. King Carol of Rumania, after his return from exile in 1930, had much trouble in exerting the full authority which he sought. His Ministry of National Unity, set up after the elections of 1931, lasted only until the summer of 1932. For a time Carol favored and subsidized the viciously nationalistic and anti-Semitic Iron Guard, then late in 1933 he turned to a liberal premier who tried to order the Guard's suppression. By 1937 Carol had swung once more to a reactionary, Octavian Goga, head of the anti-Semitic National Christian Party. He, too, did not last long. Carol proclaimed a new constitution in 1938, suspended the Iron Guard, and had its organizer arrested and shot. Then, with a new, hopefully named Party of National Rebirth, he attempted vainly to exercise power himself, until German invasion during the Second World War drove him out.

The well-intentioned King Boris of Bulgaria met very difficult times. A military dictatorship was set up in 1934 by a group of army officers. Within a year, however, Boris set up a kind of royal dictatorship which, though it refused to allow the return of political parties, seemed reasonably popular. An election was authorized in 1938 which summoned parliament for the first time in three years, but only as a purely consultative body.

The bitter tensions in Yugoslavia also continued. King Alexander, who proclaimed the end of his two-year dictatorship in 1931, issued a new constitution promising manhood suffrage. The official replacement of the old name, "Kingdom of the Serbs, Croats, and Slovenes," by the name, "Yugoslavia," and the reorganizing of the country into nine new provinces instead of the old historic divisions suggest a genuine effort toward unity. But at the same time civil liberties were suspended and royal authority remained strong. During a visit to France in 1934 Alexander was assassinated at Marseilles by a terrorist agent of the Croats—a clear indication of the continued divisions in his kingdom. The regency of Prince Paul for Alexander's young son, King Peter II, was marked by a more moderate domestic policy and by closer ties with Italy and Germany. Even so, Croat, Serb, and Slovene rivalries remained acute. Though on the very eve of the Second World War the restoration of parliamentary government was announced, it came too late for its effect to be felt.

Dictatorship in Greece was more candidly in evidence than perhaps in any other Balkan country. After eleven years of the Republic, dissatisfaction led to the restoration of monarchy in 1935 in the person of the former ruler, George II. While the king was personally eager to return to constitutional procedures, the elections of 1936, which returned 142 Republicans, 143 Royalists, and a small group of 15 Communists holding the balance of power, gave him little comfort. George II therefore appointed General Joannes Metaxas, a rightist, as premier. The regime of Metaxas was unquestionably a dictatorship. He persuaded King George to dissolve parliament, and to suspend personal liberties along with other rights guaranteed in the constitution. Ruling as a dictator, he assumed the ministries of foreign affairs, war, navy, and the air. Heavy curbs were placed on Communist and other labor leaders and the press was muzzled. Censorship was so extreme that it required the removal of certain passages regarded as politically inflammatory from the text of the *Antigone* of Sophocles. Enough was done in the way of public works and social legislation, however, to give the regime a fairly wide acceptance. Metaxas in 1938 became premier for life, and only death in 1941 brought his dictatorship to an end.

Austria and Hungary also demonstrated the growth of authoritarianism in the 1930's. Hungary had long seen such policies in effect. Julius Gömbös, who became premier in October, 1932, sought the support of both Mussolini and Hitler. Opposition came from the agrarian groups and the followers of Count Stephen Bethlen. In the elections of April, 1935, though the opposition polled 1,041,000 votes as against 1,908,000 votes for the government, they won only 51 out of 217 seats and thus remained relatively ineffective. Gömbös died in 1935. His two successors did little to moderate the existing policies. Relations with Nazi Germany, indeed, became closer and more cordial, with the result that in February, 1939, Hungary joined the Anti-Comintern Pact of Germany, Italy, and Japan.

Austria was quite typically disposed to undertake political changes with a little less ruthlessness. However, the 1930's proved to be very stormy years. Chancellor Engelbert Dollfuss,[8] who took office in May, 1932, as a Christian Socialist, was aware of the dangers threatening Austria if the Nazis came into power in Germany, for in the very first proposal of *Mein Kampf* Hitler had declared the union of Austria and Germany to be his primary goal. To strengthen his country Dollfuss used drastic methods. He suspended parliament in March, 1933, ordered Socialist, Communist, and Austrian Nazi organizations dissolved, and proclaimed his intention of unifying the Austrian people under a

8. 1892–1934. First holding ministerial office in 1931, he became chancellor a year later. He opposed the Austrian National Socialists by employing dictatorial methods himself and thus lost the support of the Social Democrats. He staked his foreign policy on friendship with Italy, although this could not save him from assassination in 1934 at the hands of Austrian Nazis in a coup which failed.

single Fatherland Front. Vigorous resistance by the Socialists was put down in February, 1934, when Dollfuss bombarded the Karl Marx Hof, a huge new Socialist housing block in Vienna, and subdued its defenders at a cost of several hundred lives. He announced plans for an authoritarian constitution that would permit the development of a corporate state, more or less on Italian lines. The Austrian Nazis, aided unquestionably by Hitler, attempted a coup in July, 1934, against the government. The tiny chancellor, whose height was one inch below five feet and whose nickname was "Millimetternich," was shot in his office at the Chancellery and left to die. The plot, however, collapsed. The new chancellor, Kurt von Schuschnigg, tried to carry on the Christian Socialist, clerical-fascist traditions of his predecessor, making use of the Father-land Front. The increasingly bitter struggles leading to the eventual surrender of Schuschnigg in 1938 and the absorption of Austria in Hitler's Greater Germany are better treated as part of the diplomatic crisis which culminated in the Second World War.[9]

Dictatorship in Poland and the Baltic countries grew more complete during the 1930's. The death of Marshal Pilsudski in 1935, on the ninth anniversary of the coup by which he had seized power, was followed by the rule of military officers, for Pilsudski had believed that the safety of Poland lay in its armed strength, buttressed by a system of favorable treaties and alliances abroad. How gravely his successor, Marshal Edward Smigly-Rydz, and his fellow officers failed in their task can best be seen later in association with the events leading to the actual outbreak of war in 1939.

The Baltic States moved still further away from their original democratic regimes. The authoritarian constitution set up by President Smetona of Lithuania in 1928 worked well enough for him to be able to deal effectively with the opposition, to be re-elected in 1931 for another seven-year term, and to dissolve in 1935 all the opposition parties. Latvia became a dictatorship in 1934, when Karlis Ulmanis seized power in a bloodless coup, arrested all prominent Socialists, and governed through martial law. Estonia, where fear of communism encouraged the growth of conservative and fascist policies, adopted a constitutional amendment giving large powers to the president in January, 1934. It had earlier been authorized by plebiscite. Konstantin Paets quickly set up a dictatorship under which parliament was prorogued and parties were dissolved. Nevertheless, in 1936 another plebiscite demanded by a three-to-one majority a return to the democratic system. Though the new constitution of 1937 seemed to guarantee democratic liberties, the elections of 1938 gave the National Front of President Paets 63 out of the 80 seats in the legislature. Dictatorship, though evidently of a mild and not unacceptable nature, continued.

9. See pp. 242–244.

Finland, too, where a democratic constitution had been in effect since 1919, ultimately developed a kind of native fascist movement stimulated by fear of Soviet Russia and urging strong, even terrorist, methods against the Finnish Communists. This was known from the village where it first flared up as the Lapua Movement. The government was able to keep both right and left wings under control, and in 1938 the Patriotic National Movement, the spearhead of fascism, was dissolved.

Spain, more dramatically than any other European country save Germany, illustrated in the mid-thirties the militant power of fascism. The Republic which was established in 1931 under the presidency of Alcalá Zamora and the premiership of Manuel Azaña was defined in the new constitution as "a democratic republic of workers of all classes." It launched heavy attacks against what it regarded as the traditional foes: the Church, the great landlords, and the army. Expulsion of the Jesuit Order, the suppression of Church schools, the granting of votes to women, and the expropriation of large estates in the interest of the peasants were accompanied by legislation granting autonomy to Catalonia. The vested interests struck back hard, one consequence being the organization in 1933 of a Fascist Party, the *Falange Española*, under the leadership of a son of Primo de Rivera. The elections of 1933 showed a swing back to the Monarchists, those of February, 1936, a counterswing to the Republicans, among whom a "Popular Front" (*Frente Popular*) government was organized. One of the marked features of the Spanish situation was the decline of the moderates and the ever sharpening conflict between a Fascist right wing and a left wing that was in substantial part Communist. The new Spanish Cortes undertook to remake a society in many respects still medieval, while parliament was under heavy pressure from the Syndicalists and Communists at one extreme and from the Catholics, Monarchists, and generally conservative interests at the other.

A military revolt broke out under these circumstances in Spanish Morocco in July, 1936, accompanied almost simultaneously by other similar revolts in various key areas of Spain. When the original organizer was killed in an air crash, another regular army officer, General Francisco Franco,[10] flew from the Canaries and took command. After some initial successes, Franco established himself at Burgos as "Chief of the Spanish State."[11]

Franco's victories led him to model his regime upon the dictatorships in

---

10. Born in 1892, he became a general at the age of thirty, soon demonstrating a strongly conservative attitude in politics. The Popular Front government of 1936 practically exiled him by making him military governor of the Canaries, whence he returned in the same year to play a leading role in the insurrection against the Republic. Though his corporate state had close affinities with Italian Fascism and German National Socialism, Franco remained nonbelligerent, though hardly neutral, during the Second World War. His subsequent policy was to establish better relations with the United States, to relax somewhat the rigors of his regime, and to keep alive the possibility of a restoration of the monarchy.

11. For details of the Civil War see pp. 239–242.

"GUERNICA." Picasso's famous mural, commissioned by the Spanish Republican government, was begun a week after Hitler's airplanes had totally destroyed the Basque village of Guernica in April, 1937, by machine-gunning and bombing. This allegorical condemnation of fascism and war depicts an assault upon women and children—the very substance of mankind.

Italy and Germany long before the fighting was over. He took the title of "Generalissimo" and, more informally, of *Caudillo,* or leader. In April, 1937, he announced a program based upon the twenty-six points of the Falange. The regime was declared to be totalitarian, one-party, unitary, based on "a military sense of life," anticapitalist, anti-Marxist, and profoundly Catholic. In place of labor unions, "vertical" syndicates of workers and employers on the Italian model were established. Much stress was placed on a dramatic program of public works, as well as upon propaganda and parade. Enormous numbers of political arrests were made, and heavy punishments meted out. There were significant differences, however, from what was done in Italy and Germany. The army, and not the party, was responsible for the seizure of power. The same old privileged groups as under the monarchy—army, aristocracy, and Church—were in positions of authority, and Franco remained on good, if somewhat ambiguous, terms with the exiled dynasty. Much Republican legislation was repealed, autonomy removed from Catalonia, and the old privileges of the Church restored. In foreign matters the links with Germany and Italy soon became close, a striking evidence being Spain's adherence in April, 1939, to Hitler's Anti-Comintern Pact.

Fascist parties were not slow to arise also in democratic countries. In the mid-thirties France, in particular, became the home of many militantly rightist groups—the *Action Française* (founded as early as 1905) being the oldest. Others, in the 1930's, included the *Jeunesse Patriotes,* the *Croix de Feu,* the *Solidarité Française,* and the *Francistes.* Clubs, daggers, colored shirts, patriotic symbols, military parades, and frequent street clashes with the Communists were marks of such movements. In Czechoslovakia—widely regarded as a model of what the new postwar democracies should be—the German-speaking residents of the Sudetenland (those border areas fringing Germany) were organized by their leader Konrad Henlein into a "Home Front" (*Heimatfront*) resembling the Nazis of Hitler's Germany. And even in England during these dangerous years strollers in Hyde Park could listen to Sir Oswald Mosley's black-shirted British Fascists vainly urging their hearers to accept a regime similar to that in Mussolini's Italy. Clearly enough, the pressures of totalitarianism were in evidence everywhere.

■ EFFORTS FOR A DEMOCRATIC GERMANY

The problem of dictatorship in postwar Germany requires careful examination for several reasons. The overthrow of the imperial regime in 1918 led to the creation of the Weimar Republic, a democratic parliamentary state which in all externals was as promising as any in Europe. Defeated Germany, by virtue of its large population, its high technical efficiency in all fields, and its basic industrial capacity, soon rose to a leading position among the powers of the Continent. Hitler's National Socialist regime, nevertheless, proved to be more ruthlessly dictatorial in domestic matters and more flagrantly aggressive in foreign policy than any other European state.

The German military collapse of 1918 produced a chaotic situation. The first revolt among sailors at Kiel on October 28 quickly spread to Hamburg, Bremen, and Lübeck and then began to go inland. As workingmen, soldiers, and sailors started to form revolutionary local councils, the danger appeared imminent that groups on the extreme Left, who took the name of Spartacists from the leader of the great slave revolt in ancient Rome, might set up a German soviet regime in imitation of that in Russia. William II abdicated on November 9, and two days later the military authorities concluded an armistice.

The crisis in Berlin was mastered by the Social Democrats. When the liberal Prince Max of Baden, who had been chancellor since September, resigned on November 9, he turned over his power to Friedrich Ebert[12] and Philip Scheidemann, the leaders of the Majority Socialists, as the principal wing of the Social Democrats was then called. Anxious to forestall the Communists, who were planning to announce a soviet workers' regime in Berlin, Scheidemann proclaimed a German democratic republic on November 9.

---

12. 1871–1925. Of modest working-class origin, in 1913 he became party leader of the Social Democrats in the Reichstag. He supported the war effort, and became chancellor of the Provisional Government when monarchy collapsed in 1918. First president of the Weimar Republic (though he would have preferred a parliamentary monarchy), he suppressed both the leftist revolt of the Spartacists and the rightist "Kapp Putsch." He gave strong, moderate, nonpartisan leadership which did much to stabilize the Republic.

He quickly organized a provisional government of three Majority Socialists and three Independent Socialists with Ebert, a former saddlemaker from Heidelberg, as provisional head. Elections were announced for January to select a constituent assembly which would meet at Weimar and draft a constitution.

The answer of the Communists was to organize an uprising in Berlin in the first weeks of January, 1919. This was crushed by the Provisional Government, aided by regular troops and the Free Corps, these latter being unofficial groups, largely of war veterans, dedicated to various forms of militant nationalism. The two chief revolutionary leaders, Karl Liebknecht and Rosa Luxemburg, were murdered by army officers while being taken to prison. Though further unrest continued in various cities throughout the spring, the first crisis had been mastered.

The National Assembly which met at Weimar on February 6 was dominated by the Social Democrats, joining with the Center Party and the Democratic Party in what came to be known as the "Weimar Coalition." It was hoped that to meet in this historic center of German culture, removed from the turmoil of Berlin and associated with the memories of Goethe and Schiller, would favor the creation of a unified, liberal Germany.[13] The gathering proceeded formally to choose Friedrich Ebert as first president of the German Republic and then turned to the work of writing a constitution. Meanwhile, the government at Berlin had the problem of accepting the treaty terms drawn up by the Allies at Paris. The Scheidemann ministry, rather than sign the treaty, resigned; Gustav Bauer, another Social Democrat, took office and with it assumed the heavy responsibility of signature.

The constitution drawn up by the Weimar Assembly and largely the work of a German professor of law, Hugo Preuss, seemed to many a remarkably promising document. Germany was declared to be a republic in which authority was derived from the people. The president was to be elected for seven years by universal secret ballot. If an absolute majority was not obtained for any candidate on the first ballot, a simple plurality would suffice on the second. An upper chamber, the Reichsrat, was made up of delegates from the various state governments allotted in rough proportion to population. The lower chamber, the Reichstag, was the real source of legislative power and was chosen by universal suffrage for a term of four years under a system of

---

13. The elected deputies, among whom no Communists were found, were grouped as follows:

Social Democrats (Majority Socialists)	163
Independent Socialists	22
Center	89
Democrats (formerly Progressives)	74
People's Party (formerly National Liberals)	22
Nationalists (Conservatives)	42

proportional representation. As each party was given one deputy for every sixty thousand votes it received, the size of the Reichstag fluctuated according to the total vote in each election. The chancellor, who was appointed by the president, required also the confidence of the Reichstag to continue in office. By the famous Article 48, the president could in a state of emergency enact by decrees "the necessary measures to restore public order." In practice, the president could decide what constituted a threat to public order, and this power, sparingly used at first, was so enlarged after 1930 as to undermine some of the foundations of democratic political life.

By reducing the number of states from twenty-five to eighteen, and by substantially enlarging the field of jurisdiction of the federal government, Germany moved further than ever before in the direction of a centralized state. The second part of the constitution, with its generous guarantee of civil rights, its provisions respecting liberty of worship, the right to public education, and the rights of labor, marked it as one of the most enlightened constitutions in Europe.

The prospective dangers, for which the constitution itself could hardly be blamed, were not immediately apparent. The Treaty of Versailles, so hateful to all Germans, was accepted on June 23 by the same government which on July 31 adopted the Weimar Constitution. Unfairly or not, this association could never subsequently be broken. The emergency powers conceded to the president in time gravely undercut the authority of the Reichstag. The preceding regime left a heavy legacy of debt. The tax system was woefully inadequate. The multiplicity of parties, often held as a reproach against the Weimar Republic, must be recognized in all fairness as nothing new. Even so, the complex party system was intensified by proportional representation, so that in the elections of 1930 twenty-three parties were represented. Between February, 1919, and January, 1933, Germany had twelve chancellors, their average term being little more than one year, and twenty-one governments lasting on an average about seven months each. This succession of short-lived governments had to operate in a general atmosphere of increasingly bitter stresses and strains.

■ PROBLEMS OF THE WEIMAR REPUBLIC

The reasons for the failure of the Weimar Republic may be discovered by examining some of the highlights of its history. From the beginning it aroused the lurking misgivings of many Germans who at heart preferred a monarchy. It carried on its shoulders the heavy incubus of the Versailles Treaty. It was closely identified with the immediate postwar unrest, and was threatened by repeated outbursts of violence, such as the Spartacist revolt of January, 1919, in Berlin, the contemporaneous Communist risings in Munich, and the "Kapp Putsch"—an attempted militarist and royal coup in Berlin of March, 1920.

Another threatening feature was the wave of assassinations in which numerous public figures, most lamentably the brilliant Walther Rathenau, were destroyed.

The long struggle over reparations, in the course of which Germany's total indebtedness was again and again placed at a lower figure, has been discussed elsewhere.[14] Reparations, whatever their amount, were a constant reminder of the Versailles Treaty. The matter became closely involved with the great currency inflation which reached a climax in 1923. The German authorities have with some justice been charged with taking measures which accentuated, if they did not actually occasion, the inflationary spiral. At the same time it was easy to associate this inflation with the French occupation of the Ruhr in January, 1923, since the occupation unquestionably and perhaps deliberately contributed to Germany's economic confusions. Before the year's end the inflation had reached fantastic proportions, destroying the savings and investments of countless Germans and playing havoc with the economy. On November 15, 1923, one United States dollar was the equivalent of 4,200,000,-000,000 German marks. Though some speculators thrived, for the most part the German people, especially the workers, whose real wages declined and whose invested union funds were wiped out, suffered gravely. The psychological effect of this sudden destruction of a whole scheme of established values must be obvious.

The death of President Ebert in 1925 occasioned a presidential election which strikingly illustrated the conflicting forces in German political life. None of the seven candidates in the first balloting won the necessary majority. The Socialists then combined with the Democrats to support the Catholic Center's candidate, Wilhelm Marx. The Communist candidate was Ernst Thälmann. The Nationalists and other groups of the Right turned to the seventy-seven-year-old Field Marshal von Hindenburg, hero of the 1914 Battle of Tannenberg, whose memories went back to serving as a lieutenant in the war with Austria in 1866. The election results gave Hindenburg 14.6 million votes; Marx, 13.7 million; and Thälmann, 1.9 million. No one could question the patriotism of the old field marshal, yet how well this loyal servant of imperial Germany could lead and support the Weimar Republic remained to be seen.

The years immediately following 1925 seemed to augur well for the Republic. Germany experienced an extraordinary economic recovery, in no small measure due to the large amounts of foreign capital, especially from America, invested in her thriving industries. The provisional arrangements made under the Dawes Plan (1924–1929), followed by what were expected to be the permanent provisions of the Young Plan (ratified in December, 1929), seemed to indicate that a workable solution of the reparations problem had been reached. The long tenure of Gustav Stresemann at the Foreign Office was productive of

14. See pp. 148–151; 156–157; 161.

the Locarno Treaties of 1925, Germany's entry into the League of Nations in 1926, and her ratification of the Pact of Paris in February, 1929. By 1930 the former Allies had completed their military evacuation of the Rhineland. This seemed, indeed, to be the "Period of Fulfilment" in which a revived Germany would come to hold a large and worthy place in a new, peace-loving Europe.

In contrast to such easy optimism, it is possible to see the threat of storms. Political life had deep divisions. Powerful conservative interests were able to oppose successfully any breaking up of the great Junker estates lying east of the Elbe River. Though outwardly Germany had been disarmed by the Treaty of Versailles, disturbing signs existed. After the withdrawal of the Allied Control Commission from Berlin in 1927, it was not possible to watch closely over German armaments. The organization of a German general staff had been forbidden by the treaty, yet high officers of the old army secretly maintained some nucleus of a staff organization at Potsdam. Labor companies and special police detachments were set up in the army in excess of the 100,000-man limit stipulated in the peace treaty. The army established close links with German industry. Makers of military aircraft, forbidden to operate in the homeland, moved their plants to Switzerland, Denmark, Sweden, and Russia. After the Treaty of Rapallo (April, 1922), arrangements were made with Russia to have German officers train on Russian soil with the Red Army, using tanks and heavy artillery forbidden at home. Few Germans regarded the settlement of their eastern frontiers with Poland as definitive. A deep resentment at the complete loss of Germany's colonies persisted. Even Stresemann, the apostle of "fulfilment," cannot be altogether freed from some secret complicity in these matters of rearmament. At all events, his death in October, 1929, came just at the wrong time, for no later German statesman had links as close with the West. And the international economic crisis, sparked by the disastrous drop on the New York Stock Exchange in the very month of Stresemann's death, led within two years to a world economic depression of major proportions. Against this setting, the rise of Adolf Hitler and National Socialism has to be considered.

■ HITLER AND NATIONAL SOCIALISM

The modern world, which again and again has observed the common man rise to a position of great power, would probably see no great significance in the humble peasant origins of Adolf Hitler and the mediocrity of his early education. More deserving of comment are the neurotic, maladjusted personality of the young Hitler and the nature of his early environment. Born in 1889 in the Austrian frontier town of Braunau, Hitler was not in the narrowly national sense even a German. The self-willed child of a stormy, ignorant household, and a rebel at school, Hitler sought his fortune at Vienna, going there in 1909, at the age of twenty. The well-known stories of his failures as a student of art and architecture, of his nondescript, shiftless life in the doss houses and cafés of Vienna, are of less importance than what he picked up in the political atmosphere of the Austrian capital. Foremost, perhaps, was the violent anti-Semitism which was the stock in trade of certain powerful Viennese political figures. Another was a lurking, unformed sense of the need for a greater Germany. It is indicative of his basic German patriotism that in 1912 Hitler left Austria for Munich, the Bavarian capital, and that in 1914, though still Austrian, he volunteered for service in a Bavarian regiment.

Hitler served during the four years of war. He was wounded twice, gassed, rendered temporarily blind, decorated for bravery, and yet rose only to the rank of corporal. His ardent nationalism was intensified by the bitterness of defeat. "On November 9, 1918," Hitler later wrote in *Mein Kampf*, "I resolved to become a politician." Munich, where Hitler spent the immediate postwar years, was the center of every kind of disillusioned and disaffected group; it was a haven for discharged soldiers accustomed to violence and infected by the bitterness of defeat.

One of these small groups, the German Workers' Party, admitted Hitler in 1919; its size is indicated by the fact that his membership card was number seven. The Party had a confused program of patriotism, anti-Semitism, racial purity, and anticapitalism. By 1920 it changed its name to the National Socialist German Workingmen's Party (*National-Sozialistische Deutsche Arbeiterpartei*), soon abbreviated to the initials N.S.D.A.P., and eventually known by the appellation Nazi. It adopted a muddled Twenty-Five Point Program drawn up by one of its members, Gottfried Feder. This was violently anti-Semitic, full of talk about German soil and German blood, bitterly hostile to the Versailles Treaty, and vaguely anticapitalist, for example, in its denunciation of "interest-slavery." Rapid growth enabled it to acquire a Munich headquarters and a newspaper, the *Völkischer Beobachter*. The famous brown shirt was adopted for its storm troopers; fascist salutes, parades, mass meetings, and increasingly bitter conflicts with the Communists became standard procedure.

While the first membership seemed to come largely from the world's disinherited, other types began to join. Among them was the former German military leader Field Marshal von Ludendorff. Another quickly to gain prominence was Hermann Goering,[15] recently an ace aviator and now a soldier of fortune. Still another was Ernst Röhm, a professional soldier and disreputable

---

15. 1893–1946. A hero of the German air force in the First World War, he took part in Hitler's "Beer Hall Putsch" of 1923. He was president of the Reichstag in 1932, and became air minister and prime minister of Prussia when Hitler came to power in 1933. He founded the Gestapo and headed it for three years, subsequently leaving this post to become virtual dictator of the German economy. One of the most flamboyant and dissolute of the Nazi leaders, he made the *Luftwaffe* an enormously powerful weapon, but was unable to attain victory with it. Sentenced to death at Nuremberg, he committed suicide two hours before his scheduled hanging.

street brawler with an active career in the Free Corps Movement. There were also intellectuals or pseudo-intellectuals such as Dr. Josef Goebbels, a student at seven universities, journalist, skilled orator, and, in time, a master propagandist. Another was Alfred Rosenberg, a Baltic German, educated in Russia and convinced of the great destiny awaiting the German master race. Different again was Heinrich Himmler, once an agricultural student, a hen farmer, and an employee in a Bavarian fertilizer factory, but now destined to play perhaps the most sinister and hated role in all Germany—that of head of the Gestapo, the Nazi secret police. Others, destined to win later notoriety, who joined in these early years were Rudolf Hess, Wilhelm Frick, Robert Ley, and Julius Streicher. Their common quality was a rooted hostility to the conventional world around them, and one is also struck by the unsavory, abnormal character of almost every one.

The first major landmark came in November, 1923, when National Socialists led by Hitler and Ludendorff joined with other dissident groups in Munich and staged their famous "Beer Hall Putsch," an attempt to defy both the government of Bavaria and the Reich government in Berlin. This was to be the beginning of what Hitler proclaimed from a tabletop in a beer cellar as the National Revolution. Its failure left sixteen dead in the street—thereafter the sacred martyrs of the Nazi cause—and committed Hitler to a mild detention in the Landsberg Prison. There, though besieged with visitors, he was able to dictate the text of *Mein Kampf*—the bible of National Socialism.

As the movement grew, it became committed to political action. The elections of May, 1924, sent thirty-two Nazi members to the Reichstag; in December, 1924, the number fell to fourteen; in 1928 the party elected only twelve. Nevertheless, in 1929 the total party membership was 178,000. Hitler's oratory came to have a kind of hypnotic effect on his hearers. As he emerged in the role of unquestioned leader, he began to enunciate his creed with greater emphasis: bitter anti-Semitism; the rearming of Germany and freeing it from "the yoke of Versailles"; militant anti-Communism, this being an attractive consideration for the great German industrialists; and a policy of action intended to be far more speedy and more ruthless than any which would be possible through ordinary parliamentary methods. No one could claim, however, that by 1929 the movement commanded the allegiance of anything approaching a majority of the German people. It was still in essence a marginal, fanatical movement of dissent.

The astonishing transformation of Germany from a parliamentary state into the totalitarian dictatorship of Hitler, within a relatively short period of time, can be ascribed to a variety of reasons. In part it was the result of the unique fanaticism of Hitler and of the skill with which he and his associates seized the opportunities which came to them. It must be attributed further to the inexperience, the failures, and the inherent weaknesses of the Weimar Republic. The transformation must also be explained by the fact that the relatively prosperous years of the late twenties were followed by mounting economic difficulties. These led Herman Mueller, chancellor from June, 1928, to March, 1930, to ask President von Hindenburg for emergency powers. On Hindenburg's refusal, Dr. Heinrich Bruening, the leader of the Center, became chancellor and was very quickly granted the emergency powers denied to his predecessor. It was now possible for Hitler to enlarge his denunciations of the regime. A deadlock over the budget led to a new election (September, 1930) in which Hitler's forces won a sixth of the vote and 107 seats out of a total of 577. One will recall that two years before the Nazis had won only 12 seats. The Social Democrats had now fallen from 153 to 143; the Center rose from 61 to 68; and the Communists on the extreme Left grew from 54 to 77. By January, 1931, the Nazi Party had 400,000 members. Quite clearly the parties of moderation were the true losers; Bruening's government was in reality a minority government.

The economic crisis grew steadily worse; in March, 1931, the French took the lead in blocking the project for an Austro-German customs union. Dr. Bruening was able to govern only by making use of the emergency powers constitutionally granted him by President von Hindenburg. Unemployment rose from 2.2 million in March, 1929, to 6 million in March, 1932. The presidential elections of 1932 were extremely ominous. Hitler decided to run in competition against President von Hindenburg and Thälmann, the Communist candidate. Since Hindenburg narrowly failed to get a clear majority over the others in March, a second election was held in April. The results then were:

Hindenburg	19,300,000 votes	(53.0 percent)
Hitler	13,400,000 "	(36.8 percent)
Thälmann	3,500,000 "	(10.2 percent)

Though the vote was more than sufficient to elect Hindenburg, Hitler in one month had gained over 2 million votes, and these at the expense of the parties of moderation. As a result of some pressure by Kurt von Schleicher, one of the leading generals and an ambitious politician, Hindenburg in May, 1932, asked for Bruening's resignation as chancellor.

For eight months the atmosphere in Germany was one of intense confusion. Hindenburg's first choice as chancellor was now Franz von Papen, an aristocrat closely connected with big industry, a monarchist at heart, and a man with an enormous capacity for intrigue. Von Papen's one achievement in the eyes of the public was the agreement at Lausanne in July, 1932, that

HITLER MAKING A SPEECH. Oratory combined with spectacular pageantry at mass gatherings proved one of Hitler's most effective means of casting his spell over the German people.

German reparations be terminated by paying, after three years, 3 billion reichsmarks (about 700 million dollars) into a general fund for European reconstruction. Despite this, in the Reichstag elections of July the Nazis made a spectacular jump from 107 to 230 seats; and in November, when their popular vote, to be sure, dropped by 2 million, they still elected 196 deputies and were still the largest party in the Reichstag. Following the election, President von Hindenburg was persuaded by General von Schleicher that von Papen's continuation in the chancellorship would mean civil war. Thus, on December 2, von Papen was asked to resign in favor of his colleague.

Von Schleicher had incorrectly assured the president that he could split the Nazi Party. Von Papen was now secretly negotiating with Hitler, who at the opening of 1933 had raised the Nazi Party membership to 900,000; the essence of the negotiation was that Hitler would become chancellor and von Papen vice-chancellor. Hindenburg was assured that von Papen and his friends would be able to keep Hitler under control, especially if the Nazis were kept to a minority in the new ministry. On January 30, 1933—a fateful day in German history—the eighty-five-year-old president offered the chancellorship to Hitler, who accepted. Only three Nazis, Hitler, Goering, and Frick, became members of the cabinet of twelve. This was almost the same number and proportion as in Mussolini's first government of 1922, and it was an equally grim augury for the future prospects of democracy.

■ DICTATORSHIP IN HITLER'S THIRD REICH

The revolutionary techniques by which Hitler took command of Germany are a striking example of the combined use of propaganda, brute force, and intuitive skill. The huge mass meetings, long emotional speeches, and parades represented one aspect; the disciplined organization of the Brown Shirts and the Black Shirts, with their bullying tactics toward the Jews, Communists, and indeed all opposition, represent another. Yet Hitler had taken office in January, 1933, on the invitation of President von Hindenburg and according to the provisions of the Weimar Constitution. The first dramatic act of violence seemed to come from Hitler's opponents, for in February the Reichstag building went up in flames. A young Dutch Communist found in the building was quickly tried and executed for the crime. Many, indeed, suspected that the fire was a "set piece," arranged by the Nazis for their own obvious advantage.[16] At all events, Hitler quickly asked for, and received, emergency powers from the Reichstag.

The elections of March, 1933, gave the following results:

PARTY	VOTES		SEATS	
	(with percent of total)			
National Socialists	17,277,200	(43.9)	288 ⎫	
Nationalists	3,136,800	(8.0)	52 ⎭ 340	
Center	4,424,900	(11.7)	74 ⎫	
Social Democrats	7,181,600	(18.3)	120 ⎬ 194	
Communists	4,848,100	(12.3)	81	
All Others	2,474,400	(5.8)	32	
Total	39,343,000	(100.0)	647	

Even after Hitler had become the master of Germany, it is striking that less than one-half of the electorate (43.9 percent) cast their votes for him, so that only with the aid of the Nationalists, on whom, to be sure, he could confidently count, was he able to push through the measures he desired with some show of legality.

Hitler needed a two-thirds majority in order to pass an act which would give him decree powers. He therefore arrested or excluded the 81 Communist deputies, made pledges to the Nationalists and the Center Party, and thus in the last freely elected German Reichstag easily outvoted the Social Democrats —now without allies—on March 23 by 444 to 94. The Enabling Act, giving

16. Recent evidence, however, seems to confirm the assertion made by Marinus Van der Lubbe at his trial that he set the fire alone as a single-handed act of protest. This would not prevent the Nazis from making use of the fire to denounce all Communists. See ALAN BULLOCK, *Hitler: A Study in Tyranny* (rev. ed., 1962), pp. 262–263.

Hitler decree powers, suspended the Weimar Constitution until April, 1937. No other constitution was introduced to replace it, and henceforth with stark simplicity Hitler promulgated whatever new laws he thought necessary. "The national laws enacted by the national cabinet," declared Article 3 of the Enabling Act, "are prepared by the Chancellor and proclaimed in the *Reichsgesetzblatt [Gazette]*. They take effect, unless otherwise specified, upon the day following their publication. . . ."

The political changes in this Third Reich, which Hitler now regarded as the worthy successor to the medieval empire of the Hohenstaufen and that of Bismarck, can be summarized briefly. The Law for the Reconstruction of the Reich (January, 1934) abolished the legislatures in the various states (*Länder*) and subordinated their administrations to the government at Berlin. All political parties save the National Socialist Party were abolished by a decree of July 14, 1933. Bit by bit, Hitler's cabinet was made completely Nazi, though as a united body it counted for little. When it became clear to Hitler that some of the radical wing of his own followers, especially the "old fighters" who made up the core of storm troopers, were resenting what seemed to them a policy of stabilization, he secretly gathered his strength and struck savagely. All over Germany, on the "Night of the Long Knives" (June 30, 1934), dissident party members were arrested and summarily shot without trial. Among these were Ernst Roehm, storm-troop leader and one of Hitler's oldest friends; former Chancellor von Schleicher and his wife; Gregor Strasser; and hundreds of others. Von Papen, it seems, escaped by accident. At least one innocent victim died because of an unfortunate confusion of names; his body was later returned, with apologies, to his family. Though much worse was to come, this bloody event first demonstrated to Europe the ruthless savagery of the new regime. When President von Hindenburg, who had telegraphed his congratulations to Hitler after the Night of the Long Knives, died in August, 1934, Hitler solved another problem by announcing that henceforth he would combine in himself the offices of president and chancellor—choosing, however, to use a new, combined title, *Führer und Reichskanzler* (Leader and Reich Chancellor). A plebiscite, significant of the new temper in Germany, confirmed this title by 88.2 percent of the 43.5 million votes cast.

An economic transformation of Germany was also undertaken. All labor unions were abolished by a decree of July 14, 1933. Every German worker was considered to be part of one vast organization known as the Labor Front. The National Labor Law of January 20, 1934, brought state control over all businesses employing more than twenty persons. A Reich Labor Service Law of June, 1935, made labor service obligatory (for a term later fixed at six months) for all men between the ages of eighteen and twenty-five. Gradually control was exercised over large industry. Many state enterprises were launched with the goal of German self-sufficiency (*Autarkie*); foreign trade and foreign exchange were controlled and manipulated; and a Four-Year Plan was announced in September, 1936, intended to make Germany self-sufficient in basic raw materials. An outstanding example of the new economic techniques was the organization of iron and steel manufacture in the Hermann Goering Works. Created in 1937, this was the largest industrial combination in Europe.

A new and utterly ruthless police state emerged in Germany. The brown-shirted storm troopers, the *Sturmabteilungen,* elaborately organized to extend from the highest ranks of the party down to the tiny group responsible for supervising a single city block, lost much of their importance after the blood purge of June, 1934. On the other hand the black-shirted S.S. formations—the *Schutzstaffeln,* or security forces—made up an elite guard fanatically devoted to Hitler and everywhere in evidence. The Gestapo, or *Geheime Staatspolizei,* established and led by Himmler, can truly be described as one of the most vicious secret-police organizations the world had seen. A propaganda machine of enormous power was elaborated by Dr. Goebbels.

Education, from kindergarten to university, became disciplined and transformed. Boys were organized in the Hitler Youth, girls in the Hitler Maidens. School textbooks were rewritten along Nazi lines. University professors were required to wear the brown shirt and swastika, and to open their lectures with a *Heil Hitler!* Special schools were set up to train a youthful elite as leaders of the new Germany.

A concordat with the Roman Catholic Church, signed in July, 1933, during the first months of the Hitler regime, guaranteed the Church many of its historic rights, including the right to conduct parochial schools. Actually it led to persistent Nazi meddling. Many German Catholic leaders denounced Hitler's attacks on the Jews, and in 1937 Pope Pius XI issued the encyclical known, from its opening words, as *Mit Brennender Sorge* (With Burning Care), condemning doctrines of state and racial superiority. Protestant leaders, too, were opposed when Hitler tried with mediocre success to set up a so-called German Christian Movement in control of the newly united German Evangelical Church. This opposition grew even more vigorous when extreme Nazi fanatics began a deliberate policy of dechristianization and actually organized the German Faith Movement with pagan rites and ceremonies.

Anti-Semitism had been a major ingredient of the Nazi program from its beginnings. Once in power, Hitler converted his tireless denunciation of the Jews into a savage program of action. Jews were dismissed in April, 1933, from public service and the universities and were debarred from entering any profession. It sufficed, to be counted as a Jew, to have one non-Aryan grandparent. The Nuremberg Laws of September, 1935, forbade marriage between Jews and "persons of German blood" and deprived Jews of all political and civic rights and privileges. When a young Jewish boy assassinated a German embassy official in Paris in November, 1938, a wave of anti-Jewish rioting (encouraged by the Gestapo) was set off all over Germany. Synagogues were burned, Jewish businesses looted and destroyed, and many people were killed or seriously injured. Wealthy Jews had their property confiscated under various pretexts and were sent to concentration camps, which were brutal enough, though not as yet the gruesome centers of extermination that they were to become during the war.

The remilitarization of Germany in order to "break the bonds of Versailles" goes a long way to explain the strong support given Hitler by the professional officer class. New factories were built, as much to provide the essential tools of war as for any other purpose; and Hitler's famous network of new roads, the *Autobahnen,* was essentially strategic in plan. The announced goal of *Autarkie,* or self-sufficiency, likewise had a clear military implication. Unemployment in these circumstances fell from over six million in 1932 to one million in 1936, Hitler taking full credit for an achievement which had been beyond the capacities of any of his predecessors. Much of the prosperity, nevertheless, must be described as artificial, and the German economy was truly a *Wehrwirtschaft*—an economy geared to war.

That Germany would chart a new course in foreign policy was also apparent. She withdrew from the Geneva Disarmament Conference in October, 1933, protesting against the unwillingness of other highly armed states to disarm. A week later Hitler gave notice that he was withdrawing from the League of Nations itself. The 93 percent vote of approval for this withdrawal in the German general elections of November, 1933, indicates the widespread support for this new policy. Similarly, when the Saar voted overwhelmingly in January, 1935, to return to Germany, this action could also be regarded as a further victory for Hitler. His propaganda in the small but to him vital Saar Province had been intensive.

By the mid-thirties it was clear that a totalitarian state of enormous power had come into being in Germany, far surpassing what Mussolini had been able to achieve in Italy, and equaled in strength only by Soviet Russia. Beside it the lesser dictatorships seemed puny indeed, and much of Russia's military strength was as yet untested and unknown. Hitler's Germany stood out above all others as the supreme example of the repudiation of democracy and the triumph of the age-old doctrine of force.

Reading List: Chapter 7

Smith, D. M., *Italy: A Modern History* (1959), chs. 39–46. The growth of Fascism to 1925.

Carsten, F. L., "The Failure of the Weimar Republic," *History Today*, vol. VI (1956), no. 5.

Gatzke, H. W., "Russo-German Military Collaboration During the Weimar Republic," *American Historical Review*, vol. LXIII (1958), no. 3. A significant side issue.

Bullock, A., *Hitler: A Study in Tyranny* (rev. ed., 1962, also paperback), chs. 2–4. The rise to power.

Watt, D. C., "Hitler Comes to Power," *History Today*, vol. XIII (1963), no. 3.

Carsten, F. L., "The German Generals and Hitler," *History Today*, vol. VIII (1958), no. 8.

Gatzke, H. W., "Gustav Stresemann: A Bibliographical Article," *Journal of Modern History*, vol. XXXVI (1964), no. 1. Examines the recent documents to show that Stresemann was more of a "good German" than a "good European."

Epstein, K., "The Nazi Consolidation of Power," *Journal of Modern History*, vol. XXXIV (1962), no. 1. A review article demonstrating the techniques used by Hitler to establish his rule in Germany.

Chapter 8

The Development of the U.S.S.R.

The Russian Enigma
The New Economic Policy
The Constitution of 1924
The Mantle of Lenin
The Five-Year Plans
The New Soviet Society
The New Constitution of 1936, the Party, and the Purges
Russia and the World

■ THE RUSSIAN ENIGMA

Just as the Communist Revolution in Russia was the most important result in Europe of the First World War, so likewise the vigorous growth of the new Russia from the position of almost mortal weakness reached in 1921 was the most important European phenomenon of the 1920's and 1930's. For the new-found strength of the Russian state and economy was vital to the defeat of German ambitions in the Second World War, and the further development of that strength afterwards provided a very formidable rival to the world leadership of the United States. In addition, the socialist basis of the new Russia presented capitalist societies great and small with a double challenge—one being the success of Russian planning in general and the other arising from Russia's ability to avoid trade depressions accompanied by the social scourge of mass unemployment.

SIGNIFICANT EVENTS

1921	New Economic Policy introduced
1924	Death of Lenin
1927	Trotsky expelled from Communist Party
1928–1932	First Five-Year Plan
1933–1937	Second Five-Year Plan
1934	Assassination of Kirov
1935	Franco-Soviet Defense Pact signed
1936	"Stalin Constitution" approved
1936–1938	Period of the great purges

It would be quite wrong, however, to suppose that the thoughts of contemporary Europe and America were keenly and steadily directed to the Russian experiment, as it was so often called, or that its ultimate success was conceded. On the contrary, for at least ten years the final breakdown of the Soviet regime was still commonly anticipated: the United States government, for instance, did not accord formal recognition until 1933. Such expectations were encouraged by the prevalent ignorance and prejudice regarding every aspect of Russian life. Few foreign journalists were regularly stationed in the country, still fewer reported objectively, and such visitors as obtained facilities for extended study were usually prejudiced sympathizers like the English Fabian publicists, Sidney and Beatrice Webb. On the other hand, it was true then as now that Russian expatriates leaned usually in the opposite direction, denigrating everything they had left behind so as to justify their leaving it.

These facts make it difficult even now to offer a balanced picture of the internal development of a huge country in a condition of rapid change. But it is even more important to bear them in mind in relation to the external policy of the Soviet government, which was largely influenced by its awareness of a profound distrust abroad which it resented—and reciprocated. The words of an American observer, written in the very middle of the period now to be studied, describe the position clearly:

> The Soviet Government . . . may refrain from offensive tactics, but that the sympathy of its leaders is on the side of revolution cannot be gainsaid. . . . Undoubtedly, capitalist governments would be justified in boycotting and ostracizing the Soviet Union. It is an anomaly that relations exist between Moscow and bourgeois capitals. They exist because capitalist states are divided among themselves, and, more significantly, because the outside world cannot get along without Russia nor neglect her. She is a potent, realistic force to be reckoned with in practical politics. She is there. To keep her beyond the pale may be fine principle, but poor policy.[1]

■ THE NEW ECONOMIC POLICY

Russia had emerged from the Civil War in a condition of desperate poverty against which even the most loyal elements of the population were disposed to revolt.[2] The situation was made all the more dangerous by the effects of War Communism, that complete break with the whole of the capitalist economic system which Lenin had fostered since 1917 as an essential part of the Revolution. In industry, the progressive extension of nationalization to any power-using concern with more than five workers had coincided with a decline in production to less than one-seventh of the prewar level. In agriculture, by 1921 no less than one-third of the land which was tilled in 1916 had been allowed to go out of cultivation, the stock of horses and cattle had been reduced by a quarter, and the country stood face to face with the first of two famine years which cost twice as many Russian lives as the World War had cost. The last and one of the most momentous of Lenin's major acts of leadership in 1921 was to announce baldly to the Communist Party Congress his famous New Economic Policy: "Everything must be set aside to increase production."

Although Lenin suffered his first stroke in May of the following year, by that time he had given a decisive impetus to the policy which made the Russia of the 1920's into a strange hybrid of capitalism and socialism. The main feature was the conciliation of the peasantry by abolishing the levies which had in principle confiscated for government use all grain in excess of the peasant's household needs and his planting requirements. Instead, he paid an assessment

---

1. LOUIS FISCHER, *The Soviets and World Affairs* (1930), vol. II, p. 692.
2. See pp. 58–60.

in kind or, later, in money, and the rest of the crop was his to dispose of as he pleased. But if the peasant was to sell, he must also be allowed to buy. Accordingly, the New Economic Policy allowed small-scale industry and internal commerce to revert largely to private hands. The so-called "nepmen," some of whom had no doubt traded illegally before, quickly became a very numerous and active body. In 1923–1924 one-quarter of all industrial production was by private enterprise (including foreign concessions); two years later, when total production had doubled, the private enterprise sector was still almost one-fifth. To service the new system a state bank was set up and a rouble currency restored which was eventually based on gold; conversely, the state ceased to supply industry with free equipment or whole sections of the population with free goods—two practices which had been tried out under War Communism.

The result was a recovery which brought Russia back from the verge of catastrophe to somewhere near its prewar level of productivity. By 1927 the area under cultivation was almost exactly the same as in 1916. Total industrial production had a slightly increased value, and there were small rises in the quantities of coal, oil, and cotton material. Foreign trade was one of the "commanding heights" which the state had retained under its own direct control; consequently the state was itself directly responsible for concessions made to foreign capitalist interests. Other "commanding heights" were the continued state ownership of transport and heavy industry in general—including, for example, the first of the great new electric power stations which had been urgently demanded by Lenin—and overall supervision of the economy through the Gosplan, or state planning commission. The outside world, however, for the most part interpreted the adoption of the New Economic Policy as a sign of weakness, and regarded its successes as so many indications that the Russian black sheep was in process of returning to the capitalist fold.

In consequence Soviet foreign policy of these years was marked by a partial resumption of amicable relations with the capitalist powers of Europe, who were in many cases disposed to turn a blind eye to the subversive activities of the Comintern[3] if the Russian market could be redeveloped so as to stimulate the flagging European economy. Moreover, Trotsky's successor as foreign minister, Georghy Chicherin, who had been a diplomat before he became a revolutionary, was well suited to tasks of conciliation. As early as March, 1921, a trade agreement was negotiated with Britain, and in the following year a meeting of thirty-one states was held at Genoa. Here Chicherin tried to arrange full recognition of the Soviets as the lawful government of Russia and the granting of the large-scale commercial credits which they urgently needed. In return, Russia would accept responsibility for prewar debts and for the value

3. See pp. 56–58; 102; 105.

of foreign property confiscated during the Revolution. The breakdown of this first attempt at a general agreement was in two respects significant. The capitalist powers were divided among themselves, the French caring chiefly for the debts of the past and the British for the trade of the future, while the Americans (who attended the conference only as observers) objected strongly to the private scheming of the British to get a monopoly of Russian oil. Equally significant in these otherwise abortive negotiations was the unexpected rapprochement between Russia and Germany. By the Treaty of Rapallo (April, 1922) the German foreign minister, Walther Rathenau, conceded to Russia full recognition as well as credits for the purchase of German machinery and equipment. In return he secured a friendship which rescued the new German Republic from total isolation and he facilitated the elaboration of existing secret arrangements by which forbidden armaments, ranging from military airplanes to poison gas, were made in Russian factories for German use.

In February, 1924, the first British Labor government was prompt to give *de jure* recognition to the Soviet authorities, and its example was quickly followed by other European powers. Early in 1925 Russia made a treaty with the Japanese, who had stayed on in eastern Siberia for a time after the end of the Civil War and had occupied northern Sakhalin as a reprisal for a massacre by Communist guerrillas; they now relinquished this part of the island, except for coal and oil concessions, returning in general to the arrangements made at the Treaty of Portsmouth twenty years earlier. The United States was the only major power which still refused recognition, but this did not prevent the growth of Russo-American trade on an unofficial basis; by 1927 it was twice as large as before the war.

Despite these steps, however, capitalist-Communist relations did not run smoothly. On the one hand, the Soviet government remained immensely suspicious of all outside influences, even that of the American Relief Administration which supplied free food to ten million persons during the famine years from 1921 to 1923. On the other hand, the western powers were always afraid that the trade contacts which they desired to foster provided a cloak for subversive activities, conducted inside their territory by the Comintern[4] and other agents of Communist infiltration. As will be shown later, the main Communist efforts at this time were directed to the Far East; even so, support was given to the general strike and the coal strike in Britain, causing Anglo-Russian relations to be broken off again between 1927 and 1929.

It is not surprising that under the circumstances economic difficulties continued. Lenin's New Economic Policy failed to provide an adequate inflow of foreign capital. Past losses made investors hesitate, and the Russian authorities were inclined to find their projects unsuitable or inadequately financed.

4. See pp. 56–58; 102; 105.

The consequence was that the stability of the economy, not to mention the prospect of its expansion, was disturbed by a growing disparity between agricultural and industrial prices—a phenomenon graphically termed "the scissors." The recovery in Soviet agriculture had been the achievement of the richer peasants, those who commonly hired labor, and of the middle peasants, roughly equivalent to the English smallholder, while the third class, those with dwarf holdings or none, were left to survive as best they could. Throughout the period farming methods improved little; a lot of hard work was done by the peasantry for a time in order to produce a sufficient surplus for buying the manufactured goods which would give them a higher standard of life. For want of foreign capital, however, industry did not expand enough to meet their demands; industrial goods continued to be expensive. The peasant accordingly saw no benefit to himself in expanded production; instead, he hoarded his grain and began to relapse into the earlier policy of growing just enough for his own use and for his inescapable share of taxes.

The New Economic Policy had been designed by Lenin for a period of national convalescence. He had died (January, 1924) when it was barely under way. Now that this national convalescence was over, the alternatives for Russia were a period of stagnation or the agonies of a second and very different revolution. The choice of the latter alternative will be forever associated with the name of Stalin, "the Man of Steel," whose rise to power during these years is a development momentous enough to warrant separate consideration. First, however, the constitution which gave permanent form to the Soviet Union must be analyzed.

■ THE CONSTITUTION OF 1924

In the month of Lenin's death the Second All-Union Congress ratified a new constitution, which had been approved by the Communist Party in the previous year. The main object was formally to extend to the whole area now under Soviet authority the system of government set up in July, 1918, for the more restricted area of the original Russian Soviet Federated Socialist Republic. The R.S.F.S.R. was accordingly linked with the Ukraine and Byelorussia (White Russia) on its western flank and with Transcaucasia to the southward in a union of four nominally equal republics. These together formed the Union of Soviet Socialist Republics or U.S.S.R.; three other republics (Turkmen, Uzbek, and Tajik) carved out of the R.S.F.S.R. brought the total of constituent republics by 1929 to seven. The Union was designed as a centralized structure, each republic being made subject to the All-Union Congress of Soviets as a formal parliamentary authority and to the All-Union Council of People's Commissars. These were the ministers who controlled each branch of administration either directly or, in the less important cases, through other commissars appointed by the constituent republics. The central executive and legislative authority was further supported by the All-Union Political Police (Ogpu), and a new supreme court which had power to enforce the laws of the Union against those made by the different republics.

The pyramid of representation was indeed an elaborate edifice, since every village soviet took part in the first of a whole series of elections which went on successively in areas of increasing size and led ultimately to the formation of the All-Union Congress of Soviets. This body of some 2,000 members elected a bicameral Executive Committee (really much more than a "committee"), comprised of the Soviet of the Union and the Soviet of Nationalities, which were to represent population and national regions respectively and which in size were comparable to the United States Congress. The Executive Committee in turn was nominally responsible for choosing both the official head of the state, who was the chairman of its presidential body or Praesidium, and the members of the all-important Council of People's Commissars.

The underlying reality, however, was still the power wielded by the Communist Party. No other party organization could have any legal existence. Those who survived from the upper and middle classes of the old regime, ranging from private businessmen to ecclesiastics and ex-policemen—the people most likely to form a separate interest-group—remained disfranchised. The workers of the towns—the people most likely to belong to or support the Communist Party—each counted for as much as five peasant voters in the election of soviets at the higher levels. Since all elections were made by open voting, and since at all the higher levels the vote was exercised only by members of soviets, the maximum incentive existed to vote for the official candidate, who was put forward by the Communist Party. The Party Congress, which did not meet every year, was therefore a more important event than the annual meeting of the All-Union Congress of Soviets; and the Party's central committee remained the ultimate repository of power. An inner ring within that committee, the Political Bureau (Politburo), with only half a dozen members, was the final arbiter of Soviet policy, assisted in matters of organization by a second group of similar size (the Orgburo), which settled the placing of individuals inside the vast bureaucracy.

At the tenth Party Congress in March, 1921, when Lenin was about to launch the New Economic Policy, he had demanded unity in the face of crisis: "An atmosphere of controversy becomes in the highest degree dangerous and poses a direct threat to the dictatorship of the proletariat. . . . We shall not be able to act without a maximum closing of ranks."[5] The sequel was the first major purging of the Party, in which 200,000 were excluded out of a total

5. Speech of March 8, 1921, quoted by J. D. CLARKSON, *History of Russia from the Ninth Century* (1961), p. 549.

membership of 730,000. Proposals for a syndicalist system, in which the workers themselves would control industry, were completely crushed, but a paradoxical result of Lenin's call for unity was that by the time of his death less than half the members of the Party which had brought into being the dictatorship of the proletariat in Russia were themselves proletarians in the sense that they had at any period been actual workers. Thus the stage was set for a power struggle which was complicated and prolonged by the fact that the democratic façade of the constitution concealed the nature and workings of an inner conflict of ideologies, programs, and personalities.

■ THE MANTLE OF LENIN

Lenin's mantle was not quickly to be assumed by any of the contestants for power. Trotsky was unquestionably second only to Lenin in the services he had rendered to the Communist Revolution, whether in the critical days of November, 1917, in the negotiations with the Germans at Brest Litovsk, or as the commissar who turned the tide of civil war. Since 1905 he had believed in the "permanency" of revolution, its advance from the antifeudal to the anticapitalist phase, and its irresistible spread from Russia to the world. It was true that he was a latecomer to the Communist Party, that he was a typically middle-class Jewish intellectual, and that he had incurred the displeasure of Lenin by suggesting a further regimentation of the workers as an alternative to his New Economic Policy. But he was the most eloquent and incisive writer and speaker who was left to take Lenin's place; as commissar for war he enjoyed great prestige with the army; and he was in all appearance securely entrenched in power as a policy-maker in the inner ring of party leaders who constituted the Politburo. Yet in the autumn of 1923, when Lenin lay dying, Trotsky's position was already so far weakened that he had complained openly of the rigid control from above over "the broad mass of the Party, for whom every decision represents a summons or a command." The result was his condemnation by the next Party Congress for "petty-bourgeois deviation" and his own admission that it was "impossible to be correct against the Party." Trotsky had embarked upon a losing battle, which ended only with his assassination by a Party member sixteen years later in far-off Mexico City.

It is an easy oversimplification to contrast the intellectual brilliance and arrogant tongue of Trotsky with the peasant shrewdness and devious ways of his successful rival, Josef Stalin. Alone among the prerevolutionary Old Bolsheviks, as they were called, Stalin had always taken the Leninist line, with the result that this commissar of nationalities had been rewarded in April, 1922, by appointment to the new office of general secretary of the Party. He was already deeply involved in the work of party organization as being the only member of the all-powerful policy-making Politburo who had also served throughout in the irksome administrative tasks of the Orgburo. Now in his new capacity as general secretary he secured control of all Party appointments down to county level. This was the situation against which Trotsky protested in vain, while the domineering attitude which it fostered in Stalin was belatedly denounced by Lenin himself in a codicil to his will which was not officially published until thirty years later:

> Stalin is too rough, and this fault, quite tolerable among ourselves and in dealings between us Communists, becomes intolerable in the office of General Secretary. Therefore I suggest that the comrades think of some means of displacing Stalin from this position and of naming in his stead some other man who . . . will be more tolerant, more loyal, more polite and more considerate toward comrades, less capricious, etc.

When Lenin was finally incapacitated by illness, he had just embarked with Trotsky's support upon a polemic against Stalin for his unnecessarily harsh treatment of his fellow Georgians on account of their ebullient nationalism. But even before his death, power fell into the hands of a triumvirate, in which Stalin allied himself with Lev Kamenev[6] and Grigori Zinoviev,[7] two very early supporters of Lenin who had nevertheless flinched from the risks of the supreme crisis in November, 1917. These three held together against Trotsky, whose position they undermined by quoting him as an opponent of Lenin's teachings: non-Communists might have agreed with Trotsky, but he was too loyal to appeal to outside elements against the Party. When Lenin died the triumvirs further strengthened their position by filling the vacancy in the Politburo with Nikolai Bukharin,[8] who, though the leading Marxist theoretician and the editor of *Pravda*, was suitably malleable in practical affairs. Trotsky was then provoked into writing an unanswerable pamphlet, *The Lessons of October*, which in analyzing the implications of the Communist seizure of power reminded its readers indirectly of the dubious part played in it by two of the triumvirs. The resulting scandal gave the Central Committee of the Party an excuse to remove him from his post as commissar for war.

6. 1883–1936. A Bolshevik since 1903, he returned from Siberia at the outbreak of the first revolution in 1917. His arrest was ordered by Kerensky along with that of Lenin in July. He favored co-operation of all socialists rather than Lenin's coup of November, 1917, but was made president of the Moscow Soviet in 1918, an original member of the Politburo, and vice-chairman of the Council of Commissars. He married Trotsky's sister, and was eventually executed as a "Trotskyist terrorist of the Left Opposition."

7. 1883–1936. A Bolshevik since 1903, a Jew and a brilliant writer, he returned with Lenin from exile in April, 1917. His arrest was ordered by Kerensky in July. He opposed Lenin's November coup and even betrayed it to the press, but became president of the Comintern in 1919 and a member of the Politburo in 1921. He was the most important figure in the "Left Opposition" and was executed as such in 1936.

8. 1888–1938. An early Bolshevik who had edited *Pravda* in Austria and *Novy Mir* in New York City before returning to Russia during the Revolution. He was co-author of *The ABC of Communism* (1921) and changed from "Left Opposition" to "Right Opposition" in 1927. He helped to draft the constitution of 1936; he was executed after confessing to crimes of treason, espionage, diversionism, wrecking, and attempted murder.

This was the beginning of the end for Trotsky, but he was not fated to fall alone. The almost immediate sequel was an attack by Stalin upon his two helpers, Kamenev and Zinoviev, who by criticizing the favor shown to the wealthier peasantry in the interpretation of the New Economic Policy had laid themselves open to a charge of "Social-Democratic deviation." In 1927 when Trotsky and seventy-five of his principal followers were formally expelled from the Party, Kamenev, Zinoviev, and others of the "Left Opposition" quickly capitulated to Stalin's view and were duly readmitted. More surprising is the fact that a similar attack was directed soon afterwards against the "Right Opposition," as a result of which Bukharin lost his position together with two other party stalwarts who had earlier rallied with him to the support of Stalin. Thus Stalin was eventually left in unchallenged control of the Party and its beliefs, at the end of maneuvers which seem all the more ruthless because of their striking resemblance to the pattern of events in France during the Reign of Terror, when Robespierre moved first against the extremists and then against the moderates.

Nevertheless it would be a mistake to think that the conflict between Stalin and Trotsky was nothing more than a naked struggle for power. Both leaders were aware that a fully Communist society could only be established on an international basis and in a remote future; for the time being Russia must live by compromising with world conditions which had failed to change. But Trotsky as an opposition leader and brilliant theorist was disposed to maintain the disquieting proposition that somehow world revolution must come, while Stalin found the arguments for "socialism in one country" convincing because as a practical man he saw the need to give Russia a sense of achievement.

The final quarrel of Stalin and Trotsky in 1927 arose in part from the latter's denunciation of the failure to foster world revolution by what he would have regarded as appropriate action in the Far East. This episode may therefore be cited as an illustration. After the recovery of its territories in eastern Siberia, the Soviet government had succeeded in maintaining a disguised protectorate over Outer Mongolia and had made a working arrangement with China for joint control of the Chinese Eastern Railway providing a short cut across Manchuria to Vladivostok. Accordingly, Russia operating through the international machinery of the Comintern was in a good position to use for Communist ends the Chinese anti-European movement known as the Kuomintang. Though Sun Yat-sen was not a Communist, he had been an admirer of Lenin, and in the year of Lenin's death the movement was supplied with a Russian Communist adviser, Michael Borodin, together with about a thousand political and military instructors and a subsidy of three million dollars. For about two years all went well from the Communist standpoint, as the Nationalist Chinese armies advanced to Hankow and Nanking, producing formidable demonstrations against foreign goods and territorial concessions and even encouraging the Comintern to organize a short-lived rising in the Netherlands East Indies.

In 1927 the dream quickly faded. General Chiang Kai-shek challenged the ascendancy of Borodin over the Communist wing of the Kuomintang. An attempt on his part to organize a purely Communist regime was foiled in Hankow, and a second Communist rising in Canton was suppressed by Nationalist forces, which executed the leaders, including some Russians. Thus Stalin was compelled for the time being to abandon hopes of a Communist revolution in China, the failure being attributed by Trotsky to a theoretically incorrect acceptance of collaboration with a middle-class, nationally-minded leadership.

Stalin, as we have seen, met Trotsky's dogma of "permanent revolution," implying perseverance in spreading communism in foreign countries, however uphill the struggle might be, by an easier doctrine. He taught that reverses in the sphere of communist foreign policy were relatively insignificant, because it was quite feasible to establish "socialism in one country." In saying this he contradicted not only Lenin but the line he had himself taken as recently as the first months of 1924. The proposition involved many serious difficulties. One was the stubborn opposition the peasants were showing to collectivism. Another was the proven inability of Russia to catch up with the industrialization of her capitalist rivals. Still another was the improbability that a socialist Russia could survive indefinitely at a lower standard of living than that of her rivals. Furthermore, it seemed likely that under conditions of continued scarcity the growth of new inequalities between classes would defeat the whole purpose of socialism. But Stalin was not a deep thinker, interested in the intellectual validity of the propositions he advanced. He was primarily concerned with the psychological impact of a slogan which encouraged self-confidence, banished the need to rely further upon international happenings which had so often failed to help, and justified the Party in concentrating wholeheartedly upon the task of building the socialist state in what was after all one-sixth of the world.

In 1929 Trotsky was banished, and spent the remaining years of his life successively in Turkey, Norway, and Mexico. Though he tried to organize a Fourth International of anti-Stalinists, his later significance was chiefly as a traitor with whose cause it was convenient to identify every enemy of Stalinism. The main problem for Stalin was not that of his fallen opponent; it was that of the enormous contrast between the ideal of "socialism in one country" and the existing situation. In January, 1928, government purchases of grain fell two million tons below the minimum needs of the urban population. To overcome the reluctance and inefficiency of the peasants would require a second revolution, for which Stalin had made no preparations and of which he could not pause even to count the cost. Yet his prestige was such that his fiftieth birthday in December of the following year was to be greeted with the slogan, "Stalin is the Lenin of today," which for a quarter of a century continued to reverberate through Russia and beyond.

■ THE FIVE-YEAR PLANS

Since the onset of the great depression in 1929, every civilized power has come to assume wide responsibilities over the economic life of its citizens. It is therefore difficult nowadays to realize the novelty of the elaborate economic planning which Russia designed before the depression—quite unparalleled in the peacetime history of other governments, fundamental in its transformation of the existing Russian system, and comprehensive in its extension to every aspect of the economy. Moreover, the Russian state achieved more rapid changes than had proved possible for private enterprise working elsewhere under better conditions of labor recruitment and with easy access to foreign capital. In the period 1900–1906, when the increase of manufacturing production in the United States was most rapid, the annual average increase was 9 percent, whereas Russia claimed an official average of 29 percent under the first Five-Year Plan, which even sceptical foreign economists do not reduce below a cumulative rate of 13.5 percent for the whole of the period 1928–1937. As for the savings which made expansion possible, whereas in the United States these had amounted to a little more than 14 percent of income, Russia claimed to reach a peak of 31 percent in 1929–1930 and is generally agreed to have saved at least 20 percent throughout the decade then opening.

To a great extent this economic advance was the personal achievement of Stalin, who had announced, "We are fifty and a hundred years behind the advanced countries. We must cover this stretch in ten years." His will was translated into terms of economic aims and methods by a state planning commission (Gosplan) dating from 1921, which in the period of the New Economic Policy had been chiefly concerned with computing results year by year so as to control the activities of state enterprises. Its objective now was to change the balance between production and consumption, so as to accumulate at home the capital which Russia had proved unable to obtain from abroad and which was nevertheless essential for any large-scale purchase of industrial equipment. Capital had to be obtained from the Russian people by rigorously curtailing the satisfaction of their most urgent needs. Two-thirds of the resulting increase was to be in the basic machinery of production, one-third only in consumer goods. So far, so good, but when the planners went on to reduce their expectations through taking account of the probable incidence of crop failure, friction over foreign trade dealings, and the need to keep up quality while increasing quantity of output, Stalin swept aside their provisos; he required the plan to be based on ideal conditions which everybody knew could not be fulfilled. In other words the plan, which the Russians flippantly called *piatiletka* ("five-yearie"), emerged as a psychological device or propaganda trick, designed to fire the imagination and encourage an unlimited effort over a limited period. This period, as the sequel showed, could be lengthened, shortened, or renewed at the government's discretion.

The program of industrialization, launched in October, 1928, was preceded in the summer of the same year by the commencement of emergency measures against the *kulaks*, or wealthier peasants, to force them to disgorge hoarded supplies of grain for the use of the towns. In the plan this movement found expression in a modest proposal for converting up to 20 percent of farms to collectivization by 1933. But Stalin was carried away by the tide of events, with the result that the agrarian struggle came to be the aspect of the first Five-Year Plan on which its success seemed to turn. The poorest peasants stood to gain from admission to a collective farm or *kolkhoz*, the richest stood to lose, a middle group was undetermined in its attitude. The government at first believed that its wishes were generally acceptable, then found that the *kulaks* were practicing passive resistance, which it resolved to crush.

The secret police led minor military operations in disaffected regions; *kulak* families were dispossessed of their property and sentenced to forced labor or deported to unpeopled districts in Siberia. Not surprisingly the *kulaks* took what revenge they could by destroying their produce, implements, and especially livestock, of which the total supply was reduced in five years by more than half. In March, 1930, the situation was so desperate that Stalin temporarily released the pressure, issuing a statement which reproached his subordinates with excesses which had been caused, he said, by "dizziness with success." He soon resumed his intended course, so that in spite of a serious crop failure and famine in 1932, by the following year collectivization had triumphed, at an estimated cost of some five million human lives.

Between the agricultural and the industrial changes, many links are to be noticed. The organization of the collective farm, to be described in detail later, brought the life and outlook of the peasant into closer harmony with those of the worker in the town. The larger unit being easier to control, the flow of grain from the country to the towns could at last be properly organized. As collective agriculture was in the main more efficient, it was possible to provide enough food for the towns while transferring a large part of the rural population to urban industrial employment. Finally, direct interaction occurred between agriculture and industry through the dependence of the farms upon a supply of tractors as the chief step in the drive for efficiency. The provision of tractors and other agricultural machines, of which the first year's output was thirty thousand, was regarded as an important industrial objective, and the concentration of the hiring-out of tractors in the hands of a special state agency made it easy to influence the work done in agriculture. At one time 25,000 urban Communists were sent to work with the state tractor stations in order to excite the rural population to maximum efforts; by 1933, 200,000 tractors were in use and the principal grain districts had 25,000 combines.

In industry the first Five-Year Plan proposed to invest in economic expansion a sum nearly twenty times as large as the entire prewar investment of Russian industry; this amount was about two and a half times what had been spent on economic expansion in the five years before the plan came into force. The main object was to be a threefold increase in heavy industry and a fivefold increase in electricity, while the supply of consumer goods would increase much more slowly. The plan was nominally completed in four and a half years, with 92.5 percent of the planned quantities achieved. All did not run smoothly, however. The deficiency was probably rather greater than stated, and certainly a marked falling-off occurred in the quality of goods produced. Moreover, the persecution of the *kulaks* had its counterpart in the towns. Relief payments to able-bodied unemployed were ended. As real wages declined, trade-union activities were diverted from defending workers' interests to developing incentives for higher output. Whatever the cost in hidden frictions, the results were impressive. In the key industry of steel, whereas output in leading capitalist countries had fallen below prewar levels in the depression, Russia's output in 1932 was 40 percent above that of 1913 in the same area. In the earlier year she stood just ahead of France; but by 1932 she had also passed both Germany and Britain, and was making nearly half as much steel as the United States.

A second Five-Year Plan ran from 1933 to 1937, and a third plan was in its fourth year of operation when the Germans invaded. In theory the lack of provision for consumer goods, causing very great hardship, was remedied when the second plan restored the proportion of investment, namely 23 percent, which had originally been allocated to this purpose in the first plan but had subsequently been reduced. However, the allocation had later to be reduced again, with the result that over the whole period 1928–1941 light industry grew only about half as fast as heavy industry. The third plan was partly concerned with the spread of industry to new focal points from the lower Volga east of the Urals, and from 1936 onward much of the effort was necessarily diverted to armaments. Nevertheless, by 1941 about 70 percent had been completed of a program requiring a higher tempo of execution than either of its predecessors.

The overall results can be viewed in many ways. What had always been a predominantly agrarian country became 50 percent industrialized. Gigantic power stations, such as that which the American engineer H. L. Cooper designed on the Dnieper River, proclaimed the realization of Lenin's famous slogan: "Socialism is a Soviet government plus electrification." Steel mills such as Magnitogorsk in the Urals, the numerous heavy machinery and tractor plants, the oil pipeline from Grozny to the Black Sea, the Baltic-White Sea Canal, and the Turkestan-Siberian Railway were visible memorials of great struggles triumphantly carried through. More than 90 percent of peasants had become members of collectives. In town and country alike millions of workers were aware of a public achievement which stirred the imagination and made private hardship easier to bear: the new Russia was clearly something to be proud of. The limits of this indubitable success are perhaps shown best by comparing the rates of growth of heavy and light industry in the years from 1932 to 1938, when light industry made its best showing:

INDUSTRY	UNIT OF MEASUREMENT	1932	1938	GROWTH
Coal	million tons	64	132	×2
Oil	million tons	22	32	$+\frac{1}{2}$
Steel	million tons	6	18	×3
Tractors	thousands	50	176	$×3\frac{1}{2}$
Chemicals	billion roubles	2	6	×3
	(1926–1927 price level)			
Cotton textiles	million meters	2,694	3,491	$+\frac{1}{3}$
Woolen textiles	million meters	88	114	$+\frac{1}{3}$
Footwear	million pairs	94	213	$×2\frac{1}{3}$
Paper	thousand tons	479	834	$+\frac{3}{4}$
Granulated sugar	thousand tons	828	2,530	×3

■ THE NEW SOVIET SOCIETY

In the period of the Five-Year Plans the Russian people experienced the strains and stresses, triumphs and disasters, and even the loss of life which other countries experienced only during a major war. They endured six years of rationing both of food and other "goods of wide consumption," and even after this came to an end in 1935 it seems probable that the standard of life of the average worker stayed below the very modest level of 1913, which had been approximately regained in 1928. While the persecution of the *kulaks* attracted world-wide attention, partly perhaps because the peasant farmer and his family were natural objects of sympathy, the plight of the new industrial workers was scarcely better. They were liable to dismissal for a single day's absence, could not be re-employed without a clearance certificate from the previous employer, and were liable to be directed to work in pioneer industrial centers in distant regions to which the capitalists of the tsarist era had never been able to attract a labor force. An American who had personally experienced the hazards involved in erecting and operating heavy industrial plants without technically expert supervision claimed that building the Magnitogorsk steel works had cost as many lives as the Battle of the Marne. Altogether it is a very remarkable fact that the Russian people, so soon after their sufferings in the First World War and the Civil War, proved capable of surviving this third ordeal without a complete collapse; the experience could not fail to leave a lasting impress on their society.

Although the government owned and managed some state farms of great size, highly mechanized and highly specialized, containing cattle by the thousand or arable fields of vast dimension, these proved uneconomical except as training and research institutions. Instead, the dominant feature in the changed countryside was the collective farm or *kolkhoz*, a unit of agrarian production round which might center the activities of anything from sixty to two hundred peasant households. As finally organized in 1935, the *kolkhoz* represented a remarkable combination of collectivism in principle with individualism in detail. The members of a *kolkhoz* were collectively the permanent possessors of the land, with individual possession of their homes, of a small patch of land, and of a small quantity of livestock. Their basic function, however, was the sale of about 90 percent of grain—more in the case of such special crops as sugar beet, flax, or cotton—to the state at fixed prices. They were also required to pay the nearest machine tractor station for the use of the technical equipment on which the new agricultural efficiency mainly depended. The nature of the crop and the rate of payment were fixed by an overall plan, and the elected chairman of the *kolkhoz* was responsible for its fulfilment. The individual members were remunerated from the proceeds of the sale of the main crop in proportion to the quantity and level of skill of the work they had put in.

By 1939 the sown area in Russia was one-third larger than in 1913, and the crop three times as large; the farms produced twice as much meat and milk, about half of it coming from individually owned resources. Since there was still considerable inefficiency, expulsion had to be prescribed for peasants who failed to do a reasonable minimum of work on the collective crops. Nevertheless, the results were becoming satisfactory both for the rural producer and the town consumer, particularly because the growth of the machine-making industry inside Russia made it less necessary to export grain in order to pay for agricultural machinery from abroad.

If the character of peasant society was transformed, industrial society was almost a new creation of this period. The effect of the first plan was to double the number of wage earners, with a further addition of nearly 50 percent in the next four years, so that in 1936 there were 27,800,000 employed as compared with 11,600,000 in 1928. A large part of this labor force was necessarily engaged for construction projects and newly established workplaces where accommodation and even the food supply were hopelessly inadequate. The result was that skilled workers were constantly on the move in search of better conditions. Wherever they went, the pressure to learn at high speed the habits which other industrial nations had acquired by slow degrees was enormous. The program was assisted by huge developments in technical education. Four times as many engineers completed their training in 1938 as in 1933, and the average number graduated from universities and polytechnics rose from 92,000 a year under the first plan to 199,000 under the second. Every such specialist was allocated to a job, which he could be punished for leaving.

For the lower grades of labor there were other incentives. The chief of these was the adoption wherever possible of piecework wage rates, graded according to degrees of skill. An attempt also was made to promote what was called "socialist competition" by giving extra rations and other privileges to members of shock brigades of workers, who set their fellows a possibly unwelcome example of unremitting toil, careful handling of tools, and eagerness to find scope for technical improvements. In 1935 a Donetz miner named Stakhanov with only unskilled assistance managed to hew 102 tons of coal in one six-hour shift; he thereby earned nearly a month's normal wages and inspired the cult of Stakhanovism. By 1938 nearly half of all industrial workers were claimed to be Stakhanovites, though there were also cases in which resentful workers disposed of Stakhanovites by murder. The general result was to raise minimum standards of production, both because Stakhanovite achievements could be used in calculating the norm and also because attention was drawn by this publicity to the desirability of performing a task in the most efficient manner. As Molotov[9] explained blandly in a pamphlet entitled *What is Stakhanovism?*, "It is not a question of *overstrain* on the part of the worker but of a *cultured* attitude towards work." No explanation was offered of the relationship between Stakhanovite rewards and the Communist principle of "To each according to his needs."

At the time of the Five-Year Plans new efforts were made to transform popular culture in the direction of "social realism," and to overthrow what was left of traditional religious life. The spasmodic efforts which had been made in the preceding ten years to shake the hold of the Christian religion upon the peasants, to banish illiteracy, and to make all the arts serve purposes of political indoctrination became much more systematic. In 1929 religious bodies were

9. Born 1890. Editor of *Pravda* in 1917 and a Party secretary since 1922. He was promoted to the Politburo at the time of Kamenev's demotion, president of the council of commissars, 1930–1941, and foreign minister, 1939–1949. He was a steady supporter of Stalin throughout, though Stalin in his last years turned against him. He became foreign minister again after Stalin's death, but was demoted in 1956, and sent next year as ambassador to Outer Mongolia, Khrushchev having belatedly discovered that he was a "saboteur of peace."

MOSCOW UNIVERSITY. The towering buildings are in the official classical style which has become standard in the Soviet Union.

forbidden to engage in any function except acts of worship. The League of the Militant Godless, first founded in 1925, rose rapidly to a membership of several million and easily turned its anti-God propaganda into positive persecution of the clergy. Some famous churches were turned into antireligious museums; many more were closed, and the introduction of a six-day week including one rest-day made it easy for habits of worship to be abandoned. The schools, vastly expanded, were now required to adopt a sterner discipline and to see that their teaching was sufficiently impregnated with Communist doctrine to "guarantee the political and social conquests of the Revolution." There were even "shock brigades" of authors, formed to boost the Five-Year Plans under a Russian Association of Proletarian Writers, though this was disbanded when planned literature was found to be hopelessly lifeless and mechanical.

Lastly, it must be recorded that the execution of the plans depended to an indeterminate extent upon penal sanctions which passed by degrees into a veritable reign of terror. The Ogpu turned its attention from the watch over surviving political opponents to the very much larger class of *kulaks*, private traders, and bourgeois engineers and technicians who might be suspected of hostility to the plans. From 1928 onward there were trials of "counterrevolutionary wreckers," a few of whom may have been what they were alleged to be. In most cases the victims were persons picked out to be treated with unjust severity for minor offences, so as to galvanize a mass of other workers into feverish activity, or were ruthlessly sacrificed as scapegoats for some perhaps unavoidable breakdown in the plan. To soothe injured national pride and restore confidence the so-called wreckers were freely stated to be in foreign pay. This claim was rendered less implausible by the presence in Russia of many technicians from the United States and the more industrialized countries of Europe. In 1933 the British government for a time suspended trade relations when two engineers from the firm of Metro-Vickers were sent to prison with their Russian "accomplices" on a charge of sabotaging the electric power stations which they were employed to construct.

Such episodes pale into insignificance by comparison with the sinister event in December, 1934, when Sergei Kirov, the principal Communist leader in Leningrad, was murdered there by a fellow Party member. Stalin's professions of grief were extreme and well publicized. So were his reprisals, which included the execution of more than a hundred alleged counterrevolutionaries who were already under arrest at the time of the murder. Stalin, however, had been under unwelcome pressure from some of his colleagues to bring Kirov as a liberalizing influence to Moscow, and it seems likely that the assassination plot was not unknown to the secret police beforehand, or unwelcome to their supreme master. Be that as it may, the death of Kirov proved to be the prelude to an era in which the political history of Russia was once more heavily stained with blood.

■ THE NEW CONSTITUTION OF 1936, THE PARTY, AND THE PURGES

The new era was ushered in by the adoption of a revised and seemingly progressive constitution. Early in 1935, in accordance with plans which had been mooted before the death of Kirov, a constitutional commission was set up with Stalin as chairman. A rough version of what it advocated was made available in June, 1936, for public discussion and criticism. After the commission had given some consideration to such amendments as were proposed, the final draft was adopted unanimously by a special Congress of Soviets held in the following December. Since this revision is still in force throughout the expanded territory of the postwar U.S.S.R., and since the constitution of Soviet satellites, to say nothing of present-day China, has been largely modeled upon it, an examination of a few of the salient features is essential to this story.

The theoretical bases of the Soviet state are clearly enunciated in the following articles:

Article 4

The economic foundation of the U.S.S.R. is the socialist system of economy and the socialist ownership of the instruments and means of production, firmly established as a result of the liquidation of the capitalist system of economy, the abolition of private ownership of the instruments and means of production, and the elimination of the exploitation of man by man.

Article 12

Work in the U.S.S.R. is a duty and a matter of honor for every able-bodied citizen, in accordance with the principle: "He who does not work, neither shall he eat." The principle applied in the U.S.S.R. is that of socialism: "From each according to his ability, to each according to his work."[10]

The Soviet Union remained federal in form, but highly centralized by reason of the strength of its central institutions, which again included an elected Praesidium whose chairman would be the nominal head of the state, a supreme court, an executive council of people's commissars, and a bicameral legislature to which they were to be in theory responsible. One change was in the character of this legislature, still composed of a Soviet of the Union and a Soviet of Nationalities but having its members chosen in each case by direct election; the lower levels of the soviets lost their elective functions and survived only to legislate and administer locally. This big move towards democratic methods was strengthened by three other provisions: voting was to be by secret ballot, urban and rural votes were to have equal weight, and all categories of citizens were henceforth admitted to the franchise. The appearance of democracy was further strengthened by the enumeration of fundamental rights of citizens, which included freedom of conscience, of speech, of meeting, and of publication, together with the right to education, to leisure, and to security in sickness and old age, and the guaranteed equality of sexes, nationalities, and races. These rights were matched by fundamental duties, including not only obedience to the law and acceptance of military service, but the special obligations of disciplined labor and vigilant protection of socialist means of production appropriate to a constitution dedicated to the preservation of a socialist economy.

The other new feature of the constitution, however, was probably more significant than all the rest: unlike its predecessor of 1924, it made explicit reference to the role of the Communist Party. Stalin argued that all classes had disappeared from Russian society save an unexploited (and therefore non-proletarian) class of workers, "an absolutely new peasantry, the like of which the history of mankind has never known," and a new intelligentsia which existed only to serve the people. Russian society therefore had no need for rival parties, because parties are an expression of a class struggle. If there were to be

10. *Constitution (Fundamental Law) of the Union of Soviet Socialist Republics, Information Bulletin*, Embassy of the U.S.S.R., Washington, December, 1947.

no parties, then the right to nominate candidates at elections must be reserved for public organizations and societies of workers. But would youth organizations, for example, or cultural societies necessarily make the right nomination for an election in which only one candidate could be nominated? That is the point at which Article 126 of the constitution formally acknowledges the role of the Communist Party:

Article 126
The most active and politically conscious citizens in the ranks of the working class and other sections of the working people unite in the Communist Party of the Soviet Union (Bolsheviks), which is the vanguard of the working people in their struggle to strengthen and develop the socialist system and is the leading core of all organizations of the working people, both public and state.[11]

The Party, it will be remembered, had been reduced in 1921 to a total of half a million members. In view of its commanding position, there was always a tendency for it to expand. It had a quite popular youth movement, the Komsomol, and a system of probationary membership for so-called "candidates." While it was true that whoever secured the Party label was expected to appear to be more active, more industrious, and more self-sacrificing than the ordinary run of humanity, such an exclusive selection based upon civic virtue seems unlikely. The prospect of power would outweigh every possible disadvantage in the eyes of ambitious persons, good and evil alike. By the beginning of 1933 there were 3.5 million members, including "candidates," and in spite of a careful check of qualifications the number still stood at 2.3 million in December, 1934. The murder of Kirov and the investigations which followed then posed the problem of the reliability of Party members and others, to which the constitution could provide no direct answer. The sequel was the "Great Purge," which began simultaneously with the drafting of the new constitution and continued until the later months of 1938.

In the course of four years the number of the victims who suffered death, imprisonment, or banishment to labor camps is believed to have totaled at least seven million and was possibly twice as many. These were swept away in several distinct waves of terror, each far more formidable than the French Terror of 1793–1794 on which so much attention has been lavished by historians. The murder of Kirov in Leningrad was followed in 1935, not merely by the executions already mentioned, but by the dissolution of the Society of Old Bolsheviks and the imposition of prison sentences on their two main leaders, Zinoviev and Kamenev; the secret trial of nearly forty members of Stalin's bodyguard; the tightening up of the conditions of punishment for all political prisoners; and the deportation to northern Siberia of tens of thousands of suspects from Leningrad and other cities. Then in August, 1936, Zinoviev,

11. *Ibid.*

Kamenev, and fourteen other Old Bolsheviks of the left wing confessed in court to having organized a terrorist group under the direction of Trotsky, who was seemingly safe in exile, and were condemned and executed. All this was the work of an All-Union police force, which had replaced the Ogpu in 1934 and is generally known as NKVD, from the Russian initials of the Commissariat of Internal Affairs by which it was controlled. By 1941 this ubiquitous body had its own frontier troops, but as early as the close of 1936 the appointment of Yezhov as its head marked the beginning of the period of maximum repression known as the *Yezhovshchina*. His reign of terror terminated only when Beria[12] took his place in control of the police in December, 1938. Yezhov himself and other so-called "witnesses" then shared the fate of their victims, presumably because they knew too much.

The purges, if the accusations made by Soviet authorities were true, revealed enormous and treasonable dissensions in high circles. First of the three most dramatic episodes of the period was the "Trial of the Seventeen," of whom thirteen were shot, accused of plotting the restoration of capitalism. Second, in June, 1937, Marshal Tukhachevsky[13] and seven other commanders were shot after secret trial by court-martial for acts of "espionage and treason." Third, early in 1938 Bukharin[14] and two other ex-members of the Politburo were included in a group of twenty-one right-wing Communists who perished after making multitudinous and often implausible confessions. When the Communist Central Committee came up for re-election at the Party Congress in 1939, only twenty-four names reappeared out of one hundred and thirty-nine members and "candidates" elected five years before. In the same short period the armed forces had lost two out of their five marshals.

The reality of the plots and the genuineness of the evidence which so many of the plotters gave against themselves and each other were, and still are, open to the gravest doubt. Where opinion outside Russia went wrong was in concluding that such sinister revelations must presage the fall of the Stalinist regime. Instead, Stalin emerged as an absolute autocrat, stained with some of the cruelty of Peter the Great but commanding much the same obedience. Though Stalin never appeared in the foreground of any trial, his cruel will was the driving force which determined the fate alike of old comrades from the heroic days of 1917 and of the nameless thousands who might happen to ob-

12. 1899–1953. Organizer of a Bolshevik group in college at Baku in 1917, he served for ten years in the Ogpu in the Caucasus, and then became party secretary in Georgia. He was vice-president of the State Committee for Defense during the Second World War; he was shot soon after the death of Stalin.

13. 1893–1937. A lieutenant in the tsarist army and a German prisoner-of-war, he had commanded Communist armies since 1918 and led the attack on Warsaw in 1920; latterly he had been chief of the Military Academy and assistant chief of staff. He was the best-known organizer in the Soviet forces.

14. See p. 210.

struct the course he had chosen. As for the obedience, two special factors helped him to create the monolithic state which was to survive the most terrible of all wars.

One factor lay in the ease with which Stalin could replace from a more pliable younger generation the people, and in particular the leaders, whom he destroyed. A new professional class, half a million strong, had received its education since 1933 and had been exposed throughout its course to a propaganda which taught them to hail Stalin as the father of his country. Even in the immediate entourage of the autocrat a new type of subordinate had come to the fore, the *Apparatchiki,* men who won their place in the Politburo or other organ of power not by their capacity for independent judgment but by their ability to manage the apparatus of the Party and the Soviets so as to carry out smoothly the policy determined by Stalin. Aptitude of this kind provided the basis of the careers of such men as Malenkov and Khrushchev, whose fortunes will be studied in a later chapter. Here it is necessary only to notice the link between their submissiveness and the second of the special factors which strengthened Stalin's position. Throughout these years the constant pressure of a hostile outside world lent color to every report of Trotskyist plots and gave to the worst excesses of the autocrat the justification, or at least the excuse, of patriotic necessity.

■ RUSSIA AND THE WORLD

The shadow of Stalin, which fell so heavily upon the whole of the U.S.S.R., was felt also in the outside world, where the Communist fervors of the first Five-Year Plan were supposed to presage a forward policy on behalf of world communism. Nothing could be further from the facts of the situation. For one thing, Stalin was not a particularly keen or well-informed observer of events outside Russia. More important, he was committed to the slogan of "socialism in one country" and to its counterpart, his campaign against the Trotskyite proposition of world communism. Most important of all, Stalin's preoccupation with domestic problems confirmed him in his disregard for the activities of the Comintern. Its record was disappointing. It had failed in the Ruhr, made only slight headway in Bulgaria, and had proved unable to surmount the barrier which religion interposed to the progress of communism in the Islamic countries of the Middle East. Stalin therefore valued the Comintern only as a means of advancing Russia's domestic interests by undercover propaganda abroad. Instead, he promoted Litvinov, the Russian representative at the World Disarmament Conference, to the post of commissar for foreign affairs, long held by Chicherin, thereby advertising in 1930 a policy of avoiding provocative action. This change of attitude had already brought about a renewal of Anglo-Russian relations and was to have its eventual reward in *de jure* recognition of the Soviet government by the United States.

As long as his relations with Germany continued to be governed by the arrangements made at Rapallo, Stalin was able to turn his back on the West and concentrate upon the more directly troublesome affairs of his neighbors in the East. The transfer of much of Russian heavy industry and the rapid general development of her Asiatic provinces emphasized this trend. In 1929 a Chinese attempt to sweep away Soviet influence in Manchuria led to an invasion by the Russian Far Eastern army at both ends of the Chinese Eastern Railway. Receiving support from dissenting Chinese generals in league with the radical wing of the Kuomintang, the Russians were able to ignore protests offered by the United States and other powers on the basis of the recently signed Kellogg Pact and successfully reasserted their claim to share in the control of the all-important railway. But the unexpected sequel to this Russian venture was the Japanese incursion into Manchuria, beginning in 1931 and resulting in the occupation without any effective resistance first of the southern and then of the northern region. The latter had been recognized by Japan as a Russian sphere of influence since 1907, and the Japanese advance there endangered the whole military and economic position of the Soviet government in the Far East. For the time being, however, the situation was met by the recognition of the puppet state of Manchukuo, to which in 1935 the Soviet half-share in the Chinese Eastern Railway was sold for the modest price of fifty million dollars.

When the Japanese launched their full-scale invasion of China in July, 1937, its significance for Russia was underlined by the fact that less than a year earlier Japan had become linked with Germany and Italy in the Anti-Comintern Pact.[15] To give effective indirect support to Chinese resistance was difficult for the Russians since the main Chinese leader, Chiang Kai-shek, was still engaged in a bitter internecine struggle with the Chinese Communists, and the alternative of an all-out open war against Japan was one from which the Russian government shrank because of the rapidly deteriorating situation in Europe. Accordingly unofficial aid in material, military instructors, and advisers was made available to the Chinese Communist army, which had somehow survived its long march in 1934–1935 into the north, and also on a less generous scale to the right-wing forces under Chiang. At the same time a war of satellites was developed between Manchuria and Mongolia, culminating in 1939 in a full-scale battle by the border river, the Khalkin-Gol, in which a Russian defeated a Japanese army. No official war followed because the Japanese still had their hands full with the Chinese resistance. The Russians, having double-tracked the Trans-Siberian Railway in 1937, when they feared the worst, wisely preferred to wait.

In the early days of Hitler's accession to power Stalin watched the extinction of the German Communist Party with an indifference which betrayed

15. See p. 239.

not only his lack of sympathy with the Comintern but his inability to measure the importance of the new phenomenon of National Socialism in Germany. For at least a year he hoped against hope to be able to retain the alliance with Germany made at Rapallo. But the German-Polish nonaggression pact renewed Russian anxieties regarding the Ukraine, which were intensified by Germany's rejection of a Russian proposal for a joint guarantee of the integrity of the Baltic States. When this was followed by German economic and political penetration of the Danubian and Balkan states on Russia's other flank, Stalin's attitude finally changed. He began instead to play the same difficult and dishonest game as did other alarmed and threatened neighbors of the Third Reich. He prepared reluctantly for a war which he would have preferred not to contemplate. He sedulously cultivated friendships which would be dropped on the instant if they proved disadvantageous. Above all, he hoped against hope to see German militarism diverted against other foes.

From September, 1934, when Soviet Russia joined the League of Nations, until the signature of the German-Soviet Pact almost exactly five years later, Russian relations with the West form an integral part of the chain of events which seems in retrospect to have led inexorably to the outbreak of the Second World War. They form the subject of the next chapter of this book. Here it will be enough to indicate briefly the main stages in the development of Soviet foreign policy.

Russia's membership of the League and the League Council, where Litvinov earnestly espoused the view that "peace is indivisible," led naturally to closer relations with the principal League powers. In March, 1935, Anthony Eden, the future British prime minister, was received with marked cordiality by Stalin in the Kremlin. Later in the same year Russia made an alliance with France, then made a further alliance with Czechoslovakia, by which Russia undertook to join in any French action for its defense. These moves were accompanied by a dramatic change of policy at what proved to be the last congress of the Comintern, where it was agreed to form "popular fronts" with middle-class parties in all parliamentary countries so as to promote a firm stand against fascism.

It seems probable that these actions were straightforwardly founded on a calculation of Russia's immediate interests. But the intricacies of the Spanish Civil War involved Russia as well as Italy and Germany in the elaborate sham of nonintervention. Russia was further involved in an internal struggle to oust the Anarchists and Trotskyites from any share of control in the Spanish Left. Such events, along with the disastrous outcome of the war, showed how hard it was to produce effective collaboration among mutually distrustful allies. The fall of Blum in France in 1937 and the rise of Chamberlain in Britain likewise served to reopen the gap which the Popular Front movement had temporarily closed. Nor is it easy to blame the ministers of the western powers for regarding with suspicion and scepticism a Russia which the great purge seemed to be reducing to a sheer political tyranny precariously dependent upon an army which had been deprived of all experienced leaders.

Stalin may always have kept a line open to Berlin to provide for contingencies. What is certain is that the Munich settlement of September, 1938, can only have confirmed his worst suspicions. When this crisis came, Russia had been carefully excluded from the counsels of Europe; from this it was a natural inference that, if Germany could make Russia her victim, Europe would view such an aggression with indifference. In all the circumstances it is remarkable that political and military negotiations with the West were continued by Stalin for so long. It is not at all surprising that at 3:15 p.m. on August 19, 1939, he gave Molotov the instruction which brought Ribbentrop to the fateful pact negotiations in the Kremlin and all the powers sooner or later to the ordeal of war in which Russia, like the others, paid a grievous price.

Reading List: Chapter 8

Clarkson, J. D., *A History of Russia from the Ninth Century* (1961), chs. 29–31.

Dmytryshyn, Basil, *USSR: A Concise History* (1965, also paperback), chs. 5–6.

Fischer, L., *The Soviets in World Affairs* (2 vols., 2nd ed., 1951), conclusion. The problems of a revolutionary foreign policy.

Sumner, B. H., *Short History of Russia* (1943), ch. 3(1), ch. 7(4). The Soviet revolution in agriculture and industry briefly described.

Pares, B., *Russia* (1941, also paperback), chs. 12–14. Industrial planning; agriculture collectivized; antireligion.

Hindus, M., *Red Bread* (1931), ch. 19. An enthusiastic description of the early form of *kolkhoz* or collective farming.

Scott, J., *Beyond the Urals* (1942), pt. III. The story of the development of the steel industry at Magnitogorsk.

Deutscher, I., *Stalin: A Political Biography* (1949, also paperback), ch. 9. A careful study of the purges and trials of 1934–1939.

Chapter 9

Democracy on the Defensive

The Challenge of Dictatorship
The Italian Invasion of Ethiopia
The Remilitarization of the Rhineland
Fencing for Position: Europe and the War in Spain
The Absorption of Austria in Germany
The Dismemberment of Czechoslovakia
War for Poland?
Responsibility for the Outbreak of War

■ THE CHALLENGE OF DICTATORSHIP

The Second World War cost the human race far greater losses than had the First, whether this cost be measured in terms of the dead and maimed, the squandering of material resources, or the immeasurable damage done to the spirit of man. Its effects, involving a drastic reorganization of the European and indeed the world balance, still overshadow the lives of all men. Thus the question of why a span of only two decades following one devastating world conflict should have had as its outcome another even more terrible war assumes major importance.

In retrospect, the war can be seen to have cast the shadow of its coming from far back in the decade of the 1930's. As early as September, 1931, the authority of the League of Nations had been directly challenged by Japanese aggression in Manchuria, the first of several direct challenges to which its

SIGNIFICANT EVENTS

1935   Italian invasion of Ethiopia (October)
1936   German military reoccupation of the Rhineland (March)
        Outbreak of the Spanish Civil War (July)
        Anti-Comintern Pact between Germany and Japan (October)
        Rome-Berlin Axis announced (November)
1937   Renewed Japanese attack on China: occupation of Peking (July)
1938   German annexation of Austria (March)
        Munich Agreement for separation of Sudetenland from Czecho-
            slovakia (September)
1939   German seizure of Czechoslovakia (March)
        British guarantee for territorial integrity of Poland
            (March)
        Russo-German nonaggression pact (August)

members failed to make any effective reply. From January, 1933, onward the vast latent strength of Germany was at the disposal of a ruthless visionary, whose dreams showed him by what arts he might build up a country more prosperous, better disciplined, and more formidable in her relations with other Continental powers than the Empire of Bismarck or Kaiser Wilhelm II had been.

Hitler knew little and cared less about overseas colonies. In Europe, where his ambitions lay, the projects for disarmament which the world had been half-heartedly pursuing since the Peace Conference in Paris were by 1935 significantly abandoned. Instead, the governments of France and Soviet Russia, ignoring the recent past, had drawn together for mutual protection. Mussolini, after championing Austrian independence at the time of Hitler's attempted coup in 1934, was increasingly disinclined to thwart German ambitions again in Austria or elsewhere. The British authorities, too, showed their uncertainty about future prospects when they signed a naval treaty with the new Germany (June, 1935), for they chose to ensure for themselves a three-to-one superiority in tonnage of ships, rather than to attempt any further stand with their allies of the First World War in defense of the Treaty of Versailles which the Germans were stage by stage repudiating.

It is therefore tempting to regard the diplomatic events of 1935–1939 as leading inevitably to a renewal of war between Germany and the western powers in circumstances far less favorable to the latter than in 1914. To be sure, many people on both sides did regard the coming of this war as inevitable. It is also true that Hitler's policies were directed toward war, in the sense that he would choose to fight rather than abandon his general program of national aggrandizement. On the other hand, he expected, with some justification, that a policy of bluff and the adroit adaptation of his program to suit a rapidly changing situation might carry him far without any major armed conflict necessarily arising. Thus it is wrong to regard Hitler and Nazi Germany as the embodiment of a demonic force which proceeded inevitably from one success to another while its victims, both actual and impending, helplessly watched the unrolling of events to their inescapable denouement. This is to attribute too much to Hitler, whose evil genius is well remembered, while his opponents' weaknesses which gave him his chance are often conveniently forgotten.

The years which had elapsed since the last-round triumph of the Allied and Associated Powers in the First World War had not placed Britain and France in a stronger position to confront Germany a second time. Both countries had grave political and economic problems. In February, 1934, France seemed on the verge of revolution, and the continuing split between Left and Right made a further upheaval likely at any time in the following five years. Though Britain was ruled by a Conservative government with a safe parliamentary majority, the unemployment problem was still unsolved and there were good reasons for avoiding any unnecessary strain upon the unity of the Commonwealth. In 1937 the renewal of Japanese aggression in China necessarily distracted the attention of Britain from the Continent to her world interests. Moreover, both countries were disillusioned by the results of such efforts as they had made since the end of the war to rectify external situations by force. Little, if anything, came of their joint intervention in the Russian Civil War, the British stand in Asia Minor against the Turks, the French occupation of the Ruhr, and their respective embroilments in Syria and Palestine. Above all, the two powers looked back upon the "Great War" as a traumatic experience which they had barely survived and of which they dare not risk a repetition, especially when they found that they had lost the support of Italy and failed to attract that of the United States.

Hence the ambiguous and unsatisfactory part played by the League of Nations, in which Britain and France might have been expected to offer strong leadership. Its fifty members, each of whom had acceded to the terms of a Covenant designed for the preservation of world peace, might seem to constitute a formidable organization for curbing an aggressor state. But the great majority were small powers bitterly aware that their lack of heavy industry made them hopelessly inadequate to the needs of modern war. As was said at the time, "50 × 0 = 0." They could fight only as auxiliaries of the great powers who knew this and therefore made use of the League for only two purposes. One was to secure strong moral support and propaganda-backing for the denunciation of aggressors and treaty breakers, so that right would always demonstrably be on the side of Britain and France. The other use was to provide a kind of screen, enabling the great powers to retreat from decisive action by referring matters to the League, where a thousand technically valid reasons could be found for doing nothing. The man in the street found it fatally easy to combine support for "League ideals" with faith in pacifism and disarmament, in the ingenuous belief that aggressors could be deterred by world public opinion or, at all events, by world actions falling short of war.

The use of the term "world opinion" commonly concealed another weakness which was well known to potential aggressors. In League of Nations discussions and elsewhere Britain and France spoke only for what would nowadays be called their satellite states in Europe and elsewhere. Japan, Germany, and Italy resigned from the League when their policies were seriously challenged. The adhesion of Soviet Russia, unfortunately, did not redress the balance, since her government was regarded with enormous suspicion as a kind of Trojan horse bringing with it into the camp of the beleaguered democracies new possibilities of treachery and dissension. Even more unfortunate was the abstention of the United States from any share in decisions which have affected all later history. The Democratic electoral victories of 1932 and 1936 did little to alter the conventional policy of isolationism. In some sense they seemed even to intensify isolationism, for America's principal impact in this period came in the purely negative Neutrality Acts of 1935 and 1937, which did all that Congressional ingenuity could contrive to avoid encouraging resistance to aggression or any implication in Europe's troubles.

■ THE ITALIAN INVASION OF ETHIOPIA

In April, 1935, one month after Hitler had announced the reintroduction of conscription in Germany, the Stresa Conference had reaffirmed the intention of Britain, France, and Italy, the Allies of the First World War, to stand together against any further repudiation by the Germans of their treaty obligations. It is rather ironical that the failure of the British and French at this same conference to mention the subject of Ethiopia, then becoming critical because of border clashes with Italy, was later claimed by the Italians as implying Franco-British approval for the imminent war in Africa. The campaign resulted in the definitive transfer of Italian support to the German side. That support, which played a large part in Hitler's calculations in the succeeding European crises of 1936–1938, had as its natural consequence Italy's belated entrance into the Second World War as a German ally, which spread the area and probably prolonged the duration of the conflict. Consequently, what had been planned as an old-style imperialist campaign in long-suffering Africa proved to be an important step toward the general ruin of Europe.

The Ethiopian war had a complicated background. The Kingdom of Italy had regarded the defeat of its forces by the Ethiopians at Adowa in 1896 as a serious blemish upon its military reputation. The location of Ethiopia between the two Italian colonies of Eritrea and Somaliland made access easy. In Italy the prevalence of unemployment during the great trade depression tempted Mussolini to restore the fortunes of the Fascist Party by a venture which might ultimately provide land for settlers and scope for commercial development, and would certainly solve the immediate problem by absorbing men into the forces and creating a big demand for munitions and other supplies. A border dispute at the obscure oasis of Walwal (December, 1934) accordingly provided a pretext for large-scale Italian preparations, against which Ethiopia appealed in vain to the League of Nations.

When, however, the campaigning season arrived in October, 1935, and Mussolini without a declaration of war launched a full-scale invasion aimed at the capital, Addis Ababa, the League acted promptly. Its Council declared Italy to be an aggressor, and the Assembly with some four exceptions voted to apply economic sanctions. Since the United States government enforced its new neutrality regulations, forbidding trade with either combatant, and the Germans fought shy of the economic risk of sales to the Italians, it looked for a moment as though the principle of collective security would be vindicated. Such hope was momentary. As soon as it was proposed to extend the trade embargo to oil, without which the Italians would be unable to continue their war, Mussolini declared that he would regard this as an "unfriendly act," to be met presumably by whatever force was at his disposal. Since none of the smaller powers offered to make any military move, it was left to Britain and France to settle the issue in the Mediterranean. The British had reinforced their fleet, but expected to lose Malta and some important naval units in any conflict with the Italian navy and air force. If the British government was half-hearted about running a risk which its experts almost certainly exaggerated, the French was directly hostile to taking any action which might alienate Italian sympathies, at a time when Italy had the choice of supporting either France or Germany.

The result was a series of actions suggesting the moral bankruptcy of all concerned—except the emperor of Ethiopia,[1] who put his trust in the League to the bitter end. In December the French premier and the British foreign secretary proposed a partitioning of Haile Selassie's empire, which would have left about one-third to continue in independence. These Hoare-Laval proposals were loudly and scornfully rejected by public opinion both in Britain and in France. Though Hoare was forced to resign, the indignation evaporated without either government being goaded into an enforcement of the proposed oil sanctions and in March, 1936, attention was distracted from this issue by the German action in the Rhineland.[2] Thus Mussolini who, though from very different motives, had also scouted the idea of any partition, was able to complete the conquest in a single season. Ethiopia's ill-trained native levies had no chance against an organized army using modern equipment and stooping to resort to mustard gas, sprayed on their helpless victims from the air. In May the emperor fled from Addis Ababa to exile in England, pausing at Geneva to make a last appeal to the shamefaced Assembly of the League of Nations. It had taken only seventeen years to extinguish the bright hopes which President Wilson had set before mankind at the close of the first "war to end war."

> It is a question of collective security [Haile Selassie declared], of the very existence of the League; of the value of promises made to small states that their integrity and independence shall be respected and assured. . . . In a word, it is international morality that is at stake. . . . God and history will remember your judgment.

Though none could foresee it, what fortune had in store for the speaker was a triumphant re-entry into his Ethiopian capital on the fifth anniversary of his withdrawal, by which time almost every small state in Europe lay under the heel of a conqueror and the League itself had passed into limbo. The record of the Italian administrators had been marred in the meantime by much bloodshed. Nevertheless, they had worked hard at the economic development of their "fascist empire," made up of Ethiopia and the earlier colonies of Eritrea, Somaliland, and Tripoli. Perhaps it was in some sense inevitable that the last of the ancient native states of Africa should fall into European hands before the nationalist renaissance of the Dark Continent began. The history of their own dealings with the peoples of Africa certainly hampered the British and French in applying League principles regarding the sacrosanctity of a state's territory to the undeniably backward and loosely controlled empire of Haile

1. Born in 1891, Haile Selassie, great-nephew of the Emperor Menelek, the victor at Adowa, became regent in 1916 on the overthrow of Menelek's pro-Moslem successor, and emperor on the death of Menelek's daughter in 1930. He secured the admission of Ethiopia to the League of Nations under French sponsorship in 1923. His policy aimed at the establishment of a strong central authority and modernization without sacrificing independence.
2. See pp. 234–237.

Selassie. Whatever the extenuating circumstances, the episode had an undeniably disastrous influence upon the course of events in Europe. Economic sanctions, even when backed by a virtually unanimous world opinion, had been proved to be incapable of restraining a major power from a course of aggression; hence the League of Nations was no longer to be reckoned with as a deterrent. At the same time Britain and France had forfeited some of the prestige which had attached to them as victors of the First World War, for they had shrunk from a trial of strength against Italy, which had ranked for two decades as their weaker partner. Finally, the fact that they had been "willing to wound, and yet afraid to strike" was not lost upon Mussolini, who now brought Italy over to the German side, or upon Hitler, who could now make the inference that a policy of bluff might carry him far. It did.

■ THE REMILITARIZATION OF THE RHINELAND

Hitler's rearming of Germany in defiance of the Treaty of Versailles had complex and ominous consequences. His announcement in March, 1935, that he was about to reintroduce conscription made clear some of his already partly executed purposes. France, Britain, and Italy met at the Stresa Conference, where they tried to establish a common front which would demonstrate their unity, condemn Germany's unilateral repudiation of a treaty obligation, and (less explicitly) indicate the likelihood that next time they would take appropriate action to defend their rights. Yet exactly twelve months later Hitler issued a further challenge when he announced that German troops were reentering the demilitarized Rhineland. This time not even a demonstration of unity occurred. Italy was at loggerheads with Britain and France regarding Ethiopia and, being on the verge of success, was in no mood to fulfill the Locarno pledges. Instead of acting at once, the French and British indulged in speeches—in their separate conclaves, in joint consultations, and in the Council of the League of Nations. The total effect, unhappily, was to mollify public opinion, which had at first been affronted by Hitler's unilateral action. Nothing whatever was done, and on the first anniversary of the re-entry into the Rhineland Hitler was able to announce that the demilitarized zone was effectively refortified.

Since Hitler's action was clearly a major turning point in the history of contemporary Europe, the event must be examined more closely. Could a different course have been followed, with a reasonable prospect of restraining German aggression? Why was the remilitarization of the Rhineland a crucial issue? Why was its importance not clearly appreciated?

The first question admits of a very brief answer. Since historians are agreed that the Germans employed at most 35,000 men in the initial coup, that their generals forecast six weeks as the longest period for which they could

TERRITORIAL CHANGES
in EUROPE, 1935-1939

JAN.1935 . . . . SAAR RETURNED
TO GERMANY
AFTER PLEBISCITE

MAR.1936 . . . . DEMILITARIZED
GERMAN ZONE REENTERED
BY GERMAN FORCES

MAR.1938 . . . . AUSTRIA SEIZED
BY GERMANY

OCT.1938 . . . . SUDETENLAND
DISTRICTS OF
CZECHOSLOVAKIA
OCCUPIED BY
GERMANY

OCT.1938 . . . . TESCHEN SEIZED
BY POLAND

NOV.1938 . . . . SLOVAK BORDER
AREAS SEIZED
BY HUNGARY

MAR.1939 . . . . BOHEMIA-MORAVIA
MADE A GERMAN
PROTECTORATE

MAR.1939 . . . . SLOVAKIA MADE AN
INDEPENDENT STATE
UNDER GERMAN PROTECTION

MAR.1939 . . . . RUTHENIA SEIZED
BY HUNGARY

MAR.1939 . . . . MEMELLAND
SEIZED BY GERMANY

APR.1939 . . . . ALBANIA SEIZED
BY ITALY

expect to hold out against French and British forces in any part of the country, and that Hitler's authority could not have survived the failure of a policy for which he had made himself directly responsible, a firm military policy would have had a very good chance of success. Nothing can appear more absurd in the light of later knowledge than the assertion of the French commander in chief, General Maurice Gamelin, that in the first twenty-four hours the Germans had poured 300,000 men into the Rhineland, unless it is the spectacle of the British prime minister with tears in his eyes assuring a French emissary that Britain had no forces with which she could help at this juncture.

The second question is that of the crucial issues at stake in remilitarizing the Rhineland. The basic importance of the demilitarized zone was that it had been instituted at the peace settlement in 1919, when the French were denied their claim to annex the territory outright, in order to deter the Germans from any future war of aggression. In the event of war, this part of Germany would fall immediately as a hostage into French hands. The arrangement had acquired a special degree of sanctity by its incorporation at the suggestion of the German negotiators in the Treaty of Locarno, to which Hitler had specifically declared his adherence less than twelve months before. Thus it was made clear that Hitler's contempt for treaty obligations and his own pledged word was not confined to the peace terms of 1919, which he could claim were imposed on Germany by *force majeure*.

The remilitarization of the Rhineland had other, more immediate repercussions on the network of alliances with which France had hoped to preserve a balance of power in Europe. She herself could still adopt a purely defensive role behind the fortifications of the Maginot Line, but if France were required to support her allies against a resurgent Germany, the Rhineland was no longer available as an easy conquest. Poland and Czechoslovakia were therefore visibly weakened by the change. Far worse were the effects upon Belgium, who had signed a defensive military agreement with France in 1920, and for whom the existence of the demilitarized zone was the main safeguard she had obtained against a repetition of the unprovoked German attack of 1914. In addition to suffering the same setback as other allies of France through the general weakening of their position, she was now directly exposed to German forces that could be poised as in 1914 along the Belgian frontier. Belgium accordingly withdrew from the Locarno system into a precarious policy of complete neutrality, the outcome of which was to be the debacle of May, 1940.

The third question concerns the general failure of the world to realize the importance of this Rhineland issue. What, then, were the reasons? One was certainly the shortsightedness which led even an eminent British politician to profess that the Germans were only "going into their own back-garden" and enabled *The Times* of London to assure its readers that this was the moment "not to despair, but to rebuild." Another was the psychological skill with which Hitler, not for the first or last time, combined the sudden shock of his challenging action with insubstantial offers which soothed, bewildered, and divided his opponents. On this occasion he offered both Britain and France a nonaggression pact valid until 1961, coupled with an assurance that he had no more territorial demands in Europe, thus implying that a formal and more general European pact was hardly necessary. But underneath all else there was the reluctance of two satiated powers, who knew that they had only just succeeded in surmounting the trials of one war, to run the risk of a second such trial in which even victory would not enable them to stave off ruin. When General Gamelin found a pretext for inactivity in doubting whether the German entry into the Rhineland constituted "flagrant aggression" within the meaning of the Treaty of Locarno, or when a British Labor Party leader said that public opinion in his party would not support the application of economic, let alone military, sanctions to eject the German aggressors, they were finding reasons for an inactivity which was very widely welcomed. Idealists hated war on principle, realists hated it because Britain and France were unprepared—partly because the idealists had called upon them to disarm. Thus Hitler throve on their disunity and divided purposes.

■ FENCING FOR POSITION: EUROPE AND THE WAR IN SPAIN

The Rhineland reoccupation of March, 1936, marked for western Europe the end of the period of tranquillity secured by the Locarno Treaties and the beginning of a period in which German ambitions supported by German arms might be expected to challenge the existing order, even at the risk of another major war. What followed was an interval of exactly two years in which Germany made no move towards direct territorial aggression, an interval felicitously named by Sir Winston Churchill "the loaded pause" and remembered chiefly at the present day for the lingering tragedy of the Civil War in Spain. The Civil War, as will be seen, became closely entangled with European rivalries, but in its origins it was an independent phenomenon of the age. We shall therefore examine first the ways in which Germany continued to gain strength as a sequel to the events already narrated, and then we shall consider separately the situation in Spain, which presented Germany and other unscrupulous powers with an unexpected chance to fish in troubled waters.

German rearmament had acquired considerable momentum as early as 1935. Hitler was able to build upon the important skeleton structure of the Reichswehr organization and a disguised general staff, upon the illicit training arrangements with Russia, which dated from the early 1920's, upon the physical basis afforded by the biggest steel industry in Europe, and upon the moral basis of nationwide resentment against the armament restrictions imposed at

Versailles. But these advantages did not mean that the Germans could regain, as it were overnight, the military strength they had forfeited in 1918. Hitler's speeches sought to cover up by vehemence and rhetoric the deficiencies and failures inevitable in a period of rapid growth. Such propaganda also helped to create an enthusiasm for discipline, hardness, and self-sacrifice which sped the reconstruction of a conscript army. By the autumn of 1936 the system was already functioning so smoothly that an extra class was called up, thus increasing by a whole age group the number of trained men who would be available in two years time. Even so, neither the promised peacetime army of more than half a million men, nor the new *Luftwaffe*, which was to grow out of the existing civil air lines, nor the new navy, for which the British had given their consent, could be built up until German war industries were completely restored. This restoration was to be among the fruits of a gigantic four-year plan under Goering's management, which was designed to achieve all-round self-sufficiency by 1940. According to a careful calculation made for Churchill, expenditure on armaments in the first year approximated one billion pounds. Unemployment was consequently cured, and the German working week rose to sixty hours. For each year that passed, Germany's war potential increased both absolutely and in relation to that of her democratic and nonmilitarist neighbors and future victims.

At the same time Hitler was busy reorganizing his relations with some of those neighbors, so as to rescue his country from the isolation to which her unprincipled actions, loudly denounced by Britain and France and formally condemned by the League of Nations, might be expected to relegate her. His nonaggression pact with Poland, signed in 1934, was more than counterbalanced by the treaty of mutual assistance between France and Soviet Russia, signed in May, 1935. The treaty was finally ratified in the following March when Hitler made it serve as a convenient if flimsy pretext for his spectacular breach of the Locarno agreements. But Italy's confrontation by Britain and France with the threat of oil sanctions, not yet formally renounced at the time of Hitler's Rhineland coup, had done much to realign Italy with Germany. Then in July, 1936, came a German agreement with Austria. On the one hand Hitler specifically recognized the sovereign independence of Austria. On the other hand she was obliged to agree that her policy should always be based on the principle that "Austria has acknowledged herself to be a German state." This agreement removed Mussolini's qualms regarding the German threat to the independence of his small neighbor across the Brenner Pass, which he had championed as vital to the interests of his own country at the time of the assassination of Dollfuss. The older dictator now felt free to enter upon a close agreement with his younger counterpart, a relationship in which he fondly believed that he would always keep the upper hand. In November, 1936, Mussolini proudly proclaimed the "Berlin-Rome Axis," which the events of the Spanish Civil War, by then at its height, did much to emphasize as a constant factor in the affairs of Europe.

In the same month Hitler announced the establishment of a link with a third unsatisfied power, geographically remote from Germany but akin in ideology and ambitions. This was achieved by the Anti-Comintern Pact, in which he joined forces with the Japanese in opposition to world communism. A year later, when Italy adhered to this pact, it was made clear that the three powers hoped in due course to establish a "great world-political triangle" for the benefit of their respective interests. Fortunately for the rest of mankind, no full co-ordination of their efforts was ever accomplished. In the meantime Germany was doubly strengthened: directly, by the weakening of Russian pressure in Europe through increased apprehensiveness regarding the possibility of concerted attack in the Far East; indirectly, by the weakening of British and French pressure because of a belief in many circles that whoever was "anti-Comintern" was their friend, even if a friend in disguise.

Events in Spain were creating an acute problem of choice for political leaders in both Britain and France. It seemed impossible for them to save the Republic without aiding and abetting the formation of a new communist state in the heart of western Europe. The second Spanish Republic, indeed, was an independent native growth, the removal of King Alfonso XIII in 1931 having been the result of a deep-rooted and widespread aspiration among the under-privileged classes to establish political and economic democracy. This they would do by the overthrow of the great landowners and their two citadels of power, the Catholic Church and the army. Bitter political conflict ensued, and in the third year of the Republic the elections went in favor of the Right. In 1936, however, a Popular Front was formed on the French model, a union of Liberals, Nationalists, Anarchists, and Communists, which gained a two-to-one majority in the elections and proceeded to carry out its mandate from the Spanish people to complete the original Republican program. This did not suit the defeated parties of the Right, which acted in accordance with the tradition of a century or more in plotting to recover their lost power by a military coup. In mid-July, 1936, General Francisco Franco organized a mutiny of the army in Morocco, which spread quickly through the mainland garrisons, though it had no success in Madrid or Barcelona. The stage was set for a war of lightning offensives and wearisome delays, which took nearly three years to end and left Spain, with Portugal, as the surviving stronghold of fascism in contemporary Europe.

An American historian laconically describes the struggle as "a class struggle in which the rich defeated the poor."[3] It was both more and less than

3. H. STUART HUGHES, *Contemporary Europe* (1962), p. 294.

this. The Basques and Catalonians fought for the Republic to a considerable extent in defense of what might fairly be called states' rights, based on a long and not inglorious record of independence and separatist aspirations. Catholics, on the other hand, in many cases supported the rebellion as a crusade against atheism rather than for the defense of private property, and scions of noble families were inspired to offer their lives "for Spain" from a romantic patriotism as well as a desire to hold fast their wealth. The sum of the deeds of heroism performed on both sides is matched, however, by the long tale of murder and massacre, wanton sacrilege and plunder, deliberate perfidy, and horrible practices of torture and mutilation which detailed study proves to have amounted to much more than the commonplace of journalistic war propaganda. Left to themselves, the two sides were not unevenly matched. Though the Republican government had the advantage of operating from the seat of authority, the Fascists were less disunited: as early as April, 1937, Franco's Falangists, founded in 1933, were able to absorb their monarchist rivals. The government had greater potential resources of manpower, but the rebels included nearly all the senior army officers and fully trained, seasoned troops. The government had the navy and small air force and the official representation in foreign countries; the rebellion was backed from the outset by the wealth of great industrialists. As for territory, in the north the government even at the outset held little more than the Basque provinces and the coastal districts to the west of them, and this area was completely lost by October, 1937. Madrid remained Republican to the very end, even though it had a narrow escape from capture in the first autumn of the war, when Franco had counted confidently on a "fifth column" inside the city. From Barcelona the Republicans controlled the whole of eastern Spain and the Mediterranean coastline, to which Franco's forces did not penetrate until April, 1938.

Foreign intervention in the war began at such an early stage that it is impossible to say with confidence what the final result would have been if the Spaniards had been left to their own devices. It seems likely that the Republic would have survived the initial shock and had time to train sufficient forces to smother the rebellion. Ultimately, however, the Second World War would almost certainly have rekindled the ashes. As it was, Mussolini hoped to strengthen his position in the Mediterranean through the establishment of a subsidiary Fascist power in Spain. Italian airplanes therefore helped in the initial transfer of troops from Morocco to the peninsula, and within a year a total of about 100,000 Italian soldiers were assisting the rebels, who also received support from more than 1,000 Italian aircraft and considerable sums of money. Hitler, who in this matter followed the Italian lead, was apparently well satisfied that the Italian commitment should be greater than the German. He saw no particular advantage in putting an end to a situation which embroiled so many powers that Germany must eventually reap a profit from their distraction. His contribution was therefore smaller in quantity though higher in quality than the Italian. In addition to shipments of arms, it comprised eleven squadrons sent from the new German air force largely for experimental purposes, and a single tank battalion for training Franco's own mechanized forces.

The help which reached the lawful government of Spain from outside the country was by comparison grudgingly given and intermittent. Soviet Russia sent in the first supplies of military equipment within ten days of the outbreak of the rebellion, and was an important source of fighter aircraft, technicians, and military advisers. But the value of Russia's help was seriously diminished by her interference in Spanish domestic politics as the champion of the Communists against their Anarchist and Trotskyite rivals, while in the last year of the war events in Russia and the Far East caused her to lose all interest in the fate of the western peninsula. For additional men the government had to fall back upon the volunteer international brigades, bands of left-wing sympathizers from many lands, who never numbered more than about 60,000 men and were not conspicuous for military discipline. The governments of Britain and France, though not their peoples, regarded the struggle in Spain from first to last as a tiresome and dangerous distraction from domestic problems and the international crisis elsewhere. The British National government also had a class prejudice against the left-wing regime in Spain, which the French Popular Front did not share. The result was the long and futile history of the Nonintervention Committee, which the two powers sponsored and to which they secured the nominal adherence of every European power. A strict watch was to be kept to prevent outside help from reaching either side in Spain. Such an agreement in any case bore hard upon the lawful government of the country, since the rebels were placed on a footing of equality with it. Much more serious was the fact that the British and French authorities showed themselves to be more concerned to avoid an open breach with Germany or Italy than to have the agreement properly enforced. For a time some help continued to reach the government side in Spain from Russia. But Mussolini and Hitler flouted the committee more openly and much more persistently; the main force of Italian "volunteers," to whose presence Mussolini alluded quite freely, did not begin to withdraw until 1938, by which time Spain had been effectively conquered for fascism.

It is believed that the Civil War cost Spain a million of her citizens dead or in exile, to say nothing of ruined cities and the ruined lives of those of the losers who stayed behind. This was a struggle of ideas and ideals, which had engaged the sympathies of the young and the intelligent in Europe and beyond: Americans fought, for example, in the International Brigades. But when the fate of Spain was conveniently forgotten in the onrush of other problems, there remained three important results. The two dictators had imposed their solution upon the problem, and in doing so had become firm friends, as witnessed by the Berlin-Rome Axis. Britain and France conversely had failed, and in the course of the tortuous proceedings over nonintervention had increased rather than diminished their suspicions of Russian policy, suspicions which could not but be reciprocated. Lastly, the awkward prospect emerged that, in the event of a general European war, France was now likely to find her southwestern frontier exposed to attack for the first time since Wellington passed the Pyrenees in 1813.

■ THE ABSORPTION OF AUSTRIA IN GERMANY

The *Anschluss*—to use the convenient German word for the incorporation of Austria in Germany—had been discussed ever since 1919 and almost certainly had, for a time at least, the support of a majority of the Austrian people. The economic condition of the smaller country was unsound, while party and regional feuds seemed incapable of reconciliation. Although Austrians customarily regarded the Germans of the Reich as uncouth and unattractive, they were bound to feel the influence of Hitler's dominant role in European affairs and be affected by all the propaganda in their common language about the greatness of the new Germany. For all the rest of Europe the *Anschluss* clearly meant an unacceptable change in the balance of power, and the prospect of the further aggrandizement of Germany through the virtual encirclement of Czechoslovakia and the access Germany would have gained to the Balkans. Both diplomatic and military preparations were therefore more important than the agitation conducted by Nazi adherents inside Austria; both types of preparation were concealed according to Hitler's practice by the treaty of July, 1936, explicitly promising that he would not attempt to tamper with the independence of Austria. This was followed in January, 1937, by an announcement that he had finished with the "policy of surprises."

Before the end of the year, however, Hitler was ready for action. In November the closer relationship with Italy which had grown out of their common involvement in the Spanish Civil War led to her ceremonial inclusion in the Anti-Comintern Pact, on which occasion Mussolini indicated that his interest in the Austrian question had declined. Immediately before this Hitler had held a secret meeting with the heads of the foreign office and the armed services, at which he purported to expound his long-range plans for German territorial expansion in Europe. Germany's problem, he declared, could only be solved by means of force and the use of force involved attendant risk. Several alternative hypothetical situations were then discussed, none of which exactly resembled the situations which did in fact arise. Some historians therefore maintain that this was not a firm agreement to wage aggressive war (as was afterwards claimed at the Nuremberg trials), but merely a device to stimulate demand for the continued expansion of the arms industries, which Hitler considered essential to keep unemployment down. However, it shows at the very least that Hitler envisaged the deliberate running of risks by the employment of a policy which depended on the use of force, if not in actual practice then certainly as a threat. Such a policy was to bring him its first easy success in Austria only four months later. Hitler used the intervening period, significantly enough, to get rid of the independent-minded war minister, Werner von Blomberg, on the flimsy pretext of a socially unsuitable marriage. He then placed the three services directly under his own command, exercised through the subservient General Wilhelm Keitel and a defense staff.

Events then moved quickly. On February 12, 1938, the successor to Dollfuss as chancellor of Austria, the rather colorless moderate reactionary, Kurt von Schuschnigg,[4] was summoned to Hitler's presence and ordered to appoint the Austrian Nazi leader, Artur von Seyss-Inquart, as minister of the interior. He meekly agreed, but almost a month later decided to try to arrest the drift into Nazism inside the country, and perhaps win support for its existing status from outside, by holding a nationwide plebiscite on the desirability of continued independence. Taken by surprise, Hitler demanded the cancellation of the proposal, the resignation of Schuschnigg, and the appointment of Seyss-Inquart to succeed him. Since neither France nor Britain nor Italy would promise any support for Austria, the president of the Republic was compelled to accept the first two demands, stubbornly refusing, however, to appoint Seyss-Inquart. An immediate crisis developed. At the end of a hectic series of telephone conversations, Seyss-Inquart appointed himself chancellor and asked for German assistance in restoring law and order. At this time the German army was already on the march. Though nearly three-quarters of the German military vehicles broke down on the road to Vienna, a show of force sufficed. When Hitler himself entered Austria in the wake of the army, enough enthusiasm was displayed to cause him to make Austria a part of Germany rather than a German satellite. A month and a day after Schuschnigg's visit to Hitler, his successor decreed his country out of existence, and a plebiscite of "Greater Germany" gave a 99 percent vote in support of his action.

The Saar, the Rhineland, and now Austria—the shadow of the new Germany on the march fell far across the frontiers of neighbor states, although no non-Germans (except the many Jews now trapped in Vienna) had as yet been brought under Hitler's rule. Governments made the best they could of

4. Born 1897. Member of the Catholic Party and founder of the rightist *Sturmscharen;* minister of justice under Dollfuss. As chancellor he continued a pro-Italian foreign policy and an internal policy of clerical fascism, based on the Fatherland Front. He was imprisoned during the German annexation of Austria, 1938–1945; he became a professor in the United States in 1948.

the changed situation. In France the Center groups, which were beginning to prevail over those of the Popular Front, were inclined to write off eastern Europe as fated to pass under German dominance. In Britain the new prime minister, Neville Chamberlain, considered that territorial claims based on possessing common nationality were in the long run undeniable, especially when the claimant was a strong man like Hitler. In Italy Mussolini, who had had some forewarning, accepted the German action without demur, not because he liked it but from a shrewd perception of the true relative strength of the two ends of the Berlin-Rome Axis. He had his reward, for Hitler in gratitude promised Mussolini that he would be "ready to go with him through thick and thin—through anything," and in this instance kept his word.

The peoples of western Europe, on the other hand, including the Italians, were not so much reassured by the calm attitude of their governments to the *Anschluss* as they were disquieted by the contrast between Hitler's record of successes and the supineness of other governments. This disquiet did not, however, lead to any great stepping-up of the rate of rearmament. The British and French peoples still thought of war in terms of self-defense—as still only a very remote possibility, though less remote than it had been five years earlier—not in terms of a crusade to maintain the liberties of other peoples. To keep Hitler in check, was anything more required than a firm and farsighted diplomacy, securely based on the principle of collective security? When, however, a further test followed quickly, too quickly perhaps for the lessons of the Austrian crisis to be properly assimilated, it resulted in the discomfiture and humiliation of peoples as well as governments.

■ THE DISMEMBERMENT OF CZECHOSLOVAKIA

Within a month of the inclusion of 6,750,000 Austrians in Germany, Hitler was launching a campaign to bring in the 3,000,000 so-called "Sudeten" Germans from Czechoslovakia. From this the further advantage to him of the elimination of that state as a factor in European affairs would presumably follow. Three ways of looking at Czechoslovakia, indeed, were possible, involving divergences of interest upon which Hitler counted to prevent the establishment of any united support in Europe for its defense. First, from a liberal standpoint its creation had been the most satisfactory consequence of the breakup of Austria-Hungary, for Prague was the capital of a financially stable, solidly bourgeois, convincingly parliamentary state. Its universally respected first president had been Thomas Masaryk, succeeded in 1935 by his right-hand man and fellow sociologist, Eduard Beneš. Second, however, from a strictly nationalist angle, Czechoslovakia was a country of disharmonious nationalities, a deliberately created anachronism in an age of nation-states. Not only were the grievances of a German-language minority of more than 20 percent echoed by appreciable percentages of Magyars, Ruthenians, and Poles; an undercurrent of national resentment also existed among the overwhelmingly rural and partly illiterate Slovaks over a system of government in which the urban, industrialized Czechs were inevitably the predominant partner. To political realists Czechoslovakia had a third significance. They stressed the military value of its army of thirty-four divisions, its armaments industry, and fortifications. Together these made Czechoslovakia the most important element in the network of alliances built up by France in eastern Europe to secure her position after the First World War. More recently the Franco-Soviet Pact had been accompanied by a treaty binding Russia to support French action in defense of Czechoslovakia.

In April, 1938, the Nazi leader in Czechoslovakia, Konrad Henlein, announced his Karlsbad program. It consisted of a series of demands for Sudeten autonomy the details of which have little significance, since Henlein was acting on instructions from Hitler to increase the demands whenever any serious risk arose of the Czechoslovak government accepting them. A war of nerves began, as a result of which Sudeten grievances received a kind of recognition through the dispatch of a British investigator, Lord Runciman, to study the situation. Beneš met this by formally conceding every autonomist claim that had been advanced by Sudeten spokesmen. Hitler then made a vague but impassioned speech about the alleged grievances of "these tortured and oppressed creatures," in response to which the Sudeten Germans rioted in favor of union with Germany. The revolt having been suppressed within twenty-four hours, the world waited for Hitler to march into the disputed territory, whereupon Czechoslovakia's allies would be bound to intervene.

On the contrary, what followed was the capitulation at Munich. A quarter of a century later, the share of the few participants who survive still besmirches their reputation. Its very name, moreover, has passed into the language of politics as a synonym for the sacrifice of principle to a shortsighted and cowardly expediency. In particular, blame has been attached to the British prime minister, Neville Chamberlain. Unlike the two French leaders, Edouard Daladier and Georges Bonnet, he had very strong parliamentary support. Earlier in the same year he had substituted Lord Halifax for Sir Anthony Eden at the British Foreign Office because the latter opposed a reconciliation with Mussolini; Chamberlain now believed that the proper course was to make a deal with Hitler at the expense of Czechoslovakia—"a far-away country," as he declared in a broadcast, "of which we know nothing." The result, so he hoped, might be a lasting peace.

Convinced that the German army might move at any moment, Chamberlain flew to interview Hitler at Berchtesgaden and secured a promise of delay pending negotiation. This was no sacrifice for Hitler, since no military action

SIGNATORIES OF THE MUNICH AGREEMENT, 1938. Prime Minister Neville Chamberlain of Great Britain and Premier Edouard Daladier of France meet with Adolf Hitler and Benito Mussolini in the Fuehrer's House at Munich on September 29, 1938. On the extreme right is Count Ciano, Mussolini's son-in-law.

was contemplated before October; what Chamberlain conceded was the principle of a partitioning of Czechoslovakia. Returning to London, he won the consent of the French by agreeing to guarantee the remainder of the country, thus imposing a theoretical barrier to further German aggression. The French in turn wrung acceptance from the Czechs by saying that they would not be able to fulfill their obligation to defend Czechs against German aggression for lack of British support. Hitler, however, in a second meeting with Chamberlain at Godesberg on the Rhine raised his terms. Since the Hungarians and Poles were also beginning to clamor for self-determination, he may have thought that Czechoslovakia would disintegrate of its own accord. More probably, his contempt for the western powers encouraged him to demand the right of military entry into the disputed territory not later than October 1. Less than a week remained, during which it became increasingly clear to Hitler that, if driven into a corner, France and Britain would support the Czechs in fighting. A slightly less spectacular triumph, however, was his for the asking. Accordingly, on September 28 he acceded to a request from his ally, Mussolini, to whom Chamberlain, Daladier, and Roosevelt had all appealed, to hold a four-power conference at Munich on the following day. Only nine hours of negotiation were required to produce an agreement, under which German troops began to occupy the Sudetenland, zone by zone, on October 1 as intended. In addition, there was to be a face-saving interval of one week for adjudication of German claims to a fifth zone. The Czechs had no alternative but to submit. Germany in the end received approximately the amount of territory claimed at Godesberg, and other, smaller cessions were promptly exacted by Poland and Hungary.

"Good man!" wired Roosevelt approvingly to Chamberlain when he heard of his intention to go to Munich.[5] Though Roosevelt quickly reappraised the situation, his words found abundant echo on both sides of the Atlantic when the participants returned to their capitals bearing, as Chamberlain claimed, "peace for our time." But the increased though still insufficient vigor with which plans for rearmament were now pursued by the democratic powers suggests that the mood of optimism among responsible statesmen was both superficial and ephemeral. In retrospect, it seems surprising that a Czechoslovak state which had been partitioned, humiliated, and deprived of its main frontier defenses could ever have been considered likely to survive. In November a new Czech government attempted to placate separatist feelings by converting the country into a federal state of "Czecho-Slovakia," in which Slovakia and Ruthenia controlled their own internal affairs. With German encouragement the new Slovak government thus created demanded a greater and greater degree of independence, until the Czech authorities were finally provoked into intervening in order to preserve the new federation from complete disruption. When the Slovaks appealed for Hitler's help against the Czechs, German troops marched into both territories, and the new Czech president was browbeaten at a stormy interview in Berlin into a most reluctant request for the establishment of a German protectorate of Bohemia-Moravia. The Hungarians having at the same time seized Ruthenia, the dismemberment of Czechoslovakia was completed by March 16, 1939, though another week passed before Slovakia too passed formally under the protection of Germany.

Chamberlain was at last completely disillusioned as to the value of any promise made by Hitler, with whom he had tried to deal as a fellow businessman. Viewing the events in retrospect, we may conclude that Britain was a little less to blame for the final catastrophe than France, the pledged ally of the Czechs. Perhaps both peoples were led or misled at this time by governments of poorer moral and intellectual quality than they deserved. In any case the destruction of Czechoslovakia cost the western powers dear, above all because one obvious means of attempting its preservation had been persistently rejected.

In March, 1938, immediately after the *Anschluss,* the Soviet government

5. U.S. Department of State, *Foreign Relations of the United States. Diplomatic Papers,* vol. I (1955), p. 688.

had proposed a meeting with the British, French and United States govern-ments to discuss collective action in the event of further aggression. Chamber-lain rejected the proposal as "inimical to the prospects of European peace." During the following six months the Russians had nevertheless consistently asserted their readiness to support action by France under the terms of the French and Soviet pacts with Czechoslovakia. The confused situation in the U.S.S.R. at the time made it easy to argue that this assertion was mere bluff, a matter regarding which historians still lack evidence for passing judgment. But the fact that no Russian representative was invited to the meeting at Munich, at which the fate of their Czech allies was determined, was clear evidence that neither Russia's entry into the League and its Council nor the ratification of the Franco-Soviet Pact had overcome the invincible distrust of a class enemy. Powerful elements in European society still judged Hitler's ag-gressions as involving a smaller threat to their interests than any westward infiltration of communism.

■ WAR FOR POLAND?

"Is this the last attack upon a small state, or is it to be followed by an-other?" The rhetorical question posed by Chamberlain in a speech at Birming-ham on March 17, 1939, marks the moment of disillusionment. While he was reluctantly realizing that Hitler had tricked him, the people of Britain were swept by a more complete revulsion of feeling against the whole spirit of the Munich Agreement, when, as they now saw, the existence of an inoffensive smaller power had been bartered for a shameful peace which was not even a lasting peace. Henceforth Britain carried France along with her, silencing the doubts of her more sceptical and more exposed neighbor across the Channel by a token measure of peacetime conscription, which imposed six months service upon men aged twenty and twenty-one. The sense of urgency was strengthened by news of Germany's exaction of Memel from the hands of Lithuania and the landing of Italian troops to take possession of Albania on Good Friday. Accord-ingly, guarantees were quickly made available to any European state which believed its territorial integrity to be threatened—to Poland first, but also to Greece, Rumania, and Turkey.

The Polish Republic had been governed under a semi-fascist regime since Pilsudski's coup d'état of 1926; it was consistently anti-Russian and also anti-Semitic in outlook; and it enjoyed the protection of a ten-year nonaggression pact, signed by Hitler five years previously. With nearly three times the popu-lation of Czechoslovakia, Poland had fewer trained men and she had virtually no up-to-date military equipment. However, the facts of her geographical posi-tion made a clash with a resurgent Germany sooner or later almost inevitable. By preaching the superior rights of the German nation as a "master race," or

Herrenvolk, Hitler had practically committed himself to the re-annexation of the German-inhabited Free City of Danzig and to some change of regime in the Polish Corridor. This was the territory containing a substantial German population which had changed hands in 1919 in order that the new Poland should have access to the sea. Believing that Danzig was in imminent danger, Chamberlain on March 31 offered an unconditional guarantee in the event of "any action . . . which clearly threatened their independence, and which the Polish government . . . felt obliged to resist." From that moment Britain and France were formally committed to calling Hitler's bluff.

This time there was no bluff. On April 3, Hitler ordered his forces to be ready for an attack on an isolated Poland by September 1, the actual date of the attack. Next he repudiated his treaty with Poland and the naval treaty with Britain. In May the so-called "Pact of Steel" bound Italy more closely to the German alliance, though Mussolini inserted a stipulation that he could not be required to participate in a war within the next three or four years. If Poland refused to let at least Danzig pass into German hands, she was to be struck down; and if France and Britain, contrary to Hitler's expectation, persisted in supporting her, then German forces must be ready "to fall upon the West and finish off Poland at the same time." After his long list of successes, there was only one risk Hitler was still not prepared to run. This was the possibility of serious and immediate intervention by Soviet Russia on the side of his opponents.

On the face of things Stalin's government might reasonably be expected to take sides with France and Britain, having been driven into their camp (and that of the League) by the violence of Hitler's polemics against communism and his long-cherished designs against Russian territory. For the author of *Mein Kampf* was on record as regretting the failure of the kaiser's Germany "to start marching along the road of the [Teutonic] Knights of former times to give, with the help of the German sword, the soil to the plow and the daily bread to the nation." He had roundly proclaimed that the goal of German foreign policy should be "an eastern policy signifying the acquisition of the necessary soil for the German people."[6] On the other hand, throughout the period of estrangement which resulted from Hitler's rise to power, a link through trade had been carefully maintained. Moreover, it was not difficult for Germans to infer that reconciliation with Russia was still possible, for in each of a series of crises Britain and France had preferred to be worsted by Germany and even by Italy rather than call upon Russia for help. As late as the winter of Munich, Chamberlain had eagerly though ineffectually courted the goodwill of the Italians. The Russians, however, he still regarded not only as politically uncongenial, but also as militarily unreliable on account of the

6. A. HITLER, *Mein Kampf*, eds. John Chamberlain, Sidney B. Fay, *et al.* (1939), pp. 182–183, 966.

The uniqueness of Hitler's achievement and the potential menace of the Nazi "New Order" are brought out by comparison with Napoleon's empire at the height of the Continental System. See *Europe: 1450–1815*, p. 665.

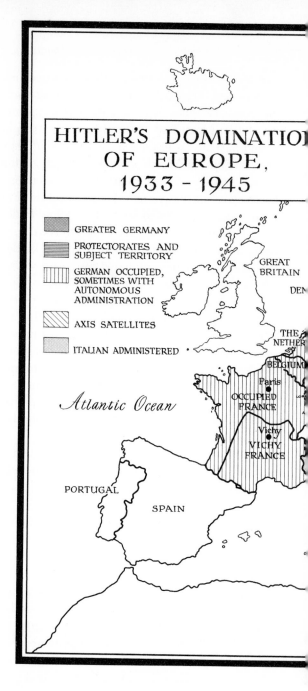

HITLER'S DOMINATION
OF EUROPE,
1933 - 1945

GREATER GERMANY

PROTECTORATES AND SUBJECT TERRITORY

GERMAN OCCUPIED, SOMETIMES WITH AUTONOMOUS ADMINISTRATION

AXIS SATELLITES

ITALIAN ADMINISTERED

Atlantic Ocean

GREAT BRITAIN

DEN

THE NETHER

BELGIUM

Paris
OCCUPIED FRANCE

Vichy
VICHY FRANCE

PORTUGAL

SPAIN

purges and, in addition, as geographically rather remote from the contested regions in central Europe. Now that a struggle for Poland was in view, Russia was in a position to act and had an obvious interest in acting: both sides had a correspondingly strong inducement to contrive that her action was in their support.

250

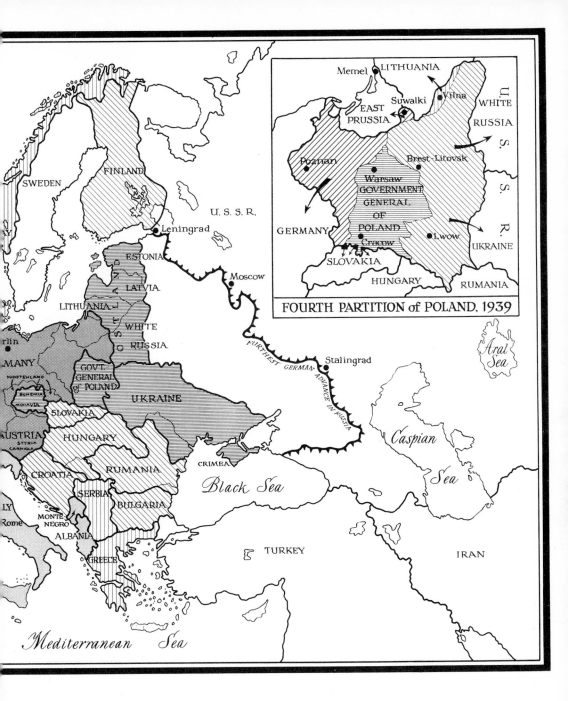

FOURTH PARTITION of POLAND, 1939

Since no Russian documents have been published, it is impossible to apportion the blame or even the responsibility for the tragic shift of alliances which took the peoples of western Europe completely by surprise. For the summer in which Hitler's battle of nerves against the Poles engrossed public attention and created something like a general expectation of war in the autumn

251

was also the time when Soviet Russia, unnoticed because unwelcome, returned from an absence of more than two decades to resume her role as a major power on the European scene. As such she had no intention of signing any agreement which might leave her to fight Germany alone. Yet, although the western powers had no means of bringing military assistance to the Poles other than through an agreement with Russia, they persisted in treating her as an ally on sufferance only. They demanded that her intervention should not take place unless and until it was asked for by France, Britain, and Poland together. They held that Rumania and the Baltic States must also agree, in the event that it was desired to march across their territory.

The replacement of the genial, westernized Maxim Litvinov as foreign minister by the brusquely efficient Vyacheslav Molotov in early May could be read as a danger signal for the West. The deadlock nevertheless remained unbroken, and when it was eventually decided on July 23 to proceed to military talks in the hope that the political difficulties would somehow settle themselves, the British and French military missions took nineteen days to get organized and make the journey to Moscow. By then it was too late. Although one or two overtures had been made earlier by the Germans, they did not begin to find the Russians conciliatory until the first week in August. Where the western powers were slow, the Germans were prompt: on August 19 they were told that Joachim von Ribbentrop could be received in Moscow in a week's time; he arrived on August 23, and the nonaggression pact was signed the same day.

The published terms provided that neither signatory would join any third party in war against the other; those kept secret promised reciprocal benefits of a kind which no democratic power would contemplate offering. "In the event of a political and territorial rearrangement," Poland was to be divided into two spheres of influence along the line of the rivers Narew and San. Lithuania was to be included in the German sphere, and Finland, Estonia, Latvia, and Bessarabia in the Russian. By this stroke Hitler, whose contempt for the men with whom he had negotiated at Munich was unbounded, probably expected once again to get his way without a war.

The Poles, however, were taught by the fate of Czechoslovakia to resist any compromise over Danzig and the Corridor, where the Germans were now alleged by Hitler to be suffering tremendous persecution. The British were not much interested in maintaining the integrity of Poland for its own sake, but they regarded the fulfilment of their guarantees as a matter both of duty and expediency, from which they were not to be deterred by an unprincipled diplomatic revolution aimed at their discomfiture. The French, while they would still have welcomed any kind of compromise between Germany and Poland, were led by their awareness of declining strength to follow the British lead, as they had done for the past three years. The Poles accordingly offered resistance to the German invaders, who entered their country at dawn on September 1.

On the evening of the next day the strong feeling of the House of Commons caused Chamberlain to give up the idea of a further conference, proposed at the last minute by Mussolini at French instigation. Britain declared war after a two-hour ultimatum next morning; a few hours later France followed suit.

■ RESPONSIBILITY FOR THE OUTBREAK OF WAR

Since the circumstances in which Hitler eventually launched war were so predominantly in his favor, the failure to make any major effort to stop him at an earlier stage appears in retrospect very remarkable. The explanation seems to lie in the fact that he began with a psychological advantage, which served him well until it could be replaced by practical advantages. The psychological advantage has appeared so often in this narrative that it needs only a very brief recapitulation. The Germans had a number of plausible and to a large extent genuine grievances: the severities and humiliations of the Treaty of Versailles; the refusal to treat Germany as equal in the matter of armaments; the existence of large German minorities under alien governments; the denial of colonies; and in general the reluctance to acknowledge the return of Germany to the rank of a great power. At the same time there were conspicuous weaknesses in the attitudes of other peoples which enabled this German sense of grievance to take full effect. These included not only the widespread sense of guilt regarding the peace settlement but also the desire to avoid a new war at almost any cost and a consequent readiness to put off difficult decisions. Hitler's opponents were disposed to take soothing statements at their face value, and to be readily distracted from international complexities to more pleasant considerations nearer home. It might not be too much to say of both the British and the French people that declining strength caused them to find their international responsibilities an irksome burden, and that they secretly envied the United States, whose withdrawal into isolationism they were wont to denounce.

By trading on these tendencies Hitler contrived to be taken at his word, which he systematically broke. By the time his promises that one more concession meant peace for all Europe were disbelieved, he had acquired the means to negotiate from strength. In his early days of power he had boasted freely of armaments he did not possess, and it had several times been a matter of touch and go whether the army leaders would not refuse to run the risks which he required them to take. But the unity of policy inside the Reich, which he had enforced by methods of sheer terrorism, had each time prevailed over the divided counsels of his opponents: France and Britain never cooperated wholeheartedly, and each country was weakened by vociferous internal rivalries. Thus Hitler was enabled to reach the period most favorable to his plans, when big threats could be backed up by military measures if the blackmail which he had found so congenial failed to show a profit.

It is a commonplace to say that the growth of armaments is a cause of war. The statement is on the whole less true of the catastrophe of 1939 than it had been in 1914 because the improvement of static defenses and uncertainty regarding the effectiveness of the novel mechanized formations had made attack by land seem more of a gamble from the technical standpoint. Concurrently, the rapid development of the airplane in the interwar period had introduced a new major factor which was almost wholly incalculable. Nevertheless, from 1938 onward Europe had clearly entered upon a period when, even though the particular problems of Danzig and the Polish Corridor had never existed, it would still have been likely for military reasons that the conflict between Germany on the one hand and Britain and France on the other would somehow be brought to what Churchill expressively termed "the crunch." By that time the concentration of effort upon the arms industries as part of the German four-year plan, to which reference has already been made, was achieving results which the rest of Europe could not ignore. In particular, the expansion of the *Luftwaffe* had an almost hypnotic influence upon the public mind, especially since at Guernica in Spain Goering's bombers had translated Hitler's boasts into brutal realities. On the eve of the Munich crisis it was chiefly the feverish activity in building the West Wall, or Siegfried Line, to block a hypothetical French offensive which implied that German preparations were not yet too complete to be challenged. But the moment was allowed to pass: a large part of the Czech industrial potential fell into German hands in the Sudetenland, and the final liquidation of Czechoslovakia in March, 1939, gave Hitler also the Skoda arms works, one of the most important in Europe.

Although the German high command, from motives of professional caution rather than political opposition, persisted in claiming that Germany was not yet ready for a general war, it is clear that German military strength mounted steadily year by year. Indeed, Hitler was not merely daydreaming when he suggested at his famous conference in November, 1937, that 1943 would be his ideal moment for some final showdown with the western powers. In spite of the fact that by 1939 his opponents had to some extent changed both their attitude to war and the tempo of their preparations for it, when war broke out the Germans were still well in the lead. The biggest advance on the side of the Allies was almost certainly made by the British air force, which since 1936 had set to work to rival the German in quality and technical efficiency, though not in quantity, and with a determination which recalled the naval rivalry before 1914. Britain had modernized its navy to some extent, though the army remained small and undermechanized. France, in spite of the more advanced military doctrine preached by the brilliant Jewish politician Georges Mandel and a certain Colonel Charles de Gaulle, still based her defense upon wishful thinking about the value of her impregnable Maginot Line, a steel and concrete network of fortifications begun as early as 1930. Her system of alliances in eastern Europe, designed for the protection of France without a thought of involving Frenchmen in a reciprocal obligation to defend the territory of others, had been reduced to nothing. In September, 1939, Poland was to suffer alone; after Dunkirk, France.

In conclusion, the extent of Germany's military preparations constitutes a strong argument for Hitler's essential war guilt. The delays on the part of Britain and France are evidence of innocence as well as weakness. Since the ultimate results are known, it is clear that rearmament came only just in time; what is less clear is whether Britain and France gained by making their final stand in 1939, with a weaker ally and a weaker cause, rather than in 1938, when both had been stronger.

To what extent does the contemporary condemnation of Hitler as a fanatical warmonger still stand? The recent publication of British and German documents has led some historians to qualify the sweeping denunciations so prevalent in 1939 of Hitler's actions.[7] Nevertheless, the words of a distinguished scholar whose views on the origins of the First World War have commanded world-wide attention can well be cited here:

> Historians may legitimately dispute as to the relative responsibility of the various countries and their leaders for the catastrophe of 1914. No such dispute is possible for reasonable and well-informed persons in regard to the Second World War.[8]

Reading List: Chapter 9

Thomson, D., *Democracy in France* (4th ed., 1964, also paperback), ch. 5. The modern challenge.

Thomas, H., "The International Brigades in Spain," *History Today,* vol. XI (1961), no. 5.

Joll, J., *The Anarchists* (1964), ch. 9(3). Their part in the Spanish Civil War.

Watt, D. C., "The Reoccupation of the Rhineland," *History Today,* vol. VI (1956), no. 4.

Brook-Shepherd, G., *Anschluss, The Rape of Austria* (1963), ch. 8. Hitler comes home.

Namier, L. B., *Diplomatic Prelude, 1938–1939* (1948), ch. 5. A vivid though not un-challenged account of Anglo-Russian negotiations in April-August, 1939.

Sontag, R. J., "The Last Months of Peace, 1939," *Foreign Affairs,* vol. XXXV (1957), no. 3.

Schmitt, B. E., "1914 and 1939" (revision article). *Journal of Modern History,* vol. XXXI (1959), no. 2. Emphasizes the differences.

7. This is particularly true of A. J. P. TAYLOR in his *Origins of the Second World War* (1962).
8. SIDNEY B. FAY, "How the War Came," *Events* (October, 1939), p. 241.

Chapter 10

The Second World War

The Emergence of Total War
The First Blitzkrieg and the German Breakthrough to the Atlantic
The British at Bay
The German Invasion of Russia
The Japanese Conquests in East Asia
Mounting the Counterattack of the Western Allies
The Destruction of Hitler's Europe
The Counterattack on Japan

■ THE EMERGENCE OF TOTAL WAR

Although the vast conflict which began on the plains of Poland on September 1, 1939, and was concluded aboard U.S.S. *Missouri* in Tokyo Bay six years and one day later, deeply involved many non-European interests, the war at its beginning seemed to be essentially European. Hitler had long looked to the grain fields of the Ukraine as a conquest that would make Germany an economic force easily able to dominate her satellite states elsewhere in Europe. France and Britain were therefore regarded by him primarily as deterrents to the eastward expansion of the German frontiers. Poland, to be sure, was Germany's immediate victim, and well worth swallowing, but the U.S.S.R., with

256

SIGNIFICANT EVENTS

1939   German and Russian invasion of Poland (September)
        Russian invasion of Finland (November)

1940   Germans invade Denmark and Norway (April)
        Germans invade Low Countries and France (May)
        Battle of Britain begins (July)

1941   Germans invade Yugoslavia and Greece (April)
        Germans invade Russia (June)
        Japanese attack Pearl Harbor (December)

1942   Japanese capture Singapore (February)
        American victory at Midway Island (June)
        British victory at El Alamein (November)

1943   Russian victory at Stalingrad (February)
        Allied landings in Sicily (July)
        Commencement of Russian counteroffensive, near Orel (July)
        Tehran Conference (November)

1944   Allied landings in Normandy (June)
        American victory at Leyte Gulf (October)
        Failure of last German counterattack in western Europe (Battle
           of the Bulge) (December)

1945   Yalta Conference (February)
        Unconditional surrender of Germany (May)
        Potsdam Conference (July)
        Atomic bombs dropped on Hiroshima and Nagasaki (August)
        Unconditional surrender of Japan (September)

which Hitler had just signed a nonaggression pact, was intended as the ultimate victim of his ambitions. The world outside Europe meant remarkably little to Hitler; even the British and French colonies never gripped that vivid but limited imagination as more than the acceptable trophies of victory.

The new war was in a sense a resumption of the old. Once more the forces of a militant Germany were to strike savagely at France, whose chief support was again a Britain, strong by sea and at the outset weak by land. Once more the Germans planned to avoid fighting simultaneously on two fronts: after they had disposed of Poland, they would direct their second lightning attack or Blitzkrieg against France and Britain, leaving Russia to be dealt with last. Once more the Germans were in a position to secure reinforcement for their cause. A large part of the old Dual Monarchy was already included in the Reich; Italy could be brought in during the first year of war, as the Ottoman Empire had been in 1914; and Germany had a strong but distant and independent ally in Japan, destined to play a leading role in the later stages of the struggle. Once more Germany discounted both the ability and the inclination of the United States to intervene in the affairs of Europe, only to be disappointed again in due course, although this time with far more deadly consequences. Once more the upshot of the war was a defeat of the German bid for hegemony in Europe, and once more Europe paid a heavy price, both materially and in things of the spirit, for its liberation.

Despite these similarities, the differences between the two wars are on the whole more striking and more significant. The Kaiser's armies suffered a strategic defeat at the battle of the Marne in September, 1914, from which their fortunes never wholly recovered, whereas Hitler's enjoyed more than two years of virtually unbroken success before the Russian winter caught them unprepared in front of Moscow. Moreover, Hitler's successful war of aggression in Europe was soon linked up with a Japanese war of aggression in Asia which brought about and also to some extent limited the intervention of the United States in the war in Europe. Indeed, the objectives of the struggle between Japan and the United States and the scale of the forces engaged both show that this was no mere extension of the European war, as had been the case with the colonial and maritime warfare outside Europe in 1914–1918. Mankind was for the first time experiencing what could properly be termed global war. Lastly, an even more significant novelty was the fact that war between 1939 and 1945 began to deserve the epithet "total" by the depth of its penetration through human society.

Total war was in a sense the natural sequel to the growth of totalitarianism in time of peace. In Germany, Italy, and Japan, as in Communist Russia, propaganda and force had been used to imprint the pattern of a state whose control over its citizens extended from the political sphere to every aspect of life. By September, 1939, as the world learned to its cost, the Germans at least were prepared for a rapid transition to total war. The history of the next six years is largely concerned with the steps by which the democratic powers—in association for two-thirds of that period with Communist Russia—also learned to wage total war, until they eventually outstripped the members of the Axis, who had had so long a start.

The change is most clearly to be seen in the overwhelming demands which war made on the economy. By 1939 munitions industries in the widest sense of the term had already taken on a new dimension. This was a result of such factors as the huge growth in importance of the air arm, increased reliance upon artillery and automatic weapons, the use of motor transport throughout the armies, and experiments with special tank forces. In all these instances the Germans held a temporary superiority: they had reached the stage of mass output from sufficiently up-to-date designs, approved as blueprints when Hitler began his armaments drive. In Britain and France the business of switching industry to new purposes was begun later, and such processes as retooling of machinery could less easily be speeded up to meet an emergency. Even so, in the later years of the war, when it has been estimated (for the Pacific campaigns) that the weight of munitions and supplies of all kinds required for each fighting man was ten times what it had been in 1917, the United States alone had a greater output of war material than all the rest of the world combined. This meant the transfer of nine-tenths of America's huge industrial resources from the civilian to the military sector, while the other combatant powers from their more restricted resources were forced to concentrate to an even greater extent upon the economic needs of total war.

The involvement of civilian man power and woman power to an unprecedented extent in tasks of military supply provided some excuse for another feature of total war: the virtual disappearance of the distinction between combatant and noncombatant which civilized man had hitherto observed. Though air raids, for example, were directed nominally to military objectives, these included almost every major industrial complex; and if it was legitimate to bomb factories because their output contributed to the enemy war effort, could not the same result be achieved with equal legitimacy by bombing the factory workers in their homes? About thirty thousand British civilians were killed by the German air force in the winter of 1940–1941, a blood bath which neutral opinion in America and elsewhere regarded with horror. By 1945 a far higher civilian death rate caused by Allied raids on German industrial towns, to say nothing of the atom bombing at Hiroshima and Nagasaki, was being regarded as an inevitable concomitant of total war. Civilians were also made to feel the full impact of war in other ways: as refugees fleeing on a scale previously unknown in advance of hostile armies; as conscripted workers brought to Germany in millions to serve under inhuman conditions in munitions factories; or as sailors in merchant navies, running the gauntlet of attack from the air as well as by the submarines which had already drowned so many innocent victims in 1914–1918.

■ THE FIRST BLITZKRIEG AND
THE GERMAN BREAKTHROUGH TO THE ATLANTIC

The first campaign of the Second World War was a triumph for the German air force. The British and French governments naturally though self-centeredly preferred not to risk the overwhelming retaliation which would come if they used their own air forces to distract German attention from the Poles. On the other hand, the Poles had less than forty-eight hours in which to mobilize, and it was relatively easy for a German air force three or four times as powerful as their own to destroy Polish machines from the ground. The *Luftwaffe* was then free to range over the country, acting as the eyes of the advancing armies and creating panic in front of the advance. Meanwhile, under the capable direction of General Heinrich von Brauchitsch,[1] motorized formations, followed up by infantry, penetrated deep into enemy territory. Within a week the German forces were beginning to converge on Warsaw, which bravely withstood a destructive siege until the end of the month. Meanwhile, well before the German forces administered the coup de grace, the Russians, in accordance with the secret terms of their recent pact with Germany, entered and overran the eastern half of the country practically unresisted.

The fifth partition of Poland followed approximately the Curzon Line of 1919.[2] The Russian half, which included the Galician oil field, was populated mainly by White Russians and Ukrainians and was fairly easily absorbed into the White Russian and Ukrainian Soviet Socialist Republics, to which it still belongs. The German half was divided into two portions. Danzig, the disputed Corridor, and most of the industrial region were annexed to the Reich, and used for the resettlement of Germans from the Baltic States and other parts of Europe. The Poles, unless required as slave labor in Germany, were to be concentrated for exploitation in the other portion, which became a kind of protectorate under a Nazi governor general.

At first Hitler seems to have regarded the Polish Protectorate as a useful item for the peace discussions by which he still hoped to avert a head-on collision with Britain and France, who had done nothing effective to save their ally. However, the British and French pinned their faith to the economic blockade of Germany, which they had made as effective as they could in the absence of Russian support, and to the gradual mobilization of Britain's full military and industrial strength in preparation for an eventual decisive campaign in the west. His overtures having met with no response, Hitler nevertheless allowed one month of Blitzkrieg to be followed by six of *"Sitzkrieg,"* the period of the so-called "phony war" in which it seemed possible that hostilities would somehow peter out.

The sense of unreality was strengthened by the distraction of the

1. Born in 1881. A general staff officer in First World War and commander in chief since February, 1938, he was inclined to resent Hitler's interventions in military decisions, but remained in charge of all important operations until the Russian campaign failed to reach its objectives in December, 1941, when he was superseded by Hitler himself.
2. This was the result of a supplementary agreement, dated September 28, which moved the dividing line eastward to Brest Litovsk and added Lithuania to the Russian share. See pp. 57, 272.

Russo-Finnish War, a winter campaign (November 30–March 12) which originated in the refusal of the Finns to accept their inclusion along with the little Baltic States in the Russian military defense zone, as provided in the secret clauses of the Russo-German pact. Their spirited resistance aroused enormous enthusiasm in all the western democracies. Soviet Russia as an aggressor power was solemnly expelled from the League of Nations and preparations were made to send an Anglo-French expedition across unwilling Scandinavia to assist the Finns. Indeed, up to the moment when Finnish resistance unexpectedly collapsed, it looked as though some politicians of the Right, and even the French commander in chief, General Maurice Gamelin, were hoping somehow to exchange an unreal and unwelcome war against Germany for a general anti-Soviet crusade.

When the spring of 1940 came, Hitler's audacity quickly converted a war of political maneuver into a struggle for survival. He moved by land, sea, and air against Scandinavia. The Germans overran Denmark without difficulty, so that their reinforcements could reach Norway by a very short sea crossing. Even so, the initial attack on the Norwegian ports on April 9, from Oslo up to Narvik, was an immensely daring enterprise, since the German ships risked interception by the overwhelmingly stronger British navy while at sea and were also extremely vulnerable to the Norwegian coast defenses. Two factors turned what might have been a disastrous adventure for Hitler into a resounding success. The planning of the Germans was meticulous, enabling them to operate among the snowbound mountains of Norway at the same Blitzkrieg tempo that had carried them across the plains of Poland. The other factor was their many-sided use of air power.

To an even greater extent than in Poland, air operations dominated the entire campaign. By their ability to bomb bases and harass enemy troops from the air the Germans drove out the Anglo-French forces which were sent to support Norwegian resistance in central Norway. Their air power served also as an effective counterweight to British sea power. For as soon as German aircraft were able to operate from bases in Denmark and Norway, it became evident that naval antiaircraft armament gave insufficient protection to the larger units of the British fleet. Control of the eastern seaboard of the North Sea passed inevitably into German hands, and after a two-months struggle, even Narvik in the far north was abandoned by the Allies after its recapture, because of the desperate situation nearer home.

The German armies meanwhile on May 10, 1940, launched their great attack on France and the Low Countries. Britain was indeed fortunate in that, as a result of general dissatisfaction brought to a head by the failures in Norway, Winston Churchill at this critical juncture replaced Neville Chamberlain as prime minister and formed a strong, interparty government. The need was urgent, for, though the total numbers of the two sides were not unequal, Germany's ten armored divisions, strongly supported by the *Luftwaffe,* provided the spearhead for an overwhelmingly successful onslaught on the Allied armies. These now included the British expeditionary force of 400,000 men serving under the French high command.

One decisive factor was certainly the brilliance and ruthlessness of German strategy, both in planning and execution. As in the invasion of Denmark and Norway, the Germans took full advantage of the reluctance of small neutral powers to risk provoking an attack by adopting any advance measures for their own protection, especially such measures as involved any sort of collaboration with Britain or France. The first onslaught was directed against the unoffending Low Countries. Holland was reduced to submission in five days. Though the Belgians were on the whole better prepared for war, the British and French advancing into their country for its defense met not only the Belgian army already in rapid retreat but also a vast horde of hapless refugees fleeing from the bombs of the invader. Meanwhile the vital gap was opened farther south, where the strongest group of German armies was commanded by the very capable General Karl von Rundstedt.[3] On the fifth day of the fighting a bombing attack enabled them to secure a passage over the Meuse, and soon some five hundred tanks were moving freely toward the Channel coast in the rear of the Belgians, the British, and the left wing of the French armies.

The tactics of the Blitzkrieg were then practiced to produce almost the same sweeping successes as in Poland. Within a week the fast-moving German armor had reached the coast and was turning east to invest Boulogne and Calais. Gamelin was replaced as commander in chief by the aged veteran, General Maxime Weygand, who organized an attempt to close the rapidly widening gap between the British forces and the main French armies to the south of them. This failed, and when the Belgian king a few days later surrendered his entire army in the field the Germans were free to advance along the Belgian coast and complete the encirclement. The British were able with difficulty to battle their way back to the port of Dunkirk, where an improvised evacuation scheme rescued an almost miraculous total of 366,000 men, one-third of them French.

Since the British expeditionary force, however, had lost the whole of its equipment, no more than two British divisions took part in the rest of the fighting in France. The first week in June, which had seen the completion of the Dunkirk evacuation, witnessed the beginning of a whole series of further

---

3. Born in 1875, and chief of general staff in an army corps in the First World War. He commanded an army group against Poland, France, and in southern Russia, and became commander in chief in France and the Low Countries, 1942. He was dismissed as a failure in July, 1944, but was reinstated in September and carried out Hitler's counteroffensive in the Ardennes. He was dismissed again after the loss of the bridge at Remagen in March, 1945.

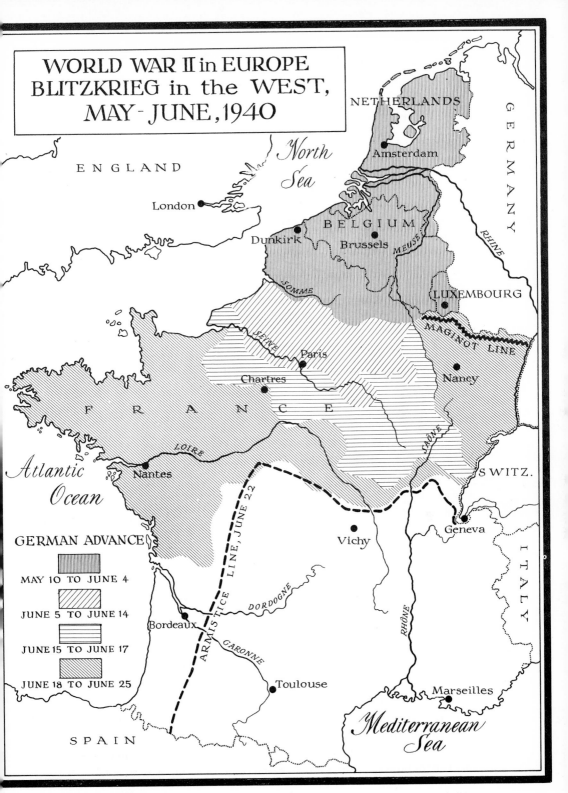

WORLD WAR II in EUROPE
BLITZKRIEG in the WEST,
MAY - JUNE, 1940

NETHERLANDS

GERMANY

ENGLAND

North Sea

Amsterdam

London

BELGIUM

Dunkirk

Brussels

MEUSE

RHINE

LUXEMBOURG

SOMME

MAGINOT LINE

SEINE

Paris

Chartres

Nancy

F R A N C E

SAÔNE

LOIRE

Atlantic Ocean

Nantes

SWITZ.

GERMAN ADVANCE

ARMISTICE LINE, JUNE 22

Vichy

Geneva

MAY 10 TO JUNE 4

ITALY

JUNE 5 TO JUNE 14

DORDOGNE

RHÔNE

JUNE 15 TO JUNE 17

Bordeaux

GARONNE

JUNE 18 TO JUNE 25

Toulouse

Marseilles

SPAIN

Mediterranean Sea

Apart from the unparalleled speed of successive Nazi thrusts, the most notable feature is the negligible strategic value of the Maginot Line on which the French had pinned great hopes.

penetrations by the German armor, which swept across northwestern France to the Bay of Biscay, took the Maginot defenses from the rear, and advanced steadily southward on a broad front. Mussolini then, on June 10, judged it safe to declare war on France and Britain. The French government fled to Bordeaux, Paris was surrendered as an open city, and the French resistance rapidly collapsed. An armistice came into effect on June 25.

The downfall of France as a great power was complete. More than half of the country, including the whole of the north and the Atlantic coast right down to the Spanish frontier, passed under direct German occupation. The rest was to be disarmed and brought within the German orbit, to which a new and semi-fascist French government, established shortly before the armistice under the eighty-four-year-old Marshal Pétain at Vichy, might safely be expected to gravitate. All that was left of the old France was a remnant of refugees in Britain and in some of the French colonies, headed by a junior minister from the fallen regime, General Charles de Gaulle.

■ THE BRITISH AT BAY

For the next twelve months the British faced the victorious Germans almost alone. A successful German invasion of their island would have made a reversal of the decision which had been so quickly reached on the Continent extremely difficult. Moreover, events had already shown the limited value of sea power—the only sphere in which the British were supreme—when it could be challenged, as in the Strait of Dover, by shore-based aircraft. The methodically minded Germans, however, devoted the month of June to the completion of the conquest of France before Hitler ordered Operation Sea Lion, the code name for the invasion of Britain, to be formally planned. Its execution was then set back several times by short stages until September 17, when it was postponed indefinitely because, in a month-long struggle known as the Battle of Britain, the *Luftwaffe* had failed to win the essential control of the sky over the Channel and southern England.

Though the enemy had done serious damage, eliminating almost one-quarter of Britain's total of one thousand fully trained fighter pilots, they had failed to knock out the fighter bases and were suffering losses nearly twice as heavy as they inflicted. The British owed much to the fact that improved types of Hurricane and Spitfire fighter aircraft had recently come into mass production; much to the political wisdom which had refused to expend the whole of that force in a vain attempt to stem the tide of defeat in France; much also to the scientific skill which had given their country a long lead over the Germans in the use of radar. But there was truth in Churchill's superb encomium on the British fighter pilots engaged in this epic contest: "Never in the field of human conflict was so much owed by so many to so few."

Short of invasion, there were several other forms of attack to which the people of the island were exposed. One of these, the massive bomber onslaughts upon crowded industrial cities, had already been begun in the London area, which was raided on eighty-two out of eighty-five consecutive nights and altogether had more than a million houses destroyed or damaged. From November until May the bigger provincial cities and especially the ports suffered similar though less continuous attacks. The morale of the public stood up to the novel strain remarkably well, and the hits on vital targets were never frequent enough to cause irremediable disaster.

If the island could not be invaded or bombarded into surrender, it could still be reduced by isolating it from the outside world. U-boats could now operate from bases situated anywhere between north Norway and the southernmost point in the Bay of Biscay and had the help of shore-based aircraft. Moreover, Italy threatened the use of the Mediterranean and the route to the east. Two highly successful actions, at Taranto in November, 1940, and off Cape Matapan in the following March, soon secured the Mediterranean Sea against Italian fleet attack. Merchant shipping, too, was in short supply and neutrality legislation forbade American shipping to enter any combat zone, a designation which included both eastern Atlantic and Mediterranean waters. So desperate was the immediate situation that, on July 4, the Royal Navy even attacked the French at Oran to keep their ships out of German hands.

Neither the permission to purchase supplies in America on a cash-and-carry basis, as enacted in November, 1939, nor the immensely fruitful Lend-Lease scheme, which was enacted by Congress in March, 1941, could have saved Britain if the U-boats had annihilated the transatlantic convoys made up of the British, Norwegian, and sundry smaller mercantile marines. Realizing the gravity of the position, President Roosevelt in September, 1940, exchanged fifty overage American destroyers for the lease of six bases on British territory in the Western Hemisphere. In the following year the United States Navy itself took an active part in patrolling the North Atlantic from other new bases in Greenland and Iceland. This action gained an invaluable respite for Britain until the disaster at Pearl Harbor confronted both the Atlantic sea powers with a new emergency.

While the British in their island home remained imperiled though unsubdued they sought to strengthen their position elsewhere. This meant chiefly a duel with their new foes, the Italians, in North and East Africa. Even in the critical August of 1940 Churchill had sent a large part of his small total supply of tanks round the Cape of Good Hope to strengthen the British base in Egypt. The sequel was a two-months campaign, in which General Sir Archibald Wavell drove the Italians back halfway across Libya, putting ten Italian divisions out of commission with a force which never exceeded two divisions. Meanwhile other British forces advanced into Ethiopia and restored Haile Selassie to his throne. So far, so good. However, in March, 1941, when Wavell was obliged to send part of his troops on a forlorn hope of sustaining the Allied cause in Greece,[4] a German armored force under General Erwin Rommel,[5] which had been sent to stiffen the Italians in Libya, quickly re-entered Egypt. Although driven back across the frontier before the end of the year, this force remained a standing threat to the British hold on the Middle East.

The Germans consolidated their position on the European continent by diplomacy as well as by a further employment of Blitzkrieg methods. In the summer of 1940 they seized the chance to realign the states of southeastern Europe when the Russians, having finally absorbed all the Baltic States, went on to demand the restoration of Bessarabia. This border province had been re-annexed to Rumania at the end of the First World War. Rumania then passed under the rule of a Fascist dictatorship in strict obedience to the Axis powers, and both Hungary and Bulgaria likewise joined the Axis. By March, 1941, without striking a blow, German armies had penetrated southeastward as far as the Bulgarian capital of Sofia. The rest could only be obtained by fighting. In expectation of an easy triumph Mussolini had already invaded Greece from Albania, only to be driven back across the Albanian frontier. Yugoslavia, too, decided at the last moment to resist German demands. The sequel, however, was a series of dazzling German military successes. Yugoslav resistance was crushed in eleven days. Though the Greeks had the help of a British expeditionary force hurriedly sent from North Africa, a three-weeks campaign ended in its evacuation, half of the force back to Egypt and half to the island of Crete, leaving the Greek mainland at the mercy of the Axis. Thereupon, before the end of May, 1941, the Germans successfully directed against Crete the first predominantly airborne invasion in history.

The fall of Crete left the defeated British in a most precarious situation. The Germans had advanced so far across the eastern Mediterranean that the whole of the British position in the Middle East was directly threatened. Again, the rapid fall of Crete suggested that Britain itself might very soon have to face the invasion which was believed to have been postponed, not abandoned. Even without that final stroke, the debacle in the Balkans could well induce the peoples of Europe to settle down to a resigned acceptance of Germany's "New Order."

In September, 1940, on the occasion of the signature at Berlin of a ten-

4. See p. 269.

5. 1891–1944. A winner of the Prussian order Pour le Mérite, and an early member of the Nazi Party, he became commander of the Afrika Korps, April, 1941–March, 1943, and a popular hero in Germany. He was appointed to command defenses from the Netherlands to the Loire under von Rundstedt, December, 1943; was wounded in air attack, July, 1944; and, having been implicated in the movement to make peace without Hitler, was ordered to commit suicide, October, 1944.

year military pact between Germany, Italy, and Japan, "the establishment of a New Order" was formally announced as the grand objective alike in Europe and East Asia. In Asia this bore a clear relationship to the weakening of the French and British position by events in Europe. French Indochina was passing by stages under Japanese military control and the British had withdrawn their garrisons from Shanghai and other Chinese treaty ports. In Europe, a huge Greater German Reich, in which industry would obviously be concentrated, might still make possible some degree of prosperity to producers of food and raw materials elsewhere. German technical efficiency would certainly work wonders in the exploitation of the natural resources of an area which had never before been unified. Political liberty had almost everywhere been supplanted either by a German or Italian authority or by a native fascist regime, as in Vichy France, where Marshal Pétain accepted collaboration with Germany. As the murder of six million Jews and of uncounted political prisoners and other victims began to cast its sickening shadow all across Europe, in each country people could be found to aid and abet such cruelties. Meanwhile, in far wider circles the growth of the will to collaborate was powerfully strengthened by the argument that democracy had failed in the supreme test of war. A different system, so it was held, might also deal successfully with peacetime problems of class war, strikes, and mass unemployment.

In reply to such counsels of defeat the British strove to keep the war alive by occasional commando raids at isolated points on enemy-held coasts and by a small-scale bomber offensive. They also maintained a flow of propaganda through such media as the radio and leaflets dropped from the air. Their only truly effective answer, however, as Churchill well knew, was the prospect of support from the United States.

If America went to war, the impact would be far more immediate than in 1917. Yet even after the initial successes of the German invasion of Russia in the summer of 1941 had lent additional color to the picture of the Nazi New Order for Europe, President Roosevelt lacked public support for any new counterstroke more directly militant than the proclamation of the Atlantic Charter. This document, agreed upon with Churchill at a rendezvous off the coast of Newfoundland in August, 1941, asserted their common principles and a common faith:

> After the final destruction of the Nazi tyranny they hope to see established a peace which will afford to all nations the means of dwelling in safety within their own boundaries, and which will afford assurance that all the men in all the lands may live out their lives in freedom from fear and want.

At that moment, when three groups of German armies were driving in seemingly irresistible strength eastward deep into Russia, it needed great faith to foresee the final destruction of the Nazi tyranny, let alone that total freedom from fear and want which is still far out of human sight. Only the greatness of the American achievement in peace and war made such an aspiration even credible.

■ THE GERMAN INVASION OF RUSSIA

The Russo-German pact of 1939 had enabled both signatories to reap great gains. Within eighteen months Hitler had won an empire comparable to Napoleon's, while Stalin had recovered nearly all Russia's losses from the First World War. The latter, however, was justifiably alarmed by the demonstrations of German military prowess in Poland and the west and sought to temporize by discussing terms for Russia's admission to the Axis. In November, 1940, Stalin's foreign minister, Molotov, went to Berlin, but the German suggestion that in the forthcoming liquidation of the British Empire Russia should acquire India meant nothing to the Russians in comparison with measures of self-protection against the Germans nearer home. In particular, Molotov demanded that Germany should keep her hands off Bulgaria, so that Russia could be sure of her Mediterranean flank and of the approaches to the Middle Eastern oil supplies, control of which would effectively counterbalance German gains elsewhere. No agreement was achieved.

Though Stalin was given specific warnings by the United States government in January, 1941, of an impending attack, and later by the British, it is evidence of the fear inspired by German arms that he continued to fulfil trade obligations, recognized German conquests, and avoided making possibly provocative counterpreparations. His only important countermeasure was the signature of a neutrality treaty with the Japanese, who had been left in the dark regarding the German intentions.

The German attack on Russia was launched on June 22, 1941. In the initial stages the German armies under von Brauchitsch, who with his principal military colleagues had been reluctant to precipitate the war, were so successful that a Japanese diversion would have been almost superfluous. The Germans rapidly gained the ascendancy in the air, and then employed the well-tried methods of the Blitzkrieg in three powerful thrusts, which were intended to carry them to Leningrad, Moscow, and the lower course of the Volga. In five successive months they overran 175,000, 125,000, 65,000, 80,000, and 50,000 square miles of enemy-held territory. By the end of November Leningrad was under siege; the towers of the Kremlin were visible to the forces smashing their way into outlying Moscow suburbs; and in the south the armies which had conquered Kiev and all the rich countryside of the Ukraine were contesting possession of Rostov-on-Don, within three hundred miles of the Volga and its great city of Stalingrad. Yet by a very narrow margin—perhaps no more than the period lost to Hitler through the heroic obstinacy of Greeks and Yugoslavs—the Germans failed to capture Leningrad and Moscow before they were halted by the weather. In trying to avoid that failure they became fatefully involved in winter campaigning, for which they lacked both equipment and experience.

During the winter the Russians recaptured about one-tenth of their lost territory. Although this included only one of the half-dozen "hedgehog" fortresses used by the Germans to stabilize the front at key positions, what mattered most was the fact that the tide of German advance had at last been stemmed and that the Russians had obtained a respite. This enabled them to expand their war production farther east in preparation for the next year's campaigns, while in western Russia behind the enemy's lines guerrilla activities were organized of a formidable and ferocious character.

In the first phase of this titanic struggle, involving larger armies and greater armaments than Europe had ever seen before, hopes and fears alike rose to new heights. Finland, Hungary, Rumania, and Slovakia all joined in the fight on the German side, and in all the satellite and German-occupied lands propaganda for Hitler's anti-Communist crusade had the practical object of recruiting foreign workers to replace the Germans now required for the armies; its long-term failure is shown by the resort to other pressures, which by the last year of the war had filled the factories of the Reich with slave labor from many lands, eight million souls in all.

On the Allied side, Britain under Churchill's guidance was prompt to welcome a mighty ally.[6] At the same time the United States government demonstrated its goodwill by agreeing to extend the Lend-Lease system to the Russians, who for their part hastened to pay lip service at least to the aims of the Atlantic Charter. Since American shipments could not be increased immediately, what the Russians received was a share in British munitions imports and production, conveyed precariously to the Russian Arctic ports, until joint pressure by Russia and Britain opened up a much safer alternative route across Iran. Even when the German and Italian declarations of war on the United States in December, 1941, ranged her fully on Russia's side in the great struggle in Europe, the immediate effect on Russia's fortunes remained small. The flow of supplies could not be increased very much while the United States was arming herself at top speed for the war against Japan in the Pacific as well as for direct participation in the Mediterranean theater. In spite of bitter Russian complaints, no additional front anywhere in Europe relieved the pressure on their armies until the summer of 1943. Even the arrival of the American air forces at British bases increased the weight of bombs dropped on Germany in 1942 to no more than 50,000 tons as compared with 33,000 tons in 1941.

6. See p. 271.

In May, 1942, the Germans mounted a massive attack from their positions in the Ukraine, aiming at the Caucasus for its oil supply and at Stalingrad for its industries and the control of the Volga. Victories here would complete the isolation of Moscow and Leningrad. The key position of Rostov-on-Don, held briefly and then lost in the winter, passed into German hands again in July. In August Sebastopol fell after a tremendous eight months siege, and naval control of the Black Sea helped the Germans to seize the Kuban oil field, which lies near the coast. But the Grozny and Baku fields were still out of reach. Meanwhile the northern prong of the German attack, an army of a third of a million men, veterans from the conquest of France, signalized its arrival at Stalingrad by a record bombardment, which flattened three-quarters of the city in a single day. What followed, however, was a long-drawn-out and immensely bloody battle in the rubble, where the German superiority in tanks availed little against the Russian capacity for sheer physical endurance. Hitler, who had committed himself to the capture of the city, would hear of no retreat. For the Russians, who were equally determined, Stalingrad was the key to the defense of the great valley of the Volga. Winter found Hitler's army still heavily engaged, and with winter came counterattacks on both sides of the city, planned by Marshal Georgi Zhukov,[7] the hero of the defense of Moscow a year before. These enclosed in a narrow pocket both the Germans and what was left of their Rumanian allies on the flanks.

The agony was prolonged–again by Hitler's orders–until the end of January, 1943, when Field Marshal von Paulus, with fifteen generals and a remnant consisting of one hundred and twenty-three thousand men, tendered his surrender in the basement of a department store. The Russians had sacrificed more men to save one ruined city than the Americans were to lose in combat during all the campaigns of the war. In so doing they had made the defense of Stalingrad a turning point in the history of Europe, if not of the world. Hitler's first important failure was also the greatest defeat in the history of the German army, a disaster which could not be concealed or glossed over: in the stark words of Stalin, "146,700 dead Germans were picked up on the field and burned."

It is true that the German forces in the Caucasus made a timely and skillful withdrawal. Nevertheless, the second Russian winter offensive achieved the raising of the blockade of Leningrad after a sixteen months siege and a clearance to a depth of two hundred and fifty miles in front of Moscow. In

---

7. Born in 1894. A peasant who was conscripted into the tsarist army in 1915, he commanded Soviet forces against the Japanese in Mongolia in 1938–1939 and became chief of staff in February, 1941. His popularity and prestige caused him to be thrust into the background during Stalin's lifetime. As minister of defense he became, in 1957, the first professional soldier to enter the Party presidium, but after his demotion by Khrushchev even his achievements at Stalingrad were belittled in official publications.

early July, 1943, the Germans opened their third summer offensive against a seventy-five-mile-wide salient in the center, around Kursk, but failed to breach the enemy line. Instead, the Russians surged forward on both flanks of the salient, commencing an attack which continued almost uninterruptedly in one part or another of the vast front until the invader became in turn the invaded.

When this final reversal of fortune came about in July, 1943, the western Allies were only beginning the first of their European landings, in the island of Sicily. The Russians, nevertheless, owed a great deal to Allied supplies, the provision of which had to some extent cramped the British war effort and had occasioned heavy losses in the Arctic convoys. In the spring of 1943 Lend-Lease shipments direct from America to Vladivostok were becoming a major source of transport equipment of all kinds: tanks and airplanes, machinery, and even food and clothing. The flow continued for the rest of the war to a total value of eleven billion dollars, a sum equal to the overall war expenditure of the United States for a period of six weeks. The fact remains that it was Soviet manpower that stemmed the tide of German conquest while Europe was still helpless in the German grip. Thus there is a large substratum of truth in Stalin's bitter gibe to the effect that the British contribution in Europe's extremity was time, the American, goods, and the Russian, human lives. And these Russians did not die only in the merciful heat of battle: their captors have admitted that 3,700,000 perished as prisoners of war in German hands.

■ THE JAPANESE CONQUESTS IN EAST ASIA

On December 7, 1941, the Japanese launched without warning a devastating air attack upon the American Pacific Fleet at Pearl Harbor. In spite of the similarity of political outlook between the Japanese militarist leaders and the rulers of Germany and Italy, which found expression in the pact of September, 1940,[8] the intervention of Japan in the war was not correlated with its two allies, either for the initial attack on Pearl Harbor or in the critical months when a juncture of forces might have been achieved in the Middle East. The signature of the nonaggression treaty between Japan and Russia (April, 1941) on the eve of the German invasion of the Soviet Union suggests that the Japanese were seeking their own opportunity for gains in Pacific waters rather than sharing with Germany the Russian spoils. They were tempted to imitate in the east the Blitzkrieg which had scored such successes in the west for various reasons. They wished to shut out aid and round off their conquest of China. They sought further advantages at the expense of the European colonial powers, from one of whom they had already wrested control of Indochina. They wished to escape the economic sanctions by which the United States was trying to force Japan to a compromise, and consequently they were tempted to strike

8. See pp. 266–267.

a sudden, overwhelming blow against the American Pacific Fleet. The blow fell, and within six months the Japanese won three million square miles of territory, based on their naval supremacy in the Western Pacific Ocean. This was to form their Co-Prosperity Sphere, with 95 percent of the world's natural rubber and 70 percent of its tin included in their resources.

From the European standpoint the crippling of one-half of the United States Navy by the air attack which preceded the Japanese declaration of war was of much smaller importance than the fact that the United States, so long hovering on the edge of the general conflict, had now been precipitated into the heart of it. The British had announced a fortnight earlier that they would join with the Americans in any conflict with Japan, and their possessions at Hong Kong and in Malaya were in fact attacked by the Japanese almost simultaneously with the American. Germany and Italy declared war on the United States within four days in nominal support of their Far Eastern ally, but President Roosevelt had reacted immediately to the Pearl Harbor attack by saying to Churchill, "We are all in the same boat now."

Three decisions quickly followed which largely determined the shape and outcome of the war. First, the United States government quickly resolved to fling the main weight of the nation's war effort into the struggle against Germany. Notwithstanding the gravity of the involvement with Japan, General George Marshall, the American chief of staff, informed his British colleagues, "Our view is that Germany is still the prime enemy and her defeat is the key to victory. Once Germany is defeated, the collapse of Italy and the defeat of Japan must follow." Second, the working out of the immensely complicated strategic problems involved was helped by the establishment of a Combined Chiefs of Staff organization in Washington, which under the general direction of Roosevelt and Churchill provided a joint Anglo-American command over operations in all theaters. It was here that the vexed questions of priorities in men, transport, and supplies were settled, often after bitter controversy but with loyal adherence to decisions once taken. Third, anticipating what lay beyond the war, on New Year's Day, 1942, a pact accepting the principles of the Atlantic Charter and promising full cooperation in the war effort was signed by Roosevelt, Churchill, and representatives of Soviet Russia and the Chinese Republic. Of the twenty-two other powers which immediately adhered, nine were small American states following the lead of their mighty neighbor and five belonged to the British Commonwealth, while no fewer than eight were European states whose governments led a fugitive existence in England. At this time France had not even a fugitive government to be included, since the anti-German movement headed by De Gaulle from outside the country did not receive full recognition from the Allies until the final stages of the war. Meanwhile, these rather modest beginnings marked the origin of the United Nations, which was greeted by Churchill with an apt quotation from Byron's verses celebrating the field of Waterloo:

> Here, where the sword United Nations drew,
> Our countrymen were warring on that day!
> And this is much—and all—which will not pass away.

In the early months of 1942, as disaster followed disaster, Allied fortunes were at a very low ebb. The Japanese had struck successfully at Clark Field, the American air base in the Philippines, within a few hours of the initial attack on Pearl Harbor. Guam and Wake Island were taken in the next two weeks, and although the last Philippine fortress, Corregidor, was not surrendered until May, the Americans under General MacArthur[9] had no means of reinforcing their army, which even with Filipino support was fighting a losing battle against odds of five to one. The positions held by the British collapsed still more rapidly. Three days after Pearl Harbor the only two capital ships which they had in eastern waters were sunk by air attack off the east coast of Malaya, where the British were faced with a Japanese landing. A Japanese alliance with Thailand also foreshadowed an invasion of Burma, and even Hong Kong, no longer safeguarded by the sea power to which it owed its rise, was surrendered on Christmas Day.

At Singapore the British possessed a great modern fortress whose guns, unhappily, were designed to protect the naval base only from attack by sea. When the Japanese came at it overland, outmatching the British in jungle warfare, the siege of Singapore Island, with a crowded population and a vulnerable water supply, took them no more than a fortnight. The surrender of the garrison of seventy thousand men, including many Australians, was an imperial catastrophe.

The Japanese also advanced from Thailand into Burma, where they again showed their skill in jungle warfare. Here, although the British fought on until May and made good their withdrawal to India, they left in enemy hands not only the whole of their former colony but also the vital terminus of the Burma Road, the link with China on which the government at Chungking depended for the means of continuing its campaign. In the circumstances the Netherlands East Indies proved no more defensible than Singapore, and for a time it looked as though Japan's sea and air power might enable her armies to continue to go forth conquering and to conquer.

In case the enemy might move forward across the Indian Ocean, a British expedition was sent to occupy the French island of Madagascar. Feverish

9. 1880–1964. The son of a former military governor of the Philippines, he commanded a division in France in 1918 and was recalled to active service as commander of the U.S. forces in the Far East, July, 1941. He was supreme allied commander in the Southwest Pacific, 1942–1945, and commanded United Nations forces in Korea, 1950–1951.

preparations were also made for the defense of India, where the Japanese pene-trated from Burma into Assam and raided the Bay of Bengal with their naval forces. Their main thrust, however, proved to be directed against Australia, which the Japanese felt, as a result of their sweeping victories, might fall an easy prey, once its communications with America were cut. They therefore ob-tained a lodgment in eastern New Guinea, based on Rabaul, and in the Solo-mon Islands where they established an airfield on Guadalcanal. To meet the crisis General MacArthur had been transferred from the Philippines to organ-ize the defense of Australia, where American troops soon arrived to fight alongside Australian forces hurriedly sent home from the Middle East.

The immediate danger was relieved, however, by the successes of the restored American Pacific Fleet in the battles of the Coral Sea and Midway. The first of these was a drawn encounter between aircraft carriers fighting at distances which far exceeded the range of any naval artillery. Nevertheless, the important consequence was that the Japanese gave up the attempt to land at Port Moresby at the southeastern extremity of New Guinea. This battle of May, 1942, was followed by a decisive victory at Midway Island in June, when American carriers combined with land-based planes to repulse an armada aiming at the capture of Midway Island and Hawaii. The result showed clearly that the carrier was now the capital ship which counted. The Japanese had lost five of them, which they could not quickly replace, the Americans, two, which they could. Consequently no landing was made by the Japanese on Australian soil. Instead, a bitter struggle quickly developed in New Guinea, the Solomons, and other island groups. Thus the position in the Pacific theater after twelve months of war was that the advance of Japanese power had been checked; but its outer perimeter, which now included Burma and the Netherlands Indies, was so distant from the center that an eventual counterattack upon the Japa-nese homeland by the Allies appeared a most formidable task. Moreover, in the warfare of the jungle and the coral atolls, America could not easily take advan-tage of her ten-to-one industrial superiority over the Japanese. New tactical methods were needed to overcome what the enemy gained by his determina-tion to die to the last man rather than to yield.

Although the United States continued to support the "Hitler First" strat-egy, the still critical situation in the Far East, where the United States govern-ment by agreement was in direct charge of all Allied operations, caused Roose-velt and his advisers to scrutinize most carefully the provision they were making for the European theater. Though the savage struggle which developed for the Pacific islands did not engage a very high proportion of American soldiers, it absorbed a big share of the United States Navy and Air Force and required a huge volume of supplies. This fact was all the more important since in 1942, while the main armies of the United States were being formed and trained, her impact upon Europe was chiefly through the flow of supplies. The flow was naturally increasing at a great pace now that the great arsenal of democracy was in full action as a belligerent; but where the build-up for the war against Germany was concerned, the shipping requirements of the campaign in the Pacific, including the defense of Australia against possibly imminent invasion, already constituted a serious limiting factor. Between the summer of 1943 and that of 1944, when the war against Germany was approaching its climax, the limitation became still more serious. By then the war in the Pacific absorbed 40 percent of all American army cargoes moving overseas.

■ MOUNTING THE COUNTERATTACK OF THE WESTERN ALLIES

Before the great counterattack in the west could be mounted, the dimensions of the German submarine menace had to be reduced. In the later months of 1941, when the German U-boats had extended their activities from the western approaches of Great Britain into the Mediterranean and along the west coast of Africa, anti-submarine forces were spread too thin to provide adequate protection for the main convoys crossing the North Atlantic from the United States and Canada. Then in 1942 the drain on merchant tonnage was enhanced by the deadly onslaughts which the Germans now organized against the Arctic convoys, to which reference has already been made. Even more important results were achieved by shifting the main force of U-boats to the Western Atlantic, where American precautionary measures were at first ineffective. When these tactics ceased to pay off, the Germans concentrated their U-boat fleet in "wolf packs," which hunted together in mid-Atlantic in cooperation with aircraft. Not until May, 1943, when the immense increase in the output of American shipyards caused the total of Allied shipping for the first time to rise, while the sinking of U-boats also for the first time exceeded their rate of replacement, did the fatal balance change. Well might Churchill write in retrospect, "The Battle of the Atlantic was the dominating factor all through the war."[10] If the Atlantic lifeline had been severed, Britain could not have survived, effective aid could not have reached Russia in time, and the liberation of Europe from the west could not even have been attempted. In the particular period now to be described, the burden of this battle was the main factor which delayed the frontal assault upon Hitler's empire far beyond the time required to muster and train the armies of America and to provide the necessary stockpile of munitions. It was also very far beyond the original sanguine calculations of General Marshall.

The only form of attack on Germany to which these considerations did not apply was the bomber offensive, which had been the only counterthrust available to the British on any large scale after the fall of France. This had been

10. WINSTON S. CHURCHILL, *The Second World War*, vol. V, *Closing the Ring* (1951), p. 6.

The six-months campaign in North Africa, following a critical struggle of more than two years for the control of Egypt, made possible the Allied invasion of Italy in the summer of 1943.

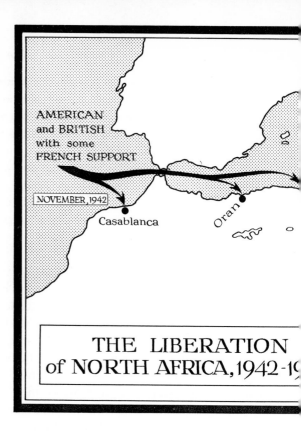

AMERICAN and BRITISH with some FRENCH SUPPORT

NOVEMBER, 1942

Casablanca

Oran

THE LIBERATION of NORTH AFRICA, 1942-19

built up through a great training scheme for pilots in Canada, a massive effort by British industry, and huge purchases from manufacturers in the United States of a form of armament which made no demand on Atlantic shipping for its transportation. By 1942 the British were able to send a force of a thousand bombers against a single objective in a single night. In 1943 these efforts were complemented by the American Superfortresses, which carried heavy defensive armament and were therefore able to raid Germany by day. Postwar investigations show that German powers of organization and repression and the high morale of the German workers prevented the effects of mass bombing from proving at all decisive until the last winter of the war. This fact is the more remarkable as the raids soon imitated those of the Germans by ceasing to be confined to legitimate military objectives: Berlin, for example, though a much smaller city than London, ended the war with a ten times larger area obliterated by bombing.

The only other way in which the British by themselves had been able to take the offensive was through the initially very successful exploitation of their position in Egypt. There, however, in the summer of 1942 a second great attack by Rommel was threatening Alexandria. Its loss would have made the whole British position in the Middle East untenable and might even have led to the cutting of the supply route to Russia across Iran. This unpromising situation

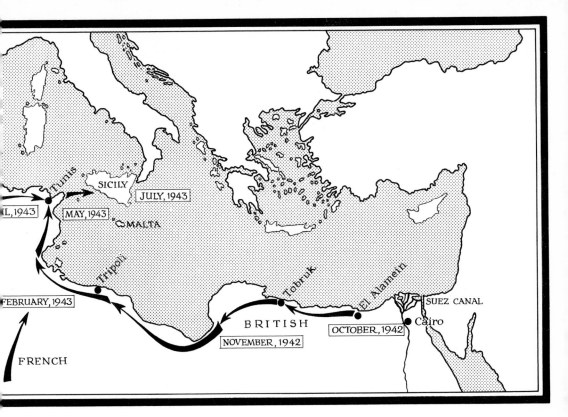

was completely transformed by an interallied cooperation which took full advantage of American resources. With the help of a patiently accumulated superiority in material, including an American tank which outclassed the German, General Sir Bernard Montgomery[11] outmaneuvered Rommel in winning his first and most brilliant victory at El Alamein.

While the Germans were falling back westward along the coast of Italian North Africa, American and British forces under General Dwight D. Eisenhower[12] landed on the other side of them in French North Africa. The French authorities there capitulated more or less readily to the Americans, with whom they had no quarrel, on orders given by leaders smuggled out from Vichy France. The Germans at once took over direct control of the unoccupied south of France, though the French fleet at Toulon was scuttled in time to avoid cap-

11. Born in 1897. He commanded the British 8th Army, 1942–1944, was commander of land forces under Eisenhower in the invasion of France, June–August, 1944, and commanded British and Canadian armies in western Europe, 1944–1945. He was created a viscount in 1946, and became deputy supreme allied commander, Europe, in NATO, 1951.
12. Born in 1890. Appointed chief of war plans division, U.S. general staff, in February, 1942, he became supreme allied commander in succession in North Africa, western Mediterranean, and western Europe, and was also supreme commander, NATO forces in Europe, 1950–1952. Churchill, who knew what problems Eisenhower had had to contend with, placed on record in April, 1945, his "admiration of the great and shining qualities of character and personality which he has proved himself to possess in all the difficulties of handling an Allied Command." In 1953 he became the thirty-fourth president of the United States.

277

ture. They were also prompt to occupy Tunisia, where a second army came to the rescue of Rommel's force. All this German effort was in vain. The Allied forces closed in from east and west, with the result that in May, 1943, six months after the initial stroke at El Alamein, the surrender of a quarter of a million Germans and Italians signalized the conquest of the entire southern shore of the Mediterranean from the Axis powers.

Though North Africa was a very long way from Berlin, the British were strongly in favor of exploiting the Mediterranean approaches. British troops were still in the majority in North Africa and relatively few United States troops had as yet acquired battle experience. In addition, an experimental landing at Dieppe in August, 1942, had been repulsed with the loss of more than half the forces engaged. Since these men were mainly Canadians of very high quality such losses suggested that Hitler's "Fortress Europe" needed to be approached with caution, careful preparation, and no less careful choice of strategy. On the whole, it was probably fortunate that at the Casablanca Conference in January, 1943, Roosevelt accepted Churchill's proposal that the next objective should be the island of Sicily.

Having the mastery of the air, a British and an American army were successfully put ashore in July, 1943, in the extreme south of the island, which was held by German as well as Italian troops. The invaders took less than six weeks to clear it of the enemy, though the majority of the Germans made good their escape to the mainland. While the invasion was in progress, the accumulation of disasters caused Mussolini to fall from power, whereupon his successor, Marshal Badoglio, was authorized by the king of Italy to start secret negotiations for an armistice.

The sequel was disappointing, for the Allies were not sufficiently quick nor the Italian anti-Fascists sufficiently resolute. Although an armistice was duly signed in September, 1943, the Germans were able to take over the defense of the peninsula and to set up a rival Italian government. In early September, on the day of the signature of the armistice, the British landed in the toe of Italy, and a week later the Americans went ashore farther up the west coast, within reach of Naples. The south was quickly overrun and the city of Naples was taken. However, by the beginning of November the Germans had organized the first of a series of defense lines based upon the mountains and strongpoints such as Monte Cassino, each of which was stubbornly contested. Although another beachhead was established at Anzio, south of Rome, it was June before the capital fell, and the Allied armies did not finally break through into the valley of the Po until the last month of the war in Europe.

The fact that large numbers of Allied troops, about two-thirds of them British, were bogged down in this way in Italy had important consequences. It fostered impatience among Americans as well as Russians, who thought that attention was being distracted from the need to open a second front in north-western Europe, whence Berlin could be directly threatened. Moreover, the slowness of the advance delayed until too late the situation to which Churchill looked forward, when the Allies would be able to move eastward from Italy into the Balkans.

The Russians had not waited for the second front before launching their great counteroffensive. The advance which began in July, 1943,[13] just before the Allied landings in Sicily, and was continued through the winter, cleared almost the whole of Russian soil from the enemy, though at tremendous cost. Kiev was liberated in November, Odessa in April of the following year, and the ruins of Sebastopol in May, by which time the Russians already stood on enemy soil in Rumania. When the Allied leaders met at Tehran at the close of 1943, Stalin was in a strong enough position to demand that any resources left over from the struggle for Italy should be used in southern France, not in the Balkans, where he needed no help. He also promised to synchronize the Russian advance against Germany from the east with the proposed Allied landing in Normandy. The second front was planned accordingly to include a diversionary operation striking northward from Marseilles.

■ THE DESTRUCTION OF HITLER'S EUROPE

At the close of 1943 the German armies had fallen back many hundreds of miles from their farthest advance eastward. Yet the Europe of the Nazi New Order, as it had taken shape up to June, 1941, still stood intact, except for Sicily and a part of Italy, which had been sealed off south of Rome. Though month by month a heavier weight of bombs was being dropped upon targets in Germany itself and in most parts of German-occupied Europe, the effect was nowhere overwhelming and the Germans had yet to bring into play their V-1 and V-2 pilotless aircraft and rockets, for which preparations were known to be well advanced. The Combined Chiefs of Staff had therefore every reason to expedite the attack across the English Channel.

Broadly speaking, the British were inclined to delay the establishment of the second front for two reasons. Psychologically, they dreaded the possibility of a second withdrawal from the Continent, which might be more catastrophic and more final than that in 1940. Practically, they wished the preparations to be as complete as possible before a frontal attack was made on a heavily fortified coastline where their coming would be expected. The Americans, on the other hand, pressed all along for a very early date, partly because a roundabout strategy seemed to them to be wrong in principle and more especially to hasten the transfer of America's main strength to the war in the Far East. At the previously mentioned Tehran Conference of November, 1943, Roosevelt,

13. See p. 271.

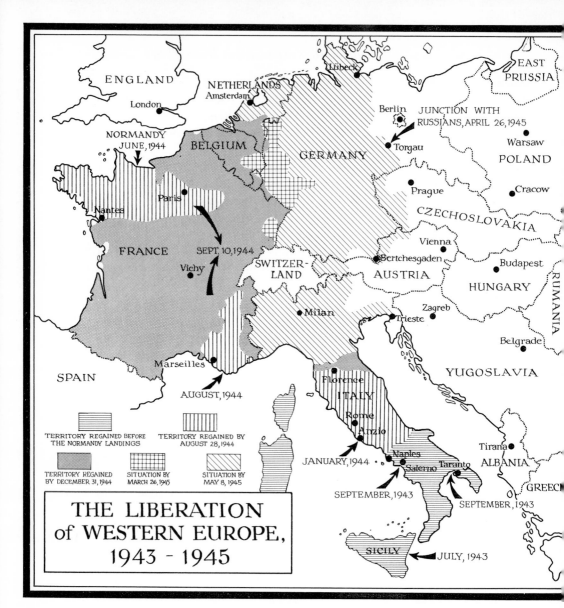

ENGLAND
NETHERLANDS
Amsterdam
London
EAST
PRUSSIA
Lübeck
Berlin   JUNCTION WITH
RUSSIANS, APRIL 26, 1945
Torgau
Warsaw
NORMANDY
JUNE, 1944
BELGIUM
GERMANY
POLAND
Paris
Prague
Cracow
Nantes
CZECHOSLOVAKIA
FRANCE   SEPT. 10, 1944
Vienna
Vichy
SWITZER-
LAND
Bertchesgaden
Budapest
AUSTRIA
HUNGARY
Milan
Zagreb
Trieste
RUMANIA
Belgrade
Marseilles
YUGOSLAVIA
SPAIN
Florence
AUGUST, 1944
ITALY
Rome
Anzio
Tirana
JANUARY, 1944
Naples
Salerno
Taranto
ALBANIA
SEPTEMBER, 1943
GREECE
SEPTEMBER, 1943

TERRITORY REGAINED BEFORE
THE NORMANDY LANDINGS

TERRITORY REGAINED BY
AUGUST 28, 1944

TERRITORY REGAINED
BY DECEMBER 31, 1944

SITUATION BY
MARCH 26, 1945

SITUATION BY
MAY 8, 1945

SICILY   JULY, 1943

THE LIBERATION of WESTERN EUROPE, 1943 - 1945

Once the Normandy landings were successful, it was clear that the Germans were fighting a losing campaign. The advance up the Rhone valley prevented the Germans from contesting southwest France.

eager to establish the best possible relations with Stalin at their first meeting, came down decisively on the Russian side when Stalin coupled his demand for a second front to be set up no later than May, 1944, with the assurance that after the final defeat of Hitler Russia would join in the war against Japan. Therefore 1943 ended with a firm decision to make the invasion of France an objective to which all else must give way. Eisenhower was to be transferred from the Mediterranean to the supreme command of this larger project, and enlarged and intensified preparations would be made for crossing the English Channel in the face of heavier opposition than had confronted any previous invasion in history.

The initial Normandy landings were made, with the help of paratroop drops in the rear and a prodigious naval bombardment, on open beaches just east of the port of Cherbourg in the early morning of D-Day, June 6. The Allies had the advantage of surprise, for the Germans had been led to think that the attack would be in the region of Calais. A more important factor in limiting their reinforcement of defenses in the landing area was the systematic destruction of communications throughout France, achieved by a long series of bomber raids and by French sabotage. A quarter of a million men were put ashore in the first twenty-four hours, but losses were heavy and it was not until the end of the third week that the Americans on the right captured Cherbourg, the first main objective. Even then, the thorough destruction of the port meant that supplies had still to be landed from an artificial harbor, which had been towed across the Channel in sections, or on the open beaches. The British on the left flank did not capture their objective at Caen until several weeks later. Nevertheless, they had attracted most of the German armor to that area and so wore down the German defenses.

The next phase was a great encircling movement, when the Americans at the end of July broke out into open country south of Cherbourg and swung quickly eastward. In the course of August a large part of two German armies was trapped, so that the Allies were at last able to advance rapidly. Paris was surrendered without any serious fight on August 25, and Brussels and Antwerp fell a week later. Meanwhile, the launching sites of the pilotless aircraft or V-1's, used since the middle of June against the London area, had also been overrun. The capture of Rome two days before D-Day enabled the Allies to make a second landing in mid-August near Marseilles. The result was that in early September an American army and an army of anti-Vichy French, formed originally in North Africa, joined hands with the forces of the first invasion not far from the Franco-German border north of Switzerland.

Meanwhile on the eastern front the Russian offensive began at midsummer with a breakthrough in the center on a front of two hundred miles. Soviet armies, which now totaled about five million men against their two million opponents, swept across the Baltic States and into East Prussia, so that in September they stood for the first time on German soil. The new gigantic onrush isolated the Finns, who quickly sued for peace; it brought down fortress after fortress in Poland, until Warsaw itself was threatened; it drove Rumania out of the war and Bulgaria into it on the Russian side. The sequel in Warsaw was tragic, for the Partisan forces organized by the exiled Polish government in London, though encouraged by the Russians to rise, received no Russian help.

Note that the siege of Leningrad had begun in November, 1941, and that Moscow was threatened in the same month. The great battle of Stalingrad, which began in the autumn of 1942, ended with the German surrender in February, 1943. At the war's end all the capitals of central and eastern Europe except Athens were in Soviet hands.

THE WAR IN
EASTERN EUROPE,
1941 - 1945

GREATEST EXTENT OF GERMAN ADVANCE
IN RUSSIA , NOVEMBER, 1942

RUSSIAN LINE, JULY, 1943

RUSSIAN LINE, APRIL, 1944

RUSSIAN LINE, FEBRUARY, 1945

ARMISTICE LINE, MAY, 1945

Leningrad

Moscow

Vitebsk

U.   S.   S.   R.

Kursk

Kharkov

Kiev

Stalingrad

Rostov

Caspian
Sea

Odessa

Sebastopol

Bucharest

Black Sea

ria

The result was the slaughter of a quarter of a million Poles. This showed clearly enough what would be the political consequences if further Russian advances were not at least paralleled by the progress made in the west. Meanwhile, news of the carefully staged though unsuccessful plot against Hitler's life in July suggested that the whole edifice of Nazi power might suddenly crumble.

Critical decisions affecting the conduct of the final campaign in the west now had to be made. The British general, Montgomery, who had been in command of the original Normandy landing under Eisenhower's supreme direction, tried to establish the principle that the main weight of the Allied reinforcements and supplies should be employed in his part of the line for a quick breakthrough into Germany to end the campaign before winter. Eisenhower, however, was supported by the Combined Chiefs of Staff in his decision to maintain an even pressure all along the line from the North Sea coast to Switzerland, with a view to exploiting each opportunity as it arose. It is impossible to determine whether Eisenhower's strategy was right or wrong, but it is clear that its full implementation was made more difficult by friction and misunderstandings.

The sequel was a series of disappointments, as a result of which there was no large-scale penetration into Germany from the west until February of the following year. One disappointment was the delay of three months before the port of Antwerp could be made into a main channel for supplies, because the Germans held out with great determination on the island of Walcheren. Another check was the failure of a surprise attack by a complete airborne army, intended to cut a way across the lower Rhine at Arnhem. But the biggest disappointment was the fact that in the December fogs the enemy proved capable of mounting a large-scale counteroffensive, which for a few breathless days seemed likely to achieve its immediate objective of a breakthrough to Antwerp. German armored forces advanced fifty miles, until they were held back by the stubborn American defense of Bastogne while troops were rushed up to contain the bulge in the Allied line.

Meanwhile the Russians during the last months of 1944 had completed the occupation of the Balkans except for Greece, which was cleared by a British seaborne expedition. Soviet forces had also penetrated into Croatia and Slovakia, and even into Hungary, which was bitterly defended. But Poland from Warsaw westward still lay between them and any part of Germany except the isolated province of East Prussia. Against these areas they struck a new and devastating blow in mid-January; three weeks sufficed for them to overrun most of East Prussia, to liberate the rest of Poland, to cross the German frontier all along the line, and to press on to within forty-five miles of Berlin. Farther south, they were suppressing the last elements of resistance in the Hungarian capital and were within eighty miles of Vienna.

In the west, on the other hand, the advance was delayed by the near catastrophe of the German December offensive. Not until early February, when the Russians had completed the great thrusts described earlier, was Eisenhower able to press forward on a broad front against the West Wall, to make the Rhine crossings, and to approach the vital industrial area of the Ruhr. The first blow was struck in the lower Rhineland by the British. Then the Americans penetrated the West Wall and by a series of enveloping movements cleared the area up to the river, and seized a bridge at Remagen in a brilliant exploit on March 8, just one month after the start of the attack. The Ruhr area was encircled, and eventually yielded the largest bag of German prisoners taken in any operation of the war, including that at Stalingrad.

German troops were surrendering in April at the rate of fifty thousand a day. By this time German transport, industry, and government were at last beginning to disintegrate, both as a result of incessant bombing by the air forces of the western Allies and because of the onward march of the Russians. The latter created, not without reason, a panic which the Germans vainly attempted to stem by the transfer of remaining reserves to the eastern front and overtures for negotiations in the west. The Russians entered Vienna on April 13, the day following the sudden death of President Roosevelt. Churchill wanted Eisenhower to press on at all costs to Berlin as a political counterweight to the Russian advance. But the Supreme Commander, in accordance with the program of a Soviet-American entente cordiale which his dead master had latterly favored, halted his armies at the line of the Elbe and its tributary, the Mulde, and inside the western frontier of Czechoslovakia. This was roughly the line along which the American and Russian armies had met.

The end came quickly. Hitler committed suicide in Berlin on April 30, two days before its surrender to the Russians; Mussolini had already been done to death by Italian Partisans. Finally, on May 7, the residual Nazi government which had been nominated by Hitler surrendered unconditionally and jointly to the western Allies and the Soviet Union. Peace reigned among ruins, and for a while all men of good will looked forward to rebuilding Europe in harmony.

■ THE COUNTERATTACK ON JAPAN

The divergence of outlook and policy among the Allies, which, hidden below the surface, had so largely determined the shape of the military operations just completed in Europe, was still more marked in relation to the Far Eastern operations which in 1945 were approaching their climax. The Americans regarded this war as their personal concern. The British, whose views were shared by the Dutch government-in-exile and by the Free French, were anxious to play a full part, once the danger in Europe had abated, so as to ensure some recovery of their lost colonial and commercial standing. This objective they suspected, not without reason, lacked a high priority with the Americans. The Russians, whom President Roosevelt was very anxious to bring into the war in order to save American lives, agreed to come in within three months of the end of the fighting in Europe for quite specific objects—the restoration of what had been lost to Japan in the war of 1904–1905, together with the sovereignty of the Kurile Islands and a return to the status quo in Outer Mongolia. This last provision would be greatly to the detriment of the Chinese Republican government under Chiang Kai-shek, whose wishes Roosevelt had disregarded in his pursuit of cordial relations with Stalin. Such was the agreement made at the Yalta Conference in February, 1945, two months before the President's death.

The advantages held by the Japanese in the Pacific were substantial, yet in time they were offset by those of the United States. Japan had the control of a vast, cheaply won empire, the outer perimeter of which could be used as a defensive screen for the vital areas, and a national character which stoically accepted a casualty rate quite disproportionate to the value of a contested territory. Against these elements of strength were set the ability of the United States, even without the support of her allies, to outstrip the Japanese in the production of every class of war material. In the third year after Pearl Harbor a hundred American aircraft-carriers were afloat in Pacific waters, while the Japanese lacked even the merchant shipping to maintain communications in their newly acquired maritime empire with its shrinking perimeter of defense. It had proved possible for American and Allied forces to make simultaneous progress from 1943 onward in two theaters; the main one stretched from the Solomon Islands past New Guinea to the Philippines, while the subsidiary theater consisted of the widely scattered outer archipelagos which the Japanese had occupied.

Guadalcanal was the scene of the first tremendous struggle in the main Southwest Pacific theater, where the supreme commander was General MacArthur. This ended in complete victory for the American arms in February, 1943, six months after the marines first landed there and at the cost of six naval battles, including an initial American defeat off Savo Island. The very costly campaign had the character of a defensive measure, undertaken in order to safeguard the supply route to Australia and undertaken before American naval and air resources were fully developed. Henceforth the general plan was to secure control of the enemy-held archipelagos by very powerful onslaughts on key positions, trusting to the severance of communications to neutralize other positions. These would then be left to "wither on the vine" far in the rear as the attack passed on toward the heart of the Japanese empire. This method, which has been compared with the German Blitzkrieg, took full advantage of the restored ability of the United States to provide and safe-guard the convoys required for these huge amphibian operations. Naval guns, bombers, tanks, and every type of armament were thus concentrated in support of the men, mainly American but including some Australian troops, who were put ashore to face heavy odds. For they had to fight a very determined enemy in terrain which varied from dense jungle to bare rock and which almost everywhere assisted the defense.

Rabaul in the Bismarck Islands, the base for Japanese operations in New Guinea, was neutralized in this way by landings close at hand. This move enabled a series of leapfrogging actions to be planned along the New Guinea coast, with the result that by May, 1944, the struggle in the Solomon Islands and New Guinea was virtually finished. In the same period similar selective landings in the subsidiary theater where Admiral Nimitz was commander in chief secured possession in turn of the Gilbert and Marshall Islands. The struggle could now be transferred without any lull to Japan's inner defense area. Truk was successfully bypassed by a landing farther north, at Saipan in the Mariana Islands, only fifteen hundred miles from Tokyo, a landing which the Japanese navy vainly contested in a carrier engagement known as the Battle of the Philippine Sea. Other landings, at Guam and in the west of the Caroline Islands, were then made to strengthen the American hold on the waters east of the Philippines. MacArthur, meanwhile, in the main theater completed the immobilization of scattered Japanese forces in New Guinea (a country larger than Germany, with a much more difficult terrain) and in September, 1944, advanced to Morotai in the Moluccas, only three hundred miles from the southern extremity of the Philippines.

The two-pronged American advance across the Pacific clearly converged on the Philippines, and here the Japanese were bound to meet the challenge by a full use of their navy. Accordingly, the first landing at Leyte in October brought three Japanese fleets to the scene. These the American naval forces defeated very heavily, sinking two battleships and four carriers for the loss of one carrier; they failed, however, to cut off the enemy's retreat, so that Japan was left with a "fleet in being." The conquest of Leyte proceeded, and was followed by landings in the other islands, which culminated in the liberation of Manila at the end of February, 1945. Clearly the Japanese had suffered a major strategic disaster. United States sea power was now in a position to cut them off from the oil and other resources of their overseas conquests and American air power could prepare the way for further thrusts northeastward toward Formosa, the occupied Chinese ports, and Japan itself.

The Japanese, however, had an important asset in their Chinese conquests. In 1944, while they were on the retreat in other theaters, in China they renewed their large-scale offensive, which had been virtually suspended

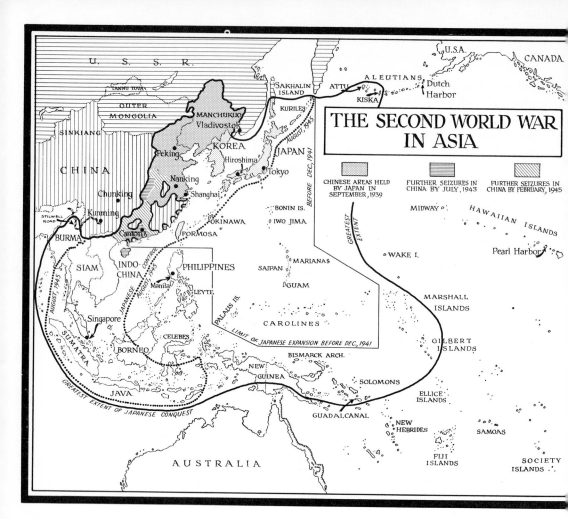

The enormous distances must be kept in mind in studying both Japanese expansion and the American advance along two lines from the Solomons to the Philippines and from the Gilberts to Okinawa.

for several years. A determined advance along the Hankow-Canton railway had as its prime object to cut off the Chinese Republicans in the coastal areas from Chiang Kai-shek's principal base round Chungking. The operation was largely successful. However, Chiang Kai-shek, who had been given considerable American air support, was able to save the immediate situation by bringing south the forces which he normally employed as security against the Chinese Communists; he also reorganized the Chinese Republican government in the direction of liberalism and efficiency.

The only long-term military remedy that could help the Chinese was still for the Allies to consolidate their rear by clearing the Japanese out of Burma. More than one false start had been made in this difficult task, which appealed strongly to the British because of its bearing on the safety of India and the future of the Empire; it had been entrusted to Admiral Mountbatten, a cousin of King George VI. As late as June, 1944, the Japanese were pressing an attack across the Burmese frontier into India, which British and Indian forces drove back. Then, with the help of American air transport and engineers, the British launched a counterattack which brought them to Mandalay in March, one month after American and Chinese forces operating farther north had enabled the first supplies to flow safely over the reconstructed Burma Road. A series of British and Indian landings from across the Bay of Bengal completed the reconquest.

The Co-Prosperity Sphere of Greater East Asia had ceased to function as an economic base for Japanese power as soon as the naval defeats severed sea communications with the Netherlands East Indies and Malaya. No lasting refuge could now be found in the Chinese mainland, and Japan itself had been under intense air attack since November, 1944. Though the war was irrevocably lost, the whole Japanese ethos forbade recognition of the fact. The grim struggle therefore continued. In March American marines landed on Iwo Jima: its capture proved to be the worst ordeal in the history of the Corps. Then it was the turn of Okinawa, whose capture was twice as expensive in time and men. Since the Japanese home islands contained an army of two million men and a reserve of about eight thousand planes, the two-stage invasion planned to begin in the fall of 1945 would clearly involve a heavy toll in American lives.

Such was the setting for the decision which ended the war and marked the beginning of a new era in human history. On August 6, after an ultimatum to surrender, the first atomic bomb destroyed rather more than four square miles of Hiroshima and killed upward of seventy thousand persons. Since the Japanese high command still ignored the ultimatum, a second and more powerful bomb was dropped three days later on Nagasaki, destroying six square miles and killing an unknown number. These two holocausts were on about the same scale as an Anglo-American triple air raid on Dresden, which had been undertaken in support of the Russian winter offensive in February, 1945. The new bomb was, however, decisive because it appeared capable of limitless, pitiless, irresistible repetition. The Japanese government resolved to submit before a third bomb fell, leaving the conquerors to wrestle with the problem of atomic weapons which still darkens the thoughts of mankind.

The atomic bomb originated to some extent in rivalry with the Germans, who in 1942 were known to be attempting to adapt the prewar discoveries of their own atomic physicists to produce the military results which American and British scientists succeeded in obtaining. The decision to use it in August, 1945, on a once-only basis may have been influenced somewhat by the fact that Russia, the uncertain ally, had no counterpart. Stalin's promised declaration of war on Japan, which his allies no longer desired, followed two days after the destruction of Hiroshima. Although the devastated Soviet Union was entitled under the Yalta agreement to some territorial advantages in the Far East, its full participation in the final campaign would presumably have meant greater claims and larger influence. But the great decision to use the bomb was motivated primarily by the desire to avoid the huge casualties which the United States and her allies would otherwise have sustained in a final campaign. Then they would also doubtless have inflicted casualties far exceeding the total taken of Japanese lives at Hiroshima and Nagasaki. As it was, on September 2, 1945, General MacArthur in the presence of Allied officers received the unconditional surrender of a Japanese delegation on the deck of U.S.S. *Missouri*. In both hemispheres, for victor and vanquished alike, the six years war was over.

Reading List: Chapter 10

Flower, D., and Reeves, J. (eds.), *The War 1939–1945* (1960), chs. 5, 12, 19, 30. Documentary.

Jacob, I., "Statesmen and Soldiers in War," *Foreign Affairs*, vol. XXXVIII (1960), no. 4.

Cairns, J. C., "Great Britain and the Fall of France: A Study in Allied Disunity," *Journal of Modern History*, vol. XXVII (1955), no. 4.

———, "Along the Road Back to France, 1940," *American Historical Review*, vol. LXIV (1959), no. 3.

Toynbee, A. and V.M. (eds.), *Hitler's Europe* (1954), pp. 47–73. The New Order.

De Conde, A., *A History of American Foreign Policy* (1963), chs. 23–24.

Feis, H., *Between War and Peace: The Potsdam Conference* (1960), ch. 41. An illuminating summary.

P A R T I I

A WORLD
IN FERMENT
1945–1964

"In every sphere—the social and economic,

the political, and the cultural—

it seems as if a great human flood

were surging up for the attack,

and beginning to batter, with its hurrying waves,

a civilization whose pride it has been

to affirm the greatness of human personality

by the creation of aristocratic hierarchies."

SIR ERNEST BARKER in *The European Inheritance, 1954*

Prologue: World Order or World Disorder

The two decades which follow the Second World War inevitably invite comparison with the two following the First. The resemblances, however, are much less fundamental than the differences. In the 1920's and the 1930's, men for the most part still saw the problems of their day as existing within the general framework of nineteenth-century institutions. They were hardly aware, for example, of the full revolutionary implication of the changes going on in Russia. They visualized the League of Nations as little more than a European system making what contributions it could to world order. In the field of imperial relations the victors of 1918, while ready to accept many adjustments, were certainly not prepared to reject imperialism as an outworn concept. Even with respect to the most striking development of the 1930's—the rapid rise of totalitarian dictatorship—such rise was widely held to be a kind of understandable aberration which in time would be toned down and adjusted to more conventional patterns of social organization. The warning conveyed by the German writer Hermann Rauschning—that National Socialism must be characterized as "The Revolution of Nihilism"—was heard too late and by too few. Finally, it is clear that both Hitler and Mussolini, who prided themselves upon being the spokesmen and champions of the world of the future, were abysmally ignorant of the new trends affecting imperial and colonial problems.

The contrasts to this picture to be found in the years following 1945 are striking. Though the Second World War had been fought in one sense as a struggle against the dictatorships of Germany, Italy, and Japan, the outcome produced problems of vastly larger scope. Compared to these new prospects, the downfall of Mussolini's Italy seems in retrospect almost episodic. True, the collapse of Hitler's Third Reich was a veritable Twilight of the Gods—a

293

tragedy played out amid the rubble of burning cities, the miseries of millions of displaced persons, and the appalling legacy of the concentration camps. Yet very quickly a new Germany was to arise, one-half of it closely linked to the West and displaying an economic strength that would soon outrival either that of imperial Germany or of the Weimar Republic. In the Far East, similarly, the total defeat of Japan did not long delay her from assuming an important new place in the postwar world.

The really striking developments did not arise as an immediate outcome of the victory over the Axis. The true significance of the two post-1945 decades is that they brought to the surface deep-rooted changes, some of which had been in the making even before the nineteenth century closed. Basically these involved a transformation in the overall power structure and a profound shift in the relations between the European and the non-European world. This latter phenomenon has been well described by a British historian as follows:

> The years between 1890 and 1960 confront us with two interlocking processes, the end of one epoch and the beginning of another. . . . What we have to ask is whether historians who have made Europe the pivot of their story have not concentrated too exclusively on the old world that was dying and paid too little attention to the new world coming to life.[1]

This "new world coming to life" will occupy an important place in the ensuing chapters. To be examined with it are further shifts in the relations of those powers to whom the appellation "great" has traditionally been given. One such power bloc, headed by the United States with the support of Great Britain, West Germany, Italy, and to a much smaller degree France, is now loosely labeled "the West" or "the Free World." The other power bloc, dominated by the Soviet Union, operates behind the Iron Curtain and exercises its control over the satellites, that is, the Soviet-dominated countries of eastern Europe. Much of the history of the post-1945 years is concerned with the mobilizing of strength by these two opposing blocs. For the West some of the great landmarks were the Marshall Plan; the Truman Doctrine; various defensive arrangements such as NATO, SEATO, and CENTO; proposals for the political integration of western Europe; and economic developments such as Benelux and the European Coal and Steel Community. On the opposing side the Soviets displayed their hand in Poland, East Germany, Czechoslovakia, and Hungary; in the propaganda activities of the Cominform; and in the creation of a counterpart to NATO, the Warsaw Pact. The Soviet Union impressively demonstrated its vast technological and scientific progress, its new industrial strength, and its equally great military power. Under such

---

1. G. BARRACLOUGH, *An Introduction to Contemporary History* (1964), p. 33.

circumstances the development of new atomic weapons, the failures to agree upon measures of disarmament, and the inability to find means for controlling nuclear power were almost predictable.

A new dimension was quickly given to these rivalries, the roots of which lay in the power struggles of an earlier age. This new dimension arose from the dramatically heightened role of the non-European peoples. Four of the world's six largest states (China, India, Indonesia, and Japan) are found in Asia, and a fifth (the Soviet Union) is almost as much Asiatic as it is European. If the trends in world population lead to the anticipated figure of six billion by the year 3,000 A.D., then Asia, Africa, and Latin America will account for five-sixths of the total. The diminishing role of Europe could not be more dramatically illustrated.

Asia in particular appears as the leader in this pattern of change. The imperial commitments of Britain, France, and the Netherlands dissolved after 1945 with startling rapidity. The Communist China of Mao Tse-tung, with a population approaching 700 million, soon showed its determination to transform and modernize itself at almost any cost in human effort, yet certainly not under the wing of the Soviet Union. Indonesia and parts of Indochina also demonstrated strong communist leanings. India with its 400 million soon displayed a new trend of noncommitment to either side which came to be known as neutralism.

Africa also saw in these years a disruption of the old imperialism and the widespread assertion of a new spirit of independence. The states which had sprung up almost overnight by 1964 provided along with Asia an absolute majority in the membership of the United Nations. They were participants in what was aptly called "the revolution of rising expectations," craving social and economic advances that would go far beyond the mere facts of political liberty. Though the new non-European nations were as yet too inexperienced and too scattered to create any close-knit organization, they were not slow to realize the many interests which they had in common. Observers, indeed, have been led to speak of a possible "third force" which some day might appear alongside the two power blocs headed by the United States and the Soviet Union.

As these new problems presented themselves, civilized man found himself superbly equipped with the instruments of a new science and a new technology. In all that relates to animate and inanimate nature his power has grown both to produce the weapons of destruction and to attack hunger, disease, scarcity, and ignorance. Progress here has come at a rate for which earlier times offer no parallel. The evidence of the concluding sections of this study demonstrates that both hazards and rewards present themselves to man on a larger scale than ever before in his history.

Chapter 11

The Transformation of Western Europe, 1945–1950

Transition from War to Peace
Germany, 1945–1950
Postwar Britain
Reconstruction in France
Italy and the Lesser Democracies
The Twilight of Colonialism
First Steps Toward European Cooperation

■ TRANSITION FROM WAR TO PEACE

The problems facing Europe in 1945 were in many respects far more acute than those of 1919. Actual war devastation had been much greater, and the proportion of civilian lives lost had been much higher than in the First World War. German surrender was unconditional. The Allied armies originally landing in Normandy had advanced within Germany as far as the River Elbe, where they met powerful Russian forces that had swept through Poland, Austria, and East Prussia to end the war amid the rubble of an appallingly devastated Berlin. No government could speak on behalf of Germany; for other Continental countries the various governments-in-exile raised no more than uncertain voices to champion the cause of the peoples whom Hitler had

SIGNIFICANT EVENTS

1945   German surrender (May 7)
       United Nations Charter signed (June 26)
       Potsdam Conference (July 17–August 3)
       Japanese surrender (August 14)

1946   Constitution of the Fourth French Republic approved (October)

1947   Peace treaties signed with Italy, Finland, Rumania, Bulgaria,
           and Hungary (February)
       Fifty-year Dunkirk alliance between Britain and France
           (March)
       "Truman Doctrine" announced (March)
       "Marshall Plan" proposed (June)
       Paris meetings to organize European Recovery Program (July)
       Communist Information Bureau (Cominform) created (October)
       End of British rule in India (August)

1948   Benelux Customs Union (January)
       France, Britain, and Benelux organize Western Union by the
           Brussels Treaty (March)

1949   NATO agreements signed in Washington (April)
       Constitution of German Federal Republic adopted at Bonn
           (May)
       German Democratic Republic proclaimed in East Germany
           (October)
       Independence of Indonesia recognized by the Netherlands
           (November)

enslaved. Some of these refugee governments were closely aligned with Britain and the United States; others had turned to the Soviet Union.

Various general statements concerning the postwar settlement had been made during the war. In his message to Congress in January, 1941, President Roosevelt had struck an idealistic note with his vision of the Four Freedoms ("Freedom of Speech, Freedom of Worship, Freedom from Want, and Freedom from Fear"). Meeting with Prime Minister Churchill off Newfoundland in the following August, he had joined in proclaiming the Atlantic Charter described in Chapter 10.[1] After America had entered the war, twenty six states opposing Hitler signed the United Nations Declaration of January,

1. See p. 267.

THE YALTA CONFERENCE, FEBRUARY, 1945. Meeting in the Crimea to make decisions affecting the fortunes of the entire world, Churchill, Roosevelt, and Stalin pose with their staffs for a photograph of high dramatic interest.

1942, adhering broadly to these principles. At Casablanca in January, 1943, Churchill and Roosevelt had announced their policy of unconditional surrender.

One great problem for Britain and America was to find common ground with the Soviet Union. At a Moscow meeting of foreign ministers in October, 1943, the Russians had accepted the formula of unconditional surrender; they had agreed to form a general international organization for keeping peace; they had also agreed to bring war criminals to trial. The meeting of Roosevelt, Churchill, and Stalin at Tehran, in Persia (December, 1943), brought the three leaders together for the first time to hear the vigorous Russian view, succinctly summarized in an American memorandum, that "Germany is to be broken up and kept broken up."[2]

More explicit agreements were reached by the Big Three at Yalta, in

2. HERBERT FEIS, *Churchill, Roosevelt, Stalin* (1957), p. 275. See also p. 279.

the Crimea (February, 1945), when the European war was nearing its close. A special meeting of the states associated in the war against Germany and Japan was planned for San Francisco to ratify a charter for the United Nations Organization, the main outlines of which had been drawn up. Tentative agreement was reached on some details such as voting procedure in the prospective Security Council and the admission of the Ukraine and White Russia to full separate membership. A stern note was apparent in decisions concerning Germany and eastern Europe. The signatories declared themselves ready to disarm, demilitarize, and dismember Germany "as they deem requisite for future peace and security." France would be invited to join the other three in having a zone of occupation, and reparations in kind would be imposed. The figure of 20 billion dollars, with 50 percent going to the Soviet Union, was accepted as a basis for discussion. The trials of war criminals were to be pursued. The Communist-dominated provisional governments actually established in Poland and Yugoslavia were to be enlarged by adding further spokesmen from the countries themselves and from their citizens still in exile. Poland's eastern frontier would follow roughly the Curzon Line of 1919, thus permitting the Soviet Union to regain the four million White Russians and Ukrainians lost by the Treaty of Riga in 1921.[3] Poland would receive "substantial accessions of territory in the North and West," though these final delimitations were to "await the Peace Conference." A Declaration on Liberated Europe promised that the three powers would aid formerly subjugated peoples in "the earliest possible establishment through free elections of governments responsive to the will of the people"—a pledge which proved to be capable of varied interpretations.

Thus, on the eve of the German surrender, the signature of which came on May 7, 1945, very substantial progress seemed to have been made; it had been achieved, moreover, with considerable outward show of unanimity. The United Nations Charter was completed at San Francisco and approved on June 26, 1945. Economic problems had also been faced. The urgent question of large-scale relief measures had been anticipated as early as November, 1943, when the United Nations Relief and Rehabilitation Administration (UNRRA) had been set up. UNRRA was a collective international agency financed by contributions supposedly from all members, though actually two-thirds came from the United States. It provided food, clothing, and medical supplies, principally in central and southeast Europe and to Communist and non-Communist countries alike. Nor was its work limited to Europe; it is noteworthy that of the seventeen major recipients of aid, China was given the most. Between the spring of 1944 and the close of 1947, UNRRA distributed more than twenty-two million tons of supplies.

3. See pp. 54, 77.

Hopes for a comprehensive and definitive peace settlement were only partly realized. Italy, whose government had signed an armistice in September, 1943, had actually joined the war against Germany—in Churchill's phrase, "working her passage." Rumania and Finland signed armistices in September, 1944; Bulgaria surrendered in October, 1944, and Hungary in January, 1945. Austria, whom the Allies regarded neither as a genuine satellite of Hitler nor a liberated state, underwent a four-power occupation at the war's end.

Discussions concerning peace treaties with Italy, Rumania, Finland, Bulgaria, and Hungary were begun by the Allied Council of Foreign Ministers at Paris in 1945 and were later enlarged to include spokesmen of sixteen smaller allied states. A formal conference was opened at Paris in July, 1946, where the defeated powers were also invited to present their views at length. Ultimately, however, Great Britain, the United States, the Soviet Union, and France had the primary responsibility of converting the tentative work of the conference into formal treaties to which everyone agreed on February 10, 1947. An unofficial poll of journalists from twenty-seven countries produced the following verdict on the conference: a success, 31; a failure, 56; a farce, 33. Their concern was no doubt due to the rift between East and West, first apparent here, to which the name "Cold War" was soon applied.

Disarmament and reparations were specified in all the treaties. Italy lost small border areas to France, the Dodecanese Islands to Greece, and some Adriatic islands and the Istrian Peninsula (without Trieste, which was to become a free territory) to Yugoslavia. She also renounced all her colonies. Hungary surrendered her gains made since 1938, giving a small border area to Czechoslovakia and a larger area to Rumania. Rumania lost Bessarabia and northern Bukowina to Russia, and the southern Dobruja to Bulgaria. To offset this she now regained northern Transylvania, restored to her by Hungary. Finland ceded a very substantial 12 percent in border areas to the Soviet Union, running from Petsamo in the extreme north to part of Karelia in the south. While these treaties were being drawn in 1947, both Germany and Austria still had the status of occupied territories.[4]

■ GERMANY, 1945–1950

Germany at the time of surrender in 1945 was a country marked by political anarchy and economic chaos. Kassel, Nuremberg, Cologne, Mannheim, Darmstadt, Essen, Coblenz, and Würzburg gave the appearance of almost complete destruction. Next in order came Berlin, Dresden, Munich, Hamburg, Mainz, and Frankfurt-am-Main. "Berlin," wrote a *New York Times* correspondent in May, 1945, "can now be regarded only as a geographical location

4. See map on facing page.

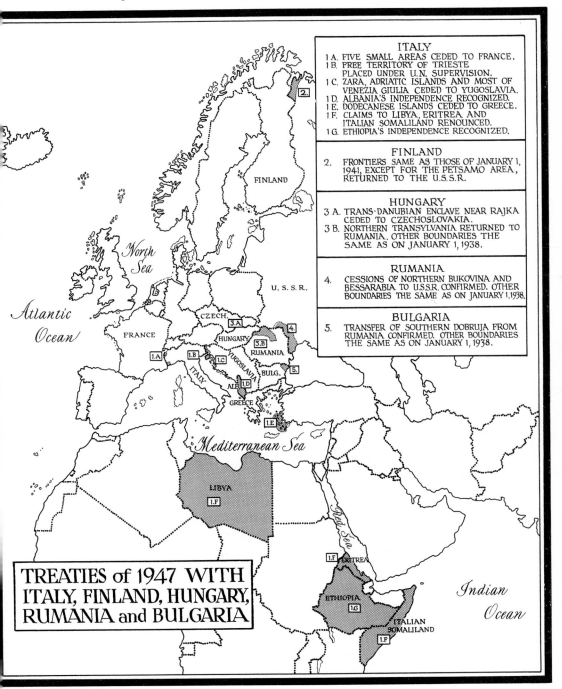

ITALY
1 A. FIVE SMALL AREAS CEDED TO FRANCE.
1 B. FREE TERRITORY OF TRIESTE PLACED UNDER U.N. SUPERVISION.
1 C. ZARA, ADRIATIC ISLANDS AND MOST OF VENEZIA GIULIA CEDED TO YUGOSLAVIA.
1 D. ALBANIA'S INDEPENDENCE RECOGNIZED.
1 E. DODECANESE ISLANDS CEDED TO GREECE.
1 F. CLAIMS TO LIBYA, ERITREA AND ITALIAN SOMALILAND RENOUNCED.
1 G. ETHIOPIA'S INDEPENDENCE RECOGNIZED.

FINLAND
2. FRONTIERS SAME AS THOSE OF JANUARY 1, 1941, EXCEPT FOR THE PETSAMO AREA, RETURNED TO THE U.S.S.R.

HUNGARY
3 A. TRANS-DANUBIAN ENCLAVE NEAR RAJKA CEDED TO CZECHOSLOVAKIA.
3 B. NORTHERN TRANSYLVANIA RETURNED TO RUMANIA. OTHER BOUNDARIES THE SAME AS ON JANUARY 1, 1938.

RUMANIA
4. CESSIONS OF NORTHERN BUKOVINA AND BESSARABIA TO U.S.S.R. CONFIRMED. OTHER BOUNDARIES THE SAME AS ON JANUARY 1, 1938.

BULGARIA
5. TRANSFER OF SOUTHERN DOBRUJA FROM RUMANIA CONFIRMED. OTHER BOUNDARIES THE SAME AS ON JANUARY 1, 1938.

TREATIES of 1947 WITH ITALY, FINLAND, HUNGARY, RUMANIA and BULGARIA

The smallness of the changes shown here as compared with those of 1919–1921 (see map, p. 74) suggests that the main national claims had been satisfied at the earlier date.

heaped with mountainous mounds of debris." To make confusion worse, eight million people, largely foreign, were freed from forced labor or concentration camps, while a new problem appeared in the ten million Germans who were soon expelled or fled from Poland, Czechoslovakia, and other lands. Shortages of food and housing seemed unsurmountable. Allied military government, and not merely occupation, was a necessity. As agreed at Yalta and confirmed at the Potsdam meetings in July, Germany was divided into four occupation zones; Berlin itself, lying well within the Russian zone, was similarly divided into sectors under Allied control.[5]

The Potsdam Conference (July–August, 1945), where President Truman, Churchill, Clement Attlee (who succeeded him as British prime minister during the Conference), and Marshal Stalin met, took some fateful steps with respect to Germany's eastern frontiers. The Conference agreed "in principle" to the transfer of the northern half of East Prussia, including Königsberg, to Russia; Poland was to get the southern half of East Prussia; and Poland's western frontier was to be extended to the Oder River and its tributary, the Neisse,[6] subject to later decision. This arrangement gave Poland Pomerania, most of Silesia, and the former Free City of Danzig. Stettin, an old Hanseatic city on the west bank of the Oder and therefore within the Russian zone, was independently and arbitrarily given by the Russians to Poland. All these lands were to be "under the administration of the Polish state" and were to remain so "pending the final determination of Poland's western frontier." Presumably the final settlement would be at a future peace conference dealing also with Germany. In the view of the Polish and Russian spokesmen, however, the 1945 agreement was definitive, and hence the "final determination" would be no more than a concluding legal formality. An immediate consequence, which rendered all the more unlikely any restoration of these lands to Germany, was a huge expulsion of former German-speaking landholders who swelled the flood of homeless refugees pouring into Germany.

The general guidelines for the treatment of Germany agreed upon at Potsdam have been summed up as "the five d's": demilitarization, denazification, decentralization, de-industrialization, and democratization. Demilitarization of Germany proved relatively simple. The further stipulation of denazification was not as easy. One of the tasks of the occupying authorities was to see that former Nazis did not reappear in local government. Another was to bring war criminals to justice.

An agreement to prosecute war criminals had been signed by the four occupying powers at London in August, 1945. All countries who had suffered

5. See map on facing page.
6. See map on facing page.

POSTWAR ARRANGEMENTS for GERMANY & POLAND | **GREATER BERLIN**

Note the closeness of Berlin to the eastern frontier of Germany. Extensive transfers of population have strengthened the actual position of Poland and the Soviet Union in former German territory.

from the Nazis could, of course, prosecute war criminals in their own courts. In addition, a special International Military Tribunal was authorized, with instructions to consider: (1) crimes against peace, i.e., planning and waging aggressive war; (2) war crimes, i.e., violation of the accepted rules of war; and (3) crimes against humanity. This plan involved many new departures, especially since crimes against humanity could not be measured against any well recognized code of international law; their inclusion led some experts to raise serious questions about the validity of such ex post facto law. The principal trials were held at Nuremberg, under a panel of judges from the victorious powers; a British appeal-court judge presided, and a justice of the United States Supreme Court acted as chief prosecutor. The trials lasted from November, 1945, to October, 1946. Twelve leading Nazis were sentenced to be hanged, among them Ribbentrop, Keitel, Rosenberg, and Streicher. Many others, including Hitler, Goebbels, and probably Himmler, had committed suicide earlier to avoid arrest; Goering took poison on the eve of his execution; some were sentenced to life imprisonment or to lesser terms; Dr. Hjalmar Schacht, Franz von Papen, and Hans Fritsche were acquitted. Thousands of less spectacular trials were held by local military tribunals and later by German courts throughout the four zones.

Other techniques of denazification had mixed success, for it was all too evident that hundreds of thousands of Germans, whether willingly or under pressure, had worn the swastika and held minor office. Procedure differed in the several zones. In the American zone alone thirteen million Germans were required to fill out questionnaires. By 1950 nearly 960,000 cases had been submitted to German courts. About 350,000 individuals were exonerated; some 23,000 major offenders were declared ineligible for public office and in certain cases imprisoned; nearly 600,000 were given nominal fines. The more constructive method of re-education of the younger Germans through the schools and with the aid of new textbooks was also undertaken, though many observers have questioned the results.[7]

The Potsdam Conference had stipulated decentralization as a guiding principle for the occupying and governing powers. Here it may be recalled that some earlier plans had gone much beyond a mere decentralization. The Morgenthau Plan, once proposed by the American secretary of the treasury and given tentative approval by Roosevelt and Churchill in their Quebec meeting (September, 1944), had envisaged a de-industrialized, "pastoralized" Germany permanently partitioned into several political units.[8] During 1946 Britain, France, and the United States authorized the subdivision of their zones into provinces (*Länder*), each with an elected local assembly; the Russians eventually did the same. The ten western *Länder* were: Schleswig-Holstein, Bremen, Lower Saxony, North Rhine-Westphalia, Hesse, Rhineland-Palatinate, Baden, Württemberg-Baden, Württemberg-Hohenzollern, and Bavaria. The five eastern *Länder* were Mecklenburg, Brandenburg, Saxony-Anhalt, Thuringia, and Saxony. It had been agreed that Prussia would not reappear. This move in the direction of local autonomy could be regarded as at least a beginning of the complicated process of democratization.

---

7. The verdict of a competent American scholar is as follows: "The zeal of Allied, especially American, educators, social workers, and youth leaders soon was dissipated against the hard realities of the long tradition of German history, of the political and moral apathy of postwar Germany, of the lack of a sufficient number of energetic and effective German workers in the program, and above all against the tensions and difficulties created by the cleavage between the East and the West in the international arena." KOPPEL S. PINSON, *Modern Germany, Its History and Civilization* (1954), p. 545.

8. Note also the proposal for a Germany divided into three independent states put forward by Sumner Welles, American undersecretary of state, in his book, *The Time For Decision* (1944), and especially his map, p. 342.

The impetus for the modification of the first occupation arrangements was largely economic. No long-range plans for reparations were undertaken after the occupying powers had made their first sweeping seizures of German industrial plants, capital equipment, and external assets. It had originally been agreed that Germany, denied any war industries, should be treated as an economic unit; yet with the divergent interests of the powers this was not easy. In January, 1947, the British and American zones were merged for economic purposes. Though the French continued to urge a weak, decentralized Germany, an American directive sent to General Lucius Clay in July, 1947, defined the basic objective as being "to create those political, economic, and moral conditions in Germany that will contribute to a stable and prosperous Europe." A decisive landmark came with the February-June negotiations of 1948, when the French, British, and American foreign ministers agreed at London to merge the three western zones economically and to proceed with the establishment of a single German government for these areas.

Political developments, linked with economic changes, then followed fast. The introduction in June, 1948, of a new Deutsche mark in the western zones was opposed by the Russians, who banned it in their zone. The Soviets cut off all land access to Berlin from the west. The result was the famous Berlin airlift, in which for over eleven months enormous quantities of supplies (including large amounts of coal and potatoes) were ferried into the city by a steady procession of American and British planes. At the peak of the airlift eight thousand tons of supplies were brought in daily. The Soviets in the end raised their blockade, leaving the division between East and West sharper than ever. During this tense period a constitutional convention of delegates from the West German state governments met at Bonn; by May, 1949, their constitutional draft was completed, ratified by the state governments and approved by the occupying powers. These, meanwhile, had drafted a new Occupation Statute, redefining their relations with this newly emerging West Germany.

The constitution of the Federal Republic of Germany (*Bundesrepublik Deutschland*) was proclaimed at Bonn, the new Rhineland capital, on May 23, 1949. A lower chamber, the Bundestag, was to be elected for four years by universal direct suffrage. The upper chamber, the Bundesrat, was to be made up of delegates from the state governments. The president, elected for five years by a special federal assembly, had mainly ceremonial and some appointive duties. The chancellor, who was elected by the Bundestag, had to command majority support within it. Careful efforts were made to provide a strong central government and at the same time to safeguard states' rights. It is significant that Britain, France, and the United States now proceeded to replace their former military governing authorities in Germany with civilian high commissioners although, to be sure, military occupation continued. It is also significant that not only was West Berlin made a part of the Federal Republic, but that the new title of the state (loosely known as "West Germany") implied an authority extending over all Germans. The elections of August, 1949, produced a victory for the Right-Center. Konrad Adenauer,[9] a Catholic, formerly mayor of Cologne and now leader of the Christian Democrats, became chancellor, and Theodor Heuss, a Free Democrat, was elected president.

The Russians took parallel action in their zone. By 1947 the Social Unity Party, a fusion of Communists and Social Democrats which the Russians sponsored, had in effect obliterated all other parties. In October, 1949, the German Democratic Republic was proclaimed after the unanimous approval of a German People's Congress. It provided for a president, a prime minister, and a popularly elected one-chamber legislature. Wilhelm Pieck was elected president and Otto Grotewohl, head of the Social Unity Party, became premier, with Walter Ulbricht as his deputy. To most observers it seemed as if the German Democratic Republic (which like its rival claimed an authority over all Germany) was in essence another Soviet satellite.

The three most striking aspects of Germany in these postwar years were the remarkable economic recovery, the quick emergence of democratic constitutional government in West Germany, and the seemingly hopeless cleavage between the two halves. The large-scale rebuilding which the western powers more and more encouraged and approved and the vigorous growth of industrial output in West Germany were a far cry from what had been proposed in the Morgenthau Plan. This recovery, indeed, soon came to be known as the "economic miracle." Whereas France and Britain leaned in the direction of nationalization, the German minister of economics, Dr. Ludwig Erhard, stressed free enterprise at home and free trade abroad. A new German industrial plant began to emerge out of the rubble of the old. By 1950 the level of industrial output equaled that of 1936, and by 1957 it was to be more than double. Such progress made nonsense out of the various efforts to keep the German level of industry from rising above that of her neighbors. As new moves were made abroad to stimulate a general European economic recovery, it was apparent that West Germany must be a major partner and pacesetter in economic life, as she would be also in any organized system for the defense of western Europe. All this made it necessary, from the Soviet point of view, to keep the direction of East German affairs in their own hands.

9. Born in 1876. Chief burgomaster of Cologne and member of the Prussian upper house, 1917–1933, he lost all office under Hitler, was twice arrested, and briefly held in a concentration camp. He became leader in 1947 of the Christian Democratic Union, successor to the Catholic Center Party, and played a large role in creating the German Federal Republic. Elected chancellor in 1949 by a majority of one vote, he held this office until 1963, retiring at the age of 87. A feature of his foreign policy was close collaboration with De Gaulle in reconciling French and German aims in Europe.

■ POSTWAR BRITAIN

Britain's history after 1945 is that of a country which, having rallied magnificently under Winston Churchill's leadership to meet the enormous burden of the Second World War, was then faced with a postwar situation of almost baffling economic problems. Six years of conflict had brought about heavy losses in shipping and other major resources, had tripled the public debt, and had seen the disappearance of more than four billion dollars in foreign investments. Air attacks had destroyed 25,000 homes, made 300,000 uninhabitable, and damaged about 4,000,000 more. The postwar elections of July, 1945, brought the Labor Party for the first time into full power.[10] Churchill's defeat implied no criticism of his superb war leadership; the public was concerned chiefly with the Conservatives' ability to tackle the staggering problems of peace. Yet Churchill's feelings were understandable. "All our enemies," he wrote, "having surrendered unconditionally or being about to do so, I was immediately dismissed by the British electorate from all further conduct of their affairs."[11]

The mandate from the British people was promptly accepted by the new prime minister, Clement Attlee. During the war Sir William Beveridge, a distinguished public servant and scholar, had submitted to the government his famous *Report on Social Insurance and Allied Services* (1942). How uncompromisingly the goal was set in the Beveridge *Report* may be seen from the following: "The aim of the Plan for Social Security is to abolish want by ensuring that every citizen willing to serve according to his powers has at all times an income sufficient to meet his responsibilities." In a space of fifteen months, eighty-four acts of parliament went far to secure these goals. Several measures—the National Insurance Act, the Health Service Act, the Industrial Injuries Act, and the National Assistance Act—dramatically changed the general social pattern. Accident, sickness, unemployment, maternity, old-age, and death benefits became available on a larger scale than ever before. A National Health Service provided medical, hospital, and dental care on the basis of contributions by employees, employers, and the state to a general fund. A new impetus was given to the wartime Education Act of 1944 which had undertaken to provide a complete national system of education from kindergarten through university. The compulsory school age was to be raised to fifteen, and eventually to sixteen, with wide provisions for scholarships and enlarged grants to universities. The New Towns Act and the Town and Country Planning Act of 1946 pro-

---

10. The previous Labor governments of 1924 and 1929 had been dependent upon Liberal support. Now the figures were: Labor, 395 seats; Conservatives, 213 seats; Liberals, 12 seats; others, 19 seats. This was the first time that a socialist party won a majority in a major western European country.
11. *The Gathering Storm* (1948), p. 667.

vided for elaborate rebuilding projects and for new, model communities stra-
tegically located in the fringes of great cities and with carefully planned areas
for residence, business, education, and recreation.

The declared purpose of the Labor Party also required the government
to act in the fields of industry and commerce, where the necessities of wartime
control had familiarized the public with techniques of planning and regulation.
Railways, civil aviation, canals, and much road haulage were nationalized.
The production and retail distribution of electricity and gas became big public
undertakings. The coal mines—a sick industry for more than two decades—
were taken over in 1947. The already government-dominated Bank of England
was nationalized in 1946. Further proposals to nationalize the iron and steel
industry seemed less welcome and contributed to the loss of seats for the Labor
Party in the elections of 1950. Labor then fell from 395 to 315 seats; the Conservatives rose from 213 to 297. Yet the voting percentages showed that Labor
had dropped only from 48.5 to 46.4 percent, while the Conservatives had risen
from 40.4 to 43.5 percent of the total vote.

In spite of Britain's slow but determined and impressive recovery from
the burdens of two world wars, many problems remained. An austerity program of rationing and controls was continued in the first postwar years. A large
loan from the United States helped matters, but did not obviate the need for
substantial Marshall Plan assistance. The need to export limited the availability of British products on the domestic market; the income tax was so heavy
that only sixty people in Britain retained after taxation a net annual income
of six thousand pounds or more. The balance of trade continued unfavorable;
and in September, 1949, the pound sterling was devalued from $4.03 to $2.80
to relieve Britain's dollar shortage by making it easier for America to purchase
British goods. In the general election of October, 1951, the Conservatives won
a close victory, with 321 seats to Labor's 295. The vagaries of the electoral system did this although Labor polled some 13.9 million votes, or 48.9 percent of
the total, and the Conservatives 13.7 million, or only 48.0 percent of the total.
Winston Churchill returned to office as prime minister—a post which he was
to hold until his retirement from public life in April, 1955. Britain meanwhile
had been obliged to assume important commitments abroad as a partner in the
various schemes being devised for the economic health and political security of
western Europe.

Concurrently Britain had to accept sweeping changes in her Commonwealth and Empire, to be examined in a later chapter. The one problem to be
considered here is that of Ireland. Since 1936 Ireland, or Eire, had regarded
itself as an independent state, loosely associated with the British Commonwealth under the External Relations Act of that year. The continued existence
of Northern Ireland, however, as part of the United Kingdom still rankled.

This was one reason why in December, 1948, the Irish parliament passed the Republic of Ireland Act, breaking the last link with Britain and officially ending the use of the name Eire. The Republic formally came into existence in April, 1949.

■ RECONSTRUCTION IN FRANCE

The problems confronting France in 1945 were not simply those of a country that had been devastated by the recent war. Some had deeper roots, associated with the basic weaknesses of the Third Republic and made all the more complex by the four years of German occupation and exploitation. During the war Marshal Pétain had urged his people to accept the authority of his Vichy regime. Many Frenchmen had perforce listened to him, others had not. Consequently much bitterness arose in the first difficult months of peace and considerable punitive action was taken against "traitors."

The French resistance to the Germans had taken two forms. Within France a movement, which at first was scattered and disorganized, gradually became better co-ordinated. A National Resistance Council was secretly created in May, 1943, containing outlines of the new France which the underground hoped to achieve after liberation. Another rallying point of opposition was provided outside France by General Charles de Gaulle.[12] Escaping in the desperate days of 1940, De Gaulle was able to begin broadcasting from London to occupied France and to undertake the laborious task of building an organization. This body, eventually known as the Free French, was made up of volunteers who had escaped and others who had organized in scattered parts of the French Empire. For a long time Britain and the United States were reluctant to recognize officially the French National Committee, choosing instead to wait until it could give evidence of having a mandate from the French people. After the successful North African landings of November, 1942, the London Committee was able to join with the French authorities in Algeria to form the French Committee of National Liberation (June, 1943), and set up a nominated Consultative Assembly which had actual links with the resistance movement in France. Thus, by the time of the Normandy landings in June, 1944, General de Gaulle had become the head of a substantial organization. His rigidity in insisting that France was still to be counted as a great power made

12. Born in 1890, the son of a professor of philosophy and literature in a Jesuit college at Lille, he became a professional soldier. He was wounded and captured in the First World War, and subsequently wrote an important monograph on mechanized warfare, more highly regarded by the German than the French general staff. After commanding a mechanized division in the Second World War, he refused to obey the Pétain government and became the dominant figure in organizing the Free French and the Committee of National Liberation. He was head of the Provisional Government, 1944–1946, and again took office in 1958. As president, he was chiefly responsible for the new constitution of that year, for giving independence to Algeria, and for seeking to make France a nuclear power.

many difficulties. He was not permitted to go ashore in France until the ninth day of the Normandy landings, and his Provisional Government was not recognized by the Allies until October, 1944.

Enthusiastically welcomed by the French people when he entered Paris on August 25, 1944, De Gaulle found no difficulty in establishing the Provisional Government of the French Republic. All political groups save collaborationists held posts in his cabinet, even including the Communists who had played a vigorous and indeed leading role in the resistance after June, 1941. By October, 1945, conditions were considered stable enough to hold a general election—one in which women for the first time voted. The three largest voting blocs were the Communists, the Socialists, and the new Popular Republicans (*Mouvement Républicain Populaire,* or M. R. P.). This last was Catholic and liberal in tendency, drawing strongly from the resistance. Disagreements over military appropriations led De Gaulle to resign as provisional president in the following January. His tenure of office had lasted for nearly sixteen months.

The constitutional draft prepared by the Assembly of the Provisional Republic having met defeat, a new election and a new assembly made possible a second draft, strongly opposed, as the earlier had been, by De Gaulle. He considered that both left the executive power too weak. The French, nevertheless, ratified this in October, 1946, thereby giving public sanction to the constitution of the Fourth Republic. About nine million Frenchmen were in favor, about eight million opposed, and another eight million simply stayed away from the polls.

This constitution, under which France lived until 1958, and which many had hoped would end the political weaknesses of the Third Republic, turned out to be an almost exact duplicate of its widely criticized predecessor. Under it the average life of a ministry down to 1951 proved to be about five and a half months. Some attempts were made to recognize new trends in overseas affairs by adopting the new title, French Union, within which citizen status was granted to all natives of overseas territories. Increased overseas representation was promised in the National Assembly, and elected local assemblies were to be set up overseas. Finally, there was to be an elected, advisory assembly for the entire French Union. Yet real progress was slow, and native demands for independence in many areas increased rather than subsided.

A striking feature in the political development of these years was the relatively equal balance between the larger groups, which asserted themselves in such a way as to preclude truly strong leadership. Some semblance of unity was provided by what the Socialist leader Léon Blum called "The Third Force"—a fluctuating coalition of Socialists, M.R.P., and Radicals who had enough in common to oppose the extremes of either Right or Left. Yet it was not enough for success.

In 1947 General de Gaulle emerged from temporary retirement to launch his Reunion of the French People (*Rassemblement du Peuple Français,* or R.P.F.). This he hoped would be no ordinary party but a genuine "rally" of all Frenchmen for the purpose of giving France stronger political leadership. The results in the general election of 1951 were disappointing to De Gaulle's hopes, for six roughly equal parties produced a "hexagonal assembly" in which effective government would be as difficult as ever before. The shift in politics, clearly, was to the Right.

The economic recovery of France was far more impressive than the political recovery. Despite the war damage and the heavy German financial levies, which have been estimated to total between $8 billion and $10 billion, industrial production by 1948 surpassed that of the best prewar years. Much assistance, to be sure, came from the United States, principally in the form of Marshall Plan aid. Steps were taken in 1946 to nationalize the coal mines, the gas and electric companies, the Bank of France and other large deposit banks, and the major insurance companies. Railways had long been a government enterprise. Though public housing lagged, some success came in modernizing the techniques of French agriculture. In January, 1947, France officially announced the Monnet Plan, a four-year blueprint devised by the brilliant economist Jean Monnet for agriculture and industry, with carefully planned goals set for coal, steel, cement, power, transport industries, and agricultural machinery. By 1950 the basic objectives of this Monnet Plan had largely been reached, and it is doubtless significant that the French population, stationary for nearly a century, now began to show a real increase.

In these years France also made important commitments abroad, first through the growth of closer economic ties with Belgium, the Netherlands, and Luxembourg, then through the larger working of the European Recovery Program. She also moved in the direction of still further important political and military commitments. These foreign interests will be the subject of a later section.

■ ITALY AND THE LESSER DEMOCRACIES

The transition from war to peace in Italy had unique features. Following Mussolini's overthrow in July, 1943, the Badoglio government made an armistice with the Allies in September and attempted, though with limited success, to mobilize Italian forces against Hitler. The Allies received the unconditional surrender of all Hitler's forces in Italy on April 29, 1945, nine days before the surrender of Germany.

Such a course of events made Italy a quite different problem from Germany. By January, 1946, practically all Italy had come under the control of Italian authorities. In June a national referendum favored by 12.7 million votes to 10.7 million votes the creation of a republic, which was immediately proclaimed. The peace treaty, officially signed in February, 1947, took away from Italy all her colonies but little in Europe save the Dodecanese Islands and the Trieste area.[13] A Constituent Assembly drafted a constitution which, save for the absence of a king, was not unlike the pre-Mussolini system of government. It provided for a president elected for a seven-year term, a chamber of deputies elected for five years, a senate elected for six years, and a ministry responsible to the majority in both houses. The country was organized into twenty-four semiautonomous regions, with a considerable emphasis, however, on the power of local prefects responsible solely to the central government.

Between April, 1944, and May, 1948, Italy had fifteen governments. Political life in Italy was marked by a struggle for power between three major parties complicated by the presence of many small groups. The Communist Party, led by Palmiro Togliatti (d. 1964), who had spent nearly the entire Fascist period in Moscow, based its strength both on the industrial workers and on a considerable number of intellectuals. The Socialists, of whom the largest group was led by Pietro Nenni, had played an important role in the resistance. They shared in some of the immediate postwar governments and by 1947 were closely aligned with the Communists. Principal power, as it turned out, was exercised by the Christian Democrats, a Catholic, clerical party favoring liberal reforms which was a successor to the *Popolare* Party of Don Sturzo, and was at that time led by Alcide de Gasperi.[14] He actually was in power at the time when the constitution of 1947 was completed. In the first elections held under this constitution in April, 1948, the government won an absolute majority (307) of the seats, although it was heavily criticized by the Left. The Communists were able to elect only 135 and their allies, the left-wing Socialists, only 33. The Christian Socialists had the firm backing of the Church. Despite the vigorous efforts of the Communists, who had captured an impressive 31.0 percent of the vote as against the Christian Democrats' 48.7, they were able to dominate the legislature during the five years of its existence.

As elsewhere in Europe, recovery in Italy was rapid and substantial, thanks in considerable degree to Marshall Plan aid. War damage, though great, was limited largely to two areas: between Naples and Rome and between Florence and Bologna. The northern industrial centers, though they had been heavily bombed, soon returned to vigorous activity. Though some reason

13. See map, p. 301.

14. 1881–1954. Born in part of unredeemed Italy, he first served in the Austrian parliament. After the First World War he joined the Italian *Popolare* Party, opposed Mussolini, and spent sixteen months in jail, being freed on the intercession of Pope Pius XI. A member of the wartime resistance, he subsequently became leader of the Christian Democrats, favoring government through democratic coalitions. One of the chief restorers of Italy and a strong supporter of European integration, he was prime minister from 1945 to 1953. He died of a heart attack shortly after learning that France had turned against his favorite scheme for a European Defense Community.

existed to question the fundamental soundness of the economy, the business revival, together with the extraordinary boom in the tourist trade, brought Italy through the first precarious postwar years, and in the view of some observers headed off the threat of a Communist take-over.

Belgium and the Netherlands can be very briefly treated. Liberation meant the return of the governments-in-exile; in Belgium a regency was set up with Prince Charles, and in the Netherlands Queen Wilhelmina came back from England. The immediate problems were to provide food for a population that in some cases was quite literally starving, to rebuild bombed cities, and to begin the revitalization of agriculture, industry, and commerce. As elsewhere, the Communists and other parties of the extreme Left sought to capitalize on the situation, but with little success. The two major phenomena in these postwar years were the crises in overseas relations, both for the Belgians and the Dutch, and the considerable integration of the economic life of the two countries into a larger European framework. In Scandinavia, the return of King Haakon to Norway and the freeing of Denmark from the German occupation permitted the previous regimes to re-establish their authority with no basic alterations. Sweden and Switzerland, who both had kept their neutrality during the war, saw no political changes.

■ THE TWILIGHT OF COLONIALISM

Twilight, rather than total extinction, best characterizes the fortunes of colonialism, as the peoples of Africa and Asia broke away from their long dependence upon Europe in the years following the Second World War. This movement towards freedom must count in its ultimate significance as one of the largest consequences of that great conflict. Even though the process can be presented here in no more than summary outline, this significance must be kept clearly in mind.

Britain, whose empire was the largest, made the earliest and most dramatic moves. She could point with much justification to the steady and substantial advances made during the prewar years in her treatment of India. Renewed agitation by Nationalist leaders after Mohandas Gandhi's release from prison in 1944, and the presence in power of a Labor government in Britain with a long commitment to ultimate freedom for India, led to the formal announcement in August, 1947, of the end of British rule and the recognition of India and Pakistan as dominions. Subsequent negotiations in India and two Commonwealth conferences held at London in 1948 and 1949 resulted in a redefinition of status, so that India and Pakistan became republics while retaining their membership in the Commonwealth, symbolized by their recognition of the British sovereign as its "Head." The first bitter conflicts between India and Pakistan, occasioned in part by the existence of a Moslem minority of forty million in the preponderantly non-Moslem Union of India, and the conflict over the fate of Kashmir, which both parties claimed, subsided sufficiently so that by 1950 something in the nature of a *modus vivendi* had been established.

Other areas in the Far East showed considerable ferment. Conferences with the British led to a political reorganization of the states composing Malaya in January, 1948, establishing a new federation which later was to be granted Commonwealth status. Ceylon in the same year was given similar recognition. Burma, on the other hand, chose complete independence, Britain reserving only a few special rights under the treaty which came into effect in January, 1948. The Sudan in the first postwar years continued as a condominium under joint British and Egyptian administration; and the British continued to garrison the Suez Canal for the twenty-year period stipulated in the treaty of 1936. Britain surrendered, with evident relief, the Palestine mandate in 1948, retaining, however, a special position in Transjordan.[15]

These changes in Britain's overseas possessions were clearly of major significance. They reflected in part the considered views and policies of the Labor government, which differed in many respects from those held by Churchill and his advisers. They also were the product of forces long at work in the history of Britain's overseas possessions. Even more, they grew out of the critical atmosphere of the postwar years when the entire colonial world was moving into a new era. In rapidity of operation they were to constitute changes in the British Empire for which the past could offer no parallels.

France, too, was compelled to accept important overseas changes. The mandated territories of Syria and Lebanon, to which France in 1941 had promised independence, entered the United Nations in 1946. In the older French colonial possessions a new policy of "association" was announced, under which natives were to be encouraged to develop along the lines of their traditional culture patterns. The constitution of 1946 envisaged, as we have seen, a new French Union in which all natives would have the status of citizens and the pattern of self-government would be steadily enlarged.[16] Yet in these first years the difficulties in seeking to retain the links with France were evident. Algerian nationalism began to assert itself in the "Democratic Union of the Algerian Manifesto," while in Tunisia similar aspirations were voiced by the *Neo-Destour* Party. A less vigorous independence movement emerged in Morocco.

By far the greatest trouble, however, developed in Indochina, one of the richest of all France's overseas possessions. In March, 1945, the French Provisional Government promised a new federal status within the French Com-

15. See pp. 366–367.
16. See p. 310.

munity to Annam, Tonkin, Cochin China, Cambodia, and Laos. This was unsatisfactory to Ho Chi-minh, the leader of the independence movement, who in September, 1945, tried to unite Annam, Tonkin, and Cochin China. The outcome was that in March, 1946, the new state of Vietnam was recognized by France as a free state within the Indochinese Federation. Difficulties, nevertheless, continued. The essence of these difficulties was that the French sought to impose the former Emperor Bao Dai of Annam as ruler of Vietnam, and that Ho Chi-minh continued to resist any such solution.

The Dutch, more perhaps than any other colonial power, seemed reluctant to abandon the reins of imperialism. In August, 1945, the Republic of Indonesia, with then nearly ninety million people and having been armed by the Japanese, proclaimed its independence. After some negotiation and compromise offers, the Dutch chose to fight, with the result that a war dragged on until a final agreement of November, 1949, transferred sovereignty from the Dutch to "the Republic of the United States of Indonesia" of which Dr. Achmed Sukarno, long a leader of the independence movement, was soon elected president. In September, 1950, Indonesia became the sixtieth member of the United Nations. The Philippines, it should be noted, had a long-standing promise of independence from the United States. This was honored in July, 1946, when freedom was finally achieved.

Thus, not without bloodshed, and with many frustrations and half-victories, the colonial world in the postwar years moved into a new era.

■ FIRST STEPS TOWARD EUROPEAN COOPERATION

The problems of western Europe as a whole were not easily defined and were even less easily handled. It was possible to hope that the period of reconstruction following the second of two world wars might make the goal of European unity seem somewhat less visionary. Actually, the immediate problems were so pressing that little more than provisional answers could be found for them. The long-range problems remained largely unanswered. Earlier in this chapter were described the large-scale emergency measures to deal with the ravages of war which had been started late in 1943 by the United Nations Relief and Rehabilitation Administration. This association of forty-four nations carried on until the close of 1947, when much of its continuing work was channeled into specialized agencies of the United Nations such as the Food and Agriculture Organization, the World Health Organization, and the International Refugee Organization. The Council of Foreign Ministers of the "Big Five" set up at Potsdam did not develop into an effective agency. The United Nations, too, moving from one provisional headquarters to another in London and the United States, was too inexperienced to take strong action.

Some students of international affairs have held that the best prospects

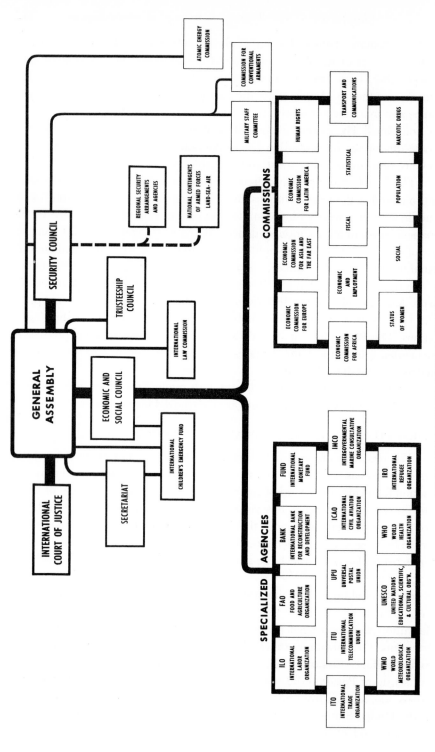

ORGANIZATION OF UNITED NATIONS, 1946

for the growth of international co-operation are found when states are confronted with urgent and specific problems such as the hunger, disease, and misery consequent upon a great war. Yet, whatever the pressing need for co-operative action among the states of postwar Europe, it was soon painfully apparent that grave rifts were developing. The powerful hand of the Soviet Union was seen in Rumania, Bulgaria, Hungary, and Albania. Disagreement about occupation policies in the four zones of Germany soon made it clear that East Germany, too, was a puppet state. The process took a little longer in Poland and in Hungary, and the Communist take-over in Czechoslovakia did not occur until February, 1948. Even so, Winston Churchill was able to summarize the stark trend of events in his pronouncement at Westminster College at Fulton, Missouri, in March, 1946: "From Stettin in the Baltic to Trieste in the Adriatic an iron curtain has descended across the Continent." Against this ominous background the noncommunist world had to make its plans.

What was soon known as the Marshall Plan stands with the Truman Doctrine as the first great constructive economic measures of the postwar years. Prospects of a Communist take-over in France and Italy seemed very real. Proposed by Secretary of State Marshall in an address at Harvard University in June, 1947, the plan began essentially as an offer by the United States to finance the recovery of Europe through grants and loans, on condition that European countries would organize themselves and engage systematically in the joint tasks of reconstruction. Though the Soviet Union forced its satellites to abstain, sixteen European countries met in Paris in July and worked out their particular programs which were then to be co-ordinated with a program of financial aid from the United States.[17]

The operation of the Marshall Plan can be given only the briefest analysis. The European countries established their Organization for European Economic Cooperation (OEEC). In Washington President Truman set up the Economic Cooperation Administration (ECA) to implement the European Recovery Program (ERP). Congress authorized the spending of $6.8 billion in the first fifteen months, with three further annual grants to follow. Thus, by 1950 Congress had raised its total authorizations to more than $12 billion. The European countries were not to be mere recipients of aid. They were required to prepare and put into effect specific programs for recovery. They were also to set up "counterpart funds" in their own currency out of the proceeds of the sale to their nationals of American food and materials, and to use these funds (with American approval) for further productive developments. There can be little question of the basic effectiveness of these programs for the revival of

17. The original sixteen were: Austria, Belgium, Denmark, Eire, France, Greece, Iceland, Italy, Luxembourg, the Netherlands, Norway, Portugal, Sweden, Switzerland, Turkey, and the United Kingdom. West Germany came in later.

Europe's economy. After 1950, however, the problems continued to be much more those of European defense and much less those of European economic growth. The United States Congress continued its annual voting of funds— now much more on a world-wide basis than on a European basis toward "un-developed" countries—through what came to be called the Mutual Security Agency (M.S.A.); such funds continued to provide substantial military assist-ance, though as the years went by this was a decreasing percentage of the total.[18]

Still another aspect of these immediate postwar years was the reappear-ance of a pattern of defensive alliances. The rapid extension of Soviet authority over the satellite countries in eastern and southeastern Europe was of anxious concern to the western powers. Nor could the specter of a revived Germany, no matter how badly beaten in 1945, be altogether ignored. Thus, in March, 1947, Britain and France signed the Treaty of Dunkirk—a fifty-year defensive alliance against a possible new German danger. The treaty was expanded just a year later by adding the three Benelux countries. This Brussels Treaty, known also as "Western Union," visualized economic, social, and cultural col-laboration along with commitments to collective self-defense in the event of "an armed attack in Europe," the danger, obviously, being expected to come from the Soviet Union.

Meanwhile President Truman, concerned at the Soviet threats to Greece and Turkey, had enunciated the "Truman Doctrine"; by a special message to Congress of March, 1947, he requested and obtained a grant of $500 million to give military and economic aid to Greece and Turkey, with the further and much broader stipulation that "it must be the policy of the United States to support free peoples who are resisting attempted subjugation by armed minori-ties or by outside pressure." The close collaboration of the United States and Britain in the Berlin airlift (June, 1948, to May, 1949) which successfully re-buffed the Russian blockade of Berlin is another example of joint action against the threat of force.[19]

In May, 1949, ten western European states, with France, Britain, and Italy as the principal members, organized the Council of Europe as the first step towards the political consolidation of the Continent. In its beginnings, with headquarters in Strasbourg, it consisted of a Committee of Ministers and a Consultative Assembly. By 1950 Greece, Turkey, and Iceland had also joined. West Germany followed in 1951 and Austria in 1956. It may be doubted whether any of its members realistically expected this Council of Europe to achieve much in the way of actual European integration. Yet the

---

18. In 1962, for example, total grants, credits, and other assistance had risen to $5,136,000,000 of which the military grants were approximately one-third.
19. See p. 305.

annual meetings provided a forum where European issues could be discussed by foreign ministers and by representatives from various parliamentary bodies, and no less a person than Sir Winston Churchill gave the Council his cordial and repeated endorsement.

In this first postwar period one other politico-economic development deserves comment, the formation in January, 1948, of Benelux. This was an agreement of Belgium, the Netherlands, and Luxembourg to integrate their tariff rates on a compromise basis against outsiders while still preserving excise taxes at different rates in the three countries concerned. More significantly, Benelux held out hopes for future economic integration with neighboring states, such as France and Germany.

The most striking outcome of the movement toward closer co-operation among the western powers was the creation in April, 1949, of the North Atlantic Treaty Organization against the threat from the East. The Brussels Treaty had set up a permanent organization to carry on its work. Now, to the five original members (Britain, France, Belgium, Luxembourg, and the Netherlands), were added seven others (the United States, Canada, Iceland, Norway, Denmark, Italy, and Portugal).[20] They were joined in a formal military alliance, based on the right of collective self-defense stipulated in Article 51 of the Charter of the United Nations. The signatories agreed that "an armed attack against one or more of them in Europe or North America shall be considered an attack against them all," against which any necessary action, "including the use of armed force," would be taken. To this end a NATO council was set up and by 1950 an integrated defense force had been established, the largest components being American and British, with General Eisenhower as the first supreme commander in Europe. NATO, particularly because of its possession of nuclear weapons, proved to be a deterrent of undeniable substance.

A few final observations are now in order concerning the critical five years in which Europe and the world moved from a state of war to that of uneasy peace. By February, 1947, peace treaties had been completed with Italy, Bulgaria, Rumania, Hungary, and Finland. Though no treaty could be made with a divided Germany, the western powers had helped to bring into existence the Federal Republic of Germany ("West Germany") even as the Soviet Union had sponsored the German Democratic Republic ("East Germany"). Peace with Austria was not to be completed until May, 1955, and that with Japan not until September, 1951. The states of western Europe, however, had made creditable efforts toward their own economic recovery, spurred on most notably by the operation of the Marshall Plan.

One serious flaw in the general fabric of European life was the instability of domestic politics in some of the major countries. When France, and to a

20. Greece and Turkey joined in 1952, West Germany in 1955.

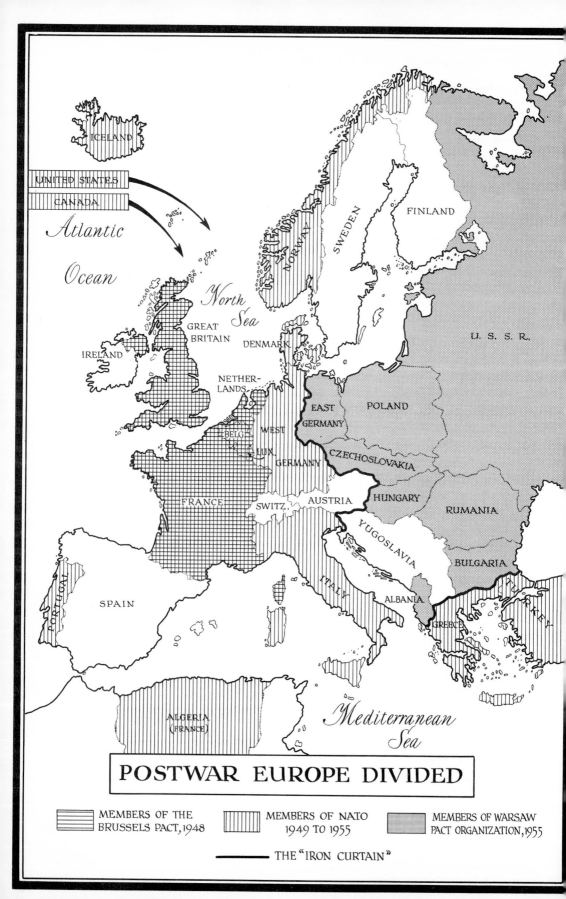

POSTWAR EUROPE DIVIDED

MEMBERS OF THE
BRUSSELS PACT, 1948

MEMBERS OF NATO
1949 TO 1955

MEMBERS OF WARSAW
PACT ORGANIZATION, 1955

——— THE "IRON CURTAIN"

lesser degree Italy, saw government after government trying with little success to exercise strong leadership, the international outlook remained of necessity clouded. Another flaw was the rapid currency inflation in France and Italy which became a factor in social and political instability. By 1950 very little in the way of genuine European integration had been achieved. Over and above the European Recovery Program, such joint activities as had developed were largely military, and in response to threats from behind the Iron Curtain. The Truman Doctrine of military and economic aid to Greece and Turkey soon grew to an annual policy of American assistance (part military, part nonmilitary) supplied to a steadily increasing number of states. And, finally, NATO, though weak in comparison to the armed might of the Soviet Union, showed that western Europe, fortified with powerful assistance from the New World, was able to organize in substantial measure for its own military defense.

Reading List: Chapter 11

Dickinson, R. E., *Germany: A General and Regional Geography* (2nd ed., 1961), ch. 15. Post–1945 Germany.

Aron, R., *France Steadfast and Changing* (1960), ch. 3, "Myths and Realities." Demonstrates the vigor of the economic revival in France.

Thomson, D., *Democracy in France* (4th ed., 1964, also paperback), chs. 7–8. The Fourth and Fifth Republics.

Wiskemann, E., *Italy* (1947), ch. 11. Italy at the end of the war.

Titmuss, R. M., *Essays on the Welfare State* (1958), chs. 8–10. A careful account of the British health service for American readers.

Worswick, G. D. N., and Ady, P. H. (eds.), *The British Economy 1945–1950* (1951), ch. 22. The international aspect.

Lumby, E. W. R., *The Transfer of Power in India, 1945–7* (1954), ch. 7. Some significant conclusions.

Mansergh, N., *Survey of British Commonwealth Affairs, 1939–1952* (1958), ch. 8. The Commonwealth at the accession of Elizabeth II.

The persistent diversities of European life are illustrated by the exceptional position of Finland, Sweden, Austria, Switzerland, Ireland, Spain, and Yugoslavia in relation to the major political alignments.

Chapter 12

The U. S. S. R. and Satellite Powers

The Breach Between East and West
Postwar Russia
The New Communist States of Eastern Europe
Cold War from Behind the Iron Curtain
The Succession to Stalin
Russia and the World

■ THE BREACH BETWEEN EAST AND WEST

This chapter traces the astonishing history of the rise of Soviet power in the postwar world, as seen in internal developments and in external relations with Europe. The story has all the elements of intense drama, for since 1945 the world has been divided and thrown into a conflict of rival ideologies, communist and non-communist. Such rivalry recalls the period of the Wars of Religion, when Catholics and Protestants also opposed each other on the basis of absolute loyalty to theories affecting every aspect of life which appeared to be totally incompatible. The seriousness of the twentieth-century clash is obviously greater because of the stupendous technological developments making destruction possible on a scale which the fanaticism of the sixteenth century never dreamed of. Moreover, for the first time the civilization of the Far East has become fully involved in issues originating in the European world, and no

SIGNIFICANT EVENTS

1945 Yalta Conference (February)
1947 Truman offer of aid to Greece and Turkey (March)
      Cominform organized (November)
1948 Communist coup in Czechoslovakia (February)
      Berlin Blockade. Expulsion of Yugoslavia from Cominform
        (June)
1949 Soviet A-bomb (September)
1950 Korean War begun (June)
1953 Death of Stalin (March)
      Soviet H-bomb (August)
1955 Warsaw Treaty Organization established (May)
1956 Revolutionary outbreaks in Poland and Hungary (October)
1957 First sputnik launched (October)
1958 Khrushchev becomes President of Council of Ministers (March)
1961 First cosmonaut (April)

precedent makes it possible to judge how decisive the role of Communist China ultimately may be. But if the triumph of the creed of Marx and Lenin in China is the biggest novelty in the world situation, an almost equally rapid transformation in the Russian-dominated Communist bloc which stretches from central Europe to the Behring Sea has also upset western calculations.

Soviet armies in the last eight months of the war won a series of huge victories which carried the hammer-and-sickle flag into every capital along Russia's western borders from Berlin to Sofia. Yet though the prestige of Russia was great, in 1945 other factors still seemed likely to limit her influence. The sacrifice of twenty million lives and about one-quarter of the entire wealth of the nation, which had been the price of Russia's survival and triumph, weakened her most seriously in comparison with the United States. This was quite apart from the fact that America was in sole possession of a weapon newly demonstrated to be supreme. At the same time, the countries which momentarily lay at the disposal of the Russian army were for the most part inhabited by peoples who for generations had based their way of life upon association with the West. It was difficult to believe that this link could be decisively broken by the experiences of a single decade.

The events of these years are too recent for us to speculate about what different outcomes there might have been. The striking consideration is that the Soviet Union, having won its military victories at an appalling cost in lives and treasure, then went on to win a further series of political victories in eastern Europe. Some of the factors making for this success deserve notice. The geographical situation at the end of the war left Russian armies in possession of most of the politically uncertain territory whose inhabitants were ripe for further revolutionary change. Russia was also in a strong position to threaten the sectors held by her allies in Berlin—a city lying deep within the Soviet occupation zone. Politically, too, the Russians profited from the fact that they alone of the major powers underwent no change of leader at the end of the war. Furthermore, the autocratic ruthlessness of the Stalin regime made it possible to pursue the interest of the state without necessarily paying even lip service to such ideas as international good faith or rights of self-determination.

Lastly, it is important to bear in mind that nearly all the events to be described were influenced by the weakness and divisions which characterized the attitudes of the central European countries and America's European allies. Moreover, along the frontiers of many of these countries Russian forces, political no less than military, operated on interior lines. Contacts between, say, Warsaw and Moscow were direct, immediate, and, if necessary, forceful. The United States, on the other hand, did not at first anticipate serious conflict and, subsequently, when its character and gravity were recognized, was exerting her influence from across the Atlantic upon a number of powers which regarded the right to bicker and disagree as the hallmark of national sovereignty and self-government. Most western Europeans had political principles which prevented them from suppressing Communists in their midst with anything like the vigor shown by the Russians in dealing with their political opponents. At the same time the military resources of western Europe were diverted in large measure to ineffectual struggles for the preservation of colonial empires. Thus the astonishing successes of the Russians were to a considerable extent attributable to equally astonishing failures on the part of those European nations which had been in the van of mankind's onward march for so long.

■ POSTWAR RUSSIA

On the fourth anniversary of the German invasion of Russia a dramatic military pageant was staged in Moscow's Red Square. Victorious troops cast the banners of Hitler's armies at the feet of Stalin in conscious imitation of their ancestors who had cast Napoleonic banners at the feet of Alexander I. But no past comparison was possible with the trail of ruined industries and shattered towns, broken communications and devastated countryside which marked the advance and retreat of the biggest and most bitterly contested invasion known to history. The Five-Year Plans, by encouraging the accumulation of a disposable agricultural surplus, by their rapid development of heavy industry, and above all by providing a new industrial base in Siberia, had increased the economic strength of Soviet Russia to the point at which the help of Lend-Lease supplies had made bare survival possible. Since Lend-Lease was brought to an end in August, 1945, and proposals for a Russian reconstruction loan came to nothing, it is clear that for the Russians of 1945, of whom twenty-five million were completely homeless, awaiting the next winter in caves, trenches, and mud huts, domestic recovery was the essential task.

In two respects, indeed, internal and external policies were directly related. Since 1943 Stalin had urged Russia's claim to reparations from Germany, which he eventually put at ten billion dollars, but the western allies, remembering the experience of the 1920's, were unenthusiastic. Instead, each occupying power was left free to take what it could from its own zone of Germany. Russia therefore obtained some immediate relief by ransacking eastern Germany and other territory occupied by her armies, especially Hungary and Rumania, receiving in addition a proportion of confiscated machinery from western Germany because this was the biggest industrial area. Of much more lasting importance was the decision to strengthen the Soviet economy by including within its orbit as many as possible of Russia's smaller European neighbors, which had been partly industrialized at an earlier date than Russia and could meet many of her immediate needs. This meant that Stalin was discarding the principle of "Socialism in one country" in favor of "Socialism in one group of countries." However, the results inside the Soviet Union, where his right to govern was no longer challenged, differ from the results outside, where Stalin's claims might still be subject to challenge by his wartime allies.

The victory of 1945 made Stalin's position in Russia down to his death in 1953 impregnable. Dissident elements had existed, to be sure, especially among the Ukrainian separatists and minority peoples in the Crimea and Caucasus, who greeted the Germans as liberators in 1941 and paid heavily for their miscalculation later on. Yet the hostility felt toward the German invader

THE SOVIET UNION: ECONOMIC RESOURCES. See pp. 326–327.

Note the continued spread of industry eastward from its older centers in European Russia. The Kuzbass coalfield around Stalinsk in central Siberia rivals those of the Don basin and the Urals. Oil is now obtained chiefly from the "second Baku field" east of the Volga.

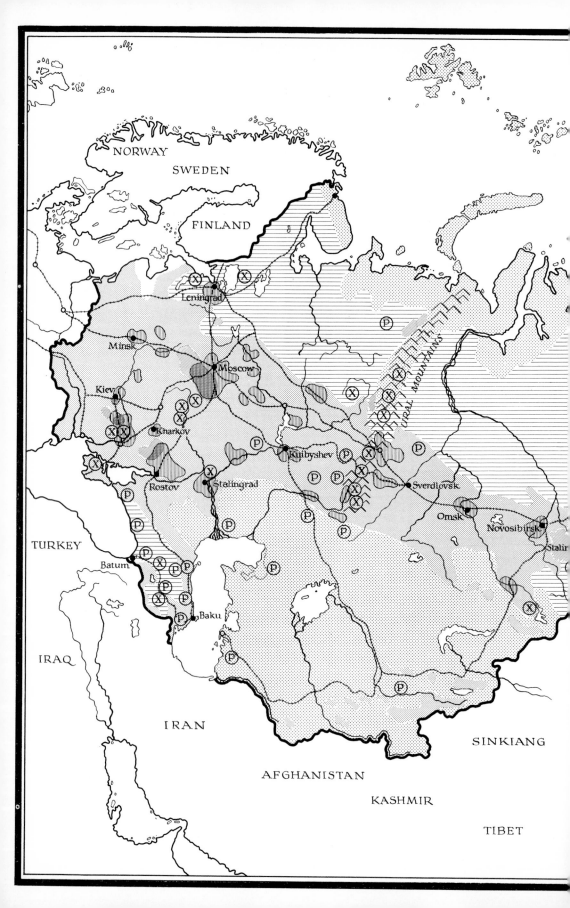

NORWAY
SWEDEN
FINLAND
Leningrad
Minsk
Moscow
Kiev
Kharkov
Rostov
Stalingrad
Kuibyshev
Sverdlovsk
Omsk
Novosibirsk
Stalir
URAL MOUNTAINS
TURKEY
Batum
Baku
IRAQ
IRAN
AFGHANISTAN
KASHMIR
SINKIANG
TIBET

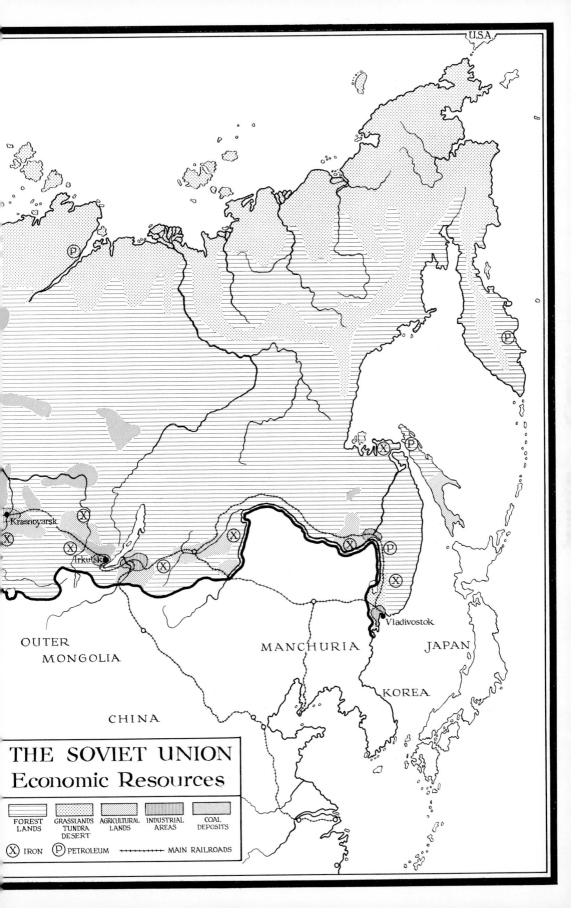

THE SOVIET UNION
Economic Resources

FOREST LANDS · GRASSLANDS TUNDRA DESERT · AGRICULTURAL LANDS · INDUSTRIAL AREAS · COAL DEPOSITS

Ⓧ IRON Ⓟ PETROLEUM ┼┼┼┼┼┼ MAIN RAILROADS

U.S.A.

Krasnoyarsk

Irkutsk

OUTER
MONGOLIA

CHINA

MANCHURIA

KOREA

JAPAN

Vladivostok

had stimulated a great increase in nationalist feeling, and this tended to obliterate the effects of the purges and to give the government a broad basis of popular support. The Communist youth movement, or Komsomol, for example, was built up to a membership of fifteen million, or one-half of the eligible age-group. The Orthodox Church, after more than two decades of partial persecution, received some degree of official recognition and the right to appoint a new patriarch in return for its spiritual and financial support of the war effort and its adulation of Stalin, "the God-given leader of genius." The alliance continued after the war, when the Church in the western provinces received a spectacular reward in the forced return to the Orthodox fold of the five million Uniates of Poland-Lithuania. These were Orthodox Christians who since 1596 had accepted the authority of the pope.

The war had also caused a revival of interest in the heroic figures of pre-Communist Russia, from Ivan the Terrible to Brusilov, who were represented as predecessors of Stalin in the defense of their country. After the war this developed into a cult which denied that the arts and sciences of Russia could owe any debt to western influences. In literature, music, the graphic arts, or even educational theory whatever was Russian was held to be inherently best, and vice versa. The same principle was applied to science and technology, including earlier as well as contemporary advances: Russians were said to have discovered almost everything. In some ways the crudities of the cultural outlook recalled the Russia of the 1930's or even the anti-western bias of the Slavophiles a century earlier.

Elections held early in 1946 produced the same type of results as on the previous occasion, in 1937. Less than one percent of the votes were cast against the single official candidate named on the ballot paper. Stalin's principal assistant at this time was Andrei Zhdanov, a militant Party secretary who championed the application of a strictly Communist ideology to politics and the arts alike. His death in 1948 was the signal for a return to the spirit of the prewar purges. The attack was directed first against Zhdanov's followers, who had failed to bring the satellite countries sufficiently to heel, then against satellite leaders deemed guilty of nationalist deviations, and finally against anyone who was unfortunate enough to arouse Stalin's suspicions. The Communist Party Congress did not meet after the war until a few months before Stalin died; then the membership of the Praesidium of its Central Committee was reorganized in a manner which showed that Georgi Malenkov,[1] who made the principal report to the Party, was Stalin's chosen heir. The other lieutenants, through whom Stalin's wishes continued to be carried out even when he

1. Born in 1901, he served as a Red Army volunteer, 1919–1922. He was later a personal secretary to Stalin and from 1946 onward one of eight deputy premiers. He was premier, 1953–1955, then was demoted to the ministry for electric power and afterwards to the management of a single power plant in Kazakhstan.

GOVERNMENT IN THE SOVIET UNION. In an austere modern setting and backed by the members of the Praesidium, Aleksei N. Kosygin, premier after the ouster of Nikita Khrushchev in October, 1964, addresses the Supreme Soviet of the U. S. S. R. Dominating the assembly is a statue of Lenin.

lay on his deathbed, were Nikolai Bulganin,[2] a civilian who had become a fighting general in the war, Nikita Khrushchev, who had for a long period controlled the troubled Ukraine, and Lavrenty Beria, whom Stalin had brought from Georgia to head the police at the end of the purges.

The political façade of postwar Russia, however, was clearly less important than the economic measures by which Stalin strove to remedy a truly desperate position. The total production of iron and steel and of gasoline had sunk by fully one-third during the war years, and if coal and electricity had suffered

2. Born in 1896 and served in the Cheka, 1918–1922. He was chairman of the State Bank in 1938, but was made a lieutenant general for his services on the Moscow front in 1941, rising to full general in 1944. He was minister of defense in 1947–1949 and again before his period as premier in 1955–1958; he was then relegated to the chairmanship of the State Bank and later to a minor post in the Caucasus.

less severely, the output of agriculture and the main consumer-goods industries had been reduced by at least one-half. Elaborately framed Five-Year Plans were launched in 1946 and 1951, which seem, like their predecessors before the war, to have fallen short of complete fulfilment but to have served their purpose of galvanizing the whole community into strenuous and purposeful activity. Although they failed quite clearly to redeem Stalin's promise to overtake the United States, which he made before the 1946 elections, it seems probable that the Plans were more successful than the gentler methods of western Europe in overcoming the lethargy of a people exhausted by a long war.

By 1950 the index of industrial production had risen from the immediate prewar level by 71 percent, the output of machinery was up by 60 percent, and that of chemicals by 80 percent. But the production of consumer goods was admitted to be 5 percent below the level proposed by the Plan, while agricultural production was as much as 16 percent below. The fifth Plan, which came into operation in 1951, likewise began to lag seriously in relation to consumer goods and agricultural products, the difficulties being accentuated by the Korean War. The Plan was therefore reconstructed to lay greater emphasis on consumer goods, and by 1955 an increase in the average size of the collective farms and the increased proportion of trained technicians among their managers were resulting in a big increase in the area sown with grain crops. Though cotton and sugar beet areas had also been made more productive, there was still a deficiency in meat, wool, and dairy produce. The gross national product was variously estimated at between 18 and 36 percent of the American. The French economist Alfred Sauvy nevertheless prophesied that "The point of junction between the American and Russian economies as regards the total production of energy may be placed about 1975."

In view of this prophecy, it is interesting to note one or two of the special trends in Soviet development after the war. In the immediate postwar period some use was made of prisoners of war, whose repatriation was deliberately delayed, as well as of the forced labor of persons subjected to so-called "political re-education" at the hands of Beria's police. These included the dissident minorities of the war period, already mentioned. Actually, the maintenance of a forty-eight-hour week for all workers and the abolition of food rationing, so that every Russian had to find work in order to buy food at market prices, did more to provide the labor force. The allocation of bonuses and "fringe benefits" was used in the manner of capitalist industry to improve the quality of the work done.

Another general trend which was accentuated after the war was the shift in the location of Soviet industry toward the east. Only a modest increase of output was expected by the fourth Plan from the recently restored heavy industries of the invaded western areas. The new phenomenon was that by 1950 more than half of all coal and steel was to come from Kazakhstan, the Urals, and Siberia. Five years later, more than half of the oil, too, was to be drawn from the wells of the "second Baku Field" between the Volga and the Urals. Lastly, the Russian programs of afforestation and irrigation deserve mention because of the vast possibilities of development by such means in a country where climate interposed the main barrier to an urgently needed expansion of agriculture. As it was, the great towns were accommodating the bulk of the annual population increase of three and a half million. In fifteen years the number of urban centers with more than half a million inhabitants rose from eleven to twenty-two.

■ THE NEW COMMUNIST STATES OF EASTERN EUROPE

Although the revolutions which took place in eastern Europe in 1945–1948 may be regarded as achievements of Russian foreign policy, aimed at the establishment of an economic zone to serve the urgent needs of war-stricken Russia, the historian sees in so tremendous an upheaval the operation of many different factors. One is certainly the generally undemocratic character of the prewar regimes in nearly every one of the countries bordering upon Russia, sustained or at least tolerated by the great western democracies as a barrier to the advance of communism. Poland and Hungary had undergone no large-scale land reform, power being shared between a class of landed magnates and those elements of former gentry who had gone into the services and professions. In the Balkan states, on the other hand, after 1918 the peasants held the land, but the general standard of life and education was still so low that the bureaucracy and petty businessmen were able to lord it over a predominantly rural society: governments could rely on officials to "make" elections. Rumania, with its oil wells and abundant wheat crops, was an exception as regards wealth but not as regards the low quality of its political life. The only true exception was Czechoslovakia, where the manufacturing industries were big and gave support to a large middle class, which in turn enabled cabinet and parliament to function as effectively as in the western democracies. Each of the five Balkan monarchies played an active part in politics and was bitterly opposed by a considerable section of its subjects. In general the sympathies of the kings were with the antidemocratic forces, even when such forces did not lean to a royal dictatorship such as Alexander had established in Yugoslavia in 1929. The Regency of Hungary and the Republic of Poland were no better served by presidents and cabinets of quasi-fascist outlook.

The war had worsened the democratic prospects. In Poland and to a smaller extent in the Czech lands German rule aimed at the destruction of the educated middle class as the potential nucleus of resistance. Here, as well as in

Yugoslavia and Greece, the governments in exile had been drawn mainly from the upper classes, for whom escape was easier. Such governments did not find it easy to command the loyalty of the masses who had remained to suffer at home. In Hungary, Slovakia, and Rumania the former upper-class governments had to a large extent co-operated willingly with the German invasion of Russia. This put them in sharp contrast with the lower classes almost everywhere in eastern Europe. These, under Communist leadership, had formed the van of the resistance movements and fought with determination to support the advance of their liberators, who in almost every case pressed forward from the east. A significant exception was the disastrous rising in Warsaw in August, 1944,[3] when the Russians failed to advance to the aid of a resistance movement sponsored chiefly by noncommunist elements and an anticommunist government in exile. To this general heritage of trouble must be added the loosening of the whole social fabric during the long war period, to the detriment of old loyalties and to the advantage of new men and new movements.

In the last twelve months of the war Churchill had frequently drawn attention to the precarious position of Russia's western neighbors. In view of the huge contribution of the Russian armies to the common cause it would have been impracticable as well as ungenerous to deny satisfaction of Russia's direct territorial claims. These involved mainly the territory lost since 1918, except for Poland west of Brest Litovsk and most of Finland, which the Russians did not reclaim; they included in addition one-third of the former German province of East Prussia and, at the opposite end of the frontier, Bessarabia from Rumania and the easternmost part of Czechoslovakia (Ruthenia). Churchill struggled hard to maintain the constitutional rights of the exiled Polish government against a rival Polish authority, set up by the Russian armies as they advanced and correspondingly pliant in relation to Russian demands. In the Balkans, too, when Churchill proved unable to carry the day for an Allied expedition which might have forestalled the Russian liberators, he struck a bargain with Stalin in October, 1944. The effect of this bargain was to trade a Russian predominance in Rumania and to a less extent in Bulgaria for western predominance in Greece and an equal share of influence in Yugoslavia and Hungary.

Despite Churchill's efforts, by the time of the Yalta Conference, and still more by the time of the conference at Potsdam, Stalin's armies were securely in possession of the debatable territory. The exception was Greece, where he made no immediate attempt to harass the British military intervention which established a royalist government. Therefore the western allies contented themselves with a very imprecise agreement, framed at Yalta, which linked Stalin with them in requiring that a democratic regime should be set up in every

3. See pp. 281, 284.

liberated territory. No attempt was made at a common definition of democracy. Instead, it was agreed explicitly that the great power in control of territory might itself appoint "interim governmental authorities broadly representative of all democratic elements" and implicitly that the new governments of eastern Europe would have to maintain generally friendly relations with Soviet Russia.

The sequel was a phase of postwar political experimentation which proceeded at a variable pace to a single conclusion—the establishment in each east European country of so-called "popular democracy." This was a form of communism modified in accordance with the conditions which gave rise to it. The peace treaties with the five lesser enemy states (Italy, Finland, Bulgaria, Rumania, and Hungary), which were signed by the Allies at Paris in February, 1947,[4] made little difference to the Russian pressure in eastern Europe, since Hungary and Rumania were still required to provide a corridor for Soviet occupation troops proceeding to and from Austria. The failure of the Russians to secure a foothold in the Italian colonies in Africa must also have confirmed them in their intention to hold on elsewhere. Yugoslavia, where Marshal Tito[5] had led the most determined and most determinedly Communist of the resistance movements, and its tiny neighbor, Albania, were the first states to become completely Communist, while Czechoslovakia, which had suffered much less severely than most during the war and had the strongest social, economic, and cultural ties with the West, was revolutionized last.

The pattern of events was everywhere roughly similar. In each case the postwar era was inaugurated by a kind of Popular Front government, in which a number of parties combined to win initial support at an election for a big program of reconstruction. Only those parties which were alleged to have collaborated with the enemy were excluded from the coalition, and one result of that exclusion was commonly the disappearance of the prewar monarchy. More important was the fact that, even at this stage, the Communist Party usually secured for itself the "levers of power," such as the ministry of police, the command of the army, and the control of propaganda. In the second stage the peasant parties and the bourgeois parties were eliminated from the government coalition, a censorship would be instituted, and methods of violence employed wherever necessary to destroy freedom of meeting and association. Finally, the time would be judged ripe to establish a one-party state on the Russian model.

4. See p. 300.
5. Born in 1892, Josip Broz, the son of a Croat locksmith. Taken prisoner by the Russians in the First World War, he later joined the Red Army and returned to Yugoslavia as a Communist in 1923. He was an organizer of the International Brigades in the Spanish Civil War and the successful leader of Partisans in Yugoslavia from 1941 onward. A self-appointed marshal, he became premier in 1945 and president under the new Yugoslav constitution in 1954.

Czechoslovakia in 1948 provided a denouement so dramatic that it made a deep impression on western countries, which had regarded the slower succession of changes elsewhere almost with resignation. The fact that Beneš was president of the restored republic, just as he had been before the war, seemed to many outsiders more important than the allocation of the premiership to a Communist, Klement Gottwald, since five other parties were represented in the government and only a third of the members of the legislature were Communists. The first blow to the survival of democracy in the western sense fell in July, 1947, when the government found it necessary to withdraw from participation in the Marshall Plan[6] as a result of a menacing demand from Stalin. After that an attempt was made to force the Social Democrats to coalesce with the Communists so as to create an extremist majority. The former, however, preferred to preserve the existing interparty relationships, which kept the middle-class parties also in the government. These last forced an issue in February, 1948, over the packing of the police force by the Communist minister of the interior. When they rashly resigned office, it took only a few days of demonstrations by Communist-controlled "action committees" to induce Beneš, who in the absence of any very strong support from the West could not possibly risk a quarrel with Russia, to authorize the formation of a new cabinet.

Henceforth all the key posts in Czechoslovakia were held by Communists or by their Social-Democratic allies, and other parties were represented only by carefully picked "stooges." The foreign minister, indeed, was still Jan Masaryk, who was not a party representative and who stayed on at the request of Beneš in the hope that the presence of the son of Czechoslovakia's founder and national hero might have a moderating influence. His death a few weeks later is attributable at best to suicide under an impossible strain. In May, 1948, elections were held, which gave a return of nearly 90 percent of the votes in favor of the single list of candidates; Beneš then resigned and was succeeded as president by Gottwald. Less than ten years after the fiasco of the Munich agreements it was hardly surprising that the Czechs, when the choice had to be made, were prepared to side with Russia, now their direct neighbor across their eastern frontier.

It was fortunate for the morale of the West that, only a few months after the defection of Czechoslovakia to the East, Yugoslavia quarreled with Russia and was excluded from the "Communist Information Bureau," or Cominform, established one year earlier with its headquarters in Belgrade. The reason for the split lay very largely in the dominant personality of Marshal Tito, who would have liked to form his own federation of smaller Communist states. The Serbs also had much self-confidence as a result of the large part they had played under Tito's leadership in their own liberation. The fact that the under-

6. See pp. 317–318.

FROM FINLAND, 1940-47

EXPANSION
OF THE SOVIET UNION
TO THE WEST SINCE 1940

PETSAMO
Murmansk

NORWAY

SWEDEN

FINLAND

1939 FRONTIER

U. S. S. R.

Helsinki

Leningrad
ESTONIA, 1940

Tallinn
Stockholm *Baltic*
Sea

Gorki

Riga

LATVIA, 1940

Moscow

Kuibyshev

FROM GERMANY
1945

Kaunas

LITHUANIA, 1940

Tula

Vilna

Minsk

Voronezh

Danzig

POLAND

Berlin

Warsaw

Brest-
Litovsk

FROM POLAND, 1940-45

1939 FRONTIER

Cracow

Kiev

Prague

Lwow

FROM CZECHOSLOVAKIA, 1945

CZECHOSLOVAKIA

Rostov

Vienna

Budapest

Kishinev

Caspian
Sea

AUSTRIA

HUNGARY

Odessa

RUMANIA

Sevastopol

Black
Sea

Baku

YUGOSLAVIA

Bucharest

Belgrade

FROM RUMANIA,
1940, 1945

Batum

This map should be related to the map showing Soviet domination of the satellite countries (see map, p. 416). As a result of these gains the Soviet Union acquired direct territorial contact with Norway, Czechoslovakia, and Hungary in addition to its previous contact with Finland, Poland, and Rumania.

ground movement had received considerable help from the British may also have encouraged the Yugoslavs to show less gratitude to Russia than was commonly expected. In any case Yugoslavia did not cease to be Communist, continuing to solve the problems of her economy along Communist lines in spite of the handicap imposed by a falling-off in trade with Russia.

The political developments described above were greatly influenced by economic problems common to the various countries. Because they had all been exploited by Germany, all save Bulgaria fought over, and all save Albania held by Russian armies whose recent privations made the temptation to loot overwhelming, the countries in question emerged from the war in a state of ruin and desolation. Poland mourned the death of about six million of her citizens, half of them Jews slaughtered with the utmost barbarity. Yugoslavia had lost about the same proportion of her population. Both states had had correspondingly heavy economic losses, including about one-half of all livestock and means of transportation. Albania, small as the country was, had a material loss estimated at 600 million dollars. Though important initial help was provided by UNRRA for Poland, Yugoslavia, Czechoslovakia, and Albania, in these countries it could cover no more than 4 percent of what was lost. Accordingly, it would leave a false impression not to mention here, however briefly, the economic policies which must have affected the man in the street (perhaps camping out literally amid the ruins) more closely than the most fundamental of purely political changes.

The first stage was the nationalization of large-scale industry and banks, for which expropriation by the Germans had often paved the way. This was an activity which tended to strengthen the position of the Communist elements, who made it their business to see that the smaller manufacturing concerns and wholesale and retail commerce were likewise taken over, step by step. By 1947 short-term recovery plans had also been launched, which at the end of two years are estimated to have raised total private consumption of goods to a level above that of 1938 in Czechoslovakia, Bulgaria, and Poland, but not in Hungary or in Yugoslavia. The last of these countries was seriously impeded by an economic blockade which followed its breach with Russia.

The long-term plans which were now entered upon followed the basic policy of concentrating at all costs upon the creation of heavy industry as the proper way to "build the foundations of socialism." The growing possibility of war between East and West meant that military requirements also had to be taken into account. Such requirements soon became an active concern of the Russian advisers and planning teams sent to all the satellite capitals. Whatever the ultimate goals, the immediate effects were remarkable. It is claimed that the rate of investment rose to 23 percent of national income for the whole group of countries, and that the annual rhythm of increase in both industry and agriculture exceeded anything in their past experience. Certainly the evidence of western visitors to Yugoslavia, whose political complexion made it more accessible than the others, suggests that the necessary popular enthusiasm was generated to carry through a rapid economic revolution. A new society, more urban, more literate, and more egalitarian was being built on the ruins of the old. Though the upper classes and the elderly of all classes suffered as in Russia in the 1920's, it is probable that by 1953 or thereabouts resources were growing faster than population. Measured in such terms as the production of steel or coal, the advance has been continuing ever since.

Two observations may be offered in conclusion. The ruthless drive to industrialization, coupled with big public works developments and the mechanization of agriculture, was an appropriate method for reducing the appalling poverty which had disfigured the society of these countries from time immemorial. Furthermore, the concentration of exports—with the exception of Yugoslavia—almost exclusively upon the Russian market gave the stimulus to production that these countries needed. By 1952 the trade of Poland, for example, was double what it had been before the war, that of Czechoslovakia was half again as great, and the overall growth was accompanied by an important increase in the subdivision of labor between the different members of the eastern bloc. Poland was in 1955 Europe's third-largest producer of coal and seventh of steel, while Czechoslovakia came sixth in both categories. Even so, only the future could show what would be the fate of these satellite states if and when a more completely industrialized Russia no longer had an interest in supporting and developing their economies.

■ COLD WAR FROM BEHIND THE IRON CURTAIN

A previous chapter has shown how the revival of strength and prosperity in western Europe came to be stimulated and directed from across the Atlantic as part of the defense policy and program of the United States. The present chapter has shown so far how the revival of strength and prosperity in eastern Europe came to be controlled by the U.S.S.R. in the period when she was herself struggling to repair the havoc of war within her own borders. What has next to be examined is the build-up of rivalry between the two blocs, a state of affairs which began by the two blocs defining their limits and ended by their creating a frontier darkened by the perpetual shadow of impending war. The examination is of a peculiarly difficult kind, because the point of view of Russia and her satellites can never be studied as can that of the western powers through the "revelations" of a free press or television network or the calculated indiscretions of a parliamentary opposition which cannot be silenced. As long as Stalin lived, the motives which lay behind the policies of Soviet Russia were to be learned only by uncertain inference from her actions and those of her satellites, with some fitful illumination from the inevitably prejudiced disclosures of refugees. Since his death, though a little more information is available regarding his now discredited regime, his successors still prefer to work in the twilight.

"Cold War" is a term which recognized the fact that warring groups with incompatible goals were nevertheless reluctant to employ the terrifying new weapons in their possession, for the simple reason that these modern weapons were capable of destroying all mankind. Recognition of the existence of the Cold War is often dated from the denunciation of Soviet policies by Winston Churchill in the presence of President Truman at Fulton, Missouri, in March, 1946. It was indeed that speech which popularized the term "Iron Curtain" for a barrier stretching across the European continent, behind which the attitude shown to the West was not merely uncommunicative but hostile. Churchill had, however, used the same expression in a letter to Truman written immediately after the termination of hostilities in Europe, an indication that the uncertainty about Russian intentions was of longer standing:

> What is to happen about Russia? . . . Like you I feel deep anxiety . . . What will be the position in a year or two? . . . An iron curtain is drawn down upon their front. We do not know what is going on behind.[7]

The course of events in eastern Europe may be more easily understood if one examines first the general factors which created clouds of suspicion on both sides of the Iron Curtain. Jan Masaryk with some reason claimed as the root cause of the defection of Czechoslovakia to the Soviets, which he saw to be approaching, that "The Americans knew nothing about the new Russia; the Russians knew even less about the New World."[8] Both the United States and Russia reached the end of the war in a mood of justified elation and awareness of paramount power, the Americans because they had won through to victory in a hard-fought struggle in both hemispheres, the Russians because the new Communist state had reversed the bitter experiences of two lost wars and had more than made good the losses of the treaties of Portsmouth in 1905 and Brest Litovsk in 1918. But in setting up the United Nations, in establishing zones of occupation in Germany and Austria, and in preparing to make peace with the lesser enemy states the two world powers had assumed a compatibility of purpose which could not possibly exist.

The possession by the United States of the atomic bomb, even if it was known in advance through spies, placed Russia in a position of military inferiority which made her deaf to any proposal for atomic disarmament until she had drawn level, when such proposals might be too late. The tendency of all great powers to expand throughout their geopolitical region until resistance hardens gave Russia, on the other hand, a natural impetus toward seizing control of her smaller neighbors, wherever Britain and France were no longer strong enough to prop up the façade of capitalist parliamentarism. In these difficult circumstances, a struggle between the two powers could only have been avoided by the creation and maintenance of mutual confidence. They were both equally unable to create or reciprocate such confidence, partly be-

7. W. S. CHURCHILL, *The Second World War* (1954), vol. VI, pp. 498–499 (letter dated May 12, 1945).
8. Quoted by D. F. FLEMING, *The Cold War and Its Origins, 1917–1960* (1961), vol. I, p. 495.

cause of their conflicting ideologies of competitive capitalism and Marxian socialism, and partly because of the tradition of suspicion and hostility dating from the period of the Russian Civil War, which had been submerged only temporarily by the common peril.

In spite of Churchill's Fulton speech, the fact that by October, 1946, peace treaties had been negotiated—though not yet actually signed—with the two westward-facing ex-enemy states of Italy and Finland, as well as with the three (Hungary, Bulgaria, and Rumania) which lay behind the Iron Curtain, suggested that co-operation for specific purposes was still feasible. Early in 1947, however, the skies darkened when it became apparent that Russia and her Balkan satellites were instigating a left-wing rebellion in Greece. Here the forces of political discontent and social misery had been held at bay by the British since 1944 at a cost which they now declared their weakened economy could no longer afford. If Greece fell, Turkey might be expected to follow, and the way would be open into the Mediterranean via the Straits, and also for that larger Russian expansion into the Middle East to which German agreement had been vainly sought in 1940.[9] President Truman thereupon decided that America should take the place of Britain in underpinning the existing governments and economies of Greece and Turkey. In asking a predominantly Republican Congress to provide the necessary funds, he enunciated the far-reaching Truman Doctrine.[10] This constituted a direct challenge to Soviet expansionism, now liable to be confronted with the principle of containment by American arms at any point of the compass, wherever the collapse of the old social order or the growth of a native Communist Party or mere proximity might give Russia its chance.

The Truman Doctrine saved Greece and Turkey, in the sense that the western nations retained an outpost in the Balkan Peninsula and the Russians were prevented from securing the control of the Turkish Straits. It also led directly to the Marshall Plan, which shored up the economy of western Europe so effectively that the strength of the Communist Party in Italy and France ceased to be a direct menace to the existing social order. By March, 1948, Britain, France, and the Low Countries had created a defensive alliance against Russia through the Treaty of Brussels. This implied that they had the will, even though they clearly lacked the means, to oppose a hypothetical thrust to the Atlantic; hence the growth of opinion which in little more than a year created the twelve-power military pact of the North Atlantic Treaty Organization.[11] Meanwhile, the Soviet bloc had not waited passively to be contained.

In one sense the changed attitude of the West may have been welcome

9. See p. 268.
10. See p. 318.
11. See p. 319.

to Stalin, since it enabled him to restore the strict separation from western contacts which had formerly prevented Russians from making invidious comparisons between a socialist and a capitalist standard of life. Millions of Russian soldiers who found themselves after the war occupying what had been capitalist lands were disposed to admire as well as to plunder. Now, however, it was possible to break contacts and rekindle old antagonisms. It is even suggested that Stalin tried to set up a second Iron Curtain by reducing to a minimum the interchange of personnel between the U.S.S.R. and her new satellites, at least until the last traces of the old capitalist society had been obliterated. The obvious reaction by the East to what the West was attempting was to counterorganize. In September, 1947, the Cominform provided all the east European Communist parties with a common front under the transparent disguise of an information bureau. It also provided the party in Italy and France with a valuable link; a Communist victory in the elections in either of those countries would present an awkward problem for an enemy who was committed to the support of parliamentary democracy. Two years later the Molotov Plan was established to rival the economic achievements of the Marshall Plan. It offered Russian help of many kinds, from credits to technicians, to the satellites, while a Council of Mutual Economic Assistance (or COMECON) was also set up for the general co-ordination of economic policies. Finally, in 1955 the military arrangements of NATO were paralleled by the Warsaw Pact, a twenty-year treaty of mutual defense, based on a pooling of resources by Soviet Russia and its seven associates, from East Germany to Albania.

Public attention was caught more readily by direct clashes. Mention has already been made of the brief struggle over Czechoslovakia, when it vainly attempted to avail itself of the Marshall Plan, and of the expulsion of over-independent Yugoslavia from the Cominform. But logically enough the main trial of strength came over Germany with its immense strategic potential which, in the absence of any final peace settlement, invited the great powers to maneuver for control or influence. The division into four occupation zones could not be preserved indefinitely. Indeed, a rift developed at the outset, because the Russians (and French) drained away all native resources, so that the Americans (and British) had to bring in resources from outside to keep the people from complete starvation. The obvious remedy was to treat the country as a single economic, and ultimately as a single political, unit. Neither side, however, dare run the risk that an eventual united Germany might carry its strength into the other camp. The western powers therefore decided in 1948 to unite their zones and to establish a parliamentary government there, to which full sovereignty might later be conceded. Since the resources of the eastern zone, though by this time thoroughly communized, were much smaller, the result was a net gain to the anti-Communist bloc.

Soviet Russia sought to combat this by scoring a spectacular triumph in Berlin. The airlift undertaken by the western powers between June, 1948, and April, 1949, has been described in Chapter 11. From this trial of strength between East and West several results emerged. The Soviet challenge had been successfully faced; the people of Berlin and, indeed, of West Germany had been assured of explicit western support, even if at a very high cost; and the rift between the two worlds had become greater than ever.

Communism had been successfully contained at one point, only to erupt in the following year at another, and in that short interval, too, its prospects of ultimate victory had been greatly enhanced. In May of 1949, it was discovered that the Russians had achieved an atomic explosion at least three years ahead of expectation. Although it was promptly announced that the Soviet atomic bomb would be completely outclassed by the American hydrogen bomb, the manufacture of which was now ordered, it was apparent even to the unthinking that Russia would again catch up and be able to hold the world to ransom, if she chose, by threatening to provoke a nuclear holocaust. At about the same time it was reluctantly realized that Chiang Kai-shek had been finally defeated on the mainland of China by the Chinese Communists. The almost untapped resources of Chinese territory and man power and the long-disputed inheritance of the Manchu Empire were cast on the Communist side. In the circumstances it was almost inevitable that the new problem of containment should arise at the opposite end of what was now a continuous Communist bloc stretching from the southwest corner of the Baltic Sea to the shores of the Pacific, with a population of 900,000,000.

Although the Korean War[12] was launched with Russian connivance by a Soviet-trained and Soviet-equipped army, the importance of the conflict lies primarily in the intervention of Chinese "volunteers." These scored a big initial success and ensured a final stalemate by showing that the new China would not shrink from world war in defense of its territory. The whole Korean episode requires to be judged in the context of the general transformation of the Far East. A struggle which lasted for three years (1950–1953) and traded nearly 157,000 American dead or wounded for maintaining virtually the prewar frontier was not all loss to the anti-Communist powers. If the war had seemed to strengthen the Sino-Soviet alliance, this effect did not last long. On the other hand, the Americans had for the first time acted as the major element in a force officially operating for the United Nations. Moreover, this force had achieved the limited objective of containing Korean Communism, and although the Koreans had suffered the enormous loss of about three million lives or one-tenth of their total population, the outbreak of a third world war had been avoided.

12. See pp. 360–361.

■ THE SUCCESSION TO STALIN

The death of Stalin, which occurred in March, 1953, shortly before the completion of the long-drawn-out negotiations in Korea, clearly marked the close of an era in Russian affairs. Since the end of the war the Marshal had been almost deified, whatever was lacking of patriotic enthusiasm being supplied by the effects of widespread propaganda and abject fear. His place was taken by a group of the younger men who had risen to power in Stalin's shadow, the indispensable *Apparatchiki* who survived the great purges.[13] Malenkov, once a personal secretary to Stalin and subsequently his most important subordinate, became chairman of the Council of Ministers; Beria, for many years chief of police, became minister of the interior and of state security; and Bulganin became minister of defense, the post he had previously held. More gradually, over a period of six months Nikita Khrushchev,[14] a coal-miner's son from the often troublesome Ukraine, took over the all-important post at the head of the Party secretariat which had formerly been held by Stalin and most recently by Malenkov. Although Khrushchev at this stage had no ministerial appointment, his hold on Party affairs already made his position more significant than that of such ministers as Molotov. This veteran Bolshevik resumed the portfolio of foreign affairs, holding it for nearly five years, until he fell in 1957 as soon as he attempted to oppose Khrushchev's Party policy in the name of true Stalinism.

Other important changes had preceded Molotov's fall. Beria was sacrificed in December, 1953, his execution after a secret trial forming part of a general attack on the rigors and injustices of Stalin's police system. Malenkov, having been outmaneuvered by Khrushchev with the support of military opinion, resigned early in 1955 and was rewarded for "going quietly" by his continuance in a minor office. His place as premier was taken by Bulganin, and the vacancy at the ministry of defense was entrusted to Marshal Zhukov, whom Stalin had long relegated to the background because of his popularity as a victorious commander.

The triumvirate of Khrushchev, Bulganin, and Zhukov, which had replaced the original quadrumvirate, lasted about two years. Then in 1957 Zhukov was removed from all his offices for having fostered the "cult of the individual" in the army, the individualist voting meekly for his own removal.

---

13. See pp. 222–224.
14. Born in 1894 near Kursk. As a child he worked on farms in summer, had very little schooling in winter, and was later employed as a fitter on mining machinery. He studied at the Stalin Industry Academy in Moscow, 1929–1931; later he became Party secretary in Moscow and in the Ukraine, where he reorganized agriculture. A member of the Politburo since March, 1939, he controlled Partisan warfare in the Ukraine and took charge of reconstruction as premier of the Ukrainian S.S.R. after its liberation from the Germans. His fall from office came in October, 1964.

Finally, in March, 1958, Bulganin resigned the premiership to Khrushchev, the sole survivor, and after a decent interval confessed to the crime of membership in an "anti-Party fractional group," of which his successor had already announced the "unanimous defeat." Even at a much earlier date, Khrushchev had been consolidating his position by placing his chosen subordinates in key Party offices and by asserting himself more prominently and vigorously on big occasions at home and abroad. In particular, it was he who denounced Stalin's excesses in the frankest terms at the Party Congress of 1956. The denunciation, though bearing most severely upon his associates who had stood closer to Stalin, placed his own career in a despicable light as that of an accessory to crimes of gross injustice and vindictive cruelty. Such an attitude could only have been adopted by a leader who felt very sure of his position.

In domestic affairs the immediate effect of Stalin's death was a general policy of softening the regime. The fall of Beria was preceded by the punishment of other police authorities for faking a recent plot against the lives of Stalin and his chief associates, allegedly by certain Jewish doctors employed in the Kremlin. A large number of other innocent persons were released from prison by a general amnesty. Minor political deviations ceased to involve any harsher penalty than loss of office, and in cultural matters some freedom of opinion was allowed. The changing climate was suggested by the symbolic title, *The Thaw*, which the well-known Soviet writer, Ilia Ehrenburg gave to his new novel. Most encouragingly, perhaps, Malenkov promised to find the means of providing more food and consumer goods for a population which, as it toiled to fulfil the fifth Five-Year Plan, could see little improvement in its standard of living. The promise was fulfilled for a time by the simple expedient of doubling imports, but after two years the fall of Malenkov was the signal for cutting the planned increase in consumer goods by half.

The big Plans continued to be the dominant feature of the Soviet society. The only major change was the delegation of most of the control work of the central authorities to a hundred or more Regional Economic Councils; the collective farms also obtained a considerable degree of autonomy in being allowed to own the machinery they used. But neither the new Five-Year Plan of 1956 nor the Seven-Year Plan, which was substituted for it at the twentieth Party Congress in 1959, offered to allow any remission of effort in such basic requirements as steel production, with its target of 100 million net tons per annum.

The Russian economy still labored under grave handicaps. Steel production suffered from a chronic scarcity of scrap metal, except for a short period after the great German retreat of 1943–1945. To tap the resources of coal and iron ore and to further the general development of heavy industry in eastern regions called for an enormous initial expenditure on transport. The man power required for expanding industry, on which everything else depended, could no longer be readily achieved from a rural surplus, for as the 1959 census showed, the size of the Soviet family was declining. Thus in agriculture and industry alike the emphasis on productivity increased. Russians showed a great interest in technological developments of all kinds, from icebreakers to irrigation dams, from quick-growing strains of seed for pushing the margin of cultivation northward to cheap oxygen for beating the American rate of output from open-hearth steel mills. Yet this interest was inevitably counterbalanced to some extent by the fact that the new methods were being operated by a peasant people, whose natural tempo of life was very slow.

By the 1960's the available statistics suggested that life was on the whole easier and the supply of food and consumer goods in general above the level of Russia in the past. They were corroborated by the impressions of foreign visitors, who were noticeably more welcome in Khrushchev's Russia than they had been in Stalin's or Lenin's. Yet the general standards were much below those of western Europe, not to speak of the United States. A particular effort was being made to catch up with housing requirements, where Russia had always lagged behind. But what mattered most to the rest of mankind was the continuance, and the purpose, of Russia's concentration upon the production of capital goods. In Khrushchev's own words:

> The economic might of the Soviet Union is based on the priority growth of heavy industry; this should insure the Soviet victory in peaceful economic competition with the capitalist countries; development of the Soviet economic might will give communism the decisive edge in the international balance of power.[15]

The death of Stalin in 1953 was inevitably a landmark also in Russia's relations with the European satellite powers, for whom he had long been the paramount authority. Only a few months later, rioting broke out in East Germany, with the result that reparation payments and the exploitation of German prisoners of war were at last brought to an end. It was also decided to convert this territory from the status of a Russian zone of occupation to that of a nominally independent Russian satellite, a "German Democratic Republic" in name as sovereign as the "Federal Republic of Germany" established by the western powers.[16] Though the new East German state was far from being economically viable, such weakness would help to make it politically more dependent than its West German counterpart. This new departure was followed by a compromise arrangement with Yugoslavia after a formal apology had been made in 1955 for the seven-year-old quarrel, conveniently blamed on

15. Quoted in T. FITZSIMMONS, P. MALOF, and J. C. FISKE, *U.S.S.R., Its People, Its Society, Its Culture* (1961), p. 250.
16. See pp. 305–306.

Beria, whose testimony was no longer available. The Cominform was dissolved, Yugoslavia agreeing in return to abandon her project for a Balkan alliance which would have benefited NATO. Both sides won important economic advantages: Russia gained access to bauxite and other much needed raw materials, while Yugoslav trade enjoyed the stimulus of both a credit and a loan. In the long run, however, Tito largely disappointed his powerful neighbor by the skill with which he preserved a middle position, balanced between East and West.

The most crucial developments in Russia's relations with the rest of eastern Europe occurred in 1956, when Khrushchev's dramatic attack on the memory of Stalin suggested that the decisions which the latter had imposed were all now open to review. In June a revolt among industrial workers in the Polish province of Poznan was quickly suppressed by Soviet forces. This was followed by the withdrawal of the Polish-born Marshal Rokossowski, who had earned undying hatred by his failure to help the Warsaw rising in 1944. Political power was eventually transferred to Wladislaw Gomulka,[17] this rehabilitation of a native Communist leader who had been imprisoned for nationalist deviationism being in itself remarkable. So was the independence of the policy which Gomulka introduced, because he moderated the rigors while retaining the essentials of communism. The Catholic Church, for example, had its liberty restored, subject only to abstention from politics, and no attempt was made from Moscow to force the pace towards collective agriculture and intensive industrialization. In foreign policy, however, Poland was not tempted to deviate, since the western powers had never approved the advance of her frontier to the line of the Oder and Western Neisse rivers, which the Soviet armies had established in 1945.

The Polish example of independent action was followed with less restraint in Hungary. In October, 1956, the month of Gomulka's rise to power in Warsaw, students launched a demand for the reinstatement of Imre Nagy,[18] a moderate Communist who had been installed as premier after the death of Stalin, only to be removed by Khrushchev early in 1955. The formidable strength of the demonstration brought Nagy into office, and after some confused street fighting the Russian troops, who had been called in by native Communists, were withdrawn from Budapest. Nagy then decided to include

17. Born in 1905. He led the Communist underground resistance to the German occupation of Poland. He was deputy prime minister in 1945-1949, but was imprisoned from 1951 to 1954 for "non-appreciation" of Russian control of Poland. He returned to power as first secretary of the Communist Party in October, 1955.
18. 1895-1958. By trade a locksmith, he was a prisoner of war in Russia at the Revolution. He then held minor office in Hungary under Bela Kun, fled, and returned with the Red Army. He was responsible for land reforms, and in 1953-1955 he was prime minister, but was ousted as a "right deviationist." After his final fall from power he was abducted by Soviet troops and shot after secret trial by a Hungarian "people's court" in June, 1958.

non-Communists in his cabinet and announced his intention of holding free elections. These would certainly have been won by the non-Communist parties with the support of the Catholic primate, Josef, Cardinal Mindszenty, who had been dramatically freed after nearly eight years of imprisonment by the fallen regime. The outcome would doubtless have been a rapprochement with the West. Russian troops, however, returned to suppress the revolution by naked force and at the cost of about thirty thousand Hungarian lives, not counting the broken lives of another two hundred thousand Hungarians who fled into exile.

Though the preoccupation of the western powers with the Suez crisis[19] no doubt encouraged the Russians to act ruthlessly, the main factor was their determination to keep eastern Europe at all costs from deserting to the West. The execution of Nagy, one year after he had been induced to leave the sanctuary of the Yugoslav embassy in Budapest under a safe-conduct, marked the flaring-up of a new quarrel between the Russians and Tito. This was made the occasion also for a recantation by Gomulka of any claim for the Poles to think independently on international issues. More generally, the execution served to underline the evidence that in the last analysis the Khrushchev regime, no less than that of Stalin, rested upon a basis of power politics, disregarding the claims of humanity.

■ RUSSIA AND THE WORLD

No contrast could be more striking than that between the forbidding isolation in which Stalin kept himself, going no farther afield than Tehran, and the readiness of Khrushchev and his colleagues to visit and be visited. Britain, India, and the United States each in turn feted the Soviet leaders, but when the shouting died down it was generally felt that more important results followed the return visits. These gave such astute politicians as Vice-President Nixon and Prime Minister Macmillan a chance to present something of a different viewpoint to an eager Russian public, cut off from any presentation of a world outlook at variance with their own. It was a mistake, however, to draw the inference, as some did, that the recurring clashes of East and West could be eliminated through a renewal of those top-level meetings which had come to an end in July, 1945.

Exactly ten years after the Potsdam Conference President Eisenhower and the British and French prime ministers, Eden and Faure, met the Russian leaders at Geneva. No progress was made with any of the three main problems discussed: disarmament, the reunification of Germany, and the improvement of contacts of all kinds between the Communist and noncommunist world. All that could be claimed was that Eisenhower's genial personality made a favor-

19. See p. 370.

able impact on the Russians, and that the holding of the conference in itself tended to reassure world opinion. It might be hoped that a deliberate resort to nuclear war had become unthinkable and therefore perhaps impossible. Even this limited claim could not be advanced for the second "summit conference," which collapsed without formally meeting. President Eisenhower arrived in Paris in mid-May, 1960, a fortnight after an American plane on a photo-reconnaissance mission had been shot down twelve hundred miles inside the Soviet frontier. The existence of such flights was first denied by the American authorities and then defended. The result was that before Eisenhower had promised to forbid their renewal, Khrushchev had gone on to make further demands for retribution and apology which were unacceptable. So far from producing even formal gestures of amity, the affair led to an alert of U.S. strategic forces at all their world-wide stations. When President John F. Kennedy convened with Khrushchev for two days at Vienna in the following year, no one was surprised at the absence of any agreement, the public being satisfied to hail their mere expression of a desire to get to know each other better and their common interest in disarmament.

The new and infinitely menacing position that had been reached in the arms race was one of the two realities underlying Russia's apparent power over mankind. Whereas it had taken the Russians four years to catch up with the atomic bomb, only nine months separated the first American hydrogen bomb explosion, which was at ground level, from the first Russian hydrogen bomb explosion in the air. Thereafter Russia appeared to the rest of the world to be setting the pace in the quality, though not as yet in the quantity, of her thermonuclear armament. Her possession of an intercontinental ballistic rocket was announced in August, 1957, after which the claims of both sides to weapons of increasing power and sophistication for both offensive and defensive purposes bewildered all except the technological experts, who were sworn to secrecy. On the one hand, the generally superior performances of Russian designs for the exploration of outer space gave the world a series of convincing demonstrations of inventive talent and technical efficiency. On the other hand, the high standard of living of the United States, and the existence of a great surplus from which she ministered to the needs of poorer countries, made it a safe inference that measures adopted for her own protection, such as the highly secret stockpiling of missiles, were being carried out on a gigantic scale.

Another extended crisis over Berlin caused many people to believe that Russia had a powerful psychological weapon in her armory, because a dictatorship as compared with a democracy could maneuver more readily on the very brink of war. This seemed to be the meaning of the new crisis over Berlin's future, which the Russians stirred up in 1958, when they announced the intention of withdrawing their occupation forces from what they proposed to treat as a demilitarized "free city." Access to it would then require negotiations with the German Democratic Republic of East Germany, which the western powers did not recognize as sovereign, let alone as having any right of control over their routes to Berlin.

When the United States showed clearly that she would preserve the western position in Berlin by force if force was used against this position, the Russians agreed to postpone the issue until 1961. It was then raised again at the Vienna meeting referred to (p. 347), producing renewed tension. This caused East Germans in increasing numbers to vote against the regime "with their legs," for they crossed into West Berlin at a rate which rose to more than two thousand a day. Consequently a twenty-eight-mile wall was built to keep them in, dramatizing for the whole world the oppression that lay behind it. Once again American determination to accept the risk of war, if risk it was, caused the threat to recede, as it was also to recede in the more extreme crisis over Russian rocket installations in Cuba.

The second underlying reality of Russian power was its capacity for raising new issues in other continents. Imperialism was everywhere on the retreat before nationalism. New nation-states were making their debut on the world stage, handicapped by extreme poverty and ignorance but impatiently eager to cut an independent figure and to advance their economies, whether by communist or by capitalistic methods. In Asia and Africa, to which the reader's attention will next be directed, it seemed that the world might yet be won for communism, if not by the forces of Khrushchev then by those of Mao Tse-tung. For one of the ironic results of Soviet Russia's impact upon the world had been the emergence in Asia of a rival Communist state of enormous potential power.

Reading List: Chapter 12

Windsor, P., "The Berlin Crises," *History Today,* vol. XII (1962), no. 6.

Florinsky, M. T. (ed.), *McGraw-Hill Encyclopedia of Russia and the Soviet Union* (1961), articles on foreign policy since 1945 and space science.

Khrushchev, N. S., "Peaceful Coexistence," *Foreign Affairs*, vol. XXXVIII (1959), no. 1.

Auty, P., *Yugoslavia* (1962), chs. 7–9. Communist leadership and mass participation illustrated.

"X," "The Sources of Soviet Conduct," *Foreign Affairs*, vol. XXV (1947), no. 4. The famous article by G. F. Kennan defining United States policy as "a long-term, patient but firm and vigilant containment of Russian expansive tendencies."

Chapter 13

The New Asia
and the New Africa

National Aspirations: Retrospect and Prospect
India and Pakistan in the New Age
Japan: From Defeat to Recovery
Conflict in China and Korea
The New Nationalism in Southeast Asia
The Middle East: Israel, Turkey, and Iran
The Middle East: The Arab States
African Independence
Continuing Stresses in Asia and Africa

■ NATIONAL ASPIRATIONS: RETROSPECT AND PROSPECT

The striking advances toward freedom which the peoples of Asia and Africa had made by mid-twentieth century constitute a dramatic chapter in the history of Europe's relations with these areas. In no other parts of the world had nineteenth-century European imperialism been more powerful. Yet ultimately the reaction came. Some stirrings of unrest and some demands, if not for independence at least for self-government, had appeared here and there after the First World War.[1] The answer of Europe at this time had been to grant concessions, but never total freedom.

1. See ch. 5, pp. 123 ff.

SIGNIFICANT EVENTS

1949   People's Republic of China proclaimed at Peiping (September)
        United States of Indonesia officially independent (November)

1950   Republic of India formally proclaimed, replacing Dominion of
            India within Commonwealth (January)
        Treaty of friendship between the People's Republic of China
            and the U.S.S.R. (February)
        Outbreak of the Korean War (June)

1951   Colombo Plan in effect to develop South and Southeast Asia
            (July)
        Treaty of peace with Japan signed (September)

1952   King Farouk overthrown in Egypt (July)

1953   Egypt proclaimed a republic (June)
        Korean armistice signed (July)
        Southeast Asia Treaty Organization established (September)

1955   Baghdad Pact launches Middle East Treaty Organization
            (March)
        South Vietnam declares itself a republic (October)

1956   Suez Canal crisis (July-November)

1957   "Eisenhower Doctrine" proposes aid against Communism to
            Middle East states (January)
        Ghana the first African state to achieve independence within
            Commonwealth (March)

1958   Communist China inaugurates the "Great Leap Forward"
            (January)
        United Arab Republic formed (February)

1959   Central Treaty Organization established (March)

National ambitions were affected by the military campaigns fought in Africa and Asia during the Second World War. The long struggle in North Africa between the Italians and Germans on the one hand and the British, Australians, New Zealanders, Indians, and Americans on the other dramatized the strategic significance of the whole Middle East; its outcome paved the way for an invasion of Europe through Italy and later through the south of France. Japan's overrunning of China, the South Pacific, and Southeast Asia necessitated large-scale warfare in Burma, Malaya, New Guinea, the Philippines, the Pacific islands, and in China itself. Moreover, in order to bring aid to the Soviet Union and China, strategic links had to be developed by rail and truck routes through Iran, by air over "the Hump" from Assam, and, until its closing in 1942, by the seven-hundred-mile Burma Road from Lashio into China.

The inevitable changes brought about by these huge campaigns, the passions that were aroused, and the new perspectives that were opened all contributed to the heightening of already powerful national aspirations in Asia and Africa. When the Japanese occupation of Indonesia collapsed in 1945, it was hardly likely that the leaders of the independence movement to whom the Japanese handed over the country would countenance a return to the former Dutch rule. Similar attitudes prevailed in the areas long subject to the French or to the British. The immediate outcomes, chiefly regarding the rapidly declining role of the European states as imperial powers in the first five years of peace, have been briefly outlined in Chapter 11. It remains now to consider these areas in the decade of the 1950's, and more specifically from the point of view of the native peoples. For in a global age no history of Europe can possibly be meaningful or complete in itself; indeed, the reaction of Asia and Africa to the old European dominance may well count as one of the most significant developments in the entire history of the twentieth century. For Europe has exported its ideas of nationalism, self-government, and human welfare, as well as its science and technology.

Some notable differences existed with respect to the problems of Africa and Asia. The total population of Africa has been estimated (1963) at 296 million; that of Asia, with 1,802 million, would be fully six times as large. India alone, with 449 million, has 1.5 times Africa's population; China, with 686 million, has nearly 2.5 times the population of the Dark Continent. Nowhere in the world has the population explosion manifested itself more dramatically than in Asia. Unlike "Black Africa," most parts of Asia have ancient and complex cultures, with long political traditions and rich developments in art, literature, and philosophy. In both cases population is growing apace, but whereas the economy of Africa is preponderantly peasant or nomadic, that of Asia has a significant industrial segment. And, finally, it can be observed that the impact of communism in Asia, whether Russian or Chinese, has so far been greater than in Africa.

■ INDIA AND PAKISTAN IN THE NEW AGE

The critical year for both India and Pakistan was 1947, when both were launched on the stormy sea of independence. Pakistan, with a population then under ninety million, had the enormous drawback of being divided into two parts, the larger in the northwest and the smaller a thousand miles distant in East Bengal. India had then a population of some four hundred million, with an annual increase of some six million—this being roughly equivalent to the entire population of Switzerland.[2] A few indications of the difficulties of these new countries may be suggested. In Pakistan some 88 percent of the population was Moslem, with most of the rest Hindu. The literacy figure at the time of independence has been given at 14 percent, the average life expectancy twenty years, the annual per capita cash income fifty dollars. India, with some beginnings of industrial growth, had similar social problems, while the appalling slum conditions in Calcutta and Bombay were among the worst in the world. India had the further complication of 14 main languages and several hundred dialects. Hindi, the state language, was spoken by only about 50 percent of the people, and Urdu, the prevalent Moslem language, by about 10 percent. An offsetting factor was the presence in both countries of at least the nucleus of a trained civil service—the product of years of British administration. One result, interestingly enough, was the persistence of English as a second language in educational and government circles; by a law of 1963 English may be used for official purposes until 1975. India was fortunate in having a leader of the caliber of Jawaharlal Nehru,[3] Gandhi's colleague and successor, who was prime minister from the achievement of independence in 1947 until his death in 1964. Pakistan likewise was guided in its beginnings by the strong hand of Mohammed Ali Jinnah,[4] the principal architect of the new state who, unhappily, died in 1948.

Both India and Pakistan had the problem of developing a constitutional structure in keeping with the democratic trends of the modern world. The Indian constitution, completed in 1950, was roughly similar to that of the United States, with a bill of rights, an elected legislature of two houses, and a president chosen for a five-year term. Pakistan completed its constitution in 1956, though widespread illiteracy made its operation difficult. In 1958 the constitution was annulled, the consequence of a military take-over by General Mohammed Ayub Khan, who in 1960 was elected president. Pakistan's second constitution came into effect in 1962, with provisions for a single-chamber legislature and a stronger presidential regime.

While India sought by various means to introduce wide schemes of so-

2. For 1963 the estimated population figures were: India, 449 million; Pakistan, 98.6 million.

3. 1889–1964. Born of a substantial Brahmin family and educated in England at Harrow, Cambridge, and the Inner Temple, he returned to India to become a follower of Gandhi after the Amritsar massacre of 1919, and eventually his principal deputy in the fight for independence. A student both of Marxism and Taoism, he spent eighteen of the years between 1921 and 1946 intermittently in jail, where he wrote *Letters from a Father to His Daughter* and *Glimpses of World History*. He then held the office of Indian prime minister, combining a foreign policy of peaceful coexistence and nonalignment with a domestic program of social reforms and industrial progress.

4. 1876–1948. Admitted to the bar in England, he returned to India where he supported the National Congress. From 1910 to 1916 he was a member of the viceroy's legislative council and a strong advocate of Hindu-Moslem unity. He long served as president of the Moslem League, seeking an independent Pakistan. During the Second World War he supported the British. He was first governor-general of the Dominion of Pakistan and president of its Constituent Assembly.

cial amelioration, to strengthen the industrial aspects of its economy (United States aid in this decade totaled in all some two billion dollars), and to raise the level of its peasant economy, serious crises came from without. The first bitter conflicts with Pakistan resulted in much bloodshed and dislocation. The problem was to transfer some part of the Moslem minority from India to Pakistan and of the Hindu minority from Pakistan to India (these transfers together numbering an estimated twelve million). Such an undertaking proved impossible without brutality and even massacre on both sides.

Another issue was that of Kashmir, a native state in the far north, preponderantly Moslem but ruled by a Hindu maharaja who tried in 1947 to unite his state with India. Pakistan sent in troops, as did India, and conflict followed. Not until 1949 was it possible for the United Nations to negotiate a cease-fire, and even then no solution proved acceptable; the plebiscite which was promised never actually was held. Both India and Pakistan remained in partial occupancy of Kashmir.

While Pakistan, by membership in the Southeast Asia Treaty Organization and the Middle East Treaty Organization,[5] flung in her lot fully with the West, India chose the path of neutralism or nonalignment. The "five principles" enunciated by Nehru in 1954 stressed essentially nonaggression and peaceful coexistence in foreign affairs. He favored admission of Red China to the United Nations and on some issues leaned more to the Soviet Union than to the West. Yet he was concerned at the Red Chinese take-over in Tibet between 1951 and 1959 and at the expulsion of the Dalai Lama, who sought refuge in India. He was equally concerned at Communist China's threat in 1959 to Kashmir and to part of India's northeast frontier. On balance it would seem that Indian sympathy was moving away from both China and the Soviet Union, though not so far as to end the policy of nonalignment.

■ JAPAN: FROM DEFEAT TO RECOVERY

The two atom bombs which fell on Japan (August 6 and 9, 1945) were followed by notice of unconditional surrender on August 14, formally signed on September 2. Earlier, at Yalta, Britain and France had agreed that the Soviet Union should regain southern Sakhalin, acquire the Kurile Islands, and be given special rights in Manchuria as a condition of its joining the war in the Far East. It had also been agreed at Potsdam that Japan should be occupied, demilitarized, and shorn of all its imperial possessions. Thus, when General MacArthur assumed the position of Supreme Commander of the Allied Powers, Japan was reduced in area to no more than the four main islands from

5. See pp. 366, 367.

which her imperial adventures had been launched in 1895, and in numbers to a population of 78 million.[6] During the war she had conquered an area with a population of 450 million.

Few countries have undergone such drastic changes as did Japan under what turned out to be essentially an American occupation. Few supreme commanders have exercised such powers as did General MacArthur, for the rule of the emperor and any Japanese cabinet was made directly subject to his authority. Demilitarization was easily achieved within a year. A new, democratic constitution, drafted by American and Japanese experts and combining elements from British and American practice, created a limited monarchy with universal suffrage and a bicameral parliament. The peerage was abolished. One clause stated that Japan had "forever renounced war as a sovereign right of the nation, and the threat or use of force as a means of settling international disputes." Troops were to be retained only for self-defense. Overwhelmingly approved by the Japanese Diet, the constitution came into effect in May, 1947. As in Europe, the major war criminals were brought to trial, and in December, 1948, former Premier Tojo and six other war leaders were hanged by the occupying authorities. Others were tried and executed in the Philippines.

A peace treaty with Japan was not signed until September, 1951. It was then accepted in San Francisco by forty-nine nations, only the Soviet Union, Czechoslovakia, and Poland abstaining. Yugoslavia, India, Burma, and the two Chinas were not present. The Soviet objection to the treaty was that its terms sought to align Japan against the communist world. Japan agreed to the losses of territory already stipulated, renounced any special rights in China, and agreed in principle to pay reparations. Allied occupation forces were to be withdrawn within ninety days of the coming into effect of the treaty, subject to special bilateral arrangements.

Along with the peace treaty the United States signed a defense agreement with Japan (modified in 1960) on the strength of which some American forces and American bases were to be retained indefinitely. Japan, for her part, provided defense forces which by 1964 amounted to 171,000 ground troops, 37,000 naval personnel, and an air force of 1,000 planes. Beginning in 1954 the United States included Japan in its Mutual Security Assistance program.

A dramatic series of economic reforms had also been sponsored by the occupying authorities. An attack on the large industrial and financial combines (*zaibatsu*, or "money cliques"), which had such a large influence on Japanese prewar policy, was only partly successful, although four, including the famous Mitsui and Mitsubishi concerns, were dissolved. Efforts were also made to strengthen the trade-union movement. In agriculture, a long-standing problem

6. This figure of 1947 includes repatriations, and had risen in 1963 to 96 million.

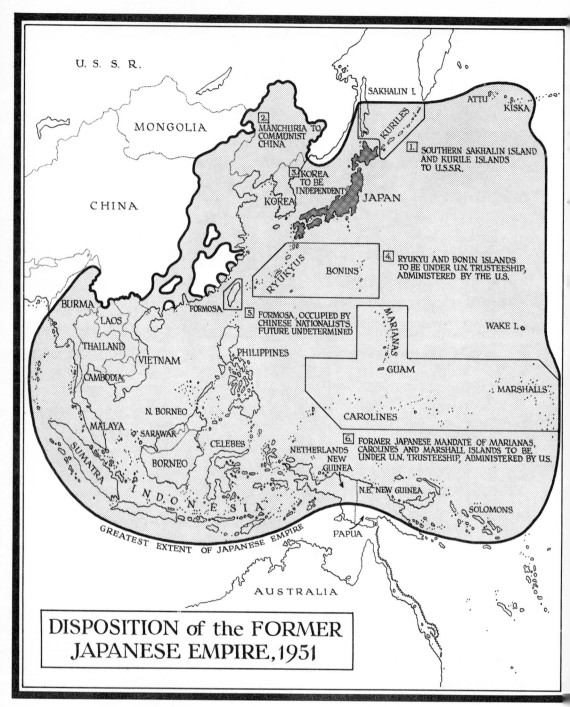

DISPOSITION of the FORMER JAPANESE EMPIRE, 1951

Note that Japan has returned to the four main islands, Honshu, Hokkaido, Kyushu, and Shikoku, from which its imperial program had first been launched in 1895. The reduction of Japanese territory to its nineteenth-century dimensions has been accompanied by an astonishing economic expansion.

was the absentee landlordism which dominated the life of the predominantly rice-growing Japanese peasants. Under pressure from General MacArthur a law of October, 1946, required absentee landlords to turn over their farmland to the government in return for long-term bonds. This land was made available to peasant cultivators on easy terms, with the result that ultimately 90 percent of such acreage was transferred to former tenants.

In a larger Asiatic sphere Japan became associated in 1950 with the beginnings of the Colombo Plan[7] for the cooperative economic development of the countries of South and Southeast Asia. She also obtained substantial credits from the United States through its Export-Import Bank and other agencies. Altogether, American aid to Japan between 1945 and 1951 amounted to some two billion dollars. After 1948 American policy was to play down the original intention of reducing and decentralizing Japanese industry. The contrary program of letting Japan develop as the industrial center of the Far East was stressed. The index of Japanese industrial production, taking the period 1935–1937 as averaging at 100, rose from 26 in 1946 to 109 in 1951. American economic aid, together with a defensive alliance, quite clearly aligned the Japanese with the anti-Communist forces in Asia, although on occasions violent public demonstrations indicated that some segment of Japanese opinion was prepared to denounce what it considered American imperialism in the Far East.

■ CONFLICT IN CHINA AND KOREA

At the war's end in 1945 the uneasy alliance between the Chinese Nationalists and the Chinese Communists exhibited ominous weaknesses. Yet in August of that year a Sino-Soviet treaty pledged Russian economic and military help to the Chinese Nationalist government. Outer Mongolia was to be independent; the Soviets agreed to withdraw their armies forthwith from Manchuria; and for thirty years they would share the operation of the Chinese Eastern and the South Manchurian railways, as well as the use of bases and ports. While this seemed favorable, in other respects troubles for the Nationalist government were mounting. Actual conflict between the Nationalist and Chinese Communist forces had broken out even before the Japanese surrender. American efforts at mediation by General Marshall failed, and although the Nationalists had returned from Chungking to Nanking in May, 1946, they were unable to stem the growing series of Communist successes. By January, 1949, the Red Chinese were in Peiping and soon after they had captured Nanking. The climactic moment came in September, 1949, when the Chinese People's Republic was proclaimed at Peiping by General Mao Tse-tung.

7. See p. 366.

ECONOMIC GROWTH IN COMMUNIST CHINA, 1949-1960

These graphs are based on official Communist statistics which are highly
suspect. The 1960 output refers in each case to planned amount.

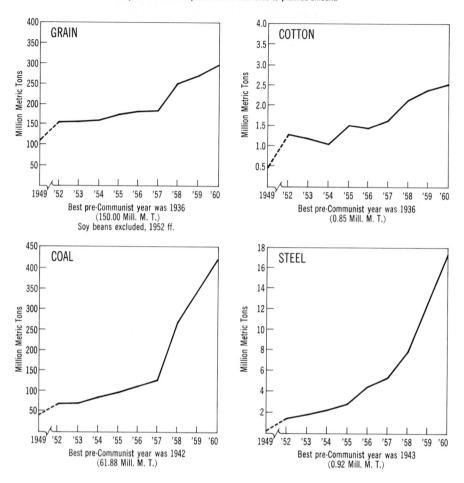

GRAIN

Million Metric Tons

Best pre-Communist year was 1936
(150.00 Mill. M. T.)
Soy beans excluded, 1952 ff.

COTTON

Million Metric Tons

Best pre-Communist year was 1936
(0.85 Mill. M. T.)

COAL

Million Metric Tons

Best pre-Communist year was 1942
(61.88 Mill. M. T.)

STEEL

Million Metric Tons

Best pre-Communist year was 1943
(0.92 Mill. M. T.)

The fortunes of Generalissimo Chiang Kai-shek,[8] who now of necessity
transferred his government to the island of Taiwan (Formosa) where, ruling
nearly ten million people, he claimed a legal if highly unrealistic authority over

8. Born in 1887 and trained for a military career, he served two years in the Japanese army before
taking part in the Chinese Revolution of 1911. He joined Sun Yat-sen in 1918, studied Marx and
Lenin, and by 1925 was in command of the Nationalist army. Within three years he had broken with
the Communists, had become a Christian, and was head of the central government at Peking. During
the long resistance to the Japanese (1937–1945), he renewed an alliance with the Chinese Communists and was able to win a place for China as one of the Big Five at the end of the Second World
War. Driven to Taiwan (Formosa) after the success of the Chinese Communists on the mainland in
1949, he relied upon close support from the United States. His long record as a revolutionary patriot
was mingled with much evidence of ruthless inflexibility, favoritism, and tolerance for administrative
corruption in his own regime.

six hundred and fifty million. True, Nationalist China held its permanent seat (with veto power) in the Security Council of the United Nations, where it relentlessly opposed the admittance of Communist China. Some of its strongest support came from the United States. Between 1937 and 1947 economic aid to China has been calculated at 3.5 billion dollars. In 1955 the United States signed a mutual defense treaty with Nationalist China, following this with regular military and economic assistance. When the Red Chinese renewed their threat in 1958 to seize the offshore islands of Matsu and Quemoy, President Eisenhower ordered units of the United States Seventh Fleet to the Formosa Straits. Despite all this, it seems clear that Chiang Kai-shek's power and prestige had undergone a substantial decline.

The Chinese People's Republic, on the other hand, quite evidently had developed imposing force. Its principal leader, Mao Tse-tung,[9] with lifelong experience as a militant revolutionary, was satisfied, like Stalin, not to become the official head of the government. He held, instead, the post of chairman of the Communist Party. His closest associate, Chou En-lai, was elected and re-elected premier. The Red Chinese role in the Korean War (1950–1953) will be considered later. In February, 1950, the Chinese People's Republic signed a thirty-year treaty of friendship and alliance with the Soviet Union, the latter promising substantial help both with the army and with China's industrial development. The Chinese constitution of 1954 had many similarities to the Soviet constitution of 1936—it provided for a "National People's Congress," for example, of 1200 members much like the Supreme Soviet in the U.S.S.R., and for a Communist Party machine with which real power lay. Authority was exercised with ruthless force; in 1957 Mao admitted the execution of 800,000 opponents in the first five years of the People's Republic—a figure which some critics would be disposed to multiply at least tenfold.

In domestic matters the most striking phenomenon—again similar to the policy of the U.S.S.R.—was the Chinese determination to bring about an economic transformation and modernization of China at almost any cost in human rights and liberties and even lives. To accomplish this end the decade of the 1950's proved critical. How striking the economic advance was, the accompanying graphs will show. Serious food shortages were but one of many gaping defects of the economy. To meet the problem three successive five-year plans were envisaged, according to the aim defined in the constitution: "to bring about step by step the socialist industrialization of the country." The first of

9. Born in 1893 of peasant origin, his first position was as assistant librarian at Peking University. He helped to found the Chinese Communist Party in 1921, working among the peasants and later organizing guerilla warfare against the Nationalists. In 1934 he led the "Long March" of the Communist forces to Yenan Province in northwest China. He headed the postwar opposition to General Chiang, and was the principal architect of Red China. He wrote *The New Democracy* in 1940, but did not go abroad until 1949, when he first visited Moscow.

such plans, running from 1953 to 1957, involved large-scale collectivization of peasant farms, together with a general increase in industrial output. The second, beginning in 1958, concentrated upon steel, coal, and hydroelectric power, all under the slogan of the "Great Leap Forward." Without any doubt basic production did witness a remarkable increase, though the Chinese, still woefully short of mechanical equipment, were compelled to use human labor on a massive and wasteful scale in building dams, roads, and other foundations of the economy. During the winter of 1957–1958 no less than a hundred million peasants were said to have been mobilized for work on these vast construction projects.

Still another feature was the large-scale merging of peasant households and collective farms into the "people's communes," averaging nearly five thousand households. These communes were intended to organize agriculture according to large-scale methods. Perhaps even more, they sought to create a new kind of communist society—a people provided with home and sustenance, educated, drilled, and disciplined in accordance with the program of the party leaders.

The foreign policy of the Chinese People's Republic was marked from the first by a total hostility to the regime of Generalissimo Chiang Kai-shek on Taiwan. It was scarcely less hostile to the United States, whose consistent policy was to refuse recognition and to spearhead the opposition to the admission of Red China to the United Nations.

The postwar problem of Korea brought the attitude of Communist China into sharp focus. At Cairo in November, 1943, it had been agreed that Korea, annexed by Japan in 1910, should be "free and independent." At Potsdam it was agreed that the 38th Parallel should be the dividing line between the Soviet and American occupying forces. In May, 1948, the South Koreans formed the Republic of Korea, with Dr. Syngman Rhee as president. About the same time the Russians in the northern half encouraged the formation of the People's Democratic Republic of Korea. Each government, more or less as in the case of a divided Germany, claimed authority over the whole land and refused to recognize the other.

In June, 1950, when Russian and American occupation forces had been for some time withdrawn from their respective areas, a crisis developed. Powerful North Korean forces crossed the 38th Parallel into South Korea. The United States immediately brought the matter to the Security Council of the United Nations which, in the absence of Soviet Russia (temporarily withdrawn as a protest against the continued presence of Nationalist China), authorized assistance to the South Koreans. The ensuing war, for which the United States provided the United Nations supreme commander and the overwhelming majority of the armed forces, lasted until 1953. General MacArthur recovered all of South Korea, crossed the 38th Parallel, and entered North Korea. When, however, he drove toward the northern boundary—the Yalu River—massive Chinese Communist forces entered the conflict (November, 1951). The outcome was a retreat, a stalemate at the 38th Parallel, which could be broken only at the risk of world war, and disagreement on strategy leading to the removal by President Truman of General MacArthur.

The end of the war, brought about by tedious negotiations lasting until July, 1953, was really no more than a truce. Since no progress was possible toward unifying Korea, the northern and southern regimes could do no more than continue their separate ways. The sympathies of the United States for South Korea were apparent; equally significant were the pacts of military and financial assistance signed by North Korea in 1951 with Communist China and the Soviet Union.

A final development—as profoundly significant, surely, for Europe as for Asia—was the rift that developed between Russia and Communist China. Although the two had signed a thirty-year treaty of alliance and mutual assistance in 1950, disagreements quickly developed. Communist China was not prepared to imitate the usually docile behavior characteristic of the Soviet Union's European satellites. It sought the leading role in Asia. On the world scene the Chinese declared themselves militantly against capitalism and imperialism. Soviet policy was now less rigidly disposed. By 1960 it had become clear that Communist China had little sympathy with any Soviet program hinting at even the possibility of "peaceful coexistence."

■ THE NEW NATIONALISM IN SOUTHEAST ASIA

The great area of Southeast Asia witnessed during the 1950's an almost complete destruction of the old European political connection. With a population of some 200,000,000, these lands were responsible for about five-sixths of the world's natural rubber production, one-half of its tin, two-thirds of its coconut products, and two-thirds of its exportable rice. Marked by a general economic backwardness, by a complex racial and religious diversity, and great political instability, the whole area still remained subject to many outside pressures. On the one hand there was the influence of the Soviet Union and Communist China; on the other hand there existed the continued presence of the non-Communist world—at first principally the Netherlands, France, and the United Kingdom, but later and in increasing measure the intervention of the United States. For, almost without exception, these lands sought, and received, American economic assistance.

The areas where legal independence already existed or was attained with the least trouble may be considered first. Thailand, the former Kingdom of Siam, quickly resumed its independent course after the Japanese wartime occu-

Burma became independent in 1948. Cambodia became independent in 1953. North Vietnam was set off from South Vietnam as a result of the armistice with France in 1954, when Laos also became independent. The Federation of Malaysia was created in 1963, retaining its link with the British Commonwealth.

pation. Its problems arose chiefly from economic backwardness, from some Communist disturbances in its northern regions, from political inexperience in trying to operate the interim constitution proclaimed by King Aduldet in 1959, and from a fairly large amount of administrative corruption. The Philippine Republic formally proclaimed its long-promised independence on July 4, 1946. Under leaders such as Carlos Romulo, Ramón Magsaysay, and Carlos Garcia,

362

SOUTHEAST ASIA, 1963

FEDERATION OF MALAYSIA

UNITED STATES OF INDONESIA

TAIWAN

PHILIPPINES

Pacific Ocean

NORTH BORNEO

HALMAHERA

CELEBES

WEST NEW GUINEA

NEW GUINEA
(WEST IRIAN)

NORTH-EAST NEW GUINEA

PAPUA

FLORES

PORTUGUESE TIMOR

TIMOR

AUSTRALIA

it made substantial progress. A treaty of 1947 guaranteed to the United States
naval and military bases; another of 1952 linked the two countries in a mutual
defense arrangement. Burma, formerly a British colony with powers of self-
government, chose the path of complete independence in January, 1948. Under
an alternation of military and civilian rule, it adopted, like the Republic of
India, something of a neutralist path with leanings to the western powers.

The various princely states making up Malaya, which after the Japanese occupation returned to their former status within the British Empire, were seriously disturbed by the native Chinese Communists. The Federation of Malaya sponsored by the British in February, 1948, provided no final answer to its problems; the country in 1957 became an independent member of the Commonwealth, relying specifically on British aid for its defense. An even further enlargement which takes us beyond the decade with which this chapter is concerned was the inclusion of Singapore, Sarawak, and North Borneo into what became in 1963 the fourteen-member Federation of Malaysia, a sovereign entity still with Commonwealth membership.

Indonesia, with a larger extent than that of the territorial United States and with a population (1962) of 97.8 million, could claim in this respect to be the world's fifth largest state. It won its formal independence from the Dutch in 1949, after four years of struggle, although the Netherlands-Indonesian Union then created as an attempt to maintain a link with the Netherlands was not dissolved until 1954. Much trouble arose, for example over the confiscation of Dutch capital assets and over the Dutch attempt to retain Netherlands New Guinea (West Irian). Although the United States supplied economic aid on a generous scale, strong Communist sympathies existed in the country, and the Soviet Union fostered these by providing Indonesia with large contributions of arms. President Sukarno's[10] glibly worded program of "guided democracy" meant in effect a dictatorial regime marked by the total suspension in 1960 of the elected parliament and its replacement by a nominated assembly.

Some of the most dramatic events of these years, particularly in their impact upon the non-Asiatic world, occurred in Indochina. This area, once described by a French minister of colonies as "the most important, the most developed, and the most prosperous of our colonies," experienced a rise of national assertiveness which had as its first outcome, in 1949, the acquisition by the monarchies of Cambodia and Laos of the status of "associated states within the French Union." By 1953 their independence was complete, though Laos, more than Cambodia, continued to feel the impact of the strife between Communist and non-Communist political factions.

A much larger and more critical area of conflict developed in Vietnam—the thousand-mile-long eastern half of Indochina running from the Chinese border to the Gulf of Siam. Bisected roughly by the 17th Parallel, it had a population of some thirty million and was composed of the former states of Tonkin, Annam, and Cochin China. The French postwar efforts to set up Bao Dai,

10. Born in 1902, the son of a Javanese schoolmaster and trained as a civil engineer and architect, he early became a revolutionary, founding the National Party of Indonesia in 1927, and spending nine years in prison. In 1945 he became first president of the Indonesian Republic and was formally elected again in 1949. Ruling with a dictatorial hand, he won strong support from the three million members of the Indonesian Communist Party, and became a bitter opponent of any surviving western European interests.

former Emperor of Annam, as puppet ruler over this whole area were quickly challenged by Ho Chi-minh, the Communist leader of the Vietminh, or the League for the Independence of Indochina. By 1950 Ho Chi-minh had won the recognition of the U.S.S.R. and Communist China and had established effective rule of North Vietnam from his capital of Hanoi. France, meanwhile, had sought to reconstitute all of Vietnam as an associated state existing within the framework of the French Union. In reality, French authority existed only in the southern half, below the 17th Parallel, with its capital at Saigon.

The enormous military efforts made by France to reassert her position throughout all Vietnam were unavailing. In eight years some 71,000 French troops were killed, while the annual officer loss in killed and wounded roughly equaled the annual number of graduates from St. Cyr, the famous French military academy. The disastrous defeat and surrender at Dien Bien Phu in the extreme northwest (May, 1954) was quickly followed by a cease-fire (July) in which both sides accepted the 17th Parallel as a line of demarcation. France, in simple terms, had decided to cut her losses. In the northern half the "Democratic Republic of Vietnam" adopted a constitution in 1959 which called for the unification of all Vietnam. The final withdrawal of all French forces from South Vietnam took place in 1956. This area had declared itself a republic in 1955, severing all ties with France, repudiating the authority of Bao Dai, and accepting the presidency of Ngo Dinh Diem, who in 1961 won re-election. With the departure of the French and the continued efforts of North Vietnam to win control through guerilla tactics south of the 17th Parallel, the role of the United States became increasingly important, for by an extension of the Truman Doctrine this country stood ready to assist those countries of Asia who themselves were prepared to resist the spread of communism.

In essence the United States had become the only great power generally opposing communism on the Asiatic mainland. What this came to mean in terms of American economic aid may be seen from the tabulation of United States nonmilitary grants to Southeast Asia for the calendar year 1963.

U. S. NONMILITARY GRANTS FOR THE CALENDAR YEAR 1963[11]

COUNTRY	AMOUNT (*in millions*)
Burma	$10
Cambodia	20
Indonesia	77
Laos	31
Philippines	8
Thailand	29
South Vietnam	210

11. *The World Almanac* (1965) p. 775. Military grants, for security reasons, are not specified by country, but can be estimated as somewhat less in total amount.

In this Asiatic world further attempts were made during the decade of the 1950's to establish political security and economic order. In 1951 Australia, New Zealand, and the United States signed a tripartite agreement (ANZUS) pledging joint military defense for mutual security. In 1954 the Southeast Asia Treaty Organization (SEATO) brought together the United States, Australia, New Zealand, Great Britain, France, the Philippines, Thailand, and Pakistan to co-ordinate defense arrangements against aggression and subversion. Unlike NATO in western Europe, there was no specific obligation to undertake military action and in general SEATO remained a shadowy organization with no permanently established forces or well-defined system of command.

A promising development in the field of economics came in 1951 with the Colombo Plan or Plan for Co-operative Economic Development in South and Southeast Asia. Representatives from the states of this area (including India and Pakistan) met at the capital of Ceylon along with the delegates from Japan, the United States, Britain, Australia, Canada, and New Zealand. The general intention was to improve the economies of the various states through jointly planned capital investments, and to this end a sum of more than five billion dollars was projected for the first six years. The programs, which visualized the development of agriculture, transport, and electrical power, were in fact limited chiefly to technical assistance and some economic aid.

■ THE MIDDLE EAST: ISRAEL, TURKEY, AND IRAN

The problems of the Middle East during the 1950's resulted in some major crises. With a concentration here of seventy million Moslems, with more than one-half of the world's known oil reserves, and with a strategic position that could be described as the crossroads of the world, the Middle East had an importance not restricted to its own territorial limits. The state of Israel, on weathering the first storms of independence, had close ties with the West. Turkey, a non-Arab state critically poised on the frontier of the Communist world, became a part both of the North Atlantic Treaty Organization in Europe and of the Middle East Treaty Organization in Asia. France and Britain found their surviving interests as imperial powers rudely attacked, and the United States at one point found herself so far involved in the politics of the Middle East as to land marines in the Lebanon. Soviet influence was apparent in more countries than one. And during these years the Egypt of Gamal Abdel Nasser took the lead in the attempt to mobilize and direct the forces of the Arab world.

The new Zionist state of Israel was proclaimed in May, 1948, after Britain had formally given up her mandate. The first scheme of partition into separate Jewish and Arab states with Jerusalem administered by the United Nations had proved unacceptable to both sides, the sequel being armed conflict between

Israel and the states of the Arab League.[12] Thanks to superiority in equipment and morale, together with unofficial aid from abroad, the Israelis were able to defend themselves successfully. United Nations mediation efforts, headed first by Count Bernadotte of Sweden (who was assassinated in Jerusalem) and then by the American, Ralph Bunche, led to the armistice of 1949, though to no definite peace. One outcome was the expulsion or flight of over 900,000 Arabs, who took refuge in Syria, Lebanon, Jordan, or in the "Gaza Strip," an adjacent Egyptian territory where they dragged out a miserable existence in conditions of extreme poverty. In spite of these losses the population of Israel had risen by 1958 to over two million, of whom only a tenth were then Arab—a striking contrast to the earlier statistics.[13]

Israel's internal development, both political and economic, was spectacular. Land reclamation projects, industrial growth, and vigorous cultural advances were among the successful achievements of this minuscule state, less than two hundred miles in length, having for much of its extent a width of only from thirty to fifty miles, and actually smaller in area than the state of New Hampshire. Between 1948 and 1960 Israel admitted more than a million immigrants. A second crisis flared up in 1956 when at the time of the Suez conflict Israel sent its troops into the Sinai Peninsula, seeking in conjunction with the military activities of Britain and France to break Egypt's military power. The United Nations was able soon to effect a cease-fire, which, unhappily, left the old tensions between Israel and the Arab world still in existence.

Turkish problems in the decade of the 1950's illustrated the critical importance of the country's position on the borders of two conflicting worlds. With a population then approaching thirty million, and with some beginnings of an industrial economy, this Moslem and yet non-Arab land had an important international role to play. The Truman Doctrine of 1947 had recognized Turkey's critical strategic importance to the West. Under heavy pressure from the Soviet Union to cede some Black Sea areas and to revise the Montreux Convention of 1936, which had allowed Turkey to fortify and in effect control the Straits in wartime, she stood firm. In 1950 she "emphatically and conclusively" rejected such demands. Turkey's membership in NATO, effective in 1951, her receipt of very substantial aid from the United States, and her membership in the Middle East Treaty Organization, or Baghdad Pact (1955)—all are evidences of her new status. When METO—the defensive association of Turkey, Iraq, Iran, Pakistan, and Britain—fell apart with the defection of Iraq, Turkey supported the former mutual security objectives by associating herself with Iran and Pakistan in the Central Treaty Organization (CENTO) of 1959, which had the backing of both Britain and the United States.

12. See p. 314.
13. See table, ch. 5, p. 133.

Much of the historical significance of neighboring Iran—like Turkey, on the frontier of two worlds—came from her critical strategic location. In the nineteenth and early twentieth centuries, for example, Russia and Britain maneuvered for the control of Persia, as this land was known until 1935. Inescapably, Persian oil became an important element in the world contest for vital economic resources.[14] The western-educated young Shah Reza Pahlevi, who succeeded his father in 1941, successfully resisted the Soviet attempt in 1946 to set up two "autonomous" regions in the Kurdish and Azerbaijan areas of northwestern Iran as a first step toward their conquest. In October, 1950, the United States concluded with Iran the first of a new series of foreign-aid agreements, with the consequence that in the next ten years some $880 million were provided by America for economic development and defense, the latter category including tanks and jet aircraft.

A matter which clearly rankled in Iranian ruling circles was the powerful position of the Anglo-Iranian Oil Company, despite the fact that in 1949 this company had paid $38 million in royalties to the government. In 1951 Premier Mohammed Mossadegh secured a law providing for the nationalization of the properties of the Anglo-Iranian Oil Company. The ensuing conflict, which because of the loss of oil revenues worked an immediate hardship on the nation's economy, had as a first result the overthrow and imprisonment of Mossadegh in 1953. A second and much more striking result was an agreement in 1954 by which the National Iranian Oil Company took over the production of oil in return for half the net profits, selling this to an international consortium in which Anglo-Iranian had only a minority holding.

A partial result of this enlarged source of national revenue, which the Shah estimated would soon reach a billion dollars annually, was the inauguration of a Seven-Year Plan in 1956 to develop communications, power, social services, agriculture, and industry. Already considerable progress had been made in transferring land to the peasants, yet the complex requirements of the Seven-Year Plan in a backward country made it extremely difficult for the government to show quick or substantial results.

Another major problem for Iran was its position in world affairs. Fear of the Soviet Union made Iran well disposed toward the West. The Tudeh, a Communist group led by Persians trained in the U.S.S.R., was banned in 1949. In November, 1955, Iran adhered to the Baghdad Pact, bringing together, as we have seen, Turkey, Iraq, Pakistan, and Britain in a defensive agreement of dubious strength. Iraq's withdrawal in 1959 led to the creation of CENTO, a similar but even weaker structure. In March, 1959, Iran and the United States signed a military agreement of mutual defense against aggression. Links through trade helped to bind Iran to Great Britain, Italy, and West Germany.

14. See ch. 5, pp. 127–129.

It can be noted, too, that Persian was spoken in parts of Afghanistan and Pakistan, both neighbors; this is perhaps a minor aspect, yet it underscores the importance of what has been called "the Northern Tier"—Turkey, Iran, Afghanistan, and Pakistan—as a kind of buffer area between the Soviet world and the Arab states to the south. In summary, it seems clear that attempts to set up a defensive organization in the Middle East in any way comparable to NATO in western Europe had, though persistent, fallen far short of genuine effectiveness.

■ THE MIDDLE EAST: THE ARAB STATES

The most complex segment of the Middle East remaining to be discussed is the area of the Arab states—first of all Egypt, then Syria, Lebanon, Jordan, Iraq, Saudi Arabia, and Yemen. The other Arab areas of the Sudan and Libya, as well as the more distant Tunisia, Algeria, and Morocco, are left for treatment later in this chapter. Moreover, the various sheikdoms and protectorates of the Persian Gulf region, though masters of enormous oil wealth, did not truly count as states.[15]

The internal history of the Arab lands, where economic and political developments for the most part were equally backward, can be sketched only briefly. More significant are the attempted linking together of various states in the Arab League and Egypt's drive to create the United Arab Republic. An aspect of these moves was the Arab reaction to the policies of the four outside powers most closely concerned: Britain, France, the Soviet Union, and the United States.

Egypt, with an estimated population (1962) of 27.3 million and a substantial economic development, counted unquestionably as the leading state of the Arab world. To be sure, the independence which it had won in 1922 was limited by the treaty arrangements with Britain which have been previously described.[16] Egypt's fortunes were further hampered by the incompetence of the dynasty, most especially by King Farouk, who ruled from 1936 to 1952 in an atmosphere of dancing girls, gluttony, and public dissipation. However, a military revolt then overthrew the regime, and by 1954 a thirty-six-year-old colonel, Gamal Abdel Nasser, exercised almost absolute power.[17] A strong opponent of the old European imperial tradition, Nasser quickly moved to

15. However, one of them, Kuwait, joined the Arab League in 1961 and was admitted to the United Nations in 1963.
16. See p. 127.
17. Born in 1918, a professional soldier who fought in the 1948 war against Israel, he was there disillusioned by the incompetence of the monarchy. He helped to found a secret revolutionary movement which in 1952 overthrew King Farouk. Two years later Nasser ousted Colonel Naguib, his former leader, and in 1956 was elected president under the new constitution. His regime combined ruthlessness in action with skillful diplomacy and an astute sense of Arab interests throughout the Middle East.

secure a treaty with Britain by which the latter agreed to withdraw its garrison from the Suez Canal in two years. He also pushed ahead with plans for building the huge new Aswan Dam and power station intended to transform the economy of Upper Egypt. Nasser's leanings in the direction of the Soviet Union led the United States and Britain to withdraw their first offers of financial assistance for the great irrigation projects. Nasser retorted by nationalizing the Suez Canal in 1956, one month after the stipulated British troop withdrawal, claiming that Egypt needed the canal revenues for the Aswan Dam project. This act clearly violated the International Convention of 1888, including the rights of the international company which operated the Suez Canal and in which Britain and France held important interests. The crisis had other repercussions, for Israel had good reason to believe that Egyptian control would make impossible any shipments through the canal destined for its ports. Consequently in October, 1956, Israeli troops, as we have already noted, invaded the Sinai Peninsula, and the old war, quiescent since 1948, flared up again.

Britain and France also took dramatic action against Egypt, bombing airfields and landing troops from the air and from the sea at the north end of the canal. Whatever the provocation from Nasser, the military policy of Britain and France brought them much criticism—and this criticism was not limited to the Arab world. Vigorous opposition by the United States as well as Russia in the United Nations soon led to a cease-fire and withdrawal of the occupying troops. In the end, therefore, Nasser had his way: the Suez Canal operated under Egyptian control, France and Britain were discredited, and Nasser became even more of a hero in the eyes of the greater part of the Arab world.

The phenomenon of Pan-Arabism now played a part. An Arab League had been organized at Cairo in 1945 with the seven states of Egypt, Saudi Arabia, Iraq, Syria, Lebanon, Jordan, and Yemen as members. Politically the League did very little, although later it attracted the adherence of the new states of Libya and Sudan, as well as Kuwait and the former French North African territories of Tunisia, Algeria, and Morocco. The League was divided, however, by the threefold rivalry of the Hashemite rulers in Jordan, the adherents of Ibn Saud in Saudi Arabia, and the followers of Nasser's leadership in Egypt. Yet despite its weakness it provided a certain rallying point for Arab aspirations.

The new Arab policies soon seemed to be achieving results. Syria and Egypt in February, 1958, announced their merger into the United Arab Republic, with which Yemen for a time also associated itself. In July of the same year a military revolt in Iraq, led by General Abdul Karim Kassem, resulted in the bloody assassination of the pro-western King Faisal II and his premier, followed by a declaration that Iraq was "part of the Arab nation." The consequences were immediate, for Kassem withdrew his country from the Middle

East Treaty Organization, whose purposes were hostile to those of the Arab League, and aligned it instead with the United Arab Republic. In Saudi Arabia, where the great Ibn Saud had died in 1953, his successors gradually drifted into a pro-Nasser and anti-western position. Egyptian pressure in 1958 upon the tiny states of Jordan and Lebanon to strengthen their ties with the Arab world led to the arrival of British paratroopers in Jordan and American marines in Lebanon. This dramatic American action exemplified the operation of the "Eisenhower Doctrine" enunciated in January, 1957, promising economic and military aid to those Arab states requesting support against Communist aggression. After weeks of crisis, tensions subsided somewhat. Yet the American sponsorship of the weak Central Treaty Organization of 1959 (Britain, the United States, Turkey, and Iran) as a successor to the Baghdad Pact could hardly be regarded by its members as a genuinely reassuring move.

Such tensions in the Middle East had international repercussions. The Soviet foreign minister, Andrei Gromyko, denounced the American intervention in Lebanon as unprovoked aggression stemming from greed for "oil, oil, and again oil." Even so, by 1960 no great confrontation had occurred. Moreover, the United Arab Republic soon was to fall apart, and the state of Jordan, once under pressure from Egypt, soon was to announce the merging of its military forces and economic policies with those of Saudi Arabia. In this complex situation Nasser, though still a powerful force in Egypt and the Arab world, was far from having realized his full ambitions.

■ AFRICAN INDEPENDENCE

The continent of Africa had been one of the great areas of European imperialism in the nineteenth century. It was the source of three-quarters of the world's gold, nearly all its industrial diamonds, three-quarters of the world's palm oil, much uranium, one-fourth of its manganese, and one-fifth of its copper and tin. It had been the scene of military operations in both world wars; in the second of these the conflict had extended across the whole Mediterranean coastal area in major campaigns. Nationalism was now making itself felt here as in Asia. Even so, as late as 1950 only four sovereign states existed: Ethiopia, claiming a history going back to the time of the Queen of Sheba; Liberia, founded by freed American Negroes and their sponsors in 1822; Egypt, granted its independence by Britain in 1922; and the Union of South Africa, a British Dominion in 1910 and to all intents a sovereign state since the First World War. By far the greater part of Africa, therefore, was still dependent upon Europe after the Second World War. And Europe was not then ready to give up its claims. Yet out of a population estimated in 1963 at 296 million, only a few million were white. To take still another illustration of difference, about one-third of the African population was Moslem in religion and only one-seventh

Christian; the larger proportion adhered to one or another of the extraordinarily variegated primitive tribal faiths. This was the continent upon which the impact of the Second World War came with a shattering force.

The first impact, as might be expected, was seen in the Mediterranean areas lying to the north of the Sahara—"Brown Africa" as distinct from the "Black Africa" of the sub-Saharan region. The position of Egypt has already been studied in relation to the problems of the Middle East and need not be considered here. Libya, the former Italian colony which was its neighbor and also the scene of some of the severest wartime fighting, was first divided between French and British administrations, then given independence in 1951. Though many questioned the viability of a country with hardly more than a million people, few roads, no industry, a literacy rate of about 40 percent, and little that could be called modern culture, Libya stumbled forward, becoming a member of the United Nations in 1954 and receiving a spur to its economy through the discovery of oil in 1957. Preponderantly Moslem, Libya joined the Arab League in 1953.

The Sudan, long an Anglo-Egyptian condominium, became independent in January, 1956, the year of the Suez crisis. Having an agricultural economy based largely on cotton and millet, and with a population of nearly thirteen million, the Sudan, which joined the Arab League in 1958, held a strategic situation at the air crossroads of Africa which heightened its prospective importance.

The two other North African areas to be briefly noted are Tunisia and Morocco. Both of them originally French protectorates, they were clearly dissatisfied with the proposed status of "independence within the French Union" offered to them as a goal under the French constitution of 1948. Agitation followed by armed conflict led ultimately to the French conceding full independence to Morocco in 1956 and to Tunisia in 1957. In Tunisia Habib Bourguiba, a leader of remarkable abilities, had emerged. The Algerian struggle for independence will be considered later.

The year 1960 was momentous for Africa. In the case of France, the new constitution of 1958 and the new leadership of General de Gaulle made it possible for her at last to face the realities of an expiring colonial world. Although the hope was expressed that French African possessions now winning their freedom would combine this freedom with some continuing association with the French Community, only a minority—Senegal, Malagasy (the former Madagascar), the Chad, Gabon, the Central African Republic, and the Republic of the Congo—elected to do so. The others—Guinea, the Ivory Coast, the Upper Volta, Togo, Niger, Dahomey, Cameroun, Mauritania, and Mali—chose complete independence.[18] The same choice was made by the former Italian colony

18. See map, p. 428.

THE NEW AFRICA AT THE UNITED NATIONS. President Kwame Nkrumah of Ghana addresses the General Assembly of the United Nations in September, 1960. Behind him are U.N. Secretary-General Dag Hammarskjöld; President of the Assembly Frederick Boland of Ireland; and Andrew W. Cordier, Executive Assistant to the Secretary-General.

of Somaliland, which after a period under trusteeship, now joined with the former British Somaliland to form the independent Somali Republic. How difficult the problems of these small and ill-equipped countries were to be, with little public education, no trained administrative cadres, and no political experience, the history of the next few years would make clear.

Many changes of status occurred in this decade among British African colonies which remained within the Commonwealth. Ghana, the former Gold Coast, won independence within the Commonwealth in 1957; three years later, under the presidency of Kwame Nkrumah, it became a republic, though still retaining the Commonwealth link. Nigeria passed through the same stages in 1960 and 1963. Both these states professed neutralist policies in relation to the outside world.

Kenya, where British settlers had dominated the land for three generations, experienced some of the most violent explosions. The Kenya Africa Association, led by Jomo Kenyatta, who had received his education in London, sought agrarian reform. Its activities were soon superseded by the savagely terrorist activities of the Mau Mau, beginning late in 1952. Kenyatta became the leader of this native movement, and four years of struggle followed, in which the British authorities jailed more than sixty thousand terrorists. Though order of a sort was ultimately restored, the new leadership of Tom Mboya at the close of the decade made it clear that independence could not long be postponed.

Further south, the two Rhodesias had long been areas where the supremacy of the British white man seemed unchallenged. In 1953, in the face of strong African opposition, Northern and Southern Rhodesia and their neighbor, Nyasaland, joined to form the Central African Federation. The Federation did not work well, and in ten years fell apart.

Some of the most acute tensions between white and Negro emerged in the Union of South Africa, where some three million whites dominated the lives of thirteen million nonwhites. Among the whites the older Dutch (Boer) settlers had long fostered a policy of *apartheid*, or separate development of the nonwhite population groups. The Nationalist Party, victorious in the election of 1958, sponsored such a program. In 1959 it passed the Bantu Self-Government Act, laying down the principle of completely separate residential areas and social development for the nonwhites. Though the native Bantus could be employed in white areas, they would enjoy no civil rights there. It is clear that such a program, running utterly counter to the prevailing trends in the rest of Africa, severely strained the relations of the Union with the Commonwealth, and would in the end intensify the difficulties, if not lead to a catastrophe of major proportions.

In the Belgian Congo, a land with long and bitter memories of exploitation, trouble erupted on a large scale and with world-wide repercussions. Here, in June, 1960, King Baudouin of Belgium formally proclaimed independence for the Republic of the Congo. The great financial difficulties with former Belgian concessionaires, the civil war which followed, the savage attacks on the whites, and the attempts at secession by dissident native groups, together produced a chaotic and bloody situation which caused the problem to be taken to the Security Council of the United Nations. The tangled sequel must be reserved for a later chapter.[19]

■ CONTINUING STRESSES IN ASIA AND AFRICA

The emergence of young nations in Asia and Africa had resulted by 1960 in the creation of as many new problems as had been solved. Independence, with all its accompanying responsibilities and dangers, had become the great reality. The problems which followed independence were both domestic and international. New states, deprived of the experienced political leadership, the

19. See p. 429.

financial backing, and the military strength of their former rulers, as well as having no trained personnel for administration, found the domestic going very hard. Yet the price of such freedom, it must be conceded, the new states were willing to pay, and in the long run no insuperable obstacles remained for European investors still willing to put their money into countries over which their flag no longer flew.

One indication of the new trends in Afro-Asian affairs was the Bandung Conference, sponsored by India, Pakistan, Ceylon, and Burma in April, 1955, and meeting at Bandung, in Java. Altogether twenty-nine new or newly emerging states of Asia and Africa sent representatives. The Conference, while confining itself largely to general statements, showed a remarkable sense of unanimity and purpose. It denounced the two extremes of communism and colonialism, and advocated a "third force," based upon "neutralism." It would oppose racial discrimination and would work for economic co-operation and for general disarmament.

The international situation produced even greater tensions than the domestic. Some countries, most notably India, were intrigued by the policy of neutralism—an unwillingness to be committed to the Cold War growing up between the Communist and noncommunist worlds. Yet, as in the case of Indonesia, North Vietnam, and the Congo, communism could and did make a strong appeal. The Soviet Union provided North Korea with ultra-modern weapons during the Korean War, and Red China actively committed her troops. In some cases the older colonial powers, on the other hand, did not let go easily or willingly. France, for example, kept some troops in Vietnam until 1956; she maintained the fight in Algeria until 1962. Britain landed paratroopers at Suez in 1956 and in Jordan in 1958.

The United States also found herself increasingly committed. From the modest beginnings in the Truman Doctrine in 1947, she moved steadily forward to an elaborate pattern of foreign aid, both military and civil, reaching to all continents and involving annual Congressional appropriations of anywhere from three to five billion dollars. American troops fought a three-year war in Korea. American marines went ashore in Lebanon in 1958 in accord with the Eisenhower Doctrine of aid to anticommunist powers. In addition, America became deeply involved in the defense of the free countries of Southeast Asia.

Regional arrangements such as ANZUS, CENTO, and SEATO made further complications. Though designed to keep the peace and though generally weak, these treaties did emphasize commitments by non-Asiatic powers in a very complex Oriental world. Hence tensions, instead of being relaxed, continued. The implications of such commitments will be considered in the final chapter of this book.

Reading List: Chapter 13

Langer, W. L., "Farewell to Empire," *Foreign Affairs,* vol. XLI (1963), no. 1.

Griffiths, P., *Modern India* (3rd ed., 1962), ch. 16. India and the world.

Nehru, J., "Changing India," *Foreign Affairs,* vol. XLI (1963), no. 3.

Ayub Khan, M., "Pakistan Perspective," *Foreign Affairs,* vol. XXXVIII (1960), no. 4.

Calvocoressi, P., *Survey of International Affairs 1949–1950* (1953), pp. 466–516. The opening phase of the Korean War.

Monroe, E., *Britain's Moment in the Middle East, 1914–1956* (1963), ch. 8. The Suez affair and its consequences.

De Conde, A., *A History of American Foreign Policy* (1963), ch. 30. The emergence of Afro-Asian nationalism.

Chapter 14

The Cultural Revolution

The "Two Cultures": Developments in Contemporary Society
The World of Nature
The World of Man
Religious and Philosophical Trends
Contemporary Trends in the Arts
Technology and Culture

■ THE "TWO CULTURES":
DEVELOPMENTS IN CONTEMPORARY SOCIETY

The enormous complexity of our contemporary life must be as apparent, surely, in man's intellectual achievements as in any other respects. The schools and universities, the great research centers and hospitals, the art galleries, museums, publishing houses, lecture halls, theaters, and even the areas of public recreation all attest to the versatility of man's interests. Their variety illustrates his endless capacity both for building upon his past and for venturing creatively into the future. In many respects it is true that the culture of the twentieth century has flung down sharp challenges to the preceding ages. The scientists have erected "indeterminacy" and "probability" into principles, the artists

SIGNIFICANT EVENTS

1922	T. S. Eliot, *The Waste Land*
	James Joyce, *Ulysses*
	Discovery of insulin
1924	Alban Berg's opera, *Wozzeck*
	Development of Arnold Schönberg's twelve-tone musical scale
1925	Walter Gropius, Bauhaus at Dessau
1928	Completion of Marcel Proust's *Remembrance of Things Past*
1929	Discovery of penicillin
1931	Electronic microscope
1935	First practical application of radar
1936	Discovery of cortisone
	Keynes, *General Theory of Employment*
1937	Pablo Picasso, "Guernica"
1939	First jet airplane
1943	Jean Paul Sartre, *Being and Nothingness*
1944	Discovery of streptomycin
1945	First nuclear bomb
1948	Organization of World Council of Churches
1952	First hydrogen bomb
1955	Development of polio vaccine
1959	Frank Lloyd Wright's Guggenheim Museum

have seemed anxious to abandon tradition, the philosophers have spoken of a "transvaluation of values," many voices have been raised in warning against an ominous disintegration of morals, and the historians have written of the Decline of the West. Vitality and confusion in contemporary intellectual life have gone hand in hand.

Scientific developments do not proceed in isolation from other aspects of the life of societies; and, as the establishment of UNESCO would suggest, the interconnections in our own day have frequently seemed close. Such connections exist even though some people have warned against the danger of the intellectual life of modern society being split into two polar groups, scientific and nonscientific. The spread of education and the popularization of knowl-

UNESCO HEADQUARTERS IN PARIS. The strikingly modern Secretariat and Conference buildings, erected between 1953 and 1957, are the work of three architects, Marcel Breuer, Pier Luigi Nervi, and B. H. Zehrfuss. The reclining figure in the piazza is by the English sculptor Henry Moore.

edge have meant the dissemination of ideas on a far greater scale than ever before. The role of government has become very large. What Thomas Hobbes in the seventeenth century called the Great Leviathan has become the modern state with its enormous demands upon those who compose it. With respect to learning, and particularly with respect to the sciences, the official pressures have been insistent. And the scientists in response to the demands made on them have shown the way to new economic, social, and even political advances. What is true of the physical scientists holds also for the social scientists. New theories have been converted by political leaders into programs of action. Elaborate research projects have been sponsored and financed by governments as a specific means to human betterment. The prospect of consciously directed growth thus exceeds in many ways the dreams of progress held by the *philosophes* of the eighteenth-century Enlightenment.

With respect to the arts, involvement in contemporary life is equally apparent. Enormous social pressures and technological skills have combined to create the new monuments of contemporary architecture. It would be impossible to ignore the social content of modern art, even in some of its most abstract forms, or of contemporary literature. In the field of music, which is hardly "committed" to the problems of modern society in the way that the novel or the drama would be, one sees the vogue for revolt or experimentation and, in the case of electronic music, the very immediate impact of modern technology.

To treat these complex adventures of the human mind as if they went on in a world separated from politics and statecraft would be to falsify history. Though what follows is of necessity a summary, it should be regarded as still another approach made by the historian to the two basic problems with which he has to deal: man's efforts to master his environment, and man's efforts to understand more deeply the mysterious world of which he is a part.

■ THE WORLD OF NATURE

While the great scientific revolution of the nineteenth century had been in the field of biology, that of the twentieth came in the field of physics. The historical importance of this advance was not simply that it transformed man's understanding of matter but also that it enormously enlarged his means of action. By releasing the energy locked up within the atom he would in theory have control of an almost unimaginable force. This could be used for constructive purposes; it could also, quite literally, destroy the world.

The new physics grew out of certain advances of the late-nineteenth century. Radioactivity had been discovered by Henri Becquerel in 1896. In the following year J. J. Thomson showed that submicroscopic particles, the negative charges of electricity which were later named electrons, were a common constituent of atoms. In 1897 Mme. Curie had presented the view that radioactive atoms, having unstable nuclei, underwent a steady disintegration in the course of which they released energy. The element radium, which emits what later were called alpha, beta, and gamma rays, was isolated from pitchblende by the Curies in 1898. Max Planck's quantum theory of 1901 held that light energy is emitted and absorbed by matter not in a steady stream but discontinuously in discrete energy packets called quanta. Furthermore, both light and electrons could sometimes be looked upon as particles and sometimes as waves. From this Niels Bohr's[1] investigation led him to formulate the first plausible theory of atomic structure which was modified in 1927 by Werner Heisenberg, who invented quantum mechanics. Albert Einstein's famous paper on the special theory of relativity (1905) had proposed that the notions of time and space could no longer be considered as absolutes, since man had no fixed platform from which to measure, no stationary points between which to calculate the elapsing of an absolute period of time.

---

1. 1885–1962. Trained in Denmark, he also studied in England with Thomson and Rutherford. As early as 1913 he made the revolutionary assumption that atomic processes could not be explained by classical laws alone. As founder of the Institute of Theoretical Physics at the University of Copenhagen he became one of the greatest authorities on atomic physics and received the Nobel Prize in 1922. He encouraged American scientists to proceed with the attempts to split the uranium atom and helped in producing the first nuclear explosion in 1945 at Alamogordo.

Such statements were closely associated with changing views of matter—more precisely with the new concept of the atomic particle. Thomson in 1897 made, as we have noted, the suggestion that the electron was a subparticle of the atom. The view later was developed that the number of electrons within the atom gave the "atomic number" of any particular element. Other subparticles were soon discovered. One of these, with a positive charge, was identified by Ernest Rutherford in 1906 as the proton. He visualized the atom as having a positively charged nucleus made up of protons, containing almost all of its mass and surrounded by "a froth of electrons which takes up nearly all the volume of the atom but contains practically none of its mass."[2] As time went on other particles were discovered, among them the neutron, the positron, the meson, the anti-neutron, and the anti-proton. In the incredibly complicated world of subatomic physics twenty-seven different particles have been identified. Modern wave mechanics tended not to use mechanical models in describing the make-up of the atom, limiting itself to mathematical formulations. Thus Heisenberg enunciated in 1927 his principle of indeterminacy—that the more precisely one sought to pinpoint a subatomic particle's position the more uncertain one must be of its exact velocity, and vice versa. One could, however, make useful average statements, as one could for the general movement of a crowd, despite uncertainty as to the exact path taken by any individual.

For the layman the importance of all this lies in the implications attaching to such a changed view of matter. Atoms differ chemically because of the different numbers of protons and electrons of which they are composed. The phenomenon of radioactive disintegration demonstrates that elements undergo change. Uranium, for example, over a very long period of time slowly is transformed into lead. Einstein's equation $E = mc^2$ in which E represents energy (measured in ergs), m represents mass (in grams), and c represents the speed of light (in centimeters per second), is properly described as one of the most famous equations in the world. Scientists had now reached the point of describing matter and energy, once regarded as separate concepts, as different manifestations of the same thing. Another aspect of the basic changes coming about was that the old science, which sought to describe the universe on a completely deterministic basis, was giving way to the new science which recognized that many aspects of knowledge could only be stated in terms of "the most probable" situation.

The associated phenomenon of radioactivity made it possible for scientists to demonstrate new powers. They could describe the origin of the different elements, account for the heat of the sun, and determine by "radiocarbon count" the date of any organic remains for as far back as thirty thousand years. Nuclear chemistry made it possible for Enrico Fermi in 1936 to bombard

2. ISAAC ASIMOV, *The Intelligent Man's Guide to Science* (1960), vol. I, p. 226.

heavy bodies with neutrons and thereby produce heavier bodies which actually constituted different elements. Of chief practical importance was the vital question of the atomic energy that could be released by the fission of the atom. By 1939 it had been found in Germany that one of the special qualities of uranium—the heaviest element known—was that by bombarding it with neutrons it could in fact be split. Albert Einstein wrote a letter to this effect in 1939 to President Roosevelt; Fermi set up the atomic pile at Chicago in 1942; and on July 16, 1945, the first atomic bomb was exploded at Alamogordo, in New Mexico. The further outcomes, including those in the field of electronics, must be reserved for later discussion under the heading of technology rather than of pure science.

Biology, though it could claim nothing quite so dramatic as the splitting of the atom, did not fall far short of physics in its actual achievements. Many unsolved problems remained in the field of evolution, where the debate was concerned hardly at all with the *fact* of evolution but very much with the *method*. Before the close of the nineteenth century biologists had amended Darwin's theory which regarded natural selection as working upon small continuous variations in living things. The newer view meant reviving the theories of the Austrian monk Gregor Mendel, who in the 1860's had concluded on the basis of careful experiments with garden peas that certain determinants exist which by crossbreeding transmit "dominant" or "recessive" traits to descendents in definite mathematical patterns. His view had been very largely ignored. It was revived in 1900 by Hugo de Vries and others who described as mutations the sudden changes or "sports" which occur occasionally in nature. They were to be explained by the presence of substructures known as chromosomes —threadlike bodies existing within the nuclei of cells and containing hereditary factors known as genes. In every individual there exist various pairs of genes, coming one from each parent and capable of combining in different ways. Such hereditary units instead of blending thus retain their particular identity, either dominant or recessive. A dominant characteristic would be at once apparent, but recessive characteristics could be simply passed on from one generation to another, only showing a striking change, or mutation, when combined with a similar gene inherited from the other parent. Through these random mutations the environment could operate and, in a sense, "select." Thus the old theory of Lamarck that acquired characteristics could be inherited was shown to be untrue.[3]

It is clear that such developments gave added importance to cytology, the study of cell structure. The discovery that mutations could be stimulated

3. Lamarckianism was dead save apparently in the Soviet Union where, in order to give "scientific" validity to the political view that conscious modifications of society would, so to speak, become part of the evolutionary process, the Lamarckian theories were upheld for a time by the Soviet biologist Trofim Lysenko, with full official support. His decline came soon after the fall of Khrushchev.

by radioactivity had various consequences. One was the terrifying prospect that the radiation from atomic explosions might so affect the genes as to produce in future generations mutations which would be monstrosities. On the other hand scientists undertook the conscious stimulation of mutations by the use of x-rays and other forms of radiation, as yet with more or less random results. Study of cell structure led to the discovery of DNA (deoxyribonucleic acid), the substance which carries genetic patterns in the nucleus of cells. Biochemistry in dealing with nucleic acid molecules seemed to be approaching close to understanding the basis of life itself, and offered the startling prospect of man being able consciously to influence and direct the actual progress of human evolution.

Other aspects of biology and biochemistry were hardly less important. The study of photosynthesis, or the process by which green plants transform the radiant energy of the sun in the formation of carbohydrates, gave a vastly important clue to understanding the nature of the world's food supply. Closely related to this was the study of metabolism in the human body—the myriad reactions by which a balance is maintained during the intake and consumption of all that maintains the living organism. A related study concerned itself with chemical agents such as enzymes, which accelerated the specific transformations of material in plants and animals. Still another key approach was through the vitamins—those "accessory food factors" without which an otherwise ample diet would not maintain health. The classic example had been that of ship's crews which, though copiously fed on sea biscuit and salt pork, developed scurvy until their diet was supplemented with a substance such as lime juice. First discovered in 1912, the long list of vitamins now known indicates the complexity and subtlety of their operation.

The study of organic growth also involved knowledge of the hormones— secretions produced in the ductless glands and carried in the bloodstream to their point of action. These secretions could be directly employed to counteract disease: adrenalin, for example, discovered in 1901, could be used to treat heart disease; insulin, discovered in 1922, for diabetes; and cortisone, discovered in 1936, for rheumatoid arthritis. These were only a few of the outcomes of the enormously complex field of hormone research.

Still another field was that of the sulfa drugs and the antibiotics—the new drugs with the property of being deadly to bacteria and to other disease-causing organisms. The first of these was salvarsan, a specific treatment for syphilis, discovered in 1909. Sulfanilamide, discovered in 1932, could truly be called a "wonder drug" for it was highly effective against many kinds of bacterial disease. A much greater advance came with the antibiotics—penicillin, discovered in 1929, streptomycin in 1943, and the long list including aureomycin, terramycin, and many others. These drugs proved to be almost miraculously effective against diseases such as bacterial pneumonia and childbed fever. In still another area, that of the vaccines, the cultivation at the Harvard Medical School of the poliomyelitis virus made large-scale experimentation with it possible. The outcome was the development by Dr. Jonas Salk in the mid-1950's of the vaccine which at last brought the scourge of polio under effective scientific control.

In addition to studying the body, scientists continued their efforts to probe and understand the workings of the mind. The foundations of a science of psychiatry established by Freud and Jung provided the basis for further studies. Without much question the clinical approach held the largest place, for the student could make use of the related fields of physiology, medicine, and even sociology. The use of special drugs for the treatment of mental illness became as significant as the use of "wonder drugs" and antibiotics in the general field of medicine. Indeed, the professional use of reserpine, long known in India for its tranquilizing effects and now employed for schizophrenics and patients with very high blood pressure, became the starting point in 1952 for the widespread and no doubt dangerous use by the general public of tranquilizers for all manner of human ailments and cares.

■ THE WORLD OF MAN

It is proper to ask in a history that deals with the contemporary age whether we can determine any general outlook which is characteristic of thinking man in the twentieth century. The eighteenth century had professed its optimistic confidence in human nature and in ordered progress. The nineteenth re-inforced this confidence by turning to the evidence on every hand of widespread scientific advance and, in large parts of Europe and America, of enormous material gains. Sobered by a certain Victorian caution, this optimism thrived to the very threshold of the First World War.

The impact of the war years, 1914–1918, and of the revolutionary years which followed was shattering. Perhaps the book by C. E. Montague, for many years on the staff of *The Manchester Guardian*, entitled *Disenchantment* (1922) best conveyed the spirit of these years. Novels such as *All Quiet on the Western Front* (1928) by the German Erich Remarque, or *Le Feu* (1916) by the Frenchman Henri Barbusse, or *A Farewell to Arms* (1929) by the American Ernest Hemingway, suggested the prevalence of a similar disenchantment. The welcome given to such writings makes it clear that many people were receptive to these critical and even bitterly disillusioned views.

It is also striking that a large audience existed for the German historian, Oswald Spengler, the two volumes of whose *Decline of the West*, appearing in 1918 and 1920, sought the widest possible interpretation of civilized man's fortunes on this planet. Spengler, who had begun writing his grim history long before 1914, saw not one linear history in an upward ascendant but instead an indeterminate number of civilizations each with a life-span of roughly a thousand years and with its own pattern of identity. The various cycles, which nothing could delay, ran through a sequence of spring, summer, autumn, and winter. Western man, the inheritor chiefly of the Classical (Apollonian) and Arab (Magian) cycles, was now in the last stage of the Western (Faustian) cycle from whose collapse nothing could save him. Spengler saw in this "Decline of the West" only the grim prospect of an age of iron in which reason would recede and some ruthless Caesar would exercise power amid a dying world.

The sociologist Pitirim Sorokin, a Russian who in 1922 fled from the Communist regime established under the dictatorship of Lenin, put forth in the four volumes of his *Social and Cultural Dynamics* (1937 ff.) the thesis that various "systems of culture" could, broadly speaking, be identified as either "ideational" or "sensate." In the former, a culture is "based upon the principle of a supersensory and superrational God." It is dominated by a sense of abstract values superior to itself. In the latter, the major principle is that "the true reality and value is sensory." According to Sorokin, the culture under which Western man has lived for the past several hundred years is increasingly sensate, and has now reached the point where it is "empirical, utilitarian, hedonistic, materialistic, economically minded, divorced from any other-worldliness, . . . and rooted entirely in the reality of a sensory world." Though a sensate culture may at one stage rise to genuine greatness, that of our age has become materialistic, decadent, and corrupt. Whatever the accuracy of the diagnosis, Sorokin's views made much of the deep unrest in the Western world and led him to forecast the imminent transformation of its present institutions. An abridged version of Sorokin's work, published in 1941, also appeared in Portuguese, German, Spanish, Dutch, Czech, Norwegian, Finnish, and Japanese translations. This popularity gave impressive evidence that a wide audience existed for views such as the following:

> As to the material well-being of our society, we have seen that the twentieth century is an insane destroyer of the well-being created by the previous centuries of the sensate era, but not its creator or promoter. Like a profligate son, it has squandered and turned into ruins what its forefathers created and accumulated.[4]

Still another work, conceived on a grander scale than the studies of Spengler or Sorokin, was Arnold Toynbee's *Study of History*, the ten volumes of which appeared between 1934 and 1954. Like Spengler, to whom he was obviously indebted, Toynbee refused to see any single linear history of man. Instead he saw in various parts of the globe and in various periods of time a

4. P. SOROKIN, *The Crisis of Our Age* (1941), p. 168.

number of "intelligible units of historical study" which he called societies of the species. Altogether Toynbee found eighteen (or by his later revised reckoning twenty-six) such societies. Most of them—for example the Egyptiac, the Hellenic, and the Sinic—were dead. Only five still lived: the Far Eastern, the Hindu, the Moslem, the Orthodox Christian, and the Western, and only the very last of the five retained much vital force. Toynbee did not try to write a world history covering all these societies of the species. He sought chiefly to discover the uniformities relating to their genesis, growth, breakdown, prolongation in new forms, and ultimate disintegration. Unlike Spengler, he did not postulate any set length of time or any mechanical cycle of spring, summer, autumn, and winter. He argued that Western society, though showing many marks of disintegration, might find a "reprieve" through the path of religion. Man therefore was not altogether a pawn. Though severely attacked by many historians for what they regarded as unwarranted deductions from insufficient and even distorted evidence, Toynbee's views had a remarkable impact, in part because of his efforts to see the drama of history on a world scale and in part because of his rejection of complete fatalism in an age when the darkening clouds were all too evident.

A number of distinguished theorists in the fields of sociology, political science, and economics set their mark on this period. In France the great tradition of Emile Durkheim, who died in 1917—that sociology and anthropology should combine in a scientific study of society—long outlived its founder. In Germany Max Weber, who died in 1920, and Werner Sombart, who died in 1941, were the giants. The former sought to understand a given society by finding some major concept which best characterized it. He was profoundly impressed, for example, by the close association between the growth of Protestantism and the rise of modern capitalism, arguing in his *Protestant Ethic and the Spirit of Capitalism* (1920) that the typical Calvinistic virtues of thrift, industry, and sobriety were what made modern capitalism possible. By establishing such major concepts on the basis of an elaborate study of precise evidence, Weber could then compare one period or situation with another. Sombart's studies were also directed toward finding key concepts. One of these was the role of nationalist, large-scale warfare in dynamizing the modern state and determining its political and economic character. Another was his view that a unique form of German socialism—antiliberal, anticapitalist, and anti-Semitic —could be distilled from the German past.

Two Spaniards should also be included in this atmosphere of critical thought. Miguel de Unamuno's *Tragic Sense of Life* (1913) had early challenged the optimistic assumptions of the nineteenth century on the basis of searching explorations of the irrational elements in modern man. A thinker of a later generation, José Ortega y Gasset, in his *Revolt of the Masses* (1930) described a declining society in which the masses were producing a barbarization of culture. The only salvation, he felt, would come through the leadership of a genuinely cultured elite.

Powerful minds, too, had their impact in Italy. As early as 1916 Vilfredo Pareto in his *Trattato di Sociologia generale* (later translated as *Mind and Society*) had tried to understand society by separating its rational and nonrational components. He held that a great part of human behavior was the expression of nonrational sentiment ("residues" and "derivations") and involved justifications which could not be verified by the methods of natural science. (One "dies for the flag," for example.) Out of all this theorizing emerged a deep distrust of liberal reformers and optimistic planners; the drift everywhere, so Pareto thought, was toward a totalitarian society in which a skilled politician could manipulate the crowd which in the intellectual sense and on the basis of reason alone he could hardly expect to lead.

Another Italian, Gaetano Mosca, in the revised edition of *The Ruling Class* which he issued in 1923, stressed the importance of a governing class which furnishes the dominant traits of the civilization of a given society in a given period. He visualized his chosen elite, nevertheless, as operating through a constitutional, representative framework of government, and therefore opposed the crudities of the Mussolini regime. An even greater Italian figure was the philosopher-historian Benedetto Croce.[5] His monumental studies of aesthetics and the philosophy of history, the latter frequently oversimplified in his aphorism that all history is contemporary history, must be set aside here in favor of his much briefer *History as the Story of Liberty* (1938) where in contrast to much current opinion he saw the positive and dominant feature of history as being the inevitable victory of liberty over tyranny.

While these represent some of the major aspects of social thought in mid-twentieth century one also heard the shrill voice of unreason preaching doctrines which broke away from the idealistic trends of preceding ages. Arthur Moeller van Broeck's *Third Reich* (1922) pleaded for a new Germany to emerge from the ashes of defeat, rid itself of Jewish elements, and base itself on a creed oriented away from the conventional liberal traditions. The first volume of Hitler's *Mein Kampf* appeared in 1925. Alfred Rosenberg's *Myth of the Twentieth Century* (1930), with the subtitle, *An Estimate of the Conflict of Spiritual Economic Values of Our Time,* also attacked the liberal and Christian traditions as myths, substituting for them the racist and barbarous doctrines of blood and soil.

Probably no writer made his points more effectively than the Cambridge

5. 1866–1952. One of Italy's most distinguished philosopher-historians, he lived principally at Naples, founding (1903) and editing for over forty years the distinguished review *Critica*. Made a senator in 1910, he was minister of education, 1920–1921, then became a strong opponent of Italian Fascism, but was too distinguished a figure for Mussolini to persecute. He served briefly as provisional head of state in 1945 in Italy.

scholar John Maynard Keynes.[6] He first won his popular reputation with *The Economic Consequences of the Peace* (1919), the outcome of his experience at the Paris Peace Conference, in which he devastatingly exposed the fallacy of large-scale German reparations.[7] In matters of general economic policy he believed neither in socialism nor laissez-faire. The great depression of 1929 produced an economic crisis in the face of which the American New Deal, for example, seemed to offer at best improvised solutions. Keynes's *General Theory of Employment, Interest, and Money* (1936) provided so large an analysis that his theses have been taken to constitute "the Keynesian Revolution." He attacked the orthodox view which accepted the gold standard as a self-regulating mechanism for international trade. In its place he would substitute a managed currency, as he would require management in other sectors of the economy. Only government could provide the necessary manipulative controls. Interest rates should be raised or lowered; in times of depression deficit spending should be boldly initiated, budgets left unbalanced, public works undertaken, and rates of taxation deliberately reduced. All this did not imply a total governmental control of the economy in the Russian sense, but rather the specific exercise of authority at critical points so that a liberal capitalistic economy could still continue to function. It is clear that the acceptance of his views has been widespread.

■ RELIGIOUS AND PHILOSOPHICAL TRENDS

The complex movements in contemporary religion and philosophy can be fitted only with difficulty into a summary picture of Europe at mid-century. In both fields sharp challenges were made to the principal views emerging from the nineteenth century. Many of these challenges, moreover, were inconsistent with each other, some seeking a return to an older orthodoxy, others plunging boldly ahead. To reduce all this to order and, even more, to seek uniformity is quite clearly an impossible task. One can at best turn the spotlight upon what seem to be major figures and characterize tentatively the major trends.

Philosophic thought in general reacted very sharply against the idealism of the nineteenth century. Such a reaction could take various forms; for example, Alfred North Whitehead and Bertrand Russell sought in their *Principia Mathematica* (1910–1913) to establish a philosophy that could be reconciled

6. 1883–1946. A product of Eton and King's College, Cambridge, and for a time in the Civil Service, he wrote on mathematics and philosophy as well as economics. A devotee of the Bloomsbury circle of esthetes, he married the Russian ballerina, Lopokova, and was a distinguished patron of modern French painting. He played a leading part in Anglo-American financial relations throughout the Second World War, and was created Lord Keynes in 1942.

7. Keynes's views did not go unchallenged. In 1946 the French scholar, Etienne Mantoux, wrote his indictment, *The Carthaginian Peace; The Economic Consequences of Mr. Keynes,* claiming that Keynes had had a powerful effect in undermining confidence in the Treaty of Versailles and thus contributed to the coming of the Second World War.

with science through logic. The American John Dewey elaborated the earlier pragmatism of William James which had revolted against "systems" and had stressed experience. Truth, to Dewey, was not simply that which works; it must work in relation to the social complex of which the individual is a part. A distinguished Austrian scholar, Ludwig Wittgenstein, who eventually taught at Cambridge University, went much further. He enunciated in his *Tractatus Logico-Philosophicus* (1921) a "logical positivism" which repudiated all traditional ethics and rational metaphysics. By analyzing the ambiguities of ordinary language one ought to be able to sort out those statements which are expressive of an emotional state on the part of the speaker ("non-sense") and those statements which have some reference to the objective world. Thus it would seem that philosophy ran the risk of becoming simply a debate over the meaning of words. Anything which could not be verified in sense experience must be labeled non-sense—a term which could apply to the views of theist and atheist alike.

Easily the most striking creed of the 1940's was existentialism, associated particularly with Jean-Paul Sartre and the band of disciples who gathered daily with him at the Café des Deux Magots in the Place Saint-Germain des Près in Paris. Although existentialism became the philosophic mood which best typified the post-1945 European world, as a philosophy it had a much longer history and a much wider range than this. It went back to the Danish thinker of the early nineteenth century, Soren Kierkegaard, who in struggling with the tormenting difficulties of a mysterious universe had stressed the immediacy of personal experience, insisting that all genuine thought must be that of a particular person in a given situation. Nietzsche had emphasized will as the essential driving power in both man and the universe. Sartre also showed the influence of the contemporary German thinker, Martin Heidegger, whose approach to the problems of human suffering and despair led him to abandon the rational solutions associated with the orderly, logically consistent world traditionally visualized by the scientist.

Sartre wrote a novel, *Nausea*, in 1938 which attracted little attention; in 1943 he published *Being and Nothingness*, a long and difficult exposition of his philosophy. Returning (1941) from a period of German captivity to live in occupied Paris he produced two powerful plays, *The Flies* (1943) and *No Exit* (1944). The three corrupt and degraded figures in *No Exit* find themselves together in Hell, each person being nothing more than the sum of what he has done. No answer to the question, "Why?" is possible. Thus Inez says to the collaborator, Garcin, who has been shot for treason, "You are no more than the sum of your acts!" Instead of a man doing something because of what he *is*, Sartre says man is because of what he *does*.

Sartre's adoption of Marxism as a political creed placed him in one current of radical, revolutionary thought. More significant, however, was his intellectual and philosophic position. Here Sartre broke with much of the great intellectual legacy of the West. Man must take his stand alone in what is essentially a meaningless world ending in the ultimate absurdity, death. "Man is condemned to a liberty as absurd as it is absolute." Sartre's philosophy is one of action, for man is "committed," yet this is a kind of action that can find no justification in any ethical or rational superstructure of the universe. Sartre's views gave him a perhaps inflated prestige in the postwar world, for in addition to arousing the enthusiasm of his devotees he required his opponents to look into the grounds and evidence of their faith. His writings were to lead to the offer in 1964 of a Nobel prize for literature which, in the interest of his own individualism, he chose to refuse. By the 1960's, however, existentialism seemed to be something of a declining creed.

Religious developments can be set alongside some of these movements of philosophic thought. During the course of wars and revolutions the Roman Catholic world had experienced many blows and weathered great storms. In the Iron Curtain countries, for example, churches had frequently been closed; high dignitaries had been removed from office and sometimes even imprisoned. Hitler's dictatorship had brought many conflicts with the Roman Catholic hierarchy in Germany. Yet the Church rallied from such blows. It was vigorously interested in the social problem. As early as 1931, on the fortieth anniversary of Leo XIII's famous *Rerum Novarum*, Pope Pius XI had issued his encyclical *Quadragesimo Anno*. He dealt directly with economic and social issues. The exploiting side of capitalism came under attack, as did liberalism for its failures and socialism for its extreme solutions. The encyclical called for an end to conflict and for state intervention to cope with the intolerable abuses of an industrial society, all being done on the basis of harmonious, co-operative action between the various classes.

Roman Catholicism in actual practice dedicated itself widely to political action. In West Germany Chancellor Adenauer, himself a Catholic, governed with the backing of the Christian Democratic Party, as did De Gasperi with a similar party in Italy. In post-1945 France the Popular Republican Party (M.R.P.) was strongly supported by those Catholics dedicated to a democratic program of progress and reform. And when General de Gaulle returned to power in 1958 as an apostle of discipline and order he made no secret of his devout Catholicism.

Catholic belief was not immune to debate. Attempts by some Church writers to reinterpret doctrine in modern terms met papal reproof in the encyclical *Humani Generis* of 1950, and a number of distinguished teachers were removed from office. At a period when unreason loomed large, the efforts of distinguished lay scholars such as Etienne Gilson and Jacques Maritain were directed toward reviving the rationalism of St. Thomas Aquinas. These "Neo-Thomists" reaffirmed the traditional faith, declaring that it was adequate to find answers to the problems of modern democratic society. Maritain's *Degrees of Knowledge* (1932) claimed that modern science could be explained from the standpoint of St. Thomas's theory of knowledge.

Protestant thought and activity also reflected the times. The modern Protestant ecumenical movement—the view that Christians of various faiths have a common ground which it should be the purpose of all to define and accept—grew out of a long series of interdenominational conferences. These began at Edinburgh in 1910 and culminated in the organization of the World Council of Churches at Amsterdam in 1948. One striking consequence was that the Orthodox churches of eastern Europe began to display an interest in their common religious ground with the West. A similar new concern also arose within the Roman Catholic Church, most notably during the pontificate of Pope John XXIII (1958–1963).[8] His summoning of the Vatican Ecumenical Council at Rome in 1962 boldly sought to bring the Roman Catholic Church abreast of modern problems.

Despite the ecumenical movement within the Protestant churches, many thoughtful observers could not conceal their grave concern. The distinguished philosopher, Albert North Whitehead, wrote in 1933 as follows:

> Protestant Christianity, so far as concerns the institutional and dogmatic forms in which it flourished for three hundred years . . . is showing all the signs of a steady decay. Its dogmas no longer dominate: its divisions no longer interest: its institutions no longer direct the patterns of life.[9]

Many men were concerned at the startling indications of decline in church attendance and the lack of a vital message in what religion taught. Some revitalization came through the neo-orthodoxy of the Swiss theologian, Karl Barth, one of the most powerful thinkers in the contemporary Protestant world. Barth turned from a modern philosophical theology to one conservatively rooted in the Protestant doctrines of the sixteenth century. In reacting against rational religion and liberal Protestantism, Barth invoked the teachings of St. Paul, saying also that the dangerous situation of crisis in the modern world required men to commit themselves to the actual practice of a dedicated Christianity inspired by faith. Though efforts to further a movement toward unity in the Protestant churches had some success in the United States and Canada,

---

8. 1881–1963. Of peasant stock, ordained in 1904, he served during the First World War in the medical corps and as an Italian army chaplain. He acted as papal representative in Bulgaria, Turkey, Greece, and France. In 1944 he became cardinal and patriarch of Venice, and was elected pope in 1958. His pontificate was notable for a vigorous promotion of social reform and for the summoning of the Second Vatican Council in 1962 to promote the cause of Christian unity.
9. *Adventures of Ideas* (1933), p. 205.

they had very little in Europe. Looking at the general picture of the Christian European world in 1960, a distinguished student ventured the following summary which mingled deep concern with a most cautious and tentative optimism:

> One has the sense of a growing loss of confidence in the universe. The sombre vision which Hardy projected at the beginning of our period has not been dissipated —it has spread and deepened. The world has appeared to be less intelligible and less friendly to human aspirations than our fathers imagined. . . . To the historian of the future the age will be deeply interesting not only for the shattering events which mark its course but for the extraordinary ferment of ideas which opened new paths for the mind.[10]

■ CONTEMPORARY TRENDS IN THE ARTS

Few thoughtful observers would find twentieth-century trends in the arts any less revolutionary than those in other fields. What one critic has called "the jettisoning of the inherited baggage of European culture"[11] may be too sweeping a verdict, yet the fact of novelty and insistent change was inescapable. If the culture of the nineteenth century had been essentially a bourgeois synthesis, then that of the succeeding age turned significantly in new directions. Many of the great names familiar to those who lived through the First World War— Hauptmann, Chekhov, Shaw, or Pinero in the theater; Conrad, Hardy, Galsworthy, Wells, Thomas Mann, or Anatole France as novelists; Richard Strauss, Rachmaninoff, or Sibelius as late romanticists in music; or even painters like Matisse and Rouault, once linked with the "madmen" of 1905—soon took on a certain dated quality in comparison with what the new age was bringing forth. Though many of these older figures, to be sure, had been leaders in the revolt against tradition, other names were to supersede them in the experimental decades of the 1920's and the 1930's. The field is so vast that only a few illustrations in literature, art, architecture, and music can be presented.

Prose writing was much influenced by a new relativism and a questioning of established values. Perhaps this uncertainty was an inevitable sequel to war; whatever the reason, the shift could be seen in various ways. The eleven volumes of Marcel Proust's *Remembrance of Things Past* (1913–1928) had a quality all their own. In order to escape from the purposeless world of the present they evoked by the most delicate and subtle techniques of suggestion a world existing only in memory. The two posthumous novels, *The Castle* and *The Trial*, of the German-Czech writer, Franz Kafka, anticipated the worst outrages and terrors of Hitler's dictatorship. In *The Trial* (1925) he drew a picture of nameless court officials performing the required little segment of their duties

10. W. R. MATTHEWS, Dean of St. Paul's, in *The New Cambridge Modern History*, vol. XII, p. 148.
11. G. BARRACLOUGH, *An Introduction to Contemporary History* (1964), p. 240.

unaware of the deadly consequences of their actions, and of men testifying supposedly on behalf of a defendant only to find their evidence used to destroy him. Nearly a generation later such moods of terror, pessimism, or hopelessness were treated with a lighter, satirical touch in George Orwell's *Animal Farm* (1945) and *Nineteen Eighty-Four* (1947), books which devastatingly exposed the inhumanly mechanized life of a communist society.

The psychoanalytical impact of Freud and Jung made itself felt very emphatically in James Joyce's *Ulysses* (1922), which quickly became one of the most influential prose works of this age. The eighteen episodes, covering a mere twenty-four hours in the lives of Stephen Dedalus, Leopold Bloom, and his wife Molly and giving an extraordinary picture of modern Dublin, were built upon the Ulysses legend. The stream-of-consciousness techniques, the fantastic tricks played with words, and the richness of Joyce's allusions led the poet, T. S. Eliot, to characterize him as the greatest master of the English language since Milton. *Ulysses* also reflected the chaos in modern society. Edmund Wilson, himself a searching critic of the contemporary age, identified Joyce's views with similar ideas outside the realm of literature:

> Like Proust's or Whitehead's or Einstein's world, Joyce's world is always changing as it is perceived by different observers and by them at different times. . . . Such a world cannot be presented in terms of such artificial abstractions as have been conventional in the past. . . . Everything is reduced to terms of "events" like those of modern physics and philosophy—events which make up a "continuum" but which may be taken as infinitely small.[12]

The mood of prose writers in the years following 1945 suggested a great ferment of ideas. The fantasy-ridden plays of the German Berthold Brecht were written in the Marxist idiom. The existentialist trend, as we have seen, required man to be "committed" though it was hard to say to what. In France the novelist Albert Camus, a heroic figure of the French Resistance, used his novels to find some elements of human dignity and moral purpose in the surging drama of events around him. Meanwhile, the "angry young men" of postwar England—Kingsley Amis in his novel, *Lucky Jim* (1954), or John Osborne in his play, *Look Back in Anger* (1957)—made their protests against the trivial social snobbery and the empty culture of the time.

The new trends had been made evident also in poetry. Few modern works have had a larger impact than T. S. Eliot's *The Waste Land* (1922). His elegantly composed verses, with their ironic tone and eminently quotable passages, decried the emptiness of a barren age and became the manifesto of a whole generation. Along with Eliot the French symbolist poet, Paul Valéry, assumed a leading place. Valéry created a private world of imagination apart from the intrusions and accidents of everyday life, the essence of which he tried to convey to his readers by the subtlest of poetic means. The revolt against the ma-

12. *Axel's Castle* (1936), pp. 221–222.

chine age was also seen in the Spanish García Lorca. In Germany, Rainer Maria Rilke sought through poetry to turn his back on a world torn apart by uncertainties—a world in which, under the influence of Nietzsche, he saw no great distinction between the operation of good and evil. This cult was carried even further by Stefan George, one of Germany's greatest modern poets, who pictured the world as little more than the arena of the strong.

Only with the greatest difficulty is it possible to compress the visual arts and music within the confines of a brief summary. Here, too, one has the impression of a rich legacy from the nineteenth century which had been so bountiful in its bequests and yet was followed by widespread revolt. In painting, for example, it is striking to realize that Pablo Picasso,[13] a leader of experiment in almost every subsequent school, had painted his "Demoiselles d'Avignon," the point of departure for modern cubism, as early as 1907. The new effort to represent three-dimensional bodies on a two-dimensional canvas abandoned the classic devices of optics and perspective and instead broke up a single body into a large number of geometric planes. Essential "reality" could be demonstrated by showing the upper and lower side of an object simultaneously, by painting a moving figure in successive positions, or by giving two eyes to a face shown in profile. Picasso's "Three Musicians" of 1921, or Marcel Duchamp's "Nude Descending a Staircase," painted as early as 1912, are famous examples.

Another aspect of the revolt came with the German expressionists of the 1920's. The most distinguished member was the Russian-born Wassily Kandinsky. Since the members of the group believed that actual sense perceptions of specific objects could not give truth, they dealt with color alone, or with lines and geometric shapes, holding that color and lines have their own inherent psychological qualities. The Swiss-German Paul Klee associated himself with the Kandinsky group, becoming famous for combining geometric and abstract elements with warm colors so as to create canvases with a powerful evocative quality. Klee, very interestingly, taught at the Bauhaus in Dessau where so much attention was given to the architectural element in art, and he was also a violinist dedicated to the intricately form-conscious works of Bach and Mozart.

The experimentalism of modern art has produced numerous vogues and trends. Surrealism, as expounded by a superegotist such as Salvador Dali, could better be described as a mood, or even a pose. Meticulously painted objects that convey a sense of reality were combined in such strange fashions or so distorted—as in the case of Dali's limp watches hanging from the limbs of dead trees—as to suggest a morbid world of madness brooding over the daily life of man. The technique of *collage,* by which scraps of paper, cloth, wood, or

13. Born in Spain in 1881, his spectacular career has made him one of the foremost figures in twentieth century art. His fame began with the painting, "Demoiselles d'Avignon" (1907), the herald of modern cubism. Noted for bold experimentalism and superb technical abilities, Picasso has worked in sculpture, ceramics and the graphic arts as well as in painting.

metal could be assembled on canvas so as to produce with the aid of the painter's traditional brush and paints a new type of art, was popularized by Picasso as early as 1912. It never since has failed to have its devotees.

The school winning the greatest vogue in contemporary painting was that of abstract art, associated with the further term either of "expressionism" or "impressionism." The American Jackson Pollock discovered the possibilities of esthetic expression in dripping and flicking paint upon a canvas laid on a floor. Thus he was able to create patterns and rhythms arising basically from color and motion. Willem de Kooning, a leader of the abstract expressionists, has been described as a painter who "reaches the point where he may express himself best by attacking his canvas vigorously while improvising abstractions of form and color, painting without schematic preparations [and] drawing spontaneously upon all that he has learned of shape and color as expressive means."[14] Another outstanding example was the Dutch artist, Piet Mondrian, who advanced beyond the geometric patterns which he first saw in trees, houses, and canals to an abstract art in which he "respected the dignity" of a flat canvas by filling it with elegantly spaced lines and rectangles marked out by pure, vivid colors.

Sculptors, too, sought new methods to convey what they felt. The powerful modeling of Jacob Epstein seemed to many observers at first sight to be a clumsy distortion and caricature; only gradually were they convinced of its strength. Similarly, Constantin Brancusi's "Bird in Space" (1925), though like no possible bird, overwhelmingly conveyed the feeling of upward-soaring motion. The majestic sculptures of Henry Moore, though distorted and hollowed out like the trunk of an old tree, suggested very powerfully the juxtaposition of mass and space inherent in nature itself.

Perhaps architecture was the field in which man's creative genius most effectively came to terms with a new age where an industrially oriented society found means through technology to meet the enormous demands made upon it. Engineers demonstrated that they could build bridges to span the widest rivers, ships to crisscross the oceans, and aircraft to master the skies. Such an age of steel, concrete, and glass could hardly fail to express itself in some new forms of architecture. The skyscraper had developed out of the inventive skill of the late nineteenth century, working with wrought iron and steel. The great genius of Walter Gropius,[15] whose Bauhaus at Dessau, in Germany (1925–

---

14. JOHN CANADAY, *Mainstreams of Modern Art* (1959), p. 448.

15. Born in 1883, he became an architect, insisting as early as 1910 upon the principle of functionalism in designing all buildings. He became head of the Weimar School of Art in 1910, moving to Dessau in 1925, where the name Bauhaus became a synonym for the new functional style. He came to the United States in 1937, heading the school of architecture at Harvard until 1952. He wrote extensively, also undertaking many important architectural projects in collaboration with young architects whom he had trained.

1926), inaugurated a whole era of functional architecture, set the pattern for modern design, not without the dangers, to be sure, of cheap stylization and imitative clichés. The famous definition of the French architect, Le Corbusier, that a house is "a machine for living," brought the same principle of functionalism into modern domestic architecture. Similarly, the techniques involved in building modern bridge spans and cantilevered structures made it possible for the Italian Pier Luigi Nervi to design soaring concrete roofs of breathtaking beauty. The American Frank Lloyd Wright and the Dutch Miës van der Rohe were those who best combined advanced structural techniques (the use, for example, of the "module," or standardized building unit) with the classic traditions that stipulate beauty and harmony of design and, above all, imagination.

Music, like the other arts, entered the twentieth century in a mood of revolt. The German Gustav Mahler—one of the great names in modern music —who died in 1911 stood astride two worlds, being one of the last in a great tradition and also the prophet of a new age. He encouraged, for example, the young Schönberg. Claude Debussy (d. 1918) and Maurice Ravel (d. 1937) were musicians who after the collapse of the romantic tradition set up a form of musical "impressionism" which was not apart from other historic European tendencies in music. Debussy also had a special influence upon the Russian composer, Igor Stravinsky, the performance of whose *Rite of Spring* at Paris in 1913 had provoked wild demonstrations of protest. Stravinsky had been called, along with Paul Hindemith, a neoclassicist who put great stress on musical technique, "objectivity," and "form." Béla Bartók, who created no school, was a natural musician of great power and an innovator constantly seeking different forms of musical expression.

To find the development in music which is most closely related to trends in other fields of the arts one must turn to Arnold Schönberg,[16] whose work deeply shook the entire edifice of musical thinking and forced a re-evaluation of the whole musical tradition. His revolutionary influence has been compared to that of Richard Wagner in the nineteenth century—and indeed Schönberg's twelve-tone scale, first used in 1924, owed much to the chromatic musical style of Wagner's *Tristan*. Schönberg held that all twelve notes in the chromatic scale were of equal importance, and that none was a tonal center. Thus he produced a new musical line and abandoned the traditional patterns of harmony for a new atonality. Such musical expression, like the forms of abstract painting, clearly bore the stamp of a revolutionary age.

16. 1874–1951. Born in Austria, he composed music and taught in Vienna and Berlin until 1933, when he came to the United States. For a time in Vienna he directed a Society for Private Performances at which neither critics nor applause were allowed. His twelve-tone scale and his use of atonality make him one of the most powerful influences in modern music.

■ TECHNOLOGY AND CULTURE

Few periods have been so exposed to change on so widespread a scale and at so rapid a pace as the first half of the twentieth century. Advances in pure science and bold experimentation in the arts came at a time when new technological marvels magnified man's power and enabled him to broadcast his achievements literally to the ends of the earth. What the printed word had done for the fifteenth and sixteenth centuries, thousands of ultra-modern devices have done for the twentieth. The main aspects of this contemporary diffusion and application of ideas and skills must be briefly indicated.

In the physical sciences the revolutionary discoveries about the nature of atomic structure gave man the ability to release atomic energy. The atom bomb of 1945 was followed by the hydrogen bomb of 1951, and this in turn led to the prospect of the even more lethal cobalt bomb. On the other hand, nuclear power derived from atomic reactors was quickly employed to drive submarines and surface ships, to generate electricity, and to serve various new purposes in the field of medicine. The new theoretical knowledge available in chemistry and the biological sciences quickly opened vistas of progress for the great research foundations, the universities, and the industrial laboratories. In the general field of health—for example in the prolongation of human life—spectacular advances were either achieved or were clearly impending.

The social implications of man's new technological powers are so vast as almost to defy analysis. An electronic computer can perform in a fraction of a second mathematical calculations that might have occupied Newton for years. Automation can so transform the operation of a factory as to reduce the number of employees to a fraction of what they formerly were. Such developments could mean a grave immediate problem of "technological unemployment," or perhaps in the long run a most fruitful opportunity for men to enjoy a more abundant leisure. Electronic devices have begun to scan the pages of foreign books, producing by completely mechanical means rough but moderately serviceable translations. Motion pictures, radio, television, and jet propulsion in travel have all vastly widened man's horizons and helped to bring the continents closer together. Huge rockets have enabled men to orbit the earth and to make contact with the surface of the moon. Nothing, surely, in the imagination of Jules Verne could surpass what modern man has actually proved able to do.

One of the widely accepted goals of the nineteenth century was to bring education, self-government, and some minimum standard of social well-being to the peoples of Europe. Though they remain far from accomplishment, such goals have now been set for the entire world. Technology has so vastly aided the process of mass education that if, as Le Corbusier wrote, a house is a machine for living, then a school or university today runs the risk of becoming a machine for instruction. Precisely what mechanized mass education could mean in the way of a general standardization or even a debasement of culture many critics—not the least of them George Orwell—were quick to point out.

A world so full of change will create new problems almost as rapidly as it disposes of the old. The pace of change and the impact of scientific doubt helped to produce a new relativism in philosophy and led to a considerable uncertainty about moral standards. Though the historian may express his concern, he must be reluctant to pass judgment. He may point out that on the evidence of the past the mass culture of today, in which leaders seek to amuse, instruct, and exhort the widest possible audience, is exposed to grave risks. As the history of the Late Roman Empire has shown, the acceptance of a steadily declining level of culture can in the end lead to destruction. On the other hand the superb technical equipment of today, even though it may at times be employed for trivial, vulgar, and even hideously destructive ends, is also available to the world's best and most dedicated minds. The technicians, the scientists, the artists, the teachers, and the philosophers have it within their power to use the vast inheritance from the past for the genuine betterment of man.

Reading List: Chapter 14

Mumford, L., *The Human Prospect* (1955, paperback), pp. 227–260, "Program for Survival." A vigorous critic traces the moral disintegration accompanying the use of atomic weapons and pleads for a "dedication to life."

Barraclough, G., *An Introduction to Contemporary History* (1964), ch. 7, "The Ideological Challenge." Considers the impact of communist theories on the West.

The New Cambridge Modern History, vol. XII (1960), ch. 5, "Science and Technology." Very good on both aspects.

The New Cambridge Modern History, vol. XII (1960), ch. 6, "Literature, Philosophy, and Religious Thought." A provocative essay by the dean of St. Paul's on the trends of the twentieth century, not always hopeful in its conclusions.

Abell, W., *The Collective Dream in Art* (1957), ch. 17. Deals with the place of art in the cultural conflicts of the twentieth century.

Johnson, Edgar N., *An Introduction to the History of the Western Tradition,* vol. I (1959), pp. 700–716. An interesting brief survey of contemporary culture with excellent illustrations.

Wilson, E., *Axel's Castle* (1936, also paperback). Chs. 4 and 6 on T. S. Eliot and James Joyce are a brilliant exposition of these major figures.

Barraclough, G., *An Introduction to Contemporary History* (1964), ch. 8, "Art and Literature in the Contemporary World."

Orwell, G., *Nineteen Eighty-Four* (1949, also paperback). Any part of this novel of the future will convey the atmosphere of the regimented world in which "Big Brother" is always watching.

Wright, Frank Lloyd, *An Autobiography* (1943). A few chapters should be read to capture the spirit of this combative genius of modern architecture.

Chapter 15

Unity and Disunity, 1949–1960

A World Divided, or a World United?
The Role of the United Nations
Regional Efforts to Establish Political and Military Order
Plans for Economic Integration
Disarmament and the Problem of Atomic Weapons
Tensions Between Eastern and Western Europe

■ A WORLD DIVIDED, OR A WORLD UNITED?

This chapter, which pursues the complex course of events through the decade of the 1950's, is concerned primarily with the efforts of the western powers to promote their common interests, political and economic, and to organize militarily in defense of them. At the same time the countries behind the Iron Curtain were being similarly mobilized, yet in a sense largely hostile to the West. The domestic policies of the European states in this decade experienced no such dramatic internal changes as those which, in the earlier cases of Mussolini or Hitler, had profoundly affected the course of events. Substantial economic progress was the general rule. Changes in the overseas world did, to be sure, have their effect upon the European powers. One consequence seems to have been that in a period of increasing prosperity western Europe could

1949   NATO agreements signed (April)
        Council of Europe established (May)
1950   United Nations takes action against aggression in Korea (June)
1952   Turkey and Greece join NATO (February)
        European Coal and Steel Community established (July)
        United States explodes hydrogen bomb (November)
1955   Warsaw Pact between the Soviet Union and its satellites (May)
        Geneva Summit Conference (July)
        West Germany admitted to NATO (October)
1956   Hungarian Revolution (October)
1957   Saar becomes tenth state of West Germany (January)
        Sputnik I launched in Soviet Union (October)
1958   European Economic Community, or Common Market, estab-
            lished by "The Six" (January)
        Nuclear testing suspended for one year by Britain, United States,
            and Soviet Union (October)
1959   General de Gaulle president of Fifth Republic of France
            (January)
1960   European Free Trade Community established by "The Seven"
            (January)

not be certain that many of the basic values which it had long held were still acceptable to the larger, non-European world. Nor could it feel certain that many of these values would not continue to be militantly challenged by the Communist world of eastern Europe.

A very quick glance at the internal policies of the various states will show some of the basic trends. In Great Britain, Winston Churchill returned to office after winning the general election of 1951. The Labor Party, which had been responsible for the huge body of social legislation of the immediate post-war years, seemed to have shot its bolt, so that a succession of Conservative prime ministers, first Churchill, then Anthony Eden, and then Harold Mac-millan, held office. Though a halt was called to the vigorous reform program, the general effectiveness of the welfare state was an undeniable fact, and Prime

Minister Macmillan, pointing to high wages and full employment, could tell the British people during the general election of 1959 that "they never had it so good."

France experienced an economic recovery called by some a "miracle"; in any case its success was in striking contrast to the realm of French politics, where (with only one or two distinguished exceptions) a lamentable succession of premiers came and went at intervals of rarely more than a few months. A rightist rebellion of French settlers and army leaders in Algiers brought a threat of actual civil war to France itself in 1958; the immediate outcome was for the president of France to summon General de Gaulle from retirement and offer him emergency powers for six months. The more permanent outcome was the drafting under De Gaulle's leadership of a new constitution, overwhelmingly ratified in 1959, which provided for a very much stronger executive power. The election of General de Gaulle in 1959 to a seven-year term as president under this constitution and the conclusion of the long Algerian war with the official recognition of independence in 1962 gave further support to the view that stability at long last had come to France.

In West Germany and Italy, similarly, economic prosperity and an orderly political life were two aspects of a generally promising picture. Chancellor Adenauer was re-elected in 1953, again in 1957, and again in 1961. As German cities emerged from the rubble of war, the new vigor was so great that the gross national product rose from $23.1 billion in 1950 to $88.7 billion in 1962. So also in Italy the Christian Democrats remained in power through the decade, though when De Gasperi retired in 1953 no leader of equal stature took his place. Communism remained as a vocal and militant minority cause, and a form of neo-Fascism began to appear which by 1960 seemed actually to threaten Italian democracy. Yet a booming prosperity helped to keep a major political crisis from developing.

The problem of the Saar Territory had long evaded solution and had been a constant irritant to Franco-German relations. This border area, with a population of nearly a million, had a valuable productive capacity in steel and coal sufficient to tip the economic balance in this respect to the advantage of France as against West Germany. After the Second World War the Saar was part of the French occupation zone. With the approval of Britain and the United States, the French arranged in 1947 to set apart the Saar as an "autonomous state," incorporated, however, into the French customs and monetary system. This arrangement met the combined protests of West Germany, the Soviet Union, and, apparently, a majority of the Saarlanders. In October, 1954, therefore, France and West Germany agreed to "Europeanize" the Saar within the framework of the Western European Union then being established.[1]

1. See p. 411.

FRANCO-GERMAN RECONCILIATION. Premier Charles de Gaulle meets with West German Chancellor Konrad Adenauer at Bad Zreuznach in November, 1958, shortly before his election to the French presidency. Their agreement to defend "with vigor" the status of Berlin marks the beginning of a sympathetic collaboration of the two leaders.

A Saar Statute to this effect was, however, decisively rejected by the Saar-landers in a plebiscite of October, 1955, and the subsequent December elections gave an emphatic victory to the parties favoring reunion with Germany. Nego-tiations between France and West Germany in 1956 led to an agreement that the Saar should be incorporated in West Germany and that France should re-tain special economic concessions for at least three years. When the Saar be-came the tenth state of the German Federal Republic in January, 1957, this persistent irritant to Franco-German relations seemed at long last to have been removed.

The smaller countries of Europe were confronted with no great crises. In Belgium, the Netherlands, and the Scandinavian countries a steady eco-nomic growth went along with a general orderliness of democratic political life and a substantial measure of state socialism. In Spain and Portugal, on the other hand, the respective dictatorships of General Franco and Dr. Salazar showed no signs of relaxing. Yet American relations with Spain improved markedly when in September, 1953, agreements known as the Pact of Madrid made available $226 million in military and economic aid. The United States in return was permitted to build and use naval and air bases in Spain for the general defense of western Europe. These became operational in 1958. It could be added that the treaty of May, 1955, which at long last recognized Austrian independence, made no very great change in a country where for ten years a "Provisional" Government had operated under only the mildest of restrictions on the part of the occupying authorities. In Switzerland a referendum of February, 1959, rejected votes for women in federal elections.

The general domestic progress in the states of western Europe was not accompanied by developments of equal promise in the field of political international affairs at the beginning of this decade. Clearly, no direct solution had been found for the larger political issues, although there were significant achievements in economic integration to be described later in this chapter. The sharp division between East and West Germany was a principal source of trouble, and was held by many observers to be the real key to the problem of European order. The baffling problem of disarmament was another. The control of atomic energy was a third. The existence of an ideological cleavage between the Soviet world and the West presented still another problem. And while some progress toward European integration had been made,[2] this progress was at best slow and uncertain. The situation became more ominous because of certain new considerations. One terrifying fact was the detonation in 1952 of the first American hydrogen bomb, followed by the announcement in August, 1953, of its Russian counterpart. Rapid developments in rocketry made possible the intercontinental ballistic missile, against which no defense was assured.

In the light of such developments it is hardly surprising that Winston Churchill should declare in the House of Commons: "I am of the opinion that we ought to have a try for peaceful coexistence—a real good try for it." It was no less significant that in these years of the Cold War some wise observers should agree that the only practical policy was not a militant "confrontation," but rather, as far as Communism was concerned, a policy of "containment." This was the view advocated as early as July, 1947, by "X," eventually identified as George F. Kennan, a high official in the United States Department of State, in a widely discussed article which appeared in the influential quarterly *Foreign Affairs*. The essence of such a policy of containment was that an unflagging military alertness would have to continue for an indefinite period of years. And such, in a general sense, has been the policy which western Europe followed.

■ THE ROLE OF THE UNITED NATIONS

The United Nations, the general wartime origins of which have already been described, quickly showed remarkable growth.[3] When the Charter came into effect in 1945 fifty-one nations were members. In 1955 sixteen states

2. See pp. 315–318.
3. See pp. 272–273; 298–299; 315–316.

were added, ten from Europe, five from Asia, and one from Africa. Of the seventeen added in 1960 all, with the one exception of Cyprus, came from Africa. By the close of that year the United Nations totaled one hundred members, the striking increase coming from the new states of Africa and Asia. These were so numerous as to constitute very nearly a majority in the General Assembly. A combined Afro-Asian majority became assured by 1961. What was the effect of this shift? Article 24 of the Charter had placed upon the Security Council the prime responsibility for maintaining the peace. Apart from the paralyzing possibilities of the veto, which could be exercised by any one of the five permanent members on a "substantive" issue, the powers of the Council seemed very large. They were indeed much stronger than those of the old League Council. How effectively were these powers used?

Issues were not long in coming before the United Nations. The Israeli-Egyptian war beginning in December, 1947, created a thorny problem. The Security Council sent out Count Bernadotte of Sweden as its official mediator. After his assassination by a Zionist terrorist in the following September, mediation efforts were continued under the direction of an American expert, Dr. Ralph Bunche.[4] By July, 1949, an armistice had been secured, though the subsequent United Nations Conciliation Commission had no success in bringing about a permanent peace between Israel and the Arab states. The United Nations Relief and Works Agency was principally responsible for the continuing care of the Arab refugees living miserably in the Gaza Strip and elsewhere. When Israel's war with Egypt was renewed in 1956, at the time of the Suez crisis, the United Nations was able to negotiate a cease-fire and to maintain a substantial United Nations supervisory force on the Israeli-Egyptian border to prevent the kind of incident that might cause the war to be resumed.

An even greater crisis developed in Korea in 1950, already briefly mentioned as part of the history of the Far East in these years.[5] From the point of view of the United Nations, the salient facts are these. In the temporary absence of the Soviet Union, the United States obtained a unanimous vote of the Security Council that North Korea was guilty of a breach of the peace. This was possible because of a prior legal ruling that abstention from voting did not constitute a veto. The action of the Security Council in recommending "that members of the United Nations aid the Republic of Korea in repelling the armed attack . . ." came one day after the United States had made its own decision to use force. The overwhelming number of troops committed were in fact American: General MacArthur was appointed United Nations commander in chief, and the contingents sent by other members were largely token forces. Thus the Korean War was in fact much more an American than a

4. See p. 367.
5. See pp. 360–361.

United Nations operation.[6] Although the outcome was a deadlock and a truce rather than genuine peace, the United Nations, if only through the fortunate accident of the Soviet Union's absence when the first vital action was taken, had not shirked its responsibilities.

One significant modification of United Nations procedure arose from the Korean War. When the Soviet Union did return as rotative president of the Security Council in August, 1950, its representative was in a position to prevent effective action by the Council on the Korean issue. Consequently the General Assembly passed a resolution in the following November, invoking Article 10 of the Charter and declaring in part as follows:

> If the Security Council, because of lack of unanimity of the permanent members, fails to exercise its primary responsibility for the maintenance of international peace and security . . . the General Assembly shall consider the matter immediately, with a view to making appropriate recommendations to members for collective measures including . . . the use of armed force when necessary, to maintain or restore international peace and security.

To some extent, therefore, by this "Uniting for Peace" resolution a two-thirds vote of the Assembly could bypass a Security Council veto. It is to be noted, however, that whereas under Articles 41 to 43 of the Charter the Security Council can "call upon" members who must "undertake" to make armed forces available, this latter resolution, in accord with Article 10 of the Charter, recognizes that the General Assembly can do no more than "make appropriate recommendations."

Still another crisis facing the United Nations was that of Suez in 1956, when, after President Nasser had seized the Suez Canal, the British and French undertook military action against Egypt by landing paratroopers and other forces on Egyptian soil.[7] Appeals to the Security Council were nullified by a Franco-British veto. The matter then went to the General Assembly where in the end a cease-fire was arranged and United Nations forces were sent in as a guarantee of it. British and French intervention had been denounced. On the other hand, when a Russian veto prevented Council action regarding Soviet intervention in Hungary in 1956, the General Assembly's efforts to devise some sort of action on behalf of the Hungarians met with lamentable failure. The western powers could no longer count, as they had tended to do in the past, on a sympathetic majority to support their views, to say nothing of the two-thirds backing needed for any important decision.

One of the most difficult crises encountered by the United Nations arose in 1960 in the former Belgian Congo.[8] Order broke down following the procla-

6. American battle deaths numbered 33,629, as compared with less than one thousand from any other single nation.
7. See p. 370.
8. See pp. 374, 429.

mation of independence in June. Premier Patrice Lumumba blamed the Belgians and asked the United Nations to send a force to hasten their departure. United Nations contingents from Canada, Sweden, and the Irish Republic finally succeeded in getting the Belgians to withdraw, though powerful European financial interests in Katanga Province were reluctant to see the new state established. Lumumba, meanwhile, who had aroused considerable discontent among his followers, showed pro-Communist leanings. He was removed from office by President Joseph Kasavubu and was subsequently murdered in Katanga Province. The Soviet Union, sympathetic to Lumumba, strongly opposed United Nations intervention, as did President de Gaulle, who did not wish to see any international control of these new African states. The confused sequel, which placed an almost intolerable strain upon the workings and the finances of the United Nations, will be considered briefly in the Epilogue. One of the most tragic aspects of the crisis was that Dag Hammarskjöld,[9] secretary-general of the United Nations, was killed (1961) in a plane crash while on his way to seek a cease-fire between the United Nations and the Katanga secessionists.

Such were the varied fruits of men's first efforts to find through the United Nations peaceful solutions for the world's critical problems. A further observation can be made. The 1950 resolution seeking to give a larger authority to the General Assembly in the case of a deadlock in the Security Council had one somewhat unexpected result. The flood of new African memberships could hardly have been foreseen; even less could one have predicted the sudden impact of these new states—inexperienced, ill-equipped, and susceptible to pressures from the Communist world. Yet in the General Assembly they, along with some of the equally inexperienced new Asiatic states, could on occasion determine the outcome of an important issue before the Assembly.

The other work of the United Nations, particularly as it affects Europe, must be considered here. The Economic and Social Council, consisting of twelve members elected by the General Assembly for three-year terms, directed a number of functional commissions, such as the Statistical Commission, the Population Commission, and the Commission on Narcotic Drugs. It also controlled certain regional commissions, such as the Economic Commission for Europe and others for Latin America, Asia, the Far East, and Africa, as well as directing UNICEF, the United Nations Children's Fund. In 1948 its Com-

9. 1905–1961. A civil servant and economics specialist, whose father was prime minister of Sweden during the First World War, he was chairman of the Board of Governors of the Bank of Sweden, 1941–1948, and member of several cabinets. Having served as a Swedish representative to the Organization for European Economic Cooperation and delegate to the United Nations, he was elected secretary-general in 1953 as "the darkest of dark horses." Re-elected in 1958, he described himself as "curator of the secrets of eighty-two nations." Three years after his tragic death in 1961, his private diaries, strongly mystical in tone, were published under the title *Markings*. He was posthumously awarded the Nobel Peace Prize in 1961.

mission on Human Rights completed a "Universal Declaration on Human Rights." The value of such work did not consist in meeting a specific crisis, but rather in mobilizing expert attention in the face of long-range and continuous problems.

The Trusteeship Council, carrying on the work of the old League Mandates Commission, did not, of course, directly affect Europe. Some of the trust territories were former mandates. Five areas in Africa—Togoland and the Cameroons (Britain and France); Tanganyika (Britain); Ruanda-Urundi (Belgium); and Somaliland (Italy)—were established as trusteeships. Between 1957 and 1962 all of them achieved independence. Four areas in the Pacific— Western Samoa (New Zealand); North East New Guinea with New Ireland, New Britain, and the Solomons (Australia); Nauru (Australia, New Zealand, and Britain); and the Marianas, Carolines, and Marshalls (United States)— became trusteeships. In 1962 one of these, Western Samoa, with a population of only 119,000 inhabiting a mere handful of Pacific islands, became an independent state.

A great deal of work done through the Specialized Agencies of the United Nations contributed to the peace and order of the world. The operation of UNRRA, between 1943 and 1947, has already been discussed.[10] The International Refugee Organization, set up in 1948, took over much of UNRRA's work until in turn it was superseded by the Office of the United Nations High Commissioner for Refugees in 1951. It is a commentary upon the persistent dislocation and unrest in eastern Europe and the Middle East that the authority of this Office was regularly renewed. Some much older bodies, such as the International Telecommunication Union (1865), the Universal Postal Union (1874), and the International Labor Organization (1919), were accepted as Specialized Agencies and continued to function in association with the work of the United Nations.

New Specialized Agencies emerged in accordance with the stipulation of Article 57 of the UN Charter:

> The various specialized agencies, established by intergovernmental agreement and having wide international responsibilities as defined in their basic instruments, in economic, social, cultural, educational, health, and related fields, shall be brought into relationship with the United Nations. . . .

The Food and Agriculture Organization (FAO), set up in 1945, undertook technical duties concerned with raising nutritional levels and living standards through improvements in the production and distribution of agricultural products. Of necessity the work of providing technical assistance was slow, though in some instances, for example in Pakistan, the increases in productivity in cer-

10. See pp. 299, 315.

tain fields were spectacular. The World Health Organization (WHO), similarly, did basic work intended to combat epidemics, improve general living conditions, and promote maternal and child welfare.

A particular comment should be made about the United Nations Educational, Scientific, and Cultural Organization (UNESCO), probably as well known through its spectacular new building in Paris as any branch of the United Nations. The constitution of UNESCO begins as follows: "Since war begins in the minds of men, it is in the minds of men that the defenses of peace must be constructed." Thus it was held that the improvement of human understanding could be furthered by encouraging the co-operation of scholars in all fields, by enlarging appreciation of the arts of alien lands, and by sponsoring such publications as the numerous volumes of a *World Art Series,* a three-volume *World Survey of Education,* a quarterly *Journal of World History,* and a six-volume *History of Mankind* of which the first impressive volume appeared in 1963.

The most concrete work of the Specialized Agencies (constitutionally not a part of the United Nations though closely linked) was done in the field of economics. The International Bank for Reconstruction and Development (World Bank) was launched in 1945, the membership eventually growing to include 102 nations. Its purposes were to assist members by facilitating investment of capital for productive purposes and by making loans available. The Bank derived its funds chiefly from paid-in capital subscriptions and the sale of its own bonds. By 1964 it had made 372 loans totaling over $8.2 billion to 72 countries or territories. The International Monetary Fund (IMF) was also launched in 1945 and operated on a more modest scale. Its aim was to promote exchange stability by providing short-term credit to any country experiencing difficulties in its balance of payments, thereby reducing the risk of sudden currency devaluations. Though the International Trade Organization, proposed in 1947, was never ratified, an international commercial treaty, the General Agreement on Trades and Tariffs (GATT), was signed by an eventual total of thirty-five states, and had considerable success in lowering and stabilizing tariff rates as a result of many regional and bilateral agreements.

In summary, the political work of the United Nations, along with the social and economic achievements of the Social and Economic Council, the Trusteeship Council, and the various Specialized Agencies, suggests the existence of a substantial reservoir of goodwill, and some modest advance in the face of continuing problems of major size. On the other hand, the International Court of Justice, continuing the work of the former Permanent Court, though potentially of the greatest significance, fell far short of the hopes of its proponents. According to Article 94 of the United Nations Charter, "Each member of the United Nations undertakes to comply with the decision of the International Court of Justice in any case to which it is a party." But the Court did not have automatic jurisdiction save when stipulated in the explicit terms of treaties. Moreover, since the Charter had defined the United Nations as being "based on the principle of the sovereign equality of all its members," states could decide when they would or would not refer disputes to the International Court, and in most cases they chose not to refer them. While the Security Council was empowered to refer disputed matters to the Court, it rarely did so. Thus the immediate effectiveness of the Court was in fact very slight.

■ REGIONAL EFFORTS TO ESTABLISH POLITICAL
AND MILITARY ORDER

The Council of Europe was the only political effort to work for some degree of European order on a regional basis. Its beginnings in 1949 have already been described.[11] To the ten original members were later added Greece, Turkey, Iceland, West Germany, and Austria. Yet the Consultative Assembly and the Council of Ministers gathering annually at Strasbourg proved disappointing, though having the vigorous support of Europe's most internationally minded statesmen, including Paul-Henri Spaak of Belgium.[12] Communist membership seemed automatically excluded by the provision that a member must "accept the principles of the rule of law and the enjoyment by all persons within its jurisdiction of human rights and fundamental freedoms." Though sponsoring debates on issues of European policy, the Council of Europe surrendered most of its initiative to other organizations—military or economic in nature—where concrete achievements could more easily be expected.

In the well-tried realm of military commitments, European co-operation was much more in evidence. The fifty-year military alliance, the Dunkirk Treaty, sealed by Britain and France in 1947, was quickly followed by the Brussels Treaty in 1948 which brought in the three Benelux countries (Belgium, the Netherlands, and Luxembourg) and had a wider scope. This was the basis of the much more elaborate fifteen-member North Atlantic Treaty Organization, the beginnings of which have already been described.[13] Greece and Turkey were added in 1952, West Germany in 1955. The rearming of Germany and its admission to NATO, after the failure to create a European Defense Community (see pp. 411–412), inevitably caused some misgivings, yet it

---

11. See pp. 318–319.
12. Born in 1899 and entering parliament in 1932, he was Belgium's first Socialist premier, holding office in 1938 and 1939. He served the Belgian government-in-exile as foreign minister, 1940–1945, and again, 1954–1957. He was president of the first General Assembly of the United Nations, 1946; president of the Consultative Assembly of the Council of Europe, 1949–1951; chairman of the Organization for European Economic Cooperation, 1948–1950; an organizer of NATO, and its secretary-general, 1957–1961; an organizer of Benelux, Euratom, and the Common Market; and president of the Common Assembly of the European Coal and Steel Community, 1953–1954. A leader of the movement for European unity, he won the nickname, "Mr. Europe."
13. See p. 319.

was indisputable that German manpower and German industry were essential to the defense of the West. The five signatories of the Brussels Treaty had established, to be sure, an "inner ring" of defense commitments. When West Germany and Italy were invited to join the Brussels powers in 1955, the new arrangement took the name of Western European Union. This Union brought pressure upon the leading western European powers to concert their policies in various ways. The clauses of the Brussels Treaty in which the signatories promised "elimination of conflict in their economic policies," "the attainment of a higher standard of living," and "a better understanding of the principles which form the basis of their common civilization" implied that the association was intended to be much more than merely military.

With respect to the larger NATO association, the going was not always easy nor the growth of military strength all that could be desired. An impressive NATO headquarters (SHAPE) was set up outside Paris, and in 1951 the very popular General Eisenhower became supreme Allied commander in Europe (SACEUR). A council, made up of the sixteen foreign ministers of the participating countries, was to meet regularly; four subordinate commands were set up; and a high degree of staff integration and standardization of operational procedures was established.

The difficulties of NATO were of various kinds. The actual numbers of available troops fell far short of those in the Iron Curtain countries, though the possession of tactical atomic weapons at first did much to offset this disparity. The contingents which had been pledged did not always materialize in full strength. Public opinion both in Britain and the United States began to turn against the policy of keeping large numbers of troops (for the United States something like 250,000) regularly abroad. France under President de Gaulle's leadership was emphatically unwilling to surrender her initiative in various military matters—most notably in creating her own nuclear striking force. She chose deliberately to send large numbers of her troops, supposedly pledged to NATO, to Algeria. Under such circumstances more than a little doubt arose as to what the actual value of NATO would be in the event of an acute military crisis. The rise in its forces from about twelve available divisions in 1949 to about forty divisions in 1958 was impressive, yet seemed no real assurance of much more than a delaying capability if war came.

Attempts between 1952 and 1954 to create a European Defense Community were inspired to some degree by French fears of what a rearmed Germany might do if not integrated more fully into the general European community. In October, 1950, the French premier, René Pleven, put forward a plan for a European army under a European minister of defense and a joint council. This army would have "combat teams" from various countries combined into "European divisions," thereby removing the danger of very large

The basis of this map is 1960. Syria, which became part of the United Arab Republic in 1958, withdrew in 1961. Kuwait joined the Arab League in 1961. West New Guinea (West Irian) became part of Indonesia in 1963. Europe is no longer the main source of world divisions.

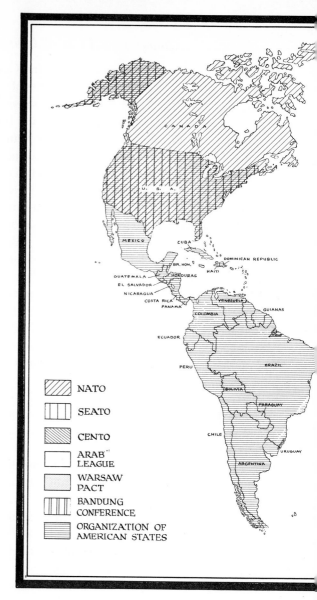

NATO

SEATO

CENTO

ARAB" LEAGUE

WARSAW PACT

BANDUNG CONFERENCE

ORGANIZATION OF AMERICAN STATES

German components making up a German army. Despite many French misgivings, the plans went ahead, but when the French premier, Pierre Mendès-France, submitted them to the National Assembly for ratification in August, 1954, they were rejected through dislike of their supranational character. Thus, by a considerable irony, plans originally advocated by France to keep West Germany from becoming too large a military power were in the end defeated by a vote in the French Assembly.

A relatively minor military reorganization at this time was the Balkan Pact of 1954. Greece, Turkey, and Yugoslavia joined in a defensive agreement

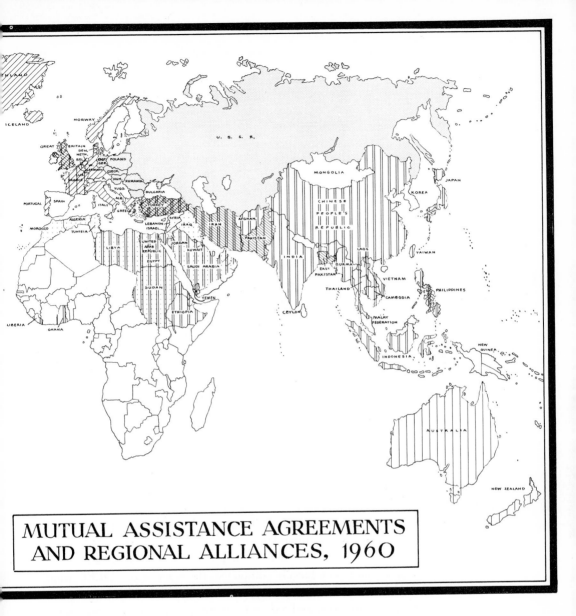

MUTUAL ASSISTANCE AGREEMENTS AND REGIONAL ALLIANCES, 1960

against the threat of outside attack, quite clearly meaning a threat from the Communist world. It is hardly surprising, therefore, that the Soviet Union should likewise have sought to mobilize the support of the various Iron Curtain countries. A series of bilateral agreements culminated in the Warsaw Pact of May, 1955, a treaty of "friendship, collaboration, and mutual assistance," in which the U.S.S.R. joined with Albania, Bulgaria, Czechoslovakia, East Germany, Hungary, Poland, and Rumania in a twenty-year mutual defense agreement.[14] Announcement of the Warsaw Pact followed within a week West Ger-

14. See p. 340.

many's entrance into NATO and was widely regarded as a reply to it, though in fact it confirmed existing treaty relationships. Marshal Ivan Konev, a distinguished Soviet soldier, became supreme commander, with a political consultative committee from the signatory countries to assist him. At the time it was estimated that the Warsaw Pact involved 170 Soviet divisions and about 80 divisions (on paper, at least) from the satellite countries. In 1963 the United States secretary of defense calculated the armed forces of NATO countries at 5 million, Russia's at 3.3 million, and its satellites at 1.2 million.

■ PLANS FOR ECONOMIC INTEGRATION

The efforts at economic integration which went along with corresponding efforts of a political and military nature could, perhaps, be rated as more important than either of the other two. The first striking example in the economic realm came in January, 1948, when Belgium, the Netherlands, and Luxembourg announced the formation of Benelux—a customs union establishing a common tariff against outside nations and removing many, but not all, customs barriers separating the three.[15] The ultimate goal was stated to be that of complete free trade. Agreements of 1958, establishing the Benelux Economic Union, came very close to achieving this end, one of the striking features being the completely free movement of workers back and forth from one country to another. An Inter-Parliamentary Advisory Council of forty-nine members and a Committee of Ministers were set up to administer the agreements. Benelux, with reason, was the model on which other economic agreements were based.

When the Marshall Plan was launched, the sixteen European member-states set up in April, 1948, the Organization for European Economic Cooperation (OEEC), already described.[16] Although its essential purpose was to carry out the work of the European Recovery Program, the OEEC Council was empowered to make further recommendations, agreements, and decisions binding on all its members. Thus, even when the original purposes of the European Recovery Program had been largely completed, the work of the OEEC went on. The United States and Canada associated themselves with it in 1950; West Germany had joined in 1949; and a decade later Spain also became associated with it. The OEEC encouraged financial and trade agreements, working to increase production and wherever possible to reduce tariffs. Perhaps in part because of the large number (twenty) of its members it did not have the same tightly organized growth as had the smaller Benelux organization.

A much more striking example of economic integration had its beginnings in 1951 with the European Coal and Steel Community. Generally regarded as the most successful effort of this kind, its success was attributable in part to the

15. See p. 319.
16. See p. 317.

clear necessity for co-operative action and in part to the precisely delimited nature of the program drafted. The proposals put forward in the spring of 1949 owed much to the fertile brain of the brilliant French planner Jean Monnet[17] and much to the persuasive skill of France's foreign minister, Robert Schuman. The complicated distribution of coal mines, iron ore, industrial plants, railways, canals, and urban populations over a large and continuous area encouraged the willing participation of France, West Germany, Italy, Belgium, the Netherlands, and Luxembourg in the European Coal and Steel Community. The members were to pool and allocate their resources, regulate prices, and jointly to control their output.

The wording of the preamble to the draft treaty initialed at Paris in April, 1951, rose to the point of eloquence:

> The High-Contracting Parties, considering that world peace may be safeguarded only by the creative efforts which measure up to the dangers which menace it. . . . Being resolved to substitute for historic rivalries a fusion of their essential interests; to establish, by creating an economic community, the foundation of a broad and independent community among peoples long divided by bloody conflicts; and to lay the bases of institutions capable of giving direction to their future common destiny; have decided to create a European Coal and Steel Community. . . .

An elaborate constitutional machinery was devised, including a High Authority of nine directors with headquarters in the city of Luxembourg, a Common Assembly of seventy-eight delegates from the participating parliamentary bodies, a Consultative Committee of producers, workers, and consumers, a Council of Ministers, and even a special Court of Justice. Described as Europe's first genuinely supranational authority, the Coal and Steel Community provided a functional approach to the problem of European unity, and could truthfully be characterized as one of the most original and constructive of the postwar regional organizations.

The very significant development arising from the Coal and Steel Community was the European Economic Community. The same six participants signed a treaty at Rome in March, 1957, pledging themselves to work toward a customs union making possible the free flow of goods and services. This union came into effect in January, 1958, with the name, "Common Market," applied to what was intended to develop over a planned period of fifteen years into a completely free-trade area. It would include something like 175 million people,

17. Born in 1888 and entering the French civil service in 1914, he served as deputy secretary-general of the League of Nations, 1919–1923. During the Second World War he became one of the seven members of the French Committee of National Liberation. He helped to organize UNRRA, was one of the principal advocates of economic planning in postwar France, and first president of the High Authority for the new Coal and Steel Community. He also was president of the action committee for a United States of Europe.

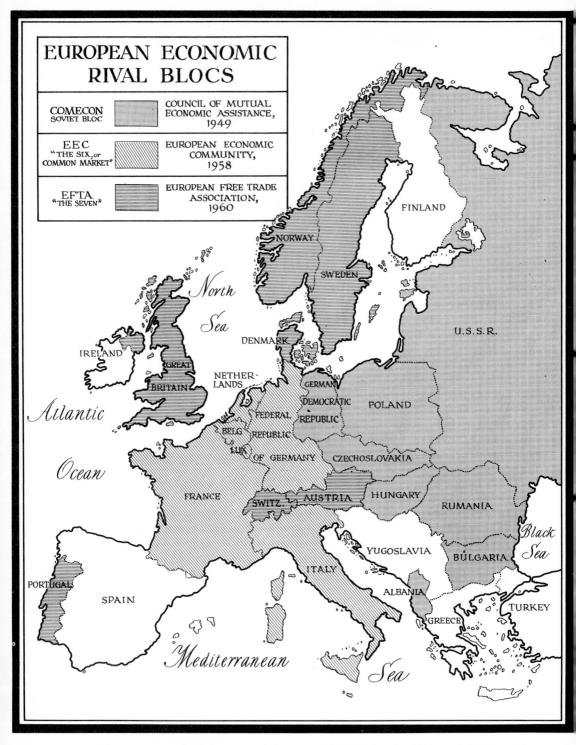

EUROPEAN ECONOMIC
RIVAL BLOCS

COMECON
SOVIET BLOC — COUNCIL OF MUTUAL
ECONOMIC ASSISTANCE,
1949

EEC
"THE SIX, or
COMMON MARKET" — EUROPEAN ECONOMIC
COMMUNITY,
1958

EFTA
"THE SEVEN" — EUROPEAN FREE TRADE
ASSOCIATION,
1960

The percentages of European population are: COMECON, 40%; EEC, 31%; EFTA, 16%; unattached, 13%.

for whom ultimately there would be a standardized system of social security and an equalized system of wages. To this inner grouping of members the name of "The Six" soon came to be applied. Still another aspect was the forming by the Six of an Atomic Energy Community (Euratom) for the peaceful exploitation of atomic energy.[18] This would be achieved by sharing information, by joint research, and by establishing a common market for fissionable materials and equipment.

The response to all this activity was an attempt at concerted action by other nonincluded European powers. Great Britain took the initiative in establishing (January, 1960) the European Free Trade Association; the members in addition to herself were Norway, Sweden, Denmark, Austria, Portugal, and Switzerland. This "Outer Seven" association could not claim the same population as "The Inner Six" (the total being in the neighborhood of 92 million people), and it covered only trade in industrial products. Yet it was a formidable combination in the light of the industrial, commercial, and banking experience and potentialities of its members. One clause of the agreement declared the readiness of the signatories to initiate negotiations with the European Economic Community. The unavailing efforts of Great Britain in 1961 and 1962 to establish such a connection with the Inner Six will be considered in the Epilogue.[19]

■ DISARMAMENT AND THE PROBLEM OF ATOMIC WEAPONS

Article 26 of the United Nations Charter declared that "The Security Council shall be responsible for formulating . . . plans . . . for the establishment of a system for the regulation of armaments." Not total disarmament, therefore, but regulation seemed to be the key to the problem as it was first, and no doubt realistically, envisaged by the makers of the Charter. A Commission for Conventional Armaments was set up in February, 1947, but in actuality did very little.

Since atomic weapons presented by far the greatest potential danger, the problem of their control and elimination quickly occupied a central position. The General Assembly established an Atomic Energy Commission in January, 1946, to which the United States almost immediately submitted its plan. Known from the name of the American representative as the Baruch Plan, it proposed: (1) the ownership and operation of all atomic facilities and all sources of nuclear fuel by an international authority; (2) an elaborate system of inspection; (3) the denial of a veto to any member of the international authority. The scheme was totally rejected by the Russians, who proposed instead the destruction within three months of all atomic weapons and the prohibition of their

18. See pp. 418–419.
19. See p. 424.

subsequent manufacture. They would agree to international inspection only after all atomic bombs had been destroyed. In view of the fact that the Russians possessed an overwhelming preponderance in military manpower and conventional weapons, it is clear why the western powers were highly skeptical of such a proposal. When the Baruch Plan came before the General Assembly in July, 1948, it passed by a vote of forty to six, with four abstentions. Immediately following, however, it was vetoed by the Soviet Union in the Security Council. It is hardly surprising that in this atmosphere the Atomic Energy Commission soon voted to suspend its work. Similarly, a new Disarmament Commission established by the United Nations in 1951 found itself able to do very little.

The renewed concern over disarmament arose from the growing sense of danger. The Soviet Union detonated its first atomic bomb in September, 1949. Then the United States detonated a hydrogen bomb in November, 1952; the Russians followed suit within a year (August, 1953). The significance of the new H-bomb must be stressed. The atomic bomb that had caused over 70,000 deaths at Hiroshima in 1945 was the equivalent of twenty thousand tons of TNT—the standard explosive of the Second World War. In the new language of atomic science, this would be called a twenty-kiloton bomb. But a single hydrogen bomb had the explosive force of twenty megatons, which is twenty *million* tons of TNT. What this means may be indicated by a comparison: during the entire period of the Second World War the United States Air Force dropped the equivalent of 1.5 million tons of TNT on Germany.[20] And the hydrogen bomb of this force, which on impact would have a lethal radius of eight miles, was designed to be carried in the new B-52 bomber of much greater range and power. In the eyes of responsible men, such a weapon could be acceptable only for its deterrent effect rather than its actual use for destructive purposes.

In 1953 President Eisenhower made his "Atoms for Peace" proposal— that men's efforts be turned to developing peaceful uses for atomic energy. A British-French memorandum of 1954 advocated the acceptance by all countries of the prohibition of atomic weapons "in principle," to be followed by a general disarmament taking place in three stages. When a summit conference met at Geneva in July, 1955, President Eisenhower tried to force the pace with his "open skies" proposal that the United States and the Soviet Union exchange full information about their military establishments and permit unlimited aerial inspection of them. The Russian reply was to bring up their old proposal that a total ban on all nuclear weapons must precede any system of inspection.

Still another attempt on a more modest scale was the Rapacky Plan of "disengagement." The proposal of the Polish foreign minister was that East

20. The "blockbuster" of the Second World War contained about one ton of TNT.

and West Germany, Poland, and Czechoslovakia should together constitute an area in which nuclear weapons were neither to be manufactured nor stockpiled, and that the use of nuclear weapons *against* this area should also be forbidden. First submitted to the United Nations in October, 1957, and then circulated as a memorandum in February, 1958, the Rapacky Plan met the firm opposition of the West German government. The German foreign minister, von Brentano, declared that "by such a partial solution of the question we would decisively weaken the defense potential of the West in comparison with the aggressive potential of the East."

Little genuine advance was made toward disarmament during the decade. The "Great Thaw" at the summit meeting in 1955 was scarcely more than superficial and did not result in any major achievement. In 1958, to be sure, when public concern over the dangers of atomic fallout increased, the United States and the Soviet Union agreed to a year's suspension of nuclear testing—an agreement extended in 1959 for still another year. At the United Nations Khrushchev called once more for general and complete disarmament. On the other hand, when the United Nations Disarmament Commission resumed its discussion at Geneva in 1960, the Soviet delegation walked out. In essence the position was that Russia would not agree to inspection and controls until complete disarmament had been undertaken, whereas the West insisted that inspection should accompany every phase of step-by-step disarmament.

It is hard to say that by 1960 any truly substantial progress toward genuine disarmament or the regulation of atomic weapons had been achieved. In the major countries national budgets for armaments seemed to be increasing rather than decreasing. The launching of the first Russian Sputnik, or space vehicle, in 1957 was followed by the launching of an American satellite in 1958, and ultimately by a series of manned space vehicles.[21] This development created a new dimension to the aspirations of nations and implied new rivalries and new dangers. Nuclear-powered submarines that could circle the globe underwater, first built by the United States and operational in 1954, were being equipped in 1959 to launch rocket missiles without surfacing. The Polaris rocket for this purpose became operational in 1961. In 1960 France detonated its first atomic bomb, and since Great Britain had already reached the point of detonating a hydrogen bomb in 1957, the grimly named "Atomic Club" now had four members. In 1960 the further advances in rocketry meant that intercontinental ballistic missiles, capable of delivering an atomic explosive from one continent to another and extremely difficult to intercept, were an alarming

---

21. Russian progress in this field was substantially ahead of the American. They launched their Sputnik I in October, 1957; the Americans launched their Explorer I in January, 1958. The first Russian-manned space vehicle was launched in April, 1961; the first American-manned space vehicle, in the following May. The Russians hit the moon in September, 1959; the Americans, in April, 1962.

reality. Thus, the modest advances which Europe had made in the direction of political or economic integration had to be balanced against the ever growing dangers of nuclear war. This was the kind of war which few men could wish for, and yet which none could be sure of avoiding.

■ TENSIONS BETWEEN EASTERN AND WESTERN EUROPE

Russian domination of eastern Europe has been discussed in the chapter dealing with the postwar problems of the Soviet Union. It suffices here to point out that this domination was far from complete. Marshal Tito of Yugoslavia, for example, who joined the Cominform in 1947, left it in 1948, making it clear that his particular brand of communism did not accept domination or direction from the Soviet Union. A Council of Mutual Economic Assistance which included the Soviet Union, Poland, Bulgaria, Czechoslovakia, Hungary, and Rumania had been set up in January, 1948. Though Yugoslavia was excluded, the boycott directed against her lacked any true effectiveness. However, when others among the "People's Democracies" began to show some sympathy for Tito, the strong hand of the Soviet Union was soon apparent, as we have seen. Wladislaw Gomulka, secretary of the Polish Communist Party, was removed in 1948; Traicho Kostov, who held a similar position in Bulgaria, was removed and executed in 1949. Three years later Anna Pauker was removed from office in Rumania. Two Czechoslovak Communist dissidents, Rudolf Slansky and Vladimir Clementis, were removed and shot in this same year.

Such Soviet procedures led to murmurings—and indeed more than murmurings—of unrest. Mass protests were repressed in Czechoslovakia in 1953, and in the same year protests in East Berlin were put down by Russian tanks. In Poland Gomulka, who had been removed from office by the Russians, returned to power as prime minister in October, 1957, and was able to resist Khrushchev's attempts to dominate him.

The two failures of opposition to Soviet Russia were seen in Hungary and in East Germany. In the former, the heroic risings of October, 1956, met disaster in the face of ruthless Soviet intervention with armed force followed by the failure of the United Nations to act. In East Germany, the steadily increasing difficulties with the West led to the crisis of August, 1961, in which the border between the two parts was closed, and in Berlin itself a wall was erected to divide one half of the city from the other. This wall symbolized, not only for Germany but perhaps also for Europe, the deep divisions which at this date the goodwill of man had been unable to overcome.

If, in conclusion, one returns to the question with which this chapter began: "A World Divided, or a World United?" it must be clear that in 1960 the forces of disunity were still alarmingly powerful. Though men of goodwill had labored hard, and the results of their labors were not inconsiderable, the continuing dangers were enormous. One has but to look at the titles of books published—*The Political Collapse of Europe, Darkness at Noon, The Twenty-fifth Hour, Animal Farm, Escape From Freedom, The Age of Overkill, The Predicament of Democratic Man, Neither War nor Peace, Winds of Revolution, The Century of Total War*—to realize the enormous tensions which beset this "Age of Anxiety." On balance, however, one must be impressed by the general steadiness with which both European peoples and their leaders faced the problems of the mid-twentieth century. Such steadiness must be kept in mind as the Epilogue to this volume brings us to the close of the fifty-year period which began in 1914 with the sound of the guns of August.

Reading List: Chapter 15

Harris, H. R., "Communism and Asia: Illusions and Misconceptions," *International Affairs,* vol. XXXIX (1963), no. 1. By the Far Eastern expert of the London *Times.*

Aron, R., "French Public Opinion and the Atlantic Treaty," *International Affairs,* vol. XXVIII (1952), no. 1.

Spaak, P., *Why NATO?* (1959). A pamphlet on the need for NATO by one of its organizers.

Lindsay, K., *Towards a European Parliament* (1958), ch. 1. The Council of Europe in perspective.

Kulski, W. W., *International Politics in a Revolutionary Age* (1964), ch. 9. International organizations.

Curti, M., *American Philanthropy Abroad: A History* (1963), ch. 19. On "attacking the causes of mass misery."

Nef, J. U., *War and Human Progress* (1950), ch. 18. The material road to total war.

Gatland, K. W., *Astronautics in the Sixties* (1962), ch. 5. The military uses of space.

Barker, Sir E., and others, *The European Inheritance,* vol. III (1954), pp. 346–355. A brief profession of faith in the continuing role of Europe by a distinguished historian.

Epilogue: New Perspectives in Western History

The five years which began in 1960 and closed in 1964 round off a fifty-year period which opened in 1914 with the great battles of northeastern France and East Prussia. Only in the chronological sense can these final years claim completeness, for it is clear that the unresolved conflicts besetting mankind found no easy or quick solution. During this whole period science and technology had enlarged man's power to a frightening extent. Rarely, it would seem, had the pace of change been so rapid, and never before, perhaps, in human history did new critical areas arise so speedily in distant continents to challenge the authority of a long-established center such as European civilization had provided. A brief résumé of recent developments in Europe itself, followed by a. similar account of those in the non-European world, will relate the patterns of the immediate present to the events which preceded them.

A point of departure can be found in the May, 1960, summit meeting in Paris of Eisenhower, De Gaulle, Khrushchev, and Macmillan. Their professed purpose was to reduce world tensions, especially with respect to two persistent and threatening problems: disarmament and the future of Germany. However, the diplomatic crisis arising from the shooting down of a United States U-2 reconnaissance plane over Russia quickly led, as has been shown, to a breakdown of the meetings. Two months later the Soviet Union also walked out of a formal session of the Disarmament Conference at Geneva. And in this same year 1960 Premier Khrushchev, addressing the fifteenth General Assembly of the United Nations in New York, denounced the United Nations, expressed contempt for its secretary-general, and in every way showed a complete indifference to orderly democratic procedure. Such an attitude was clearly a bad omen for the future.

The basic difficulty for men of goodwill arose from the continuing lack of confidence between East and West, hardly allayed when the newly elected President Kennedy met with Premier Khrushchev at Vienna in June, 1961.

Little was accomplished. Indeed, within two months a crisis of the first order developed in Berlin. Because of continuing disagreements with the West, the East German authorities, who could make no move without Soviet approval, began the construction of the Berlin Wall. This improvised barrier soon reached formidable enough proportions to seal off completely one-half of the great city of Berlin from the other, and thereby symbolized the total impasse that had developed in the relations between East and West Germany. The situation was rendered all the more discouraging by the failure of Britain, France, and the United States to take any strong action against this clear violation of their rights, to say nothing of those of West Germany.

The resumption of nuclear testing, which had been in abeyance since 1958, was still another troubling development. Soviet scientists in October, 1961, produced two hydrogen bomb explosions, one having a strength of twenty-five megatons and the other fifty megatons. These set a new record in man's efforts to harness the explosive power of nature. In response, American scientists also undertook to resume testing. Such a situation gave added urgency to the negotiations on the general subject of disarmament. In the summer of 1962 an eighteen-nation Disarmament Conference met at Geneva and continued its sessions until September, 1964, with much basic disagreement and very little accomplishment.

The general situation was made worse by lack of harmony among the western powers. The year 1963 saw France veto Britain's entrance into the Common Market. Since 1959 Great Britain had been a member of the seven-nation European Free Trade Association (the "Outer Seven"), discussed earlier. In 1961 she had obtained permission from her EFTA colleagues to approach the six-nation Common Market (the "Inner Six") in order to discover on what terms she might also join the Six. It was hoped that a successful move of this sort would in time lead to a single economic community resulting from a combination of the two groups. Although Britain met with serious objections from other members of the Commonwealth, the main obstacle was the attitude of President de Gaulle, who feared that France might lose her leading position in the Common Market. France's veto in January, 1963, of Britain's admission came as a cruel blow to those who believed that the new member could have contributed substantially to the continued growth of the European Economic Community. The veto was particularly unfortunate since President Kennedy and his advisers had made it clear that a greater degree of political and economic unification in western Europe would have made the United States more willing to share in an enlarged European trade program.

President de Gaulle's actions created difficulties for the rest of the world in other respects. Mistrusting the proposals of President Kennedy and Prime Minister Macmillan in December, 1962, to increase Britain's nuclear power and to enlarge Anglo-American co-operation in NATO, he sought instead to establish closer ties with West Germany. Negotiations begun in January, 1963, resulted in the ratification by June of a Franco-German treaty of friendship pledging collaboration in military, economic, political, and cultural matters, including consultation at least twice yearly of the two heads of state. If De Gaulle could now claim to have contributed substantially to reducing the long antagonism between France and Germany, he could not avoid the charge of having seriously—perhaps, indeed, fatally—weakened NATO. Always jealous of French sovereign rights, he withdrew the French Atlantic fleet in June, 1963, from NATO command, and in August he refused to adhere to the Nuclear Test-Ban Treaty just signed in Moscow by the Soviet Union, Great Britain, and the United States.

The Test-Ban Treaty forbade nuclear explosions in the atmosphere, under water, and in outer space. Though many other nations adhered to the Treaty, both France and Communist China—the two other states with nuclear capabilities—refused. West Germany, acting in close association with France, reserved its decision. This was all the more disappointing because Pope John XXIII, a spiritual leader who had shown a remarkable capacity to arouse world-wide admiration and affection, had recently issued his encyclical *Pacem in Terris*. This document pleaded eloquently for a world peace based on universal justice.

Chancellor Adenauer retired in October, 1963. His successor, Dr. Ludwig Erhard, had been a key figure in West Germany's remarkable economic recovery, and he recognized that the continuance of German prosperity involved the maintenance of good relations with Britain, the United States, and indeed the whole Atlantic Community of which NATO remained the symbol. The hope was, therefore, that West Germany might avoid the skeptically hostile attitude toward NATO that was so characteristic of De Gaulle. Thus at the opening of 1964 the European picture was, to say the least, mixed.

Trouble meanwhile had broken out in Cyprus. This island, though still a member of the Commonwealth, had won its independence from Britain in 1960. Constitutional changes subsequently proposed by its president, Archbishop Makarios, were bitterly resented by the Turkish minority, who began active opposition. The danger was that Turkey would intervene on behalf of the Cypriot Turks and Greece intervene on the other side. This might well produce the classic situation out of which a major war could erupt. The United Nations therefore authorized a peace-keeping force in March, and this fortunately was successful enough that by August, 1964, both sides agreed to accept a cease-fire.

Means to stimulate the flow of trade remained an important concern. Greece became an associate member of the Common Market in 1962, and Turkey in 1963. Economic aid from the United States to Europe had been administered since 1961 through the Organization for Economic Co-operation and Development. Though declining in amount, such aid to all western Europe in 1963 still totaled $469 million. The Trade Expansion Act passed by the United States Congress in 1962 had authorized the president to negotiate for tariff reductions of as much as 50 percent. Between March and July, 1964, the United States joined with sixty-five other countries meeting at Geneva to seek tariff reductions. Yet specific difficulties in one country after another made progress very limited.

The Soviet Union, not for the first time, continued to baffle the calculations of statesmen. In January, 1964, Premier Khrushchev appealed for an international agreement to renounce the use of force in questions about territory and frontiers. His own domestic position seemed to have become the stronger when in April three of his former close colleagues, Malenkov, Molotov, and Kaganovich, were expelled from the Party, ostensibly on account of their disagreements with Khrushchev. On his visits to Hungary, the United Arab Republic, and East Germany, he spoke and acted with confidence. He negotiated in June, 1964, for example, a twenty-year treaty of co-operation and friendship with East Germany. Yet within four months he was out of office. In October the announcement came from the Kremlin that Khrushchev, "in view of his health and age," had requested to be relieved of his duties as first secretary of the Communist Party, as premier, and member of the Praesidium. If Khrushchev's work during the preceding eleven years had entitled him to have his name attached to this period in Soviet history, no one quite knew how to evaluate the two solid Party men who succeeded him. Leonid Brezhnev became Party secretary and Alexei Kosygin became premier. The fact that Khrushchev was neither exiled, imprisoned, nor shot, but was allowed to live in comfortable retirement in Moscow suggested an unusual and certainly welcome relaxation in one aspect of Soviet practice.

Restlessness seemed to have become increasingly the mark of the Soviet satellites. Hungary and Bulgaria, to be sure, remained docile. In East Germany, to judge by the continued large migration into West Berlin, the people were obviously less willing than their leaders to accept the close domination of Moscow. Czechoslovakia, which during the 1950's had enjoyed considerable prosperity, encountered an economic slump in 1961 from which COMECON, the Council for Mutual Economic Assistance set up by Moscow, gave little relief. Rumania struggled with some success to build up her foreign trade outside the satellite orbit. And, finally, Albania proved to be so resistant to Khrushchev's demands that by 1961 she had been dropped from membership in the Warsaw Pact and from COMECON and had been roundly denounced by Moscow. Yugoslavia under Tito was somewhat less aloof from the Soviet Union than formerly, but quite clearly had no major role to play in Khrushchev's diplomatic and economic plans.

In summary, Europe in these five years had weathered many storms and witnessed some dramatic turns of fate—most notably the tragic assassination of President Kennedy and the removal from office of Premier Khrushchev. With the retirement of Chancellor Adenauer, only President de Gaulle remained as a major European figure whose public career spanned the whole postwar period. The successes in the field of European economic integration had been much greater than those in the political field. The European economy was thriving. In country after country the general health and well-being were demonstrably improved. Yet the United Nations suffered increasingly from weakness and divisions in a way that discouraged even some of its warmest supporters. The deadlock in Berlin, the failure of the long series of disarmament conferences, and the limited effectiveness of the Test-Ban Treaty would have to be listed as major disappointments.

The most dramatic development of these years was the appearance of the astronaut as a new figure of incalculable portent for the future. During the Second World War the Germans were chiefly responsible for scientific advances in rocketry. Both the Soviet Union and the United States, aided by German experts, were subsequently able to build on this knowledge with spectacular success. In April, 1961, the Russians put Yuri Gagarin into one orbit of the earth, following this with a seventeen-orbit flight by Gherman Titov in August. Though the American Alan Shepard was successfully rocketed for a distance of 116 miles in the same month, it remained for his colleague, John Glenn, to make a flight of three global orbits in February, 1962. From this point flights of greater extent and complexity followed rapidly, including that of the first woman astronaut, Valentina Tereshkova. Unmanned vehicles were landed on the moon, and the world eventually witnessed with the aid of television the astonishing phenomenon of a man leaving his capsule and walking in space. With such success, it was apparent that man's actual landing on the moon was a realizable possibility in the near future.

Within our world, problems outside Europe had reached the point where they seemed almost to dwarf those within. This is true both with respect to the areas and populations involved and the complexity of those matters crying out for solution. Christianity, for example, which commands the adherence of something less than one-third of the world's population, looked forward with less assurance than formerly to the ultimate conversion of those outside the fold. Mohammedans, Hindus, Confucians, Buddhists, Taoists, and Shintoists together make up nearly one-half of the world's people. When one looks at Africa, the Middle East, the Far East, and many parts of the Western Hemisphere, the generalization as to the declining role of Europe would seem to hold good.

For Africa the years from 1960 to 1965 were phenomenal. In 1960 alone

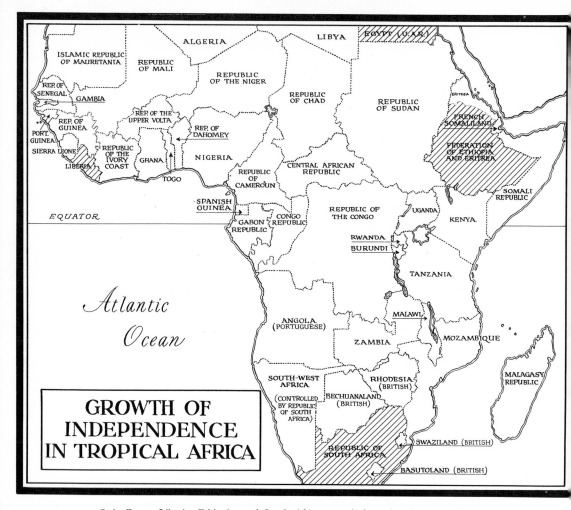

Only Egypt, Liberia, Ethiopia, and South Africa were independent in 1950. The admission of Gambia, Malawi, and Zambia to the United Nations at the beginning of 1965 brought the number of independent African states to 37.

sixteen new African states became members of the United Nations, and by the close of 1964 the thirty-five African states constituted about one-third of its membership. Combined with the Asian members they made up a clear majority in the General Assembly. African leaders such as Moise Tshombe of the Congo, Kwame Nkrumah of Ghana, Julius Nyerere of Tanzania, and Jomo Kenyatta of Kenya had become figures widely recognized outside their own borders. In contrast to the time half a century earlier, when European imperialism completely dominated Africa, it is impossible at this later point not to be struck by the fragmentary extent of the possessions left in European hands. Spain controlled the Spanish Sahara, Ifni, and Rio Muni. France held the small area of French Somaliland on the Red Sea. Britain held Bechuanaland, Basutoland, Swaziland, and Southern Rhodesia, this last being a self-governing colony. Unprogressive Portugal seemed to have hung on best of all, maintaining its historic possessions of Portuguese Guinea, Cabinda, Angola, and Mozambique. The Republic of South Africa, separated since 1961 from any ties with Great Britain, still held stubbornly to South-West Africa which it had acquired in 1921 as a mandate. Though some of the newly independent African states chose to retain membership either in the British Commonwealth or the French Community,[1] in general Africa was free to an extent which few men a generation earlier would have thought possible.

The winning of freedom was accompanied by much violence in which the outside world was deeply involved. In North Africa, for example, Algerian independence was finally realized only after a cruel struggle which cost France heavily in manpower and aroused deep bitterness. The negotiations undertaken by President de Gaulle in 1960 to end the miserable six-years' war led to a revolt of French army officers in Algeria and to terrorist activities in France which threatened the life of De Gaulle and challenged the very continuance of the Republic. In the end, after an overwhelmingly favorable plebiscite, Algeria won complete independence in July, 1962.

Another area full of trouble was the former Belgian Congo, where, as previously outlined, independence became a fact in June, 1960. The sequel was a nightmare of confusions with one tribal group or province taking up arms against another, with white mercenaries defending the interests of the big companies whose investments were at stake, and with European men and women senselessly murdered. The efforts of the United Nations to re-establish order were sharply challenged both by the Soviet Union and by France. A United Nations force, authorized in July, 1961, was sent to the Congo. Secretary-General Dag Hammarskjöld of the United Nations, on a mission to negotiate with Moise Tshombe, leader of the secessionist Katanga Province, was killed in September, 1961, when his plane crashed. By 1964 United Nations forces were finally withdrawn after some semblance of order had appeared, and President Joseph Kasavubu decided to appoint Tshombe as premier of what still was a country torn by factional conflicts and the subject of bitter disagreements among the great powers.

Still another problem which made itself felt in the United Nations arose in the Republic of South Africa, which seceded from the British Commonwealth in 1961. The policy of the South African Dutch leaders toward the natives was that of *apartheid,* which meant that only the three million whites had full civil and political rights, while a program of segregation and separate de-

---

1. Senegal, the Malagasy Republic, Chad, the Central African Republic, the Republic of the Congo, and Gabon, though independent, still retained membership in the French Community. Zambia, Malawi, Kenya, Uganda, Tanzania, Ghana, Nigeria, Gambia, and Sierra Leone similarly retained membership in the British Commonwealth.

velopment with a definitely inferior status was applied to the great majority (some fourteen million) comprising the nonwhites. Such a policy, coming just at the time when the rest of Africa was moving toward full political independence, had consequences that could have been expected. Protests and riots in South Africa were echoed at the United Nations where in August, 1963, the Security Council adopted a resolution formally condemning *apartheid*.

The emerging African states quite naturally had much sympathy for the new nationalism of Asia. As early as 1955 those then existing in Africa had been represented at the Bandung Conference, where colonialism was roundly condemned. Other "solidarity conferences" of representatives from the two continents followed. Since the attitude of the new states tended on the whole to be anti-Western it was natural that Communist pressures, whether from Russia or China, should be in evidence, and in many places be welcome.

The Africans sought a greater degree of cohesion among themselves, in addition to a rudimentary Afro-Asian bloc which existed in the General Assembly of the United Nations. The outcome of various regional meetings in Africa was the "Summit Conference on African Unity" meeting in May, 1963, at Addis Ababa, the capital of Ethiopia. Here the Organization of African Unity was set up, with a permanent secretariat and provisions for annual meetings of heads of state and for biennial meetings of foreign ministers. At Cairo in July, 1964, the Organization of African Unity called for a boycott against Portugal and South Africa because of their racial policies. In the following September it sent a conciliation commission headed by Prime Minister Jomo Kenyatta of Kenya to the Congo. Despite such evidences of co-operative action, the prospects of any genuine African unity movement appeared to be still remote.

The Middle East in these years showed parallel trends toward nationalism and modernization. A Turkish army junta in 1960 overthrew the democratically elected Adnan Menderes, charging him with undemocratic policies. The victor, General Cemal Gursel, proclaimed a new constitution in 1961, and by a "democratic" election where he was the sole candidate became president, with Ismet Inonu, a long-time protégé of Kemal Ataturk, as premier.

In Iran, Shah Reza Pahlevi continued the struggle to modernize his backward country. A principal aspect of his six-point reform program of 1963 was the government assistance which made it possible for peasants to become landowners—a move given impetus by the shah's distribution of part of his own vast holdings. Students with high-school education were allowed to teach in the villages instead of doing their army service. Among the further efforts to spur industrial production were three hydroelectric dams built between 1961 and 1963.

A still unsolved question in the Middle East was whether the Arab states

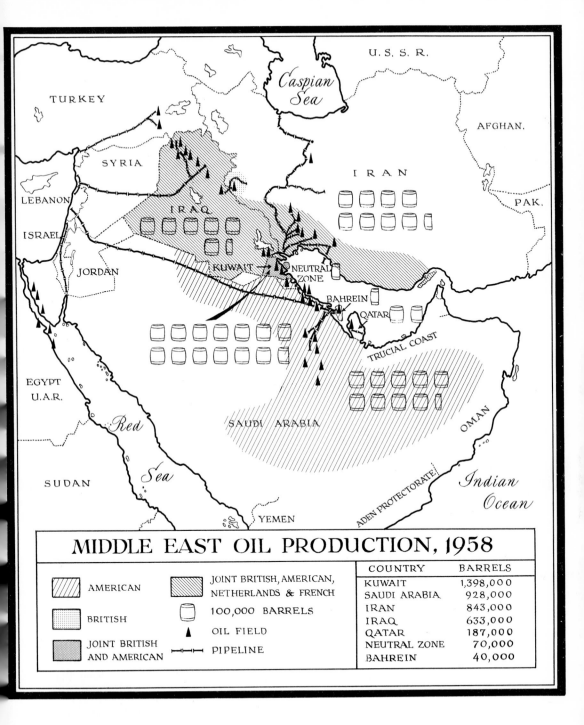

MIDDLE EAST OIL PRODUCTION, 1958

[AMERICAN hatch] **AMERICAN**	[JOINT hatch] **JOINT BRITISH, AMERICAN, NETHERLANDS & FRENCH**	
[BRITISH dots] **BRITISH**	[barrel] **100,000 BARRELS**	
[JOINT dots] **JOINT BRITISH AND AMERICAN**	▲ **OIL FIELD**	
	├─┼─┤ **PIPELINE**	

COUNTRY	BARRELS
KUWAIT	1,398,000
SAUDI ARABIA	928,000
IRAN	843,000
IRAQ	633,000
QATAR	187,000
NEUTRAL ZONE	70,000
BAHREIN	40,000

Production figures are for comparative purposes. Note the strategic importance of the Eastern Mediterranean and the Persian Gulf as the beginning of oil tanker routes. The Middle East has been estimated to contain 60 percent of world oil reserves.

could combine in a genuinely effective Arab League.[2] President Nasser's United Arab Republic, formed in 1958 by the union of Egypt and Syria, with Yemen for a time a federated member, fell apart in 1961. Syria used military action to regain its independence, charging that Nasser had exercised too strong a hand. Leaders of other Arab states, notably King Hussein of Jordan and Premier Abdul Karim of Iraq, were similarly opposed to Nasser's leadership. When, however, in 1963 new governments took over by force in both Iraq and Syria, they spoke for parties which combined some belief in socialist doctrines with a desire for greater Arab unity. Yet the various meetings of the Arab League in 1962, 1963, and 1964 were unimpressive and were marked by considerable confusion of purpose, the one common feature being the continued and general hostility to the state of Israel. Late in 1964 plans were announced for an Arab Common Market that would comprise Egypt, Jordan, Syria, Iraq, and Kuwait, this last state having achieved full independence in 1961.

Israel continued its struggle for modernization amid the menace of this great sea of Arab nationalism. The government estimated the population in 1964 at 2.4 million. By contrast, the total population of the eleven Arab League countries was estimated at 97 million. In 1963 it was reported that 98 percent of Jewish children, boys and girls alike, were in school. Some 90 percent of Arab boys in Israel were being educated, yet apparently, in deference to Arab custom, no girls. The distinction of sexes is significant. As part of the great emphasis on technical progress, Israel opened its first atomic reactor in 1960 and sent a solid-fuel rocket fifty miles into the atmosphere in 1961. Plans to divert water from the River Jordan to irrigate the southern desert area of the Negev occasioned violent threats from Israel's Arab neighbors, Syria and Jordan. Such threats well illustrate the continuing tensions in Israel's foreign relations.

Communism in alliance with nationalism combined to create a situation in the Far East which the European world regarded with great concern. Pakistan, whose membership in SEATO and CENTO as well as mutual defense agreements with the United States were evidences of its western orientation, adopted a new constitution in 1962. This provided for a strong presidential government with an elected legislature in which democratic control remained a promise for the future rather than a present reality. A border agreement with Communist China in 1962 concerning Kashmir, and economic agreements with the Soviet Union suggest some degree of realignment. A Five-Year Plan introduced in 1960 was intended to create self-sufficiency in food, raise the national income by 26 percent, and promote the growth of small industries.

2. To the seven original members of 1945 (Egypt, Syria, Lebanon, Jordan, Iraq, Saudi Arabia, and Yemen) six others (Libya, Morocco, Sudan, Tunisia, Algeria, and Kuwait) were eventually added.

India, where neutralism had been the announced policy, met troubles with Red China which in 1962 led to actual armed conflict along the northeast frontier. This conflict, indeed, caused India to be somewhat less receptive than previously to professions of friendship from the Soviet Union. India's seizure of the ancient Portuguese colony of Goa in 1961 was a small but characteristic example of the new Asian nationalism. The complexity of the situation is evidenced by the fact that a resolution in the United Nations Security Council condemning India's unilateral military action in Goa failed because of a Soviet veto. Prime Minister Nehru, second only to Gandhi as the architect of India's independence, died in May, 1964, and was succeeded by Lal Bahadur Shastri.

Other areas in Asia also had their troubles. Burma experienced a military coup in 1962 as a result of which General Ne Win ruled with dictatorial powers. Indonesia, after long conflict with the Dutch, obtained West Irian (the former Netherlands portion of New Guinea) in consequence of mediation offered by the United States and the United Nations. Dr. Sukarno, named president of Indonesia for life in 1963, showed a marked hostility to the new Federation of Malaysia, which was established as a free member-state of the British Commonwealth in 1963. Sukarno's attitude was strengthened by a promise from the Soviet Union of large supplies of modern arms. Communist pressure was also apparent elsewhere. In the independent state of Laos, for example, both the Soviet Union and North Vietnam provided arms for the Pathet Lao, or native Communist movement, which kept the country in a turmoil. Ceylon, an independent nation within the British Commonwealth, also showed some drifting toward the Soviet sphere. In 1962 the government took over one British and two United States oil refineries, announcing plans to purchase oil from the Soviet Union and the United Arab Republic.

By far the most threatening developments in the Far East were the growing strength of Communist China and the effect of this strength upon its neighbors, especially in Vietnam. By 1960 it was apparent that the Soviet Union and China, though dedicated to the same goals and employing very similar methods to reach them, were diverging sharply in their actual policies. Chinese leaders had no intention of playing a satellite role or of accepting Russian leadership in Asia. When Russia denounced Albanian unco-operativeness at the twenty-second Party Congress in 1961, China protested. At the time of the border conflicts with India in 1962, China accused the Soviet Union of helping India. The most striking fact, however, was the renewed economic growth of Red China, following temporary setbacks. After modifying the rigors of the "people's commune" system in 1961, the government resumed in 1964 the emphasis upon collective farming, by which time vast hydroelectric, irrigation, and canal projects had also been started.

France gave diplomatic recognition to Communist China in 1964, as about a score of other states already had done. The repeated refusal of the United States to grant such recognition, her trade embargo, her leading role in opposing Red China's admission to the United Nations, and her continued military and economic support to Nationalist China all combined to mark the United States as Red China's principal opponent.

This state of affairs became particularly significant because of developments in Southeast Asia, where Red China sought to play a major role. The situation in Indochina after the departure of the French in 1954 has already been sketched. When President Ngo Dinh Diem became head of South Vietnam in 1955, he received economic and military aid from the United States which continued after his re-election in 1961. When he was overthrown in 1963 by a military coup, American aid was continued under the new regime of General Nguyen Khanh. Concern quickly arose in the United States and Europe about the narrowly selfish nature of this government and the allegedly "imperialist" character of the role which the United States had come to play in Southeast Asia. The situation became all the more critical when President Ho Chi-minh of North Vietnam, long identified with the Communist cause in Southeast Asia, intensified his guerilla support to the political organization of South Vietnamese Communists known as the Vietcong. This explosive situation led the United States late in 1964 to employ far more than the military "advisers" and technicians who hitherto had been training and assisting the South Vietnamese forces. The year closed with vigorous United States naval, air, and infantry operations, the landing of marine battalions, and a steady enlargement of hostilities for which "escalation" was now the accepted term.

Only brief mention need be made of Japan, where a spectacular economic growth in the decade since the end of the Allied occupation in 1952 more than doubled the yearly national output. A new security pact with the United States was signed in 1960, under which American forces were to remain in Japan to guarantee her security. Despite leftist protests, some 45,000 United States troops were stationed there. It is striking to observe the extent to which Japan, in sharp contrast to her earlier policies, avoided major involvement in the problems of the Asiatic mainland.

As the United States increased her role as a global power, some developments in the Western Hemisphere took on a world significance that they probably would not have done at an earlier period. In 1961 President Kennedy announced the Alliance for Progress—a continuance and enlargement of earlier undertakings now setting as its goal "the maximum levels of well-being, with equal opportunities for all, in democratic societies adapted to their own needs and desires." Though the scheme was disappointingly slow in developing, and met many obstacles, it continued as an important component of

United States foreign policy. President Lyndon Johnson, for example, announced in May, 1964, that in the preceding four months the United States had extended more than $430 million in assistance to Latin America for schools, agriculture, health, and food programs.

A principal source of trouble for the United States was Cuba, where Fidel Castro, who had overthrown General Fulgencio Batista in 1959, remained firmly established in power. The Communist tendencies of the Castro regime grew increasingly apparent as the Soviet Union and its satellites, for example, bought large quantities of sugar and provided Cuba with large shipments of arms. United States secret support to a small force of Cuban exiles that landed in the Bay of Pigs in April, 1961, proved a disastrous and embarrassing failure. When, however, late in 1962 the United States learned that the Soviet Union was delivering nuclear missiles and other weapons to Cuba, providing technicians, and building rocket bases there, President Kennedy took strong action. By imposing a "quarantine" on all military shipments to Cuba, and by threatening full retaliation on the Soviet Union in the event of a missile attack from Cuba on the United States, he was able to have the bases dismantled and the missiles removed. The episode illustrated how a revolutionary regime in a small state of the Western Hemisphere could fan the flames of rivalry between the United States and the Soviet Union, even as a not dissimilar situation in Southeast Asia could threaten a major conflict between the United States and Red China.

This Epilogue, which can be no more than a brief sketch of current events, may well end with a recapitulation which includes some of the dominant material factors. The United States and some other countries have achieved the highest level of material well-being in the world's history, so as to justify for them the title of "the affluent society." Elsewhere, however, it is possible to talk even of a declining standard of living, for since 1945 in many parts of the world population has increased faster than the food supplies. If it is true that half the world's population is undernourished and that the "average man" on this planet does not have a shirt to his back, then truly "the revolution of rising expectations" has hardly begun. Widespread skepticism has become evident among native peoples concerning the role of the prosperous nations. It was the West, wrote Kwame Nkrumah with some bitterness, "which set the pattern of our hopes." Only with the greatest difficulty, and only in small part, have these hopes yet been realized.

The growing importance of Asia and Africa on the world scene can be illustrated in various ways. China, India, Pakistan, and Indonesia together account for nearly half of the world's population. Their bursting population growth—as yet relatively uncontrolled—renews the melancholy forecasts of

Malthus that population will surely outrun food supply. In India, for example, where the average increase under cultivation is expected to be about 0.2 percent per year, the population increase runs at over 2 percent—in other words, ten times as fast. It seems hardly likely that measures to increase productivity per acre or to control the increase in population can quickly remedy so critical a situation. The industrial growth of Communist China, of India, and to a lesser degree of other non-European countries calls to mind the remarkable economic transformation of Japan at the close of the nineteenth century. Such economic growth inevitably affects the balance of power and in another sense generates the complex social problems with which Europe has long been familiar.

Another striking phenomenon in the world today is what has been called "nuclear proliferation." The United States, the Soviet Union, Great Britain, France, and Communist China have all demonstrated their capacity to achieve nuclear fission and to produce nuclear weapons. It is estimated that altogether some twenty states have the industrial and technological resources for such weaponry. Within the European orbit one would first include West Germany, Italy, Sweden, Spain, Switzerland, Belgium, the Netherlands, and Canada. In the Asiatic world the first possibilities are India, Israel, and Japan. Clearly, the tensions and dangers arising from such likely proliferation could be enormous.

In a volume which with its predecessors has given first attention to the role of Europe, it is fitting in conclusion to ask once more what this European role continues to be. If, unhappily, the principal dangers to world peace seem to come from the explosive forces being generated in Asia and to a lesser degree in Africa, it is still not clear that Asia and Africa are in a position to solve their own problems. The most significant shift in the actual center of political, economic, and military power has been from Europe to the United States, with the Soviet Union firmly established as a rival center in the Old World. But these two do not stand alone. It is inevitable that a larger measure of responsibility must be put into the hands of the Asiatic and African peoples along with those of the New World. As for the Europeans, with their great legacy from the past and their possession of great knowledge and skill, the opportunity remains for them to use these gifts wisely. Perhaps the authors of this book do not depart too far from their historian's role if they observe in conclusion that for all men everywhere danger and opportunity in this age go hand in hand.

BIBLIOGRAPHY

Bibliography

This Bibliography is designed to cover the period from 1914 to the present. Many of the general works listed in the Bibliography to the preceding volume, *Europe: 1815–1914,* are still relevant here, and consequently the reader is referred to them.

General

BIBLIOGRAPHIES

Council on Foreign Relations, *Foreign Affairs Bibliography, 1919–1932* (1933); *1932–1942* (1945); *1942–1952* (1955); *1952–1962* (1964). Extremely thorough.

American Universities Field Staff, *A Select Bibliography: Asia, Africa, Eastern Europe, Latin America* (1960). Carefully annotated.

Grierson, P., *Books on Soviet Russia, 1917–1942* (1943).

The Atlantic Community, An Introductory Bibliography, vol. I (1961).

Scott, F. D., *The Twentieth Century World: A Reading Guide* (11th rev. ed., 1959, paperback).

REFERENCE WORKS

Elliott, F., and Summerskill, M., *A Dictionary of Politics* (4th ed., 1964). Up-to-date, short summaries.

Pryce-Jones, A. (ed.), *The New Outline of Modern Knowledge* (1956).

Keesing's Contemporary Archives. A most useful British weekly loose-leaf service, beginning in 1931, which is fuller than the comparable U. S. *Facts on File,* beginning in 1941.

ATLASES

Boyd, A., *An Atlas of World Affairs* (5th ed., 1964, also paperback).
Horrabin, J. F., *An Atlas of Current Affairs* (7th ed., 1939).
Kingsbury, R. C., and Pounds, N. G. J., *An Atlas of Middle Eastern Affairs* (1963).

COLLECTIONS OF SOURCE MATERIAL

Baltzly, A., and Salomone, A. W. (eds.), *Readings in Twentieth Century European History* (1950).
Wishy, B. (ed.), *The Western World in the Twentieth Century* (1961). Wide-ranging excerpts illustrative of contemporary civilization.
Langsam, W. C. (ed.), *Documents and Readings in the History of Europe Since 1918* (rev. ed., 1951).
Mendel, A. P. (ed.), *Sources in Western Civilization: The Twentieth Century* (1965, paperback).
Royal Institute of International Affairs, *Documents on International Affairs, 1928–*. An important annual publication, now reaching 1958.
Snyder, L. L. (ed.), *Fifty Major Documents of the Twentieth Century* (1958, paperback).

CONTEMPORARY WORLD HISTORIES

Royal Institute of International Affairs, *Survey of International Affairs*. These annual volumes, beginning with 1920, are indispensable.
Chambers, F. P., Harris, C. P., and Bayley, C. C., *This Age of Conflict: The Western World, 1914 to the Present* (3rd ed., 1962).
Barraclough, G., *An Introduction to Contemporary History* (1964). Eight essays designed to show what are "the distinguishing marks of the contemporary era."
Thomson, D., *World History from 1914 to 1961* (2nd ed., 1961, paperback). A conspectus of world changes.
Gatzke, H. W., *The Present in Perspective* (3rd ed., 1965, paperback). Latest edition covers very recent events.
Jackson, J. H., *The Post-War Decade: A Short History of the World, 1945–1955* (1955, paperback).
Crouzet, M., *L'époque contemporaine: à la recherche d'une civilisation nouvelle* (1957). Vol. VII of *Histoire générale des civilisations*.
Propyläen Weltgeschichte, vols. IX, X (1960, 1961). Superbly illustrated, with text by international specialists.

WORKS DEALING WITH SPECIAL ASPECTS OF EUROPEAN HISTORY

Geographical

Cole, J. P., *Geography of World Affairs* (1959). Highly informative.

Economic

Alpert, P., *Twentieth Century Economic History of Europe* (1951).
Ashworth, W., *A Short History of the International Economy, 1850–1950* (1952).
Svennilson, I., *Growth and Stagnation in the European Economy* (1954).

Diplomatic

Gathorne-Hardy, G. M., *A Short History of International Affairs, 1920–1939* (4th ed., 1950). A very careful, detailed survey.
Carr, E. H., *International Relations Between Two World Wars, 1919–1939* (rev. ed., 1948).
Craig, G. A., and Gilbert, F. (eds.), *The Diplomats, 1919–1939* (1953, also paperback). Some penetrating studies.
Baumont, M., *La faillite de la paix, 1918–1939* (2 vols., rev. ed., 1961). In the *Peuples et civilisations* series.

Renouvin, P., *Les crises du XXe siècle* (2 vols., 1957, 1958). By a distinguished authority.

Örvik, N., *The Decline of Neutrality, 1914–1941* (Engl. tr., 1954). The standpoint of a small power.

Military and Naval

Howard, M. (ed.), *Soldiers and Governments* (1957).

Huntington, S. P. (ed.), *Changing Patterns of Military Politics* (1962).

Kissinger, H. A., *Nuclear Weapons and Foreign Policy* (1957, also paperback). Very influential.

Liddell Hart, B. H., *Deterrent or Defense: A Fresh Look at the West's Military Position* (1960). By the doyen of British military writers.

Scientific and Technological

Dingle, H. (ed.), *Century of Science, 1851–1951* (1951).

Dunsheath, P. (ed.), *Century of Invention, 1851–1951* (1951).

Gartmann, H., *Science As History* (Engl. tr., 1960). By a German engineer with special interests in space exploration.

Sociological, Intellectual, and Legal

Beloff, M., *Europe and the Europeans* (1957).

Oakeshott, M., *The Social and Political Doctrines of Contemporary Europe* (1939). A valuable collection of readings.

Hayes, C. J. H., *Nationalism: A Religion* (1960). The summing up of a lifetime's study.

Shafer, B. C., *Nationalism: Myth and Reality* (1955).

Brogan, D. W., *The Price of Revolution* (1951).

Arendt, H., *The Human Condition* (1958, also paperback).

Goodspeed, E. S., *The Nature and Functions of International Organizations* (1959).

Carr, E. H., *The Twenty Years Crisis: An Introduction to the Study of International Relations* (rev. ed., 1946, also paperback).

Brinton, C., *The Temper of Western Europe* (1953). Reflective and generally optimistic.

By Chapters

CHAPTER 1   The First World War

MILITARY HISTORY

Cruttwell, C. R. M. F., *A History of the Great War, 1914–1918* (2nd ed., 1936). A classic narrative by a distinguished British historian who had served as an infantry officer.
Edmonds, J. E., *A Short History of World War I* (1951). Based on a unique knowledge of the British and other official histories of the war on land.
Falls, C., *The First World War* (1960, also paperback). A well-balanced, up-to-date survey.
Churchill, W. S., *The World Crisis, 1911–1918* (abridged and revised ed., 1931). "A contribution to history strung upon a fairly strong thread of personal reminiscence."
Baldwin, Hanson W., *World War I: An Outline History* (1962, also paperback). By the military analyst of *The New York Times*.
Snyder, L. L., *Historic Documents of World War I* (1958, paperback).
Liddell Hart, B. H., *The Tanks* (2 vols., 1959). An exhaustive study.

POLITICAL ASPECTS

Chambers, F. P., *The War Behind the War: A History of the Political and Civilian Fronts* (1939).
May, E. R., *The World War and American Isolationism, 1914–1917* (1958). Stresses the influence of German submarine policy.
Lutz, R. H., *The Causes of the German Collapse in 1918* (1934). Documents.
Zeman, Z. A. B., *The Break-Up of the Hapsburg Empire, 1914–1918* (1961).
Maurice, F., *The Armistices of 1918* (1943).
Hankey, Maurice, Lord, *The Supreme Command 1914–1918* (2 vols., 1961).
Rudin, H., *Armistice, 1918* (1944).

CHAPTER 2   The Russian Revolution, 1917–1921

GENERAL HISTORIES

Chamberlin, W. H., *The Russian Revolution, 1917–1921* (2 vols., 1935). A detailed study based on accessible Russian records, by a correspondent of the *Christian Science Monitor* stationed in Russia from 1922 onwards.
Hill, C., *Lenin and the Russian Revolution* (1947). A sympathetic introduction.
Carr, E. H., *The Bolshevik Revolution, 1917–1923* (3 vols., 1950, 1951, 1953). An advanced text of great authority.
Moorehead, A., *The Russian Revolution* (1958, also paperback). Readable, though overstressing the German role in bringing Lenin into power.
Treadgold, D. W., *Twentieth Century Russia* (1959). Places the revolution in its chronological setting.
Dobb, M., *Soviet Economic Development Since 1917* (1948).

EYEWITNESS ACCOUNTS OF THE REVOLUTION

Bunyan, J., and Fisher, H. H. (eds.), *The Bolshevik Revolution, 1917–1918. Documents and Materials* (1934).
Trotsky, L., *The History of the Russian Revolution* (Engl. tr., 3 vols., 1932–1933, also paperback, abridged). Partly a polemic against Stalin.

Sukhanov, N. N., *The Russian Revolution, 1917: A Personal Record* (abridged ed., 1953).

Reed, J., *Ten Days that Shook the World* (1926, also paperback). An enthusiastic account by a young American journalist in Petrograd.

Lockhart, R. H. B., *Memoirs of a British Agent* (1932). Acting consul-general and head of a special mission to the Soviet government.

Kerensky, A., *Russia and History's Turning Point* (1965). A re-examination of events by Kerensky in his eighty-fourth year.

FOREIGN POLICY AND THE CIVIL WAR

Wheeler-Bennett, J. W., *Brest-Litovsk: The Forgotten Peace* (1938, also paperback).

Footman, D., *Civil War in Russia* (1961). A clear, short account by an expert.

Kennan, G. F., *Russia and the West under Lenin and Stalin* (1961, also paperback). Masterly lectures.

——, *Soviet-American Relations, 1917–1920*, vols. 1 and 2 (1956, 1958). A fascinating but very detailed study.

Ullman, R. H., *Anglo-Soviet Relations, 1917–1921*, vol. 1 (1961). Based on hitherto unpublished British official sources.

Bunyan, J. (ed.), *Intervention, Civil War, and Communism in Russia, April–December, 1918. Documents and Materials* (1936).

NOTABLE BIOGRAPHIES

Shub, D., *Lenin: A Biography* (1948, also paperback).

Deutscher, I., *The Prophet Armed* (1954, also paperback). Trotsky in power. The first of three volumes.

——, *Stalin: A Political Biography* (1949, also paperback).

CHAPTER 3   The Resettlement of Continental Europe

EVENTS AND EVALUATION OF THE PEACEMAKING

Marston, F. S., *The Peace Conference of 1919: Organization and Procedure* (1945).

Nicolson, H., *Peacemaking, 1919* (1939, also paperback). A vivid account by a minor participant.

Tillman, S. P., *Anglo-American Relations at the Paris Peace Conference of 1919* (1961).

Keynes, J. M., *The Economic Consequences of the Peace* (1920). A highly effective criticism by a British Treasury representative at the Conference.

Birdsall, P., *Versailles Twenty Years After* (1941).

McCallum, R. B., *Public Opinion and the Last Peace* (1944).

Carnegie Endowment for International Peace, *The Treaties of Peace, 1919–1923* (2 vols., 1924). Texts of the treaties.

THE LEAGUE OF NATIONS AND PEACE PRESERVATION

Walters, F. P., *A History of the League of Nations* (2 vols., 1952). By a League official of long experience.

Zimmern, A. E., *The League of Nations and the Rule of Law* (1936). A penetrating study of the origins of the League and of its practical achievements and limitations.

Rappard, W. E., *The Quest for Peace Since the World War* (1940). A Swiss study.

Ferrell, R. H., *Peace in Their Time: The Origins of the Kellogg-Briand Pact* (1952).

Myers, D. P., *World Disarmament* (1932). Concise.

Shotwell, J. T., and Slavin, M., *Lessons on Security and Disarmament: From the History of the League of Nations* (1949). A critical appraisal.

Hall, H. D., *Mandates, Dependencies and Trusteeships* (1948).

THE GREAT POWERS OF WESTERN EUROPE

Wolfers, A., *Britain and France Between Two Wars* (1940).

Knapton, E. J., *France Since Versailles* (1952, paperback).

Wright, G., *France in Modern Times, 1760 to the Present* (1960).

Eyck, E., *A History of the Weimar Republic* (Engl. tr., 2 vols., 1962, 1963). A classic and reasonably dispassionate account.

Halperin, S. W., *Germany Tried Democracy: A Political History of the Reich, 1918–1933* (1946, also paperback).

Bretton, H. L., *Stresemann and the Revision of Versailles* (1953).

Turner, H. A., *Stresemann and the Politics of the Weimar Republic* (1963).

Craig, G. A., *From Bismarck to Adenauer: Aspects of German Statecraft* (1958, also paperback). Interpretative biographical sketches.

Wheeler-Bennett, J. W., *Wooden Titan, Hindenburg in Twenty Years of German History, 1914–1934* (1936).

Sprigge, C. J., *The Development of Modern Italy* (1944).

Macartney, H. H., and Cremona, P., *Italy's Foreign and Colonial Policy, 1914–1937* (1938).

Albrecht-Carrié, R., *Italy from Napoleon to Mussolini* (1950, also paperback).

THE SMALLER POWERS OF CENTRAL AND EASTERN EUROPE

Seton-Watson, H., *Eastern Europe Between the Wars, 1918–1941* (2nd ed., 1946). Reliable.

Stavrianos, L. S., *The Balkans Since 1453* (1958).

Wolf, R. L., *The Balkans in Our Time* (1956).

Macartney, C. A., and Palmer, A. W., *Independent Eastern Europe: A History* (1962). Covers the interwar period very usefully for countries lying between the U.S.S.R. and Germany and Italy.

Schlesinger, R., *Federalism in Central and Eastern Europe* (1945).

Seton-Watson, R. W., *Twenty-Five Years of Czechoslovakia* (1945). By the English scholar and publicist who helped to found it.

Kerner, R. J. (ed.), *Czechoslovakia* (1940).

Gulick, C. A., *Austria from Habsburg to Hitler* (2 vols., 1948). A detailed study with socialist sympathies.

Macartney, C. A., *A History of Hungary, 1920–1944* (2 vols., 1956, 1957).

Mitrany, D., *The Land and the Peasant in Rumania* (1930). An important economic study.

Kerner, R. J. (ed.), *Yugoslavia* (1949).

Markham, R. H., *Meet Bulgaria* (1931).

Royal Institute of International Affairs, *South-Eastern Europe: A Political and Economic Survey* (1939). Compact and remarkably complete.

———, *The Balkan States* (1936). Largely economic.

———, *The Baltic States* (1938). A dependable factual examination.

CHAPTER 4   Conservative Britain

POLITICAL HISTORY

Mowat, C. L., *Britain Between the Wars, 1918–1940* (1955). Comprehensive, interesting, and accurate.

Somervell, D. C., *British Politics Since 1900* (1950). The achievements of the political parties during the half-century.

Cole, G. D. H., *A History of the Labour Party from 1914* (1948).

Havighurst, A. F., *Twentieth-century Britain* (1962). An up-to-date American text.

ECONOMIC AND SOCIAL HISTORY

Youngson, A. J., *The British Economy, 1920–1957* (1960).
Pollard, S., *The Development of the British Economy, 1914–1950* (1962).
Graves, R., and Hodge, A., *The Long Week End: A Social History of Great Britain* (1940, also paperback). Despite its title, a study in depth.
Symons, J., *The General Strike* (1957). A well-balanced account.
Spinks, G. S., *Religion in Britain Since 1900* (1952).

IMPERIAL RELATIONSHIPS

Barker, E., *The Ideas and Ideals of the British Empire* (1941). By an English political theorist of international reputation.
Wheare, K. C., *The Statute of Westminster and Dominion Status* (5th ed., 1953). The legal structure of the Commonwealth authoritatively examined.
Hancock, W. K., *Survey of British Commonwealth Affairs* (2 vols., 3 parts, 1937–1941). A comprehensive work by an Australian, interestingly written.
Mansergh, N., *The Irish Free State: Its Government and Politics* (1934).

FOREIGN POLICY

Seton-Watson, R. W., *Britain and the Dictators: A Survey of Post-War British Policy* (1938). Critical.
Foot, M. R. D., *British Foreign Policy Since 1898* (1956).
Monroe, E., *Britain's Moment in the Middle East, 1914–1956* (1963).
Medlicott, W. N., *British Foreign Policy Since Versailles, 1919–1939* (1940).

CHAPTER 5   Europe and the World East of Suez

GENERAL HISTORIES OF ASIA

Thomson, I., *The Rise of Modern Asia* (1957). A general survey of the transformation in the twentieth century.
Panikkar, K. M., *Asia and Western Dominance* (abridged ed., 1959). By a prominent Indian diplomat and historian.
Edwardes, M., *Asia in the European Age, 1498–1955* (1962).

MIDDLE EAST

Lenczowski, G., *The Middle East in World Affairs* (2nd ed., 1956).
Kirk, G. E., *A Short History of the Middle East* (1949, also paperback).
Fisher, S. N., *The Middle East: A History* (1959).
Badeau, J. S., *The Lands Between* (1958, paperback).
Lewis, B., *The Emergence of Modern Turkey* (1961). By a leading historian of the Middle East.
Lewis, G. L., *Turkey* (2nd rev. ed., 1960). Primarily deals with the Republic.
Kinross, Lord, *Ataturk: A Biography of Mustafa Kemal, Father of Modern Turkey* (1965).
Atiyah, E., *The Arabs* (1955, paperback).
Lipsky, G. A., and others, *Saudi Arabia: Its People, Its Society, Its Culture* (1959).
Patai, R., *The Kingdom of Jordan* (1958).
Khadduri, M., *Independent Iraq, 1932–1958* (2nd ed., 1960).
Hitti, P., *Lebanon in History* (1957).
———, *Syria: A Short History* (1959, also paperback).

Bernstein, M. H., *The Politics of Israel* (1957). A survey of the first ten years of independence.
Royal Institute of International Affairs, *Great Britain and Palestine, 1915–1945* (1946).
Issawi, C., *Egypt: An Economic and Social Analysis* (1947).

INDIA

Griffiths, P., *The British Impact on India* (1952).
Wallbank, T. W., *India: A Survey of the Heritage and Growth of Indian Nationalism* (1948).
Brown, W. N., *The United States and India and Pakistan* (rev. ed., 1963).

SOUTHEAST ASIA

Hall, D. G. E., *A History of Southeast Asia* (1955). Detailed and up to date.
Harrison, B., *Southeast Asia: A Short History* (1954).
Allen, G. C., and Donnithorne, A. G., *Western Enterprise in Indonesia and Malaya* (1957).
    Examines the pattern of European investment.
Palmier, L. H., *Indonesia and the Dutch* (1962). An able analysis.

FAR EAST

Michael, F. H., and Taylor, G. E., *The Far East in the Modern World* (1956).
Hudson, G. F., *The Far East in World Politics* (1937). A scholarly study.
Lattimore, O., *The Making of Modern China* (1944).
Snow, E., *Red Star Over China* (1938, also paperback). Not unprejudiced.
Latourette, K. S., *The Chinese: Their History and Culture* (2 vols., 1934). Authoritative.
Tawney, R. H., *Land and Labour in China* (1932). A work of lasting value by a leading economic historian.
Cressey, G. B., *Land of the 500 Million: A Geography of China* (1955). By a distinguished authority.
Jones, F. C., *Manchuria Since 1931* (1949).
Borton, H., *Japan's Modern Century* (1955).
Storry, R., *A History of Modern Japan* (1960, also paperback). A balanced survey.
Reischauer, E. O., *The United States and Japan* (rev. ed., 1957, also paperback).

CHAPTER 6   Europe and the World Economy

Lewis, W. A., *Economic Survey, 1919–1939* (1949).
Day, J. P., *Introduction to World Economic History Since the Great War* (1939).
Yates, P. L., and Warriner, D., *Food and Farming in Post-War Europe* (1943).
Sturmthal, A. F., *The Tragedy of European Labour, 1918–1939* (1943).
Carr-Saunders, A. M., *World Population: Past Growth and Present Trends* (1936).

THE AFTERMATH OF WAR

Bowley, A. L., *Some Economic Consequences of the Great War* (1930).
Wheeler-Bennett, J. W., *The Wreck of Reparations* (1933).
Moulton, H. G., and Pasvolsky, L., *War Debts and World Prosperity* (1932).

THE GREAT DEPRESSION AND ITS CONSEQUENCES

Hodson, H. V., *Slump and Recovery, 1929–1937: A Survey of World Economic Affairs* (1938).
Galbraith, J. K., *The Great Crash, 1929* (1955). The starting point in America.
Robbins, L. C., *The Great Depression* (1934). By a leading English economist.
Condliffe, J. B., *The Reconstruction of World Trade* (1940). A clear account of the collapse of world trade and of the attempts to revive it up to the outbreak of war.

Gordon, M. S., *Barriers to World Trade: A Study of Recent Commercial Policy* (1941).
Ropke, W., *International Economic Disintegration* (1942).
League of Nations, *The Network of World Trade* (1942).

CHAPTER 7   The Rise of the Dictatorships

For general histories of countries from 1919 onwards, see pp. 444–446.

TOTALITARIANISM IN GENERAL

Arendt, H., *The Origins of Totalitarianism* (2nd ed., 1958, also paperback).
Cobban, A., *Dictatorship: Its History and Theory* (1939).
Friedrich, C. J. (ed.), *Totalitarianism* (1954, also paperback).

ITALY

Kirkpatrick, I., *Mussolini: Study of a Demagogue* (1964). A full account by a British diplomat of wide experience.
Chabod, F., *A History of Italian Fascism* (Engl. tr., 1963). Traces the movement from its earliest years.
Schneider, H. W., *The Fascist Government of Italy* (1936). An analysis.
Borgese, G. H., *Goliath: The March of Fascism* (1937). Polemical.
Binchy, D. A., *Church and State in Fascist Italy* (1941).

GERMANY

Hitler, A., *Mein Kampf* (complete Engl. tr., 1939, also paperback).
Bullock, A., *Hitler: A Study in Tyranny* (rev. ed., 1962, also paperback). A masterpiece.
Waite, R., *Vanguard of Nazism: The Free Corps Movement* (1952). A study in origins.
Gatzke, H., *Stresemann and the Rearmament of Germany* (1954).
Wheeler-Bennett, J. W., *The Nemesis of Power: The German Army in Politics, 1918–1945* (1953). Hitler's all-important relations with the army from 1920 to 1944.
Heiden, K., *A History of National Socialism* (1935). Based on first-hand knowledge.
Roberts, S. H., *The House That Hitler Built* (1937). Clear and readable.
Shirer, W. L., *The Rise and Fall of the Third Reich* (1960, also paperback). A detailed popular account which has received considerable scholarly criticism.
Butler, R. D'O., *The Roots of National Socialism* (1941). A study in depth.
Neumann, F. L., *Behemoth: The Structure and Practice of National Socialism* (1942).

OTHER DICTATORSHIPS

See also the references on pp. 448–450.

Brenan, G., *The Spanish Labyrinth* (3rd ed., 1960, also paperback).
Derrick, M., *The Portugal of Salazar* (1939).
Fryer, P., and Pinheiro, P. M., *Oldest Ally: A Portrait of Salazar's Portugal* (1961). A British critical evaluation.
Machray, R., *The Poland of Pilsudski* (1936).
MacDonald, M., *The Republic of Austria, 1918–1934: A Study in the Failure of Democratic Government* (1946).
Bullock, M., *Austria, 1918–1938: A Study in Failure* (1939).
Graham, S., *Alexander of Yugoslavia* (1939).
Webster, D. E., *The Turkey of Ataturk* (1939).

CHAPTER 8   The Development of the U.S.S.R.

GENERAL WORKS

In addition to the references on pp. 442–443:

Carr, E. H., *A History of Soviet Russia.* Vols. IV–VI (1954, 1958, 1960) cover the period 1923–1926. These follow the volumes, *The Bolshevik Revolution, 1917–1923.*
Deutscher, I., *The Prophet Unarmed* [1921–1929] (1959, also paperback); *The Prophet Outcast* [1929–1940] (1963, also paperback). These enable the later years of Trotsky's life to be studied side by side with the same author's account of Stalin.
Dmytryshyn, B., *USSR: A Concise History* (1965, also paperback).
Reshetar, J. S., *A Concise History of the Communist Party of the Soviet Union* (1960, also paperback).
White, D. F., *The Red Army* (1944).
Kohn, H., *Nationalism in the Soviet Union* (1933).
Florinsky, M. T., *Toward an Understanding of the U.S.S.R.* (rev. ed., 1951).

ECONOMIC

Baykov, A., *The Development of the Soviet Economic System* (1946).
Jasny, N., *The Socialized Agriculture of the U.S.S.R.* (1949).
Hubbard, L. E., *Soviet Labor and Industry* (1942).
Hindus, M. G., *Humanity Uprooted* (rev. ed., 1930). The effect of revolution on the life of the individual.
Chamberlin, W. H., *Russia's Iron Age* (1935).

EXTERNAL RELATIONS

Beloff, M., *The Foreign Policy of Soviet Russia, 1929–1941* (2 vols., 1947, 1949).
Borkenau, F., *World Communism* (1962, also paperback).
Carr, E. H., *German-Soviet Relations Between the Two World Wars, 1919–1939* (1951).
Dallin, D. J., *Soviet Russia and the Far East* (1948).
———, *The Rise of Russia in Asia* (1949).
Mosely, P. E., *The Kremlin and World Politics* (1960, paperback). By a leading American authority.

CHAPTER 9   Democracy on the Defensive

RIVAL DIPLOMACIES

Wiskemann, E., *The Rome-Berlin Axis* (1949). A history of the relations between Hitler and Mussolini.
Furnia, A. H., *The Diplomacy of Appeasement: Anglo-French Relations and the Prelude to World War II, 1931–1938* (1960).
Jordan, W. M., *Great Britain, France and the German Problem, 1918–1939* (1943).
Cameron, E. R., *Prologue to Appeasement: A Study of French Foreign Policy* (1942).
Rowse, A. L., *Appeasement: A Study in Political Decline, 1933–1939* (1961). A study of British leaders, very critical.
Langer, W. L., and Gleason, S. E., *The Challenge to Isolation, 1937–1940* (1952, also paperback). A study of American foreign policy.
Gantenbein, J. W. (ed.), *Documentary Background of World War II, 1931–1941* (1948). Excellent.

THE ETHIOPIAN AND SPANISH AFFAIRS

Monroe, E., *The Mediterranean in Politics* (1938).

Jones, A. H. M., and Monroe, E., *A History of Ethiopia* (new ed., 1955). The Italian invasion seen in perspective.

Thomas, H., *The Spanish Civil War* (1961, also paperback). A definitive history.

Van der Esch, P., *Prelude to War: The International Repercussions of the Spanish Civil War* (1951). A comprehensive Dutch account.

THE GERMAN ANNEXATION OF AUSTRIA AND CZECHOSLOVAKIA

Gedye, G. E. R., *Betrayal in Central Europe* (1939). An eyewitness account of the fall of both countries, written with passion and insight.

Gehl, J., *Austria, Germany, and the Anschluss* (1963). Detailed and useful.

Wheeler-Bennett, J. W., *Munich: Prologue to Tragedy* (1948, also paperback). A masterly study.

Eubank, K., *Munich* (1963). Argues that Hitler settled at Munich for less than he really wanted.

Wiskemann, E., *Czechs and Germans: A Study of the Struggle in the Historic Provinces of Bohemia and Moravia* (1938).

Namier, L. B., *Diplomatic Prelude, 1938–39* (1948).

———, *Europe in Decay: A Study in Disintegration, 1936–40* (1950). Both books are based on very wide knowledge, but some of the conclusions have been challenged by later writers.

Taylor, A. J. P., *Origins of the Second World War* (1962). A learned book which has aroused a storm of controversy by insisting that the diplomacy of these years was "without heroes, and perhaps even without villains."

THE OUTBREAK OF WAR

Hofer, W., *War Premeditated, 1939* (1955). An excellent Swiss study of the immediate causes of the war.

Toynbee, A., and Ashton-Gwatkin, F. T. (eds.), *The World in March 1939* (1952). An examination of the powers and their comparative strength on the eve of the war.

CHAPTER 10   The Second World War

GENERAL HISTORIES

Snyder, L., *The War, 1939–1945: A Concise History* (1960). Comprehensive.

Churchill, W. S., *The Second World War* (6 vols., 1948–1953). A mine of information and opinion.

Wilmot, C., *The Struggle for Europe* (1951). The pattern of Allied planning.

Werth, A., *Russia At War, 1941–1945* (1964). Based on Russian sources, including official history.

Hall, W. P., *Iron out of Calvary: An Interpretative History of the Second World War* (1946).

Fuller, F. J. C., *The Second World War: A Strategical and Tactical History* (1949). Strongly maintained personal views.

Falls, C., *The Second World War* (3rd ed., 1950). A safe outline.

Langsam, W. C., *Historic Documents of World War II* (1958, paperback).

SPECIAL MILITARY ASPECTS

Goutard, A., *The Fall of France* (1959).

Office of the Chief of Military History, *Command Decisions* (1959).

Puleston, W. D., *The Influence of Sea Power in World War II* (1947).

Eisenhower, D. D., *Crusade in Europe* (1948).

Ryan, C., *The Longest Day* (1959). A vivid account of the Normandy landing.

Allen, W. E. D., and Muratoff, P., *The Russian Campaigns of 1941–1943* (1944); *The Russian Campaigns of 1944–1945* (1946).

Jones, F. C., Borton, H., and Pearn, B. R., *The Far East, 1942–1946* (1955).

POLITICS OF THE GRAND ALLIANCE

Langer, W. L., and Gleason, F. E., *The Undeclared War, 1940–1941* (1953).

Feis, H., *The Road to Pearl Harbor: The Coming of the War Between the United States and Japan* (1950).

McNeill, W. H., *America, Britain and Russia: Their Co-operation and Conflict, 1941–1946* (1953).

Feis, H., *Churchill, Roosevelt, Stalin: The War They Waged and the Peace They Sought* (1957).

———, *Between War and Peace: The Potsdam Conference* (1960).

———, *Japan Subdued: The Atomic Bomb and the End of the War in the Pacific* (1961). Three very important volumes.

THE ENEMY

Hinsley, F. H., *Hitler's Strategy* (1951). Based on Hitler's naval conferences.

Wheatley, R., *Operation Sea Lion* (1958). Plans for the invasion of England.

Freidin, S., and Richardson, W. (eds.), *The Fatal Decisions* (1956). Essays by German generals.

Liddell Hart, B. H., *The Other Side of the Hill* (new ed., 1951). Statements of German officers in captivity.

Toynbee, A. and V. M. (eds.), *Hitler's Europe* (1954). A full analysis of the New Order and of German controls in Vichy France, Italy, and occupied territories.

Deakin, F. W., *The Brutal Friendship* (1962). Hitler's relations with Mussolini between 1942 and 1945.

Trevor-Roper, H. T., *The Last Days of Hitler* (1947). Investigations made in Berlin and elsewhere in 1945.

Reitlinger, G., *The Final Solution: The Attempt to Exterminate the Jews of Europe, 1939–1945* (1953).

Aron, R., *The Vichy Regime 1940–1944* (1958).

CHAPTER 11   The Transformation of Western Europe, 1945–1950

For works on interstate relations, see pp. 439–441; for works on the disintegration of colonial empires, see pp. 452–454.

GENERAL

United States Department of State, *Making the Peace Treaties, 1941–1947* (1947).

Toynbee, A. and V. M. (eds.), *The Realignment of Europe* (1955).

Holborn, H., *The Political Collapse of Europe* (1950). Basically pessimistic.

White, T. H., *Fire in the Ashes: Europe in Mid-Century* (1953). Optimistic.

Harris, S. E., *The European Recovery Program* (1948). By a distinguished economist.

Freymond, J., *Western Europe Since the War: A Short Political History* (1964, also paperback). A thoughtful and moderately optimistic view by a Swiss scholar.

GERMANY

Freund, G., *Germany Between Two World Wars* (1961).
Balfour, M., and Mair, J., *Four-Power Control in Germany and Austria, 1945–1946* (1956). A thorough study based on participation.
Meinecke, F., *The German Catastrophe* (Engl. tr., 1949). Reflections of a leading German historian.
Clay, L. D., *Decision in Germany* (1950). The experience of a top-level American official.
Davison, W. P., *The Berlin Blockade* (1958). An excellent analysis of the 1948 crisis.
Golay, J. F., *The Founding of the Federal Republic of Germany* (1958). By an American official.
Merkl, P. H., *The Origin of the West German Republic* (1963, also paperback).
Grosser, A., *The Federal Republic of Germany* (1964, paperback).
Weymar, P., *Adenauer* (1957). A competent, authorized biography, translated from the German.
Stolper, W. F., *The Structure of the East German Economy* (1960). An adverse report.

FRANCE

Wright, G., *The Reshaping of French Democracy* (1948).
Luethy, H., *France Against Herself* (Engl. tr., 1955, also paperback). A penetrating Swiss study.
Pickles, D., *The Fourth French Republic* (1956).
———, *The Fifth French Republic* (rev. ed., 1962, also paperback).
Aron, Robert, *France Reborn* (1964). The liberation.
Aron, Raymond, *France: Steadfast and Changing* (1960).

ITALY

Grindrod, M., *The Rebuilding of Italy: Politics and Economics, 1945–1955* (1955). A thorough examination.
Einaudi, E., and Goguel, F., *Christian Democracy in Italy and France* (1952).
Hughes, H. S., *The United States and Italy* (1953).
Kogan, N., *Italy and the Allies* (1956). From the overthrow of Mussolini to 1956.
———, *The Government of Italy* (1962, also paperback).

BRITAIN

Watkins, E., *The Cautious Revolution* (1951).
Morrison, H., *The Peaceful Revolution* (1949). A collection of addresses by a leading socialist minister.
Clarke, C. F. O., *Britain Today* (1951). Exposition for American audiences.
Stewart, M., *The British Approach to Politics* (4th ed., 1958). By a future foreign secretary.
Middleton, D., *The British* (1957). Appraisal by an experienced American journalist.
Spearman, D., *Democracy in England* (1957, also paperback).
Bruce, M., *The Coming of the Welfare State* (1961).
Mansergh, N., *Survey of British Commonwealth Affairs, 1939–1952* (1958).
Woodhouse, C. M., *British Foreign Policy Since the Second World War* (1962). By the former director of the Royal Institute of International Affairs.

OTHER COUNTRIES

Matthews, H., *The Yoke and the Arrow: A Report on Spain* (rev. ed., 1961). By a veteran *New York Times* correspondent.
Hiscocks. R., *The Rebirth of Austria* (1953).
Helmreich, E. C. (ed.), *Hungary* (1957). A useful handbook.

CHAPTER 12   The U.S.S.R. and Satellite Powers

THE SOVIET UNION

In addition to the references on p. 448:

Schwartz, H., *Russia's Soviet Economy* (1950). The postwar situation.
Calvocoressi, P., *Survey of International Affairs, 1953* (1956). Section I on the death of Stalin.
Crankshaw, E., *Khrushchev's Russia* (1959, also paperback). "Sketches the sort of society which seems to be emerging under Stalin's successors."
Mellor, R. E. H., *Geography of the U.S.S.R.* (1964). Based on Russian sources and recent travel.
Tomasic, D., *The Impact of Russian Culture on Soviet Communism* (1953).
Seton-Watson, H., *The New Imperialism* (1962). A concise account of Soviet imperialism.
Shulman, M. D., *Stalin's Foreign Policy Reappraised* (1963, also paperback). Deals largely with 1949–1953.
Kulski, W. W., *The Soviet Regime—Communism in Practice* (1963, paperback).
Kellen, K., *Khrushchev: A Political Portrait* (1961).
Barghoorn, F. C., *The Soviet Cultural Offensive* (1960). A study of cultural diplomacy.

SATELLITES

Seton-Watson, H., *East European Revolution* (3rd ed., 1956, paperback). The most satisfactory account.
Halasz, N., *In the Shadow of Russia: Eastern Europe in the Postwar World* (1959).
Wolff, R. L., *The Balkans in Our Time* (1956).
Korbel, J., *The Communist Subversion of Czechoslovakia* (1959). Goes to 1948.
Táborsky, E., *Communism in Czechoslovakia, 1948–1960* (1961).
Roberts, H. L., *Rumania: Political Problems of an Agrarian State* (1951).
Spulber, N., *The Economics of Communist Eastern Europe* (1957).
Staar, R. F., *Poland, 1944–1962: The Sovietization of a Captured People* (1962).
Brzezinski, N., *The Soviet Bloc: Unity and Conflict* (rev. ed., 1961, also paperback). Events of 1956.
Betts, R. R. (ed.), *Central and South-Eastern Europe* (1950). An accurate and comprehensive survey which is still of value.
Hungary Today (1962). By the editors of *Survey*.
Skendis, S., *Albania* (1961). A handbook.

YUGOSLAVIA

Armstrong, H. F., *Tito and Goliath* (1951). The avoidance of satellite status.
Auty, P., *Building a New Yugoslavia* (1954). A Fabian Society study.
Maclean, F., *The Heretic: The Life and Times of Josef Broz-Tito* (1957). Based on personal contact. Also paperback as *The Man Who Defied Hitler and Stalin.*
Hoffman, G. W., and Neal, F. W., *Yugoslavia and the New Communism* (1962). An appraisal of Titoism in practice.

CHAPTER 13   The New Asia and the New Africa

For general histories of Asiatic countries, see pp. 445–446.

GENERAL

Easton, S. C., *The Twilight of European Colonialism: A Political Analysis* (1960). Substantial.
Emerson, R., *From Empire to Nation: The Rise to Self-Assertion of Asian and African Peoples* (1960).

Toynbee, A., *The World and the West* (1953). Important radio series.
Benham, F., *The Colombo Plan and Other Essays* (1956).
Hodson, H. V., *Twentieth Century Empire* (1948).
Fairbank, J. K., Reischauer, E. O., and Craig, A.M., *East Asia: The Modern Transformation* (1965).

INDIA AND PAKISTAN

Griffiths, P., *Modern India* (3rd ed., 1962).
Gandhi, M. K., *An Autobiography* (1949).
Wallbank, T. W., *India in the New Era* (1951).
Lamb, B. P., *India: A World in Transition* (1963, paperback).
Dean, V. M., *New Patterns of Democracy in India* (1959).
Sheehan, V., *Mahatma Gandhi: A Great Life in Brief* (1958).
————, *Nehru: The Years of Power* (1960).
Tinker, H., *India and Pakistan: A Political Analysis* (1962, paperback).
Campbell, R. D., *Pakistan: Emerging Democracy* (1963, paperback).
Symonds, R., *The Making of Pakistan* (1950).
Spate, O. K. H., *India and Pakistan* (2nd ed., 1957). A geography text with wide ramifications.
Spear, P., *India, Pakistan and the West* (1949). Cultural relationships.
Ward, B., *India and the West* (1961).

JAPAN

Maki, J. M., *Government and Politics in Japan* (1962, paperback).
Storry, R., *A History of Modern Japan* (1960, paperback).
Jones, F. C., *Japan's New Order in East Asia: Its Rise and Fall* (1954).
Cohen, J. B., *Japan's Economy in War and Reconstruction* (1949). Covers the period from 1937.
————, *Japan's Postwar Economy* (1958).

CHINA AND KOREA

Schwartz, B. I., *Chinese Communism and the Rise of Mao* (1951).
Osgood, R. E., *Limited War* (1957). Diplomatic impact of military policy in Korea.
Fairbank, J. K., *The United States and China* (rev. ed., 1963, also paperback).
Barnett, A. D., *Communist China and Asia* (1960, also paperback).
————, *Communist China in Perspective* (1962, paperback).
Boyd, R. G., *Communist China's Foreign Policy* (1962, paperback).
Floyd, D., *Mao Against Khrushchev* (1963, paperback).
Pentony, D. E., *China the Emerging Red Giant—Communist Foreign Policies* (1962, paperback).
Snow, E., *The Other Side of the River: Red China Today* (1962).
Leckie, R., *Conflict: The History of the Korean War, 1950–1953* (1962, paperback).

SOUTHEAST ASIA

Fifield, R. H., *The Diplomacy of Southeast Asia, 1945–1958* (1958).
Kahin, G. McT. (ed.), *Governments and Politics of Southeast Asia* (1959).
————, *Nationalism and Revolution in Indonesia* (1952).
Lancaster, D., *The Emancipation of French Indochina* (1961). By a British embassy official in Saigon.
Brimmell, J. H., *Communism in South East Asia: A Political Analysis* (1959).
King, J. K., *Southeast Asia in Perspective* (1956).
Buss, C. A., *Southeast Asia and the World Today* (1958, paperback).

MIDDLE EAST

Kirk, G., *The Middle East, 1945–1950* (1954).
Berger, M., *The Arab World Today* (1964, paperback).
Upton, J. M., *The History of Modern Iran* (1960).
Glubb, J. B., *Britain and the Arabs* (1959).
Schwarz, W., *The Arabs in Israel* (1959).
Heller, A. M., *Israel's Odyssey* (1959).
Halpern, B., *The Idea of the Jewish State* (1961). A study of Zionism.
Lacouture, J. and S., *Egypt in Transition* (Engl. tr., 1958).
Wheelock, K., *Nasser's New Egypt: A Critical Analysis* (1961).
Cremeans, C. D., *The Arabs and the World: Nasser's Arab Nationalist Policy* (1963, paperback).
Campbell, J. C., *Defense of the Middle East: Problems of American Policy* (1960).

AFRICA

Gillespie, J., *Algeria: Rebellion and Revolution* (1960).
Kraft, J., *The Struggle for Algeria* (1961).
Ashford, D. E., *Political Change in Morocco* (1961).
Cameron, J., *The African Revolution* (1961). A brief survey of events in twenty-six African countries by an English correspondent.
Hunter, G., *The New Societies of Tropical Africa* (1962).
Hailey, Malcolm, Lord, *An African Survey* (rev. ed., 1957). An outstanding study, first published in 1938.
Hodgkin, T., *Nationalism in Colonial Africa* (1956, also paperback). A sympathetic study.
Bowles, C., *Africa's Challenge to America* (1957). Lectures by a former ambassador.
Kimble, G. H. T., *Tropical Africa* (2 vols., 1960, also paperback).
Wiedner, D. L., *A History of Africa South of the Sahara* (1962, also paperback).
Burke, F. G., *Africa's Quest for Order* (1964, paperback).
Carter, G., *Independence for Africa* (1960, paperback).
Lipsky, G. A., and others, *Ethiopia: Its People, Its Society, Its Culture* (1962).
Thompson, V. M., and Adloff, R., *The Emerging States of French Equatorial Africa* (1960).
Legum, C., *The Congo Disaster* (1961, paperback).
Nkrumah, K., *Ghana: The Autobiography of Kwame Nkrumah* (1957).
Wood, S., *Kenya: The Tensions of Progress* (1962).
DeKiewiet, C. W., *The Anatomy of South African Misery* (1956). A brief account of *apartheid*.
Paton, A., *Hope for South Africa* (1959).
Carter, G., *The Politics of Inequality: South Africa Since 1948* (1958). An important study.
Legum, C., *Pan-Africanism: A Short Political Guide* (1962, also paperback).
Abraham, W. E., *The Mind of Africa* (1962). An important study by a native professor of philosophy at the University of Ghana.

CHAPTER 14 The Cultural Revolution

HISTORY, POLITICAL THOUGHT, PHILOSOPHY

Hughes, H. S., *Consciousness and Society: The Reorientation of European Social Thought, 1890–1930* (1958). Principally Durkheim, Pareto, Croce, Sorel, Bergson, Freud, and Weber.
Geyl, P., *From Ranke to Toynbee* (1952). Lectures on Spengler and other historians.
Barraclough, G., *History in a Changing World* (1956). An interpretation of the contemporary world in the light of history in general.

Popper, K. R., *The Open Society and Its Enemies* (1950). A distinguished study of democracy in modern society.

Ebenstein, W., *Today's Isms* (2nd ed., 1958, paperback). An excellent analysis of communism, fascism, capitalism, and socialism.

Runes, D. (ed.), *Twentieth Century Philosophy* (1942). Essays from various fields.

White, M. G. (ed.), *The Age of Analysis: Twentieth Century Philosophers* (1955, paperback). Selections and commentary.

Bridgman, P. W., *The Way Things Are* (1959). The philosophic outlook of a distinguished scientist.

SCIENCE

Asimov, I., *The Intelligent Man's Guide to Science* (2 vols., 1960). Systematic and up to date.

Mason, S. F., *Main Currents of Scientific Thought* (1953).

Skinner, C. P., *Science and Human Behavior* (1956). Behaviorist psychology.

Heisenberg, W., *Physics and Philosophy: The Revolution of Modern Science* (1958, also paperback). A distinguished essay by one of the greatest contemporary scientists.

Guardini, R., *The End of the Modern World* (1957). Discusses the impact of the new scientific outlook upon accepted views of the cosmos.

Snow, C. P., *The Two Cultures and the Scientific Revolution* (1961). Lectures on the great gulf developing between scientists and nonscientists.

LITERATURE AND THE ARTS

Wilson, E., *Axel's Castle: A Study in the Imaginative Literature of 1870–1930* (1931, also paperback). A classic of modern literary criticism.

Colum, M., *From These Roots: The Ideas That Have Made Modern Literature* (1944).

Canaday, J. E., *Mainstreams of Modern Art* (1959). A comprehensive and distinguished survey, superbly illustrated.

Casson, J., Pevsner, N., and Langui, E., *Gateway to the Twentieth Century: Art and Culture in a Changing World* (1962).

Read, H., *A Concise History of Modern Painting* (1959, also paperback).

Jaffe, H. L. C., *Twentieth Century Painting* (1963).

Daix, P., *Picasso* (1965). By a distinguished critic and close friend.

Read, H., *A Concise History of Modern Sculpture* (1964, also paperback).

Giedion, S., *Space, Time, and Architecture: The Growth of a New Tradition* (4th rev. ed., 1962). The classic statement of the new architecture.

Gropius, W., *The Scope of Total Architecture* (1955). By its most distinguished exponent.

Hartog, H. (ed.), *European Music in the Twentieth Century* (1957, paperback). Valuable essays on all major composers.

Copland, A., *Our New Music* (1941). By a distinguished modern composer.

REFLECTIONS ON THE CONTEMPORARY WORLD

Heller, E., *The Disinherited Mind* (1961, also paperback). An examination of today's uncertain world.

Muller, H. J., *Issues of Freedom, Paradoxes and Promises* (1960).

Boulding, K., *The Meaning of the Twentieth Century: The Great Transition* (1964).

Whitehead, A. N., *Alfred North Whitehead: His Reflections on Man and Nature* (1961). Selections chosen by Ruth Nanda Anshen.

CHAPTER 15   Unity and Disunity, 1949–1960

THE COLD WAR

Fleming, D. F., *The Cold War and Its Origins, 1917–1960* (2 vols., 1960). An ample narrative, with a massive indictment of the West.

Lukacs, J. A., *History of the Cold War* (1961, also paperback). Brief but stimulating.

Deutscher, I., *The Great Contest: Russia and the West* (1960, also paperback).

Luard, E. (ed.), *The Cold War: A Reappraisal* (1964). A regional and topical treatment.

Leonhard, W., *The Kremlin Since Stalin* (1962, also paperback). A good account of recent changes.

Ripka, H., *Eastern Europe in the Postwar World* (1961). By a Czech journalist and former diplomat.

NATO

NATO Information Service, *NATO: Facts about the North Atlantic Treaty Organization* (1962). A careful analysis of structure and activities.

Ismay, Hastings, Lord, *NATO: The First Five Years, 1949–54* (1955). An account by the first secretary-general.

Osgood, R. E., *NATO: The Entangling Alliance* (1962). Military and strategic aspects.

Lichtheim, G., *The Future of the Atlantic Community* (1963).

Buchan, A., *NATO in the 1960's: The Implications of Independence* (1963, paperback).

UNIFICATION OF WESTERN EUROPE

Royal Institute of International Affairs, *Britain in Western Europe: WEU and the Atlantic Alliance* (1956).

Benoit, E., *Europe at Sixes and Sevens: The Common Market, the Free Trade Association, and the United States* (1961, also paperback).

Beloff, M., *The United States and the Unity of Europe* (1963, paperback). A survey of events from the Second World War to the Common Market.

Price, H. B., *The Marshall Plan and Its Meaning* (1955).

Hallstein, W., *United Europe: Challenge and Opportunity* (1962).

European Organizations, 1959 (1959). A survey and appraisal of the eight principal associations set up in Europe since 1945.

Mason, H. L., *The European Coal and Steel Community* (1955). A concise summary.

Clark, Colin, and others, *Plain Facts About the Common Market* (1964, paperback).

Krause, L. B. (ed.), *The Common Market: Progress and Controversy* (1964, paperback).

Robertson, A. H., *The Council of Europe: Its Structure, Functions, and Achievements* (1961). A comprehensive study by an official of the Council.

THE UNITED NATIONS

U. N. Office of Public Information, *Everyman's United Nations* (7th ed., 1964).

Goodrich, L. M., *The United Nations* (1959).

Nicholas, H. G., *The United Nations as a Political Institution* (1960, also paperback).

Huxley, J., *UNESCO: Its Purposes and Philosophy* (1947).

Boyd, A., *United Nations: Piety, Myth, and Truth* (1962, paperback).

Beckel, G., *Workshops for the World: The Specialized Agencies of the United Nations* (1954).

Laves, W. H. C., and Thompson, C. A., *UNESCO: Purpose, Progress, Prospects* (1957).

THE PRECARIOUS BALANCE

Aron, R., *The Century of Total War* (Engl. tr., 1954, also paperback).

Barraclough, G. (ed.), *Survey of International Affairs, 1956–1958* (1962). Section VII is on Sputnik and strategy.

Crankshaw, E., *The New Cold War: Moscow v. Peking* (1963, paperback).

Kahn, H., *On Thermonuclear War* (1960).

Seton-Watson, H., *Neither War Nor Peace: The Struggle for Power in the Postwar World* (1960, paperback).

Friedmann, W., *An Introduction to World Politics* (5th ed., 1965). Part III discusses the challenge to mankind of population pressures, the call for economic aid, and the threat of nuclear war.

Brodie, B., *Strategy in the Missile Age* (1959, also paperback). A scholarly study of the influence of new weapons on strategy.

Beloff, M., *The United States and the Unity of Europe* (1963, paperback).

Hauser, P. M., *The Population Dilemma* (1963, paperback).

Martin, L. W. (ed.), *Neutralism and Nonalignment—The New States in World Affairs* (1963, paperback).

Parry, A., *Russia's Rockets and Missiles* (1960). An attempted appraisal.

INDEX

Aaland Islands, 89
Abdul Karim (1914–1963), 432
Abdullah, of Jordan (1882–1951), 134–135
Addis Ababa, 232, 233, 430
Adenauer, Konrad (b. 1876), 306, 391, 402, 403, 425
Adowa, Battle (1896), 232
Aduldet, of Thailand (b. 1927), 362
Afghanistan, 57, 137, 369
Africa: population, 352, 371; First World War, 22, 37; to 1939, 37, 57, 232, 233; Second World War, 265, 266, 276–278; since 1945, 11, 295, 313, 314, 348, 350–352, 369–375, 405–407, 427–430
Agriculture, improvements in, 11, 86, 155, 157, 163, 176, 207, 214, 217, 311, 337, 360
Air warfare (see also Nuclear weapons): First World War, 18, 35; to 1939, 233, 241; Second World War, 259–261, 262, 264–266, 269–271, 273, 275, 276, 278, 279, 281, 284–286, 289, 290
Airplanes, 18, 34, 37, 148, 163, 165, 254, 264
Albania, 89, 180, 248, 266, 333, 336, 340, 426, 433
Alexander, of Greece (1893–1920), 179
Alexander I, of Russia (1777–1825), 325
Alexander I, of Yugoslavia (1888–1934), 181, 183, 331
Alexandra, Tsarina (1872–1918), 42
Alfonso XIII, of Spain (1886–1941), 179–180, 239
Algeria, 137, 309, 314, 370, 375, 402, 411, 429
Allenby, General Sir Edmund (1861–1936), 33
Alliance for Progress, 434
Allied Supreme Council, 32, 89
Alsace-Lorraine, 3, 67, 72
Amanullah, of Afghanistan (b. 1892), 137
America, see United States, Canada, Latin America
American economic aid and relief: First World War, 28, 148; to 1939, 148–149, 206; Second World War, 265, 271; since 1945, 299, 308, 318, 355, 364, 403, 425–426
Amis, Kingsley (b. 1922), 394
Amritsar massacre (1919), 111

Anarchism, 239, 241
Anatolia, 77, 120–122, 179
Angell, Norman (b. 1874), 145
Anglo-Egyptian treaty (1936), 127, 369
Anglo-German naval treaty (1935), 116, 230
Anglo-Iranian Oil Company, 128, 129, 368
Anglo-Japanese Alliance (1902), 4, 115
Ankara, 121, 122
Annam, 315, 364, 365
Anschluss, 76, 181, 242–244
Anti-Comintern Pact, 184, 187, 225, 239, 242
Anti-Semitism, 131, 133, 181, 183, 193, 194, 199–200, 248, 267, 336, 387, 388
Antwerp, 281, 284
ANZACS, 24
Anzio, 278
ANZUS treaty (1951), 366, 375
Apartheid, 429
Apparatchiki, 224, 342
Arab League, 367, 370, 372, 432
Arab Legion, 135
Arab peoples, 33, 65, 120, 123–127, 131–136, 366–367, 369–371, 405
Arabia (see also Saudi Arabia), 33, 121, 124–126
Archangel, 41, 54
Architecture, 12, 378, 396–397
Arctic convoys, 269, 271, 275
Armaments (see also Disarmament projects, Nuclear weapons, and sub-entry under names of major powers): 5, 79, 165, 183, 192, 215, 237, 238, 254, 255, 258–259, 275, 286
Armenia, 76
Armies (numerical data): First World War, 5, 19, 23, 25, 31–34, 37, 41, 170; to 1939, 52–53, 72, 141, 234, 240; Second World War, 262, 269–271, 273, 278, 281, 289
Armistice (1918), 35, 36, 67
Armored formations, see Tank warfare
Arnhem, Battle (1944), 284
Arras, Battles (1917, 1918), 31–32
Arts, developments in the, 12, 328, 380–381, 385–391, 393–397
Asia: population, 295, 352; First World War, 22, 27, 32–33, 35; to 1939, 70, 76, 137–142;

Second World War, 258, 267, 271–275, 285–290; since 1945, 295, 313–315, 350–371, 375, 405, 430–433
Asquith, Herbert (1852–1928), 28, 96, 97, 101
Astronauts, 427
Aswan Dam, Egypt, 370
Ataturk, *see* Kemal
Atlantic, Battle of the, 275
Atlantic Charter (1941), 267, 269, 272, 297
Atomic bomb, *see* Nuclear weapons
Atomic energy, *see* Nuclear energy
Atomic Energy Commission, 417–418
Australasia, *see* Australia, New Zealand
Australia: First World War, 16, 24; to 1939, 112, 158; Second World War, 273, 274, 275, 286, 287; since 1945, 366, 375
Australian and New Zealand Army Corps (ANZACS), 24
Austria (*see also* Austria-Hungary): population, 75, 181; to 1945, 72, 83, 152, 181, 238, 242–244, 284–285; since 1945, 300, 317, 319, 333, 403–404, 417
Austria-Hungary, 3–6, 19, 21, 23, 27, 32, 35–37, 41, 66
Autarky (*Autarkie*), 165, 199, 200, 238
Automobiles, 148, 153, 163
Axis powers, 239, 244, 266, 278
Ayub Khan, Mohammed (b. 1907), 353
Azaña, Manuel (1880–1940), 186

Badoglio, Pietro (b. 1871), 278
Baghdad, 27, 32
Baghdad Pact, *see* Middle East Treaty Organization
Balbo, Italo (1896–1940), 180
Baldwin, Stanley (1867–1947), 101, 103, 107, 116, 117
Balfour, Arthur (1848–1930), 112, 131, 136–137
Balfour Declaration (1917), 66, 131, 134
Balfour Note (1922), 149
Balkan Pact: (1934), 123; (1954), 412
Balkan states, 3, 5, 6, 23, 183, 331
Balkan Wars (1912–1913), 6
Baltic States, 53, 86, 182, 185, 260, 261, 266, 281
Bandung Conference (1955), 375, 430
Banks (*see also* World Bank), 105, 159, 357, 409
Bao Dai, of Annam (b. 1913), 315, 364, 365
Barbusse, Henri (1873–1935), 385
Barcelona, 179, 239, 240
Barth, Karl (b. 1886), 392
Bartók, Béla (1881–1945), 397
Baruch, Bernard (1870–1965), 417
Baruch Plan, 417–418
Bastogne, 284
Batista, General Fulgencio (b. 1901), 435
Baudouin, of Belgium (b. 1930), 374
Bauer, Gustav (1870–1944), 189

Bavaria, 56, 69, 304
Becquerel, Henri (1852–1908), 381
"Beer Hall Putsch" (1923), 194
Belgian colonial empire (*see also* Congo), 313, 374, 406–407
Belgium: First World War, 5, 6, 20, 37; to 1939, 72, 87, 91, 236; Second World War, 262, 281; since 1945, 313, 319, 403, 407, 410, 414, 415
Bell, Gertrude (1868–1926), *quoted*, 135
Benelux, 319, 410, 414
Beneš, Eduard (1884–1948), 80, 244, 334
Berenguer, General Dámaso (1873–1953), 180
Bergson, Henri (1859–1941), 170
Beria, Lavrenty (1899–1953), 329, 342, 345
Berlin, 189, 276, 296, 300, 302, 305, 306, 324, 347–348, 420, 426
Berlin airlift (1948–1949), 305, 318, 341
Berlin Wall, 420, 424
Bernadotte, Count Folke (1895–1948), 367, 405
Bernhardi, Friedrich von (1849–1930), 170
Bessarabia, 51, 56, 252, 266, 300
Bethlen, Count Stephen (1874–1947), 178, 184
Bethmann-Hollweg, Theobald von (1856–1921), 28
Bismarck, Otto von (1815–1898), 4
Bismarck Islands, 287
Black and Tans, 99
Blitzkrieg, 257, 260, 261, 268, 286
Blockade: 1914–1920, 22, 26, 34, 36, 55, 56, 58, 69, 96; 1939–1945, 260, 265, 275
Blomberg, General Werner von (1878–1946), 243
Blum, Léon (1872–1950), 310
Bohemia (*see also* Czechoslovakia), 36
Bohemia-Moravia, 247
Bohr, Niels (1885–1962), 381
Bolsheviks (*see also* Communism), 33, 42, 45–51, 61
Bonn, 305
Bonnet, Georges (b. 1889), 245
Boris III, of Bulgaria (1894–1943), 181, 183
Borodin, Michael (1884–1953), 211–212
Bosnia, 5, 6
Bourgeoisie, *see* Middle classes
Bourguiba, Habib (b. 1903), 372
Brancusi, Constantin (1876–1957), 396
Bratianu, Ion (1864–1927), 181
Brauchitsch, General Heinrich von (1881–1948), 260, 268
Brecht, Berthold (1898–1956), 394
Brentano, Heinrich von (b. 1904), 419
Brest Litovsk, Armistice (1917), Treaty (1918), 33, 50–51, 53, 61, 72, 338
Brezhnev, Leonid (b. 1906), 426
Briand, Aristide (1862–1932), 28, 90–92
Britain, *see* Great Britain
Britain, Battle of (1940), 264

British colonial empire, 95, 110–111, 126, 127, 136–137, 164, 286, 295, 313–314, 352, 428

British Commonwealth (*see also* Dominions): to 1945, 90, 112, 116, 136–137, 164, 272; since 1945, 313–314, 373–374, 424, 425, 429, 433

Broeck, Moeller van den (1876–1925), 388

Brown Shirts, 193, 197, 199

Bruening, Heinrich (b. 1885), 195

Brusilov, General Alexei (1853–1926), 27, 30, 328

Brussels, Treaty (1948), 318, 339, 410, 411

Budapest, 345, 346

Bukharin, Nikolai (1888–1938), 210, 211, 223

Bukowina, 75, 300

Bulganin, Nikolai (b. 1896), 329, 342–343

Bulgaria: First World War, 23, 35; to 1939, 76, 83, 165, 181, 183, 224; Second World War, 266, 281; since 1945, 300, 332, 333, 336, 420, 426

Bulge, Battle of the (1944–1945), 262, 284

Bunche, Ralph (b. 1904), 367, 405

Burma, 273, 288–289, 314, 363, 365, 433

Burma Road, 273, 289, 352

Byelorussia, 57, 77, 207, 260, 299

Cairo Conference (1943), 360

Cambodia, 315, 364, 365

Cambrai, Battle (1917), 18, 32

Camus, Albert (1913–1960), 394

Canada: First World War, 16, 22, 31; to 1939, 111, 112, 158, 164; Second World War, 276, 277, 278; since 1945, 319, 407, 414

Canton, 141, 212

Caporetto, Battle (1917), 32

Carmona, General Antonio (1869–1951), 180

Carol II, of Rumania (1893–1953), 181, 183

Caroline Islands, 82, 287

Casablanca Conference (1943), 278, 298

Castro, Fidel (b. 1927), 435

Catalan separatism, 179, 186, 187, 240

Caucasus (*see also* Transcaucasia), 270, 325

Center Party (Germany), 189, 191, 195, 197

Central Powers, 18, 22, 24, 28, 29, 34–36, 41

Central Treaty Organization (CENTO), 367, 368, 371, 375, 432

Ceylon, 314, 366, 433

Chadwick, James (b. 1891), 164

Chamberlain, Austen (1863–1937), 90

Chamberlain, Joseph (1836–1914), 110

Chamberlain, Neville (1869–1940), 103, 106, 107, 110, 244–249, 253, 261

Chanak crisis (1922), 101, 111, 121

Charles, Prince, of Belgium (b. 1903), 313

Charles, *see* Karl

Cheka (Soviet secret police), 49, 52, 59, 329

Chekhov, Anton (1860–1904), 393

Chiang Kai-shek (b. 1886), 140–142, 225, 286, 288, 341, 358, 360

Chicherin, Georghi (1872–1936), 224

China: population, 7, 295, 350; to 1931, 4, 66, 70, 72, 139–141, 211–212, 225; to 1949, 141–142, 225, 271–273, 286–289, 299, 357; People's Republic, 11, 220, 295, 323, 341, 354, 357–361, 425, 432–434, 436; Nationalist Government, 358–359, 434

"China Incident" (1937), 141

Chinese Eastern Railway, 211, 225, 357

Chou En-lai (b. 1898), 359

Christian Democratic Party: Germany, 306, 391; Italy, 312, 391, 402

Christian Socialist Party (Austria), 181, 184–185

Christianity (*see also* Protestantism, Roman Catholic Church), 115, 130, 131, 372, 391–393, 427

Chungking, 142, 273, 288, 357

Churchill, Winston Spencer (1874–1965): to 1939, 18, 106, 107, 132, 238; to 1945, 261, 265, 267, 269, 272, 278, 285, 298, 302, 304, 307, 332; to 1964, 308, 314, 319, 401, 404; *quoted*, 91, 114, 237, 254, 264, 273, 275, 277, 307, 317, 338, 404

Clay, General Lucius (b. 1897), 305

Clemenceau, Georges (1841–1929), 66, 68, 73

Clementis, Vladimir (1902–1952), 420

Cochin China, 315, 364

"Cold War," 7, 337–339, 375, 404

Collective farming, *see Kolkhoz*, People's communes

Colombo Plan, 357, 366

Colonialism, *see* Imperialism

Combined Chiefs of Staff, 272, 279, 284

Cominform, 334, 340, 345, 420

Comintern, 56–57, 205, 206, 212, 224, 226

Commissars, 49, 207–208

Common Market, *see* European institutions

Communism (*see also* Communist Parties), 60–62, 169, 183, 333, 338–339

Communist Parties (*see also* Communist Party, Russian): Austria, 184; Belgium, 313; Bulgaria, 224; China, 140, 142, 211–212, 225, 288, 359; Finland, 186; France, 310, 339, 340; Germany, 55, 56, 188, 195, 197, 225; Great Britain, 103; Greece, 184, 339; Hungary, 56, 76; Indochina, 138, 295; Indonesia, 139, 295, 364; Italy, 171, 312, 313, 339, 340, 402; Iran, 368; Netherlands, 313; Russian satellite states, 331–338, 345–346; South Vietnam, 434; Spain, 186, 239, 241

Communist Party, Russian, 51, 56, 59–61, 208–209, 221–224, 328, 341–343, 426

Concentration camps, 200, 267, 294, 306

Concert of Europe, 79

Congo, 374, 406–407, 428, 429

Conrad, Joseph (1857–1924), 393

Conrad von Hötzendorf, Franz (1852–1925), 19

Conscription, 4, 6, 96, 234, 248
Conservative Party (Britain), 96–97, 100–107, 307, 308, 401
Constantine I, of Greece (1868–1923), 179
Constantinople, 42, 122
Cooper, Hugh Lincoln (1865–1937), 216
Co-Prosperity Sphere, 272, 289
Coral Sea, Battle (1942), 274
Corfu bombardment (1923), 89, 115
Coronel, Battle (1914), 22
Corporative State, 175–176, 185
Corregidor, 273
Council of Europe, 318–319, 410
Council of Mutual Economic Assistance (COMECON), 340, 420, 426
Covenant, see League of Nations
Crete, 266
Crimea (see also Sebastopol, Yalta Conference), 325
Croats, 180, 181, 183, 284
Croce, Benedetto (1866–1952), 388
Cuba, 348, 435
Curie, Marie (1867–1934), 381
Curie, Pierre (1859–1906), 381
Curzon Line, 57, 77, 260
Cyprus, 77, 122, 425
Czech Legion, 52, 54
Czechoslovakia: to 1945, 66, 83, 86, 244–248, 254, 285, 331; since 1945, 300, 332–334, 336–338, 420, 426

Daladier, Edouard (b. 1884), 245, 246
Dali, Salvador (b. 1904), 395
Damascus, 35, 130, 135
D'Annunzio, Gabriele (1863–1938), 77, 171
Danzig, 72, 90, 249, 252, 260, 302
D'Arcy, William (1849–1917), 128
Dardanelles, see Straits
Dardanelles Campaign (1915), 24
Darwin, Charles (1809–1882), 383
Dawes Plan (1924), 89, 107, 151, 191
Debussy, Claude (1862–1918), 397
Democracy, 7, 84, 97, 169, 179, 182, 267, 333, 347, 355, 434
Denikin, Anton (1872–1947), 54
Denmark, 261, 313
Depression, world economic, 109–110, 157–163
De Valera, Eamon (b. 1882), 98–99, 113
Dewey, John (1859–1952), 390
Dictatorship, 8, 84–85, 168–201, 293, 347
Dien Bien Phu, 365
Dieppe Raid (1942), 278
Disarmament projects: 1919–1939, 9, 72, 79, 89, 115–116, 200, 237; since 1945, 417–419, 423, 424
Dobrudja, 300
Dodecanese Islands, 76, 77, 300, 312
Dollfuss, Engelbert (1892–1934), 184–185, 238

Dominions, British self-governing, 90, 100, 110–113, 136, 153, 164, 313, 371
Dreadnought battleships, 5, 26
Dresden, 289, 300
Drugs, see Public Health
Dual Alliance (1879), 4
Dual Monarchy, see Austria-Hungary
Duchamp, Marcel (b. 1887), 395
Dulles, John Foster (1888–1959), 73
Duma, 42–44
Dunkirk evacuation (1940), 262
Dunkirk, Treaty (1947), 318, 410
Durkheim, Emile (1858–1917), 387
Dyarchy, 113, 114
Dyer, General Reginald (1864–1927), 111

East Germany, 306, 317, 340, 344, 348, 404, 420, 424, 426
East Prussia, 21, 72, 281, 285, 302
Ebert, Friedrich (1871–1925), 188, 189, 191
Economic Cooperation Administration (ECA), 317
Eden, Anthony (b. 1897), 226, 245, 346, 401
Education: European, 378–379, 398; Britain, 97, 100, 307; Germany, 190, 199, 304; India, 353; Israel, 432; Italy, 177; Russia, 218, 219, 328
Edward VIII, of Britain (b. 1894), 116
Egypt: population, 127; to 1945, 4, 27, 33, 111, 126–127, 265–266, 276; since 1945, 314, 366, 369–372, 406, 432
Ehrenburg, Ilia (b. 1891), 343
Einstein, Albert (1879–1955), 381, 382, 383
Eire, see Ireland
Eisenhower, General Dwight D. (b. 1890), 277, 280, 284, 285, 319, 346–347, 359, 411, 418
"Eisenhower Doctrine," 371, 375
El Alamein, Battle (1942), 277
Eliot, Thomas Stearns (1888–1965), 394
Emigration overseas, 153–154
England, see Great Britain
Entente Cordiale (1904), 4
Epstein, Jacob (1880–1959), 396
Erhard, Ludwig (b. 1897), 306, 425
Eritrea, 232, 233
Estonia, 54, 57, 66, 85, 86, 182, 252
Ethiopia, 231–234, 266, 371
Europe: number of states, 84; political weaknesses, 10, 37, 258, 294–295, 324; economic difficulties, 144–146, 153, 159, 166, 296, 315–318, 323, 329; loss of empire, 313–315, 350–352
European institutions: Atomic Energy Community (Euratom), 417; Coal and Steel Community, 414–415; Defense Community, 312, 411; Economic Community (Common Market), 415, 417, 424, 425; Free Trade Association (EFTA), 417, 424; Recovery Program (ERP), 311, 317, 318, 321, 414

Fabian Society, 203
Faisal I, of Syria and Iraq (1885–1933), 130, 135, 136
Falange, 186–187, 240
Falkenhayn, General Erich von (1861–1922), 21, 23, 25
Falkland Islands, Battle (1914), 22
Far East, 4, 139–142, 206, 211, 225, 239, 290, 314, 322, 341, 357, 433
Farouk, of Egypt (b. 1920), 369
Fascism, 172–178, 180, 183
Fascist Parties: Italy, 56, 77, 172–175, 278; Spain, 186, 240; France, 187, 267; Britain, 107, 188
Faure, Edgar (b. 1908), 346
Ferdinand I, of Rumania (1865–1927), 181
Fermi, Enrico (1901–1954), 382, 383
Finland: to 1939, 45, 47, 50, 89, 161, 186; since 1939, 269, 281, 300, 333
First World War (1914–1918): causes, 3–6; character, 14–19; campaigns, 19–36; loss of life, 37, 41, 147, 170; economic effects, 146–148; peace treaties, 64–76
Fiume, 77
Five-Year Plans, Russian (see also Planning), 202, 213–220, 325, 330, 343
Foch, Marshal Ferdinand (1851–1929), 33–36, 37, 78
Food supply (see also Agriculture, improvements in; Blockade), 408, 436
Formosa, 139, 358–359
"Four Freedoms," 297
Fourteen Points, 36, 66–67, 152
France: population, 311; First World War, 14, 18–21, 23–25, 28, 30–37; to 1939, 67–68, 75, 187, 230, 242, 252; Second World War, 259, 261–265, 277, 281, 309; since 1945, 300, 304–305, 309–311, 321, 370, 372, 402, 429; constitution, 264, 310, 402; parties, 187, 230; economic life, 159, 160–165, 311; foreign policy, 3–6, 9, 87–88, 90–92, 238, 241, 245–249, 252, 318–319, 402, 411–412, 415, 424, 425; armaments and armed forces, 5, 19, 236, 254, 262
France, Anatole (1844–1924), 393
Francis Ferdinand, Archduke (1863–1914), 6
Francis Joseph, of Austria-Hungary (1830–1916), 28
Franco, General Francisco (b. 1892), 186–187, 239–241, 403
Franco-Russian Alliance: (1894), 4; (1935), 226, 238, 248
Free Corps, 189, 194
Free French, 309
Free Trade (see also Tariff systems), 100, 110, 159, 162, 415, 424
Freedom of the seas, 66, 67
French, General Sir John (1852–1925), 20, 23

French alliance system (1920–1926), 87, 236
French colonial empire, 137–138, 295, 309–310, 314–315, 352, 364–365, 372, 428
French Community, 429
French Union, 310, 314, 364, 372
Freud, Sigmund (1856–1939), 385, 394
Frick, Wilhelm (1877–1946), 194, 196
Fuad, of Egypt (1868–1936), 127

Gagarin, Yuri (b. 1934), 427
Galicia, 21, 24, 30, 75
Gallipoli, see Dardanelles Campaign
Galsworthy, John (1867–1933), 393
Gamelin, General Maurice (1872–1958), 236, 261, 262
Gandhi, Mahatma (1869–1948), 114, 139, 353
Gas Warfare, 23, 233
Gasperi, Alcide de (1881–1954), 312, 391
Gaulle, General Charles de (b. 1890), 87, 254, 264, 272, 309–311, 391, 402, 403, 407, 411, 427, 429
Gaza Strip, 367, 405
General Agreement on Tariffs and Trade (GATT), 407
General strike (Great Britain), 103–104, (Italy), 173
Geneva, 79
Geneva Conference (1955), see Summit Conferences
Geneva Protocol (1924), 90, 115
Gentile, Giovanni (1875–1944), 172
George II, of Greece (1890–1947), 179, 184
George V, of Britain (1865–1936), 99, 100, 105, 112
George, Stefan (1868–1933), 395
Georgia, 54, 58, 210
German colonial empire, 72, 81, 192, 229, 257
German Democratic Republic, see East Germany
German Federal Republic, see West Germany
Germany (see also East Germany, West Germany, Nazi Party): population, 72; First World War, 14–37; to 1939, 71–75, 188–200, 229–231, 234–240, 242–253; Second World War, 256–271, 275–285; since 1945, 294, 300–306, 340; constitution, 189–190, 197–199, 305–306; parties, 189, 190, 193, 197, 306; economic life, 8–9, 147, 150–152, 156–157, 159, 164–165, 191, 198–199, 305–306; foreign policy, 3–6, 22, 28, 51, 67, 71, 91, 192, 200, 206, 229–230, 234–255, 266–267, 318; armaments and armed forces, 18, 19, 33, 72–73, 193, 200, 237–238, 255, 259
Gestapo, 193, 194, 199, 200
Ghana, 373
Ghazi I, of Iraq (1912–1939), 136
Gilbert Islands, 287
Gilson, Etienne (b. 1884), 391
Giolitti, Giovanni (1842–1928), 171

Gladstone, William (1809–1898), 120
Glenn, John (b. 1922), 427
Glubb, John (b. 1897), 135
Goebbels, Joseph (1897–1945), 194, 199, 304
Goering, Marshal Hermann (1893–1946), 193, 196, 254, 304
Goga, Octavian (1881–1938), 183
Gold standard, 106, 108, 110, 145, 154–155, 159–162, 164, 165, 389
Gömbös, Julius (1886–1936), 178, 184
Gomulka, Wladislaw (b. 1905), 345, 420
Gottwald, Klement (1896–1953), 334
Gouraud, General Henri (1867–1946), 130
Government of India Act (1935), 115
Great Britain (see also British colonial empire, British Commonwealth): First World War, 14–18, 20, 22–37, 96–97; to 1939, 94–95, 97–117; Second World War, 256–269, 272–281, 284, 285; since 1945, 307–309, 401; parties, 96–97, 100–107, 307, 308; economic life, 96, 103–110, 145, 147, 152, 155, 157–161, 163–164, 308, 402; foreign policy, 3–6, 28, 53, 66–70, 73, 79, 90–91, 115–117, 148–150, 230, 233, 237, 239, 241, 244–249, 252, 318, 370, 424; armaments and armed forces, 5, 18, 23, 115, 117, 254
Greece: to 1945, 6, 23, 35, 76, 83, 86, 165, 179, 184, 266, 284; since 1945, 318–319, 332, 339, 425
Green Revolution, see Land reform
Greenland, 265
Gromyko, Andrei (b. 1909), 371
Gropius, Walter (b. 1883), 396
Grotewohl, Otto (1894–1964), 306
Guadalcanal, 274, 286
Guam, 273, 287
"Guernica," 187, 254
Gursel, Cemal (b. 1895), 430

Haakon VII, of Norway (1872–1957), 313
Hague Conferences (1899–1907), 23, 81
Hahn, Otto (b. 1879), 164
Haig, Field Marshal Douglas (1861–1928), 23, 25, 32, 33, 36
Haile Selassie, of Ethiopia (b. 1891), 233–234, 266
Halifax, Lord (1881–1959), 245
Hammarskjöld, Dag (1905–1961), 407, 429
Hankow, 140, 141, 211, 212
Hankow-Canton Railway, 288
Hapsburg Empire, see Austria-Hungary
Hardy, Thomas (1840–1928), 7, 393
Hauptmann, Gerhard (1862–1946), 393
Hawley-Smoot tariff (1930), 162
Heidegger, Martin (b. 1889), 390
Heimwehr, 181
Heisenberg, Werner (b. 1901), 381
Hejaz, kingdom of the, 124, 125
Helgoland, 73

Hemingway, Ernest (1898–1961), 385
Henderson, Arthur (1863–1935), 116
Henlein, Konrad (1898–1945), 188, 245
Herzl, Theodor (1860–1904), 131
Hess, Rudolf (b. 1894), 194
Heuss, Theodor (1884–1963), 306
Himmler, Heinrich (1900–1945), 194, 199, 304
Hindemith, Paul (1895–1963), 397
Hindenburg, Field Marshal Paul von (1847–1934), 21, 26, 191, 195–198
Hindenburg Line, 31, 35
Hinduism, 115, 353–354, 427
Hiroshima, 259, 289, 290, 418
Historical studies, 385–388
Hitler, Adolf (1889–1945) (see also Mein Kampf), 192–200, 229–231, 234–255, 260, 261, 268–270, 284, 285, 293, 304
Ho Chi-minh (b. 1890), 315, 365, 434
Hoare, Samuel (1880–1959), 233
Hoare-Laval Proposals (1935), 233
Hong Kong, 139, 272, 273
Hoover, Herbert (1874–1964), 148–149, 161
Horthy, Admiral Miklos (1868–1957), 178
Hungary (see also Austria-Hungary): to 1945, 56, 76, 83, 85, 86, 165, 178, 184, 246–247, 331; Second World War, 266, 269, 284; since 1945, 300, 325, 332, 333, 336, 345–346, 406, 420, 426
Husein, of Mecca (1856–1931), 123–125, 130, 134
Hussein, of Jordan (b. 1934), 432
Hydrogen bomb, see Nuclear weapons

Ibn-Saud, Abdul-Aziz (b. 1880), 124–126, 371
Iceland, 265
Imperialism, 5, 10, 47, 57, 292, 295, 348, 350
India: population, 7, 295, 351, 352; to 1939, 24, 27, 111, 113–115, 136; since 1939, 273, 274, 313–314, 346, 352–354, 433, 436
Indochina, 138, 267, 271, 295, 314–315, 364–365
Indonesia, 7, 295, 315, 364, 365, 433
Inflation, 150–151, 161, 166, 191, 321
International, Third, see Comintern
International Bank, 409
International Brigades, 241, 333
International investment, 109, 145, 148, 151, 158–159, 409
International Justice, Permanent Court of, 81, 409
International Labor Organization (ILO), 80–81, 408
International Monetary Fund (IMF), 409
Invergordon Mutiny, 106
Ionescu, Take (1858–1922), 168
Iran, 4, 57, 127–129, 269, 276, 352, 368
Iraq (see also Mesopotamia), 83, 135–136, 368, 370–371, 432
Iraq Petroleum Company, 136

Ireland, 98–100, 110, 113, 308, 407
Irish Rebellion (1916), 98
"Iron Curtain," 317, 338–340
Iron Guard, 181, 183
Islam, *see* Mohammedanism
Ismet Pasha, Inonu (b. 1884), 121, 123, 430
Israel (*see also* Palestine), 366, 367, 370, 432
Israeli-Egyptian War (1947–), 369, 370, 405
Istanbul, 122
Italian colonial empire, 177, 232–233, 300, 312, 333
Italy (*see also* Fascist Parties): First World War, 22–23, 32, 36, 37, 65; to 1939, 75, 76, 77, 170–178, 231–234; Second World War, 264–266, 277–278, 285; since 1945, 300, 311–313, 402; constitution, 175–176, 312; parties, 170–171, 312; economic life, 171, 175–176, 312–313, 321; foreign policy, 3–4, 22–23, 65, 68, 70, 77, 79, 91, 177–178, 232–234, 238, 240, 244, 246, 253, 264–266, 278; armaments and armed forces, 170
Iwo Jima, 289

James, William (1842–1910), 390
Japan: population, 295, 355; First World War, 22, 52, 66, 139, 140; to 1939, 140–142, 153; Second World War, 258, 271–274, 280, 285–290; since 1945, 294, 319, 354–358, 434; constitution, 355; economic life, 8, 153, 355, 357; foreign policy, 4, 22, 52, 54, 66, 68, 70, 79, 80, 82, 139–142, 225, 239, 258, 267, 271, 273–274, 286, 352; armaments and armed forces, 289, 355
Japanese colonial empire, 66, 82, 139–142, 225, 272, 286, 355
Jellicoe, Admiral Sir John (1859–1935), 26
Jerusalem, 33, 366, 367
Jesuit Order, 186
Jewish religion and people (*see also* Israel, Anti-Semitism): 45, 66, 131–134, 199–200, 267, 366–367
Jidda, Treaty (1927), 135
Jinnah, Mohammed Ali (1876–1948), 353
Joffre, General Joseph (1852–1931), 19, 30
John XXIII, Pope (1881–1963), 392, 425
Johnson, President Lyndon (b. 1908), 435
Jordan (*see also* Transjordan), 370, 432
Joyce, James (1882–1941), 394
Jung, Carl Gustave (1875–1961), 385, 394
Jutland, Battle (1916), 26

Kafka, Franz (1883–1924), 393
Kaganovich, Lazar (b. 1893), 426
Kamenev, Lev Borisovich (1883–1936), 210, 211, 222–223
Kandinsky, Wassily (1866–1944), 395
"Kapp Putsch," 85, 190
Karl, of Austria-Hungary (1887–1922), 28, 35, 178

Karlsbad program, 245
Károlyi, Count Michael (1875–1955), 178
Kasavubu, Joseph (b. 1917), 407, 429
Kashmir, 314, 354, 432
Kazakhstan, 331
Kazan, 52, 53
Keitel, General Wilhelm (1882–1946), 243, 304
Kellogg, Frank Billings, (1856–1937), 92
Kellogg Pact, *see* Paris, Pact of (1928)
Kemal, Mustafa (Ataturk) (1881–1938), 77, 120–123, 430
Kennan, George Frost (b. 1904), 404
Kennedy, President John (1917–1963), 347, 423, 424, 427, 434, 435
Kenya, 373–374, 428
Kenyatta, Jomo (b. 1921), 373, 428, 430
Kerensky, Alexander (b. 1881), 29, 44, 45, 47–49
Keynes, John Maynard (1883–1946), *quoted*, 68; 150, 389
Khalkin-Gol, Battle of the (1939), 225
Khrushchev, Nikita (b. 1894), 329, 342–347, 422–423, 426
Kierkegaard, Sören (1813–1855), 390
Kiev, 54, 268, 279
King-Crane Commission, 130
Kirov, Sergei (1888–1934), 220, 222
Kitchener, Field Marshal Lord (1850–1916), 20, 96
Klee, Paul (1879–1940), 395
Kolchak, Admiral Aleksandr (1874–1920), 53–54
Kolkhoz (collective farm), 214, 217, 330, 343
Konev, Marshal Ivan (b. 1897), 414
Kooning, Willem de (b. 1904), 396
Korea, 4, 360
Korean War (1950–1953), 330, 341, 360–361, 375, 405–406
Kostov, Traicho (1897–1949), 420
Kosygin, Alexei (b. 1904), 426
Kronstadt, 45, 59, 60
Kulaks, 214–216, 219
Kun, Bela (1885–1939), 56, 76, 178, 345
Kuomintang, 139, 140, 211, 212, 225
Kurile Islands, 286, 354
Kut-el-Amara, 27
Kuwait, 125–126, 369, 370, 432

Labor Party (Britain), 97, 101–106, 307–308, 314, 401
Labor Unions, *see* Trade Unions
Lamarck, Jean (1744–1829), 383
Land reform, 45, 49, 85–86, 171, 178, 186, 331, 357, 430
Länder (German states), 189–190, 198, 304
Lansing-Ishii Agreement (1917), 140
Laos, 138, 315, 364, 365, 433
Lapua Movement, 186

Lateran Treaty (1929), 177
Latin America, 153, 154, 158, 295, 435
Latvia, 57, 66, 83, 85, 86, 182, 185, 252
Lausanne, Treaty (1923), 77, 121
Laval, Pierre (1883–1945), 233
Law, Andrew Bonar (1858–1923), 101
Lawrence, Thomas Edward (1888–1935), 33
League of Nations (*see also* International Justice, Permanent Court of, International Labor Organization, Mandates, Sanctions): origins, 66–67, 78; Covenant, 67, 70, 71, 78–81; organization, 78–80; membership, 78, 80, 81–82, 91, 111, 116, 192, 200, 226, 233, 261; main activities, 82, 89–90, 115–116, 157, 160, 231–234, 261, 292
Lebanon, 130–131, 314, 366, 369–371
Le Cateau, 20
Le Corbusier (1887–1965), 397, 398
Left Social Revolutionaries, *see* Social Revolutionary Party
Lend-Lease, 265, 269, 271, 325
Lenin, Nicolai (1870–1924), 46–52, 55–57, 60–61, 204–207, 210
Leningrad (*see also* Petrograd), 220, 268–270
Leo XIII, Pope (1810–1903), 175
Leopold III, of Belgium (b. 1901), 262
Ley, Robert, (1890–1945), 194
Leyte Gulf, Battle (1944), 287
Liberal Party (Britain), 96–97, 101–102, 105–106, 307
Liberia, 371
Libya, 265–266, 370, 372
Literature, 12, 385–395
Lithuania, 57, 66, 72, 77, 83, 86, 89, 182, 185, 248, 252
"Little Entente" (1921), 87
Litvinov, Maxim (1876–1951), 224, 252
Lloyd George, David (1863–1945), 23, 28, 29, 56, 66, 68, 70, 73, 75, 96–101, 147
Locarno Treaties (1925), 90–92, 112, 115, 192, 236, 237
London, 265
London, Treaty (1915), 23, 65
Lorca, García (1899–1936), 395
Lubbe, Marinus van der (1910–1934), 197
Ludendorff, General Erich von (1865–1937), 21, 28, 33–35, 193, 194
Lumumba, Patrice (1925–1961), 407
Luxembourg, 319, 410, 414, 415
Lvov, Prince (1861–1925), 29, 43, 44
Lysenko, Trofim (b. 1898), 383
Lytton, Lord (1876–1947), 141

MacArthur, General Douglas (1880–1964), 273, 274, 286, 287, 290, 354, 355, 360–361, 405
MacDonald, James Ramsay (1866–1937), 56, 90, 102, 103, 105, 106, 115
McMahon Pledge (1915), 65, 123, 129, 134

Macmillan, Harold (b. 1894), 346, 401, 402, 424
Madagascar, 273
Madrid, 239, 240
Madrid Pact (1953), 403
Maginot Line, 236, 255, 263, 264
Magnitogorsk, 216, 217
Magyars, *see* Hungary
Mahler, Gustav (1861–1911), 397
Majority Socialist Party (Germany), 188–189
Makarios III, Archbishop (b. 1913), 425
Malaya, 272, 273, 289, 314, 364
Malaysia, 364, 433
Malenkov, Georgi (b. 1901), 328, 342, 343, 426
Malthus, Thomas (1766–1834), 436
Manchukuo, 141, 225
Manchuria, 139–141, 211, 225, 354, 357
Mandates, 72, 76, 81–82, 129–136, 139, 171, 314, 408, 429
Mandel, Georges (1885–1943), 254
Manila, 287
Maniu, Juliu (1873–1951), 86, 181
Mariana Islands, 82, 287
Maritain, Jacques (b. 1882), 391
Marne, Battle of the: (1914), 20, 258; (1918), 34
Marshall, General George (1880–1959), 272, 275, 317, 357
Marshall Islands, 82, 287
Marshall Plan, 308, 311, 312, 317–318, 319, 339, 340, 414
Marx, Wilhelm (1863–1946), 191
Marxism, 40, 61
Masaryk, Jan (1886–1948), 334, 338
Masaryk, Thomas (1850–1937), 244
Matapan, Battle of Cape (1941), 265
Matisse, Henri (1869–1954), 393
Matsu, 359
Matteotti, Giacomo (1885–1924), 173–174
Max, Prince, of Baden (1867–1929), 35, 188
Mboya, Thomas Joseph (b. 1930), 374
Megiddo, Battle (1918), 35
Mein Kampf, 184, 193, 194, 249, 388
Memel, 72, 89, 248
Mendel, Gregor (1822–1884), 383
Menderes, Adnan (1899–1961), 430
Mendès-France, Pierre (b. 1907), 412
Mensheviks, 61
Mesopotamia (*see also* Iraq), 27, 33, 135
Metaxas, General Joannes (1871–1941), 184
Metro-Vickers, 220
Mexico, 28
Michael I, of Rumania (b. 1921), 181
Michael, Grand Duke (1878–1918), 43
Middle Classes, 49, 58, 103, 166, 331, 333
Middle East, 118–136, 224, 351, 366–371, 430–433
Middle East Treaty Organization (METO), 354, 366–371

Midway, Battle (1942), 274
Miliukov, Paul (1859–1943), 42, 43
Mindszenty, Joseph, Cardinal (b. 1892) 346
Minorities, national, 78, 82–84, 122, 244–247, 325, 330, 354
Mobilization, 4–6, 19, 260
Mohammedanism, 115, 119, 124, 128, 130, 131, 135, 313, 353–354, 366, 371, 427
Molotov, Vyacheslav (b. 1890), 46, 218, 227, 252, 342, 426
Molotov Plan, 340
Moltke, General Helmuth von (1848–1916), 20, 21
Moluccas, 287
Mondrian, Piet (1872–1944), 396
Monnet, Jean (b. 1888), 311, 415
Monroe Doctrine, 79
Mons, Battle (1914), 20
Montagu, Edwin (1879–1924), 111
Montague, Charles (1867–1928), 385
Monte Cassino, 278
Montenegro, 23, 181
Montgomery, General Bernard (b. 1897), 277, 284
Montreux Convention (1936), 77, 123, 367
Moore, Henry Spencer (b. 1898), 396
Morgenthau Plan, 304, 306
Morocco: 4, 179, 370, 372; Spanish, 186, 239, 240
Morotai, 287
Mosca, Gaetano (1859–1941), 388
Moscicki, Ignacy (1867–1946), 182
Moscow, 43, 47, 48, 51, 54, 219, 258, 268–270, 324
Mosley, Oswald (b. 1896), 107, 188
Mossadegh, Mohammed (b. 1881), 368
Mosul, 90, 123, 130
Mountbatten, Admiral Louis (b. 1900), 114, 289
Mouvement Républicain Populaire (MRP), 310, 391
Mueller, Hermann (1876–1931), 195
Munich, 193, 194, 300
Munich Agreement (1938), 227, 245–247
Music, 12, 380, 397
Mussolini, Benito (1883–1945), 169, 171–178, 229, 232–234, 239, 240, 241, 242, 244–246, 249, 253, 264, 266, 278, 285, 293
Mutual Security Agency (MSA), 318, 355

Nadir, of Afghanistan (1880–1933), 137
Nagasaki, 259, 289, 290
Nagy, Imre (1895–1958), 345–346
Nanking, 140, 141, 211, 357
Nansen, Fridtjof (1861–1930), 80, 122
Nasser, Gamal Abdel (b. 1918), 366, 369–370, 432
National Socialist Party, *see* Nazi Party
Nationalism, 5, 66, 68, 75, 84, 98, 142, 170, 348, 351, 371, 432

Nationalization of industry, 58, 102, 103, 204, 308, 311
Naval warfare: First World War, 5, 18, 22, 24, 26–29, 33, 36; Second World War, 259, 261, 265, 269, 273, 274, 275, 277, 286, 287
Nazi Party, 184–185, 193–200, 302–304
Ne Win, General (b. 1911), 433
Nehru, Jawaharlal (1889–1964), 353, 354, 433
Nenni, Pietro (b. 1891), 312
Neo-Destour Party, 314
Neo-Fascism, 402
Nepmen, 60, 205
Nervi, Pier (b. 1891), 397
Netherlands, 262, 313, 319, 403
Netherlands colonial empire, 138–139, 212, 273, 289, 295, 313, 315, 352
Neuilly, Treaty (1919), 76
Neutralism, 354, 363, 373, 375
Neutrality Acts, U.S.A. (1935, 1937), 231
New Economic Policy (1921), 60, 204–207, 211, 213
New Guinea, 274, 286–287; Netherlands, 364, 433
New Order, Nazi, 266–267
New York Stock Exchange crisis (1929), 146, 192
New Zealand, 16, 24, 111, 366, 375
Ngo Dinh Diem (1901–1964), 365, 434
Nguyen Khanh, General (b. 1928), 434
Nicholas II, of Russia (1868–1918), 6, 42–43, 52
Nietzsche, Friedrich (1844–1900), 170
Nigeria, 373
"Night of the Long Knives" (1934), 198
Nimitz, Admiral Chester (b. 1885), 287
Nitti, Francesco (1868–1953), 171
Nivelle, General Robert (1856–1924), 30–32
Nixon, Richard (b. 1913), 346
Nkrumah, Kwame (b. 1909), 373, 428, 435
NKVD (Soviet secret police), 223
Nobel prizes, 80, 90, 381, 391, 407
Nonaggression pacts, 237, 238, 248, 252, 271
Nonintervention Committee, 241
North Atlantic Treaty Organization (NATO), 319, 321, 339, 345, 366, 367, 369, 410–411, 414, 424, 425
Northern Ireland, *see* Ulster
Norway, 261, 313
Nuclear energy, 11, 164, 381–383, 398, 417, 432
Nuclear Test-Ban Treaty (1963), 425, 427
Nuclear weapons, 7, 259, 289–290, 295, 338, 341, 347, 384, 398, 404, 411, 417–419, 424, 435, 436
Nuremberg Laws (1935), 199, 200
Nuremberg Trials (1945–1946), 243, 303–304
Nyasaland, 374
Nyerere, Julius (b. 1921), 428

Odessa, 56, 279
Ogpu (Soviet secret police), 208, 219, 220, 223
Oil: sources of supply, 54, 66, 120, 121, 123, 124–126, 206, 216, 260, 270, 366; production and use, 109, 128, 136, 216, 232, 238, 331, 368, 371, 433
Okinawa, 289
Old Bolsheviks, 209, 222, 223
Open Door Policy, 140
Operation Sea Lion, 264
Optional Clause, 81
Oran, 265
Organization for Economic Cooperation and Development (OECD), 425–426
Organization for European Economic Cooperation (OEEC), 317, 414
Organization of African Unity, 430
Orgburo, 208, 210
Orlando, Vittorio (1860–1952), 68
Ortega y Gasset, José (1883–1955), 387
Orwell, George (1903–1950), 394, 399
Osborne, John (b. 1929), 394
Ottawa Conference (1932), 110, 164
Ottoman Empire (see also Turkey), 4, 65, 67, 81, 120, 121, 258
Outer Mongolia, 57, 139, 211, 286, 357

"Pact of Steel" (1939), 249
Paets, Konstantin (1874–1943), 185
Painting, 12, 396
Pakistan, 313–314, 352–354, 367, 368, 369, 432
Palestine (see also Israel), 66, 131–135, 314
Pan-Arabism, 370
Papen, Franz von (b. 1879), 195, 196, 198, 304
Pareto, Vilfredo (1848–1923), 388
Paris, 264, 281, 409, 411
Paris, Pact of (1928), 92, 192
Paris Peace Conference: (1919), 67–75; (1946–1947), 300, 333
Parties, political, see names of parties and sub-entry under names of major powers
Passchendaele, Battle (1917), 32
Pauker, Anna (1893–1960), 420
Paul, Prince, of Yugoslavia (b. 1893), 183
Paulus, Field Marshal Friedrich von (1890–1957), 270
Pearl Harbor, 271, 272
Peasants, 42, 44, 45, 49, 59, 84–86, 122, 154, 170, 207, 212–217, 221, 331, 333, 344, 360
Peiping, see Peking
Peking, 141, 357
People's Communes, 360
People's Republics, see "Popular democracy"
Permanent Court, see International Justice
Pershing, General John Joseph (1860–1948), 35
Persia, see Iran
Pétain, Marshal Philippe (1856–1951), 25, 32, 264, 267, 309

Peter II, of Yugoslavia (b. 1923), 183
Petliura, Simon (1879–1926), 50, 54
Petrograd (see also Leningrad), 42–48, 51, 54, 59
Petroleum, see Oil
Philippine Islands, 142, 273, 286, 287, 315, 355, 362, 365
Philosophic studies, 389–391
"Phony war," 260
Piatiletka, see Five-Year Plans
Picasso, Pablo (b. 1881), 187, 395, 396
Pieck, Wilhelm (1876–1960), 306
Pilsudski, Josef (1867–1935), 182, 185
Pinero, Arthur (1855–1934), 393
Pius XI, Pope (1857–1939), 177, 199, 312, 391
Pius XII, Pope (1876–1958), 177
Planck, Max (1858–1947), 381
Planning, economic (see also Five-Year Plans): to 1945, 166, 198–199, 213–216; since 1945, 308, 311, 340, 359, 368, 389, 415, 432
Pleven, René (b. 1901), 411
Poison gas, 18, 23, 148, 233
Poland (see also Galicia): First World War, 21, 24, 30, 66, 67; to 1939, 54, 70, 75, 77, 83, 85–86, 87, 89, 182, 185, 192, 246–247, 248–251, 331; Second World War, 259–260, 281, 284; since 1945, 299, 302, 332, 336, 337, 345, 420
Polish Corridor, 72, 249, 252, 260
Politburo, 208, 209, 224
Pollock, Jackson (1912–1956), 396
"Popular democracy," 333
Popular Front, 186, 226, 239, 333
Popular Party (Italy), 171, 177, 312
Population (see also sub-entry under names of major powers), 7, 11, 15, 435
Population transfer, 82, 122, 302
Portsmouth, Treaty (1905), 338
Portugal, 33, 180, 403, 429
Portuguese colonial empire, 429, 433
Potsdam Conference (1945), 304, 315, 332, 354, 360
Preuss, Hugo (1860–1925), 189
Primo de Rivera, see Rivera
Proletariat, 46, 56, 104, 208, 209, 219
Propaganda, 28, 55, 183, 199, 200, 224, 258, 267, 333
Protection, see Tariff systems
Protestantism, 199, 392
Proust, Marcel (1871–1922), 393
Prussia (see also East Prussia), 193, 306
Public Health, 11, 37, 69, 163–164, 176, 384–385
Pu-yi, Henry, of China and Manchukuo (b. 1906), 141

Quebec Conference (1944), 304
Quemoy, 359

Rabaul, 274, 287
Rachmaninoff, Sergei (1873–1943), 393

Radar, 163
Radek, Karl (b. 1885), 55
Radich, Stefan (1871–1928), 181
Radio, 155, 163, 183
Railways (*see also* names of railways), 163
Rapacky, Adam (b. 1909), 418
Rapacky Plan, 418–419
Rapallo, Treaty (1922), 147, 192, 206, 225, 226
Rasputin, Grigori (1871–1916), 42
Rassemblement du Peuple Français (R.P.F.), 311
Rathenau, Walther (1867–1922), 87, 147, 191, 206
Rationalization, 155, 163
Rauschning, Hermann (b. 1887), 293
Ravel, Maurice (1875–1937), 397
Reed, John (1887–1920), 48
Reichstag Fire (1933), 197
Reinsurance Treaty (1887), 4
Religion (*see also* names of religions and churches), 12, 427
Remagen, 285
Remarque, Erich (b. 1898), 385
Reparations: First World War, 67, 70, 73, 75, 76, 87–89, 107, 148–150, 161, 191, 196; Second World War, 299, 300, 305, 325, 355
Republicanism, 84, 113, 180, 312, 333
Reza Pahlevi, Mohammed, of Iran (b. 1919), 368
Rhee, Syngman (1875–1965), 360
Rhineland, 70, 73, 88, 91, 192; remilitarization, 234–237
Rhodesia, 374, 428
Ribbentrop, Joachim von (1893–1946), 227, 252
Riga, Treaty (1921), 54, 57, 77, 299
Rilke, Rainer Maria (1875–1926), 395
Rivera, Miguel Primo de (1870–1930), 179–180, 186
Riza Pahlevi, of Iran (1877–1944), 128
Rocco, Alfredo (1875–1935), 172
Rohe, Ludwig Miës van der (b. 1886), 397
Rohm, Ernst (1887–1934), 193, 198
Rokossowski, Marshal Konstantin (b. 1896), 345
Roman Catholic Church, 176–177, 186, 187, 239, 240, 345, 391
Rome, 173, 278, 281
Rome, Treaty (1957), 415
Rommel, General Erwin (1891–1944), 266, 276–278
Roosevelt, President Franklin (1882–1945), 246, 247, 265, 267, 272, 274, 278, 279, 285, 286, 297, 298, 304, 383
Rosenberg, Alfred (1893–1946), 194, 304, 388
Rothschild, Lord (1868–1937), 131
Rouault, Georges (1871–1958), 393
Ruhr, 88, 115, 150–151, 191, 285
Rumania: First World War, 23, 35; to 1939, 65, 76, 83, 86, 165, 181, 183, 331; Second World War, 266, 269, 270, 279, 281; since 1945, 300, 325, 331, 333, 420, 426
Runciman, Lord (1870–1949), 245
Rundstedt, Field Marshal Gerd von (1875–1953), 262
Russell, Bertrand (b. 1872), 389
Russia (*see also* Satellite states, Union of Soviet Socialist Republics): population, 295, 331; First World War, 19, 21, 22, 24, 27, 29–30, 41–42, 45, 50; to 1939, 40–62, 66, 202–227; Second World War, 268–271, 279, 281, 284–285, 286, 323; since 1945, 294, 297, 324–331, 342–344, 347, 348, 426; constitution, 49, 207–208, 220–222; parties, 8, 43, 45, 50, 52, 61, 208; economic life, 8, 42, 45, 49, 58–60, 204–207, 213–218, 324–331, 343; foreign policy, 3–6, 42, 45, 205–206, 224–227, 249–252, 337–341, 354, 357, 360–361, 364, 406; armaments and armed forces, 7, 41, 52, 281, 347, 414, 424
Russian calendar, 43
Russian famine (1921), 60, 80, 148–149, 204
Russian police forces, *see* Cheka, Ogpu, NKVD
Russian Soviet Federated Socialist Republic (RSFSR), 207
Russo-Finnish War (1939–1940), 261
Russo-German Pact (1939), 252, 260, 261, 268
Russo-Japanese War (1904–1905), 139, 141, 338
Russo-Polish War (1920), 54, 87
Ruthenia, 76, 245, 247, 332
Rutherford, Ernest (1871–1937), 382
Rydz-Smigly, Marshal Edward (1886–1941), 185

Saar, 70, 72, 90, 200, 402–403
Safeguarding of Industries Acts (1922, 1925), 100, 110, 152
St. Germain, Treaty (1919), 75, 181
Saint-Mihiel, Battle (1918), 35
Saipan, 287
Sakhalin, 139, 206, 354
Sakkaria, Battle of the (1921), 121
Salazar, Antonio (b. 1889), 180, 403
Salk, Jonas (b. 1914), 385
Salvemini, Gaetano (b. 1873), 176
San Francisco Conference (1945), 299
San Remo Conference (1920), 120, 124, 130, 132
Sanctions, 80, 90, 232–233
Sarajevo assassination, 5, 6, 71
Sarrail, General Maurice (1856–1929), 130
Sartre, Jean-Paul (b. 1905), 390–391
Satellite states (Russian), 220, 306, 317, 318, 331–339, 344–346, 420
Saudi Arabia, 124–126, 370, 371
Sauvy, Alfred (b. 1898), 330
Savo Island, 286

Scandinavia (*see also* Denmark, Norway, Sweden), 261, 403

Schacht, Hjalmar (b. 1877), 304

Scheidemann, Philip (1865-1939), 71, 188, 189

Schleicher, General Kurt von (1882-1934), 195, 196, 198

Schleswig, 71, 72

Schlieffen Plan, 5, 6, 20

Schönberg, Arnold (1874-1951), 397

Schuman, Robert (1886-1963), 415

Schuschnigg, Kurt von (b. 1897), 185, 243

Schutzstaffeln (SS), 199

Scientific studies, 11, 295, 328, 380-385

Sebastopol, 270, 279

Second Front demand, 269, 279, 280

Second World War (1939-1945): causes, 228-231, 234, 242-255; character, 256-259; campaigns, 259-290, 351-352; loss of life, 259, 265, 270, 289, 290, 323; economic effects, 299, 300, 302, 307, 311, 312, 323, 325; peace treaties, 300, 355, 403-404

Security Council, *see* United Nations

Seipel, Ignaz (1876-1932), 181

Serbia (*see also* Yugoslavia), 5, 6, 19, 23, 180, 181

Sèvres, Treaty (1920), 76, 120

Seyss-Inquart, Artur von (1892-1946), 243

Shanghai, 141, 267

Shastri, Lal Bahadur (1904-1966), 433

Shaw, Bernard (1856-1950), 393

Shepard, Alan (b. 1923), 427

Siam, *see* Thailand

Sibelius, Jan (1865-1958), 393

Siberia, 45, 52-54, 59, 206, 222, 325, 331

Sicily, 271, 278

Siegfried Line, *see* West Wall

Silesia, 71, 72, 90, 302

Simon, John (1873-1954), 114

Singapore, 273, 364

Sinn Fein, 98

Slansky, Rudolf (1901-1952), 420

Slavophiles, 328

Slovakia, 76, 245, 247, 269, 284, 332

Slovenes, 183

Smetona, President Antanas of Lithuania (1874-1944), 185

Smuts, General Jan Christiaan (1870-1950), *quoted*, 1; 113

Smyrna, 120-122

Social Democratic or Socialist Party: Austria, 181; Britain, 307; Czechoslovakia, 334; Germany, 189, 195, 197, 306; Italy, 312; Russia, 45, 61

Social reform, 9, 84, 102, 107, 156, 307, 398, 401, 417

Social Revolutionary Party (Russia), 45, 49, 50, 52, 61

Socialism, *see* Communism, Social Democratic or Socialist Party

Solomon Islands, 274, 286, 287

Somaliland (Somali Republic), 232, 233, 373, 428

Sombart, Werner (1863-1941), 387

Somme, Battle of the (1916), 25

Sorel, Georges (1847-1922), 170, 171

Sorokin, Pitirim (b. 1889), 386

South Africa, 113, 371, 374, 429-430

South Manchurian Railway, 141, 357

Southeast Asia, 361-366, 434

Southeast Asia Treaty Organization (SEATO), 354, 366, 375, 432

Southwest Africa, 429

Soviet (*see also* Union of Soviet Socialist Republics), 43, 44, 47-48, 59, 61, 207-208, 221, 331

Spaak, Paul-Henri (b. 1899), 410

Space vehicles, 419, 427

Spain, 179-180, 186-187, 403, 414

Spanish Civil War (1936-1939), 183, 186, 237, 239-242

Spanish colonial empire, 179, 428

Spartacists, 188, 190

Spengler, Oswald (1880-1936), 385-386

Sputnik, *see* Space vehicles

Stakhanov, Aleksei (b. 1905), 218

Stalin, Joseph (1879-1953), 45, 47, 207-227, 268, 270, 271, 279, 280, 289, 298, 302, 324-330, 332, 337, 340, 342-346

Stalingrad, Siege (1942-1943), 270

Stambolisky, Alexander (1879-1923), 181

Stahremberg, Prince (1899-1956), 181

State farms (Russia), 217

Sterling currency, 159, 308

Stettin, 302, 317

Stimson, Henry (1867-1950), 141

Storm troopers (*Stürmabteilungen*), 193, 199

Straits (Bosphorus and Dardanelles), 24, 42, 67, 76, 77, 120-123, 339, 367

Strasbourg, 410

Strasser, Gregor (1892-1934), 198

Strassmann, Fritz (b. 1902), 164

Strauss, Richard (1864-1949), 393

Stravinsky, Igor (b. 1882), 397

Streicher, Julius (1885-1946), 194, 304

Stresa Conference (1935), 231, 234

Stresemann, Gustav (1878-1929), 91, 191, 192

Sturzo, Luigi (1871-1959), 171, 312

Succession states, 84

Sudan, 127, 314, 370, 372

Sudetenland, 245, 247, 254

Suez Canal, 27, 127, 314, 370

Suez conflict (1956), 367, 370, 405, 406

Sukarno, Achmed (b. 1901), 139, 315, 364, 433

Summit Conferences (1955, 1960), 346-348, 418, 422-424

Sun Yat-sen (1866-1925), 139, 140, 211, 358

Sweden, 89, 108, 313, 367, 407

Switzerland, 313, 404, 417

Sykes-Picot Agreement (1916), 66, 129
Syndicalism, 175, 186
Syria, 129–131, 314, 369, 370, 432

Taiwan, *see* Formosa
Tajik SSR, 207
Tanganyika (*see also* Tanzania), 81
Tank warfare; First World War, 18, 25, 26, 32, 34; Second World War, 259, 260, 264, 265, 266, 270, 277, 309
Tannenberg, Battle (1914), 21
Tanzania, 428, 429
Taranto, Battle (1940), 265
Tariff systems, 100, 110, 122, 138, 152, 157, 162, 409, 426
Taylor, Frederick Winslow (1856–1915), 155
Technology, developments in (*see also* Armaments, Nuclear energy): to 1945, 109, 148, 155, 156, 161, 163–164, 199, 213, 215, 216; since 1945, 295, 311, 336, 344, 347, 383, 396, 398, 427
Tehran, 128, 298, 346
Tehran Conference (1943), 279, 298
Television, 163
Tereshkova, Valentina (b. 1937), 427
Thailand, 273, 361–362, 365
Thälmann, Ernst (1886–1944), 191, 195
Thrace: eastern, 76, 121; western, 76
Three Emperors' League, 4
Third International, *see* Comintern
Tibet, 354
Tito, Marshal Josip (b. 1892), 333, 334, 420, 426
Titov, Gherman (b. 1935), 427
Togliatti, Palmiro (1893–1964), 312
Tojo, General Hideki (1885–1948), 355
Tonkin, 315, 364
Total war, 258–259
Totalitarianism, 388
Towns, *see* Urbanization
Townshend, General Sir Charles (1861–1924), 27
Toynbee, Arnold Joseph (b. 1889), 386–387
Trade (*see also* Depression, Free Trade, Tariff systems), 8, 37, 153, 157, 160, 162, 164, 165, 409
Trade Unions, 45, 49, 59, 97, 102–104, 173, 215
Transcaucasia, 27, 207
Trans-Iranian Railway, 128
Transjordan (*see also* Jordan), 132, 134–135, 314
Transport, *see* Airplanes, Automobiles, Railways
Trans-Siberian Railway, 52, 225
Trentino, 75
Trianon, Treaty (1920), 76, 178
Trieste, 75, 77, 300, 312, 317
Triple Alliance (1882), 4

Triple Entente (1907), 4
Trotsky, Leon (1877–1940), 46–54, 60, 61, 209–212, 223
Trotskyites, 210, 212, 213, 226, 241
Truk, 287
Truman, President Harry (b. 1884), 302, 317, 318, 338, 339, 361
"Truman Doctrine," 317, 318, 321, 339, 365, 375
Trust Territories, 408
Tsarina, Alexandra, *see* Alexandra
Tshombe, Moise (b. 1919), 428, 429
Tukhachevsky, Marshal Mikhail (1893–1937), 223
Tunisia, 4, 278, 370, 372
Turkestan-Siberian Railway, 216
Turkey: First World War, 22, 24, 27, 32, 35; to 1945, 76–77, 83, 120–123, 165; since 1945, 318, 339, 366, 367, 425, 430
Turkmen SSR, 207
"Twenty-One Demands" (1915), 66, 140
Tydings-McDuffie Act (1934), 142

Ukraine, 34, 50, 53, 56, 57, 59, 66, 77, 207, 226, 327, 329, 342
Ulbricht, Walter (b. 1893), 306
Ulmanis, Karlis (1877–1940), 185
Ulster, 99–100, 113
Unamuno, Miguel de (1864–1936), 387
Unemployment, 104–108, 110, 157, 158, 159, 165, 166, 195, 202, 307
Uniates, Greek Catholics, 328
Union of Soviet Socialist Republics (for history, *see* Russia), 61
United Arab Republic, 370–371, 432, 433
United Nations (*see also* Trust Territories): origins, 272–273, 297, 298, 299, 338; Charter, 299, 405, 406, 409, 410, 417; organization, 315, 407–409; membership, 11, 295, 314, 315, 359, 369, 372, 404–405, 428; main activities, 341, 354, 360, 366–367, 370, 405–409, 425, 429, 430; peace-keeping forces, 405, 406, 429
United Nations Educational, Scientific, and Cultural Organization (UNESCO), 379, 380, 409
United Nations Children's Fund (UNICEF), 407
United Nations Relief and Rehabilitation Association (UNRRA), 299, 315, 336, 408
United States: First World War, 28–29, 33–36, 37, 43, 66–67, 140, 152; relations with Europe, to 1939, 8, 67–75, 79, 80, 92, 105, 140, 146, 148–149, 153, 154–162, 165, 231, 241, 247; Second World War, 258, 265, 267, 269, 271–290; relations with Europe, since 1945, 10, 294, 297, 308, 311, 317–321, 401; relations with Communist Russia, 7, 52, 206, 216, 220, 224, 294, 317, 338; relations with

Middle and Far East, 126, 140, 141, 142, 315, 357, 359–361, 367–371, 405–406; armaments and armed forces, 7, 28, 34, 36, 269, 272, 286, 287, 347, 411

Urbanization, 308

Uzbek SSR, 207

Valéry, Paul (1871–1945), 394

Vatican City, 177

Vatican Council (1962–1965), 392

Venizelos, Eleutherios (1864–1936), 80, 179

Verdun, Battle (1916), 25, 30

Versailles, Treaty (1919), 71–75, 78, 190, 193, 234, 238, 389

Vichy government (France), 264, 267, 277, 309

Victor Emmanuel II, of Italy (1820–1878), 170

Victor Emmanuel III, of Italy (1869–1947), 173, 278

Vienna, 75, 156, 185, 192–193, 243, 285, 347–348

Vienna Meeting (1961), 347, 423

Vietnam, 315, 365, 375, 433; North, 365, 433, 434; South, 365, 434

Vilna, 77, 89

Vimy Ridge, Battle (1917), 31

Vladivostok, 52, 54, 211, 271

Vries, Hugo de (1848–1935), 383

Wages and purchasing power of workers, 96, 110, 156, 165, 191, 215, 402

Wagner, Richard (1813–1883), 397

Wake Island, 273

Walwal, 232

War Communism, 58, 204, 205

War criminals, 73, 298, 302–304

War debts (see also Lend-Lease), 107, 148–150, 161

War guilt, 73, 76, 78, 255

Warfare, see Air warfare, Armaments, Armies, Naval warfare, Nuclear weapons, Tank warfare

Warsaw, 21, 24, 54, 260, 281, 284, 324, 332, 345

Warsaw Pact (1955), 413

Washington Treaties (1922), 89, 115, 140

Wassmuss, Consul, 128

Watt, Robert Watson (b. 1892), 163

Wavell, General Sir Archibald (1883–1950), 265–266

Webb, Beatrice (1858–1943), 203

Webb, Sidney (1859–1947), 203

Weber, Max (1864–1920), 387

Wehrwirtschaft, 9, 200

Weimar, 189

Weizmann, Chaim (1874–1952), 132

Welfare state, 9, 107

Welles, Sumner (1892–1961), 304

West Germany, 305–306, 344, 402, 403, 404, 412, 413, 414, 415, 419, 424, 425

West Irian, see New Guinea

West Wall, 254, 285

Western European Union, 402, 411

Westminster, Statute (1931), 112

Weygand, General Maxime (1867–1965), 130, 262

White Russia, see Byelorussia

White Russians (counterrevolutionaries), 52–55

Whitehead, Alfred (1861–1947), 389, 392

Wilhelmina, of the Netherlands (1880–1962), 313

William II, German Emperor (1859–1941), 4, 6, 35, 73, 188

Wilson, Edmund (b. 1895), 394

Wilson, President Woodrow (1856–1924), 27, 56, 66–71, 75, 78, 79, 152

Wirth, Joseph (1879–1956), 87

Wittgenstein, Ludwig (1889–1951), 390

Woman suffrage, 84, 97, 105, 186, 404

Working classes, see Peasants, Proletariat

World Bank, 409

World Council of Churches, 392

World Health Organization (WHO), 409

Wrangel, Baron Peter (1878–1928), 55

Wright, Frank Lloyd (1869–1959), 397

Yalta Conference (1945), 286, 290, 298, 302, 332, 354

Yemen, 370, 432

Young Plan, 156, 191

Youth organizations, 174, 199, 222, 328

Ypres, Battles (1914, 1915, 1917), 21, 23, 32

Yüan Shih-kai (1859–1916), 139, 140

Yugoslavia: to 1945, 66, 76, 77, 83, 86, 165, 180–181, 183, 266, 331; since 1945, 300, 332–337, 340, 344–346, 420, 426

Zhdanov, Andrei (1896–1948), 328

Zhukov, General Georgi (b. 1896), 270, 342

Zinoviev, Grigori (1883–1936), 57, 210, 211, 222–223

Zionism, 131, 132

Zog I, of Albania (1895–1961), 180

Illustration Acknowledgments

PAGE

26 Brown Brothers

46 Sovfoto

69 Library of Congress

104 Culver Pictures

126 Arabian American Oil Company

151 United Press International Newspictures

174 Brown Brothers

196 Keystone

219 Sovfoto

246 United Press International Newspictures

298 Imperial War Museum, London

329 Sovfoto

373 United Nations

380 Unesco/Dominque Lajoux, 1959

403 Wide World Photos